Why You Need This New Edition

1. Strong focus on the "Third Age", the healthy active years around retirement before old age sets in.
2. A new chapter on demography places aging in the U.S. in a world context.
3. Coverage of the increased research on exercise, diet, and new ways to cope with physical change in later life.
4. Inclusion of the latest research on mental potential in later life. Terms like "reserve capacity," "plasticity," "adaptability" in the literature all describe a new, more positive view of mental ability in old age.
5. Detailed exploration of minority aging.
6. Chapter 7 reports on the 2010 federal government health care reform bill, the "Patient Protection and Affordable Care Act."
7. A thorough discussion of funding for the Social Security program and reform proposals such as private retirement accounts and defined contribution pension plans.
8. Reports on the latest trends in workforce participation. Recent data show a reversal in a decades-long trend toward early retirement. A number of social and economic forces, including a drop in stock market values, the recent recession, and longer life expectancy, all encourage people to postpone retirement.
9. Examination of the latest trends in senior housing, including the development of green homes, universal design (to suit people of all ages), and smart homes. This leads to a discussion that appears in several earlier chapters—the use of technology to support successful aging.
10. New information on gay couples, widowhood, couples that live apart, and dating.
11. Exploration of how different cultural groups in the U.S. look at death and dying.

PEARSON

THIRD EDITION

ISSUES IN AGING

Mark Novak
San Jose State University

PEARSON

Boston   Columbus   Indianapolis   New York   San Francisco   Upper Saddle River
Amsterdam   Cape Town   Dubai   London   Madrid   Milan   Munich   Paris   Montreal   Toronto
Delhi   Mexico City   Sao Paulo   Sydney   Hong Kong   Seoul   Singapore   Taipei   Tokyo

Executive Editor: *Karen Hanson*
Editorial Assistant: *Joseph Jantas*
Executive Marketing Manager: *Kelly May*
Marketing Assistant: *Janeli Bitor*
Production Manager: *Meghan DeMaio*
Creative Director: Jayne Conte
Cover Designer: Karen Salzbach
Cover Image: © Yuri Arcurs/Fotolia
Editorial Production and Composition Service: *Aptara®, Inc.*
Printer/Binder: Edwards Brothers
Cover Printer: Lehigh-Phoenix Color

Library of Congress Cataloging-in-Publication Data

Novak, Mark
  Issues in aging/Mark Novak.—3rd ed.
    p. cm.
  ISBN-13: 978-0-205-83195-1
  ISBN-10: 0-205-83195-8
  1. Gerontology. 2. Aging. 3. Older people—Social conditions. 4. Older people—United States—Social conditions. I. Title.
  HQ1061.N883 2012
  305.26—dc23

                                2011035053

10 9 8 7 6 5 4 3 2 1   15 14 13 12 11

ISBN-10: 0-205-83195-8
ISBN-13: 978-0-205-83195-1

CONTENTS

10   HOUSING AND TRANSPORTATION 292

11   LEISURE, RECREATION, AND EDUCATION 324

Some years ago I attended a sociology department meeting to present my first proposal for a course on aging. After some questions from the committee, the committee chair (a professor of comparative culture) leaned forward and squinted at me. "I have no objection to you teaching this course," he said. "You have an interest in the subject and knowledge of the area. But, tell me, what in the world will you talk about for an entire semester in a course on aging? People get old, then they die. What else is there to say?"

This colleague wouldn't ask these questions today. Every day newspaper and magazine articles bring us new knowledge about aging and our aging society. In the United States today there are more older people in the population than ever before. Studies report findings on diet, exercise, pensions, family life, and housing. Televised reports suggest ways to stay healthy and live a long life. Almost everyone knows something about aging today, and the growth in popular books on this subject suggests that people want to know more.

Issues in aging will grow in importance as more people enter middle and later life. Most university and college students today will face these issues in their careers. For example, the Baby Boom generation has entered middle age and will move like a glacier into old age in the next few years. This mass of people will want services from professionals who understand their needs and concerns. Students in gerontology classes, whatever their major or field of study, will need to know about this aging population.

This book presents facts and information about aging today. It covers the issues that most older people and their families will face. And it deals with issues that an aging society will raise for all of us. Whether you are older yourself, have older parents, relatives, and friends, or plan to work with older people, the information in this text will help you understand aging today.

SPECIAL FEATURES

This book has an underlying theme: successful aging. The text presents a full picture of aging—problems and all. But it emphasizes the opportunities and advantages of later life. This theme makes more sense today than ever before.

Longer life and more years of activity and good health have changed the landscape of later life. Late old age still brings physical decline. But better health and nutrition at every stage of life along with advances in medicine extend the active years of middle age. The saying "60 is the new 40 and 70 the new 50" may have begun as clever remarks. But they describe the reality of aging today for more and more people. Relatively few older people today (aged 65 and over) fit the stereotypical image of the poor and decrepit senior. Better pension plans, better health, and more opportunities for personal expression and social engagement all have transformed later life. This book documents that transformation and the new ecology of aging today.

Some years ago French gerontologists used the term *the Third Age* to describe this new stage of life. This concept defines a time of life between adulthood (the Second Age) and old age (the Fourth Age). It refers to the healthy active years around retirement before old age sets in. Researchers Moen and Spencer (2006, p. 128) define this as a time of transition, a "*midcourse* between the career- and family-building tasks associated with adulthood, but before any debilitating infirmities associated with old age." This stage may begin in the 50s and go on to age 80 or more.

Two phenomena led to the emergence of the Third Age today. The first is demography. More people than ever before (the Baby Boomers) have entered the Third Age. This group will soon fit the traditional age category of old age (aged 65 and over). Baby Boomers will look and act more like people in middle age than like the stereotypical older person. The second factor is longevity. People, on average, live longer today than ever before. And they will live these added years, sometimes called the "longevity bonus," in better health than past generations (Moen & Spencer, 2006, p. 128). Add to this changes in technology that allow people to stay productive longer, opportunities to stay engaged through volunteer work, and the practice of lifelong learning. All of these changes mean that Third Agers will remain active and engaged in second careers, leisure, and social service. They will redefine the concept of retirement and of later life.

Moen and Spencer (2006, p. 134) call the traditional view of old age "outdated" and "obsolete." The old model no longer fits the complexity and emergence of the Third Age. The rapid social change at the start of the 21st century—technological change, a globalized economy, unstable work careers, demographic change, convergence of male and female career opportunities—calls for new models to fit new patterns of social experience.

The existence of the Third Age as a large-scale phenomenon causes some rethinking of assumptions about aging. The Senior Olympics, for example, have existed for a number of years. But, in the past, people who took part in these events seemed like odd specimens. Today, large numbers of people in their 50s and older run marathons, take up surfing, and climb mountains (a 71-year-old Japanese man summited Mount Everest in the spring of 2007). These Third Agers shatter the stereotype of the older person. They force a new look at what we call old age.

Social institutions such as business and industry need to adapt to this new population of Third Agers. As Baby Boomers retire from the workplace, they will leave behind a labor shortage. The smaller age groups behind them will provide fewer workers to the labor force. This will change the way that business and industry view retirement and the retiree. Some companies will rehire retirees, others will give people incentives to delay retirement.

On my campus an interim president came out of retirement for 2 years to manage the campus while we searched for a new leader. The campus then hired our administrative vice president, who delayed retirement, to serve as our new president. He then brought back a retired senior administrator to serve as vice president to manage a troublesome unit. These administrators all had many years of successful experience. This pattern will occur more and more often in varied industries and institutions in the years ahead.

Third Agers will engage in activities that express their interests and passions. And they will create institutions to meet these needs. They will form programs like the Osher Life-long Learning Institutes (a nationwide consortium of education programs) and Civic Ventures (a nationwide volunteer group) (both described in Chapter 12).

This third edition of *Issues in Aging* also links the generations through the life course perspective. The emergence of the Third Age demands this approach.

The Third Age blurs the meaning of retirement and old age. It asks for a view of aging that looks at the whole of adult life—the discontinuities (e.g., retirement) and the continuities (e.g., lifelong learning). A life course perspective shows where and how a person's life has continuity. It also shows how the generations depend on one another. Many Boomers will play the role of caregiver to their aging parents and to their children and grandchildren. They will deal with their own retirement and health issues as they age. And they will affect the younger generations through their use of services, their social contributions, and their ability to improve society as they age.

Finally, as Baby Boomers enter the Third Age they will put pressure on existing programs and services. The Social Security system, corporate pension programs, and the health care system will have to adapt to this large number of older people. Some of these changes have begun already. For example, the Social Security program raised the age for entitlement to full benefits. In general, these systems and others may shift the cost of a program or service to the individual. This marks a change from the way that programs and services developed during the 20th century. During the past century, government and corporate programs provided greater benefits to older people. The 21st century will ask people to take more responsibility for their own pension planning and health care costs.

Novelli and Workman (2006, p. 12) list five threats to the well-being of the big generation entering the Third Age:

1. Lack of preparation by Boomers for their long period in retirement
2. The shift of pension risk and responsibility to workers by corporations
3. Poor financing and organization of government programs, including health care, Social Security, and social services
4. A health care system that focuses on paying bills but not on health promotion
5. Lack of clear options and opportunities for a well-educated, healthy, and active Boomer population

Each of these threats puts the Boomer generation at risk. These items point to weaknesses in America's preparation for an aging society.

This book looks at these and other issues related to aging and society today. For example, all older people encounter negative stereotyping, many minority older people face low incomes, and some older workers retire without sound pension plans due to economic change. Rising health care costs threaten to bankrupt individuals and burden society. All of us need to understand these and other issues. This calls for knowledge that sorts the myths from the realities of aging.

I have designed this book for easy use and enjoyable reading. Each chapter presents issues around a single theme—for example, housing, health care, or income security. I present the facts on that theme, the issues related to that theme, and creative responses to these issues.

Chapters also include graphs and tables for the display of complex information. In almost every case, these displays have an accompanying explanation. I have also tried to give the meaning of new concepts in the text so that students can read along without constant reference to the Glossary. I have included photos and case studies of older people. Some of these people I have met informally or through my research. Other cases come from insightful articles in the popular press. These additions show the human side of aging. The various boxed features show the diversity of older people and their unique circumstances. Cartoons are also included to show the lighter side of aging.

The end of each chapter includes a summary of main points, questions for discussion or study, suggested readings, and relevant high-quality Web sites. These resources will help students explore a topic and begin independent research.

ORGANIZATION

Issues in Aging first looks at large-scale social issues—social attitudes, the study of aging, and demographic issues. It then explores how these conditions affect individuals and social institutions. The book concludes with a look at political responses to aging and how individuals can create a better old age for themselves and the people they know.

This edition has made some changes in chapter structure, organization, and content. Chapters 1 and 2 introduce students to the study of aging. Chapter 1 looks at attitudes toward older people. It corrects many of the myths about aging. It also examines the origins of negative attitudes toward older people and ways to change these attitudes. Chapter 2 looks at how best to study aging. It reviews the theories and methods gerontologists use in their research.

Chapter 3, a new chapter on demography, places aging in the United States in a world context. The chapter first reviews aging in underdeveloped, developing, and developed societies. It then presents information about aging in the United States. Chapter 3 looks at the increase in the number and proportion of older people in the U.S. population. This is the foundation for the chapters that follow.

Chapters 4, 5, and 6 discuss how individuals age. Chapter 4 covers the issue of biological aging, its causes, and its effects, including the changes that take place in personal health and illness. This edition reports the increased research on exercise, diet, and new ways to cope with physical change in later life.

Chapter 5 discusses psychological and developmental issues related to aging. This chapter reviews changes in memory and intelligence. This edition reports the latest research on mental potential in later life. Terms in the literature such as *reserve capacity*, *plasticity*, and *adaptability* all describe a new, more positive view of mental ability in old age. Researchers have also begun to explore the effects of training, physical exercise, and creative activity on mental ability. This edition highlights this new thinking about mental ability.

Chapter 6 examines race, ethnicity, and culture. It looks at discrimination and societal barriers to good aging. This chapter looks at many of the challenges that older minority members face throughout their lives. This edition takes a fine-grained look at minority aging. It points out the differences *between* minority groups and the differences *within* minority groups. The Hispanic group of older people, for example, includes people from Mexico, Cuba, Puerto Rico, South America, Spain, and other countries. These people bring different traditions and experiences with them into later life. The same thing applies to older people referred to as Asian. A Chinese elderly woman in San Francisco, whose family arrived here in the 1800s, differs from a Hmong elderly woman who arrived in the United States from Vietnam a few years ago, Both of these women show up as "Asian" in census reports. But their backgrounds lead to very different experiences of aging in the United States.

Chapters 7 through 10 explore current issues related to health care, income security, retirement, and housing. These chapters show that problems related to population aging and to individual aging exist in all these institutions.

Chapter 7 reports on the 2010 federal government health care reform bill, the "Patient Protection and Affordable Care Act." This chapter looks at how this legislation affects health care for older people. Controversy over this legislation continues as this edition goes to print. And some parts of this law may get changed in the years ahead. But this act shows the direction the Obama administration feels health care should take. In particular, this chapter looks at the expansion of the Medicaid program to cover middle class families. The lack of a long-term care system in the United States makes Medicaid (formerly a program for the poor) the only option for many families. This will pose funding problems in the years ahead.

Chapter 8 includes a discussion of funding for the Social Security program. It provides up-to-date information on the current and future solvency of Social Security. (Hint: The program will likely survive and be around for future generations.) The chapter also looks at reform proposals such as private retirement accounts and defined contribution pension plans. These approaches to retirement funding shift the investment risk from the government and corporations to the individual. The chapter looks at recent data on pockets of poverty—minority group members, widows—that exist within the older population. The chapter includes a discussion of the recent economic recession and its effect on older people's incomes.

Chapter 9 reports on the latest trends in workforce participation. Recent data show a reversal in a decades-long trend toward early retirement. A number of social and economic forces, including a drop in stock market values, the recent recession, and longer life expectancy, all encourage people to postpone retirement. The recent recession and corporate closures have also led some older workers to leave the workforce early. The chapter documents the problems older workers have in finding new jobs if they get laid off. The chapter concludes with a discussion of new career options for older workers and retirees.

Chapter 10 looks at some of the latest trends in senior housing. This includes the development of green homes, universal design (to suit people of all ages), and smart homes. This chapter picks up a theme that appears in several earlier chapters—the use of technology to support successful aging. The use of technology in homes includes video monitoring devices, computerized lighting systems, and safety devices like anti-scalding water systems. This chapter reports on the growth of the "Aging Friendly Communities" movement. These communities provide social and health care support to members who otherwise live independently. Technology will also change the way older people drive cars. Auto safety features include video cameras to help people back up and alarms to warn a driver if he or she gets too close to a car in front. Improvements to road signs will make driving safer for older people (and everyone else).

Chapter 11 tracks the growing interest in recreation and education among older people. In particular, studies show a growth in the use of computers among older people. This includes participation in online communities, communication with family and friends, and the use of the Internet for education. Future advances in technology will open new educational opportunities for older people. It will especially benefit homebound older people or those who live at a distance from their families.

Chapters 12 through 13 look at the personal lives of older people. This edition presents separate chapters on family life and social supports. Each of these topics has its own large literature and deserves its own focus. Chapter 12 looks at intimacy and our relationships with those we love. This chapter presents new information on gay couples, widowhood, couples that live apart, and dating. It describes older singles' use of Facebook and Twitter to meet new people. It also looks at grandparenting—an experience common to most older people today. Chapter 13 looks more closely in this edition at the differences between male and female caregivers. It also expands the discussion of caregiver burden.

Chapter 14 raises questions and issues related to the treatment of older people at the end of life. It explores topics such as physician-assisted suicide and prolonging life through technology. This edition looks at how different cultural groups in the United States look at death and dying. This discussion returns to the theme of diversity within the older population. It urges sensitivity to cultural differences around end-of-life care. The chapter also describes new ways to communicate end-of-life preferences.

Chapter 15 provides information on politics and social policy. It deals with the current political system and how it might address the issues raised in earlier chapters. This chapter shows the potential and limits of public response. The chapter also criticizes the "merchants of doom" who predict generational conflict due to population aging. More moderate voices call for intergenerational cooperation and support.

Taken together, these chapters give an overview of aging in American society. This edition traces changes first noted in earlier editions. These include a more positive view of aging, new responses to an aging society, and the entry of new cohorts of people into later life.

Instructors and students who want to keep up with developments in the field of aging can go to the blog I've created for this book. You can find it at **issuesinaging.org.** I am starting this blog because I continue to discover and collect great material for instruction and learning. Through this blog I can share these sources immediately, rather than wait for the next edition of this text.

This blog will provide instructors with new material to use in their courses. It will include new sources of information, links to videos, audio sources, charts, government reports, and so on. This blog will also provide activities for students to try, so they can deepen their knowledge and experience of aging.

ACKNOWLEDGMENTS

Authors often say that a book takes a team effort. It's certainly true for a complex work like this. The team at Pearson has given me support and encouragement from the first day. They also supplied expertise in fields that an author can never master. My colleagues include copyeditors, photo archivists, marketing specialists, and designers. Some of these people I got to know well. Others worked behind the scenes to produce this work. These people have all earned my gratitude and respect. A few people deserve special mention.

First, thanks to Jeff Lasser at Pearson who saw the potential in this book from the start. Thanks also to Karen Hanson, Christine Dore, and Roberta Sherman, who oversaw this third edition. Kristin Landon deserves thanks for her careful copyediting. The errors that remain are my responsibility alone.

Special thanks to an outstanding group of reviewers, including Esther S. Brannon, West Virginia State Community and Technical College; Betty Hicks, Truckee Meadows Community College; Jennifer Keene, University of Nevada, Las Vegas; Naomi Schlagman, State University of New York, Brockport; Mary Francis Stuck, State University of New York, Oswego; Diane Zablotsky, University of North Carolina, Charlotte; Eldon Wegner, University of Hawaii at Manoa; Maria Claver, California State University, Long Beach; and Wei Zhang, University of Hawaii at Manoa.

They spent hours on the review of a text by an anonymous author. This puts the ideal of colleagueship to the test. They passed the test with honors. They raised questions, provided detailed comments, and suggested sources that improved this work. I thank each of them for the time and effort they put into helping me. The students who use this book

will benefit from their advice. I alone take responsibility for the book's shortcomings.

Students in my Sociology of Aging courses told me what they would want to see in a gerontology text. Debra David, a colleague and friend at San Jose State, gave me the opportunity to use material from this text in the classroom. We've had many good conversations about the topics presented here. I appreciate her support and friendship.

I would also like to thank my Canadian colleagues at Nelson/Thomson Canada. I have worked with them on gerontology projects for many years, and they have always given me their support. My colleague and coauthor on other works, Lori Campbell, deserves special thanks. We've worked together on several projects over a number of years. I value her humor, her positive outlook on life, and her good wishes for this project.

The librarians at the Martin Luther King Memorial Library at San Jose State helped me with interlibrary requests and database searches. Dean Ruth Kifer supervises an exceptional staff, who worked hard to get me the resources I needed to complete this text. I thank them all for their support.

Devansh Bavishi, my research assistant, spent many hours tracking down permissions for the text. He's a geology graduate student who now understands what it takes to produce a sociology text. I thank him for his careful work.

A few people serve as my support group every day. Nadia Elliott, my administrative assistant, helped me find time to work on the text. She cleared my calendar and rearranged meetings so I could finish the text as the deadline approached. She relentlessly tracked down obscure permissions. I thank her for her patience and good cheer.

Dr. Steve Zlotolow, associate dean of International and Extended Studies at San Jose State, works in the next office. We interact throughout the day. His frequent "No problem. Everything's gonna be OK" helped me keep focused on this work. Steve often held the wheel of the ship on days when I had to give full attention to completing the text. He's a great colleague, friend, and fellow mountain climber. I appreciate his willingness to help me find time for this work.

My mentor and good friend Hans Mohr inspires all of my work. I can never repay him, only thank him for his support and friendship.

My wife, Mona, helped prepare the study material for students at the end of each chapter. All of this took time from her already busy schedule. Some of this work went late into the night in order to meet publication deadlines. She worked as a colleague and scholar to make this a better book.

My son Daniel assisted at points along the way. He helped gather sources from the library and the Internet and generally encouraged the work. He's the genius behind the blog at issuesinaging.org. He's watched me work on this book for several years. Now he has become a scholar himself and plans an academic career. Someday I may help him with one of his books.

I dedicate this book to my sister Lynne and my mother-in-law Sylvia Kravis. For several years Lynne looked after our mother near the end of her life. I lived half a continent away. She did this while she cared for her own young family. She knows too well the meaning of the term *woman in the middle*. No dedication can fully thank her for her devotion. Let this be a small token of my love and esteem.

My mother-in-law, Sylvia Kravis, now in her late 80s, is a great-grandmother many times over. She still drives her own car, and she recently went on a Hawaiian cruise with one of her granddaughters. She has raised a happy and productive family. A recent photo shows her surrounded by her children, their spouses, her grandchildren, their spouses, and her great-grandchildren. She beams with pride at the camera, her youngest great-grandchild in her lap. She's a role model of successful aging. And I thank her for the support she's given all of us through the years.

SUPPLEMENTS FOR THE INSTRUCTOR

The following supplements are available to qualified instructors who have adopted this textbook.

The Instructor's Manual and Test Bank (ISBN 0205001076): has been prepared to assist teachers in their efforts to prepare lectures and evaluate student learning. For each chapter of the text, the Instructor's Manual offers different types of resources, including detailed chapter summaries and outlines, learning objectives, discussion questions, classroom activities and much more.

Also included in this manual is a test bank offering multiple-choice, true/false, fill-in-the-blank, and/or essay questions for each chapter. The Instructor's Manual and Test Bank is available to adopters at www.pearsonhighered.com.

MyTest (ISBN 020500105X): This computerized software allows instructors to create their own personalized exams, to edit any or all of the existing test questions, and to add new questions. Other special features of this program include random generation of test questions, creation of alternate versions of the same test, scrambling question sequence, and test preview before printing. For easy access, this software is available at www.pearsonhighered.com.

PowerPoint Presentations (ISBN 0205001068): The Lecture PowerPoint slides provide an overview and outline of key topics for each chapter. They are available to adopters at www.pearsonhighered.com.

SUPPLEMENTS FOR THE STUDENT

MySearchLab: **MySearchLab** is a dynamic website that delivers proven results in helping individual students succeed. Its wealth of resources provides engaging experiences that personalize, stimulate, and measure learning for each student. Many accessible tools will encourage students to read their text, improve writing skills, and help them improve their grade in their course.

Features of MySearchLab

Writing—Step by step tutorials present complete overviews of the research and writing process.

Research and citing sources—Instructors and students receive access to the EBSCO ContentSelect database, census data from Social Explorer, Associated Press news feeds, and the Pearson bookshelf. Pearson SourceCheck helps students and instructors monitor originality and avoid plagiarism.

Pearson eText—An e-book version of **Issues in Aging** is included in MySearchLab. Just like the printed text, students can highlight and add their own notes as they read their interactive text online.

Chapter quizzes and flashcards—Chapter and key term reviews are available for each chapter online and offer immediate feedback.

Gradebook—Automated grading of quizzes helps both instructors and students monitor their results throughout the course.

Blog—A blog maintained by the author keeps the text up-to-date with discussions of current issues.

1

AGING TODAY

Jessie Taylor called for a cab and headed downtown for her last appointment of the day. She works for the state office on aging. She monitors nursing-home standards and teaches staff ways to improve patient care. Jessie is 63 years old. She has a pear-shaped figure, a pixie grin, and a mop of gray hair. As she got out of the cab, the driver got out too. He grabbed her elbow, ushered her across the street, and deposited her on the sidewalk. "You can't be too careful crossing the street these days," he said, then smiled and waved good-bye. Jessie says that when she goes to her local supermarket, the checkout clerk often asks other customers to wait a moment while she checks Jessie's things through. Then, one of the workers helps her to her car with her groceries.

All of this used to surprise Jessie. After all, she works at a job like everyone else, drives her own car when she travels out of town, and serves as a leader in her profession. Yet sometimes people treat her like a frail old woman. People see her kind face, gray hair, and wrinkles and they want to help her. They imagine that she needs help doing simple things because of her age. I asked Jessie whether she ever tells people that she doesn't need their help. She said that sometimes she does, but she doesn't want to discourage these people from helping someone in the future, so often she goes along and grins to herself.

Jessie knows that stereotypes can be useful. They help us get along in a complex world where we know only a fraction of the people we see and meet every day. But stereotypes can lead to problems. Jessie sees **stereotyping** every day in her work. She listens as nursing-home aides call patients "dearie" and "sweetie." She watches as workers use baby talk with their adult patients.

Stereotypes can lead us to misjudge people, to treat them inappropriately, and in the case of older people to assume that they need help.[1] Stereotyping can also lead to **prejudice**, a negative attitude toward a person, and to **discrimination**, unfair treatment based on prejudice rather than merit. **Gerontology**, the systematic study of aging, attempts to counteract stereotyping and prejudice. It presents a more balanced view of later life. This chapter looks at (1) the benefits of studying aging, (2) the social basis of age stereotyping, and (3) changes in society that will lead to new images of later life.

WHY STUDY AGING?

Everyone can benefit from the study of aging. First, gerontology can help you understand current social issues. A society with an increasingly older population, for example, will experience changes in **social institutions**. Consider the following changes that will occur in three institutions: the family, the health care system, and recreation programs.

- More people than ever before will live in what some gerontologists call *beanpole families*. These families have three, four, or more generations alive at the same time. Each generation has relatively few members due to smaller numbers of children being born. Older people in these families will live into late old age. Some of them will need caregiving help from their younger family members. Others will live independently or with some formal help in late old age.
- Older people will get more of their health care services in the community. Programs such as visiting nurse services, Meals on Wheels, and foot clinics at senior centers will help keep seniors in their homes longer.

- Older people will take part in more active recreation programs, including fitness programs, adventure travel, and university courses.

These changes will lead to different social service needs, and this will require a shift in economic resources. Should the government give more money to older people? Will this mean less money for other age groups? Will it lead to tensions between the generations? Answers to these questions will shape public policy in the future. The study of aging allows you to understand and respond sensibly to such issues.

The second reason for studying aging is that you might plan to work in a field that serves older people. Students in nursing, social work, or physiotherapy will almost certainly work with older people. Students in recreation studies, architecture, or family studies will also benefit from understanding aging. Even students in business programs need to know about aging. Companies, from banks to restaurants to travel agencies, now see older customers as an important part of their clientele. You will work with older people in almost any field you choose. Knowledge of aging will give you a better understanding of your clients and their needs.

Third, most of us live in families with older members. Your parents and grandparents will soon face many of the issues discussed here. You can help them deal with the issues of later life by studying aging.

Jeanne, a student in one of my classes, used her knowledge of aging to help her grandmother stay involved in family life. She noticed that her grandmother had begun to avoid Sunday family dinners. Jeanne discovered that her mother had told her grandmother not to bother making the potato salad for dinners anymore. Jeanne's mother wanted to make life easier for her grandmother, whose arthritis had gotten worse.

The grandmother felt that she had lost an important role in the family. If she couldn't help cook the family dinner, she decided she wouldn't come at all. Jeanne explained the situation to her mother, and they arranged for Jeanne to work with her grandmother in preparing the potato salad. The grandmother enjoyed teaching Jeanne her recipe, Jeanne got to know her grandmother in a new way, and her grandmother started coming to Sunday dinners again. Greater awareness of aging issues can make you a resource to your community, your family, and yourself.

Most people know something about aging before they study the subject. They know about aging from

---

[1]The terms *old, elderly,* and *aged* in this book refer to people 65 and over unless another age is given. This fits the definition of the elderly used by the U.S. Census Bureau, the Social Security Administration, and many pension plans. Be aware, however, that many differences exist among people in this age group. Older people differ by race, gender, and region of the country. Older people also differ by age. Some older people today were 40 years old when other older people were children. The term *old people* and other related terms refer at best to a typical older person, not all older people.

their personal experiences, from their contact with older people in their families and neighborhoods, and from the media. Still, this gives a limited view of aging, one that sometimes mixes truth with bias and myth. A person who has watched a relative or friend die of Alzheimer's disease, for example, may fear aging. But relatively few people contract this disease. Most older people are healthy into late old age.

Likewise, the media present many negative images of older people. But older people form a diverse group. Some people have problems, while others report high life satisfaction. "Apart from dementia," Zarit says, ". . . older people have lower rates of mental disorders than other adult age groups and generally report higher emotional well-being. . . . This is a finding supported by virtually every epidemiological survey" (2009, pp. 675–676). Zarit concludes that "older people may, in fact, be somewhat better off—happier, less depressed, and even less lonely than the other adult age-groups" (p. 678).

Gerontologists work to replace myths and stereotypes with facts and knowledge. They have conducted many studies that look at current images of aging and attitudes toward old age.

AGEISM

Some years ago Robert Butler (1969) coined the term **ageism** to describe these negative attitudes toward aging. The International Longevity Center (2006, p. 21) defines ageism as "Ideas, attitudes, beliefs, and practices on the part of individuals that are biased against persons or groups based on their older age." Ageism "reflects a deep seated uneasiness on the part of the young and middle-aged—a personal revulsion to and distaste for growing old, disease, disability; and fear of powerlessness, 'uselessness,' and death" (Butler, 1969, p. 243). Palmore (2001) reports that, in one sample of older people, 77% said they had experienced more than one incident of ageism. They most often reported disrespect or the assumption that they had an illness.

Hess (2006, p. 384) reviewed the psychological literature on aging stereotypes. He found that overall "the literature suggests an underlying negative component to most categories of older adults." Laboratory studies of attitudes about aging show a consistent bias against older people (Hummert, Garstka, & O'Brien, 2002). Nosek, Banaji, and Greenwald (2002) compared subjects' attitudes toward race, gender, and age. They found stronger negative associa-

tions with age than with race or gender. They also found that older adults showed just as strong an age bias as did younger adults.

Older people may even try to distance themselves from being old. Cohen (2001) says that some older adults buy into the negative stereotypes, reject aging, and try to stay middle-aged forever. Nancy Perry Graham (2010, p. 4), editor of *AARP—The Magazine*, tells the following story. She and fellow editors attended a Bruce Springsteen concert in New Jersey in October 2009. A woman approached them and asked, "Why would you wear an AARP [American Association of Retired Persons] T-shirt to a Springsteen concert?" Graham explained that she worked for AARP and that, by the way, Springsteen himself was 60 years old. The woman took this in, then asked, "But why would you want people to know you're *old?*" Graham says this response would make sense from a teenaged Springsteen fan. But this woman was in her 60s. Graham says a friend of hers calls this attitude "chronological racism."

A national study of perceptions of aging in the United States found that fewer than half of older people reported "very serious" or "somewhat serious" problems with health, crime, income, and loneliness. But this same group of older people thought that nearly all older people had "very serious" or "somewhat serious" health, safety, income, or relationship problems (Cutler, Whitelaw, & Beattie, 2002) (see Table 1.1).

Some older people, for example, refuse to use bus passes that give discounts to seniors. They would rather pay the higher fares than admit their age. A 72-year-old man I met on a bus told me he was going to visit the "old folks" at a local nursing home. He does not see himself as an old person. Most people, it seems, feel that "old" is 5 years older than they are.

Some years ago, Kalish (1979) and Estes (1979) described a **new ageism**. This refers to the desire to help older people who need special treatment due to poor health, poverty, or lack of social supports. Although this positive form of ageism tries to do good, it supports the stereotype of old age as a time of decline and loss. Binstock (1983, 2005a) calls this a **compassionate stereotype** or compassionate ageism. This stereotype attempts to create sympathy for older people, but it doesn't give a true picture of later life.

Estes found that a federal bureaucracy to care for older people, what she calls the **aging enterprise**, grew out of compassionate stereotyping. Supporters

TABLE 1.1 "Very Serious" or "Somewhat Serious" Problems Facing Older People, 2000: A Survey of American Older People

	A Problem for Me (%)		A Problem for Other Older People (%)	
	1974	*2000*	*1974*	*2000*
Health	54	42	96	92
Fear of crime	50	36	84	82
Not having enough money to live on	46	36	92	88
Loneliness	36	21	94	84

This nationwide study found that, compared with 1974, in 2000, a smaller proportion of older people reported very or somewhat serious problems. Older people's subjective sense of well-being improved over the 25 years. But older people's view of other older people stayed roughly the same. Older people continue to think that nearly all other people their age suffer from health, crime, money, and personal relationship problems. Older people have a stereotyped view of other older people. Further analysis of the data in this study showed that middle-aged people (ages 35 to 53) had an even more negative view of older people. More than 90% of the Baby Boom group thought that older people today had serious problems with the items on this list.

How do your friends feel about aging? How do you think they would answer if asked about the "very serious" or "somewhat serious" problems that older people face?

Source: Adapted from N. E. Cutler, N. A. Whitelaw, & B. L. Beattie, *American Perceptions of Aging in the 21st Century: A Myths and Realities of Aging Chartbook* (Washington, DC: National Council on the Aging, 2002), Figure 1–1, p. 2, and Figure 1–2, p. 4. Used with permission of the National Council on the Aging.

of older people created the stereotype of older people as poor, frail, and dependent. This image created sympathy for older people and led to programs such as **Medicare,** the **Older Americans Act,** and improved **Social Security**. These programs did improve older people's lives, but they also set the stage for the current round of **scapegoating**.

People now question whether the old deserve such apparently lavish treatment. Some policy analysts and the press declare that older people have plenty of money and political power and they cost too much to care for. Stereotyping, whether negative or compassionate, in the end decreases public support for the older person who really needs help.

CULTURE AS A SOURCE OF AGEISM

At a conference a few years ago, a sales representative gave me a page of comments about getting older. The page had his name and phone number in the outside margins. I suppose he thought that people would pass this page along to colleagues. They would share this

bit of humor and his name as well. The page said:

You know you're getting old when . . .

- Everything hurts and what doesn't hurt doesn't work.
- Your pacemaker makes the garage door go up every time a pretty girl walks by.
- Your back goes out more often than you do.
- The last time you helped a little old lady across the street it was your wife.

I've read these lines to many audiences and classes of students, and people find them funny. But at the risk of ruining the fun, I suggest that all of these jokes foster ageism. For one thing, they all make older people seem physically and psychologically weak. They also make older people seem less able to do things or imply that they cannot control their bodily functions.

The man who gave me this list saw no harm in the humor, and since then I have received copies of this list from other sources. One copy of this list appeared in *Reader's Digest*. Imagine that a similar list had a racial or ethnic bias. Would you pass it along to your customers or show it to your professor? Would it be published in a national magazine? Few people see these jokes as ageist at first. All of us have grown up with the stereotype of older people as run-down and decrepit. Jokes like these and many other sources in our culture support ageist beliefs.

Great writings from the past, for example, present ageist images of older people. Aristotle's (1941, Bk. II: Ch. 13, pp. 1405–1406) image of aging shows many of the biases people express today. Old men, he says,

are sure about nothing and under-do everything. . . . They are small-minded, because they have been humbled by life: their desires are set upon nothing more exalted or unusual than what will help them to keep alive. . . . They live by memory rather than by hope. . . . This, again, is the cause of their loquacity; they are continually talking of the past, because they enjoy remembering it. . . . Their sensual passions have either altogether gone or have lost their vigour.

Machiavelli presents the old man in his play *La Clizia* as a lecher. Shakespeare, at the start of *King Lear*, presents the king as a fool. Children's stories throughout history feature rag men, bogeymen, and wicked witches, all caricatures of old people. Montepare and Zebrowitc (2002) report that children get exposure to attitudes and views of aging and older people in preschool. Psychologist Becca Levy (2003, cited in Dittmann, 2003; also Calasanti, 2006) reports, "Age stereotypes are often internalized at a young age—long before they are even relevant to people," and early attitudes tend to be reinforced over their lifetimes.

BOX 1.1
WHAT'S IN A NAME?

Every group has its preferred name for itself. Do we call someone an American Indian, an Aboriginal Person, a Native American? Groups generally adopt and promote a term that presents them in a positive way. However, no acceptable term has evolved to refer to the older population, and anyone who writes about older people or speaks to groups about aging faces a dilemma. What should we call people age 65 and over?

I have not found a term that all the older people I meet will accept. This poses a dilemma for someone who needs to write about older people as a group.

Canadians, for example, feel comfortable with the term *seniors*, as in "senior centre." But in the United States, senior center directors want to find a new term for

their organizations. They feel that the word *senior* turns off new generations of older people. Likewise, terms such as *Gruppies* (Graying Urban Professionals) seem silly. Beck (1990b) reports on several other options: "Whoopies (Well-Heeled Older People), OPALS (Older Persons with Active Lifestyles) and Grumpies (Grown-up Mature People)." None of these has caught on.

"The real problem," Beck (1990b) says, "is that any term associated with *old* is still considered derogatory." And until we tackle and overcome our societal rejection of aging, someone will be offended no matter what term we choose.

If you know some older people, ask them what term they use to describe their age group.

The Media as a Source of Ageism

The media provide more up-to-date examples of ageist treatment. The cartoon show *The Simpsons* depicts Grandpa Simpson as ignorant, forgetful, and timid. In one episode he and his nursing-home friends break out of the home to freedom. They make it to the sidewalk, look around, get scared, and shuffle back inside.

Studies of prime-time television shows, television commercials, and children's shows have generally found that television underrepresents older people (Signorielli, 2001). Donlon, Ashman, and Levy (2005) found that fewer than 2% of prime time TV characters were age 65 years or older (though the older population makes up nearly 13% of American society). Studies of television commercials also find an underrepresentation of older people in advertisements (Miller, Levell, & Mazachek, 2004). When television does portray older people, as in commercials, it often puts them in stereotyped roles.

In 2003, the Screen Actors Guild (SAG) reported that only 27% of all women's roles on prime-time television went to women over age 40, and they were typically cast as victims: betrayed, abandoned, and abused. The SAG also reported that more than twice as many roles are available for actors under the age of 40 as for actors older than 40 (International Longevity Center, 2006). Older people express concern about these negative stereotypes (Robinson, Popovich, Gustafson, & Fraser, 2003).

Levitt and Dubner (2005, p. 79), in their book *Freakonomics,* describe a TV show called *The Weakest Link.*

On this show, contestants vote to eliminate other players. In the early rounds, weak players are eliminated because they lack the information needed to help the others succeed. In the later rounds, players are eliminated if they know too much because they increase the competition. Levitt and Dubner found that "elderly players [on the show] . . . are victims of taste-based discrimination: in the early rounds *and* late rounds, they are eliminated far out of proportion to their skills. It seems as if the other contestants—this is a show on which the average age is thirty-four—simply don't want the older players around."

Most studies show that the print media also underrepresent older people. A study of pictures in magazines and newspapers in the United Kingdom (Whitfield, 2001), for example, found that they included relatively few pictures of older people. Older people make up 16% of that society. But pictures of older people made up 3% or fewer of pictures in newspapers and magazines. The study found that even magazines for seniors showed relatively few pictures of older people.

De Luce (2001, p. 40) reviewed advertising and articles in 31 American popular magazines, including *Time* and *Newsweek*. She found that a number of magazines (e.g., *The New Yorker* and *The New York Times Magazine*) had no ads targeted at people age 50 and over. Nineteen publications in her study had only one to five ads targeted to older people. De Luce says that these findings reveal the "invisibility" of older consumers. Ads that did have older people in them included ads for cancer survivors, for sufferers of memory loss and for loss of sexual vigor.

A study titled *Ageism in America* (International Longevity Center, 2006, p. 55) reports that the TV show *Murder She Wrote* "starred the legendary stage and film actress Angela Lansbury. Having run successfully for ten years, the show was canceled at the height of its popularity because the audience was deemed too old and therefore the time sold not sufficiently profitable."

Krueger (2001) says that only about 50 newspapers in the United States have a reporter dedicated to reporting on aging issues. He says that the lack of stories on older adults supports stereotyping. It also limits the amount of useful information that the public needs to understand aging. Kleyman (2002) says that, even though few newspapers put resources into reporting on aging, the topic will grow in interest. The aging of the Baby Boom generation, the aging of senior news managers, and a growing interest in topics related to aging will lead to more stories on older people.

Studies have found signs of ageism in magazine articles (Whitfield, 2001), country music (Aday & Austin, 2000), and jokes. Bowd (2003) reviewed 4,200 jokes and found eight categories of negative stereotypes, including the impotent male, the unattractive female, the sick older person, and the forgetful older person.

Thornton and Light (2006, p. 276) describe the use of **elderspeak** and its effect on older people. Elderspeak refers to "a specialized speech register resembling baby talk in addressing older adults." This form of speech uses fewer clauses, shorter phrases, more filler phrases (e.g., *like* or *you know*), words with fewer syllables, slower speech, and longer pauses. In other words, elderspeak sounds like baby talk. It also includes the use of words such as *dearie, cutie,* and *sweetie.* Institutional workers may use words like these to address residents (for example, "Good morning, dearie, it's time for breakfast") (Hess, 2006). Thornton and Light say that stereotyping drives elderspeak. The speaker assumes that the older person has low mental ability or some other impairment.

Elderspeak has a negative effect on the older person. It creates low self-esteem, it reduces a person's ability to communicate effectively, it decreases the quality of interaction, and it reduces the older person's sense of control (Thornton & Light, 2006).

Ageism even influences retail sales. One student, as part of an assignment to study ageism, entered a women's clothing store with her mother and grandmother.

The store sold moderately priced clothes for women of all ages. The three women walked around the store separately to see whom the sales staff would approach first. The staff approached the student first to offer help and the grandmother last.

Ruth Reichl, former *New York Times* food critic, conducted a similar experiment. She went to lunch at Tavern on the Green in New York with two older women. One was an acting coach, the other a wealthy older woman dressed in cashmere and fur. Reichl dressed in disguise for the lunch in order to remain anonymous to the restaurant staff. She wore the clothes and took on the personality of a poor old woman.

She reports that the waiters either ignored their table or appeared impatient when serving them. Their table seemed to get slower service than others. Reichl writes,

> The service was so slow that after a great deal of small talk and five pots of tea, I felt compelled to apologize. "I always seem to get bad service," I told Helen [the wealthy woman]. "I don't know why." "Well, I do," she [Helen] snapped. "You look like an old lady. And waiters consider old ladies their natural enemies. They think that they will complain constantly, order the cheapest dishes on the menu, and leave a six percent tip. I have found that it is essential to appear prosperous when going out to eat." (Reichl, 2005, pp. 211–212, 215)

Obvious poverty or low income compounds the ageism that an older person faces. In her disguise as an old and poor woman, Reichl became invisible. "As I walked up Riverside Drive," she says, "not one of the many people walking dogs, wheeling strollers, or carrying briefcases glanced my way. No doorman tipped his hat as I went by. By the time I got to the corner, I felt as insubstantial as the wind; when people looked my way they saw only the buildings at my back. When I waved my hand the taxis hurtled past as if I were not there. I finally resorted to stepping into the middle of the street."

When she finally got a cab, the driver hit the gas so hard it threw her against the back of the seat. When she protested and asked him to slow down, he ignored her. "Perhaps it was how he always drove," she says, "but it made me feel like an old boot, a piece of junk that he was desperate to deposit at its destination."

Reichl experienced a sudden entry into the world of an older person. But many older people experience ageism daily.

One woman, in a study of attitudes toward older people, said, "Salespersons can be impatient if you are choosing something and are not swift enough." Another woman said, "Salespeople will talk to me rather than to my mother who is 85" (National Advisory

---

BOX 1.2
DISGUISED
The Story of Patricia Moore: A Woman Who Disguised Herself as Old

How does it feel to be an older person? Most of us will have to wait many years to find out, but knowing what it feels like might give us each new insights into aging. Patricia Moore, a 26-year-old industrial designer at the time, decided to turn herself into an 85-year-old woman.

Her journey into old age began with a custom-made latex mask and a white wig. She dressed the part with her mother's purse, canvas shoes, and a cane. She wore bandages on her legs, support stockings, and a cinch to flatten her chest. Old glasses and a pillbox hat completed the disguise.

Pat put her disguise on almost every week for 3 years. She played the role of an old woman in 116 cities in 14 states and 2 provinces in Canada. She says that geography made little difference in how people treated her as an older person. Some people offered her help and treated her kindly. Other people ignored her. Sometimes she faced overt ageism.

Pat gave up her disguise after 3 years, but not before she got mugged, met poor and abused older people, and also met kind strangers who helped her on her way. She counts older people among the kindest strangers she met during her time as an old woman.

Does Pat Moore, the young one with the smooth skin and the pretty eyes, ever miss the "old lady"?

"Oh, I miss her," Pat answers without hesitation. "She was a good friend. We meant a great deal to each other, but for now we've said good-bye.

"It's not a sad parting, though," she adds with a mischievous smile, "I expect to see her again—in the mirror—in about 50 years!"

Below, you can see how Pat looked in and out of her disguise at the time.

Pat Moore in her disguise as an old woman and as she looks today.

Source: Patricia Moore, *DISGUISED—The Story of Patricia Moore: A Woman Who Disguised Herself as Old.* Used with permission.

Council on Aging, 1993, p. 20). Ageism negatively affects older people's self-images and lowers their status in society. It makes everyday life less pleasant and in some cases more difficult.

Writer Malcolm Cowley (1980) describes the effects of ageism on his self-image. "We start by growing old in other people's eyes," he says, "then slowly we come to share their judgment." He recalls the time he backed out of a parking lot and nearly collided with another car. The driver got out, ready to fight. "Why, you're an old man," he said after seeing Cowley. Then he got back in his car and drove away. Cowley bristles when he remembers the event.

Some years later, he says, "a young woman rose and offered me her seat in a Madison Avenue bus. That message was kind and also devastating. 'Can't I even stand up?' I thought as I thanked her and declined the seat. But the same thing happened twice the following year, and the second time I gratefully accepted the offer, though with a sense of having diminished myself. 'People are right about me,' I thought. . . . All the same it was a relief to sit down and relax" (Cowley, 1980, pp. 5–6).

Gladwell (2005) shows that exposure to negative views of aging can have a subtler—but no less damaging—effect on the person. One psychology experiment gave subjects five scrambled words and asked them to make a four-word sentence—for example, "shoes give replace old the." (Replace the old shoes.) The study asked subjects to complete 10 of these sentences. Most people found the job easy and completed all 10 sentences. But, Gladwell says, "After you finished that test—believe it or not—you would have walked out of my office and back down the hall more slowly than you walked in" (p. 53). Why? Because the researchers included in the sentences words that referred to aging—*old, lonely, wrinkle*, etc.

Gladwell says that in this study, subjects' unconscious minds began to think about old age. As a result, their bodies responded as if they had aged. Their minds, he says, "took all this talk of old age so seriously that by the time [they] finished and walked down the corridor, [they] acted old. [They] walked slowly" (p. 53). In other words, in this study mere exposure to words related to aging had a subliminal effect. It led to stereotypical negative behavior.

Lack of Knowledge as a Source of Ageism

Some of what looks like ageism comes from ignorance. Few people know much about aging today except what they see and hear in the media and popular culture. Gerontologist Erdman Palmore (1977) created a Facts on Aging Quiz (FAQ) to explore people's knowledge about aging. Palmore designed the quiz to test physical, mental, and social knowledge as well as common misconceptions about old age. The FAQ has led to a small explosion of studies as researchers from around the world criticized, validated, and modified the original quiz (Palmore, 1998; Pennington,

Pachana, & Cole, 2001; Seufert & Carrozza, 2002).

Palmore himself published Part Two of the quiz in 1981. He later developed a multiple-choice quiz (Harris, Changas, & Palmore, 1996). Here is a brief FAQ that draws on Palmore's quizzes.[2] Read the questions and answer them either true or false.

1. All five senses tend to decline in old age.
2. Over 20% of the U.S. population is now age 65 or over.
3. The life expectancy of African Americans at age 75 is about the same as that of whites.
4. The majority of older people have incomes below the poverty level (as defined by the federal government).
5. Older workers have fewer accidents than younger workers.
6. People tend to become more religious as they age.
7. Lung capacity tends to decline in old age.
8. At least 10% of the aged are living in long-stay institutions (i.e., nursing homes, mental hospitals, homes for the aged).
9. Over three fourths of older people can carry out their daily activities without help.
10. The aged have higher rates of criminal victimization than persons under age 65.

How did you score? (The answers appear on page 9.)

Palmore (1998, p. 43) reports a "most disturbing general finding" from the use of the FAQs. "Most people know little about aging and have many misconceptions . . . the average person appears to have almost as many misconceptions about aging as correct conceptions." He found that people scored better on some questions than on others. The questions most often missed included the proportion of older people in long-term stay institutions, the older person's inability to change, and the proportion of older people below the poverty line.

A study by the AARP (formerly the American Association of Retired Persons) and the University of Southern California (2004) found similar results. This national study of almost 1,500 Americans found that people answered about half the items on a 25-point quiz correctly. Sixty-four percent of respondents mistakenly thought that a majority of older people lived in poverty, 73% percent mistakenly thought older people were lonely, and 85% mistakenly thought that 10% of older people live in nursing homes.

---

[2]*Source:* Adapted from Palmore, E. B. 1977. Facts on Aging: A short quiz. *The Gerontologist, 17,* 315–320; and Palmore, E. B. 1981. The Facts on Aging Quiz: Part two. *The Gerontologist, 21,* 431–437.

Palmore (1998) found that test takers tended to assume a negative view of older people. He also found that even people with expertise in aging missed many of the FAQ questions. Graduate students and professionals who worked with older people missed about one third of the true/false questions. Gerontology students and faculty members missed from 10% to 30% of the items. These findings suggest that most people have an uneven knowledge about aging. In general, people seemed to have more knowledge of physical changes that come with age and less knowledge of social facts about aging.

Both the Palmore research and the study by the AARP and University of Southern California show that the most frequent misconceptions about aging come from negative views of old age. Palmore found that people with more education scored better on the FAQ. People with a high school education averaged between 52% and 60% correct, undergraduates averaged between 55% and 69%, graduate students scored 65% to 76% correct, and gerontology students and faculty scored 66% to 92% correct. Finally, specialists in the field of aging scored 90% or better (Palmore, 1998).

Hess (2006) reviewed the research on attitudes toward older people. He found that people with more knowledge about aging had a more positive view of later life. They could see things from the perspective of the older person. Also, people who had personal contact with older adults tend to stereotype less. Negative stereotypes come into play most often when we know little about a person or group (Funderburk, Damron-Rodriguez, Storms, & Solomon, 2006).

BOX 1.3
TO DYE OR NOT TO DYE: THAT IS THE QUESTION

"I had light streaks put in my dark hair when I was younger," Genie says. "Now I do the opposite. I have dark streaks put in my gray hair.

"As I got older," she says, "I had my hair colored its original black. I had it done every 3 or 4 weeks. It cost a fortune. But I made it part of my budget. Had to have it done. I couldn't stop. If I stopped, I'd have a line across my head where the gray would grow in and where the black color stopped."

"Then I got sick and they shaved my head. That was my opportunity. I stopped coloring my hair. I let it go silver. But one day I looked in the mirror and I thought, 'Gosh, she looks old.' So I started again, but this time with dark highlights in the gray."

Genie faced the dilemma that many women (and men) face as they age—to dye or not to dye. In a society that idolizes youth, gray hair marks a person as old and less desirable. Hair dye covers one sign of aging and allows a person to appear more youthful.

Anne Kreamer (2007) reports that a Procter & Gamble survey found that 65% of women dyed their hair in 2004—many times the proportion in the 1950s. This, Kreamer (p. 72) says, "is why going gray has become a difficult . . . choice for modern women to make." A gray-haired older woman now stands out from her age group.

A 2007 *Time* magazine poll asked people whether they thought gray hair is an advantage or disadvantage today. Nearly four fifths of respondents (79%) thought gray hair disadvantaged a person in personal or social life, and 67% thought it disadvantaged a person in the workplace.

Nora Ephron (2006), in her book *I Feel Bad About My Neck*, says, "There's a reason why forty, fifty, and sixty don't look the way they used to, and it's not because of feminism or better living through exercise. It's because of hair dye. . . . Hair dye has changed everything, but it almost never gets the credit. It's the most powerful weapon older women have against the youth culture" (p. 36).

The new role of women in the workplace plays some role in women's decisions to dye their hair. The workplace values a youthful look, and women may feel pressured by social attitudes to use hair color. But this poses a dilemma. The independent working woman represents a liberation from the past definitions of femininity.

The women's liberation movement promised freedom from narrow (male-dominated) views of female beauty. A woman who dyes her hair to appear younger seems to give in to the stereotypical images of youth and beauty that women wanted to escape.

Will new generations of women, the Baby Boomers, continue to dye their hair? Boomers created the "do your own thing" ethic of the 1960s. Will they reject social convention and stop coloring their hair as they enter the third age? Will Boomers let their inner gray show?

What do you think about the tendency of women (and some men) to color their hair? Should people dye their hair as they age in order to look younger? Or should they allow their gray hair to show? Does hair coloring give in to societal ageism? Does it encourage the continuation of negative attitudes toward getting older?

Note: Answers to the FAQ on p.8: Odd numbered items are true. Even numbered items are false.

SOME FACTS ON AGING TODAY

Consider some of the correct answers to questions on the FAQ. You will find more details on these questions and the other questions on the FAQ in later chapters. For now, consider the facts presented here and think about why people might have missed these items.

True or False: Over 20% of the U.S. population is now age 65 or over.

False. The proportion of older people in the United States has grown over the past 100 years. In 1900, about 4% of the population was age 65 or over. By 2010, the proportion of older people had more than tripled to 12.97% (U.S. Census Bureau, 2008b). The proportion of older people in the population will continue to grow. By the year 2050, when the last Baby Boomers reach late old age, the U.S. Census Bureau projects that older people will make up 20.17% of the population. This aging of the population will transform U.S. society. It will transform policies and programs for older people, open new opportunities for people of all ages, and change our views of later life.

True or False: The majority of older people have incomes below the poverty level (as defined by the federal government).

False. In 2007, 9.7% of people age 65 and over had incomes below the government's poverty line (U.S. Census Bureau, 2010a). This proportion has dropped from the early 1960s, when more than 30% of older people had incomes below the poverty line. Older people today get more of their income from work or pensions than in the past.

In addition, a number of government programs provide a stronger economic safety net than ever before. This net consists of improved Social Security benefits, yearly cost-of-living increases in Social Security, and a Supplemental Security Income program. Some groups of older people still suffer from high rates of poverty, as we will see. But Schulz (2001, p. 2) concludes that overall, "older people today are *economically much better off than they were a little more than two decades ago*" [emphasis in the original].

True or False: At least 10% of the aged are living in long-stay institutions (i.e., nursing homes, mental hospitals, or homes for the aged).

False. On any given day, about 5% of people age 65 and over live in an institution. Some will stay for a short time and return to their homes. Most older people today and in the future will live on their own or with family members in the community. Most have reasonably good health and manage to care for themselves.

Those older people who have physical problems and need help often use community care programs that range from Meals on Wheels to visiting nurse services. Older people who need help rely mostly on family and friends. People who live in institutions, in most cases, are very old, have poor health, and have few informal supports to help them stay in the community.

True or False: The life expectancy of African Americans at age 75 is significantly less than that of whites.

False. African Americans, compared to whites, have a lower **life expectancy** at birth. An African American child born in 2005 could expect to live to age 73.2. A white child born in that year could expect to live to age 78.3. These figures mean a difference of 5.3 fewer years of life expectancy for the African American child.

But this question asks about life expectancy at age 75. In 2002, the life expectancy for African American men and women at age 75 was 86.4 years. The life expectancy for white men and women age 75 in that year was 86.9 years, a difference of only half a year or about the same (National Center for Health Statistics, 2009). These figures show the effects of high African American **mortality** in childhood and young adulthood. Poverty, poor health care, and unhealthy living conditions put many African American infants and children at greater risk than whites. Once African Americans reach age 75, they have survived most of these harsh conditions.

True or False: Compared to people under age 65, the aged have higher rates of criminal victimization.

False. Older people have the lowest rates of criminal victimization across all crime categories. (See Table 1.2.) Older people, compared with younger people, have a much lower risk of violent crime or property crime. In addition, rates have fallen by one third since the 1970s (Federal Interagency, 2004). However, older people do have a high risk for certain types of crimes—for example, larceny with personal contact, such as purse snatching and pocket picking. Older people show some of the highest rates for these types of crimes in urban settings.

Doyle (1990) used an opportunity framework to explain patterns of crime against older people. *Opportunity* refers to the attractiveness of a target, the exposure of the target, and the guardianship or protection of the target. Older people have less exposure to criminals. They tend to stay at home at night and to live in relatively safe neighborhoods. Retired people spend

TABLE 1.2 Estimated Personal Violent Victimization Rates by Type of Victimization at Selected Ages, per 1,000 persons, United States, 2009

Age	Total	Rape/Sexual Assault	Robbery	Aggravated Assault	Simple Assault
12–15	36.8	0.9*	3.1	6.9	25.9
16–19	30.3	0.6*	5.2	5.3	19.3
20–24	28.1	0.8*	3.5	7.5	16.3
25–34	21.5	0.8*	2.8	4.5	13.4
35–49	16.1	0.4*	2.0	2.6	11.1
50–64	10.7	0.3*	1.1	1.9	7.5
65+	3.2	0.2*	0.4*	0.3*	2.2

*Based on 10 or fewer cases.

This table shows the decrease in violent criminal victimization that takes place from middle-age onward. Older people show extremely low rates of violent victimization. Except in the case of simple assault (e.g. purse snatching) data show less than 10 cases per 1,000 older people.

Source: Adapted from Truman, J. L., and Rand, M. R. (2010). *Criminal victimization, 2009. National Crime Victimization Survey.* Washington, DC: U.S. Department of Justice. Office of Justice Programs. Bureau of Justice Statistics. Table 5. Retrieved October 19, 2010, from http://bjs.ojp.usdoj.gov/content/pub/pdf/cv09.pdf

more time at home and so protect their property more. At the same time, they do offer an attractive target for purse snatchers and pickpockets on the street.

Other studies support this framework. Many minority older people live in high-crime neighborhoods and have more exposure to criminals. African American men, for example, show high rates of assault and intimidation against them. Older men in these neighborhoods may look like easy targets to criminals.

Victimization by Fraud

Older people seem more susceptible to certain types of crime than others. Con artists and swindlers, for example, tend to target this population. Older people have savings that make them attractive targets. They also may have fewer social supports to help them steer clear of bogus deals such as home repair and medical and insurance scams.

Cons and swindles take many forms. Con artists often use the "bank examiner" swindle on older people. In that case, a con artist calls an older person, often a woman who lives alone, and says that someone is embezzling money from her bank. The caller asks if she will help catch the thief. The caller tells her to withdraw money from her account and give the money to a bank messenger who will arrive at her door. The caller explains that the messenger will take the money back to the bank. The bank will then check the serial numbers and catch the crooked teller. The messenger, of course, works for the con artist and gets away with the money.

"'Once you hand over your money, there is no recovery,' says Melvin L. Jeter, southern regional security director for NationsBank. 'There's no way any money's going to get back'" (McLeod, 1995, p. 14).

Home repair con artists also target older people. They look for homes that need repairs—loose shingles or a broken eaves trough. The swindler then knocks on the older person's door and offers to estimate the cost of repairs. He or she gives a low estimate and says that the older person will have to pay for the work right away to get this deal. The con artist usually asks for cash payment before any work gets done.

Some crooks even drive the older person to the bank to withdraw the money. Once the swindler has the money, the work may never get done, or it is done poorly with cheap materials. Con artists of this type may come back again and again to do more repairs. They may even try to borrow money from the older person once they have a relationship.

No exact figures exist on the cost of fraud to older people. But a report from the City and County of Denver, Colorado, gives some idea of the losses older people face. One criminal case filed with the Denver District Attorney's Economic Crime Unit found that older victims lost $20 million to fraud. In another case, an investment advisor swindled older clients out of $17 million. In still another case, a probate attorney stole more than $3.5 million from older people or their estates (Curtis, 2006).

Swindlers have increased their use of technology to bilk older people. *Slamming*, for example, switches a person's phone to another provider without the owner's permission. *Cramming* occurs when a person gets charged for phone services that he or she never ordered. Money offers from Nigerian sources often come as email messages. They promise to transfer funds to a person's bank account. The victim will supposedly receive part of these funds as a reward for helping with the transfer. But after the person has agreed to help, further letters demand money for transfer fees and other expenses. The victim never receives the promised funds or any reward.

These and other electronic schemes use technology to play on a person's ignorance or greed. Older people who have little experience with electronic media serve as easy targets for thieves. Greisman (2005), in a presentation on behalf of the Federal Trade Commission, estimated that Internet auction scams, identity theft, and lottery, prize, and sweepstakes scams cost older Americans $152 million in 2004. The FTC estimates that Internet scams account for about two fifths of fraud complaints. The Federal Trade Commission (2010) and the FBI (2010) provide fraud prevention information on their websites.

Effects of Victimization

Barbara Barer, an anthropologist at the University of California, San Francisco, found that fraud can lower an older person's self-image. She reports the case of a 96-year-old woman cheated out of money for an emergency alert system. The woman felt so embarrassed about losing the money that she never reported the crime. She felt that if her friends or family knew, they might question her competence.

Barer says that older people also feel that if they report crimes, they may face further victimization. One man arranged for car repairs with a neighbor. The neighbor never did the repairs. The man feared that the neighbor's children would smash his car windows and slash his tires if he reported the crime.

Barer says that crimes like these against older people can lead to feelings of inferiority and loss of self-esteem. Crimes against very old people can lead to a loss of independence and possibly institutionalization. Barer says that with most crimes, society sees the criminal at fault, but "when a crime is committed against an elderly individual, the victim is implicated for being at fault for allowing it to happen. The mistake is unforgivable. Thus it is preferable to conceal the shame" (Unreported Crime, 1994, p. 4).

The AARP (1999) conducted a study of consumers age 18 and over. The study found that compared with younger people, older people were more vulnerable to unfair or deceptive business practices. The oldest age group, age 75 and over, had the highest proportion of vulnerable people. Older people with low education

levels and low incomes had the highest rates of vulnerability. These people also can least afford the cost of unfair business practices.

Older people, compared with younger people, had less knowledge of consumer rights. Younger people, compared with older people, tended to take a less trusting attitude toward businesses. These differences between older and younger consumers make older people more susceptible to con artists. Police often have special pamphlets prepared to alert older people to schemes directed at them. Twenty states share information to foil fraud schemes. Other states sponsor consumer hotlines for older people, train police, and scan junk mail for current scams.

Fear of Crime

A national study in 2000 by the National Council on Aging (Cutler et al., 2002) found that 36% of older people felt that fear of crime was a "very" or "somewhat" serious problem for them. This figure dropped from 50% in 1974. But it still means that more than one older person in three considers crime a serious problem. Also, specific groups may fear crime more than others. Acierno and Kilpatrick (2004) asked 106 adults age 55 and over about their fear of crime. The researchers found that women, visible minority group members, people who felt depressed, and socially isolated people reported the most fear of crime.

Some fear of crime may have a sound basis. Older people who live in urban areas with high crime rates, for example, report a greater fear of crime than those in rural areas. They do in fact face a greater risk of victimization than suburban older people. Likewise, older people may fear crime because a purse snatching can lead to personal injury. Older people who live on fixed incomes may fear the effects of petty theft on their ability to pay their bills. The topics of fear of crime and ways to reduce this fear need more careful study.

Ageism and the Workplace

The U.S. Age Discrimination in Employment Act (ADEA) prohibits mandatory retirement at any age (except in cases where age influences ability). Congress (29 U.S.C. 621(b)—1967, cited in McCann & Ventrell-Monses, 2010) enacted the ADEA "to promote the employment of older persons based on their ability rather than age; [and] to prohibit arbitrary age discrimination in employment." The act attempts to reduce discrimination against older workers.

But researchers have a hard time judging the success of this legislation or the extent of discrimination. Employers who discriminate on the basis of age cannot admit it for fear of legal action. Schulz and Binstock (2006, p. 158) say that the law has driven most discrimination "underground." McCann and Ventrell-Monses (2010, p. 356) say that "more than 40 years after the ADEA's enactment, age discrimination continues to impede the achievement of equal treatment for older persons in the workplace."

The number of formal complaints lodged by workers gives a glimpse of the problem. Older workers filed 19,103 discrimination complaints with the Equal Employment Opportunity Commission (EEOC) in 2007. This figure increased by 29% to 24,582 in 2008—the highest figure in 15 years. The economic recession and layoffs in 2008 in part accounts for this spike in complaints (Levitz & Shishkin, 2009).

An AARP study (Groeneman, 2006) found that 60% of workers age 45 and over believe that age discrimination exists in the workplace. Among this group, 95% think it is "very common" or "somewhat common." A majority of this group felt that age discrimination began after age 50. One worker told the Conference Board (Parkinson, 2002, pp. 17, 33), "After about (age) 45, the company does not continue to recognize one's contribution, and further advancement is denied if one is not already at the VP level." Another worker said, "All meaningful assignments or other opportunities are given to employees who are the same age as, or younger than, the boss—who is most often in his or her 40s."

"I do not expect to retire for approximately 6 years," one worker said. But his supervisor denied him opportunities for advancement due to his age. Haralson and Parker (2003) found that 63% of job seekers said they would leave dates off their resumes to hide their age.

Even before the recent recession, middle-aged workers worried about age discrimination at work. In an AARP (2008a) study 60% of workers age 45–74 said they believe age discrimination exists in the workplace. Of those who believed age discrimination exists at work, nearly all (90%) consider it very common or somewhat common. Most of them felt that age discrimination begins at age 50. Thirteen percent of workers in this study said they experienced some form of age discrimination during the past 5 years. This included not getting hired, being passed over for promotion, being denied access to training, or being passed up for a raise.

Another survey by the AARP (2007b, p. 59) found that, compared to younger workers, workers age 50 and over had much less confidence in their ability to find a job. "Age discrimination," the report says, "is viewed as the single largest barrier to finding jobs for workers over age 50."

A Merrill Lynch (2006) survey supports these findings. The study found that only 25% of people age 60 and over who wanted to work said they had a problem finding a job. But of those who could not find work, 80% said that they faced age discrimination.

A number of experimental studies document age discrimination in the workplace. The studies found that "younger job applicants were favored over older applicants who were identical in all respects save age" (Rix, 2004, p. 15). Lahey (2006, cited in Herd, 2009), for example, sent out resumes for equally experienced older and younger workers. The resumes went to 4,000 companies in Florida and Massachusetts. She found that the people presented as younger applicants in their resumes had a 40% greater chance of getting called for an interview.

What sorts of things do employers believe about older workers? And what are the facts about older workers?

Cooke (2006) says that employers view older workers as more expensive and less effective than younger workers. They believe this "despite anti-discrimination laws and evidence that older workers are indeed capable of learning new tasks and tend to have higher loyalty and less absenteeism" (p. 396). Firms that want to retire older workers will do so through "voluntary buy-outs" even where states make mandatory retirement illegal.

The AARP (2007a, p. 59) sponsored a study of seven developed nations. The study found that "age discrimination in hiring practices continues to be a serious concern around the world." People age 50 and over, compared to younger workers, said they felt less confident about their ability to find a new job. They also felt that age discrimination posed the single greatest barrier to finding a job. In this AARP study, 28% of people age 50 and over said that they had experienced age discrimination. Sixty percent of these people said that they experienced age discrimination when looking for a job. More than 35% reported age discrimination in promotion decisions.

McMullin and Berger (2006, pp. 211–218) conducted in-depth interviews with 30 unemployed women and men ages 45–65. All of these people actively tried to find work—and they all reported overt and covert ageism in their job search. "No one will tell you; no one will admit it," one 60-year-old woman told the researchers. "But I have a friend who owns his own company and he said, 'If I interview three people, even though you have the experience, if I think I can get more years out of another one, I would hire another person.' And you know, they don't have to say that, that's just the way it's done."

In answer to a question about age discrimination, one 45-year-old woman made reference to the role that gender plays in age discrimination. "Well definitely because I am a woman and because of my age. They want young, attractive women, not women who are forty-five, fifty or older." Men in this study also experienced rejection based on their age. One 62-year-old man said, "I went to two interviews there. They finally rejected me. . . . I, as they put it, was 'overqualified.' . . . But I couldn't get anyone to hire me."

McMullin and Berger found throughout their research that employers often used euphemisms in order to reject older workers. Some companies say that they feel the work is too fast-paced for an older worker, instead of saying the person is too old for the job. The authors say that these phrases and excuses try "to avoid charges of ageism and age-based discrimination." Employers "seem to disguise their ageist hiring practices by rejecting older applicants with the use of more age neutral terms."

Employers use years of experience to identify a person's age. Workers find that their strong resumes may work against them. They signify the age of the worker and that alone may eliminate them from consideration. One worker, a woman of 60, said: "They don't say anything, but you know when there is absolutely no reason why you shouldn't be considered—to just look at my resume, they know how many years I've been in the business and they can sort of deduct that I'm not thirty-five or forty."

These workers report the effects of ageism and (in the case of the women) sexism in later life. Ageism in these cases affects more than a person's self-image. It can lead to low wages when a person does find a job (Rix, 2006). This can keep a person from living a decent life.

McCann and Ventrell-Monses (2010) trace the presence of discrimination to weak legislation. These authors say that, compared to legislation that prohibits racial or gender-based discrimination, the law takes a weak stand against age discrimination. For example, a person discriminated against based on race or gender can sue for compensatory or punitive damages due to discrimination. The law does not give the older worker this same right. "Congress's failure to provide for such damages in an age case implies that the older victim does not deserve a remedy" (McCann & Ventrell-Monses, 2010, p. 360).

The courts have taken a similar stand and "have been consistently unsympathetic to constitutionally based claims of age discrimination." For example, the courts do not support claims based on ageist comments. A U.S. Court of Appeals for the Fifth Circuit considered ageist statements irrelevant when presented as evidence of discrimination. One court ruling said, "Ageism is not a vice, or at least not enough of an evil to warrant judicial intervention" (Eglit, 1986, cited in McCann & Ventrell-Monses, 2010, p. 362).

The legal system views age discrimination as less harmful than other forms of discrimination. But the effects of ageism equal those of racial or gender discrimination. Discrimination against an older worker leads to loss of a job, loss of income, and personal humiliation. It has the same damaging effects as other forms of discrimination. But for the older worker fair treatment often depends on corporate policy and practice rather than legal support.

Some companies do a better job than others at reducing age discrimination. Deutsche Bank, for example, developed a task force on age diversity led by senior managers. The National Health Service in the United Kingdom conducts training on the value of older workers and promotes intergenerational mentoring. Danny Green, Human Resources Director of Merck Frost in Quebec, says, "Frankly, it's good business for government and employers to make it easier for over-50 employees to continue working. It's a win-win all around—it adds to the GDP of the country" (AARP, 2007a). These companies and others recognize the experience and dedication that many older workers bring to their jobs. They also recognize that a company must take a proactive stance to overcome age discrimination in the workplace.

The Ageless Self: Another Form of Ageism

Aging celebrities such as George Clooney or Cher serve as role models for Baby Boomers. They make aging look glamorous, and they challenge negative stereotypes. But they may create a new stereotype of the sophisticated, successful, beautiful senior. These new images of aging may lead to a new form of ageism: the ageless self.

Katz and Marshall (2003), for example, note that our consumer society pressures older people to use drugs and products to remain sexually and physically youthful. The authors say that this promotes an impossible ideal, one that ignores other ways to age. Many of the new images of aging, they say, marginalize the very old, older people with disabilities, and older people with a different view of aging.

Some authors see the current interest in longevity, the increases in surgery to alter the effects of aging, and the desire to act young into old age as a rejection of aging. Calasanti and Slevin (2006, p. 3) say that successful aging, when it promotes the image of eternal youth "means not aging not being 'old,' or, at the very least, not looking old."

Women may feel especially vulnerable as they age. Holstein (2001–2002) says that throughout life women get social approval for their looks. The ideal older woman according to the ageist stereotype, Calasanti and Slevin (2006) say, is "healthy, slim, discreetly sexy and independent."

Clarke, Griffin, and Maliha (2009) interviewed 36 women ages 71–93 about their clothing choices. These women used clothing to mask changes in their bodies that signaled aging. They opted for traditional styles and clothing that masked flabby underarm skin (referred to as bat wings), wrinkles, pear-shaped bodies, and loose skin at their necks. One woman said she wears turtlenecks because, "Most women as they get older, they get the turkey wattle here you know . . . the fat sinks from here, goes to under your chin and you'll find that older women have a bunch of fat hanging down here. . . . I like things with a turtleneck because they hide that ugly part" (p. 718). Their comments hint at the underlying anxiety that affects most older people as they age in American society.

BOX 1.4
THE BOOMING BOOMER MARKET

Boomers take a unique view of later life. Market researchers have begun to track the habits and preference of this big generation. Here are some of their findings:

- Boomers look forward to the future. They plan to begin some big new experiences. Many Boomers plan to start new businesses after they retire. Others want to give back to their communities through volunteer work. They want to find meaning in their post-retirement years.

- Boomers feel concerned with their physical well-being, and they plan to do something about it. Rich Kelleher, age 60, jogs daily. He had an operation on his knee recently that sidelined him for a while. But now he plays tennis daily with the retirees in his condo complex. He and his wife bicycle along the boardwalk near their home in Florida. Rich also owns a kayak that he uses for trips into the mangrove swamps near his home. He's training to run a half-marathon. Rich lives a more active lifestyle now than when he was in college. Like many Boomers, Rich wants to stay in good health as long as he can. He's begun to take care of his body through diet, weight control, and exercise.

- Boomers represent a relatively young and wealthy market. They go out for dinner to fast-food and to fine restaurants, they enjoy luxury cars, and they spend money on grandchildren. Some even buy new homes that reflect their new lifestyle in retirement. Studies show that Boomers also like to travel. They take vacations, and they include vacation expenses in their financial plans. Willens (2003, p. 45) says that "60 percent [of Boomers] have taken at least one vacation trip in past 12 months and plan for another next year." Novelli and Workman (2006) report that the 50 and over age group accounts for 70% of cruise passengers and accounts for 72% of all trips in a recreational vehicle.

- Myers and Nielson (2003, pp. 55, 57) say that "Boomers want unique life experiences." They report that 40% of travelers age 50 and over hold passports (compared to only 17% for all Americans). Also, "Among all travelers, people aged 50 and over use 80 percent of all luxury travel—e.g., vacations that cost at least $350 per day, they average 3 trips per year (more than the young), they stay places almost 1.5 times longer when they go somewhere, [and] they spend 75 percent more money at a vacation site than people aged 18–48."

- Boomers have embraced computer technology. They used technology at work, and they continue to use it in their private lives. Boomers use computers for email, trip planning, medical advice, shopping, and financial management.

Can you detect any other trends in the media that show the influence of the Baby Boom generation? Consider advertising, consumer products, and changes in attitudes toward aging.

Baker and Gringart (2009, p. 989) found that older men also expressed dissatisfaction with their physical appearance as they aged. The researchers found that men tended to engage in physical fitness activity to stay in shape. The researchers propose that men (particularly those under age 70) "engage in physical activity . . . to maintain a certain body-shape ideal." Men at older ages lose their interest in fitness as they age, possibly because they can no longer maintain the ideal of a youthful body. This study found that men become "progressively dissatisfied with their physical appearance" as they age. The researchers conclude that "cultural pressures to conform to youthful ideals are experienced by both genders" (p. 990).

Catherine Mayer (2009) coined the term *amortality* to describe the ageless self. Amortals, she says, obey no age norms. "The defining characteristic of amortality," she writes, "is to live the same way, at the same pitch, doing and consuming much the same things, from late teens right up until death." Amortals deny aging. In their most extreme pronouncements they deny death itself—hoping for a scientific breakthrough before they meet the reaper. A National Consumers League (2004) survey, for example, estimates that about 90 million Americans each year buy products or undergo procedures to hide physical signs of aging. In 2004 alone, the antiaging industry reported more than a $45.5 billion gross in products and services (Business Communications, 2005).

Katz (2001–2002) found that advertisements for retirement communities focus on active lifestyles and make life seem problem free. Older people in these ads appear to live in a paradise of mature adulthood. These ads promote a lifestyle for healthy, ageless older people. Katz says that these images can make the problems of aging—such as poverty, poor health, or the frailty of late old age—seem deviant. Stoller and Gibson (2000, p. 76) say that "recommendations to join an exercise class, learn ballroom dancing, or take up lap swimming imply sufficient discretionary income to purchase lessons or gain access to appropriate facilities."

Likewise, the move to a retirement paradise implies that the person has enough money to live in one of these communities. These models of aging create new problems for older people. "We find ourselves yearning to be like people in these pictures," one older woman writes, "and belabor ourselves for failing these role models" (Preston, cited in Stoller & Gibson, 2000).

This image of the ageless self ignores the diversity among older people and the fact that the body declines with age. Holstein (2005, p. 28) cautions that the ideal of "successful aging" "can also serve to threaten the self-esteem of people who cannot or choose not to live up to those new norms." Cruikshank (2003, p. 168) proposes that older people and American society show "frankness about decline and loss of capacity." She argues against the "false cheerfulness" of the ageless self.

This critique of popular images of aging points to the diverse experiences of aging in the twenty-first century. It also shows the need for older people to confront ageist stereotypes. Clarke (2002), for example, studied the attitudes of older women toward beauty in later life. The women in this study felt pressure from the fashion industry to stay thin. But they rejected the current ideal of extreme thinness. They preferred a more rounded body shape for themselves.

These women emphasized the importance of inner beauty. They found beauty in a person's personality, a person's relationships with others, and a person's inner happiness. Clarke (2002, p. 440; also Clarke et al., 2009) concludes that social ideals shape an older woman's view of herself and that "ageist norms . . . denigrate older women and older women's bodies." But, she says, older women can and do challenge these norms. "Many of the women in my study," she says, "provide an important example of how oppressive social values can be resisted and how individuals may . . . offer alternatives to ageist interpretations of later life" (Clarke, 2002, p. 440).

We need to allow for many ways to grow old. Some people want to engage in energetic activities that we associate with youth. Other older people define later life as a time to use their wisdom, share their memories, and offer community leadership. Some people live vibrant, healthy lives into late old age. Others live with chronic illnesses. Some seem youthful to us; others look old. No single right way to grow old exists. And none of these ways should meet with social rejection.

RESPONSES TO AGEISM

A study by Cutler, Whitelaw, and Beattie (2002) found that 45% of older people believed that their later years were "the best years of my life." Sixty-one percent of the people in this survey said they would feel "very happy" if they knew they could live another 10 years. People in this survey said that the key to a meaningful old age lies in having close family and friendships, good health, and a rich spiritual life. Middle-aged people in this sample agreed that these three items held the keys to a good old age. In this same survey, 68% of the older people said that as they grew older, "things seem better than I thought they would be." And 89% of the older people said that as they looked back on their lives they felt "fairly well satisfied."

People with good incomes, married couples, people with a secure pension, and healthy people report some of the greatest life satisfaction in later life (Holden & Hatcher, 2006). But as this survey shows, nearly all older people feel satisfied with life in general and they look forward to the years ahead. George (2006) reviewed the literature on life satisfaction.

She says that in both short-term and long-term studies, life satisfaction in old age remains high. This view from old age contradicts many of the stereotypes of aging.

Research shows that stereotypes exist because of ignorance about later life and the fear of aging. Even positive stereotypes can lead to prejudice and discrimination against older people. Authors suggest a number of ways to produce a more balanced view of aging. These include the use of the media, education programs, intergenerational programs, and legislation that prohibits discrimination based on age.

BOX 1.5
THE LIFE EXPERIENCES OF TODAY'S CENTENARIANS VIEWED THROUGH HISTORICAL EVENTS

Year	Age in That Year	Event
1914	1	World War I begins
1918	5	World War I ends
1929	16	Stock market crashes; Great Depression begins
1931	18	Penicillin discovered
1935	22	Social Security Act passed
1937	24	U.S. Housing Act passed; establishes public housing
1941	28	Pearl Harbor; United States enters World War II
1945	32	Yalta conference; Cold War begins
1946	33	Baby Boom begins
1950	37	United States enters Korean War
1955	42	Nationwide polio vaccination program begins
1964	51	United States enters Vietnam War; Baby Boom ends
1969	56	First man on the moon
1980	67	First AIDS case is reported to the Centers for disease control and prevention
1980	67	Era of the personal computer begins
1989	76	Berlin wall falls
1990	77	United States enters Persian Gulf War
2000	87	Dot-com stock market bubble bursts
2001	88	September 11 attack on the World Trade Center; terrorist threat worldwide increases
2003	90	United States enters Iraq war
2006	93	Broadband Internet, the World Wide Web, and mobile communications create a global community; concern about global warming takes hold
2008	95	First baby boomers turn 62, eligible for Social Security retired worker benefits
2008	95	Housing market bubble bursts; economy declines

One stereotype of older people says that they are rigid and inflexible. But older people have adapted to a wide range of challenges and opportunities throughout their lives. And most older people continue to successfully adapt today. This chart shows some of the social, political, and technological changes a typical older person has experienced in his or her lifetime. What changes have occurred in your grandparents' lifetime? Your parents' lifetime? In your own? Create a chart that lists the changes you have witnessed in history, technology, and society. How have you responded to these changes? Can you guess what changes you will witness in the future? How do you think you'll respond?

Source: Adapted from the Federal Interagency Forum on Aging-Related Statistics. *Older Americans 2008: Key Indicators of Well-Being.* (Washington, DC: U.S. Government Printing Office, 2008). Retrieved December 21, 2009, from http://www.agingstats.gov/agingstatsdotnet/Main_Site/Data/2008_Documents/OA_2008.pdf

CHANGE ON THE HORIZON

The Media

Some improvement in attitudes toward older people may be taking place. Janelli and Sorge (2001) reviewed 61 children's storybooks published between 1991 and 1999. They found that most authors presented realistic stories. These stories showed both grandmothers and grandfathers as affectionate toward their grandchildren.

Magazines and television ads now feature famous seniors. Hall of Fame football player and coach Mike Ditka and former U.S. Senator Bob Dole promote drugs to correct erectile dysfunction. Jack Nicklaus promotes a ceramic and titanium hip replacement. Fashion model Lauren Hutton, now over 60 years old, wears a low-cut gown to promote a soy-based cereal that "may reduce the risk of heart disease." They send the message that they have control of their lives. They actively respond to the physical challenges that come with aging.

Luttropp (1995) reports that Oil of Olay skin lotion launched an ad campaign that presented healthy, happy women in their 40s. The campaign also responded to the diversity of the older population. It depicted African American as well as white women who feel content with their age. An African American woman in the ads says she is "looking forward to being the best-looking grandmother on the block" (Luttropp, 1995, p. 5). Other cosmetics companies, such as Clinique, have removed ageist language from their ads, and companies such as Nike target some of their ads to a middle-aged audience.

Unilever, the maker of Dove beauty products, has taken a bold step to attract older consumers. It created a new line of products called "Pro Age" that help people look good without denying their age. The advertising for the Dove products feature full-figured women, nonmodels, over age 50. Unilever takes a risk in promoting a product that helps people look their age (rather than deny it). After all, millions of Americans get Botox treatments each year, use antiaging makeup, and buy toothpaste to whiten aging teeth.

The Unilever (2010) company conducted a global study of women ages 50–64 and found that 91% of these women "believe it is time for society to change its views about women and ageing." Nancy Etcoff, a psychologist at the Harvard Medical School, consulted on a study that led to the new Dove products. She may be optimistic when she says, "We're seeing a real shift in how people are approaching beauty. Up to now, it's been about fighting aging with everything you have. Now you have a chance not to" (cited in Tsiantar, 2007).

Today the mass media also present an image of healthier, more active older people than in the past. *Time* magazine ran a story (complete with an ad for Levitra, an erectile dysfunction drug) titled "Still Sexy After Sixty" (Golden, 2004). The article presented vignettes that described the happy sex lives of seniors. Some years ago the TV comedy series *The Golden Girls* broke ground when it featured four older women who lived together. The series portrayed the women as active, engaged, and involved in complex relationships with men. It gained a wide audience and ran for several seasons.

Betty White, age 88 in 2010 and one of the Golden Girls, continues to entertain Americans. She starred in a 2010 Super Bowl commercial for Snickers candy where she played a football player. She also hosted *Saturday Night Live* on May 8 that year. Her show received the highest ratings of the past 18 months.

Architect Frank Gehry, when he was in his 70s, designed and oversaw construction of the Disney Concert Hall in Los Angeles. The concert hall has gotten critical raves. Gehry's Guggenheim Museum in Bilbao, Spain, and now the Disney Concert Hall mark him as one of the most creative men of our time. Pulitzer Prize–winning author Toni Morrison, now past 80, continues to write, teach, and influence our culture.

Astronaut John Glenn returned to space flight at age 77. David Bowie, at age 57, performed through a 112-date tour in 2004. Bob Dylan, now past 70, spends as much as 20 weeks touring on the road and continues to produce new music, as do the Rolling Stones. Frere-Jones (2005, p. 94) says, "In 2004, many of the best shows came from older groups who—perhaps owing to experience, new sobriety, humility, or all three—improved their repertory through performance, in ways that their juniors can't."

The Senior Market: A New Image of Aging

A few years ago a young market researcher sat down with three senior executives: one from a cosmetics firm, one from an egg-producing plant, and one from a pantyhose company. She explained that she wanted to study the spending patterns of older people. The executives laughed at her idea. None of them could understand why she wanted to do this. They each explained that they couldn't see this as relevant to their companies' future.

Some marketing directors still hold these views (Lippert & Scott, 2003). But the growing aging market has changed many advertisers' minds and will soon change many more. **Demographers** trumpet the aging of society, and economists tell us that older people today make up the richest generation of older people in history. As a group, they sit on a pile of wealth that includes their homes, pensions, savings, investments, and in some cases income from work.

Novelli and Workman (2006, p. 145) report that Baby Boomer households "pull in more than $2 trillion in annual income, account for 50% of all discretionary income, and are house-rich." Boomers hold 40 million credit cards, nearly half of all the credit cards in the United States. This group controls a large majority of the country's financial assets (Lippert & Scott, 2003).

The older market will grow in the future, but few companies have an idea of how to attract this older consumer. So far, attempts to target this market have had mixed results. Beck (1990a) notes that Kellogg's, for example, changed the name of "Bran Flakes" to "40+Bran Flakes" to capture the older market. She says that Kellogg's dropped the "40+" six months later when the name change failed to help sales.

Marketing experts say that people do not want a cereal that reminds them of their age. Other products, such as a line of gourmet foods called "Singles" (for people who live alone), have also failed to attract older consumers. In this case, experts say that people don't want to be reminded that they eat alone. Bradley and Longino (2001) report that pureed food for seniors and shampoo for people with gray hair both failed to sell.

Products that play on disabilities or problems turn people off. George Moschis, a researcher at the Center for Mature Consumer Studies at Georgia State University, found that older people will avoid a product if they think the company negatively stereotypes their age group (cited in Beck, 1990a; also Bradley & Longino, 2001). Success in attracting older consumers demands knowledge of what motivates them.

Ambrosius (1994, p. 11), for example, says that younger and older consumers want different things. Younger people focus on building families, careers, and success in their social roles. Older people want psychological fulfillment (rather than social-role fulfillment) and want to achieve life satisfaction. Ambrosius says, "We need to be more concerned with personal development . . . and deeper values. . . . Remember, no one buys anything merely because of age."

Baby Boomers will pay for quality and service when they buy a product. But they want products that fit their lifestyles and needs. Novelli & Workman (2006, p. 143) says that "Good Grips," a line of kitchen tools, "ease household tasks and boast a smart,

---

BOX 1.6
SOME MODELS OF GOOD AGING

Do people lose their abilities with age? Is aging a constant downhill course? Some well-known people should cause us to question our beliefs about old age. They show that people can continue to excel long past the normal retirement age. The following cases show the potential of later life.

- As of April 2009, the average age of the Supreme Court justices was 69 years.

- As of October 20, 2010, 4 senators are in their 80s, 23 are in their 70s, 34 are in their 60s (61% are age 60 or over).

- Former Senator John Glenn, the first American to orbit Earth in 1962, returned to space at age 77. He served as a payload specialist.

- Former Federal Reserve chairman Alan Greenspan oversaw the U.S. economy from age 61 to age 80.

- Actress Betty White starred on *Saturday Night Live* at age 87 and has had a career revival in her late 80s.

- Hugh Hefner, age 83, continues to oversee the Playboy empire.

- Pete Seeger, renowned folk-singer, released a new CD at age 90.

- Leroy "Satchel" Paige was the oldest baseball player, age 59. He pitched three scoreless innings in 1965 for the Kansas City Athletics. When asked about the secret of a good age, Paige said:

  - Don't look back. Something might be gaining on you.

  - Avoid fried meats which angry up the blood.

  - Age is a question of mind over matter. If you don't mind, it doesn't matter.

ageless design." All of these products support a new model of later life. They meet the needs of older people who see themselves as active, energetic, and engaged. This view of later life rejects the image of aging as a decline.

Advertisements have also begun to take a more positive view of older people. Investment companies, such as Smith Barney Transamerica and E*Trade, use full-page magazine ads to target Baby Boomers. An E*Trade ad plays on Boomers' concerns for their income in retirement. The ad says, "You're still working. Is your retirement account?" These companies want to offer investment advice to this rich and expanding market. Retail companies have also begun to target the older consumer. Ikea, the assemble-it-yourself furniture company, now offers delivery and assembly to attract older customers.

The September 2010 issue of the AARP *Bulletin* contained articles on Alzheimer's disease, health insurance for people with a preexisting condition, and retirement. You might expect to see these articles in a magazine for seniors. But it also contained articles on travel, smartphone use, and Harry Potter. These articles reflect the diverse interests and lifestyles of older people today.

Harris (2003b, pp. 2, 5) says, "In the same way that not every automobile is a Ford, not every member of the Boomer generation is the same. It is a diverse group, consisting of multiple sub-groups, with each sub-group having its own wants and needs." The Boomer generation, for example, stretches over 20 years. Boomers in their early 50s still hold their mid-career jobs and have children in college. Many older Boomers have retired from their first careers and may have begun second careers. People in each of these life stages have different interests and will respond to different products and services.

According to the International Longevity Center (2006, p. 57, citing Dobrow, 2005), "Products targeting baby boomers are set to become the next big ad category in the coming years." Each year new people enter the ranks of the old. These people have better education, better financial resources, and better health than past generations of older people. They lead active, engaged lives until late old age, and they will reshape our ideas about aging.

Education Programs

Gerontology and geriatric education courses exist for professionals who work with older people. But some professions provide more education than others. And education programs need to improve enrollment rates.

Lee (2002) studied graduate schools of social work in the United States. The study found that 81.6% of schools offered courses on aging (an increase from 74% in 1992). About one quarter of the schools offered a concentration in aging. The field of social work recognizes the need to train more geriatric social workers. A grant from the John A. Hartford Foundation has funded a major effort to strengthen social workers' competencies in gerontology. Projects

---

BOX 1.7
TOWARD AN AGE-IRRELEVANT SOCIETY

Historian Andrew Achenbaum (1983) says that we may go too far in giving preferred treatment to older people. This amounts to a reverse form of discrimination. It gives one group access to special programs and services based on their age. In an age-irrelevant society, should older people get special benefits?

Achenbaum says we need to look at whether age should serve as the basis for a policy or practice. Mandatory retirement, for example, discriminates against older people because age alone cannot predict ability on the job. On the other hand, he says, shelter allowances should be based not on age, but on need. Many age groups need help with housing costs.

This logic could apply to seniors' discounts as well. A young family of four may have as much need for a discount at a restaurant as a senior couple. A review of age-based policies would sometimes benefit older people and other times not. "Programs that unduly favor or disfavor people because they happen to be 'old,'" Achenbaum says, "should be reconsidered, and then either scrapped or reformulated" (p. 171).

The cry of ageism can play on our guilt about our negative feelings toward aging. Achenbaum asks us to use a rational basis for deciding how we treat all people.

Do you agree with Achenbaum's view? Do older people deserve discounts? Or should people get discounts only if they can show they are needy?

funded under this grant developed competencies and guidelines for generalist social workers and specialists in geriatrics. Schools of social work will have the option of adopting and implementing these guidelines (Greene & Galambos, 2002).

The Alliance for Aging Research (2010) reports that fewer than 10% of medical schools require unique course work or a rotation in geriatrics. Fewer than 3% of medical school graduates have taken elective courses in geriatrics. Only 9,000 geriatric specialists practice in the United States, and this number could fall to 6,000 as a result of retirements and declines in recertification. This will take place as the older population doubles in the next 20 years.

The International Longevity Center (2006, p. 70) sums up the problem that older people face: "Physicians and other health care providers, including nurses and social workers, are not adequately trained to understand the specific conditions of old age, so that high-quality affordable care has not been available by well-trained health care providers in the field of geriatrics."

Those who work directly with frail older people (e.g., nurses' aides) may have less factual knowledge about aging than supervisors and administrators (e.g., registered nurses). Direct-care workers often get the least gerontology education. Their heavy workloads and low pay make continuing education more difficult. They rarely have professional development funds they can use for courses or conferences. In-service gerontology programs for these workers can increase their knowledge and give them a more balanced view of their patients.

The Alliance for Aging Research (2010) calls for the "restoration and expansion of federal funding for Title VII programs including Geriatric Education Centers, Geriatric Health Professions Training and Geriatric Career Awards." The Alliance predicts that the lack of training "will have a tremendous impact on the quality of care older adults receive."

Studies show that fact-based programs alone will not change ageist stereotypes (Stuart-Hamilton & Mahoney, 2003). A study of medical school students (MacKnight & Powell, 2001), for example, found that home visits had little positive effect on attitudes toward older people. And on some measures the students showed a less positive attitude toward aging. Students in the health sciences who see only ill and institutionalized older people may have a negative attitude toward aging at the end of their studies.

A study of college students (Ragan & Bowen, 2001) found that only groups that got reinforcement for their knowledge showed a change in attitude after 1 month. Gerontology curricula for health professionals need to balance a problems focus with information about successful aging. Health care workers such as doctors, nurses, and physiotherapists especially need to learn about successful aging. They need to understand the possibilities for wellness and growth in their patients.

Intergenerational Programs

Research by Becca Levy and her colleagues at the Yale School of Public Health (Levy, Slade, Kunkel, & Kasl, 2002; also Hess, Auman, Colcombe, & Rahhal, 2003) report that Americans develop stereotypes of aging in childhood. Society reinforces these stereotypes throughout life. People then enter later life with the same prejudices toward older people as others in the population. These stereotypes can lead to decreased mental ability and poor cardiovascular responses to stress, and they can even shorten life. On the other hand, one study showed that people who hold positive views of aging lived an average of 7.5 years longer than people who held negative views.

Studies show that social contact between older and younger people can reduce stereotyping. My first contact with older people outside my family, for example, led to my career in gerontology. In 1973, a colleague asked me to speak to a group of older people in a university-sponsored discussion group. I decided to speak on school reform (my main interest at that time).

Thinking I would shock the group with a criticism of traditional schooling, I told them about open

"Elizabeth Lasley, 85, tells a story to Sherri Dahl, 21. Sherri's creative writing class finds their inspiration from a group of seniors who live down the street."

classroom structures, new concepts of learning, and the new role of the teacher as facilitator. After I finished, the group looked at me in silence. Then one woman said, "You know, I was the principal at Pine Ridge Elementary School until two years ago when I retired. I brought in most of the changes you've just told us about." She then told me how she put these innovative programs in place. Other group members also had taught in the public schools until they retired. They spoke about the administrative and day-to-day problems that new programs posed for teachers.

I left the room stunned. These people had calmly shattered my stereotype of old age. They knew as much as I did about my topic. They were articulate and had a great sense of humor. They had just taken me through one of the most enjoyable seminars I had ever led. I resolved to learn more about older people and spend more time with them. This seminar launched me into the next 30 years of my career.

My own experience convinces me that contact between older and younger people can remove ageist stereotypes. But contact alone does not guarantee more knowledge about older people or less bias against them. Studies of education programs show that positive attitudes arise from balanced contact and guided reflection.

Knapp and Stubblefield (2000) asked students in a psychology of aging course to work with older people in the community. The students also interacted with fellow classmates age 55 and over. Students kept a journal and discussed their experiences in class. The researchers compared these students with a control group in a criminal justice course. The researchers concluded that interaction with older people in class and through service learning led to more realistic and positive views of older people.

Roth (2005) describes a volunteer program for university students. Students spent time interacting with residents of a nearby long-term care facility. The program asked students to learn about the residents' views of life. Students wrote weekly reports that reflected on their experience. The researchers conclude that the students developed a more positive view of frailty and later life.

A study of Experience Corps volunteers, who work with children in schools, found that older people gain benefits from intergenerational programs, too. Compared to nonvolunteers, volunteers took part in more social interaction, read more books, and watched less television. Other studies show that older people who volunteer with children burn more calories and do better on memory tests (Rebok et al., 2004).

A program in Salem, Oregon, paired chronically truant teenagers with homebound seniors in a friendly visiting program. The students visited the seniors 1 day a week. Butts and Lent (2009, p. 154) say that many of the seniors would get dressed up and open their curtains only on the day that their visitors arrived. Likewise, the teachers could count on these students to attend school on their visiting day. "They both had to be there for each other. They knew they were needed."

These programs show the value of interaction between the generations. "One antidote to ageism," Butler (1993, p. 77) says, "is knowledge, the primary intervention." He reports that knowledge and satisfying contact with older people lead to a more positive view of aging. Butts and Lent (2009, p. 153) say that "thoughtfully planned intergenerational programs that engage the generations in a purposeful way with clear goals have positive outcomes."

Legislation and Social Action

Education can help reduce ageism. But discrimination can also be fought directly through legislation. Past success includes passage of the Age Discrimination in Employment Act of 1967 and the Age Discrimination Act of 1975. Under the 1967 Employment Act (amended in 1974 and 1978), an employer cannot fire someone because of age, cannot refuse to hire someone because of age, and cannot discriminate in pay because of age.

This kind of legislation, like other kinds of antidiscriminatory legislation, will not end discriminatory acts. Nevertheless, antidiscrimination laws clearly state society's values and the intent to allow workers to stay at work if they choose.

An end to ageism, prejudice, and discrimination will require all of the strategies proposed here: education, balanced contact, and social action. It will require that we develop a society that judges people by who they are and what they can do, rather than by their ages. The seeds of this kind of society may already exist. Some years ago, Sharon Curtin (1972, p. 50) said, "Almost everyone has someone they know, they love, who is also old. But they regard these loved ones as rather special cases. They may be the rule rather than the exception."

CONCLUSION

Ageism can lead to stereotyping, prejudice, and discrimination against older people. It can lead us to misjudge them, to treat them inappropriately, and to assume that they have less ability than they do. Alex Comfort writes:

> We can't take the pain out of the facts that humans aren't immortal or indefinitely disease-proof, or that illnesses accumulate as we age. We can, however, wholly abolish the mischievous idea that after a fixed age we become different, impaired or nonpeople. The start of this demystification has to be in our own rejection of it for ourselves, and then in our refusal to impose it on others. (1976, pp. 32–33)

Novelist and travel writer Paul Theroux (2003) says this about aging and old age:

> What all older people know, what had taken me almost sixty years to learn, is that an aged face is misleading. . . . I now knew: the old are not as frail as you think, and they are insulted to be regarded as feeble. They are full of ideas, hidden powers, even sexual energy. Don't be fooled by the thin hair and battered features and skepticism. The older traveler knows it best: in our hearts we are youthful, and we are insulted to be treated as old men and burdens, for we have come to know that the years have made us more powerful and streetwise. Years are not an affliction. Old age is strength enough.

These writers point the way to the future, toward a fuller understanding of age and aging—one that includes the reality of physical change. But one that also includes the potential for wisdom and continued engagement with the world.

George Burns (1896–1996) worked as a comedian into his late 90s. He smoked, drank, and stayed out late. Someone once asked him, "What do your doctors say about all this?" Burns answered, "They don't say anything; they're all dead." George Burns presented a new model of old age: active, purposeful, joyful, and enviable.

Gerontology focuses on older people, but it also asks us to look at ourselves. It asks us to look at our beliefs, values, and actions. Some people want to study aging for the joy of learning something new, but many people have a practical or professional interest in aging. We are all aging, and we have friends, relatives, and neighbors who are now in or will soon enter old age. Alex Comfort gave one of the best reasons for studying aging: self-interest. After all, he said, old age is a minority group nearly all of us will join one day. The more we know about aging, the better our ability to create a good old age for ourselves and the people we love.

SUMMARY

- Gerontology is the systematic study of aging. This chapter explains the benefits of studying aging, the social basis of age stereotyping, and the changes that will lead to new images of aging.
- Robert Butler used the term *ageism* to describe negative attitudes toward aging. New ageism tries to do good by advocating for policies and programs to help older people. But it also supports the stereotype of old age as a time of decline and loss.
- Ageism leads to stereotyping, prejudice, and discrimination against older people.
- The media, advertising, literature, and popular culture are common sources of ageism in our society.
- Ageism results from ignorance about aging and misconceptions about old age. The Facts on Aging Quiz (FAQ) suggests that people with more education have fewer misconceptions about aging.
- Gerontologists gather and teach facts about aging. This creates a better understanding of later life and a better quality of life for people of all ages.
- Ageism in the workplace leads to discrimination against older workers. Legislation attempts to prevent this. But it still takes place. Older workers often find it hard to reenter the workplace, or they have to take jobs at low pay.
- The promotion of the ageless self rejects the reality of aging. This creates another form of ageism. It promotes ideal of a youthful appearance and an active lifestyle. People who don't fit this ideal can appear as failures.
- Gerontologists suggest that the media, education, intergenerational programs, and legislation can produce a more positive and balanced view of aging.
- The Baby Boom generation will change our image of later life. This group will challenge the stereotype of aging as a time of decline. At the same time, an increase in older people of all ages will lead to acceptance of diversity in later life. This will include acceptance of physical changes that come with age.
- An acceptance of aging as a normal part of life will help end ageism in the future. It may lead to an **age-irrelevant society**. This type of society judges people by who they are and what they contribute, rather than their age.

DISCUSSION QUESTIONS

1. Define *ageism* according to Robert Butler. Explain how it can lead to social and personal problems.
2. Discuss the effects of ageism on older people and propose several strategies to discourage (or end) ageism in our society. How does compassionate stereotyping lead to scapegoating older people?
3. What are some common sources of ageism? Can you list several examples of ageism in your environment?
4. List some common misconceptions about old age today. Did you believe some of these misconceptions yourself, or did you have a more accurate view of aging?
5. How does the "ageless self" lead to ageism? How can we promote a good image of aging without rejecting people who do not conform to a youthful ideal of old age?
6. What industries, besides those listed in this chapter, could target the older market?
7. How can younger people and university or college students increase their social interactions with older people? How would this benefit society?
8. How will the Baby Boomers change our view of aging? Will society and individuals stop denying aging and accept normal changes that come with age?
9. Do you think American society in the future will provide a better opportunity for successful aging?

SUGGESTED READING

Cohen, Gene D. (2000). *Creative Age: Awakening Human Potential in the Second Half of Life*. New York: Avon Books.

This book counteracts the myth of decline in later life. The author refers to historical examples, scientific research, and case studies to support the idea that older people can live creative lives. The book shows that age, experience, and creativity can lead to inner growth and new potential in later life. The book also suggests ways that older people can enhance their creativity in everyday life.

Martz, S. H. (1994). *If I Had My Life to Live Over I Would Pick More Daisies*. Watsonville, CA: Papier Mache.

This is a classic collection of fiction, poetry, and photos on what it means to age as an older woman. It provides insight into the experience of older women from their own perspectives. The book offers a dose of reality to combat the myths that lead to ageism.

Morrow-Howell, N., Hinterlong, J., & Sherraden, M. (Eds.). (2001). *Productive Aging: Concepts and Challenges*. Baltimore, MD: Johns Hopkins University Press.

This collection of essays by well-known gerontologists advances the concept of productive aging. The essays explore the personal, psychological, social, and economic meaning of productive aging in America today. Race, gender, age, and education all influence productive aging. Several of the essays describe programs that provide opportunities for productive aging.

Palmore, E. B., Branch, L. G., & Harris, D. K. (Eds.). (2005). *Encyclopedia of Ageism*. Binghamton, NY: Haworth.

This book takes a comprehensive look at negative attitudes and behaviors toward aging and older people. Topics include elder abuse, inequality, the cost of ageism, and human rights of older people. An understanding and awareness of ageism can lead to better treatment of older people.

Websites to Consult

The Third Age—The Age of Change
www.thirdage.com

A website that focuses on Baby Boomer health, retirement, and lifestyle topics. Think of yourself as an anthropologist studying a newly discovered tribe. This site offers a look at topics of interest to the tribe we call Baby Boomers. This site has a magazine-style format. It tells us about the culture of this new generation of older people—what issues they face (e.g., caregiving to parents) and what keeps them going (e.g., sex in long-term relationships).

National Academy on an Aging Society—Selected Resources
www.agingsociety.org/agingsociety/links/links_ageism.html

This provides a short reference list of articles on aging in the media, age discrimination, and ways to fight ageism.

AARP Magazine
www.aarpmagazine.org

The AARP Magazine is the premier magazine from America's largest association of older people. This website contains human-interest stories, case studies, and information about aging in U.S. society. Articles on technology, relationships, and cooking show the range of interests of older people today. Check back frequently for updates.

chapter 2

THEORIES AND METHODS

I visited Frances Kennedy, 68 years old, in her apartment on a cool autumn afternoon. I had just begun a study of how people make **transitions** in later life. Frances agreed to take part in the study, and I arranged to visit her home. She had lived alone since her youngest son moved out several years ago. I wanted to understand how she had adapted to living by herself.

"Oh, I love it," she said. "At first I had to adjust. For instance, I couldn't understand how the toothpaste spray got on the bathroom mirror now that I lived alone. I had always blamed that on Jimmy, my son. Finally, I had to admit that it must have been at least partly me all along.

"I love the idea that I can leave a chicken leg or a half container of milk in the refrigerator and find it still

there the next day. I can sleep late on Saturdays if I want to, and I can have quiet suppers alone after work.

"I've also developed some tricks to make life interesting. You know, it's not much fun every night coming home and making your own supper. There's no surprise in it. So I found a way to surprise myself. One Sunday a month I prepare a batch of dinners—things like eggplant parmigiana, beef stew, lasagna. Then I put them in containers, seal the lids, and put them in the freezer. I don't label them.

"In the morning, before I go out, I take out two containers and put them on the counter to defrost. When I come home at night I open the containers, pop them in the microwave, and surprise myself with whatever's for dinner.

"I have other ways to make living alone more fun. For instance, I hate to clean house. But there's no one to share the work with now. So I put on a 20- or 25-minute piece of fast music. I have to clean the whole house before the music ends. I've got a whole lot of these games (like putting a label on the window cleaner bottle with the date when I think it will be used up) to make life interesting."

Frances has a creative streak that makes play out of the simplest jobs. Living alone allows her to express this creativity. My afternoon with her showed me why she enjoys living alone. It also gave me insight into why many older women prefer to live on their own.

Research on aging can take many forms. My meeting with Frances took the form of an in-depth interview. I used a few leading questions to guide our discussion, but mostly I wanted her to talk about her life in her own words. The open-ended interview method allowed Frances to reveal her private world to me.

Other research methods help to answer different research questions. And they produce different results. Research methods provide guides on how to collect information, ways to analyze research findings, and ways to report findings so other researchers can verify the results.

Some researchers, for example, use survey methods. They mail questionnaires to hundreds or even thousands of people, then they analyze the results on a computer. Other researchers conduct controlled studies in laboratories. They ask people to take a paper-and-pencil test or they test a person's reaction time. Historical researchers study diaries and letters. Researchers who want to understand a group's culture or everyday life spend many hours doing field research.

No single method can answer all research questions. Gerontologists choose the methods and theories that best suit their research questions. Sociologists define a *theory* as a "conceptual model of some aspect of life" (Online Dictionary, 2004). Theories try to make sense out of a complex reality. They link concepts and ideas into a single pattern. Scientists use theories to develop hypotheses about the way the world works. They then test these hypotheses through their research.

Gerontologists use many theories to guide their research. Some theories apply to individuals and their personal relationships. A gerontologist, for example, might want to understand whom older people turn to for help. The researcher might theorize that older people turn to family members for help before they turn to government services. This theory of social support says that people use informal supports before they turn to formal helpers.

Each theory and method has its limits and its strengths. This chapter looks at (1) theories that guide gerontologists in their research; (2) methods that gerontologists use to gather their data; and (3) future trends in aging research in the United States.

THE STUDY OF AGING IN THE PAST

Historians trace the study of aging to the ancient scriptures of the Far East, the Bible, and the work of Greek philosophers such as Plato and Aristotle. Before the 17th century, authors based their writings on their own experiences. The writings reflected writers' fears and the biases of the time.

In the 17th century, writers began to base their studies on scientific methods and systematic observations. Most of the early researchers who studied aging were trained in the natural sciences and medicine. By the 18th century, scientists began to use mathematical techniques to study aging. Sir Edmund Halley, the discoverer of the comet named after him, created the first table of life expectancy. Benjamin Rush, in 1793, published the first American geriatrics work, *Account of the State of the Body and Mind in Old Age*. This started a modern period in which researchers saw aging as something other than disease. It also marked the start of the medical study of aging.

Quetelet in the mid-19th century proposed a "social physics"—a science that would study human facts and events, express them in numbers, and locate cause-and-effect relationships. Quetelet, for example, collected physical and social data on people of different ages. He studied birth and death rates and looked at how crime and suicide varied by age. His study, *On the Nature of Man and the Development of His Faculties* (1835), described how human strength and weight varied by age. By the late 19th century, the social sciences—sociology and psychology—had also begun to study aging.

Historians credit Elie Metchnikoff of the Pasteur Institute in Paris with the first use of the term *gerontology* in 1905 (Freeman, 1979). Metchnikoff wrote the first gerontology text, *The Problem of Age, Growth, and Death*, in 1908. A short time later, in 1912, the Society of Geriatry—one of the first groups to study aging in North America—was formed in New York. G. Stanley Hall wrote *Senescence, the Last Half of Life* in 1922, one of the first scientific studies of aging in the United States. Hall used survey data to understand religious beliefs and attitudes toward death among older people. He and other writers at this time focused on the problems of old age (Achenbaum, 1987).

GERONTOLOGY RESEARCH TODAY

Research output on aging grew rapidly after World War II. Research on aging in the 1960s moved beyond a study of problems to include studies of normal aging. This included studies of positive developments in later life. Major journals in the United States began to be published after 1946.

Today, dozens of academic journals around the world publish research on aging, and new ones start all the time. Journals such as *The Journals of Gerontology*, *The Gerontologist*, and *The International Journal of Human Development* serve a wide audience. Other journals target specific groups such as nurses, social workers, or recreation professionals. A series of handbooks in biology, psychology, and the social sciences synthesize knowledge on key topics.

A bibliography of sources on aging for the years 1954 to 1974 listed 50,000 entries (Woodruff & Birren, 1975). This list contained more sources than all the writings on aging in the previous 100 years. Today, a complete bibliography would contain many times this number of sources. Computerized bibliographies such as *AGELINE* (a general database) or CINAHL (focused mostly on health-related sources) attempt to keep track of the thousands of sources published on aging each year. A search for even one keyword in a database can turn up hundreds of sources published in the past 20 years.

IS GERONTOLOGY A DISCIPLINE?

The varied approaches that researchers take to aging (biological, psychological, social) raise some questions: Is gerontology a discipline, or is it a subfield within existing disciplines (such as sociology or biology)?

Some years ago the Gerontological Society of America (GSA) sponsored the Foundations Project (Foundations Project, 1980). This project asked experts to reflect on the status of gerontology as a discipline. A *discipline,* the project said, has "a distinct body of knowledge, requiring the establishment of a separate academic unit" (p. 6). A number of leaders in the field of aging at that time thought that gerontology met this criterion. They proposed that universities and colleges develop gerontology departments with their own faculty members and with administrative status.

Few schools, however, have taken this route. Gerontologists almost always belong to traditional disciplines such as sociology, psychology, or biology. In most cases gerontology programs exist within a social science department, although some schools offer an interdisciplinary option that spans more than one field.

The status of gerontology as a discipline rests on whether gerontology has claim to a "distinct body of knowledge." The GSA put this to a test. The GSA asked 111 experts on aging from fields as varied as biomedicine and economics whether gerontology has a distinct body of knowledge (Foundations Project, 1980). The study asked them to define the core and scope of the field. Although the experts differed on the exact content and boundaries of the field, they did agree that three areas made up the core of aging studies: biomedicine, psychosocial studies, and socioeconomic-environmental studies.

Biomedicine studies look at the changes in the body that come with age, including studies of DNA, the cells, the body's systems, stress, and dementia. The experts showed the most agreement on the content of this subfield. This may be due to the long history of biomedical research on aging. Geriatrics, the medical specialty that deals with older people, draws heavily on biomedical knowledge of aging. Geriatricians, physicians who treat older people, also contribute to this body of knowledge through clinical research.

Psychosocial studies look at the changes that take place inside the individual and between individuals and groups. Researchers study memory, creativity, and learning. They also study personality, relationships, and death and dying.

Socioeconomic-environmental studies look at the effects of aging on social institutions. Sociologists define a *social institution* as a pattern of social interaction that has a relatively stable structure and persists over time (Online Dictionary, 2004). Institutions include the economy, the family, and the health care system. Socioeconomic-environmental studies ask, for example, how an aging society will affect the health care system or the economy. These studies also look at the effect of social institutions on aging individuals. For example, how does the U.S. retirement income system (pension plans and retirement policies) affect the experience of aging?

Social gerontology makes up a part of the total body of gerontological knowledge. It includes the psychosocial, socioeconomic-environmental, and practice-related studies of aging. Clark Tibbitts first introduced the idea of social gerontology in 1954.

Social gerontology views aging from the perspective of the individual and the social system. When social gerontologists look at biomedical issues, they focus on the social effects of physical aging. For example, they ask how changes in a person's ability to walk affect that person's needs for social services. Or they ask how physical aging differs by race and ethnicity. Do older African Americans and whites have the same diseases at the same rates and from the same causes? Social gerontologists also look at changes throughout the life course. They study changes in family life, relationships, and activities. Social gerontology has grown in importance in the past 20 years.

THEORIES OF AGING

My grandmother used to keep her eyeglasses pushed up onto her head. I remember one day watching her walk around the house with a puzzled look on her face.

"Grandma," I asked, "what are you looking for?"

"My glasses. I can't find them anywhere."

"They're on your head," I said with a laugh.

"Oh," she said, as she patted her head. "I must be getting old."

In that moment my grandmother expressed a theory of aging: When you get old, you forget things, like where you put your eyeglasses. She didn't think of this as a theory; she didn't know anything about theories. But she had one. When she forgot where she put her glasses, it confirmed her belief that you forget things when you age.

Many psychologists use this same theory in their research. They suspect that memory declines with age, and they have produced volumes of literature to test this theory. In this way researchers differ from my grandmother. They suspect that memory decreases with age, but they try to prove or disprove this idea.

Theories often start with beliefs, commonsense ideas, or hunches. But scientific theories differ from everyday theories in that scientists try to state a theory clearly. A theory may contain formal propositions linked to one another. The theory will also produce testable hypotheses that can guide research. Social scientists then study their research findings to see whether they support, reject, or modify the theory.

Bengtson, Gans, Putney, and Silverstein (2009, p. 5) say, "Theories are like lenses. Look at an object through one kind of lens, and the viewer will see one thing; look at it through another lens, and the viewer will be able to see something different." Theories help researchers to organize and give focus to their work. For example, you can think of a family in terms of power, authority, and kinship relations. Or you can think of the family as an economic unit related to the larger economy. In each case theory leads to a different description and explanation of family life.

Gerontologists have developed many theories to explain aging. These range from biological theories of why the skin wrinkles to theories of why some societies revere their elders. Some gerontologists borrow theories from sociology and psychology and apply them to the study of aging. For example, psychologists have applied theories of mental function to the study of memory (Dixon, Backman, & Nilsson, 2004). Social psychologists use theories of stress to study the buffering effects of social relations (Antonucci, Birditt, & Akiyama, 2009). Sociologists have applied political economy theory to the study of pensions (Quadagno, 2005).

Gerontologists create theories to help them explain a set of facts. For example, research shows that older people may need housing with more physical and social supports as they age. The theory of person–environment fit, first advanced by Lawton and Nahemow (1973), explains this trend. This theory says that the supports a person needs depend on two things: a person's ability and the demands of the environment. As ability decreases, demand increases, and a person needs more support. This theory interprets the facts and puts them in a framework. It allows researchers to test the relationship between different forces that shape housing needs. It also allows service providers to offer supports that improve an older person's quality of life.

Each theory contains a set of assumptions about people and the world. For example, exchange theory focuses on what people give and get from one another. It helps explain caregivers' service to their spouses or parents. But it has its limits. For example, it says nothing about the impact of modern industrial society on the family, or about state policies that limit home care benefits to older people. Gerontologists use other theories, such as modernization theory or political economy theory, to understand social change and social policy.

Gerontologists differ in the kinds of theories they favor. The choice of a theory depends on a researcher's training, the subject under study, and even personal preference. The study of gerontological theories shows the scope of gerontological research and the ways that gerontologists think about aging.

TWO LEVELS OF THEORIES

Social gerontologists use theories to explain everything from child–parent relations to the treatment of older people by the government. The following discussion arranges some of the major theories in a framework and gives examples of how gerontologists have applied them in their work. Gerontologists use at least two types of theory: micro-level theories and macro-level theories.

Micro-level theories describe people and their relationships. They focus on small-scale events such as interactions between staff and patients in a nursing home, changes in personality with age, and choice of leisure activities. These theories encompass studies of how individuals change as they age. They include the study of memory and intelligence, as well as the study of adjustments to retirement or widowhood.

Macro-level theories look at social institutions (such as the family), social systems (such as health care or housing), and whole societies. These theories examine the way that social institutions shape experiences and behavior. These theories focus on large-scale events such as historical changes in family size and structure, health care policies, and how industrial or agricultural societies treat their older people.

Modernization theory serves as an example of a macro-level theory.

THREE THEORETICAL PERSPECTIVES

Micro-level and macro-level theories look at different phenomena. Taken together, they show the scope of gerontological study. Researchers can choose from three major theoretical perspectives within these two levels of study: the interpretive perspective, the functionalist perspective, and the conflict perspective.

Interpretive Perspective

The interpretive perspective most often focuses on the micro-level of social life. It looks at how people relate to one another, how they define situations, and how they create social order. Theories within this perspective include social constructionism, social exchange theory (Homans, 1961), the symbolic-interactionist perspective, social phenomenology, and ethnomethodology (Garfinkel, 1967), as well as an even earlier tradition pioneered by Max Weber (1905/1955). A relatively small number of gerontologists have used this perspective.

BOX 2.1
THEORIES OF AGING

Levels of Theory

Micro (individual social interaction)		*Macro* (social structures, social processes)

Theoretical Perspectives

Interpretive (how individuals define and create social world)	*Functionalist* (social order based on cooperation and consensus)	*Conflict* (society based on conflict between social groups)

Theories

Social constructionism	Structural functionalism	Political economy
Symbolic interactionism	Modernization	Moral economy
Social phenomenology	Disengagement	Feminist theories
Ethnomethodology	Continuity	
Social exchange	Activity	
	Age stratification	
	Life course	

This chart presents the most influential theories in the study of aging. It summarizes the discussion in the text.

Source: Aging and Society, A Canadian Perspective, Fifth Edition by NOVAK/CAMPBELL. © 2006. Reprinted with permission of Nelson, a division of Thomson Learning: www.thomsonrights.com. Fax 800-730-2215.

Symbolic interaction, based on the work of George Herbert Mead (1934), and social phenomenology, based on the work of Alfred Schutz (1967), fit this perspective. Symbolic interactionists study how symbols such as clothing, body language, and written words shape social relations. For example, an older man in a derby hat with a pipe and an umbrella gives one impression. A young woman in jeans and a bustier and with platinum-colored hair gives another. We would address each of these people differently and make different assumptions about their backgrounds and interests. People learn to read and respond to the symbols around them.

Social phenomenologists take a more extreme view. They speak of "the social construction of reality" (Berger & Luckmann, 1967). They view social order as a creation of everyday interaction (Longino & Powell, 2009). Social phenomenologists often look at conversation to find the methods people use to maintain social relations. For example, if I ask, "How are you?" you understand that I don't want to hear about your athlete's foot. You answer, "Fine." We smile and move on.

A doctor who asks this same question wants to know about your health. You give a different answer to this question in a doctor's office. If you answer, "Fine," the doctor may probe and ask some very personal questions. You will play along and assume that this is part of the doctor's job. A social phenomenologist studies the way that a doctor's conversation builds and creates a social reality that we call "the medical exam."

The interactionist perspective sees the person as an actor and a creator of social life. People do more than live in social groups and organizations. They play a part in creating and maintaining them. They do this every day and in every interaction. People negotiate who goes through a door first, who sits where at the dinner table, and what kind of clothes to wear to a job interview. All of these actions have meaning, and people learn to read and interpret these meanings. People also take these actions for granted and rarely notice their impact.

Symbols come loaded with meaning. I once asked a graphic designer to create a brochure for a gerontology program that I planned to offer. I explained that I would send the brochure to health care professionals. The designer came back with a brochure that had an abstract image on it. The image looked like a bent and crooked figure leaning on a cane. This image reflected the designer's idea of aging. It presented an image that he felt the public shared. I could have used this brochure cover in the program, but only as a case study in ageism.

Gray hair, wrinkles, a walker—all symbolize aging. Symbols or images can have a strong influence on us. The wheelchair symbolizes sickness, weakness, and dependence. Wheelchair designers have worked to change this image. Some wheelchairs now have angled wheels, high-performance tires, and special seats for athletic use. Some physically challenged older people prefer indoor scooters to wheelchairs.

One older woman I know, who owned a wheelchair, says that her scooter changed her self-image. She felt helpless and stigmatized in her wheelchair. She now rides around her local shopping mall with confidence and self-esteem. Why does the image of a scooter differ from that of a wheelchair? The wheelchair symbolizes illness. The scooter symbolizes freedom and an active lifestyle. People attach different meanings to each. Sociologist W. I. Thomas summed this up in what sociologists call the **Thomas theorem**: "If people define situations as real, they are real in their consequences" (Thomas & Thomas, 1928, p. 572).

The interpretive perspective can give a good understanding of how people interpret their social world, how they interact with one another, and why they do what they do. Studies that focus on language, for example, "can 'give voice' to people as individual informants" (Coupland, 2009, p. 851). For example, a report on conversations with people who live in retirement communities shows how these people understand their own condition (Norrick, 2009). Interviews with older Japanese women (Matsumoto, 2009) and a study of the self-expression of poor older women in Detroit (Onolemhemhen, 2009) give insight into these people's social world. Gerontologists have used this approach to study how people adapt to retirement, loss of a spouse, and changes in health (Koch, 2000).

Schaefer (2010) studied the experience of older adult students who attended college classes. The students' children had grown up and they no longer needed to spend time on childrearing. This allowed them to return to school. Schaefer conducted in-depth interviews and used reflective questionnaires with nine of these students ages 50 to 62. She felt that higher education institutions do not necessarily meet the needs of older learners, so she set out to understand these students' experiences in college. She wanted to understand what was "personally meaningful" to them.

This study explored students' past education experiences and their future goals, what brought them to higher education, and what supports they found useful in their program. Schaefer locates her study within the tradition of social phenomenology. This allows her to understand what is "real and meaningful" in the minds of these students.

Schaefer found that the Baby Boomers in her study attended school to develop their careers (rather than for personal enrichment); they were first-generation students who needed a better understanding of the higher education process; and they had complex support needs. Schaefer reports the students' experiences in their own words.

One student said, in explaining her return to school, "I think I went through a big, serious empty nest problem there. It was just this loss—what do I do now? The being isolated, children were gone, and what am I here on earth [for]—what is my purpose anymore?" (p. 77).

Another student expressed emotions related to her role as homemaker. "I felt so isolated," she said. "I think that's primarily what it was. I felt so isolated at home day in, day out taking care of children, taking care of the home, and not getting out in the real world because, you know he wouldn't let me work either outside the home."

These students discovered a new role for themselves through a return to school. School helped them deal with existential crises. It helped them develop a new sense of self. Schaefer also discovered that the students faced unique challenges. One student said, "This was walking through a whole new door I hadn't been to in years, and things had changed considerably. There was a lot of confusion of what I needed to do to start, the fear of getting started."

These expressions of doubt and uncertainty give a rich understanding of these students' lives as they enter the institution. The interpretive perspective allows us to see and understand the world from the student's point of view. This type of study provides rich information for students of life transitions. Administrators of higher education can use these insights to create more responsive programs for older learners.

Kaufman (1993) used an interactionist theory to guide her study of stroke patients because she thought "the voices of individual old people were deemphasized or lost in the conduct of . . . [scientific] research" (p. 13). She wanted to explore the meaning older people gave to their lives. She found that stroke patients experience a sharp break with past life patterns. She also found that people try to maintain continuity in their lives. They interpret the past and link it to the present. Kaufman determined that stroke patients worked hard to build links from their past to their future. People who completed this task recovered, even if they still had physical disability. Stroke patients needed to show that they were the same people after their illness as before.

Kaufman (1993) places her work within a phenomenological framework. "Phenomenology," she says, "attends to the reality of experience" (p. 15). It studies a phenomenon—sickness, rehabilitation, health—from the subject's point of view. This type of research requires a close collaboration between the researcher and the subject. The subject's story and the way the subject comes to create that story become the research finding. This approach to research opens the researcher to the world of the subject. The researcher in a well-crafted study learns to see the world through the eyes of the subject and to understand the meaning the subject gives to the world.

Gubrium points to a growing interest in the interpretive perspective. He reports a "decided surge of interest in the place of personal meaning, the unstandardized, and the emergent in everyday life" (Gubrium, 1993, p. 60; Gubrium & Holstein, 1999). But Gubrium cautions against romanticizing this experience. The interactionist perspective, he says, must include an awareness of culture and history. This allows the researcher to see how people create and maintain the meaning of old age in a specific social setting.

Critique of the Interpretive Perspective

Like every perspective, the interactionist perspective gives only one view of social life. Critics of this perspective say, first, that it overlooks the links between the individual and larger social institutions. For example, an interactionist view of older students' self-understanding misses the impact of the school bureaucracy—paperwork, deadlines, fees—on students' lives. It also misses the effects of hospital bureaucracy on stroke patients.

Second, the interactionist perspective does not look at the impact of social policies on people or groups. For example, policies may restrict the number of courses students can take. This can affect the older student's ability to move through the curriculum. Policies can also affect the kinds of rehabilitation services that a stroke patient receives.

Third, the interactionist perspective does not discuss power and conflict between social groups. The interactionist perspective would not, for example, study the effects of race on educational opportunity for older students in America. Likewise, stroke patient

Rembrandt van Rijn (1606–1669) began painting self-portraits in the 1620s. He completed his last self-portrait the year of his death, 1669. Here we see him in late middle age. In all, he painted more than 90 self-portraits. Experts have called his self-portraits a "visual diary." They stand as one of the great achievements in the history of Western art.

Does Rembrandt's self-portrait count as a "research study" of aging? If not, why not? If so, why do you consider it a research study? How does it differ from studies done by social scientists? What do artists discover through their "research"? What can an artist's work teach us about aging?

ethnicity and social class influences the treatment they receive. The functionalist and conflict perspectives focus on these issues.

Functionalist Perspective

The functionalist perspective includes structural-functionalist theory (or *functionalism*) in sociology. Emile Durkheim promoted this theory in the 19th century in *The Division of Labor in Society* (1893). Talcott Parsons developed this theory further in *The Social System* (1951). Functionalism views society as a system made up of many parts. These include religion, the family, education, and politics. Changes to one part of the system lead to changes in the whole system.

Functionalism sees society as an organism that tries to stay in equilibrium. Biologists refer to this as *homeostasis*. Society regulates itself in the same way your body keeps a steady temperature. When you exercise, you overheat your body. Sweat cools you down. A change in one part of the system brings into play mechanisms that reestablish order.

An increase in the number of older people in society, for example, leads to more government money directed to programs for the elderly. More support to older people can create a dysfunction (e.g., a fear that too little money exists for other age groups). This may lead to political backlash and reduced support. The system tries to stay in balance through changes in policies and programs.

Functionalism can explain large-scale political change as well as the way small groups maintain their structure. Functionalism says that norms (shared rules of behavior) and roles (expectations for behavior in a certain social status) shape behavior. People learn these norms and learn to play social roles as they grow older. People conform to these norms through social pressure, but also through belief in society's underlying value system. The values expressed in the commandment "Honor thy father and mother" show up in everyday behavior and in social policies. Failure to honor a parent may lead to informal sanctions, such as criticism from a sister or brother. Extreme neglect may lead to the charge of abuse and legal sanctions.

Informal and formal sanctions create a smooth-running society. People know what to do and what others expect of them. Functionalism focuses on consensus and social order. It assumes that society changes or evolves in a positive direction. It explains social problems as dysfunctions, and it proposes to correct these dysfunctions through the use of experts in planning and the helping professions.

Historically, gerontologists used the functionalist perspective more than any other perspective in their study of aging. Gerontology's most influential early theories are disengagement theory (Cumming & Henry, 1961), activity theory (Neugarten, Havighurst, & Tobin, 1968) (both discussed in Chapter 7), and modernization theory (Cowgill & Holmes, 1972). All three rely on structural-functionalist assumptions. Riley and colleagues (Riley, 1987; Riley, Foner, & Waring, 1988) also produced a dominant theory based on structural-functionalist principles: age stratification theory.

Age Stratification Theory: An Example of the Functionalist Perspective

Age stratification theory, or its more recent identification as the "aging and society paradigm" (Riley, Foner, & Riley,1999), links individual aging to social institutions. The theory discusses individual aging, societal aging, and **cohort flow** (Riley et al., 1988). Age stratification theory describes a "dynamic interplay between two interdependent processes: individual aging and social change" (Riley, 1985, p. 371).

Individual Aging

Age stratification theory views aging as a lifelong process. People experience biological changes with age. They also experience changes in roles and social positions. Each society sets out a series of roles that people enter and leave as they age. These include the role of child, student, spouse, parent, worker, retiree, and grandparent. These roles and the norms that go with them change over time. Many older people, for example, learned that a person should not have sex outside of marriage. Some of these people now find themselves widowed. If they want to have an active sex life without marrying again, they will have to rethink their childhood beliefs about marriage, sex, and old age. This can lead to a broader change in social values and behavior. In this way individuals and cohorts can create social change.

Societal Change

Every society has a set of age grades that stratifies its members. Societies attach certain rights and responsibilities to each age grade. Age grades in the United States include childhood, adolescence, young adulthood, middle age, and old age. These age grades may change over time. Today, for example, gerontologists

speak of the Third Age (young retirees) and the Fourth Age (the very old). More people now live in the Third and Fourth age grades than ever before.

The U.S. Census Bureau often divides statistics on older people into two or more groups (e.g., ages 65 to 74, 75 to 84, and 85 and over). This division recognizes that people move through different stages in later life (e.g., many people have to cope with increased frailty after age 85). Gerontologists can learn about a society by studying its age stratification system.

Cohort flow describes the dynamics of the age stratification system. People belong to an **age cohort**, a group of people born at about the same time. People born between 1950 and 1959, for example, form an age cohort. Age cohorts move through society's age grade system together. They go through the same age grades and transitions at about the same time.

People in their 80s today experienced the end of World War II in their early adult years. Many of them married just after the war, and they produced the Baby Boom generation. These people share memories of the postwar years as young parents. They also share the memory of the Big Band era, the first television shows, and early commercial air travel.

The Baby Boom generation will remember some of these events, but they may recall more about the first cartoon shows than anything else on television. The Baby Boomers will recall little of the McCarthy hearings or Dwight Eisenhower's presidency in the 1950s. Historical events affect each cohort, but each cohort experiences these events differently because they go through the event at a different time in the life cycle.

Each age cohort moves through life as if on an escalator. One group leaves an age grade, and the next group enters it. Each age grade places expectations on its members and offers members new roles to play. At the same time, each cohort brings into an age grade a new set of norms and values that lead to changes in social life.

New cohorts and historical events can lead to changes in the age grade system itself. For example, each generation brings into later life unique shared experiences. World War II shaped the worldview of my father's generation. The Viet Nam war and Woodstock shape Baby Boomers' thinking, philosophy, and worldview today. Elder (1999, p. 15) says that "individuals are thought to acquire a distinct outlook and philosophy from the historical world, defined by their birth date, an outlook that reflects lives lived interdependently in a particular historical context."

Older people today as a group enter old age with more income than older people in the past. The Social Security system, corporate pension plans, and good nutrition allow them to live more active lifestyles and to engage in new activities. The current generation of older people has begun to change our notion of old age. They travel, take courses, and exercise. These new seniors have given rise to new education programs, new travel options, and new products that cater to their needs. Gerontologists now speak of the young-old (age 65 to 74), the old-old (age 75 to 84), and the oldest-old (age 85 and over) because the single age grade "old age" has lost its meaning.

Age stratification theory relies on many of the assumptions of the structural-functionalist approach to aging. First, it assumes that norms and values influence individual aging. Second, it describes the relationship between the individual and society as a feedback loop. Change begins with the individual cohort or with large-scale historical or social change. These changes then lead to change in other parts of the social system. Third, the theory tends to see society as a homogeneous set of structures and functions that all people in a cohort experience in the same way.

Age stratification theory has a number of strengths. First, it has helped to separate age differences (between cohorts) from age changes over the life course (aging). Second, it highlights the impact of historical and social changes on individuals and cohorts. Third, it highlights the relationship between aging and social structures. Bengtson, Burgess, and Parott (1997, p. S82) say that age stratification theory "provides new ways to explore differences related to time, period, and cohort."

Critique of the Functionalist Perspective

Criticisms of age stratification theory show the limits of the functionalist perspective. First, age stratification theory tends to see society as a homogeneous set of structures and functions that all people in an age cohort experience the same way. This approach focuses on the differences between cohorts, but misses the diversity within them. For example, people in the same cohort differ by gender, race, and ethnicity.

Age stratification theory puts little focus on how gender, social class, race, and ethnicity create inequalities within age cohorts. For example, it says little about the differences between growing old as a lower-class woman and growing old as a middle-class man. Income differences within a cohort may have a greater influence on a person's life than the norms and values related to his or her age grade.

A person's race or gender leads to different behaviors and to different responses to sociohistorical events. A person's race or gender also determines the choices available as the person ages. For example, compared to a poor older woman, a wealthy older man will have more opportunity to invest in an Individual Retirement Account (IRA). This will increase the gap in income between these two people.

A second criticism is that the age stratification theory overlooks the person's interpretation of the social world. It emphasizes the impact of society and history on the individual but says little about how the individual makes sense of these conditions and responds to them. People in the same age cohort interpret the world and respond to events in unique ways. A war may turn one person into a patriot and another into a pacifist. An elderly Chinese woman who has just arrived in California from Hong Kong will see the world differently from a retired New England farmer. Age stratification theory overlooks how each of these people interpret the world. It makes little reference to individual control or action.

Third, functionalist theories have a conservative bias. Functionalism sees equilibrium and social order as preferred social conditions. Age stratification theory, for example, focuses on cohorts, norms, and social order, but it fails to account for conflicts and tensions between social groups in society or for issues of power. These conflicts often shape a person's life. Race, gender, social class, and ethnicity create unequal access to a good life in society. Older African Americans today, for example, have poorer health than whites. Racial inequality may explain more about African Americans' life changes than do the norms and values of their age cohort.

Functionalist theories, like the age stratification theory, have their shortcomings. Still, they order the complex changes that take place over the life course.

The *life course approach*, also a functionalist approach, bridges both the micro-level and macro-levels of analysis. It incorporates social interaction and social structure within its framework (Settersten, 2006). Idler (2006, p. 283) says the life course perspective "focuses on timing, sequencing, and duration of roles or periods" of life.

Elder and Johnson (2003) describe five principles of the life course perspective:

1. Human development and aging take place throughout life.
2. History and location shape an individual's life.
3. Life transitions and events vary depending on when they take place in a person's life.

4. Individuals are linked to others and live interdependently.
5. Individuals give shape to their lives by taking action and making choices.

Researchers use the life course approach to explain (1) the changes that take place in an individual over time, (2) age-related and socially recognized life transitions, and (3) the interaction of social life, history, culture, and personal biography (Moen & Spencer, 2006; Settersten, 2006). At the micro-level or individual level, the life course approach looks at how events and conditions early in life affect later life.

Zarit (2009) gives the example of how earlier experiences affect mental disorder in later life. Major depressive disorder (MDD) shows up in about 1% to 5% of older people. But research shows that usually this problem started earlier in a person's life. Rarely does MDD show up for the first time in old age. New cases, Zarit says, steadily decline after age 30 (with a slight increase after age 75). Anxiety disorders show the same pattern. Most people face this disorder first in adolescence or young adulthood. These mental disorders form a lifelong pattern of disturbance.

At the macro-level or societal level, the life course approach shows how social change and historical events can create differences between cohorts (Elder, 2000). For example, teenagers and adults in New Orleans will feel different effects from the damage caused by hurricane Katrina. The hurricane caused some university students to drop out of school. This may influence their earning power for many years to come. Older adults experienced a different kind of loss. They lost homes and businesses that they may never have time or resources to replace. The life course approach studies the impact of macro-level events on individual lives.

The life course approach overcomes some of the limitations of age stratification theory. It recognizes variety in life course patterns and differences between age cohorts. It also recognizes differences within age cohorts due to differences in race, ethnicity, social class, and gender. This approach takes into account the diversity of roles and role changes across the life course. It recognizes aging as a lifelong, dynamic, interactive, and multidirectional process. For example, an older woman may maintain good relations with her children, she may have trouble walking up stairs, but she may take up a new hobby such as painting. Aging involves stability in some areas of life, decline in others, and improvement in others.

The life course approach looks at transitions and trajectories. Transitions refer to changes in social status or social roles (in particular, when transitions occur, how long they last, how people get through the transitions). Transitions include marriage, divorce, remarriage, widowhood, and parenthood. Work-related transitions also occur—for example, getting a first job or retiring.

Trajectories refer to long-term patterns of stability and change. They may include many transitions. One marital status trajectory may involve the transition to marriage, a subsequent divorce, then a remarriage, and finally a transition to widowhood. Another marital status trajectory may involve only one marriage for life. This involves only the transition to a first marriage and, for one of the couple, the transition to widowhood. The life course approach has made a number of contributions to the study of aging.

First, it bridges the macro-level and the micro-level of analysis by recognizing the importance of social structures and historical context, as well as individual experiences and meanings. It helps us understand the diversity within and between cohorts.

Second, the approach brings together sociological, psychological, anthropological, and historical approaches to the study of aging.

Third, the life course approach understands aging as a dynamic process that takes place throughout life.

The life course approach in particular appreciates the link between earlier stages of adulthood and later life. Research on topics such as diet, health and illness, family life, and work all show the impact of earlier life conditions on later life. For example, women more often than men show a broken work history. This leads to lower incomes for women in midlife, but also poorer pensions and lower incomes in old age. Likewise, a divorce or the decision to stay single may lead to fewer family supports in later life. Even conditions such as poor nutrition in childhood have an impact on old age.

This approach has some limitations. It puts the greatest emphasis on social structures and on individual responses to those structures. It focuses less on how individuals or cohorts create social change. Like most functionalist theories, it puts the greatest emphasis on social stability. Also, its broad focus on society, history, culture, and the individual makes it hard to define as a single theory.

Some researchers say that no unified, systematic approach to the life course exists. Rather, the life course approach merges theoretical approaches from many disciplines, including sociology and psychology (Settersten, 2006). Bengtson and colleagues (1997, p. S80) say, "It is very difficult to incorporate into a single analysis the many contextual variables . . . that this approach identifies." Still, the life course approach encourages us to think about the many individual and social forces that affect aging.

Conflict Perspective

Conflict theory looks at the tensions that exist between groups in society. It grows out of the work of Karl Marx (1867–1895/1967), who viewed society as a struggle between social classes. Conflict theorists look at the ways socially powerful groups or the government (as a tool of these groups) shapes the lives of others. Few gerontologists have used the conflict perspective in their work. Those who do often look at how the economy or state policies influence old age.

In the early 20th century, for example, new machines demanded faster work. Older workers faced greater stresses than ever before. They often found it hard to keep up with the pace of the new machines. Many companies at this time replaced slower older workers with younger workers. The conflict perspective views these social tensions as part of a class struggle. The owners of factories exploited workers to increase their profits. Older people became victims of the system.

Gerontologists also make use of *political economy theory*, a type of conflict theory that looks at the state, the economy, social class, and their impact on people. The political economy approach traces the origins of older people's problems to the political and economic structure of capitalist society (Kail, Quadagno, & Keene, 2009). It looks at how the market economy and public policies produce inequality. The economic order and social programs and policies for older people can reinforce class, gender, and racial inequalities in later life. The political economy of aging framework sees old age as a social construction that mirrors the unequal distribution of resources in youth and middle age.

Cumulative disadvantage theory (a type of conflict theory) focuses on the lifelong effects of inequality. This theory says that disadvantages earlier in life accumulate and are magnified over the life course. "Thus, the more disadvantages individuals experience, the more likely they are to accrue subsequent and greater disadvantages" (Kail et al., 2009, p. 557)

For example, compared with men, women in their younger years are more likely to earn less income, work part time, or have disrupted work histories due to child care or care for other family members. Public and private pension programs tend to reward those with higher incomes and stable work histories. This means that, compared with older men, older women find themselves with fewer pension benefits and less savings.

Researchers have begun to study the causes of poverty in later life, women and gender discrimination, the ideology of aging as a social problem, and pensions and policies. Gerontologists have looked at the impact of retirement and pensions on the quality of life in old age (Moen & Spencer, 2006), the social structures that influence retirement for women (Zimmerman, Mitchell, Wister, & Gutman, 2000), and social policy in an aging society (Hudson, 2004).

Early work by Estes (1979) took a political economy approach to the study of welfare programs in the United States. She found that these programs tended to stigmatize older people. They defined the needs of older people as a need for services. This justified the expansion of the social service bureaucracy. Within the social welfare system, older people have little control over the services they can get or the ones they receive. Control lies in the hands of middle-class service workers. These workers define the older person's needs (e.g., for homemaker services or Meals on Wheels) and dole out services based on their assessment. Estes concluded that those who run the welfare state gain more than those served by it.

Estes's work shows the strength of the political economy approach. First, it places the study of aging in the context of large political, historical, economic, and social forces. Second, it views public pensions and income in later life as the outcome of a struggle between competing groups. Third, it predicts that economic and political forces will shape future changes in public pensions.

The political economy approach emphasizes the impact of history and economics on individuals. It shows how the state and social policies can increase or decrease social inequalities. But the political economy approach tends to overemphasize the poverty and problems older people face. It also tends to view the individual as the product of political and economic forces. It pays little attention to individuals' interpretations of social life. It says little about the ways that individuals shape their world through interactions with others. As Bengtson and colleagues (1997, p. S83) say, this perspective too often "paints a picture of all elders as powerless, forced to exist under oppressive structural arrangements with no control over their own lives."

Within the conflict perspective, *feminist theories* bridge both the micro-level and macro-level of analysis. They recognize the importance of social interaction and social structure in the study of aging. Feminist theories hold that society is gendered by nature. Feminist social gerontologists believe that gender defines social interaction and life experiences, including the experience of aging.

A feminist approach recognizes gender as a social organizing principle, not just a category on a census form (Calasanti & Slevin, 2006). Furthermore, within a patriarchal system (such as North American society), gender-based inequalities are created and perpetuated (for example, through pay inequality in the workplace). This results in social advantages for men (for instance, higher wages and better pensions) and disadvantages for women (higher rates of poverty in old age).

Feminist gerontologists criticize other theories of aging and other gerontologists for not focusing enough on gender relations or on older women's experiences (Calasanti, 2009; Allen & Walker, 2009). Feminist scholars also criticize the positivist assumption that social scientists stand outside the social world they study. Feminist theory and research includes a commitment to social change. Quadagno and Reid (1999, p. 344) say that "the challenge for social gerontology is not simply to understand how people interpret their private troubles but rather to consider also how these private troubles become public issues, thereby generating a societal response."

Feminist research in aging has focused on many unique issues: sexual relations in later life (Connidis, 2006), "double-duty care" by female health professionals who care for older parents (Ward-Griffin et al., 2005), the health of older men (Calasanti, 2004a), and identity and the aging body (Slevin, 2006).

Feminist theories make an important contribution to the study of aging. First, feminist theories, like the life course approach, recognize the importance of social structure, social interaction, and individual characteristics (primarily gender, but also race, ethnicity, and social class). Second, feminist theories present a more inclusive picture of aging and older adults, by focusing on the majority of the older population— women—and on issues that are relevant to women's lives. Third, feminist theories of aging challenge the traditional focus on men in research and the ageist biases in mainstream feminist theories that ignore

issues of age (Calasanti, 2004b; Calasanti & Slevin, 2006). Fourth, feminist theories challenge political economy studies that focus on the labor market and inequality related to work. These studies continue to devalue caregiving for children, spouses, and parents.

There are some limitations to feminist theories. For example, some gerontologists see gender as too narrow a focus for the study of aging. They say that feminist theories attempt to feminize the study of aging and that they ignore the experiences important to older men (Calasanti, 2004a). Critics also say that feminist theories dwell too much on social problems. They overlook the positive experience many women have in later life and women's contributions to society. Still, feminist theories of aging contribute to our understanding of aging. They have made gender an explicit theme in the study of aging and later life.[1]

Critique of the Conflict Perspective

Conflict theories ask questions neither of the other perspectives can. Conflict theories link individual problems to larger social issues of the economy and the state. Still, conflict theories have their limits. First, they overemphasize the poverty and problems that older people face. Second, they overemphasize the effect of social structures on individual aging. Third, they tend to see the person as the product of social and political forces. Conflict theories pay little attention to the responses older people make to social pressures.

Gerontologists need theories to make sense of the mass of detailed information that researchers gather. A statement made more than a decade ago by Bengtson and his colleagues (1997, S84) remains true today. They say that "theory is not a marginal, meaningless 'tacked-on' exercise to presenting results in an empirical paper. Rather, cumulative theory-building represents the core of the foundation of scientific inquiry and knowledge" (see also Biggs, Hendricks, & Lowenstein, 2003).

Gerontological theories offer many explanations of aging. Their variety reflects the many dimensions of gerontological research. Gerontologists have borrowed theoretical perspectives from most of the social sciences. They have modified these theories to fit the study of aging. In some cases, they have developed new theories (such as age stratification theory and the life course approach) to fit the issues that gerontologists study. Gerontologists can select from the theories presented here and from many more specific

[1] I thank my colleague, Professor Lori Campbell, McMaster University, for developing this review of feminist gerontology.

theories in their attempts to understand aging. Each of these theories and perspectives gives us a different insight into what it means to age.

New Developments in Theory

What theoretical ideas have emerged in social gerontology in recent years? What approaches will emerge or grow in the years ahead? Some researchers and theorists support the wider use of interpretive frameworks for studying aging. Narrative gerontology offers one new framework (Randall & Kenyon, 2004). This approach seeks to understand the "inside" of aging. It studies the stories that people tell in order to organize and make sense of their lives. These stories create meaning around their experience of aging. Becker (2001) used the narrative approach to study older people who live with chronic pain. Other writers have studied the life stories of people with dementia and terminal illness (Basting, 2003; Kuhl & Westwood, 2001). Narrative gerontology shows that people "compose" their lives through their life stories. These stories are retold, revisited, and reinterpreted as people age.

Moral economy theory, a complement to political economy theory, grew out of the work of E. P. Thompson in England. Political economy theorists and researchers have begun to use this perspective to explore issues such as retirement, long-term care (Minkler & Estes, 1999), and community volunteerism (Narushima, 2005). This approach to the study of aging looks at the shared moral assumptions held by members of a society. Studies that use this approach look at values such as justice and fairness in society and how they affect social policies. The moral economy theory is concerned with the social consensus that underlies issues such as justice between the generations, pension entitlements, and access to health care.

Critical gerontology emerged to address limitations in mainstream gerontological theory. Ray (2003, 2008) makes the distinction between "theory" and "critical theory." Theory helps to guide research and interpret research findings. Critical theory questions these findings. It reminds "us that all theories are partial, that other meanings are always possible, that meaning-making itself is an exercise in power and authority, and that we promote some meanings at the expense of others" (Ray, 2003, p. 34).

Estes (2003; also Katz, 2003), for example, criticizes mainstream theory for not "looking within" to examine and question its underlying and "taken-for-granted" assumptions about aging. This view asks gerontologists to look at "what is missing, ignored, or denied" within aging theories and research. This approach has produced some fresh insights from gerontologists who reflect on their own lives.

Stephen Katz (2008, p. 141), for example, traces his thoughts and feelings about old age to his youth in Toronto's Jewish quarter in Kensington Market. There he identified "old" with "the majority adults; Yiddish; rye bread; barrels of pickled and salted foods. . . ." His warm reflections on his youth show the roots of his interest in aging today. "Indeed," he says, "if one probes the career of any author or thinker or critic, one will find a narrative of life whose experiences, revelations, and suffering are the voice and soul of their work" (p. 145).

Bengtson and colleagues (2009) see a trend toward novelty as they look across the field of theory in gerontology. They note that theories today differ in their origins, their scope, and their focus of interest. But these writers also recognize "an integration of theoretical perspectives both within and across disciplines." For example, they see a growing awareness in all disciplines of aging as a lifelong process. In psychology and biology this takes the form of life-span development. It takes the form of the life course approach in sociology. It takes the form of a life-cycle model in the economy of aging.

They see similarities across disciplines in an interest in: (1) the study of cumulative advantages and disadvantages of aging; (2) the interrelationship of the environment and the person; (3) the variability that comes with aging; and (4) the need for cross-disciplinary thinking.

New theoretical approaches will include biological and genetic approaches to aging as well as an interest in the effects of globalization on aging.

Theory will remain central to studying aging. Bengtson, Rice, and Johnson (1999) say that "theory is the compass with which to navigate through vast seas of data. It is the means by which data are transformed into meaningful explanations, or stories, about the processes and consequences of aging." Gerontological theories offer many explanations of aging. Their variety reflects the many dimensions of gerontological research. Each of these perspectives gives us a different insight into what it means to age.

RESEARCH ISSUES AND METHODS

Gerontologists use many different methods to study aging. Methods vary by discipline, by subfields within a discipline, and by the question under study. Methods range from the laboratory work of biomedical scientists to the intelligence tests of psychologists, from studies of diaries and literature, to surveys such as the U.S. Census. Some studies use more than one method. The U.S. Health and Retirement Study (U.S. Department of Health and Human Services, 2007), for example, used face-to-face interviews in people's homes, telephone interviews, and physiological measurements to study the retirement process. The proper use of research methods ensures that gerontologists end up with reliable and valid results. The following discussion looks at some of the methodological issues that gerontologists face.

Experimental Designs

Social gerontologists want to understand the changes that take place in individuals over time. For example, a gerontologist might want to know how drinking milk in childhood affects bone density in old age. An experiment could answer this question. A researcher could divide a group of children into two groups in childhood. One group would drink milk. The other would not. After 60 years, the researchers would measure the effects of milk drinking on bone density. Of course, gerontologists cannot conduct this kind of experiment. They could not risk the health of a group of children. Even if they could do the experiment, they would have to wait nearly a lifetime to get the results.

Instead, social gerontologists more often work with groups that already exist. For example, a gerontologist might study bone density in two groups of women born at different times. These groups might differ naturally in the diet they ate. Women who grew up during the Great Depression, for example, may have had a poorer diet than women born 10 years later. A gerontologist could compare the bone density in these two groups of women in old age.

Gerontologists often conduct this kind of study. These studies take the place of formal experiments and often serve as the quickest, least expensive way to gather information. But this type of study presents problems for the researcher. For instance, imagine a researcher who conducts a study of diet and bone density in older women in 2010. She looks at bone density in two groups of women—one group born in 1940 (70 years old) and the other born in 1930 (80 years old and born during the Great Depression). The researcher finds that women born during the Depression (who had poor diets) have less bone density than women born after the Depression.

Does this mean that poor diet in childhood leads to less bone density in old age? Not necessarily. The researchers want to know whether one variable (diet) causes a change in another variable (bone density). They have found a **correlation** or regular relationship between these two variables, but a high correlation between two variables (such as childhood diet and bone

---

BOX 2.3
TIMING AND THE LIMITATIONS OF SURVEY DATA

The AARP conducted a survey titled "Staying Ahead of the Curve: The AARP Work and Career Study." The AARP conducted the study in the spring of 2007. The survey sample included 1,500 workers between the ages of 45 and 74. All had jobs at the time or were looking for work. The researchers included the following note at the start of their report.

A NOTE ON THE TIMING: When respondents were interviewed for this survey in the spring of 2007, the economy was relatively strong and unemployment was lower than at the time that the writing of this report was being completed in the spring of 2008. If the survey were taken during the current economic slowdown, it is possible that responses to questions would be different—especially those concerning job security, age discrimination, and motivations to work.

This comment shows the sensitivity of data to changing social conditions. Think about a survey that asks 65- to 69-year-olds about their attitudes toward retirement and their financial resources. Five years later a survey asks these same people the same questions. Will they give the same answers that they gave the first time?

A change in Social Security policies, a downturn in the housing market, or an economic boom could change their answers. Likewise, a new cohort of 65- to 69-year-olds at the time of the second survey might give answers very different from those of the first cohort five years ago. Readers of survey reports need to keep in mind that surveys provide a snapshot of a population at one point in time.

density in old age) does not prove that one caused the other. Consider some other possibilities.

First, the 1930 group is 10 years older than the 1940 group at the time of the study. Bone density may decrease with age. The two groups may differ because bone density decreases between ages 70 and 80. Diet in childhood may have little or nothing to do with this.

Second, the two groups may have begun life with different bone densities due to differences in their mothers' diets. Children born during the Depression may suffer throughout their lives from the effects of their mothers' poor nutrition.

Third, historical events may have influenced these two groups differently. For example, older women from both the 1930 and 1940 groups have begun to exercise in the past few years. This increase in activity will increase bone density, but it may have less effect on older women. This effect makes it unclear whether childhood diet led to the differences in bone density that the researcher found.

These examples show the kinds of problems gerontologists face when they search for the causes of change in later life. Gerontologists generally place changes in old age into one of three categories: age effects, cohort effects, or period effects.

Age effects, due to physical decline, appear with the passage of time. They include an increase in the body's fat-to-muscle ratio, a decrease in lung elasticity, and decreases in bone density. They also include environmentally caused changes such as wrinkled skin and cataracts caused by the sun.

Cohort effects are related to the time of a person's birth. A *cohort* refers to a group of people born around the same time (usually within a 5-year period). People born in a certain cohort often share a common background and view of the world. People born just after World War II, for example, were the first cohorts exposed to large doses of television. This shaped their entertainment habits, values, and lifestyles.

Period effects are due to the time of measurement. This would include historical effects on measurement, such as an ongoing war, or changes in health habits, such as increased exercise. These effects have different influences on different age cohorts.

Gerontologists try to disentangle these effects to understand the causes of aging. Maddox and Campbell (1985, p. 20) called this the "age/period/cohort (APC) problem." Gerontologists use a number of research designs to look at these three effects and understand change in later life.

Cross-Sectional Designs

A cross-sectional study takes place when a researcher studies several age groups at one point in time. Many studies use this approach (Neuman & Robson, 2009). Brach and colleagues (Brach, Simonsick, Kritchevsky, Yaffe, & Neuman, 2004), for example, used data from a questionnaire study to compare the physical functioning of older people who exercised or stayed active with those who were inactive. The researchers found that people in the exercise group had significantly better physical functioning than the active group and the inactive group. They conclude that twenty to thirty minutes of exercise most days leads to better physical functioning.

Bond and colleagues (2003) studied the relationship between alcohol consumption and depression among Japanese Americans and white Americans between the ages of 65 and 101. The study analyzed data from more than 4,000 people. The study found that the younger people in the study consumed more alcohol and had lower depression scores.

Researchers use cross-sectional designs for a number of reasons. First, cross-sectional data sets may already exist. This saves time and money. The cross-sectional exercise and activity data used by Brach and colleagues (2004), for example, came from a larger longitudinal study, the Aging and Body Composition (Health ABC) study. This information cost thousands of dollars and many weeks to collect. The researchers wanted to compare the responses of several age groups at one point in time, and the data from this already completed study could answer this question.

Second, cross-sectional designs control for environmental events that might affect the study. For example, if the season of the year affects answers on a housing study, then a one-time study can get responses from everyone in the same season. Third, cross-sectional designs allow the researcher to gather data about many age groups in one study.

Cross-sectional studies show differences between age groups. However, they may confuse differences between age groups (differences due to when a person was born) with changes due to aging. For example, many cross-sectional studies done in psychology until the 1960s found that older age groups had lower intelligence scores than younger age groups. This led to the conclusion that intelligence decreases with age.

But other things could explain this apparent decline in intelligence with age. For example, educational differences between the older and younger groups account, at least in part, for the cross-sectional findings. Older cohorts with less education tended to do less well on paper-and-pencil tests and felt more test anxiety. This led to lower intelligence scores.

Most researchers who study aging still use cross-sectional designs. They often do this for practical reasons. Cross-sectional studies cost less to conduct, and researchers can analyze the data immediately. But cross-sectional studies can lead to errors in interpretation. They confound aging and cohort effects. They rely on the untested assumption that between-person differences reflect within-person changes over time. Researchers try to overcome this problem. They can combine results from a number of cross-sectional studies. This gives a picture of change over time. It allows gerontologists to study social trends and to assess the impact of social policies. The use of more than one cross-sectional study creates a longitudinal design. Longitudinal studies correct for some of the problems that cross-sectional studies face.

Longitudinal Designs

Longitudinal studies look at age cohorts or individuals over time. Longitudinal studies of intelligence, for example, help untangle the effects of background and environment (cohort effects) from changes due to age. A longitudinal study, for example, can compare a person's test scores at age 45, 50, and 55. This provides a record of how a person's mental ability changes over the years. Hofer and Sliwinski (2006) report the existence of more than 40 large-scale longitudinal studies of people aged 50 and over. These studies took place in the United States and in other countries. They offer information about changes within individuals over time.

The Health and Retirement Study (National Institute on Aging and National Institutes of Health, 2007) conducted in the United States offers a good example of a longitudinal study. Researchers collected a first round of data from 12,600 people aged 51 to 61 in 1992. Researchers also drew an oversample of people from Florida, people of African American descent, and people with Hispanic heritage. Follow-up waves of this study take place every 2 years. A second study, the Study of Assets and Health Dynamics Among the Oldest Old, began in 1993, and the data from the two studies were merged into a single study. The study also added two new groups in 1998. It included age groups not in the two original studies, and it included a group in their 50s to replace people in the original group who had aged.

This study looks at the retirement experience, savings, health insurance coverage, and economic condition of older Americans. The study focuses on health and economic transitions in later life. It also looks at the role that families play in the economic support of older people. The longitudinal design follows the same people over many years (at 2-year intervals). Researchers can use these findings to see what events influence retirement decisions and how people manage the challenges of later life.

One study based on these findings, for example, found that, over time, education level best predicted a person's retirement decision. People with high levels of education and good emotional health tended to stay on the job. The researchers say that the current trend toward early retirement could end as more educated cohorts enter the retirement years (Boeri & Baunach, 2002). These and other findings will help policy makers plan for an aging society.

Longitudinal studies pose practical problems. First, they take many years to complete. The researcher, the funding agency, or the public may want faster results. Second, they cost more money than cross-sectional studies. A longitudinal study requires a number of tests or surveys. Third, fewer grants exist for longitudinal studies than for cross-sectional studies. Longitudinal studies depend on a stream of funding over many years that granting bodies and the government find hard to promise.

Fourth, longitudinal studies lose members over time (through dropouts or death) (Alwin, Hofer, & McCammon, 2006). This may lead to confusing findings. For example, if lower intelligence leads to shorter life, then, over time, as less intelligent people die off, the average intelligence score for a group may improve. This confounds the study results (Hofer & Sliwinski, 2006). The same holds true for studies of disease (Vogler, 2006). Those who die during a study leave a healthier, less diseased group behind. This group no longer represents the original sample's characteristics. Some longitudinal studies try to overcome this problem. They bring new people into the study as people die off or drop out.

Longitudinal studies also have other drawbacks. They confound age effects (due to aging) with period effects (due to the time of testing). For example, intelligence test results reflect economic, social, and political conditions at the time of the test. A war or other stressful social event may affect results. Also, people may improve their test scores with practice as they get tested many times. This reflects a change unrelated to aging.

BOX 2.4
THE BALTIMORE LONGITUDINAL STUDY OF AGING

Longitudinal studies take time, money, and management skill. A lack of any of these will cause a study to fizzle and die. Studies that have lasted many years stand as a tribute to the planning and dedication of their creators and current researchers.

The Baltimore Longitudinal Study of Aging (BLSA) (National Institute on Aging, 2010a), begun in 1958, celebrated its 50th anniversary in 2008. It is the longest-running scientific study of human aging in the United States. The study aims to (1) measure biological and behavioral changes as people age, (2) relate these measures to one another, and (3) separate universal aging processes from disease and the effects of the environment. Researchers have produced more than 800 articles and reports using the data from this study. These findings have shaped scientists' and practitioners' thinking about the aging process.

People in the study come to Baltimore every 2 years for a battery of tests and measurements. In 2010, the BLSA included 1,400 men and women (women first entered the study in 1978). People range in age from their 20s to their early 100s. The oldest person is 102. Many people have taken part in the study for most of their adult lives. The study has included more than 2,500 people in its history, and it adds new people every year. Some people are fourth-generation BLSA volunteers.

All longitudinal studies face the problem of dropouts. How does the BLSA manage to keep so many of its volunteers in the study over so many years? The BLSA, from the start, treated the people in the study as coworkers. One volunteer said the study "made me feel not like a guinea pig, but like a human being who is part of a great scientific enterprise."

Louise Capone, a 47-year-old woman in the study, who has been tested seven times so far, says:

> This is really what keeps me coming back. . . . We get the results of our own tests, which are nice to have, but also we learn what the study is learning, overall. There is a real sense of being a partner in the study, of working with the researchers toward a goal. (U.S. Department of Health and Human Services, BLSA, 1993)

The BLSA has produced many breakthroughs and supports for our understanding of aging. Consider the following findings:

- Differences between individuals increase with age.
- People can reduce the decline in oxygen use that comes with age, if they stay active.
- Disease-free older people at rest have cardiac output similar to that of younger people.
- Until at least age 70, problem-solving ability shows little or no decline.
- Personality remains stable through most of life. A cheerful person in youth will stay that way in old age.

These longitudinal findings present a clearer picture of the changes that come with time, and they suggest how people can improve functions that decline through neglect or misuse.

Paul Costa, a personality psychologist, says that the BLSA gives us a new view of aging. "We need not worry that we will become crotchety with age or that only firm resignation can save us from despair and fear of death. . . . We need not dread our future" (U.S. Department of Health and Human Services, 1993).

Source: National Institute on Aging. (2010a). *Baltimore Longitudinal Study of Aging*. National Institutes of Health. Retrieved October 25, 2010, from www.grc.nia.nih.gov/branches/blsa/blsanew.htm

---

A third method, time-lag comparison design, tries to overcome the problems raised by simple cross-sectional and simple longitudinal designs. Time-lag studies look at groups of people of the same age at different points in time (e.g., 65-year-olds in 1990, 2000, and 2010; 60-year-olds over this same time period). This type of study tries to measure differences between cohorts.

Like cross-sectional and longitudinal methods, the time-lag method also presents problems. It confounds cohort effects with environmental effects. If a research study finds that 70-year-olds in 2005 visited doctors less often than 70-year-olds did in 1985, this difference

may be due to the better health of 70-year-olds in 2005 (a cohort effect). Or it may be due to a change in the health care system, perhaps higher costs to users that discourage visits to doctors (an environmental effect).

Each of these designs attempts to understand the effects of aging on individuals, and each design has its place in the researcher's tool kit. (See Figure 2.1.) Gerontologists must use these methods to get a clearer picture of how people change over time. Longitudinal studies prove especially useful in studies of health over time. This approach can track the influence of behaviors (such as smoking or exercise) on health.

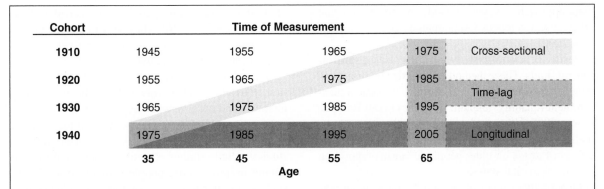

Cohort	Time of Measurement				
1910	1945	1955	1965	1975	Cross-sectional
1920	1955	1965	1975	1985	
					Time-lag
1930	1965	1975	1985	1995	
1940	1975	1985	1995	2005	Longitudinal
	35	**45**	**55**	**65**	
		Age			

This chart shows the different approaches used in three types of study design.

The hypothetical cross-sectional study took place in 1975 and studied four age groups (35, 45, 55, and 65) in that year. It compared findings across age groups. This study took a snapshot of age differences at one point in time.

The longitudinal study also began in 1975, but it went on for 30 years. It measured the 1940 cohort four times (in 1975, 1985, 1995, and 2005) at four different ages (35, 45, 55, and 65). The study had fewer people in it at each time of measurement due to dropouts and deaths. (Some research studies of this type replace people who die or leave the study.) This study could follow age changes in the 1940 cohort.

The time-lag study measured 65-year-olds at four times (1965, 1975, 1985, and 1995). This study had different people in the sample at each time of measurement. It could show how 65-year-olds differed at each time of measurement.

FIGURE 2.1   Cross-Sectional, Longitudinal, and Time-Lag Designs

Source: Adapted from P. B. Baltes, H. W. Reese, and J. R. Nesselroade, *Life-Span Developmental Psychology: Introduction to Research Methods*, 1977, Monterey, CA: Brooks/Cole.

Longitudinal studies can also assess the influence of early life experiences on health in later life.

Salthouse (2006) says that only longitudinal studies allow researchers to assess the long-term effects of interventions. For example, it may take years for an exercise program to affect health in later life. An immediate effect of the exercise program (e.g., an improved self-image) might lessen and disappear over time. Salthouse admits that long-term studies cost a lot and consume time and energy. But they provide the only accurate assessment of an intervention's effect on the process of aging.

Complex methods such as time-lag designs help sort out the effects of age, cohort, and period. But these results still leave unanswered questions (Alwin et al., 2006). For example, a longitudinal design may clearly show that lung elasticity decreases with age. And it may show that this holds true for all age cohorts and at different points in time. But this study says nothing about why the lung changes. After studies sort out these effects, the gerontologist's work has only begun. "Separating the confounds," Botwinick says, "is not the end of the line, it is but the beginning" (1984, p. 400). Whatever method the researcher chooses, researchers must look closely to find the causes of the change.

Quantitative and Qualitative Methods

Paradigms are frameworks used to think about and organize an understanding of natural or social phenomena (Online Dictionary, 2004). They define what questions scientists ask and how scientists conduct their studies.

Gerontology has a long history of using a natural science paradigm. This began with studies of physiology and disease. Later, social scientists followed biomedical science in using mathematical measurement. Today, gerontologists often apply the methods of natural science—mathematical measurement, statistical methods, cause-and-effect models—to the study of aging.

Philosophers refer to this type of science as **positivism**. Positivism seeks to control natural events like aging. It underlies the work in the biology and physiology of aging. Positivist science has led to many of the breakthroughs in medicine in the past century. It has also led to a more detailed understanding of the aging process.

Positivism assumes a nonreflexive object of study. Hormones, muscles, and vitamins fit this picture. The successes of positivist study in biology and physiology have led to its application to other fields—recreation, family life, and creativity. Positivism has become the main approach to scientific study in gerontology and other social sciences (Achenbaum, 2000a; Cole & Ray, 2000).

Positivist scientific study typically uses **quantitative methods**. These methods emphasize relationships between and among variables through numerical measurement (quantity, amount, frequency) (Del Balso & Lewis, 2008; Neuman & Robson, 2009). Quantitative methods range from pharmaceutical research on the effects of drugs on older people to census reports on income or marital status.

Quantitative studies often take the form of surveys or questionnaires. Researchers then summarize responses into numerical values for statistical analysis.

This model of scientific rationality serves certain ends. It discovers the facts about income, health care services, recreation, and other subjects of interest to gerontologists. It also suggests ways to improve later life (e.g., by showing the need for more health care services). But this approach may apply less well to understanding why people do what they do. A study might show that a high percent of people quit exercise programs after they sign up for a gym. But this finding doesn't say why people quit. Census data may provide information on mortality rates for men and women. But they can't tell us why, compared to women, men tend to marry again shortly after widowhood. Positivism limits the study of aging to certain topics and approaches. It rules out other questions and methods.

Critical gerontology questions the ideals of positivist science. Critical gerontologists say the positivist approach creates a system that dominates older people (Moody, 1993). For example, medical science turns the older person into a patient. It prescribes drugs, plans treatment, and controls access to health services. It does all this in the name of health care. But to provide this care, medical science turns the older person into a passive object. Critical gerontology exposes the effects of positivism on older people. Critical research seeks to empower people by giving them an understanding of the forces that shape their lives.

Critical gerontologists often use **qualitative methods** such as in-depth interviews, life histories, case studies, analysis of the content of documents or artifacts, and observation. Qualitative methods use an interpretive theoretical approach to understand these data. "Qualitative research is characterized by a verbal or literary presentation of data" (Del Balso & Lewis, 2008, p. 40).

The use of qualitative methods in research on aging has grown significantly in recent years. Qualitative researchers "look at social life from multiple points of

view and explain how people construct identities" (Neuman, 2003, p. 146). They seek to understand the social world and social experience of individuals from the subjects' own perspectives.

Qualitative methods include participant observation. Participant observers spend time with group members and observe what they do. Researchers want to learn as much as possible about social life from the participants' points of view. Participant observation studies include studies of national identity formation among minority older people (Tammeveski, 2003), studies of how spouses respond to caregiving (Calasanti, 2006), and studies of older people in assisted-living facilities (Ball et al., 2004). Neuman (2003, p. 146) says that "instead of trying to convert social life into variables or numbers, qualitative researchers borrow ideas from the people they study." Researchers try to understand the meanings people bring to social interactions. Qualitative research wants to give voice to the study participants. Studies often report results in the subjects' own words.

Beard (2004) conducted a participant observation study of people diagnosed with Alzheimer's disease. She also used in-depth interviews and focus group discussions to study the experience of memory loss. The study took place over 6 months. Like many researchers who use this method, Beard used unstructured interviews and accounts of the participants' experiences. She found that, in spite of memory loss, participants found ways to manage the effects of the illness and preserve their sense of self.

Saarnio and Isola (2009) conducted an observational study of elderly people in institutions in Finland. The researchers wanted to study the use of physical restraints in these settings. The researchers collected data on restraints for 4 months. They spent between 6 and 16 hours each week in the institutions. They observed staff and patients on all shifts. The researchers took notes during their time in the institutions and kept a journal of their emotions during the research.

The study found that the staff frequently used restraints to control patients. Staff used belts to keep people in their chairs, they tied patients to beds with linens, they used physical force, and they issued sharp verbal commands.

Sometimes staff reduced patients' mobility through passive restraint. For example, they restrained patients by removing a person's walker or wheelchair. They sometimes intentionally removed alarm bells so patients could not call for help. Nurses even kept patients underdressed so they would be less likely to appear in public.

A field note from this study gives an example of what one researcher observed: "The elderly patient is sitting in a wheelchair in his underpants and tells me right away that he hasn't been given any trousers by the nurses although he has asked for them. He says that he's too embarrassed to walk around in the corridor without his trousers on" (p. 283).

The researchers conclude that this environment does not serve older patients' needs. Staff systematically ignored patients and kept them immobile to decrease their workload. This frustrated patients and created a dangerous and unpleasant environment. These conditions raise ethical questions about the treatment of patients and the quality of care they receive.

Participant observation allowed the researchers to observe the actual conditions in the nursing home. It's doubtful that the researchers could have gotten this information any other way.

This study also shows the amount of time and effort it takes to do participant observation research. Participant observation researchers need to get the permission to enter the organization they plan to study. They must carefully observe and document what they see and hear.

Because entering and working in the field takes a lot of time, relatively few researchers use this method. But this study shows that participant observation produces unique and insightful results.

Critical gerontology looks for those places and moments where alternative models of aging would improve the lives of older people. The interests of critical gerontology and positivist gerontology differ. Positivist gerontology wants prediction and control over aging. Positivist studies produce knowledge that the state or experts in the field of aging can use to cure disease, improve housing, or develop effective fitness programs. This takes the form of control by professionals, government agencies, and policies. Critical gerontology, on the other hand, has a different agenda. It works to "open up possibilities of communication, mutual understanding, and coordinated social action" (Moody, 1993, p. xxiii). It aims to empower older people and enhance their freedom.

Quantitative and qualitative methods each have their strengths and limitations. Quantitative methods allow researchers to gather a great deal of information on a wide range of issues. Moreover, they can analyze a large sample and generalize their results to a larger population. But quantitative researchers structure their research questions and give respondents limited choices. This kind of research offers little opportunity to capture the rich description of individuals' subjective experiences or their perceptions of their social world (Lincoln & Guba, 2000; Neuman, 2003).

Qualitative methods allow researchers to appreciate the complexity of social interactions and behaviors. These methods study how individuals understand and give meaning to their lives (Del Balso & Lewis, 2008; Neuman & Robson, 2009). They allow the words and subjective experiences of participants to be heard.

Qualitative research also has its limits. Researchers often use small sample sizes. This limits generalization to a larger population. Some researchers combine both quantitative and qualitative methods in one study (Neuman & Robson, 2009).

BOX 2.5
STRENGTHS AND WEAKNESSES OF QUALITATIVE AND QUANTITATIVE METHODS

	Quantitative Methods	*Qualitative Methods*
Strengths	• Data can be quantified, standardized, and measured	• Hear voice of participants
	• Generalizable to larger population	• Captures subjective experiences
	• Can study wide range of topics	• Data detailed, rich, in depth
	• Study can be replicated	• Suitable for "sensitive" topics
Weaknesses	• Data general and lacks depth	• Not generalizable
	• Cannot capture subjective experience or meanings	• Interviewer effect
	• Responses forced into "tick boxes"	• Unintentional subjectivity or bias of researcher
	• Not suitable for "sensitive" topics	• Time and labor intensive

This table summarizes some general advantages and disadvantages of qualitative and quantitative methods, based on Neuman and Robson (2009).

Source: From *Basics of Social Research: Qualitative and Quantitative Approaches, Canadian Edition,* by W. L. Neuman and K. Robson, 2009, Toronto, ON: Pearson Education Canada. Reprinted with permission.

The Humanities

The study of aging has grown to include the humanities (e.g., literature, philosophy, fine arts) as well as biomedicine and social science (Cole & Ray, 2000). Frankel says, "The humanities are that form of knowledge in which the knower is revealed . . . when we are asked to contemplate not only the proposition but the proposer, when we hear the human voice behind what is said" (cited in Moody, 1988b).

Scholars in the humanities use many methods to study aging. Vesperi (2002) shows how literary interpretation opens up new ways of thinking about aging. Yahnke (2000), for example, studied the portrayal of aging in films and videos. He looked at how these media presented the themes of intergenerational relations and regeneration in later life. He found that most films give a positive view of aging by showing satisfying relationships and fulfillment in old age.

Shenk and Schmid (2002) list the use of photo archives, self-portraits, photocollage, and photography as resources and methods for studying aging. Winkler (1992) studied pictures of aging by great artists, selecting examples from Ghirlandaio (15th century) to Käthe Kollwitz (20th century). These pictures guide us, she says, to reflect on the end of life. Historians have studied population trends, church records, and diaries (Haber, 2000). These studies allow us to compare aging today with old age at other times and in other places.

Some gerontologists have written autobiographical sketches (Katz, 2008; Calasanti, 2008) to expand their own understanding of aging. This goes against the positivist bias of gerontology research, but it fits well within a humanistic approach, and it reveals the human face of aging.

Aging studies in the humanities stand on the margins of gerontology today, but interest in this approach continues to grow (Achenbaum, 2000a). The Gerontological Society of America, for example, at its annual meetings sponsors an interest group in the humanities, and the second edition of *Handbook of the Humanities and Aging* appeared in 2000 (Cole & Ray, 2000). Studies in the humanities reflect on the universal experience of aging. They show us the value that great writers, artists, and scholars place on old age. They expose us to new ways of thinking about aging and offer us new ways to explore our own lives.

Information Literacy: The Challenge of the Internet

Anyone with a computer can now read and download volumes of information about aging. Web sites offer everything from complex government documents (e.g., census data) to infomercials (e.g., investment advice). How can a person assess the quality of information available today?

The American Library Association's (ALA) *Presidential Committee on Information Literacy: Final Report* (1989) states, "To be information literate, a person must be able to recognize when information is needed and have the ability to locate, evaluate, and use effectively the needed information." Information literacy is a vital skill for anyone who wants to understand aging today.

Consider a request for health information. I just typed the word "arthritis" into the Google search engine (December 18, 2010). The first page of Web sites retrieved included the Arthritis Foundation, Wikipedia (the free encyclopedia), WebMD, a Mayo Clinic site on rheumatoid arthritis, the U.S. Centers for Disease Control and Prevention (CDC), and a site related to the U.S. National Institutes of Health (NIH). These sources provide a range of information on arthritis. But the quality of information on these sites varies.

The government sources, the CDC (2010) site, for example, links to information about research grants, scientific findings on this topic, and practical information on personal care. It also links to research reports and information on government agencies. This site provides a high standard of information quality. For example, the scientific reports have passed inspection by top scientists.

But all information has a bias. The government site takes Western scientific method and knowledge as a cornerstone of truth. Someone questioning the government's goals, someone skeptical of scientific methods and findings, someone who wants a more personal view of aging will question the value of this site.

Wikipedia (2011) on the other hand, provides this disclaimer: "Older articles tend to grow more comprehensive and balanced; newer articles may contain misinformation, unencyclopedic content, or vandalism. Awareness of this aids obtaining valid information and avoiding recently added misinformation."

Wikipedia, an encyclopedia created by a community of users and changed constantly by those users, does not claim to offer true or valid knowledge. The managers of the Wikipedia site admit bias in the listings. They warn readers about potentially misleading information.

Wikipedia shows sensitivity to the quality of the information it provides. This is good. But it leaves the reader to sort out the truth from the misinformation. For example, a section on the cognitive effects of aging takes up only one paragraph, though it links to many other submissions. A link to memory provides only four paragraphs, but again provides many links to other articles. And these entries have many further links.

Wikipedia shows the strengths and the weaknesses of Web-based information. It allows a reader to surf from one topic to another according to his or her needs, and it offers a lot of information from a wide range of authors. But it offers no expert review or screening of the information. The Wikipedia community members can change information they consider inaccurate. But Wikipedia leaves it to the reader to decide on the validity and reliability of the information. Wikipedia might serve as a starting point for research, but it can mislead a naïve reader who has little experience in a field.

A site called WebMD (2010) provides a third example of information available on the Web. It sits somewhere between the government sources and Wikipedia on the reliability scale. The site provides up-to-date information on arthritis and health tips designed to inform the general public. But a close look at the site shows that it accepts advertising. And this could bias the information presented. For example, the editor of this site chooses what information to present. Does the editor subtly or overtly choose news items to attract or keep advertisers? Would the editor leave out an item that reflected badly on an advertiser? The reader needs to keep these questions in mind. A serious student of this subject would not use this source alone for information on arthritis.

Today you have more information available to you than ever before. And you can get that information at the touch of a button. Blogs, wikis, YouTube, and Twitter all offer opportunities for people to express and publish their views. Web sites that can seem informational (sites put up by financial advisors, insurance agents, etc.) may actually be infomercials for a product. These sites exist side by side on the Web with U.S. government studies and scholarly reports. This places a greater burden than ever before on your ability to assess the quality of the information you receive.

To understand this issue firsthand, try a Google search on some aging-related topics (e.g., retirement, pensions, or arthritis). Look carefully at the types of sites retrieved (government, for-profit, nonprofit, individual, etc.). Go to a few of these sites and consider the variations in the quality of information provided.

Also, go to Wikipedia and enter the same keywords as you did in the Google search. Explore the topic by reading a section and then going to related links in the article. Note how easily you can gather information as you go from topic to topic. But think about the sources of the information. Critically evaluate the information you gather. Look at the variation in the completeness of entries, in the types of references given, and in the content of the entries. These exercises will sharpen your thinking and build your information literacy skills.

ETHICAL ISSUES IN RESEARCH

Research studies on human subjects face ethical challenges. And studies of certain frail or vulnerable groups pose unique problems. Researchers need to consider the ethical implications of studying institutionalized older people, those living in poverty, the socially isolated (Russell, 1999), and people with Alzheimer's disease or other cognitive impairments (Karlawish, 2004; Sevick et al., 2003). They also need to consider the ethics of doing field research where the researcher observes people (e.g., in a nursing home) without their permission.

Saarnio and Isola (2009) in their study of physical restraints, for example, had to get permission to conduct their research. They report the following method for getting permission: "After obtaining the permits to conduct the study, an information session was organized for the staff working on the units; after the session they could decide whether to take part in the study. The decision about taking part in the study was collective, and the head nurse of each unit passed on the information about the unit's participation to the researcher (R.S.)."

Note that first the researchers needed to get "permits" to conduct the study (it's unclear from their report who issued these permits). They then took care to inform participants (nurses) about the research and its purposes. Participants could opt out of the research if they chose. Note also that they got group consent. It appears that a nurse who did not want to participate had no choice once the group made its decision. Also, note that the patients had no say in this decision. Should the patients have been consulted? Did the researcher need their permission to proceed? An ethics committee would have to consider these issues before granting permission for the research to go ahead.

Most professional associations have a code of ethics that they require members to follow. (See Box 2.6.) Universities also have ethical guidelines and standards for research. They often have a research ethics committee that reviews proposed projects. The ethics review board must approve each study, weigh the potential risks and benefits, and then give permission for research to proceed. Research committees today demand informed consent from the people under study. They also require full disclosure to the subjects of the researcher's intent.

Universities do this for several reasons: to protect themselves from lawsuits, to ensure that subjects understand the studies they take part in, and to protect subjects from harm. My own university requires ethical review for all faculty and student projects that involve an older person. This includes class projects such as interviewing an older person or observing activities at a senior center.

BOX 2.6
ETHICAL PRINCIPLES OF PSYCHOLOGISTS AND CODE OF CONDUCT

Most professional associations have a code of ethics that guides members' conduct. The American Psychological Association, for example, has an ethics code titled *Ethical Principles of Psychologists and Code of Conduct*. This ethics code sets standards of practice for members and states penalties for violating the code.

Standard 8, entitled "Research and Publication," discusses the need for institutional approval, informed consent from participants, and the use of deception in research.

8.01 Institutional Approval

When institutional approval is required, psychologists provide accurate information about their research proposals and obtain approval prior to conducting the research. They conduct the research in accordance with the approved research protocol.

8.02 Informed Consent to Research

(a) When obtaining informed consent as required in Standard 3.10, Informed Consent, psychologists inform participants about (1) the purpose of the research, expected duration, and procedures; (2) their right to decline to participate and to withdraw from the research once participation has begun; (3) the foreseeable consequences of declining or withdrawing; (4) reasonably foreseeable factors that may be expected to influence their willingness to participate such as potential risks, discomfort, or adverse effects; (5) any prospective research benefits; (6) limits of confidentiality; (7) incentives for participation; and (8) whom to contact for questions about the research and research participants' rights. They provide opportunity for the prospective participants to ask questions and receive answers. (See also Standards 8.03, Informed Consent for Recording Voices and Images in Research; 8.05, Dispensing With Informed Consent for Research; and 8.07, Deception in Research.)

(b) Psychologists conducting intervention research involving the use of experimental treatments clarify to participants at the outset of the research (1) the experimental nature of the treatment; (2) the services that will or will not be available to the control group(s) if appropriate; (3) the means by which assignment to treatment and control groups will be made; (4) available treatment alternatives if an individual does not wish to participate in the research or wishes to withdraw once a study has begun; and (5) compensation for or monetary costs of participating including, if appropriate, whether reimbursement from the participant or a third-party payer will be sought. (See also Standard 8.02a, Informed Consent to Research.)

Other subsections of the ethics code include guidelines on deception in research, debriefing subjects, offering inducements to take part in studies, and maintaining confidentiality. The ethics code requires psychologists to pay special attention to the rights of their subjects.

Ethical issues arise, in particular, when researchers study cognitively impaired older people. These people cannot understand the meaning of the research or their role in the studies. Researchers need to take special care to protect the rights of these participants. They need to get consent from family members, institution officials, or other responsible parties before proceeding with their research.

Source: American Psychological Association. (2010). *Ethical Principles of Psychologists and Code of Conduct. 2010 Amendments.* Retrieved October 22, 2010, from www.apa.org/ethics/code/index.aspx. Copyright © 2010 by the American Psychological Association. Reprinted with permission.

Researchers want to safeguard their subjects, but they also have a selfish reason for keeping high ethical standards. Unethical studies sour the public on research. A few years ago, I visited some senior centers to speak about a study I had begun. A woman raised her hand at the end of my talk.

"You're not the fellow that went around a little while ago asking people about sex, are you?" she asked.

"No, I'm not," I said.

"Well," she said, "that guy asked a lot of questions he had no business asking."

A number of other people in the audience nodded agreement. I met the same question in two or three other groups I visited. I learned that someone had done a questionnaire study on sexuality several years before. This person had not explained the study to the subjects and had left questions unanswered in their minds. I never found out who did this research, but I know that the study upset older people in the community and made it harder for me to gain their trust and support.

Researchers need to consider at least three ethical issues: (1) the need for informed consent, (2) the need to guard subjects against harm or injury, and (3) the need to protect individuals' privacy (Neuman, 2003).

Informed consent means that the researcher tells the subjects the facts about the research and gets written permission from them before they take part in a study. Older people who live in long-term care facilities and socially isolated people may feel some pressure to take part in a study. Individuals must freely give their consent, without any coercion. They need to understand that they can decide not to answer any questions without explanation. And they need to know that they can withdraw from the study at any time.

Researchers must also guard against doing harm or injury to study participants. This includes physical harm and psychological harm. Some people might feel embarrassed or upset at some questions they feel they have to answer. Researchers need to minimize risk to participants throughout the research process. Researchers also seek to protect participants from potential harm by keeping the participants' identities private. Researchers can do this by making sure that data analysis cannot reveal an individual's identity. The researcher should also promise to keep personal information private.

Older people with Alzheimer's disease or other types of dementia present special challenges in research. For example, they may not be able to give true voluntary informed consent (Bravo et al., 2005; Neuman & Robson, 2009). If the mental competency of an individual is in question, the researcher must get written permission from someone who has the legal authority to make such decisions. A family member or staff member in a nursing home may have this authority. Permission from a substitute decision maker allows for research at all stages of the disease (Karlawish, 2004).

THE FUTURE OF GERONTOLOGICAL THEORY AND METHODS

What theories and methods will gerontologists use in the future? Some or all of the following trends will create new theories and methods in the years to come.

- Gerontologists will create new and more sophisticated quantitative methods. These include structural equation models, longitudinal factor analysis, and multivariate effects models. These methods will emerge as computer power increases and as gerontologists apply methods used in other social sciences. They will allow gerontologists to test new and more complex theories.
- Gavrilov and Gavrilova (2001) propose the use of recent models from natural science—chaos theory and catastrophe theory—to explain aging. These theories and models question the assumptions of linear, probabilistic analyses that gerontologists use today. Hendricks (1997, p. 205) challenges gerontology "to develop mind-sets and measures that address the possibility of non-linear processes." This approach would include the study of unpredictable and dramatic changes in individuals' lives and in their families, work, and neighborhoods. It would also include a study of how people modify their life courses through their own interpretations of their lives.
- Gerontologists would like to link the micro-levels and macro-levels of theory. The age stratification theory, the life course approach, and feminist theories come closest to doing this now, though each has its limits. These approaches and theories look at the intersection of individual biography and history. They also look at the influence of earlier life experiences on old age. These approaches point to the need for multidisciplinary and interdisciplinary studies.
- Researchers will further develop political economy and phenomenological theories, as well as feminist theories, and life course approaches. These approaches

reveal hidden sides of aging. They challenge the myths of aging and explore ways to create a good old age.

- Qualitative methods will continue to play a role in gerontological research. Qualitative methods can explore the experience of aging at a time when more and more people want to know about that experience. Qualitative methods can also reveal the diversity of later life.

- Studies in the humanities will add new methods to gerontological research, such as linguistic analysis, the study of paintings and photos, and autobiographical analysis. New topics of interest in the future will lead to new approaches to the study of aging. Achenbaum (2000a) says that cross-disciplinary studies show promise. These studies blend social science with the studies of art or history.

- Technology will expand research opportunities. Laptop computers, for example, allow researchers to enter interview data in the field. Researchers can use video technology to study behavior problems in long-term care settings. Video recording technology permits researchers to observe behavior without a researcher present. This method allows researchers to gather data throughout the day, and a number of researchers can observe and analyze the same data. Researchers have used this technology to study wandering behavior and the causes of falls in nursing homes.

Researchers will use all of these approaches and more as they explore new topics in the study of aging.

CONCLUSION

Gerontologists use a variety of theories and methods to study aging. Theories range from micro-level studies of individuals and interaction to macro-level studies of whole societies. Researchers use interactionist, functionalist, and conflict theories. Methods range from laboratory studies in the biological sciences to surveys and observation studies in the social sciences. Researchers choose the theories and methods that best help them answer their questions.

The range of theories and methods reflects the varied interests of gerontologists. Gerontologists traditionally came from the biological and social sciences. In the past few years, scholars from the humanities have turned to the study of aging. These scholars have added the study of art, literature, and history to the traditional methods of gerontological research.

The increase in the older population will lead to greater interest in aging and more research in the future. Researchers will come from ever more varied disciplines. They will create new methods and develop new theories as they explore new questions in the field of aging.

SUMMARY

- Gerontology has three subfields: biomedicine, psychosocial studies, and socioeconomic-environmental studies.
- Gerontologists create theories to help explain sets of facts. They use micro-level theories to describe people and their relationships, and they use macro-level theories to describe social institutions.
- The micro-level and macro-level of theory can each take an interactionist, functionalist, or conflict perspective.
- New developments in theory include narrative gerontology, moral economy theory, and critical gerontology. Also, different disciplines have begun to use similar theoretical models—for example, variability among aging populations and the link between the person and the environment.
- Gerontologists use a variety of research methods to study aging. These include experiments, mailed surveys, face-to-face interviews, participant observation, and studies of historical documents. The proper use of these methods ensures reliable and valid results.

- Age, period, and cohort effects influence people as they age. Researchers use a variety of methods to disentangle these effects.
- Cross-sectional, longitudinal, and time-lag designs each have strengths and weaknesses. Researchers try to use the approach that best answers their questions, given the resources they have available.
- Quantitative methods allow researchers to test theories and hypotheses. They look at relationships between variables and typically use numerical measures. They use a positivist approach to social phenomena, an approach similar to the study of natural science.
- Critical gerontology tries to understand the forces that shape people's lives. Researchers in this tradition often use qualitative methods, such as in-depth interviews and participant observation, in their studies.
- Historians and researchers in the humanities, such as classicists and English scholars, bring new theories and

methods to the study of aging. The multidisciplinary study of aging brings richness to gerontology and to our understanding of later life.

• The tremendous amount of information available on the Internet places new demands on students of aging. Information available online varies in quality and reliability. Everyone needs to improve their information literacy to make the best use of information available today.

• Researchers need to consider ethical issues related to their research. Professional associations and universities provide ethical standards, guidelines, and review committees to ensure ethical treatment of subjects in research.

• New theories developed in the natural sciences, interdisciplinary studies, and new technologies will all influence gerontological theories and methods in the future.

DISCUSSION QUESTIONS

1. List the three areas that make up the field of gerontology. Describe the kinds of questions each area asks and the kinds of things each area studies.
2. Explain the difference between micro-level and macro-level theories. Give examples of each. State the benefits and limits of each type of theory.
3. What are the three theoretical perspectives that gerontologists use in their studies? Explain the advantages and disadvantages of each perspective. Give at least one example of a study that uses each perspective.
4. What is the age/period/cohort problem? How can it influence research results? How do gerontologists try to overcome this problem?
5. Why do gerontologists use cross-sectional, longitudinal, and time-lag designs? Explain the advantages and disadvantages of each type of design.
6. Define the term *critical gerontology*. What methods do critical gerontologists use in their studies? Give an example of a study done using this approach.
7. What is information literacy? How has the use of the Internet made information literacy more important than ever before?
8. What safeguards exist to ensure ethical treatment of older subjects in research?
9. What are some of the future directions that gerontology theories and methods may take?

SUGGESTED READING

Biggs, S., Lowenstain, A., & Hendricks, J. (Eds.). (2003). *The need for theory: Critical approaches to a social gerontology.* Amityville, NY: Baywood.

The editors have collected a series of essays on the applications of critical theory to the study of aging. Studies look at personal meaning in gerontology theory, the ways that people negotiate identity in later life, and the family in the context of modernization. A student new to the field may find these essays difficult, but they show how some gerontologists think.

Bengtson, V. L., Gans, D., Putney, N., & Silverstein, M. (2008). *Handbook of theories of aging*, 2nd ed. New York: Springer.

This book contains chapters written by 67 prominent gerontologists. It reviews developments in gerontological theories over the decade prior to its publication. The chapters cover biological, social, and psychological theories. The book also includes a section on theory and social policy. It offers an excellent summary of major theories and provides references that you can follow up for in-depth study.

Gubrium, J. F., & Holstein, J. A. (Eds.). (2000). *Aging and everyday life*. Malden, MA: Blackwell.

This book contains essays by 30 gerontologists on the subject of the aging experience. The essays span a range of topics, including the cultural construction of aging, changing age consciousness as a person ages, and grief among daughters who have lost a parent. Other essays present examples of aging experiences, including the management of aging among exotic dancers, life in a single-room occupancy hotel, and the experience of the body through autobiography. The essays show the variety of studies that qualitative researchers have conducted.

Websites to Consult

The Gerontological Society of America—Journals
www.geron.org/Publications

This Gerontological Society of America website presents a list of the peer-reviewed journals and other publications sponsored by the GSA. These are among the premier academic publications in the field of aging. The journals cover a broad range of topics. They include articles on biological, psychological, and social facets of aging. The site offers free abstracts of articles from the association's journals. Check with your school's library to see if it provides access to physical or electronic copies of these journals.

AgeLine
www.ebscohost.com/thisTopic.php?marketID=1&topicID=23

This site contains a database of academic and high-quality popular writings on aging. The database includes journal articles, books, chapters, research reports, dissertations, and educational videos from more than 200 sources. You can search AgeLine by topic, author, keyword, date, or a combination of these methods. AgeLine provides detailed bibliographical information for each source it retrieves. It also provides abstracts of each of its entries. Some entries offer the full text of the item online. AgeLine is an invaluable research tool. You may need to access this site through your university library in order to make full use of its resources. If your library does not have access to AgeLine, request that it subscribe.

AARP's Database on Internet Resources
www.aarp.org/research/internet_resources/

This site links to more than 1,200 of the best sites for people age 50+. You can browse this site or search for resources using the URL given here.

National Institute on Aging
www.nia.nih.gov

This site offers a brief description of 250 health care and aging organizations. The site gives contact information for these organizations. Some of these sources will overlap with sources found in the AARP Web site database, but it offers another way to search for information you need.

Federal Interagency Forum on Aging-Related Statistics
www.agingstats.gov

This portal contains links to census data, current government studies, and discussions of aging-related topics. It is a great resource for data and research topics.

chapter 3

DEMOGRAPHY

Astrid Thoenig, 100 years old, lives in Parsippany, NJ. She says she's lived so long because she comes from "good stock." She spent her life as an office worker in a variety of businesses. Now she works 40 hours a week in her son's insurance agency. She reads, she knits. She says that having a purpose in life keeps her happy.

Like Ms. Thoenig, more Americans than ever before live past the age of 100. Long life has become the norm as average life expectancy has increased. And not just in the United States. We may be blessed to have more 90- and 100-year-olds than ever before. But in countries throughout the world, popula-

tions have aged. The average life expectancy has increased worldwide. In particular, more people live to old age and late old age than ever before (Hobson, 2010, p. 36).

In 2000, for example, the world had 421 million people age 65 years and over. The United Nations projects that by 2050 this figure will more than triple and the world will have almost one and a half billion people age 65 and over (United Nations, 2002b; Davidson, 2009). In 2050, the population of older persons will be larger than the population of children (0–14 years) for the first time in human history.

Population aging will affect different societies in different ways. The United Nations divides the world's nations into two groups—the more developed and the less developed—based on their demographic and socioeconomic characteristics. "The less developed regions include all regions of Africa, Asia (excluding Japan), Latin America and the Caribbean, and Oceania (excluding Australia and New Zealand). The more developed regions include all other regions plus the three countries excluded from the less developed regions" (United Nations, 2002a, p. iv).

The **developed nations**, such as France, Sweden, and the United States, will have large proportions of older people in their populations. The proportion of older people in most of these countries has increased gradually over many decades. Their populations will get older in the future. Some developed countries, such as Japan, had relatively young populations until recently. They have seen rapid population aging in recent years.

The **less developed nations**, such as China and Viet Nam, already have large numbers of older people. In 2000, for example, the majority of the world's older persons (54%) lived in Asia (Kinsella & Velkoff, 2001). These countries also have large numbers of young people (due to high **birth rates**). For this reason, compared with the developed nations, they will have lower *proportions* of older people in their populations. Still, the *large numbers* of older people will put new demands on these societies.

The less developed nations also include very undeveloped nations, such as the countries of Africa, Oceania, parts of the Caribbean, and parts of Latin America. These **least developed nations** will have large numbers of older people in their populations. They will have the least resources to cope with the demands of population aging.

Each type of society will face population aging in the years ahead. Each will face different challenges as their older populations grow. And each will need to make different responses to the challenge of population aging.

This chapter (1) looks at population aging in three types of societies, (2) describes some of the challenges created by population aging, and (3) considers population aging in the United States and its impact on American society.

THE CHALLENGE OF POPULATION AGING

What Is Population Aging?

When we talk about aging we generally refer to a person or even an animal or a thing. But what do we mean when we say that populations age?

Demographers, experts in the study of population change, use at least three measures to describe population aging: (1) the **absolute number of older people** in a population, (2) the **median age** of the population, and (3) the increased proportion of older people. These measures allow comparisons between societies and between a single society at two points in time. A population ages when any of these measures increase. Populations with large numbers of older people or with high proportions of older people are said to be old or aging societies.

The following discussions of societies will often make reference to the number or proportion of older people in the society. Be aware that a society can have a large number of older people, but still have a relatively small proportion of its population in old age. The less developed nations show this pattern. This kind of society will have a high birth rate and a large number of young people. More developed nations will have a low birth rate and a high proportion of older people. Each of these types of societies faces different challenges as they respond to population aging.

THE DEMOGRAPHIC TRANSITION

The **demographic transition** describes a pattern of population change that took place in Western nations over the past 250 years. The **developing nations** will probably go through this transition, and some of these nations have already started the process. Figure 3.1 shows the population trends over time that created the transition.

The developed nations that have gone through the demographic transition—from high to low birth and **death rates**—face new issues related to a large older population. For one thing, the demographic transition leads to a new perspective on the life cycle. Nearly all children can now expect to live to old age. Most middle-aged people can expect to live a decade or more in retirement, and many older people will live to late old age. A larger population than ever before will live more than 100 years.

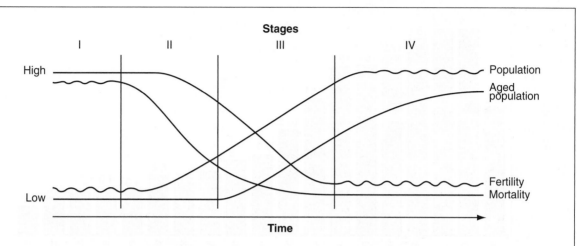

Stages

I II III IV

High — Population

Aged population

Low — Fertility
Mortality

Time

Stage I: High fertility and high mortality. Small population. Slow and varied population growth. High proportion of young people, small proportion of older people.

Stage II: High fertility; mortality begins to decline. Population begins to grow as more children survive. Population explosion may occur and society may get younger. Small proportion of elderly people.

Stage III: Fertility declines and mortality declines further. Population growth begins to level off at larger size. *This is the stage of the transition from a young high-growth to an older low-growth population.* Older population begins to grow as a proportion of the population.

Stage IV: Low fertility, low mortality. Low population growth and large proportion of older people in the population.

FIGURE 3.1   Stages of the Demographic Transition

Source: Reprinted from "Demography of Aging" by G. C. Myers, in R. H. Binstock & L. K. George, Eds., *Handbook of Aging and the Social Sciences,* 3rd ed. (p. 25). Copyright 1990, with permission from Elsevier.

The developing nations that go through this transition will experience similar benefits and challenges as their populations age (see Figure 3.2).

THREE TYPES OF SOCIETIES AND POPULATION AGING

The Less Developed Nations

The less developed nations of Africa, Asia, Oceania, the Caribbean, and Latin America make up three quarters of the world's population. Most of these nations have young populations with a small proportion of older people. In some cases they have as few as 2% of their populations age 65 and over. These countries will age in the years ahead, though they will still have relatively small proportions of older people.

African nations (some of the least developed nations) will average only a little over 4% age 65 and over in the year 2025. Overall the developing nations will average only about 8% in that year (United Nations, 2002a). High birth rates will keep the *proportion* of older people relatively low in these countries, but these nations will see explosive growth in the *number* of older people.

"By the year 2025," Myers (1990, p. 27) says, "over two-thirds of the world's older population will be found in the developing countries." Asia will gain over a quarter of a billion older people. China alone will have 194 million people age 65 and over by 2025. (By comparison, the entire U.S. population will be about 346 million people in that year [United Nations, 2002b].) High **fertility** in the past and greater survival of older people in the present will produce this explosive growth.

An increase in older people in developing nations will strain current social, health, and economic programs. Sennott-Miller (1994) says that developing nations need more information about their older populations, and they need to plan for an aging society. Countries with

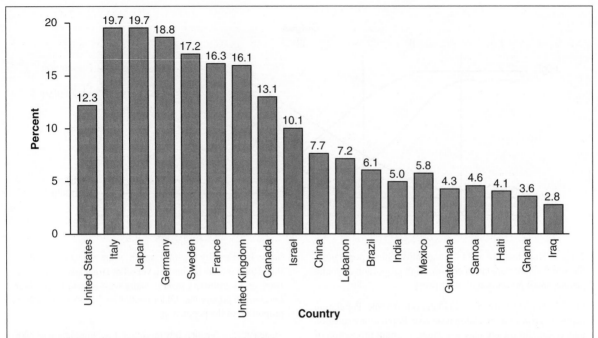

This chart reveals that the developed countries of Europe and North America have the largest proportions of older people. The developing nations (e.g., Brazil and China) have smaller proportions of older people. These proportions will increase if their birth rates decline and life expectancy increases. The least developed nations have the smallest proportions of older people, the highest birth rates, and the highest death rates.

FIGURE 3.2 Elder Populations in Selected Countries, 2005, Age 65 and Over

Source: Population Division of the Department of Economic and Social Affairs of the United Nations Secretariat, *World Population Prospects: The 2006 Revision* and *World Urbanization Prospects: The 2005 Revision,* http://esa.un.org/unpp. Retrieved November 15, 2007, from http://esa.un.org/unpp/p2k0data.asp.

TABLE 3.1 Elder Population Increases, Age 65 and Over from World and Major Regions, 2000 to 2050

	Population (in millions)			*Increase (2000 as base = 100)*	
	2000	*2025*	*2050*	*2025*	*2050*
World	421.4	832.2	1,464.9	197	348
More developed[*]	171.0	260.3	320.7	152	188
Less developed[**]	250.3	571.8	1,144.2	228	457
Africa	26.6	56.9	128.8	214	484
Latin America	29.1	70.1	143.7	241	494
North America	39.0	70.0	92.6	179	237
Asia	216.2	480.6	910.5	222	421
Europe	107.4	148.5	180.1	138	168
Oceania	3.0	6.1	9.2	203	307

[*]More developed: Europe, Japan, North America, Australia, and New Zealand.

[**]Less developed: Africa, Asia (excluding Japan), Latin America/Caribbean, Melanesia, Micronesia, and Polynesia.

The absolute number of older people given in this chart: (1) shows the distribution of older people worldwide; (2) allows for a comparison of the size of older populations that each country and region will have to deal with; and (3) shows the growth rate of the older population in each region. This growth rate gives an idea of how much demographic change each society will undergo.

   This table shows that, worldwide, the less-developed countries have a larger number of older people than the more developed countries (although they have smaller percentages of older people). It also shows that the older population will increase in the less developed countries at a faster rate than in the more developed countries.

   In 2000, for example, Asia had five and a half times more older people than North America. This reflects the larger size of the total Asian population. Projections show that the Asian older population will increase at a faster rate than the North American older population. This reflects increased life expectancies in Asian countries. By the year 2050, compared to North America, Asia will have more than nine and a half times more older people.

Source: Medium variant data in Population Division of the Department of Economic and Social Affairs of the United Nations Secretariat, *World Population Prospects: The 2004 Revision* and *World Urbanization Prospects: The 2003 Revision.* Retrieved April 14, 2005, from http://esa.un.org/unpp

social programs and pension plans in place will need to adapt these programs to serve more older people. China provides a good example of a developing nation that faces the challenge of population aging.

China: A Case Study of Population Aging in a Developing Nation

China had a total population of 1.3 billion people in 2000. Demographers expect the population to grow to almost 1.5 billion people by 2050. Over these same 30 years, the population age 65 will grow from 88 million in 2000 to 341 million in 2050 (United Nations, 2002b). Retirees at midcentury (people between the ages of 50 and 60, depending on their jobs) will make up about one third of China's population or 430 million people (*New York Times,* 2007).

Researchers trace this rapid increase in population aging to a decrease in China's **fertility rate.** The one-child policy begun in 1979 accounts for much of this decline in fertility. Due to this fertility decline (a rate of 1.8 in 2000) China will age sooner and more rapidly than other developing nations (Kinsella & Velkoff, 2001). Zhang (2001, p. 12) says that "China has a population that is aging . . . so fast that it has outpaced **industrialization** and **modernization**." Experts call this "one of the greatest **demographic changes** in history" (French, 2006).

At current rates of population change, China will get old before it gets rich. It will have to deal with the issues of a developing nation, such as feeding its people. And it will have to deal with issues of a developed society, such as caring for the elderly. It will also have to develop the pension and health care systems to care for its older population at the same time that it privatizes industry and grows its economy.

China today has the largest population of older people in the world. It also has the largest share of the world's oldest old (age 80+). These figures raise questions about China's ability to respond to its rapidly aging population. For example, the **elderly support ratio** (the number of people age 65 and over per 100 people ages 20 to 64 years old) between 2000 and 2030 will double from 12 to 26. And its parent support ratio (the number of people age 80 and over per 100 people ages 50 to 64) during those same years will more than quadruple from 3 to 14. These crude figures suggest that Chinese society and its members will need to provide more support for its older population in the years ahead. Most of these older people (about 76% of all older Chinese) live in rural areas.

In the cities many older people get a pension. But in rural areas older people depend mostly on family financial, social, and health care support (Peng & Hui, 2009). This can cause stress, and sometimes it leads to family breakdown. Also, younger people often move away from their families to find work in the cities. This further reduces the support for rural older people.

Older people in cities face a different set of challenges. More older people than ever before in China live on their own, especially in cities. The Chinese Association of Senior Citizens reports that more than 25% of older people in China live alone or with only their spouse (Zhang, 2001). These people face poverty, and they may lack a family support network. Osnos (2007, p. 7A) interviewed Zhang Junrui, a 79-year-old who retired from a state-owned factory in Beijing. Zhang says that "for elderly people, the biggest issue is to avoid getting sick. . . . Because savings might not be enough."

Chinese tradition puts the responsibility for elder care on the family. But in urban centers, this can also lead to burden and burnout. A study in Beijing found that 50% of families report financial, emotional, or other hardship in caring for their older relatives. This pressure will grow in the future as small young families with one child care for four or more older relatives.

An increase in the very old population (80+) will put a further burden on the young. The very old population will increase almost sixfold from 16 million in 2006 to 94 million people in 2050 (Johnson, 2006). Li Bengong, the executive deputy director of the China National Committee on Aging, says, "The situation is very serious. . . . We have weak economic capability to cope with the aging of the population" (Johnson, 2006, p. 20A).

China, like other developing nations, will find it hard to meet the needs of its growing older population. The high cost of building and running long-term care institutions will limit the growth of nursing homes. Also, older people in China prefer to stay at home and get support from their families. China has begun to develop home care options that fit its culture and that meet the needs of its aging population.

The increased number and proportion of older people in China and their need for support will lead to social change. Kinsella and Velkoff (2001, p. 79) say that in the near future China "may anticipate a social and economic fabric radically different from that of today."

The Least Developed Nations

The least developed nations face unique challenges due to population aging. Older people in parts of Africa, for example, face hardships because urban life, wage labor, and national political movements have lowered their status. Some countries in Africa will experience sudden demographic aging due to the HIV/AIDS epidemic. Botswana, for example, has seen a decrease in life expectancy from around 60 years in the 1950s "to a low of 42 years for females and 45 years for males" in the 1990s. The deaths of middle-aged and younger people will lead to rapid societal aging (Oduaran & Molosi, 2009, p. 123; also Wolff, Kabunga, Tumwekwase, & Grosskurth, 2009).

Cattell (1994), in a study of older people in Kenya, says that "delocalization," the shift of power outside the community and family, has occurred. This leads to loose family bonds and loss of authority for older people. A study of groups near Lake Victoria found that, in the past, grandmothers played a vital role in raising granddaughters. Today, granddaughters spend most of their day at school, and some live away during the school term. Schoolteachers and more worldly ideas now replace grandmothers and their teachings.

Older people in African countries often lack basic services. A study of South Africa, for example, found that only 47% of urban black older people and 15% of rural black older people had access to conveniences such as running water, sanitation, and electricity. A study of southern Africa found that in Botswana, Lesotho, Namibia, Swaziland, and Zimbabwe, few older people get a pension. For this reason most work into their 70s and 80s (Gist, 1994; Martin & Kinsella, 1994).

Many of these older people still give support to their families. Some give direct financial support to younger people. Kinsella calls pension sharing "the norm." Others provide services (such as babysitting) that allow younger people to work outside the home.

Very old people in these countries rely on family support for their well-being, but lower fertility, the movement of young people to find jobs, and deaths due to AIDS among the young will reduce the amount of family support older people can count on. This occurs at a time when the older population in southern Africa will nearly triple between 2000 and 2025 from 1.2 million to 3.5 million people (United Nations, 2002a). The country of Ghana provides a good example of the challenges facing the least developed nations.

Ghana: A Case Study of Population Aging in a Least Developed Nation

The number of older people (60+) in Ghana will increase from 1.3 million in 2005 to almost 5.6 million people in 2050. During this same time people age 80+ will increase six times from 100,000 to almost 600,000 in 2050. Once people in Africa enter old age, their life expectancy mirrors that of people throughout the world. This means that this large older population will live longer than ever before.

These demographic facts challenge Ghanaian society to provide support for older people. African nations in general have few social security programs for older people. These societies face "economic stagnation, heavy indebtedness, severely constrained public resources and sustained pervasive poverty of populations" (Aboderin, 2006, p. 19). The United Nations (UNDP, 2003, cited in Aboderin, 2006) reports that in Ghana 45% of the people live below $1 per day. And 79% live below $2 per day. Under these conditions welfare programs for the young and middle aged compete with the needs of the elderly for scarce resources.

People in Ghana cannot depend on social security in later life. Nor can they save enough during their working years to provide for themselves in old age. This leaves the responsibility for their care on the family.

Aboderin (2006, p. 108) found that current economic and social conditions undermine traditional models of family support. Today, for example, support for an older person falls mainly on adult children. In the past, the entire community shared in the care for older members. One respondent told Aboderin, "In the olden days older people were cared for not just by the children but also the relatives. Everybody was sharing food and so on but now . . . only the children look after the old person."

Adult children find it difficult to support their parents and pay their own family expenses. For this reason support for older parents has declined and in some cases has ceased. Older people who lack support from their children sink deep into poverty. One respondent says, "If I usually chop [eat] three times a day, [some] days I will chop only once. . . . So I will force to tighten my belt because *there is nowhere for me to go*" (Aboderin, 2006, p. 110, emphasis added by author).

Aboderin (2006, p. 111) found that "the middle aged child often has to choose between support for their own children or support for their parents." And people tend to choose support for the young. Aboderin summarizes the comments of the people she interviewed. *"The . . . older generation has no right to stand in the way of—or absorb resources that are needed for—the future life and well-being of the younger generations.*" One person told Aboderin, "Right now I can't help my mother how I want because I don't have" (p. 113, emphasis in the original).

Some people propose that governments find ways to support the family in its traditional role. Other planners argue for laws that would force middle-aged children to care for their aging parents. The lack of funds makes either of these options unlikely in the near future.

This case study shows the challenges that face the least developed nations as they try to plan for an aging population. Older people can no longer rely on support from their children. And the wider community no longer provides support to older members. Poverty among young adults undermines their ability provide support for their parents.

Older people in a least developed nation have little or no social security. They have no savings. And they have only tenuous support from their adult children. As more people enter old age in Ghana and as they live longer in old age, this lack of support could turn into a crisis. "The major single cause of the decline [in support for elders]," Aboderin (2006, p. 146) says, "without doubt . . . has been a reduced resource capacity of the middle generation." And unless the economic conditions in the country improve, older people cannot count on support from any source. This makes old age an uncertain and painful time for many people in Ghana.

Summary of Aging in Developing and Least Developed Nations

The ability of a country to help its older people largely depends on its economy. A country with a strong economy can make more resources available to its older people. But few developing nations have strong economies. Responses that fit Western industrialized societies will not fit developing nations.

The developing nations need solutions that fit their cultures and current economic conditions. Developing nations such as India, cannot afford expensive pension programs. India's large population (1.3 billion people, about 3.6 times that of the United States) and its developing economy challenge its ability to care for people of all ages. More than one quarter of the population lives below the poverty line.

India uses most of its public resources for poverty alleviation, job creation, and food subsidies to the poor. India provides pension relief only to its poorest elders (about 5.3 million people), and then only 75 rupees per month (about $1.50 U.S. in 2010) (Rao, 2001).

Sokolovsky (2000) concludes that the family remains the primary source of support for older people throughout the world. Where public supports exist, especially in developing nations, they can, at their best, support traditional family commitments to the old. He cites Nana Apt, an African sociologist, to support this point. "It is not enough," she says, "to talk about the bind of tradition, and it's not enough to talk about its

---

BOX 3.1
REFLECTIONS ON AGING IN AFRICA

Novelist and travel writer Paul Theroux traveled by land from Cairo to Cape Town. He detailed his journey in his book *Dark Star Safari: Overland from Cairo to Cape Town* (2003). During his travels he passed his 60th birthday. This caused him to examine the meaning of age and aging—for him and for the people he met. In the excerpt below, Theroux reflects on what aging means in the African context.

I decided to avoid any birthday celebration. I was so self-conscious of my age that I often asked Africans to guess how old I was, hoping—perhaps knowing in advance—they would give me a low figure. They always did. Few people see elderly in Africa. Forty was considered old, a man of fifty was at death's door, sixty year olds were just crocks or crones. Despite my years I was healthy, and being agile and resilient I found traveling in Africa a pleasure. I did not seem old here, did not feel it, did not look it to Africans, and so it was a great place to be, another African fantasy, an adventure in rejuvenation.

"You are forty-something," Kamal had guessed in Addis. The highest number I got was fifty-two. Little did they know how much they flattered my vanity. But no one was vain about longevity in Africa, because the notion of longevity hardly existed. No one lived long and so age didn't matter, and perhaps that accounted for the casual way Africans regarded time. In Africa no one's lifetime was long enough to accomplish anything substantial, or to see any task of value completed. Two generations in the West equaled three generations in African time, telescoped by early marriage, early child-bearing, and early death. (pp. 197–198)

disintegration. We must find ways and means of transforming it into a modern form that will make multigenerational relationships much more viable" (Apt, 1998, p. 14, cited in Sokolovsky, 2000).

Sokolovsky (2000, p. 44) goes on to say that traditional systems work best when they fit into local economic and cultural systems. "These systems need to give both youth and elders reason to support each other."

THE DEVELOPED NATIONS

The United Nations (2002a) reports that the developed nations of the world will see increases in their proportions of older people. The U.N. projects that these countries on average will have more than one quarter of their populations age 65 and over by 2025. And they will have one third of their populations over age 60 in that year. Population aging will extend a trend that, for some of these countries, began in the 19th century.

Increased population aging will create challenges for the developed nations. For example, all of these countries will face the issue of rising health care and pension costs. These societies may need to shift funds from other types of programs to serve older people. Or they may develop new programs that better fit an older population.

Societies like those of Western Europe, Canada, Japan, and the United States today have relatively few people who work in manufacturing and food production. Instead, most people work in the service sector. This includes nurses, teachers, and investment counselors. These people sell their technical expertise. People in a **postindustrial society** generally have a high standard of living. These societies have high social mobility, a concern for equality and individual rights, and long life expectancies.

Christensen and colleagues (Christensen, Doblhammer, Rau, & Vaupel, 2009) say that if the increase in life expectancy in developed nations continues, "most babies born since 2000 . . . will celebrate their 100th birthdays."

The high proportion of older people in developed nations and the large number of very old people will pose challenges to their pension and health care systems. Japan shows the challenges that face developed nations today.

Japan: A Case Study of Population Aging in a Developed Nation

Japan had a population of 84 million people in 1950. By 2000, the population had increased to 127 million

Korea has modernized rapidly. This Korean woman sells vegetables at the indoor market in Gyeongjus, South Korea. Many older people in Korea keep shops. Others sew and sell their goods. They help their extended families with the income and they stay active in the community.

(United Nations, 2002b). Over these same 50 years the population age 65 and over increased more than five times. The Japanese today have one of the longest average life expectancies in the world. According to the United Nations (2002b), at birth a Japanese female can expect to live 85 years, a Japanese male, 77.8 years.

In the year 2006, Japan had 21% of its population age 65 and over (the highest percentage in the world) (Chandler, 2006). Low fertility rates and low death rates will lead to continued population aging in the future. Projections to the year 2050 show that in that year nearly two of every five people in Japan will be age 65 or older (Maeda, 2009). Myers (1990, p. 26) calls this "a spectacular growth" in the proportion of older people. And Chandler (2006) calls the pace of population aging in Japan "without precedent in the industrial world."

The large increase in the oldest old (age 80+) poses unique problems for Japan. This population will grow to over 17 million people by 2050, a 2.7-fold increase from 2005. Nearly one person in five in Japan will be age 80 and over in 2055. This large increase in the very old will place heavier demands on government, community, and family support systems.

The Japanese call this *koreika,* societal aging. A 1995 survey conducted by the Ministry of Health and Welfare in Japan (National Institute of Population, 2004) found that 57.3% of the respondents considered population aging "a trouble" or "a serious trouble." And 68% of the respondents said that Japan should increase its birth rate to slow population aging. Knight and Traphagan (2003, p. 13) say people in rural communities use low birth rates and population aging to explain all kinds of problems. They use this "depopulation consciousness" to explain poor treatment of older people, problems at work, and the inability to find a bride.

Japan has a history of providing social security and health care to its older people. The government has provided a national pension plan and a universal health insurance program since the 1960s. A report by the National Institute of Population and Social Security Research (2002–2003) says that these two programs "have become the two main pillars of Japanese social security system." Population aging will strain the capacity of these systems in the years ahead. This will require new responses from individuals and the government.

Japan faces challenges similar to those of other developed nations. These challenges include higher costs for pensions, more chronic disease, and the need to rethink health care services for an older population. Japan differs from other developed nations in the speed of its transition to an aging society. In only 26 years (1970 to 1996), the Japanese older population grew from 7% to 14% of the population. By contrast, some European societies took as long as 115 years to see this kind of change (Kinsella & Velkoff, 2001). Japan will have to make changes quickly to meet the needs of its aging population and to maintain its standard of living.

Mass retirement in the next few years also poses a threat to Japan's prosperity. More than 2 million people age 60 retired in 2007. These experienced workers will leave the labor force, but fewer young people will be there to take their place. And this will mean fewer people to pay into the national pension system. Ibe (2000, p. 8) concludes that a "revision of pension benefits and payments is therefore inevitable."

Proposed changes that might solve this problem include increasing the birth rate, raising the retirement age (now age 60), encouraging women to enter the labor force to increase productivity, and allowing more immigrant labor in order to boost the national economy (Chandler, 2006; Doi, 2007). Some combination of these options will be needed to manage societal aging in Japan.

Population aging affects nations and people throughout the world. The developed nations will have greater proportions of older people in their populations in the future. The developing nations will have larger numbers of older people than ever before. These changes will take place in the context of rapid **urbanization**, industrialization, globalization, and changes to the environment. We cannot look back. New conditions call for new responses. The large number of older people in the world today "remains irreducibly novel," Laslett (1976, p. 96) says, and "it calls for invention rather than imitation."

POPULATION AGING IN THE UNITED STATES

Increased Numbers of Older People

In 2006, 37 million people age 65 and over lived in the United States. Older people accounted for just over 12% of the total population. Over the 20th century, the older population grew more than 10-fold from 3 million to 37 million. Projections show that it will more than double again from the year 2006 to 2050, from 37 million to 86.7 million people.

The oldest-old population (those age 85 and over) grew from just over 100,000 in 1900 to 5.3 million in 2006. The U.S. Census Bureau projects that this group could grow to nearly 21 million people by 2050. Some experts predict an even faster growth of this older population due to lower death rates at later ages (Federal Interagency Forum, 2008). (Figure 3.3 shows the actual and projected increase in the number of older people in the United States from 1900 to 2050.)

This growth in the older population will take place unevenly over the forty-year period from 1990 to 2030. From 1990 to 2010, the older population grew relatively slowly by about 1.3% per year. This reflects the relatively small number of births during the 1930s. But from 2010 to 2030, when the large Baby Boom cohorts enter old age, the older population will grow by as much as 2.8% per year.

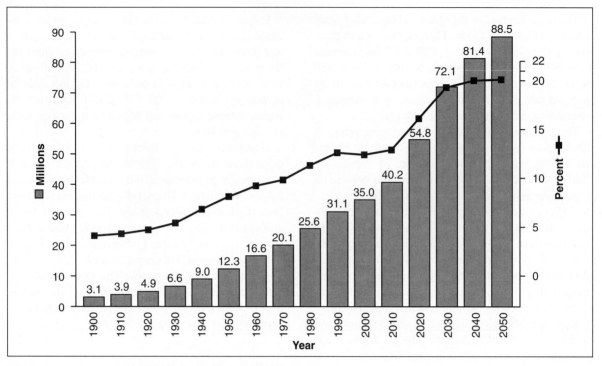

FIGURE 3.3   U.S. Elder Population, Age 65 and Over, 1900–2050*

*The projections presented here reflect the U.S. Census Bureau's "middle series" projections. The U.S. Census Bureau makes a number of projections based on a number of fertility, mortality, and migration assumptions. The middle series assumes a fertility rate in 2050 of 2,150 births per 1,000 women, life expectancy at birth in 2050 of 79.7 years for men and 85.6 years for women, and an ultimate net migration of 880,000 per year.

  The 1900 to 1980 data are tabulated from the Decennial Censuses of the Population and exclude Armed Forces overseas. Projections (1990 onward) are middle series projections and include Armed Forces overseas.

Sources: Adapted from L. Hetzel & A. Smith, *The 65 Years and Over Population: 2000–Census 2000 Brief,* 2001. Retrieved on March 21, 2004, from www.census.gov/prod/2001pubs/c2kbr01-lo.pdf. F. Hobbs & N. Stoops, *Demographic Trends in the 20th Century,* U.S. Census Bureau, Census 2000 Special Reports, Series CENSR-4 (Washington DC: U.S. Government Printing Office, 2002). Retrieved on January 19, 2004, from www.census.gov/prod/2002pubs/censr-4.pdf. National Center for Health Statistics. (2010a). Health, United States, 2009: With Special Feature on Medical Technology. Hyattsville, MD. 2010. Figure 1, p. 15. Projected 2010–2050 figures.

Demographers rarely use the absolute number of older people in a society alone to analyze population aging. They rarely use it to compare aging in different societies. This figure, if used alone, can mislead a researcher. For example, a doubling or tripling of the older population can seem like an overwhelming change to a society, but its effect will depend on many things, including the society's economy, its policies, and its total rate of population growth.

Increased Median Age of the Population

Half the population is older and half younger than the median age. Median age gives a rough estimate of a population's age structure. It offers a sensitive measure of increases or decreases in population aging.

An increase in the median age means that the population has gotten older. Note in Figure 3.4 that the median age has more than doubled over the years, from seventeen years in 1820 to a projected thirty-nine years in 2050. Note also that the increase halted during the 1960s and 1970s. This signals a reversal in the process of population aging for those years.

Why did this occur? These declines in median age mark the effects of the Baby Boom that took place after World War II. The median age increased again between 1970 and 2000 from twenty-eight to thirty-five years. The U.S. Census projects a further increase in median age to 39 years by 2030 (He, Sangupta, Velkoff, & De Barros, 2005). Demographers rarely use the median age alone as a measure of population aging. The median age says little about the relative size of age groups within the population, or about changes in the size of age groups relative to one another.

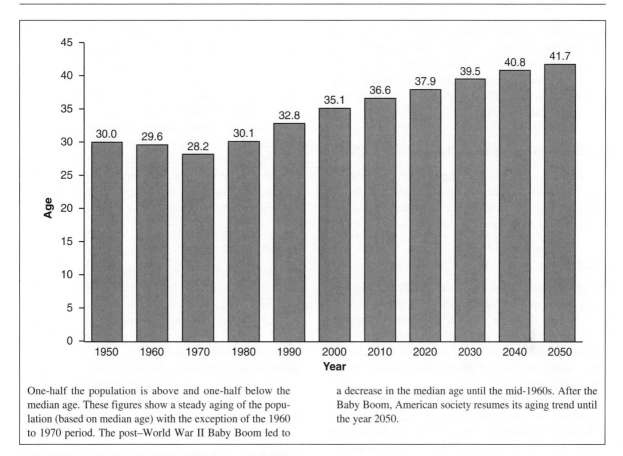

One-half the population is above and one-half below the median age. These figures show a steady aging of the population (based on median age) with the exception of the 1960 to 1970 period. The post–World War II Baby Boom led to a decrease in the median age until the mid-1960s. After the Baby Boom, American society resumes its aging trend until the year 2050.

FIGURE 3.4 Median Age of U.S. Population, 1950–2050

Source: Population Division of the Department of Economic and Social Affairs of the United Nations Secretariat. (2009). *World Population Prospects: The 2008 Revision*, http://esa.un.org/unpp. Retrieved: November 05, 2010—http://esa.un.org/unpp/p2k0data.asp

Increased Proportion of Older People

Gerontologists most often use the proportion of people age 65 and over in the population as a measure of population aging. This measure shows the relationship between the older group and the rest of society. An increase in the proportion of older people, for example, means a decrease in the proportion of other age groups. It gives an indication of how much influence the older group will have on social life. Figure 3.3 shows the proportion of people age 65 and over in the United States for the years 1900 to 2050. Note that the proportion increases from 4% in 1900 to 20% in 2050 when the last of the Baby Boom generation reaches late old age.

Measuring Trends

Each of these measures of population aging shows the same trend: *the aging of the U.S. population*. Each measure gives a unique perspective on this phenomenon. For example, the absolute number of older people gives an idea of how many people will enter retirement at a certain time. It also gives some idea of the number of customers who might want to invest in condominiums or buy cars. The median age points to shifts in the political interests of the population. A higher median age means more people interested in programs and policies for later middle-aged and older adults.

The proportion of older people shows the relationship between older and younger age groups. For example, in 1900, older people made up 4% of the population, but people under age 18 made up 40% of the population. In 1980, older people made up 11% and young people made up 28% of the population. By the year 2050, older people (age 65 and over) will make up 20.6% and younger people (ages 0 to 14) will make up only 18.5% of the population (Hetzel &

Smith, 2001; United Nations, 2002b). These figures suggest that societal resources will need to shift to serve older people in the future. Gerontologists use these measures to assess various impacts of population aging on social life and to project social changes due to population aging.

THE CAUSES OF POPULATION CHANGE

A population can change in three ways: people move into or out of a society, people die, and people are born. Demographers study migration, death rates, and birth rates to understand population aging.

Migration

Migration has played a relatively small role in population aging in the United States and will likely play a smaller role in the future. Because immigrants typically arrive in the United States as young adults, their presence tends to lower the country's median age. They also tend to have children, which further lowers the median age.

Migrants who come of age in the United States have an impact on population aging 45 or 50 years later. This delayed effect accounts for some of the increase in the older population until 1960. Many of the people who came of age before 1960 immigrated to the United States between 1905 and 1914. Between 1901 and 1910, for example, nearly 9 million immigrants arrived in the United States, by far the highest rate of immigration in the past 100 years (U.S. Census Bureau, 2002).

Immigrants have less impact on population aging today than at certain times in the past. First, the immigrants from earlier in the last century have died off. Second, more restrictive immigration laws have kept the group of foreign-born older people relatively small. (Immigration averaged around 700,000 people per year of all ages in the 1980s.) This has relaxed somewhat. In 1990, the government lifted quotas on family reunification, which led to larger numbers of immigrants than in the 1980s (some of them older people).

Still, the numbers remain relatively small. For the years 2007–2009, for example, about 1.1 million people became legal permanent residents of the United States each year. New arrivals totaled less than half a million people each year (Monger, 2010).

Third, projected low immigration levels in the future will mean small proportions of foreign-born older people. The U.S. Census Bureau middle series projections put immigration in the year 2050 at about 880,000,

a number similar to the recent past, but a relatively small proportion of the total U.S. population.

Changes in immigration laws, the quality of border control, and the flow of immigrants make future migration figures uncertain. Illegal immigration, mostly by young people, would slow population aging in the short run, but demographers find it hard to assess the impact of this group. Zopf (1986, p. 5) concludes that "the largest impact of immigration on the aging of the population has probably passed." For this reason, death rates and birth rates will have the greatest impact on population aging in the years ahead.

Death Rates

Death rates fell throughout the past century for whites and nonwhites and for men and women. (See Table 3.2.) This means that more people survived into old age than ever before. Life expectancy at birth in 1900 was 47.3 years. It reached a record high of 77.7 years in 2006 (Heron et al., 2009; Arias, 2010). These gains in life expectancy largely reflect decreases in infant mortality. The National Center for Health Statistics (2003; Xu, Kochanek, & Tejada-Vera, 2009) reports that from 1960 to 2001, infant mortality fell

TABLE 3.2   U.S. Life Expectancy at Birth (in Years)

	White		African American	
	Male	*Female*	*Male*	*Female*
1970	68.0	75.6	60.0	68.3
1980	70.7	78.1	63.8	72.5
1990	72.7	79.4	64.5	73.6
2000	74.7	79.9	68.2	75.1
2010	76.5	81.3	70.2	77.2
2020	77.7	82.4	72.6	79.2

This table shows the increase in life expectancy at birth for whites and African Americans in the United States for selected years from 1970 to 2010. All four groups show an increase in life expectancy. African American men and women, from 1970 to 2000, have narrowed the gap in life expectancy with their white counterparts. Whites of either sex continue to have longer life expectancies than African Americans. But the projection to 2020 shows an increase for all groups and a narrower gap between whites and African Americans.

Source: Adapted from U.S. National Center for Health Statistics, National Vital Statistics Reports (NVSR). (2009). *Deaths: Final Data for 2006*, Vol. 57, No. 14, April 17, 2009. Retrieved: October 19, 2010, from http://www.census.gov/compendia/statab/2010/tables/10s0102.pdf

U.S. Census Bureau, Statistical Abstract of the *United States* (Washington, DC: U.S. Government Printing Office, 2002b). Retrieved March 21, 2004, from www.census.gov/prod/www/statistical-abstract-02.html; Arias, E. (2004). United States life tables, 2001, *National Vital Statistics Reports, Vol. 52*(14) (Hyattsville, MD: National Center for Health Statistics, 2004). Retrieved March 21, 2004, from www.cdc.gov/nchs/data/nvsr/nvsr52/nvsr52_14.pdf.

steadily. The rate decreased from 26.0 (per 1,000 live births) in 1960 to 6.77 in 2007.

This is the lowest rate ever recorded in the United States. Both African Americans and whites showed a decline in infant mortality from 1960 to 2007. African Americans showed a decline from 44.3 in 1960 to 12.92 in 2007 for both sexes. Whites showed a decline from 22.9 in 1960 to 5.72 in 2007 (National Center for Health Statistics, 2003; Xu et al., 2007).

Both races show improvements in infant survival, but the 2007 figures show that African Americans have an infant mortality rate 2.3 times the rate of whites. This reflects lower incomes, poverty, and less access to high-quality medical care for African Americans.

The United States could see further decreases in infant mortality. Countries such as Hong Kong, Japan, and Singapore have rates below 4 per 100,000. But these countries have small, homogeneous populations.

Demographers also project increases in life expectancy for people over age 65. They project these gains for whites and nonwhites, men and women. The trend that supports these future gains already exists. For example, between 1980 and 2006, life expectancy at age 65 increased from 14.2 years to 17.1 years for white males, from 18.4 to 19.8 years for white females, from 13.0 to 15.1 years for black males, and from 16.8 to 18.6 years for black females (National Center for Health Statistics, 2009; Arias, 2010).

Changes in life expectancy will affect the size and structure of the older population in the years ahead. By the years 2045–2050, men at age 65 can expect on average to live another 18.8 years, and women at age 65 can expect to live another 23 years (United Nations, 2002b).

The conquest of cancer or further declines in stroke and heart disease death rates could lead to further increases in life expectancy in old age. This will mean, among other things, continued increases in the number and proportion of the oldest old people in the population, and a greater proportion of women in the old and very old population.

In the past, population aging took place because of decreased infant mortality. Today and in the future, population aging will occur mostly because of increased longevity.

Birth Rates

The decline in the **fertility rate** and the **birth rate**, more than any other cause, explains population aging during the past century. This may surprise you. Why should the rate of children born influence aging?

Demographers define the fertility rate as the number of live births per 1,000 women ages 15 to 44; they define the birth rate as the number of live births per 1,000 population. A high fertility rate (many births) will increase the proportion of younger people in society. This will keep the population relatively young. A low fertility rate will mean a proportionately greater number of older people. Couple a low fertility rate (fewer children) with a low death rate (people living longer), and you get population aging in the United States today.

At least three specific changes in birth rate influenced population aging in the United States. First, an increase in births took place before 1920 (Easterlin, 1987). The end of World War I in part accounts for this increase. The same may be said for the large number of young immigrants in the early 1900s, who began having children at this time. These people (the children born around 1920) entered old age in the mid-1980s. They will make up the very old population in the United States in the early years of this century.

Second, an explosion in births, the Baby Boom, took place after World War II, between 1946 and 1964. The first Baby Boomer, Kathleen Casey-Kirschling, was born 1 second after midnight on January 1, 1946. Between her birth and the end of 1964, America added one new baby to its population every 8 seconds. This meant a total of 78.2 million people added to the population during these years. Boomers formed the largest generation in U.S. history. In 2006, Baby Boomers totaled 78 million people or 26.1% of the population (U.S. Census Bureau, 2006e).

Nearly all of this group will have entered old age by the year 2030. In that year the United States will have an estimated 72 million older people (around 20% of the population at that time). This will come to more than twice the number of older people alive in 2000 (He et al., 2005). The oldest-old population will grow rapidly after 2030, when the Baby Boomers move into this age group.

The Baby Boom generation has shaped U.S. society and culture since the 1950s. The education system built schools for them in their childhood; the housing industry built homes for them as young adults; and the travel, leisure, and health care industries await their arrival into old age. This group, compared with past generations, has greater expectations for its living standards in later life. The size of the older Baby Boom generation will reshape the marketplace, social services, and politics in the next century. (See Box 3.2.)

BOX 3.2
THE BABY BOOM

One of my earliest memories is from 1951. I'm sitting in a car on a hot summer day with my uncle and grand-mother. We're waiting outside a gray brick building. I can see the steps that lead to the front door far away. My uncle sits in the driver's seat. I see my mother coming down the step. She's carrying a blanket in her arms. A woman dressed in white walks beside her. The car door opens. My mother gets in and everyone in the car cranes their necks to look at the blanket.

The bundle was my sister Lynne. I was 3 years old at the time. I wasn't the only child with a new sister. Throughout my neighborhood and across the country boys and girls welcomed newborn sisters and brothers into their homes. The Baby Boom was in full swing.

During World War II my father and my uncles left their fiancées and girlfriends at home and went off to war. When the men came home they picked up where their lives had left off. They got jobs, got married, and moved to the suburbs. They also started families. And they did this with vigor.

The returning soldiers and their new brides made up for time lost during the war. They began to produce children at a furious rate.

The United States had a fairly steady number of births each year before the Baby Boom—hovering around 8 to 10 million children born per year. The Baby Boom years saw roughly double these numbers of births for two decades (between 1946 and 1964). This burst of children affected every American institution.

I was born in 1948, at the "leading edge" of the Baby Boom, so I know. Builders created suburbs to house us. Communities built schools to educate us. And industries (such as the food industry) created new products—first, prepared baby foods, then shelves of sugared cereals—to feed us. The streets in my neighborhood teemed with kids on Saturdays and during summer vacations. Every family it seemed had at least two children, some more. On my father's side of the family, for example, my sister and I have eight cousins. On my mother's side we have thirteen cousins—most of them born during the Baby Boom years.

The Baby Boom continued to shape American culture as we grew up. Boomers brought a new mindset to the country. If society didn't meet our needs, we changed society. Elvis. The Beatles. Bob Dylan. The Civil Rights Movement. Marijuana. LSD. Free love. The antiwar protests of the 1960s and early 1970s. All of this social unrest said "We'll have it our way."

Boomer influence continues today. As the first Boomers reached age 60, some radio stations dedicated themselves to "classic rock." Translation: rock music from the 60s and 70s that Boomers like. These stations play to the largest and one of the wealthiest groups in America.

The Baby Boom will continue to shape American culture, economics, and politics in the years ahead. The population pyramids show that by the middle of this century, Boomers will make up the largest older population ever. For example, between 2000 and 2030, the older population will more than double, from 35 million to 72 million, and almost one in five people will be age 65 or older (He et al., 2005).

"Every day," Myers and Nielson (2003, p. 56) say, "more than 10,000 Leading Edge Baby Boomers in the U.S. reach 55 years of age." Between 2011 and 2030, the years when the Baby Boom cohorts enter old age, the older population will grow by as much as 2.8% per year. The U.S. Census Bureau projects a population of 69 million people ages 50 to 59 in the year 2010 (cited in Harris, 2003). The Census Bureau (1996, pp. 2–5) calls this a "massive increase" in the number of older people.

The sheer number of older people in the future will influence economic and social life. As they enter later life, Baby Boomers will place demands on the retirement income system, the health care system, and every other system in U.S. society. They will also serve as a market for new goods and services—travel tours, education, electronic gear, housing, and more.

Health clubs, once the home of yogurt-loving, wheat germ-eating eccentrics, now exist in most hotels and shopping malls. An entire genre of books focuses on later-life issues and lifestyles—retirement, relationships, parent care, and personal growth. This interest in health and well-being in later life will accelerate in the years ahead. The cosmetics industry, the pharmaceutical industry, and business in general will shift attention to this growing market of affluent Boomers.

Russell (2001, p. 3) sums up the influence of the Boomer generation: "Boomers continue to be the most powerful generation the nation has ever experienced. Not only is . . . [this] group large, but its influence extends into the younger and older generations as it guides its children and aids its parents."

Third, fertility has declined from the mid-1960s to the early years of this century. The U.S. birth and fertility rates began to fall after 1960 (with a birth rate of 118 per 1,000 births to women ages 15 to 44) and hit an all-time low of 61 in 2002 (Downs, 2003). This has led to a sharp increase in the median age and an increase in the proportion of older people. Zopf (1986, p. 24) says, "The birth rate has fallen so significantly in virtually all parts of the nation that the aging of the population is one of [America's] universal demographic phenomena."

Will birth rates stay low in the future? Will the population keep getting older? No one can say for sure. For example, a surprising increase in births in 2007 led to the highest number of births ever registered in the United States in 1 year (more than 4.3 million). The general fertility rate in that year increased by 1% to 69.5—the highest level since 1990 (Hamilton, Martin, & Ventura, 2009).

This increase in fertility rates reverses a U.S. decline in fertility rates and bucks a worldwide trend among developed nations. Other developed nations have seen sharp decreases in fertility rates. Sweden, Japan, and Italy have birth rates far below the rate needed to replace their populations. Some countries, such as Sweden and Japan, have tried to reverse this trend, but they have had little success.

Birth rates reflect changing social and demographic conditions. Consider the following social forces that lead to a decreased birth rate:

1. New methods of birth control allow couples to choose how many children they will have. Gee (1982, p. 61) called population aging an "unplanned by-product of planned parenthood."
2. Young people in developed nations spend more years in school and in starting their careers than ever before.
3. Most young women today, compared with the past, work outside the home. They start families later and want fewer children.

These trends point to lower birth rates in the future. But no one can predict the direction of future rates. For example, the recent increase in birth rate took place even though more American women work outside the home than ever before.

Also, birth rates differ for various ethnic and racial groups. The Hispanic population has historically had a birth rate higher than the white population and other ethnic/racial groups. This young population will play a future role in the politics of population aging, especially in states with large Hispanic populations (e.g., California and other southwestern states).

Gerontologists point to the potential for conflict between the relatively large older white population and the large younger Hispanic population. For example, this young group may resist paying for benefits to the older white population through taxes and other state subsidies. We will discuss this issue further in Chapters 7 and 15.

If birth rates stay high, this will moderate the aging of the population. An increased birth rate will decrease the proportion of older people in the population and will lower the median age. Still, it won't reduce the large effect of the aging Baby Boomer population on American society.

THE CHALLENGES OF AN AGING POPULATION

The older group will grow over the next 50 years or so, but it will not grow steadily. For example, population aging will slow and in some years will reverse itself. Myers (1990, p. 32) calls this the "metabolism of the population."

Between 1990 and 2000, for instance, the proportion of older people in the population decreased. The slow growth in the 65- to 74-year-old group accounts for this trend. But this will change in the early to middle years of the 21st century when the Baby Boom cohorts enter old age. These new cohorts will bring with them better health, better incomes, and a new view of later life.

At the same time, a larger number of people than ever before will live into late old age. These people, some of them over 100 years old, will have unique health and social service needs. The composition of the older population (the number of younger and the number of older seniors) can tell us about the challenges the United States will face as the population ages.

The Aging of the Older Population

Settersten and Trauten (2010, p. 143) call old age "life's longest period, extending three or more decades." Demographers divide the older group into subgroups. In the past, gerontologists defined the group ages 55 to 74 as the young-old and those age 75 and over as the old-old. But population aging has led to a refinement of this scheme. Research reports now often divide the older population into three groups: 65 to 74, 75 to 84, and 85 and over. All of these groups have grown in size.

He and colleagues (2005) report that the 65- to 74-year-old age group in 2000 was 8 times larger than in 1900, the 75- to 84-year-old age group was 16 times larger, and the 85 and over age group was 35 times larger. These groups will all grow in size in this century. But the oldest age group will be among the fastest-growing groups in the population. For example, between 1990 and 2000 the oldest age group increased by more than one third (from 3.1 million to 4.2 million) (He et al., 2005). (See Box 3.3 and Figure 3.5.)

People age 85 and over form a unique group within the older population. This group will grow about five times in size between 2000 and 2050 (Gonyea, 2010, citing Federal Interagency Forum on Aging-Related Statistics, 2006). By 2050, nearly a fifth of the older population (age 65 and over) will be 85 years old or over. This makes the oldest old population one of the fastest growing age groups in the country. Better health care and disease prevention have led to longer life in old age, and they will extend the lives of more people in the future. (See Figure 3.6.)

The oldest old population (age 85 and over) looks very different demographically from the young-old population (ages 65 to 74). Dunkle, Roberts, and Haug (2001) analyzed data from a longitudinal study of people in their 80s and 90s who lived in the Midwestern United States. They found that many of these people had small social networks. Although more than half the men in their study (52.2%) had spouses, only 11% of women were married. One third of the people in this study had no living children. The researchers found that the social networks of these people declined over time. (See Box 3.4.)

BOX 3.3
CENTENARIANS

Peter Keating (2010), writing for *Smart Money Magazine*, reports the following cases of centenarian achievement:

> Last year Emma Hendrickson, 101, became the oldest person ever to compete in the U.S. Bowling Congress Women's Championships, when she rolled a 318 series in Reno, Nev.
>
> Harriet Ames, 100, of Concord, N.H., earned her bachelor's degree in January, then died the next day.
>
> Frank DiPaolo Jr., 103, Providence political operative, still holds down his job as a doorman at the Rhode Island State House.

These people represent the leading edge of a population explosion of centenarians. The U.S. Administration on Aging reports that in 2008 the United States had 92,127 people age 100 and over (one quarter of one percent of the total 65+ population). This is a 147% increase from the 1990 figure of 37,306.

The Census Bureau predicts that by the year 2080, the United States will have over 1 million people age 100 or over. This will be a 10-fold increase over current figures. Vierck (2002, p. 2) calls this a "centenarian boom." Never in history have so many people reached their hundredth birthday.

What is it like to live to 100 years old? Will more centenarians mean more chronic health problems such as Alzheimer's disease? Will it mean more years of suffering for more people? Thomas Perls (1995), associate professor of geriatrics at Boston University School of Medicine, directed the New England Centenarian Study.

He thinks that people who live to age 100, as a group, will have better health than people 20 years younger. His pilot work found low proportions of centenarians with Alzheimer's disease. These people had better cognitive ability and health than expected. Perls says, "Centenarians disprove the perception that 'the older you get, the sicker you get. . . . They teach us that the older you get, the healthier you've been" (Keating, 2010).

Perls (1995) found that men in their 90s have better mental functioning than men in their 80s. Also, he has found what he calls a "gender crossover." Women tend to outlive men, but men who live beyond age 80 live healthier, more independent lives than women. Men who survive to late old age have greater physical and mental resources than expected.

Alfred Benedetti, age 101, serves as a model for the old age Perls describes. Benedetti performed in the Senior Olympics for the past 11 years, entering the javelin, shot put, and basketball free throw events. He bowls twice a week. He said that his health and long life came from avoiding tobacco and alcohol—except for the shot of port wine he drank every day. He stayed busy reading, writing, and working with his hands.

Genetics may explain part of the reason for long life and well-being in late old age. Those who live long may have genes that protect them from routine physical decline. They may also have genes that increase their ability to overcome disease and keep organs functioning well. Good health and a strong physical system lead to survival into late old age.

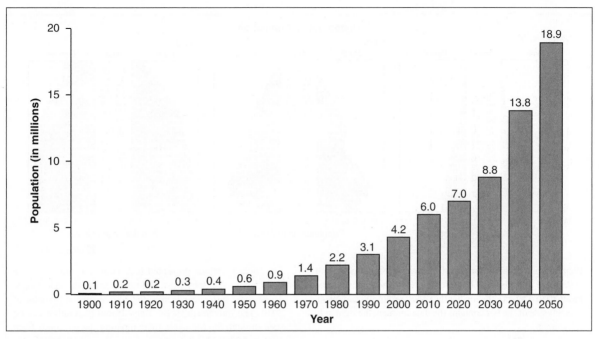

FIGURE 3.5 Population 85 Years and Over, 1900 to 2050

Source: U.S. Census Bureau. (1993). *Decennial censuses for specified years* and *population projections of the United States by age, sex, race, and Hispanic origin, 1993 to 2050,* Current Population Reports, P25-1104. Washington, DC: U.S. Government Printing Office. The data for 1990 are from He, W., Sangupta, M., Velkoff, V. A., & De Barros, K. A. (2005). *1990 census of population and housing,* CPH-L-74, *Modified and actual age, sex, race, and Hispanic origin data, 65+ in the United States: 2005,* U.S. Census Bureau, Current Population Reports, P23-209. Washington, DC: U.S. Government Printing Office.

BOX 3.4
A GERONTOLOGIST REFLECTS ON LATE OLD AGE

Elaine Brody, at age 88, provided a 50th anniversary feature article for *The Gerontologist* in 2010. Brody is one of the best-known gerontologists of her generation. Among other achievements, she coined the term "women in the middle" to capture the caregiving demands on middle-aged women.

In this article she provides a personal view of late old age. Below you will find some excerpts that focus on her experience.

My present perspective, then, is that of an 86-year-old woman who, I suppose, was prepared for old age intellectually but not emotionally. Even my children are growing into the stages of life I studied. Common experiences of old age, such as illness and losses, were unexpected, even though expectable. . . .

I do not remember becoming old. All of a sudden, I was there. Others perceive me as old. Cars stop to let me cross. People offer to help carry my packages. My grandchildren "check up" on me when my children are out of town and hold my arm when we cross a street. People my age walk more slowly and fatigue more quickly. Our waistlines thicken and our hair thins. Our balance is not great. We develop lots of wrinkles. One of my granddaughters is observant in detecting which of my friends have had what she calls "a little work done" on their faces (though having such "work" is by no means limited to the old). Some have had to give up driving—with the accompanying loss of independence and feelings of competence that entails. . . .

Our perspective on age has changed. One day, three people in succession said to me, "Did you hear about poor Harold? He was too young to die. He was only 83." A 92-year-old man died suddenly. Until that moment, he had been a regular member of his Neighborhood Security Patrol. As Jerry Seinfeld said, "Who dies at 70 anymore? It's old-fashioned.". . .

Source: Adapted from Brody, E. M. (2009). On being very, very old: an insider's perspective. *The Gerontologist, 50*(1), pp. 2–10.

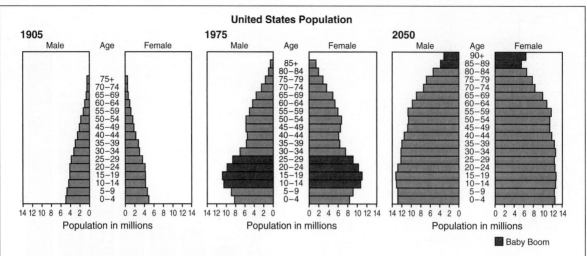

FIGURE 3.6 Images of Aging: Population Pyramids for the United States, 1905, 1975, 2050

Sources: U.S. Census Bureau. (1965). *Estimates of the population of the United States, by single years of age, color, and sex: 1900 to 1959,* Current Population Reports, Series P-25, No. 311. Washington, DC: U.S. Government Printing Office. U.S. Census Bureau. (1982). *Preliminary estimates of the population of the United States, age, sex, and race: 1970 to 1981,* Current Population Reports, Series P-25, No. 917. Washington, DC: U.S. Government Printing Office. Day, J. C., & U.S. Census Bureau (1993). *Population projections of the United States, age, sex, race, and Hispanic origin: 1993 to 2050,* Current Population Reports, Series P2-1104. Washington, DC: U.S. Government Printing Office, middle series projections.

Gonyea (2010) says that people age 80 and over have the lowest average income of all age groups over age 65. Median income in 2006 for people age 80 and over came to $15,462 compared to $20,518 for people ages 64 to 69. More than 1 person in 10 among the oldest old lives in poverty (11.4%) and 3 in 10 live near poverty. Women and minority members of the oldest group report the lowest incomes.

African American women age 75 and over and Hispanic women age 85 and over have the lowest incomes of all. For example, older white men age 75 and over have a poverty rate of 4.4%. African American women in this age group have a poverty rate of 30.2%—more than seven times the rate of older white men. These figures reflect a lifetime of low income for minority women, lack of pensions and savings, and time out of

the workforce taken to raise a family. These low-income groups rely most heavily on Social Security for their income.

The oldest old people have multiple chronic conditions and high rates of disability. They also consume large amounts of services, considering their numbers. Freedman, Aykan, Wolf, and Marcotte (2004) studied the amount of care services people age 75 and over used each month during a 3-year period. The researchers found that over the 3 years this group increased its care hours by 38%.

Wang (2004) reports that the 85 and over population accounts for 1.5% of the population, but uses 16.1% of Medicare fee-for-service payments. This group also uses the most nursing home services. He and colleagues (2005) report that in 2000, 18.2% of people age 85 and over lived in institutions compared with only 1.1% of people ages 65 to 74 and 4.5% of those ages 75 to 84. This represents a decrease in nursing home use from 1990. But it shows the continued need for heavy health care services for the very old.

The increase in the very old population in the years ahead will lead to an increase in the use of long-term care services. Some of that care will take place in institutions. But where possible, long-term care will take place in the community. In either case, increases in the oldest old population will have a large impact on national health care costs and policies.

Ethnic and Racial Variations

The racial and ethnic composition of the older population changes as new people enter old age. Today, for example, the nonwhite population of the United States is younger than the white population. Older people make up only 8% of the African American and 5% of the Hispanic American populations compared with 13.4% of the white population (National Center for Health Statistics, 2003). This difference reflects higher fertility rates (more young people in minority populations) and higher mortality among nonwhites. However, these rates may change in the years ahead, and this would lead to changes in the older population.

He and colleagues (2005) say that the proportion of non-Hispanic Whites in the older population will decrease from 83% in 2003 to 72% by 2030. During this same period the population of older African Americans will increase from 8% to 10% of the older population. Hispanics will increase from about 6% to 11% of the older population. And the proportion of Asians in the older population will increase from 3 to 5% of the older population. These changes will lead to greater ethnic and racial diversity in the older population.

Regional Distribution

Internal migration (**in-migration**) in the United States in the past several decades has led to decreases in the proportion of older people in the Northeast, increases in the proportion of older people in the Midwest, and increases in the proportions of older people in the South and the West. These findings reflect three trends that lead to an older population: accumulation, recomposition, and congregation (Longino, 2001).

Accumulation

Accumulation takes place when older people stay behind and young people move out of an area. Midwestern states (Iowa, Missouri, Nebraska, North Dakota, and South Dakota) made up 5 of the 15 states with the highest concentrations of older people in 2000 (He et al., 2005). The **out-migration** of younger people accounts for this. Young people leave this region to find work, often in the Sunbelt states. Projections show that northeastern states like Maine, Pennsylvania, and Rhode Island will age in the future in part because of out-migration. If present trends continue, they will rank among the 10 oldest states in the year 2020 (U.S. Census Bureau, 1996).

Recomposition

Recomposition takes place when older people move into an area that younger people leave. For example, some older people move to rural areas to retire. These areas may offer little opportunity for young workers. But they offer a low cost of living and beautiful scenery that suits older people (Hunt, Marshall, & Merrill, 2002). Arkansas and Missouri fit this pattern. They had large numbers of older people in 2000. Projections show that they will have some of the highest proportions of older people in the country in 2020 (19.3% and 17.5% of the population, respectively).

Congregation

Congregation takes place when people of all ages move to an area, but older people arrive at the fastest pace. Florida, Arizona, and North Carolina fit this pattern. The large number of older people who have moved to Florida made this the oldest state in the country in 2000 (with 17.6% of its population age 65 or over). Only Arkansas and Arizona will reach this level by the year 2020. By that time, Florida is projected to have over one quarter of its population age 65 and over.

Other Sunbelt and Western states (e.g., California and Texas) with a large number of older people also attract a large number of young people. This keeps the proportion of older people relatively low. Both California and Nevada rank in the bottom 10 states by proportion of older people, with 10.6% and 9.9% age 65 or older, respectively (He et al., 2005).

The movement of many Baby Boomers to the Sunbelt has delayed population aging in that region until later in this century. But Longino (2001, citing Frey,

"The kids are grown before you know it, aren't they?"

1999) says, "This pattern should continue to fuel the aging of the Sunbelt in the early decades of the 21st century." Only Florida has both a large number and a large proportion of older people. Florida in 2000 had 6 of the 10 cities in the United States with the highest proportions of older people. Clearwater, Florida, in that year had 21.5% of its population age 65 and over (Hetzel & Smith, 2001).

Interstate Migration

Willa Reich lived in Manhattan all of her adult life. When she was in her 60s, her son and his family moved to Florida, but her daughter and her daughter's family remained in the city, a few minutes away by car. Willa's apartment was a short subway ride from her job, and with her daughter nearby, she felt content where she was.

Nevertheless, when Willa retired at age 65, she began to consider a move. She had a good pension from the city, Social Security, and some savings. The neighborhood had gotten worse, the winters felt more severe, and her son in Florida kept asking her to move south. She went to look at a condominium apartment north of Miami during one visit to her son. The complex had a clubhouse, swimming pools, a lake, a transportation system, and recreation activities. Her son lived only an hour away by car. She decided to move. Two years later her daughter and family moved to a town a few miles away. Willa now has her children and grandchildren nearby, and she enjoys the lifestyle she wants. Willa will probably live in her new community for the rest of her life.

Willa's decision to move to a southern small town fits a pattern similar to that of many older people today. Demographers find that migration patterns follow the life course. Studies done in the 1980s found a stable pattern that has lasted for decades. The tendency to move peaks at around age 20 to 24. This coincides with students leaving school and with marriage. Younger people move to find jobs and set up their own families.

From age 35 on, the tendency to move declines slowly until retirement. Children, a job, and community ties all limit the tendency to move during the middle years. Migration picks up again for some people between ages 60 and 70 after people retire. An increase in migration occurs again at the end of life due to declines in health (Longino, 2004).

Amenity Migration

The first type of move, at retirement, Longino (1992) calls **amenity migration**. People move to enjoy a new lifestyle, to be with friends who have moved, or to establish a new identity as a retiree. He also describes another kind of amenity move: a move back to a person's childhood home state. People who do this often moved in their youth to find work. They then return to their roots in retirement.

Kadlec (2007) cites the U.S. Census when he reports that "nearly 18% of people over 60 who moved across state lines say they are returning to their home town." African Americans have a relatively high rate of this type of migration. Migration researchers say that retirees often have "'remote thoughts' or daydreams about moving before they make a move. They also gather information about new locations that shape their decision to move" (Longino & Bradley, 2006, p. 77).

Longino (2001) says that people tend to move for three reasons in old age: retirement, moderate disability, and major chronic disability.

Retirement

Longino (1990, p. 52) says that people who make their first move after retirement look for "places of natural beauty and more pleasant climates." Studies in Canada, Great Britain, and the United States show that

---

BOX 3.5
LIFE IN A RETIREMENT COMMUNITY
Pro and Con

I recently visited a friend who lives in a retirement community near Fort Lauderdale, Florida. At the main entrance, a line of cars waited to get in. A security guard walked up to my car with a clipboard and asked whom I was visiting. I told him and said that my host had called ahead to clear my arrival. He went into a guardhouse to check the guest list. When he returned, he asked to see my driver's license, then walked around the car to check the license plate and jot down the number. Finally, he waved me through. By this time I felt hot, bothered, and ready to turn around.

I have had an easier time crossing national borders than getting into this community. The delay may have annoyed me as a visitor, but the person I visited loves living here. She has made new friends and keeps busy with exercise classes, mah jong, and movies. She also likes the sense of security she gets from the high fence and the guardhouse at the entrance.

Many other older people feel the same way about their retirement communities. These enclaves attract more people every year. They offer a lifestyle that many older people want in retirement. Sun City in Arizona, one of the largest retirement communities in the United States, has 50,000 residents and its own banks, shopping plazas, golf courses, and restaurants. Retirement communities offer a self-contained world. They offer convenience, social activity, and security.

Critics see a downside to retirement communities. Kastenbaum (1993b) says these communities can create a "fortress mentality." They often cut themselves off from the local community and from local social issues. Some communities refuse to pay taxes for the local school system. People in these settings may even cut themselves off from their families. "An old man and woman move down here and build a mansion," Jim Martin, retiree and social activist says. "Then he dies and she's left living in his mausoleum. Then what? They cut all their lifelines to everybody!" (cited in Crispell & Frey, 1994).

Some communities limit the length of stay of anyone under age 18. Some communities discourage visits by families with young children. Gerber and colleagues (1989) quote one of the rules at a retirement community in Florida: "Children require the constant supervision of those responsible for them. They must be kept from interfering in any way with the quiet and comfort of residents."

What are the pros and cons of retirement community living? Would you want to live in a community like this? Would you want your parents or grandparents to move to one? Would you like to visit them there?

---

retirees tend to migrate to specific areas. Mobile older people tend to move to places with a mild climate, often by the coast. They also look for places with a reasonable cost of living (Walters, 2002).

An active senior couple at the Snowbird Ski Resort, Utah. People will often visit a place for a vacation before they decide to move there full or part-time.

"The pattern is never random," Longino (1990, p. 52) says, "nor are migrants randomly selected from among all older people." Hazelrigg and Hardy (1995) found that most migrants are retired, married, and generally have higher incomes than peers in their new location. They also have more education and better health than older people who stay put. Migrants are also "overwhelmingly Anglo" (Longino, 1990, p. 53).

Research shows that destination characteristics tend to determine the place people choose, more than nearness or distance from the preretirement home. Some states in the United States have a great attraction for retirees (e.g., Florida and Arizona) (Longino & Bradley, 2006). Ten states received 54.3% of out-of-state migrants age 60 and over in 2000.

The recession following 2008 may have had a moderating effect on interstate migration. Longino and Bradley (2006) note that the top receiving states lost some share of interstate migrants between 1990 and 2000. Also, California slid from 13.6% of all older migrants in 1960 to 6.1% in 2000. The high cost of living, the loss of jobs, and relatively high taxes in California help explain this decrease in migration.

Still, the Sunbelt and Western states get the largest share of migrating retirees. Mild winter temperatures and scenic beauty lead people to the South and West (Stafford, 2009). Florida, California, Arizona, Texas, and North Carolina get the largest streams of older migrants from states outside their regions. Longino (2001, p. 111) calls these "national destination states." Florida, the lead destination state, adds more older migrants each year than Arizona, California, and Texas combined (Longino & Bradley, 2006).

Longino (2001, 2004) notes some counterintuitive trends. For example, many retirees migrate to attractive places in neighboring states. New Yorkers and people from Pennsylvania often migrate to the New Jersey shore. Cape Cod, the Wisconsin Dells, and the Pocono Mountains of Pennsylvania also attract retirees. Some older people move out of Sunbelt states. Florida, for example, contains the 100 top counties that send migrants out of state. Disability and the need to live near their children motivate these moves. Los Angeles County seniors often move to Arizona, Nevada, or Oregon. Relief from the high cost of living and a more relaxed lifestyle draw them to these locations.

Often, migrants have visited a place before. Some have even lived in the place for part of the year in the years before they move. Some never move permanently. They live in a Sunbelt location until the weather turns hot. Then they head back to their northern homes.

A case will illustrate this pattern. Jack Exeter owns a computer services business in Connecticut. His company creates websites for local businesses. He and his wife wanted an escape from the cold northern winters. They enjoyed vacationing in Florida, so they began exploring housing options there. They visited a number of condominium complexes, compared prices, and looked for a community that felt comfortable. They finally found a setting that offered the amenities they liked. Jack, an outdoors type, could play tennis, kayak, and hike on nearby trails. His wife Josie wanted warm weather and a chance to relax with a good book in quiet surroundings.

They bought a condo, but they didn't move there all at once. For one thing, their children and grandchildren still lived in Connecticut. And they enjoy summers at nearby beaches. They use the condo only during the winter. Josie spends most of the cold months there—from Thanksgiving to Easter. Jack commutes there for 2-week stints throughout the

winter. He works hard with his staff when he's in Connecticut. He runs his business by phone and via email while he's away.

Jack's not ready to retire yet. He needs to keep working. But when he does retire, he'll spend all winter in Florida with Josie. They'll come back for the summer and for holidays and special events with their kids. Their winter home also offers a place for their family and friends to gather during winter vacations.

Longino (2001) refers to people like Jack as "seasonal" or "cyclical" migrants. As many as 80% of these migrants never settle permanently in their seasonal homes. These people live a lifestyle different from that of permanent migrants. When their health declines they make fewer and shorter visits to their seasonal location. Eventually they give up their seasonal visits.

Some permanent migrants take part in community life. Others remain aloof and bond with other migrants, never becoming part of the community. A person who plans to migrate should think about social needs as well as the climate before they make a move. The charm of golf or fishing, Longino says, will wear off in a year. People need to think about the community life, the culture, and the kinds of services they use (e.g., a library or a theater). "Long-term satisfaction," he says, "is more strongly determined by whether or not they can do the things they want to do and be the person they want to be in retirement" (Longino, 1992, p. 30).

The migration of older people to Sunbelt states after retirement sometimes creates tension between the migrants and the long-time residents. Some Sunbelt communities fear that older migrants will increase health and social service costs. But when Longino (1990) reviewed the data on health, transportation, and service use in host communities, he found no evidence for the supposed high costs of older people.

In the South, for example, except for Florida, most older migrants came from the region or were returning to their native states. Local residents saw them as natives. Longino (2001) reports that Florida's income from older migrants came to $8.3 billion between 1985 and 1990 (up from $4 billion in 1975 to 1980). Sastry (1992) found that retiree migrants had large positive economic effects on the Florida economy. Retirees contribute by spending their pension funds and paying taxes. This benefits older and younger people. The migration of older people also creates jobs in host communities.

Experts still disagree on the benefits of older people's migration to an area. Research shows that older people create economic growth in smaller towns and retirement settings. But as these older people age, they may place new demands on their communities. The long-term cost to a community may outweigh the short-term benefit of older migrants. Continued migration by younger retirees will offset this cost in some cases, as will out-migration that often takes place late in life. The complexity of migration decisions and trends makes it difficult to predict future costs or benefits.

Moderate Disability

The second type of move is what Wiseman and Roseman (1979) call "kinship migration," or what Walters (2002) calls "assistance-seek migration." This takes place when the older retiree moves back near his or, more often, her children. Illness, disability, or widowhood lead to this move (Stoller & Longino, 2001). People who live in rural areas will move to more urban centers at this time so they can get the health care and support they need from their children and from social services.

Roberts (2007, no page) gives some examples of this trend. Ida Kotowitz, age 88, says, "I was failing in health, most of my friends have passed away and I was alone." She moved to a retirement home in the Bronx, New York, after 22 years in Florida. "Friends are all right when you're well," she says, "but when you're not, you need family." Al Petzke, age 82, tells a similar story. After his wife died he continued to live in their home in Houston. But "it didn't make one bit of sense," the retired steelworker says, "[for his son] to be spending all that money every month flying down to see me." Al left Houston and moved back to Ohio in order to live near his son. Kadlec (2007) says that "even if you have plenty of money, eventually you are going to want the support of the people you know best."

Major Chronic Disability

The third move comes near the end of life. Meyer and Speare (1985) call this a move in "preparation for aging." Older people move from a community setting (their own home, an apartment, or living with their children) to an institution. This move often takes place within the person's local community. Generally, it coincides with increased disability and the need for institutional health care. A person who needs nursing home care may migrate to a nursing home from a location with few nursing home beds. This applies especially to people with severe disability (Walters, 2002).

Urban–Rural Distribution

In the United States, about three-quarters of older people live in metropolitan counties (with a city of 50,000 or more people) (He et al., 2005). Longino (2001) says that from the 1950s onward, older people have tended to live in suburbs of these cities. Central cities have attracted more young people. Older populations in suburbs have increased proportionately as children move out and older people age in place.

Two trends explain the presence of older people in cities. First, many older people in the city centers have always lived there and will age in place. They have close friends in the neighborhood. They see neighbors and friends when they shop or go to church. Those who live in cities tend to be nonwhite, have the least money, have low mobility, and live alone.

In 2000, for example, elderly Hispanic Americans had a nine times greater likelihood of living inside than outside a metropolitan area. Elderly African Americans had a five times greater likelihood of living in a city than outside one. Whites had only a three times greater likelihood of living in a city than outside one. Older minority group members in cities sometimes have problems getting to and using social and health care services. Barriers such as language, poverty, poor transportation, and lack of knowledge about services may keep people from using programs.

These problems and the desire to live a simpler life help explain why some African Americans over age 60 return to southern states in retirement (Longino & Bradley, 2006). These moves fit into a historical cycle. African American workers move North in their younger years and return to their roots in later life. Hispanic Americans today who move to northern cities for jobs may show this pattern in the future.

The second trend, described by Smith (2004a, b), is the tendency for educated former suburbanites to move back to the city in later life. She reports that this group of older people enjoys the culture and services that big cities offer. One couple who moved from the Washington suburbs to a downtown neighborhood said that the museums and cultural events only partly explain their move. "It's the restaurants, it's the stores, it's the sense of vitality on the streets, the diversity of age and ethnic groups. It's a lively atmosphere to live in."

This trend may grow as the Baby Boom ages and some of its members choose the excitement of city living. Smith reports that Del Webb, the company that pioneered the Sun City lifestyle in the Southwest, has begun to develop city-oriented properties. They have considered developing an urban high-rise retirement community for active people who want to live downtown.

Suburban communities also show an increase in older people and in the proportion of older people. At least three trends account for this increase. First, suburbs attracted young couples after World War II. As these people age in place, they increase the number and proportion of older people in the suburbs. This trend accounts for most of the increase in older people in suburbs today.

Second, the children of these older people grow up and move away. This leads to a greater proportion of older people in certain suburbs. Third, some older people move to the suburbs when they retire (Longino, 2001). These people tend to be married, have more money, and live in their own homes. They may move into suburban or small-town retirement communities. Preston (1993) projects an increase in the size of smaller centers when Baby Boomers retire.

Changes in the Sex Ratio

The **sex ratio** shows the proportion of men to women in the population. The formula for the sex ratio looks like this:

$$\text{Sex ratio} = \frac{\text{Number of men} \times 100}{\text{Number of women}}$$

A ratio of 100 for people age 65 and over would mean an older population with one man for every woman. The lower the ratio, the smaller the proportion of men in the older population.

In 1900, men age 60 and over in the United States outnumbered women in that age group 105 to 100 (Hobbs & Stoops, 2002). These figures reflect the high rates of female deaths due to childbirth at the turn of the century. This ratio declined throughout most of the 20th century. In 2000, the older population (65 and over) had a ratio of 70 men for every 100 women. The ratio ranged from 86 for those ages 65 to 69 to 41 for those age 85 and over (He et al., 2005).

At least two trends account for the increase of women over men in later life: (1) better health care for women during their childbearing and middle years and (2) increases in cigarette smoking and work-related diseases among men in the 20th century. But recently, this trend has begun to reverse itself. Between 1980 and 2002, the gap in life expectancy

between men and women narrowed. A girl born in 1980 could expect to live 7.4 years longer than a boy born in that year. But a girl born in 2002 could expect to live only 5.2 years longer than her male counterpart (National Center for Health Statistics, 2004b).

These figures show a convergence of life expectancies for men and women. This may be due to increased cigarette use by women. Pampel (2002) reports that cigarette smoking among women from the 1960s to the 1980s accounts for *all* of the narrowing in mortality figures for men and women. Also, large numbers of women have entered the workforce, and they now face the same working conditions as men.

Table 3.3 shows the sex ratio at various ages. Notice that the ratio declines with each older age group. In 2001, the group ages 95 to 99 has a ratio about one third that of the 65- to 69-age group. This reflects the greater life expectancy of older women compared with older men.

This low sex ratio points to another characteristic of the older population today. Compared to men, women face a greater chance of being single in later life. Several factors account for this. First, women tend to marry older men. Second, men have a shorter life expectancy than women in later life. Third, whereas men

TABLE 3.3 U.S. Sex Ratios by Age for Selected Years

	Year			
Age	*2001*	*2030*	*2050*	*2070*
65–69	85.2	89.1	90.2	91.7
70–74	80.1	85.9	87.5	89.9
75–79	72.1	80.6	83.4	87.7
80–84	62.2	72.9	77.9	82.9
85–89	49.5	63.2	70.2	75.9
90–94	37.5	52.8	60.6	67.5
95–99	28.9	43.0	51.0	58.7
100+	22.0	33.1	40.9	49.4

The sex ratio is the proportion of men to women in the population. The figures in the table represent the number of men for every 100 women. In any given year, compared with younger age groups, older age groups show lower sex ratios. This occurs because the proportion of men in an age cohort decreases over time. Note that demographers expect more men to survive in each age group in the future. This leads to higher sex ratios. Demographers predict that the life expectancies of men and women will come closer together in the future. This will mean a decrease in the rates of widowhood and more married couples in the older population.

Source: U.S. Census Bureau. (2000). *Projections of the total resident population by 5-year age groups,* and *Sex with special age categories: Middle series, 2001 to 2005, 2025 to 2045, 2050 to 2070,* Population Projections Program, Population Division. Washington, DC: U.S. Government Printing Office. Retrieved April 26, 2004, from www.census.gov/population/projections/nation/summary/np-t3-b.pdf and np-t3-f.pdf, and np-t3-g.pdf.

tend to remarry, women tend to stay single. In 2002, for example, only 13.9% of men age 65 and over were widowed; in that same year and age group, 45.5% of women were widowed (U.S. Census Bureau, 2004).

The higher proportion of women in later life and their greater chance of widowhood makes old age a different experience for women and men today. Women, more than men, have to adapt to a singles lifestyle. They need to create social supports outside of marriage. And they have a greater stake in the quality and availability of services and supports in later life.

The future of aging for men and women may look different due to the increases in the life expectancy of men. Married couples in happy marriages will live more years together. And women who experience widowhood will typically do so at a later age. This will provide women as well as men with more in-home (spousal) support in later life.

THE IMPACT OF POPULATION AGING

Support (or Dependency) Ratios

The aging of the older population will lead to change in what demographers call the **total dependency ratio**. This is the ratio of the 0 to 14 and 65 and older age groups to the rest of the population (ages 15 to 64). This ratio gives a crude measure of how many middle-aged (working) people exist to support younger and older people in the population.

Demographers express the total dependency ratio in the following formula:

$$\text{Total dependency ratio} = \frac{\text{Population 0 to 19 plus Population 65+}}{\text{Population 20 to 64}} \times 100$$

Table 3.4 introduces the concept of the elderly and youth dependency ratios. The **elderly dependency ratio** refers to the number of people age 65 and over divided by the population ages 20 to 64, multiplied by 100. The **youth dependency ratio** refers to the number of people ages 0 to 19 divided by the population ages 20 to 64, multiplied by 100. These ratios show how these two subgroups contribute to the total dependency ratio.

Table 3.4 gives a good summary of recent demographic change in the United States. The total dependency ratio decreases from 1990 to 2000 and picks up again into the middle of this century. In 2030, it reaches a level similar to that of 1930.

TABLE 3.4 Dependency Ratios: 1980 to 2050

Year	Total	Youth	Older
1980	76.2	56.4	19.9
1990	70.2	48.8	21.4
2000	69.6	48.5	21.1
2010	66.5	44.8	21.7
2020	74	46	28
2030	83	48	35
2040	85	48	37
2050	85	48	37

The old age dependency ratio measures the relationship between the population age 65 and over and the general population (ages 20 to 64). The youth dependency ratio measures the relationship between the population under age 20 and the general population (ages 20 to 64). Addition of these two ratios gives the total dependency ratio. These figures provide an indication of how many people in the general population exist to support younger and older people in the population.

Note that the composition of the total ratio changes over time. In 1980, young people made up about three quarters of the total ratio. This means that in 1980, compared to older people, younger people (by this measure) required more support from the middle-aged population. At the middle of this century (2050), older people will make up almost half (44%) of the total dependency ratio. Older people will have almost doubled in their need for support by the middle-aged population between 1980 and 2050. The traditional view of the old age dependency ratio holds that older people make large demands on society's resources. But as healthier, better educated, and active older people enter old age, they may not follow this traditional pattern.

Note: The reference population for these data is the resident population.

Sources: U.S. Bureau of the Census. (1983). *1980 census of population, vol. 1, Characteristics of the population, Chapter B, General population characteristics, Part 1, United States summary,* PC80-1-B1. Washington, DC: Government Printing Office, Table 42. U.S. Bureau of the Census. (1991). *1990 census of population and housing summary tape file 1* (STF1). Washington, DC: Government Printing Office. U.S. Census Bureau. (2001). *Census 2000 summary file 1* (SF1). Washington, DC: Government Printing Office, Table QT-P1; Table PCT12; 2010 to 2030. U.S. Census Bureau, International Programs Center, International Data Base. (2004). U.S. Department of Commerce Economics and Statistics Administration. www.census.gov/ipc/www/idbnew.html. Vincent, G. K., & Velkoff, V. A.. (2010, May). *The next four decades: The older population in the United States: 2010 to 2050. Population estimates and projections.* Current Population Reports. P25-1138. U.S. National Center for Health Statistics. (2009, April 17). National Vital Statistics Reports (NVSR), *Deaths: Final data for 2006,* Vol. 57, No. 14. Retrieved October 19, 2010, from www.census.gov/compendia/statab/2010/tables/10s0102.pdf

Several considerations are worth noting.

• First, the elderly and youth dependency ratios make up different proportions of the total dependency ratio at different points in time. Until 1950, for example, the youth dependency ratio made up almost the entire total dependency ratio. In 2030, older people account for almost half the total dependency ratio.

• Second, the elderly dependency ratio generally increases throughout this period. But it makes a sudden jump after the year 2010.

- Third, the youth dependency ratio stays roughly the same from 1990 to 2030.
- Fourth, the ratio of working people ages 20 to 64 to those age 65 and over decreases dramatically in this century. By 2030, the United States will have only 2.5 younger adults for each older person.

This table shows that the increase in total dependency ratio is due to an increase in older people in the population. Some see this as a sign of trouble in the future. They see this as a shift from lower-cost programs for younger people to high-cost programs for older people. Kotlikoff (1993), for example, warns about increased costs for health care and potentially less investment in long-term programs such as care for the environment, infrastructure improvements (roads and bridges), and education.

A smaller number of children may reduce the costs for schooling. This could allow local and state governments to meet the higher costs of an aging population. But, not counting the costs for public schools, children rely mostly on private support from their parents. An older population depends more on public sources of support. This means that the same total dependency ratio, but with a higher elderly dependency ratio, may mean greater public cost in the future.

Programs such as Medicare and Social Security depend on intergenerational support. They assume that society will transfer some funds from the younger generation to the older generation. This works well today with a large working-age population and a relatively small older population. But the future will see a large group of older people depend on a smaller group of younger people. Peterson (1999, cited in Korczyk & Public Policy Institute, AARP, 2002) takes a gloomy view of the future. He calls the increase in older people a "global hazard" that "may actually do more to shape our collective future than deadly super-viruses, extreme climate change or the proliferation of nuclear, biological and chemical weapons."

Not everyone agrees with this conclusion. A look at other countries with populations older than the United States suggests how the United States can adapt to an aging population. Many societies have greater elderly dependency ratios than the United States. Sweden and Austria, for example, already have dependency ratios similar to those projected for the United States later this century. These countries have not faced a crisis due to their aging populations. They have well-developed social support systems and some of the highest standards of living in the world. This suggests that the United States can adapt to an older population in the future without crisis or social upheaval (Schulz & Binstock, 2006).

Jackson and colleagues (2003) studied old age dependency ratios in twelve countries. The study assessed, among other things, the public burden of an aging population. The study placed the United States (along with Australia and the United Kingdom) in a low-vulnerability category. The authors say that the modest dependency ratio in the future and a pension system balanced between public and private sources will allow the United States to adapt to its aging population. These authors and others (Korczyk & Public Policy Institute, AARP, 2002) take a close look at dependency ratios and fail to see an economic crisis due to population aging.

Critique of Dependency Ratios

The conclusions drawn from dependency ratios seem self-evident. The word *dependency* itself leads to the conclusion that an increase in older people will place a greater burden on society. Some reports use the less loaded term *support* ratio, although this refers to the same measure (He et al., 2005). A closer look at this measure raises questions about its ability to predict the future.

For example, this formula assumes that all people in an age group behave the same and have the same needs. Dependency ratios assume that all people ages 20 to 64 work, support themselves, and support the older and younger populations. But many people ages 20 to 64 (college students, for example, or people who are disabled or unemployed) depend on others or public funds for their income.

Dependency ratios also assume that all people age 65 and over depend primarily on younger people (or public support). But this doesn't fit the facts today and will be less true in the future.

First, studies show that Baby Boomers plan to stay active in their retirement. A Harvard University–MetLife (2004) study reports a trend toward later retirement ages. The report predicts that Baby Boomers will likely increase this trend. An end to mandatory retirement for most workers, an increase in the age for receiving full Social Security benefits, and the need for more labor all point toward later retirement ages in the future.

Attitudes toward retirement have also changed. Many Boomers now plan to work part-time for interest, enjoyment, or extra income. In addition, the recent economic downturn has led workers to rethink early retirement plans.

Many Baby Boomers also plan for second careers as entrepreneurs, teachers, or workers in nonprofit agencies. These people prefer new career opportunities and income to government pensions (Reynolds, 2004). If this trend continues, these people will stay at work long past the current retirement age of 65. This group will continue to add to the economy as they age.

Second, health care experts expect that, compared to past generations of older people, Baby Boomers will enter later life in better health. Willens (2003) reviewed the research on Baby Boom health practices. He summarizes three national random samples of Boomers done in 2001–2002. He reports that they are "highly concerned with their physical well-being and doing something about it" (p. 43).

Fifty-five percent of Boomers in these studies say they try to cut back on unhealthy foods and on the quantity they eat. Fifty-two percent take vitamin and mineral supplements, 49% walk for exercise three to five times per week, 32% have exercise equipment at home and use it, 13% belong to a health club, and 10% belong to a commercial weight reduction program. Willens (2003, p. 44) concludes, "Boomers . . . have decided to begin taking care of their bodies—bodies that in many instances have been neglected over the years."

Third, Boomers plan to stay engaged in social life as they age. They look forward to retirement, actively plan for it, and want to do more than recreation. Willens (2003, p. 40) says that "this group is ready to begin some big new experience." The dependency ratio may serve as an easy way to look at the cost of an aging society, but it fails to predict the impact of the older population today. And it will do an even worse job of predicting the impact of the Baby Boom generation.

The use of this ratio does damage when it creates a sense of crisis or panic about societal aging. The dependency ratio creates a fiction based on weak assumptions. It assumes that an older population will only increase societal costs. But more older people in society may lead to a better use of resources. An older society, for example, may have a lower crime rate, a lower auto accident rate, and an increased concern for fitness and disease prevention.

Older people, many with good incomes, will spend their pensions and savings on travel, restaurants, and professional services. Many older people will help support their younger family members and will give to their communities as volunteers. These trends will make better use of social resources and create a better quality of life for all age groups.

Korczyk and Public Policy Institute, AARP (2002) says that the characteristics of older people (e.g., their health) and social policies have the greatest effect on the cost of an older population. Many retirement policies today, for example, encourage retirement at age 65. Ironically, countries with the highest elderly dependency ratios encourage older people to leave the workforce early. They appear to demand economic dependency by the older population.

In the future, these countries may rethink these policies. The United States has already taken action. Over the next few years, it will gradually raise the age of eligibility for full Social Security payments. The government must also control Medicare and other health care costs. Marmor (2001) shows that practices like the use of Diagnosis Related Groups, begun in the 1980s, helped control and reduce hospital fees. Projections of current health care costs, based on an aging population, create the demand for change.

A stronger economy and improved private pension plans would reduce the impact of an older population on public funds. Korczyk and Public Policy Institute, AARP (2002) says that society's economic stability and growth would expand the job market. It would allow people to save for retirement, and it would provide young people with good salaries. This will help them pay for services that will support an older population. Better private pension plans would help people stay financially independent in later life.

Friedland and Summer (1999, p. 5) say that "society can and will adjust [to an aging population] as it has done before. But adjustment will be easier if the challenges are addressed in a rational manner today." How well the United States manages this shift will depend on how well people understand population aging and how well our society prepares for change. Much of this planning has begun, but more will have to take place in the years ahead. Preparation for the future will take planning, thought, and creative social action, and all of us will play a part in this societal transformation.

CONCLUSION

I worked for some years at a university campus in a northern city. I headed home one day in January and noticed my wife about a block ahead of me, pushing one of our children in a baby carriage. She reached the corner of the busiest intersection in town and began to cross when the light changed. The slush from the cars slowed the wheels of the carriage in the street and she only made it to the center island. There she climbed the snow bank and hauled the carriage (and our child) up to safety.

As she caught her breath, she noticed that an elderly woman had just reached the bottom of the snow bank and was trying to climb up. The traffic had started and the woman looked scared. My wife reached down and helped the woman to safety. They stood breathing hard in the cold air with a look of weary triumph. They had both braved the city streets and won a small victory.

People imagine that more social services, longer traffic lights, or new architectural designs to serve an older population will inhibit social life. The demographic doomsayers imagine that an older population will bring only higher costs. But an older society can benefit all of us. In this story, the older woman needed a longer red light to cross the street, but so did my wife and our baby. And I wouldn't mind if I didn't have to climb over snow mountains to get on the bus or risk a concussion when the bus whips into traffic just as I move toward my seat. An older society might be a more humane society. And a more enjoyable place for all of us.

The world will face population aging in the years ahead. The developing and the developed nations will face challenges due to the costs associated with an aging population. In every case societies will need to review past practices and think of new ways to support their aging populations.

The United States cannot copy any other society as it moves into the future. It cannot look back to recover a golden age of the past. But it can learn from other societies about a good old age. Throughout the world, older people do best when they can give to their society. They get the highest esteem when they contribute to society and express themselves.

Some societies make this possible. Older people served as matchmakers in China and Japan; they served as spiritual and community leaders in early America. They still serve as ritual leaders among the Coast Salish Indians in the Pacific Northwest. When older people play useful roles, they contribute to society and receive respect. The United States can create policies and social opportunities for older people with this in mind.

SUMMARY

- The developing nations still have relatively young populations. They will have increased numbers of older people in the years ahead due to decreased death rates. An increase in the number of older people in these societies will strain current social, health, and economic programs for older people.
- The developed nations of the world have increasing proportions of older people in their populations. They also have growing proportions of very old people (age 85 and over). Societal population aging, and the aging of the older population, will create new economic and social challenges for these nations.
- The U.S. population aged steadily during the last century and will continue to age in the future. Social scientists believe that population aging will lead to social change, but they do not think that it will lead to conflict, crisis, and more social problems.
- Demographers study the aging of society and the impact of societal aging on social institutions. Demographers use three measures of population aging: the absolute number of older people in a society, the median age of the population, and the increased proportion of older people.
- Population change occurs due to migration, deaths, and births. The decline in the fertility rate is the major cause of population aging in the United States today.
- Demographers divide the older population into subgroups. They refer to young-, middle-, and old-old. Each of these groups has unique needs.
- Internal migration has led to a shift in the proportions of the older population in different parts of the United States. We see decreases in the proportion of older people in the Northeast and increases in the proportion of older people in the South, Midwest, and West.
- People tend to move for three reasons in old age. Gerontologists call the first type of move a retirement move, the second type a moderate disability move, and the third type a major chronic disability move.
- Two things account for the greater number of women to men at every age in later life. First is better health care for women during their childbearing and middle years. Second are the increases in cigarette smoking and work-related diseases for men. Current trends show an improvement in life expectancy for men. This may lead to similar numbers of men and women in old age in the future.
- Demographic studies show an increase in the elderly dependency ratio. Some researchers believe that this increase will lead to a future crisis in the cost of services for older people. Other researchers believe that the older population will lead society to a better use of resources. Most gerontologists agree that U.S. society needs to pre-

pare for an aging population. New policies and new approaches to services can meet the challenges of population aging.

- The oldest members of the Baby Boom generation turned 60 in 2005. This generation will enter old age in large numbers in the next 30 years. They will change the meaning of later life during their Third Age (between ages 60 and 85).

- U.S. society will need to change to meet the needs of older people. Many of these changes will lead to a better quality of life for all age groups.

- The past cannot give answers to the new challenges that aging societies will face. But history can teach us one thing. When older people have a useful role to play in society, they live a good old age. And society benefits from their contributions and their wisdom.

DISCUSSION QUESTIONS

1. Compare and contrast the challenges facing the developed and developing nations as a result of the increase in the proportion and number of older people in their societies. Discuss some responses each type of society can make to these challenges.
2. What are the stages of the demographic transition? Describe the changes in birth and death rates at each stage. What impact do birth and death rates at each stage have on social institutions? What impact do they have on everyday life?
3. List the measures that demographers use to describe population aging. Give the strengths and weaknesses of each measure.
4. State three changes in social institutions that will come about due to population aging.
5. What are the three causes of population change in the United States today? What effect does a declining birth rate have on population aging? Why does it have this effect?
6. List some of the pros and cons of having children today. Do you think that young people in the United States today want to have many or few children? Think for a moment about how many children you would like to have. What about your friends and other people your age? What effect will today's decisions about having children have on the future age structure of the U.S. population?
7. How long do you expect to live? How does that influence your decisions with respect to diet, exercise, relationships, career, and any other important component

of your life? What if life expectancy was 120 years or 150 years? How would you think differently about your life? What differences would it make in planning your future?
8. Describe the migration patterns of older people in the past 20 years or so. Do you know anyone who has migrated within the United States after retirement? Where did they move from? Where did they move to? Why did they move? Were they satisfied with their move?
9. Look at the three population pyramids presented in this chapter (Figure 3.6). Compare the size of the older population (age 65 and older) with the younger population (age 14 and under). What do you see? Compare the ratio of men and women in the three oldest age groups. Now compare one pyramid with another and look at the total size of the three oldest age groups. What accounts for the different shapes of these pyramids?
10. Give three reasons why an older woman stands a greater chance than an older man of living without a spouse. What social changes may make widowhood for women less common in the future?
11. Present the pros and cons of using dependency ratios to project future social conditions. What can the United States do now to prepare for an aging society in the years ahead?
12. Give three reasons why the "Merchants of Doom" are likely to be wrong in their predictions of a social crisis due to population aging.

SUGGESTED READING

Carmel, S., Morse, C., & Torres-Gil, F. (Eds.). (2007). *Lessons on aging from three nations*, Vol. I and Vol. II. New York: Baywood Press.

The editors look at aging in three multicultural modern societies: the United States, Israel, and Australia. Each of these countries faces issues related to immigration, social diversity, and population aging. The articles in these volumes show how each of these societies develop unique policies and programs for older people. The authors draw on their own experiences in

each society to suggest improvements in programs and practices. A rare study that allows cross-cultural and cross-national comparisons.

Palmore, E., Whittington, F., & Kunkel, S. (eds.). (2009). *The international handbook on aging* (3rd ed.). Santa Barbara, CA: ABC-CLIO.

A collection of articles by social scientists in 47 countries. Each author provides the social, political, and economic backdrop to population aging. The articles describe the challenges that each country will face as its population ages. The handbook also contains overview essays on world regions (e.g., Asian-Pacific Region) and a directory of gerontological and geriatric associations worldwide. A good reference volume.

Korczyk, S. M., & Public Policy Institute, AARP. (2002). *Back to which future: The U.S. aging crisis revisited.* Washington, DC: Public Policy Institute, AARP. Available online at http://research.aarp.org/econ/2002_18_aging.pdf.

This paper looks at many of the issues presented in this chapter. It also assesses the impact of population aging on health and income in later life as well as the cost of health care. The paper concludes that **demography** is not destiny. The effect of population aging on society will depend on the health and abilities of the older population as well as on public policy.

Websites to Consult

HelpAge International
www.helpage.org/Home

This site contains information about aging in an international context. If you need information about how other countries and cultures confront the physical, social, and economic challenges associated with aging, HelpAge can provide it.

AARP AgeSource/AgeStats Worldwide
http://www.aarpinternational.org/database/

These two databases support the exchange of policy and program information around the world. AgeSource Worldwide offers several hundred information sources in 25 countries. Sources include libraries, databases, major reports, and other Web meta-sites. AgeStats Worldwide provides access to comparative statistical data on older adults across countries or regions. You can browse by country, topic, and type of information (e.g., report, text, reading list). The database provides some projections as far ahead as 2050.

International Association of Gerontology and Geriatrics
www.iagg.info

This site contains links to international collections of information as well as a photo bank that depicts active, healthy seniors from around the world. It is an excellent resource for presentations and access to international news on aging.

The U.S. Census Bureau
www.census.gov

Reliable and updated regularly, the U.S. Census Bureau produces the most reliable demographic data and information on population changes. It also releases periodic aging-related studies.

The U.S. Census Bureau's DataFerrett
http://dataferrett.census.gov

DataFerrett is an advanced search program that downloads, organizes, and stores datasets from a number of government programs. If you need to cross-reference data from a number of government programs, DataFerrett can help you find and organize the information. Topics include race and ethnicity, social security data, and economic data.

National Institute on Aging Demography Centers
http://agingcenters.org/

The NIA's Demography Centers provide links to a wide variety of aging-related databases and publications. On this site, you can find demographic data from a number of organizations and archives. You can also find information about the latest demographic studies being conducted at each of the Institute's centers.

chapter 4

PERSONAL HEALTH AND WELL-BEING

Jeanne Calment of Arles, France, died in 1997 at the age of 122 years and 164 days. At that time, she had lived the longest reliably documented life in human history. Ms. Calment claimed to have met Vincent Van Gogh in her father's store and to have attended Victor Hugo's funeral. For her 121st birthday she released a four-song CD and videotape entitled "Maitresse du Temps" ("Time's Mistress"). The songs include rap and techno numbers that back up stories from her life.

On September 21, 2010, Walter Breuning (114 years old) claimed the title of the world's oldest man. (He is the fourth oldest person. Three women born

earlier in the same year hold the top three positions.) Breuning replaced Henry Allingham, of Great Britain, who died in July 2010 at 113.

How did these people live so long? For one thing, Ms. Calment stayed active throughout her life. She lived on her own in a second-floor apartment until age 110 and she rode a bicycle until age 100. Other centenarians also attribute their long life to an active lifestyle. Henry Allingham attributed his long life to "Cigarettes, whisky and wild, wild women—and a good sense of humor." Some people say they like regular sex and never worry. One 100-year-old man claimed that he lived so long because he ate a pound of peanuts a day. Someone once said that to live 100 years, you should eat a hot bowl of oatmeal every morning for 1,200 months.

The United States today has more 100-year-olds than ever before. As biologists and physiologists work to extend life expectancy even further, more and more people will live close to the maximum human **life span** of about 120 years.

This chapter looks at the biology of aging and health in later life. It describes (1) biological theories of aging; (2) how aging affects health, activity, and life satisfaction; and (3) how people can respond to physical changes that come with age.

BIOLOGICAL AGING

Biologists and physiologists study aging in everything from one-celled animals to human populations. Austad (2009, p. 147) defines biological aging as ". . . the gradual and progressive decay in physical function that begins in adulthood and ends in death in virtually all animal species."

Intrinsic aging includes decreases in lung capacity, loss of brain cells, and hardened arteries. **Extrinsic aging** includes changes in the body due to sunlight, smoking, or noise. Scientists try to separate out the effects of these two causes of aging.

Strehler (1977) lists four criteria for intrinsic (or true) aging. First, true aging is universal. It occurs in all members of a species if they live long enough. Wrinkled skin in humans fits this definition. Second, true aging is basic to the organism. A person cannot undo it or stop it. Decreased lung elasticity falls into this category. Third, true aging is progressive. Debris accumulates in the cell over time until the cell stops working. Fourth, true aging is deleterious. It leads to decline in physical function. This puts the person at risk of illness and leads to death.

These criteria describe *senescence*, normal functional decline that takes place in the human body over time. If you have any doubt what senescence means, do a simple test. Gently pinch the skin on the back of a baby's hand, then pinch the skin on your hand, and then the skin on a 70-year-old's hand. Notice that you can hardly get a grip on the chubby skin of a baby. Your skin and the older person's skin will feel thinner and less elastic. Notice that the baby's skin pops back into place immediately. The older person's skin may form a slight peak that remains after you take your hand away. The effects of senescence will differ from person to person (due to genetics and variation in body functions), but in general, skin elasticity declines with age.

Scientists want to know why this and other intrinsic changes take place over time. They want to know what causes intrinsic aging. Why, for example, does skin become less elastic? Why don't cells in the human body live forever? Scientists have developed a number of theories to explain intrinsic aging.

THEORIES OF BIOLOGICAL AGING

Aldwin and Gilmer (2004) say that more than a dozen biological theories of aging exist today. Biological theories of aging often reflect the methods and models of researchers and their disciplines as much as the basic processes of aging. This chapter presents a variety of theories. Each gives some insight into how the body ages.

Schneider (1992) places these theories in one of two groups:

1. Programmed theories. These locate the cause of aging in the action of inherited genes.
2. Error theories. These locate the cause of aging in the normal function of the body over time.

Probably both of these causes play some role in aging. These two causes, working together, lead to a decrease in the body's ability to fight off internal and external threats. This in turn leads to an increased chance of death as the body ages.

Programmed Theories

Programmed theories say that the same processes that cause animals to grow and thrive also lead to senescence and death. Scientists have found the strongest evidence for programmed senescence in the body's cells.

Programmed Senescence

Human life begins with a single fertilized cell. This cell divides many times to form the human body. Some cells—such as those in the spinal cord—stop dividing in youth. Other cells—such as intestinal cells and blood cells—divide throughout life. Until the 1960s, scientists thought that cells could divide an unlimited number of times, but Hayflick and Moorehead (1961) found that cell division had a limit and that this limit differed for each species. Scientists refer to this as the **Hayflick limit**.

Tortoise cells, for example, divide 90 to 125 times before they die. Chicken cells divide 15 to 35 times, and human embryo cells 40 to 60 times. The older the cell donor, the fewer times the cell could divide before death. Cells from young people, for example, could divide about 50 times before they stopped. Cells from adults could divide only about 20 times more before they died. Based on these findings Hayflick and Moorehead estimated the human life span at 110 to 120 years.

Hayflick and Moorehead took their research a step further and looked inside the cell to see why cell division stopped. They found that before cells die, their structure and function change. Hayflick and Moorehead discovered that cells showed signs of aging after a year of active division in the lab. These cells took a longer time to double, gradually stopped dividing, accumulated debris, and in the end totally degenerated. Cells produced less energy, made enzymes more slowly, and allowed waste to pile up inside them. Eventually cells stopped dividing. Biologists call this the **phase III phenomenon**.

These results show that (1) cells undergo programmed decline, (2) the rate of decline differs for each organism, and (3) genetic differences play a role in determining an organism's life span (Hayflick, 1996). To understand these changes at the cellular and systemic level, some scientists look to the molecular and genetic structure of the cell. Recent research helps explain the Hayflick limit. Studies find a relationship between "telomere shortening" and aging of cells.

Telomeres exist on the ends of chromosomes. Every time a cell divides, part of the end of the chromosome (or telomere) gets removed. The cell loses a protective effect that the telomeres provide. Gatza and colleagues (Gatza, Hinkal, Moore, Dumble, & Donehower, 2006, p. 160) say that the "gradual erosion [of telomeres] is believed to be the primary factor for the Hayflick Limit."

Aldwin and Gilmer (2004; also Sinclair & Howitz, 2006) provide further insight into the limit on cell division. They describe the process of *apoptosis*, a genetic process that switches off the cell's ability to divide. This process controls growth and produces normal development. But it also leads to cell death and breakdown in the body over time.

Gavrilov and Gavrilova (2006) describe another genetic process that leads to physical aging. Researchers find that some genes serve a positive function early in life, but damage the system later. Scientists call these **pleiotropic genes**. A gene, for example, might order calcium production in a 10-year-old. A young person's body needs calcium to build bones and teeth. This same gene might lead to too much calcium in a 60-year-old. This could produce calcium deposits in the person's arteries. Scientists refer to this as "antagonistic pleiotropy" (Austad, 2009). Apoptosis and pleiotropy suggest that aging occurs as a by-product of normal human development. More knowledge of genes' actions might allow scientists to turn genes on and off as needed. This could prevent or reverse aging.

Endocrine and Immunological Theory

Glandular tissues make up the endocrine system. They include the hypothalamus, pituitary gland, adrenal glands, ovaries, and testes. These glands secrete hormones into the bloodstream. The hormones then act on specific sites in the body. The endocrine system responds to both internal and external changes in the body and controls growth, metabolism, reproduction, and responses to stress.

Researchers have known for some time that the production of the sex hormones estrogen and testosterone tends to decrease as we age (Harman et al., 2000). Also, the timing of hormonal release and the responsiveness of tissues to hormones decline with age (Bartke & Lane, 2001). These changes in hormonal activity can lead to changes in sexual response.

A number of endocrine glands affect sexual function, and these functions decline with age. The adrenal glands, for example, secrete hormones, including androgens and estrogens that produce secondary sexual characteristics. Likewise, the pituitary gland in women at around age 55 stops producing hormones to stimulate the ovaries.

As males age they will experience a 35% decrease in testosterone levels between ages 21 and 85. Harman and colleagues (2000) report low levels of testosterone in 20% of men over age 60, 30% of men over age 70, and 50% of men over age 80. This leads to a gradual decrease in sexual function from the teens to old age. In men, for example, as they age it takes more time and physical stimulation to gain sexual arousal. Also, with age a man needs a longer time before he can perform again.

Studies show that replacement of hormones in both men and women can help prevent some signs of aging. Harman and colleagues (2000), for example, say that a decrease in testosterone in older men can lead to osteoporosis and broken bones. They report that in some studies of older men, testosterone replacement therapy improved lean body mass, muscle strength, and grip strength. Still, this treatment remains controversial. Harman and colleagues propose further research to explore the benefits of this treatment. A report from the International Longevity Center–USA (2003) supports the need for more research on testosterone replacement. The report proposes a large-scale ($100 million) study to assess the effects of testosterone replacement on older men.

The immune system also ages. T and B cells play the most important role in the immune system's adaptive function over time. Each of these cells has a receptor that identifies a foreign substance called an "antigen" (Effros, 2009). B cells secrete antibodies that inactivate pathogens in the blood. If a pathogen enters the cell from the blood, the T cells take over and attack the foreign substance. T cells, because they must replicate to respond to pathogen attack, will come up against the Hayflick Limit. They will become senescent and unable to reproduce beyond a certain point. This decreases the body's ability to resist attack. Studies that compare senescent T cells in younger and older people find that older people have significantly higher amounts of senescent T cells (Effros, 2009).

The immune system goes into a decline as early as age 20 as the thymus gland begins to shrink. By age 50 this gland has almost ceased to exist. The decline in T cells from the thymus gland and their decline in function lead to a reduced ability to fight infection and disease. This kind of programmed change in the body may lead to age-related problems such as a higher risk of Alzheimer's disease, increased risk of cancer, and hardening of the arteries (Effros, 2001, 2009). Even in cases where the number of antibodies stays high, their quality decreases and they lose their effectiveness. Effros (2001) reports that infections cause most of the deaths in people over age 80.

Programmed theories view aging as a normal part of growth and development. They link senescence to growth, development, and the body's normal func-

---

BOX 4.1

MENOPAUSE: THE SOCIAL CONSTRUCTION OF BIOLOGICAL CHANGE

Bones, muscles, and blood change as we age. Most people accept this as a natural process. But physical change takes place in a social context. How we view a physical change like menopause—as a loss, as illness, as something to treat or overcome, or as a sign of normal aging—depends on the meaning we attach to the change. Menopause offers a case study in the interpretation and reinterpretation of physical change.

Feminist writer Germaine Greer (1991) calls it *The Change*. Popular author Gail Sheehy (1992) calls it *The Silent Passage*. Whatever it is called, menopause has played a role in the mythology of female aging for centuries, and much of this mythology created fear and shame. Today, writers present a more balanced view of this change. The Mayo Clinic (2010a), for example, states, "Menopause is a natural biological process, not a medical illness."

Menopause means the end of regular menstrual bleeding. It comes about as estrogen decreases in a woman's body around the age of 50. This marks the end of a woman's childbearing years. Menopause has two common symptoms—hot flashes and vaginal dryness. Some women complain of other symptoms such as insomnia, headaches, irritability, and depression. These symptoms cause physical discomfort and may cause psychological distress.

Tulandi and Lal (1985) note that between 50% and 85% of menopausal women feel some sort of hot flash. The decrease in estrogen in the body or changes in blood vessel size may cause this feeling. These problems decrease as a woman's body adjusts to new hormonal levels.

Some studies show that hormone replacement therapy, treatment with both estrogen and progesterone, can reduce the symptoms of menopause. Controversy exists, however, about the effectiveness of treating menopause with estrogen. Some studies show harmful side effects of estrogen treatment, such as increased rates of uterine and breast cancer and heart disease. Other studies suggest that women in their 50s could use this therapy, but only to control night sweats and hot flashes.

Weg (1987) says that medical science too often uses the disease model to describe menopause. Clinical descriptions create a picture of a sick woman at this time of life. This view led in the past to many unnecessary hysterectomies and to removal of women's ovaries in order to cure the illness. It also led to the mass prescription of hormone replacement drugs. The disease model of menopause may change in the future. Studies show that most women cope well with menopausal symptoms.

The National Institute on Aging (2010d) suggests simple methods to cope with problems like hot flashes—wear layered clothing, sleep in a cool room, and drink cool liquids. About 20% to 40% of women have few or no problems due to menopause.

Women in societies that value youth over age tend to report more menopausal symptoms. This is also true for women whose lives focus on child rearing and the family. Society and culture play an important role in shaping a woman's feelings about menopause.

The Mayo Clinic (2010b) says that many women find menopause liberating. Instead of an end to childbearing years, it can signal a "time to stop worrying about pregnancy." This can free a woman to further enjoy her sexuality.

tions. Any attempt to slow or stop these processes will require more knowledge of the body's cellular and genetic functions.

Error Theories

Error theories view aging as a by-product of errors or mistakes within the body. Some of these errors come from inside the cell, others from outside the cell. In both cases, they lead to declines in cellular and physical function.

Somatic Mutation Theory

Mutation theories link aging to mistakes that take place in the synthesis of proteins. The cell nucleus contains deoxyribonucleic acid (DNA) and ribonucleic acid (RNA). These chemicals help maintain the body's structure and function. To do this, DNA gets transcribed to messenger RNA (mRNA), and mRNA in turn oversees the creation of proteins that structure the cell, fight disease, and keep the body in balance. Scientists suspect that some of what we call aging comes about due to mutations or changes in DNA (Masoro, 2006; Steams & Partridge, 2001).

DNA, RNA, and proteins face constant attack from inside and outside the body. Radiation from X-rays, for example, can damage DNA, as can chemicals in the body. Schneider (1992) says that the cell has to cope with 100,000 oxidative lesions (due to chemical attack) each day, in each cell.

Damage to DNA can lead to mutations when the cell divides. This can lead to changes in mRNA and in turn to damaged proteins. Because mRNA and proteins help produce more proteins, errors compound. A large number of defective proteins would lead to cell and tissue death. Some studies have found increased DNA lesions and increased somatic mutations with age (Vijg, 2000).

Cross-Linking Theory

The long-term exposure of proteins to glucose (sugar) molecules leads to a process called **glycation**. Glucose molecules attach themselves to proteins. This results in proteins binding together, or **cross-linking** (Gafni, 2001). This process increases with age. Cross-links toughen tissue and cause some of the damage associated with aging, including stiffened connective tissue, hardened arteries, and loss of nerve and kidney function. Foreign chemicals (such as glucose) can set up links between the DNA strands. This may stop the strands from dividing. Pollutants such as lead and smoke can also cause cross-link damage.

The body does have a way to combat cross-links. Immune system cells called **macrophages** seek out glucose molecules, engulf them, destroy them, and send them to the kidneys for elimination. However, this defense breaks down with age as kidney function declines and macrophages become less active (Effros, 2001). As a result, cross-links increase over time. The accumulation of cross-links in the body ultimately leads to physical system breakdown.

Researchers have experimented with methods to delay or prevent cross-linking. These methods include tests of a drug called amino-guanidine to inhibit cross-links and enhance the body's repair system. Cross-links may cause only a part of aging, but medicine may one day be able to prevent this process.

Free Radicals Theory

Grune and Davies (2001, p. 25) describe the "oxygen paradox." Human beings need oxygen to live. Oxygen allows us to take energy from our foods. But oxygen can also damage cells and their contents.

Free radicals due to oxygen production in the body serve as one source of damage that leads to aging. Free radicals are molecules that have an unpaired electron, a large amount of free energy, and a tendency to bond with other molecules. Normal cell metabolism produces free radicals. These molecules can damage tissues and other molecules (such as DNA, RNA, and cell proteins) (Austad, 2001; Sinclair & Howitz, 2006). Shringarpure and Davies (2009, p. 238) call the free radical theory of aging "a major aging theory."

Free radicals act in three phases. First, the body produces free radicals. It does this when, in the course of metabolism, an extra electron gets attached to molecular oxygen. Second, the free radical roams through the body and takes an electron from another molecule. This creates a new free radical. This chain reaction produces harmful chemicals in the body. Third, free radicals react with molecules like DNA or RNA. This ends the process but damages the cell.

Many sites in the cell are damaged by free radicals. The DNA in mitochondria (where oxidation takes place) faces a high risk of damage (Sinclair & Howitz, 2006; Shringarpure & Davies, 2009). Studies show that free radical damage to DNA increases rapidly with age. It can lead to diseases such as late-onset diabetes, arthritis, cataracts, hypertension, and atherosclerosis.

Cells in the heart, brain, and skeleton face a high risk of free radical damage because of the oxygen in their environments. Free radical attack can also damage proteins. This causes a change in the protein's structure and makes it unable to perform its function. Repair systems in older cells become less efficient and older cells produce fewer antioxidants (Aldwin & Gilmer, 2004).

Free radicals also lead to an accumulation of chemical by-products in the cell. They create large fatty molecules in the cells, called **lipofuscin**. These molecules show up as brown liver spots on the skin. Lipofuscin makes up about 6% to 7% of the human heart muscle and nearly 75% of the volume of nerve cells by age 90 (Strehler, 1977). As lipofuscin takes up more room in the cell, it may interfere with the cell's ability to create enzymes, release energy, and get rid of wastes. This leads to more sluggish performance—a sign of aging. Researchers find that lipofuscin blocks cell reproduction and leads to cell death (von Zglinicki, Nilsson, Docke, & Brunk, 1995, cited in Aldwin & Gilmer, 2004).

The body must repair free radical damage or replace damaged cells. Fortunately, chemicals in the body, called *antioxidants,* bind and neutralize free radicals. Antioxidants include such nutrients as vitamins C and E and beta carotene, as well as enzymes in the body such as superoxide dismutase (SOD) (Grune & Davies, 2001; Shringarpure & Davies, 2009). Research on food supplements suggest that certain foods (e.g., green tea, broccoli, and cauliflower) may have an antioxidant effect. These antioxidants may prevent some, but not all, oxidative damage. Some damage still accumulates with time and contributes to the deterioration of tissues and organs.

Other Theories

Programmed and error theories provide some explanations of why aging takes place. Other approaches explain aging through population dynamics (Gavrilov & Gavrilova, 1991), the life history of the organism (Arking, 1991), and the theory of natural selection (Gavrilov & Gavrilova, 2006; Gonidakis & Longo, 2009).

Darwin, for example, said that natural selection selects genes that support the survival of an animal up to the age of reproduction. Animals that survive to the age of reproduction pass their genes on to the next generation. Animals that have characteristics that work against survival do not live long enough to pass on their genes. These genes get selected out of the gene pool. In other words, the fittest animals survive and pass on their traits to the next generation. This ensures the survival of the species.

But genes that have an effect after the reproductive age (genes that might cause arthritis or cancer) don't get selected out. Animals that have these genes lived to reproductive age and pass them on to the next generation. The next generation will also suffer from these later life problems (Masoro, 2006).

Michael Rose at the University of California at Irvine put this simply: "We are genetic garbage cans, for genes that produce bad effects at later ages" (cited in Schmidt, 1993, pp. 72–73). Rose tested this theory. He delayed reproduction in 70 generations of fruit flies. His older flies could then pass on longevity genes to the next generation. His research extended the flies' life expectancy by 80% and produced healthier flies.

Rose (1993) believes that a theory of aging based on natural selection will eventually replace other theories of aging. But right now gerontologists have many

---

BOX 4.2
THE EFFECTS OF AGING ON SELF-IMAGE

The effects of intrinsic aging can damage our self-images as well as our bodies. Author Ann Domitrovich (1986, pp. 131–132) reflects on changes in her skin and on what those changes meant to her:

And then there was my face. Oh God, my face. The lines, the wrinkles, the sags and bags. Every few months it got worse. Makeup only accentuated it, and, unlike my body, I could not cover it up. Your face simply cannot be hidden. Your eyes, your smile, your expressions—all right out there for the world to see and react to. And the world began to react to this middle-aged woman. My status as a citizen of this world we all live in began to waver. Middle-aged women lose rank fast just because they are not young. They are tolerated if they are bright enough, successful enough, and—this is most important—if they do not appear to be middle-aged. . . . If she looks thin enough, pretty enough, young enough, she can still be accepted. As long as she doesn't look like what she naturally is. For all those who have yet to travel that road, it is very frightening because you know the next day can only bring more of the same. And it will be that much harder because nature is taking her course. You can never catch up. Never. But I continued the chase because I didn't know what else to do.

theories of aging to choose from. Each tells us something about aging, but no single theory accounts for all the changes that occur with age. Scientists currently view aging as the result of many interactive and interdependent processes. These ultimately determine life span and health in the individual.

THE EFFECTS OF AGING ON BODY SYSTEMS

Intrinsic changes take place in the cells as we age. Over time these changes compound and lead to changes in the body's systems. All of the body's systems decline or lose reserve capacity with age, but each system, and the organs and structures in the system, declines and deteriorates at different rates after maturity.

This section looks at how some of the body's systems change with age. The limits of space make it impossible to give a full picture of physical changes due to aging. You can find more complete discussions of physical change in reference books such as *The Handbook of the Biology of Aging* (Masoro & Austad, 2006). The discussion here focuses on two systems that change with age and influence an older person's ability to function in everyday life: the musculoskeletal system and the senses.

Musculoskeletal System

Muscle and bone content decrease with age. Physiologists call this **sarcopenia**. With age the number of muscle fibers declines and the remaining neurons become less efficient. This leads to muscle weakness. A person has to make more effort to carry out a task. Some studies report that muscles begin to lose strength by age 20 or 30. Other studies show more stable strength until 50 or 60. Lovell, Cuneo, and Gass (2010) report that after age 70 muscle strength drops by more than 3% per year. Muscle power (a combination of strength and speed) after age 70 drops by as much as 5% per year. Muscle mass can decrease by 50% by age 80 (Digiovanna, 2000). This decline in muscle strength and power can lead to decreased mobility and increased dependence in later life.

Resistance and aerobic training can reduce these losses and reverse some of this decline. Researchers find that even the oldest-old people improve muscle mass and strength with weight training. People who took part in a strength training program in a nursing home (some as old as 98) showed an average strength increase of 174%. Some disabled people began to walk without the help of a cane. One 93-year-old in the study said, "I feel as though I were 50 again. . . . The program gave me strength I didn't have before. Every day I feel better, more optimistic. Pills won't do for you what exercise does!" (Haber, 2010, p. 173).

Lovell and colleagues (2010) conducted a controlled study of healthy older men ages 70 to 80. The men worked out on an exercise bicycle for 35 to 40 minutes three times per week. The study found an increase in muscle strength of 21%. Because muscle burns more calories than fat, muscle-building exercise can also help a person lose weight.

The skeletal system also changes with age. The body replaces about 10% of its bone content each year. Bones reach maximum density between ages 25 and 35. From then on, the bones lose more cells than they replace—as much as half a percent per year (Duque & Troen, 2008). This causes bones to lose hardness and density. They lose the ability to twist and bend without breaking. The loss of bone mass increases the older person's risk of a fracture. Murray (1996) reports that women lose between 20% and 25% of their bone mass during the 10 years after menopause. Men also lose bone mass, but at a slower rate than women.

Compared with men, this puts women at higher risk of a fracture in later life. In 2000 more than 10% of men and women age 50 and over suffered from osteoporosis—porous bones. Aldwin and Gilmer (2004) say that 60% of women age 65 and over have some amount of osteoporosis. And 90% of women past the age of 80 have serious amounts of bone loss.

Osteoporosis increases the risk of fracture. The Osteoporosis and Related Bone Diseases National Resource Center (cited in Aldwin & Gilmer, 2004) reports that half of women age 50 or over will suffer from a fracture (often of the wrist or hip) due to osteoporosis. These injuries cause hospitalization, reduce a person's social contacts, and often lead to further illness.

The Centers for Disease Control and Prevention (CDC) estimates that fractures related to osteoporosis lead to direct care costs of between $12 and $18 billion per year. Research shows that exercise can slow the rate of bone loss (Koncelik, 2003). Weight-bearing exercise—such as lifting weights—increases bone density. Exercise helps a person maintain the appropriate weight and improves balance. Exercise also lubricates the joints and reduces the risk of arthritis. All of these outcomes improve bone strength, improve health, and help prevent fractures.

Sensory Changes

All five senses—smell, taste, touch, hearing, and sight—change with age. Some senses show more dramatic changes than others. Even with one sense, such as smell, sensitivity decreases for some smells earlier than for others.

Taste, Smell, and Touch

Scientists call taste and smell the chemical senses. A person has about 9,000 taste buds. They sense sweet, salty, sour, and bitter. By ages 40 to 50 in women and ages 50 to 60 in men, the number of taste buds declines. Also, the taste buds decrease in size. Still, studies find only a small decline in the sense of taste with age. The taste sensitivity to salty and sweet foods tends to decrease first. Adding herbs and spices to food may increase enjoyment and promote better eating habits.

Taste and smell go together. Aldwin and Gilmer (2004, p. 164) say that "most of what we consider taste is actually a function of smell." Studies show some loss in the sense of smell with age, especially after age 70. Sensitivity to some smells, for example the smell put in natural gas, declines earlier than sensitivity to others, such as the smell of roses (Rawson, 2003). A decrease in the sense of smell can lead to a loss of interest in food. This can lead to weight loss and poor health. Poor smell can also put people at risk if they can't smell a gas leak or rotten food.

The sense of touch also declines with age. Receptors for touch, temperature, and vibration decrease in sensitivity. Controversy exists about whether sensitivity to pain decreases or increases with age. Decreased blood circulation to the skin and degeneration of receptors to the brain may account for the loss of the sense of touch. A decreased ability to feel sensation can lead to injury from burns and slower reaction time to pain.

Sight

Changes in sight and hearing have the greatest effect on a person's ability to function in later life. Changes in vision can begin as early as age 30. By age 55, most people need glasses for reading. Schieber (2006) presents a detailed summary of the many changes that take place in the eyes as people age. This discussion here presents only a few of the changes in vision that affect everyday life.

With age, the eyes produce fewer tears, and older people may feel discomfort due to dry eyes. Also, the eye's pupil, compared with its size at age 20, decreases by about two thirds by age 60. Eye muscles weaken and limit the eye's rotation. This reduces the older person's visual field. The eye's lens also yellows and turns cloudy with age. Gawande (2007, p. 52) says that "the amount of light reaching the retina of a healthy sixty-year-old is one-third that of a twenty-year-old."

People also have a harder time seeing a contrast between light and dark as they age. Some older people also report a loss of color sensitivity. Changes in vision include slower adaptation when moving from a brightly lit to a dark area, decreased ability to see fine detail, problems adapting due to glare, and a decline in peripheral vision (Schieber, 2003, 2006).

These changes can limit how well a person can see under certain conditions. Drivers encounter many of these conditions at night. For this reason some older people reduce the amount of night driving they do (MedlinePlus, 2004a). Better lighting and better road signs would help older drivers. Schieber (2006) reports that 1 in 28 adults in the United States cope with visual impairment.

Most people adapt to changes in sight as they age. They correct for normal changes by wearing glasses, using large-print books, and using better lighting. Still, many older people suffer from poor vision. The National Center for Health Statistics (2009, p. 287) reports that 17.4% of people age 65 and over say they "have trouble seeing, even with glasses or contacts."

Three diseases account for most visual impairment in later life: cataracts (clouding of the lens), degeneration of the retinal structure, and glaucoma (increased pressure within the eye). Surgery can correct more extreme problems such as cataracts or a detached retina. Retinal degeneration remains incurable at this time. Drug therapy can treat glaucoma. Early detection of glaucoma can prevent some loss of function (National Institute on Aging, 2009a).

Hearing

A person loses some hearing each year after age 50. Most people don't notice the change, but by age 60 about 30% of people suffer from some noticeable hearing loss. This figure increases to 50% for people age 85 and older (National Institute on Aging, 2004a). Men lose hearing at twice the rate of women after age 30. Most people notice hearing loss when they have trouble hearing low-frequency tones—the kind common to speech. This starts to occur on average between ages 60 and 70. The National Center for Health Statistics (2009, p. 287) reports that 11.4% of people say they have "a lot of trouble hearing" or are deaf.

A hearing problem can lead a person to withdraw from social contacts. It can lead friends and family to label the older person as confused or unhelpful. Older people may come to distrust others who won't speak up or who seem to whisper in their presence. Hearing problems can also lead to isolation and depression.

Hearing loss can take several forms:

1. Presbycusis, or age-related hearing loss, develops gradually. A person may find it hard to hear conversations or callers on the phone. Work-related damage, heredity, loud noise, or prescription drugs can all lead to this form of hearing loss. A doctor can diagnose and treat this problem.
2. Tinnitus, another type of hearing problem, is a ringing or roaring in the ear. Loud noises, medicines, or other health problems can lead to tinnitus. People with tinnitus should avoid loud noises. Music can soothe this problem.

3. Conductive hearing loss comes from a blockage in the ear canal. Wax buildup can cause this problem. A doctor can clean out the ear and solve this problem.
4. The National Institute on Aging (2009b) gives the following advice to people who work with or know someone with a hearing problem:
   a. Speak low and slow. Take your time when you talk to someone with a hearing loss. Do not speed up your speech or shout.
   b. Stand or sit in front of the person. Speak at a distance of three to six feet so the person can see you clearly. Have the light on your face (not behind you).
   c. Let the person see you before you start speaking. Use facial and hand gestures to emphasize what you say.
   d. Do not cover your mouth or chew while speaking.
   e. Rephrase what you say. Use different words if the person did not understand you.
   f. Have presenters at large events use a public address system.
   g. Include the person in all discussions about him or her. This will reduce feelings of isolation.

No medical cure exists for loss of hearing due to deterioration of the hearing mechanism (Fozard & Gordon-Salant, 2001). But technology today can help older people deal with hearing loss. Hearing aids, telephone-amplifying devices, adapters to televisions and radios (so that the person can increase the volume without disturbing others), and even electrical implants under the skin can help a person deal with hearing loss.

The Internet can also help a person cope with hearing loss (Scialfa & Fernie, 2006). Cummings, Sproul, and Keisler (2002) studied an online support group for older people with hearing impairments. They found that people with the least offline support got the most benefit from the online group.

PERSONAL HEALTH AND ILLNESS

Changes in Health Status

Today older Americans have a longer life expectancy and live more years in good health than ever before. They live more active lives than seniors in the past, and they have more opportunities to enjoy recreation and leisure activities. But a longer life expectancy also means that more people suffer from the chronic diseases in old age.

The shift from a young to an older population in the United States has led to a change in the pattern of disease. The rate of acute illness (e.g., diphtheria, typhoid, and measles) has decreased during this century. More children now live, grow to adulthood, and enter old age. This leads to an increase in the rate of chronic illness (e.g., arthritis, diabetes, and heart disease). Scientists refer to this as the *epidemiological transition* (Land & Yang, 2006).

Chronic diseases currently account for 70% of all deaths in the United States. They lead to activity limitations and cost 70% of the U.S. $1 trillion health bill (U.S. Department of Health and Human Services, CDC, 2004). Nearly every major chronic disease (except certain cancers) increases in frequency and severity with age. The leading chronic illnesses that account for deaths in the United States include (in order of prevalence) heart disease, cancer, stroke, chronic lower respiratory disease, accidents, diabetes,

and Alzheimer's disease (Kung, Hoyert, Xi, & Murphy, 2008).

The CDC (2009a) reports that chronic disease accounts for 7 of 10 deaths among Americans each year. In particular, heart disease, cancer, and stroke account for more than 50% of all deaths each year. The death rates from these illnesses have declined over the past decade. But other chronic illnesses like Alzheimer's disease show an increase in prevalence and a "rapid increase" in death rates (CDC, 2009a, p. 9).

Older people also suffer from a variety of nonlethal chronic diseases. These include arthritis, hearing impairment, and cataracts. This means that decreases in death rates due to the major killers in old age—heart disease, cancer, and stroke—may have a paradoxical effect. Decreased death rates lead to longer life, but possibly also to more years of life with nonlethal chronic illness. A number of gerontologists have debated this possibility. You will read about this later in a discussion on the compression of morbidity hypothesis.

BOX 4.3
LEADING CAUSES OF DEATH IN THE UNITED STATES

1900	2002–2003
Pneumonia-influenza-bronchitis	Heart disease
Tuberculosis	Cancer
Diarrhea and enteritis	Stroke
Heart disease	Chronic lower respiratory disease

In 1900, acute diseases of childhood and youth led to most deaths in the United States. Today, chronic diseases of old age lead the causes of death. (The first two items on the list for 2002–2003—heart disease and cancer—account for nearly half of all deaths each year) (Xu, Kochanek, Murphy, & Tejada-Vera, 2010).

Gerontologists refer to such a shift in the leading causes as an *epidemiological transition*. This refers to the transition a society makes from having a high proportion of deaths due to infectious, acute diseases to having a high proportion of deaths from degenerative chronic diseases (Land & Yang, 2006). This change in the causes of death brings about corresponding changes in the health care system. Different types of illness require different types of treatment and can change the organization of health care service. Chronic diseases

most often occur in later life. They require long-term treatment and the development of long-term care resources (e.g., nursing homes, home care, and respite care programs).

Novelli and Workman (2006, p. 25) report, for example, that "more than half of all people aged 50 and over have diabetes, high blood pressure, heart disease, or some other chronic condition." An older population will need care for these long-term illnesses. Yet few doctors today specialize in geriatric medicine. In 2005, Congress removed support for training geriatricians in U.S. medical schools from the federal budget (Novelli & Workman, 2006). The shortage of trained physicians and the growing need for care of chronic illness will challenge the health care system in the years ahead.

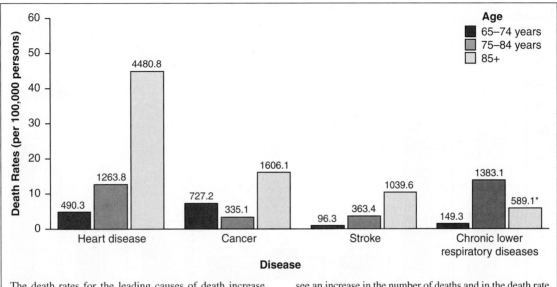

FIGURE 4.1   The Four Leading Causes of Death by Age Among People Age 65 and Over, United States, 2006.

Source: M. P. Heron. (2010). *Deaths: Leading Causes for 2006. National Vital Statistics Reports, 85,* no. 14 (Hyattsville, MD: National Center for Health Statistics, 2010), pp. 22–23.

Some rates of chronic illness differ by race and gender. African Americans age 65 and over, compared with whites, for example, have only about two thirds the rate of emphysema and about two thirds the rate of heart disease. But older African Americans, compared with whites in 2001, had about a 30% higher rate of hypertension and more than one and a half times the rate of diabetes.

Older women, compared with older men, have higher rates of hypertension and arthritis. Older men, compared with older women, have higher rates of diabetes, cancer, and heart disease (National Center for Health Statistics, 2004a, b; He, Sangupta, Velkoff, & De Barros, 2005; Federal Interagency Forum, 2010a). Older women live longer than older men, but they have poorer health. Differences in income, work-related stress, and habits such as smoking and drinking account for most of these differences in illness rates.

Limits on Activity Due to Physical Decline

National studies in the United States show that chronic conditions lead to functional loss. And this leads to disability and activity limitations in older people. The National Center for Health Statistics (NCHS) (2009; CDC, 2009a) reports that in 2006 one-third of Americans age 65 and over reported some activity limitation due to a chronic condition.

Activities of daily living (ADLs) include bathing or showering, dressing, eating, getting in or out of bed or chairs, using the toilet, including getting to the toilet, and getting around inside the home. Rates of limitation on activities of daily living

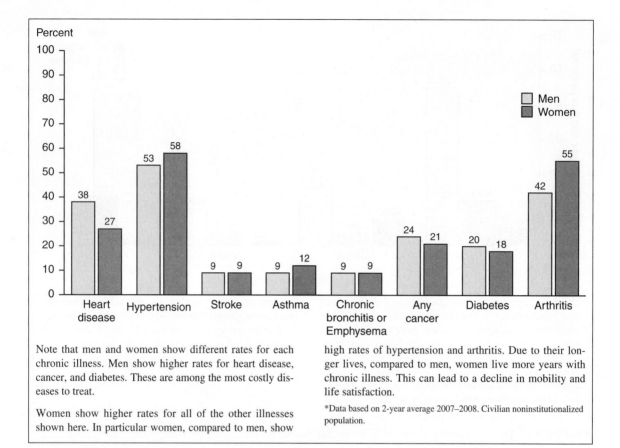

Note that men and women show different rates for each chronic illness. Men show higher rates for heart disease, cancer, and diabetes. These are among the most costly diseases to treat.

Women show higher rates for all of the other illnesses shown here. In particular women, compared to men, show high rates of hypertension and arthritis. Due to their longer lives, compared to men, women live more years with chronic illness. This can lead to a decline in mobility and life satisfaction.

*Data based on 2-year average 2007–2008. Civilian noninstitutionalized population.

FIGURE 4.2   Chronic Health Conditions Among the Population Age 65 and Over, by Sex, 2007–2008

Source: Federal Interagency Forum on Aging-Related Statistics. (2010a). Indicator 16: Chronic health conditions. *Older Americans 2010: Key indicators of well-being*. Washington, DC: U.S. Government Printing Office, p. 27. Citing Centers for Disease Control and Prevention, National Center for Health Statistics, National Health Interview Survey.

BOX 4.4
BOOMER HEALTH: TROUBLE AHEAD?

Gerontologists often assume that, compared to older people today, older people in the future (the Boomers in particular) will have better health. But some recent data question this assumption. For example, Putnam (2009, citing Soldo, Mitchell, Tfaily, & McCabe, 2006) says that "boomers self-report lower health status levels than did their parents at the same age. . . . Boomers have higher rates of chronic illnesses and conditions such as diabetes and obesity than prior generations."

In 2005 aging Baby Boomers made up more than one-third of the 47.5 million adults who reported a disability (CDC, 2009a). The National Health Interview Survey reports that in 2005–2007 more than 40% of people ages 50–64 had problems with at least one basic physical function. The study found an increase in the number of people in this age group who had trouble walking a quarter-mile or climbing 10 steps.

Dr. Richard Suzman, who directs the Division of Behavioral and Social Research at the National Institute on Aging, said, "If people have such difficulties in middle age, how can we expect that this age group—today's baby boomers—will be able to take care of itself with advancing age? If it continues, this trend could have a significant effect on the need for long-term care in the future" (LiveScience, 2010). And this could make the Boomers one of the least healthy and costliest generations (in long-term care costs) in U.S. history.

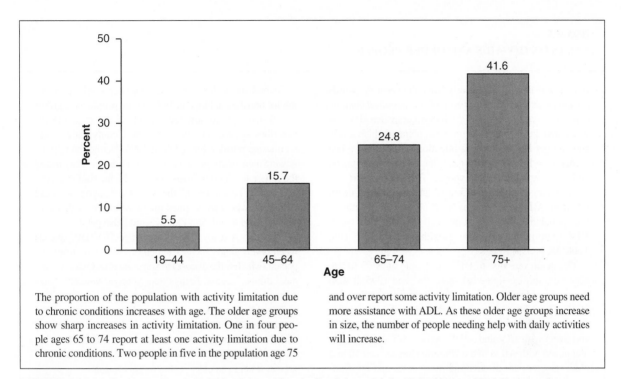

The proportion of the population with activity limitation due to chronic conditions increases with age. The older age groups show sharp increases in activity limitation. One in four people ages 65 to 74 report at least one activity limitation due to chronic conditions. Two people in five in the population age 75 and over report some activity limitation. Older age groups need more assistance with ADL. As these older age groups increase in size, the number of people needing help with daily activities will increase.

FIGURE 4.3   Limitation on Usual Activities Due to Chronic Conditions, Adults, United States, 2006 (Percent of persons with any activity limitation due to one or more chronic conditions)

Source: Adams, P. F., Lucas, J. W., & Barnes, P. M. (2008). *Summary health statistics for the U.S. population.* National Health Interview Survey, 2006. *National Vital Statistics Reports, 10*(236), Table 4, p. 16. Hyattsville, MD: National Center for Health Statistics. Retrieved November 5, 2010, from http://www.cdc.gov/nchs/data/series/sr_10/sr10_236.pdf

(ADL) increased from 3% for people ages 65–74 to almost 18% for people age 85 and over. Nearly 10% of people age 85 and over need help with three or more ADLs.

Older people also report limitations in **instrumental activities of daily living (IADLs)**, including everyday household chores, shopping, or getting around for other purposes. The CDC (2009a) reports that about 12% of people age 65 and over report some limitation on IADLs. The rate of IADL limitation increases from 6.2% for 65- to 74-year-olds to 35.3% for people age 85 and over. ADL and IADL limitations may range from a mild problem such as trouble dialing the phone to more serious problems such as the inability to eat or use the toilet. A decrease in the ability to care for oneself signals a drop in quality of life and in the number of active years a person will live (Prohaska, Mermelstein, Miller, & Jack, 1993).

These findings show that ADL and IADL problems increase with age. Most older people in their early retirement years report few limitations on their activities even if they have chronic illness. But by their 80s and 90s health and mobility decline. In later old age, activity limitation increases the chance that a person will need health, social services, and institutionalization.

Some groups more than others face higher rates of disability in old age. African Americans, compared with whites or Hispanic Americans, for example, report a higher proportion of ADL and IADL limitation (U.S. Department of Health and Human Services, 2003) (Figures 4.4 and 4.5). Some research shows that higher rates of disability for African Americans begin early in life and continue into old age (Kelley-Moore & Ferraro, 2004). Socioeconomic differences account for these higher rates. Women at every age, compared with men, report a higher proportion of ADL and IADL limitations. One third of older people with a disability (most of them women) live alone. They need help with everyday chores and face the greatest risk of institutionalization.

BOX 4.5
FACTS ON HIV/AIDS AND OLDER PEOPLE

Few people think of the elderly when they hear the words *human immunodeficiency virus (HIV)* or *acquired immune deficiency syndrome (AIDS)*. AIDS occurs when HIV has weakened the immune system to the point at which a person can get life-threatening infections and cancers. The media have linked HIV to gays, intravenous drug users, and sexually active young people. The data support this view. Young people ages 25 to 54 have the highest death rate from AIDS. People ages 65 to 74, compared with the total population, have about one-half the death rate due to HIV (National Center for Health Statistics, 2010a, Table 38, p. 229).

The death rate due to HIV for people ages 65 to 74, however, almost tripled between 1987 and 1995. It then dropped suddenly and began to climb again to the year 2006. The National Institute on Aging (NIA) (2008c) reports an increase in the number of older people (age 50 and over) with HIV and AIDS. About 19% of all people diagnosed with AIDS in the United States are age 50 and older. Doctors are discovering more cases and are finding that people with the disease live longer due to better treatments. The NIA goes on to say, "There may even be many more cases than we know about."

The NIA (2008c) goes on to say that women and people of color run a higher than average risk of getting AIDS. African Americans and Hispanic Americans make up 52% of people age 50 and over with AIDS. African American and Hispanic American men make up 49% of the male population age 50 and over with AIDS. But African American and Hispanic American women make up 70% of the female population age 50 and over with AIDS.

Older women of all races show higher rates of infection than older men. The NIA (2008c) reports an increase in AIDS cases among women age 50 and over. Most of these women got the virus from having sex with an infected partner or by sharing a needle. The NIA reports that HIV and AIDS cases continue to grow in number in communities of color and among women. The NIA encourages older people at risk to get tested.

The older population in the future may show an increase in deaths and illness from HIV and AIDS. Why is there a projected increase in AIDS among older people? First, a person can have HIV for 10 years or more before the body's immune system breaks down and AIDS appears. Intravenous drug users, for example, may become infected with HIV in their younger years but may not show signs of the disease until old age. More people in the future will enter old age with the HIV virus. The NIA (2008c) says that "people age 50 and older may not recognize HIV symptoms in themselves because they think what they are feeling and experiencing is part of normal aging."

Second, the health care system only began AIDS screening for transfusion blood in 1985. Some people have gotten AIDS from contaminated blood. Kellerman (1994) describes an older couple in Nassau County, New York, who tested positive for AIDS in 1993. Neither had affairs outside their marriage and neither used drugs. They traced the illness to blood transfusions that the husband received in 1982. "If I could get it," the wife said, "anyone who had a husband who was operated on, or who slept with someone who had it and didn't know, could also get it."

Third, any sexually active adult can get HIV. HIV spreads when bodily fluids such as semen or blood pass from one person (who has the disease) to someone else. Older women have thinner vaginal linings than younger women. Abrasions in these linings can open the way for infection. This makes older women more susceptible to HIV if they have sexual contact with an HIV carrier. Kellerman (1994) indicates that older people may stand a greater chance of getting HIV because they have weaker immune systems. AIDS progresses faster in an older person for this reason.

The National Institute on Aging (2008c) gives an example of how HIV can develop in an older person:

Grace was a happily married woman with a family and a career. After more than 20 years of marriage, her husband left her. After her divorce, she began dating George, a close family friend she had known for years. They became lovers. Because she was beyond childbearing years, she wasn't worried about getting pregnant and didn't think about using condoms. And because she had known George for years, it didn't occur to her to ask about his sexual history or if he had been tested for HIV.

At age 55 she had a routine medical checkup. Her blood tested positive for HIV. George had infected her. She will spend the rest of her life worrying that the virus will develop into life-threatening AIDS—that any cough, sneeze, rash, or flu would, in fact, indicate AIDS and perhaps the beginning of the end of her life.

The NIA (2008c) proposes that older people use condoms when having sex, avoid sharing needles, ensure that their partners do not have HIV, and get tested if they or their partners have had a blood transfusion between 1978 and 1985 or a transfusion in a developing nation. Early detection and treatment offers the best hope of keeping the virus in check. Older people who do not get the disease may still find their lives affected by it. Perhaps they will serve as caregivers to their adult children with AIDS, and some will have to play the role of parent to grandchildren whose parents have AIDS. Also, as more AIDS patients enter the long-term care system, they will compete with older people for services, such as home care. The AIDS epidemic in the years ahead will affect older people by affecting policies for health care delivery.

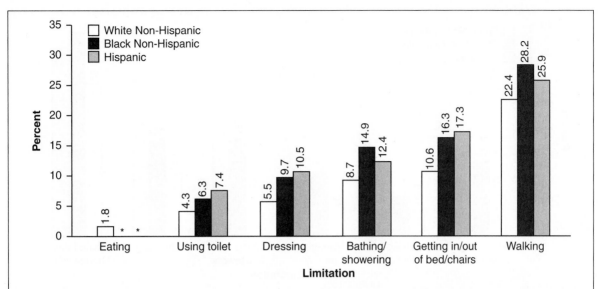

These figures show that older people have the greatest problems with mobility, transferring in and out of chairs or bed and walking. The proportion of people who experience ADL limitations differs by race/ethnicity. Whites, for example, have the lowest proportion of people with any ADL limitations. Blacks and Hispanics, compared with whites, have one and one-half to two times the proportion of older people with ADL limitations. These figures show the effects of poverty, health care treatment, and life-style choices over a lifetime.

These figures also show that the large majority of older people in the community live without ADL limitations. But, people with limitations in ADLs need support to live on their own in the community. The lack of this support can lead to institutionalization. Compared with whites, a higher proportion of older blacks and Hispanics will need assistance in order to stay in the community.

*Sample size under 50, too small to report results.

FIGURE 4.4   Activity of Daily Living (ADL) Limitations, Community-Dwelling People, Age 65 and Over, by Race/Ethnicity, 2004

Source: National Center for Health Statistics. (2007). *Trends in health and aging. Functional status and disability.* Difficulty performing activities of daily living, by age, residence, sex, race and ethnicity: Medicare Beneficiaries from the Medicare Current Beneficiary Survey, 1992–2004. (MAADL04). Retrieved November 15, 2007, from http://209.217.72.34/aging/ReportFolders/ReportFolders.aspx.

An increase in the older population and in the very old population could lead to more people with disabilities in later life. Will a longer life mean more years of suffering? This concern led researchers to the concept of disability-free life expectancy. This concept measures the number of years of life a person can expect to live without a disability.

In 2002, for example, the United States ranked 24th in the world for healthy life expectancy. In that year men age 60 could expect to live on average another 15.3 years in full health. Women age 60 could expect to live another 17.9 years in full health (Hu et al., 2005). Manton and Gu (2001) report a steady decline in disability rates among older people.

The National Long Term Care Survey supports this view. The study reports that disability rates fell by 1.52% each year between 1982 and 2004/05 (Manton, Gu, & Lamb, 2006). In total, from 1982 to 2004–2005, the nondisabled prevalence increased from 73.5% to 81% (or a decrease in chronic disability from 26.5% to 19% over the 22 year period). The researchers report that the rate of decline in disability increased over time, and the oldest age groups showed the fastest rate of decline in disability. This suggests that disability rates may decrease further in the future.

Manton and colleagues (2006) discuss some possible causes for the decline in disability rates. They propose that more assisted living options, more home care services, better rehabilitation techniques, and regenerative medicine all play a role in this decline. Also, better public health, improved treatment of diseases in later life, fewer smokers, and better education play a role in decreasing disability. Manton and colleagues (2006) look to improvements in basic medical science and medical care for future declines in disability. They foresee an important role for biomedical research and cellular and molecular understanding of chronic diseases.

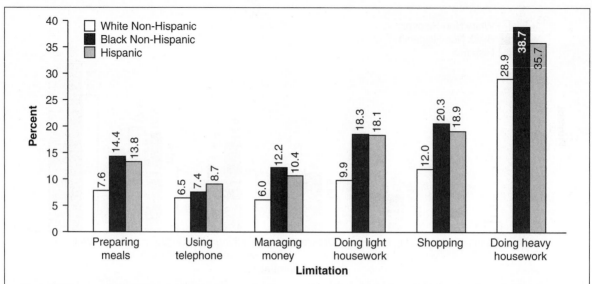

The inability to perform IADLs leads to a decrease in the quality of life. These figures show that most older people who live in the community have no limitations on their primary (IADL) activities. People need the most help with strenuous activities such as light housework, shopping, and heavy housework. Homemaker supports (e.g., help with shopping or cleaning) will improve the quality of life for people who have these limitations. A high proportion of older people in all groups need help with heavy housework. But, compared with white non-Hispanics, black non-Hispanics and Hispanics have higher rates of limitations in all categories. This points to a need for support for minority elders with specific activities for them to maintain a high quality of life.

FIGURE 4.5 Instrumental Activity of Daily Living (IADL) Limitations, Community Dwelling People, Age 65 and Over, by Race/Ethnicity, 2002

Source: National Center for Health Statistics. (2004). *Trends in health and aging. Functional status and disability.* Difficulty performing instrumental activities of daily living, by age, residence, sex, race and ethnicity: Medicare beneficiaries from the Medicare Current Beneficiary Survey, 1992–2004. (MAADL04). Retrieved November 15, 2007, from http://209.217.72.34/aging/ReportFolders/ReportFolders.aspx.

Gene therapy in the future, for example, could have a profound effect on health and illness in later life. Genes make up a part of the DNA in every cell. They hold the code for more than 100,000 proteins that keep the body working. Gene therapy will allow a researcher to replace a defective gene and reverse a state of illness or physical decline. Researchers would use recombinant DNA methods to (1) multiply the gene in a bacterial culture, (2) use a benign virus to place the gene in the host's cell, and (3) allow the gene to produce a needed protein. Scientists may use this technology to cure immune system breakdown, Parkinson's disease, and cancer.

Some studies show that people with disabilities can improve their health in later life. A study in Canada (Statistics Canada, 2000a), for example, reports that about 20% of older people developed a long-term activity limitation over the 5-year period 1994–1999. But about one third of older people with long-term activity limitations (31% of men and 37% of women) overcame their limitations during this time.

An 8-year longitudinal study in the United States found that nearly a quarter of people who aged successfully improved their physical function during the study (Rowe & Kahn, 1998). "Activity limitations and dependency are not necessarily long-lasting. . . . This may reflect the natural resolution of some conditions (back problems, for example) and effective treatment of others (such as arthritis), resulting in improvements in functional ability" (Statistics Canada, 2000a, p. 29). Health promotion, disease prevention, and effective management of disability can reduce the need for health services. They can even lead to rehabilitation and restored good health.

Disability in later life deserves researchers' attention. First, older people with disabilities need informal and sometimes formal support to maintain a high quality of life. Some disabled older people will rely on the health care system for service. An increase in the number of disabled seniors will increase costs and will affect the types of resources that the health care system needs to provide.

Second, some older people cope well with their disability and some get their functioning back. This group can help us understand how to encourage and rehabilitate disabled seniors. Third, exercise and self-care can prevent, ease, or reverse disabilities. Studies show that even people with chronic illness can improve their functioning.

COPING WITH PHYSICAL CHANGE

Chronic conditions do not always turn into functional disability or the need for assistance. Many older people adapt and cope with their conditions. For example, people change their habits (e.g., they drive less at night to deal with poor vision or take a yoga class to ease arthritis pain). They also use devices such as hearing aids and grab bars in the bathroom. Improvements in technology, the environment, self-care, and lifestyles can all lead to better functioning in later life.

Improvements in Technology

Both low-tech and high-tech devices can help older people cope with disabilities. For example, an older person can use a handheld magnifying glass to read a newspaper (low tech). Or the person can download the newspaper to a computer and use an enlarged font (high tech). Computers can now control hearing aids so that they filter out high- or low-pitched sounds or reduce background noise (Koncelik, 2003). New technologies can also allow families to visit with and watch television with a relative in a nursing home thousands of miles away.

New medical technologies will keep older people healthy and active longer. Doctors already use kidney dialysis to treat older people with kidney failure. Insulin pumps dispense a steady dose of insulin to improve the length and quality of diabetics' lives. New drugs for care after a stroke reduce vascular spasms and increase survival rates. Other technologies include rehabilitation programs, simple devices such as large rubber grips for spoons, and prosthetics like hip replacements.

Computers allow people to order groceries online, use email to keep in touch with friends, and play Scrabble with a grandchild across the country. Older people use the Internet for online banking. Computer databases and Web sites provide information on disabilities, coping methods, and even support groups online. All these

TABLE 4.1   Persons Using the Internet in and Outside the Home, by Age, United States, 2009

Age	Percent	
	Used in Home	*Used Anywhere*
Under 25	60.99	67.89
25–34	70.83	78.75
35–44	72.85	78.52
45–54	69.85	74.44
55+	50.84	54.00

This table shows Internet use at home and anywhere for 10-year cohort groups. Use at home and anywhere decreases markedly for the oldest age group. This may reflect an effect due to age. For example, people feel less comfortable using computers as they age. Or it may reflect a cohort effect. Older age groups had less familiarity with computers throughout their lives and so tend to use them less in old age.

The findings probably reflect some combination of these two effects. But future generations of older people will come into old age as active computer users. About three quarters of middle-aged cohorts use computers anywhere. This will make computer use more common among older people in the future. It will allow more people to access health care information and resources.

Source: National Telecommunications and Information Administration. (2010). *Current population survey (CPS) Internet use 2009.* Table 1. U.S. Department of Commerce. Retrieved November 5, 2010, from http://www.ntia.doc.gov/data/CPSTables/t11_1lst.txt.

resources will increase in the future. Email, chat rooms, instant messaging, and video links allow older people to develop and maintain social contacts.

Studies of online support groups, for example, show that they have a good effect on health and well-being. One study looked at the effects of an Internet support group on family caregivers for people with Alzheimer's disease. Caregivers in the group reported reduced strain. Spousal caregivers gained the most from this support group (Bass, McClendon, Brennan, & McCarthy, 1998). Other studies find that online support groups reduce depression and anxiety (Mahoney, Tarlow, & Jones, 2003). Ford and Ford (2009) studied Internet use among a national sample of 7,000 people age 50 and over. They found that Internet use led to about a 30% reduction in depression.

Still older people lag behind the general population in Internet use. Seventy-nine percent of the general population reports using the Internet. But only 42% of people age 65 and over report Internet use. Declines in physical and mental ability with age may account for part of this difference in use. Computer use demands physical skill (e.g., use of the mouse and keyboard) and mental ability.

Scialfa and Fernie (2006) say that computer use taxes verbal and spatial working memory. Computer users need to keep information about search paths and previous Web pages in mind as they browse and search. They also have to contend with pop-up ads and windows that draw attention from the person's main task. Multiple Web page links, information presented in hard-to-read fonts, and poorly organized Web sites can make computer use a challenge. A search on Wikipedia, for example, can quickly lead to confusion as the reader (at any age) wanders from one link to another.

Today, some people can't afford a computer or the cost of Internet service. This creates a "digital divide" within the older population. As a result, some people have access to electronic information and social networks while others do not. Also, some people feel comfortable using the latest technologies and some don't (Liu & Park, 2003). Web-site designers and manufacturers can design tools that make computer use easier for older people. For example, some Web sites of interest to older people have buttons that users can click to increase font size. Simple techniques like this encourage older people to use computer technology.

Designers now understand the need to include users in the development of new products. Gandy and colleagues (Gandy, Westeyn, Brashear, & Starner, 2008, p. 321), for example, say that "the first step in the design process is to determine who the target users are." Developing a product for an average user "is a pitfall that results in numerous users whose needs are overlooked." Once researchers have identified a target population, they can then focus on understanding the users' abilities and needs. Sixsmith (2008) calls this "user-centric" analysis and design.

A Web site called NIHSeniorHealth.gov (http:// nihseniorhealth.gov/) provides health information. This site shows how designers can make computer technology accessible to older adults. The design team for this site set three criteria for the Web site: (1) an older person should be able to read the Web page easily; (2) an older person should be able to understand the content; and (3) an older person should be able to easily navigate through the site.

The site developers had to understand and compensate for the sensory and cognitive deficits that come with age. This led the researchers to review studies of cognitive and sensory change, to test the Web site on older people before launching the site, and to alter the site based on the response of the people in their study. Above all, this project demonstrates the need to test and adapt technology to the older person's abilities (Morrell, Dailey, & Rousseau, 2003).

Training can also help older people overcome barriers to the use of new technology (Karmarkar, Chavez, & Cooper, 2008). Effective training increases the older person's confidence and increases the use of assistive devices. Shapira, Barak, and Gal (2007) taught a group of 22 older people (ages 70–93) how to use the Internet. They compared this group to a control group that got no computer training, but took part in recreational activities. The trained group used email, browsed the Web, and took part in forums and virtual communities.

The trained group reported increased well-being and feelings of empowerment. Compared to the control group they reported less loneliness, less depression, and greater life satisfaction. The untrained group showed deterioration on these measures.

Future cohorts of older people will face fewer problems with computer technology. They will have a lifetime of experience with computers and will feel comfortable using these tools. This study and others suggest the usefulness of the computer in enhancing older people's lives.

Emerging technologies, such as the use of the mobile phone as an information medium, open worlds of information and social supports to older users. Mobile phones now access the Internet, send instant messages, and download emails. But small screens, tiny words and pictures, and minuscule keyboards all challenge older eyes, ears, and fingers. New devices with touch screens and large icons help overcome some of these barriers. Future generations of older people will face new challenges as new technologies emerge. Good design can reduce the lag between innovation and the use of technology by older users.

Surveys report that about two thirds of people with ADL limitations use one or more assistive devices (Agree & Freedman, 2000). Hoenig, Taylor, and Sloar (2003) found that technology aids decreased the number of hours of personal help a person needed. But Bryant and Bryant (2003) found that poorer people made the least use of technology devices. More financial support and training is needed for poorer people who need technological help.

Clarke and Colantonio (2005, p. 192) call assistive devices "a powerful tool to help older adults overcome functional limitations." For example, more than one third of seniors with a hearing disability use a hearing aid. Eighty-two percent of seniors with a vision disability wear glasses. And an estimated 4.6% of seniors (88,300 people) in the community use wheelchairs. These devices make it possible for many people to live active lives in their communities.

Sutton and colleagues (2002) found that 92% of older adults with disabilities used a wide range of nonmedical assistive devices, and about two thirds used a medical device. Most people used assistive devices for personal care and in-home mobility. Most often people used simple products to make life easier.

One woman, for example, bought a cordless phone so she could carry it with her around the house. Another older person uses the microwave as an assistive device. She boils water by the cupful in the microwave. This avoids the need to lift a heavy kettle.

Devices like wheelchairs, walkers, or electric scooters all increase a person's mobility. People who use assistive devices say they rely less on others. And an assistive device can help a person stay out of a nursing home. But an older person will reject a device that makes them look different or dependent. A cane or walker, for example, may make a person feel self-conscious.

Karmarkar and colleagues (2008) describe three types of acceptance of technology: reluctant acceptance, grateful acceptance, and internal acceptance. Designers try to achieve this last type of acceptance. In this case the device "is considered by users as a medium for overcoming their physical impairments and a replacement for the impaired part of their bodies" (p. 29). Sometimes a shift in design can overcome resistance to a technology. One woman rejected the use of a motorized wheelchair because it made her feel helpless. But she accepted and even bragged about a motorized scooter that served the same purpose. Designers of devices need to understand how the older person sees the world. They can then design devices that older people will use with confidence.

Engineers have begun to meet older peoples' needs through robotics. Cutler (2006) reports on the "Nursebot" project at three universities: Carnegie Mellon, the University of Pittsburgh, and the University of Michigan. Researchers at these schools want to create a personal robot to help people who have a chronic illness. Abdulrazak and Mokhtari (2008) call assistive robotics "one of the most complex technologies more recently considered in the lives of people with special needs" (pp. 355–356). A number of companies see assistive robotics as an emerging market. Companies in Japan and Korea want to create machines that will get a disabled person food, move them from room to room, or even call a doctor.

A product titled My Spoon available since 2002 assists users who need help feeding themselves. The user works a joystick to control a spoon or fork on the end of a mechanical arm. In a semiautomatic and automatic mode the user selects a desired compart-

ment that contains food. The robotic arm than automatically brings the food to the person's mouth.

A robot called the "Care-O-Bot II" developed in Germany performs household tasks. The user controls the robot through a touch screen display or through voice commands. The robot can support a person while walking, can deliver food, and can clean up after a person finishes eating. The robot stores information about the environment in its database, and in a semiautomatic mode it can move around a person's home on its own.

Shibata and Wada (2008) report on a robot named Paro in the shape of a stuffed toy seal. The researchers used the robot to develop a program of "robot therapy" similar to animal therapy for nursing-home residents. The research project explored the use of the robot as a substitute for a live animal. The researchers report that the residents spoke to the robot, stroked it, and hugged it as if it were a live animal. The study found that Paro improved the residents' moods over a 4-month period. The researchers say that "Paro was effective in improving or eliminating depression" among the residents who interacted with the electronic pet (p. 412).

Robots and other assistive technologies will increase in the future. Smart textiles, for example, can monitor a person's heart, breath rate, or EEG 24 hours a day. This creates a "wearable health care system" (Paradiso, Taccini, & Loriga, 2008, p. 687). These products and new ones in development promise to improve the quality of life for people with disabilities.

Improvements in the Environment

Changes in the environment can also improve the quality of life for older people. Improved lighting, for example, can create safer and more enjoyable living spaces. Older people take more time to adapt to changes in lighting, their eyes grow more sensitive to glare, and their color perception weakens. Koncelik (2003) says that, compared with the eyes of someone age 25, the eyes of a person age 70 take three times longer to adapt to a change in light level. Also, compared with a younger person's eyes, the older person's eyes need more light to perform the same task. Designers have created lighting that eases the transition from bright to dimly lit rooms, reduces glare in hallways, and provides more light in dining rooms (Calkins, 2003).

Architects can also use materials that cut down on glare or reduce the echo in hallways and rooms. Koncelik (2003, p. 127) says that the technique of "redundant cueing" can improve the environment. For example, elevators can emit a beep along with a change in color to signal a change in floor level. Designers now routinely include devices such as grab bars in a tub or a ramp outside a home to increase the safety and mobility of older people.

Technology can allow families to monitor older relatives at risk of falling. These technologies help older people age in place. Video technology, for example, can monitor a person's condition and report any changes to a health care center (Cutler, 2006). Some children have set up a camera in a parent's home. The camera monitors the older person's behavior. And through the Internet the system alerts the children about any changes that signal danger. For example, the family can program the camera to expect the older person to enter the kitchen in the morning. If this does not happen, the system can alert the children, who can then check for any problems. The older person can turn the camera off if they choose.

Technology can also detect wandering, a problem faced by Alzheimer's patients. Devices can note when a door opens and can track a person through GPS systems. Some people appreciate this kind of support. Others find it intrusive. Melenhorst and colleagues (Melenhorst, Fisk, Mynatt, & Rogers, 2004) found that older people will tolerate the intrusion if the technology improves their sense of safety and security.

Improvements in Self-Care

Self-care refers to exercise, good eating habits, rest, stress release, and medical checkups. The CDC says that smoking, eating a poor diet, and inactivity cause nearly a third of all deaths in the United States. "Adopting healthier behaviors, such as engaging in regular physical activity, eating a healthy diet, leading a tobacco-free lifestyle, and getting regular health screenings . . . can dramatically reduce a person's risk for most chronic diseases, including the leading causes of death" (CDC, 2007, p. 4).

People can choose from a variety of health promotion and health maintenance methods (Ferraro, 2006). These include exercise programs like t'ai chi, acupuncture, chiropractic treatment, and relaxation therapies. Haber (2010) reviewed these methods and found that a market exists for alternative therapies. He reports that in 2008, 40% of Americans used some form of alternative therapy. Relaxation techniques and chiropractic treatment had the largest following. These techniques appeal to people with chronic illnesses that do not respond to conventional medical therapy.

Trombley, Thomas, and Mosher-Ashley (2003) report on a massage therapy program offered to people in two long-term care facilities. They found that massage therapy relieved tension from pain. The study combined massage with music therapy and reminiscence therapy. These methods improved residents' general well-being.

Information can also enhance self-care. This can take the form of diet and medication checklists, computerized self-assessment programs, and communication systems that provide answers to questions. Wagner and Wagner (2003) found that older people use self-care information if they have it at hand. These authors studied the use of a self-care handbook and a telephone advice line in one community. They found that, compared with younger people, people age 65 and over made more use of the self-care handbook. This shows that low-tech interventions like information sources can encourage self-care.

Thousands of Web sites now offer information on diseases, medications, and services. Fox (2004) found that 66% of older Internet users looked for health or medical information on the Web. The quality of information varies. And some sites mix advertising, items for sale, and advice on health conditions. For instance, a site that gives advice on back pain may also try to sell back braces, exercise videos, and other services. Still, the Internet provides a good source of information for the cautious consumer.

Some studies show that self-care lowers health care costs. Wheeler (2003) conducted a controlled study of women age 60 and over with heart disease. The study taught the women how to manage their health care. Women chose a health behavior to improve—for example, exercise. A health educator then taught the women how to assess their chosen behavior, develop a plan to improve this behavior, and monitor their response. Women in the program got a workbook, videotape, and self-monitoring tools (a log book). The control group continued with their usual health practices.

The self-care group, compared with the control group, used about half the number of inpatient hospital days and had about half the inpatient hospital costs. Wheeler says that the program saved $5 in hospital costs for every dollar spent on the program. Easom (2003) believes that older people in self-care programs benefit from encouragement, contact with role models of good self-care, and a supportive environment.

Social support plays an important role in self-care programs. Miller and Iris (2002) studied members of a wellness center to understand members' views of health promotion. They found that older people want social contact and social support along with a wellness program. People want to interact with others during their program. The researchers say that program designers need to keep these preferences in mind when designing programs for older adults.

Ferraro (2006) reports a growth in the use of technology and environmental modification as methods of self-care. But he notes that when a health condition gets serious (e.g., something that might require surgery), people turn to conventional medicine. Most people will combine self-care methods with drug therapies and the approaches of modern medicine. Still, self-care plays a role in prevention, reduction of symptoms, and the promotion of well-being in later life.

Improvements in Lifestyle

Research finds that early life experiences influence health in later life. For example, childhood abuse, poverty, or a broken home can lead to drug abuse, adult obesity, and even attempted suicide later in life. Low socioeconomic status (SES) also can lead to self-destructive behavior. Compared to people with middle-class income and above, those with low SES tend to smoke, remain physically inactive, and abuse alcohol and drugs (Ferraro, 2006). Also, compared to people with middle-class income and above, people with low income may have less access to health care programs and services. In spite of these trends, studies show that people can improve their health through exercise and weight reduction and by ending risky behavior (Clark, Stump, & Damush, 2003).

Chernoff (2002) says that a program of lifestyle change should include a smoking cessation program, better nutrition, increased exercise, and stress reduction.

Decreased Smoking. Robert Kane, an experienced health care researcher at the University of Minnesota, calls smoking "the biggest threat to improving our lifestyles. . . . That trumps everything else" (in Buettner, 2009, p. 16). The Surgeon General's (2004, p. 8) report on smoking finds "that the substantial risks of smoking can be reduced by successfully quitting at any age. . . . Quitting smoking has immediate as well as long-term benefits, reducing risks for diseases caused by smoking and improving health in general."

Kane and the Surgeon General join a chorus of experts who put smoking at the top of the list of life damaging behaviors. "The good news is that older men and women in 2006 reported the lowest rates of cigarette smoking among the adult population (12.6% for men and 8.3% for women)" (National Center for Health Statistics, 2009). This came to about half the

rate of other age groups for men and less than half the rate of other age groups for women. Older men and women also reported the highest rates of former smokers (Fryar et al., 2006). Men age 65 and over, for example, have smoking rates in 2006 less than half the rate of this group in the 1960s. Older women show a less dramatic decrease because they had a rate about one third that of men at that time.

Research shows that the benefits of quitting begin almost immediately. And the benefits of quitting last into late old age. The longer a smoker stays off cigarettes, the better. Ostbye and Taylor (2004) found that people who had quit smoking at least 15 years before their study began had the same life expectancy as people who had never smoked. People who quit in their late 30s can add 3 to 5 years to their life expectancy. Someone who quits between ages 65 and 69 can add 1 year to life expectancy (Surgeon General's Report, cited in the American Heart Association, n.d.). Smoking also deepens wrinkles and can lend a leathery look to skin.

Smoking leads to a long list of physical problems. Research links smoking to heart disease, lung cancer, emphysema, high blood pressure, stroke, and other major diseases that debilitate and kill people in later life. The Surgeon General's (2004) report on smoking says,

> The list of diseases caused by smoking has been expanded to include abdominal aortic aneurysm, acute myeloid leukemia, cataract, cervical cancer, kidney cancer, pancreatic cancer, pneumonia, periodontitis, and stomach cancer. These are in addition to diseases previously known to be caused by smoking, including bladder, esophageal, laryngeal, lung, oral, and throat cancers, chronic lung diseases, coronary heart and cardiovascular diseases, as well as reproductive effects and sudden infant death syndrome. (p. 25)

Cataldo (2003) calls smoking the number one preventable cause of disability and death among older people. Unfortunately, 24.5% of men and 19.3% of women ages 45 to 64 continue to smoke (National Center for Health Statistics, 2009). And among adults over age 18, older smokers showed the lowest proportion of those who intended to quit (Schoenbom, Adams, Barnes, Vickerie, & Schiller, 2004).

Research shows that older smokers, who want to quit, have the hardest time quitting. Lantz and Giambanco (2001) report that people who try to quit have a relapse rate of 70% after 3 months and 90% after 1 year. Cataldo (2003) says that, compared with younger smokers, older smokers get less guidance and less support for quitting.

A study by Fair (2003) offers more hope. This study found the same effectiveness of a smoking cessation program for younger and older people. Health promotion programs for older adults often include sessions on smoking cessation (Cheong, Johnson, Lewis, Fischer, & Johnson, 2003). Lantz and Giambanco (2001) say that programs need to include education about the benefits of quitting, nicotine substitutes, and in some cases antidepressants.

Programs sometimes require intensive intervention. Jorenby (2001) lists a number of medicinal approaches to quitting that physicians should offer to patients who want to quit smoking. These options include the use of gum, an inhaler, a nasal spray, or a patch. They replace nicotine in the body and decrease the smoker's craving for a cigarette. Another drug, bupropion, affects the pathways to the brain involved in addiction.

Smokers face a challenge when they have an addiction to cigarettes. But Lantz and Giambanco (2001) urge professionals who work with smokers not to give up and to use all of the methods available to help smokers quit.

Better Nutrition. The Federal Interagency Forum on Aging-Related Statistics (2010e) reports that obesity (a body mass index of 30 or above) among older people age 65 and over increased between 1988–1994 and 2007–2008 from 22% to 32%. On a positive note, more recent data (for 1999–2000 and 2007–2008) show no statistically significant increase in obesity for older men or women. Still, this higher body mass index (since the late 1980s) will mean an increased risk of chronic diseases like diabetes.

Ferraro and Kelley-Moore (2003) found that obesity led to premature disability in men and women. They report that diabetes (a disease linked to obesity) is on the rise. They say that an estimated 14.6 million people already have the diagnosis and another 6.2 million are unaware they have the disease.

More than half of people age 50 and over have a chronic illness like diabetes, high blood pressure, or heart disease. Scientists agree that good nutrition can support health and limit the progress of these diseases (Bates et al., 2002). Research on free radicals, for example, has led to the hope that eating antioxidant-rich food (like carrots, broccoli, and green tea) could hold back or in some cases reverse damage to the body. Studies of walnuts, grape juice, spinach, strawberries, and blueberries have all shown reversals of the signs of aging as measured by physical and/or mental performance. Vitamins C and E also have anti-oxidant effects on the body.

Vitamins and minerals can have good effects on the older body apart from their effect on free radicals. Vitamin C may reduce heart disease by blocking the formation of fatty proteins. Increased vitamin E may reduce the risk of Alzheimer's disease (National Institute on Aging, 2002). Research shows that calcium and vitamin D in the diet increase bone density. This may help prevent osteoporosis in older women.

What do these results mean for the older person's diet? What should older people eat to stay well and delay the aging process? First, metabolic rate decreases with age. An older person has to either eat less or exercise more to maintain an ideal weight. Second, older people need to make sure that they get at least minimum adult requirements of basic nutrients. They should also follow general guidelines that apply to people of all ages (e.g., avoid refined sugars and fats). Third, vitamin supplements may help older people stay in good health. Some older people lose their appetites or find it difficult to chew food. This can lead to vitamin and mineral deficiencies. A vitamin supplement can help ensure that a person gets the nutrients needed.

The U.S. government's *Dietary Guidelines for Americans 2010* (U.S. Department of Agriculture and U.S. Department of Health and Human Services, 2010) includes the following recommendations for a healthy lifestyle and diet. The Committee bases its finding on the latest scientific research.

- Consume a variety of foods within and among the basic food groups while staying within energy needs.
- Control calorie intake to manage body weight.
- Be physically active every day.
- Increase daily intake of fruits and vegetables, whole grains, and nonfat or low-fat milk and milk products.
- Choose fats wisely for good health.
- Choose carbohydrates wisely for good health.
- Choose and prepare foods with little salt.
- If you drink alcoholic beverages, do so in moderation.
- Keep food safe to eat.

The report *Older Americans 2010* (Federal Interagency Forum on Aging-Related Statistics, 2010b, p. 38) used these guidelines to assess the dietary habits of older Americans. The report says that, based on the Healthy Eating Index—2005, older Americans need to improve their diet. They need to decrease "their intake of foods containing solid fats and added sugars, limit alcoholic beverages, and reduce their sodium (salt) intake." In addition, they need to increase their intake of "vegetables, whole grains, oils, and nonfat/lowfat milk products."

BOX 4.6
GOOD NUTRITION IN LATER LIFE

Most nutrition experts in the United States today have come to similar conclusions about eating habits that lead to good health in later life. They say that an adult past age 50, for example, needs between 2,000 and 3,000 calories per day (the exact number of calories needed depends on a person's weight, gender, unique metabolism, and activities). A woman generally needs fewer calories than a man. And most experts agree on the contents of a healthy diet. A healthy diet for an older adult should include the following:

- Plenty of fruits and vegetables (of all colors) (2 cups of fruit; 2.5 cups of vegetables per day according to the USDA and the U.S. Department of Health and Human Services (HHS)
- Cruciferous vegetables (cauliflower, Brussels sprouts)
- Whole grains (brown rice, oatmeal)—3 or more ounces per day
- Healthy oils (e.g., extra virgin olive oil)
- Sources of calcium and vitamin D to build and maintain bones and resist osteoporosis
- Fiber (e.g., wheat or oat bran) to help reduce heart disease and colon cancer; fiber also provides a feeling of fullness and good bowel function
- Less than a teaspoon of salt per day (and beware of salt hidden in prepared foods like canned vegetables)
- Lean protein and varied protein choices, with an emphasis on fish (especially oily fish such as salmon and sardines)

- Poultry (and a reduction in the amount of red meat eaten)
- Nuts (almonds, cashews, walnuts)
- A multivitamin with minerals
- 6–8 glasses of water each day
- A balance of carbohydrates, proteins, and monounsaturated or polyunsaturated fats in a ratio of about 40%–30%–30% of calories
- Tea (green, white)
- Berries and other natural foods (avoid processed foods)

A healthy diet also means portion control. The supersized plates used in many American restaurants allow for the giant portions served. Keith (2004) says that the size of plates in U.S. restaurants has grown from 10 inches to 12 or 13 inches (or 20% to 30%) in recent years.

Combine this trend toward bigger portions with the high sugar and fat content in popular foods, and you have one explanation for America's obesity crisis. A meal at one popular burger chain, for instance—a double beef burger, fries, a large Coke, and a Dutch apple pie for dessert—provides 1,929 calories. That's about the entire daily caloric allowance for an adult woman in the United States. And these calories come mostly from processed sugar, refined starch, and fat.

By comparison, a balanced diet will contain about 40% complex carbohydrates, 30% from low-fat protein, and 30% from healthy fat (olive oil, fish oil, etc.). As people age, they need to get the maximum nutrition with the least calories.

Kane (in Buettner, 2008, p. 15) adds another important point to these dietary guidelines. "What one is looking for is moderation," he says, "taking in a level of calories that is necessary and balancing those calories across carbohydrates, fats, and proteins. Taking in really what you need." A healthy diet for an older person must take into account the slowing of the system with age, the body's increased sensitivity to extremes (like hot, spicy, and rich foods), and the body's need for high-quality nutrients with a minimum of calories. Volumes of research and study support this simple formula. Jeffrey Blumberg of Tufts University says, "Proper nutrition won't abolish the aging process, but it could slow the decline and postpone the onset of disease" (Schmidt, 1993, p. 69).

Exercise. Dennis waves as he closes his door and heads out of the office at noon. He's got a gym bag on his shoulder. Along with a group of co-workers, Dennis is off to do his lunch-hour exercise program. For the next hour he'll be sweating it out on a treadmill to the sound of the Allman Brothers, Luther Allison, or some other high-energy blues band. Once or twice a week Dennis, age 60, joins some other older colleagues for a basketball game. He sometimes comes back from these sessions exhausted. But he loves the game and the camaraderie.

Beth, another Baby Boomer, who works down the hall, belongs to a nearby gym. She has a different routine. She and her staff gather after work for a yoga/ Pilates class. They twist, turn, and sweat to relieve the day's stress. "It's not that easy," Beth says. "They work you really hard. It's kind of aerobic yoga." She's now got her 20-year-old niece, who lives in another town, going to yoga classes. When she visits her niece she brings her yoga mat and workout clothes and they go to class together.

Alice started a new diet and already looks thinner. She's 60, and she's joined a "dieter's anonymous" club—similar to AA. She's sworn off junk food and extra calories. At this year's holiday luncheon she skipped the rolls and wine and ate only the turkey and vegetables. She uses all her willpower to pass the staff kitchen without stopping in. She also joined a ladies' gym that features a half-hour circuit-training program. She attends almost every day.

Millions of Boomers like Dennis, Beth, and Alice now turn to exercise programs, workout videos, and personal trainers to stay fit. The fitness industry now takes in almost $24 billion per year (IBIS World, 2009). And the industry grows bigger every year. Many Boomers realize that they need to develop a new maintenance plan for their bodies. Still, the majority of Boomers and older people today report low levels of physical activity.

The Centers for Disease Control (2011) reports that inactivity levels increase with each older age group. For example, by age 75 about one third of the men and half of women engage in no physical activity. If this trend continues, Boomers may show the same low levels of physical activity as older people today. And this could translate into a very large generation of older people in poor health.

A large literature shows that physical exercise can improve the health and well-being of older people. It can help prevent disease and reduce the risk of chronic illness. Exercise can relieve symptoms of depression, increase independence, and improve a person's quality of life. Ferraro and Kelley-Moore (2003) found that exercise reduces the incidence of diabetes and other chronic illnesses. Even frail and very old people can benefit from physical activity.

Aldwin, Spiro, and Park (2006) say that aerobic exercise improves a whole range of physical conditions. It improves cardiac output, strengthens the heart muscle, lowers bad cholesterol, raises good cholesterol, and increases lung function. Aerobic exercise also improves muscle strength, flexibility, walking, standing, and balance. Weight-bearing exercise increases muscle strength and balance. It also slows down calcium loss from bones. People show improvements from exercise even late in life. These improvements lead to better functioning in their homes and greater independence.

Exercise can reduce the incidence of chronic diseases like diabetes (Plonczynski, 2003). Today more than 20 million people (or 7% of the population) have diabetes. Symptoms include frequent urination, excessive thirst, extreme hunger, unusual weight loss, increased fatigue, irritability, and blurry vision.

The American Diabetes Association (2011) reports that compared to someone without diabetes, someone with the disease spends more than twice as much yearly on medical care costs. Dall and colleagues (2011) say "the U.S. national economic burden of pre-diabetes and diabetes reached $218 billion in 2007." The Economist (2007a) calls diabetes "an American epidemic."

Griffin (2005) reports on the Diabetes Prevention Program, a national study that looked at the effects of lifestyle change on diabetes. The study found that even people over age 60 showed improvements after they started a program of diet and exercise. The older subjects showed more benefits than younger people in the study. They reduced their risk of diabetes by 71%.

The researchers ended the study a year early because the data showed such positive results. Griffin quotes Dr. David Nathan, the Harvard Medical School principal investigator, who said, "It was completely counterintuitive. . . . We thought, they're older, their lifestyles are much more ingrained. But in fact, just the opposite occurred." The study showed that lifestyle changes lead to better health at any age. Even mild exercise like walking makes the muscles more sensitive to insulin and reduces blood sugar.

For many years researchers thought that cardiovascular ability declined steadily by about 10% per year. Recent research shows that regular exercise can reduce the rate of decline. Some studies show no decline in cardiovascular performance over a decade or more among highly trained older people. Active people tend to live longer and have better health. They show a decreased risk of falling and better functional ability than nonactive older people.

Studies show that moderate exercise offers as much benefit as vigorous exercise. A study of physical activity and the risk of stroke in women found that vigorous physical activity had no significant effect on stroke risk. But increased walking time and increased pace lowered the risk (Sattelmair, Kurth, Buring, & Lee, 2010).

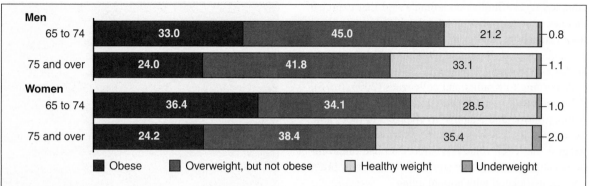

This chart shows that in 2003–2006 more than three quarters of men ages 65 to 74 were either obese or overweight. Two thirds of men in the 75 and older age group had similar weight problems. The rate of obesity and overweight drops slightly for women. About 70% of women ages 65 to 74 were either obese or overweight.

The 65–74 age group had the highest rate of obesity—1 of 3 men and almost 2 of every 5 women. The oldest group of women, age 75 and over, had the lowest rate of weight problems. But still, 60% fell into the obese or overweight category. The unhealthy weight of most older people increases their risk for many illnesses including diabetes, arthritis, blindness, amputation, heart disease, and stroke (Aldwin et al., 2006).

Troublesome as these figures may seem, the condition of the adult population in general appears just as bad. A study conducted by the Trust for America's Health (2007) found that in 2004–2006, two thirds of U.S. adults were overweight or obese. Some states had obese populations that made up one quarter to one third (Mississippi, 30.6%) of their total populations. These people will likely bring their habits and weight problems with them into later life.

*A body mass index (BMI) less than 18.5 is considered underweight. Healthy weight is defined as a BMI of 18.5 to 24; overweight is defined as a BMI of 25 to 29; obese is defined as a BMI of more than 30.

Note: The reference population for these data is the civilian noninstitutionalized population.

FIGURE 4.6 Overweight, Obesity, and Healthy Weight (as Measured by BMI) Among Persons 65 Years of Age and Over, by Selected Characteristics: United States, 2003–2006.*

Source: National Center for Health Statistics. (2010). *Health, United States, 2009: With special feature on medical technology.* Table 72, pp. 301–304. Hyattsville, MD. Also Trust for America's Health (TFAH). (2007). *F as in fat: How obesity policies are failing in America, 2007.* Retrieved: September 9, 2007, from http://healthyamericans.org/reports/obesity2007/Obesity2007Report.pdf.

Exercise can buffer risks created by smoking or by having high blood pressure (Rowe & Kahn, 1998). It can restore the age-related decline in muscle protein and increase antioxidant production in the muscles (Ji & Hollander, 2000). Sobczak (2002) reports that exercise can stop and in some cases reverse the trend toward loss of mobility and dependence that may come with age.

Franco and colleagues (2005) studied exercise data from the Framingham Heart Study. The study included men ($n = 2,336$) and women ($n = 2,873$) ages 28 to 62 years. This group has been medically reexamined every 2 years for 46 years. Franco and colleagues found that compared to men who engaged in low physical activity, men who engaged in moderate to high physical activity gained between 1.3 and 3.7 more years of life expectancy. The active group of men also lived 1.1 to 3.2 more years without cardiovascular disease. Active women showed similar gains compared to those who engaged in low amounts of activity. Active women gained 1.5 to 3.5 years of life expectancy and 1.3 to 3.3 more years free of cardiovascular disease.

The researchers conclude that an active lifestyle not only prevents cardiovascular disease but also leads to longer cardiovascular disease-free life. Many studies link exercise to better health and higher quality of life. But this study *for the first time* links exercise to longer disease-free life expectancy. And it shows that even moderate exercise can lead to a longer disease-free life. This finding should encourage people to stay active as they age.

Kramer, Babiani, and Colcombe (2006) report that exercise even improves mental ability. They say that older adults who exercise show improvements in mental tasks and show the greatest improvement in highly complex tasks. Studies on animals find that exercise increases survival of neurons, growth of new neuronal interconnections, and growth of new capillaries in the brain (Cotman & Berchtold, 2002, cited in Kramer et al., 2006; van Praag, 2009).

According to Kramer and colleagues (2006, p. 76), "The end result of exercise training then is a brain that is more plastic and adaptive to change and more able to survive the vagaries of the aging process. Results suggest that even relatively short exercise interventions can begin to restore some of the losses in brain volume associated with normal aging."

Williamson and Pahor (2010, p. 124) in a review of the research on exercise and aging say that "physical activity may be the most effective prescription that physicians can dispense for the purposes of promoting successful aging. . . . Today it is recognized that virtually all of the diseases and conditions that lead to physical disability in older adults has as part of their etiology a component of personal lifestyle choices (e.g., physical inactivity)."

Millions of people each year would avoid illness and extend their lives by adopting healthier lifestyles. This in turn would reduce health care costs. Chapter 12 discusses exercise programs for older people in more detail.

Stress Reduction. The Framingham Offspring Study tracked the health of 3,682 men and women (average age 48.5 years) over a 10-year period. The study found that tension (a type of stress) increased a man's risk of heart disease, heart rhythm abnormalities, and death from all causes. Men who had high levels of tension had a 25% higher risk of heart disease and a 23% higher overall risk of death compared to a control group. This gave men who reported feeling tension the same risk of death as men with high blood pressure. Women who reported high anxiety also showed a greater risk of death.

Eaker (cited in Reuters [Health], 2005) say that "you need to take care of the tension in addition to taking care of your cholesterol and your diabetes. . . . This should be part and parcel of the whole reduction and prevention of risk factors for heart disease and mortality."

Selye (1956) coined the term *stress* to refer to the wear and tear we experience every day as we adjust to changes in the environment. A new job, for example, can lead to excitement, anticipation, and action. Selye called this "eustress" or good stress. But if the job demands long hours, sleepless nights, travel, and impossible goals, it can lead to "distress." This can

Banana George was born January 22, 1915. He learned to water-ski at age 40 and to barefoot water-ski at age 46. In 2003, *Water Ski Magazine* named him a water-ski "icon," the International Waterskiing Federation awarded him the Order of Merit, and he was inducted into the Florida Sports Hall of Fame. His motto is, "Do It."

produce diseases like headaches, high blood pressure, heart disease, and stroke.

Many stress reduction techniques exist, from secular relaxation methods, to meditation practices, to religious retreats. Studies show that regular practice of many of these methods can improve health and well-being. Cerpa (1989), for example, studied the blood sugar levels of people with type 2 diabetes. He compared people who practiced a meditation-relaxation technique and those in a diabetes education program. He found that the meditating group showed significantly reduced blood sugar levels after participating in the program for 6 weeks. The control group showed no change in blood sugar levels. The findings support the idea that meditation-relaxation techniques can help control diabetes.

BOX 4.7
THE BLUE ZONES: NINE KEYS TO A LONG AND HEALTHY LIFE

Dan Buettner, founder of Quest Network, Inc., studied long-lived people in a variety of cultures. He produced a photo essay on his research for *National Geographic* magazine, titled "Secrets of Living Longer" (Buettner, 2005). The article and photo essay profiled long-lived people in three societies—Sardinia, Italy; Okinawa, Japan; and Loma Linda, California, USA.

The *National Geographic* essay reviewed the work of three research teams. Each team studied the habits and social conditions that best explained a group's longevity. The three studies in different parts of the world found many similarities in long-lived people's lifestyles and habits.

Buettner (2010) boils the results of these studies down to "The Power Nine: Secrets of long life from the world's healthiest humans."

1. Move (find ways to move mindlessly, make moving unavoidable)

2. Plan de Vida (know your purpose in life)

3. Down Shift (work less, slow down, rest, take vacation)

4. 80% Rule (stop eating when you're 80% full)

5. Plant-Power (more veggies, less protein and processed foods)

6. Red Wine (consistency and moderation)

7. Belong (create a healthy social network)

8. Beliefs (spiritual or religious participation)

9. Your Tribe (make family a priority)

The fast pace of life in the United States challenges a person at any age to adopt these principles and apply them. Yet they make common sense, and we would probably all enjoy life more if we practiced them.

How does your life and that of your family and friends match these nine principles of good aging? What would you have to change or what would have to change in the world around you in order for you to live according to these Blue Zones principles?

BOX 4.8
BOOMERITIS

Jay Corman, 62, carefully puts down the coffee cup. "I didn't fall off my bike once this holiday season,' he says with a laugh. "Though I cross-country skied and fell down a lot." Jay's referring to a recent accident he had when a section of trail fell out from under his mountain bike. He fell into a ravine 30 feet below and suffered a concussion and a broken rib. "When I came to sometime later," he says, "I had to climb out of the ravine with my bike and a broken rib. Then I had to ride 5 miles to the trailhead and my car."

Jay's an outdoorsman, a mountain climber, a hiker, and a backpacker. He leads treks to Himalayan mountains, rides road and mountain bikes, and plays soccer with a group of younger guys. He recently had a knee operation to repair torn cartilage. Today Jay can't hold his coffee cup straight in front of him because he has tendonitis in his elbow from weight lifting. Jay could serve as the poster child for "Boomeritis." This term refers to the illnesses caused by Boomers' abuse of their bodies as they try to engage in the sports and physical activities of their youth.

Fiona, another Boomer, likes to inline skate on the Strand in Los Angeles. A few years ago she crashed into

a sign pole while skating down a steep hill at high speed. She broke four ribs, spent the next week in the hospital, and took several months to recover. Now she only skates on flat surfaces like the path beside the beach in L.A. Still, she recently slipped on a puddle of water there, fell and hurt her tailbone and back. Older bodies take longer to heal and are more easily bruised and injured. So, even a slight fall can cause pain and demand a long recovery.

Dr. Nicholas DiNubile (DiNubile in Carrns, 2008), orthopedic surgeon and consulting physician to the Philadelphia 76ers basketball team, coined the term "Boomeritis" to describe the damaging effects of extreme exercise on Boomers' bodies. "When we are looking at the Baby Boomers," he says, "we're looking at the first generation that's really trying to stay active on an aging frame, in droves. We have doubled the human life span in the past hundred or so years. [But] we have a mismatch between longevity and durability. You're going to live longer, but your frame isn't designed to go that many years, so it's going to fail.

"Baby boomers often forget this in their zeal to stay young and active. But activity has its limits as the body ages. If you have a problem, say arthritis in the knee, you

(Continued)

BOX 4.8 (*continued*)

can have it operated on and resolve the problem. Or you can strengthen your muscles. So, even though the problem remains it's less of a problem. But if you can't resolve it or strengthen it, then you need to work around it. That might mean power walking instead of jogging if you have a sore knee. Or using an elliptical trainer rather than the treadmill."

Modern medicine has improved care for the heart, and we know more about diet and exercise than ever before (even if people don't always heed this advice). But our bones, joints, and ligaments weren't made to take a beating for our newly extended lives. DiNubile (2005, p. xxi) in his book *Framework*, warns that, "Without proper care, your bones and joints can all too easily become the limiting factor in your enjoyment of life." You can stay fit and active without damaging your bones, ligaments, and tendons. If you have a weight problem, for example, losing weight can take some of the strain off your frame. DiNubile says that "for every extra pound you're carrying, your knee thinks it's 5 to 7 pounds . . . if you lose 5

to 10 pounds, your knee thinks you lost 35 to 70 pounds" (in Carrns, 2008).

He also advises doing a variety of activities—aerobic, weight bearing, and stretching (like yoga or Pilates)—to minimize stress on joints. An older woman who wants to stay fit and healthy should balance aerobic training (swimming or jogging) with weight-bearing exercise. Swimming, for example, strengthens the cardiovascular system. But it does little for bone density. Doing one activity to an extreme may lead to the opposite of good health. As you age and stay active, DiNubile says, "You have to be open to change. Otherwise, you're going to fail."

What's the takeaway here for the older person? Moderation. Know your limits. Make sure you're prepared for the challenges you undertake. Be aware that your body now isn't the same as it was in your youth. Don't give up your favorite activities, but be sure to train for a specific challenge. And have injuries looked after soon after they occur.

Alexander and colleagues (Alexander, Langer, Newman, Chandler, & Davies, 1989) conducted a controlled study of older people who practiced Transcendental Meditation (a popular meditation technique), mindfulness training (a method of increasing awareness of reactions to the environment), and relaxation. They found that the meditation and mindfulness groups, compared to the relaxation and control groups, showed improved mental health, better cardiovascular function, and improved mental ability. These two groups also showed greater longevity. The entire meditation group and 87% of the mindfulness group were still alive after 3 years. Only two thirds of the control group was still alive after 3 years.

A later study by Alexander and colleagues (1996) further supports the value of meditation as a way to improve health in later life. This study looked at the effect of Transcendental Meditation on older African American men. The researchers found that meditation significantly decreased hypertension, obesity, and other risk factors for heart disease. Aldwin and colleagues (2006, p. 94; also Seeman, Dubin, & Seeman, 2003) say that "this accords with the growing evidence of the beneficial effect of meditation practice on cardiovascular health." Idler (2006, p. 291) reports that experimental and epidemiological studies show "direct biological pathways from religious states, particularly those induced by meditation, to health by way of cardiovascular, neuroendocrine, and immune function."

Lindberg (2005) studied the literature on meditation, spirituality, and health in older persons. She reviewed 25 years of research and found that overall, meditation reduces anxiety and depression. It improves a person's physical, emotional, and spiritual health, and it helps a person cope with problems, challenges, and stress.

Schneider and colleagues (2009; also Anderson et al., 2008) conducted a randomized controlled study of 201 African American older adults (mean age 58) with coronary artery disease. The experimental group learned and practiced meditation. The control group engaged in a health education program. The study measured survival rates of subjects, heart attack, and stroke. Secondarily, the study looked at blood pressure, body mass index, and a psychosocial stress index including depression, anger, and hostility in the experimental and control groups.

After 5 years, the researchers found a "43% reduction in risk for all cause mortality, myocardial infarction and stroke in a high-risk sample of African Americans." The researchers conclude that "a selected stress reduction approach may be useful in the secondary prevention of atherosclerotic CVD [cardio-vascular disease]." These results and many others studies in the literature showed the value of stress reduction methods for improving length of life and quality of life.

Disease prevention, health promotion, and stress management should play a role in planning for a

---

BOX 4.9
CALORIE-RESTRICTED DIET: THE SECRET TO LONGEVITY?

The study of calorie restriction has grown into one of the most active areas of aging research. Walford (1983; Weindruch & Walford, 1988) conducted some of the earliest research into the effects of calorie restriction on aging. He fed lab mice a diet with all needed nutrients, but with 30% to 60% fewer calories than normal. He found that a calorie-restricted diet in lab mice led to longer life and better health.

Bartke and Lane (2001, p. 301) say that calorie restriction of 60% to 70% of normal led to "impressive extension of life in laboratory rodents." Barzilai and Gabriely (2001, p. 903S) call calorie restriction "one of the most robust observations in the biology of aging." Sinclair and Howitz (2006, p. 63) say that "dietary restriction (DR) is the only way to reliably and dramatically extend life span in mammals without genetic interventions." Animals that live longer due to dietary restriction "remain more youthful and are somehow protected from the common diseases of aging."

The National Institutes of Health (1993, p. 27) report that "undernutrition has increased the life spans of nearly every species studied—protozoa, fruit flies, mice, rats, and other laboratory animals." Many studies now exist to support the effects of calorie restriction on longer life and a healthier old age (Masoro, 2001). And Austad (2001) says that in studies of laboratory rodents, calorie restriction lengthens life and leads to more vigor in later life. According to Sinclair and Howitz (2006, p. 63), the ability of DR to extend life span "is so remarkable that it took numerous studies to reassure the scientific community that DR is a universal effect."

Researchers have found that calorie restriction retards age-related declines in DNA repair. Calorie restriction also decreases the accumulation of mutations in the cells. Researchers have found that low-calorie diets may cut down the number of free radicals in the system (Masoro, 2001). Finally, calorie restriction lowers fat in the body and this keeps blood sugar levels in balance (Barzilai & Gabriely, 2001).

Recent calorie restriction studies have looked at humans and other primates, such as monkeys. The Comprehensive Assessment of Long-term Effects of Reducing Intake of Energy (CALERIE) study found results that point to longevity. Adults who cut their calorie consumption by 25% lowered their fasting insulin levels.

They also lowered their core body temperature. Both of these signs correlate with increased longevity in animals. Other studies with nonhuman primates report that calorie restriction reduces the incidence of heart disease and cancer (National Institute on Aging, 2010b).

How does calorie restriction affect longevity? Sinclair and Howitz (2006, p. 68) in a review of the research say that, in addition to DR, other stressors such as overcrowding or mild shock to the system can also extend life span. They say that these shocks "invoke a survival response." They propose a broad theory to explain these findings: the "hormesis hypothesis." They derived this term from the Greek word *hormaein* or "excite." It refers to the good effects that come from response to a mild stress.

This hypothesis states that DR creates a mild stress that boosts resistance to biological and chemical attacks on the body. This protects the person from the effects of aging. Sinclair and Howitz (2006) say that this response evolved to help organisms cope with poor external conditions. They report that this theory marks a major shift in thinking about DR and extended life. Earlier theories saw longer life as a passive by-product of DR (e.g., lower metabolism or less sugar in the body). But the hormesis hypothesis proposes that the body makes an active response to the threat posed by DR.

Will people take up low-calorie diets in the future? Probably not. Walford spent 2 years in Biosphere 2, a futuristic experiment in an artificial environment in Arizona. While there, he put himself on a calorie-restricted diet and lived on two thirds the average calories of a man his age.[*] Other members of the Biosphere team refused to follow Walford's diet. A spokesperson for the project observed, "They're not lab rats."

Calorie restriction may not gain wide adoption among humans. But studies of calorie restriction reveal some of the mechanisms that lead to aging and disease in later life. Sinclair and Howitz (2006) provide an excellent review of the research on DR and the theories that explain its effect on longevity. Exploration of the effect of DR, even if few humans adopt this regimen, will lead to a better understanding of biological aging.

[*]Walford died of cancer at age 80 in 2004.

---

successful age. These activities can reduce the risk of many chronic conditions of later life (arthritis, high blood pressure, and heart disease). They can also reduce the incidence of the three major causes of death in later life: heart disease, cancer, and stroke.

COMPRESSION OF MORBIDITY HYPOTHESIS

Controversy exists over the benefits of longer life expectancy. Some researchers believe that longer life will lead to more years of good health. They say that

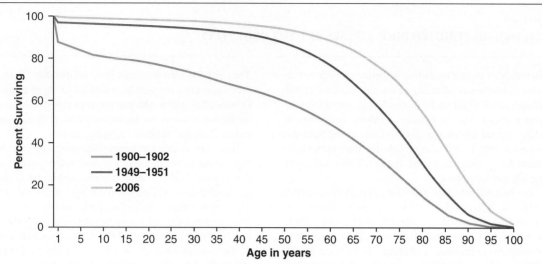

This figure shows the rectangularization of the life curve. The three curves represent survival rates for people born at three points in time. The most recent cohort, 2006, shows a projected decrease of death rates. People in this cohort tend to live longer, and fewer people die at younger ages. This leads to a more rectangular look to the life curve.

Note how the 2006 curve starts to approximate the square shape of the chart's outline. If you compare the 1900–1902 and the 2006 groups, you will see that in the 1900–1902 cohort nearly 10% of the group dies in the first year or so of

life. And 20% (one in five) have died by age 10. Note that the 2006 cohort is not expected to lose this many members until around age 75. In other words most of the 2006 cohort will live to old age and many (20%) will live to age 90.

The compression of morbidity hypothesis says that illness will also be pushed to the later stages of life. This would mean that the 2006 cohort (and later cohorts) will stay relatively healthy into late old age. They would suffer a short period of decline before death.

FIGURE 4.7   Compression of Morbidity

Source: Arias, E. (2010). United States life tables, 2006. *National Vital Statistics Reports, 58*(21), 5. Hyattsville, MD: National Center for Health Statistics. Retrieved: July 22, 2010, from http://www.cdc.gov/nchs/data/nvsr/nvsr58/nvsr58_21.pdf.

longer life will push disease and loss of function to the last years of life. Other researchers believe that people will live longer, but with more years of chronic illness.

Some years ago, Fries (1980, 1987a) predicted that as life expectancy increased, people would have fewer years of disability, suffer less from chronic disease, and need less medical care. He predicted that death would come for most people around the age of 85 after a short illness. This, he said, would create a **rectangularization of the life curve** as more people live out the full human life span. Longer life, he said, would lead to a **compression of morbidity** (illness) at the end of life. (See Figure 4.7.)

This hypothesis produced controversy during the 1980s and early 1990s. Some results at that time suggested that people would live more years with disabilities as life expectancy increased (Crimmins, Saito, & Ingegneri, 1989). Researchers reasoned that we cannot control nonfatal diseases like arthritis and

Alzheimer's. So, they said, the prevalence of these diseases would increase as more people lived longer. They predicted that the total number of people with disabilities would increase in the future (Olshansky, Rudberg, Carnes, Casse, & Brody, 1991).

But, recent research supports Fries' predictions of morbidity compression (Laditka & Laditka, 2000). Between 1997 and 2005, for example, life expectancy in the U.S. at age 65 increased from 17.7 to 18.7 years (National Center for Health Statistics, 2009). During this same period the percent of people who reported a limitation on their activity due to chronic illness fell from 38.7% to 32.6%. This decrease in disability applies to whites, African Americans, and Latino groups. This means that longer life led to more years free of disability and dependence.

More detailed studies show that some groups gain more disability-free years than other groups. Crimmins and Saito (2001), for example, found that people with higher educational status showed a compression of morbidity, but those with less education showed an expansion of morbidity. This suggests that illness in later life is not an inevitable outcome of longer life. Instead, these findings point to the plasticity of the body as it ages. The morbidity compression hypothesis supports attempts to improve health and well-being in later life by prevention and lifestyle changes.

Fries (1990) said that healthier lifestyles, exercise, and good public health would lead to healthier life into late old age. Recent research supports this view. Studies find that higher socioeconomic status (Melzer, McWilliams, Brayne, Johnson, & Bond, 2000), smoking reduction (Bronnum-Hansen & Juel, 2001), and regular physical activity (Ferrucci et al., 1999) all lead to a relative compression of morbidity. People at lower risk of illness (those who exercised, did not smoke, and had low or normal weight) faced disability at later ages (Hubert, Block, Oehlert, & Fries, 2002). These people, compared with those at high risk, also have fewer disabilities, have less serious disabilities, and face disability for a shorter time at the end of life.

Fries also said that the variation in ability among older people shows room for further compression of morbidity (Vita, Terry, Hubert, & Fries, 1998). In other words, if some people live morbidity-free lives into late old age today, more people can follow this pattern in the future. Laditka and Laditka (2000) believe that women can benefit most from this view. Women live longer than men and have a higher risk of disability due to chronic illness. Active living can lead to the compression of morbidity and more satisfying lives for older women. The potential for further improvement in well-being among older people has led to the study of successful aging.

SUCCESSFUL AGING

Rowe and Kahn's Model of Successful Aging

Cross-sectional studies show declines in most body functions with age. The older the person, on average, the poorer his or her physical function. This holds for kidney, lung, and heart function, among others. These findings led to the idea that aging takes a steady downhill course and that the body wears out on a set schedule.

But researchers have begun to question this view. Studies have looked at the effects of exercise, nutrition, and healthy lifestyles on aging (Chernoff, 2002). They find that people can maintain good health and physical function into late old age. Kahana, Kahana,

and Kercher (2003), for example, describe a variety of activities that can buffer physical decline and lead to successful aging. Activities include consumer awareness, self-improvement, access to technology, and engagement in physical activity.

According to Rowe and Kahn (1998), gerontologists have spent too much time on the study of "normal" aging (the study of illness and disability). Instead, these researchers propose that gerontologists study people who age well. For example, about three quarters of people age 65 and over and almost 70% of people age 75 and over rate their health as good to excellent (National Center for Health Statistics, 2010b).

Rowe and Kahn urge gerontologists to study this new generation of healthy older people. "There was a persistent preoccupation," they say, "with disability, disease, and chronological age, rather than with the positive aspects of aging." Researchers also underestimated the effects of lifestyle choices and other social and psychological conditions on the well-being of older people. Rowe and Kahn (1998, p. xii) set out to create the basis for a "new gerontology," a study of successful aging.

Successful aging refers to "people who demonstrate little or no loss in a constellation of physiologic functions" and who therefore "would be regarded as more broadly successful in physiologic terms" (Rowe & Kahn, 1991, p. 21). Successful aging means more than aging without disease. Rowe and Kahn (1998, p. 38) define successful aging as the ability to maintain (1) a "low risk of disease and disease-related disability," (2) "high mental and physical function," and (3) "active engagement with life."

Some researchers see a contradiction in this view of successful aging (Thompson & Forbes, 1990). If a person can avoid decline through lifestyle or environmental changes, then this decline must not be intrinsic or true aging. The biologist who wants to know the causes of true aging may find little value in the concept of successful aging, but physiologists and practitioners who work to improve well-being in later life find the concept useful.

The SOC Model of Successful Aging

Some researchers find Rowe and Kahn's view of successful aging too narrow. For example, in their model, the onset of physical decline or disability means that a person has aged unsuccessfully. Is this always the case? Minkler and Fadem (2002) worry that this model of successful aging stigmatizes and blames disabled or ill people for their problems. Also, people with low incomes or a lifetime of economic or health problems will have a hard time meeting Rowe and Kahn's standard. George (2006) raises a further problem with this model—it doesn't take into account a person's subjective view of life. Someone with a chronic illness or disability can still feel fulfilled and happy.

Researchers Paul Baltes and Margaret Baltes and their colleagues, who created the Berlin Aging Study, explain that a person with chronic illness or disability can live a successful age. They describe a process called **"selective optimization with compensation (SOC)"** (Baltes & Carstensen, 2003; George, 2006). These researchers view successful aging as a response to life's challenges.

They found in their research that people often face losses or physical distress as they age. But those who aged successfully used the SOC method. They engaged in activities that optimized their ability. When they could no longer engage in an activity, they compensated for losses by setting new priorities. For example, they dropped less important activities and relationships and focused on more important ones. Or they substituted one activity for another. A person who could no longer travel due to disability might attend travelogue sessions at a local senior center. Someone who could no longer drive at night might focus on daytime social events.

Spirduso, Francis, and MacRae (2005) say that people, as they age, compensate for changes in their bodies by anticipating and simplifying actions. They will prepare to perform an action, say, by getting up from a bus seat early enough to make their way to the door. A younger person might wait until the last minute to exit. In this case the older person's actions may look like the younger person's. But the older person has consciously or unconsciously compensated for decreased reaction time and planned a smooth exit from the bus.

Spirduso and colleagues (2005, p. 203) say, "As the passage of time blunts efficiency and reduces speed of processing individuals inevitably develop strategies to cope with these losses; thus for many years the loss of function in a highly practiced, healthy individual is so slight it is unnoticeable."

An older person may act with more caution—aware that a decrease in motor coordination increases the risk of a fall. They may also simplify an action by breaking it down into smaller parts. For example, a younger person may mount a bike by standing on one pedal, pushing off, and swinging on to the seat. An older person may get on a bicycle from a stationary position.

The body and its decreasing abilities pose practical problems for older people. And awareness of these problems can improve performance. Also, a person can consciously compensate for these limitations through practice or attention.

Clearly a model of successful aging must allow for a person's ability to cope with chronic illness, disability in late old age, and genetic diseases. Successful aging based on the SOC model encourages people, at whatever age or physical condition, to make the most of their abilities. This model supports the attempt by anyone—in whatever physical condition—to live a full and engaged life. It should also encourage professionals who work with older people to help each person reach his or her maximum potential.

A Life Course Model of Successful Aging

In the face of these facts what can or should a person do to age successfully? Ashley Montagu, ethologist and researcher, says, "The goal in life is to die young—as late as possible." Baby Boomers want to come into their 60s looking and feeling like 40 and enter their 70s looking and feeling like 50. In order to do this, they will need to (1) preserve the health they've got, (2) do as little damage as possible to their bodies, and (3) strengthen what they can. Current research shows that successful aging remains largely within a person's power.

Researcher George Vaillant (2002) studied the histories of people in the Harvard Study of Adult Development. This study tracked a group of Harvard students over their lifetimes. Vaillant found seven predictors of healthy aging:

1. Not being a smoker or stopping smoking
2. Adaptive coping style (mature defenses—e.g., turn lemons into lemonade)
3. Absence of alcohol abuse
4. Healthy weight
5. Stable marriage
6. Some exercise
7. More years of education (this led to self-care and perseverance)

Vaillant was surprised at how much a person's health and lifestyle before age 50 predicted a 70-year-old's health condition. Vaillant found that a person could control most of the conditions that led to good or poor health.

"The good news," Vaillant says, "is that most of us—if we start young and try hard—can voluntarily control our weight, our exercise, and our abuse of cigarettes and alcohol, at least by the time we are fifty. . . . Whether we live to a vigorous old age lies not so much in our stars or our genes as in ourselves" (2002, pp. 212–213). Schneider and Miles (2003, p. 1) say that for adults, "behaviors and lifestyle account for a *full 70 percent of how well you age*" (italics in the original).

These findings show that, in part, later life reflects the activities, living conditions, and lifestyle choices made in youth and middle age. Damage done to our bodies earlier in life—by reckless behavior, excessive use of drugs or alcohol, or a poor diet—can lead to disease and disability later. Longer life expectancy today makes it wise to adopt healthy activities, habits, and lifestyles as early as possible.

ANTI-AGING MEDICINE AND SCIENCE

Concern for the effects of aging and a desire to halt or reverse those effects have led to a rise in **anti-aging medicine and science**. This interest in reversing or halting aging takes many forms. Books with titles like *121 Ways to Live 121 Years . . . and More* promise longevity. Products such as hormone replacement supplements promise a reversal of the signs of aging. And an organization called The American Academy for Anti-Aging Medicine (A4M) (A4M, 2006) challenges traditional medical approaches to treatment. This association provides certification to physicians who want to promote anti-aging. It also sells anti-aging cosmetics and health supplements on its Web site. Products include pineapple enzyme (for digestion) and oregano oil to combat infection.

The International Longevity Center, an affiliate of the Mount Sinai School of Medicine (2006), reports that the U.S. market for anti-aging products and services in 2004 grew to more than $45.5 billion. This market is growing at an annual rate of 9.5%. Also, Americans spend an estimated $27 billion on dietary supplements. A U.S. Senate Hearing (2001) reported that 60% of these consumers are age 65 and older. The anti-aging industry begins targeting people as early as age 35 with advertisements to reverse the appearance of aging. Many people want to believe that a magic formula exists that will reverse or stop the aging process.

Binstock and George (2006) devote a chapter in the sixth edition of *Handbook of Aging and the Social Sciences* to the discussion of anti-aging medicine and science. They trace this movement to at least five social conditions: (1) Baby Boomers value youth and will try experimental methods to stay young. (2) New scientific findings suggest treatments that may slow or reverse the aging process. (3) People show a growing concern for the cost of a large older population that needs health care. Anti-aging proposes to keep people healthy longer (at lower cost to society and individuals). (4) Companies can play on the fear of aging to promote and sell anti-aging products. The Internet serves as a new medium for the sale and promotion of such products. (5) A trend exists to medicalize normal aging processes. Aging from this perspective looks like an illness or series of diseases that science can cure. All of these trends create a susceptibility to anti-aging promises.

In addition, some people feel disillusioned with modern medicine and medical treatment. They object to the control that modern medicine exerts over treatments and cures. And they lack trust in the medical establishment. This leads many people to look outside the medical establishment for health advice and treatment.

Binstock and colleagues (2006) note that the medical and gerontological community share common goals with the anti-aging movement. A4M (2006), for example, seeks to detect, prevent, and treat aging-related disease and to promote research into methods to retard and optimize the human aging process. A4M is also dedicated to educating physicians, scientists, and members of the public on anti-aging issues. A4M proposes that the disabilities associated with normal aging are caused by physiological dysfunction. And it believes that many of these disabilities will respond to medical treatment.

Gerontologists say that the anti-aging movement offers some helpful options—such as exercise or vitamin supplements. But the movement also poses dangers. First, it sees aging as a reversible or avoidable condition. This stigmatizes people who look "old" (Binstock et al., 2006). Haber (2001–02, 2004) says that the anti-aging movement demeans and marginalizes aging and older people. She notes that the current movement harks back to beliefs about aging at the start of the 20th century. At that time anti-aging supporters saw aging as something to be feared and avoided. Haber says that both the earlier and current anti-aging movement view aging as a disease to be overcome.

Second, people may waste money on unproven supplements. Suppliers of antioxidant supplements, for example, promise health and longevity. But the National Institute on Aging (NIA, 2007) states that "there is no proof that large doses of antioxidants will prevent chronic diseases such as heart disease, diabetes, or cataracts."

Third, people who take anti-aging medicines may miss out on the benefits of normal medical treatment or lifestyle changes. For example, the use of pineapple enzyme for stomach upset may delay the medical treatment of a serious stomach problem.

Finally, most anti-aging methods and drugs remain untested through normal scientific means. Binstock and colleagues (2006, p. 440) say that "the wares being sold and techniques being endorsed include powerful drugs that have the potential to cause serious physical and mental harm." Haber (2010, p. 27) gives an example of the risks that some anti-aging treatments pose. She reports on the use of human growth hormone (HGH) to halt or reverse the effects of aging. People pay as much as $1,000 per month for these treatments. As many as 25,000 to 30,000 people in the United States take these injections. Physicians cannot legally prescribe this drug for healthy people. But they can diagnose mild hormone deficiency to justify the treatment. Side effects can include "diabetes, hypertension, hardening of the arteries, and abnormal growth of bones or internal organs."

These hands of an older person show some of the changes in the skin that come with age. Note the leathery look, age spots, and wrinkles. Everyone's skin shows similar objective changes with age. How we see these changes (for example, as ugly, beautiful, or tragic) depends on us. I recall my grandmother's hands. I saw a lifetime of service in her weathered skin.

The gerontological and medical communities remain skeptical of the anti-aging movement's promises. Instead, the scientific community generally promotes a moderate and careful approach to health in later life. The NIA (2007), for example, proposes the following approach to aging well: "Stick to a healthy diet, exercise, keep your mind active, don't smoke, and see your doctor regularly."

SOCIAL INEQUALITY AND PERSONAL HEALTH

A healthy old age depends on personal action—diet, exercise, and self-care. But people enter later life with different chances of living a healthy old age. Some researchers trace health in old age to childhood and a lifetime of good or bad health. O'Rand (2006, pp. 154–155), for example, says that poverty in early childhood leads to a "chain of life course 'insults.' . . . Early and sustained poverty has been shown repeatedly to predict higher rates of disability and mortality in later life." Studies now link adult diseases to childhood stress, illness, and poverty (Kuh, Ben-Shlomo, Lynch, Hallqvist, & Power, 2003).

Research on the "early origins" of disease takes a life course approach to health (Ferraro, 2006). Studies find that mothers who experience famine while pregnant have children who report ill health 50 years later. Other studies show long-term effects of mothers' health-damaging behavior during pregnancy.

Not everyone agrees that a clear link exists between fatal health and health in later life. But the literature does point to some connections between health in childhood and adulthood. Low birth weight, for example, raises the risk of obesity in adulthood. And obesity, in turn, raises the risk of diabetes. So, low birth rate has an indirect, but potentially strong, influence on health in old age. Ferraro (2006, p. 241) notes that only longitudinal studies can trace these detailed connections. These studies will make an "important contribution for both maternal and gerontological health."

Research on the early origins of disease show that people come into later life with different health resources. Compared to middle- and upper-class people, people with a lower-class background tend to engage in more health-destructive behavior. This includes smoking, alcohol abuse, drug abuse, and lack of exercise (Ferraro, 2006). Compared to middle-class children, children brought up in low-income households get exposed to these poor health habits. Ferraro (2006, pp. 245 and 248) says that a childhood in a poor family may lead to "a cascade of risks. . . . A good start in life aids the chances for a good finish. . . . It is hard to overstate the influence of early disadvantages."

Socioeconomic differences mean that some older people will suffer from the effects of early health disadvantage. Other older people will build on the good health and income that they enjoyed throughout their lives. Life course studies of health make the case for public policies that improve health in childhood and middle age (e.g., health education, welfare programs, income security, child care, and public health programs).

Health promotion programs for poorer older people can also help. Exercise and weight-loss programs, for example, can improve health, functional ability, and quality of life at every age. This makes health in later life a societal issue as well as a personal problem.

CONCLUSION

Some years ago, Hayflick (1981, p. 176) said that a short-range goal of gerontology "would simply be to reduce the physiological decrements associated with biological aging so that vigorous, productive, non-dependent lives would be led up until the mean maximum life span of, say, 80 years." This he considered a feasible and worthwhile goal. And studies in the biology and physiology of aging show that more people than ever before have begun to achieve this goal.

But what of the future? Some scientists propose an optimistic scenario. Crews (1993, p. 288), for example, says that "the possibility of human life span extension is real and interventions that postpone human aging are a likely prospect." Rose (1993, p. 72) says that:

> Given enough time and resources, there is no reason to doubt that eventually we will be able to postpone human aging, at least to some extent. . . . [T]here is the further

possibility that increases in the human "health span" could likewise be open-ended. . . . [E]volutionarily postponed aging involves an enhancement in performance at later ages, not an extended period of debility. The long-term prospect, then, is more of an extension of youth than an increase in longevity, though the latter does occur.

The technical ability to extend life and improve the quality of life in old age now exists. And the future may see more life extension. But we may arrive at that point before we have worked out the social effects of this change. For example, how would personal and social life differ if people lived, on average, 120 years? How would this change our ideas about youth, middle age, and old age? Would retirement at age 65 make any sense? Would people and society adjust their life cycles and careers to meet this new schedule?

Studies of people age 100 years or more throughout the world give some clue about what a long-lived society will look like. Vogler (2006, p. 47) says that centenarians serve as "a useful human model of disease-free or disease delayed aging." Studies report that long-lived people have good genes, a purpose in life, physical activity, independence, close family ties, friends, good hygiene, a simple balanced diet, low stress, good self-esteem, and a belief in God (Vogler, 2006). In other words, centenarians live balanced lives in supportive social settings.

These findings suggest that we take the quest for a long life out of the realm of science fiction. Instead, we should place the search for a long and full life where it belongs: within the power of each of us and the society we live in. We can and will extend life through scientific research and improvements in the quality of life. But life extension will only put off the deeper question. Can we give meaning and purpose to those added years?

SUMMARY

- Gerontologists distinguish between two causes of aging: intrinsic aging due to normal physical decline and extrinsic aging due to lifestyle, the environment, and disease.
- Scientists have developed two different classes of theory to explain the cause of aging. Programmed theories locate the cause of aging in programmed actions by the genes. Error theories locate the cause of aging in external and internal assaults on the body over time. Research suggests that both of these causes play a role in physical aging.
- Bones, muscles, blood, and hormones change as we age. The five senses also decline as a person grows older, although the senses decline at different rates.
- The rate of chronic illnesses such as arthritis, diabetes, and heart disease increases as the population ages. The

rate of acute illness decreases with population aging. Chronic illnesses tend not to cause death (as do heart disease, cancer, and stroke), but they lead to long-term illness and the need for help with everyday activities.
- Most older people report no problems in performing ADLs, but the proportion of people who report limitations increases with age. By late old age (85 and over), people often need help in order to live on their own in the community.
- The use of technology will improve the quality of life for people with disabilities. The Internet, well-designed household appliances, and robots in the future will make life richer, safer, and more comfortable for older people. Older people benefit from training in the use of technology. Designers of technological devices need to

understand their use from the older person's point of view. This will produce products that older people will use and enjoy.

- Older people can use a variety of health maintenance and health promotion methods to stay healthy and active. Self-care leads to better health and less use of costly health care services.

- Decreases in smoking, better nutrition, increased exercise, and stress reduction all lead to a healthier old age. Today and in the future, older people risk increased illness due to obesity. Obesity increases the risk of diabetes, heart disease, and other chronic and life-threatening illnesses. A sensible diet and exercise offer the best ways to combat this problem. A good diet and exercise also improve health and physical function.

- Stress reduction can play a role in creating a successful age. Methods include meditation, relaxation techniques, and spiritual retreats. Any or all of these methods can improve physical function, increase well-being, and improve mental alertness.

- Compression of morbidity occurs when chronic disease comes later in life. The late onset of chronic disease compresses illness into fewer years at the end of life. This could result in decreased use of medical care and services in the future.

- Some researchers propose that the study of normal aging limits our understanding of health and well-being in later life. They propose the study of successfully aging older people. Studies of people who live in good health into late old age may give scientists clues about how to improve aging for everyone. The SOC model of successful aging expands on Rowe and Kahn's earlier work.

- A life course model of successful aging looks at the links between earlier stages of life and a good old age. Current research shows that successful aging remains largely within a person's power.

- Anti-aging and science attempt to slow, stop, or reverse the aging process. The anti-aging movement uses methods that go beyond the accepted practices of Western science and medicine.

- A lifetime of inequality can lead to poor health in later life. The life course model of aging studies the connection between health early in life (as early as infancy) and health in old age. Those who have good income and health earlier in life generally live a healthier old age.

- Scientists in the future may be able to extend the human life span. This will likely increase the number of healthy years people will live. These changes will raise the question of how to make the best use of the added years people will have available to them.

DISCUSSION QUESTIONS

1. Distinguish between intrinsic and extrinsic aging. List the four criteria for intrinsic (true) aging. Can you give examples of each type of aging in your own life? In the lives of older people you know?

2. Name the two classes of theories that gerontologists have developed to explain the causes of aging. What perspective does each type of theory take on the process of aging?

3. How do our senses change with age? What problems does this present to the older person? Suggest some things that older people, their friends, and relatives can do to compensate for declines in each of the senses.

4. What changes in the pattern of disease took place as U.S. society aged? Why did this change take place? What implications does this have for the health care system?

5. What are ADLs and IADLs? What do they tell us about older people? What causes limitations in ADLs and IADLs? How do other people help an older person cope with ADL and IADL problems? What types of people provide this help? Do you know of any people or groups in your area who provide ADL or IADL help? Who are they and what do they do?

6. What are some of the responses older people can make to the effects of aging? For example, what can older people with arthritis do to maintain the quality of their life? What other lifestyle practices would improve health and well-being in later life?

7. Explain the term *rectangularization of the life curve*. Link this term to the *compression of morbidity* hypothesis. What do these two concepts suggest about aging in the future?

8. How would personal and social life differ if people, on average, lived for 120 years? How would this change our ideas about youth, middle age, and old age? How would retirement be affected? What would society need to do to adjust to a longer life span?

9. Can you give three reasons why gerontologists do not support the anti-aging movement's activities?

10. What link do gerontologists find between health in youth and later life? What kind of studies would confirm this link?

11. What are three models of successful aging? What do each of these models add to our understanding of later life?

12. What links have gerontologists found between a person's life in childhood, youth, and middle age and the quality of that person's life in old age? How does this broaden our thinking about how to create a good old age?

13. What long-term goal do scientists propose for the study of biological and physical aging? Do you think science will reach this goal? Why or why not? How will this change social life as we know it?

SUGGESTED READING

Charness, N., & Schaie, K. W. (2003). *Impact of technology on successful aging.* New York: Springer.

This series of articles looks at many of the issues and themes raised in this chapter. Articles examine how technology can help older people deal with sensory changes, the impact of computers and the Internet on older people, and the use of assistive devices. The articles describe ways that technology can reduce dangers and provide people with the support they need to live independently in the community.

Haber, D. (2010). *Health promotion and aging* (5th ed.). New York: Springer.

The fifth edition updates this classic work. The book shows the many new approaches to health promotion that have emerged in the past few years. The book discusses exercise, nutrition, and behavior change. It also includes a section on complementary and alternative medicine.

Many of the author's insights come from his own experience working with older people. The text discusses current topics including gay aging, social networking, brain games, recent health care reform, and the use of the Wii system for rehabilitation.

Wykle, M. L., Whitehouse, P. J., & Morris, D. L. (2005). *Successful aging through the lifespan: Intergenerational issues in health.* New York: Springer.

This collection of readings applies the concept of successful aging to issues related to intergenerational relations. Articles look at a wide range of topics, including how older people can engage in productive aging, exercise and diet to maximize well-being, and the opportunities to build family relations through caregiving. The book suggests ways to make aging a positive experience and later life a time of challenge and personal growth.

Websites to Consult

The American Geriatric Association for Health in Aging

www.healthinaging.org

This site contains information about strategies for staying healthy in old age, elder care, and stories about successful aging.

Users (both elder-care patients and providers) also contribute real-life stories about their experiences with aging and personal health. Some seniors have left fascinating personal accounts of their struggles with age-related illnesses and the social challenges they face.

NIHSeniorHealth

http://nihseniorhealth.gov

This site contains up-to-date information on a number of age-related health ailments organized by condition. It includes descriptions of a wide variety of physical problems, as well as ways to treat and avoid them. The site also includes a "Trainer's Toolkit." The Toolkit includes an online course that teaches older adults how to use the Internet to get health information.

National Council on Aging

www.ncoa.org

This site displays information about many health care programs, advocacy groups, and special interests that promote physical health in old age.

Healthy Aging—Centers for Disease Control and Prevention

www.cdc.gov/aging

This site includes practical information for older adults as well as research reports, data, and statistics. It also includes information on CDC initiatives on caregiving, mental health, and end-of-life preparedness. All of this aims at creating a healthier older population. An excellent source of basic data on aging in the United States.

Healthfinder.gov

http://healthfinder.gov

A portal to the most reputable health information on the Web. The site includes information on healthy living, personal health tools to assess your health, and an index of services and information. The site also provides information in Spanish. An excellent resource for older people and for anyone interested in the many health-related resources that exist online.

What is a *good* old age? Consider these three cases. Each person shows a different response to the challenge of aging.

Elsa Bhrem Noffman, 102 years old, lives a busy and active life. At age 100 she leased a Lincoln and threw herself a giant party with plenty of orchids. One hundred eighty people attended. She lives in Hillsboro Beach, Florida, and spends her days at luncheons, shopping, and playing bridge. She played golf until about 6 years ago, when arthritis in her back made her give up the game. She recently took a cruise to South America and the Caribbean. Now she says she enjoys meeting people. "Meeting people—it seems to be as if love is radiating. It's a great feeling" (Hobson, 2010, p. 34).

Becky Reitman, age 73, reports high life satisfaction, but at a slow pace. She lives alone in a seniors housing complex in central New Jersey. She has arthritis in her legs and an unstable walk due to a broken hip that healed poorly. These problems limit her activity, but Becky takes the complex's bus to a local shopping center twice a week. The bus driver helps her with her packages. She watches television, knits, and talks to friends on the phone most mornings. After lunch she sits in the lobby with a group of other tenants. Once a month she goes to a movie in the lounge.

Pasquale Ianni, age 66, has followed a third path to a satisfying old age. He lives in his own home with two of his unmarried adult children. Seven years ago Pasquale had a heart attack that nearly killed him. His illness left him depressed and without a purpose in life. To pull himself out of his depression, he enrolled in a leadership program for seniors. The program required a community service project, so he offered to set up a meal program for the Italian community through Villa Rosa, a seniors housing complex. The program delivered meals to people who could not come to the complex for lunch. Pasquale now runs this program. His role as a community leader gives his life meaning and purpose.

Three people, three cases of high life satisfaction, yet each person shows a different pattern of aging. Elsa Bhrem Noffman has stayed active in many of the things she did during her younger years. Becky Reitman has withdrawn from most of her middle-aged activities. She lives a quiet life, content to see only a few people and limit her activity. Pasquale Ianni has found new roles to replace those of middle age. He feels good about what he has done, and he looks forward to doing more community service.

Each of these people takes part in activities and relationships that he or she finds meaningful. They have each met and overcome challenges to achieve a good old age for themselves. *Good aging* in this chapter refers to the mastery of inner and outer challenges in later life. These challenges include changes in mental ability, changes in social relations, and changes in social status. These challenges and the older person's response take place in a social context. This chapter looks at (1) mental function and self-development in later life, (2) issues raised by changes in a person's psychosocial condition, and (3) creative responses to change in old age.

MEMORY AND INTELLIGENCE

Ruth and Ray, both in their 80s, take ballroom dance lessons on Friday evenings. I met Ruth one Friday after their class. She looked worried. I asked her what was wrong. "Is there something the matter with Ray?" she asked. "Tonight, after dinner at our favorite restaurant he couldn't remember where he'd parked the car."

I said I didn't think she had to worry much about this. Ray, a former scientist, has a keen mind. He can learn and remember a complex series of dance steps in an hour and dance them a week later. I said she could put this memory lapse in the category of benign forgetfulness. A physician I know tells older patients, "You don't have to worry if you can't recall where you put your eyeglasses. You should start to worry if you don't remember that you wear eyeglasses."

Like Ruth, many older people worry about the loss of memory as they age. They assume that memory loss will take place as a part of the normal aging process. They also fear the loss of their mental abilities. But, Pearman and Storandt (2004) say that these worries often have little basis in fact. Recent research questions the idea that memory and other mental abilities decline radically with age.

The stability and adaptability of the brain allow for continuity and growth in mental potential throughout life. Research on the older brain reports that:

1. Changes in the brain take place gradually throughout life,
2. People lose more neurons in childhood than in healthy adulthood,
3. The nervous system has a remarkable ability to adapt to change,
4. Most neurons live through the entire life of the person, and
5. The body creates new neurons even in later life.

Research on memory and intelligence shows that varied changes occur in mental ability as people age. In some cases, mental ability declines. But in other cases it improves. And in most cases, older people adapt well to changes in mental function.

Memory

A hand shot up in the audience. "Doctor," the man said, "I can't remember things the way I used to. Am I getting senile?" "No, you're not suffering from dementia. And your memory may not be any worse than in the past. You're just more aware of memory lapses, so you seem to forget more." "Well, I don't know," the man went on, "I think my mind's not what it once was and I want to know what I can do about it."

Many older people would agree with this man. Some studies report that two fifths of people ages 25 to 75 report memory problems at least once a week (Lachman, 2000). McDougall (2000) says that people fear memory loss more than almost any other effect of aging. But studies of memory loss show only a weak connection between these fears and reality.

Memory refers to recall after learning has taken place. Psychologists in the field of aging have spent more time on the study of memory than on any other subject. Smith (1996, p. 236) says that studies of memory and aging made up "34% of all the published papers in the two journals *Psychology and Aging* and *Journal of Gerontology: Psychological Sciences.*" Psychologists have developed a number of theories about how memory works (and how it changes) in later life.

Researchers break the process of remembering into a series of steps. Most researchers use an information-processing model to guide their work (Schieber, 2003). This model includes the following steps: (1) a person perceives information (psychologists call this sensory memory); (2) the person acts on this information, transforms it in some way, while the information sits in short-term memory; and (3) the person stores the information in long-term memory, the storehouse of knowledge that also includes the rules for using knowledge.

Take the example of looking up and remembering a phone number. You open the phone book and see the number (sensory memory). You repeat it to yourself a few times as your eye moves from the phone book to the dial (short-term memory). You make a rhyme of the number so you can remember it later (long-term memory). The greatest mental work goes on when a person stores information in long-term memory.

Most psychological studies test memory in the laboratory. This allows the researcher to control outside influences and to compare performance between age groups. These studies often use a cross-sectional design. For example, the researcher gives subjects of different ages a list of words to remember. The researcher then tests the subjects' recall and compares the performance of young and old people.

In general, older people perform less well than younger people on this kind of test. This suggests a general decline in memory with age. But further research shows that results differ when researchers study different parts of the memory model.

For example, studies find little difference between younger and older people in sensory memory or primary memory. Young and old people perceive information (such as a phone number) about equally well. And both young and old people hold this information in consciousness about equally well.

A number of studies report a decrease in episodic memory, including **working memory**. This type of memory selects, manipulates, and stores recent information (Bäckman, Hill, & Stigsdotter-Neely, 2001). In addition, working memory processes new information while it stores other information temporarily (Schieber, 2003; Braver & West, 2008). A decline in working memory takes place in older people when irrelevant information comes between two things to be remembered. Older adults, compared with younger people, also have a harder time remembering information in a scrambled order. This requires that they hold all information in memory and then make sense of it.

Researchers find that the greater the effort required by memory, the more an older person shows decline in processing speed and recall. For example, when a topic changes, it place an extra load on working memory. Older people forget relevant information when topics change rapidly. Brown and Park (2003) find that decreases in working memory lead to poor comprehension and recall of novel medical information. Craik (2000, p. 82) says, "It is clear that older adults have particular problems in situations where they must hold, manipulate, and integrate moderate amounts of information over short time spans."

Studies have also found differences in function between young and old people in long-term memory. Researchers have looked in detail at the process of long-term memory to understand this difference. Long-term memory requires **encoding** (learning information), **storage** (putting information away), and **retrieval** (getting information back out). Psychologists believe that how someone retrieves information (how he or she searches for it and finds it in memory) depends on how the person acquired it (how he or she organized and stored it). Studies show that encoding and retrieval account for most of the memory performance differences between younger and older people.

Researchers find that, compared with younger people, older people use less efficient strategies to encode (or learn) information. Perfect and Dasgupta (1997) found that older adults could not think of encoding strategies or used less elaborate methods of encoding. The researchers believe that encoding, rather than retrieval, accounts for the lower recall rate in older adults (Schieber, 2003).

Ska and Nespoulous (1988, p. 408) concluded that "elderly subjects reproduced [put into memory] less during the encoding phase and retrieved fewer elements during the recall phase." Speeded tasks increase the gap between young and old subjects. Older people take in less information and fail to encode some items. They miss items presented rapidly, miss items late in a list, and encode some items at the expense of others. Older people may do worse on speed trials because they do not have time to encode effectively.

Older people, compared with younger people, also have more trouble with retrieval. It takes older people longer to get information out. Braver and West (2008) report that latency (the time a person takes to process or retrieve information) increases with age. Cerella (1990) says this shows a "generalized slowing" in the nervous system, and he considers this a classical finding in the field of cognitive psychology.

More recent research supports this conclusion. Madden (2001, p. 289) says that "slowing is a fundamental dimension of age-related change in cognitive function." Verhaeghen and Cerella (2008, p. 134) say that age-related slowing of mental function occurs in a wide variety of tasks among many mental systems. "Memory search, visual search, lexical decision, mental rotation, speech discrimination" and other mental processes show declines in response time with age.

Park (2000) likens the older mind to a computer. The computer has a large store of memory in the hard drive, but it has limited RAM (random access memory). This computer will process information slowly. The processor cannot efficiently use the large store of memory in the hard drive. "The computer works, but perhaps a little less efficiently than one would like" (p. 5).

According to Salthouse (1996), decreased processing speed underlies much of the age-related decline in mental ability found in research. For example, he notes that due to decreased processing speed, an earlier task slows a later activity (e.g., if someone needs to keep some figures in memory, this will inhibit later decision-making speed). And slower processing accounts for the loss of information from an earlier task as a person performs a more recent task (e.g., a person may forget figures held in memory while trying to make a decision).

Kramer, Babiani, and Colcombe (2006, p. 59) say that processing speed "can often account for a large proportion of age-related variance across a wide assortment of tasks and environments."

Hartley (2006), in a careful review of the literature on speed of processing, traces the slowing of mental functioning to breakdown in the central nervous system with age. Breakdowns in the neural network lead to more travel time within the brain before a message registers. This may explain the generalized slowing of response, and it accounts for why older people do less well on speed trials.

Many studies of memory report that sensory decline leads to a decline in memory (Lindenberger, Scherer, & Baltes, 2003; McDaniel, Einstein, & Jacoby, 2008). Researchers propose that it takes more effort to remember something if a person has to cope with a sensory deficit (like hearing loss). Lindenberger and Baltes (1997, cited in Park, 2000) found that visual and auditory ability explained nearly all age-related declines on a series of psychological tests. Further research by this team controlled for education, social class, and income. The authors still found declines in cognition based on sensory decline. They say that this points to "a common factor or ensemble of factors," the decrease in the brain's structural and functional integrity.

Recent work supports the idea that changes in the brain lead to cognitive decline. Kramer and colleagues (2006, p. 65) report losses of gray and white matter in the brain. They go on to say that losses in prefrontal gray matter correlate with reduced performance on "frontally mediated executive tasks." And they conclude that changes in brain structure over time (e.g., atrophy of sections of the brain) predict declines in cognitive performance. Hartley (2006, p. 191) says that differences in processing speed may be due to "a general reduction in the functional intactness of the central nervous system."

Raz (2000) reviewed the literature on the relationship between mental performance and neural activity in the brain. Studies of encoding found that, compared with younger people, older people showed less activation or no activation in certain parts of the brain during these tests. The studies also found differences in how older and younger people's brains functioned when they worked on harder verbal recall tasks. Researchers have begun to describe the neural sources of memory changes in later life.

The *Handbook of Aging and Cognition* (Craik & Salthouse, 2008) contains several reviews of the literature on brain function and mental performance. Psychologists have also studied genetics, cellular function, and brain physiology to understand the effects of aging on mental ability. These studies show a growing interest among psychologists in the biology and physiology of mental functioning.

New Approaches to the Study of Mental Function

It appears that both the structure and function of the brain decline with age. But recent research using some of the latest technology has begun to modify this view of mental decline. Research conducted by Patricia Reuter-Lorenz and colleagues, for example, used positron emission tomographic (PET) technology to study the brains of older and younger subjects. They gave each group short-term and spatial memory tests.

They found that, compared to younger subjects, older subjects reacted more slowly and made more errors. But older adults used both sides of their brains to complete the tasks. Younger subjects used only one side of the brain. The older subjects naturally (and without their conscious awareness) drew on more mental processing ability when they needed it.

The researchers say that this compensation allows older people to continue to act effectively as they age. Reuter-Lorenz says, "If we didn't have the ability to compensate in part for that [decline in neural and metabolic efficiency] then the effects of ageing might be much worse" (cited in Larkin, 2001).

Functional neuroimaging studies show similar compensation for losses in the aging brain. Meade and Park (2009) report that older adults, compared to younger adults, recruit more parts of the brain to help with mental processing. The researchers say, "The flexibility inherent in this compensation suggests that older adults' neural function is dynamic and that plasticity remains in the neurocognitive system in late adulthood. Moreover, a limited behavioral literature indicates that older adults utilize different and often efficient strategies to compensate for declining cognition" (p. 37).

Flexibility in brain function points to a mental reserve capacity. Christensen and colleagues (Christensen, Anstey, Leach, & Mackinnon, 2008) call this the "brain reserve hypothesis." According to this view, high intelligence, education, an active, stimulating lifestyle, genetic makeup, or a physically larger brain provide a reserve capacity. This protects the person from the decline due to aging and from diseases of the brain.

Much of the research on the aging brain and mental performance focuses on why memory declines with age. But neuroimaging and brain scanning show a more complex picture of brain function. Some mental processes decline, but the older brain compensates for these losses. Older people use strategies to function well in everyday life in spite of changes in the brain. Research on mental function in everyday life gives a more complex and a more positive view of mental potential in later life.

Memory and Everyday Life

Laboratory studies raise an important question: How well do these findings describe how an older person functions in everyday life? The answer: They don't describe it very well. We know that in the laboratory, older people, compared with younger people, do less well under time pressure or when they have to learn information that they see as irrelevant (Hess, Rosenberg, & Waters, 2001). But memory studies have poor ecological validity (they do not translate well from laboratory to life) (Park & Gutchess, 2000; Rendell & Thomson, 2002).

For one thing, everyday problems often lack a correct answer. For example, a question like "How can I best manage on my current income?" has no simple answer. Also, as Berg (2008, p. 218) says, "Everyday problem solving draws not only on the cognitive abilities of adults but also on their emotional, interpersonal, and physiological regulatory systems."

Solving a problem in everyday life may involve emotion, social sensitivity, and coping with stress. Everyday problems can occur over a long period of time (e.g., how to relate to grandchildren). Morrow (2009) says that "research rooted in meaningful, familiar situations at work and home presents a more encouraging view [when compared to laboratory studies]."

Phillips and her colleagues (Phillips, Kliegel, & Martin, 2006) studied two groups of 39 subjects each. One group ages 22–31 had a mean age of 24.8. The second group ages 60–80 had a mean age of 69.5. The researchers asked each group to engage in two computerized tasks. One was a traditional laboratory task that entailed abstract planning. The second was a planning task that entailed running a number of errands in a made-up situation with specific constraints. The researchers found that, as expected, subjects showed a decline in performance based on age for the abstract planning task. But the researchers found no relationship between age and performance on the more ecologically valid errand-planning task.

The researchers conclude that a decrease in information processing speed and education account for the decrease in performance by the older subjects on the abstract task. They say that task-related knowledge and experience helped older subjects compensate for decreases in processing speed in the errand planning exercise. In other words, in real-life situations older people draw on their experience and can perform as well as younger people.

Some studies have looked directly at what older people remember about the world around them. These studies have found less of the memory deficit reported in laboratory research. Craik (2000) reports that **semantic memory**, the store of factual information, shows little decline with age. Hoyer and Verhaeghen (2006, p. 216) say that "older adults do not show a deficit on [vocabulary] tasks, but rather an advantage." They go on to say that "vocabulary measures probably underestimate the breadth and depth of knowledge and development of word meanings and language accumulated through years of experience and use." Only after age 90 do decreases in word knowledge appear. The more automatic the recall (for example, driving a car in a person's own neighborhood), the better the older person will perform (Park & Gutchess, 2000).

Allen and colleagues (Allen, Bucur, & Murphy, 2006) report a number of studies that support a process-specific effect of aging on mental activity. They find that although complex problems lead to poorer performance by older workers, this applies to only some tasks. On tasks that have to do with word recognition, for example, older people do as well as or better than younger people. These researchers report similar findings for math problems—probably because older people have a lifetime of experience with arithmetic. The researchers conclude that some mental processes decline with age while others remain stable. "Therefore," they say, "the aging process is not comprised simply of cognitive decline."

Ackerman (2008, pp. 476–477) reports on a study of 228 adults between ages 21 and 62 with at least a bachelor's degree. The study found that "older adults tended to perform better on most of the knowledge tests, except for those in the domain of physical sciences (e.g., Chemistry, Physics)." Older adults showed superior results, when compared to younger adults, on knowledge of the humanities (literature, art, music) and civics (government, history, law). A lifetime of accumulated knowledge remains available to older adults. The research concludes that "age in and of itself is not a particularly important determinant of individual differences in domain knowledge."

Research also shows that the use of memory aids (such as the use of a notebook) can significantly improve memory performance. Park (2000, p. 11) says that "environmental supports" lead to improved recall. For example, an older person will do better on a multiple-choice test (with all the possible answers displayed) than on a free-recall test with no cues. Supports reduce the amount of mental processing or resource use. And this leads to better recall.

Research on people outside the lab gives a more complex picture of mental potential in later life. Cerella and his colleagues (Cerella, Rybash, Hoyer, & Commons,1993), for example, report compensation for decline, positive effects of physical exercise on memory, and benefits from training. Bugos and colleagues (Bugos, Perlstein, McCrae, Brophy, & Bedenbaugh, 2007) found that sensory-motor training (learning to play the piano) led to significantly improved mental function. Some studies of training programs (Nyberg et al., 2003; Draganski et al., 2004, cited in Small & McEvoy, 2008) report increased brain activation and gray matter increases. These "studies suggest that focal training can result in changes in the structure and function of the brain" (Small & McEvoy, 2008, p. 582). Other studies show that social engagement leads to improved mental ability (Stine-Morrow, Parisi, Morrow, Greene, & Park, 2007).

This research shows that physical changes measured in the lab and through tests give a limited view of mental potential in later life. Older people, in the real world, in the absence of pathology, show resilience and flexibility in the use of their minds. These findings also show that a person can modify and improve mental performance in everyday life by engaging in stimulating and challenging activity. Analyses of specific mental processes "opens the possibility for interventions to help older adults compensate in domains that do show age-related decline" (Small & McEvoy, 2008, p. 591).

Experience and Mental Function in Later Life

Studies of familiar problem-solving tasks, for example, find that older people and younger people can do equally well. Researcher Neil Charness has done some of the pioneering work on the study of mental performance outside the lab. His early work focused on younger and older chess players' problem-solving abilities. He found that older players had more difficulty than younger players at the same skill level in recalling positions accurately. He attributes this difficulty to older players' poorer retrieval ability, a finding that fits with the other lab-based studies on memory.

But when Charness evaluated game-playing performance, he found that skill level, not age, determined a player's ability. Older players did as well as younger players of the same skill level. "Given the retrieval deficits associated with aging," Charness asks, "why is there no deficit in molar [overall] problem-solving performance?" (1981, pp. 34–35).

Mireles and Charness (2002) provide an answer to this question. They found that in a chess recall task, people with a larger knowledge base achieved more accuracy on the recall task. The researchers say that preexisting knowledge can overcome the effects of systemic slowing due to neural noise. In a later study, Roring and Charness (2007) found support for this view. They compared chess players with different levels of skill at the start of their careers. Players who had a high skill level at the start of their careers showed a slower rate of decline as they aged.

Recent studies support this view. "Expert performance," Morrow reports, "depends on highly organized knowledge structures in long-term memory that enable experts to view problems at an abstract level" (pp. 50–51). Charness and Krampe (2008, p. 248) say that "having a large vocabulary of patterns linked to plausible moves can compensate for age-related declines in fluid abilities."

In the world outside the lab, nonexperts as well as experts use many techniques to perform effectively (Hoyer & Verhaeghen, 2006). Park and Meade (2006) say that a person who needs to remember to take medication may chain that activity to another routine. For example, he or she may take the medication routinely at breakfast or just before bed. Liu and Park (2003) found that people who linked the process of monitoring their blood sugar level to breakfast, for example, increased the accuracy of their monitoring.

Consider the case of Mrs. Zeno. She has just returned from the doctor. He told her she needs to take a calcium pill to strengthen her bones. She's to take the pill with breakfast. How does she remember this important task? She puts the pill bottle near the cup she uses for her morning orange juice. She uses a simple rule to guide her action: "If I place something (the pills) near something else (the juice glass), in plain view, I'm likely to remember to do something with them (the pills)."

Expert chess players do this, too. They develop rules of thumb to guide their play. The beginner at chess learns a rule of thumb like "control the center." This provides a simple rule to guide play in the complex middle of the game. Experts at chess use more and more sophisticated rules of thumb as they study the game, gain experience, and grow in their expertise.

Consider Mrs. Zeno again. She not only put the pills near her juice to build it into her routine. She wrote a note and pasted it on the refrigerator. After a month or so, the pill-taking has turned into a morning routine, and she takes the note off the fridge. She's become an "expert" at this task and no longer needs to keep this in memory. She just follows her new routine.

Nearly everyone makes lists, whether to create a shopping list or a daily "to do" list for work. This technique takes the load off working memory and frees the mind for other demands. Older people can learn this and other techniques for improving memory and performance.

The study of experts shows the plasticity or flexibility of the mind at every age. It also brings to light some of the methods experts use to compensate for the decline in mental speed and function. Krampe and Ericsson (1996) studied piano masters. They found that on standard motor tasks these masters showed the slowing in performance found in many other studies. But, as they age, on keyboard exercises piano masters show continued ability. These masters maintain their abilities through deliberate practice. They spend large amounts of time focusing on repetition and refinement of their technique.

Carstensen, Mikels, and Mather (2006, p. 344) say that "such expertise can even offset cognitive decline." On tasks unrelated to their expertise, experts show the same age-related decline in memory and performance as nonexperts. But, Liu and Park (2003) say, older people who keep up their mental abilities can compensate for losses in mental functioning. They may put more effort into a task, they may draw on experience and skill, or they may develop new skills. Charness and Krampe (2008) say that practice and pattern recognition best explain the performance of experts.

You can think of practice and repetition as a way to make a mental activity automatic. The more automatic the activity, like driving a car in one's own neighborhood, the better the older person's performance. Poon (1985, p. 435) says that "evidence to date shows minimal differences in memory for familiar discourse materials that may be found in the everyday environment." Studies find that older people can maintain their ability to remember general knowledge of the world and specific knowledge related to their expertise. These mental abilities can increase through adulthood.

Craik (2000) found that semantic memory, our store of factual information, shows little decline with age. On IQ tests, for example, older and younger people show little difference in their knowledge. Verhaeghen and Cerella (2008, p. 147) reviewed many studies of mental function in later life. They found at least three different effects of aging on mental function. "Lexical tasks [related to reading and word recognition]," they say, "are largely spared from the ill effects of aging; simple decisions show modest age-related slowing; spatial tasks are slowed to a greater degree. . . . The picture of cognitive aging that emerges from our analyses," the researchers say, "is both simpler and more positive than that painted in typical review articles: Apart from spatial processes and tasks demanding dual task set maintenance, no cognitive tasks appear to show deficits beyond those seen in simple decisions."

Older people also have a good memory for past personal events (Zacks, Hasher, & Li, 2000). The more automatic the recall (e.g., driving a car in the person's own neighborhood), the better the older person will perform (Park & Gutchess, 2000). Poon (1985, p. 435) says that "in general, evidence to date shows minimal differences in memory for familiar discourse materials that may be found in the everyday environment."

Studies also find that older people maintain their ability to remember general knowledge of the world and specific knowledge related to their expertise. These mental abilities increase through adulthood. Studies of prospective memory (the ability to remember something to be done in the future) find similar results. These studies find that older people outperform younger people. For example, older people do better at remembering to carry out a task like mailing back a postcard or telephoning the researcher in the future. In particular, when a person had to remember to do something at a certain time (e.g., take a pill before going to bed), they showed no memory deficit (McDaniel et al., 2008).

One study discouraged people from using external memory aids (Kvavilashvili & Fisher, 2007). This study still found no age-related declines in time-based memory tasks. The study asked older and younger participants on a Monday to call the researcher on Sunday at a certain time. They found that 81% of the older adults called on time. Only 68% of the younger adults did. Both groups found that cues throughout the week (e.g., a ringing telephone) reminded them of

their task. Park and Meade say that studies of everyday memory need to take into account the person, the demands of the task (e.g., whether it is a new task or a routine task), and the environment.

Dixon and Cohen (2001) say that **competence** (a person's skill at real-world tasks) can improve with age. Research shows that a simple practice such as note taking reduces the pressure on working memory and leads to better comprehension and better recall (Morrow, 2003). The researchers go on to say that older people often show more competence in daily life than psychological tests suggest.

Adams and colleagues (Adams, Smith, Pasupathi, & Vitolo, 2002) studied how well older and younger women recalled a story that the researchers asked them to tell. They found that younger storytellers showed better recall than older storytellers when they told their stories to an experimenter. But they found no differences in recall when the older and younger storytellers told their stories to children. Also, the older storytellers, more than younger storytellers, adjusted the complexity of their retelling to suit their listeners. The researchers say that memory research needs to take social context into account when comparing older and younger subjects.

Bäckman and colleagues (2000, p. 501) summarize the literature on memory and aging:

> No form of memory appears to be fully resistant to the negative influence of human aging. Thus, age-related deficits may be observed in tasks assessing implicit memory . . ., semantic memory . . ., primary memory . . ., working memory . . ., and episodic memory. . . . However it is important to note that the size of age-related deficits and the consistency with which such deficits are observed varies systematically across different forms of memory. Specifically, *age deficits tend to be large and robust for measures of episodic memory and working memory, smaller and more contingent on demand characteristics in tasks assessing implicit and semantic memory, and even smaller in primary memory tasks* [emphasis added].

Studies show that memory in old age varies by individual (education and gender), lifestyle (social activity), and health. Some people show greater decreases in memory than do others. Also, research shows that older people have a reserve mental capacity. They can improve memory performance by using memory cues and by training. Salthouse and Craik (2000, p. 701) say that researchers should look at ways that older people can put off the declines that come with age and "optimize [their] mental capacities."

Memory and Everyday Life: The Study of Reading

Laboratory research shows declines in working memory as tasks grow more complex. But Meyer and Pollard (2006, p. 237) say that studies of older people in everyday life or on the job "have failed to find predicted age by task complexity interactions." The study of reading shows some of the ways that older people compensate for losses in processing in everyday life.

Reading serves as an important skill in modern society. Older adults read newspapers, magazines, prescriptions, Web pages, and novels. Meyer and Pollard (2006) reviewed the research on reading in later life. They found that in many cases older people outperformed younger people.

Older adults performed best when they had a better vocabulary than younger readers, when the study measured broad comprehension (rather than a list of unrelated sentences), when the text related to past experience and knowledge, and when the adults could pace themselves. Longitudinal studies showed growth in comprehension through late middle age and only a small decrease after that (until late old age).

In general, older people compensate for losses in mental processing speed by using stronger lighting in everyday settings, using eyeglasses or laser surgery, changing reading speed or rereading passages, and using a reading style that emphasizes themes, concepts, and information linked to existing knowledge. Meyer and Pollard (2006, p. 238) say that this style suits "an experienced solver [of problems] with many available structures of knowledge."

Meyer and Pollard (2006) taught older readers how to recognize the structure of a text and how to use the signals writers give to readers. In one case, a 66-year-old woman improved her recall by learning these skills. Meyer and Pollard (p. 246) say that "she more than doubled her ability to remember information from her reading." This woman went on to teach this strategy to others over the next 6 years. During that time "she maintained her mastery of the strategy and high level of text recall."

Spirduso and colleagues (2005, p. 203) say, "As the passage of time blunts efficiency and reduces speed of processing individuals inevitably develop strategies to cope with these losses; thus for many years the loss of function in a highly practiced,

healthy individual is so slight it is unnoticeable." Spirduso and colleagues give the real-world example of an older person waiting to get luggage from an airport carousel. The older person positions himself or herself in order to see the luggage in advance and have time to move forward to grab it. The younger person will need less time to make this move. From an observer's point of view, the young and older person look equally competent. But the older person compensates for a slower response time and has prepared for this movement.

Meyer and Pollard (2006, p. 238) summarize the research on reading. They say that research often focuses on decline in mental ability, "but despite these declines, older adults are resilient and able to productively use information gathered from text." In some cases, when the text relies on past knowledge or holds information of special interest to the older reader, older people perform better than younger readers.

Summary of Memory Research

Laboratory studies reveal a systematic decline in memory with age. But the tests themselves in part account for these results. Studies find that differences in educational background, test conditions, and lack of experience at encoding can all influence performance. Some studies show that an older person's fear of failure on memory tests also leads to poor performance. Researchers call this "stereotype threat" (Hess, 2006). Rahhal, Hasher, and Colombe (2001), for example, found that test instructions that focus on memory remind people of declines in mental ability. This can lower a person's score. Hess (2006, p. 394) reports that "differences in performance were essentially eliminated" when test instructions said positive things about aging and memory.

Research shows that a supportive test environment leads to improvements in older subjects' ability to learn paired words. Supports can include guidance in how to encode information, testing people on familiar topics, giving people control over the speed of learning, encouraging practice, and providing external cues to help learning (Zacks et al., 2000; Carstensen et al., 2006). All of these supports lead to better performance.

Laboratory research has explored mental processes in detail. And this has added to our understanding of human development. But the results of these studies can support the stereotype of memory loss and forgetfulness in later life. Studies of memory in everyday life show that healthy older people function well throughout life. And in many cases older people display unique mental abilities (such as wisdom) as they age.

Intelligence

Intelligence refers to the mind's ability to function. Psychologists have developed tests to measure intelligence, and studies of intelligence mirror the research on memory. According to Woodruff-Pak (1989), the study of adult intelligence went through four phases. In phase I (1920 to 1950), researchers believed that intelligence declined steeply with age. In phase II (late 1950s to mid-1960s), researchers placed more emphasis on stability in intelligence in later life. In phase III (late 1960s to mid-1970s), research on improving intelligence test scores met with some success. In phase IV (late 1970s to present), researchers developed a new understanding of intelligence. This includes the study of wisdom and new methods used to explore this concept.

Most intelligence studies take place in a laboratory and compare performance of younger and older people on intelligence tests. Berg and Sternberg (2003, p. 104) call this the "psychometric perspective." This perspective has dominated the field. Studies up to the 1960s used cross-sectional methods. They showed a peak in intelligence around age 30 and a steady decline after that. Later longitudinal studies showed a decline as well, but only after age 60 (Schaie, 1990).

Intelligence tests assess a number of mental skills. These include skill in vocabulary, comprehension, and performance (e.g., the mental rotation of a figure). Studies showed that older people do less well on performance scale scores than on verbal scale scores. Botwinick (1984, p. 254) says this "classic aging pattern, relative maintenance of function in verbal skills as compared to performance skills, has been seen many times with a variety of different populations."

In the 1960s, Horn and Cattell (1966, 1967; Cattell, 1963) proposed a multidimensional model of intelligence. They described two types of mental abilities: fluid intelligence and crystallized intelligence. Their model proposed that these two types of intelligence differ in their rate of decline with age.

Fluid intelligence refers to activities like creative design, quick response to a question, or mental rearrangement of facts. This type of intelligence relies on how efficiently the central nervous system works.

Crystallized intelligence refers to abilities like vocabulary, association of past and present ideas, and technical ability. It depends on a person's education or store of information.

Researchers suggest that fluid intelligence declines after age 14. Fluid intelligence includes many of the processes linked to memory, such as organizing and storing information (Kramer et al., 2006). Crystallized intelligence, on the other hand, refers to information already learned. This increases throughout adulthood as a person gains more knowledge and skill. Studies found declines in crystallized intelligence only after age 70 (Horn, 1982).

This model explains the differences between older people's verbal and performance scores. Verbal scales measure crystallized intelligence; performance tests measure fluid intelligence. Fluid intelligence may follow the decline of the biological system from the teen years on. Crystallized intelligence shows stable intelligence scores and even increased scores with age (Park, 2000; Kramer et al., 2006).

Improving Mental Performance

Some research explores the older person's ability to improve intellectual functioning. Studies show that older people who live in good health and in a challenging environment score better on intelligence tests than those who do not. People who read books and newspapers, who travel and talk with friends, keep their minds fresh. Mental stimulation may protect the brain from decline. Or it may help the brain compensate for losses in some abilities (Snowdon, 2001).

Researchers now think that individuals can modify their intellectual functioning as they age. Baltes (1997) developed a model of mental development in later life that he calls selective optimization with compensation (SOC) (see details of this model in Chapter 4). He says that people who age well select tasks that will likely lead to success. They keep up (or optimize) the skills they have. And they compensate for losses by gaining new skills and knowledge. The SOC model recognizes that aging brings change. But it also shows that people can adapt to changes and improve their mental ability as they age. Riediger, Li, and Lindenberger (2006, pp. 296, 300) say that "people themselves influence their development within the range of available opportunities." They refer to this as "active life management." Berg and Sternberg (2003; also Zarit, 2009) say that greater use of selective optimization may lead to more successful aging and greater life satisfaction.

BOX 5.1
SUGGESTIONS FOR MENTAL EXERCISE

A number of activities can help keep mature minds sharp. Dr. Gene Cohen (2005) notes that activities like the following are based on "the latest findings from neuroscience."

- Do crossword puzzles or games that challenge the mind.
- Join a book discussion group at a local bookstore.
- Go on a trip, see and experience new foods, new sights, new cultures.
- Take a course on a new subject that could develop into a hobby.
- Read magazines or books in fields new to you.
- Volunteer at a nonprofit organization.
- Write your memoirs, start a blog, keep a diary.

- Start or maintain an exercise routine.
- Learn a new sport.
- Learn a new computer program, like Photoshop.
- Become the family historian, research your genealogy.

Most of these activities provide mental stimulation, require creativity, engage a person's curiosity, and put the person in contact with others. Some of these activities require quiet reflection and awareness of a person's inner life. By choosing varied activities, a person can maintain mental ability, develop new abilities, express his or her personality, and expand social relations as the person ages.

What activities do you think you will prefer in later life? Do you know any older people who engage in these activities? What effect does this have on their well-being, personality, and mental function?

Baltes and Willis (1982, pp. 120–121; also Willis, Schaie, & Martin, 2009) report that "people can learn to make better use of their minds at any age. The logical approach [to observed decrements in mental functioning in late life] might be the development of compensatory education programs at about the time of retirement." Kramer and colleagues (2006), in a review of studies on cognitive training, find support for this view. They say that in some cases "older adults can achieve greater gains from formal cognitive training interventions than their younger counterparts."

NEW MODELS OF MENTAL ABILITY IN LATER LIFE

Psychologists in the past tended to view life as a hill: mental ability increases, reaches a plateau, and then declines. But this view has begun to change. Researchers have conducted studies of wisdom, and this offers a different view of psychological change in later life.

Paul B. Baltes, Director of Berlin's Max Planck Institute for Human Development and Education, has conducted some of the most respected research on intelligence. He notes that two concepts have led to changes in his thinking about mental ability in later life (Baltes & Baltes, 1990). First, research shows variability between individuals. In general, younger people outperform older people on intelligence tests. But on a given measure, some older people perform better than younger people (McDaniel et al., 2008; Ackerman, 2008).

Second, research shows that people adapt and change at every stage of life. Research has found **plasticity** in brain function. Plasticity refers to a person's unexpressed potential or the ability to gain new mental abilities (Willis et al., 2009). The latest research shows that older people have reserve mental capacities. Studies show that training, practice, and education can enhance mental ability in old age. Dixon and Cohen (2001, p. 138) say that these findings offer a "cautiously optimistic perspective, with emphases on resilience and adaptation in late life."

The Study of Wisdom in Later Life

A person who displays wisdom has insight into life's conditions and shows good judgment. This person gives good advice. Younger people may do better than older people in problem solving in a laboratory or classroom. They can answer clearly structured problems faster than older people. But older people may do better at *problem finding*. Older people have a greater ability to shape and solve a problem in a less-defined situation (Shedlock & Cornelius, 2003).

"Chris Calloway working on a podcast that celebrates the music of her father, Cab Calloway, with John Biethan, a tech expert. Some older people use their own computers and inexpensive webcams to create blogs that record their personal history."

Baltes (1992) reports that older people get higher scores than younger people on problems related to real-life dilemmas. More than half of the top responses, he says, come from people over age 60.

Baltes and colleagues (Scheibe, Kunzmann, & Baltes, 2007, cited in Knight & Laidlaw, 2009) list five criteria of wisdom:

1. A store of factual information about human nature;
2. Rich procedural knowledge about handling life's problems;
3. An awareness of life's contexts and how they change over the life span;
4. Understanding the relativism of values and tolerance for others; and
5. Understanding of how to deal with uncertainty.

These abilities make wise older people good decision makers and advisors.

Montgomery, Barber, & McKee (2002) studied wisdom in a group of people ages 60 to 88. They found that wise people guided others, had knowledge and experience, and applied moral principles. Ardelt (2000) found that wisdom in older women led to greater life satisfaction, better health, and better family relationships. Kramer (2003, p. 132) says that a wise person has an "awareness of the relativistic, uncertain, and paradoxical nature of reality." This person interacts with others "in a way that does not put those others on the defensive" (p. 133).

Research on decision-making supports this view. Marsiske and Margrett (2006, p. 317) say that in the real world, when people make decisions, they "consider their own preferences, values, and feelings as well as those of their social partners and cultural context." For example, older adults used both emotion- and action-oriented coping strategies in problem solving. The researchers say that this attention to the complexity of life shows a higher order of thinking than purely rational problem solving.

Wisdom allows a person to critically view cultural illusions and to act on the basis of universal principles. A series of studies conducted by Grossman and colleagues (2010) compared the responses of younger and older people to conflict situations. In one of the studies they asked a random sample of 247 younger and older people to read stories about conflicts between ethnic groups in a foreign country. They asked the subjects how they expected the conflicts to develop or get resolved.

Compared to younger subjects, older subjects showed flexibility in their thinking and emphasized the need for multiple perspectives. They saw the value of compromise and the limits of knowledge. The researchers conclude that "social reasoning improves with age despite a decline in fluid intelligence." They say that

---

BOX 5.2
WISDOM IN LATER LIFE

Socrates, in *The Republic,* says that he likes to talk to older people. They have gone along a path that all of us will one day follow. Their years have given them knowledge about life and aging. Some might call it wisdom. Consider the following thoughts on aging by some thoughtful older people.

═══

Art Blake, a retired judge from Jamaica, says that recently he attended the funeral of a friend. He flew back to Jamaica and went directly to the church from the airport. His plane landed early, so he arrived at the church before anyone else. "I watched as the people arrived," he says. "Many of them I knew from my childhood; we went to school and grew up together. These are all old people, I thought. Then I thought, 'I too must look like this.' But I couldn't see it in myself. I shave every day and I don't see my age. But I could see it in them. . . . The mind plays tricks on you."

═══

Art serves as the legal advisor to an education program for older people and sits on the advisory board of a university certification program. "We want to be young," Art says. "We use creams to smooth out the wrinkles. But this is the most natural process. We cannot help but get old."

═══

Bertrand Russell developed new interests as he aged. He began his career as a mathematician, moved on to philosophy, then in late old age turned to political and social issues. At age 80 he said that the best way to overcome old age "is to make your interests gradually wider and more impersonal, until bit by bit the walls of the ego recede, and your life becomes increasingly merged in the universal life. An individual human existence should be like a river—small at first, narrowly contained within its banks, and rushing passionately past boulders and over waterfalls. Gradually the river grows wider, the banks recede, the waters flow more quietly, and in the end, without any visible break, they become merged in the sea and painlessly lose their individual being" (cited in Puner, 1979).

---

older people could play an important role in legal disputes, counseling, and intergroup negotiations.

Baltes and his colleagues' later work on wisdom, curiously, found little empirical support for the unique expression of wisdom by older people. They found that expressions of wisdom could occur from the teen years onward. Brugman (2006, p. 449), in a review of the research, reports that "in most empirical studies thus far no age differences [between younger and older people] have been found."

Some researchers propose that wisdom exists as a "potential" in later life—some people realize this potential and some don't. Knight and Laidlaw (2009, p. 696) say that "physical aging, societal ageism, and psychological disorders" can keep someone from developing wisdom in later life. These authors say that a person can develop a skill at making wise decisions. An encouraging environment and supportive others can promote wisdom in older people.

Cohen (2005, pp. 36–37) gives further insight into the wisdom that can develop with age. He calls the growth of wisdom in later life **developmental intelligence**. He considers this an "advanced style of cognition." Cohen describes three "styles" that characterize this type of thinking:

1. *Relativistic thinking:* An awareness that knowledge is not absolute. Context can affect knowledge and understanding.
2. *Dualistic thinking:* The ability to hold mutually exclusive ideas in the mind at the same time. A person can suspend judgment while trying to resolve contradictions.
3. *Systematic thinking:* The ability to take a broad view of a situation or a system of knowledge.

Older people who display wisdom show more skill in managing everyday life. Society could use their broad perspective and flexible thinking to redefine problems that escape technical solutions.

Plasticity and Cognitive Reserve

For many years scientists and the general public believed that the brain lost neurons with age. This seemed to explain the decline in mental function over time. Finch (cited in Guttman, 2008) says,

> Historically the subject was thought to be very simple: that brain neurons were lost from birth onwards. Now it is really clear that if you don't have a specific disease that causes loss of nerve cells, then most, if not all, of the neurons remain healthy until you die. That's a big change, and it has only come about in the last 10 years.

The most recent research shows that the body not only preserves brain cells, it can create new neurons and new neuronal connections at every age. Scientists call this *neurogenesis*. Cohen (2005) says that "our brains never lose the ability to learn . . . brain development throughout life increases coordination within the brain. This leads to more complex thinking that we call wisdom."

Cohen (2005) lists four findings from recent brain research that describe mental growth and development in later life:

1. The brain reorganizes itself in response to new information and experience.
2. Brain cells grow in later life.
3. The brain's emotional centers grow more balanced with age.
4. Compared to younger people, older people use both halves of the brain more equally.

We now know that the brain rewires connections in response to demands. Maguire, Rackowiak, and Firth (1997) report that London cab drivers show the development of neural connections in that part of the brain that makes spatial relations. Likewise, musicians show brain development in the parts of the brain related to tone and pitch (Cohen, 2005).

Stern (2002, 2007) studied what he calls the brain's "cognitive reserve." The term *cognitive reserve* originally referred to people with dementia who performed better than expected in everyday life. Stern (2002, p. 448) expanded that view. He says, "The concept of reserve should be extended to encompass variation in healthy individuals' performance, particularly when they must perform at their maximum capacity." Stern says that "how we use our brains during our lives influences the amount of cognitive reserve that we have. . . . [Cognitive reserve] is malleable and changes over the course of our life, depending on innate factors and subsequent exposures."

Education and literacy in particular seem to create a large cognitive reserve. "What we can be sure of," Stern says, "is that over a very long period of time, exposure such as education and leisure activities do contribute to reserve" (Christensen et al., 2008; De la Vega & Zambrano, 2003). But he cautions that research has yet to show what specific activities increase cognitive reserve. We can't say, for example, that a person who takes a photography class or solves Sudoku puzzles will increase his or her cognitive reserve.

Some researchers believe that cognitive reserve can protect people from the ravages of Alzheimer's disease (AD). Bennett and colleagues (2006) conducted a community-based study of people with AD. They found that some people with Alzheimer's brain pathology continue to function without impairment. The researchers propose that these people have a "neural reserve." They looked at the backgrounds of these people and found that education and social connections may create this reserve.

Willis and colleagues (2009) say that the research on plasticity (based on experiments and interventions) and the research on **cognitive reserve** (based on descriptive examples) come to some of the same conclusions: (1) Both perspectives emphasize the person's active role in developing a reserve and compensating for losses; (2) both recognize individual differences in reserve capacity; (3) both perspectives recognize that prior conditions in a person's life (e.g., education) influence reserve; (4) both recognize the limits to reserve and plasticity; and finally, (5) both perspectives believe that a person can enhance plasticity and reserve. This last point has led researchers to explore programs and activities that might draw on reserve and enhance plasticity.

Stimulating the Brain for Growth in Later Life

The research on plasticity and cognitive reserve points toward interventions that might increase or at least stabilize mental function in later life. Mentally stimulating activities like crossword puzzles, taking classes, or reading might enable the brain to compensate for disease. Barnes and colleagues (Barnes, Tager, Satariano, & Yaffe, 2004) studied literacy and mental ability in a group of white, well-educated older people (mean age 76). They found a strong relationship between literacy and all measures of mental ability in their study. The higher the rate of literacy, the higher the test scores on mental functioning.

Science has yet to find the precise connection between education and social interaction and cognitive or neural reserve. But it may be that educated people and those with strong social connections make more use of their cognitive functions. They challenge their brains with new information and creative activity. This may generate neuron growth that slows or circumvents the damage done to the brain by AD.

Carmi Schooler, a researcher at the National Institute of Mental Health, reports that "doing intellectually challenging things on and off the job are significant and meaningful" (Schooler, 2009, p. 31). Schooler concludes that "even in old age, carrying out self-directed complex tasks has a positive effect on intellectual processes."

Schooler (2009, p. 32) says that engagement in complex tasks is similar to mental aerobics. And even in later life, complex tasks "build the capacity to deal with the intellectual challenges that complex environments provide." By contrast, a focus on one activity such as working on crossword puzzles does not lead to general cognitive improvement. Puzzles and games do no harm. But more general engagement in mentally stimulating activities and relationships leads to better overall mental function. The person who focuses on only one activity does not appear to gain this broader benefit.

These findings open the door to training programs that can keep mental functioning strong as we age. Basak and colleagues (Basak, Boot, Voss, & Kramer, 2008) conducted a controlled experiment to test the effects of training, using video games to improve cognitive function. They chose a group of 40 older adults who said they had not spent any time playing video games in the past 2 years. Half the group with an average age of 70 got 15 one-and-a-half-hour training sessions with a strategy video game. The training lasted 4 to 5 weeks. The other group with an average age of 69 got no training. They served as a control for the experiment.

The experimental group showed improvements when compared to the control group on a number of psychological functions, including task switching, working memory, visual short-term memory, and reasoning. This still leaves the question of whether these results translate into better function in everyday life. But they point in the right direction.

Wilson and colleagues (2002) conducted a long-term study of nuns and priests. The researchers found that people who spent a significant amount of time on information processing activities showed about half the rate of Alzheimer's disease (AD) as those who did not. Activities included reading the newspaper and playing puzzle games. This study suggests that people who continue to challenge and stimulate their brains maintain and may even strengthen their mental function as they age. These and other mentally challenging activities may create a more responsive brain that is resistant to AD and its effects.

All of these studies show that the brain needs stimulation and challenge as a person ages. "The brain wants to learn," says Michael Merzenich (2006), a neurobiologist at University of California, San Francisco. "It wants to be engaged as a learning machine." The brain needs new challenges to stay active and to grow. Merzenich says, "The brain requires active continuous learning. . . . It requires change, and that change requires that you acquire new skills and abili-

ties, new hobbies, and activities that require the brain to remodel itself. That's the key."

Dixon and Cohen (2001, p. 138) say that the large body of research on mental plasticity offers a "cautiously optimistic perspective, with emphases on resilience and adaptation in late life."

An Effective Training Program

Willis and colleagues (2006) recently conducted the most rigorous test of training on mental function. The National Institute on Aging supported this study with a $15 million grant. Willis and her colleagues studied 2,802 people with an average age of 73 for 5 years. All of these people lived in the community, and all had normal mental ability at the start of the study. The program was called Advanced Cognitive Training for Independent and Vital Elderly, or ACTIVE.

The study randomly divided the participants into four groups. One group got memory training. This group learned methods for remembering word lists, story ideas, and details. A second group got training on reasoning. This group learned how to find patterns in a letter or word series. They then learned how to judge the next item in the series. A third group got training on speed of processing information. This group learned to identify objects on a computer screen in short time frames. At the same time they needed to locate another item on the screen. The fourth group got no training. The people in the training groups got up to 10 one-hour training sessions on a computer. The training took place over 5 to 6 weeks. About 700 of the 1,877 people took a 75-minute "booster" session after 1 year and then after 3 years beyond the training.

Researchers tested the mental function of participants before the study, just after the training, and yearly for 5 years. Just after the training, 87% of the speed-training group showed improvement, 74% of the reasoning group showed improvement, and 26% of the memory group showed improvement. These groups showed improvement after 5 years when compared to the control group.

The reasoning and speed-training groups that got the booster training showed the most benefit. Willis says that,

> The improvements seen after the training roughly counteract the degree of decline in cognitive performance that we would expect to see over a seven- to 14-year period among older people without dementia.
>
> After five years, all three intervention groups reported less difficulty than the control group in tasks such as preparing meals, managing money and doing housework.

Those who received speed-of-processing training and follow-up booster training scored better on how quickly and accurately they could find items on a pantry shelf, make change, read medicine dosing instructions, place telephone calls and react to road traffic signs.

But only the effect of reasoning training on self-reported performance of daily tasks was statistically significant. In short, the study showed real but modest results in maintaining everyday mental functioning due to training.

This study shows that training can delay or compensate for mental decline. But the study also shows the limitations of short-term training, even with follow-up sessions. The results of this study and others (Small & McEvoy, 2008, p. 581; also Ball et al., 2002) suggest that training works best when it targets a specific skill. "The main limitation of this type of intervention [ACTIVE] is the lack of transfer from the trained cognitive ability domain to other abilities." Dr. Richard Suzman, director of the NIA's Behavioral and Social Research Program, sums up the findings. He says that "relatively brief targeted cognitive exercises can produce durable changes in the skills taught." But, he says that he "would now like to see studies aimed at producing more generalized changes."

The result of this study, other studies of training (Schooler, 2009), and studies of expertise (Charness & Krampe, 2008) show that training can lead to better mental functioning in later life. But the results of training may not translate into improvements in other abilities. The wider engagement in social life and a challenging environment seems to have the best effect on a person's mental function as they age. This challenges individuals to find social activities that engage their minds. And it challenges society to provide meaningful roles to keep older people engaged in social life.

BOX 5.3
THE NUN'S STUDY

Researcher David Snowdon began one of the most unusual and creative research studies of human mental performance. In 1986 he visited the School Sisters of Notre Dame in Mankato, Minnesota. He asked whether they would take part in a research project. The project would study older Sisters' mental ability. After some consultation, the Sisters agreed to take part in this study. They felt that they could continue their mission of education by contributing to knowledge during their lives and after their deaths. The study began with 675 participants ages 75 to 102.

They agreed to have their mental function probed and studied. This project became known as "The Nun Study"—a multidisciplinary longitudinal study of mental potential in later life. In particular the study focused on the incidence of Alzheimer's disease (AD) and its potential causes. The National Institutes of Health has provided more than $5 million in grants to this project. In addition, a number of private foundations have supported the research.

The Sisters made an ideal focus for study. Snowdon explained to the head Sister that the convent provided a controlled environment. All of the Sisters lived the same lifestyle, ate the same food, did roughly the same work, lived celibate lives, and so forth. The similarity in their lives would allow him and his research team to tease out the effects of any differences in their backgrounds that might account for the emergence of AD.

Snowdon gained a unique opportunity, he says, when he discovered the convent's archives. The archives contained detailed personal data, medical records, work histories, and writings by the sisters. It documented their lives from the time they entered the convent as young women until their late old age and death. The archives gave detailed accounts of individual differences throughout their lives. Researchers could use this information to judge the impact of earlier life experiences on the nuns' mental health in old age.

Snowdon added one other advantage to this study. He got permission from the nuns to have their brains autopsied after death to assess the advance of AD. This allowed him and a team of researchers to study the life conditions that might have led to a nun getting this disease. Also, it allowed them to compare a nun's brain condition with her memory while still alive.

Snowdon reports that all the sisters showed age-related decline in mental function. But those who taught for most of their lives showed less decline than those who had spent most of their lives in service work. Intellectually stimulating activity, it seems, enhances mental activity and keeps the mind sharp and alert. It may even protect a person from the physiological effects of AD. The study found that nuns, who taught and who lived intellectually stimulating lives, functioned well in spite of AD in their brains on autopsy.

This study supports the idea that a stimulating environment and social engagement help maintain good mental functioning in later life. It offers the surprising finding that social and intellectual engagement can even overcome the damage to the brain associated with AD.

Physical Exercise and the Brain

Exercise increases cardiovascular fitness and endurance. But scientists find that exercise also leads to more connections between brain cells and growth in brain size. Poon and Harrington (2006), for example, report that even mild physical activity, like playing the fiddle, leads to increased production of brain cells. In this case, the brain cells related to the activity of the left hand. Some evidence suggests that exercise also increases blood flow that brings oxygen to the brain and increases the efficiency of neuronal function. High levels of fitness may lead to more efficient mental processing, especially for complex and demanding tasks.

Dustman and White (2006, p. 70) say that exercise leads to "improved neuronal activity, synaptic structure, and neuronal plasticity." Fitness may also restore mental abilities in less fit people. A prescription of fitness activity could protect a person from mental decline and could restore some lost mental functions in the absence of disease (Poon & Harrington, 2006).

A Canadian study compared two groups of older women (a total of 42 women) randomly chosen from the community. One group took part in aerobic exercise, the other group did not. The study measured cardiovascular health, blood flow to the brain at rest, reserve capacity of blood vessels in the brain, and cognitive functions. The active women had better vascular blood flow to the brain and lower blood pressure. Compared to the control group, they also had better cognitive functions (U.S. News, 2009).

The author of this study, Marc Poulin, says, "Being sedentary is now considered a risk factor for stroke and dementia. This study proves for the first time that people who are fit have better blood flow to their brain. Our findings also show that better blood flow translates into improved cognition. . . . The take-home message from our research is that basic fitness—something as simple as getting out for a walk every day—is critical to staying mentally sharp and remaining healthy as we age" (Alberta Heritage Foundation, 2009).

Many studies also show differences between highly fit and less fit people on working memory, reaction time, and reasoning. Etnier (2009) reviewed 11 large-scale studies that looked at the effects of physical activity on cognitive performance and clinical impairment. Nine of the studies showed that exercise led to less risk of cognitive impairment. (The other two studies took place over a relatively short time span, and this may have affected the results.) The studies that showed an effect of exercise on cognitive ability also studied the intensity of the exercise.

Etnier (2009, pp. 166–167) concludes that "'more is better' and that physical activity intensity is an important component of the dose of physical activity." A review of many other studies leads Etnier to conclude that programs that include both strength training and aerobic training best reduce cognitive impairment. She also concludes that activity should take place from 20 to 60 minutes most days.

In a review of reviews of the literature, Tomporowski (2006, p. 32) concludes that, "indeed, exercise, both acute and chronic, facilitates specific aspects of cognitive functioning." Researchers continue to study the link between exercise and mental function. For example, researchers do not have a clear idea of how physical activity acts on cognition (Spirduso et al., 2008). Nor do they know how strong the relationship is. But the research to date points toward the value of living an active lifestyle for good mental function.

Summary of Findings on Aging and Mental Potential

A few key points summarize some of the positive findings in the large literature on aging and mental performance:

1. Negative stereotypes, test anxiety, and other distractions account for some of the decline we see in lab studies of mental performance.
2. Some types of memory and cognitive function show little decline when studied in everyday contexts.
3. Some older people perform as well or better on tests and in everyday life as younger people.
4. Experts show that practice and pattern recognition in a field can lead to continued high performance.
5. Older people can display wisdom in their assessment of problems and in their advice to others.
6. Training can improve mental processes at least for the specific skills trained.
7. Physical activity can forestall mental decline and help maintain good mental function.

These findings come from a growing literature on mental potential in later life. The increase in the older population, longer life, and the desire of the Baby Boom generation to maintain an active lifestyle will drive more research on mental potential. This research will study ways that older people can maintain and improve their mental functions. Studies in the future may uncover and describe unique mental activities that only mature in old age.

Creativity

The bulk of research on psychology and aging has focused on changes in memory and intelligence with age. The word *creativity*, for example, does not appear in the subject index of the *Handbook of the Psychology of Aging* (Birren & Schaie, 2006). Creativity can refer to a great achievement, or it can be a form of personal expression.

Creativity as Measured by Great Works

Studies of creative achievement, based on the number of creative works or the greatness of creative work, conclude that creativity decreases with age. Lehman (1953; also 1968) produced the classic work in this field. He studied the ages at which scientists, philosophers, mathematicians, painters, inventors, and other creative people produced their greatest works. He found that most past and present scientists produced their greatest creative work between the ages of 30 and 40. Most famous writers produce the greatest work before age 45. Lehman found that creative achievement decreased after age 45.

Lehman's work set off a wave of controversy. Dennis (1968) challenged Lehman's conclusions. He also challenged Lehman's methods. Lehman looked at *when a person produced their greatest works.* Dennis studied creative output, *the number of works a person produced.* He, too, measured the output of artists, scientists, scholars, and dancers. He found that in almost all fields creativity, as measured by output, peaks between the ages of 40 and 49. About 10 years later than Lehman's findings. Dennis also found that creative output differed by field. Artists peaked earliest in life. Scholars such as historians showed little decline with age. They produce as much in their 70s as in their 40s.

Later studies by Simonton (1977, 1988, 1990) also found that creativity decreased with age. In general, Simonton (1990, p. 322) says, "If one plots creative output as a function of age, productivity tends to rise fairly rapidly to a definite peak and thereafter tends to decline gradually." Does this mean that creativity and innovation end in middle age?

Simonton in a later study (2006) modified his view on creativity. He says that creative people can produce great works of every age. The quantity of a person's output may decline. But the quality of their work will remain constant. This means that an older person may produce fewer masterpieces but will produce fewer mediocre works as well.

Why does creativity decrease in later life for some people? Declining health, decreasing energy, changes in a profession, and different goals and motivations in later life all explain declining creative output. A person's chosen field will also make a difference. Dancers, gymnasts, and figure skaters, for example, will naturally peak earlier than other creative artists. Painters and musicians will have longer creative careers. Historians may only come into their prime toward the end of their careers, when their knowledge and experience have ripened.

Cohen (2005) notes that a historian at age 75, for example, could outshine a 25-year-old Rhodes history scholar when it comes to discussing or interpreting history. Arnold Toynbee, the great historian, at age 77, wrote that "an historian's work is of the kind in which time is a necessary condition for achievement."

Galenson (2006) provides another view of creativity in later life. He studied the careers of great writers and artists. He discovered two types of creativity—experimental innovation and conceptual innovation. Each type of artist and writer, he says, approaches creative work differently. And these two approaches lead to creative excellence at different stages in the life cycle.

Experimental innovators, he found, focus on presenting visual perceptions. Artists like Monet and Cézanne fall into this type. They work in a tentative style and paint the same scene or object many times. They use their art to search for perfection in their work. Cézanne, said about his art, "I seek in painting." Experimentalists continue to produce great work throughout their careers.

Conceptual innovators, in contrast to experimentalists, communicate a specific idea or emotion. They know the goal of each work precisely. The great conceptual innovators break with tradition. They develop a new style or approach to art that suddenly appears. The conceptual innovator does not view art as a search for truth. They present the work of art as something already found. Pablo Picasso, one of the great conceptual innovators, said about his art, "I don't seek; I find." Picasso, like most conceptual innovators, created his most important work early in his life. He created Cubism, for example, in his mid-20s.

Galenson (2006, p. 15) summarizes his findings using Cézanne and Picasso as examples of these two approaches. "Cézanne's slow production and elaboration of his creative ideas led to a very late peak in the quality of his work, whereas Picasso's rapid production and development of his new ideas led to a very early peak."

Galenson admits that exceptions to this model exist. Some artists show more or less extreme versions of these two approaches. Some artists change their approach as they age. But Galenson's work shows that personality and creative style influence productivity throughout the life cycle.

The research on creativity shows that it can take place at any age. In some fields, such as physics, mathematics, and sports, young people show the greatest creativity. But in other fields, like history, philosophy, and art, compared to younger people, older people can produce more creative work and greater creative work. The personality of the artist, conceptual or experimental, also determines the amount and quality of an artist's work. In some fields, it takes a lifetime of learning, thinking, and integrating knowledge to make a great contribution. The most creative people continue to express themselves throughout their lives.

Creativity as Personal Expression

Creativity can be a form of personal expression. This perspective treats creativity as a source of individual satisfaction regardless of how other people judge the works produced. A program in Bergen, Norway, for example, offered courses in poetry writing and story-telling to 45 people ages 67 to 90. Researchers found that creative expression led to sharpened awareness, increased self-esteem, and good social relations in the classes (Aadlandsvik, 2007).

BOX 5.4
JOHN HOLT: A STUDY IN SELF-DEVELOPMENT

Students of educational reform in the 1970s will know the name John Holt.[*] Holt became one of the vocal and constructive critics of schools and standard methods of instruction. His books *How Children Fail* and *How Children Learn*, based on his observation of children in and out of school, described the natural learning ability of young children. Holt (1978) turned his attention to learning in later life as he aged. His last book, *Never Too Late*, chronicles his own experiences as he attempted to master the cello at age 40 and again at age 50.

"If I could learn to play the cello well, as I thought I could," he says, "I could show by my own example that we all have greater powers than we think; that whatever we want to learn or learn to do, we probably can learn; that our lives and our possibilities are not determined and fixed by what happened to us when we were little, or by what experts say we can or cannot do."

Holt's reflections on his learning show several keys to mastery in later life:

- He has a serious desire to improve and a belief that he can achieve excellence.

- He engages in serious, deliberate practice—repetition plus reflection on his learning. "Now, when home, I try to play three or four hours a day, more when I can make time for it. To become a skillful musician has become perhaps the most important task in my life."

- He creates ingenious methods of practice to provide feedback on his learning—for example, he rigs up a speaker system so he can hear his own work as a listener would hear it.

- He creates stretch goals for himself—new challenges to improve his ability. He begins teaching the cello to the child of a friend. He also plays along with students at a school where he teaches soccer. He plays with a variety of musical groups from quartets to small symphonies.

- He engages in reflection and constant assessment of his work in order to track his improvement.

- He learns through multiple channels. He explores music stores for new scores. He visits the public library to hear music he's never heard before. He attends the symphony to hear music by composers he's never heard of. He searches everywhere for more ways to understand music.

Holt holds out an optimistic and realistic message. "Countless other teachers say that if we don't learn to play musical instruments as children we will never be able to learn as adults. Again, not so. Of course it is nice, if we come freely to music, to come to it young, but if we don't come to it then . . . we can later. *It is never too late*" (p. 4, emphasis added).

[5.4]John Holt died in 1985 at age 62.

Engelman (2000) led a creativity class for 6 years with a group of women at a senior center. The class solved puzzles, engaged in brainstorming, and invented poems and stories. Engelman concluded that people at any age can display creativity, and that the act of creation brings joy to older people's lives.

Cohen (2005) reports that creativity can improve the health of older adults. He and colleagues (2006, 2007) conducted a study of a professionally led chorale group. This program included 128 people with an average age of 79. The members of the chorale group attended 30 practice sessions and gave 10 public concerts. The researchers used a control group to assess the effect of this program. The researchers found that, compared to the control group, the chorale group made fewer doctor visits, used less medication, reported less depression, and had better morale. Cohen (2005) says that challenging mental activity and the achievement of control and mastery lead to better health and good mental function.

Zarit (2009, p. 684; Fauth, Zarit, Malmberg, & Johansson, 2007) supports this point. He found that even among people ages 80 to 90, those people with a greater sense of mastery had less disability. "Mastery," he says, "remained a strong predictor of continued independence." Arts and creativity programs offer a good method of health promotion and good way to improve the quality of older people's lives.

Not everyone can or wants to join a group to express their creativity. Butler (1974) says that many older people become **autodidacts**—self-teachers. These kinds of people take charge of their own learning. They transform their world in response to their own concerns, and, in the process, create something new. Older people have more opportunities than ever before—individually and in groups—to engage in creative, rewarding activity. This view of creativity makes later life a time of potential discovery and self-renewal rather than a time of decline.

PERSONALITY DEVELOPMENT AND THE SELF

Some psychologists and social psychologists have focused on personality growth in later life. Erik Erikson (1963) developed one of the best-known models of human development. McCrae and Costa (1990, pp. 11–12) call it "the single most important theory of adult personality development." Erikson based his model of the life course on Freud's psychosexual stages. The model assumes that:

- A fixed set of stages for the life course exists.
- These stages unfold over time just as the physiology develops over time.
- At each stage the person faces a challenge with a positive and a negative pole.
- A healthy personality will achieve the goal of the positive pole and then have the resources to tackle the challenge of the next stage.

Erikson's model of the life course has eight stages. The eighth stage corresponds to old age. Erikson says that in this stage a person either achieves a sense of "integrity" or falls into "despair and doubt." This stage demands "the acceptance of one's one and only life cycle as something that had to be and that, by necessity, permitted of no substitutions" (Erikson, [orig. 1959], in Jenks, 2005, p. 324). Erikson describes this last stage as a time of inwardness and reflection. One reviews the past and accepts one's life as a product of one's actions within one's culture. This last stage sums up the other stages. A person who achieves integrity faces death without despair. This person serves as a model for the young, who learn to trust their culture and follow its prescriptions (Erikson, 1963, 1982).

A number of gerontologists have criticized the final stage of Erikson's model (Butler, 1975; Novak, 1985–86). This stage describes old age as a time to disengage from life and look back. It ignores the fact that older people go on living. Butler, for example, takes issue with the idea that people in old age can only accept who they are and what they have been.

"People are locked in by such a theory," he says. They may look healthy from Erikson's point of view, but they suffer because they are trapped by their work, marriage, or lifestyle. "Excessive or exaggerated identity seems clearly to be an obstacle to continued growth and development through life and to appreciation of the future. . . . Human beings need the freedom to live with change, to invent themselves a number of times throughout their lives" (Butler, 1975, pp. 400–401).

Research findings point to varied patterns of development that depend on social context as well as inner unfolding (Hendricks, 1999). This contextual view of life span development takes into account a person's culture, social class, educational level, and gender. It also looks at a person's sociohistorical context (Hofer & Sliwinski, 2006).

Fry (2003, p. 284) links the life course described by Erikson and others to life structured by mass education and industrialization. Fry calls this the **institutionalized life course**. The structure of this life course emerged in the late 19th and early 20th centuries. This life course fits a society where a child goes to school, a young person takes one job for life, and an older person retires with a pension. This may apply only to a limited moment in the history of western societies.

Fry (2003, p. 284) finds other life course structures in other societies. Small-scale societies, for example, often refer to a **generational life course**. "Within generational life courses, the life plan is to mature into adulthood, have a family, work in subsistence, and simply live."

Eyetsemitan and Gire (2003) studied the life course in seven nations. They found that Erikson's stages did not fit the timing of life events or the roles of older people in developing nations. They saw that stages occurred at much earlier ages than in the developed world. For example, the stage of late adulthood could occur as early as age 44 or earlier. They also found that older people in developed nations often played a "generative" role that Erikson's theory puts in middle adulthood.

Today, people marry, divorce, remarry, start businesses, leave careers, return to careers, and return to school at all ages in adulthood. Studies find many stages in the life cycle and different stages and patterns for men and women. These findings reflect the diversity of the life course in a time of social change (Ryff, Kwan, & Singer, 2001).

Self-Development in Later Life

Critics of stage models call for a more flexible model of the self in later life. Some social psychologists put this dynamic model of the self at the center of their studies.

Breytspraak (1995, p. 93) defines the self as "the ability to be aware of one's own boundaries and individuality and to reflect upon these." According to Breytspraak, two motives shape behavior as people age. First, people try to view themselves positively and to present a good image of themselves to others. Second, people try to maintain their sense of self in the face of a changing social environment. This makes the self a dynamic process more than a state of being. The self constantly shapes interaction and interprets events to achieve these two goals.

Blanchard-Fields and Abeles (1996), for example, found that older and younger people view themselves differently. Older people, compared with younger people, have a more limited view of their future selves. They reported fewer hopes and fears for their future selves. And they tended to define themselves in relation to their current concerns, especially health. This reflects the older person's place in the life course and their realistic view of the future.

"You're still the King of the Apes as far as I'm concerned, dear."

McAdams (1996, p. 134) says that identity in later life relies on a "lifestory." This story, along with the self, changes over time (Tornstam, 2005). For example, near the end of life, the self may live mostly in the present. Ruth and Coleman (1996, p. 317) reviewed studies that described a "spiritual Me." A person in later life may begin an inward journey.

Tornstam (2005) refers to this as **gerotranscendence**—the self begins to expand its boundaries and reflect on the meaning of human life. At this time, a person reviews the connection to childhood, the link to earlier **generations**, and the meaning of life and death. Gerotranscendence also refers to a shift from materialism and a practical view of life to a more contemplative, cosmic view. It includes "a deepening spirituality, and a greater sense of intergenerational continuity" (Aldwin, Spiro, & Park, 2006, p. 98). Johnson (2009, p. 669) says that with gerotranscendence, "the individual becomes less self occupied, becomes more selective about social activities, has a greater affinity with past generations, and takes less interest in superfluous social interaction . . . even developing a need for solitary meditation."

Aging poses a number of challenges to the self. These challenges come from at least three sources: social attitudes toward older people, physical decline, and the loss of social roles. Ageism, for example, poses a challenge to everyone in later life. The self's sensitivity to others' perceptions can make ageism a painful experience. It can lower a person's self-esteem. In our society a person must work to combat ageism. A strong social support network makes this easier. For example, friends and family can give a person feelings of worth and importance that combat negative stereotypes.

Physical decline also challenges a person's sense of self. People who get their self-esteem from playing sports may feel let down as their ability decreases with age. Our culture links driving a car with maturity, adulthood, freedom, and self-sufficiency. No longer being able to drive may undermine an older person's self-esteem. Even people with Alzheimer's disease, a radical loss of the self, resist giving up driving.

Definitions of successful aging (Rowe & Kahn, 1998) often emphasize physical well-being and behavior. But they fail to account for a person's response to physical change. George (2006), in a review of the literature on the quality of life, says this definition of successful aging leaves out a person's subjective perceptions. For example, many people with a physical disability report a high quality of life, happiness,

intellectual growth, and spiritual fulfillment. By contrast, some people in good health report low feelings of subjective well-being. A broader definition of successful aging recognizes that a person can give meaning to life in spite of losses that come with age. Successful aging must include personal perceptions as well as the potential for growth in the face of loss.

This growth can take many forms. For example, sports programs for elders, such as the Senior Olympics or the Seniors Golf Tour, help people maintain their self-esteem in the face of physical decline. Programs that refresh an older person's driving skills or writing classes that encourage creativity can all boost self-esteem.

Tornstam (1999) found that a health crisis can challenge views of the self that are taken for granted. A 68-year-old man who learned that he had heart disease says that his illness caused him to read books he would never have otherwise read. "I think there is so much in these new things," he says. ". . . I'm in the middle of a process where I have a lot to learn."

Finally, role loss can rob a person of self-worth. Social roles give a person status, purpose, and a sense of achievement. Loss of roles threatens a person's well-being. Retirement, widowhood, and the empty nest all challenge a person's sense of self. Most people cope with these role losses and find new sources of esteem. A widow may find self-worth in counseling other widows. A retired machinist may find self-esteem in a second career as a handyman. These new roles can lead to a satisfying sense of self. The challenge of role loss demands that the older person search for new meaning in later life. This search for new roles can take many forms.

Psychologist Viktor Frankl (1984, 1990) in his classic work, *Man's Search for Meaning*, puts the search for meaning at the center of human existence. He says that a person must have or find a purpose in life in order to feel fulfilled. In old age, for many people, the search for life's meaning grows in importance. Krause (2004b, 2009) builds on the work of Frankl and Erikson, who identified the integration of life as the central psychological task of old age.

Krause (2004b) conducted a national survey and found that meaning in life arose when a person had a strong set of values, a purpose in life, and goals. People can also discover meaning through their religious traditions. Krause says that a satisfying answer to the question of meaning entails four things: a system of values that guides behavior, a sense of purpose, goals for the future, and an ability to make sense of the past.

The search for meaning includes a supportive social context and positive relations with others, as well as an inner integration.

Krause shows that members of a person's social network can provide an older person with emotional support and comfort. Relationships themselves can provide a sense of meaning and purpose (e.g., grandparenting). Other people can support the older person by asking questions about the past and showing interest in the older person's life.

Ryff and Keyes (1996, cited in Qualls, 2002, p. 10) report six dimensions of psychological well-being in later life: "autonomy, environmental mastery, personal growth, positive relations with others, purpose in life, and self-acceptance." Ryff and colleagues (Ryff, Magee, Kling, & Wing, 1999) report that wealthier, better-educated people feel they have a purpose in life and report more personal growth in old age. Ryff and Keyes's summary of the literature shows the link between the self and social conditions such as income, education, and social class.

A person's culture also plays a role in self-development. How does one's culture (e.g., Hispanic culture or Chinese culture) view old age? What roles does the culture offer older people? Answers to these questions shape a person's sense of self in later life. Singer and Ryff (1999, cited in Ryff et al., 2001) found, for example, that people with a history of poverty showed less physical decline if they had strong social relationships. A person with more resources (e.g., education, money, health, friends) has a better chance of achieving psychological health in later life. Ryff and colleagues (2001) call for more research on the effect of social integration on health and well-being in later life.

Spirituality: The Search for Meaning in Later Life

Moberg (2001, p. 10) defines *spirituality* as a person's "ultimate concern, the basic value around which all other values are focused, the central philosophy of life." The search for successful aging can take many forms, including religious faith, service attendance, and nontraditional spiritual beliefs.

Some people see spirituality as their personal relationship to God (Moore, Metcalf, & Schow, 2006). Moore and colleagues (2006) found that spirituality and faith in God gave people a sense of purpose and enthusiasm. Other people take a more philosophical view. They see God everywhere in the natural world.

Spirituality can take place within organized religion or through personal beliefs and rituals. Some people express their spirituality outside traditional religious channels. They may feel oneness with nature or a commitment to the betterment of all life. Benjamin Franklin, for example, expressed his spiritual beliefs through service to his fellow citizens.

Some older people turn to eastern and western meditation practices to feel a sense of wholeness. They feel that yoga and t'ai chi exercises create a sense of unity within themselves and with the environment. Studies show that spiritual practices such as these can lead to better health, improved social relations, and high life satisfaction (Chan, 2003).

The diversity of American life today, with its various ethnic and cultural groups, leads to many different religious and spiritual perspectives. Most Americans claim some form of Christianity as their religious belief. Other faiths include Judaism, Islam, Baha'i, Buddhism, Hinduism, Sikhism, Confucianism, and Taoism.

American spiritual life in the past often centered on the church or synagogue. Religion gave people a common set of values, involved them in a community of like-minded people, and gave meaning to life. Churches, mosques, synagogues, and temples also provide social services and social supports to their memberships. Some congregations run nursing homes and provide hospice care. They run adult day-care programs and social clubs for older members.

Many older people today feel a strong connection to their religious communities and have a strong religious faith. A Gallup poll (Newport, 2006) found that, compared to people ages 18 to 29, a greater proportion of older people (ages 65 and over) consider religion very important to themselves (47% compared to 72%). And longitudinal research shows that many people grow more religious as they age (Aldwin et al., 2006, citing Argue, Johnson, & White, 1999).

Idler (2006, p. 294) says that lifelong membership in a congregation provides continuity in a person's life. A church, synagogue, temple, or mosque may hold collective and individual memories—of births, marriages, and deaths. "For older persons with lifelong religious observances, a thread sews through all these seasons, providing accumulating continuity and deepening memories." Idler goes on to say that in a fast-changing world, religion and religious communities provide continuity. For people who have lived "89, 90, or even 100 years," she says, "it is difficult to name any other aspect of those lives [except religion] that would have changed so little."

In the United States, "persons 65 years and over attend religious services significantly more frequently than younger adults [though this declines in late old age due to illness and disability]; engage in private religious activities such as prayer, reading sacred texts, and meditating significantly more often" (Idler, 2006, pp. 283–284). Older people also report more subjective religious experiences, increased religious experiences in daily life, and greater use of religion as a way to cope with crises.

Moberg (1997, cited in Schulz-Hipp, 2001, p. 87) says that, compared to other age groups, older people show the strongest religious belief "on almost all measures" and that "this has remained the same year after year when similar questions are asked." This commitment to religion partly reflects the past experiences of older people. In the past, religion played a bigger role in people's lives than it does today.

Spiritual practices, whether formal religious services or quiet reflection on the past, can bring fullness to later life. It helps many people cope when health, income, and social supports decline in late old age. Coping methods include prayer, faith in God, and support from clergy and the faith community. Religious belief can help a person find meaning in the face of despair.

Religious leaders and caregivers can help older people live their faith. It's important that professionals understand and respect the religious traditions of the people they serve. Professionals can help a religious community provide support to older members, and they can help older members take part in their religious communities. Support can take the form of arranging outreach religious services or carpools to places of worship.

Connections to religious organizations tend to differ by gender and race. Women, compared to men, show more participation in organized religious activity in later life (Idler, 2006). Krause (2006) reports that, compared to whites, African American older people tend to give and receive more social support from their churches. Older African Americans report that religion helps them cope with racial discrimination. Also, fellow church members tend to give African Americans emotional support (Krause, 2004b). Mexican American elders also show strong religious belief and participation in formal religious activities (Idler, 2006).

Research on the Baby Boom generation finds a decrease in religious participation in these cohorts. Boomers report less confidence in religious institutions and less interest in religion, and they are more likely to say they are neither spiritual nor religious (Hoffman, 1998; Marler & Hadaway, 2002). An AARP study found that only 47% of Boomers reported satisfaction with their spiritual and religious life (Keegan, Gross, Fisher, & Remez, 2002).

Russell (2001, p. 40) says, "Many boomers and younger adults are on a personal spiritual quest rather than following the dictates of the religion in which they were raised. This shift has emptied some traditional institutions and brought greater diversity to religious practice." Compared to older people today and in the past, Boomers will show a broader range of spiritual interest. Researchers and practitioners need to learn more about the many expressions of religion, spirituality, and personal growth in later life. They can then apply this understanding to serve the spiritual and religious needs of current and future generations of older people.

SOCIAL PSYCHOLOGICAL CHANGE

The Kansas City Studies of Adult Life in the 1960s produced a series of theories about successful aging. The Kansas City project took place in two waves. Researchers from a number of disciplines, including psychology and sociology, conducted the research, and many publications reported their findings. This study led to heated debate over the ideal way to grow old. The researchers proposed at least three ways for people to adapt to changes as they age: disengagement, activity, and continuity.

Disengagement Theory

The **disengagement theory** of successful aging says that as people age, social interaction decreases. This decreased interaction takes place, at least in part, because society withdraws from the older person (e.g., through mandatory retirement).

Cumming and Henry (1961) developed the disengagement theory of aging out of the Kansas City findings. Disengagement, they said, allows older people to naturally withdraw from social contacts and roles as their strength declines. It also allows society to remove older people from social roles before the final disengagement—death. This creates a smooth transition from one generation to the next. Disengagement theory sees withdrawal as inevitable, universal, and satisfying to the individual and society.

Critics attacked disengagement theory for at least three reasons. First, it supports the negative stereotype of older people as frail and unable to perform social roles. Second, the theory assumes that younger people perform social roles better than older people. This supports mandatory retirement based on age. Third, it assumes that all older people will (or should) respond to aging in the same way.

Activity Theory

Activity theory serves as an antithesis to disengagement theory. This theory says that activity leads to the highest satisfaction in later life. Activity theory assumes that older people have the same needs as people in middle age. It assumes that disengagement takes place against the older person's will (e.g., through mandatory retirement or the death of age mates). Satisfied older people resist the shrinkage of their social roles. They find substitutes for the roles that they lose over time.

Neugarten, Havighurst, and Tobin (1968) reanalyzed the Kansas City data used by Cumming and Henry. Using different measures, they found "moderate support for the activity theory" (Neugarten, 1987, p. 373). They also found at least three types of active people who report high life satisfaction. One group started new activities to fill in for lost roles. The researchers called this group "reorganizers." A second group stayed active and held on to middle-aged roles. The researchers said these people were "holding-on." A third group narrowed the range of their activities but stayed active. The researchers called these people "focused."

Later research and common sense suggest that both activity and disengagement theory give too simple an account of aging. Activity alone, for example, cannot ensure satisfaction in later life. Ray and Heppe (1986) found that the number of activities did not predict happiness, but a commitment to activities did. Studies show that people report the greatest satisfaction when they engage in activities that they find meaningful (Singleton, Forbes, & Agwani, 1993).

Continuity Theory

Continuity theory emphasizes continuity over the life course. Atchley (1999b) says that people age best if they can view change in later life within an existing pattern of thought or behavior. People also adapt best if they can use strategies from their past experience to cope with current challenges.

Atchley applies continuity theory to internal structures such as a person's sense of self. He also applies

"Activity theory says that people who stay active have the highest life satisfaction. This couple enjoys a bicycle ride in the country."

it to external structures like the environment, relationships, and activities. Continuity theory suggests that mildly active people in their middle years will feel most satisfied with a mildly active old age. Very active people will stay very active. Atchley says that a person's own preferences and social expectations create continuity in later life.

Atchley (1989) contrasts continuity theory with activity theory. He says that activity theory assumes that for successful aging, a person needs to balance each loss of activity with a gain, but continuity theory assumes an evolution. People integrate new experiences into their past history and move forward. Atchley uses the model of a drama to describe this process. "Everyday life for most older people," he says, "is like long-running improvisational theater in which the settings, characters, and actions are familiar and in which the changes are mostly in the form of new episodes rather than entirely new plays" (p. 185). Continuity leads to a strong self-image, good mental health, and competence in daily life.

Each of the three theories—disengagement, activity, and continuity—offers insight into how people adapt to change as they age. Some writers suggest that the disengagement theory applies best to people in late old age (Tornstam, 2005). People in this phase of life may lack the energy to keep up their past activities. They may welcome disengagement and find satisfaction in a less active lifestyle. Other studies support the activity and continuity theories (Hao, 2008; Agahi & Parker, 2006). Studies of aging in other countries using the Kansas City measures have found more patterns of successful aging. It appears that many paths lead to a good and satisfying old age.

The Life Course Perspective

The **life course perspective** is a grand view of the life cycle. It includes growth through social roles and stages of life, it takes into account social institutions, and it places all of this in a historical context (Stevens-Long & Michaud, 2003).

The life course perspective contrasts with simpler models of the life cycle. The simplest life cycle model proposes a steady decline in function with age. Shakespeare offers one view of this model, in which life ends "sans teeth, sans eyes, sans taste, sans everything." Some biological studies support this model. However, once psychologists move away from a biological model of decline, as they need to do in adult studies, they require new concepts (Stevens-Long & Michaud, 2003). These concepts link the individual to the social environment. The life course perspective offers this view.

First, the life course perspective sees development as a lifelong process. The person changes continually from birth to death. This model differs from stage models. It does not include an end point (such as ego integrity). Instead it sees crisis and change as an ongoing part of life. Riegel (1979, p. 13), an early proponent of the life course perspective, states this simply: "Developmental and historical tasks are never completed. At the very moment when completion seems to be achieved, new questions and doubts arise in the individual and society."

Second, this model sees development as a process through which the individual and society change in response to each other. This gives rise to many stages and patterns of development. People's individual life course development depends on their physical condition, intelligence, personality, coping styles, resources, gender, race and ethnicity, social class, and the social world they live in. This model turns the researcher's attention to the social context to explain the timing, direction, and length of developmental stages (Stevens-Long & Michaud, 2003; Wapner & Demick, 2003).

Third, the life course model sees development as a normal part of living at every age. The child, for example, grows physically taller and stronger. The adult gains more social influence and status with age. A person, even in late old age, can create wholeness and a sense of continuity out of past experience. This search for meaning in later life can take the form of new roles (as family advisor or confidant to the young) or through reminiscence and life review.

Settersten (2003; also Marshall, 2009) presents a summary of the life course perspective's main principles:

- *Development is multidimensional and multispheral:* People develop biologically, physically, psychologically, and socially. Development in each dimension takes place at different rates. Likewise, development takes place in many spheres of life—in the family, at work, through leisure, and so on.
- *Development is multidirectional:* People change throughout the life course. They may grow and develop on one dimension and may decline or experience stability on another dimension. For example, a person may grow in knowledge in later life, but may decline physically.
- *Development takes place from birth through death:* But development takes different forms—it occurs at different rates, on different dimensions, and within different spheres—at different times in life. Early views of human development focused on childhood and youth. The life course perspective looks at the whole of life. So, for example, a disabled older person may regain a lost ability through exercise and physiotherapy.
- *Development takes place through continuity and discontinuity:* Some development takes place at specific times in life, other developments happen throughout life. Physical growth or maturation takes place from childhood to young adulthood. But learning and the growth of wisdom occur throughout life.
- *Development takes place in a historical context:* Historical, social, and demographic events shape the lives of individuals and age cohorts. The Baby Boom generation has lived through a time of prosperity and peace in the United States. Post-WWII

prosperity, television, mass advertising, mass education, and the rebellious years of the 1960s all shaped the lives of Baby Boomers. They will bring these unique experiences with them into old age. (Adapted from Settersten, 2003.)

The Structure of the Life Course

Society sets out the structure of the life course. This structure includes life events that mark transitions from one life stage to another.

Life Events

Life events shape personal development and the lives of entire cohorts of people. They present a person with the challenge of change. They often mark a transition between one stage of life and another. Life course researchers look at three types of life events: (1) nonnormative events (unplanned events such as illness or an accident); (2) normative, history-graded events (for example, the Great Depression or World War II); and (3) normative, age-graded events (events that occur at a certain time in life, like a first marriage or retirement).

Nonnormative Life Events

Events such as accidents, illness, or a fight with a neighbor take place without warning. Society does not prescribe these events. They do not fit into the normal order of the life cycle and people cannot plan for them.

Nonnormative events often come as a shock. An illness such as a stroke, for example, can damage a person's self-image and relationships.

In one case, a husband and wife had been married for 27 years. At age 52 the husband had a stroke that paralyzed his right side. He could barely talk and needed a wheelchair to move around. He felt depressed and bitter about his illness. His wife worried about his mood, which put a further strain on their relationship. Neither the husband nor the wife had prepared themselves for this event, and society gave them little guidance about how to deal with it.

Normative, History-Graded Life Events

On the afternoon of November 22, 1963, I sat at my desk in the 10th grade in a classroom in Snyder High School in Jersey City, New Jersey. Someone called the teacher to the door. She came back into the room and told us that President John F. Kennedy had been shot. We sat in silence as we heard the news. At the time, we did not know whether he would live. We ran home that day to watch the story unfold on television.

Nearly every American alive at the time of President Kennedy's death remembers where she or he heard the news. History-graded events such as the death of a president, the Great Depression, or the Vietnam War change the lives of all the people living at that time. These events have different effects on different age cohorts. People in the youngest age

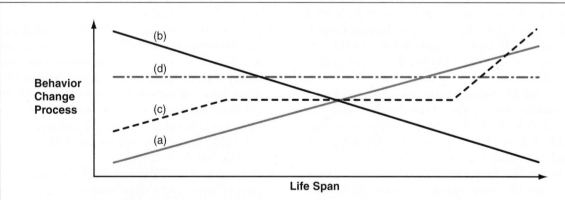

In this chart of life span development, the lines show that multidimensional and multidirectional changes can take place throughout life. A person can experience increases in some abilities (a) and decreases in others (b). Also, some abilities can take a nonlinear pattern (c). For example, a person may learn the piano in childhood, not play for many years, and then begin to play and improve again in later life. Many other patterns occur as well, including stability throughout life (d).

FIGURE 5.1 Life Span Development

Source: Adapted from P. Baltes, "Developmental Psychology," in G. L. Maddox (Ed.), *The Encyclopedia of Aging* (New York: Springer Publishing Company, 1987), pp. 170–175. Used by permission.

cohort, from birth to age 5, will not remember an economic recession. People in their early 20s will experience that same recession just as they enter adulthood. They will remember those years as a time when they found it hard to enter the job market and start their careers. A history-graded event can shape the lives of an entire generation.

Demographers label the people born between 1946 and 1964 the "Baby Boom" because of the increased number of births during this time. This history-graded event forced Baby Boomers to compete with one another for grades, jobs, and houses. Easterlin (1987) says that the large size of this group led Boomers to expect only modest economic success, and this in turn led them to have small families. These same age cohorts may face a shortage of public pensions and services in retirement due to the smaller cohorts behind them.

Cohorts that come after the Baby Boom will benefit from the size of the Boomer cohorts. Baby Boom cohorts are beginning to retire now, in the early years of this century. This may cause a labor shortage that will leave younger people with their pick of jobs. Likewise, Boomers will sell their larger homes to move to smaller retirement homes. This may create a market in which younger people can buy these homes at lower prices.

Historical events get filtered through the **age stratification system**, the system of age grades a society uses (e.g., child, adolescent, young adult). For instance, the 1900 to 1910 cohort (now largely deceased) went through the Great Depression of the 1930s in young adulthood, and the Depression affected their decisions to marry, as it did the early years of their careers. The Depression also affected the cohort born between 1920 and 1930, but it had a different effect on these people. They lived through the Depression as children. Some of them may not remember the Depression at all; others may simply have accepted the hard times as "the way things are."

Gerontologists use the term *generation* to describe people who share an awareness of their common historical or cultural experiences, but who may come from different cohorts. The Baby Boom cohorts born between 1946 and 1964 form a generation; they have all lived under the threat of nuclear war, and they have lived in a relatively affluent time in U.S. history.

Braun and Sweet (1983–84) developed a **generational event theory** of development. Generational event theory says that attitudes form for a generation in their teens. People who grow up at the same time in the same society share the same attitudes. And these attitudes shape a generation's worldview throughout life.

Like nonnormative events, history-graded events can happen without warning, and sometimes the changes they bring about do not show up until years later. The destruction of the World Trade Center on September 11, 2001, for example, had an immediate effect on American society. The president declared a war on terrorism, the government set up a new Office of Homeland Security, and everyone had to submit to more careful searches at airports. Young children today will have little or no memory of the World Trade Center tragedy. They will learn about it from their parents, watch videos of the event on TV, and read about it in their history books.

The second war in Iraq that began in the early 2000s will influence all Americans. But it will have a different effect on a 22-year-old who served in the war than on a 52-year-old who did not. Many Baby Boomers, who lived through the Viet Nam war era in their teen years, question the wisdom of fighting wars in foreign countries. A single historical event has a different effect on different age cohorts.

Normative, Age-Graded Life Events

Some years ago, Riley and colleagues (Riley, Johnson, & Foner, 1972; Riley, Foner, & Riley, 1999) developed a sophisticated model of the life cycle, the age stratification model (later termed the aging and society paradigm). This model linked individual development to the social structures that shape personal growth. Riley and colleagues said that society orders age cohorts into an age stratification system, a series of age grades through which people move as they age. They call this cohort flow.

As cohorts age (and members die), cohorts replace one another in society's age structure. As cohorts flow through the age structure, they change the size of particular age groups (e.g., the size of the group of 20- to 30-year-olds will differ in 1940 and 1970 and 2010). New groups of people enter each age grade over time. People ages 20 to 25 today will enter the age grade of old age 40 to 45 years from now.

New cohorts also bring new experiences with them as they age. Older cohorts today, for example, have less education than younger cohorts. Younger, more educated groups will probably demand more educational opportunities when they reach old age.

People experience the age stratification system as a series of life events around a certain age: high school graduation, the birth of a child, and retirement. We enter high school, flow through a series of school grades, and leave after a few years. Younger students enter to take our place.

Normative, age-graded life events often reflect the physical changes that take place as we age. Society expects a woman to have a child during the most active part of her childbearing years (ages 18 to 35). Likewise, we expect someone to graduate from high school around age 17 or 18. Society helps people make normative age grade transitions. For example, women in the United States hold baby showers to mark a woman's entry into motherhood. A high school graduation marks a passage to a new phase of life. Other events such as marriage or retirement involve rites of passage to bring closure to one life phase and help ease people into the next.

This structure of the life course includes the timing of life events such as graduation, marriage, and retirement. A 28-year-old medical school student, for example, may feel too old to be a student. Someone who retires at age 50 due to poor health may feel too young to leave the workforce. A person who gets promoted to vice president of marketing at age 25 may feel lucky to get this job so young. Social norms shape our sense of order and the timing of life events.

Settersten (2003) speaks of being **on time** or **off time** for life events. A person off time—early or late—may feel discomfort or dissatisfaction. Elder and Johnson (2003, p. 65) give the example of retired autoworkers in poor health. These workers felt dissatisfied with retirement because they believed they had to leave work too early.

A few years ago, a secretary in our office became a grandmother at age 40. She felt proud of her new granddaughter and wanted to tell everyone about her, but she also felt that being a grandmother made her an old woman, something she wanted to avoid. She therefore held back making a big announcement of the event. When she told people about her granddaughter, she would also explain how old this made her feel. By saying this, she implied that she was not old, but that she was a grandmother ahead of schedule.

Life events also differ by gender. Society has expectations for when a woman will have a first child. And more women, compared with men, experience widowhood in later life because in many cases women live longer and marry older men. A widowed woman will tend to stay unmarried. A widowed man will tend to remarry. Men, compared with women, will more likely retire on time (at age 65) due to their unbroken work careers and the likelihood that they will have a pension plan. Women have broken work careers (due to caregiving and child-rearing responsibilities). They tend to have smaller pensions or no pension at all of their own. Compared with men, fewer women have the option of a formal retirement at age 65. These differences reflect the different treatment of men and women throughout the life course.

The study of life events can make it seem like people have little influence on their own development. It seems like they can only respond to events that happen to them. But Kahana and Kahana (2003, p. 235) say that people do more than respond to the world. They call this "proactivity." People adapt and change their behavior and ways of thinking to minimize stress and maximize development.

For example, people can give up one role in order to take on another. A worker who retires early may decide to volunteer at a local youth center. Or a person may decide to take up an exercise program after reading about the effects of obesity on health in later life. Kahana and Kahana (2003) list a number of other proactive responses to the environment, including planning ahead, asking for help, and adapting a home environment in response to physical changes. People can and do respond to history and their environment as they age.

Nonnormative, history-graded, and normative life events shape our lives. They affect each of us differently as our personalities interact with the external environment. Each of us brings a lifetime of personal experience and interaction with society into later life.

PSYCHOLOGICAL DISORDERS: ABNORMAL AGING

Studies of memory, intelligence, and the life course describe normal aging. But some people suffer from psychological problems such as loneliness, depression, or thoughts of suicide in later life. Psychologists call these functional disorders because they interfere with a person's ability to function. These problems have no clear organic or biological cause. The older person may have suffered with this problem for many years. Other older people suffer from organic disorders. These include Parkinson's disease, stroke, and Alzheimer's disease. These illnesses arise due to a malfunction in the brain.

Organic Disorders: Cognitive Impairment in Later Life

Changes in the brain that come with age can lead to cognitive disorders. Writers refer to these disorders as *organic brain syndrome, senile dementia,* or simply *dementia.* These general terms describe a variety of organic brain disorders. The development of lesions, neurofibrillary tangles, and amyloid plaques in the brain, for example, lead to dementia—confusion, forgetfulness, and sometimes antisocial behavior (Berg & Sternberg, 2002). Some individuals with these disorders wander, strike out, or resist help from their caregivers. Dementia cases create stress for both professional care providers and family caregivers.

Alzheimer's disease is the most common form of dementia among older people (National Institute on Aging, 2008b). About 5% of people ages 65 to 74 have AD. This rate increases to nearly half of people age 85 and over. In total, as many as 4.5 million Americans may have AD. None of the research so far has produced a method to treat this disease. Physicians face special challenges when treating AD. They often cannot make an early diagnosis of the disease. They first try to rule out other causes of confusion and personality decline such as brain tumors, blood pressure problems, or hyperthyroidism. Caution prevents doctors from quickly reaching a conclusion of AD because a patient might have a treatable illness or a problem like overmedication or infection.

Tierney and Charles (2002) report on the development of an Alzheimer Predictive Index. Physicians can use this index to assess people who have some

---

BOX 5.5
ALZHEIMER'S DISEASE: STAGES AND SYMPTOMS

Researchers typically divide the progression of AD into a series of stages. The Mayo Clinic uses three broad stages—mild, moderate, and severe impairment. The following description gives some of the signs that appear at each stage.

Common Changes in Mild AD

- Finds it hard to remember recent information
- Repeatedly asks the same question
- Trouble solving complex tasks (e.g., balancing a checkbook)
- Poor judgment (e.g., irrational financial decisions)
- Gets lost in familiar surroundings
- Loses and misplaces things (even valuable objects)

Common Changes in Moderate AD

- Loses track of their current location
- Doesn't know the day of the week or season of the year
- Can't recognize their own things
- Takes things that don't belong to them
- Can't recognize family members, mistakes strangers for family
- Wandering that can create danger for the person
- Forgets personal history (e.g., where they live or where they went to school)
- Confabulates, makes up stories to fill gaps in memory
- Needs some help with ADLs (e.g., dressing, bathing, and toileting)

- Personality may change (e.g., a person can get suspicious, angry, restless)
- May engage in sexually inappropriate behavior, scream, or act out

Common Changes in Severe AD

- Can no longer speak coherently
- Needs assistance with nearly all ADLs (e.g., eating, dressing, toileting, and other self-care tasks)
- Inability to walk without help
- Needs help sitting up and help holding head up without support
- Abnormal reflexes and muscle rigidity
- Loss of ability to swallow
- Loss of bowel and bladder functions

Be aware that a person may not fit into a single stage. Stages overlap and each person will show unique symptoms as the disease progresses. Also, the disease progresses differently for each person. One person may pass through these stages in 4 to 6 years. Another person can live with this disease for 20 years or more. Death often comes from infection, pneumonia, or a fall.

Based on: Mayo Clinic. (2010). *Alzheimer's disease. Alzheimer's stages: How the disease progresses.* Retrieved February 20, 2011, from www.mayoclinic.com/health/alzheimers-stages/AZ00041; see also Alzheimer's Association (2011). *Stages of Alzheimer's.* Retrieved February 20, 2011, from www.alz.org/alzheimers_disease_stages_of_alzheimers.asp.

memory loss. Research shows that 89% of the time the index can predict the onset of AD within 2 years. This index and other new methods will lead to earlier diagnosis. Early diagnosis helps families cope with the disease's progress.

Researchers who study early treatment hope to develop ways to slow or stop the progress of the disease. The U.S. Food and Drug Administration has approved a small number of drugs for use in the treatment of AD (The National Institute on Aging, 2008b). Donepezil (brand name Aricept), rivastigmine, and galantamine treat mild AD symptoms. Donepezil may also be used to treat severe AD. These drugs stop or slow the action of a chemical that interferes with memory formation. They help people carry out activities of daily living and retain some memory, thinking, and speaking skill.

These drugs may also help control some problem behaviors. They do not stop or reverse AD, and they only help for a few months or years. Research continues on drugs that may slow the progress of AD in its early stages. Other drugs, such as sleeping pills and antidepressants, can control some of AD's symptoms. But, at present, nothing can stop the progress of the disease.

AD patients go through a series of changes over a number of years. On average, a person with AD lives 8 to 10 years after diagnosis. But some people live as long as 20 years with the disease. The progress of the disease differs for each person. But researchers have tried to organize the disease's progress into a series of stages. This helps caregivers assess their current situation and predict what they will have to deal with in the future.

A person in the early stages of the disease, for example, shows signs of forgetfulness. The person asks the same question over and over or repeats the same story word for word. The person may forget how to do simple tasks, such as cooking or playing cards (National Institute on Aging, 2008a). A spouse or family member may not notice these signs at first. But as the disease progresses, it has more obvious effects on behavior and social relations. The person will eventually need full-time care, often in a nursing home.

Meade and Park (2009) say that "social engagement may have a protective effect against developing dementia in old age." A Swedish longitudinal study, for example, found that the risk of dementia increased by 60% in people with a limited social network. Snowdon's (2001) study of active and socially engaged nuns supports this finding (see Box 5.3).

Other studies show an increased risk of dementia for people with limited social activities. This may take some planning as the older person's networks shrink due to loss of friends, loss of a spouse, or an illness.

AD poses problems for family caregivers. Studies of caregiver burden find that caregivers suffer from the demands of care. Caregivers often feel physical exhaustion. A caregiver may have to stay awake at night to prevent a spouse from wandering out of the house. Or the caregiver may face a physical struggle when he or she tries to bathe the person with AD.

Caregivers can also feel anger when a person asks the same question again and again or when the person damages something in the home. One woman woke up to find that her husband had filled the toilet with oranges. Another time her husband wandered into a neighbor's yard with a kitchen knife in his hand. The neighbors called the police and it took hours to calm the neighbors and get her husband back in the house.

Another woman recalls that she first became worried when her husband, a physician, lost his way home from work one night. He planned to stop at a patient's house for a short house call around 5 pm. The patient lived only a few blocks away, so his wife expected him home by 6 pm. She began to worry at eight o'clock when she still hadn't heard from him. An hour later he came in exhausted. He had spent the last 3 hours driving around their neighborhood looking for their house.

As the disease progresses, the demands of care increase. Many caregivers try to keep the relative at home as long as possible (Schulz & Martire, 2004). This leads to increased stress and can lead to illness for the caregiver. Many books and Web sites now exist to advise caregivers on how to manage their care receiver. Also, the Alzheimer's Society, local hospitals, and community service agencies offer support groups for family members.

Zarit and colleagues (Zarit, Femia, Watson, Rice-Oeschger, & Kakos, 2004) report on the development of a Memory Club. Care partners meet for 10 sessions in groups of 8 to 10 pairs. A social worker and neuropsychologist supervise the meetings. The meetings provide information about memory loss. They also provide a supportive setting for care partners to discuss their experiences. Other support programs include adult daycare facilities and overnight respite programs that give caregivers temporary relief from the demands of care.

The National Institute on Aging estimates that the direct and indirect cost of AD in the United States is about $100 billion per year. If science finds no cure for AD and if current trends continue, 13.5 million

Americans will have AD by the year 2050. This will increase the cost of caring for people with AD and will increase the burden AD places on families and the health care system. Scientists continue to work on finding a cure for AD. Vogler (2006; also National Institute on Aging, 2008b) says that researchers have found three genes that influence early-onset or familial AD. Researchers have found a fourth gene that influences late-onset AD. These results may lead to early diagnosis and treatment of the disease.

Functional Disorders

The prevalence of organic mental disorders will increase as the U.S. population ages. But older people also suffer from functional disorders such as loneliness, depression, and despair that leads to suicide. These problems have their roots in the person's social setting as well as the person's psychology.

Loneliness

Gerontologists distinguish between social isolation and loneliness. *Social isolation* refers to the decrease in social contacts that often come with age (Hall & Havens, 2002). Widowhood, the deaths of friends, children moving away—these events can lead to social isolation. *Loneliness* comes about when a person feels a relational deficit or a gap between the number of relationships desired and the number he or she has.

Older people who have lost a spouse, another family member, or a friend tend to feel lonely (Havens & Hall, 2001). Institutionalized older people with few family supports and people who live alone also report feeling lonely (Choi, Wyllie, & Ransom, 2009; Miedema & Tatemichi, 2003). Eshbaugh (2009) studied older women who lived alone. Women in this study reported less loneliness if they had close friends. This proved true even if they had family nearby.

But a person may feel lonely even if she or he has many social contacts. For example, a widow may play an active part in her bridge club, but she may feel lonely because she misses the company of her husband. Marriage tends to reduce the likelihood of loneliness. Bereavement tends to increase the risk of loneliness (Luanaigh & Lawlor, 2008). Hall and Havens (2002, citing Holmen, Ericsson, Andersson, & Winblad, 1992) say that some older people who live with their children or with siblings report high levels of loneliness.

Luanaigh and Lawlor (2008) reviewed the literature on loneliness. Studies report that between 5% and 16% of older people report feeling lonely often or always.

Kirk, Waldrop, and Rittner (2001) studied people who attended a daytime meal program in rural Louisiana. They found that although most of these people (53%) lived alone, only 30% said they felt lonely or very lonely. The researchers say that lack of social contact for these people did not necessarily lead to loneliness. Attendance at the meal program and other activities in this senior center may have decreased these participants' sense of loneliness. Participants said they attended the center because they enjoyed the social contact. A study of very old adults (age 85 and over) found that affection from and for their children reduced loneliness (Long & Martin, 2000).

A program in the United Kingdom offered a befriending service to older adults who lived alone. Visitors visited the clients 1 hour per week. The older people valued the service and the reliability of the visitors. Some of these friendships developed into personal relationships that included social activities and other types of support (Andrews, Gavin, Begley, & Brodie, 2003). Programs that promote social participation also reduce loneliness. A lunch program that brought people together to learn about health issues reduced feelings of loneliness (Sorrell, 2006).

Some nursing homes have used animal-assisted therapy (visits by a pet to the facility) to combat loneliness (Banks & Banks, 2002, 2003). The researchers found that visits of 30 minutes once a week reduced loneliness for patients who enjoyed the presence of the animals.

Technology can also help older people combat loneliness. Cell phones and the Internet can help people to stay in touch with relatives and friends. McMellon and Schiffman (2002) studied "cyber senior empowerment." The researchers asked a sample of older people about their Internet use. They found that nearly all of the people in the study (91%) used email to keep in touch with friends. People in the study who had physical limits or those who lived in social isolation felt more in control of their lives.

Research shows that loneliness and poor health often go together. Luanaigh and Lawlor (2008) report that feelings of loneliness lead to a higher risk of poor physical health and mental decline. This can lead to further problems, such as an increased risk of depression and suicide.

Depression and Suicide

Blazer (2003, p. M249) calls depression "the most frequent cause of emotional suffering in later life." Community studies of major depressive disorder (MDD) find rates of 1% to 5% (Blazer, 2003; Okura & Langa, 2010; Zarit, 2009). D'Mello (2003, p. 3) estimates that 14% of older people in the United States suffer from "significant depressive symptoms." Jones, Marcantonio, and Rabinowitz (2003) report that at least 20% of nursing home residents suffer from clinical depression. Researchers propose higher rates of clinical or minor depression.

Symptoms of depression include lack of interest, feelings of worthlessness, poor ability to concentrate, inability to make decisions, insomnia, loss or gain of weight, and suicidal thoughts. Depression can show up as withdrawal, apathy, and loss of energy. Depression can lead to further problems for the older person. Apathy can lead to poor eating habits and loss of weight and strength (D'Mello, 2003). This puts the older person at risk of frailty, falls, and broken bones. Research also links depression to other illnesses such as heart disease and inflammation (Blazer, 2003).

Older people with clinical depression show limitations on activities of daily living (Okura & Langa, 2010). One study found that depression increased the risk of mobility decline by 67% and increased the risk of ADL decline by 73% (Penninx, Leveille, Ferrucci, van Eijk, & Guralnik, 1999). Depression may also give a clue to the onset of AD or vascular dementia (Blazer, 2003).

Untreated, depression can lead a person to feel hopeless and suicidal (Cukrowicz, 2009). Suicide rates for older people decreased by half between 1950 and 2007 (National Center for Health Statistics, 2011). This may reflect improvements in pension benefits, health care programs, and other social supports.

Older people (ages 65 and over) in 2007 had a suicide rate of 14.3 per 100,000 people compared to 11.3 per 100,000 all ages. But suicide rates vary within the older age group (Figure 5.2). Older men (age 65+) had a rate more than seven times that of older women. Among the 85 and over age group, men have a suicide rate more than 13 times that of women (National Center for Health Statistics, 2011).

Non-Hispanic white men age 65 and over have the highest suicide rate of any age, gender, or racial group. They had a rate of 31.1 suicides per 100,000 people. The "old-old" white men age 85 and over had a rate in 2007 of 45.42 per 100,000. This came to 2.5 times the rate for men of all ages (18.3) (American Association of Suicidology, 2009).

Suicide statistics probably underestimate suicides among older people. The official figures miss people who fail to take medications or who overdose themselves. They also miss people who starve themselves or intentionally hurt themselves in accidents.

Older people attempt suicide less often than other age groups. But they have a higher completion rate. The American Association of Suicidology (2009) reports that for all ages the ratio of attempts to actual suicide comes to 25 to 1. For the group ages 15 to 24, the ratio is 100 attempts to 1 completion. But for people age 65 and over, 1 person succeeds for every 4 attempts.

Compared to older men, more older women attempt suicide. But men more often succeed. Szanto and colleagues (2002) report that older people who commit suicide have planned it for a long time. Those who have attempted suicide in the past also show an increased risk of successful suicide in later life.

Conwell and colleagues (2002) studied the use of firearms and the risk of suicide. They found that men who kept an unlocked and loaded gun at home showed the greatest tendency to commit suicide. This reflects the preference of men at all ages for more violent forms of suicide. The preference for the use of firearms in part accounts for the high rate of lethality among male suicide attempts. Between 2002 and 2006 (for people age 65 and over), firearms accounted for the greatest percentage of suicides (between 50% and 75%) for all race and ethnicity groups (except Asian/Pacific Islanders). The Asian/Pacific Island group most often chose suffocation (52.6%) (Centers for Disease Control and Prevention [CDC], 2009b).

What accounts for these high rates of suicide among some older people? No single cause or explanation fits all cases. Researchers find that depression, isolation, loneliness, bereavement, and physical illness all put older people at risk of suicide (CDC, 2010b). Social conditions and policies such as decreased pension benefits, reduced health care benefits, and the loss of close social ties can lead to depression and suicide.

These risk factors often build on one another. For example, a widowed person may live alone and feel depressed. Illness and lack of social supports may add to feelings of depression. Corr, Nabe, and Corr (1994) speak of "bereavement overload." A person may not have time to grieve for one loss before another one strikes.

Turvey and colleagues (2002) studied more than 14,000 people age 65 and over during a 10-year period. They found that people who committed suicide reported feelings of depression, poor self-reported

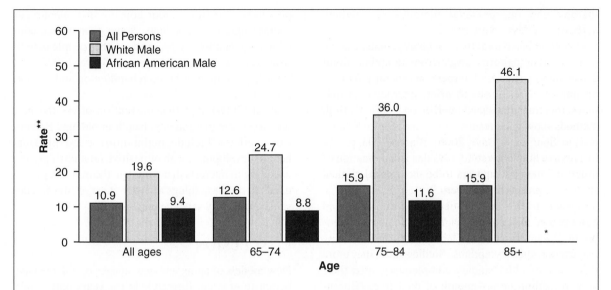

This chart compares the suicide rate for people of all ages and those age 65 and over. Note that the suicide rate increases with age for all people (regardless of race) and that the oldest age group of white males (age 85 and over) has a higher rate than any other age group.

Also, note the high rate of suicide for older white males, compared with all persons and African Americans at any age. The rate for the oldest white males is three times that of all persons in that age group. The rate for white males is

also about three times that of African American males in the oldest comparable group (75–84 years). These figures show that white males run a higher risk of suicide than other age and racial groups. And the older the white male, the higher the suicide risk.

*The low rates for African American males 85{plus} are unreliable and are not shown.

**Deaths per 100,000 resident population.

FIGURE 5.2   Death Rates for Suicide, for All People, White Males, and African American Males, Age 65 and over, 2006**

Source: National Center for Health Statistics. (2010b). *Health, United States, 2009: With special feature on medical technology* (Table 42, pp. 240–242). Hyattsville, MD: National Center for Health Statistics.

health, poor sleep quality, and the absence of a relative to talk to. Older people who want to die have often lost hope. Suicide notes will say the person feels "tired of life" (Osgood et al., 1991, p. 5).

Duberstein and colleagues (2000) found that depressed older people (age 50+) who thought about suicide had long-standing patterns of introversion and closed themselves to new experiences. Szanto and her colleagues (2002) say that antidepressants may lower the risk of suicide. Fiske and Arbore (2000–01) propose prevention programs that screen for depression and feelings of hopelessness. They say that even a small increase in feelings of depression should signal the need for support and preventive efforts.

Durkheim (1951) proposed that a lack of social integration led to high rates of suicide in modern society. Normlessness, or anomie, a lack of connection between the person and society, puts a person at risk. Current research on suicide in later life supports this view. Older people often lose the contacts and links that prevent suicide. Retirement, the deaths of friends, and a move to a nursing home weaken the older person's social network. As this network shrinks, the person may lose a sense of purpose and meaning. This increases the risk of suicide.

Conwell (2001) notes that older suicide victims often have many problems, including psychiatric illness, hopelessness, social losses, and physical decline. Professionals need to consider a number of interventions to reduce the risk of suicide.

Treatment for depression (and suicide attempts) in older people most often includes antidepressant drugs and psychological therapy (Blazer, 2003; Heisel, 2006). Some studies find that aerobic exercise and even exposure to bright light can decrease depression. Short-term psychotherapy—cognitive behavioral therapy and interpersonal therapy—can reduce depression in less severe cases.

Cognitive behavioral therapy helps patients change their thought patterns away from thoughts about depression or suicide. Interpersonal therapy focuses on improved responses to grief, interpersonal disputes, role transitions, and interpersonal deficits. Both methods show good results with older people (Knight, Kaskie, Shurgot, & Dave, 2006). Blazer (2003, p. 13), in a review of the literature, says that a combination of drugs and therapy "appears to be the optimal clinical strategy in preserving recovery."

Barriers to treatment of depression exist. Isolated older people may not get diagnosed. Some older people may want to avoid the label of depression. They underreport their symptoms. Studies show that more than 70% of older suicide completers visited their doctors within the last month of their lives (Bharucha, 2003). This suggests that physicians and other health care workers may not detect a desire to commit suicide in the older person. General or family practitioners may lack the experience with psychological disorders, or they may lack the time to diagnose the problem.

Knight and colleagues (2006) say that fewer than one older person in four with a mental disorder or substance abuse problem gets mental health care. Older people who do get help often get it from nonspecialists (e.g., their family doctors).

The cost of treatment for depression may create a barrier to care. This can include the cost of copayments and drug treatment (Kyomen & Gottlieb, 2003). Only 4% of Medicare dollars go to mental health programs (Knight et al., 2006). And half this money goes to people under age 65. Medicare also allots more money to inpatient care than to outpatient services. Medicare, a program that many older people rely on to maintain their health, continues to "fall short in promoting [mental health] service use among older beneficiaries" (Knight et al., 2006, p. 417).

Social supports (including group and personal counseling) hold a key to helping lonely, depressed, or suicidal older people. Heisel (2006) says that having a social network, a hobby, a religious practice, and feeling that life has meaning and purpose all buffer depression and suicidal thoughts. The type of support that feels best will differ for each person. Some people benefit from senior housing that encourages socializing among residents. Some people need education and counseling programs. Other people benefit from support groups. Bartels and Smyer (2002) call for more community-based rehabilitation and support programs.

Zarit (2009) says that prevention offers the best way to ensure good mental health in old age. Preventive methods include maintaining good physical health, developing a web of positive relationships, and engaging in interests that stimulate the mind. A person needs to do these things at every stage of life. In later stages, they may save the person's life.

CONCLUSION

New models of aging and new images of old age have begun to emerge. Researchers for years based their studies of memory and intelligence on laboratory studies and on a model of age as decline. Studies confirmed this decline when researchers compared the mental function of older and younger people. New models of aging study the talents that develop in later life. These include the older person's heightened ability to use practical knowledge and the expression of wisdom.

Likewise, stage models of human development have given way to multidimensional models of development. These models include many more ways to live well in old age. They better fit the diverse older population today and the complex lives of people in postindustrial society. They also recognize the potential for further growth and development in later life.

Finally, terms such as *multidimensionality*, *plasticity*, and *variability* describe the many lifestyles that older people live today. At the least, modern society can provide supports that keep people from social breakdown. But society can do more. It can create the conditions for a *good* old age. This includes supportive housing, good transportation, adequate income, and meaningful roles for older people to play. Society can take into account the individual and the cultural diversity of the older population. It can recognize the potential in older people, and it can accept and encourage many versions of a good old age.

SUMMARY

- Good aging refers to the mastery of inner and outer challenges in later life. These challenges include changes in mental ability, changes in social relations, and changes in social status.
- The stability and adaptability of the brain allow for continuity and growth in mental potential throughout life.
- *Memory* refers to recall after learning has taken place. Studies find little difference between younger and older people in sensory and short-term memory. Researchers find the greatest difference in function between younger and older people in long-term memory.
- Studies of memory find a generalized slowing with age in the search and retrieval of information. Psychologists consider this a fundamental change in mental function as a person ages. Recent research points to flexibility and plasticity in brain function as well as a mental reserve capacity.
- Studies of memory in every day life give a more optimistic view of mental potential in later life. Older people also do as well or better than younger people on real-world tasks. Experts can maintain their skills through practice.
- Longitudinal research on intelligence (the measure of mental capacity) shows a difference in intellectual performance between younger and older people. But intelligence differs less on some measures than on others. Fluid intelligence tends to decrease with age; crystallized intelligence can increase with age.
- Older people select tasks, optimize their abilities, and compensate for losses in mental function. Training can improve mental performance on specific tasks. It can help a person compensate for decline in mental ability.
- Older people have the potential to develop wisdom. Studies of wisdom describe specific criteria that describe this talent. These include the ability to deal with uncertainty and tolerance for others.
- Studies show that physical exercise can enhance mental performance. Exercise increases blood flow to the brain, and vigorous exercise may work best.
- Creativity can grow in later life. Creativity can refer to great works of art or science, or it can refer to personal expression. Creativity improves well-being and gives a sense of purpose in life. Some creative works show the benefits of lifelong experience.
- Aging poses challenges to a person's sense of self. These challenges result from social attitudes toward older people, physical decline, and loss of social roles.
- Some psychologists describe later life as a series of stages. But others disagree and see aging as a process that can take many forms according to a person's gender, race/ethnicity, and culture. Some researchers see later life as a time to search for meaning and a deeper purpose.
- Spiritual belief and membership in a religious community bring fulfillment and meaning to many older people. Some people hold traditional religious beliefs based on faith in God and church doctrine. Other people see God in the order of the natural world. Older Americans today hold many spiritual beliefs, engage in diverse spiritual practices, and belong to many different faiths. This diversity will increase in the future. Traditional religious communities can help older people take part in community life by providing supports like transportation and outreach.
- The life course perspective proposes that development is a lifelong process. A person's individual life course development depends on his or her physical condition, intelligence, personality, coping styles, resources, gender, and social world.
- Life course researchers propose that three types of events shape a person's life: nonnormative or unplanned events; normative, history-graded events; and normative, age-graded events.
- Organic brain disorders (e.g., Alzheimer's disease), loneliness, depression, and suicide are potential problems in old age. Experiences such as illness, widowhood, and retirement can create feelings of loneliness and isolation. These feelings can lead to suicide. Older people need a purpose in life and need to feel useful in order to live a good old age. Social supports and opportunities for social engagement lead to life satisfaction in later life.

DISCUSSION QUESTIONS

1. Describe the process of remembering something. How does this process differ for older and younger people? What methods do you use in everyday life to help you remember things?
2. What effect does age have on a person's intelligence? What type of intelligence stays stable or may even increase with age?
3. How do people adjust their behavior to cope with mental changes due to aging? Describe the SOC model of coping and adaptation. Give some examples that illustrate each part of this model.
4. What sorts of creative activities enhance well-being in later life? What links do researchers find between creativity and mental function in later life? What are some of the benefits of creative personal expression?
5. What challenges to the self does a person face with age? Give some examples of what people can do to maintain self-esteem as they age.

6. Define the terms *on time* and *off time* in relation to life events. Have you ever found yourself off time for a life event? Do you know someone who has experienced this? Why did this occur? What did it feel like? How did you/they deal with the experience?

7. List and explain the three types of events that shape a person's life. Which type of life event has affected you most so far in your life? Give examples of each type from your own life. How did you cope with these life events?

8. What benefits do people say they get from spiritual belief and religious practice? What changes in spiritual practice are likely to take place in the future as new cohorts enter old age?

9. What life events can lead to psychological problems in later life? What events will more likely affect women than men? How do men and women differ in their ways of coping with personal problems? Give examples of the different responses for each gender (e.g., suicide).

10. What can society do to prevent or buffer problems older people face in later life? Do you know of any prevention or support programs for older people in your community? Describe them. What prevention programs are needed in your community but don't exist at this time?

11. Do all ethnic, racial, and income groups have equal access to social supports in later life? What might inhibit someone from a minority group from seeking and using community supports? How can your community overcome these barriers?

SUGGESTED READING

Garner, J. D., & Mercer, S. O. (Eds.). (2001). *Women as they age.* New York: Haworth Press.

This collection looks at the challenges women face as they age in a male-dominated society. It includes discussions of psychological, social, and health care issues related to older women. It also looks at the challenges that many older women face. These include surrogate parenting, membership in an ethnic minority, and intimacy. The book can also serve as a resource guide for women in later life. It encourages empowerment and the development of self-determination.

Jung, C. G. (1976). The stages of life. In J. Campbell (Ed.), *The portable Jung.* Harmondsworth, England: Penguin.

This classic short essay takes a profound look at healthy aging. Jung describes the unique task of later life as a recovery of culture, a time for reflection and inner development. He says that we may need to learn how to make the most of this time of life.

McFadden, S. H., Brennan, M., & Patrick, J. H. (Eds.). (2003). *New directions in the study of late life religiousness and spirituality.* Binghamton, NY: Haworth Pastoral Press.

These essays focus on religious activity and spirituality in old age. The articles discuss the role of spirituality in providing quality health care to older people, the meaning of religion and spirituality to different racial and ethnic groups, and the role of religion in helping people cope with problems such as dementia, caregiving, and bereavement.

Weinberg, J. A. (2006). *Still going strong: Memoirs, stories, and poems about great older women.* Binghamton, NY: Haworth Press.

This is a collection of stories and creative works by and about older women. The writings show the meaning of later life as seen through the eyes of the writers or people who admire them. The book expresses the fulfillment that many older women feel in later life.

Websites to Consult

Alzheimer's Association
www.alz.org

This site contains information about Alzheimer's disease. It includes information on topics from diagnosis to coping with caregiving stress. Alz.org contains valuable information for those who must grapple with Alzheimer's in their lives. This Web site can also help you better understand the biological basis and social impact of the disease.

The American Association for Geriatric Psychiatry
www.aagpgpa.org

This Web site contains the latest news and information about the field of geriatric psychiatry. It updates regularly with new information about geriatric legislation, advances in the field, and information for caregivers.

National Institute on Aging Alzheimer's Disease Education and Referral (ADEAR) Center
www.nia.nih.gov/alzheimers

This portal contains general information on Alzheimer's disease as well as current information and studies about the illness. You can download many of the publications and datasets for free. An excellent starting place for research related to AD.

chapter 6

RACE AND ETHNICITY

Bart Hircus runs exercise classes for older people at housing complexes and recreation centers for seniors. A few years ago, a Native American senior center invited him to hold some fitness classes. They assigned him a room and announced the class in advance. He came to the center eager to work with this new group of people.

About 10 people, men and women, showed up for his session. He began with warm-up stretches and then put on some peppy music. He launched into his routine and his usual patter. But he noticed that after a few minutes his students began to drift out to a nearby patio for a smoke and some talk. People would wander in and out to see how the class was going or to watch Bart do the exercises.

This went on for about 30 minutes. Finally, Bart gave up the exercising and began talking with the center members. He found that they didn't get the point of all this jumping around. They had worked hard all their lives. Some of them had trapped, hunted, and lived in the bush. They associated exercise with hard work. They couldn't understand why anyone would get sweated up and not get paid for it. To them this looked like work, and they wanted no part of it.

After he gave up trying to get them to exercise, Bart enjoyed his experience. He says he learned a lot from listening to these people and from coming to understand their points of view. He does things differently today when he presents a program to a minority group audience. For one thing, he gets to know something about the culture and background of the group before he begins. For another, he explains the purpose of the program and its benefits in advance. Finally, he tailors the program to the background and experience of his students.

Gerontologists know that culture and life events shape an older person's worldview. For example, many older minority members face disadvantages today due to discrimination they have faced throughout their lives. Other minority members have just arrived in the United States and have little knowledge of American society, its language, and its customs.

Gerontologists have learned that cultural and economic barriers can keep minority older people from living a satisfying old age. They also know some of the things that can bring down these barriers: offering a service in a minority language, using minority staff to deliver the service, or locating services in settings that will attract minority members. The study of minority aging expands our understanding of aging today and suggests ways to improve older minority members' lives.

This chapter looks at (1) the size, composition, and socioeconomic status of minority groups; (2) the experience of aging as a minority group member; and (3) creative responses to the challenge of minority aging.

WHO ARE THE MINORITY ELDERLY?[1]

The term **dominant group** in the United States applies to the white population. Whites make up a numerical majority of the population in the United States. More importantly, this group has the most power and controls most of the social and economic resources in the country. The encyclopedia defines a *minority* as a culturally, ethnically, or racially distinct group living within a larger society. Minority group members have a sense of peoplehood and shared origins (Angel & Angel, 2006). In addition, minority group members often face prejudice and discrimination within the larger society.

Sociologists include women and gays in this definition, but here we focus on minorities based on race, eth-

nicity, and national origin. The term *minority* as we use it here applies to the four largest groups recognized by the U.S. Census: African Americans, Hispanic Americans, Asian American/Pacific Islanders (APIs), and American Indians/Alaskan Natives (see Figure 6.1).

Many people think of the United States as a **melting pot**. The U.S. takes in people from around the world and turns them into Americans. This image arose in the early years of the 20th century when European immigrants poured into this country. Many of them settled in cities on the East Coast and adapted to American customs to survive. The melting pot ideal encouraged children to leave behind their parents' language and customs. Assimilation opened the way for these people to enter middle-class American life.

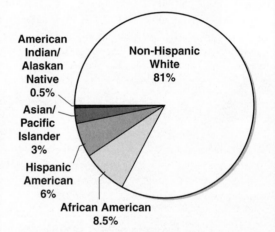

Whites make up the large majority (81%) of the older population. Some groups, such as Asian Americans and American Indians, make up a relatively small portion of the older population. Other groups, such as Hispanic Americans and African Americans, make up larger proportions of the older population. All of these minority groups will grow in size and will make up a greater proportion of the older population in the future.

By the year 2010, for example, the U.S. Census Bureau projects that the minority older population will grow to about 20% of the total older population (up from 17% in 2002). This increase in the minority older population will require new policies and programs to meet minority elders' needs.

FIGURE 6.1 Population of the U.S. by Racial and Ethnic Group, 2005

Note: The figures in the chart total less than 100% due to rounding.

Source: U.S. Census Bureau, *Statistical Abstract of the United States. Table No. 14. Resident population by race, Hispanic origin, and age: 2000 and 2005,* 2007. Retrieved: November 16, 2007, from www.census.gov/compendia/statab/tables/07s0014.xls.

---

[1]Minority groups do not agree on a single term to describe their groups. Also, government reports differ in their designation of each group. Here, I use the most commonly used terms at this time. I use the terms *African American* or *black; Hispanic, Latino,* or *Latina;* and *American Indian* or *Native American* to describe each of these groups. The term *Hispanic American* refers to people who are Hispanic or Latino. Hispanics may be any race. The term *African American* refers to people who identify themselves as African American or black. I use the term *white* to refer to whites.

This view now seems naive. Large numbers of Jews, for example, immigrated to the United States early in the 1900s. They adopted the customs and culture of the dominant population, but they held on to a strong group identity. The same can be said for Asian Americans, African Americans, and Hispanic Americans. People understand the need to assimilate in their public lives. But they often maintain their culture through religious practices, festivals, and food. Ethnic identity survives for many generations and may even grow stronger as later generations celebrate their ethnicity.

The United States today looks more like a **pluralistic society** where many racial and ethnic groups exist side by side. Angel and Angel (2006, p. 94) say that "at the beginning of the twenty-first century, the population of the United States is socially, demographically, and culturally almost unrecognizably different than it was at the beginning of the twentieth century."

For one thing, the mix of these ethnic groups looks different today than in the last century. Migrants in the early years of the 20th century came mostly from Europe. Today, migrants come from all over the world, primarily from Asia and Latin America (He, Sangupta, Velkoff, & De Barros, 2005). These new groups, compared to the majority white population, have high fertility rates. As a result, by the middle of this century one in two Americans will come from Asian, Latin America, or African American descent. The white majority of today will become one of many minority groups.

As in the past, today's migrants retain some of their original culture. Immigrants bring to American society new beliefs, new cuisines, and new customs. Even third- or fourth-generation Americans show pride in their Italian, Polish, Chinese, or other ancestry. More recent immigrants exhibit even closer ties to their original language and culture. Spanish, Chinese, and other TV stations find audiences throughout the country, as do newspapers and magazines published in languages other than English.

Ramon Valle, a sociologist at San Diego State University, said that an **assimilation continuum** exists. The continuum runs from very traditional to bicultural to very assimilated. People can fit in various places on this continuum for different areas of their lives. A minority group member may be very assimilated in the office, but adopt a traditional worldview at home.

An example or two will make this clear. A colleague of mine from India wears a suit and tie to the office every day. He speaks English with only a mild Indian accent, and he shows few outward signs of his ethnic background. But at home he carries on many traditional Indian practices. He eats a vegetarian diet, he reads his tradition's scriptures, and he performs a *puja*, or religious ritual, every morning before work. He fits in the bicultural category of Valle's continuum. He scores high on assimilation in the workplace, but he also scores high on tradition at home.

An African American friend would score high on assimilation at the office and in his personal life, but he does not want to be completely assimilated either at home or at work. At work, he stands up for the interests of African Americans and expresses views that highlight his racial identity. He also owns a cottage in rural Virginia near his birthplace. He drives there on long weekends and in the summer to enjoy the rural lifestyle he identifies with his roots.

Valle's assimilation continuum points to the complexity of ethnic and racial identity. It shows that individuals differ in how they identify with, use, and express their race and ethnicity. In part, this reflects personal preference. It also reflects the demands of U.S. society for a common public face.

The older population reflects the pluralism of U.S. society. Older people belong to a variety of ethnic and racial minorities. Some of these older people came to the United States from other countries many years ago. Other minority older people were born in the United States but have had their lives shaped by their ethnic or racial identities. Some older minority group members have just arrived in the United States. Some came by choice, to follow their middle-aged children. Others came as refugees. These new immigrants face culture shock as well as issues related to aging. They are challenged by language barriers, difficulties in making new friends, and problems using medical and social services (Longino & Bradley, 2006).

Researchers find that diversity exists even within a single minority group (Burr, Mutchler, & Gerst, 2010). Yeo (2009) notes that the Asian group, for example, includes subgroups that differ in education, English ability, and income. The 2000 Census reported an 11.9% poverty rate for the group of older Asians. But poverty rates for subgroups within the Asian group range from 5.6% for Japanese older people to 27.4% for Hmong older people. When researchers report on "Asian" older people they miss the large and important differences within this group. Yeo notes that similar differences exist within the American Indian cultures and the Hispanic population.

Hispanic Americans, for example, have come to the United States from Spain, Cuba, Puerto Rico,

South America, and Mexico. Each subgroup has a different culture and worldview, although research reports often refer to them all as Hispanic or Latino.[2] Even within a minority subgroup (such as the Mexican American group), older people differ by age, gender, personality, how long they have lived in the United States, and whether they live in an urban or rural setting.

This great diversity among the minority population makes the study of minority aging fascinating. It also makes generalization risky.

WHY STUDY MINORITY AGING?

Until the 1990s, a Gerontological Society of America report (GSA Task Force, 1994, p. vii) says, "The study of aging in America has been principally the study of the older Whites." But gerontologists now show an interest in minority aging. Why this increased interest?

First, minority older populations have begun to grow in size and in proportion to the dominant older population. This growth will continue in the future. The number of minority older people will grow from 5.7 million in 2000 to 33.5 million in 2050. Population experts expect the Hispanic older population to quadruple in size by 2050 and become the largest group of minority elders. During this same time the Asian older populations will grow by a factor of 5 (Markides & Wallace, 2007).

Between 2008 and 2050, the non-Hispanic white proportion of the older population could fall from 80% to 59%. During this same period Hispanic Americans will nearly triple their proportion in the older population (from 7% to 20%). African Americans will increase their proportion in the older population from 9% to 12%. And Asian Americans will triple their proportion in the older population from 3% to 9% (Federal Interagency Forum, 2008). This will create the most diverse older population in U.S. history. (See Figure 6.2).

Second, minority older people often have lower incomes, poorer health, and shorter lives than other older people. The study of minorities can lead to more responsive programs for older people and a better quality of life for minority elders. Third, studies show that minority group members experience aging differently than do whites. Leisure and retirement, for example, can mean something different for minority elders than for the dominant culture (Calasanti, 2002; Wilcox, 2002). Fourth, minority groups can teach us other ways of growing old. They show the strength and resourcefulness that older people bring to their communities and to our society.

Finally, older populations express the diversity of U.S. society. They keep and pass on many of the traditions of their cultures and add to the richness of American life. Native American elders, for example, often keep up the traditions of their society (Penman, 2000). Some of these elders have lived through their culture's transition from a rural to an urban lifestyle. Some African American elders keep alive family stories, recipes, and values. They provide models of strength and stability in a changing world. Japanese American elders recall key moments in the history of their group's life in North America. Some remember the deportations that took place during World War II. They know firsthand the pain of prejudice and discrimination. These elders serve as valuable resources for younger generations.

DEMOGRAPHIC CHARACTERISTICS OF DOMINANT AND MINORITY GROUP ELDERS

Whites: The Dominant Group Older Population

The elderly white population includes a variety of ethnic groups of European origin. The white subgroups with the largest numbers of people—mostly of European origin—have a long history of settlement in the United States. Compared with the national average, they also have greater proportions of their populations age 65 and over.

The older white population has more formal education and lower rates of poverty than minority group elders (He et al., 2005). For example, elderly whites have twice the high school graduation rate of elderly Hispanics and 1.7 times the rate of elderly blacks. Asian/Pacific Island elderly (referred to as *Asians* or *Asian Americans* from this point forward) also have a lower rate of high school graduation than whites. But they have a higher rate of university graduation. This,

---

[2]No single name is agreed on by all members of this group or by researchers and government officials. Members of this group who live in Texas and have a Mexican background often refer to themselves as Hispanic. Californians tend to use the term *Latino* or *Latina*. The U.S. Census and other government reports use the term *Hispanic American*. Gerontologists use all of these terms. Some people feel that the word *Hispanic* refers to a colonial past and oppression. They feel that *Latino/Latina* avoids this connotation. We will use either term here to refer to this group. In particular we will use the term *Hispanic* when we use information from government reports that use this label.

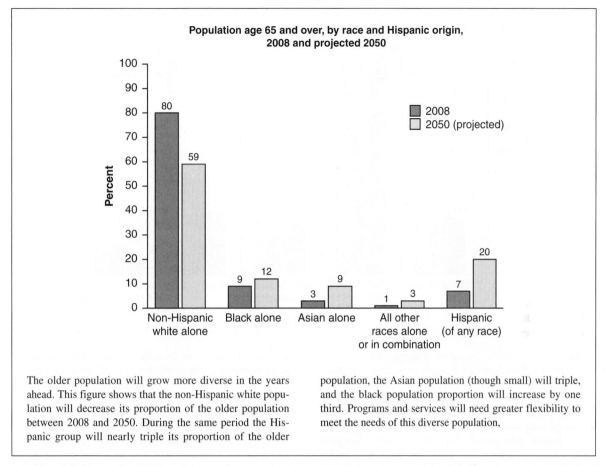

The older population will grow more diverse in the years ahead. This figure shows that the non-Hispanic white population will decrease its proportion of the older population between 2008 and 2050. During the same period the Hispanic group will nearly triple its proportion of the older population, the Asian population (though small) will triple, and the black population proportion will increase by one third. Programs and services will need greater flexibility to meet the needs of this diverse population,

FIGURE 6.2   Racial and Ethnic Composition of the Population Age 65 and Over, by Race and Hispanic Origin 2008 and Projected to 2050

Source: Federal Interagency Forum on Aging-Related Statistics. (2010). *Older Americans 2010: Key Indicators of Well-Being.* Indicator 2. Racial and Ethnic Composition. Washington, DC. Citing U.S. Census Bureau, *Population Estimates and Projections, 2008.*

in part, reflects the higher educational levels of more recent Asian immigrants when they arrived in the United States.

These differences between the majority and minority groups reflect the historical experiences of the minority elderly. Many older Hispanic Americans grew up outside the United States and, compared with whites, had fewer educational opportunities. Older blacks experienced racial discrimination and segregated schooling, and, compared with whites, they had fewer opportunities to get higher education.

Measures of poverty show results similar to those of education. Older non-Hispanic whites have a poverty rate of 7.4%. Older blacks have more than three times the rate of poverty of older whites (23.2%). Older Hispanics have about two-and-a-half times the

rate of poverty of older whites (17.1%). And Asian elderly have about one and a half times the rate of poverty (11.3%) compared to older whites (Federal Interagency Forum, 2010h).

Williams and Wilson (2001) say that when poverty figures include the near poor (those above poverty but less than twice the poverty level), the gap between whites and minority elderly grows. They report that 16% of whites fell into the poor and near poor group. But 45% of blacks, 34% of Hispanics, and 19% of Asian elderly fall into this group. Some subgroups (rural older people, women, the oldest old) within these minority groups have even higher rates of poor and near-poor elderly. And women, compared with men, in all racial groups have fewer financial resources.

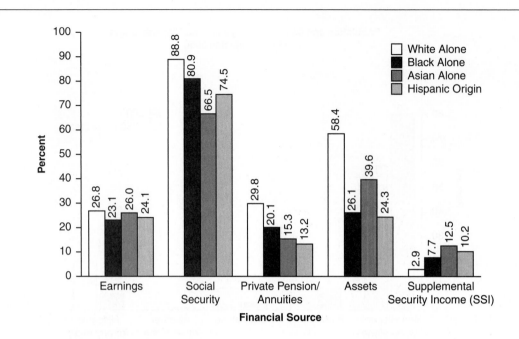

This figure shows the percentage of people in a group who get income from a particular source (e.g., 26.8% of white seniors get income from earnings compared to 23.1% of black seniors). Note that, compared to the other groups, the white population has a higher proportion of members with income from all of these sources (except SSI, a program for the poorest older people). This reflects whites' economic advantage throughout life. Their higher incomes and more stable work careers lead to better incomes and more diverse sources of income in old age.

The Hispanic group has the lowest proportion of people who draw income from any of the sources here (except for Earnings and Social Security). Some members of this group immigrated later in life, have poor English skills and low educational levels, and work in low-income jobs. All of these conditions along with racial and ethnic discrimination throughout life lead to low income in old age. The Asian group (also a group with many recent immigrants) has the lowest proportion of members who get Social Security. The Asian and Hispanic groups also have small proportions of their populations with private pensions. They have the highest rates of poverty (twice the white rate for Hispanics and one-and-a-half the white rate for Asians) and rely most heavily on SSI.

FIGURE 6.3   Percentage of a Group with Income from a Specified Source for Persons Age 65 or Older, by Race and Hispanic Origin, 2008*

*Totals more than 100% because income comes from more than one source.

Source: U.S. Social Security Administration. Office of Retirement and Disability Policy. (2009). *Income of the population 55 or older, 2008.* Table 2.A3: Percentage with income from specified source, by marital status, race, Hispanic origin, and age, 2008. http://www.ssa.gov/policy/docs/statcomps/income_pop55/2008/sect02.html#table2.a3.

Members of the white group will likely have access to and make the most use of **formal support systems**. These systems include government programs, health care services, community centers, and ethnic associations. Today, most programs for older people best fit the needs of the white group. But this relatively large and dominant older population will shrink in size in the years ahead. Indeed, this group may decrease to under 60% of the total older population by 2050.

Diversity of the Minority Population

Minority groups differ from the white population in mortality, fertility, and migration. Minority groups also differ from one another. The Hispanic American group, for example, has a young population due to high fertility and high levels of immigration. This group will show growth in its older *and* its younger population in the years ahead. Even within the

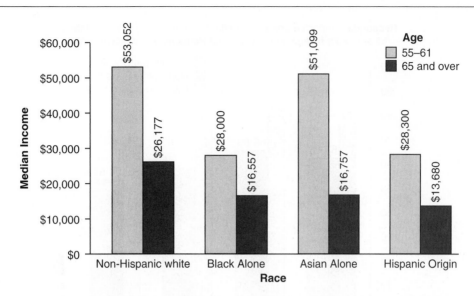

This figure shows the median income for two adult age groups for four racial and ethnic groups. The 65-and-older population for all races and ethnicities has lower incomes than the younger adult age group. Most people in the younger age group continue to earn a salary. The older group contains mostly people who live on a pension. It also contains very old people who have only Social Security income.

For both age groups, whites have higher incomes than blacks and Hispanics. The lower income for minority older people shows the effect of lower income for minority members earlier in life. Note that in the older age group, the income gap lessens between whites and blacks. Most people will experience a drop in income after retirement. This fact and income from Social Security narrows the gap in incomes in later life. All groups show about a 50% decrease in income between the younger and older age groups. Asian minority members show the greatest gap in incomes between the age groups. This reflects the higher educational status of more recent Asian immigrants (and hence the higher incomes of Asians in the workforce). Social Security provides a floor for minority group members that keeps many of them out of poverty.

FIGURE 6.4   Median Income (in Dollars) by Age, Race, and Hispanic Origin, 2008

Source: Social Security Online. (2010). *Income of the Population 55 or Older, 2008.* Table 3.A3, p. 87. Retrieved November 7, 2010, from http://www.ssa.gov/policy/docs/statcomps/income_pop55/2008/sect03.pdf.

Hispanic minority group, subgroups differ in their demography and cultural background.

Some Hispanic elderly come from Cuba. Others come from Puerto Rico, Latin America, and Europe (see Figure 6.7). Each of these groups has a unique demographic structure. Cuban Americans, for example, make up the third largest group of Hispanic elderly. Many of these people came to the United States in middle age in the 1960s as political refugees after the Cuban revolution. Cuban Americans make up only 3.7% of the total Hispanic population, but they make up 14% of the over 65 Hispanic population (U.S. Census Bureau, 2007b).

Mexican Americans made up slightly more than one-half of the older Hispanic population in 2004 (Markides & Wallace, 2007). Almost half of them live in the West (Texas and California), but they also live in many other parts of the country. Some of these people trace their family origins in the United States to colonial times. Others arrived in the 1950s to do agricultural work. Still others have just arrived as legal and illegal immigrants. This group has many young adults and a high birth rate. They have a young population today, but will add to the older Hispanic population in the future (Hayes-Bautista, Hsu, Perez, & Gambon, 2002).

Other minority groups show similar diversity. Markides and Wallace (2007) say that the Asian Pacific Island group includes 60 different nationality and language groups. Each of these groups has a unique culture, demographic structure, and history in the United States. The Chinese subgroup makes up

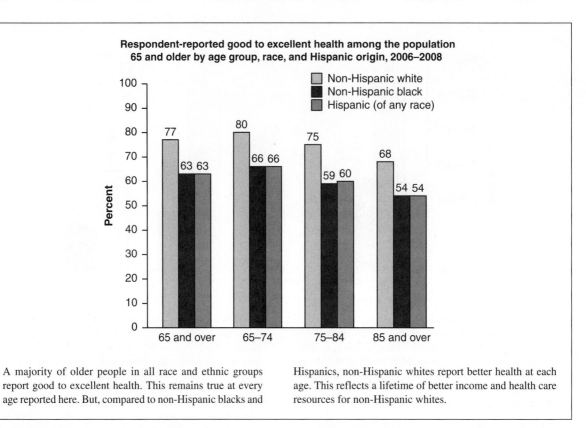

FIGURE 6.5 Respondent-Assessed Health Status.

Source: Federal Interagency Forum on Aging-Related Statistics. (2010). *Older Americans 2010: Key Indicators of Well-Being.* Indicator 18. Respondent-Assessed Health Status. Washington, DC. Citing U.S. Census Bureau, *Population Estimates and Projections, 2008.* Citing Centers for Disease Control and Prevention, National Center for Health Statistics, *National Health Interview Survey.*

30% of Asian elderly. Japanese and Filipinos each make up 24% of the Asian elderly group. Koreans make up 8% of Asian elders, Asian Indians make up 5%, and other groups make up the rest of the Asian elderly population (Williams & Wilson, 2001).

These subgroups (like those of the Hispanic population) each have their own history in the United States. Most Chinese older people, for example, were born in the United States. Their parents immigrated to the United States in the early 20th century (Williams & Wilson, 2001). Japanese American elders also have a long history in the United States. Most Vietnamese and Cambodian elderly immigrants entered the United States recently. Each of these groups has a different relationship with American culture and different access to social and economic resources (Hayes-Bautista et al., 2002). Almost two-thirds of Asian older people live in the western United States (He et al., 2005).

The African American group also has many sub-groups. Some African Americans came to the United States as slaves before the Civil War. Their descendants make up the largest proportion of African Americans today. Some of them continue to live in the South. Others live in Northern cities and suburbs. These groups may have very different cultural backgrounds and lifestyles. Other African Americans have recently arrived from Africa, South America, and the Caribbean. They bring their own cultural values and traditions. Much of the literature and research on older African Americans focuses on inequality, poverty, and the long-term effects of racism. Yet many older African Americans retire from management and professional jobs and live middle-class lives.

Gerontologists who study minority aging must keep this minority group diversity in mind. Subgroups of older minority Americans will have different

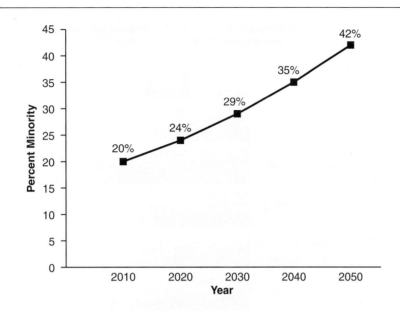

This figure shows the increase in the proportion of minority group members within the older population. It shows that the proportion of minority members in the older population more than doubles between 2010 and 2050. Several demographic forces account for the increase. Minority populations have higher fertility rates than the white population. These children will add to the older minority population in the future. Longer life expectancies for minority group members will mean more older minority elders in the future. Also, older immigrants who come to the United States with their families will increase the older minority population. Many of these immigrants will belong to the Hispanic and Asian minority groups.

FIGURE 6.6　Proportion of Minorities in the U.S. Population Age 65 and Over, 2010–2050

Source: Vincent, G. K., & Velkoff, V. A. (2010). *The next four decades: The older population in the United States: 2010 to 2050.* Table A-2, p. 11. U.S. Census Bureau. Retrieved November 7, 2010, from http://www.census.gov/prod/2010pubs/p25-1138.pdf.

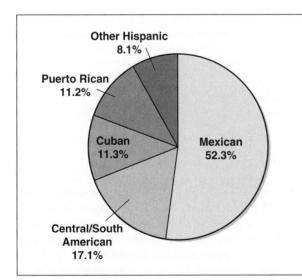

This chart shows the diversity of subgroups within the Hispanic older population. Mexican Americans, most of whom live in the southern and western parts of the United States, make up half of the Hispanic older group. The other subgroups live mostly in the eastern part of the United States. Each of these groups has a unique history, cultural heritage, and experience in the United States. These differences lead to different experiences of aging within each community.

FIGURE 6.7　Subgroups within the Hispanic U.S. Older Population (65+), 2008

Source: U.S. Census Bureau. (2009). *Statistical Abstract of the United States.* Population, Social and Economic Characteristics of the Hispanic Population: 2008. Table No. 39. Retrieved: November 7, 2010, from http://www.census.gov/prod/2009pubs/10statab/pop.pdf.

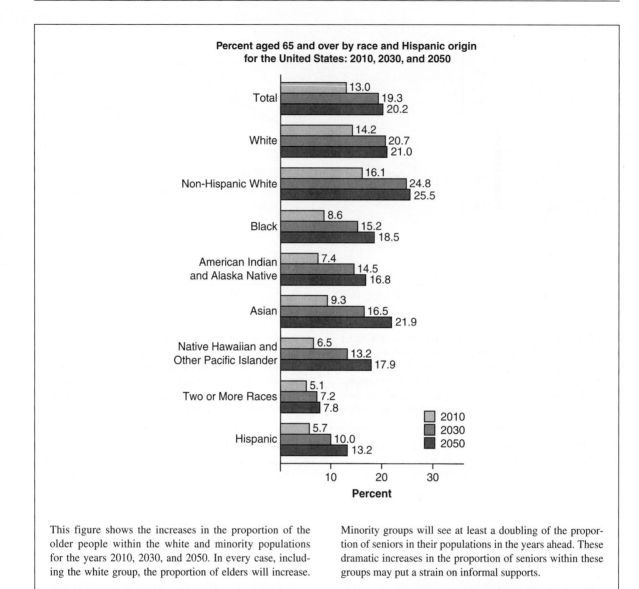

Percent aged 65 and over by race and Hispanic origin for the United States: 2010, 2030, and 2050

This figure shows the increases in the proportion of the older people within the white and minority populations for the years 2010, 2030, and 2050. In every case, including the white group, the proportion of elders will increase.

Minority groups will see at least a doubling of the proportion of seniors in their populations in the years ahead. These dramatic increases in the proportion of seniors within these groups may put a strain on informal supports.

FIGURE 6.8 Percent Age 65 and Over by Race and Hispanic Origin for the United States: 2010, 2030, 2050

Source: Vincent, G. K., & Velkoff, V. A. (2010). *The Next Four Decades. The older population in the United States: 2010 to 2050.* Figure 6. Current Population Reports, P25-1138, U.S. Census Bureau, Washington, DC.

health care and social service needs (Yeo, 2009) (see Figure 6.8).

Aging of the Minority Population

The minority older population as a whole is aging. In 2006, 5.3 million Americans were age 85 and over. This will increase to 21 million people by the year 2050—a fourfold increase (Federal Interagency Forum, 2008). Over this same time period, the number of oldest-old African Americans (85+) will increase sixfold, and the oldest-old Hispanics will increase by 12 times. Other minority groups will also show large increases in their oldest-old populations.

These dramatic increases in numbers may put a strain on informal supports. Very old minority elders who rely on family supports today may have to turn to formal supports for help. Right now, minority elders tend to underuse formal supports. These supports may not suit their needs. Formal supports will have to adapt their services and modes of delivery to meet the needs of the growing very old minority population.

THREE THEORIES ON MINORITY GROUP AGING

Gerontologists study the impact of minority group membership on aging. They ask how a minority person's experiences throughout life affect that person's experience of old age. Three theories describe the effects of minority group membership on the older person: multiple jeopardy, leveling, and the life course perspective.

Multiple Jeopardy

Societies use age, gender, social class, and minority group membership to classify people. *Young, male, upper middle-class,* and *white* place a person at the upper end of North American society. *Old, female, lower class,* and *minority group membership* place a person at the lower end. The **multiple jeopardy** perspective says that a person with more than one of these characteristics—for example, a minority member age 65 and over—will face multiple jeopardy. According to this view, people in multiple jeopardy will face an increased risk of death and illness, compared with whites, as they age.

Some gerontologists gave a broad meaning to multiple jeopardy. They viewed the poorer health and income of older minority group members, compared with dominant group members, as evidence of multiple jeopardy (Belgrave & Bradsher, 1994). But Markides, Timbers, and Osberg (1984) gave a more precise meaning to multiple jeopardy. They said that multiple jeopardy exists when (1) the minority group has poorer health or lower income than the dominant group and (2) the minority group, compared with the dominant group, shows greater declines in health and well-being with age.

This means that multiple jeopardy exists when age *adds* to the disadvantage already experienced by a minority group in middle age. According to this view, the gap between the two groups must widen with age for multiple jeopardy to exist. Markides (1987b) called multiple jeopardy the "key conceptual model in the field" of minority group studies in gerontology.

Researchers find it hard to measure multiple jeopardy. For one thing, most studies of multiple jeopardy use a cross-sectional method. They look at a minority group at one point in time. This makes it impossible to tell if things have gotten worse for minority members, compared with dominant group members, as they have aged. It could be that older age cohorts differ in some way from younger cohorts, regardless of race.

For example, African Americans have poorer health than whites in old age, in part because older African Americans had poorer health and nutrition in their youth. This has to do with poverty (and discrimination) in U.S. society. It only becomes multiple jeopardy if the gap between African Americans' health and whites' health widens as they age.

Researchers need to study people over time to test for multiple jeopardy. Longitudinal study could also control for social class differences. Multiple jeopardy may affect only lower-class minority group members. If so, then social class rather than minority group membership leads to multiple jeopardy.

Critique of Multiple Jeopardy Theory

A number of researchers find the multiple jeopardy theory limited. First, some recent studies of older African Americans' health find no evidence of multiple jeopardy. Kelley-Moore and Ferraro (2004), for example, found differences in health between older African Americans and whites. They found that African American older people had poorer health and more disability than whites. But age did not amplify differences based on race. The researchers say that this supports the "persistent-inequality" thesis. They conclude that African Americans have poorer health early in life, and that this carries through to old age (Ferraro, 2006).

Second, Jackson, Taylor, and Chatters (1993b, p. 2) reject the multiple jeopardy perspective. They believe it takes a "victim-centered" approach. It shows the negative effects of discrimination on minority older people. But it fails to study the strengths and coping abilities of minority members. This does an injustice to minority elders.

Third, Hayes-Bautista and colleagues (2002, p. 39) report data that fail to support the multiple jeopardy theory. They used California data to look at health risks and mortality among older minority group members. They found that elderly African Americans fit the model of a minority health disparity in later life. But Hispanic and Asian elderly showed the opposite of this model.

Compared with whites, Hispanic and Asian older people showed lower relative risk of death from nearly all of the major diseases of old age. Hayes-Bautista and colleagues call this an "epidemiological paradox." In other words, these two minority groups have the risk factors—low income, low English language ability, and low educational achievement—that should lead to multiple jeopardy. But these groups show the opposite of multiple jeopardy in old age. Compared to whites, they have a lower risk of illness and premature death. These findings call into question the general application of multiple jeopardy theory to all racial and ethnic groups.

Still, the multiple jeopardy theory has had some value. It has led researchers to separate the effects of age from lifelong effects of inequality. This perspective offers a framework for longitudinal studies of specific subgroups of older people.

Leveling

Some studies find that multiple jeopardy describes only some characteristics of older minority members' lives. Williams and Wilson (2001) say that ethnic identity can help a person adapt to the stress of living as a minority member. It can also offer people self-esteem and career opportunities.

The **leveling** perspective says that the health and incomes of minority and dominant group members look more alike as people age. For example, a pension rarely replaces a middle-class person's salary. Middle-class workers usually see a decrease in income when they leave their jobs. Minority members with low incomes may see no decrease in income with age. Many of these people work past age 65 because they have no pensions. The lowest earners may even see an increase in income when they receive Social Security payments. These trends lead to a smaller income gap between minority and dominant group members as they age.

Studies of the oldest old lend some of the strongest support to the leveling perspective. Studies of mortality find that minority group members show higher mortality than the rest of the U.S. population until age 65. From age 65 onward, they show lower mortality than the population as a whole. Elo and Preston (1997) found this **mortality crossover** among blacks for men between the ages of 85 and 89 and for women ages 90 to 94. N. E. Johnson (2000) reports a crossover between black and white older people in mortality at age 81. She also found a crossover at age 76 in the

total number of six potentially fatal diseases including cancer, heart disease, and diabetes.

The U.S. Census reports that black men, compared to white men at age 85, show a 0.2-year advantage in life expectancy. And black women at age 85, compared to white women at the same age, show a 0.4- year advantage in life expectancy. At age 100 black men and women have a 0.6 year advantage in life expectancy (U.S. Census Bureau, 2010e). Hayes-Bautista and colleagues (2002) found this tendency in data on Hispanic and Asian elderly in California. John (1994) reports this mortality crossover by age 65 in American Indians.

Studies of leveling, like studies of multiple jeopardy, often look at older minority group members at one point in time. This makes it hard to say exactly why the crossover effect takes place. Gerontologists think that this crossover occurs because whites gain benefits in life expectancy early in life due to better nutrition and medical care. But only the healthiest minority group members survive into late old age (Gelfand, 2003; Land & Yang, 2006). Those who do survive show extreme hardiness. They resist common causes of death in later life and so have longer life expectancies than whites.

N. E. Johnson (2000) looked at mortality and illness at two points in time. She concludes that the crossover in disease (lower for blacks than for whites at later ages) accounts for the crossover in mortality (higher mortality for whites than for blacks in late old age). This still leaves the question of why a crossover in the amount of disease occurs. Researchers will continue to study this puzzling phenomenon.

Both the leveling and the multiple jeopardy perspectives have their place in the study of aging. Research guided by these theories illustrates the resilience of older minority members at later ages.

The Life Course Perspective

Gerontologists have begun to take a broader view of minority group aging. The life course perspective begins with the idea that life unfolds from birth to death in a social, cultural, and historical context. This perspective looks at the impact of social institutions, historical periods and events, personal biography, life cycle stage, life events, and resources on the minority older person. It also looks at differences between minority groups, cultural subgroups within a minority group, and age cohorts among minority group members.

The life course perspective looks for continuities and discontinuities within minority groups. For example, it links early life experiences to actions and attitudes in later life. The life course perspective also links life experiences to the minority norms for timing life events and entering and leaving social roles.

Cumulative disadvantage theory fits the life course perspective. It says that inequalities throughout life lead to inequality in old age (Kail, Quadagno, & Keene, 2009; Burr et al., 2010). The more disadvantages a person faces earlier in life (e.g., poor education, poverty in youth), the more disadvantages they face in old age. A lifetime of work at low wages, for example, will mean modest savings and few or no pension benefits. African Americans, Native Americans, and Hispanics "are more likely to be born into families with fewer advantages than are their white counterparts, and they continue to accumulate fewer resources as they age" (Mutchler & Burr, 2009, p. 27).

Kail and colleagues (2009) report that, compared to whites, African Americans and Hispanics get only 70% of the Social Security benefits and 60% of private pension payments. This meant that in 2005, compared to older white men, older African American and Hispanic men had $10,000 less in median income. The figure came to $3,000 less for older African American women and $4,500 less for older Hispanic women (Kail et al., 2009, citing U.S. Census 2007). Older women have twice the poverty rate of older men. And older African American women have twice the poverty rate of older white women.

The researchers say that disadvantages have "a magnifying or feedback effect" (Kail et al., 2009, p. 557; Ferraro & Kelley-Moore, 2003). They accumulate and reinforce one another throughout life. For example, poor education in childhood leads to low income in middle age, and this leads to poor health in later life.

Institutional Completeness: An Example of Life Course Differences

The life course perspective proposes that gerontologists study how a group's culture and context affect aging. Each minority group provides a different context for its members. This differs for subgroups within a minority and for regions of the country. A minority group's institutional completeness, for example, can influence members' quality of life. **Institutional completeness** refers to the number of agencies, programs, family members, friendship networks, and religious institutions in an older person's environment. An institutionally complete context provides strong support for the older person.

African Americans in large cities, for example, have a wide array of services and programs available.

If they choose, they can attend an African American church, spend time in an African American adult day program, and see an African American counselor. African Americans in a large city can meet their social, health care, and personal needs within their minority communities. Service providers in these communities understand the unique needs, perspectives, and backgrounds of minority older people.

Markides and Wallace (2007) say that Mexican American cultural values encourage keeping older people in the community. So, for example, many Mexican Americans who immigrate to the United States late in life live with family members. Mexican American elders who live in the Southwest also benefit from familiar language and cultural customs in their region. Markides and Wallace (2007, p. 205) say that Mexican American elders who live in a Hispanic neighborhood report better health, less depression, and lower mortality. The researchers say that Hispanic neighborhoods "provide supportive environments that promote good physical and mental health."

A study of Vietnamese and Chinese older people in California shows the importance of social supports for minority older people. This study found that both the Vietnamese and Chinese groups lacked English language skills. This led to physical, mental, and social problems. However, poor English had less effect on the Vietnamese older people in the study. The researchers (Morton, Stanford, Happersett, & Molgaard, 1992, p. 173) concluded that "the Vietnamese community may act as an effective buffer to the stress associated with the acculturation process. Without a large community structure for support, it is probable that impairment levels would increase."

Many Vietnamese older people even give up government support to live near members of their minority group. The ethnic community provides these people with "a reservoir of collective support for economic and psychological adjustment" (Morton et al., 1992, p. 174). Kim and Lauderdale (2002) studied Korean elders. They found a similar benefit for people who lived in a neighborhood with subsidized housing and Korean stores.

Tran, Ngo, and Sung (2001) show how the lack of community supports can affect Vietnamese elders. The researchers report that many Vietnamese elders without community supports lived in poverty and isolation. And often their children had few resources to share. If the Vietnamese elder lived in a nonethnic neighborhood, the elder had few social contacts. Their isolation increased due to the absence of newspapers, television, and radio in their own language. Their lack of English also created a barrier to the use of health or social services. This report shows the importance of a supportive community to ethnic elders.

American Indian elders who live on reservations benefit from the informal supports available there. Elders live close to one another and their kin. They form a small but distinct group within the reservation. Reservations often lack formal supports (such as visiting nurse programs or Meals on Wheels), but elders call on kin, neighbors, and friends for support if needed (University of North Dakota, 2003).

American Indian elders who live in a city such as Los Angeles often lack a supportive setting. First, the people who make up this population live in a 4,000-square-mile area. A study in the early 1990s (Kramer,1992, p. 50) found these people scattered widely over the area. "The largest concentration of elders in one zip code," she says, "was 33 persons."

Second, this area had poor transportation and no intergenerational center. Third, elders came from as many as 200 tribes and spoke at least 80 different languages. Fourth, elders had little contact with one another or with younger Americans Indians. City dwellers lived socially isolated lives and got little support.

The concept of institutional completeness shows the importance of the social environment to minority older people. It also shows that members of the same minority group can experience aging differently, depending on their social context. The life course perspective encourages analyses that look at the minority group culture and social life.

Structured Inequality and Personal History

Structured inequality refers to inequalities built into the social system. *Personal history* refers to a person's passage through life. The life course perspective looks at the links between personal history (youth, middle age, and old age) and a person's social and historical context. For example, early life experiences shape African Americans' status and roles in later life. For many African Americans, low-paying jobs and low income in youth lead to low-paying jobs in middle age and poverty in later life.

African Americans age 85 in 2010 were born in 1925. They lived their childhood years during the Great Depression, and their early adult years during World War II. They had children during the Baby Boom and retired during the 1980s and 1990s. These people faced economic hard times, physical danger, and overt racial discrimination. They can trace some of their health and economic problems today to the historical time they lived through.

THE IMPACT OF MINORITY GROUP MEMBERSHIP ON AGING

A person's experience of aging depends on many things other than simply being a member of a minority group. It depends on whether members assimilate into the wider society, when they immigrated to the United States, the institutional completeness of their community, and the geographic closeness of members. It depends on how much or how little the minority culture values older people, on past and present discrimination against minority group elders, and on many other social conditions.

A person's experience depends on historical events and the resources they have available as they age. It also depends on their gender, educational background, and marital status. These conditions differ for members of different minority groups, and they differ for subgroups within a minority.

Each perspective—multiple jeopardy, leveling, and the life course—gives some insight into minority aging. The lens of multiple jeopardy highlights poor housing, poor nutrition, and low income among minority older people. The leveling perspective reports on these same issues, but it looks at the way that aging balances inequalities.

Multiple jeopardy and leveling alone miss important details about minority aging. "They do not reveal . . . important issues of group lifestyle and coping mechanisms" (Barresi, 1990, p. 249). This requires the life course perspective. It looks at how minority groups and their members adapt and survive. A full picture of minority aging requires all three perspectives.

A LOOK AT FOUR MINORITY GROUPS

The four largest U.S. minority groups are African Americans, Hispanic Americans, Asian Americans, and American Indians. These groups differ in size and in their proportion of the population. As noted earlier, they also differ by the proportion of older people in each group. And they each have subgroups. These subgroups—for example, the Vietnamese, Chinese, Korean, and Japanese groups within the Asian group—differ almost as widely from one another as they do from the dominant group.

Scott and colleagues (2010) give the example of diversity in the African American community.

Although many are low income, very large and growing segments are in the middle and upper income categories. Some are retired professionals, and many others have children with professional careers. Religious affiliations include Protestant, Catholic, Muslim, and none. Many are still living in the rural South, but more are in urban areas in the North and West. Educational levels vary from almost no years of schooling to those with doctorates. While many in their 70s and 80s are dependent on care from children, grandchildren, or **"fictive kin,"** many others are raising their grandchildren or great grandchildren.

You need to keep this diversity in mind as you read about each minority group. Where space permits, discussions of these groups point out some of the differences between subgroups of minority elders.

African Americans

African Americans have a relatively young population. The median age for African Americans in 2010 was 31.7 (compared to 41.3 for non-Hispanic whites) (U.S. Census Bureau, 2008b). The Administration on Aging (2009) projects a tripling of the African American older population to the middle of this century—from 3.3 million in 2010 to over 9.9 million in 2050. In 2007, African American persons made up 8.3% of the older population. By 2050, the African Americans will account for 11% of the older population.

Health

Markides and Wallace (2007, p. 197) say that "African American older persons consistently show the worst health status [of any group] regardless of the measure considered." Older African Americans will probably show improvement on these measures in the future as younger cohorts move into old age. But, due to continued inequality at all ages, older African Americans may still lag behind whites on measures of health. Between 2006 and 2008, for example, 65% of older African American men and 61% of older African American women reported good or excellent health. For the total older population this figure came to 76% in good or excellent health for both men and women (Administration on Aging, 2010a).

Most African American older people report at least one chronic condition. Many report more than one. For the years 2005–2007, compared to all seniors, African Americans had higher rates of hypertension (84% vs. 71%), arthritis (53% vs. 49%), and diabetes (29% vs. 18%). On the positive side, compared to all

older persons, African American elders reported lower rates of heart disease (27% vs. 31%) and lower rates of cancer (13% vs. 22%) (Administration on Aging, 2010a).

Nearly all (96%) of African American in 2006–2008 said they had a usual source of health care. And in 2003 only a small percentage (16%) said they or a family member couldn't get care or felt delayed in getting care. Still, elderly African Americans had less health insurance than the general population of older people. In 2008, for example, only a third (34%) of older African Americans had both Medicare and supplementary private health insurance. At this same time more than half (54%) of all older people had these two types of insurance (Administration on Aging, 2010a).

African American older people, compared to all older people, also spend less on health care and see a doctor less often. They have less access to quality medical care, receive fewer medical procedures, and receive more procedures for illnesses due to delayed diagnosis (Williams & Wilson, 2001). The low rate of insurance and delayed health care may explain why, compared with whites, older African Americans have higher rates of disability (Kelley-Moore & Ferraro, 2004).

Dancy and Ralston (2002) studied the barriers to health care for three groups of African Americans—rural blacks, women, and those age 75 and over. These groups all face a high risk of poor health. The researchers found that all groups faced economic barriers (poverty or low economic resources) and expressed lack of confidence in the health care system. Scott and colleagues (2010) say that, compared to whites, African Americans have less knowledge about health issues and less access to health care resources. These barriers kept them from getting the formal health care they needed.

Ferraro (2006, citing Bach, Pham, Schrag, Tate, & Hargraves, 2004) reports that, compared to whites, African Americans often get treated by doctors with less access to high-quality medical resources. Ibrahim and colleagues (2003) found, for example, that African Americans stood less chance than whites of having treatment to clear blocked arteries. This then leads to more sudden deaths among African Americans due to heart attack (Gillum, 1997).

The recent recession has led to further health problems for African American older people. Perron (2010a) studied the effects of the 2007–2009 recession on African Americans age 45 and over. The study, sponsored by the AARP, took place in January 2010 and asked more than 1,000 people about their experiences in the past year. The study contained a targeted sample of 405 African Americans age 45 and over.

African Americans in this survey reported stress and worry. Nearly one person in three (31%) said they cut back on medications (compared to 15% of the general sample). And nearly one in four (23%) lost employer-provided health insurance (compared to 13% of the general sample). These changes in health practices will have current and long-term effects on African Americans' health.

Lifelong differences in access to health care, health practices, and workplace stress account for most of the health differences between older African Americans and whites. Cumulative disadvantage theory helps explain this outcome. Poor health due to poverty or low income in childhood can lead to lower earnings during a person's working years. This disadvantage early in life carries over into old age. Discrimination throughout life takes its toll and leads to poorer health in old age.

Income

Elderly blacks face economic disadvantage when compared to whites. Households containing families headed by black persons age 65 and over in 2007 reported a median income of $32,025. The comparable figure for all older households was $41,851. The median personal income for older black men was $16,074 and $11,578 for older black women. The comparable figures for all elderly were $24,323 for men and $14,021 for women (Administration on Aging, 2009). Compared with elderly whites, twice the proportion of elderly blacks relied on Social Security for their sole source of income. On average, elderly blacks have only about one quarter the net worth of their white counterparts.

The Administration on Aging (2009) reports that 23% of older African Americans in 2007 lived in poverty. (See Table 6.1.) This rate has decreased dramatically from 65% in 1965. Still, it came to more than twice the rate for all elderly (9.7%) in 2007.

Honig (1999) studied the expected retirement wealth of 4,371 households. The measure of total wealth included financial wealth, housing wealth, pension benefits, and Social Security benefits. White households in the study had an expected total wealth in retirement of $390,950. Black households had about one half the white household expected retirement total—$189,023. On every measure of financial well-being, compared with whites, elderly blacks show a disadvantage.

TABLE 6.1 Older People Below the Poverty Level by Age and Race/Ethnicity, 2007[a]

	65+	*75+*
All races	9.7	10.6
Non-Hispanic white alone[b]	7.4	8.8
Asian alone	11.3	14.1
Hispanic (of any race)	17.1	18.0
American Indian[c]	23.5	26.3
Black alone	23.2	22.8

[a]Figures are for the civilian noninstitutionalized population.
[b]*Alone* refers to people who indicated only one racial group.
[c]Figures for American Indian/Alaskan Native are for 1999.

Whites have the lowest rate of poverty of any racial or ethnic group. Asians have the next lowest rate. In both older age groups (65+ and 75+), Hispanics have more than twice the poverty rate of whites. American Indians and blacks age 65 and over have more than three times the poverty rate of whites.

The life course perspective in part explains the inequalities that show up in these figures. For example, the older age group (75+) shows higher poverty rates for every racial and ethnic group (except the black alone group). This reflects lower salaries, the lack of pensions, and fewer years paying into Social Security programs for this oldest group. Also, widowed women in this group have the least likelihood of having a private pension, investments, or savings.

The three groups with the highest poverty rates in old age (Hispanic, American Indian, and African American) have higher poverty rates than whites throughout life. For these groups, poverty carries through into old age. Reasons for inequality in minority members' lives include overt and covert discrimination in employment, high unemployment rates, part-time work, seasonal work, low pay, poverty in middle age, and few pension plans in domestic and service jobs.

Source: Federal Interagency Forum on Aging-Related Statistics. (2008). *Older Americans 2008: Key Indicators of Well-Being.* Percentage of the Population age 65 and over living in poverty, by Selected Characteristics, 2007. Indicator 7b, p. 82. Federal Interagency Forum on Aging-Related Statistics. Washington, DC: U.S. Government Printing Office. March 2008. Citing U.S. Census Bureau, *Current Population Survey, Annual Social and Economic Supplement, 2008.*

The disadvantage that African Americans face in later life reflects career and income disadvantages earlier in their lives. For example, compared with African Americans, a higher proportion of white workers have higher-paying managerial or professional jobs. A higher proportion of African American workers, compared with white workers, work in lower-paying service, production, transportation, and material moving jobs (U.S. Census Bureau, 2003a).

Income inequality also reflects educational differences between African American and white older people. About one third of white Baby Boomers have at least one college degree. For African Americans the figure comes to less than one in five (Mutchler & Burr, 2009). Fewer years of schooling lead to lower income and to jobs that lack pension plans and benefits. This inequality will continue for Baby Boomers into later life.

Older African American women face unique hardships. For example, African American women have a lower rate of pension coverage than any other racial or gender group in the United States. They also have the lowest annual median private pension or annuity income ($6,600) (Social Security Administration, 2009).

The type of work African American women do and their family responsibilities throughout life account in part for their low pension income. A lifetime of low pay, time off from paid work to raise children, work in the peripheral sector of the economy, and poor pension plans all lead to high rates of poverty for older African American women.

African American women's median total income in 2001 came to $16,282. This put them below every other racial, ethnic, and gender group except Hispanic women (U.S. Census Bureau, 2003a). They depend heavily on Social Security and Supplemental Security Income (SSI) for their income (the SSI goes to the poorest older people). Their low Social Security benefits reflect their low income during their working years. They carry the inequalities of gender, social class, and race into old age.

African American women also have nearly twice the rate of widowhood of white women at age 65. Social Security and SSI policies favor married couples. They also favor people who live in a traditional family structure with a male breadwinner. Families with a high-income male earner and a dependent spouse receive the highest Social Security benefits (Kail et al., 2009). This further hurts older African American women, many of them single.

Black women age 65 and over have a higher rate of poverty (26.7%) than any racial or gender group. They also have the greatest percentage of people (36.6%) in near poverty (below 125% of the poverty line) (Social Security Administration, 2009).

Perron (2010a) found that, compared to the general sample age 45 and over, African Americans faced more hardship during the recent recession. They reported more problems paying for everyday expenses (such as gas, food, utilities, and rent). Nearly one person in five (18%) said they had lost a job in the past year (compared to 10% of the general sample).

Nearly a third (30%) of the African Americans in this sample had to borrow money for living expenses during the past year. More than a quarter (28%) asked for financial help from family, friends, charities, and churches. The general sample reported half these rates of borrowing to pay basic expenses. Eight percent of African Americans filed for bankruptcy (compared to only 2% of the general sample).

African Americans in this study appear to walk a tightrope of survival. A downturn in the economy can turn into a personal financial crisis. This has immediate effects on their income. But it will have long-term effects on the resources people have available in retirement.

For example, about one third (34%) of African Americans in this study said they stopped contributing to their retirement accounts during the past year. And about one quarter of this group (26%) withdrew money from their accounts during the past year. A majority of those who withdrew money (53%) used it for living expenses, and 49% used the money to pay their mortgage or rent. The loss of work, stress, and the loss of medical coverage may affect the quality of African Americans' lives in retirement. Also, a drop in retirement savings during the recession directly reduced their retirement resources.

This study shows that, compared to the general population, African Americans face a greater risk of financial hardship in an economic downturn. Inequality in the job market, relatively low wages, and little savings leaves African Americans with a fragile safety net. This translates into fewer personal resources in mid- and later life.

African Americans in the future will rely on government support to ensure a good old age. Even workers, as the AARP study shows, may find that they need government programs to top up their own resources. (See Figure 6.9.)

Family and Community Life

Most studies of African American aging take a multiple jeopardy perspective. These studies compare the minority experience of aging with the experience of aging in the dominant group. They focus on inequality and highlight minority group problems.

Stanford (1990, p. 41) objects to this approach. "Collectively," he says, "African American older persons should be viewed from the perspective of their own history, without having to suffer the indignity of being compared with those older persons who have, for the most part, had entirely different social, political, and economic experiences." A look at the African American family and community should focus on the unique experience of the African American older person and on the diversity of experiences within the African American older population.

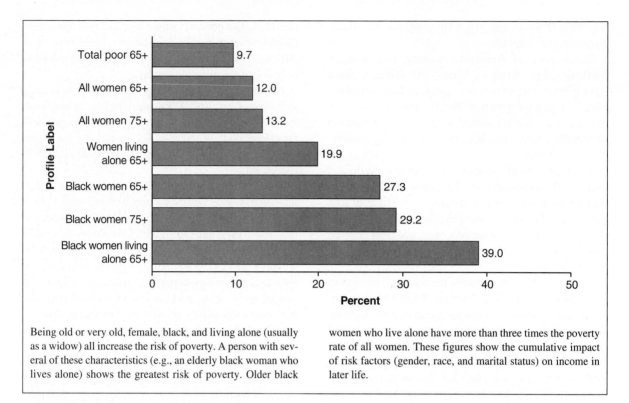

Being old or very old, female, black, and living alone (usually as a widow) all increase the risk of poverty. A person with several of these characteristics (e.g., an elderly black woman who lives alone) shows the greatest risk of poverty. Older black women who live alone have more than three times the poverty rate of all women. These figures show the cumulative impact of risk factors (gender, race, and marital status) on income in later life.

FIGURE 6.9   Profile of the Elderly Poor, 2007

Source: Federal Interagency Forum on Aging-Related Statistics. (2008). *Older Americans 2008: Key Indicators of Well-Being.* Percentage of the Population age 65 and over living in poverty, by Selected Characteristics, 2007. Indicator 7b, p. 82. Federal Interagency Forum on Aging-Related Statistics. Washington, DC: U.S. Government Printing Office. March 2008. Citing U.S. Census Bureau, *Current Population Survey, Annual Social and Economic Supplement, 2008.*

Research suggests two views of the African American family and its effect on older people. First, high divorce rates, teen pregnancies, and single-parent households lead to an unstable family. This perspective emphasizes the problems that African Americans face as they age. Second, African American families have adapted to poverty, discrimination, and social problems. These families have flexible structures that allow them to cope with a stressful environment.

This second perspective emphasizes the ability of the African American family to care for its aging members. It suggests that older African Americans in many cases have rich family and community supports, even in the face of social problems (Cantor & Brennan, 2000; Williams & Wilson, 2001).

The first National Survey of African Americans studied 581 randomly chosen older people from across the United States. Part of this study looked at African American adult children of older people. The study found that 90% of children reported that they helped their parents. One third of these children said they gave frequent help (Chatters & Taylor, 1993). When adult children face poverty and family breakdown, they may lack the resources to give help. The findings show, however, that most African American adult children give some support to their parents.

Also, compared to whites, fewer African American older people live alone. Instead they tend to live in extended families, often with children and grandchildren (Markides & Wallace, 2007). They tend to give and get help across generations. Peek, Coward, and Peek (2000) interviewed 1,200 older people in northern Florida communities. They found that, compared with whites, older African Americans with disability more often got support from their grandchildren. The researchers say that the large size of African American families and the tendency for older people to live with their children accounts for these findings.

Perron (2010a) reports that during the 2007–2009 recession, compared to the general population, African Americans (1) were more likely to have a child move in with them, (2) were more likely to move in with a child or parent, and (3) were more likely to have helped parents pay their bills. People who helped family members did so, in many cases, at the cost of hardship to themselves (such as increasing credit card balances and savings withdrawal). These findings point to the fragile financial status of many African American families. But they also point to the resilience of the family in the face of economic crisis.

Social Support

Older African Americans also develop social networks to add to their family supports. More often than whites, they interact with and get support from friends, church members, and associations (Taylor-Jones, 2006). The segregation of many African Americans in inner-city neighborhoods has led to a neighborhood focus (especially for poorer people). Older African Americans, more than whites, think of their neighborhoods as centers of personal influence (Jackson et al., 1993b). They know and visit their neighbors and use their neighbors as a resource.

Older African Americans have wide networks of friends and neighbors. Compared with other minority groups and whites, they also include fictive kin as a part of their informal support networks. Fictive kin are nonrelatives who give social support to the older person and act as confidants (Cantor & Brennan, 2000). Older African Americans refer to fictive kin as "just like family." Jordan-Marsh and Harden (2005) include "upgraded kin" in this category. This refers to cousins and other relatives who act as immediate family members.

C. L. Johnson (2000) found that women more often than men had fictive kin. These women often had no spouse or children and played an active role in their church. African Americans often used fictive kin for social support (Jordan-Marsh & Harden, 2005). Childless African American older people sometimes also adopt **play siblings** to get the support they need (Johnson & Barer, 1990). They bond with a formal care worker and consider them a "best pal" or "like a sister to me."

Friendship provides satisfying relationships for many older African Americans. Taylor, Keith, and Tucker (1993) found that 80% of African Americans said they got help from a close friend. Sixty percent got support from church members. Over half got support from extended family members. Only a small proportion of people reported social isolation with no close friend or supports. The researchers conclude that older African Americans "are embedded in support networks comprised of both family and friends" (Taylor et al., 1993, p. 62).

A recent study of African American men supports this view. Grief (2009) compared friendship patterns for middle-aged and older white and African American men. He found that both groups considered friendship important. But, compared to white men, African American men more often said they shared their thoughts and feelings with friends.

African American men also tended to see their spouse or other family members as friends. One 50-year-old told the researchers, "A friend is someone who you rely on, trust, and have faith in when you need a shoulder. This person is also someone you can call when needed and who you bond with—like my wife." None of the white men referred to family members when describing friendships.

Overall, the African American men, more often than the white men, said they needed the emotional support of friendship. This took the form of encouragement, visits when a man was in the hospital, and listening. Also, African American men, more often than white men, got financial support from friends.

This study supports the idea that African Americans value and rely on strong community and interpersonal supports for their well-being. It also shows the richness of support (emotional, social, and financial) that friends provide.

Older African American men and women give support to their families as well as receive it. Cantor and Brennan (2000) compared the care for grandchildren among different minority groups. They found that African Americans reported more ongoing care for grandchildren. Twenty-two percent of low-income African Americans and 39% of moderate-income African Americans reported day-to-day care of grandchildren (Kail et al., 2009). Only 4% of moderate-income whites reported day-to-day care.

A high proportion of African American grandparents (between 29% and 39%) said they gave care because the child's parent could not do so. Gelfand (2003, citing Lugaila, 1998) says that compared with other groups, African American grandparents had twice the likelihood of fully parenting their grandchildren.

Care for grandchildren today extends the historical role that grandparents have played in the African American family (Gelfand, 2003). "The African American grandmother is a heroic archetype, the highest status a woman can attain in the African American community" (Ovrebo & Minkler, 1993, p. 305). Gibson (1986, p. 195) says that "elderly African American women have been a wellspring of support and nurturance over time."

Religious belief, a support network, and a good self-image all make the older African American woman a source of strength in her family and community (Ovrebo & Minkler, 1993). But Jackson (1972) cautions against stereotyping all older African American women as matriarchs or mother surrogates for grandchildren. Cantor and Brennan (2000, p. 227) say that "for many [African American grandparents] such care involves burdens in terms of time, energy, finances, and emotional strain." The more demanding the caregiving responsibilities (for example, living with a grandchild in a skipped-generation household), the more likely the feeling of strain (Hughes, Waite, LaPierre, & Luo, 2007).

Cantor and Brennan (2000) studied African American older people in New York City. They found that most older people use formal supports as a complement to informal supports. The most often-used community services included hospital emergency rooms, senior centers, and religious leaders. The church also plays an important role as a social support for African American older people (Krause, 2006).

Taylor and colleagues (Taylor, Chatters, Bullard, Wallace, & Jackson, 2009) say that African American religious involvement increases with age. These researchers used a national sample to study religious participation of older African Americans. The sample contained 837 African Americans age 55 and older. Half the people in this sample said they attended services at least once each week. Another 27.1% attended services at least a few times a year.

The large majority of these two groups (82.5%) said they served as official members of their church. Three quarters (75.3%) of this group also took part in other church activities during the year. These findings support earlier research that found a strong link between older African Americans and their church. In particular they support the importance of the church to older African American women.

This research also discovered something new. The researchers found, as expected, that men went to services less often than women. But the men reported spending more *time* each week at their places of worship. The researchers wondered—What do these men do if they spend more time than women at their place of worship, but less frequently attend services? Taylor and colleagues found that men engaged in volunteer work—cleaning, cutting the grass, doing minor repairs. They also took part in activities like a men's choir or a Bible study group.

Some older men serve as deacons, stewards, and supervisors of the church's premises. Men engage in less structured church-related activities (e.g., they visit sick church members) and often serve in leadership positions (e.g., elder or lay minister).

This study gives a clearer picture of the many ways that African American men take part in their religious community. The researchers conclude, "Churches may be a primary social outlet and sphere of productive activity for older African American men, particularly those who are no longer active in the labor force" (p. 453).

Kart (1990, p. 111, citing Dancy, 1977) gives an example of how church life can provide meaning and self-esteem to an older African American man.

John Jordon worked as a baggage handler. He missed many chances for promotion during his career due to discrimination, but he found self-esteem and status in the church. There, over 25 years, "he had moved from a pew member to a deacon. Now he was also treasurer of the church—a job of enormous responsibility that required banking a thousand dollars weekly. Mr. Jordon's church appreciated his talents, and Mr. Jordon was a faithful man and loved his church. There he was somebody."

Taylor and colleagues (2009, p. 454) say that through the church, "African American men can retain, or perhaps, even achieve, important 'work' roles, status, and prestige."

African American Men

Most studies of African Americans in the United States have focused on women. Studies of African American men often emphasize the problems they face and their absence from African American family life. Those who are single (never married), separated, or divorced have the highest poverty rates among older African American men. These men risk isolation, poor nutrition, and poor health in later life. The extended family offers these men less support than it does older women (Kart, 1990).

Kart (1990) says that the image of the poor and absent older African American man overlooks the majority of older men. He reports, for example, that in 1985, 60% of older African American men were married and lived with their spouses. Married men had the lowest poverty rate among African American men (19%). Men in these married couples take part in an extended kin network.

Kart (1990) also reports that 15% of all older African American couples have a child age 18 or under living with them (about half of these are grandchildren). "Presumably," Kart says (p. 110), "the aged

Black males in these families are active in the child-grandchild-rearing activities of the families." They also can serve as role models for their male grandchildren (Hayslip, Shore, & Henderson, 2000).

Burton and DeVries (1992, p. 52) give examples of grandfather caregivers from their research.

- Simon, age 67, has looked after three of his grandchildren since their birth. The children now range in age from 7 to 13 years. "I had no idea I would be raising these children this long," he says. "I am going to be raising kids all my life, I know it. I just know it."
- Pervis, a 62-year-old grandfather, says, "I got a lot on my back. I take care of my wife who has cancer and my two grandbabies. Sometimes, I think that it's a losing battle. But I have faith in the Almighty and I have two good boys who help me."

These men and their family commitments challenge the simple image of the absent older African American man. They also show the conflicting emotions that grandfathers face in the caregiving role. Thomas, Sperry, and Yarbrough (2000) say that grandfathers give care and give advice. But, compared with grandmothers, they express less grandparenting satisfaction.

The diversity within the group of African American men should alert policy makers and service providers to their varied needs. Single men in poverty risk poor health and homelessness. Married men, who give care to their wives, children, and grandchildren, may need more home care support. A more accurate view of African American older men can target supports to meet their needs.

The Future of African American Aging

Some demographic and social trends today will influence aging in the African American family in the future. First, older people in the African American family may have fewer resources to draw on. For example, many African American women in their teens and early 20s today already have children. Children born to these young women will be old themselves when these women reach late old age. These children will have to care for frail or chronically ill parents and for themselves, yet they may have limited resources to do so.

This points to the need for more formal supports. Cantor and Brennan (2000) found that in New York City 42% of their sample said they had needed more formal support in the past year. Formal support can also free the older person from reliance on

This man, age 71, serves as a volunteer to repair a little league park in St. Paul, Minnesota.

family members or provide support in the absence of family members. Johnson and Barer (1990, p. 732) say that with more formal supports in place for inner-city African Americans, "for the first time in their lives, individuals have autonomy to withdraw from problematic family relationships and concentrate on those relationships that are more rewarding."

Second, high mortality for younger African American men will lead to relatively few men compared with women in later life. This will produce more single older women, many of whom will live alone. Jackson, Chatters, and Taylor (1993a, p. 316; also Dilworth-Anderson, Williams, & Williams, 2001) say that a growing number of older African American adults "are at severe risk for impoverished conditions and poor social, physical, and psychological health in old age." They base this conclusion on "the inevitable poor prognosis of the life experience paths into older ages of so many African Americans."

Third, current conditions for young people in different parts of the African American community will shape their lives in old age. Research shows more middle-class African Americans than ever before. Cantor and Brennan (2000) noted differences in the economic, health, and social conditions of poor and moderate-income older African Americans. In many cases, the moderate-income African Americans had an experience of aging more similar to whites than to poorer African Americans. This points to a widening gap in the experiences of poor and middle-class African Americans.

Middle-class African Americans of the future may feel they have little in common with poor African Americans. This could fragment the political power that African Americans can wield as a group. Middle-class older African Americans may feel concerned about different issues (e.g., lower taxes) than poor older African Americans (who may want higher

Social Security benefits). These two groups may press for support of their own issues, rather than issues related to poverty and race. Gerontologists, service providers, and policy makers will have to take into account the different experiences of aging within the African American community.

Hispanic Americans

Two and a half million older Americans identified themselves as Hispanic in 2007. Demographers estimate that this group will grow to over 17 million by 2050. In 2010, Hispanic persons made up 7.1% of the older population. By 2050, this percentage group will grow to 19.8% of the older population. (See Figure 6.10.) By 2019, the Hispanic population age 65 and older is projected to be the largest racial/ethnic minority in this age group (Administration on Aging, 2008c).

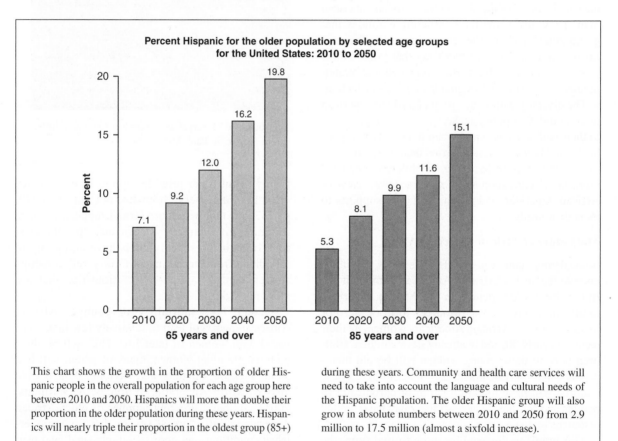

Percent Hispanic for the older population by selected age groups for the United States: 2010 to 2050

This chart shows the growth in the proportion of older Hispanic people in the overall population for each age group here between 2010 and 2050. Hispanics will more than double their proportion in the older population during these years. Hispanics will nearly triple their proportion in the oldest group (85+) during these years. Community and health care services will need to take into account the language and cultural needs of the Hispanic population. The older Hispanic group will also grow in absolute numbers between 2010 and 2050 from 2.9 million to 17.5 million (almost a sixfold increase).

FIGURE 6.10 Percent Hispanic for the Older Population by Selected Age Groups for the United States: 2010 to 2050

Source: Vincent, G. K., & Velkoff, V. A. (2010). *The Next Four Decades, the Older Population in the United States: 2010 to 2050*, 5, p. 6. Current Population Reports, P25-1138, U.S. Census Bureau, Washington, DC; also Administration on Aging (2008c). *A statistical profile of Hispanic older Americans age 65+*. Retrieved October 9, 2010, from http://www.aoa.gov/AoARoot/Aging_Statistics/Minority_Aging/Facts-on-Hispanic-Elderly-2008.aspx.

The Hispanic group is a young population compared to the general population. In 2010 it had a median age of 27.5 years compared to 41.3 years for non-Hispanic whites (U.S. Census Bureau, 2008b). Also, only 6.5% of the Hispanic population is age 62 or older compared to 15% of the total population (Burr et al., 2010; Martin, 2007). This young population and its relatively high birth rate have slowed population aging in the United States.

A number of subgroups make up the Hispanic older population. These subgroups differ in size and in their proportion of the older population. The history of each subgroup in the United States accounts for this difference. The Cuban group, for example, arrived in the United States in a wave after the Cuban revolution. Few people have migrated from Cuba since then. This group made up 11.3% of the Hispanic population in 2008. The Cuban community has had a relatively low birth rate. For these reasons, this community, among all the Hispanic groups, has the largest proportion of older people (18.1%) (U.S. Census Bureau, 2009).

In contrast to the Cubans, young Hispanic migrants continue to enter the U.S. from Mexico. Mexicans made up 52.3% of all Hispanics in 2008. These immigrants (many of them newly arrived) come for work and to raise their families. They have a relatively high birth rate and will add to the younger Hispanic population in the years ahead. Mexican immigrants have spread throughout the country as they followed work opportunities (Wallace & Castaneda, 2008).

The largest populations of Mexican Hispanics live in the Southwest and California. This group will grow into a larger proportion of the Hispanic population in the future due to immigration from Mexico.

The Puerto Rican subgroup made up 11.2% of Hispanics in 2008. This group settled on the East Coast,

---

BOX 6.1
THE OLD ONES OF NEW MEXICO

Gerontological studies of Hispanic American elders often emphasize the differences between them and the non-Hispanic white population. The Hispanic older person usually comes out second best. They look poor, uneducated, and needy. Gerontologists have begun to call for a more complete study of racial and cultural differences in later life. They suggest more study of the uniqueness of each group. This uniqueness comes through when we hear the voices of older people themselves.

Psychologist Robert Coles studied older Hispanics in New Mexico. In his work he captures the voices of the Spanish-speaking people he met. We get a glimpse of the world through their eyes.

An old woman says:

I won't let my family celebrate my birthdays anymore; and when I look at myself in the mirror a feeling of sadness comes over me. I pull at my skin and try to erase the lines, but no luck. I think back: all those years when my husband and I were young, and never worried about our health, our strength, our appearance. I don't say we always do now; but there are times when we look like ghosts of ourselves. I will see my husband noticing how weak and tired I have become, how hunched over. I pretend not to see, but once the eyes have caught something, one cannot shake the picture off. And I look at him, too; he will straighten up when he feels my glance strike him, and I quickly move away. Too late, though; he has been told by me, without a word spoken, that he is old, and I am old, and that is our fate, to live through these last years.

But it is not only pity we feel for ourselves. A few drops of rain and I feel grateful; the air is so fresh afterwards. I love to sit in the sun. We have the sun so often here, a regular visitor, a friend one can expect to see often and trust. I like to make teas for my husband and me. At midday we take our tea outside and sit on our bench, our backs against the wall of the house. Neither of us wants pillows; I tell my daughters and sons that they are soft—those beach chairs of theirs. Imagine beach chairs here in New Mexico, so far from any ocean! The bench feels strong to us, not uncomfortable. The tea warms us inside, the sun on the outside. I joke with my husband; I say we are part of the house: the adobe gets baked, and so do we. For the most part we say nothing, though. It is enough to sit and be part of God's world. We hear the birds talking to each other, and are grateful they come as close to us as they do; all the more reason to keep our tongues still and hold ourselves in one place. . . .

A man is lucky; it is his nature to fight or preach. A woman should be peaceful. My mother used to say all begins the day we are born: some are born on a clear, warm day; some when it is cloudy and stormy. So, it is a consolation to find myself easy to live with these days. And I have found an answer to the few moods I still get. When I have come back from giving the horses each a cube or two of sugar, I give myself the same. I am an old horse who needs something sweet to give her more faith in life!

Source: R. Coles, *The Old Ones of New Mexico* (Albuquerque: University of New Mexico Press, 1973), pp. 6–7.

primarily in New York City. This group stands somewhere between the Cubans and the Mexican migrants in their birth rate. Most members of this group were born in the United States. Their families have lived here for several generations and they have established themselves as part of ethnic mix on the East Coast.

Other relatively large Hispanic groups come from Central and South America (17.1% of the Hispanic population).

Health

Cantor and Brennan (2000) studied 337 Hispanic American elderly persons in New York City. They found that over half of the people in the study reported fair or poor health. Only 7% said they had excellent health. Older Hispanics also had a higher rate of physical impairment than white or African American older people.

Hispanic elders suffer from a high rate of chronic illness. For example, compared to African American and white men, Mexican American older men have a greater rate of diabetes, stroke, hypertension, cancer, and major disability. Compared to their African American and white age mates, Mexican American older women have higher rates of hypertension and cancer (Angel & Angel, 2006; Black, Ray, & Markides, 1999).

Wallace and Castaneda (2008, p. 39) find that only 2% of recent immigrants from Mexico suffer from diabetes. But 12% of long-term residents (more than 10 years in the United States) have this disease. They say that "poor eating habits acquired in the United States, combined with the lack of routine medical check-ups, have triggered the development of diabetes among this [Mexican immigrant] population."

In addition to this high rate of diabetes Hispanics get fewer tests that would help them manage this illness. This puts Hispanics at risk of complications like blindness, leg amputation, and heart and kidney diseases. Hispanics (along with African Americans) have the highest rate of admission to hospitals due to uncontrolled diabetes.

Findings from the National Health Interview Survey (2007) support these results. About 66% of Hispanic older men and women reported good to excellent health. Among non-Hispanic whites, this figure was 77% for men and 78% for women. The AARP (Johnson & Soto, 2009; also Administration on Aging, 2009) reports that 38% of Hispanics ages 65 to 69 reported fair or poor health compared to 23% of non-Hispanic whites.

Mexican immigrants show the highest rate of self-reported bad health. Nearly three older Mexican immigrants in five (58.6%) report bad health (Wallace & Castaneda, 2008). Self-reports of fair or poor health for Hispanic men and women increase with age.

Poor health has an effect on older Hispanics' lifestyles and mood. Older Hispanics, compared with whites, had more trouble with household activities and advanced activities of daily living (Angel & Angel, 2006). Older Mexican Americans, compared to African Americans and whites, show higher rates of disability related to instrumental activities of daily living. They have trouble with tasks like driving and managing finances. Eighty-five percent of older Hispanic American women say they have a chronic illness, and 45% say they have trouble with activities of daily living (Burggraf, 2000).

Older Hispanics also report high rates of depression. And this may weaken their immune system, make them less likely to take their medications, decrease their social contacts, and decrease their self-care. Older Hispanics who report a good mood show the opposite of these effects. They care for themselves, cope with their disabilities, and report less illness (Markides & Wallace, 2007).

Compared to whites, older Hispanics less often use hospitals and nursing homes (Markides & Wallace, 2007; Burr et al., 2010). They use nursing homes at about two thirds the rate of non-Hispanic whites. A high proportion of older Hispanic immigrants (particularly Mexicans) report having no regular place for medical care in the United States. These usage rates mean that older Hispanics risk having untreated illness and poor health.

Older Hispanics give lack of funds and fear of hospitals as the reasons for underuse. Lack of private health insurance may also keep older Hispanics from using formal services. Hispanics, compared with whites and other minority groups, have the highest proportion of uninsured people. About one-third of older Hispanic Americans have insurance only through Medicare. They use Medicaid to cover basic expenses (Villa & Aranda, 2000), but many older Hispanics lack even this basic coverage.

This lack of health insurance in old age reflects a lifelong lack of health insurance (DeNavas-Walt, Proctor, & Smith, 2009). Johnson and Soto (2009) report that only 49% of all Hispanic wage and salary workers ages 50 to 69 got health insurance from their employers in 2006–2008. Only 43% of Hispanic workers born outside the United States got employer health insurance. During this same time 65% of non-Hispanic whites had employer health insurance.

Immigrants who work in low-wage jobs (e.g., in construction or agriculture) rarely have health benefits through their work. But even in industries with insurance, Hispanic workers had lower coverage rates than whites. Wallace and Castaneda (2008, p. 21) say that workplace discrimination accounts for this low rate of insurance. "Mexican labor," they say, "tends to be less highly valued than that of other population groups, particularly whites."

Immigrant workers often lack the money to pay for private health insurance. These people face financial hardship if they need medical help or hospital care. This in part explains why immigrants often put off treatment. Or they go back to Mexico for treatment after their condition gets serious (Wallace & Castaneda, 2008).

Wallace, Mendez-Luck, and Castaneda (2009) studied health care use by Mexican immigrants in California. They found that nearly half a million Mexican immigrants in the United States returned to Mexico for medical, dental, or prescription services in 2001 (the year of the study). Immigrants returned to Mexico for care because of need, because they had no insurance, because they had delayed seeking care, and because they spoke little English. The researchers conclude that "access and acceptability barriers in the U.S. medical care system encourage immigrants to seek care in Mexico."

He and colleagues (2005, p. 65), in a discussion of minority health issues, say that "older people who were uninsured or had Medicare coverage only were more likely to delay or go without medical care than those who had a combination of Medicare and private insurance." Angel and Angel (2006) report that due to lack of insurance when Mexican Americans finally seek treatment, disease has caused serious damage. Long waits, impersonal service, and poor communication also create barriers to health care use. Undocumented older immigrants have no access to Medicare or Medicaid.

According to Burggraf (2000), health care providers often do not understand the culture and family lives of Hispanic elders. This leads to low service use by Hispanics and to poor health. Researchers for years reported that older Hispanics tend to rely on informal supports to look after their health care needs. In 2007, for example, 9.9% of older Hispanics needed help with personal care compared to 6.1% for non-Hispanic whites (National Health Interview Survey, 2007).

This research has created an ideal of the supportive Hispanic family. But families do not always provide the care an older person needs. In some cases, the family steps in because the community lacks formal resources to help the older Hispanic person. Researchers call for more complete formal services for Hispanic elders (Gelfand, 2003; Burr et al., 2010).

BOX 6.2
THE CHALLENGE OF SERVING ETHNIC ELDERS

Consider the following cases drawn from the files of the Administration on Aging guidebook to professional caregivers. They demonstrate the issues that ethnic elders raise for health care providers.

Case 1: Chieko is a 70-year-old foreign-born elder who recently was brought to the United States by her family. She has heart trouble, but she delays getting care. She feels confused by the health care system, speaks English poorly, and has trouble using public transit. She feels afraid due to the strangeness of American life.

Case 2: Juanita is a 68-year-old Latina. She lives in San Diego County and has lived in a Hispanic neighborhood since she came to the United States in her 30s. She consults with "curanderos" when she has a health problem. She goes back to Mexico to buy her medications. Because she lives close to the border, she has not learned English or acculturated to American society.

Case 3: Joe, an 85-year-old African American, has hypertension. He has had this condition for the past 15 years. He experiences dramatic changes in his blood pressure because he doesn't take his medication as prescribed. Joe would respond better if his doctor used the term "high blood pressure" instead of "hypertension."

Each of these cases shows how cultural barriers (language, traditional beliefs, lack of familiarity with American society) can interfere with good health care. The Administration on Aging promotes the development of cultural competence for professional caregivers. This includes the ability to use a client's or patient's language, sensitivity to cultural differences, and awareness of one's own cultural biases.

Source: Administration on Aging. (n.d.). *Achieving Cultural Competence: A Guidebook for Providers of Services to Older Americans and Their Families.* Retrieved: October 9, 2010, from http://www.docstoc.com/docs/29384529/US-Administration-on-Aging.

Elderly Hispanics: The Paradox of Poverty, Good Health, and Long Life

Elderly Hispanics, especially Mexican Americans, have less education and lower incomes than non-Hispanic whites. By these measures older Hispanics should show poorer health than whites of the same age. And on some measures they do. Compared to African Americans and whites, Hispanic older people have greater rates of diabetes, infections, and parasitic diseases (Angel & Angel, 2006).

But studies also find something unexpected. Compared to whites, Hispanics have lower death rates from cardiovascular disease, stroke, and certain types of cancer (Angel & Angel, 2006). This outcome puzzles researchers. They refer to this as an "epidemiologic paradox." And they have searched for the reasons for the relatively good health of Hispanic elders.

Markides and Coreil (1986; also Wallace & Castaneda, 2008) first proposed a "healthy immigrant" effect to explain this paradox. They suggested that Hispanics who immigrate have better health than Hispanics born in the United States. Also, immigration authorities screen out unhealthy people. Finally, people who immigrate have a good attitude toward life, and this promotes good health (Markides & Wallace, 2007).

Some studies suggest that migration patterns explain all or part of this paradox. Older Hispanics may return to their countries of origin if they become ill and near death. Researchers call this the "salmon effect" (because salmon return to their birthplace to die). These people would not show up in U.S. mortality figures. And this would artificially lower the mortality rate for U.S. Hispanics.

The puzzle deepens when researchers look at older people in other minority groups. These studies also find a minority mortality advantage over non-Hispanic whites at later ages. This suggests that migration alone cannot account for this paradox.

Markides and Wallace (2007) suggest that immigrants' behavior and culture (e.g., a non-Western diet) may promote longevity. Another theory proposes that the minority member who survives the stresses of minority mid- and later life may then have better health than white elder survivors (Heron et al., 2009). This would explain why the mortality crossover shows up in African American as well as Hispanic and other minority groups.

Wallace and Castaneda (2008) propose that statistics underestimate the amount of illness in the Mexican immigrant population. Immigrants may not seek out health care for their illnesses. These people don't show up in health statistics. Also, misclassification of ethnicity may account for low illness and mortality figures (Markides & Wallace, 2007). Finally, the lack of health insurance drives many immigrants to seek alternative services to meet their health needs. These include community clinics, non-Western healers, and churches that provide some health care (e.g., foot clinics).

The mysteries of the epidemiological paradox and the mortality crossover continue. And researchers will continue to search for the causes of these phenomena. The causes may tell us something about how to improve health and longevity for all older people.

Wallace and Castaneda (2008, p. 38) say, "Despite their good 'state of health,' empirical evidence exists to show that Latin American immigrants, particularly Mexicans, experience a high prevalence of certain chronic and infectious diseases—such as diabetes, HIV/AIDS, and tuberculosis—that require lifelong care." Wallace and Castaneda call for reform in the health care system that would provide insurance for the poorest people, including Hispanic immigrants. In addition, the health care system needs to respect and respond to the cultural needs of Hispanic elders.

Income

Hispanic Americans generally have lower incomes than African Americans or whites. Families headed by Hispanic persons age 65 and over reported a median income of $31,544 in 2007 (compared to $43,654 for non-Hispanic whites). Sixteen percent of these Hispanic households had an income of less than $15,000 (compared to 5.4% for non-Hispanic whites). Only 45% had incomes of $35,000 or more (compared to 62% for non-Hispanic whites) (Administration on Aging, 2008c).

Small or nonexistent pensions account for this low income, The AARP reports that only 38% of Hispanic employees ages 50 to 69 had access to an employer pension plan in 2006–2008 compared to 62% of non-Hispanic whites (AARP, 2009a). Throughout their work life, Hispanics, compared to whites, also face a greater likelihood of unemployment (Johnson & Soto, 2009). This reduces the buildup of pension credits. Finally, work in low-wage jobs means small pensions even for those who belong to a pension plan. In one study Hispanics ages 45 to 74 expressed worry about their pension benefits (Groeneman, 2008). These inequalities lead many older Hispanics into poverty.

In 2007, Hispanics age 62 or older made up only about 6% of Social Security beneficiaries. This reflects the marginal work that many older Hispanics did throughout their lives. As Hispanics work in more mainstream jobs, this will improve. Martin (2007) says that this figure will increase to more than 15% by 2050. Still, Hispanics (age 15 and over) now make up 13% of the SSI program. This program provides support to the poorest disabled and older people.

Low income among Hispanic elders, compared to the total population of older people, reflects their lower level of education. In 2005, for example, 41% of Hispanics age 25 and over did not have a high school diploma (compared to 16% of the total population in this age group). And only 12% of Hispanics age 25 and over had a bachelor's degree, compared to 27% of the total population age 25 and over. Hispanics born in the United States or in another country have lower educational levels than non-Hispanic blacks and non-Hispanic whites. These low levels of education lead to low-wage jobs and low Social Security and pension income in the future (Martin, 2007; Markides & Wallace, 2007).

Poverty

Older Hispanics in 2008 had two and a half times the rate of poverty of the white older group (19.3% compared with 7.6%) (Administration on Aging, 2009). But poverty rates vary within the Hispanic population. Hispanics of Dominican origin, for example, have the largest proportion of people living in poverty. For those who get Social Security, more than one third live in poverty and 56% live in or near poverty. Social Security beneficiaries who trace their origin to Spain had only 11% of their population in poverty and 27% of their population in or near poverty. Other Hispanic groups (e.g., Puerto Ricans, Cubans, or Salvadorans) fall between these extremes.

Differences in income exist among the Hispanic population. For example, younger Cubans, more than any other Hispanic group, tend to work in technical, sales, and clerical work. Nearly one person in five (18.6%) with a Cuban background has a bachelor's degree (U.S. Census Bureau, 2003a).

Puerto Ricans, on the other hand, tend to work in low-paying service jobs. They have lower incomes and higher poverty rates than Mexican Americans and Cubans (Martin, 2007). These differences in income earlier in life lead to differences in income in retirement. For example, compared with other Hispanic subgroups, Cubans have a better chance of a good income in later life. Their higher incomes during their working years allow them to save and invest for their retirement.

Puerto Ricans and Mexican Americans who work in low-paying jobs have little opportunity to save for retirement. They are less likely than Cubans to have an employer pension plan. In addition, the higher a person's payments into Social Security, the more they get in retirement. Low wages and unemployment will mean low Social Security payments in retirement.

Cantor and Brennan (2000) found in a New York City sample of Hispanic older people that between 91% (Puerto Ricans) and 62% (other Hispanic origins) received Social Security. But for one in five members of their sample, SSI (paid to the poorest older people) served as their main source of income. Most of these people live in poverty. Andrews (1989) says that more low-income Hispanic elders could get SSI. But in her study, few older Hispanics who could get SSI knew about this program.

Wallace and Smith (2009) in a study of Californian Hispanic elders found that people who live alone or with a spouse had the lowest incomes. About three quarters of those who live alone and half of those who live with a spouse report that they cannot cover basic costs. The researchers say that more subsidized housing would ease the financial burden on older people who live alone. In the long run better jobs and better wages in midlife hold the answer to reduced poverty for future Hispanic elders.

Cantor and Brennan (2000, p. 143) summarize these findings when they say that Hispanic elders (in New York City) "whether in terms of social class, occupational history, income, extent of poverty, or perceived economic well-being reveal a consistent picture of low socioeconomic status and inadequate financial resources." This also applies to groups of Hispanic elders in other parts of the country.

Martin (2007) makes a larger point about social policy based on her study of Hispanic elders. Social Security income plays an important role in the economic well-being of older Hispanics. And it will play a larger role in the future as young Hispanics enter old age.

But Social Security or other government programs reflect a person's income during their working years. Hispanics continue to lack opportunity in the workplace because of discrimination or personal characteristics (such as lack of English ability). This will lead to poverty for Hispanic elders in the future. Johnson and Mommaerts (2010, p. i) look to the future when they say about Hispanics, "Even Social Security—which tends to equalize the distribution of retirement income by paying low-income people more then they put in and wealthier contributors less—may not make them financially secure."

A January 2010 study by AARP (Perron, 2010b) underscores the importance of work for the future of Hispanic elderly. The study asked a national random sample of 1,002 adults age 45 and over about their recent financial and family obligations. The study included a targeted sample of 400 Hispanics in that age group.

The study found that the 2007–2009 recession hit Hispanic boomers (ages 45 to 64) especially hard. Perron reports that, compared to the general population, during 2009 "twice as many Hispanics 45+ lost a job than the general population (21% versus 10%)." And compared to the general population, twice the percentage of Hispanics returned to work from retirement (10% vs. 5%).

Of those who kept their jobs, 32% had their hours or pay cut. One person in five lost their employer-sponsored health insurance during this period. The recession comes at a time when these Boomers provide financial help to their children and aging parents.

These financial challenges affect Hispanic Boomers' lifestyles today. But they will also affect their retirement security. For example, the study found that 2 in 10 Hispanic Boomers withdrew money from their retirement accounts to get through the recession. And 35% of the Boomers in the study said they stopped contributing to their retirement account during previous year. Some people reported that they depleted their 401(k), 403(b), or IRA accounts in the past year.

Of those with these accounts, 28% withdrew funds and 45% stopped contributing. Compared to the general population, a higher proportion of Hispanic Boomers took these steps. Almost half of the Hispanics in this study (47%) said they felt "'not too confident' or 'not at all confident' that they would have enough money to live comfortably through their retirement years" (Perron, 2010b, p. 2).

This study shows that Hispanic workers face unequal treatment in the workplace. They face layoffs at a higher rate than non-Hispanics. Compared to the general population, they spend more of their resources caring for children and aging parents. For these rea-

sons they have trouble saving for their own retirement. Younger Boomer Hispanics will have some time to recover from the recession. But many older Boomers will need to work longer or reenter the workforce after retirement to meet their financial needs.

Family and Community Life

Hispanics show a clear disadvantage on economic measures, but they seem less disadvantaged on measures of family relations and informal supports. The Pew Research Center (2010) reports that Mexican American elders, compared with whites, tend to live in multigenerational families. Most often, when an older person lives with other family members, the older person lives in the adult child's home. Sarkisian and colleagues (Sarkisian, Prohaska, Wong, Hirsch, & Mangione, 2007) in a nationwide study of 7,929 families found that 67% of Mexican Americans lived in an extended family or within 2 miles of other family members. Only 50% of Euro-American households reported this type of family integration. The Administration on Aging (2009) reports that compared to the general population, a smaller proportion of elder Hispanics live alone. The percent of Hispanic older persons living with other relatives is almost twice that of the total older population.

Burr and Mutchler (2003) say that among Mexican American families, the tendency to live in a multigeneration household increases if the older person has poor English language skills and if the person lives in a non–Spanish-speaking community.

Wilmoth (2001) says that the tendency for older Hispanics to live with their children reflects their cultural background. A national survey of 2,352 middle-aged adults (ages 45 to 55) asked about family relationships. The survey found that, compared with whites and African Americans, Hispanics showed the most family focus. The report calls Hispanic adult children "engaged caregivers." They reported that they did more for their parents and felt guilty for not doing enough (Belden & Stewart Research/Strategy/Management, 2001, p. 89).

A study of Puerto Rican families found that support flows in two directions—to the older person from family members and from the older person to others (Sanchez, 2001). For example, older Puerto Ricans expect their children to look after them in old age. They expect their children to visit and call often. But they also give support to younger family members. Freidenberg (2000, pp. 102–103) studied Puerto Rican elders in El Barrio, Spanish Harlem, in New York

City. Eiliana, one of her respondents, describes her commitment to her family. She says:

> Yes, I continued being here with them [the grandchildren]. I rose early and I took them to school, at fourteen! Don't believe that because I saw them big I abandoned them! . . . I would take the kids to school and would leave them, and at ten in the morning I was already calling to see if they were at school.

Older Mexican Americans give advice to younger relatives and pass on cultural history. They also get health care and social support from family members (Du Bois, Yavno, & Stanford, 2001). The family often acts as a bridge between the older Hispanic person and the wider society. Children of older migrants who have close contacts with their parents often help them make use of formal social services.

Belden and colleagues (Belden & Stewart Research/ Strategy/Management, 2001) found that adult children talk to medical personnel on behalf of their parents. And a high proportion of adult children provide personal care such as bathing, dressing, and eating (21%, almost double the rate of the total group studied). Forty percent of Hispanic American adult children provide financial support to their parents (compared with only 27% of the sample as a whole). Beyene, Becker, and Mayen (2002) found that close family relations buffered the effects of aging among Hispanic elderly. People in strong family relationships reported good to excellent health and thought of aging as a blessing.

Some studies caution against stereotyping all Hispanic families as close and supportive. Studies of Mexican Americans in the Southwest, for example, have found that city life has weakened family ties. Also, caregiving responsibilities often fall to women. These women show a strong commitment to care for their aging relatives, but caregiving can create a burden for them (Kolb, 2000; Groeneman, 2008). If a family cannot give care to an older person, living together can lead to poor treatment and abuse (Gallegos, 1991).

Sarkisian and colleagues (2007) studied Mexican American families. They found that social class and income more than culture explained family closeness. Multigenerational households tended to have fewer financial resources. People with more money tended toward less family closeness.

Cantor and Brennan (2000) say that the family focus of Hispanic elders leaves them with fewer options if the family cannot give support. Compared with whites and African Americans, they have fewer friends, confidants, and neighbors to call on in an emergency. Elders who lack English skills find it hard to use formal community supports.

A study of U.S. Census data found that, compared with other Hispanic groups, Cuban immigrants showed the highest rate of independent living. Among older Cubans, married people with the most financial resources tended to live on their own (Wilmoth, 2001). Martinez (2002) interviewed 79 older Cubans

This Hispanic grandfather spends time reading with his grandson. Activities like this establish a warm bond between the generations.

immigrants in Miami. More than half (53.2%) of these people lived alone. Only 7.6% lived in multigenerational households.

These older Cubans idealized the large family that includes the old and the young. But they resigned themselves to the reality of the nuclear family. Many of these people said that they preferred to live alone. They felt that younger people thought of older people as a nuisance. The demand of jobs and the pressure to succeed in the United States leads many Cuban young people to spend less time with their families (Gelfand, 2003).

The Future of Hispanic American Aging

Hispanics form a diverse group. Some immigrated many years ago, some only yesterday. In addition, Hispanic subgroups come from different cultures. Puerto Rican elders, for example, may have a support system in Puerto Rico that they can call on if needed. They can return to Puerto Rico for support whenever they choose because they have U.S. citizenship. Other groups, such as Cubans, have to make the best of conditions in the United States. This may mean learning to live a more independent life in old age. Finally, older Hispanics in urban centers have access to more formal supports. Those in rural areas may rely almost entirely on informal supports.

Every Hispanic community could use more accessible and available support services. Differences within the Hispanic group mean that service providers need to shape programs to fit individuals' and subgroups' specific needs. The growing size and importance of the older Hispanic population calls for more knowledge about this group's service needs. This will include studies of functional ability, the impact of poverty on health, and the use of formal and informal social supports.

Asian Americans

Asian Americans make up 2.6% of all people age 65 and over in the United States. Older Asian Americans made up 8% of the total Asian American population (U.S. Census Bureau, 2003b). The Asian older population is relatively young with a median age of 36.0 in 2010; the Hawaiian and Pacific Island older population is even younger with a median age of 30.5 (compared to non-Hispanic whites at 41.3 years) (U.S. Census Bureau, 2008b). These two groups had 1.4 million older people in 2010, and they are projected to grow almost five times to over 6.8 million by 2050.

Asian Americans include people from many countries and cultures. A list of major subgroups of older Asian Americans includes Chinese, Filipino, Asian Indians, Vietnamese, and Koreans. All of these groups number more than 1 million people in the United States (Gelfand, 2003). Smaller groups include Japanese, Afghans, Pakistanis, Thais, Laotians, and Cambodians. More than two thirds of older Asian Americans live in the western United States. More than two fifths (41%) live in California and nearly 10% (9.8%) live in Hawaii (Administration on Aging, 2008a). Hawaii, of all the states, has the highest proportion of Asians in its older population (63.5%) (He et al., 2005). Each Asian subgroup has a unique history in the United States.

Health

Asian Americans in general have good health. Gelfand (2003, citing Hahn & Eberhardt, 1995) says that elderly Asian men and women have an average life expectancy 5 years longer than that of whites. Certain illnesses affect subgroups of the Asian elderly population. For example, older Asians, compared with whites, have a higher incidence of liver, stomach, and pancreatic cancer. Japanese and Filipino older people also have an increased incidence of diabetes (Gelfand, 2003).

Filipino elders report worse health than the overall Asian group. Fifty-five percent of older Filipinos report arthritis and 29% report heart disease. These rates are "substantially higher than the rates for all Asian elders" (Markides & Wallace, 2007, p. 202, citing UCLA, 2003). Genetics, diet, and lifestyles differ for each of these groups. Immigrants from poorer countries show the effects of poor health care in childhood and middle age (Burr et al., 2010). All of these conditions in part accounts for these differences in disease rates.

Few studies have looked at the health care needs of Asian Americans. Lee, Yeo, and Gallagher-Thompson (1993) report that Korean American older people need more information about illness and prevention. The researchers suggest that education programs need to offer this information in Korean (and to other groups in their own Asian languages). Research on Asian Americans needs to include enough people in a sample so that researchers can study different subgroups' use of services.

Income and Poverty

In general, Asian American elders have the highest economic status of any minority group. Compared with African Americans or Hispanic Americans, they have a poverty rate closer to that of whites. But variation in income exists within the Asian group. Married people, for example, tend to have higher incomes than single people. Married couples with two incomes explain the relatively high family income among Asians. Older Asian women have a slightly higher poverty rate than for all older women. But older Asian men have nearly twice the poverty rate of all older men (Administration on Aging, 2008a).

Economic status also differs by subgroup within the Asian American population. For example, some older people within the Chinese subgroup arrived in the United States recently and speak only their native language. They often have low incomes and rely on family members for support. Other members of the Chinese community come from families that have lived in the United States for many generations. These people live middle-class and upper middle-class lives. They work as professionals or own their own businesses.

Nearly all older people in the Filipino subgroup came to the United States as immigrants. Earlier Filipino immigrants have Social Security or pensions. More recent immigrants have to rely on their children for support. Older people in the Korean and Vietnamese subgroups have arrived fairly recently. They live mostly on the West Coast, have high rates of poverty, and rely on family members for social and economic support.

Older people in the Japanese subgroup have higher incomes and longer life expectancy than other Asian American elders. The Issei (first generation) arrived in the United States between 1870 and 1924, when laws cut off immigration. They brought traditional Japanese customs and values. The Issei celebrated Japanese holidays, honored the first-born son, and had a strong family-centered (vs. individual-centered) view of the world. They committed themselves to the upward mobility of their children, the Nisei, through education.

The Nisei were born in the United States between 1910 and 1940. Many members of this group have died. The younger members are age 70 and over today. This generation has mixed Japanese and American values. They value education, respect for authority, and investment for the future.

The Sansei, the third generation, serve as caregivers to their parents either in their parents' homes or as visitors to their parents in institutions. The Sansei vary in their commitments to traditional Japanese values and culture. The Sansei have accepted American values and culture, but may partake in traditional rituals (e.g., funerals) and holidays.

Educational level strongly predicts income at work and in retirement. And the past four decades have seen a significant increase in educational attainment among older Asian Americans. In 2007, more than 70% of the older Asian population age 65 and older had finished high school. Also in 2007, almost 30% of Asian older persons had a bachelor's degree or higher. This reflects the high value that many Asian cultures place on education. It also reflects the high educational status that many Asian immigrants bring with them when they come to the United States. Asian elders with high educational attainment will have relatively high incomes in retirement.

Family and Community Life

The Confucian value of filial piety—respect and care for elders—continues to influence Asian family relations. Belden and associates (2001) found that, compared with members of other groups, more middle-aged people of Asian background expected to care for elderly parents. Seventy-three percent of the Asian adults in their sample said they felt responsible for parent care (compared with only 49% of Americans in general). Almost this same proportion of Asian adults (72%) said they felt guilty about the amount of care they give. They felt they should do more for their parents (compared with 48% of the total sample).

Except for American Indians, Asians report the highest proportion of families living in a multigenerational household. One quarter of Asian families in 2008 said they lived in a multigenerational household (compared with only 12.7% of whites in this living arrangement). Forty-three percent of these families lived with three generations or more in the same household (Pew Research Center, 2010).

Asian adult children often work with health care professionals to arrange care, and they often give personal care themselves. Asian adults also have made adjustments in their work and personal lives to support their elderly parents. The demands of caring for an elderly parent sometimes clash with the demands of work and other activities. Asian American adults, more often than other caregivers, report stress due to the demands of care.

A Chinese colleague who works at my university maintains an active teaching and research career. At the same time she has raised her own children and cares for her aging father who lives with her. She cooks his food. And recently when she had to travel outside the country for several weeks, she arranged for a Chinese friend to visit daily and care for her father.

This creates challenges for her as she juggles her career and family responsibilities. I asked her how she

This Chinese family in New Jersey gathers three generations together to make traditional dumplings.

feels about her elder care responsibilities. She shrugs and says, "What else am I to do? He's my father and I owe it to him to care for him. He's my family. He took care of me when I was growing up. Now it's my turn." Her response reflects the Chinese culture's respect for older people and the sense of duty that the younger generation owes to parents.

Kendis (1989) studied Japanese American elders (age 60 and over) in Gardena, California. The elders in this study said they felt financially and socially secure. They also saw their children as a support system in case they needed help. One woman said, "If you get sick, you need someone to hold onto. Good friends are okay for one or two weeks, but not for longer" (Kendis, 1989, p. 103). This woman looks to her family for long-term support.

Shibusawa, Lubben, and Kitano (2001) report that adult children in the Japanese subgroup express obligation and gratitude toward their parents. For example, a high proportion of unmarried Japanese elders live with their adult children. Still, these researchers say, Japanese elders today prefer to live on their own near their children. Elders today have accepted the American values of independence.

Sung (2000, p. 235; Putney, Bengtson, & Wakeman, 2007) says that some older people in Asian communities adapt to American life by changing their expectations. They treat younger people as equals, they share their ideas with younger relatives, and they use social service agencies to meet their needs. In some cases, the demands of life in the United States and the adoption of U.S. values have weakened family support for older people.

Older people in the Chinese subgroup sometimes choose to live apart from their children, preferring to live in "Chinatowns" where they have access to other elders of Chinese heritage. They also have access to the foods and cultural life they enjoy (Gelfand, 2003). These people often live with little income and in poor housing conditions. They risk illness and isolation from their families. But they live in the community of their choice.

The Future of Asian American Aging

The Asian American group has grown faster than any other minority since 1970 (mostly through immigration), and they have a longer life expectancy at age 65 than other minority groups or whites. Although many Asian American elders get support from their families, others lack that support. These people need help from formal social services. Language and cultural barriers keep some of them from getting the help they need. Yee (1999, p. 46) calls for more "culturally competent services and health systems" to meet the needs of older Asian Americans.

Lee (1992) suggests that social service agencies recruit Asian American professionals. Also, community agency and health service boards should include Asian American community leaders. This would give agencies a clearer picture of community members' needs. Kim and Kim (1989) propose that curricula in universities should sensitize social work students to the needs of Asian Americans. Client education programs can also help Asian Americans learn to stay healthy and to use the health care system (Roberts, Takenaka, Ross, Chong, & Tulang, 1989).

American Indians and Alaskan Natives (AIAN)

The term *American Indians* or *Native Americans* from this point forward refers to American Indians and Alaska Natives (Eskimo and Aleut). In 2007, 4.3 million adults in the United States (1.5%) identified themselves as American Indian and Alaskan Natives (AIAN). This group had a median age of 29.9 years (compared to the non-Hispanic white median age of 41.3 years). The AIAN group contained 212,605 older people in 2007. This older group will grow to almost 918,000 by 2050.

In 2007, AIAN older persons made up 0.6% of the older population. By 2050, the percentage of the older population that is American Indian and Native Alaskan is projected to account for 1.0% of the total older population in the United States (Administration on Aging, 2008b). By 2050, the AIAN population age 55 and over will equal 12.6% of the AIAN total population (an increase from 5.5% in 1990) (Satter & Wallace, 2010).

Like other minority groups in the United States, the American Indian population has many subgroups. Barnes, Adams, and Powell-Griner (2010) say that the AIAN population has 569 federally recognized tribes. Many other tribes also exist without federal recognition. Many American Indians live on reservations, but others live off reservations in cities and towns. Forty percent of American Indians live in the western United States (Barnes et al., 2010). California alone has 100 recognized tribes (Satter & Wallace, 2010). Thirty-one percent live in the South. Twenty-six percent live in the Midwest and Northeast.

This variety reflects the social structure of American Indian society. And this diversity makes generalizations about this group difficult. For example, some studies of American Indians make reference to the high status of Native elders. But Baldridge (2002, p. 256) says that "the fact that elders are so highly regarded in Indian political rhetoric contrasts dramatically with their poor health and socioeconomic status and with tribes' frequent failure to provide adequate senior programs for them." A report on AIAN elders in California (Satter & Wallace, 2010) says that,

compared to whites, AIAN elders have two to three times the poverty or low income rate (49% vs. 17%).

Health and Income

Health. A lack of quality health care, unhealthy lifestyles, and genetic-based illnesses mean that older American Indians suffer from poor health. Studies of this group find high rates of heart disease, cancer, diabetes, and chronic liver disease and cirrhosis (related to alcohol abuse) (Baldridge, 2002; Rhoades et al., 2007). Gold and colleagues (2006) studied the health of more than 146,000 women between the ages of 50 and 79. They found that American Indians in the study had the greatest likelihood of lifetime health problems. Low income, low levels of education, and advanced age predicted poorer health (McDonald, Ludtke, & Muus, 2006).

Rhoades and colleagues (2007), based on their research, predict poorer cardiovascular health in the future for American Indians. For example, American Indians show increasing rates of diabetes. Twenty-four percent of American Indians over age 65 have this disease—a 25% increase between 1990 and 1997 (Gelfand, 2003, citing Burrows, Geiss, Engelgau, & Acton, 2000). In some communities, Baldridge (2002) says, more than half the people age 50 and over have diabetes. Some reservations have the highest rates of diabetes reported anywhere in the world.

A needs assessment of 83 tribes (E. Walker, 2002) found that "a greater percentage of Indian elders consider their health to be fair or poor (48 percent) than elders in the general population (34 percent)." Also, "many more Indian elders are overweight or obese (75 percent) than their non-Indian counterparts (53 percent)."

Baldridge (2002) says that Indians have a life expectancy 3.3 years less than that of whites. Indians also die of alcoholism at 4.6 times the rate of whites, of tuberculosis at 4.2 times the rate of whites, and of diabetes at 1.6 times the rate of whites.

McDonald and Muus (2006) report on a study of 9,296 AIAN people age 55 and over. These people came from 132 tribes at 88 different sites. People in this study with lower income and less education had the highest rates of chronic disease. Other studies (Garrett & Black, 2006) show a similar link between low income and poor health. People with low income who exercised and didn't use alcohol showed the least chronic disease. The researchers conclude that health promotion could reduce the incidence of disease among older American Indians.

High rates of chronic illness lead to high rates of disability. Barnes and colleagues (2010) report that over 41% of AIAN adults reported a functional limitation caused by at least one chronic condition. The researchers sum up their findings. "In general," they say, "compared with other groups, non-Hispanic AIAN adults are more likely to have poorer health, [and] unmet medical needs due to cost" (p. 1). In addition, compared to whites, they are less likely to have employment health insurance and they are nearly twice as likely to have no health insurance at all.

The quality of health care for AIAN elders varies across the country. New Mexico, for example, provides a "Consumer Directed Personal Care Option" program. This program provides services to keep people out of institutions. Services include assistance for people with cognitive impairment, meal preparation, and household care services (Sanchez, 2008).

Health care providers in Zuni Pueblo, also in New Mexico, joined together to coordinate services. They formed the "Adult Protection Team." The team members meet every 2 weeks to discuss cases and solutions to referrals. Team members give monthly updates on their activities. The team provides a 24-hour work-day follow-up to referrals. This program attempts to provide effective and efficient service to Zuni elders (Bowannie & Leekity, 2008).

These programs serve as models of community health care for American Indian elders. But not every elder has access to a health care program. Yeo (2009) says that historical agreements limit available health care to American Indians today. For example, the Indian Health Service (IHS) delivers care to patients in institutions and to people in the community. But American Indians only get this care if they live on or near a reservation.

Yeo (2009; also Satter & Wallace, 2010) notes that more than half of older American Indians live in urban areas. And few urban centers exist. Those that do exist have poor funding and don't offer a full range of geriatric care. In addition, the IHS lacks the funds to provide a complete program of geriatric or long-term care.

Satter and Wallace (2010) report that "only one in 20 (5 percent) of AIAN elders use, or are eligible, for Indian Health Service (HIS) coverage." This leaves each state and the individual tribes to provide care for AIAN older people.

As a result only 12 nursing homes exist for American Indians in the entire nation (Baldridge, 2002). This means that many AIAN elders who need institutionalization must live in nursing homes off their reservations. This can lead to isolation and culture shock.

Even when services exist, American Indian elders often choose not to use them. Many American Indians consider programs to be insensitive to their culture. Elders mistrust government services, including health care services. They prefer their own traditions of medicine (Wykle & Kaskel, 1994). They go for help only when serious illness threatens their lives. A study of elders in Los Angeles County found that American Indian elders see the social service system as "disrespectful at best or outright hostile at worst" (Kramer, 1992, p. 49).

Income.   American Indians have lower incomes than other U.S. older populations (Schweitzer, 1999). In a study of minority members (age 45 and over), the AARP (2005d) found that 60% of American Indians worried about the cost of basic items such as utilities and grocery expenses. And 44% of this group said they did not save any money.

The U.S. Census Bureau reports that between 1998 and 2000 American Indians had a poverty rate of 26%—a rate higher than whites or any other minority group (Gelfand, 2003, citing U.S. Census Bureau, 2001). A report on AIAN elders in California (Satter & Wallace, 2010) says that, compared to whites, AIAN elders have two to three times the poverty or low income rate (49% vs. 17%).

These conditions prompted the federal government's Administration on Aging to identify American Indians as a priority group. This means that American Indian elders should get special attention because they have many health, social, and economic problems. They also tend to have less access to formal support programs such as home care or respite care for Native elders (Polacca, 2001).

Family and Community Life

The poverty and social breakdown in some American Indian communities lead to problems for older people within the family. Families with good incomes, stable employment, and stable marriages can supply the most support, but some families have few resources to spare. Financial need can force generations to live together. American Indians, compared to other minorities, report the highest percentage (25.6%) of families that live in a multigenerational household (Pew Research Center, 2010).

The stress of caregiving along with financial strain can lead to elder abuse. One study found that 81% of elders expressed worry about abuse (Baldridge, 2002). Brown (1989, p. 17, cited in Baldridge, 2002) reported that abuse can occur when a family had "caregiving responsibilities thrust upon them for which they were unprepared." Schweitzer (1999, p. 15) says that "lack of money means lack of food, fuel, and housing, [which] creat[es] hardships for all members of the family. Elder abuse may result." Schweitzer says that frail elders, who need the most support, face the greatest threat of neglect or abuse.

Conditions on reservations can also lead to financial abuse. The lack of work on reservations, for example, has led older American Indian families to rely on their elders' Social Security checks for survival. This may be the only cash income a family gets. Younger people then have to rely on the older person for support.

Grandparenting. In spite of these challenges and problems, American Indian elders contribute to family life. Many studies report that American Indians respect their elders. Some authors have reported on the important role that older women play in American Indian society. Schweitzer (1999), for example, gathered reports on grandmothers' roles in a number of Indian tribes. She notes that in some cultures, such as the Hopi and Navajo, a child can have many grandmothers. The culture defines "grandmother" broadly to include many older female relatives.

In other American Indian cultures, a person becomes a grandmother by adopting a grandchild. In still other cultures, the term *grandmother* applies to any older woman. Grandmothers actively teach the younger generation about tribal customs. They do this by telling stories to their grandchildren (Marshall, 2007), by demonstrating and teaching crafts such as weaving (Hedlund, 1999), or by performing traditional ceremonies that include healing or naming children (Jacobs, 1999).

Many grandparents take an active role in raising their grandchildren. Schweitzer (1999, p. 8, citing Weibel-Orlando, 1990) says that "of all the characteristics we observed [in the research], one trait dominates: Indian grandmothers are almost universally engaged in childcare and childrearing." Elders take part in cultural renewal programs in schools, provide foster care, or actually raise their grandchildren. They may babysit a grandchild for short periods. They may care for a city-raised grandchild during summer vacations. Or they may raise a grandchild if the parents have too few resources or have a drug addiction.

These periods of child rearing allow grandmothers to pass Indian culture to their grandchildren.

Older American Indian women typically find the grandmother role appealing. But they also feel the burden of caring for a grandchild, especially if they need help themselves. Baldridge (2002) says that reports on grandparenting tend to romanticize the elders' place in modern Indian society. Grandparents who get called into the parenting role often feel they have no choice. They have to help because of a breakdown in their adult child's life.

Conway and Shuster (2007) found that grandmothers often experienced stressful relations with their daughters over care for their grandchildren. This occurred when a grandchild had emotional problems (e.g., hyperactivity) and when the child's parent abused drugs or alcohol. Grandparents reported physical stress, lack of support, and feeling tied down.

Glass and Huneycutt (2002) refer to this as *grandparenting due to the four D's:* drugs, divorce, desertion, or death. One survey of Indian elders asked how they felt about caring for grandchildren. Eighty-six percent of respondents said that younger people should not expect elders to care for young children for long periods of time. And 77% felt that it was "abusive or wrong" to have elders take on this task. Schweitzer (1999, p. 9) says that Indian elders feel "happiness . . . at the new status . . . sometimes mixed with ambivalence."

Eldercare. Similar issues arise when adult children have to care for an aging parent or grandparent. Elders ranked child, spouse, sibling, other person, grandchild, or other relative in that order as sources of support (John, 1994). Eighty percent of Native elders gave spouse or child as the most likely support. About half of American Indian elders rely on a child for support.

These findings suggest that the large majority of American Indian elders have informal support systems in place if they need them. Shomaker (1990) says that in Navajo culture, reciprocity exists between children brought up by grandmothers and grandmothers in later life. In this society grandmothers often raise their daughters' children. These women raise their grandchildren to believe in lifetime reciprocity. The children owe their grandmothers for the care they get as children. The grandchildren expect to care for their grandmothers in their old age. Older women in this culture often live on their own even in late old age. Children and grandchildren provide the supports that make this possible.

American Indian society faces many internal and external challenges—lack of jobs, alcohol and drug abuse, poverty. The treatment of elders reflects these challenges. Older people contribute to their families, but sometimes feel stress in doing so. Likewise, adult children will live with a parent, but may do so only because the family lacks money to live apart. These challenges will continue in the future as long as American Indians suffer from poverty and marginal status in the wider society.

The Future of American Indian Aging

Anthropologists say that elders get the most support when they control some resource. Navajo women control the value of reciprocity, and they pass this on to their grandchildren. Arapaho elders in Wyoming keep their prestige by controlling religious ritual (Fowler, 1990). The Coast Salish elders gain respect for their role as political leaders (Miller, 1999).

Miller (1999) describes the important role that older women play in cultural renewal among the Coast Salish tribes. Curley (1987, p. 472) reports a renewed interest by the American Indian community in its culture and tradition. The community knows that it "cannot survive without the knowledge and wisdom held by the elders—the preservers of the Indian race, culture, and history."

At the same time, Indian elders face poverty, poor health, and sometimes abuse. Schweitzer (1999) calls this the "paradox of aging" in Indian society. Studies,

---

BOX 6.3
THE COAST SALISH PEOPLE: A CHALLENGE TO MODERNIZATION THEORY

Modernization theory describes a single path from pre-modern to modern society. It also describes a single outcome for older people: a drop in status. The Coast Salish people of the Pacific coast of North America show an alternative to modernization theory. They show how people can respond to events and shape their future.

Miller (1999) researched the role of older women, grandmothers, in Coast Salish tribes in the 1980s and 1990s. He found that some grandmothers did lose status as they aged. Tribal custom speaks of respect for elders. But elders who did not control resources or who did not make a contribution to the group lost status.

But Miller also found that some grandmothers gained status with age. These women play an important role in tribal culture. Their status comes, in part, from recent changes in tribal life. And their status questions the universality of modernization theory.

Miller calls these women "political grandmothers." They hold office and play a role in the political life of the community. They also preserve traditional practices and the right to tribal membership. This gives them control of fishing rights (the key to material well-being in the tribe). All of these roles give these grandmothers power and prestige in their community.

Also, young people show a new interest in Indian identity and tribal culture. This has led to higher status for certain elders. Miller says that grandmothers "who have ritual knowledge and control (i.e., knowledge of Indian names, shamanistic abilities, or influence over the process of initiation into dancing societies) are in demand and are valued in their communities" (1999, pp. 106–107).

Political grandmothers who hold office link their political role to traditional roles held by women in Coast Salish society. They emphasize their work as teachers and mentors of children and grandchildren in the tribe. These grandmothers also speak out in public. They remind tribal members of their genealogy, traditional values, and cultural practices. These women remain active in public life until late old age. The tribe admires them for the care they gave their families, for providing income to the family, and for their knowledge of tribal customs (Miller, 1999).

Amoss (1981) says that respect for Coast Salish tradition translates into respect for older people. "Every public occasion where the elders appear . . . is punctuated by speeches that reiterate the necessity of respecting them and heeding their advice." The Coast Salish elders have managed to regain status in their changed society. "Far from being the helpless victims of change," Amoss writes, ". . . given the right conditions, elders can not only profit from it, but may even become active agents of change themselves."

Sources: Amoss, P. T. (1981). Coast Salish elders. In P. T. Amoss and S. Harrell (Eds.), *Other ways of growing old: Anthropological perspectives* (pp. 227–247). Stanford, CA: Stanford University Press; and Miller, B. G. (1999). Discontinuities in the statuses of Puget Sound grandmothers. In M. M. Schweitzer (Ed.), *American Indian grandmothers: Traditions and transitions* (pp. 103–124). Albuquerque: University of New Mexico Press.

documentaries, and public ceremonies show that elders have respect and support within Indian society. Still, the data on income, health care, and family relations show that elders face hardship. Schweitzer (1999) believes that this paradox reflects both the cultural values that give respect to elders and the current problems that Indian communities face today. She calls these two sides of a coin. "Families find themselves encountering both conditions at the same time" (p. 19).

John, Hennessy, and Denny (1999) call for better health screening and prevention. They point to the high rates of preventable diseases such as diabetes, obesity, cancer (due to smoking), and liver disease (due to heavy drinking). They propose improvements in health screening programs by the Indian Health Service. They also call for home safety improvements to cut back on injuries and accidents.

Agencies need to tailor their programs and services to the cultural needs of American Indians (Hendrix, 2003). For example, older American Indians see their health in the context of their communities. The researchers suggest that prevention programs should emphasize the good effects of health promotion on the older person's family.

Baldridge (2002) sums up the condition of aging in Indian society today. He says that improvement of elders' conditions depend on improving the conditions of Indian life in general. "Until tribes can generate sufficient revenues, or until federal and state governments provide better funding and access to programs, local improvement of these infrastructures is unlikely" (p. 265). Elders cannot live a high quality of material life if their children and grandchildren suffer from poverty and deprivation. Low incomes, poor-quality housing, lack of transportation, and poor health care affect the old as well as the young.

In recent years, some tribes have found a new source of revenue—the casino. Baldridge (2004), Director of the National Indian Project Center in Albuquerque, New Mexico, says that today "something like 200 tribes generate $17 billion annually from gaming ventures." American Indians may now have the revenue needed to create a healthier, more secure old age. But, Baldridge says, "What's missing is any semblance of parity between tribes."

Tribes vary in their wealth. On one end of the wealth spectrum, the Massantucket Pequots own a pharmaceutical company. The company employs more people than almost any other company in New England. On the other end of the spectrum, the North Slope Alaska Native village cannot dispose of solid waste. They have no access to fresh water.

Baldridge (2004) reports that "something like two-thirds of Indian tribes—because of their rural isolation and other reasons—do not have casinos. Other tribes who do operate gaming are making marginal profits, at best." The growing diversity of this population makes it hard to find a single solution to Indian elders' problems.

If the new wealth of the casinos cannot guarantee a good old age for American Indians, what can? Baldridge (2004) considers political advocacy essential to creating a good old age for American Indians. The National Indian Council on Aging (NICOA) serves as the primary advocate for Indian issues in Washington. Baldridge says that NICOA had some success in advocating for Indian needs. For example, "Title 6 of the Older Americans Act (OAA) . . . has increased from $13.5 million to $30 million. In Title 5, the Senior Community Service Employment Program, NICOA's annual share has increased from $3 million to $6 million. In the recent Family Caregiver Support Program, NICOA's advocacy directly resulted in a $5-million increase for Indian funding."

These relatively small gains came after years of advocacy work. Baldridge says that Indian elders' problems "seldom appear on the radar screen of America's consciousness. Because they are historically stoic and soft-spoken, Indians have seldom asserted themselves in a political context. Yet they remain, for the most part, the only senior population for whom healthcare is an entitlement. And they remain among the most poorly served, invisible to much of the aging network" (Baldridge, 2004).

RESPONSES TO MINORITY GROUP AGING

Local senior centers, commissions, committees, and advisory boards now give minority older people a chance to speak up on issues. A number of national associations for minority groups now exist. These include the National Caucus and Center on Black Aged, the National Association for Hispanic Elderly (Asociación Nacional Por Personas Mayores), the National Indian Council on Aging, and the National Asian Pacific Center on Aging. These associations speak for their respective minority groups to the government, they sponsor research, and they disperse information about their group. Hayes-Bautista and colleagues (2002) describe the challenges posed by an ethnically and racially diverse older population.

- First, different groups have different health and social service needs. All groups, however, could benefit from diabetes education and prevention programs. Specific groups, such as African Americans, could benefit from specific programs (in this case targeted heart disease and stroke prevention programs) (Johnson & Smith, 2002; Hummer, Benjamins, & Rogers, 2004).
- Second, diversity exists within ethnic groups. The Asian group contains American-born older people as well as recent immigrants. This group contains members from many different cultures. These subgroups speak a variety of languages and may need services delivered in their native tongue.

  The 2000 census reports that 38% of older Hispanic people and 41% of older Asians spoke little or no English. Some minority older populations report more than 80% non-English speakers (Yeo, 2009). Johnson and Smith (2002) report that one third of Hispanic patients and one quarter of Asian patients have trouble communicating with their doctors. Physicians and health care workers need to overcome communication barriers to deliver treatment.

  Yeo (2009) says that appropriate treatment of conditions such as dementia and depression depends on knowledge of the patient's language and culture. Lack of a patient's language or culture can lead to misdiagnosis and improper treatment. She recommends the use of professional interpreters to work with health providers if a language barrier exists. In too many cases, she reports, hospitals rely on family or friends to interpret for the sick person. Limited vocabulary and understanding of medical concepts as well as potential bias by family members can lead to misunderstanding.

- Third, minority members may mix traditional medicine with modern medical treatment. Chinese elders may understand health as a balance of yin and yang or the flow of chi (energy) through the body. East Indian elders may consult an Ayurvedic doctor for an herbal cure. American Indians may use the sweat lodge to maintain their health. Western physicians need to understand these preferences to gain the older person's trust and compliance. They also need to monitor interactions between Western drugs and folk medicines.
- Fourth, the time in the life cycle when a person immigrates influences his or her quality of life in

old age. People who arrive in the United States in their youth will learn English and American customs. They will also spend a lifetime in the workforce accumulating Social Security credits, pension benefits, and savings. Immigrants who arrive later in life may lack language skills and social supports. They may also lack eligibility for programs and services. For example, older people who immigrated recently may not be eligible for certain government health care and income programs (Burr et al., 2010). These people live in poverty and have unmet health and social service needs.

Legislation has tried to address this problem. The law now requires families to provide complete support to older immigrants whom they sponsor. They must agree to do this for 5 years. The older family member cannot make use of public services during this time. This policy attempts to ensure support for older immigrants. But it may discourage some families from bringing their older relatives to the United States. And it also makes the older person completely dependent on his or her family for care (Angel & Angel, 2006).

The unique needs of minority older people means that they often have less access to quality health care. Compared with whites, minority members less often have health insurance (DeNavas-Walt et al., 2009). American Indians ages 55 to 64, for example, compared to whites in this age group, have twice the rate of people uninsured (Satter & Wallace, 2010).

Minority members may also face discrimination and prejudice when they interact with the health care system. Some minority members distrust the health care system and avoid using health care services (Johnson & Smith, 2002). Garroutte and Beals (2008) studied older American Indians' perception of their health care. Patients who had the strongest association with American Indian culture felt least satisfied with the information they got from their health care provider.

Morton and colleagues (1992, p. 174) suggest that agencies create "programs designed to reinforce and preserve traditional cultural beliefs and practices, and promote respect for cultural differences." Programs that consult with members of the minority group and include them in the development of programs will have the greatest success.

Brown and Gibbons (2008) studied an assisted living facility designed and managed by an American Indian tribe. They compared the life satisfaction of residents with a group of nonresidents.

Compared to nonresidents, residents reported greater happiness, more perceived social support, and less loneliness. This study points to the value of culturally appropriate settings for older minority group members.

Yeo (2009) says that successful models of service to ethnic elders involve the elders' community. An Area Agency on Aging, for example, developed a bilingual and bicultural program for Hispanic elders. The program trained Hispanic elders to serve as "community ambassadors." The elders teach the staff of the program about Hispanic culture. The program resulted in a culturally sensitive program that encouraged Hispanic elders to use long-term care and caregiver supports.

Other programs train respected members of the community to present health services to the community. These trained community members also screen potential patients, engage in health education, and provide personal support to ethnic elders.

Another program hired an ethnic dietitian to redesign a meal program. This person held focus groups with elders to learn about their preferences. The program used traditional cooking and preparation methods that the older people appreciated (Administration on Aging, n.d.)

All of these programs provide support that respects the older person's culture. This requires service workers who are sensitive to the cultural needs of ethnic elders. The Administration on Aging (n.d.) says that a culturally competent health care worker can "work effectively in cross cultural situations."

This model goes beyond service delivery. It builds competence in older people, strengthening their ability to function in the wider society. Hendrix (2003) likewise calls for intercultural collaboration in service delivery. This approach balances the health care worker's formal approach to medical care with the cultural needs of the minority elder. It encourages humility in the health care worker and respect for the older person's culture.

Future Issues

The U.S. Census reports that in 2006, minority group members in the United States topped 100 million people—about one third of the total population. This will lead to a new kind of generation gap in the future. Minority groups—particularly Hispanic Americans—have high birth rates and a low median group age. This group will grow in size in the future.

At the same time, the older population will contain more whites. Texas, for example, has almost the same proportion of Hispanics and whites in its 5- to 9-year-old population (41% and 42%, respectively). But its 65 and older population has only 17% Hispanics and 73% whites (Angel & Angel, 2006). Mutchler and Burr (2009, p. 26) say that "the boomer generation will move through later life embedded in a population that is increasingly composed of nonwhite and Hispanic youth and younger adults. . . . These persons will make up larger shares of the labor force and thus contribute to the payroll and other taxes that support programs aimed at assisting elderly boomers."

These facts pose a vital question: Will minority group younger people finance the retirement and health care needs of the largely white older population? Angel and Angel (2006, pp. 96–97) predict that minority youth in the future, many in low-paying jobs, "will not have the resources nor likely be willing to shoulder the burden of supporting a disproportionately privileged White elderly population." They go on to say that "the potential for serious intergenerational conflict fueled further by racial and ethnic tensions . . . is quite real."

Chapter 1 discussed the issue of intergenerational equity. But the study of racial and ethnic diversity adds another dimension to this issue. Markides and Wallace (2007, p. 209) say that the increasing numbers of older minority group members "will change the dynamics of policy and intergenerational relationships in coming years . . . public policy discussions of ethics and responsibilities across generations and across ethnic groups cannot ignore the special needs as well as talents and contributions of this dynamic segment of the population."

Policy decisions in the future need to take into account the different needs of minority group elders and non-Hispanic whites. Recall also that minority group elders belong to many subgroups. Some minority elders live in good health, have solid pension plans, and look forward to a good old age. These people will want the same benefits and opportunities as majority group members.

At the same time many Hispanic and African American elders live in poverty. Compared to whites, they rely more heavily on Social Security Supplemental Security Insurance, Medicare, and Medicaid. Any reductions in Social Security benefits will disproportionately hurt minority older people. Social Security and health care reform, in particular, needs to take into account the effects that reform will have on minority elders.

CONCLUSION

Minority members make up about 10% of the older population. Researchers divide the minority population into four main groups: African Americans, Hispanic Americans, Asian Americans, and American Indians. Each of these groups contains unique subgroups. These subgroups sometimes differ as much from one another as they do from the dominant population.

Some studies show that minority membership compounds the problems that older people face. Other studies show that minority group membership can level differences in old age.

The life course perspective puts minority aging in the context of personal history, culture, world events, and the conditions in the wider society. This perspective gives the most complete understanding of minority aging. It allows researchers to look at a person's health, income, and social service needs. It also encourages researchers to look at a person's culture, family and social supports, and community life.

The minority older population will increase in the years ahead, and this population will increase in diversity. Minority group members will differ in culture, country of origin, language ability, educational background, income, family supports, and the time in the life cycle of immigration. Social policies and programs must adapt to meet minority elders' income, health care, and social service needs. More research on minority aging will help shape programs and policies that suit minority older people. Health and social service professionals need more education about minority aging. This will increase their awareness of minority elders' needs and improve services to their clients.

SUMMARY

- This chapter examines the size, composition, and socioeconomic status of older minority groups. It discusses the experience of aging as a minority group member, and it describes creative responses to the challenge of minority aging.
- The term *dominant group* in the United States applies to white people. This group makes up a numerical majority of the U.S. population and controls most of the social and economic resources in the country. Social scientists define a *minority* as a group that faces subordination and discrimination within society.
- The United States looks like a pluralistic society in which many social and ethnic groups live together. An assimilation continuum exists that runs from very traditional to bicultural to very assimilated. The older population reflects the pluralism of American society.
- Gerontologists study minority aging because (1) older minority populations have increased in size, (2) the study of older minorities can lead to more responsive programs for older people, (3) minorities experience aging differently than do whites, and (4) minority groups can teach us other ways of growing old.
- The white population makes up about 90% of the population age 65 and over. The proportion of minority people in the older population increased slowly until the year 2000 and then speeded up.
- Three theories describe the effects of minority group membership on the older person: multiple jeopardy, leveling, and the life course perspective.
- Poverty, discrimination, and social problems such as divorce, high mortality, and teen pregnancies influence aging in African American families. Older African Americans rely on strong informal support networks to deal with these problems.
- Hispanic Americans demonstrate clear economic disadvantages compared with whites, but they seem less disadvantaged on measures of family relations and informal supports. Studies show that, although industrial and city life weaken family ties, Hispanic American elders still tend to live in multigenerational families.
- Asian American elders have a higher economic status than any other minority group. They also have longer life expectancies. Many Asian American elders get support from their families. They may also need help from formal supports, but language and cultural barriers sometimes keep them from getting the help they need.
- American Indians have many health, social, and economic problems. They tend to underuse formal support programs. The lack of formal supports on reservations and long distances between reservations and support services disadvantage American Indians. Many American Indians now live in urban centers. They lack access to services on reservations and may have no government services available where they live. About one-half of American Indian elders rely on their grown children for support.
- Researchers suggest that social service workers use a **cultural competence** model of service. This model not only delivers service to the minority community but also builds competence in the older person.

DISCUSSION QUESTIONS

1. Explain the difference between a dominant group and a minority group. What racial and ethnic groups form the largest minorities in the United States today?
2. What does Ramon Valle mean by the term *assimilation continuum?* How does this continuum apply to a pluralistic society? Give an example of how a person's private and public conduct might fit into different places on this continuum.
3. What are the demographic forces that will account for the increase in the older minority group population in the future? Do the forces vary for different minority groups? If so, how? What effect will this increase have on American society?
4. Define the terms *multiple jeopardy, leveling,* and *life course perspective.* Describe the strengths and weaknesses of each approach to studying minority aging.
5. What do gerontologists mean when they speak of "institutional completeness?" How does this affect the experience of minority group elders as they age?
6. What problems face aging African American families today? How do they cope with these problems? What

future problems will African American older people face due to changes in family life?
7. Explain why diversity within the Hispanic older community leads to different experiences of aging for members of different subgroups. Give specific examples of the diverse responses to aging within the Hispanic American minority group.
8. What barriers keep Asian Americans from getting the social supports they need as they age? Do some of these same barriers apply to other minority groups? How can social service agencies overcome these barriers?
9. What unique problems do American Indians face due to geographic location? What are the pros and cons of reservation living for older American Indians? What problems do urban American Indians face?
10. What can health care and social service workers do to improve care and service to ethnic elders? Give two examples of specific changes that would improve care and service.

SUGGESTED READING

Freidenberg, J. M. (2000). *Growing old in El Barrio.* New York: New York University Press.

The author interviewed 41 Puerto Rican elders age 60 and over in New York's East Harlem (El Barrio). Most of the people in the book arrived in New York in the 1950s. The book provides an ethnographic account, through in-depth interviews, of these people's lives in old age. People describe, in their own words, their everyday lives. They discuss their relations with their families, their health and income, and their use of community resources. The book provides a detailed picture of later life in this unique community.

Gelfand, D. E. (2003). *Aging and ethnicity: Knowledge and services* (2nd ed.). New York: Springer.

This book provides an overview of aging in the United States. It includes discussions of ethnicity and gerontological theory, immigration patterns, and an overview of major ethnic groups, including African American, Hispanic American, and Asian American elders. The later chapters focus on the program and social service needs of older ethnic group members.

Olson, L. K. (Ed.). (2001). *Age through ethnic lenses: Caring for the elderly in a multicultural society.* Lanham, MD: Rowman & Littlefield.

The editor has collected essays that look at older people from diverse backgrounds. Essays discuss long-term care in relation to the racial and ethnic groups discussed in this chapter. Essays also discuss other minority groups, including Mormon, Amish, and Jewish older people. The book gives a glimpse at the variety of minority groups (other than racial and ethnic groups) that make up the older population today (including gay and lesbian older people). The essays propose ways to improve care for the wide variety of older people who make up the aging population today.

Websites to Consult

Administration on Aging—Minority Aging
www.aoa.gov/aoaroot/aging_statistics/minority_aging/Index.aspx

This page contains a variety of resources on minority aging, including breakdowns by age, ethnic group, occurrences of illness, and in-depth profiles of the aged in their social context.

Resource Centers for Minority Aging Research
www.rcmar.ucla.edu/mission.php

The University of California, Los Angeles, coordinates these centers' activities. This portal contains links to information and data from a number of government organizations and research centers. It covers a variety of topics that affect minorities and examines a number of issues that confront aging minority groups.

National Academy on an Aging Society
www.agingsociety.org/agingsociety/links/links_minority.html

This portal contains links to studies conducted by a number of minority interest groups. It contains links to studies on aging in black, Hispanic, Native American, and Asian Pacific populations.

UCLA Center for Health Policy Research
www.healthpolicy.ucla.edu

An excellent resource for policy papers and research reports on ethnic aging. The Center focuses on California data and issues. But a large number of Mexican, Asian, and American Indian elders live in California. So, the Center's research reports on health give a good understanding of these groups' conditions and needs.

chapter *7*

THE HEALTH CARE SYSTEM

In the spring of 1991, my mother fell as she walked down the steps outside her doctor's office. She had broken her hip many years before and walked with an uneven gait. When she lost her balance on the steps, she feared that she had broken her hip again. An ambulance took her to a nearby hospital for x-rays. The doctors thought she had a hairline fracture in her hip. She couldn't walk well enough to be on her own at her apartment, so the hospital discharged her to a nursing home.

I lived about 2,000 miles away at the time and arrived in town after my mother had settled into the home. My sister and I knew that she could stay in the nursing home only for a short time under Medicare. The costs

would start to mount after that. So we created a discharge plan that would allow our mother to move back to her own apartment after a short stay with my sister. To carry out this plan, we had to find the health care and social supports she needed to live on her own.

My mother had friends in her apartment building. They would visit and look after her social needs. But we knew she needed help with bathing and meal preparation, and she needed transportation to and from her doctor's office. I spent several mornings on the phone, calling agencies, community groups, religious groups, and government offices in my mother's town. Could someone help me put together a package of services that would allow her to live on her own?

I had not heard about Area Agencies on Aging at the time. They might have helped me find the resources I needed. But on my own I could find no agency or group to coordinate services for my mother. This nearly drove my sister and me crazy. Our mother needed to leave the nursing home—she needed no further medical care and the place depressed her. I had to get back to work and to my family. We felt unsure that we could get my mother the support she needed.

This prospect raised a number of fears for us. First, we saw that our mother had gotten worse in the nursing home. She felt bored and slept during the days. This kept her awake at night, so the staff gave her sleeping pills to help her sleep. The pills made her groggy and dull during the day, so she dozed all day and completed the vicious circle. Second, we knew that she could afford institutional care for a year or two, at most, before she would spend all her assets. Then she could get **Medicaid**. But this could mean a move to another institution, possibly one further from my sister's home.

In the end, my sister patched together a collection of people to support our mother. She organized friends, neighbors, relatives, a visiting nurse, someone to clean the house, and a person who made and delivered meals. My sister became our mother's **care manager**. She visited at least once a week and spoke on the phone with my mother at least once a day. She did all this while she cared for her own family.

The plan worked pretty well. We knew, however, that any decline in my mother's health would send us back to the phones again, and we feared that a further decline in health would send my mother to an institution for good.

Many families in the United States face this problem. The current health care system does best at providing medical care in hospitals, nursing homes, and doctors' offices. It does less well at helping families to keep older people at home. This means that people will find help when they get an acute illness. They will probably find financial support to help pay for radiology, x-rays, surgery, and other medical services. But people with some **chronic illness** or disability who want to stay well and live on their own may have trouble finding support, and they will probably have to pay for this support themselves.

The health care system today consists of a mixture of publicly and privately funded programs. These programs hardly form a comprehensive system of care. Schulz (2001, p. 205) calls the United States "very unusual when compared with most other countries in the industrialized world." He reports that 24 industri-

alized countries out of 29 provide government health insurance to 99% or more of their people. The U.S. government system, before recent changes to the law, covered only 33% of U.S. citizens. Most people had to rely on private health insurance through their work. But many employers do not offer health insurance. As a result, an estimated 14.8% of workers had no insurance coverage at all (Kaiser Commission, 2004).

Recent changes to the law governing health care will change some of this. The United States will not adopt the government-sponsored and -managed approach to health care common in Europe and Canada. But Congress instituted reforms in 2010. These reforms will guarantee that all Americans—regardless of their job status or prior health—will have health insurance.

This new legislation will gradually change the U.S. health care system. Note the word *gradually*. The legislation will bring in some immediate changes that will benefit individuals. But reform of the system will take time. The new law encourages experimentation with new payment methods, studies of best practices, and the development of new treatment methods.

In the meantime, older people will continue to rely on Medicare and Medicaid as their basic health insurance programs. Satisfaction with these programs remains high among seniors. The new legislation includes some small improvements to these programs, but generally leaves them unchanged.

These programs provide older people with a broad range of coverage that also includes some coverage for medications. Still, the current system of health care, even with the proposed reforms, fails to meet many older people's needs. A study of the current system will point out the places where change needs to take place. This chapter looks at (1) the structure of the health care system today, (2) the issues that this system creates for an aging society, and (3) how the system has begun to change to meet older people's needs.

THREE MODELS OF HEALTH CARE

Social scientists use three models to describe different approaches to health care in the United States today: the medical model, the social model, and the health promotion model. A model simplifies real life, but it presents a system's basic structure, activity, and values. Each model defines the goal and practice of health care differently. Each one meets different needs of the older population. A review of these models gives a picture of the U.S. health care system today.

The Medical Model

The medical model focuses on diagnosis and cure of illness. It defines health care as sickness treatment. Care most often takes place in a doctor's office, hospital, or nursing home. The medical model uses drugs, surgery, and rehabilitation to treat disease. Chappell, Strain, and Blandford (1986, p. 101) say that within this model, "medical care and treatment are defined primarily as technical problems, and the goals of medicine are viewed in terms of technical criteria, such as validity, diagnosis, precision of disease-related treatment, symptom relief and termination of disease process." Physicians control most of the treatment that takes place within this model. They also control or influence the activities of other health care professionals. Physicians learn this approach in medical school. They get little

training in other forms of treatment, such as health promotion or community long-term care.

The current system of health care services and government reimbursements supports the medical model. Government financing of health care, through Medicare and Medicaid, mostly pays for doctors' or institutions' services. Schulz (2001, p. 214) says that "most public money for long-term care currently goes for institutional care, and the inadequate **availability** of community care services . . . encourage[s] overutilization of institutional options." (See Figure 7.1.)

The Social Model

The social model of health care defines health and care more broadly than does the medical model. *Health* in this model refers to more than the absence

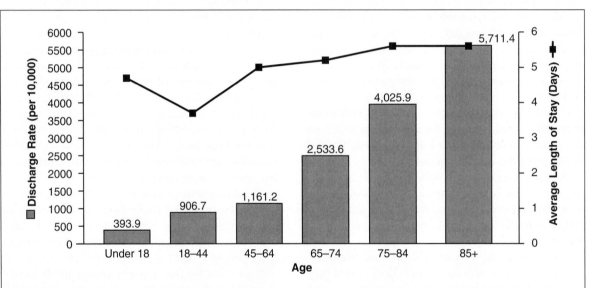

The discharge rate measures the number of hospital discharges in a year (per 10,000 population). Each time a person leaves a hospital, it counts as one discharge. A person can have more than one discharge from a hospital in a year.

This chart shows the hospital discharge rate for six age groups. Note that the discharge rate increases with age. It increases dramatically for people age 65 and over. The oldest age group (85+) has more than six times the rate of the 18- to 44-year-old age group. The oldest group also has more than twice the discharge rate of the 65- to 74-year-old age group.

This shows the diversity in health care use among members of the older population. Hospital use increases dramatically

with age. And the very old population—a group expected to grow in the years ahead—makes the most frequent use of hospital resources.

Also, the number of days a person stays in the hospital per visit increases with age after ages 18–44. The oldest age group, for example, tends to stay in the hospital almost one and one-half times longer per stay than the 18- to 44-year-old age group. These figures show the older population's (especially the oldest group's) greater use of hospital resources. The aging of the older population will increase the cost of hospital care in the years ahead.

FIGURE 7.1   Hospital Discharge Rates, 2006

Source: National Center for Health Statistics. (2010b). *Health, United States, 2009: With Special Feature on Medical Technology.* Discharges, days of care, and average length of stay in nonfederal short-stay hospitals, by selected characteristics: United States, selected years 1980–2006, Table 99, p. 356. Hyattsville, MD: Author.

of disease. It refers to a person's ability to function in the social world. A person may need medical care to do this. An older person often needs other kinds of care as well. Family counseling, home health care, and **adult day care** all form part of the social model. Health care in this model most often takes place in the community. This model includes health care professionals, but also social workers, counselors, and volunteers. The doctor, in this model, works as part of a health care team.

The social model of health care suits an older population. Today, most older people live on their own in the community. They need little medical help, but they may need social and personal supports to live on

their own. The social model of health care aims to keep older people in the community. Community care involves coordination of services among many health care professionals. It includes formal and informal care, and it involves case management and multidisciplinary assessment of needs and outcomes.

Until the 1990s, the social model got little public or private support. But the rising costs of Medicare led to a change in policy. Moon (2006) says that Medicare costs as a share of the federal budget grew from 3.5% in the early 1970s to almost 13% in 2004. The actual cost of Medicare rose between 1980 and 2009 more than 12 times from $37 billion to $502.3 billion (Centers for Medicare and Medicaid Services, 2010c).

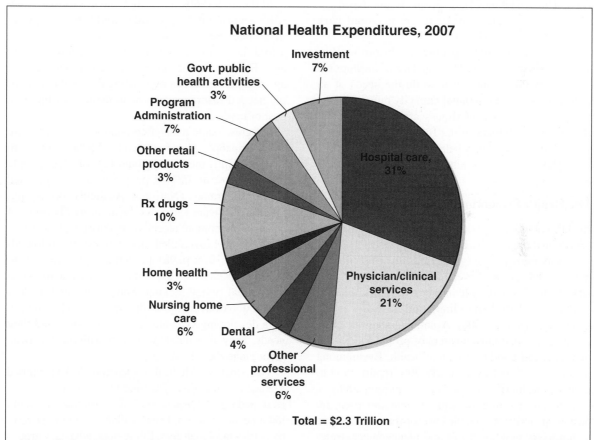

National Health Expenditures, 2007

- Investment 7%
- Govt. public health activities 3%
- Program Administration 7%
- Other retail products 3%
- Rx drugs 10%
- Home health 3%
- Nursing home care 6%
- Dental 4%
- Other professional services 6%
- Hospital care, 31%
- Physician/clinical services 21%

Total = $2.3 Trillion

The medical model dominates health care service today. You can see this in the expenditure figures in this chart. More than half the $2.24 trillion spent on health care services goes to hospital care and physician/clinical services. Only 3% of the total goes to home health care—the core of the social model of health care. Long-term care costs, including home health care and hospice care, will increase in the future as the population ages. Policies designed to reduce hospital and physician costs could lead to lower-cost services (such as outpatient and community care).

FIGURE 7.2   How Is the U.S. Health Care Dollar Spent? National Health Expenditures, United States, 2007

Source: U.S. Department of Health and Human Services. Centers for Disease Control and Prevention. National Center for Health Statistics. (2010c). *Health, United States, 2009*. National health expenditures . . . and percent distribution, by type of expenditure: United States, selected years 1960–2007, Table 126, p. 397.

The high cost of hospital care led to a shift in Medicare payments. This encouraged early discharges from hospitals and led to more care in the community. Kane and Kane (2001) say that a large portion of Medicare payments began to go toward home health care. Also, the Medicaid program encouraged states to set up community-based health care programs. Medicaid funded these programs as long as states could show reductions in nursing-home costs. Kane and Kane (2001) say that a number of states have set up statewide programs to serve people with disabilities at home.

Still, the health care payment system puts medical treatment at the center of care. Medicare and Medicaid, for example, support home health care, but they often require nursing or therapy as part of the program. This sometimes leads people to use expensive skilled nursing care in order to get **personal care** (such as help with bathing).

Health care for older people has begun to shift toward the social model. The high cost of institutional care drives this change. But so do the needs of an aging population. **Functional capacity** rather than the presence or absence of illness affects well-being. Health care providers in the future will judge their success by how well they help people manage on their own. This fits the new reality of an aging society.

The Health Promotion Model

Health promotion includes the concept of disease prevention and reduced disability. Current research shows that many older people can maintain their functioning into late old age. And even among people with some **ADL** (activities of daily living) or **IADL** (instrumental activities of daily living) limitation, 81% live in the community (Stone, 2006). A national study of older people found that three quarters of people age 65 and over reported good to excellent health. Even among people age 75 and over, nearly 70% report good to excellent health (Federal Interagency Forum, 2008).

With proper support, some people can even get back lost abilities. Health care professionals have begun to try new treatment and management strategies. These include public health measures such as flu vaccination, antismoking campaigns, diet education, and yoga classes. Health-promotion and disease-prevention professionals work to keep older people healthy and fit.

These three models form a continuum of care— from the most intensive acute medical care, to management of health conditions in the community, to activities that prevent disease and promote health. Too often, the system serves the person at the acute-care end of this continuum, and the medical model guides the choice of treatment. This leads to high costs for care and sometimes to **overmedicalized service**. Health care professionals and policy makers have begun to explore the social and health promotion models of care. These models may save the system money in the long run, and they provide the kind of care that fits older people's long-term needs.

THE U.S. HEALTH CARE SYSTEM TODAY

Older people had few health care insurance options until the mid-1960s. First, they did not form a group (like a corporation), so they could not get group insurance. Second, most older people could not afford the cost of private insurance premiums in old age. Third, insurance companies could deny coverage to a person with a preexisting illness. Older people needed insurance to protect them from the high cost of medical care.

Congress made a major commitment to health care for older people when it passed the Medicare program in 1965. Until then, only about half of older people (compared with 75% of people under age 65) had health insurance (National Academy on Aging, 1995b). Medicare came into being in part because of an atmosphere more receptive to older people's issues.

Theodore Lowi called this "interest group liberalism" (Pratt, 1976, p. 98). Lowi traces this atmosphere to John F. Kennedy's support for groups that took part in national policy making. Spokespersons for older people took advantage of this moment. They played on a developing sympathy for older people and their needs. They also allied themselves with the American labor giant, the AFL-CIO.

The American Medical Association (AMA) opposed Medicare at that time, claiming that it created "socialized medicine." Quadagno (2005) says that this claim hid a deeper concern. Doctors didn't want the government to control their fees. But seniors' advocacy groups claimed that Medicare simply extended programs like Social Security. They said that it took a "truly American" approach to the solution of a social problem. The American Medical Association in this debate looked selfish and opposed to progress. The new sympathy for older people and their needs, along with strong allies like organized labor and a shrewd campaign, led to the passage of Medicare (Gluck & Reno, 2001).

But seniors' groups won only a partial victory. The American Medical Association still managed to stop the passage of a comprehensive health care program. The program that did get passed attempted to please a variety of players. Insurance companies got to manage Medicare claims from health care providers. This brought them income. Hospital associations gained because Medicare offered hospital insurance. Physicians accepted the plan because they got a direct method of payment for services to the poor. Each of these groups saw the chance to get some profit from the system.

The Medicare program, however, created the seeds of its future problems. None of the groups that supported and provided services to Medicare had an interest in containing health care costs. The system paid for each service or procedure performed. They all benefited from more procedures, more claims, and higher-priced services. Quadagno says,

> Under Medicare the federal government poured virtually unlimited public resources into financing care for the aged and the poor, turning health care into a profitable enterprise for physicians, hospitals, and insurance companies. As what had been largely a charitable, ostensibly noncommercial enterprise became a growth industry, costs skyrocketed. (2005, p. 108)

These high and rising costs threaten to bankrupt the system today. And they drive the current interest in health care reform.

Medicare

The Structure of the Program

Medicare covered 19 million people when it began on July 1, 1966. In 2009, the program covered almost 46 million people. This makes Medicare the largest pool of insured people in the United States (Klees. Wolfe, & Curtis, 2009a; Moon, 2005). In total the Medicare programs paid out $462 billion in benefits in 2008.

The Medicare program contains two parts: hospital insurance (HI or Part A) and supplementary medical insurance (SMI or Part B and Part D). People eligible for Social Security get Part A insurance at no cost when they turn age 65. Part A includes four kinds of care: care in a hospital, care in a nursing home after a hospital stay, home health care, and hospice care.

A payroll tax funds the hospital insurance program. Employees pay 1.45% of their income; employers match this amount. The money collected goes into a Federal Hospital Insurance Trust Fund. All hospital insurance expenses come from this fund.

The hospital insurance program sets guidelines for standards of care in hospitals and other agencies that take part in the program. The program also reviews the cost of services, sets limits on cost, and, in the case of most hospitals, pays a set rate for a specific diagnosis. Medical review groups made up of doctors in each state see that care given under the program meets standards of quality and effectiveness.

People may choose to get Supplementary Medical Insurance (called Part B insurance) if they are entitled to Part A, are age 65 or older, and live in the United States. Medicare Part B helps pay for doctors' services, medical equipment, laboratory tests, radiation therapy, home health care, and other services for older people who have enrolled. Part B enrollees agree to pay a premium for this coverage.

Medicare also offers a Part C or the Medicare Advantage program. This program (formerly called Medicare + Choice) offers a Medicare Managed Care Plan and Medicare Private Fee-for-Service Plan. Private insurance companies offer these plans. By May 2009, Medicare enrollees could choose from 562 plans. These plans provide services that coordinate care or lower out-of-pocket expenses. Some plans offer prescription drug benefits (Medicare, 2004a). These plans operate under contract to Medicare and they differ from state to state. About 11 million people have enrolled in these programs or about 23% of all Medicare beneficiaries (Feder, Komisar, & Niefeld, 2001; Klees et al., 2009a).

The Bush administration in 2003 added a Prescription Drug Discount Card to the Medicare program (Medicare Part D). This benefit came into effect in 2006. Medicare Part D covered 25.4 million people in 2008. The average cost to Medicare for this coverage came to $39.86 per person in that year (Center for Medicare Advocacy, 2010).

People who want this benefit have to enroll in a private plan to get their Discount Card. The amount of discount depends on a person's income and whether the person has other insurance.

A study of Part D's effect on out-of-pocket costs found that the program lowered costs for beneficiaries (Millett, Everett, Matheson, Bindman, & Mainous, 2010). All Medicare enrollees saw an average 32% drop in out-of-pocket drug costs in the first year of Part D coverage. Those without drug coverage before Part D saw an average decrease of 49% in costs. The researchers in this study conclude that out-of-pocket costs dropped substantially for people without Medicaid coverage in the past.

But critics of the plan say that the program includes a confusing, complex set of rules, unclear premium costs, and uncertainty about the drugs covered. Critics also state that this plan involves high administrative costs (estimated at nearly 8 times the administrative cost of the Medicare program) (Schulz & Binstock, 2006, p. xi). Part D offers costly incentives to private insurers to participate in the plan. Finally, the plan covers only about one fourth of total drug spending by beneficiaries (Moon, 2006). This leaves some older people (e.g., those who don't enroll in the private plan) with high out-of-pocket drug expenses.

Millett and colleagues (2010, p. 1325) wonder "whether the high public cost of providing pharmacy coverage through Medicare is worth the substantially lower financial benefit derived by beneficiaries." The high public cost of Part D coverage comes at a time when policy makers struggle to contain health care costs.

Medicare Costs and Funding

In 2008, 44.9 million people age 65 and over (96% of all seniors) enrolled in Medicare Part A. Part A paid out $232 billion to all beneficiaries in that year (including payments to 7.4 million disabled people). This came to an average of $5,179 per person (Board of Trustees, 2009).

Thirty-five million seniors (90% of all seniors) have Part B insurance. Total government expenditures for benefits for Part B in 2008 came to $180 billion (up from $3.3 billion in 1967 and $111 billion in 1990) (Freid, Prager, MacKay, & Xia, 2003; National Committee, 2009). The average benefit per person came to $4,322 in 2008.

If a person chooses Part B, the government deducts a premium for Part B from Social Security benefits ($110.50 per month in 2010 for lower- and middle-income earners) and matches these fees from general revenues (taxes). Participants may also have to make coinsurance payments (usually 20% of charges) and payments for services above Medicare limits.

Most of the money paid out through Medicare (Part A and Part B) went to pay for inpatient hospital care and doctors' fees (Board of Trustees, 2009). The amount paid in benefits by Part A and Part B came to $412 billion in 2008. (See Figures 7.3 and 7.4.)

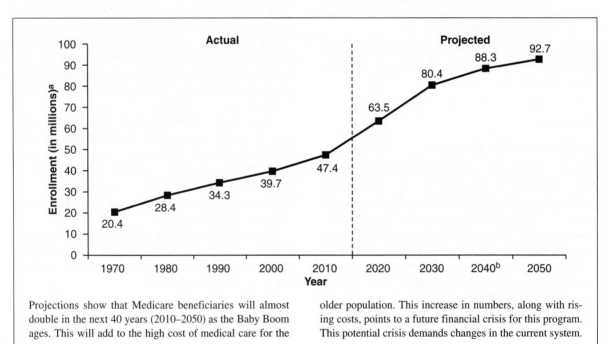

Projections show that Medicare beneficiaries will almost double in the next 40 years (2010–2050) as the Baby Boom ages. This will add to the high cost of medical care for the older population. This increase in numbers, along with rising costs, points to a future financial crisis for this program. This potential crisis demands changes in the current system.

FIGURE 7.3 Number of Medicare Beneficiaries, 1970–2050

[a]Number of beneficiaries with HI and/or SMI coverage. Figures from 2010 onward are estimates.

[b]Enrollment in Part C is not explicitly projected beyond 2030. Totals for 2040 and 2050 do not include Part C enrollments.

Source: The Board of Trustees, Federal Hospital Insurance and Federal Supplementary Medical Insurance Trust Funds. (2010). *2010 annual report of the boards of trustees of the Federal Hospital Insurance and Federal Supplementary Medical Insurance Trust Funds.* Washington, DC: Author. Retrieved November 13, 2010, from www.cms.gov/ReportsTrustFunds/downloads/tr2010.pdf.

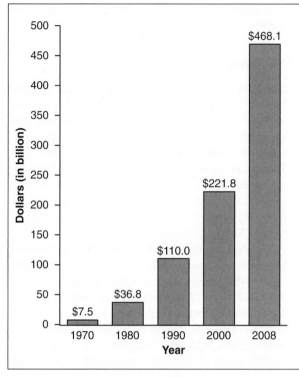

This figure shows the increase in Medicare expenses. It shows why concern exists about the cost of health care for seniors. Note that the cost more than doubles between 2000 and 2008. Policy analysts project increased costs in the future as the Baby Boom enters old age. This large group will use more health care services and will further increase costs.

FIGURE 7.4   Total Medicare Expenditures 1970–2008

Source: U.S. Department of Health and Human Services. Centers for Disease Control and Prevention. National Center for Health Statistics. (2010c). *Health, United States, 2009.* National health expenditures . . . and percent distribution, by type of expenditure: United States, selected years 1960–2007, Table 142, p. 426.

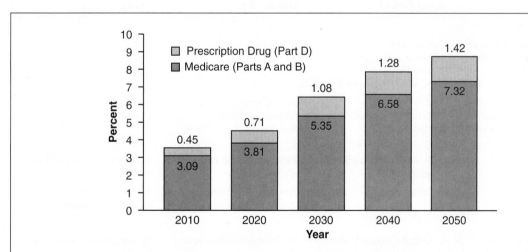

These rising costs in relation to GDP worry policy makers. The large Baby Boom generation and longer life expectancies will increase costs further. Current figures show that costs will increase two and a half times (between 2010 and 2050) as a proportion of GDP. Moon (2006, p. 31) notes that federal deficits and the wider economy will affect support for the Medicare program in the future. "Changes in Medicare," she says, "will be caught up in the pressure to limit all federal spending."

FIGURE 7.5   Medicare Costs as a Share of Gross Domestic Product (GDP)

Sources: The Boards of Trustees (2009). 2009 Annual Report of the Boards of Trustees of the Federal Hospital Insurance and Federal Supplementary Medical Insurance Trust Funds. HI and SMI Incurred Expenditures as a Percentage of the Gross Domestic Product. Table III.A2, p. 35). Retrieved: November 7, 2010 http://www.cms.gov/ReportsTrustFunds/downloads/tr2009.pdf

Physicians and other service suppliers may or may not agree to participate in the Medicare program. Those who agree accept the Medicare limits on charges. They then get payments directly through Medicare. Patients will pay only the **deductible** and the **coinsurance** payment. Patients with a doctor who does not accept assignment to Medicare Part B must pay the doctor themselves. They then get paid back for the amount of the bill accepted by Medicare.

Schulz (2001) says that only about 50% of doctors accept assignment to Medicare. Doctors who opt out of the Medicare system can charge as much as 115% of the Medicare allowable rate. This means that many older people with Medicare insurance still have to pay some costs for a doctor's care out of their own pocket.

Over time, Medicare has covered less and less of older people's medical costs. For example, the poorest people pay almost one third of their income for health care treatment (Schulz, 2001). Out-of-pocket expenses include payments for eyeglasses, hearing aids, dental care, and prescription drugs. These costs for everyday items drive up the cost of health care for individuals.

And out-of-pocket expenses increase with age. (See Table 7.1.)

Medicaid

The federal government set up the Medicaid program in 1965 along with Medicare. Medicaid serves low-income Americans of all ages. The federal and state governments jointly fund this program. Medicaid enrolled 44.8 million older people in December 2008. People age 65 and over make up 8% of all Medicaid recipients (Ellis, Roberts, Schwartz, & Rousseau, 2010; Klees, Wolfe, & Curtis, 2009b). The total cost of Medicaid services in 2008 came to $38.8 billion (Kaiser Slides, 2010).

The average Medicaid payment to an eligible older person in 2007 came to $12,499 (Statehealthfacts.org, 2010). Almost one quarter (24.4%) of Hispanic seniors and 18.8% of African American seniors receive Medicaid payments (compared to only 5.7% of white seniors). This reflects the lower incomes of minority older people. Widowed, divorced, and never-married seniors (many of them women) have the highest rates

TABLE 7.1 Medicare Payments, Original Medicare Plan, Selected Medicare Services, 2004

Service	*Period Covered*	*Medicare Pays*	*You Pay*
Medicare Part A[a]			
1. Hospitalization Semiprivate room, general nursing, services, and supplies	First 60 days 61st–90th day 91st–onward Up to 60 days over a lifetime	All but $1,132 All but $283/day All but $566/day	$1,132 $283/day $566/day
2. Skilled nursing Facility care Semiprivate room, general and skilled nursing, services, and supplies	First 20 days 21st–100th day Beyond 100 days	100% of approved amount All but $141.50/day Nothing	Nothing Up to $141.50/day All costs
3. Home health care	Unlimited as long as you meet Medicare conditions	100% of approved amount; 80% of equipment	Nothing for services; 20% for equipment
4. Hospice care	Unlimited	95% of approved amount for inpatient respite care	5% for respite care; copayment of $5 for prescription drugs
Medicare Part B[b]			
5. Medical expenses	Unlimited if medically necessary	80% of approved amount after $162 deductible	20% of approved amount plus $162 deductible
6. Home health care	Unlimited as long as you meet Medicare conditions	100% of approved amount; 80% of equipment	Nothing for services; 20% for equipment

[a]2011 Part A monthly premium: None for people who have full Social Security credits. Others can buy Medicare service for up to $450 per month (in 2011) if they have not paid into the Medicare program while working.

[b]2011 Part B monthly premium: $115.40 for couples who earned $170,000 or less in 2009. You also pay a Part B deductible each year before Medicare starts to pay its share. In 2011, the deductible amount is $162.

Source: Centers for Medicare & Medicaid Services. (2010b). *Medicare & you 2011.* Washington, DC: Department of Health & Human Services. Retrieved November 13, 2010, from www.medicare.gov/Publications/Pubs/pdf/10050.pdf.

of Medicaid use. Compared to married seniors, widowed seniors have more than three times the rate of Medicaid use (Klees et al., 2009a).

Medicaid goes to older people eligible for state public assistance, to people who get Supplemental Security Income (a federal income supplement program), or to people with incomes below a set amount. This income and asset limit differs for each state. People age 85 and over and people in poor mental and physical health make up a large proportion of the older population that uses the Medicaid program (Feder et al., 2001).

A national study found, for example, that people on Medicaid had high rates of heart disease, hypertension, stroke, chronic lung disease, diabetes, and other chronic illnesses (National Center for Health Statistics, 2007b). Also, more than a quarter (28%) of this group of poorer older people reported feelings of sadness all or most of the time in the 30 days before the interview. This came to twice the rate of Medicare recipients and two-and-a-half times the rate of people with private insurance who reported these feelings.

Medicaid also finances long-term care for eligible people. Klees and colleagues (2009b) report that Medicaid paid almost 42% of all nursing-home costs in the United States. In 2006, this came to $45.8 billion and served 1.7 million people (most of them elderly). Home health services under Medicaid came to $5.9 billion and served 1.2 million people. These costs will increase as the number of older people with disabilities increases. But funds that keep older people in the community may reduce the costs of institutional care.

In the past, spouses of Medicaid patients in an institution had to spend down all of their income and assets to get Medicaid coverage. This could leave the spouse in the community in poverty. The new policy allows spouses of institutionalized Medicaid patients a living allowance and other resources. Some people get both Medicare and Medicaid benefits. States may pay for Medicare Supplementary Medical Insurance (Part B) for Medicaid clients. The Part B program offers a number of basic services, including inpatient hospital care, physician services, and skilled nursing home services.

The amount of service clients get, how long they get the service, and the types of service covered differ from state to state and even within a state during a year. The federal and state governments give matching funds to the Medicaid program. (See Figure 7.6.)

Medicaid pays nursing-home expenses for needy older people or for people who have used up most of their own income and assets (Schulz, 2001). Without Medicaid support, most older people who now get Medicaid could not afford nursing-home care.

Medicaid now serves as the default national long-term care program. It set out to serve the poorest older people. But it now also serves middle-income people who spend down their assets before or after they enter a nursing home. For example, two thirds of people who enter a nursing home as private pay residents eventually spend down their savings in order to get Medicaid support.

President Clinton in 1995 referred to Medicaid and Medicare as a package of programs that serve middle-class as well as poor older people. Grogan and Andrews (2010) say this extends Medicaid's original mandate. Total Medicaid costs (federal and state) for 2008 came to $338.8 billion (Statehealthfacts.org, 2010). Klees and colleagues (2009b) say that, due to increasing costs for services and an aging population, program costs could reach $577.6 billion by 2014.

Employer-Sponsored Health Care Plans

Some employers provide health care coverage as part of their pension package. The employer pays part of the health care premium for retirees just as they do for employed workers. Many of these plans cover prescription drugs. The Medicare Payment Advisory Commission (2002) reports that people in these plans have the lowest out-of-pocket costs. But only those in the most generous pension programs get these benefits. The Medicare Payment Advisory Commission (2004) estimates that only about one third of Medicare beneficiaries have this type of plan. People in these plans have some of the highest incomes among Medicare beneficiaries.

Moon (2006) says that the proportion of retirees who have employer-sponsored health insurance has begun to decrease. Employers have cut back on this benefit to control costs. Employer-sponsored programs now often include cost sharing, limits on coverage, and increased premiums. Moon predicts that fewer people will have employer-sponsored health care plans in the future. One study found that the proportion of large companies that offered health care benefits dropped from 66% in 1988 to 29% in 2009 (Kaiser Family Foundation and Health Research and Educational Trust, 2009). Workers and retirees without employer-sponsored benefits will need to pay for

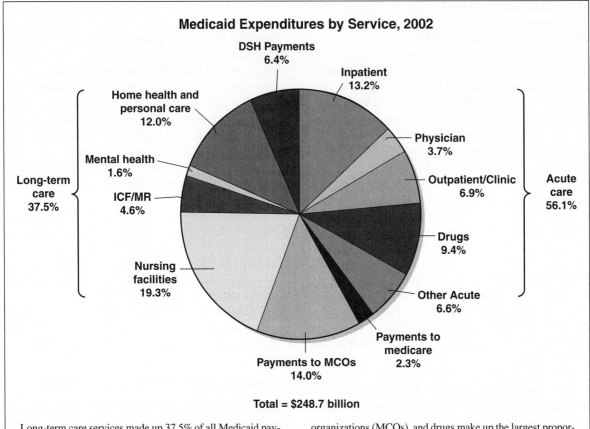

Medicaid Expenditures by Service, 2002

DSH Payments 6.4%

Inpatient 13.2%

Home health and personal care 12.0%

Physician 3.7%

Mental health 1.6%

Outpatient/Clinic 6.9%

Long-term care 37.5%

ICF/MR 4.6%

Acute care 56.1%

Drugs 9.4%

Nursing facilities 19.3%

Other Acute 6.6%

Payments to medicare 2.3%

Payments to MCOs 14.0%

Total = $248.7 billion

Long-term care services made up 37.5% of all Medicaid payments. Acute-care services made up more than half of all Medicaid expenses (56.1%). The largest proportion of Medicaid dollars devoted to long-term care (19.3%) goes to cover nursing-home costs ($48 billion). Hospitals, managed care organizations (MCOs), and drugs make up the largest proportions of acute-care payments. Medicaid helps the most needy older people. Many of them are the very old. They often need institutional care and home care support. Researchers predict an expansion of home health care services in the future.

FIGURE 7.6 Where the Medicaid Dollar for the Elderly Goes, 2002

Source: Kaiser Commission on Medicaid and the Uninsured. (2004). *The Medicaid program at a glance.* Figure 5. Citing Urban Institute estimates based on data from CMS (Form 64). Retrieved November 13, 2010, from www.state.tn.us/tenncare/forms/medicaidglance.pdf.

their own health care coverage. Those who can't afford to pay for private insurance will rely on the Medicare (and in some cases the Medicaid) program.

Medigap and Long-Term Care Insurance

The Medicare and Medicaid programs cover only a part of older people's medical expenses. Figures for nursing-home expenditures, for example, show a gap between Medicaid payments and out-of-pocket expenses. Also, older people will see increases in out-of-pocket home care expenses. This has led many older people to take out private health insurance, called *Medigap insurance*. This covers the difference in cost between government health care plans and the cost of medical treatment. Private insurance companies offer Medigap policies.

Medigap companies offer 12 standard policy options. Policies cover charges such as hospital deductibles and physician **copayments.** They also cover services such as preventive screening and outpatient drug costs. Each plan offers a different combination of services. Costs vary from plan to plan (and even plans that offer the same coverage may charge different rates).

The government sets standards for this kind of insurance. For example, companies that sell this insurance must spell out detailed benefits clearly. They

"YOUR BLOOD PRESSURE AND TEMPERATURE ARE WAY UP, BUT YOUR MEDICARE COVERAGE IS WAY DOWN. LOOKS AS IF YOU CAN GO HOME TODAY, MRS. FITCH!"

© Stayskal, 1986 *Tampa Tribune*.

cannot cancel the insurance or refuse to renew it based on a person's health.

These plans work best as a form of protection from a single year of high out-of-pocket costs. People value these programs because they put no upper limit on costs for care (Moon, 2006). But these programs also have some drawbacks.

First, the cost of most Medigap insurance increases with the insured person's age. A program that a person can afford at age 65 can become unaffordable in later old age. In other words, the person may have to drop the coverage when he or she needs it most. (See Figure 7.7.) Also, the cost of Medigap insurance means that relatively few minority seniors buy this coverage. The National Center for Health Statistics (2009) reports that 20.2% of white seniors have Medigap insurance. But only 7.3% of African American and 7.7% of Hispanic seniors have Medigap insurance.

Second, Medigap insurance covers only deductibles and copayments for Medicare services. If Medicare does not cover a service, Medigap insurance will not cover it. For example, general Medigap insurance does not cover long-term care services such as nursing-home placement and home health care. Yet older people feel the greatest concern about the costs of a long-term illness.

Third, Medigap insurers can exclude less healthy people from coverage after a basic enrollment period. This reduces their risk but it makes these policies unavailable to people who may need them most (Moon, 2005). Special long-term care insurance poli-

cies exist, but they vary widely in the services they cover and in their costs. Some policies set conditions before a person can collect on a policy. For example, a policy may pay only for nursing-home care in a **skilled nursing facility**. Or the policy will pay only if a person enters a nursing home from a hospital.

Schulz and Binstock (2006) note that a typical long-term care policy for a 65-year-old can cost almost $3,000 per year. The older the person, the higher the price. Insurance for a couple will nearly double this cost. Also, premiums can increase over time for certain classes of policy holders. Studies show that only 10% to 20% of older people can afford the cost of long-term care insurance.

A study of Baby Boomer women, for example, found that two thirds of the women said they could not afford long-term plan costs (Brown, 2009). The high cost of policies, the many conditions on coverage, the risk of increased premiums late in life, and people's different circumstances make long-term care insurance a poor option for most older people.

Employers sponsored about a third of all long-term care policies (29%) in 1998. But most employers do not want to offer this option today and only a small proportion of employees (under 10%) buy them (Stone, 2006). Some states and government agencies also offer these plans. A federal government plan offered workers a lower premium than they would pay through an individual policy. Still few people took this option. A study of the plan found that only 5% of

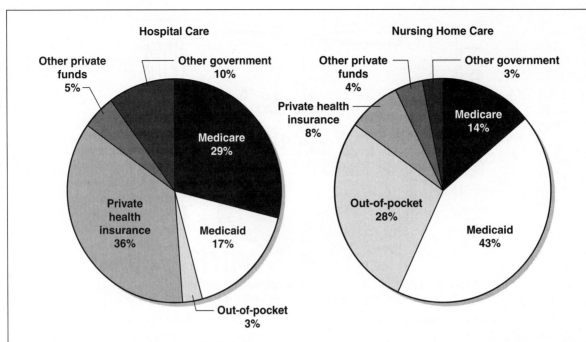

These charts show how health care costs affect individual and government health expenses. The charts show a clear difference in government and private support for hospital and nursing-home care. A combination of government and private insurance plans covers 97% of hospital costs. This provides a safety net for most people who need hospital care.

Medicare funds, however, cover only 13.9% of nursing-home care. Individuals pay one third (32%) of nursing-home costs out of their own resources (out-of-pocket plus other private funds). Medicaid pays for 43% of nursing-home costs, but only 60% of all nursing-home patients get Medicaid payments. This leaves 40% of nursing-home patients with little or no protection. Middle-income families fear the cost of long-term nursing-home care. The health care system provides them with little protection from the ruinous effects of a catastrophic illness.

FIGURE 7.7   Funding for Long-Term Care, 2004

Source: Personal health care expenditures, by source of funds and type of expenditures: United States, 2004. In *Health, United States, 2006. With Chartbook on Trends in the Health of Americans.* Data table for Figure 9. Hyattsville, MD: Centers for Medicare and Medicaid Services, Office of the Actuary, National Health Statistics Group, National Health Accounts.

government workers bought the insurance (Schulz & Binstock, 2006). Coronel (2004) reports that in 2002 only about 4 million Americans had long-term care insurance. Stone (2006) says that in 2004, long-term care insurance policies covered only about 4% of all long-term care costs for older people.

The poorest older people can rely on Medicaid to help with their long-term care costs. The wealthiest older people can afford the costs of insurance. But the absence of an affordable long-term care insurance program puts middle-income earners at risk of poverty if they have a long-term illness.

The Health Care System and the Cost of Care

Since 1960, the United States has led the developed nations in health care spending in absolute dollars per person and as a percentage of the gross domestic product. In 2008, for example, the United States spent $2.3 trillion on health care. This came to more than triple the amount ($714 billion) spent in 1990 and over eight times the amount ($253 billion) spent in 1980.

In 2008 the United States spent 16.2% of its gross domestic product (GDP) on health care, or $7,681 per person. The Centers for Medicare and Medicaid Services (2010e) projected a GDP increase to 17.3% in 2009, "the largest one-year increase in history." This amounts to one of the highest rates among industrialized nations.

Compared with most other industrialized nations, this comes to about 50% more as a proportion of gross domestic product and about two and a half times the per capita expenditure. Costs for health care now make up almost one-quarter of all federal government expenditures and about 15% of state and local government expenditures (Organization for Economic Co-operation and Development [OECD], 2009).

The Centers for Medicare and Medicaid Services (2010e) projects continued increases in health care costs. This agency projects an average annual growth of national health expenditures of 6.3% between 2009 and 2019. This means that health care will make up an estimated 19.6% of the gross domestic product by the year 2019 (up from 16.2% in 2008).

Federal, state, and local governments in the United States paid nearly half (43%) of the total health care bill in 2000. Private sources (e.g., insurance and out-of-pocket payments) made up the rest. Of the government's share, most of the money went to pay for Medicare and Medicaid programs (Centers for Medicare and Medicaid Services, 2010c).

Medicare and Medicaid (and the Children's Health Insurance Program—CHIP) accounted for 21 percent of the federal government budget in 2010 or $732 billion. Nearly two thirds of this cost or $452 billion went to pay for Medicare expenses (Center on Budget and Policy Priorities, 2011). The Congressional Budget Office (2011) projects that government health care spending on Medicare, Medicaid, and the CHIP will grow from 5.6% of GDP in 2011 to about 9% of GDP in 2035. Rising health care costs (not pension outlays) explain most of the increase in government spending on older people.

Some people point to the increase in the number of old and very old people in the United States as a cause of higher health care costs. This explains some, but not all, of the increase in costs. The very old population (age 85 and over), for example, has grown faster than other segments of the population. This age group uses more hospital and physician services than any other age group. But the increased number of older people cannot account for all the increase in health care costs. Studies show that the system itself has created higher costs.

For one thing, government programs have expanded and now cover more costs of health care for older people. This has led to an expansion of hospital care, nursing-home care, and community care. The proportion of personal health care expenses covered by government programs increased from 21.4% in 1960 to 45% in 2007. The prescription drug legislation (Medicare Part D) passed in 2003 that came into effect in 2006 added to federal health care costs.

Also, the cost of care has grown faster than the rate of growth of the older population. The population age 65 and over grew by about 80% (from about 20 million to about 38.9 million people) between 1970 and 2008. And the number of Medicare enrollees more than doubled in that time from 20.4 to 45.20 million. But Medicare payments grew more than 61 times (from $7.5 billion to $462 billion) between 1970 and 2008 (Board of Trustees, 2009).

Higher physicians' fees, more expensive treatments, and increased hospital costs all contributed to these increases. Between 1970 and 2008, for example, personal health care expenditures on hospital care grew more than 26 times from $27.6 billion to $718.4 billion. And personal expenditures on physician and clinical services grew more than 35 times from $14.0 billion to $496.2 billion (Centers for Medicare and Medicaid Services, 2009). The increase in the older population cannot alone explain these cost increases.

Health care economists, policy makers, and politicians have all raised concerns about the high cost of health care. The AARP has put health care reform at the top of its national and state agenda for change (Novelli & Workman, 2006). *The Economist* (2007b, p. 28) calls government-sponsored medical care "the source of America's biggest long-term fiscal problem." The health care system will need to change in the years ahead to control costs and meet the needs of America's older population. Each part of the system needs reform.

Cost of Care and the Older Population

Medicare Costs.   Rising health care costs threaten the Medicare program. The 2004 Annual Report of the Medicare Board of Trustees contains dire warnings about the financial state of Medicare.

> The fundamentals of the financial status of . . . Medicare remain problematic under the intermediate economic and demographic assumptions. . . . The financial outlook for the Medicare Hospital Insurance (HI) Trust Fund that pays hospital benefits has deteriorated significantly from last year, with annual cash flow deficits beginning this year and expected to grow rapidly after 2010 as baby boomers begin to retire. The growing annual cash deficits . . . will lead to exhaustion in trust fund reserves for HI in 2019. (Social Security and Medicare Board of Trustees, 2004)

The report goes on to say that the Medicare Supplementary Medical Insurance Trust Fund and the new prescription drug benefit will all need more revenue from taxes and higher premium charges. Rising costs and the need for more money to fund these programs mean that "the pressure on the Federal budget will

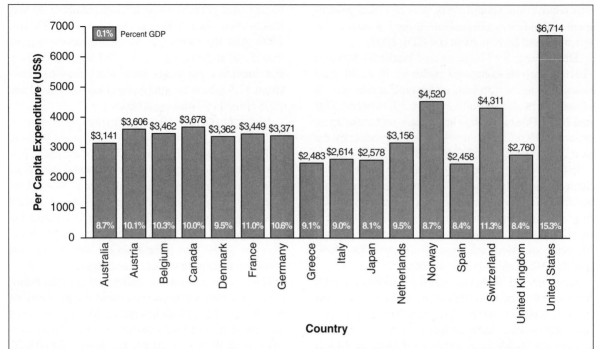

The United States spends more money on health care as a proportion of its GDP than any other developed nation in this chart. Some countries spend little on health care as a proportion of GDP because they offer less formal health care service to their people. But even among countries with a full network of formal services (like Canada or Switzerland), the United States ranks highest in cost. Physician fees, costly intensive daily hospital service, administration costs in hospitals, the use of high technology, and high insurance administration costs all add to the high cost of U.S. health care.

FIGURE 7.8 Total Health Expenditures as a Percentage of Gross Domestic Product and Per Capita Health Expenditures in U.S. Dollars, by Selected Countries: 2006

Source: National Center for Health Statistics. (2010b). Total health expenditures as a percent of gross domestic product, and per capita health expenditures in dollars, by selected countries: Selected years 1960–2006. Table 122, p. 392. Citing OECD data. *Health, United States, 2009: With Special Feature on Medical Technology.* Hyattsville, MD: Author.

intensify" (Social Security and Medicare Board of Trustees, 2004).

Five years later, in its 2009 Annual Report to Congress, the Board of Trustees increased its warning. The Board of Trustees (2009, p. 3) issued "a determination of projected 'excess general revenue Medicare funding.'" This led to a fourth consecutive "Medicare funding warning." This requires the president to submit to Congress proposed legislation to respond to the warning within 15 days after the date of the budget submission for the succeeding year (Board of Trustees, 2009, p. 3). Congress is then required to consider the legislation on an expedited basis. This dire warning and its mandated effect on both the president and the Congress show the serious condition of federal health care funding.

The Board of Trustees (2009) calls for immediate action to bring the looming health care deficit into balance. The sooner the government takes action, the board says, the more flexible and gradual the reforms. This will give health care providers and the public time to adjust to changes in the system.

This looming deficit and the high cost of health care to the federal government make Medicare a target of budget cutting. Legislators see Medicare as a place to reduce spending. Some of them see Medicare reform as a way to shift health care costs to consumers (e.g., through higher insurance payments and more copayments by users). Others suggest raising the age of eligibility for Medicare. Feder and colleagues (2001) say that the debate over Medicare has largely focused on restructuring the Medicare program to contain or shift costs.

The attempt to cap costs began more than two decades ago. In 1983, the government set up a

Prospective Payment System (PPS) to control hospital costs. The federal Health Care Financing Administration created categories of illness called **diagnosis-related groupings (DRGs)**. Hospitals then categorized patients by their medical conditions. Medicare reimbursed hospitals for a fixed number of days of care according to the patient's DRG. If a hospital kept a person longer, the hospital paid the extra cost.

The Prospective Payment System replaced an open-ended system where hospitals got paid according to how long they kept a patient and what they did for the patient. The PPS encouraged hospitals to discharge patients on schedule or sooner. Hospitals that discharged patients early got to keep the extra money allowed by the patient's DRG.

The PPS accounts in part for a decrease in the number of hospital stays by older people between 1997 and 2007, and for the continued low number of days per stay today (relative to the 1980s) (National Center for Health Statistics, 2009). Some studies report lower hospital costs and better care under the PPS (Fillit, 1994).

An increase in the use of outpatient services and community hospital use was one of the results of the PPS system. Managed care programs also contributed to decreased hospital use. They encourage alternative types of treatment to control costs (Medicare, 2004b).

The PPS poses problems for older people on Medicare. First, the system encourages hospitals to release Medicare patients early, and it may restrict the treatment a person gets. It also encourages hospitals to have more private-pay patients. These patients have no DRG limits attached to their stay.

Second, the DRG system takes no account of the person's general health or the severity of the illness. A healthy 65-year-old man and a frail 85-year-old woman who both need a hip replacement fall into the same DRG. But the 85-year-old woman may need more hospital days to recover. The hospital has an incentive to get both patients out in the same length of time. This has led to more early discharges to the community and to nursing homes (Kane & Kane, 2001).

Third, early discharges may increase costs for home health care, outpatient care, and nursing-home care (Estes, 2000). A study funded by the Health Care Financing Administration found no increase in readmissions to the hospital due to early discharges. It also found no increase in nursing-home stays. But it did find an increase in the discharge of patients with unstable conditions (Kahn, Draper, Keeler, Rogers, & Rubenstein, 1992).

A study of DRGs found that community care services had more heavy-care clients due to the PPS (Clifford, 1989). Discharge planners, nursing homes, and home health agencies said they had to provide more units of care due to the PPS (Wood & Estes, 1990). Kane and Kane (2001) note that as the intensity of care increases, the cost of care goes up. So, the early discharge to a nursing home or to a person's home may not save the health care system's money (although the cost of hospital care will go down).

The PPS attempts to cap health care costs by changing a part of the health care system—hospital Medicare reimbursements. But its focus on one part of the system leads to problems in other parts of the system. For example, the PPS focuses only on hospital care. Early or unplanned discharges can lead to further illness and greater need for medical care. Also, decreased hospital days lead to an increased need for home care, and this can end up costing as much as hospital care (Kane & Kane, 2001). The PPS system shifts more of the cost of health care to the nursing home or the community. This may also shift costs to the patient and family.

Further attempts to reform the health care system took place in 1994 and 1995. President Clinton planned a major reform of the health care system, including Medicare. His plan (and several similar plans proposed by others) moved toward coverage for all Americans. It also included some prescription-drug and long-term care benefits for older people. This met with political opposition and failed in Congress. Both parties claimed that the public did not back broad reform.

Congress finally enacted a broad reform of the American health care system in 2010. This took place after many months of public debate and political posturing. The reform makes only minor changes to the Medicare program. But it offers health care coverage to all Americans and removes many of the barriers that kept people from getting the care they needed. This will reduce the cost of caring for a large older population if people enter old age in better health.

Medicaid Costs. The Medicaid program pays for a variety of services for the poorest older people. Services include inpatient hospital care, care in a skilled nursing facility, doctors' fees, and insurance premiums (e.g., for Medicare).

Medicaid payments rose from $6.3 billion in 1972 to $338.8 billion in 2008 (Kaiser Slides, 2010). The growth rate of cost has decreased in recent years. The rate of increase dropped from 10.8% in the 1990s to 6.6% between 2000 and 2007 (National Center on Health Statistics, 2009). But costs continue to grow. Part of this increased cost over time comes from increased services. For example, the Medicaid program pays two fifths (42%) of the cost of nursing-home expenses (a total of $49.9 billion in 2008) (Kaiser Slides, 2010; Klees et al., 2009b).

Medicaid has expanded to provide more home and community-based services. These include **respite care,** personal care, and **chore services.** Home health and personal care services covered by Medicaid rose from $14 billion in 1999 to $47.7 billion in 2008 (Centers for Medicare & Medicaid Services and Office of the Assistant Secretary, 2007; Kaiser Slides, 2010). These services meet the needs of older people in the community who need long-term care and who have limitations on ADLs.

Part of the cost increase in Medicaid comes from increased doctor and hospital fees along with higher administrative costs. The system, for example, lets physicians and hospitals set their own fees. This leads to increases in health care costs over time and to fragmented reforms that try to control costs.

Again, as with Medicare, legislators propose cuts in Medicaid spending. Smith and colleagues (2005) report that all 50 states and the District of Columbia put in place cost-containment measures in 2003. And in 2004, 49 states reduced or froze payments to providers. Forty-four states put in place methods to reduce prescription drug spending.

Legislators who support cuts also call for increased user payments, options to Medicare/Medicaid payments (such as employer-sponsored plans), and more enrollments in managed care programs such as **health maintenance organizations (HMOs).**

Critics say that these proposed cuts will increase private insurance costs to individuals, increase costs for home care, and put limits on nursing-home care to the poorest older people (Hey, 1995). This debate will lead to some reform, but it will probably raise new issues related to **accessibility** of health care for poor and very old people. A look at the personal cost of health care will show why cutbacks in government support will hurt the poorest people.

The Rising Personal Cost of Health Care

Even with increased federal health care payments in the past few years, the amount paid by individuals for health care increased. The Bureau of Labor Statistics (2010) reports that, compared with younger people (ages 25–34), health care costs take a larger proportion of older people's budgets. In 2008, for example, people ages 25 to 34 spent 4.8% of their annual budget on health care. People age 65 and over spent more than twice this proportion of their income—12.9% of their budget on health care. Much of this expense goes to pay for insurance.

Medicare and Medicaid cover some health care costs. But older people had to pay out of their own pockets a high proportion of costs for long-term care, prescription drugs, physician care, dental care, hospitals, and home health services. For poorer older people this creates a burden. And some people fail to visit a doctor or take medications because of the cost.

About 9% of Medicare beneficiaries have no coverage beyond Medicare. These people run the highest risk of poor medical care. Many of them cannot afford added coverage and cannot qualify for Medicaid. Moon (2006) says that the oldest-old tend to fall into this category. They tend to delay care and fail to see a doctor regularly.

In the future, more older people will need long-term care. But very few people have long-term care insurance outside of the Medicaid program. This leaves older people and their families with little protection against the cost of a long nursing-home stay. It puts many people at risk of losing all their assets if they have a catastrophic illness. A catastrophic illness or long-term care can wipe out a lifetime of savings and throw the older person into poverty.

Public Dissatisfaction

Future increases in health care costs will place an added burden on the government and on older people. These increases might make sense if the U.S. public got more for its dollar. But the OECD (2009) says, "The United States does not do well in preventing costly hospital admissions for chronic conditions, such as asthma or complications from diabetes, which should normally be managed through proper primary care." The United States has more than twice the rate of avoidable hospital admissions for these two diseases.

According to Gladwell (2005),

American life expectancy is lower than the Western average. Childhood-immunization rates in the United States are lower than average. Infant-mortality rates are in the nineteenth percentile of industrialized nations. Doctors here perform more high-end medical procedures, such as coronary angioplasties, than in other countries, but most of the wealthier Western countries have more CT scanners than the United States does, and Switzerland, Japan, Austria, and Finland all have more MRI machines per capita. (p. 45)

Recent research by Muennig and Glied (2010) supports this comment. The researchers studied health data from 13 industrialized nations. They found that in 1950 the United States ranked fifth in female life expectancy at birth. By 1990 the United States ranked 46th for female life expectancy. And by 2010 the United States had slipped to 49th for male and female life expectancy combined. The U.S. rankings dropped even though per capita health care spending in the United States rose at more than twice the rate of comparison countries. The researchers conclude from their study that the U.S. health care system needs major repair.

Gladwell (2005, p. 45) goes on to say that "Americans, compared to people in other countries, feel less satisfied with their health care system." The high cost of care and the weak return in outcomes from the U.S. health care system largely account for the public's lack of satisfaction. Schulz (2001) reports that in an international study, 40% of people in Canada, The Netherlands, Germany, and France thought their health care system worked "pretty well." Thirty percent of people in Australia, Sweden, Japan, and the United Kingdom felt this way. But only 10% of Americans thought the U.S. health care system works "pretty well." Thirty-three percent of Americans said, "Our health care system has so much wrong with it that we need to completely rebuild it" (Schulz & Binstock, 2006).

A picture of the U.S. health care system emerges from these findings. First, taxpayers and individuals pay a high price for health care. Schulz and Binstock (2006) say that the U.S. health care system may cost as much as 19% of GDP by 2014. Second, Americans get less for their money than people in other countries. And third, young and old people feel dissatisfied with the current system.

Health Care Reform: National Legislative Action 2010

On March 23, 2010, President Obama signed into legislation the "Patient Protection and Affordable Care Act." The bill aims to provide health insurance for all Americans regardless of age, health condition, or work status. Tumulty, Pickert, and Park (2010, p. 25) call it "an achievement for the history books." Some people consider it the most important piece of social legislation since Social Security. Others take a gloomier view. Senate Minority Leader Mitch McConnell called it "Armageddon." He and other Senate Republicans swore to repeal the bill and replace it with one of their own.

A *USA Today* Gallup poll in the last week of March 2010 found that 49% of the public said they felt "enthusiastic" or "pleased" about the new law. Forty percent said they felt "disappointed" or "angry" (Page, 2010).

These two views of one law give some idea of the partisan rancor within Congress and the strong feelings in the public that led up to the passage of the bill. The bill generated debate and emotion throughout the country.

Months of wrangling and haggling over the bill's contents led to charges that the bill supported "death panels," or that the bill would increase the national

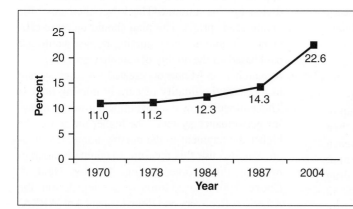

These figures show the increase in the proportion of income spent out-of-pocket on health care by older Medicare beneficiaries. The rate more than doubles over the 34 years reported here. This shows the increasing burden of health care costs older people bear outside the public health insurance program.

FIGURE 7.9   Out-of-Pocket Health Care Costs as a Share of Income of Elderly Medicare Beneficiaries

Source: Adapted from Moon, M. (2006). *Medicare: A policy primer.* Washington, DC: The Urban Institute, p. 23, Figure 1.8, her calculations.

debt. Town Hall meetings led opponents of the bill to shout their disapproval at legislators. Others saw the bill as a chance for the United States to offer all Americans a comprehensive health care plan.

Whatever the views of this health care package before passage, the bill now stands as law. And people (as well as history) will judge the bill by what it does. The legislation intends to improve health care for under- or uninsured people throughout the country. It fills a policy gap that made the United States stand out among developed nations as the only one without a national health care policy.

The legislation fills almost 2,400 pages and contains too many details to review here. I review some of the provisions that affect older people.

Some Losses for Medicare Beneficiaries:

- The bill reduces payments for home health services by $40 billion between now and 2019. Hospitals would lose about $22 billion for certain payments in that same time period.
- In 2011 Medicare Advantage plans will see a gradual decrease in benefits including eye exams, hearing aids, and in some cases gym memberships. These extra benefits cost 14% more per policyholder compared to a typical Medicare patient. The government estimates a saving of $132 billion over 10 years by reducing these extra costs. People in these plans may also see an increase in copayments. These changes will affect about 10 million people.
- In 2013 Medicare payroll taxes will increase for wealthier people. People with incomes over $200,000 and families with incomes over $250,000 will pay a 3.8% tax on unearned (investment) income.
- Until 2019 Medicare Part B beneficiaries who earn $85,000 or more ($170,000 for married couples) will pay higher premiums.

Some Gains for Medicare Beneficiaries:

- The new law maintains basic Medicare benefits.
- At present Medicare Part D covers a person up to $2,830 in medication costs each year. They then have to pay the full cost for drugs until they reach $6,440 in costs. Critics call this the "doughnut hole." People who get Medicare prescription drug benefits (Part D of Medicare) will now get a $250 rebate when they hit the current gap in drug coverage.

- This rebate will ease the burden of uninsured drug costs. This benefit will begin immediately. In 2011 seniors will also get a 50% discount on brand-name drugs when they hit the doughnut hole. They get a smaller break on generics. In 2020 the bill puts an end to the "doughnut hole" prescription coverage gap. The new bill also provides free preventive services—such as an annual checkup—to Medicare recipients. It also increases payments to primary care doctors and nurses who serve as medical coordinators.
- The new bill reduces expensive government subsidies to private insurance plans.
- Small rural hospitals will get Medicare support for the Medicare patients they serve. The bill proposes new methods to screen Medicare claims for fraud and waste. It also provides a temporary program to support companies that offer early retiree health benefits to help reduce the cost of this expensive coverage.
- The new law also makes preventive services free for most people.
- The bill requires states to expand Medicaid coverage. Beginning in 2014 it will include childless adults. This will add an estimated 16 million people to Medicaid, a program run by the states and the federal government. The federal government will cover these costs through 2016. But after that date the states will cover the extra cost of these new enrollees. Governors of the states worry that after federal subsidies end, the states will face large increases in health care costs.
- The new law encourages innovation and experimentation with care delivery. In one option, the government would set a payment for a procedure such as a bypass operation. The doctors and hospital would divide up this amount. The lower their cost, the greater their profit. The plan should increase efficiency. In another case nursing homes would get paid based on the quality of care they provide.
- Researchers in Minnesota created a scoring system to measure the quality of care in nursing homes. This tool will allow the government to set up a pay-for-performance system. The higher the score, the higher the payment to the nursing home. Consumers can also use this measure to compare nursing-home quality (Kane, Arling, Mueller, Heid, & Cooke, 2007). In addition to this legislation, the American Recovery and Reinvestment Act (ARRA) provides $22.3 billion in additional funding through

a Medicare Improvement Fund. This fund will provide bonuses or penalties to hospitals and physicians for the use of information technologies. Penalty funds will be added to this fund beginning in 2020 (Board of Trustees, 2009).

The federal government will study these and other approaches to health care delivery. The 2010 bill sets up an independent board to study pilot projects. Medicare will adopt the most successful programs. Private insurers may also adopt the most successful approaches. The new bill will use the Medicare system to lead health care reform. Medicare's size alone will encourage providers to try new care options.

Summary of the Legislation

Overall, the bill makes few changes to Medicare and Medicaid. Most seniors feel satisfied with these programs as they now exist. Tumulty and colleagues (2010, p. 28) call Medicare "one of the most popular social programs in U.S. History. . . . Lawmakers have learned the hard way that nothing is more dangerous to their survival than treading too heavily on a program that is cherished by seniors."

The effect of the new law on seniors and health care spending goes beyond changes in Medicare and Medicaid. For example, the law includes an employer-based long-term care insurance option. This will help older people stay in their homes if they need long-term health support. The law also includes money from 2010 to 2013 to help employer health plans reduce health insurance costs to early retirees (ages 55–64).

The law promises better health care for children and people in their working years. A comprehensive health care system will allow people to get medical care before a condition gets out of control. And this will mean more people coming into later life in better health. Given the rising costs for care as people age and given the wave of Baby Boomers who will enter retirement in the next 20 years, this is good news.

What will this reform cost taxpayers and individuals? The new law calls for $500 billion in cuts to Medicare over the next 10 years (out of $6.1 trillion in expected costs). Lawmakers say that efficiencies in the system (not cuts in services) will save this money. For example, the bill forecasts $150 billion in savings by cutting small amounts from reimbursements to hospitals and other institutions. The

institutions will have to deliver service at a lower cost. Barry (2010), writing for the AARP, says that the new law will keep "Medicare financially sound for nearly 10 more years [than if no law had passed] and reduces the U.S. deficit by an estimated $143 billion."

Structural Flaws in the System

As costs rise in the future and as more people enter old age, concerns about health care will grow. Some of these concerns will focus on the high cost of caring for an aging population. But a focus on population aging creates a misleading view of the increasing cost of health care. Population aging will have some effect on health care use and costs in the future, but this will occur slowly and over many decades (Orszag, 2008).

Binstock (1993) looked at the relationship between population aging and health care costs in 12 industrial countries. He found little relationship between health care costs and the proportion of people age 65 and over or 80 and over. He found that many nations with high proportions of older people do not have runaway health care costs.

Pearson (2009, p. 3) reporting on behalf of the OECD, says that population aging is "one factor which *cannot* [emphasis in original] explain why the U.S. spends more than other countries." Other countries with a larger proportion of their populations over age 65 spend less on health care compared to the United States. Lazenby and Letsch (1990) say that an increase in the older population accounts for less than one quarter of increased health care costs. Many economic and social forces create increases in health care costs. These include inflation, rising costs of professional services, and increased costs for medications and equipment (Schulz & Binstock, 2006; Quadagno, 2007). Schulz (2001) lists the causes of rising costs in order of importance:

- Expanded use of medical technology and services;
- A lack of spending limits on physicians and hospitals;
- Inflation and especially inflation in medical care costs;
- Increased numbers of people (especially the elderly) who use services; and
- High administrative costs due to a decentralized insurance system.

BOX 7.1
SETTING LIMITS

Daniel Callahan, ethicist and health care critic, proposed rationing as a way to deal with increased health care costs. His 1987 book, *Setting Limits,* focuses on the increased numbers of older people in society and on the heavy use of health care resources by older people as a group. He predicted that an older population would draw health care resources away from younger people who need them. Callahan presented three principles that the health care system could use to cut treatment for older people:

1. Medical care should not prolong life after people have passed their natural life expectancy (somewhere between 70 and 80 years).

2. After people have passed their natural life expectancy, medical care should only relieve suffering. It should no longer attempt to extend life.

3. Medical technology should not be used to extend life beyond the natural life expectancy.

Callahan said that these policies would reduce the cost of health care for older people and their families, lead to a high quality of life until late old age, and keep society's health care costs down.

Binstock and Kahana (1988) took issue with Callahan's proposal. Callahan, for example, said that physically strong and mentally alert older people could get treatment if they come down with a sudden illness. He would apply his plan only to frail older people in need of long-term care.

But Binstock and Kahana asked who would decide what care a person should get. Would a second illness lead to a withdrawal of care? A third? What about a frail older person who could live well with medical support? Why should this person get no treatment? Binstock and Kahana asked why Callahan used age as a criterion at all in deciding who should get medical treatment.

Callahan made little reference to the social, moral, and ethical changes that his proposal would bring about. He also remained vague about who would put this policy of rationing into place. Many people disagree with rationing as a solution to the rising cost of health care, but Callahan's work expresses a concern, shared by many, about health care costs in an aging society.

Sources: Callahan, D. (1987). *Setting limits: Medical goals in an aging society.* New York: Simon & Schuster; also, Binstock, R. H., & Kahana, J. (1988). An essay on *Setting limits: Medical goals in an aging society, The Gerontologist, 28,* 424–426.

Rising health care costs, in part, reflect the organization of the health care system. Smith (1992, p. 244) says that U.S. health insurance looks the way it does and costs what it does because of "professional dominance and institutional weakness." The government lacked a clear national health care policy when it set up Medicare. At the same time, the medical profession blocked changes that would lessen its power or its income. The program we have today came about in order to reduce conflict and get some program in place. The result, Smith says,

> was fragmented, in the sense that it was both a national and a state program and that it began with two schemes of payment, one for hospitals and another for the physicians. It contained, as well, numerous subsidies for and concessions to providers, designed to secure their support for the program or at least, to buy a grudging acquiescence. (p. 244)

So, from the start, the medical model shaped the U.S. health care system. Medicare, the program that pays for most of the health care services in the United States, leans toward support for doctor and institution services. Although Medicaid will pay for some home health care services, Medicare pays primarily for medical services such as skilled nursing care, physical or speech therapy, home health aides, and medical supplies. Medicare will not pay for homemaker services or meals delivered at home. All of this gives Medicare-supported home health care a medical slant and raises costs.

Doctors, hospitals, drug companies, and other health care providers benefit from a growing health care system. Lawlor (2009, p. 223) calls this the *medical-industrial complex.* These interest groups resist drastic changes. The American Medical Association, for example, discourages doctors from taking part in the Medicare program (Schulz, 2001). Medical care interest groups (e.g., drug companies and health care providers) lobby against changes that will reduce their revenue or power.

Also, the U.S. health care system has high administrative costs. A study that compared the Canadian and U.S. health care systems found that the U.S. system had higher costs for doctors and hospitals, but the two systems differed most on administrative costs (Barer,

Hertzman, Miller, & Pascali, 1992). The U.S. system has a web of government, private insurance, and individual sources of payment. The administration of this complex system drives health care costs up.

Finally, only a relatively small proportion of older people use high proportions of medical care (Kane & Kane, 1987). True, figures show that as a group older people go to the hospital more often, stay in the hospital for more days, and visit physicians more often than younger people. But these figures hide the variation in use within the older population. For example, 9% of older people will use 5 years or more of nursing-home care in their lifetime. This small group will account for 64% of the cost of care. The large majority of older people (68%) will use less than 3 months of care in a lifetime and will account for about 1% of costs (Kemper, Spillman, & Murtaugh, 1991).

According to Cohen (1994, p. 401), "It is time to turn the public debate away from its increasingly myopic and misleading focus on older people and back to an examination of real issues." This will turn attention to the system itself. The current system lacks sensitivity to the needs of older people.

Older people with chronic illnesses and disabilities need different kinds of care than do acute care patients. Chronic care patients need long-term care (Lawlor, 2009). Kane and Kane (2001, p. 406) say that chronic care "represents the equivalent of a movie as opposed to a series of [acute care] snapshots." Care for patients with chronic illnesses requires that caregivers monitor patients over time, assess their needs, and adjust care to suit the individual. This type of care typically takes place outside the acute-care setting (e.g., the hospital or doctor's office). It most often takes place in the community, in a person's home.

This type of care requires case management, a coordinated system of services, and an ongoing assessment of service outcomes. Some programs have shown that they can provide this coordinated care in a community at a reasonable cost. The On Lok program in San Francisco and Fremont, California (described in a later section on Managed Care with a Community Focus), serves as a model for community-based long-term care.

LONG-TERM CARE: A RESPONSE TO OLDER PEOPLE'S NEEDS

The image most people have of long-term care is of a nursing home, but long-term care also refers to help with shopping, bathing, or chores around the house. It includes in-home services and community-based

services, as well as institutional care. Long-term care needs increase with age. Stone (2006, citing Davis, 2004) reports that only 1.8% of younger old people (ages 65 to 74) needed help with one or two ADLs. But 8.2% of older-old people (age 80 and over) needed help with one or two ADLs. The growth of the oldest-old people in the population will increase the need for long-term care.

Quadagno (2007, p. 889) calls the need for long-term care "nearly universal" as people age. And the "costs are enormous." In 2009, for example, a private room in a nursing home cost an average of $79,935 a year. A semiprivate room cost $72,270 in that year. Rates ranged from $132 a day for a private room in Louisiana to $584 a day for a private room in Arkansas. Care in an Alzheimer's unit or wing costs about 5% more (MetLife Mature Market, 2009a).

A 2010 survey of long-term care costs reports that an assisted living facility costs on average $38,220 a year. And home care agency rates average $19 per hour for a home health aide and $18 per hour for homemaker services. This survey estimates an average yearly cost for a home health aide at $43,472 (Genworth Financial, 2010). Few people can afford these costs.

And few people prepare for this need. Instead people rely on the current system when they face long-term care costs. More middle-class people than ever before now use Medicaid as their source of long-term care support. To get Medicaid benefits for long-term care, older people must show financial need. Some older people will transfer their assets to an adult child. They then spend down their savings to qualify for Medicaid. The program was never meant to provide long-term care coverage to this broad population. But many middle-class people have no alternative.

The current system leads to unnecessary nursing-home admissions and soaring costs to state budgets. Quadagno (2007, p. 889) says that "in many states Medicaid has become the single largest expenditure."

Long-Term Care Insurance: A Good Bet?

People should not expect Medicare or Medicaid to pay for long-term care. Senator John D. Rockefeller IV, Chairman of the Subcommittee on Health Care, told the Senate Finance Health Subcommittee in March 2009: "Contrary to what most Americans believe and expect, Medicare does not provide meaningful coverage for long term care. And, help with Medicaid—the largest payer of long term care—requires individuals to spend down their income and

TABLE 7.2 Long-Term Care Expenditures for the Elderly, by Source of Payment, 2004

(Billions of dollars)

Payment Source	Institutional Care	Home Care	Total
Medicaid	36.5	10.8	47.3
Medicare	15.9	17.7	33.6
Private Insurance	2.4	3.3	5.6
Out of Pocket	35.7	8.3	44.0
Other	2.0	2.5	4.4
Total	**92.4**	**42.5**	**134.9**

This table shows that Medicare and Medicaid account for 60% of long-term care costs ($80.9 billion). Medicaid serves as the largest single funder of long-term care, covering 35% of all costs ($47.3 billion). More than three quarters (77%) of Medicaid payments go to institutional care. Sixty-eight percent of all long-term care payments go for institutional care.

Older people spent nearly as much on long-term care as the Medicaid program spent. They paid $44 billion out of pocket for long-term care, or 33% of all long-term care costs. The increasing need for long-term care will increase the need for institutional and home care. A shift in emphasis to home care could save the system money. It would also provide the kind of care that older people prefer.

Source: Congressional Budget Office. (2004). *Financing Long-term care for the elderly.* Table 1-2, p. 5. Washington, DC: Congress of the United States. Retrieved: October 11, 2010, from www.cbo.gov/ftpdocs/54xx/doc5400/04-26-LongTermCare.pdf.

assets to a level of impoverishment." (Genworth Financial, 2010, p. 9)

Personal long-term care insurance provides one way to meet long-term care needs. These policies pay from 60% to 75% of long-term care expenses. Kassner (2009) reports that in 2005 about 7 million long-term care policies existed in the United States. Nearly all policies cover home care support as well as institutional support. They usually provide a daily reimbursement for care—e.g., as $100 or $150 per day. Good policies also include inflation protection. A person must meet certain disability criteria (severe cognitive impairment or the need for help with at least two ADLs) to get this reimbursement.

Long-term care insurance can buffer the high cost of long-term care. But the high cost of this insurance keeps most people from buying these policies. In 2008 a 40-year-old would pay around $1,500 per year for a typical policy. A 60-year-old would pay around $2,300 and a 70-year-old would pay around $4,500 per year (Tumlinson, Aguiar, & Watts, 2009). As a result of these high costs, almost half of long-term care insurance purchasers had incomes over $75,000 per year.

Denial of the need for long-term care insurance and distrust of insurance companies also keep people from buying policies. People wonder, "Will the company still be in business 20 years from now when I need help?" Also, insurance companies can increase rates for entire classes of people (e.g., people age 75 and older). And this could put the cost of insurance out of reach when a person needs the coverage the most. For all these reasons few people take out long-term care

insurance. Long-term care insurance pays for only about 7% of all long-term care costs.

Today people with a high income can afford private long-term care insurance. The poor and now the middle class turn to Medicaid. Putnam (2009, p. 227) calls Medicaid "the default national long-term care insurer for persons . . . who have spent their private savings." The large majority of middle-income seniors at present have few alternatives to meet their long-term care needs. No easy solution to this problem exists.

The 2010 health care reform law recognizes the need for some affordable long-term care option. The new law includes a long-term care program that employers can join. A worker can pay a monthly premium through payroll deductions. After 5 years the employee can draw on a cash benefit. The funds will help with the cost of services and devices such as a home health aide or a wheelchair ramp. The law has yet to put this program into practice. So it remains uncertain whether this program will meet employers' and workers' needs.

Institutional Care[1]

In 2004, the United States spent about $135 billion on long-term care, or about $15,000 for each disabled person (Congressional Budget Office, 2004). Most of

---

[1]Institutional care goes by many names. These include *nursing homes, group homes, homes for the aged, personal care homes, adult homes,* and more. Some of these names refer to specific types of services offered. Nursing homes, for example, typically offer professional nursing care. Group homes most often include only shelter and meals with little nursing care. All of these types of facilities (and others not listed here) provide institutional options to living in a private residence.

this money went to nursing-home care. In 2004, the United States had 16,100 nursing homes and 1.77 million nursing-home beds (Centers for Disease Control, 2010a). On any day, 4% of the older population (about 1.5 million people) in the United States lives in a nursing home. However, at age 65 in 2000, a person has about a 44% chance of entering a nursing home at some point in his or her lifetime (Congressional Budget Office, 2004; Schulz & Binstock, 2006).

Some people stay in a nursing home only a short time—for example, as a stopping point from hospital to home. About one third of the people who spend time in a nursing home will stay for less than 3 months. Others spend the last years of their lives in nursing homes. About 20% of people who enter a nursing home spend 5 years or more there (Rich, 1991, cited in Schulz, 2001). Schulz (2001) says that about 13% of all older people account for 90% of all nursing-home costs.

People differ in their risk of entering a nursing home. For example, nursing homes tend to house older and more disabled people (Bernstein et al., 2003). The

---

BOX 7.2

DRUG ABUSE: THE LIMITS OF THE MEDICAL MODEL

Drug use increases with age. Older people take more drugs, and more kinds of drugs, than younger people. They often have multiple health problems and take many drugs at once.

Sometimes drug use can turn to abuse. Older people who abuse drugs often use tranquilizers or narcotic analgesics (pain relievers). Some people get these drugs by doctor shopping and collecting prescriptions. Other people become addicted to drugs through many years of use.

Lois Reynolds began taking tranquilizers after a nervous collapse when two of her children moved out on their own. The drugs worked well in the short run and allowed her to go back to work. But here is the rest of the story in her own words.

> It was about a month before I began to feel somewhat normal, and six months to a year before I could say I was, for sure. I did not need the drugs, but if I did not take them, I would begin to feel nervous and would become afraid I was going to have a relapse. Time marches on, and so did my ulcers and headaches. About one year after this, the doctor and I decided that it was necessary for me to have surgery for the ulcers, which consisted of removal of 75 percent of my stomach. Thus another crisis, and continuation of drugs. Now I ask some of you, does this sound familiar? I think this is the story of most prescription drug dependency.
>
> . . . During the next few years, I became sedated to the point that my blood pressure and pulse were so low, my headaches so severe, that I had to do something. To relieve the headaches, I started taking a stimulant (Dexedrine), which is a controlled substance, but was also prescribed by the doctor. Now I was 12 to 15 years down the drug road—still taking 4 tranquilizers, 4 Dexedrine, plus 8 Tylenol a day, and feeling great. I continued a normal, happy life for another 10 years until I retired from work at age 62.

> So began the "Golden Years," until boom, all of a sudden I had been home for a couple of years and had begun to get bored and depressed because my husband was still working, as were all my friends, and I was pretty much alone.
>
> Now I needed something for my depression, and the doctor gave it to me. So I had three drugs to cope with. By this time, I had slowly increased the dosage of tranquilizers and Dexedrine, each to eight a day, and the trouble really began. The drugs no longer had the same effect and I wasn't feeling as well.
>
> I began to give more thought to making a serious effort to get off drugs, and I decided to enter the hospital. This was a good start, but not quite a success. I managed in a week's stay in the hospital to cut the amount considerably, but did not follow up on the treatment.
>
> The doctor told me he doubted if I would ever be able to do without drugs completely due to the length of time I had been taking them. So I accepted that as a fact and did nothing more for five years. At that point, I began hearing news reports that made me decide that if I were really serious about wanting to get off drugs, then I could. There were so many people going through these programs that were successful. If they could, so could I.

Reynolds finally signed up for a program for drug-dependent older people. The program offered medical care and counseling for 1 year. At the time she wrote her story she had quit drug use for 15 months and vowed to stay drug free. She concludes with advice to other older people:

> I have no qualms about discussing this with anyone, as I feel no guilt about what happened. After all, I was only following the doctor's orders at all times.

Source: Reynolds, L. (1990). Drug free after 30 years of dependency. *Aging Magazine, 361,* 26–27.

older the person, the greater the chance of living in a nursing home. Schulz (2001; Jones, Dwyer, Bercovitz, & Strahan, 2009) says that the proportion of people age 85 and over in nursing homes will increase from 45.2% (in 2004) to 51% (in 2016 to 2020). Women run a greater risk than men of entering a nursing home. In 2004, for example, women age 65 and over outnumbered older men in nursing homes by more than 2 to 1. This difference reflects the fact that older men more often than older women have a spouse at home to care for them.

Any of the following conditions increase the risk of entering a nursing home: cognitive impairment, functional impairment, non-homeowner status, recent hospital release, no spouse or family member at home, poor community supports, and living in an area with many nursing-home beds.

The U.S. government in the late 1980s attempted to improve the quality of nursing homes through legislation. The Omnibus Budget Reconciliation Act of 1987 set strict standards for nursing-home quality. This act required clear care plans for patients, a declaration to patients of their rights, and a minimum number of nurses on duty each day. The legislation met problems in the field. Nursing homes got the regulations late, administrators had little training, and nursing homes got little extra funding to cover improvements in service. But once implemented, these regulations led to improvements in nursing-home quality.

As mentioned earlier, Minnesota has developed quality standards for nursing homes (Kane et al., 2007). The state intends to link those standards to financial rewards for quality management and service. Nursing-home owners support the idea in principle. But they have raised questions about definitions and scoring methods. The owners also request that Medicaid reimbursements for care increase to meet increased expenses regardless of quality measures. The program may prove too expensive if a large number of homes improve quality and deserve increased funding.

Even with a good nursing home as an option, most older people prefer to live in their own homes. They choose this option for at least two reasons: (1) they prefer the independence of living on their own and (2) they may not be able to afford a nursing home.

"Many people believe that Medicare, Medicaid, and private supplemental health insurance provide substantial nursing-home benefits. Unfortunately, due to restrictions on reimbursements, this is not the case" (AARP, 1992, p. 16; Schulz, 2001). For exam-

ple, Medicare covers nursing care only in a "skilled nursing facility," and most facilities in the United States do not offer this level of care. Medicaid pays for long-term care, but only for poor and destitute people.

Even long-term care insurance generally pays only part of the costs of nursing-home care for older people. Long-term care insurance on average covers only 70% of long-term care costs. The cost of a nursing-home stay can deplete a person's assets and leave them with few resources if they return home. It can often leave a healthy spouse with only a small allowance to live on.

Community-Based Services

Data from the National Nursing Home Survey (Jones et al., 2009) show a decline in nursing-home use. Also, over time, the nursing-home population has gotten older, and nursing homes serve people with more severe disabilities. Stone (2006; also Putnam, 2009) says that better community care programs (in-home and assisted living options) account for much of this change. In addition, a 1999 Supreme Court decision, the *Olmstead Decision,* stated that a person with a disability should have access to care in the least restrictive context (Stone, 2006).

Putnam (2009) points to "quiet revolutions" that have created a shift in long-term care availability. These include more home and community programs, programs that provide financial support for family caregivers, and changes in the law such as the Olmstead Decision. Putnam predicts that these quiet revolutions will continue within Medicaid and perhaps in Medicare (Lawlor, 2009).

Some changes in funding for long-term care point in this direction. The National Association for Home Care & Hospice (2010) reports that Medicaid payments for home care increased from $24.3 million in 2000 to $55.9 million in 2007. The report says that "states have recently begun to place a greater emphasis on providing care at home in lieu of institutions."

Leutz, Abrahams, and Capitman (1993) say that community long-term care programs have four goals: (1) keep potential patients out of nursing homes, (2) meet the social and personal care needs of older people, (3) meet health needs not covered by Medicare, and (4) link medical care and social support to keep older people in the community. Community care services range from adult day care, to respite services, to home health care.

Adult Day Care

Adult day care programs may follow the medical model, the social model, or a combination of the two models of care. Medical model programs offer rehabilitation, nursing care, and health assessment. Social model programs offer exercise, crafts, and social contacts. Almost half of adult day care programs (48%) offer a mix of these services.

These programs have increased in the United States from 300 in 1975 to more than 4,600 in 2009 (MetLife Mature Market, 2009b). More than 150,000 older people use these programs each day. Nearly 78% of these programs are nonprofit. Programs typically have about 40 members and attract people with an average age of 77.2 years. A typical program member is white and unmarried. Women make up two thirds of adult day service users. About half of all clients in adult day care have a cognitive impairment (Gaugler & Zarit, 2001).

A survey of 1,300 adult day centers in 2010 found that adult day care cost an average of $60 a day (Genworth Financial, 2010). Medicare does not cover adult day care, but nearly half of the people in these programs receive Medicaid. Studies of adult day services find that they provide caregivers with relief. Day care reduces their worry, anger, and feelings of burden (Dabelko & Zimmerman, 2008). But studies show little effect of adult day services on improvement in the physical function of participants. Studies also disagree on whether these programs keep people out of nursing homes longer or save money. This may be because these programs attract people close to institutionalization already.

At their best, adult day programs support caregivers' attempts to keep an older person in the community. Studies also show that these programs can improve the morale, mood, and life satisfaction of participants (Gaugler & Zarit, 2001; Baumgarten, Lebel, Laprise, Leclerc, & Quinn, 2002).

Respite Services

Respite services, another form of community support, also give family caregivers a break from the demands of care. These programs take many forms. Some nursing homes, for example, offer 1- or 2-week respite stays for care receivers. Other programs send someone into a caregiver's home to sit with a care receiver and give the caregiver a day off. Medicaid will cover respite costs for people at risk of institutionalization. Some states help fund respite programs. In some cases, families pay for respite on their own.

A survey of the literature on respite services (Zarit, cited in Lewin Group, 2001) found that few studies report on the effectiveness of respite services. The literature does show that caregivers often use respite late in the caregiving process, use very little service, or do not use respite at all. Still, research finds that the more use a caregiver makes of respite service, the more he or she benefits.

Home Health Care Programs

Home health care programs deliver services to people in their own homes. The National Association for Home Care & Hospice (2008) reports that 7.6 million people get home care from 83,000 agencies. People age 65 and over made up 69% of home care patients. Home care programs minimize the effects of illness and give the older person as much independence as possible. Services most frequently used include bathing and showering, dressing, moving a person from bed to chair, and using the toilet. Home health care programs also offer help with shopping (for food or clothes), light housework, medications, and meal preparation.

Home health care can have many goals. Some programs aim to rehabilitate an older person after an injury. Others focus on helping a person get well without complications after a hospital stay. Still others strive to provide a comfortable death.

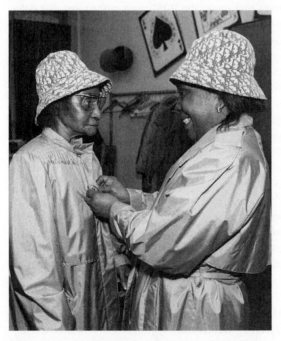

A daughter takes her mother home at the end of the day from the Central Harlem Senior Citizens Coalition Center in New York. Her mother spent the day in an activity program designed to give respite to family caregivers.

Public funding for home health care boomed when the government put limits on hospital stays. Because home care services appear to cost less than institutional placement, home health care looked like an answer to rising costs.

Research findings question this idea. Kane and Kane (2001, p. 414) say that "the debate about whether community-based long-term care is actually cheaper than nursing homes has raged for some time." They note that community care may cost less per unit to deliver, but as the amount of service to a person increases, the cost of community care can equal or go beyond the cost of institutional care. Also, available community care may lead more people to use health care services. This increases the number of people served and raises the total cost of health care. The Medicaid program allowed states to pay for home care as long as the states could show comparable savings in institutional care.

The 1981–1982 National Long-Term Care Channeling Demonstration Project, a study still cited in the literature (Caro, 2003; Kane & Kane, 2001), looked at the costs of home care services for disabled and frail older people. The study involved 6,000 older people with severe disabilities. These people lived in the community. The project substituted case-managed long-term care for nursing-home care. Case-managed care provides care designed for the individual. A case manager assesses a person's needs, arranges for care, and monitors outcomes.

The project researchers studied the cost of community care and satisfaction with this type of service. The researchers found that the cost of care went up by about 18% due to added services. Nursing-home use fell very little (Wiener & Harris, 1990). However, people in the project said they had fewer unmet needs, felt increased satisfaction with the care they got, and had higher overall life satisfaction (Carcagno & Kemper, 1988).

Home health care may not save the system money, but it provides older people with the kind of care they want and need. A New Jersey survey of AARP members (Stowell-Ritter, 2005) found that 80% to 90% of respondents considered government financial and policy support for community-based, long-term care a top or high priority. Clients' preferences for these programs make the primary argument for offering them.

Changes in Funding to Control Costs

The government has tried to control home care costs. The Balanced Budget Act (BBA) of 1997, for example, changed the way Medicare reimburses for home care. Medicare shifted away from a cost-based reimburse-

ment system to a PPS. This meant that providers got paid a set amount for a specific client need (rather than an amount based on the company's cost to deliver the service). This led to large declines in the use of home health services by Medicare/Medicaid beneficiaries.

For example, the number of home health care visits per 1,000 Medicare enrollees increased from 3,822 in 1992 to 8,376 in 1996. Increased Medicare benefits for home care explains this increase. But visits declined sharply after 1997 to 2,295 enrollees in 2001. The Balanced Budget Act of 1997 PPS policy explains the drop in visits. An evaluation of the PPS "found that prospectively paid home health agencies significantly reduced the length of time patients remained in home health care as well as the average number of visits" (Bernstein et al., 2003, p. 40).

One study (Murtaugh, McCall, Moore, & Meadow, 2003) reported a 60% decline in average annual home health visits. Another study (McCall, Petersons, Moore, & Korb, 2003) found a 22% decrease in the percentage of Medicare beneficiaries using home health services after the change to PPS. They also found a 39% decrease in the number of visits per year.

These researchers say that this reduction in services put vulnerable groups, such as nonwhites, women, and people age 85 and over, at risk. Pagan (2002) notes that under the PPS many companies that delivered home care either sold out or closed down. Schulmerich (2000) estimates that 30% of home health agencies closed their Medicare services when they could not operate within the new guidelines.

The rate of home care visits increased again slowly to 3,409 per 1,000 enrollees in 2007. But this remains far below the 1996 rate of service. This brief history of home care use shows the effect of government policies on the use of health care services. Older people rely on government funding and sound policy in order to get the care they need (and prefer).

The new prospective payment system may lead to better control of expenses. But it may also reduce the amount of home care available to older people. The government and care providers will need to find a balance between the cost of home care and the growing need among older people for home care services.

Managed Care: Alternative Delivery Methods

Managed Care with a Medical Focus

Managed care plans promise some control of health care costs and usage rates. These plans are based on

capitated payments. This means that a payer (Medicare, Medicaid, or a private insurer) prepays a set amount per person per month for care. An organization then manages care to stay within this budget and earn a profit. Most managed care programs take the form of HMOs or competitive medical plans (CMPs). These programs have expanded in the past few years. An HMO contracts with Medicare to provide services. People join the plan and pay a monthly premium. They also make small copayments for services.

Health maintenance organizations offer some advantages over regular fee-for-service Medicare. They take an interdisciplinary approach to care and coordinate all services to a client. This allows them to keep track of a person's health record, past contacts with specialists and therapists, and use of prescription drugs. Also, HMOs can help with early long-term care planning and can provide community care after hospital discharge.

Some of these plans focus on rehabilitation and even have rehabilitation teams that provide services in a person's home. Some HMOs offer preventive care, items like eyeglasses and hearing aids, and dental care. **Social health maintenance organizations (SHMOs)** put together an array of services that suit the needs of older people. This includes basic Medicare, extra benefits (such as prescription drugs and eyeglasses), and added care (such as homemaker services and chore services).

The staff of Brandeis University started the first SHMO in 1985 as part of a national demonstration program (Van Ellett, 1993). Like HMOs, SHMOs assume the total cost of care for a person for a set monthly fee. The agency bears the risk of high costs. SHMOs combine medical care with social supports. They use case management to arrange services and control costs. This kind of program targets people who need help with ADLs, but do not need skilled nursing care or therapy.

A report by the Medicare Payment Advisory Commission (2003) to Congress reviewed the results of four SHMO demonstration projects. These projects received 5.3% more funding per person than a comparable Medicare+Choice plan. Two studies of these projects found no support for improvements in seniors' health or function. In addition, the studies found no reduction in hospital use or long-term nursing-home use. The commission recommended ending the projects' special funding.

Kane (1991) cautions that some people (including the government) may not want to pay for these extra benefits and some people cannot afford to pay. Also, some SHMOs limit enrollment to low-risk clients. These two conditions protect the SHMOs from heavy costs, but limit the program to select, relatively healthy people.

Newcomer, Harrington, and Kane (2002) say that coordinating medical and social care in these programs creates a challenge. For example, in the pilot SHMO projects, doctors and case managers failed to set up good working relationships. The doctors continued their usual method of practice and remained uninvolved with the rest of the delivery system (Medicare Payment, 2002). Newcomer and colleagues (2002) say that it can take years for a program to mature and to show benefits. The researchers caution against short-term assessments of these programs.

The SHMO demonstration project shows one attempt to improve care and limit the costs of health care to older people. It also shows how research and careful study can assess the costs and benefits of a program. This type of research takes time to conduct and assess. But it helps policy makers develop innovations in health care delivery. The 2010 government health care reform legislation recognizes the importance of assessment. It includes support for research on innovative programs and an independent board to assess research findings.

Managed Care with a Community Focus

On Lok, Inc., a community long-term care program located in the San Francisco Bay Area, has served as a model for community care programs throughout the United States. On Lok means "peaceful, happy abode" in Chinese. The program began in 1972 as a drop-in center that served warm meals. About three quarters of On Lok's participants (On Lok's term for clients) have Chinese ancestry. Many of On Lok's workers speak Chinese. The program also serves other minorities, including Filipino, Italian, and Hispanic older people.

On Lok combines medical services with adult day care, home care, and transportation. The program describes itself as "specifically designed to provide total long-term care for the frail elderly." On Lok's Lifeways program provides a comprehensive health plan that includes full medical care, prescription drugs, home care, adult day health, transportation, and other services. On Lok works to keep members in their homes as long as possible (On Lok, Inc., 2010).

On Lok receives monthly capitated payments from Medicare, Medicaid, and individuals. In 1983, Congress allowed On Lok to get a set fee from Medicare and Medicaid for each person in the program. On Lok took 100% of the risk, paying for all of the clients' services out of this amount. The program now serves mentally and physically frail older people—a high-risk, high-cost group (On Lok, Inc., 2010). Without On Lok, most of these people would live in an institution.

On Lok contracts with health care professionals and institutions for services. It also runs 10 senior centers in San Francisco and nearby communities, an intergenerational social and educational program, an intergenerational program, and three housing units. In 2005 On Lok created an on-site mental and behavioral health team. This includes a bilingual psychologist, a psychiatric social worker, and a marriage and family therapist (Ginsburg, 2009).

On Lok tailors its services to each family's needs and to its ethnicity. It assesses a family's ability to give care and discusses family members' roles in the caregiving process. This assessment provides families with services to relieve their stress.

The program also builds caregivers' knowledge and skills at managing the older person's disabilities. On Lok workers teach caregivers to notice signs of decline in a frail older person. Social workers in the program help families cope with changes such as institutionalization and death. The program also includes the participant in care planning. Professionals help patients express their "health wishes" or preferences for treatment (Der-McLeod & Hansen, 1992, p. 72). This includes decisions about resuscitation and tube feeding. A study of the program found lower costs for hospital and nursing-home services and more use of community services (Zawadski & Eng, 1988). Care usually lasts until a person's death.

On Lok has inspired the start of programs in other states. It now belongs to the national long-term care demonstration project called Program of All-Inclusive Care for the Elderly (PACE). These programs believe that older people with chronic care needs and their families get better care when served in the community (On Lok SeniorHealth, 2007). On Lok advised on the creation of the PACE program model. PACE programs serve nursing-home–eligible people age 55 and over who can live safely in the community. A person who enters a nursing home from a PACE program (about 7% of PACE enrollees live in nursing homes) continues to get coordination of his or her care from the PACE program.

PACE began by serving frail older people at eight sites in eight states. Today, 70 PACE sites exist under Medicaid (Centers for Medicare, 2010a). Each site has about 200 enrollees. A person who wants to take part in PACE voluntarily enrolls. The participant must be 55 years old or older, live in the PACE service area, have a screening by a team of health professionals, and agree to terms of enrollment.

The PACE programs follow the original On Lok method of payment. The programs get a fixed amount each month per enrollee from Medicare and Medicaid. All Medicare and Medicaid services in that state are included. The programs also include at least 16 other services, including social work support and nursing facility care. PACE day centers provide meals, transportation, recreational therapy, and other support services. The programs provide many of these services 24 hours a day, 7 days a week, 365 days a year.

Enrollees can get services at day centers, at referral services, or in their own homes. This includes hospital care, nursing-home care, and treatment by a medical specialist. A medical team decides on a person's need. Today more than 70 organizations in 30 states are in various stages of the PACE model, from start-up to full operation (On Lok SeniorHealth, 2004).

Rich (1999) says that PACE programs lead to more community care, fewer hospital days, and a low rate of nursing-home use. Also, people in the PACE programs report high satisfaction and excellent care ratings. Chatterji and colleagues (Chatterji, Burstein, Kidder, & White, 1998; also Eng, Pedulla, Eleazer, McCann, & Fox, 1997) found that PACE programs provided community care at a cost comparable with other approaches. They also showed improvements in health and functional ability similar to other approaches (cited in Kane & Kane, 2001).

Today, relatively few older people in the United States have access to this type of coordinated service. Huttman (1987, p. 146) says that barriers exist throughout the country to the use of community services. Services "are scattered, limited in the number of people they can serve, and are often exclusively for the poor, or for the rich, and seldom for the large middle income group."

A system of community-based, long-term care does not exist in the United States at present. Community care programs such as On Lok and the other PACE programs offer promise for the future. These programs show that managed community care can control costs and provide quality care to an older population (Dobell & Newcomer, 2008; Hirth & Dever-Bumba, 2009). Kane and Kane (2001, p. 419) say, "We know much more about how to deliver good chronic care for older persons than we are willing to put into practice."

DISEASE PREVENTION AND HEALTH PROMOTION

Disease prevention and health promotion programs provide other ways to manage illness in an aging society. Some of these methods have caught on in the United States. For example, some cities ban smoking in restaurants, bars, public places, and even outside near a public place. Some airlines brag about smoke-free flights worldwide. Magazines on fitness, running, and dieting appear on every newsstand. Even fast-food restaurants offer salads and low-fat dishes to a more health-conscious public. Disease prevention and health promotion include things we take for granted, such as water and air quality standards, vaccinations, and regular medical checkups.

Researchers describe three types of disease or disability prevention: primary, secondary, and tertiary (Kane & Kane, 2001). *Primary prevention* refers to stopping new problems from arising. For example, warnings on cigarette packs try to discourage smoking and thus prevent heart disease. *Secondary prevention* refers to screening to detect problems. Doctors do this when they take your blood pressure. *Tertiary prevention* refers to stopping current problems from getting worse. For example, doctors use surgery or drug therapy to treat cancer.

Some studies of health promotion programs show promising outcomes. For example, Wheeler (2003) describes a program, titled Women Take PRIDE, for older women with cardiac disease. This program

This exercise-swim program takes place in Cerritos, California. The program promotes health and attempts to prevent illness through exercise.

encouraged a group of 233 women to engage in self-management of their heart conditions (219 women served as a control group and received the usual care for their conditions). Each woman in the experimental group selected a behavior to focus on (based on her physician's suggestions). Behaviors included exercise, medication use, diet, and so on.

The women met in groups with an educator to learn a process for monitoring and managing their behaviors. The women got instructional material, diaries to keep notes, and a number to call with questions they might have. The study showed that, compared with the control group, women in the program made significantly less use of hospital inpatient services. This led to significant cost savings and better health for these women.

One large study of primary prevention gives some idea of the potential for prevention programs. Hughes and Bazzarre (2009) conducted a study of 544 older adults (mean age 66) at three sites. The study provided a best-practice physical activity program for 60 minutes three times a week to 289 of the participants. The others did not participate in this program and served as a control. They could take part in other programs offered by these sites or at other locations.

The study found significant health benefits in the treatment group after 5 and 10 months. The activity program group showed better adherence to an exercise program, increased upper- and lower-body strength, and more exercise participation. The authors conclude that public policy should support relatively inexpensive exercise programs like this.

Health promotion programs go beyond preventing illness; they attempt to improve health. Health promotion includes programs that improve nutrition, lifestyles, and fitness. People can take part in health promotion even though some of their physical functions decline. For example, a person with arthritis can improve health with moderate activity. Someone with diabetes can switch to a low-carb, low-sugar diet.

The best health promotion programs allow older people to play a role in program design. These programs enhance the older person's well-being. For instance, a person develops a sense of self-efficacy, a sense of being able to control events in his or her life (Easom, 2003). Many studies now support the value of active lifestyles. Iso-Ahola (1993), a pioneer in the field of health promotion, reports that an "active leisure lifestyle" does at least two things: It directly benefits health, and it helps to buffer the influence of life events and illness.

Other studies support this view. Swinburn and Sager (2003) report that physical activity reduces the incidence of diabetes and hypertension and increases bone density. Orsega-Smith, Payne, and Godbey (2003) note that improved fitness leads to greater endurance and flexibility. Even programs as short as 6 months can produce good results (Fitts & Phelan, 2008).

Disease prevention and health promotion should play an increasing role in health care in the future. Health promotion and disease prevention can decrease three of the major chronic conditions of old age (arthritis, high blood pressure, and heart disease). They can also reduce the incidence of the three major causes of death in old age (heart disease, cancer, and stroke).

The Surgeon General's report in 1964 and anti-smoking publicity explain much of the significant decrease in cigarette smoking in the United States between 1965 and 2007 (National Center for Health Statistics, 2009). The proportion of male smokers age 65 and over dropped by almost two thirds from 28.5% to 9.3% during this period. The proportion of female smokers age 65 and over during this period began at 9.6% in 1965, rose to 13.5% in 1985, and dropped to a low of 7.6% in 2007 (National Center for Health Statistics, 2009). Decreases in smoking among older people will lead to longer life expectancies and better health as they age. These changes show the effectiveness of health promotion campaigns.

Some barriers exist to an increase in health-promoting behavior. First, middle-aged and older people expect less benefit from exercise than do younger people (Sarkisian, Prohaska, Wong, Hirsch, & Mangione, 2005). They may carry this attitude into later life and may resist health promotion programs.

Second, older people tend to live sedentary lives, and relatively few show a desire to be more active (National Center for Health Statistics, 2009). Health promotion programs have to overcome lifelong habits and negative attitudes toward exercise. Many programs and professionals offer advice to older people about health promotion, but relatively few older people change their habits. Bradshaw and Klein (2007) report that older people generally know the value of exercise. But they give a host of excuses for not exercising, including fear of a heart attack, trouble catching their breath, and the need to relax.

Third, many older people who join exercise or fitness programs drop out. And many people who could benefit most from these programs never join. Some people told AARP researchers that they felt discouraged by photos of fit and active older people.

Some people felt that exercise would cause them pain and discomfort. Programs face information barriers, beliefs about the causes and cures of illness, and economic barriers. Poor older people have less money and time than middle-class people for health promotion activities. Health promotion programs must find ways to attract older people and keep them coming back.

Chapter 12 discusses fitness and exercise programs in more detail. It describes the benefits of these programs, the challenges they have to meet, and some ways to overcome these challenges. In the case of poor people, this means designing programs that take their budgets and social context into account.

A program in Corpus Christi, Texas, the Latino Education Project (LEP), shows what it takes to meet the health promotion needs of older minority members. This program exists as part of a nationwide project—Racial and Ethnic Approaches to Community Health (REACH 2010). REACH supports innovative community-based programs that reduce disparities in health between white majority and minority older people (Centers for Disease Control and the Merck Company Foundation, 2007). REACH 2010 programs create community commitment to better health care for minority older people. They also bring together older people, health professionals, and government officials to tackle this problem.

The LEP program in Corpus Christi focuses on midlife and older Latinos. This population shows high rates of diabetes. The LEP program serves small, rural, and isolated communities. These communities have 80% to 95% Hispanic residents. Nearly half are age 60 or older.

Through the LEP program, local community organizations address the problem of diabetes. The program uses health forums that bring together health professionals, media representatives, and local leaders. They work to find prevention, diagnosis, and management methods for the disease. The program uses small study groups to advise people on a healthier diet and healthy behavior. The program also uses "lay health educators (promotores de salud)" to help the community and individuals use available resources.

Results from the program show that "LEP participants have increased their levels of physical activity and consumption of water, fruits, and vegetables, as well as improved communication with their health care providers" (Center for Disease Control, 2007, p. 3). This program shows the need for local leadership, local control, and integrating a program into community life.

Beyond Fitness and Personal Health Promotion

Much of the research on health promotion focuses on individuals' behaviors and lifestyles. Programs typically focus on individual habit and lifestyle change. But McKinlay, a health policy analyst, uses a political economy perspective to show how our economic system produces illness.

He calls health promotion programs "downstream endeavors" (McKinlay, 1985, p. 485). They ignore the social context that leads people to get sick. For example, air pollution, solvents in water and food, and pesticides all do greater damage to older people than to people in middle age. Also, drug companies encourage the use of drugs such as estrogen to reduce menopause symptoms, but research questions the wisdom of estrogen use. This drug may increase a person's risk of cancer.

McKinlay (1985, p. 485) says that business and industry often profit at the expense of people's health. The tobacco, fast-food, and soft-drink industries come to mind. The health promotion focus on the individual overlooks the economic forces that lead to ill health. McKinlay admits the value of individual health promotion and disease prevention activity. But too often, he says, the "beginning point in the process [the marketing and production of products that create illness] remains unaffected by most preventive endeavors, even though it is at this point that the greatest potential for change, and perhaps even ultimate victory, lies" (p. 493). Health promotion and disease prevention must have an impact on the production of illness to have their greatest effect.

Watson and Hall (2001) also look at the social environment as a source of health risk. They say that a person's social class, employment status, and level of education all influence health and well-being. Likewise, poverty leads to anxiety, insecurity, stress, and poor social networks. These conditions threaten good health. The REACH program that targets minority health attempts to address this issue. But it too focuses on individual responses to social conditions.

Research findings show that a healthy older population depends on a supportive social environment. A program in Oakland, California, and Alameda County focuses on environmental change to promote health. A local seniors agency—United Seniors of Oakland and Alameda County (USOAC)—recognized that seniors in some neighborhoods feel unsafe walking around. The program developed safe walking routes and walking groups to encourage seniors to stay active (Hooker & Wicks, 2007).

Models of a quality health care system need to include improvements in the environment and decreases in social inequality.

FUTURE ISSUES IN HEALTH CARE

Availability

Availability refers to the existence of services. Some parts of the country have many services for older people. Other regions have few.

Rural areas offer fewer services to older people than do metropolitan areas.[2] Bull and Bane (1993) give three reasons for this lack of service. First, rural hospitals have fewer patients, make smaller profits, and get lower reimbursement from Medicare. Second, rural hospitals have fewer high-tech services. This means younger old people go to urban centers for care. Third, rural settings have fewer health care professionals such as doctors, nurses, and pharmacists (Brown, 2006). In addition to these challenges, professionals in rural settings need to travel to deliver services (Kaufman, Scogin, Burgio, Morthland, & Ford, 2007). Still, older people in these areas need medical help as much as or more than their urban peers.

Brown (2006) suggests a number of ways to improve the availability of health care in rural and nonmetro settings. First, rural areas need to hire skilled health care generalists who can provide many types of care. These professionals need to shift the focus of care from providing care to teaching people to care for themselves.

Second, the government needs to offer more incentives to encourage current health professionals to move to rural areas. Incentives can take the form of start-up grants for rural practices, tax credits, and subsidies to help health professionals avoid burnout. The National Health Service Corps (NHSC) has had some success at this. Begun in 1972, it offers medical school scholarships in return for 2 to 4 years' work in "Health Professional Shortage Areas." More than 30,000 clinicians have served in the Corps since it started. Almost 80% of them stay in the underserved area at the end of their commitment. In a typical year 3,500 NHSC professionals serve 4 million people (Health and Human Services, 2010).

---

[2]The U.S. Office of Management and Budget defines *rural* as an area of low residential density and size (under 2,500 people). The term *nonmetro* refers to counties that lie outside metropolitan areas. The Office of Management and Budget defines *metropolitan* as an urbanized area of 50,000 or more people and a total population of 100,000 or more that includes adjacent counties.

Third, health professionals can use technology to bring health care to rural settings. Technology cannot overcome the absence of health professionals or hospitals, but it can overcome some barriers due to distance. For example, people can get health screenings by phone or by computer. Fax machines can send prescriptions to a distant pharmacy and arrange for delivery of the medicine (Brown, 2006).

Accessibility

Accessibility refers to whether a person can get the services that exist. Barriers to services can include lack of knowledge, eligibility, money, transportation, bad weather, or geography. People in rural settings, as well as minority group members, often face more than one barrier to access.

Distance and isolation present barriers to access for rural older people. Better roads and transportation would make it easier for older people to get to services and vice versa. Attempts to improve access must overcome the effects of blizzards, floods, and heat waves on health care delivery.

The Kaiser Family Foundation (2003) conducted a study of health care access in Washington, DC. Results of the study showed that 19% of poor or near-poor older people said they had not visited a doctor in the past 12 months (compared with 4% of higher-income older people). Not surprisingly, the poorer people reported poorer health. The report also found that 22% of poor or near-poor older people failed to fill a drug prescription in the past 12 months because of the cost. Only 7% of higher-income seniors reported this.

Takamura (2002) notes that a gap in health care access exists between whites and minority older people. Latino American and African American people (of all ages), compared with whites, gave the lowest ratings to the health care service they received (Kaiser Family Foundation, 2003).

Also, minority older people have lower rates of health care insurance than do whites. Thirty-seven percent of Latinos (of all ages) have no health insurance. Nearly one quarter (23%) of African Americans have no insurance. One in five (21%) Asian Americans and Pacific Islanders have no insurance. The cost of copayments, deductibles, and dissatisfaction with service leads poorer and minority old people to underuse health care resources. These findings suggest that, compared to whites, poorer and minority-group older people have less access to health care.

Changes in service to minority elders could include better office hours, a more convenient location of the doctor's office, more minority physicians, and home care. Health promotion programs could take place in churches and should include older people in program planning.

Coordination

The United States needs better coordination of health care services (Kane & Kane, 2001). Often, older people and their families become case managers. They find and contact specialists, let specialists know about other medical services they use, and follow up on treatment. Kane and Kane call this a "client-driven" system.

Information about the patient can get lost as patients move from one health care provider to another. Good care from one doctor can interfere with treatment prescribed by another doctor. Let me give a personal example. I recently wrenched my left shoulder lifting a suitcase. I went to an orthopedic specialist where I got a cortisone shot to ease the swelling and pain. This doctor recommended that I get an MRI and see a sports medicine specialist. That doctor reviewed the MRI, suggested rest, and offered to ease my pain with a cortisone shot. I declined his offer.

Two cortisone shots in a very short time can damage muscles and tendons. The second doctor did not have the records from the first doctor to show my recent history. The lack of coordination could have resulted in further damage to my shoulder. In other cases a person can receive prescriptions for medicine from one doctor that can interfere with medicine prescribed by another. No central record exists to track a person's full medical history. In the case of an older patient, for example, no system exists to let the home health nurse know about a physician-specialist's findings.

Area Agencies on Aging offer long-term care planning help, as do hospital discharge planners, some senior centers, and some social agencies. A doctor may also help set up a long-term care plan. Some people have turned to private care management services. They help decide what services a person needs, where to find them, and how to coordinate them. Care management within a larger service (e.g., a hospital) may come free of charge. A private care management firm will charge a monthly fee. No public or private insurers will cover the charge of private care management.

Stone (2006, citing Booth, Fralich, & Sucier, 1997) lists five characteristics of an integrated service system:

1. It provides broad and flexible services.
2. It includes community-based care as well as institutional care.
3. It uses care planning methods, teams, and other approaches to integration.
4. It provides quality control and a single responsible party.
5. It offers flexible funding that rewards efficient and effective service.

Little successful innovation in health care service delivery has occurred in the past 25 years (Stone, 2006). The fragmented system and many funding sources limit integration. Programs such as On Lok and other PACE programs focus on coordination of services. But they largely serve the poorest older people, and they exist only in pockets throughout the country.

The AARP (1992, p. 1) summed up the problems with the long-term care system a decade ago. The problems still exist today. "It's not always easy to find these services," the AARP said, "and when found, they often are costly. Some options are not universally available and many forms of care are not covered by insurance."

CONCLUSION

Health care costs have increased in the recent past, and projections suggest that costs will go up in the future (Moon, 2006). Some writers point to an aging society as the cause of these increases. They say that older people use more health care services and that an increase in the number of older people will drive health care costs through the roof.

A closer look at the health care system shows that the system itself accounts for most of the increase in costs. The current system relies on the medical model to serve an aging population. This model developed and had its greatest successes in response to **acute illness**. But an older population has more chronic than acute illnesses. The medical model often provides older people with costly care that sometimes fails to meet their needs.

The current anti-tax mood of the public will limit future expansions of government-funded health care programs. Medicare will come under fire as a way to cut federal spending. Programs will do well if they maintain their current benefits in the face of proposed rollbacks. To stay solvent, the system can increase premiums, it can provide better information about care and coordination of care, and it can encourage cost-saving programs like PACE and other long-term care options (Moon, 2006).

Older people have varied needs, complex medical histories, many chronic conditions, and uncertain outcomes from treatment. They need long-term care services. These services help with a variety of supports that range from medical care to help with activities of daily living. Community care and home health supports often suit the older person better than institutional care and expensive medical treatment.

Health promotion may create a healthier older population in the future. This approach fits a society that values activity and engagement in social life. But many reports on programs simply describe the programs or report on positive program outcomes. Researchers need to conduct more controlled studies of health promotion programs. Studies need to look at whether these programs improve health and save health care dollars as they claim.

Researchers and practitioners have begun to apply research findings to program development (Blackburn & Dulmus, 2007). They also collect data to improve existing programs and create new ones. These programs now exist throughout the country. They can serve as models for more and better programs in the future.

The current health care system will need to change to serve an aging society. It will have to offer a broader range of services, it will have to provide more community care and offer nonmedical supports to help older people stay in the community, and it will have to recognize the value of prevention and health promotion. It will also have to provide coordinated services with fewer barriers to access. Some movement in this direction has begun. Reports on Medicare spending show a shift from hospital- and physician-based care to community care.

Changes to the health care system will take place in a time of funding cutbacks. At the same time, the system must continue to deliver service. Someone said this is like trying to change a tire while driving down the highway at 60 miles per hour. This will take skillful management and public support. But the outcome will be a health care system that better fits the needs of an aging society.

SUMMARY

- Social scientists use three models to describe the approaches to health care in the United States: the medical model, the social model, and the health promotion model. The medical model focuses on diagnosis and cure of illness. The social model focuses on helping a person function in everyday life. And the health promotion model focuses on prevention and well-being. The health care system in the United States today favors treatment using the medical model. But this model best fits treatment of acute illness. Chronic illnesses, the type most common among older people, can better be served through the social and health promotion models.

- Congress established the Medicare program in 1965. Until then, only about half of all older people had health insurance. The Medicare program contains two parts: hospital insurance (or Part A) and medical insurance (or Part B). People who receive Social Security get Part A insurance at age 65. People with Part A can pay extra for Part B insurance.

- Medicare offers a Part C. This option allows a person to choose an alternative to Medicare Part A and Part B. Under this option a person can choose a private "Medicare Advantage" health insurance plan that contracts with Medicare. This option provides enhanced benefits.

- Medicare Part D offers subsidies for drug costs. It offers this option to all Medicare beneficiaries, and it offers cost-sharing supports to low-income people.

- Congress also set up the Medicaid program in 1965. This program serves low-income Americans of all ages. Older people make up about 12% of Medicaid recipients. Few people can afford private long-term care insurance. For this reason Medicaid now serves as a default long-term care program. It now serves many middle-class seniors.

- The high cost of the U.S. health care system results from costly hospital service, hospital administration costs, high insurance administration costs, and advances in high-cost technology. An aging society plays some role in increasing costs. But it plays a minor role compared to other forces.

- In an attempt to control hospital costs, the federal government set up the Prospective Payment System. The PPS led to a drop in older persons' length of stay in hospitals, but this method poses problems for older patients. It encourages hospitals to release Medicare patients early (because Medicare pays less for care than private patients do), to restrict their treatment, and to increase the number of private patients they accept.

- Congress enacted a broad reform of the American health care system in 2010—the "Patient Protection and Affordable Care Act." This legislation makes only minor changes to the Medicare program. But it offers health care coverage to all Americans and removes many of the barriers that kept people from getting the care they needed.

- Health care expenses have increased, and they take up a large part of the older person's budget. Most of this money pays for insurance, medical supplies, and prescription drugs. Catastrophic illness and long-term care in an institution can wipe out a family's savings. Future increases in health care costs will affect government programs and older people.

- Community-based services link medical care and social supports to help keep older people out of institutions. Community services range from adult day care programs to home care and respite services.

- Health maintenance organizations take an interdisciplinary approach to care and coordinate all services for a client. An HMO gets a certain amount of money per person (a capitated payment) to provide that person with health care. The HMO has an incentive to stay within its budget and earn a profit. This type of plan promises some control of health care costs. At the same time, it provides comprehensive care to its clients.

- The national PACE demonstration project shows that community health care programs can provide high-quality service and control costs. Research shows that PACE programs, such as On Lok in San Francisco, reduce hospital and nursing-home stays. This kind of program also gets high marks from clients and patients.

- Disease prevention and health promotion can lead to lower health care system costs. People who do not smoke, drink moderately, exercise, and wear seatbelts have lower health care costs than others. Health promotion and disease prevention programs can create a healthier society.

- The health care system needs to improve by making services widely available, removing barriers to access, and coordinating services.

DISCUSSION QUESTIONS

1. List the three different approaches to health care. Define the goals and practices of each.
2. Explain how Parts A, B, C, and D of the Medicare program work and how the government funds each part of this program.
3. Who can receive Medicaid? What services does Medicaid support?
4. The Medicare and Medicaid programs cover only part of an older person's medical expenses. State two ways that older people cover the rest of the costs. What forces have driven Medicaid to serve middle-class citizens?
5. List the major reasons for the increase in health care costs for the elderly. What effect does this increase in costs have on the Medicare program?

6. How does the PPS attempt to control hospital costs? What problems does this approach pose for older people?

7. Why are some people dissatisfied with the U.S. health care system? Suggest some approaches the government can use to reduce the cost of health care for older people and their families.

8. Describe how the health care reform legislation of 2010 will improve health care for seniors. What are the long-term benefits that may come from this legislation?

9. What types of services must the medical system develop to respond to the increase in chronic medical conditions? Describe how adult day care, respite, and home health care programs each work.

10. On Lok serves as a model for other HMOs throughout the United States. Describe how On Lok operates. Discuss the benefits that PACE programs offer to older people.

11. What types of programs do disease prevention and health promotion include? How can these programs benefit older people physically, psychologically, and financially?

12. How must the current health care system change to serve the future needs of an aging society?

SUGGESTED READING

Haber, D. (2010). *Health promotion and aging* (5th ed). New York: Springer.

The fifth edition updates this classic work. The book reports the variety of approaches to health promotion that have emerged in the past few years. Many of the author's insights come from his own experience working with older people. The text discusses current topics including gay aging, social networking, brain games, recent health care reform, and the use of the Wii system for rehabilitation.

Quadagno, J. (2005). *One nation, uninsured: Why the U.S. has no national health insurance.* New York: Oxford University Press.

The author provides a history of the struggle over national health insurance in the United States. She describes the players, the interest groups, and the issues that have kept the United States from having health care for all. The lack of a national health insurance program in the United States affects more than the elderly. The lack of a national health care system means that many people earlier in life will suffer from illnesses and fail to get care they need. This will affect their health in old age. This book is an excellent analysis of a chronic American problem.

Tepper, L. M., & Cassidy, T. M. (Eds.). (2005). *Multidisciplinary perspectives on aging.* New York: Springer.

This collection of essays looks at the health care needs of older people and how the health care system can best meet those needs. The essays cover a range of topics, including the impact of an aging society on the health care system, financing health care, and health promotion. This collection present the latest thinking on these and other topics related to health care for older people.

Websites to Consult

The Official U.S. Medicare Website
www.medicare.gov

This site contains information for Americans with Medicare. It includes information on Medicare costs, availability, and the quality of available health care by location.

The Eldercare Locator
http://www.eldercare.gov/Eldercare.NET/Public/Index.aspx

This site, a service of the U.S. Administration on Aging, contains information about elder care organized by location. It also contains information about Medicare, elder abuse prevention, legal assistance, and other health care issues.

U.S. Department of Health and Human Services Centers for Medicare and Medicaid Services
www.cms.hhs.gov/home/medicaid.asp

This site contains official information about the various services provided by Medicare and Medicaid. It includes information about legal issues and services for seniors. It provides links to other useful government Web sites.

Kaiser Commission on Medicaid and the Uninsured
http://facts.kff.org

This site contains a wealth of facts, slides, and online tools for learning about Medicaid and other health care issues. You can download the slides and create your own slide presentation or print off the slides for other purposes. An excellent source of current data on health care issues.

chapter 8

FINANCES AND ECONOMICS

A glance through the *Bulletin,* a newsletter published by the AARP, shows the interests of older people today. Articles focus on Medicare and **Social Security (OASDI)** policies and on issues such as career changes in later life. Advertisements describe rental car bargains, investment funds, vacation options, and exercise equipment.

The AARP sends the *Bulletin* to about 25 million older people in the United States. Readers include retirees from all parts of the country, from all social classes, and from different racial and ethnic groups. The articles, investment tips, and advertisements for travel suggest that older people today have educated tastes, good health, and sound incomes.

In the past 30 years or so, older people's finances have improved dramatically. A travel section banner for a newspaper aimed at seniors reads: "If you don't go first class, your heirs will."

Social Security provides people with a financial safety net, and this has decreased **poverty** in old age. Retirees have better private pensions than ever before. And older people have assets, such as investments and mortgage-free homes, that increase their net worth.

Today, though income disparities exist, most older people have enough money to cover their basic expenses and still have some left over for recreation and leisure. A national survey found that between 1974 and 2000, the proportion of older people who

TABLE 8.1   Distribution of Older Population's Average Annual Income, by Source and Gender, 2009

Source	Men: Income	Men: Percentage	Women: Income	Women Percentage
Total income	$37,509	100.0%	$21,519	100.0%
Social Security	$13,461	35.9%	$10,552	49.0%
Pensions	$7,948	21.2%	$3,571	16.6%
Assets	$3,798	10.1%	$2,753	12.8%
Earnings	$11,304	30.1%	$4,269	19.8%
Other	$998	2.7%	$375	1.7%

This table shows that older men have an average yearly income nearly twice that of older women. Also, note that the sources of income differ for men and women. Compared to older men, older women rely more heavily on public sources of income. For example, Social Security makes up one half of the income of older women (49%). But Social Security makes up only one third of the income of older men (35.9%). Men, by contrast, draw more than half of their income from pensions and earnings. Women draw only 36% of their earnings from these sources. Lifetime differences in income and employment in part explain these differences in income sources.

Note: The EBRI tabulations are based on the latest available data on the elderly population's income, from the U.S. Census Bureau's March 2010 Current Population Survey. Percentages may not total to 100% due to rounding.

Source: Employee Benefit Research Institute (EBRI). (2010c). *The sources of income of elderly men and women (age 65 and older).* Fast Facts. Retrieved: October 23, 2010, from www.ebri.org/pdf/FFE176.30Sept10.IncEld-Gndr.Final.pdf.

said money was a "serious personal problem" for them decreased from 44% to 29% (Cutler, Whitelaw, & Beattie, 2002).

Things have improved so much in general that some critics wonder whether older people do too well. They call the new generation of seniors "greedy geezers" (Salholz, Clift, Thomas, & Bingham, 1990). These critics ask whether the United States should continue to support this affluent older population through public pension plans. Some writers see a conflict between this high cost of caring for an older population and the needs of children (who have the highest poverty rates in the country). They ask whether support for older people has gone too far.

Critics of public income security programs for older people ignore the fact that government programs created the older population's current well-being. Schulz, for example, shows what it would take to save for a comfortable old age. He says that if a person wanted to replace 60% to 70% of his or her preretirement income, the person would need to save about 20% of his or her *"earnings each and every year"* (Schulz, 2001, p. 105, emphasis in original). Most people could not or would not save at this rate.

Without public pension plans, a large proportion of older people would live in or **near poverty**. (See Figure 8.1.) Hudson (2010a) says that without public pensions (mostly Social Security) the poverty rate would be five times the current rate. Public pension plans ensure that everyone will have income security in old age. Private pension plans help people replace the income lost when they retire.

The current system still does not provide an adequate income for everyone. The U.S. government in 2009 set the poverty threshold at $10,289 for a person age 65 and over. It set the threshold at $12,968 for a

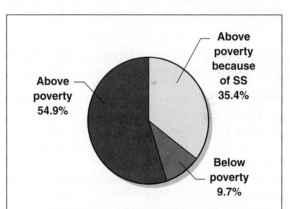

This chart shows that Social Security keeps more than a third of older people (35.4%) above the poverty line. Without Social Security support, nearly half of older people (45.1%) would live in poverty. These figures come from reports of family income (including nonsenior members). Caldera (2009) says that if you look only at individual seniors' incomes, then 61% of older people rely on Social Security for at least half their income. This group includes 36% of people who rely on Social Security for 90% of their income.

FIGURE 8.1   Social Security Keeps Older People Out of Poverty, 2007

Source: U.S. Bureau of the Census, March 2008, Current Population Survey; Caldera, S. (2009, April). *Social Security: Ten facts that matter.* Fact Sheet 154, April. Washington, DC: AARP Public Policy Institute. www.aarp.org/ppi.

household with two older adults (U.S. Census Bureau, 2010d). In 2009, 9.7% of older people lived below the poverty threshold. This came to 3.7 million older people who lived in poverty.

Very old people, minorities, and disabled older people face the greatest risk of poverty. Very old women have some of the lowest incomes in the country. Women age 75 and over had a poverty rate in 2009 of 13.3%. Those who did not live in a family had a rate of 18.8% (nearly double the rate for all older people) (U.S. Census Bureau, 2010f). Income inequality reflects a lifetime of discrimination and limited opportunities in the workforce.

Pockets of poverty such as these call for better pension funding, not cutbacks. Controversy exists about the amount of money that older people receive, about the costs of federal pension programs, and about whether the government should reduce the funding to pension programs in the future. To get at the truth of aging and pensions today, we first need to separate fact from myth.

This chapter looks at (1) the structure of the U.S. retirement income system and how it works, (2) the flaws in the system and ideas for reform, and (3) the future of retirement income in the United States.

HISTORICAL DEVELOPMENT OF THE U.S. PENSION SYSTEM

The change from an agricultural to an industrial society caused great upheaval in society wherever this occurred. People moved to the cities and took jobs in industry. This led to new risks for workers and less support from traditional sources. In an agricultural society, people did as much as they could, given their health and strength. They relied on younger family members to take up the heavier work.

In the cities, injuries, unemployment, and old age could put a sudden end to a worker's career. This led to discontent among unemployed and retired workers and caused a crisis for many older people who had no means of support. State governments realized that some groups of people, such as the old, needed help to survive. Governments often started pension plans and unemployment insurance to win loyalty to the existing government.

Otto von Bismarck, Chancellor of Germany, put the first national pension plan in place in 1889. He used pension reform to combat socialism and the discontent of the working class (Myles, 1984). The German

pension plan combined old-age and unemployment insurance. Workers and employers paid into the plan. Unemployed workers and older workers at age 65 could draw benefits.

By the early 1900s, Denmark, New Zealand, and Britain all had old-age security programs. By the early 1930s, 34 nations had some form of social insurance (Social Security Administration, 2010b). The United States was one of the last industrialized nations to create a national old-age insurance plan. Koff and Park (1993) give one reason for this delay. Industrialization came late to the United States. The U.S. frontier allowed people to move out of industrial work if they chose. This meant that a large part of the U.S. workforce in the 19th century still lived an agricultural lifestyle. In 1870, for example, one half of adult workers in the United States worked on farms (Social Security Administration, 1997, 2010b).

This changed in the early 20th century as more people moved to the cities and industrialization increased. In 1900, for example, nearly one third of men said they had retired. Many of them left work due to health problems. These workers had to rely on their own savings, relatives, or charity for survival.

By the late 1920s, the number of older people out of work had grown, and local laws related to the poor and families could not care for these needy older people. The state and federal governments responded to this problem with the first U.S. social insurance programs. These programs offered a subsistence income to the neediest people.

The Great Depression of the 1930s created a national economic crisis. The Depression left many older people and people near retirement without any savings for their old age. For example, fewer than 10% of older people who died during this time left any estate at the time of their death (U.S. Department of Health, SSA, ORS, 1993). Haber (1993) says that at this time older people began to fill the poorhouses. Twenty-eight state welfare programs for older people existed. Also, charities and religious groups provided help to older people. These programs offered mostly food and shelter, but little cash.

The Social Security Administration (2010b) says that the average benefit from state welfare programs during the Depression came to about 65 cents a day. And only about 3% of older people got these benefits. The Depression spread state funds to the limit and provided too little help for older people. No state had an old-age insurance program, and no state had plans for one (Koff & Park, 1993).

The Depression convinced many people that a person could fall into poverty due to circumstances beyond their control. Healthy younger people as well as the old and disabled needed help. The Great Depression of the 1930s, Schulz (2001) says,

> went a long way toward exposing the great political lie of American welfare debates: that poverty was generally the result of the laziness or personal unworthiness of particular individuals. . . . Millions of jobless workers and their families suffered severe financial problems because of an economic catastrophe caused by factors unrelated to their own personal activities. (p. 105)

At the start of 1933, 12 to 14 million people in the United States had no jobs, and 19 million people (about 16% of the population) signed up for state relief (U.S. Department of Health, SSA, ORS, 1993). In 1937, nearly half of all people age 65 and over (47.5%) had no income (Social Security Administration, 1997).

These conditions fed workers' discontent. Populist and socialist movements sprang up across the country. "There was even some concern," say Koff and Park (1993, p. 149), "that the unhappy condition of workers across the country could lead to riot and anarchy." General labor strikes in San Francisco and Minneapolis, for example, created concern for the social order.

The federal government passed the Social Security Act on August 14, 1935, in part as a response to these conditions. Like the program developed in Germany, Social Security responded to social and economic distress. The Social Security Act created a social insurance program that protected workers in business and industry from unemployment and poverty in retirement.

President Roosevelt summed up the importance of this legislation as he signed the Social Security Act into law:

> We can never insure one hundred percent of the population against one hundred percent of the hazards and vicissitudes of life, but we have tried to frame a law which will give some measure of protection to the average citizen and to his family against the loss of a job and against poverty-ridden old age. (Social Security Administration, 2010b)

Today Social Security serves as a financial safety net for most retired workers and their families. The government offers this program "to replace, in part, the income that is lost to a worker and his or her family when the worker retires in old age, becomes disabled, or dies" (U.S. Department of Health, SSA, ORS, 1993, p. 7). Former Senator Moynihan said that Social Security "put an end to what was the great terror of life—growing old and having no income and getting ill" (Rovner, 1995).

Workers paid into the program according to their earnings. Employers matched workers' payments. These payments created a pool of money that workers could draw on when they retired. Workers received benefits linked to the amounts they paid into the system. The poorest older workers got added benefits to boost their income in retirement. The act also included a plan for the federal government to pay one half of the cost of state benefits to the neediest older people.

The system began collecting payments in a reserve account in 1937 and began paying pensions to workers in 1940. The first benefits ranged from $10 to $85 per month (U.S. Department of Health, SSA, ORS, 1993). The program in those early days covered 56% of all workers. It did not cover the self-employed, casual laborers, or domestic workers. The program also excluded railroad workers, who had their own plan.

Today the Social Security program covers nearly all workers in the United States. In 2009, for example, the Social Security program covered 159 million workers, or 94% of the U.S. labor force (Social Security Administration, 2009). Social Security includes programs for the disabled, for widows and orphans, and for the very poor. Social Security today has the official title of Old-Age, Survivors, and Disability Insurance (OASDI). It forms part of a retirement income system that provides an income replacement system for middle-income retirees and a safety net for the poorest older people.

In 2003, for example, about two thirds of people who received Social Security benefits said that these benefits made up more than half of their total income. Twenty percent of people who received Social Security in that year claimed it as their only source of income (Social Security Administration, 2004a). Today, Hudson (2007, p. 274) says, roughly 30% of the U.S. budget goes to programs and services for people age 65 and over. "That the United States has what amounts to an old-age welfare state," he says, "is beyond controversy."

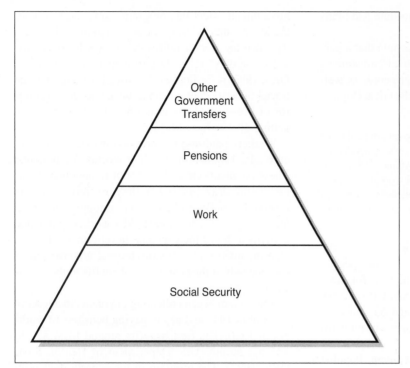

FIGURE 8.2 Tiered U.S. Retirement Income System

THE U.S. RETIREMENT INCOME SYSTEM TODAY

The retirement income system in the United States consists of a combination of public and private income sources. These include government pension programs, **employment pensions**, and private savings. Think of these income sources as tiers in a pyramid. (See Figure 8.2.) Government programs make up the broad base of the pyramid. Over 90% of people age 65 and over receive Social Security benefits. And Social Security forms the only income for about 20% of older people. Social Security, on average, makes up the largest part of older people's income. It makes up 49% of the total income of older women and 35.9% of the total income of older men (Employee Benefit Research Institute [EBRI], 2010c).

Income from work makes up about another 19.8% of income for older women and 30.1% of income for older men. A large number of people have pensions from their employers. These private (or employment) pensions make up about 16.6% of income for older women and 21.2% of income for older men. Finally, a smaller number of people have assets and other

government transfers that make up another 12.8% of income for older women and 10.1% of total income for older men (EBRI, 2010c). (Less than 3% of seniors' income comes from other sources.)

Gerontologists often refer to this mix of (1) public pensions and other government transfers, (2) work and assets, and (3) private pensions as the **three-legged stool** of the retirement income system. Most people will need income from each part of the system to maintain their preretirement lifestyles.

Level One: Social Security

The U.S. government offers the OASDI (the Federal Old-Age, Survivors, and Disability Insurance) program, better known as Social Security, to retired workers, disabled workers, and surviving spouses of workers who have paid into the program. (See Figure 8.3.) In 2010, workers and employers each paid 6.2% of the worker's covered earnings (a total of 12.4% of earnings) as a Social Security tax. A self-employed person pays the entire 12.4% of earnings.

Employers withhold this tax from workers' pay and submit it with their own portion to the Internal Revenue Service. This money goes into a trust fund to pay only for these programs. Benefits get paid out to people today from payments made by current workers (economists call this a **pay-as-you-go plan**).

In December 2008, 51 million people got Social Security benefits (including children, retired workers and their dependents, survivors of deceased workers, and disabled workers and their dependents). They received a total of $615.4 billion in payments in that year. Sixty-nine percent of these payments went to 35.2 million retired workers and their dependents, another 13% went to survivors of workers, and 18% went to disabled workers and their dependents (Office of Retirement and Disability Policy, 2009; Social Security Online, 2010a). This makes Social Security the largest income maintenance program in the United States. Williamson (2007, p. 327) calls Social Security "the nation's most popular social program."

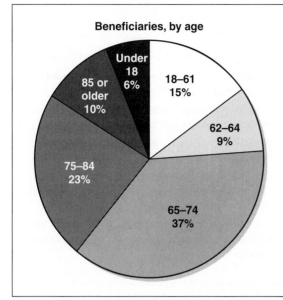

Beneficiaries, by age

The OASDI program has two parts: The Old Age Security Income (OASI) program that serves retirees, and the Disability Insurance (DI) program that serves disabled workers and their dependents. This figure shows that the Social Security program benefits people of all ages. One third of all beneficiaries are under age 65.

"Almost 50 million Americans—nearly one in four households—receive monthly Social Security checks. In addition to the over 31 million retirees who collect Social Security, the program is the nation's largest children's program. Dependent children of workers who have died, become disabled, or retired receive monthly wage-related benefits as a matter of right until their late teens. Social Security is also the nation's largest disability program, providing disabled workers and their families wage-related benefits, also as a matter of right" (Altman, 2007).

FIGURE 8.3   OASDI Beneficiaries by Age, 2009

Source: Social Security Administration. Office of Retirement and Disability Policy. Office of Research, Evaluation, and Statistics. (2010). *Fast Facts & Figures about Social Security, 2010,* p. 16. Citing Social Security Administration, Master Beneficiary Record, 100 percent data. Retrieved: November 17, 2010, from www.ssa.gov/policy/docs/chartbooks/fast_facts/2010/fast_facts10.pdf; also Altman, Nancy J. (2007). *Protecting Social Security's beneficiaries: Achieving balance without benefit cuts.* The Economic Policy Institute, Briefing Paper No. 206. Retrieved November 23, 2007, from www.sharedprosperity.org/bp206.html.

BOX 8.1
BASIC PRINCIPLES OF THE SOCIAL SECURITY PROGRAM

The U.S. Department of Health lists five principles of the Social Security program:

1. *Work-related benefits.* Workers pay into the program and receive benefits according to the amount paid in. The higher the income, the greater the amount received. The program weights benefits to help poorer workers.

2. *No means test.* A worker earns credits toward Social Security benefits and receives benefits regardless of other income, pensions, or savings. The program expects workers to save for retirement through other sources such as private pensions. A retirement test does exist that reduces benefits for people with incomes over a certain amount.

3. *Contributory.* A payroll tax for Social Security pays for benefits and at times has built a reserve fund. Payment into the program creates a commitment from workers to the Social Security system.

4. *Compulsory coverage.* Workers (with only a few exceptions) must pay into the program. This spreads the risk of social insurance among the workforce. It also means that workers and their families will have a guaranteed base income in retirement.

5. *Rights defined in law.* The law guarantees the right to Social Security for a worker who has paid into the system. A person may appeal a decision through the courts if necessary.

These principles ensure that nearly all workers and their families in the United States will have at least a basic income in retirement. In 2008, Social Security provided at least half the income to 64% of older people. The Social Security program has removed the threat of poverty from millions of older Americans.

Sources: U.S. Department of Health and Human Services, Social Security Administration, Office of Research and Statistics. (1993). Social Security programs in the United States. *Social Security Bulletin, 56*(4). Washington, DC: U.S. Government Printing Office; also Social Security Administration. Office of Retirement and Disability Policy. Office of Research, Evaluation and Statistics. (2010). *Fast Facts & Figures about Social Security, 2010.* Retrieved November 17, 2010, from www.ssa.gov/policy/docs/chartbooks/fast_facts/2010/fast_facts10.pdf.

BOX 8.2
SOCIAL SECURITY'S BENEFIT TO THE INDIVIDUAL AND SOCIETY

Discussion about Social Security often focuses on the cost of the program and, by implication, the high cost of older people to American society. But Social Security serves young people as well as older people. Here are some of the benefits that Social Security provides to all age groups.

Social Security:

- provides a variety of benefits that include life insurance, disability insurance, and survivor benefits for spouses and children.

- provides younger family members with a sense of security. They know that older members will have a pension and will not need to rely on younger members for support.

- provides coverage for nearly all American workers.

- ensures pension payments to beneficiaries regardless of the economic climate, such as declines in the stock market.

- adjusts benefits to the cost of living; this provides protection against inflation.

- provides guaranteed payments for life; funds cannot run out (as they can with personal savings).

- provides a guaranteed pension for spouses if a beneficiary dies.

- guarantees a base income that a person can rely on. This allows people to make riskier investments with other portions of their income if they choose.

- provides more support to lower income earners; low-income earners get a larger proportion of their income replaced.

Source: Based on Diamond, P. A., & Orszag, P. R. (2007). A summary of *Saving Social Security: A balanced approach.* In R. A. Pruchno, & M. A. Smyer (eds.), *Challenges of an aging society: Ethical dilemmas, political issues* (pp. 346–395). Baltimore: The Johns Hopkins Unive rsity Press.

At times, money has gathered in the Social Security fund. For example, the federal government increased payroll tax rates in 1977 and 1983 to provide a 3-year benefit surplus by 2015. The government increased this tax to build up reserves for the Baby Boomers from the year 2010 on. This led to Social Security surpluses of over $1 trillion beginning in 2000. The trust fund came to $2.5 trillion at the end of March, 2010, more than at any time in the fund's history (Social Security Online, 2010d).

But the Social Security Administration says that even a $2.5 trillion surplus cannot cover the program's future benefit obligations. Fears that the Social Security system will go bankrupt in the short run have no foundation. But, Social Security's Chief Actuary says that over the longer term—75 years or more—the fund will face a massive and growing shortfall. If current payroll tax rates stay the same, the shortfall will begin in 2017 and the trust fund will be exhausted by 2037 (Social Security Online, 2010b).

Diamond and Orszag (2007) trace the shortfall to three conditions: (1) increasing life expectancy; (2) increasing inequality of earnings; and (3) the legacy debt burden. Increasing life expectancy means that people will collect Social Security for more years than originally projected. The inequality of earning refers

to an increase in the share of earnings above the maximum amount taxable for Social Security. In other words, the Social Security program today has access to a much smaller amount of the total income earned by workers. Finally, the benefits paid to nearly all current and past beneficiaries exceed the amount they paid into the program. All workers today and in the future need to repay this debt.

The total shortfall over the 75 years (from 2009 to 2083) will amount to $5.3 trillion. Payments into the system at that time will only cover at best 75% of expected benefits. The OASDI Trustees Report (2009) proposed four ways to deal with this growing problem. I discuss these later under the topic of pension reform.

Who Gets Social Security?

Workers who have paid into the system and were born before 1938 get full Social Security benefits at age 65. (The full-retirement age increases for those born after 1938 because people live longer today than in the past. A person born in 1960 or later, for instance, collects full benefits at age 67.) Workers can begin to get benefits as early as age 62, but at that age retirees get reduced benefits because they will draw a pension for more years. A person who delays retirement past their full benefit age will get higher payments. These come to about 8% more for each year a person delays collecting benefits.

A person born after 1929 must have at least 40 quarters of earnings (or about 10 years of work covered by Social Security) to get benefits (Social Security Online, 2010c). The Social Security program bases benefits on a person's highest earnings of all years worked after 1950. The program indexes a person's earnings and gives greater weight to people with low incomes. This provides the poorest people with proportionately higher benefits.

Social Security also provides a pension for workers' spouses. A woman who worked as a homemaker, for example, would have made no Social Security payments. She would have no Social Security pension of her own. Instead, she receives 50% of her husband's benefits. This gives the couple 150% of the husband's pension. A person entitled to Social Security benefits also gets Medicare (Part A) hospital insurance and may buy Medicare (Part B) medical insurance. A married woman who has worked only in the home gets the same Medicare benefits as her husband.

A widow can get benefits after age 60 (or at age 50 if disabled). The amount of benefit depends on the widow's age and her husband's entitlement. A widow's benefit ranges from 71.5% of her husband's benefit amount if she takes the pension at age 60, to 100% of his pension if she begins at age 65. A widow will get Medicare coverage if her husband would have.

She continues to get payments even if she remarries. Or she can apply for benefits based on her new husband's pension. But she cannot draw two Social Security pensions. The program contains an "anti-duplication" rule. A person entitled to more than one benefit gets only the largest benefit. If a woman, for example, has pension entitlements of her own based on years she has worked, she will get either her spousal entitlement or her own, not both.

An increase in the number of older people and longer life expectancies will lead to more retirees in the future. The government has raised the age of retirement to cope with this change and to encourage people to work longer. The age for the payment of full Social Security benefits started to increase in the year 2003 and will reach age 67 in 2027 (Social Security Administration, 2004b, 2007). The government also began taxing Social Security benefits in 1984 to reduce the cost of the program. From that year onward, a couple or single person paid tax on their adjusted gross income over a certain amount. The higher a person's total income, the more the person pays back to the Social Security system.

The Social Security program accounts for the sharp decrease in poverty rates for older people since the 1950s. The program adjusted benefits to reflect increases in the consumer price index. This helped protect retirees' incomes from inflation. But recent changes in the law have put the brakes on Social Security increases. And many older people will feel financially pressed by rising costs. Also, people who did not work, who had low-paying jobs, or who did not pay into the system (e.g., older immigrants) get low or no Social Security benefits. These people need further assistance to bring them at least near the poverty line. (See Figure 8.4.)

Individual Retirement Accounts: The Cure Worse Than the Disease?

In 2005, President George Bush began a campaign to privatize Social Security. He claimed that the current system "was headed for disaster—that it soon would be 'flat bust' . . . and that it was 'headed toward bankruptcy'" (Binstock, 2007, citing Bush, 2005; and Bumiller, 2005). A group called the Concord Coalition (2004) proposed that Social Security move toward a fully funded system (versus the current pay-as-you-go system that exists today). Schulz and Binstock (2006, p. 19) call these fear-mongers the "Merchants of Doom."

In a privatized or partially privatized Social Security, people would invest all or part of their Social Security taxes in their own accounts. Accounts could include treasury notes or stocks and bonds. Supporters of this system say that workers would have more control of their funds, would gain the benefit of stock market growth, and would end the supposed crisis in Social Security financing. The plan would invest "tens to hundreds of billions of additional dollars in the private sector" (Binstock, 2007, p. 297).

This proposal got support from the banking and investment community. It would inject massive amounts of capital into the market. The proposal gained public attention in the late 1990s and early 2000s as stock market values soared. The lure of high returns on individual accounts made this seem like a good idea.

Herd and Kingson (2005) and others describe the drawbacks to privatization:

1. Transfer costs to set up accounts and pay for current Social Security obligations would offset any increases in returns. Depending on the plan put in place, couples would see between a 10% to 30% cut in benefits.

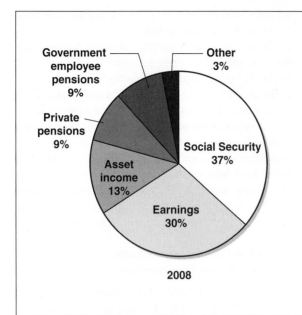

The proportions of older people's income from various sources have remained largely unchanged over the past 46 years. Social Security income grew from 30% of older people's income in 1962 to 37% in 2008. Earnings, asset income, and government employee pensions income changed by 3% or less over this time period.

Compared with 1962, older people now get a larger share of their income from private pensions (9% in 2008 compared with 3% in 1962). This reflects the tendency for employers in the last half of the 20th century to provide pension plans to their employees. During this time period, the share of income from "Other" income dropped from 16% to 3%.

Private pensions accounted for only 9% of older people's incomes in 2008. But this share tripled from 3% in 1962. People have more diverse sources of income today than in the past. Still, Social Security still makes up the largest share of older people's incomes. And it has done so for the past half century. It forms the core of income security in later life in the United States.

FIGURE 8.4   Income Sources of People Age 65 and Over, 2008

ᵃTotal does not equal 100% due to rounding.

Source: Social Security Administration. Office of Retirement and Disability Policy. Office of Research, Evaluation, and Statistics. (2010). *Fast Facts & Figures about Social Security, 2010,* p. 6. Retrieved November 17, 2010, from www.ssa.gov/policy/docs/chartbooks/fast_facts/2010/fast_facts10.pdf.

2. Administrative costs to manage private accounts would eat into benefits. The more choices given to investors, the more costly the administration of the system.
3. Dramatic fluctuations in stock market returns would put savings at risk. Stock market returns average 5.5% over many years (compared to 3% for Social Security investment in government bonds). But this average hides wild swings in the market. A retiree who retired in March 2001, for example, would get benefits one third smaller than a retiree who retired a year earlier (citing Aaron, Blinder, Munnell, & Orszag, 2001).

  People with 401(k) accounts and other stock-based portfolios in 2008 saw their savings decrease by as much as 37%. People already retired and those near retirement learned with a shock that investments can go down as well as up. And when it comes to retirement, the loss of a lifetime's savings can force a person back to work, force a person to postpone retirement, or lower a person's standard of living. "In a nutshell," Walker (2006, p. 355) says, [in a privatized system] "the risks associated with old age will be increasingly individualized."
4. Few people have the knowledge to invest successfully over the long run. Gosselin (2005, cited

in Schulz & Binstock, 2006, p. 117) reports that even Nobel prize winners in economics fail to plan properly for retirement. Almost half the experts Gosselin interviewed admitted that they "failed to regularly manage their retirement savings." And many of them said they took too conservative an approach to investing. They had large amounts of their savings in low-interest money market funds.
5. Few people have the discipline to save over many years and to leave their retirement funds untouched. A study by Hewitt Associates reported in *The New York Times*, for example, found that "45 percent of American workers cash out their retirement plans when leaving a company, rather than 'rolling it over' into a new one to keep the money accumulating and available for retirement" (cited in Schulz & Binstock, 2006, p. 135).
6. Poorer people and average earners would gain the least from a privatized system. Those with large assets to invest could take greater risk and get the best return. Wealthier people would also know more about investing. But a low-income person could afford to lose less. They would hold a more conservative portfolio and would stand to gain less.

A person, rich or poor, who made bad investments would find themselves with little or no retirement savings—and nowhere to look for support as they age. A privatized system would change Social Security from a broad program that spreads the risk and rewards in retirement among all workers to a program that perpetuates midlife income inequalities.

In addition to these drawbacks, privatization would lack the many benefits of the Social Security system. It would offer no disability insurance to workers, it would offer no guaranteed payments to workers' widows and children, and it would not redistribute revenue to support low-income beneficiaries (as the current system does). Schulz and Binstock (2006, p. 19) summarize the problem with private retirement accounts. "Instead of today's financial security in old age, the Merchants' [of Doom] approach could lead us in the direction of massive financial insecurity."

Today the proposal to privatize Social Security gets little support from the public or from most legislators. Recent stock market and housing market crashes have decreased the enthusiasm for personal risk. Studies of public attitudes toward Social Security continue to support the program.

Wright and Davies (2007) on behalf of the AARP surveyed Americans' attitudes toward Social Security. Sixty-eight percent of the respondents rated Social Security as the most important government program. The researchers report that "an average of 84% [of the public] now agree[s] with the statement, 'Even though I might be able to do better on my own, I think it is important to contribute to Social Security for the common good.'" Also, 83% of nonretired persons agree with the statement, "Maybe I won't need Social Security when I retire, but I definitely want to know it's there in case I do."

Still, controversy and debate over Social Security will continue in the years ahead as legislators take on the challenge of reform. And the plan to create individual retirement accounts will probably arise again (Herd, 2009).

The Social Security system needs reform to remain viable. Most analysts agree on this (Herd & Kingson, 2005; Binstock, 2007). But the Social Security Trust Fund Trustees report that Social Security can continue to meet its obligations to 2037. After that time it can meet about three quarters of its obligations if nothing is done.

But many options exist to create a strong and solvent Social Security system for at least the next 75 years. Options fall into three categories—(1) raise revenues, (3) reduce benefits, and (3) invest part of the Social Security trust fund assets in equities and/or corporate bonds. Shelton (2008b, Introduction) says that "these alternative reforms can be packaged together in a many different ways to achieve long-term solvency." And these changes can take place over many years (e.g., through modest increases in payroll taxes or some reduction in future benefits).

The trustees show that reform of the current system can create stable funding into the distant future. And the sooner reform takes place, the smoother the transition to long-term stability of the Social Security program.

Herd (2009) says, "In this recession, middle-class retirees and near-retirees have faced some of the largest financial losses and were likely hit with the realization that Social Security was the only source of retirement income they could count on to ensure their economic security in old age."

Supplemental Security Income

Social scientists use two definitions of *poverty:* **relative deprivation** and **absolute deprivation**. Relative deprivation refers to people's feelings of poverty in relation to people like themselves.

Absolute deprivation refers to the minimal income needed to survive—to buy food, clothing, shelter, and health care. People who lack this minimum income are defined as poor. The U.S. government sets poverty levels each year based on this minimum. Discussions of poverty in the United States usually refer to a standard of absolute deprivation. The U.S. government in 2009 set a yearly income of $10,289 as the poverty threshold for an aged individual. The poverty threshold was set at $12,968 for a household head age 65 or over (U.S. Census Bureau, 2010d).

Congress approved the **Supplemental Security Income (SSI)** program in 1972 to help older people and others in need, whose incomes fall below the official poverty threshold. In 2008, 9.7% of older people lived in poverty (3.7 million people) (O'Brien, Wu, & Baer, 2010; U.S. Census Bureau, 2010c).

Congress kept the SSI program separate from Social Security. People pay into Social Security and it has its own trust fund, but SSI gets paid out of general revenues. The SSI program provides a safety net to elderly, blind, and disabled people with little or no income. It offers direct and uniform payments to people who meet the program's requirements. The program guarantees an income at 75% to 90% of the poverty level. This is the largest cash assistance

---

BOX 8.3
SUPPORT IN RETIREMENT: A SOCIAL COMPACT OR A SOCIAL CONTRACT?

The phrase *social contract* refers to legal obligations between parties in society—for example, citizens and the government. People use this term to describe Social Security and Medicare. Acts of Congress established these programs. They stand on firm legal ground.

A compact, however, lacks the legal standing of a contract. Employers, for example, do not have a legal obligation to provide benefits to workers (e.g., health care subsidy or contributions to a retirement plan). Some writers see the government moving from a contract with its citizens to a (much looser) compact.

William A. Galston (2009, p. 6) of The Brookings Institution says, "Every element of this social contract is now under intense pressure." The public sector faces challenges in paying for Social Security and especially Medicare. The private sector has moved away from providing pensions security and health care. These challenges tend to shift risk from large organizations (government and industry) to the individual.

Galston says, "To the greatest extent possible, individuals and families will be expected to take the lead in providing for their own futures through personal savings and the purchase of insurance against low-probability, high-cost events."

Herd (2009, p. 13) says, "This shift toward individualized risk has for all practical purposes reshaped the three-legged stool into a two-legged stool. One leg, which individualizes risk, is composed of personal savings, employer-provided defined-contribution pensions

(that do not guarantee a set pension), and earnings. The other leg, which collectivizes risk, is composed of Social Security." The three-legged stool provided employer pensions (with a guaranteed pension) along with Social Security to balance the risk of private savings and income from work (riskier ventures).

Today the older person bears most of the risk through defined contribution pension plans, savings, and hard-to-find employment. An investment misstep or an economic downturn can sink a person's retirement portfolio and wipe out a lifetime's savings. People at the bottom of the income scale will have the least opportunity to save and will find it hardest to find work in a down economy.

How do you feel about this society-wide shift in responsibility for income security and health care in old age? Do you believe that the government will honor its obligations to provide Social Security and Medicare over the next 75 years? Do you think the private sector will support workers' retirement security in the future? Do you feel confident that the contracts and compacts in place today will be there for you when you retire?

Source: AARP Public Policy Institute. (2009). *The social compact in the twenty-first century.* Washington, DC: AARP Public Policy Institute; Galston, W. A. (2009). My view. In AARP Public Policy Institute. *The social compact in the twenty-first century* (p. 6). Washington, DC: AARP Public Policy Institute; Herd, P. (2009). The two-legged stool: The reconfiguration of risk in retirement income security [Part of a special issue: *The Great Recession: Implications for an aging America*]. *Generations, 33*(3), 12–18.

---

program in the United States for older people in need. Most states supplement the SSI payments. About one third of SSI recipients get a state supplement (Social Security Administration, 2010a).

To receive SSI benefits, a person must have an income that falls below the federal maximum SSI benefit level. If single, a person must have resources or assets less than $2,000 ($3,000 for a couple). Assets include property but exclude the home a person lives in, a car worth up to $4,500, food stamps, life insurance (up to $1,500), and personal household goods.

A person can earn up to $20 a month from any source without loss of SSI benefits (sources include Social Security, pensions, and donations of food and clothing). The program also allows a person to earn $65 per month from work without loss of benefits. After the $20 basic deduction and the first $65 from

work income, a person loses 50 cents of SSI for every dollar earned (Social Security Online, 2011).

The average SSI benefit in 2009 came to $674 per month for an individual and $1,011 per month for a married couple. The federal government made SSI payments to about 7.8 million older people in 2010. Overall, women made up 58% of people who got benefits. The proportion of older people who receive SSI has declined from 60% of all SSI recipients in 1974 to 34% in 2010. This reflects better incomes from Social Security for the poorest older people (Social Security Administration, 2010d).

Level Two: Employment Pensions

The Social Security program has worked well to keep many older people out of poverty. It provides a safety net for the disabled, widowed, and low-income older person. But it works less well as a way of maintaining pre-retirement income. The middle-class worker cannot rely on Social Security as a means of income replacement in retirement. The average Social Security payment in 2010 for a retired worker age 62 or over and a spouse came to $1,743 per month, $20,916 per year (Social Security Administration, 2010d).

In the future (2040), a person in the upper-income bracket, who paid the maximum amount in Social Security taxes, can expect only a 29% income replacement. The average wage earner will see income replacement of about 39%. People who earned low wages will see a 65% replacement of income (Biggs & Springstead, 2008; also Munnell & Quinby, 2009).

Middle- and upper-income people cannot maintain their preretirement lifestyles on Social Security benefits alone. Private pensions supplement Social Security and help middle-income and upper-income earners maintain their lifestyles.

Private pension coverage grew after World War II. The Employee Benefit Research Institute (Copeland, 2009) reports that in 2008 just under 55% of all full-time, full-year workers ages 21–64 belonged to a pension plan. This varied by income and type of work. Only 25% of workers who earned $15,000 to $19,999 belonged to a private pension plan. But 68.8% of workers who earned $50,000 or more belonged to a private plan. Likewise, 62% of professionals belonged to a private pension plan. But only 13.9% of farm, fishing, and forestry workers belonged to a private plan.

Among full-time year-round workers, compared to men, women had a higher participation rate in private plans (56.2% compared to 53.7%). But among all workers, women, compared to men, had a lower rate. This reflects the tendency of women to work in part-time, low-wage jobs. Hispanic workers at all income levels showed the lowest rate of participation in a private pension plan. Whites showed the highest participation rates at all income levels.

About 35% of all people age 65 and older in 2007 got a pension either from their own or from a spouse's employer (EBRI, 2010a). Schulz (1988) notes that private pension plans often say they guarantee a 25% replacement of income (higher in industries such as manufacturing), but this applies to people with a long service record. In the best case, private pensions and Social Security together provide between 50% and 80% of workers' preretirement income.

These figures express ideal conditions. Many people will get less than these replacement rates. The Employee Retirement Income Security Act (ERISA) of 1974 regulates pension plans to protect workers. This act sets standard rules for participation in pension plans and rules for the eligibility of workers. Schulz (2001, p. 253, emphasis in original) says that ERISA's principal focus *"was on expanding the supervision and regulation of private plans."*

For example, ERISA ensures that vesting of pension benefits takes place. Vesting means that workers will get all or part of their earned benefit from a company when they leave. They will get this benefit even if they have moved to a different company. Full vesting now takes place after 5 years for most covered workers (Schulz, 2001). ERISA also guarantees workers the right to choose a joint and survivor option, which provides a pension for a spouse after a worker dies.

Vesting does not guarantee a good pension for workers who change jobs. For example, the value of vested money left in a plan does not increase if a plan improves benefits for continuing workers. Also, some companies link a pension to the person's salary. If a person leaves this type of firm, his or her benefits will reflect only the salary the individual had when he or she left the company. The person will have a smaller pension than someone who has stayed with the company until retirement. Finally, inflation will erode the value of this vested pension.

Portability helps solve this problem. Portability allows a person to transfer the money value of his or her vested pension to another plan. This option requires complex administration. For this reason, few portable pension plans exist. But some multiemployer plans do offer portability. A plan that serves many U.S. university professors, for example, manages pension savings from professors and employers across the country. This allows professors to move from one school to another throughout their careers without losing accumulated pension savings.

Individual Pension Plans

The Internal Revenue Service (2009b) believes that the high cost of running pension plans and reporting on them has led some employers to cancel them. Many employers have taken a less drastic route. They changed the type of pension plan they offer. This led to a decrease in *defined benefit* plans and the increase in *defined contribution* plans. This change will have an effect on retiree benefits in the years to come. (See Box 8.4.)

BOX 8.4
DEFINED BENEFIT (DB) AND DEFINED CONTRIBUTION (DC) PLANS: A COMPARISON

Defined Benefit (DB) Plans
These plans offer the most security to workers. A DB plan:

- Promises a pension at retirement based on years of service and salary.
- Provides a dependable, guaranteed outcome and makes planning easier.
- In some cases indexes to inflation.
- Often provides a contribution match by the company.
- Is insured through the PBGC under ERISA in 1974 and protects workers' pensions.
- Along with Social Security, spreads the risk over the entire population and gives poorer people a safety net in retirement.
- Pays out over time as an annuity (annual payout over lifetime of worker or last survivor of a married couple).
- Helps retain workers in a competitive employment market because people stay to collect their pensions.

But DB plans create some problems for companies. A DB plan:

- Creates an uncertain outcome for company—the company can't know for certain the costs of pension payouts in the future (e.g., due to life expectancy uncertainty and market uncertainty).
- Costs the company money in matching funds and potentially high payout in the future.
- Can lead to financial problems for the firm—companies may lose their competitive edge in the market due to high costs of pension obligations. Pension obligations can lead to higher costs of goods and services (U.S. auto manufacturers and airlines face this problem).

Defined Contribution (DC) Plans
These plans offer the most benefits to the company and some benefits to workers. A DC plan:

- Creates certainty for the company—a company may agree to contribute a set amount to a plan during an employee's working years or the company may make no contribution at all.

- Vests immediately; employees own their account and can track the amount in their accounts.
- Rich people gain the most from these plans—they have the extra money to invest in them and they gain the most from the tax advantages.

But these plans create some problems for workers. A DC plan:

- Makes the pension payout uncertain—it depends on the amount saved, management fees, and the return on the investment over time.
- Makes participation optional—this leads to more freedom for the worker, but lower participation than in DB plans.
- Can lead to lower returns because workers don't have investment knowledge. Left on their own, people often make investments that are too conservative or too risky.
- May encourage investment in company stock. This puts retirement at risk because it ties the person's salary and pension to the same firm. If the company closes, workers face a double loss. (Many workers lost their jobs and their entire pension savings in the Enron scandal a few years ago.)
- May lead to low pensions due to poor investments or low rates of savings.
- Allows workers to take their money out and spend it if they switch jobs.
- Often has high management and administrative costs. These costs reduce the pension payout.
- Allows employers to reduce or eliminate matching funds in an economic downturn.
- Allows workers to take a lump sum at retirement and spend the money too quickly.
- Can lead to loss of funds if brokers, companies, or planners take advantage of workers' lack of investment knowledge.
- Offers limited pension payout because the law limits the amount that a worker can save in a DC plan.

Defined benefit plans promise a set amount to workers when they retire. These plans often base this figure on a person's salary (often the highest 3 or 5 years) and his or her number of years of service. Most companies, especially large ones, offered defined benefit pension plans in the past. The Pension Benefit Guarantee Corporation (2009b) (PBGC)—the government agency that insures defined benefit plans—reported that more than 44 million workers took part in 29,000 defined benefit pension plans. Full-time, union members show the greatest participation in defined benefit pension plans (U.S. Census Bureau, 2010b).

The Employee Retirement Income Security Act (ERISA) in the mid-1970s attempted to protect workers and provide more secure retirement pensions, but this led to the opposite effect. Due to ERISA's policies, many companies chose to move away from defined benefit programs (Schulz & Borowski, 2006). Rebecca Miller, a pension consultant, told an Internal Revenue Service hearing, "Every time the rules changed, clients say, 'I'm going to junk this thing'" (cited in Schulz & Binstock, 2006, p. 108). Smith, Soto, and Penner (2009) report that defined benefit plan coverage fell from 38% in 1980 to 20% in 2008. AON Consulting (2007, p. 1) says that "more than 168,000 pension plans were terminated between 1975 and 2004."

Some large companies may have started a trend. They no longer pay pension benefits to their management workers. The law allows this because companies have no obligation to offer nonunion employees a pension. Companies may freeze pension plans for managers in order to save money. Workers at these companies can see their pensions drop by hundreds of thousands of dollars. In one case, a 51-year-old manager at IBM saw her pension cut by 25% (Gross, 2006). Some companies in industries such as airlines, steel, or coal have declared bankruptcy and have ended their defined benefit pension plans completely. Gross (2006, p. 10) says, "It's hard not to conclude that defined benefit pensions are under assault."

Many companies (large and small) now opt for **defined contribution plans**. Defined contribution plans say how much workers have to pay into the plan, but they do not guarantee a specific return. The return depends on the investments the worker has made with the money paid in. These programs have spread. Between 1980 and 2008, worker participation in

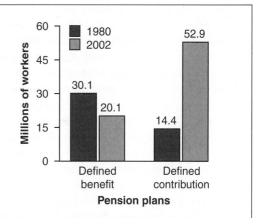

This figure shows the decline in the number of workers (in millions) who have a defined benefit (DB) pension plan. It shows, over the same time period, the increase in the number of workers (in millions) who have a defined contribution (DC) pension plan. The number of workers in DC plans grew by 250% over the 22 years reported here. The number of workers in a DB plan decreased by 33% over this same period. This figures shows that in the past two decades, retirement risk has shifted from employers to workers.

FIGURE 8.5   The Transition from Defined Benefit to Defined Contribution Pension Plans

Source: Based on AON Consulting. (2007). *Retirement and the aging workforce*, p. 2. Citing U.S. Department of Labor. Retrieved June 6, 2010, from www.cfo.com/whitepapers/index.cfm/download/10492691.

defined contribution plans increased from 8% to 31% (Smith et al., 2009). Smith and colleagues (p. 1) say, "This trend is likely to continue in the future."

Defined contribution plans shift pension responsibility to the worker (Herd, 2009). Companies choose defined contribution plans for a number of reasons. First, they find it hard to plan for the costs of defined benefit plans. A company has to make complex and uncertain predictions about workers' life expectancies and about financial markets in the future. Many companies today, in the automobile and airline industries, for example, find it hard to compete because of their pension obligations. EBRI (2009) reports that the proportion of workers in private pension plans who have a defined contribution plan rose from 26% in 1975 to 64% in 2005.

Second, the government regulates defined benefit plans. This gives companies fewer options in how they design and fund these plans. Finally, some companies say that employees prefer defined contribution plans.

The programs vest immediately and workers know exactly how much they have in their accounts. This type of plan appeals to workers who switch jobs often. The savings in the plan goes with the worker when he or she moves from company to company.

Most defined contribution plans take the form of a 401(k) (or 403(b)) program. The Revenue Act of 1978, section 401(k) (and 403(b) for education and nonprofit organizations) allows employees to save money in tax-deferred employer-sponsored savings plans. The company may match some or all of the employees' contributions. The law puts a cap on how much a person can save in a 401(k) (also called a "safe harbor") account each year. In 2009–10, for example, an employee could save up to $16,500. The amount may increase each year according to a price index. Other regulations apply to high-income employees and employees over age 50 (Internal Revenue Service, 2009a; Schulz & Borowski, 2006).

Participation in 401(k) plans has grown since the program started. The U.S. Government Accountability Office (2007) reports that more than 47 million workers belonged to 401(k) programs in 2005 (compared to 7 million in 1983). The EBRI estimates that 417,000 pension plans offered a 401(k) feature (95% of all defined contribution plans in 2005). And total assets in all plans came to $2.5 trillion in 2005.

A 401(k) plan relieves the company of long-term pension obligations, and it makes the worker responsible for the plan's performance. Critics of defined contribution plans say that they create more risk for the worker. Most workers have little financial knowledge and cannot make informed investment decisions (Novelli & Workman, 2006; Schulz & Borowski, 2006). For example, workers tend to put all of their savings into their 401(k) plan. Or they may invest all of their money in their employer's company stock. This leaves them without savings if their company runs into trouble.

Also, workers who manage their own funds may choose riskier investments than they should late in their careers. Many people near retirement lost large amounts of money in the 2000–2002 and 2008 stock market crashes. The EBRI (2009) reports that workers who made regular contributions into their 401(k) plans from 2003 to 2008 saw their savings drop 24.3% on average in the 2008 market crash. Some of them had to postpone retirement to make up for these losses. Schulz and Borowski (2006, p. 368) conclude that "DC [defined contribution] plans place major risk manage-

ment burdens on financially unsophisticated individuals." They go on to say that "adequate education in financial affairs is difficult, if not impossible to find (assuming most people would be willing to take the time to learn)."

Herd (2009) says,

> Finally, there is evidence that employers are decreasing their contributions toward 401(k) plans. In 1997, company contributions toward 401(k) plans as a portion of payroll were 3.2%. By 2001, this proportion had fallen to 2.5% (Munnell & Sundén, 2004). And the recent recession has led employers to suspend or reduce matching contributions for 401(k) plans. Almost fifty large companies, including Ford, General Motors, Motorola, Sprint, Sears, and UPS, suspended their matches (Munnell, 2009).
>
> Another survey of 245 large companies found that 12 percent had cut their matches and another 12 percent planned to do so in the next twelve months (citing Laise, 2009). The responsibility for private pension funding is being transferred even more fully from employers to employees. Reduced subsidization of retirement income is particularly problematic for low earners, who lack resources to save. (p. 14)

Compared to men who retire over the next 15 years, Even and MacPherson (2004) say, women and low-wage workers will have half the 401(k) savings. One economist called defined contribution plans a "lottery ticket" to retirement. The growing emphasis on 401(k) plans creates some problems. In 2004, for example, only 30.2% of workers took part in a 401(k) plan (Copeland, 2007a). And those who do take part in a plan often have only a small amount saved.

Hacker (2006, pp. 122–123) says,

> We are told that the "average" American has tens of thousands of dollars socked away in a 401(k), but in fact roughly three-quarters of account holders have less than the widely cited average of $47,000. The median among account-holders—which is a better measure of what's typical—have around $13,000. And all these figures include only those who *have* 401(k)s. . . . Overall, around 70 percent of defined-contribution pension and IRA assets are held by the richest fifth of Americans. (emphasis in original)

Some companies help their employees make the most of 401(k) options. For example, some companies now automatically enroll employees in their plans. Also, some companies have cut back on the number of plan options. Studies find that having too many choices leads to confusion. A simpler set of choices leads to more participation in a plan. Some companies opt for lifestyle funds that diversify investments and suit the investments to a person's age and time to retirement. And some companies hire advisors to help employees make sound decisions (Boyle, 2005).

Individual Retirement Accounts (IRAs) and Keogh Plans for self-employed people also encourage saving for retirement. These accounts allow people without a company pension plan to save a defined amount of money tax-free each year. For earnings in 2009, the tax-deductible amount came to $5,000 ($6,000 for people age 50 and over). Workers with pension plans can also set up IRAs. They do not get a tax deduction for the amount they put in, but their money gains tax-free interest until they draw it out.

About 23% of all workers in the United States had IRA accounts in 2005 (Copeland, 2008). EBRI reports that in 2005 these accounts held $3.67 trillion (Copeland, 2007b). Copeland (p. 11) says that IRAs will likely be "the largest non-Social Security asset in retirement for many in the next generation of retirees (baby boomers and beyond)." IRA accounts (like 401(k) plans) encourage personal savings for retirement and give workers control over a part of their retirement income.

Still, Copeland (2007b) says, only about 10% of taxpayers who could make use of an IRA account do so. And the average household with a head age 60 and over in 2006 has only a small amount saved. On average a household with a moderate income held just over $52,000 in an IRA account (Smith et al., 2009).

Lower-income earners make less use of this program than people with higher incomes. Schulz and Borowski (2006) report that only 7% of families with incomes under $10,000 had IRA or Keogh accounts. However, two-thirds of families with incomes over $100,000 had these accounts. This means that a large part of the deferred taxes on IRAs go to support the retirement savings of people with high incomes. Critics argue against this type of program because it offers a tax loophole to the wealthy. It also perpetuates inequality in later life. Still, it encourages people at all income levels to save for retirement.

The Cost of Living (a Long Time)

Pension plans for workers in federal and state government jobs (also the military) often have cost-of-living increases built in. These plans adjust to inflation automatically but place caps on the amount of increase. Some private companies adjust pensions periodically. But most private sector pensions (especially defined contribution pensions) drop in value over the years.

According to Schulz, "Almost no employer-sponsored plan in the private sector *automatically* adjusts the pensions being paid in retirement for increases in the cost of living" (2001, p. 263, emphasis in original). He reports that during the high inflation period of 1983 through 1988, for example, private pensions increased by only 10% of the inflation rate. People with defined contribution plans risk the greatest loss of income due to inflation (Schulz, 2001).

Longer life for more workers in the future may mean more years of decreasing pension value due to inflation. Combine this with the choice of early retirement (more years drawing a pension) and some people with private pensions will find that they slip into poverty as they age. (See Figures 8.6 and 8.7.)

Level Three: Personal Assets and Other Income

Financial assets and earnings from work make up the third largest source of income for older people. Schulz (2001) cautions that many people underreport their income and liquid assets (e.g., interest revenue). People with higher incomes tend to underreport the most. This makes it hard to assess the exact incomes of older people from assets and earnings.

Fifty-two percent of older people claimed some asset income in 2007. Older people have three major sources of asset income: (1) savings and checking accounts, (2) financial investments (stocks and bonds), and (3) other investments such as bank deposits, art, or rare collections.

Twenty-five percent of older people report earnings as part of their total income (Administration on Aging, 2009; Wu, 2003). Younger old people (under age 75) tend to have the most income from earnings. Many people in this age group still work part-time. Older-old people (age 75 and over) tend to rely on public pension programs for their income.

Older people also have other sources of income. They include other in-kind government transfers (e.g., Medicaid, Medicare Part D Low-Income Subsidy, Supplemental Nutritional Assistance Program [SNAP]). Some older people get housing subsidies and may get in-kind help from their children. These

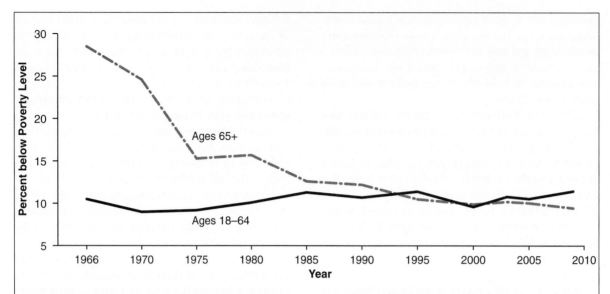

The poverty rate decreased for the younger adult population through the mid-1970s in the United States. It then rose again with some variation to 2009. The poverty rate for people ages 18–64 in 2009 reached the highest level (12.9%) since the mid-1960s. The poverty rate decreased dramatically for older people from 1966 to the mid-1970s. It then continued to decline with some variation to the lowest point (8.9%) on record in 2009. The rate of poverty among older people is two thirds that of adults ages 18–64 today.

This chart excludes the poverty rate for children (under 18 years). That rate came to 20.1% in 2009. This high rate of poverty among children raises the nonelderly poverty rate. This gives older people a significantly lower poverty rate than children and a lower rate than the younger population as a whole.

Munnell, Wu, and Hurwitz (2010), at the Boston College Center for Retirement Research, give three reasons for this decline in poverty among seniors. The government decreased the poverty threshold, provided an "enormous" cost of living adjustment (COLA), and gave seniors a one-time $250 payment.

FIGURE 8.6   U.S. Poverty Rates, by Age, 1966–2003

Source: U.S. Census Bureau. (2010). *Poverty.* Table 3. Poverty status of people, by age, race, and Hispanic origin: 1959 to 2009. U.S. Bureau of the Census, Current Population Survey, Annual Social and Economic Supplements. Retrieved November 20, 2010, from www.census.gov/hhes/www/poverty/data/historical/people.html; DeNavas-Walt, C., Proctor, B. D., & Smith, J. C. (2010). *Income, poverty, and health insurance coverage in the United States: 2009.* U.S. Census Bureau, Current Population Reports, P60-238. Citing U.S. Census Bureau, Current Population Survey, 1960 to 2010 Annual Social and Economic Supplements. Washington, DC. Retrieved: November 20, 2010, from www.census.gov/prod/2010pubs/p60-238.pdf.

resources improve a poor older person's standard of living.

Older people (age 65 and over) also have other assets they cannot quickly convert to cash. These assets provide no income but add to the older person's total wealth. For example, 80.6% of people age 65 and over own their own home. The increase in home equity during the 1990s and early 2000s helped increase the net worth of older homeowners. People ages 65 to 69, for example, saw median home values increase from $100,000 to $140,000 from 1998 to 2004 (Sinai & Souleles, 2007). (The decline in housing values in the mid- to later-2000s led to a reduction in net worth—though housing values in most cases still showed an increase over time.) Nearly half of the total net worth of older households comes from owning a home (Orzechowski & Sepielli, 2003).

In 2007, the group ages 55 to 64 had the highest median net worth in the country ($253,700) followed by the group ages 65 to 74 ($239,400) (U.S. Census Bureau, 2010a). People ages 35 to 44, by comparison, had a net worth of only $86,600. This makes sense because older people, compared with younger people, have had more time to accumulate wealth and assets (including a mortgage-free home). These averages, however, hide large differences in net worth within the older population. Many old people have limited financial resources.

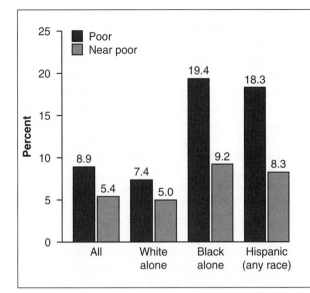

This figure shows that large pockets of poverty exist within the older population. The overall poverty rate for older people is the lowest of all age groups. And it has decreased even during the recent recession. This improvement in economic condition applies to all of the racial and ethnic groups presented here.

Still, as this figure shows, pockets of poverty exist within the older population. Though only 7.4% of whites fall below the poverty line, they make up more than half of all older people in poverty (due to the large size of the white population).

Both blacks and Hispanics have more than twice the poverty rate of whites. And blacks have the highest poverty rate of the three groups. This chart includes figures for people near poverty. The addition of the near poor to poverty figures shows that more than 1 in 4 older minority group members live in poverty or on a very low income.

FIGURE 8.7 Poverty Status, by, Race, and Hispanic Origin, Age 65 and Over, 2009

Note: The near-poor group lives between the poverty line and 125% of the poverty line.

Source: U.S. Census. (2010). *Poverty.* Table 12. Persons 65 and over with incomes below 125 percent of the poverty threshold, and the near poor, by race: 1975 to 2009. U.S. Bureau of the Census, Current Population Survey, Annual Social and Economic Supplements. Retrieved November 20, 2010, from www.census.gov/hhes/www/poverty/data/historical/people.html.

THE IMPACT OF THE RETIREMENT INCOME SYSTEM ON OLDER PEOPLE'S INCOMES

The 1960s and early 1970s saw the greatest improvements in income for older people. Poverty rates for older people dropped by one half, from 28.5% in 1966 to 14.6% in 1974. Families with heads age 65 or over saw a large increase in their incomes during this time (on average an increase from $14,000 to $19,000). What accounts for this improvement in older people's finances?

First, compared to retirees in the past, new retirees had paid into Social Security and pension plans longer. These retirees get better benefits than older retired workers. Second, Congress added a cost-of-living increase to Social Security between 1968 and 1971. This increased benefits by 43%. Prices during this time rose only 27%. Third, the government added another 20% increase to Social Security benefits in 1972.

Older people's finances continued to improve during the late 1970s and 1980s. The poverty rate for older people dropped from 35% in 1959 to 10.2% in 2000. In 2007, older people had a poverty rate lower than all other age groups (9.7% compared with 12.5% for other groups combined) (National Center for Health Statistics, 2009).

Clearly, older people's incomes showed a marked improvement from 1960 to the present. Still, retirement almost always leads to a long-term decline in income, though not necessarily to poverty. Even among relatively well-off older people, Schulz (2001) says, "Many [find] themselves faced with a sharp decline in income relative to their pre-retirement levels and a consequent decline in their living standards" (p. 42).

An example shows the impact of declining income over time. Robert O'Connor worked as a registrar at a university for 26 years. He and his wife planned for retirement. "We took steps to reduce economic problems as far as we could," he says. "We paid off our mortgage, we bought a new car—anything so we could go into retirement as well-equipped as we could."

Still, a drop in their living standard came as soon as he retired. "When I was working, I'd say to my wife, 'Well, come on, where will we go for dinner?' Now we don't go out to eat as much. And when we do go, it's more likely we go to Sizzler's Steak House with a discount coupon than to our favorite restaurant.

"We don't talk much about it. But we've faced a lowering of our social standards. We can't say, 'Let's go back now and look at Scotland.' We say, 'Let's renew our subscription to *Britain in Pictures*.'

"One of the problems when you retire is to build up a small nest egg, but even relatively fortunate people like myself often watch it disappear. Six weeks ago we had to put a roof on our house—$5,000. Last week our washing machine broke down. There we had to dip into our bank account. The time is coming when it's not imprudent to contemplate almost the virtual exhaustion of our savings."

Schulz (2001) reports that in retirement a one-worker couple would need between 68% and 82% of his or her preretirement income to maintain their standard of living. And "only 6 percent to 8 percent of new retired workers replaced at least two-thirds of their highest earnings" (p. 152). Single people, minority group members, and women do less well. A look at inequality in later life will show the impact of retirement on people with different social histories.

INEQUALITY IN LATER LIFE

Overall, older people have better incomes today than in the past. Public pensions, private pensions, and cash and noncash assets have all improved for most older people.

Better public pensions account for much of the income security among the older population today. They ensure a good old age for more people than ever before.

But this good news hides differences within the older age group. For example, the older population shows a more unequal distribution of income than younger age groups (Holden & Hatcher, 2006). Compared to younger groups, the older group tends to have a higher proportion of wealthy members. For example, in 2000, the richest fifth of the older population had a median net worth more than 10 times that of the poorest fifth.

Even here the numbers can hide variations in income. For example, many older people who have a high net worth have little cash. An increase in the value of an older person's home will increase the person's net worth, but he or she still has little money to spend. The person lives house rich and cash poor. If the figures exclude home equity, then the richest fifth has a median net worth of almost 100 times the poorest fifth ($328,432 versus $3,500) (Orzechowski & Sepielli, 2003).

Some groups within the older population have much lower incomes than others. The older group has significant pockets of poverty. Older people have different work histories and different amounts of past

income. They also have different racial, ethnic, and gender backgrounds that shaped their past and influence their present incomes.

Women, compared with men, for example, show higher rates of poverty at every age. But the greatest disparity between men and women shows up in later life. In 2007, older women, compared with older men, had almost twice the rate of poverty (12.0% compared with 6.6%) (U.S. Census Bureau, 2008a).

The oldest-old have the lowest incomes of any older people. Over 12% of people age 85 and over lived in poverty in 2008 compared to 8.4% for people ages 65 to 74 (O'Brien et al., 2010). People with more than one characteristic (e.g., minority women) have an increased chance of poverty. Most poor older people will live in poverty for the rest of their lives.

The economic conditions of older people differ by age, gender, marital status, and minority status. A closer look at these differences gives a better understanding of how income varies within the older population.

Age Differences and Income

The older the person, the greater the chance of a low income. In 2008, families headed by a person age 65 or over had a median income of $29,744, slightly more than half the median income of households with heads under age 65 ($56,791) (DeNavas-Walt, Proctor, & Smith, 2009). But in 2006, families with heads age 75 or over had a median income only 82% of the income of all older people in that year ($24,592) (U.S. Census Bureau, 2007a). People age 75 and over in 2007 had a poverty rate of 10.6%. This was higher than the rate for people ages 65 to 74 (8.8%) (U.S Census Bureau, 2008a).

Poverty figures do not include people who live in institutions or with other relatives. These hidden poor individuals, if counted, would increase the poverty rate of older people. Schulz (2001, p. 17) says, "All evidence to date shows this group (ages 75 to 80 and older) to be economically less well-off than the younger aged."

The young-old and old-old also spend their incomes in different ways. The young-old entered adulthood after World War II and lived more affluent lifestyles. Compared with the oldest-old, for example, the young-old spend more money on travel and restaurant food. This in part reflects their better health, but it also reflects their greater resources. The young-old entered old age with better pensions and have had fewer years to see their pensions decline in value. Also, some new retirees work past the age of 65 to add to their incomes.

Very old people grew up during the Depression and World War II. They have fewer resources than the young-old. Widowhood, poor pensions in the past, and the declining value of fixed pension payments leave the oldest-old to rely mostly on Social Security. Very few can earn money to raise their incomes. Compared with the young-old, the oldest-old spend more money on health care. These expenses can eat up a large share of a very old person's income and savings. This makes the oldest-old vulnerable to cuts in public pension plans and decreases in Medicare or Medicaid benefits.

Gender and Income

A look at income by gender shows that older women have lower incomes than older men. The Administration on Aging (2007a) reports that older women in 2006 had a median income only 58% that of older men. And they had a lower income at every age after age 65. Also, women make up 60% of the older population, but make up 70% of older people in poverty (International Longevity Center and AARP, 2003).

Women who worked outside the home often worked as part-time or temporary help. Generally, these jobs offer low pay and no benefits. Stone (1989) calls this the "feminization of poverty" among older people. Women also report different sources of income than men. A greater proportion of women (46.3%), compared with men (30%), relied on Social

Security for 90% or more of their income (Wu, 2006a). Fifteen percent of women got spousal benefits and 24% got adult survivor benefits. More men than women (82% versus 58%) got retired worker benefits (Institute for Women's Policy Research, 2005).

Men also got larger Social Security pensions than women. These figures point to past inequities between men and women and their different work histories. Many older women today worked as homemakers. They relied on their husbands' incomes during their middle years and now they rely on their husbands' pensions in old age. Women whose husbands had no private pension, widows who no longer receive a spousal private pension, women with small spousal pensions, and the oldest women, whose pensions or savings have lost value with time, have the lowest incomes. They often find themselves in poverty. Many of these women face poverty for the first time in old age.

Older women often have little experience coping with the financial problems they face. They may also have little knowledge of the social welfare system and the programs that might help them. Some women in poverty, for example, could qualify for SSI benefits. But often these benefits go unclaimed because people

This woman retiree in Amsterdam, New York, delivers a newspaper on her afternoon paper route. She uses the money she earns to meet her expenses.

A poor older woman reads a grocery store flyer.

do not know about the program. Or they may not qualify due to strict earnings and asset tests (Meyer, 2010).

This pattern has begun to change as more women work outside the home. In 2009, 59.2% of women worked for pay (or were looking for work), an increase from 37.7% in 1960 (U.S. Department of Labor, 2009). Likewise, more women than ever before claim benefits from their earnings as well as their husbands'.

More women in the future will have their own pensions and Social Security benefits. They will have worked for many years and will have better education than women in the past. This will lead to better-paying jobs and improved incomes for older women (MetLife Mature Market Institute, 2007). More women in the workforce today will lead to a narrower income gap between men and women in old age in the future. But a gap will probably still exist. At least four conditions will lead to lower retirement incomes for women in the future.

First, Social Security bases its benefits on yearly earnings over 35 years. This suits men who spend all their adult years in the labor force. But women often have shorter work careers than men. In 1999, for example, of people who got pensions for the first time, women had 32 years of paid work. Men had 44 years of paid work (International Longevity Center and AARP, 2003).

Many women take time out of the labor force to care for their families. Social Security averages these zero-income years into a woman's lifetime earnings to arrive at 35 years of earnings. This will give her lower average earnings than if she had worked for 35 years or more. Compared with a typical man in the labor force, a woman with these lower earnings will get a smaller pension. Women who care for their families now and in the future will face this same inequity. A projection to the year 2030 found that only one third of women ages 62 to 69 would have a complete work record (Fierst & Campbell, 1988).

Chen (2001) notes that women who rely on their husbands' employment pensions may also face problems. Some of these pension plans stop payments on the death of the retiree. And even in cases where the pension continues, it loses buying power over time.

Second, women tend to work part time and in small businesses. These jobs rarely provide pension plans. Also, a woman who enters and leaves the workforce due to family care will not work long enough to accumulate a large private pension. Women who start their own businesses (a growing trend) seldom have pension plans. This means a woman can work for a

lifetime and still have little or no private pension coverage of her own.

Third, lower pension benefits for retired women reflect the fact that women work in the lowest-paying jobs. This leads to less income, lower Social Security payments, and lower benefits in retirement. The U.S. Department of Labor (2009; U.S. Department of Labor, Women's Bureau, 2007) reports that in 2009, the top 20 occupations for women included secretaries and administrative assistants, registered nurses, cashiers, elementary and middle school teachers, retail salespersons, maids, housekeepers, and nurses. Women made up the majority of workers in these jobs (e.g., 97% of secretaries and 91% of nurses).

Women continue to work in traditionally female occupations and receive low earnings (Women's Institute, 2006). Women in service sector jobs often find they have few or no pension or health benefits. More women today work in managerial or professional jobs. But many of these women worked in lower-paying professions within the professional ranks, such as teachers or registered nurses. They may get pensions, but those pensions are based on relatively low pay.

Fourth, discrimination leads to lower pension benefits for women. Compared to a man in the labor force in 2009, a woman in the labor force, on average, earned only 80% of his salary (U.S. Department of Labor, 2009). Rayman, Allshouse, and Allen (1993, p. 143) traced only one half of the earnings gap to characteristics of workers (such as differences in education or time out of the labor force). Instead, the study found that the income gap is due to "sex discrimination, compounded for older women and women of color by race and age discrimination."

Perkins (1993) agrees. She sorted out the effects of class, race, gender, and age to explain poverty among women in later life. She found that job segregation by sex and discrimination best explained women's low pay. Employers discriminate in hiring, placement, and promotions. The Women's Institute for a Secure Retirement (2006) says that a "typical 25-year-old woman with a college degree in 1984, who is now in her mid 40s, has lost a total of $440,743 in wages over her lifetime—an amount that could add up to a comfortable retirement nest egg."

Perkins (1993) challenges other theories of low pay for women, like the human capital theory. This theory says that women lose their skills when they stay home to raise children. For this reason, the theory says, they get lower pay. Perkins compared African American and white women. She found that African American women spend less time than white women out of the workforce raising children, but they still get low pay due to discrimination at work. Perkins sees poverty in later life as the outcome of unfair practices in the workplace throughout a woman's career.

The effects of past inequality will affect the current generation of older people. But some reports suggest improvements in women's pay. The U.S. Department of Labor (2009) reports that young women ages 16 to 24 get pay equivalent to 93% of young men's pay. If this pattern continues, younger cohorts of women will have better incomes in old age.

Malveaux (1993, p. 168) says, "The economic status of older women is a map or mirror of their past lives, reflecting their education, employment history, and marital status. The economic problems that older women face are extensions of the problems and choices they faced earlier in their lives."

Marital Status and Income

Like married people of all ages, older married couples have lower rates of poverty and better incomes than nonmarried people. Older husband-and-wife families had a median income in 2008 of $43,087. In that same year, single people age 65 and over had a median income of $16,757. In 2008, 1 in 5 older men (20.6%) and 1 in 4 older nonmarried women (27.7%) lived below 125% of the poverty line. In that same year only 7.8% of married couples lived below 125% of the poverty line (Social Security Administration, 2010c).

These figures show, once again, the income gap between married and single older people, and the gap

"If we take a late retirement and an early death, we'll just squeak by."

between older single men and women. They also show the negative effect of widowhood on an older woman's income. Some private pension plans stop when the former employee dies. A widow with only Social Security will get only 71.5% of her husband's pension benefits if his benefits began at age 60.

In addition, a husband's illness can deplete the couple's resources. This can lead the surviving spouse into poverty even though the couple lived a comfortable life. McGarry and Schoeni (2005) found that lower income and higher costs accounted for most of the difference between married and widowed older people. The younger the age of people at widowhood and the longer they live as widows, the greater the chance of poverty (Sevak, Weir, & Willis, 2004). Gillen and Kim (2009, p. 320) say that "widowhood greatly decreases income from every source."

Compared to widows, divorced older women have fewer financial safeguards. For example, a divorced older woman has a legal claim on a former husband's defined benefit pension plan. But she has no legal right to control how a former husband's 401(k) plan gets paid. This puts her at risk of poverty even after many years as a partner in this savings plan. "A woman can wind up losing her share of her spouse's pension if she is unaware of her rights, has an uninformed attorney, or a judge who is not familiar with the division of pensions" (Women's Institute, 2006). The Social Security Administration says that among older women, the proportion of never-married and divorced single women will double by the year 2030. This will put a large group of older women at risk of losing their retirement security (Women's Institute, 2006).

Couples have higher incomes than an unmarried person for at least three reasons. First, some couples benefit from having had two incomes for all or part of their married life. This allowed for more savings and in some cases two pensions. Second, in the case of a two-earner couple, the couple can get the highest earner's Social Security benefits. The spouse of the pensioner then gets 50% of that benefit as a spousal pension. Third, widows make up a large proportion of single older people. They often experience a decrease in income after a spouse's death (Women's Institute, 2006).

Couples and single older people will have better incomes in the future due to Social Security and better private pension plans today. But differences due to marital status will still exist. In part, this will occur because the married group includes younger old people. They will enter old age with more resources, and

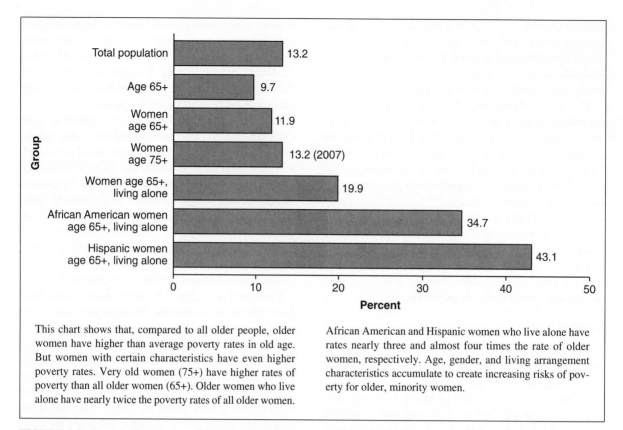

This chart shows that, compared to all older people, older women have higher than average poverty rates in old age. But women with certain characteristics have even higher poverty rates. Very old women (75+) have higher rates of poverty than all older women (65+). Older women who live alone have nearly twice the poverty rates of all older women.

African American and Hispanic women who live alone have rates nearly three and almost four times the rate of older women, respectively. Age, gender, and living arrangement characteristics accumulate to create increasing risks of poverty for older, minority women.

FIGURE 8.8   Poverty Rates Among Selected Vulnerable Groups, Percent of Population in Poverty, 2008

Sources: Administration on Aging. (2009). *A profile of older Americans: 2009.* U.S. Census Bureau, Current Population Survey, Annual Social and Economic Supplement, 2008. Retrieved November 20, 2010, from www.aoa.gov/AoARoot/Aging_Statistics/Profile/2009/10.aspx; Federal Interagency Forum on Aging-Related Statistics. (2010). *Older Americans 2010: Key indicators of well-being.* Table 7b. Percentage of the population age 65 and over living in poverty, by selected characteristics, 2007, p. 82. Washington, DC.

some will work in their early retirement years. Older unmarried people will include very old, widowed women who live alone. These women will rely on public sources of income in the future. These sources have improved in recent years but still provide relatively low benefits. (See Figure 8.8.)

Minority Status and Income

Minority older people have lower incomes than non-Hispanic whites. Households headed by African American persons age 65 and over had a median income in 2008 of $35,025. This came to about three quarters of the median income for all older households ($44,188).

The median income of African American men came to $19,161 in that year, about two thirds the income for all older men ($25,503). African American women show a similar pattern. They reported a median

income of $12,499 compared to $14,559 for all older women (Administration on Aging, 2010b).

Households headed by Hispanic persons age 65 and over had a median income in 2008 of $33,418. This came to about 70% of the median income for all non-Hispanic whites. The Administration on Aging (2008c) reports that 16% of older Hispanic households had an income of less than $15,000 (compared to only 5.4% of non-Hispanic white households).

Wong (2002) says that migration patterns (how long a person has lived in the United States) affect the incomes of Mexican older migrants. She found that those who had lived in the United States longest had the highest individual and household incomes (although they had a low rate of health care coverage).

The Women's Institute for a Secure Retirement (2000) reports that "only 15 percent of older black women and 8 percent of Hispanic older women received [private] pension income in 2000." Housell and Riojas (2006, p. 7) say that "despite an overall decline in poverty levels for elders in recent decades . . . more than 40% of African American and Latina women who live alone have incomes below the federal poverty line, compared with 17.9% of single, older white women and only about 10% of elderly white men."

According to the Women's Institute for a Secure Retirement (2000), in 2000 only "38 percent of black women, 26 percent of Hispanic women and 38 percent of Asian/Pacific Islander women [were] covered by any sort of pension in the workplace." Minority women tend to rely on Social Security for their income in later life. Wu (2006a) reports that 48.6% of older Hispanic and 43.8% of older African American Social Security recipients got all of their income from Social Security (compared with 20.3% of older white people). Social Security provides minority older people with a basic income and tends to level racial and ethnic income differences in later life. But it also provides only a basic income that provides little extra for luxuries or emergencies.

Minority members bear a higher burden of poverty in old age than do whites. African American and Hispanic American older people in 2007 had a poverty rate of 23.2% and 17.1%, respectively—more than two-and-a-half times the white rate of 7.4% (National Center for Health Statistics, 2009; O'Brien et al., 2010). A longitudinal study tracked the economic status of women in their retirement years (Sunhwa & Shaw, 2008). The study found that African American women had three times the poverty rate of white women (42% compared to 14%). Compared to white women in this study, African American women also had fewer assets.

Older minority women who live alone have more than three times the poverty rate of those who live with families. Older Hispanic women who live alone face the highest poverty rates (47.1%) (Administration on Aging, 2003). For many of these women, poverty in later life reflects a lifetime of disadvantage. Chapter 7 gives more detail on inequalities in later life due to race and ethnicity.

The U.S. government reports data on poverty rates in later life for African Americans, whites, and Hispanics, but few data exist on Asian older people. Asian Americans have higher median incomes than whites, but they have a poverty rate in old age about one and a half times that of whites (11.3%) (National Center for Health Statistics, 2009). Some studies report higher poverty rates among groups within the Asian community.

Reeves and Bennett (2004), for example, report that Hmong and Cambodians have the highest poverty rates among Asian minority group members (37.8% and 29.3%, respectively). The Vietnamese, Laotian, and Pakistani groups all have poverty rates over 15%. These high rates will translate into low incomes in later life. Older Asian women who outlive their husbands face unique challenges. These widows often have little education and speak little English. They have trouble applying for programs such as SSI, and few of them have private pensions. This puts them at risk of poverty.

Older African American women worked in a double employment ghetto. They worked in typically female jobs and in typically African American female jobs such as dietitian, file clerk, lab technician, and cleaning and health service worker (Women's Institute, 2000). These jobs pay low wages and offer poor pension benefits.

The income gap between older African American and white women may decrease in the future. African American women have begun to take on jobs in administration and management. These jobs offer pension plans and health insurance. Still, discrimination exists and an income gap between older African American and white women will probably remain.

A study by the Administration on Aging (2003) summarized the effect of gender, race, and ethnicity on income in later life. The study found that older women had a higher poverty rate (12.4%) than older men (7.7%) in 2002. Older persons living alone were much more likely to be poor (19.2%) than were older persons living with families (6.0%). The highest poverty rates (47.1%) were experienced by older Hispanic women who lived alone.

A person with more than one of these characteristics faces a high risk of poverty. These facts and others call for pension reform that focuses on the income needs of poorer older people.

Further Effects of Poverty

Government programs now keep more than 90% of older people out of poverty. But those who live in poverty, regardless of their ethnicity, race, or gender, face common problems.

For example, poor people have worse health than the nonpoor. They have more chronic illnesses and more disability. They also spend more money on health care than nonpoor older people. O'Brien and colleagues (2010) say that in 2006 a poor older person on average spent nearly one fifth (19.6%) of their income on health care. A wealthy person (with an income over four times the poverty level) spent only 6.1% of their income on health care. Half of poor older people face unaffordable health care costs (more than 20% of their income).

Poor older people also spend more on housing than their nonpoor age mates. More than two fifths (40.6%) live in rental housing. On average a poor household in 2008 spent 60% of their income on housing. This makes housing unaffordable for more than half of poor households. A high proportion of poor older people live alone (58%). This subgroup of the older poor bears the full cost of their housing (O'Brien et al., 2010).

In 2008 nearly a quarter (22.1%) of low-income older households (with incomes below 130% of the poverty line) lived "food insecure." They faced an uncertain supply of healthy and safe food. Poor older people have few assets to buffer the costs of food and housing. Excluding the value of their homes, in 2005, a poor older person on average had only $5,310 in assets. People at the upper end of the poverty scale had on average $29,355 in assets. Those with bank accounts or other assets can use them to meet basic needs. Those without savings face hardship (O'Brien et al., 2010).

Many writers propose measures to close the poverty gap between an older family's income and the federal poverty level. An end to poverty in old age would require increases in Supplemental Security Income (SSI), increases in Social Security payments, better health insurance, and more affordable housing, among other policy reforms. O'Brien and colleagues (2010) say that it would have cost $12.3 billion in 2008 to raise all older people to the federal poverty line. This would cost $3,350 per older poor person. This would come to almost three times the cost of Supplemental Security Income (SSI) for that year, and almost twice the cost of the federal subsidy for Medicare Part B.

These changes seem unlikely at this time. Critics of government programs already propose decreases in support for the elderly. O'Brien and colleagues (2010, p. 57) say that in the current environment, "there is a risk that budget reform will increase rather than decrease the number of older adults living below the poverty line." Reforms should at least protect the poorest older adults from further hardship.

PENSION REFORM

"The key to reducing poverty in old age," gerontologist Beth Hess said, "is to eliminate income disabilities at earlier life stages. If affirmative action for women, blacks, and Hispanics ensured equal opportunities for education, jobs, and promotions throughout their lives, they would enter old age with a more secure income base and higher pension entitlements than is now the case" (1987, p. 532). Reports on income and inequality in later life continue to support Hess's comment. The need for pension reform points to the need for societal reform. Pay equity, an end to segregation of women in low-paying jobs, and an end to racial discrimination would all create better pensions for minority older people. Pension reform can at least try to make up for some of these inequities.

Social Security Reform

Social Security forms the bedrock of income for older people today. People who worked outside the labor force (e.g., homemakers) or people who had low-paying jobs rely almost entirely on Social Security payments. Wu (2003, p. 27) says that "nearly 38 percent of Social Security beneficiaries receive 90 percent or more of their income from Social Security." This figure increases to 59% of poor older people (O'Brien et al., 2010). See Figure 8.9.

Increases in Social Security benefits and indexing Social Security to the cost of living account for the decrease in poverty among the older population in recent years. Wu (2006b, p. 55) estimates that "without Social Security benefits, the poverty rate would increase from 9.8% to 47.9% for all older persons and from 11.4% to 59% for those age 80 and older."

This makes Social Security reform a key to ensuring a strong pension system in the future.

The current system assumes that older people fall into two types: single workers or married couples. And it assumes that married couples consist of a worker (usually the husband) and an unpaid homemaker. Schulz (2001, p. 157) says that "the social security benefit structure reflects a pattern of marital life and family obligations which is no longer typical in the United States." For example, most women now work for at least part of their middle years and many women now enter old age divorced or separated.

Also, women have a widowhood rate in later life five times that of older men. And an older woman married less than 10 years and divorced gets no spouse's or widow's Social Security pension. Social Security needs to create a set of policies that reflect the reality of marriage today and women's current work patterns and careers. The following reforms

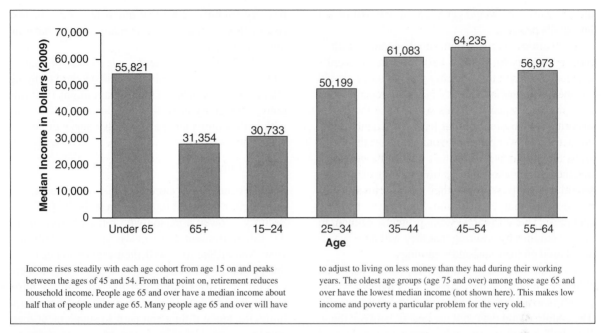

Income rises steadily with each age cohort from age 15 on and peaks between the ages of 45 and 54. From that point on, retirement reduces household income. People age 65 and over have a median income about half that of people under age 65. Many people age 65 and over will have to adjust to living on less money than they had during their working years. The oldest age groups (age 75 and over) among those age 65 and over have the lowest median income (not shown here). This makes low income and poverty a particular problem for the very old.

FIGURE 8.9   Median Income of Households

Source: DeNavas-Walt, C., Proctor, B. D., & Smith, J. C. (2010). *Income, poverty, and health insurance coverage in the United States: 2009.* Income and earnings summary measures by selected characteristics: 2008 and 2009, Table 1, p. 5. U.S. Census Bureau, Current Population Reports, P60-238. Citing U.S. Census Bureau, Current Population Survey, 1960 to 2010 Annual Social and Economic Supplements. Washington, DC: U.S. Government Printing Office. Retrieved November 20, 2010, from www.census.gov/prod/2010pubs/p60-238.pdf.

would bring Social Security policies in line with a woman's life course today.

Family Care

The current Social Security system gives no credit to homemakers who spend years and sometimes a lifetime out of the labor force. These people, mostly women, either have no Social Security pension of their own in later life or have to depend on their spouse's pension. Women who spend some time as a homemaker and then enter the labor force get a smaller pension because they have smaller lifetime earnings.

Some authors (Malveaux, 1993; Rix, 1993) propose a dropout allowance of 10 years. This would allow a homemaker (or other type of family caregiver) to drop these years in the calculation of average yearly earnings. This dropout allowance would recognize a woman's role as family caregiver and would increase her pension in retirement. A lower-cost version of this policy could apply this 10-year dropout allowance only to people with low incomes.

A more costly approach to improved pensions for homemakers would provide them with **homemaker credits**. A person would get credits based on an estimated income for this work. Either this plan could pay

pensions out of general revenue, or homemakers could pay into the plan.

Countries such as Japan, the United Kingdom, and Germany allow homemakers to contribute to the government pension plan. Disagreement exists over how to finance this option in the United States and how much homemakers should get. Still, this proposal points to the value of women's work and the lack of recognition it receives.

Spousal Pensions

A married woman who paid into Social Security, but whose benefits come to less than one half of her husband's, will get benefits based on her husband's pension. She will get 50% of her spouse's income (or an amount to bring her pension up to 50% of her husband's amount if she has a small pension of her own). A woman who has a pension greater than half of her husband's pension will get her own pension amount.

The Social Security Administration gives an example of this. If a wife worked and will receive a Social Security pension of $850 per month and her husband worked and will receive a Social Security pension of $1,450 per month, they will each get their own pensions (Social Security Administration, 2004e). If she did not work, she would get $725, or one half of her husband's pension.

Some critics say the system should do away with or reduce benefits for women based on the husband's pension. They say that working women today should get their own Social Security pensions regardless of their husband's pension. This would save the Social Security system money on at least two counts. First, women with lower pensions would not have their pensions topped up at half of their husband's pensions. Second, homemaker spouses of wealthier pensioners would not get pensions of their own. Critics of this proposal say that it would hurt women who had low incomes. The current system protects women in poorer families by ensuring that they will have a pension based on their husband's earnings.

Some authors suggest a pension policy based on shared earnings (Schulz, 2001). This method would pool a married couple's benefits into a total benefit. The couple would then split the benefit between them. One half would go to each spouse in the case of divorce or widowhood. This would give homemakers an earnings record they could draw on regardless of divorce.

This policy would cost more than the present policy. Also, it would mostly benefit two-earner couples and divorced women. It might disadvantage some people, like widows and divorced men (Rix, 1993). Some version of this plan might arise in the future as more working women lobby for a change in the current policy. But at present even supporters of the idea worry that it would increase benefits to some, while decreasing benefits to others.

Another proposal, one that would follow the German model, suggests that homemakers get direct coverage and benefits. This would recognize the work of homemaking as a contribution to a family's and society's economic well-being. This proposal would cost more money. And given current concerns about the national debt, any increase in Social Security costs will get little support in Congress.

Widows' Benefits

When a retired worker dies, the spouse loses the spousal benefit and gets only the full worker's benefit. This means that a surviving spouse will continue to get only two-thirds of the predeath income. But economists say that a single person needs about 80% of a couple's income to maintain his or her standard of living. The decrease in income after widowhood can throw a surviving spouse into poverty (Schulz, 2001). Women face the greatest risk of this decrease because many women have no other pension income.

Social Security needs to provide a better pension to widows to help them maintain their standard of living after a spouse's death. The program might fund this policy change by providing smaller spousal benefits with both spouses alive and a higher survivor benefit when one spouse dies.

Income Limits

Social Security puts earnings limits on retirees who retire before their full retirement age. In 2010, Social Security allowed a person who retired before his or her full retirement age to earn up to $14,160 in a year. Social Security will then reduce benefits for this person $1 for every $2 earned above this amount (Social Security Online, 2010h). This policy hurts people who had low incomes in the past because it limits the amount they can earn to supplement their pension.

This policy ignores the fact that women, for example, get 25% lower Social Security benefits on average than men. They also have smaller personal savings and less likelihood of a private pension than a man. This policy forces some women to limit their income if they retire before their full retirement age and want to collect a Social Security pension.

Social Security could raise the earnings limit to help people keep more of their earnings. Or it could allow no limit for people who have low pensions because they did little or no paid work in the past due to family care.

Schulz (2001) says "the biggest obstacle to social security reform for women is the inability to devise a reform plan at reasonable cost without lowering benefits for some retirees." Ross and Upp (1993, cited in Schulz, 2001), two experienced policy researchers, note that "these conflicts [between different group needs] appear insoluble." Still, Social Security needs to adapt to current social conditions (e.g., divorce, widowhood, women's pay, and caregiving).

Supplemental Security Income Reform

Critics of SSI point to three problems with the program. First, its benefits do not bring people up to the poverty line; second, state supplements vary widely; and third, the program enrolls only about half the people eligible. This leads to varied levels of support across the country.

Improved Benefits

Federal SSI payments now ensure an income of only about 75% of the poverty line for the poorest older people (Social Security Online, 2010e; Administration for Children & Families, 2010). A panel created to review the SSI program recommended increased benefits to bring all older people to at least the poverty line. The panel also recommended that the Social Security Administration increase the amount of assets a person can have and still get SSI benefits.

A person with a life insurance policy with a face value of $2,500, for example, would top the SSI minimum asset allowance. But this person would get little cash income from this policy. This type of asset leaves them in poverty and with no SSI help. An increase in the allowance for assets would open SSI to more low-income people.

Improve State Supplements

States differ in the SSI supplements they give. For example, in 2010, the monthly federal and New York state SSI payment added $761 to Social Security for poor people who live alone; an eligible person living alone in California would receive $845 (Social Security Online, 2010f,g).

These differences reflect local conditions, such as the cost of living in each state. But supplements also reflect the state economy and the local political climate. State benefits can get cut more easily than federal benefits. This puts poor older people, especially minorities, at risk of reduced income. More stable and generous state SSI supplements would provide a better income to poor older people.

Higher Enrollment Rates

All people below the poverty line can receive SSI and Medicaid coverage. Unfortunately, about 40% of people eligible for SSI do not take part in the program (Schulz, 2001). Many of these people have never heard of SSI. Others believe they have to give up their homes or stop working to get SSI payments. The paperwork puts off frail older people and those who speak a language other than English. And many people avoid SSI because it links them to poverty.

The Administration on Aging has increased outreach to older people eligible for SSI. It has funded outreach projects, including a computerized screening program to match people with programs and a toll-free number to take applications by phone. But even a direct letter from the Social Security Administration encouraging people to apply led to only a 3% response (Schulz, 2001).

The asset test associated with SSI keeps many older people from getting SSI benefits. Most poor older people have few assets. But, Schulz (2001, p. 239) says, "The asset test for SSI is so stringent that some people with inadequate incomes are denied assistance because of small amounts of savings and other resources." A less stringent test would allow more poor older people to take advantage of SSI.

Private Pension Reform

Private pensions also need reform. In 2008, for example, only about half of all workers in the United States (51%) had private pension coverage. This means that about half of all workers at that time gained no pension credits other than Social Security. IRAs, 401(k)s, and other defined contribution plans have not closed this gap (Schulz & Borowski, 2006).

The higher a person's income, the more likely they are to have a pension. The U.S. Bureau of Labor Statistics reports that 68% of people in white-collar jobs have a company pension plan, and 52% of blue-collar craft and repair workers have company pensions. But in service jobs, only one quarter of all workers paid into a pension plan (U.S. Census Bureau, 2010d).

The data show that poorer people in low-paying jobs tend not to have pensions. Low-income workers tend to work for smaller companies, work part time, and have less money to pay into a pension plan. This forces them to rely almost entirely on Social Security. And this leads to low income in retirement. The government never intended the Social Security system to serve as a full replacement for preretirement income.

An expansion of private pensions to more workers will provide a better income for older people. But pension plan expansion seems unlikely at present. Many companies have cut back on pension programs or have shifted to defined contribution plans. This shift from defined benefit to defined contribution plans will put more responsibility for retirement savings on individual workers. And it will increase the risk of low retirement incomes for workers.

At the least, the government needs to continue its oversight of private pensions (through the Employee Retirement Income Security Act—ERISA). This helps ensure that those people who pay into a company pension plan will get a pension when they retire.

Vesting

Vesting refers to an employee's entitlement to his or her pension payments plus the payments of the employer. Pension plans often require 5 or 10 years of employment for full vesting. The federal government, through the ERISA of 1974, ensures that workers will have access to their pensions through vesting. But a long vesting period works against workers who change jobs often, who lose their jobs, or who take time out for family care. A worker can work for a lifetime in a variety of jobs and still have no vested pension funds. The federal government could legislate a shorter vesting period. This would ensure that more workers get their full pension entitlements at retirement.

Portability and Indexing

Most private pension plans lack **portability**. Lack of portability limits a worker's ability to change jobs and can limit the pension a person gets in retirement. Portability requires cooperation between employers with different pension plans. Given the number of plans and their different policies, portability proves difficult. Portability will probably not increase in the near future.

Few pension plans index payments to the cost of living. But indexing pensions would protect workers from inflation. This would cost workers more money when they pay into a plan, but it would ensure a better pension in retirement.

Better Private Plan Insurance

Another cloud sits on the pension horizon: underfunded pensions. Companies often place their retirement funds in the hands of insurance companies. These insurers invest the money and guarantee the company's retirees a pension for life. Most insurance companies take modest risks for stable returns, but some have taken extreme risks with this money. They have invested in junk bonds and unsound real estate deals. Executive Life, a company in California, lost retirement fund money that left thousands of people with smaller pensions than they had expected (Malveaux, 1993).

Underfunded pension plans have too little money in them to pay their workers' pensions in the future. The federal government set up the Pension Benefit Guaranty Corporation (PBGC) under ERISA to insure private defined benefit pension plans. People in these plans would look to the PBGC for help if a pension plan could not pay benefits.

Revell (2003) reports that pension plans owe $1.2 trillion in benefits to current and future retirees. But they fall short by $240 billion in meeting these commitments. The millions of people in these plans would look to the PBGC for help if a pension plan could not pay benefits.

The PBGC covers more than 44 million workers in 29,000 pension plans (Pension Benefit Guaranty Corporation, 2010a). But the PBGC has faced deficits for 29 of its 35 years. Company closures and bankruptcies created deficits that congress acted to cover.

But the PBGC faces rough times ahead. For example, low interest rates and the weak economy in 2009 led to the collapse of 144 private-sector plans (compared to 67 plans in 2008). In 2009, the PBGC declared a deficit of $22 billion (about twice the 2008 deficit of $11.2 billion).

The PBGC's annual report in 2009 also projected a $1.64 billion cost in the future from 27 large pension plans that could fail. Its exposure to losses increased from $47 billion in 2008 to $168 billion in 2009 (Pension Benefit Guaranty Corporation, 2009). This has led some critics to call for review of the PBGC's future solvency. There have also been calls for action to shore up the PBGC's role as guarantor of defined benefit pension plans (Healey, 2010).

A person who gets pension help from the PBGC may get less than they hoped for. For example, in 2010 the PBGC paid only up to $54,000 per year (for a 65-year-old) if a company fails and cannot pay its pensions. Some people will get much less than this. A 55-year-old would get only $24,300 (Pension Benefit Guaranty Corporation, 2010b). Underfunded pension plans, even with PBGC insurance to back them up, will lead to pension losses for many people.

ERISA required that companies have enough funds to pay workers' pensions, but it gave companies 30 years to meet this requirement. Some of these companies will close before they can meet their pension obligations. Unless reform takes place, many workers will find themselves with less income than they expect, and the taxpayers will have to bail out pensions through the PBGC.

The PBGC wants the law to require employers to have the funds in place to meet workers' future pensions. But legal requirements for companies to fully fund plans (within, say, 7 years) could have a paradoxical effect. It will provide more security for workers in companies that abide by this legislation. But it will also encourage companies to move to defined contribution plans or no plans at all. These options will give workers even less security (Gross, 2006).

The U.S. retirement income system provides a decent standard of living for most older people and keeps most of the poorest older people out of poverty. But financial analyst Harold Evensky (2005, p. 42) says that the three-legged stool no longer exists. "Social Security is questionable. Defined-benefit pensions are not going to be there. And as a country we have very little in personal savings." He goes on to say that "a lot of baby-boomers are not going to be able to afford to retire, but instead of saying they can't afford it, they are going to redefine it as a positive, to keep working." Each part of the retirement income system needs improvement. These improvements will help people in the most need now, and they will ensure a better old age for everyone in the future.

THE FUTURE

Weinstein (1988, p. 7) called retirement at the end of the last century the "golden age of the golden years." This golden age in part reflects planning and hard work by older people in the past, but it also reflects economic growth in the years after World War II, a low dependency ratio, and improved pensions. All of this could change in the future. Already, politicians and policy analysts project hard times ahead for future generations of older people.

Will the Social Security program go broke as some critics claim? Will today's workers have a pension to count on when they retire? The OASDI trust fund had a surplus of $2.4 trillion in 2009. And the fund expects to grow to $3.9 trillion at the start of 2018 (OASDI, 2009). The trustees of the Social Security trust funds say that the funds "are adequately financed over the next ten years."

But the system pays out money as it comes in (a pay-as-you-go system). And this system will face problems in the future. The large size of the Baby Boom generation, a low birth rate with smaller numbers of workers, and people living longer than ever before will all strain the Social Security system. The OASDI Trustees say that if income and benefits continue at the expected rate, then by the year 2016, Social Security will need to dip into its surplus. And by 2037, the surplus will be gone. The program will be unable to make its payments as promised. This could lead to a 27% reduction in benefits for retirees from 2037 onward. Unless the system brings in more funds, by the year 2079, benefits could be as low as two thirds of promised benefits.

The Social Security Administration sums up the problem: "Social Security is not sustainable over the long term at present benefit and tax rates without large infusions of additional revenue. There will be a massive and growing shortfall over the 75-year period [2004–2079]" (Social Security Administration, 2004d; Board of Trustees, 2011). Social Security's Chief Actuary projects a $4.6 trillion shortfall over the next 75 years.

The Social Security Trustees and other government experts, such as the Chairman of the Federal Reserve Board, say that we need to make changes now. The independent, bipartisan Social Security Advisory Board has said, "As time goes by, the size of the Social Security problem grows, and the choices available to fix it become more limited" (Social Security Administration, 2004d).

The trustees' report for 2009 (OASDI Board of Trustees, 2009) urges immediate action. They say, "The projected trust fund deficits should be addressed in a timely way so that necessary changes can be phased in gradually and workers can be given time to plan for them. Implementing changes sooner will allow their effects to be spread over more generations."

Bill Novelli, former executive director of the AARP, says,

> The system is neither broke nor broken. It does not need a radical overhaul. What it needs are reasonable, incremental adjustments to make it solvent and maintain guaranteed benefits of future generations . . . "Wait and see" and "muddle through" are not good strategies, whether you're managing a business, raising a family, pursuing a career, or working to make your community and country a better place. (Novelli & Workman, 2006, pp. 79 and 234)

The report of the OASDI Board of Trustees (2009) says that "with informed discussion, creative thinking, and timely legislative action, present and future Congresses and Presidents can ensure that Social Security continues to protect future generations." The Trustees proposes four actions that the system needs to take immediately:

1. The system needs to immediately and permanently increase payroll taxes by 14.4%; or
2. The system needs to immediately and permanently reduce benefits by 13.3%; or
3. The government could transfer funds from the general fund to cover Social Security costs; or
4. Some combination of these actions.

If the government waits until 2037, then Social Security will need more drastic changes to keep it solvent. For example, payroll taxes will need to increase to 16.26% of wages in 2037 and will increase to 16.74% in 2083. Or the system could reduce benefits by 24% to 26% from 2037 onward. Making adjustments sooner creates a smoother transition to the future (OASDI Board of Trustees, 2009).

Some writers propose further changes to the system. Schulz and Binstock (2006), for example, favor increases in the normal retirement age as life expectancy increases. They propose small reductions in the annual cost-of-living increases. And they would raise the ceiling on the payroll tax. This would increase revenue from more affluent workers. They would shift revenues from estate taxes to cover Social Security obligations. Schulz and Binstock also propose that the government put changes in place gradually in order to gain public support.

These and other proposals show that modest and timely changes to Social Security policies can create a stable system into the future. All reforms will need political action. This will mean enlisting the support of interest and lobby groups as well as legislators. The path to a strong Social Security system seems clear. We need to start on this path now.

CONCLUSION

Critics of the public pension system today say that public pensions cost too much. They warn that a large older population will lead to higher costs in the future. And they say that these costs will burden the younger generation with an increased national debt. But other policy analysts believe that action today to reform the system can forestall a crisis in the future. Most workers, young and old, will benefit from a strong (if more costly) public pension system.

Today and in the future, older people will rely on the Social Security system for their well-being. In 2009, Social Security served 52 million beneficiaries (young and old) and 160 million workers and their families. Social Security programs provide a safety net for the poorest older people. Some of these people have no other source of income. Social Security led to the large decrease in poverty rates among older people since the 1960s. Even young people today benefit from the OASDI disability and survivor pension benefits.

The current climate of retrenchment in policies for older people leads to uncertainty and doubt among all generations. Meyer (2010, p. 36) says that "preoccupation with shifting risk and responsibility from the government onto individuals has prompted U.S.

policy makers to reshape the old age welfare state." These changes, she goes on to say, dilute "the protective features of welfare state programs" and increase inequality that already exists due to gender, race, and marital status.

An AARP study (2010) found that two thirds of the people surveyed showed a lack of confidence in the future of Social Security (though 92% of adults consider Social Security an "important government program" or one of the "very most important government programs"). Alice Rivlin (2010), a member of the President's Commission on Fiscal Responsibility and Reform, says "the right reason for saving Social Security is to reassure all Americans that this hugely successful program is solidly funded and will be there for the millions who depend on it when they need it." A strong Social Security system provides a safety net for older people and their families.

Better private pensions have also improved the standard of living of older people. The combination of private pensions, income and savings, and Social Security can replace as much as 50% to 80% of income after retirement. People with these resources have many housing and lifestyle options. A national survey of attitudes toward aging, for example, shows that the general public appreciates the importance of a strong pension system.

Still, the United States retirement income system needs reform. Many older people live in or near poverty. Cutler and colleagues (2002) found that 76% of older whites had saved for later life, compared with only 43% of African Americans. And about 40% of older whites considered money a problem, compared with over 60% of older African Americans.

Women, minorities, and very old people make up a high proportion of poor older people. People with broken work records or women who worked in the home may not get enough from Social Security to keep them out of poverty. These people rarely have private pensions, and they get poorer as they age. Minority members run the greatest risk of poverty in old age.

Gerontologists and economists have proposed reforms for each part of the retirement income system. Reforms include increased payments into the Social Security system to prepare for more retired people in the future and better benefits for family caregivers, homemakers, and widows. Private pensions could offer better portability and vesting. They could also cover more workers. The government needs to help guard against the misuse of pension funds and corporate defaults on pension payments.

A strong retirement income system will benefit everyone (Myles, 2010). Older people will live free of the fear of poverty and will have more resources to enjoy old age. Younger people can feel secure that their parents will have enough resources to live on. And younger people can look forward to a good income in their own old age.

The United States will have to make changes in its public pension program. But it should support a balanced approach to pension planning that includes a strong public pension system as well as private pensions and savings. If the government and people adopt this approach, the country can enter the future without a crisis in its retirement income system.

SUMMARY

- Controversy exists over the cost of federal retirement income programs for older people. Some writers think that the high cost of federal old-age pensions leads to less money and fewer programs for other age groups. These writers propose reduced funding for programs that serve older people. Other writers argue against reduced funding. They say that the public pension system accounts for improvements in older people's financial well-being. And poorer people, who gain the most from a strong public pension system, would suffer the most if the government cuts funding.

- In the early 1900s, both the change to an industrial society and the Great Depression created an economic crisis. This left many older people jobless and destitute. In response to these conditions, the federal government passed the Social Security Act. It established a social insurance program that protected workers from unemployment and gave people some income in retirement.

- The U.S. retirement income system consists of a combination of public and private income sources. These include Social Security benefits, personal savings and assets, and employment pensions.

- Social Security benefits ensure that all workers and their families will have at least a basic income in retirement. This program removed the threat of poverty from millions of older Americans.

- Older people's finances improved during the 1960s and 1970s. This came about because (1) new retirees had paid into Social Security for a longer time than retirees in the past, (2) Congress added cost of living increases to Social Security benefits, and (3) in 1972 the government increased benefits by 20%.

- Research shows that rich and poor older people differ in more than the amount of money they have. The sources of their income differ as well. The poorest older people rely heavily on public sources of support. Wealthier older people receive less than one fifth of their income from public support. They get most of their income from private sources. A government policy that cuts public pension benefits hurts the poorest older people most.

- Some policy analysts propose individual retirement accounts as an alternative to Social Security. This option gained some attention prior to 2008, when the economy took a downturn. Individual accounts place more risk on the individual. Poor investments or a stock market decline could leave many people with little or no retirement income. This option has lost support given the recent declines in stock market values and the losses many people experienced in their stock portfolios.

- Many companies have moved from defined benefit to defined contribution plans. These plans reduce the exposure of the companies to high pension costs in the future. But they put the responsibility on the worker to ensure good returns on invested pension savings. This increases the risk of poor pensions for workers.

- Age, gender, marital status, and minority status all affect retirement income in later life. African American and Hispanic American elders, for example, have many times the poverty rate of whites in old age. A lifetime of inequality for minority group members explains these differences in later life.

- The government needs to create a new set of Social Security policies that reflect changes in the life course today. Reforms would include changes in family care policies, spousal pensions, widows' benefits, and income standards. In addition, private pension rules that govern vesting, portability, and pension plan insurance all need reform.

- The Social Security system needs to change its policies now in order to remain solvent in the future. The system can increase revenue, reduce benefits, or transfer funds from the federal General Fund. It could also raise the retirement age for full benefits and make a number of small adjustments to current policies. The sooner the system puts changes in place, the milder the impact on retirees and workers.

- Future economic policies should encourage a balanced approach to retirement income. This approach includes balancing public supports with private pensions, savings, and work.

DISCUSSION QUESTIONS

1. What two major socioeconomic conditions resulted in the need to develop a federal old-age security system? Briefly describe the system that the Social Security Act established in 1935.
2. Define and describe the three-tiered retirement income system.
3. List the five basic principles of the Social Security program. What do these five principles ensure?
4. Who is eligible to collect Social Security? When are Social Security benefits taxed? What happens to the money collected as tax?
5. List the major reasons that the finances of older people improved during the 1960s and 1970s.
6. What effect would a decrease in Social Security benefits have on poorer older people? How would it affect the wealthier retiree?
7. What is the difference between a defined benefit and a defined contribution pension plan?
8. What are the major factors that affect a person's retirement income?
9. Describe the effect of work history, gender, and marital status on retirement income.
10. Explain why and how Social Security policies must change to meet the needs of older people today.
11. What approach might a younger person use to best prepare financially for retirement?

SUGGESTED READING

Schulz, J. H., & Binstock, R. H. (2006). *Aging nation: The economics and politics of growing older in America*. Baltimore: The Johns Hopkins Press.

These authors, two of the leading thinkers in the field of gerontology, cover the major issues related to our aging society. The authors begin by debunking the "phony threat of population aging." They go on to report in detail on pension plan issues, health in later life, and the politics of aging. An excellent introduction to these important issues.

United States, Congressional Budget Office. (2004). *Outlook for Social Security*. Washington, DC: Congressional Budget Office. Full text available at www.cbo.gov/ftpdocs/55xx/doc5530/06-14-SocialSecurity.pdf.

This short but challenging work presents the details behind the current concerns about Social Security's resources. The study gives an overview of the current system and policies governing the system. It also projects revenue and expenses for the next 100 years—an exercise in futurology. Still, this work gives a sense for how government experts look at the Social Security system. The text includes charts and graphs for easier comprehension of the issues.

O'Brien, E., Wu, K. B., & Baer, D. (2010). *Older Americans in poverty: A snapshot*. AARP Public Policy Institute. Retrieved May 9, 2010, from http://assets.aarp.org/rgcenter/ppi/econsec/2010-03-poverty.pdf.

Websites to Consult

AARP Financial Planning
www.aarp.org/money

This site contains detailed advice and tips for seniors who want to take control of their finances. It includes information about money management, online banking, and socially responsible investing for older Americans.

International Monetary Fund
www.imf.org

Among its tasks, the IMF monitors international economic changes related to aging. Use the site's search engine to look for articles and data about how other countries are dealing with the economic changes caused by population aging. For example, type "aging" and "France" in the search box to learn about the financial challenges facing that country as it ages.

National Bureau of Economic Research
www.nber.org/aging.html

This site contains links to the NBER's "Economics of Aging" program. "The Economics Of Aging Program involves research on the health and economic circumstances of individuals as they age, and on the implications of population aging on the well-being of older persons." This site contains reports on how aging affects health care systems, economic structures, and government programs.

Bureau of Labor Statistics, United States Department of Labor
http://www.bls.gov/data/inflation_calculator.htm.

This inflation calculator allows you to input an amount of money (e.g., $1,000) and a date to see the buying power of that amount in a given year that you select. For example, you would need $1,665.12 in 2010 to equal the buying power of $1,000 in 1990. This tool gives some idea of how inflation can eat away at a fixed pension.

The Social Security Administration
www.ssa.gov/history/briefhistory3.html

The SSA provides a concise history of Social Security on its Web site. The site includes access to electronic copies of original documents such as the full text of the 1935 Social Security Act. Fascinating details about aging throughout American history. The site contains graphs, photos, and links to other resources.

chapter 9

RETIREMENT AND WORK

Reverend Sam Wong felt bitter and angry when his church asked him to retire. "At age 65," he says, "you're no longer needed. You're no longer important. It doesn't matter what you were in your active years. You're nothing now. You don't have a place."

Rev. Wong's father had worked as a lay priest in the Chinese community on the West Coast, and Rev. Wong took up his father's work. He had spent his life in the church and derived his sense of self-esteem from his work.

When the church asked him to stay on part time after he retired, he refused. "Once you retire," he says, "they don't base your pay on your experience or on how much you know. I heard the person interviewing me say, 'Well, you know, there is really no standard for paying retired people.' In other words, 'We'll pay you what we decide to pay you. And you can take it or leave it.'"

Mandatory retirement forced Rev. Wong to give up his career for no reason other than his age. The federal Age Discrimination in Employment Act (ADEA) makes an exception for people like Rev. Wong. A person age 65 or older may face mandatory retirement if they hold an "executive or high policy-making position for at least two years prior to the retirement date" (AARP, 2006c, p. 5). Professionals faced with this sudden break in their careers often find it hard to adjust to retirement. Given the choice, many would prefer to keep on working.

Wes Weston chose an early retirement. He worked in the state land titles office for 17 years and then in the Department of Mines until age 63. "I retired early," Wes says, "because I had sufficient funds to do the things I've always wanted to do. My work with the government was far from what I wanted to do. I wanted to be able to sit down and systematically while away my time with these." He points to a bookcase filled with philosophy books.

Wes gets three pension checks a month—a small pension for work he did before the war, his Social Security check, and his civil service pension check. Wes has few money worries and spends his free time on his hobbies. His living room, for example, contains a piano and an electric organ. "I want to think, maybe write my memoirs. I also want to improve the little knowledge I have of music. I've got a number of works that I want to explore more thoroughly."

Wes has only one problem. He's still too busy. "I'm busier now than ever," he says. He serves on the board of directors of three seniors organizations, and he and his wife have designed a tabletop golf game that he hopes will sell well enough to create a legacy for his grandchildren.

Pat Larmond, a professor of classics, shows a third way to retire. She eased into retirement. She took her pension at age 65, but continued to teach one course in her specialty, Greek theater, for the next 3 years. At age 68, she gave up this course to a younger professor. She now has the title Professor Emeritus. The university gives her an office that she shares with another retired professor. She comes in two or three times a week to do research, give guest lectures, and have lunch in the faculty club. She keeps in touch with colleagues and her field of study.

Professor Larmond adjusted to retirement without a hitch. She found that she could leave work a little at a time over a period of a few years. Flexible retirement offers an option to the shock of sudden retirement at a fixed age.

These three people show three different responses to retirement. One person experienced retirement as a shock, another as a relief, and the third as an easy transition. These older people show some of retirement's pitfalls and possibilities. They also show that retirement today offers more options than ever before.

Savishinsky (2000, p. 13) says that "one size—and one theory—does not fit all." Responses to retirement differ by personal preference. They also differ by gender, social class, and race. The more people know about retirement, the more they can plan for it and shape it to suit their needs.

This chapter looks at (1) retirement policies and trends, (2) the decision to retire and options to retirement at age 65, and (3) the future of retirement in the United States.

THE SOCIAL ORIGINS OF RETIREMENT

Retirement in the United States today forms a normal part of the life cycle. Most people will spend some time in retirement. In 2005, for example, 33.6% of men and 23.7% of women ages 65 to 69 worked in the labor force (up from 32.2% of men and 20.8% of women in 2002). But for 70- to 74-year-olds, these figures drop to 16.3% of men and 12.8% of women still in the labor force (Rix, 2006).

Myles (1984; also Schulz & Binstock, 2006) traces retirement as a life stage to two factors. First, industrial societies developed and applied the "retirement principle." This principle proposed that people should leave work at a fixed age regardless of physical or mental ability. Until this principle came into play, people worked as long as they could. In agricultural societies, landowners withdrew from work as they grew more frail. Then, in late old age, they gave their property to their children. They would still work in the household if they had the strength.

Economists say that a fixed retirement age began with Bismarck's national pension plan in Germany in the 1880s. Bismarck first set the age of retirement at 70 years, then lowered it to 65. This then became the standard age for retirement. In the United States, the retirement principle served an economy that valued faster, stronger, younger workers. It allowed companies to let older workers go without firing them.

Employers and unions both supported a fixed retirement age. Employers supported retirement because they could retire high-priced older workers and hire cheaper younger workers. Also, younger workers could work faster. Companies wanted to speed up production and get more out of workers. Unions agreed to a faster work pace if workers could get a shorter workday. Older workers had a hard time working at this faster pace. Retirement gave them a graceful way out of work.

Unions also wanted companies to bring in a seniority system (first hired, last fired) in deciding layoffs. Seniority gave the oldest workers the most job security. This forced companies to keep the oldest, most expensive workers the longest. Retirement solved this problem. It offered seniority rights only up to the age of retirement. At retirement age, companies could let older workers go. The unions traded older workers' rights to a job for job security in middle age. The retirement principle opened the door to retirement, but few workers walked through. The absence of private pension plans for most people kept them at work.

The second factor that made retirement almost universal, Myles (1984) says, was the "retirement wage." In the United States this took the form of the Social Security program begun in 1935. The retirement wage at first provided only small benefits. Later, increases in benefits meant that Social Security replaced a larger part of a person's preretirement income.

"You're fired!"

The American Labor Legislation Review, 19 December, 1929.

The retirement wage makes it possible for nearly everyone (even people with very low incomes) to retire. Myles (1984, p. 21; also Hudson, 2007) traces current high rates of retirement at age 65 or earlier to the retirement wage. "It was the rising entitlements made available by the state," Myles says, "that increasingly allowed [workers] to withdraw from the labor market before they wore out. . . . By 1980, the institution of retirement had been consolidated and old age had become a period in the life cycle defined and sustained by the welfare state."

RETIREMENT IN THE UNITED STATES TODAY

The retirement principle and the retirement wage have led to changes in work patterns in the United States. Hudson (2009a) says that in all industrial countries the retirement age set by the national pension system best predicts workers' retirement age. Coile (2003), for example, found that in the United States both men and women show retirement spikes at ages 62 and 65. These choices of retirement age reflect the ages when Social Security and private pension plans encourage older workers to retire. These age spikes show the impact of pension policies and finances on a retiree's decision to leave work.

But men and women differ in their labor force participation. Participation for older men, for example, dropped between 1950 and 1985 (Rix, 2004). In 1950, 49.6% of men age 65 and over worked in the labor force. By 1960, this figure decreased to 35.9%, and by 1985, it dropped to 17.1%. This trend toward decreased labor force participation hit bottom in the mid-1980s.

The participation rate for men stayed around 16% to18% until 2002. By 2009 it had increased to 22%. The participation rate for women stayed around 7% to 9% from 1986 to 2000. The rate for women began to rise after 2000 to 13% to 14% in 2009 (Administration on Aging, 2009; Pynoos & Liebig, 2009). Copeland (2010b) projects a continued upward trend in labor force participation for older workers.

An AARP study conducted in 2007 found that 70% of workers age 45 and over said they planned to work into their retirement years. Responses differed for men and women. Compared to 66% of women, 77% of men said they planned to work in retirement (Groeneman, 2008). The need for income, due to the loss of savings in the recent recession, the need for health insurance that often comes with a job, and a desire to work reported by educated workers will all fuel this trend. People also work to maintain social contacts. Smyer, Besen, and Pitt-Catsouphes (2009, p. 9) report that 70% of workers age 45 and over "think of their co-workers almost as family."

Women and Retirement

Women in 2009 made up 47% of the total labor force (U.S. Department of Labor, Women's Bureau, 2009).

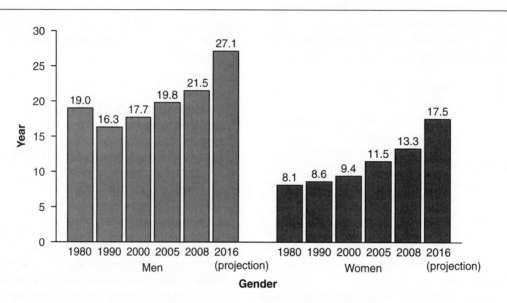

This chart shows a decrease in labor force participation for men from 1980 to 1990. In the past, many older male workers could leave the workforce because they had employment pensions. For a number of reasons—the trend toward defined contribution pensions, better health, longer life expectancies, and so on—labor force participation began to increase after 1990. The Census Bureau projects further increases in labor force participation for men.

Older women increased their labor force participation from 1980 onward. More opportunities for older women to work, better education, more women in the workforce in their middle years, and the need to work longer to earn money help explain this trend. Older widows may remain at work, return to work, or begin work to maintain their standard of living. The Census Bureau projects a doubling of labor force participation for women from 1980 to 2016.

The Bureau of Labor Statistics (2008a) says "The number of workers between the ages of 65 and 74 and those aged 75 and up are predicted to soar by more than 80 percent. By 2016, workers age 65 and over are expected to account for 6.1 percent of the total labor force, up sharply from their 2006 share of 3.6 percent."

Many Baby Boomers say that they plan to stay at work after age 65. Some will do this by choice, because they enjoy the challenge or the camaraderie of work. Others, with little savings and weak pension plans, will have to work to pay the bills. A recent survey by the Employee Benefit Research Institute (EBRI) (2010b), for example, found that more than a quarter of workers (29%) said they have delayed retirement due to a poor economy. Twenty-two percent said they delayed retirement because their employment situation changed. Sixteen percent said they can't afford to retire, and 12% said they needed to work to make up for losses in the stock market.

The small growth in the labor force for 25- to 54-year-olds and the decrease for 16- to 24-year-olds may lead to labor shortages in some industries and regions (Piktialis, 2009). This may encourage employers to hire or keep older workers. Boomers who work longer will relieve some of the pressure on the Social Security system.

FIGURE 9.1 Civilian Labor Force and Participation Rates, 65+ Population, with Projections: 1980 to 2016.

Source: U.S. Census Bureau. (2010g). *The 2010 statistical abstract. The national data book.* Labor force, employment, & earnings: Labor force status. Civilian labor force and participation rates with projections: 1980 to 2016. Table No. 575. Citing U.S. Bureau of Labor Statistics. (2009, January). Employment and Earnings Online. www.bls.gov/opub/ee/home.htm; *Monthly labor review*, November 2007; and www.bls.gov/emp/emplab1.htm. Retrieved November 20, 2010, from www.census.gov/compendia/statab/2010/tables/10s0575.pdf.

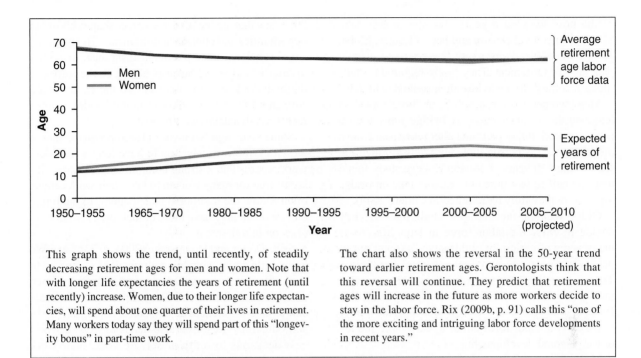

This graph shows the trend, until recently, of steadily decreasing retirement ages for men and women. Note that with longer life expectancies the years of retirement (until recently) increase. Women, due to their longer life expectancies, will spend about one quarter of their lives in retirement. Many workers today say they will spend part of this "longevity bonus" in part-time work.

The chart also shows the reversal in the 50-year trend toward earlier retirement ages. Gerontologists think that this reversal will continue. They predict that retirement ages will increase in the future as more workers decide to stay in the labor force. Rix (2009b, p. 91) calls this "one of the more exciting and intriguing labor force developments in recent years."

FIGURE 9.2   Estimated Average Age of Retirement and Expected Years of Postwork Retirement, Selected Periods

Source: Adapted from Gendell, M. (2008, January). Older workers: Increasing their labor force participation and hours of work. *Monthly Labor Review,* 42. Retrieved May 22, 2010, from www.bls.gov/opub/mlr/2008/01/art3full.pdf.

The proportion of women ages 55 to 64 in the labor force doubled from 1950 to 2009 (from 28.2% to 46.8%). From 1975 to 2008, older women (age 65 and over) showed an increase in labor force participation (from 8.2% to 11.9%) (Howard & Woodring, 2009). This increase in participation reflects the lower pension benefits received by older women and their need to earn money in later life.

Women, compared with men, follow more varied career paths. Some women work, then take time off to raise a family, then return to work. Others work during their childrearing years. Others never enter the labor force (U.S. Department of Labor, 2004). Single women often show unbroken work records similar to those of men. Hill (2002) found that older women who had worked spent only a little over half of their adult years in the labor force. These different work histories make it hard to describe one retirement pattern for women.

Beehr and Adams (2003; also Szinovacz, 2006) believe that the study of women and retirement must take into account a woman's life cycle. This includes her history in the workforce and childrearing responsibilities. It also includes her marital status. Divorced women, for example, plan to retire later than married women. Widows without private pensions also plan

for later retirement. These findings show that life course experiences affect finances. And finances in turn shape a single woman's retirement plans.

Earlier research found that married women often timed their retirement to their husbands' retirement (Weaver, 1994). And husbands' resources and opportunities still have a strong influence on retirement decisions of wives (Pienta & Hayward, 2002). For example, McBride (1988) reported that women with an older spouse and a high income tended to retire early or at age 62. But, Coile (2003) says, as more women spend more years in the labor force, husbands and wives have a mutual influence on their decisions to retire. The practice of couples retiring together may increase in the future as two-earner couples decide to leave work at the same time.

A woman who relies on her husband's pension may fall into poverty if she faces widowhood, divorce, or separation in later life. A divorced woman age 68 told Denton and her colleagues (2004, p. S80), "I assumed I would be in my house until I died and the house was going to be paid for when my husband retired so I thought we were . . . that was going to be our life. We were going to be all set you know, not have to worry about anything."

She now lives on a yearly income of less than $20,000. In general Denton and her colleagues (2004, p. S81) found that women with fewer resources could plan less for retirement. They "were required to 'take life as it comes', living as best they could day to day."

Many women work past age 55 at "bridge jobs" to lengthen their work careers. A **bridge job** allows a person to work full or part time after retirement from a midlife career. A person typically holds a bridge job for less than 10 years. A Boston College study found that one half to two thirds of workers take on bridge jobs before they fully retire (cited in Cullen, 2006).

Older women face unique challenges if they decide to enter the labor force in later life. After many years of caring for children and staying out of paid work, a woman may feel unsure of her ability. Time out of the labor force for a woman can mean more than just the loss of income or pension credits. It can also mean the loss of confidence in the ability to reenter the labor force either to earn more money or for personal development.

McMullin and Berger (2006) conducted in-depth interviews with 30 unemployed older men and women. One woman in the study said:

> I was probably too chicken to get a job. I guess really, I didn't feel confident that I can get a job in my field because I haven't been in it for so many years. I left to raise my kids, and then when I wanted to go back to work I was too afraid. (p. 214)

For the woman who needs to work in order to pay her bills, the internal and external barriers to work (like age and gender discrimination) can lead to poverty.

Family responsibilities throughout life shape women's retirement decisions. For example, women more often than men retire because they have family caregiving responsibilities (caring for an infirm parent or spouse). Dentinger and Clarkberg (2002) report that both men and women engage in caregiving for older parents. But women tend to retire so they can stay at home to provide direct care. Men tend to stay at work to provide financial support to family members. Women, compared to men, more often retire to care for a spouse.

A lifetime of gender differences and discrimination in the workplace also affects women's retirement decisions. For example, poor pensions, low pay, and broken work careers due to family caregiving all lead to low income in retirement for women. These facts have a great impact on women's retirement decisions. Moen and Spencer (2006, p. 134; also Szinovacz,

2003) say that a person's work career shapes his or her opportunities and choices in retirement. "Health insurance, pensions, unemployment insurance, disability insurance, and Social Security all rest on the edifice of the male lock-step life course." To the extent that a woman's life course differs from this model, women face a disadvantage in retirement.

Some years ago Szinovacz (1983) predicted that in the future more women would have longer unbroken work records and a strong commitment to work. This seems true for many women today. Their work careers often follow the traditional male pattern. In the future older women may have more of their own resources to draw on in retirement.

Still, Taylor and Doverspike (2003, p. 73) say, "We know little about women's retirement as compared to men." Researchers need to compare men and women in retirement. This would include research on male and female differences in resources, coping methods, and outcomes. Research also needs to look at women's decisions to retire or stay at work, their work options in later life, and the effects of family life on retirement decisions.

McDonald (2006, pp. 135–136) sums up the need for more research and a new view of women and retirement. She says, "The time has come for scholars to go back to the drawing board. . . . At minimum, a life course perspective with revised definitions of retirement that include gender/family/work linkages would be valuable in reflecting the experiences of people."

Minorities and Retirement

African Americans show a variety of retirement patterns. For one thing, they make up a diverse group. The African American community contains professionals, executives, blue-collar workers, and people in poverty. People in each social and economic class respond to retirement differently.

The 2007 Minority Retirement Confidence Survey found that African-American and Hispanic workers are at least as likely as American workers overall to feel confident about their retirement security. But preparation for retirement differs by income within minority groups. For example, savings for retirement increase as household income goes up. Also higher income minority workers tend to have a workplace pension plan (Helman, Greenwald & Associates, Van Derhei, & Copeland, 2007).

Most minority workers have fewer resources than workers overall. Minority retirees tend to have poorer

Edith Irby Jones, MD (age 65 when this photo was taken), practices internal medicine in Houston, Texas. She also serves as Clinical Assistant Professor of Medicine at Baylor College of Medicine and at the University of Texas School of Medicine, Houston. Dr. Jones served as the first president of the National Medical Association. She has focused her practice on poor people, minorities, and the elderly. Patients age 65 and over make up 70% of her patient load. Professionals such as Dr. Jones often work into late old age.

pensions than other workers. They tend to have broken work careers due to lower education levels, lower income levels, and racial discrimination. This keeps them from building up large private or public pension benefits. They often must work in their later years to survive.

The 2007 Minority Retirement Confidence Survey (Helman et al., 2007) raises some doubts about the financial readiness of minority members for retirement.

The study found that 70% of African American and Hispanic American workers feel confident about their retirement security. This matches the proportion of workers overall who feel this way. But compared to all workers, minority members have less savings and report poorer preparation for retirement. For example, compared to findings in a 2003 study, a smaller proportion of minority members in 2007 report saving for retirement. And half of minority members say they have saved less than $10,000 (compared to one third of other workers).

Compared to workers in general and to Hispanics, a greater proportion of African Americans say they will rely on a defined benefit pension as their major source of income. Minority members, compared to other workers, tend to expect health benefits and long-term care benefits in retirement. Among the poorest workers, those who earn $25,000 or less, minority members show the greatest confidence in their retirement security.

The Employee Benefit Research Institute (EBRI, 2007, p. 11) considers these expectations and this confidence unwarranted. The EBRI warns that "many African-Americans and Hispanics are counting on employer-provided retirement benefits they may not receive." In addition about three quarters of minority workers have not tried to calculate their retirement needs.

The 2007 Minority Retirement Confidence Survey results suggest that many minority workers will need to work past their expected retirement age. Other research supports this view. Cook and Welch (1994) studied the coping strategies of middle-aged and older women with low incomes. They conducted focus groups with 56 low-income women in Chicago. They found that white women rarely mentioned paid work, but nearly all of the African American women did part-time and in some cases steady work "off the books."

A 68-year-old woman named Lena, for example, made floral corsages and centerpieces to bring in extra money. She also helps another woman sell Avon products. Winfred, 81, works in a variety store and a Laundromat 2 or 3 days a week. These women use this money to pay basic expenses like utility bills.

African Americans tend to work in the **secondary labor market** in retail work and service jobs. These jobs offer low pay, few benefits, and often lead to disability. Taylor and Doverspike (2003) found that, compared with whites, African American older men show high disability rates and poor health. Poor

TABLE 9.1 Reasons for Retiring

Cutler and colleagues (2002) on behalf of the National Council on the Aging asked the following question of retirees in a nationally representative sample: "How important was _____ in your decision to retire—very important, somewhat important or not important at all?" The following table gives the proportion of men and women who responded "very" or "somewhat important" to this question.

Reason for Retiring	Men	Women
Social Security	74	71
Money saved	77	66
Specific age	60	43
Family reasons	44	47
Health decline	39	40
Employer pressure	25	16

These responses show that employer pressure to leave work least often influenced the decision to retire (although it did influence one-quarter of the men in the sample). Financial reasons most often influenced the retirement decision—Social Security and money saved. The mention of a specific age also relates to eligibility for public or private pension benefits.

Men and women about equally report health as a reason for retirement. Some people use poor health as a graceful way to explain their exit from work. And some retirement plans take this as a legitimate reason to begin benefit payments.

Family reasons clearly play a role for some people in their decisions to retire. The influence of family depends on personal circumstances such as caregiving demands of a family member or the retirement of a spouse.

Source: Adapted from N. E. Cutler, N. A. Whitelaw, & B. L. Beattie, *American Perceptions of Aging in the 21st Century* (Washington, DC: The National Council on the Aging, 2002) Table 3-2, p. 23. Used with permission of The National Council on the Aging.

pensions and disability lead to fewer options in retirement for African Americans.

Corley (2009) in a report for National Public Radio says that the 2008 recession hit African American male workers especially hard. Some call it the "he-cession" because of its impact on men. Corley presents the case of Randolph Smith, a 53-year-old African American man, who manages "logistics, inventory and supplies for large companies." Smith lives outside Chicago in a middle-class suburb. He got laid off from the Caterpillar Tractor Company in 2008 and still hasn't found a job a year later.

Smith copes by playing racquetball with friends at a local health club a few times a week. Just "to be around some good friends where there's camaraderie. To exercise and get the stress off my life." Outside of the gym he spends his time looking for work. The Smiths converted a bedroom into a home office where he conducts his job search.

Smith says he follows up job leads, works with agents, and even considers temp agency work. But after a year of searching he still has no work. "Since the beginning of the year [2009]" he says, "it's been dry."

Linton Weeks (2009) tells the story of Paul Taylor, a 53-year-old African American man, who worked as a printing press operator near Richmond, Virginia. He made nearly $60,000 a year as a skilled worker. He lost his job in 2008 when his company downsized. Now he works as a part-time security guard at half his former salary. He does extra work as a bartender, waiter, and car valet. He tries to piece together a salary that will help his family pay their bills.

"'I'm looking for a job every day," he says. "I'm up early every day. So it's almost like a nonstop thing. It's almost like a full-time job—looking for a job."

African American older men also face the challenge of age discrimination. The recent recession has forced many middle-class African American men to face unemployment in a weak economy. Some of these men may decide to retire (if they can afford to), rather than continue with a punishing job search.

Gibson (1987) says that the concept of retirement may not apply to poorer African American workers. She reviewed the meaning of *retirement* in major studies in the literature. These studies assume that people retire at age 65, that a clear line exists between work and nonwork, that retired people draw income primarily from retirement sources, and that they view themselves as retired. She says that older members of minority groups such as African Americans and Hispanics often don't fit these criteria. Gerontologists need to expand the meaning of *retirement* in light of minority experiences.

For example, Gibson (1993) found that some older African Americans form a category missed by traditional views of retirement. She calls these people the "unretired-retired" (p. 277). This term refers to people age 55 and older who do not work, but who do not think of themselves as retired. These people make up about one quarter of African Americans age 55 and over who do not work. Few studies have looked at this group. But, Gibson says, they face greater disadvantage than any group of African American older people.

Gibson (1991, 1993) explored why some older African Americans do not see themselves as retired. First, poorer African Americans' broken work records may blur the line between retirement and work. Older African Americans may not view a lack of work in later life as a new phase of life. African Americans who still work part time have even less reason to see themselves as retired. For many of them, this pattern of work carries on from their middle years.

Second, Gibson notes that older African Americans more often take on the sick role than the retired role. A person without a pension, for example, may find disability pay the only way to get retirement income. This finding accounts in part for the strong link between poor health and retirement (Taylor & Doverspike, 2003). Gibson's work shows how inequality affects poorer African Americans' work patterns in middle age and their economic opportunities in later life. "Poor health and disadvantaged labor force experiences," Gibson (1993, p. 282) says, "are more influential for blacks, whereas financial readiness is more influential for whites."

Retirement patterns within the African American group differ. A small proportion (15%) of older African Americans, many with very low incomes, work past the age of 70. These people may end up working until they die. Another group (about one half the older people in the National Survey of Black Americans) retired early, before age 64. This may be due to choice or the lack of jobs.

Flippen and Tienda (2000) used large-scale survey data to study work and retirement among minority workers. They focused on the preretirement work experience of minority and female workers. They found that black, Hispanic, and female older workers, compared with white workers, faced more involuntary joblessness just before retirement. The loss of a job late in a minority worker's career often meant retirement or the end of the person's labor force participation.

According to Flippen and Tienda (2000), black men and Hispanic women, compared with similar white workers, showed the greatest likelihood of work loss in later life. The researchers trace the loss of work to racial and ethnic discrimination in the workplace, poorer health, less education, and fewer job skills. They say that a broken work record in youth makes it hard for these workers to stay in the labor force as they age. The loss of work late in life increases the risk of poverty in retirement. It also increases the risk of poor mental and physical health (Gallo, Bradley, Liegel, & Kasl, 2000).

Zsembik and Singer (1990) conducted one of the few studies on retirement among Mexican Americans. They say that "given the lifetime work patterns of Mexican Americans, it is unclear how best to define retirement, identify when it occurs, and determine what retirement means" (p. 750). Many Mexican Americans, for example, fit Gibson's unretired-retired

type. They work at part-time and seasonal jobs throughout their lives. And this leads to unclear lines between work and non-work.

The 2007 Minority Retirement Confidence Survey (EBRI, 2007) captures some more information about Hispanic American workers and their views on retirement. The study showed that, compared to all workers, Hispanic workers show less confidence that they will have enough money to take care of basic expenses in retirement (40% vs. 29%). They report less confidence that they are doing a good job preparing for retirement. And they report less confidence that they will have enough money to pay for long-term care (EBRI, 2007).

This finding reflects the large number of poorer workers in the Hispanic population. Only 22% of respondents felt "very confident" in their financial preparation for retirement. Only 15% felt "very confident" that they would have money for long-term care expenses if they needed it. Hispanics say that they will rely primarily on Social Security for their retirement income.

Non-native-born Hispanics, compared with native-born Hispanics, report one half the rate of employers paying into a pension plan for them (22% compared with 41%). Poorer Hispanic workers, compared with the non-Hispanic poorer population, reported less chance of having an employer-sponsored pension plan, and less chance that an employer paid into a plan on their behalf. These findings reflect the part-time work that poorer Hispanics do and the small companies they work for.

The research to date shows that discrimination, low education levels, language barriers, and broken work careers all shape minority members' work experiences. These experiences lead to retirement options and decisions for many minority members that differ from those for the white population.

Compared with what we know about whites in retirement, we know little about whether older African Americans retire, why they retire, or what they do in retirement (Taylor & Doverspike, 2003). Gibson (1993) says that future research needs to recognize that many types of retirement exist. For example, current definitions exclude the unretired-retired from research studies. This leads to little knowledge about a large group of African American older people.

Also, researchers know almost nothing about African American professionals. This group has grown in recent years and will increase in the future. Gerontologists know little about their pension arrangements, career stability, or views of retirement. A study of 50 retired African American professional women ages 53 to 86 found that many of them engaged in volunteer work (Slevin, 2005). They often worked with disadvantaged people in their community. They said they felt the need to give back to others. The 2003 Minority Retirement Confidence Survey (EBRI, 2004) found that middle-class African Americans tend to hold attitudes and behave in ways similar to the overall middle-class population.

Minority groups other than African Americans pose unique problems to the study of retirement. Gerontologists know relatively little about retirement among minorities such as Hispanic Americans. Many members of this group work as migrant laborers and speak little or no English. This makes research on this population difficult.

Almost no research exists on the retirement experience of Asian Americans. Many subgroups make up this population, from well-educated high-tech workers to poor refugees from developing nations. Research on this population (and on American Indian elders) can help policy makers and service providers create programs to serve their needs.

ALTERNATIVES TO RETIREMENT

People retire for many reasons: poor health, loss of a job in later life, eligibility for Social Security, a good private income, the retirement of a spouse, or the desire for leisure activity. Cutler, Whitelaw, and Beattie (2002) conducted a national survey for the National Council on the Aging (NCOA). Sixty-nine percent of the people in the survey said that having enough savings motivated them to retire. Forty percent said that eligibility for Social Security would motivate their retirement. Fifteen percent of retirees in this study reported that they worked full or part time, and another 35% said they did volunteer work.

These findings point to a shift in the meaning of retirement for the older worker. Early research on retirement saw retirement as a life crisis and a time of disengagement. But today, retirees typically have good mental and physical health along with high life satisfaction. This leads to many alternatives in retirement. Neal Cutler, the director of the NCOA survey, says:

> We will see more and more people who describe themselves as retired but continue to work. Many of these people are working by choice, not because they have to. In the 21st century, retirement will encompass a wide range of options. We will see some 75-year-olds working

---

BOX 9.1
FORCES LEADING TO RETIREMENT

Individual Reasons	Institutional Forces
Finances	Working conditions and employer policies
Health	Retirement age policies, pension policies, and rules
Attitudes to work and retirement	Societal economic conditions
Social supports or pressures	Historical events and social values

The table presents the broad forces that lead to retirement. Pension policies, working conditions, and discrimination influence men, women, and minority workers differently. This leads to different paths to retirement for members of these groups.

Source: Adapted from Robinson, P. K., Coberly, S., & Paul, C. E. (1985). Work and retirement. In R. H. Binstock & E. Shanas (Eds.), *Handbook of aging and the social sciences* (2nd ed., p. 513). New York: Van Nostrand.

---

two jobs and some 40-year-olds lounging poolside. Retirement used to be defined by what one was no longer doing—not parenting, not working, not actively involved. Increasingly, it will be defined by what one does do— **second career**, volunteer work, travel, sport activities. (National Council on the Aging, 2000)

James Firman, President and CEO of the NCOA, says,

> Sixty-five may be meaningful as a speed limit, but it means less and less as a retirement age. . . . The stereotypical notion of working until age 65, moving to a warm and sunny climate and rocking on the porch has gone the way of the gold retirement watch. . . . We are in the midst of a fundamental reformulation of retirement. (National Council on the Aging, 2000)

Peter Drucker (2001), one of the most astute observers of the business world, comments,

> What has not yet sunk in is that a growing number of older people—say those over 50—will not keep on working as traditional full-time nine-to-five employees, but will participate in the labor force in many new and different ways.

In an economic history of retirement in the United States, Costa (1998, p. 133, cited in Rix, 2004, p. 3) says that retirement now looks like a "time of personal discovery and fulfillment rather than one of withdrawal, a situation made possible by rising incomes and the abundance and declining cost of leisure activities."

Moen and Spencer (2006, p. 129) say, "The emerging third-age concept differentiates retirement, along with the years preceding and following it, from conventional notions of old age." This change reflects longer life expectancy and better health of retirees today. But it also reflects a different understanding of work and of the life course.

The diversity of retirement experiences today shows that the middle-class white male life course no longer describes the complexity of work or retirement. Rapid changes in the economy—mergers, acquisitions, bankruptcies, international trade, outsourcing—make work careers unstable. Even white male middle-aged workers can find themselves unemployed due to any of these forces (Moen & Roehling, 2005). Today, the traditional model of retirement exists alongside many other patterns of work and post-work life in the third age.

Schulz and Binstock (2006, p. 147) say, "The notion that most people are forced to retire and suffer in retirement from boredom and psychological distress is a myth." Most middle-class people adjust well to retirement. And middle-income retirees now have many options. They range from early retirement, to partial retirement, to work at second careers. Moen and Spencer (2006, p. 132) refer to these activities as "second acts."

Early Retirement

Why do some older workers retire early? First, people quit work when they can get their best deal on retirement benefits. Second, they leave work because they do not enjoy working.

The reasons for early retirement differ by ethnicity. Early-retired whites, for example, tend to come from white-collar jobs. They take early retirement because of their good pension programs. Early-retired African Americans and Mexican Americans tend to come from blue-collar and service jobs. Minority group members tend to retire due to poor health or physical impairment (Taylor & Doverspike, 2003).

Recent changes to Social Security rules attempt to remove some of the incentive to retire early. First, Social Security will raise the age for full benefits from age 65 today to age 67 by the year 2027. Second, Social Security will reduce benefits at age 62 from 80% to 70%. Third, workers will get increased Social Security benefits for putting off retirement. These changes may decrease the rate of early retirements (Rix, 2008).

Recent changes to private pension plan benefits could also lead to fewer early retirements in the future. Defined benefit pension plans pay out a defined amount at a set age according to a formula. These plans encourage retirement at a prescribed age or earlier. But companies have begun to shift from defined benefit to defined contribution plans. For example, more than 100 companies dropped defined benefit plans during 2009 (Callahan, 2009).

This continues a decade-long pattern. Defined contribution plans, an increasingly common option, offer less incentive to retire at a set age. These plans work like a savings account. The longer people work, the more money they add to their plan and the more they will have when they retire. If a person in a defined contribution plan puts off retirement, he or she will have more money to use over fewer years in retirement.

These changes to pension plan rules and policies will affect workers' retirement decisions. Changes to pension rules may make early retirement less attractive. Also, the recent economic recession has forced many older workers to postpone retirement (MetLife, 2010a; Helman, Copeland, & VanDerhei, 2010). The trend toward labor force participation for older workers points to a shift away from early retirement. Though workers might still prefer this option if they can afford to retire.

Partial Retirement

Gendell (2008) divides the post–World War II years into two periods. The first 30 years after the war, he says, favored early retirement. The second period from the mid-1980s onward produced incentives for workers to stay at work. The trend toward workforce participation past traditional retirement ages continues today and will likely continue into the future. The Merrill Lynch Retirement Survey (Merrill Lynch, 2006a), for example, found that 76% of Baby Boomers plan to work in retirement. And the Bureau of Labor Statistics estimates that by 2014, 41% of adults age 55 and older will still be in the workplace (Toossi, 2005).

Many of these "retired" workers will engage in *partial retirement*. Definitions of partial retirement differ. Some researchers say people have partially retired if they earn less than half their past maximum yearly income. Other researchers say people have partially retired if they earn less than 80% of their past maximum monthly income. Still other researchers define partial retirement as work in the 2 years after a person begins to get Social Security benefits.

Hardy (2006, p. 207) says that only about half of retirees today experience retirement as a once-in-a-lifetime break with their past. Many workers, she says, "retire from one job and begin collecting pension benefits as they search for new jobs." Wannell (2007, p. 19) says that people with private pension plans "are increasingly finding their way back into paid jobs in their 60s." Today many retirees cycle in and out of retirement—sometimes more than once.

Studies find that, depending on the definition used, between 5% and 30% of retired wage workers work at some time during retirement. A U.S. Department of Labor report (2000) found that 25% of retirees said they worked part time. And 67% of workers said they expected that they would work in retirement. (See Figure 9.3.) Partial retirement allows a retiree to ease out of the workforce.

Sara Rix (2006), in a study for the AARP, reports an upswing in labor force participation for older workers (age 55 and over). The growth of the 55-and-over workforce, she says, "is expected to be large and rapid—an increase of nearly 50 percent through 2014." The entry of the large Baby Boom cohorts into the older age groups in part accounts for this increase. But all age groups age 55 and over showed increases in labor force participation. This reflects the decision of many older people to remain at work either full- or part-time.

Rix (2009b) projects that if this trend continues, 1 worker in 4 will be age 55 or over in 2016. People who choose partial retirement often choose to work because it provides them with a sense of purpose. They may work at a special project for their former employer, as a consultant, or as a part-time employee.

Walt Jamieson, historian, former dean, former provost, author, and emeritus professor, took on a major research project several years after he retired. His university called on him to update the university's official history. Walt published a book from this project that now serves as the best recent history of the campus. This past year the school's Continuing Education unit asked Walt to create a history of continuing education for the university's 150th anniversary. Walt spent a year visiting libraries, interviewing staff members, and tracking down historical documents.

Walt's study came out as a companion book to the university history. He says, "The project gave me a reason to get up in the morning. I thoroughly enjoyed

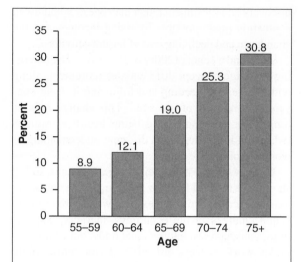

Older workers, who return to work, tend to work part-time after retirement. The proportion of older workers (those still in the labor force) who work part-time increases with age. Older workers may work because they need the money, to stay engaged in meaningful activity, or to stay socially connected. But by later old age a large proportion of older workers (30.8%) only work part-time. These figures with some variation have remained stable over the past two decades.

Copeland (2010b) further reports that 17.7% of female workers age 55 and over, compared to 9.4% of male workers in that age group, work part-time. Male workers may continue in their primary job after age 55. Many men can then fully retire with a pension. Women may have fewer work options after age 55. (For example, only 58% of older women, compared to 69.2% of older men, work full-time, full-year). Those who have not worked in the past may only have access to part-time work. Also, many women worked part-time throughout their lives. They may maintain this pattern in later life.

FIGURE 9.3   Part-Time, Full-year, Workers by Age, 2008

Source: Copeland, C. (2010a). *Employment status of workers ages 55 or older, 1987-2008.* Percentage of workers age 55 or older working part-time, full-year, by age, 1987–2008. Figure 4. Vol. 31(3), p. 4. Notes. Employee Benefit Research Institute. Retrieved November 20, 2010, from www.ebri.org/pdf/notespdf/EBRI_Notes_03–Mar10.EmptStat.pdf.

engagement with the Dean of the unit and his staff. It was one of the best years of my retirement." The project led to publicity, requests for public lectures, and a new interest in Walt's earlier book. He's now begun a new research project that will explore the lives of 19th-century female graduates.

Walt has clearly retired. He works at his own pace from his home. He employs his wife as a research assistant. He stays involved in academic life through projects that use his expertise, and his institution benefits from this engagement. Walt also serves as a role model to younger scholars who may wonder what the future holds for them.

Rix (2004) reports that 60% of retirees, who still worked, saw partial retirement as the ideal. Moen and colleagues (Moen, Erickson, Agarwal, Fields, & Todd, 2000, cited in Rix, 2004) found that most older workers preferred less than full-time work. According to Novelli and Workman (2006, p. 88), "Workers who retire in phases, or steps, are more likely to have a positive view of work and may stay in the workforce longer."

Elder and Pavalko (1993) studied 517 men from the Stanford-Terman longitudinal study of high-IQ children. This study began in 1922 and collected 12 waves of data until 1986. Most of the men in this study had managerial or professional jobs. The researchers found three retirement patterns: abrupt, sporadic, and gradual retirement.

About one third of the group (30%) made a single *abrupt* exit from work. These people tended to leave work at age 62. Another 16% showed a *sporadic* pattern. They left work fully, then returned to the workforce. These people made more than five work transitions and about half of them made two or more exits from the labor force. On average, they first left the labor force at age 61. Nearly half (46%) of the sample showed a *gradual* pattern of retirement.

Gradual retirees either reduced their work time or had at least two transitions out of work. They averaged three to four transitions between their career and retirement. On average, they left the labor force for the first time at age 63. About half of these men worked between 16% and 75% of full-time in their first jobs after retirement. They fully retired on average at age 70, later than any other group.

In the national Health and Retirement Study (U.S. Department of Health and Human Services & National Institute on Aging, 1993, cited in Rix, 2004), about three fourths of workers ages 51 to 61 said they would like to work part-time. They said they would like to stay at their current jobs with fewer hours per week. Workers say that more flexible work options would allow them to stay in the labor force longer. But few of them thought that their employers would agree to this. Most people find that they either have to work full-time or retire (Moen et al., 2000).

A Cornell University study of phased retirement among white collar workers found a variety of options and some barriers (Hutchens, 2003, 2007). More than three quarters of the firms studied had an informal policy that allowed phased retirement. But this option depended on the specific type of work done and the needs of the company. An Ernst & Young (2006) study reports, "State and local governments have the most experience with one form of phased retirement—the deferred retirement option program (DROP)." A DROP allows eligible older workers, often teachers, to work for a government employer beyond the normal retirement age. Workers in these plans add to their retirement plan income.

A California secondary school administrator told Hutchens (2003), "Teachers and administrators can stay in the profession for as long as they want. We are always looking for experienced people." The California State University system in cooperation with the

---

BOX 9.2

BEST PRACTICES FOR ATTRACTING AND RETAINING OLDER WORKERS

Merrill Lynch studied companies that try to attract and retain older workers. The study found that these companies use at least two of the following practices:

1. Use technology to allow older workers to work from home;

2. Encourage older workers to coach and mentor younger workers;

3. Offer health care coverage to people who work seasonally or part-time;

4. Provide new assignments to challenge older workers;

5. Allow older workers to transfer to jobs that offer reduced hours/pay;

6. Allow workers to phase into retirement;

7. Provide new options that substitute other benefits for compensation;

8. Allow more flexible work schedules.

Source: Adapted from Merrill Lynch. (2006b). *The 2006 Merrill Lynch New Retirement Study: A perspective from individuals and employers.* Washington, DC. Retrieved August 14, 2010, from www.ml.com/media/66482.pdf. Reprinted with permission.

California Faculty Association offers faculty members a "faculty early retirement program" (FERP). Faculty members eligible for retirement can work up to half-time—one semester full-time or two semesters half-time. Faculty members in this program can collect their pensions while they continue working.

This gives faculty members a financial boost as they enter retirement. It also reduces the cost of high-priced faculty members to the system while it retains their talent. Faculty members can choose to FERP for up to 5 years after they retire.

Industries outside government and education take a more cautious view of phased retirement. A Wisconsin bank executive said, "There might not be a part time position available, there might be work that needs to be picked up because fewer hours are being worked."

Some companies see phased retirement as a tool they can use to keep experienced workers on the job (Hewitt Associates, 2008, p. 9). But rather than create phased retirement policies, companies prefer to work out details with individual retirees. Some companies hire retired workers to help with training or to work on special projects. The Argonne National Laboratory, for example, offers temporary positions to retirees with unique technical expertise.

Procter & Gamble, Eli Lilly, and more than 50 other corporations work with a company called YourEncore. These companies hire scientists and engineers for short-term projects (Pope, 2008; YourEncore, 2010). YourEncore has more than 4,000 experts in its database. Pope (2008) says that most of AARP's "Best Employers" have a "retiree relations specialist." This person keeps in touch with former employees, invites them to events, and keeps their names in a database. A company can then call on these former workers to help short-term projects.

Companies that want to keep their older workers offer job-sharing, flex-time, telecommuting, reduced hours without loss of benefits, and adjustment of hours as needed (Pope, 2008). Bon Secours Richmond Health System in Richmond, Virginia, has 90 nurses and other employees who work part-time in retirement. They collect their partial salary and benefits as long as they work 15 hours or more per week (Galinsky, Eby, & Peer, 2008).

Some companies have developed unique programs to fit older workers' lifestyles and preferences. Borders, the bookstore company, has a "passport" system that allows workers to move between stores. Older workers can work summers in Maine and winters in Florida (Novelli & Workman, 2006). Home Depot

offers a similar program. Some health care corporations offer this option to nurses. Mercy Health System sponsors a "Work to Retire Program." This allows workers age 50 and over to work fewer hours, share work, or work from home.

Some retired workers move to jobs outside their industry. These new jobs often demand lower skill levels than the job a person held before retirement. The jobs often involve routine work, perhaps as a counter worker in a fast-food chain, as a bank teller, or as a part-time factory worker.

Days Inn, McDonald's, and Sears all hire older employees. These companies offer flexible schedules and part-time work. But they also offer low pay. Workers who move into these jobs face a cut in wage rates of 30% or more. Some people decide to retire rather than work at these rates. Others see these jobs as ways to earn extra money and stay socially active. Rix (2002) says that the sudden transition to retirement in the past has begun to change into a more gradual process of withdrawal from work.

Second Careers

A *New Yorker* cartoon shows an older man across the desk from a retirement counselor. The counselor says, "So, what sort of work will you want to do now that you're retired?" Like a lot of humor, this cartoon contains a kernel of truth. Policy makers and gerontologists predict that many Baby Boomers will work past the traditional retirement age of 65. The AARP (2005e, p. 10) says that "younger retirees and baby boomers . . . view retirement as a transition of lifestyles rather than the abrupt end of a job, a new opportunity rather than the conclusion of a career. Indeed, nearly 70% of Boomers report that they expect to continue working in their 'retirement' years."

The Merrill Lynch (2006a, p. 4) *New Retirement Study* found:

> The ideal retirement for 71% of adults surveyed is to work in some capacity, and almost half of those U.S. adults who plan to work in retirement (45%) say they don't plan to stop working—ever. On average, people expect to retire at age 61, but they see themselves working an average of nine years in retirement. The average age at which they will stop working completely is over 70. (p. 4)

Stern (1993, p. 52) says that retirement used to mean an end to productive life. "Now," she says, "it's more likely to mean 'the day on which you take your first pension and move on to something new.'" For many people this means starting a second career. A

BOX 9.3
WHAT DO OLDER WORKERS WANT IN A JOB?

The AARP conducted a study of what older workers look for in a job (AARP, 2006c, p. 11). The workers listed the following features of an ideal workplace:

- Positive work environment
- Respect from their co-workers
- Opportunities to use their talents
- Opportunities to use their skills to do something worthwhile
- Learn something new
- Help others
- Do what they "have always wanted to do"

Workers at every age would agree that these items describe a good job. Piktialis (2009, p. 25) adds that older workers "want the respect of other generations and to be valued by their managers and supervisors."

Older workers list items that express their unique life-stage goals—their desire to do "something worthwhile" and to "help others." Psychologist Erik Erikson calls this "generativity"—the desire to give back to society and care for the younger generation. Many older workers want more than a job and paycheck. They want to make a contribution to their workplace and to society as a whole. They also want to realize some unfulfilled dreams—do something they "always wanted to do." These findings suggest that work can mean different things at different points in the life cycle.

What would you list as features of your ideal workplace today (aside from a huge salary)? Ask your parents and/or grandparents what they consider the ideal workplace. What similarities and differences do you notice in these responses? Why do you think people differ in what they look for in a job?

---

second career means working at something you love to do or something you have always wanted to do.

A second career differs from leisure or from a person's midlife career. It also differs from a return to work part-time. A second career stands outside the hierarchy of corporate life. In a second career, people set their own goals, use their own approaches to solving problems, and express their own identities.

Savishinsky (2000, p. 144) gives the example of Zoe, a retired woman in her 60s who became a t'ai chi enthusiast. (T'ai chi is an ancient Chinese spiritual practice and exercise program.) She gained skill in the practice of t'ai chi after about 18 months of training. She then apprenticed to her instructor and became a teacher of t'ai chi. She said she had wanted to teach for decades. So this new role fulfills one of her dreams. "What they're paying me is nice," she says, "but the money's incidental." Zoe believes in the good that t'ai chi does for her students. And this gives her new role a deeper meaning.

Sadler (2006) interviewed retirees to learn about their activities. "Contrary to what I expected to learn from people who were approaching retirement age," Sadler says, "I found that work was becoming more, not less, important." Sadler gives the example of Marty, a primary school teacher who quit his job in his late 50s. He told Sadler, "I have learned that my work is not my job." Sadler reports that after Marty retired, he "expanded his creative work, making stained glass and graphic designs, learning to prepare gourmet meals, and at 65 serving two years in the Peace Corps. In his seventies he has added to his work portfolio by participating in Habitat for Humanity."

These activities express the personalities, interests, and in some cases the fantasies of their creators. For many people, a second career opens a new life. As Paul Tournier (1972, p. 130) says, a second career "has a goal, a mission, and that implies organization, loyalty, and even priority over other more selfish pleasures—not in the line of duty, since professional obligations are not involved, but for the love of people. It is, therefore, not an escape, but a presence in the world."

Encore Careers

An organization called Civic Ventures has further developed the idea of a second career. It enlists older volunteers for specific projects. Civic Ventures sponsors the Experience Corps, a program that recruits older people to serve as tutors and mentors in the schools. Civic Ventures also helps community groups develop projects served by older volunteers. It gives awards to older social entrepreneurs to encourage their work. And it helps people prepare for new careers in their Third Age.

Marc Freedman (2007), CEO of Civic Ventures, supports what he calls "**encore careers.**" An encore career has the following features: First, it takes place after a midlife career ends. Second, it could last as long as 10 or 20 years and it accomplishes something important. Third, it pays a salary and offers benefits. Fourth, it allows a person to give back to society (Bank, 2009; Ruffenach, 2007).

Freedman says many Baby Boomers "are searching for a calling in the second half of life." As an example, consider "someone who—after spending 30 years as a money manager—decides in his or her 60s to become a math teacher or to launch a second career with an environmental organization" (Ruffenach, 2007, n.p.). This work won't pay as much as a person's midlife job. But, Freedman (2007, p. 5) says, an encore career swaps "income for impact."

Freedman foresees a time when Baby Boomer retirees would take a 1- or 2-year sabbatical at the end of their midlife career. They would travel, fix up their homes, take up a hobby—the things that people expect to do in retirement. Then they would reengage in an encore career. Some people would train for this new career. Other people would use the skills and experience they gathered in their first career.

Ed Speedling went from being a health care executive to serving as an advocate for the homeless. "When I walked into St. John's [a homeless shelter]," he says," it was love at first sight. It was really the fulfillment of a deep desire to work with the poor, to align myself with people who are vulnerable." As his encore career evolved, Ed went on to do other work with the homeless. He's worked on the streets talking with homeless people and helping them get the services they need. He's also used his first-career skills in the boardroom, advising organization executives. Freedman (2007, p. 5) uses this case to show the power of what he calls "the 'experience economy.'"

Freedman (2007, p. 12) envisions retirement as a "freedom *to* work" instead of "freedom *from* work." He describes a future corps of a few million older people engaged in work to improve society. This corps, like the Peace Corps that attracted many Baby Boomers in their youth, will attract Baby Boomers in retirement who want to create a better world. Boomers would leave a legacy of social service and societal improvement. This, he says, "could be one of the greatest accomplishments of the 21st century."

The encore career offers an added option to partial retirement and bridge jobs. It provides fulfillment for the individual. It also allows society to reap a "windfall of talent" (Freedman, 2007, p. 22). Goggin (2009) says that nearly half of people ages 44 to 70 not engaged in an encore career see this as a high priority for themselves. Members of the biggest generation can throw their weight into solving some of society's biggest problems.

Could meaningful work also lead to better health and longevity? A number of studies point in this direction. Researchers at Johns Hopkins University Medical Centers, for example, studied older people who tutored elementary school students in reading. Half the people in the study worked 15 hours a week in Baltimore helping students learn to read. The other half of the group did not work at all. The researchers found improved "'physical, cognitive, and social activity'" in the tutor group. The study found decreases on these measures in the control group (Freedman, 2007, p. 82). This study and others suggest that work in later life can lead to good health, longer life, and successful aging.

PERSONAL RESPONSES TO RETIREMENT

Cohen (2005, p. 144) conducted a series of in-depth interviews with retirees. He found that if people plan for retirement at all, they tend to do financial planning. Few people plan for "how you will be socially engaged, how you will spend your time, what larger goals you want to pursue, and how you can take full advantage of the extra time available in this phase of life."

Crowley and Lodge (2004, pp. 296–297), describe the social pressure one of them felt when he retired from work:

> It occurs to me that my greatest fear then was not that I would fall apart—although I worried plenty about that. It was that I would be useless and idle and bored. And ashamed because I was not doing anything. When I first retired and found myself walking along the streets of New York at midday with nothing to do, I felt as if I'd just walked out of a porno movie. I didn't want my friends to see me, because they'd know I had no job, that I wasn't doing anything. I felt that weird guilt for a long time. In retrospect, that was silly, but I think a lot of men see retirement that way. We can't bear the idea of doing nothing, but we don't know what to do.

A *BusinessWeek* report (Gutner, 2004, p. 88) described the case of Bernard Salevitz. He retired at age 65 from a busy medical practice in New York. He and his wife moved to a new home in Scottsdale, Arizona, where one of their children lived. Salevitz says that after a period of golf and travel, "I mentally and physically collapsed. . . . There was no challenge or stimulation in my life, and that was a big mistake." He went back to work at the Mayo Clinic in Scottsdale. Three days a week he sees patients and teaches residents. He says, "It brought me back to civilization."

These examples point to the importance of planning for social engagement in retirement. Denton and colleagues (2004), in a Canadian study, looked at how people planned for retirement. They conducted qualitative interviews with 51 men and women age 45 and over. They found that a small group of people (about 20% of their sample) did little planning. These people lived from day to day and hoped for the best. Widowed, divorced and separated women made up a large proportion of these "day-to-dayers." Compared to people who planned for later life, they had lower incomes and fewer choices in later life.

The majority of people in this study planned for later life. They made financial plans, intentionally led healthy lifestyles, and planned for social engagement. These people had a positive view of life and felt in control of their future. The planners "envisioned a lifestyle of their choice and actively sought, through planning and preparation, to achieve their goals" (Denton et al., 2004, p. S79). The researchers say that people with more education and resources see later life as a time of leisure, enjoyment, recreation, and activity.

Ekerdt (1986), in a classic essay, says that many retirees subscribe to what he calls "the **busy ethic**." This ethic values an active life. Retirees who subscribe to this ethic often carry electronic organizers and have telephone answering machines, so they won't miss messages. Ekerdt says that the busy ethic helps retirees ease into retirement.

The busy ethic allows retirees to maintain the same values they held while working—engagement in community affairs, an active social life, and self-development. Retirees legitimate their retirement through "involvement and engagement . . . [the busy ethic] esteems leisure that is earnest, occupied, and

"Have you given much thought to what kind of job you want after you retire?"

filled with activity" (Ekerdt, 1986, pp. 239–240). The busy ethic domesticates or tames retirement. It supports energetic activity and healthful lifestyles, two long-standing North American values. The busy ethic keeps retirement and retirees in the mainstream of life.

Cohen (2005, p. 138) adds a caution to enthusiasm for the busy ethic. "No one," he says, "should feel pressured to be more active than they want to be." Most people, Cohen adds, want to stay busy and active. People in the third age want to engage in activities that they define as meaningful. Most people today don't want to retire to a life of idleness.

Cohen (2005, p. 138) feels that activity in the third age "is a natural outgrowth of inner desires we all have for learning, social relationships, a sense of meaning, and giving something back to society." People in the third age have a chance to choose what interests and motivates them.

Cohen (2005, p. 146) talks about creating a "balanced social portfolio." This "portfolio" of activities might include a mix of creative expression, family and other relationships, community service, and learning. Cohen emphasizes balancing active with quiet activity, social with personal time, short-term and long-term projects and commitments. Like a financial portfolio, the social portfolio needs periodic review. If a social activity like a volunteer position ends, a person may want to substitute something new. Part-time work may offer a more satisfying social outlet.

The social portfolio demands reflection—awareness of one's total life experience. And it offers a structure or context for thinking about and anticipating the future. A person may serve as a volunteer on a nonprofit board before they retire, knowing that they will retire in a year or so. The board membership will provide a social outlet that will substitute for the social relations that exist at work.

Corbett (2007) created the concept of the **life portfolio**. A life portfolio consists of a person's commitments to specific activities and relationships. These include family, community service, spiritual development, recreation, and in some cases work. Imagine these items placed in a pie chart. The size of each slice will depend on a person's commitment to each activity, group, or individual that the pie slice represents. A retiree decides how much time and energy he or she will commit to the segments of their portfolio. A portfolio approach gives a person control over their future. And it encourages action.

Corbett (2007, p. 107) gives an example of an exercise that helps people create their life portfolio. "Think about the dreams, talents, projects, achievements, loves inside of you that would be unexpressed or unrealized if your life ended today. If, at the end of the day you are still alive, and you have done this exercise faithfully, you have the first draft of a portfolio plan." Corbett also encourages people to write a personal mission statement. This statement helps a person define what he or she cares most about. From there, the person can set goals and begin to take action.

Preretirement Planning (PRE)

A study by Ernst & Young (2006) found that nearly half of corporations in the study (47.1%) offered a broad financial planning program for their employees. Only 16.5% said they had a preretirement program for older workers. More than one third of companies (36.5%) offered no preretirement program. And yet a **preretirement education (PRE)** program can help workers transition smoothly into retirement.

A good program will help people understand their financial options. This part of the program needs to start early in a person's career. Financial planning comes too late if it takes place a year or two before retirement. A PRE program will include a review of employee retirement benefits. It will help employees calculate the amount of their monthly pension. It will also let employees know about pension plan options (e.g., pension benefits for a spouse).

Corporations in the Ernst & Young (2006) study said that preretirees valued seminars and workshops, online tools (such as Web-based calculators), print publications, and personalized projections of benefits. Less than 1 company in 5 (17.4%) offered individual counseling in person.

Good preretirement program go beyond finances. They include a variety of health and lifestyle topics, including legal issues, information on housing, work after retirement, fitness, and relationships. Programs should involve the spouse of the retiree. Spouses can then discuss their retirement plans and goals. A PRE program can help a couple look at their lifestyle, decide what changes they want to make (if any) after retirement, and help them plan how to make the transition (Feldman, 2003).

Compared to men, women have less opportunity to plan their retirement. Women tend to hold service, wholesale, and retail jobs at low pay with poor pensions. These jobs seldom offer PRE. Women in professional positions have a better chance to get retirement advice than nonprofessionals. But even women who have access to a PRE program may find that it ignores their specific concerns.

Deren (1990) says that women's programs have a content, design, and sensitivity to women's issues that other programs lack. Sessions in programs for women focused on finances, a major concern. But these

---

BOX 9.4
DOUBLE-DIPPING SWEETENS RETIREMENT FOR STATE WORKERS: BUT IS IT RIGHT?

Arizona teachers by the hundreds return to teaching after they retire. They reenter the classroom by working for a private company called SmartSchoolsPlus. This company contracts with the school system and sends these teachers back to work—often at the same jobs they had before retiring. The teachers then collect their pensions and a salary. Arizona law requires teachers to wait a year before taking up their same jobs. But they get around this law by contracting with companies like SmartSchoolsPlus.

State legislatures have tried to stop this "double-dipping," but they have had little success. Most states need more teachers and other employees. Retirees who return to work fill a need in industries that face a labor shortage. *The Economist* (2007c, p. 83) says that "double-dippers save the states money because they do not have to be trained. Moreover, state employers often have early pensionable ages—sometimes as low as 55—so the newly retired still have plenty of vigor they might otherwise lavish on the private sector."

Retirees may serve a function in a labor-starved economy. But the idea of a retiree collecting a state pension and a salary for the same job he or she just left rankles the public, the press, and state legislators. Some states (e.g., New York, California) cap the amount of money a retiree can earn in a state job after retirement.

Should the public or the states care that a retiree returns to work? They contribute their skills to the workplace and improve the economy. "As long as they earn their salary," *The Economist* (2007c, p. 83) writes, "adding more to the economy than they take from it, double-dippers are helping to solve the demographic problem. Delaying their retirement by raising the pensionable age might make sense. But to ban them and berate them seems doubly dippy."

What do you think? Does double-dipping raise ethical as well as economic problems? Is it right for people to get paid twice for the same job? Is *The Economist* right in supporting this activity because it helps the wider economy?

programs found that women also needed to discuss issues with their spouses, like task sharing after retirement, sexual relations, and lifestyle changes.

Deren calls for programs that will meet the needs of Hispanic and other minority women. These programs, she says, must do more than translate English language programs. They must contain information relevant to minority women, and they should show sensitivity to their cultures.

SOCIAL STRUCTURES AND RETIREMENT

Retirement studies since the 1940s and 1950s have focused on the individual experience of retirement. Studies have looked at retirement planning, activities in retirement, and retirement satisfaction. Researchers often take disengagement, activity, or continuity theory as the basis for their analyses. They assume that retirement will cause problems and that people need to cope with and respond to these problems. Most importantly, these theories view retirement as a personal problem that the individual must solve. These theories (and others like modernization or age stratification theory) take social structures as given.

A **political economy** view of retirement looks at the effect of social structures on individuals' retirement options. *Social structure* refers to the economy, the social stratification system, and social institutions. The political economy view assesses how social structures enhance or limit retirement options. For example, second careers best fit the backgrounds of middle-class workers. Executives, engineers, and technicians have the privilege of retirement due to their good pension plans, good health, and education. They also have skills that they can use as consultants for pay or as volunteers to community groups.

Middle-class and upper-middle-class workers with orderly work careers and good pensions report high satisfaction in retirement. People with less orderly careers, low incomes, and few skills have less opportunity.

The Dual Economy

Some social scientists divide the economy into the goods-producing and the service sectors. The goods-producing, or core, sector includes agriculture, mining, construction, and manufacturing. (The government sector has many of the characteristics of the core sector.) The service or periphery sector includes personal care, food services, general office work, and child care. Dowd (1980, p. 77; Bulow & Summers, 1986) says that the core sector is "highly organized and characterized by high wages and pensions systems, and the other [the periphery sector] is marked by low wages and few, if any fringe benefits." These sectors offer unequal opportunities to retirees.

Workers in the core sector (with higher wages and pensions) tend to follow traditional retirement patterns. Core sector companies (mostly large firms) offered workers good pension plans in retirement. Hogan, Perrucci, and Wilmoth (2000) found that white men in core sector jobs had higher incomes than others in their sample, including women in the core sector.

White men also had much larger incomes in retirement. These trends reflect the tendency for workers in the core sector to work for larger firms and to have more stable work careers. Core workers' pension plans encourage and allow retirement from the labor force.

Those in the periphery sector (with lower pay and no pensions) show less traditional patterns of retirement. Women more often than men work in this sector. They tend to have broken work records and less chance of having a pension. This, in part, explains why single older women have some of the poorest incomes. It also explains why they often work past age 65. The type of work they do gives them few resources in retirement.

Quinn, Burkhauser, and Myers (1990) found that the poorest and richest workers tended to stay in the labor force: the richest (many of them professionals) because they chose to work; the poorest, many in the service sector, because they needed the money. Low-wage men and women showed the greatest likelihood of working.

Even within a sector, the type of job a person does influences retirement options. Ruhm (1991) studied *bridge jobs* among retirees ages 50 to 64. Bridge jobs (jobs after a life career but before full retirement) included part-time work, second careers, and self-employment that a person held after retirement.

Ruhm found that people who held bridge jobs most often had worked in higher-status jobs in the core sector. They worked as professionals, managers, or technical workers. More than half of these people (57%) judged their bridge jobs as the most enjoyable job they had ever held.

Ruhm discovered that women, nonwhites, and people with little education who left work before the normal retirement age had trouble finding bridge jobs. Their lack of marketable skills made it hard for them to find work after retirement.

Displaced Workers

Large shifts in the economy can also affect retirement options. Recently, many workers have been laid off due to changes in the economy. Even white male workers with seniority in union jobs find themselves out of work when an industry declines. The restructuring of the economy has led to plant closures in core industries such as steel, textiles, and auto manufacturing.

This change in the economy creates long-term unemployment for large numbers of people. The U.S. Department of Labor, Bureau of Labor Statistics (2002, cited in Rix, 2004), reports that between January 1999 and December 2001 almost 10 million workers lost their jobs due to displacement. People age 55 and older made up 1.2 million of these workers. Older workers (age 55 and over) made up 18% of long-tenured workers (in their jobs at least 3 years) who lost their jobs.

Jobs for high-tech professionals and low-paying service jobs open up due to restructuring. But economic restructuring often leads to the loss of middle-income jobs. Older workers in the middle often lack the skills to fill jobs in fields such as computers and electronics.

Displaced factory workers who want to stay in their communities may have little choice but to move into service jobs. These jobs pay much less than many **displaced workers** made in union manufacturing jobs. Hardy (2006, p. 206) says that "older workers have the lowest rates of reemployment. For those who find

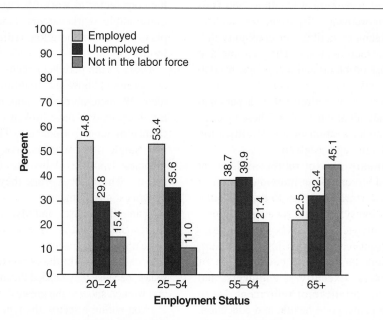

This figure shows the different experiences of displaced workers based on their age. Note that by January 2010 the younger the worker, the more likely that they had returned to work. The oldest workers (age 65 and over) have less than half the reemployment rate of the workers under age 55.

Workers ages 55 to 64 show high rates of exit from the labor force. One in five of these workers (21.4%) has exited the labor force. The oldest group shows more than twice this rate of labor force exit. Nearly half (45.1%) of the oldest workers (age 65 and over) had left the labor force after losing their jobs.

Older workers tend to get discouraged looking for work. Compared to younger workers, older workers take longer to find a job after displacement. The recession that took place during the period of this study made it more difficult for older workers to find a job. Some older workers face (or feel they face) age discrimination in their job searches. Or they may simply get discouraged. Many displaced older workers opt for retirement rather than continue to look for a job. In this way, displacement in later life effectively ends many workers' careers.

FIGURE 9.4 Employment Status in January 2010, by Age of Workers Displaced from Jobs between January 2007 and December 2009[a]

[a]Data refer to persons who had 3 or more years of tenure on a job they had lost or left between January 2007 and December 2009 because of plant or company closings or moves, insufficient work, or the abolishment of their positions or shifts.

Source: Bureau of Labor Statistics. (2010). Economic news release. Table 1. Long-tenured displaced workers(1) by age, sex, race, Hispanic or Latino ethnicity, and employment status in January 2010. United States Department of Labor. Retrieved November 20, 2010, from www.bls.gov/news.release/disp. t01.htm.

new jobs, older workers have high rates of reemployment in only part-time positions and the largest wage losses."

Some of the new jobs created through restructuring require a move to another part of the country. For example, many companies in the Midwest closed at the end of the last century as manufacturing shifted overseas. At the same time new high-tech industries opened in the South and West. Older workers with paid-off homes and roots in their communities found it hard to move. Structural changes in the economy partially account for individual choices in retirement today. "In a growing number of cases," Moody (1988b, p. 217) says, "'retirement' actually becomes a euphemism for discouraged or dislocated workers in the U.S. economy." Among the oldest displaced workers (65 and over), compared to those who choose to work, twice as many choose to retire (Rix, 2004).

Fleck (2010) reports that between 2007 and 2010 the number of **discouraged workers** rose from 53,000 to 287,000. Nearly a third (32%) of the oldest workers faced long-term unemployment (Rix, 2009a). Many of these workers give up looking for work. Some older workers with long work records prefer to retire on their pensions. Other workers leave the labor force because they can't get the kind of jobs they like. Still others want to avoid age discrimination in the hiring process.

Retirement and the Great Recession

The year 2008 saw a sharp downturn in the economy. The aftereffects of this will last for many years—possibly decades. The stock market decline, for example, affected 401(k) plans and employment opportunities. It caused retirees and near-retirees to rethink their retirement options. Many retirees returned to work as their investment revenue dried up. Many near-retirees decided to spend more years at work—to increase their savings and wait for market values to return (MetLife, 2010a).

Herd (2009; Johnson, 2008) reports that people age 50 and over hold three quarters of the total assets in 401(k) and Individual Retirement Accounts. By the end of 2008 the value of these investments fell by $2.8 trillion from their high the year before. Middle-class retirees and near-retirees, most of whom had invested their savings in stocks, saw their accounts plummet. (Poor older people suffered smaller losses because they had less saved in these accounts.)

Older men and women of every race and ethnicity lost jobs during this recession. But men suffered more than other groups. Pynoos and Liebig (2009, citing Zielenziger, 2009a) say that the jobless rate for men age 55 and over more than doubled "from 3.3 percent in December 2007 to 6.7 percent in April 2009. Women in this same age group, during this same period, saw an increase from 2.9 percent to 5.4 percent." Stettner and Wenger (2003), writing for the Economic Policy Institute, report that during a recession people age 45 and over make up a large percentage (25.6%) of the long-term unemployed.

The Bureau of Labor statistics reported that in July 2009, 2 million workers age 55 and over had no jobs. This was the highest rate of unemployment since the Bureau started collecting data in 1948. An AARP poll found that a quarter of workers ages 45 to 64 reported a drop in hours, and nearly a third reported unpaid furlough days. Among older workers, one fourth of those ages 55 to 64 faced pay cuts, and 16% lost their jobs (Zielenziger, 2009b).

Fleck (2010) says that the average time for a 55-year-old to find work after a layoff went from 20 weeks in December 2007 to 36 weeks in February 2010. A recession, increased competition for jobs, and age discrimination in the labor market account for this high rate of unemployment. People with a college education stood the best chance of finding work (Herd, 2009). But the recession created a crisis for low-income workers. These workers have the highest rate of disability and illness.

Many early retirees who faced layoffs in the recession took money from their savings and in some cases from their 401(k) accounts. Others began to draw Social Security pensions as early as age 62. Moody (2009) calls this an "ominous trend." "By retiring at age 62 instead of 66 [the normal retirement age]," he says, "the oldest boomers will find their benefits reduced by as much as 30 percent."

Pynoos and Liebig (2009, citing Consumer Reports, 2008) make this clear with an example. A worker who retires early at age 62 instead of age 66 loses $403 in Social Security benefits per month for life. The 62-year-old also does not get Medicare and has to pay his or her own health insurance (until age 66). This could cost from $6,000 to $45,000 depending on coverage for the 4 years before they can get Medicare. But, as Moody says, "these older boomers, now out of the labor force, and faced with declining home equity and lower stock market returns, will have few alternatives."

An out-of-work computer service employee, Steve Stanislowsky, 61, says he's "pretty much resigned to retiring." He plans to claim Social Security benefits when he turns 62. But, he says, "I'm very worried about running out of money. . . . My whole retirement plan has crumbled" (Fleck, 2010).

Another case shows the long-term cost of a forced early retirement. Fleck (2010, p. 4) tells the story of Jan Gissel, 63, a small business owner. She owned a franchise that provided technical support to small businesses. The recession shrank business to the point where she couldn't make payments to the franchise company. She decided to retire rather than fight for a job. "Unfortunately," she says, "I'm too old to snag one of the few jobs available in this economy. Who's going to hire me at 63?"

The economy forced Gissel into retirement. She had to give up her health insurance when her business folded. She trimmed her cable bill and reads the newspaper online to save money. She's also decided to collect Social Security and she's taken a reverse mortgage on her home. But this strategy will cost her in the long run. Taking early Social Security benefits will reduce her lifetime income. And taking a reverse mortgage at her early age puts her at risk of running out of money late in her life. "I had great plans for what retirement was going to look like," she says. "This isn't it."

Current retirees have little chance of recovering lost savings or home equity in the short term. Munnell (2009, cited in Lynch, 2010, p. 92) says that people in their 50s "simply don't have time to increase their savings by an amount that would be sufficient [to make up for losses]. Your savings rate would have to be so high that you wouldn't have enough to live on. The only option is to stay in the labor force longer."

Some people will stay at work and others will try to reenter the workforce to replace lost pension income. But reentry may prove difficult. They will compete for jobs with the large number of younger unemployed workers. Older workers even in a strong economy take longer to find work and often give up. The current high unemployment rates for all ages will make it more difficult for older workers to find a job. The oldest-old people will have little choice but to cut expenses. Some may fall into poverty.

The recent recession shows how large economic forces can shape individual retirement options. Even the best plans can come undone due to social and economic change. Retirement planning can at least buffer the shock of unexpected social and economic crises.

THE FUTURE OF RETIREMENT

Gerontologists, economists, and other social scientists predict changes in retirement in the future. First, very soon the U.S. population will have more people of retirement age than ever before. These people will form diverse groups based on age, ethnicity, race, region, work history, life experience, and income. No single pattern of retirement will describe how future retirees will end their work careers. Individual choice, the economy, marital status, and personal finances will shape workers' retirement decisions.

Second, longer life expectancy and better health for older workers will encourage many people to stay at work longer. They will need to add to their pensions (public or private) to maintain their lifestyles for more years. Bridget A. Macaskill, president and CEO of OppenheimerFunds, Inc., says that "the estimate of 70% of pre-retirement income built into many planning models may fall short, particularly given emerging healthcare concerns and the changing nature of retirement lifestyles. Even if these levels prove sufficient, they will be required for more years than most people plan for" (National Council on the Aging, 2000). Retirees in the future may decide to delay drawing their pensions so that they can get higher payments into later old age.

Third, older workers will have more options in later life than ever before. Their choices will depend on their resources, skills, and experience. Options will include gradual retirement, flexible hours, bridge jobs, part-time work, second careers, or remaining at their current jobs.

Fourth, future changes in the economy—such as a shortage of workers as the Baby Boom generation ages, the need for more service workers, and electronic offices that allow people to work from home—will open new work options for older people. This will encourage more workers to stay on the job or to find bridge jobs before they retire.

Partial retirement—flexible retirement, part-time work, job sharing, self-employment, and many other options—questions the concept of retirement itself. Retirement in the future will depend not on age but on how well people can perform a job, whether they can afford to retire, and whether they want to work.

The variety of people in old age, due to differences in social class, gender, minority group status, and occupation, leads to varied choices and opportunities in retirement. Vierck (2002) says that due to longer life expectancies, some people will work into their 80s. These people may have two or three careers.

Retirement policies and the changing structure of the economy also influence retirement options. Researchers and policy makers see longer work lives as a way to avoid a crisis in financing pensions for long-lived Baby Boomers.

CONCLUSION

Economists trace old age in modern society to the retirement principle and the retirement wage. These two social inventions created a stage of active life beyond work. Workers earn an income from the state and can devote their time to leisure activities. Increases in public pensions have led to higher proportions of people who choose retirement. Retirement now exists as a normal part of the life cycle.

The research on retirement in the past focused mostly on white men. But studies of women and minorities show that they have unique patterns of work and retirement. Women, compared with men, often have broken work records and less pension income. Many women stay at work into later life because they need the money. Minority members, too, have broken work records, and they may have a unique view of retirement. They also have fewer retirement options because they lack private pensions or savings. Researchers need to do more studies of female and minority workers' retirement.

Researchers also need to do more work on alternatives to retirement. Changes in Social Security rules and changes in the economy have led to more retirement options for older workers. These include early retirement, partial retirement, and second careers. Structural changes in the economy create challenges for many older workers. They may face forced retirement due to plant closures and layoffs.

Most of us will experience some of these changes. People will create the retirement of the future as they meet these challenges. The more we know about retirement, the more we can plan for a successful retirement transition.

SUMMARY

- Today, retirement is an established social institution. The trend toward retirement results from two historical events: the development of the retirement principle in industrialized societies, and the creation of the retirement wage or Social Security.
- Studies of the labor force show a reversal of the long-term trend toward early retirement. Workers today tend to stay at work longer. And workers project even longer work careers for themselves. Longer life expectancies, changes in pension plan policies, personal preferences, and a variety of other social forces all lead to increases in older workers in the labor force.
- A large proportion of men still choose to retire between the ages of 62 and 65 because of the retirement principle and the retirement wage. Because women follow more varied career paths than men, they do not show the same retirement pattern. Many women work past the normal retirement age in order to increase their pensions and because they need the income.
- Minorities tend to have poorer pensions, fewer benefits, and fewer options in retirement because of lower education levels, lower income levels, and racial discrimination. The recent recession has hit minority older workers and retirees harder than other workers in the labor force. Retirement may have a different meaning for minority workers who have nonstandard work careers.

- Retirees can now receive Social Security benefits at age 62. Also, many companies encourage retirement by offering early retirement packages to older workers. These incentives account for the trend toward early retirement, partial retirement, second careers, and encore careers. Today, the traditional model of retirement exists alongside many other patterns of work and postwork life in the third age.
- People who plan for their retirements tend to enjoy their retirements more. They report high life satisfaction and better financial resources. Some companies offer PRE programs, seminars for workers and spouses, and counseling.
- A person's position in the social structure influences his or her retirement options. The dual economy perspective demonstrates this. Workers in the core sector of the economy have the most choice. Those in the peripheral sector have fewer options.
- The recent recession has caused many workers to rethink their retirement plans. Many workers lost pension savings in the stock market downturn. Many lost value in their homes. This led some workers to stay at work longer than they had planned. It led other workers to return to work after retirement.
- Some workers lost their jobs due to layoffs and industry downsizing. Many of these workers opted for retirement

after a fruitless job search. Others retired rather than face the current weak job market.

- In the future, ability rather than age will decide a person's retirement status. Older workers in the future may move in and out of the labor force more than once as their interests, abilities, and financial resources change.

- The diversity of the older population—men, women, minorities, younger old people, older old people, rich, and poor—will lead to many models of retirement. The needs of the labor force and individual needs for income or meaningful work will lead to many paths to retirement.

DISCUSSION QUESTIONS

1. Define the term *retirement*. How and why did our society develop the institution of retirement?
2. Discuss the reasons for the reversal in the long-term trend toward early retirement. What are the social and individual forces at work that led to this reversal?
3. How do retirement patterns for men and women differ? What are the major reasons for these differences?
4. Why is retirement different for African Americans than for whites? Explain the term *unretired-retired* as it applies to older African Americans and Hispanic workers. What effect has the recent recession had on minority older workers?
5. List and describe some of the options older workers now have in retirement today.

6. What benefit do workers gain from planning? Give an example of a good PRE program. Describe the topics covered in a good program. How does this type of information help a person plan for retirement?
7. How does a person's position in the social structure influence their retirement options? What categories of people occupy different places in the social structure?
8. What effect has the recent economic recession had on older workers and retirees? How has this economic downturn influenced people's retirement decisions?
9. Describe some of the trends in retirement that gerontologists predict for the future. What social forces will shape these trends? What individual needs and preferences will shape these trends?

SUGGESTED READING

Adams, G. A., & Beehr, T. A. (Eds.). (2003). *Retirement: Reasons, processes, and results.* New York: Springer.

The authors organized this collection around three phases of the retirement process: preretirement, the retirement decision, and postretirement. The articles cover many of the topics discussed in this chapter. The writings discuss financial, social, and psychological issues that people face in retirement, as well as current trends such as bridge jobs, early retirement, and extending work life.

Bauer-Maglin, N., & Radosh, A. (Eds.). (2003). *Women confronting retirement: a nontraditional guide.* New Brunswick, NJ: Rutgers University Press.

Thirty-eight women from many professions and life conditions look at retirement. The authors discuss the need to find a new self-image beyond work, the need to balance work with recreation, and the need to shape public policies to create better opportunities in retirement. Many of these women played an activist role in the 1960s and 1970s. They continue to challenge the system as they work to overcome their negative views of retirement. This book offers a chance to learn what retirement looks like through the eyes of these articulate and socially aware women.

Freedman, M. (2007). *Encore: Finding work that matters in the second half of life.* New York: Public Affairs.

The author, CEO of Civic Ventures and a social entrepreneur, describes the reinvention of work in the second half of life.

Many Boomers will need to work to pay the bills. Others will work because they want to stay engaged in the world. But, the author says, Baby Boomers will want to work at something meaningful. "They are searching for a calling in the second half of life." The author tells the story of this reinvention of work through a series of case studies. This readable and inspiring work shows what work can mean in the third age.

Websites to Consult

Social Security Administration
www.ssa.gov/retire2

This is the SSA's retirement planning website. It includes income and benefits calculators, information about the retirement process, and preretirement information.

CNN.com Retirement Page
http://money.cnn.com/pf/retirement
    and

New York Times Retirement Page
http://topics.nytimes.com/your-money/retirement/index. html?emc=eta2

CNN and *The New York Times* have Web sites that address retirement issues such as investments, pension plans, retirement strategies, and retirement lifestyles. They are updated regularly and include human-interest stories and information about changes in retirement policy.

Senior Corps

www.seniorcorps.gov

Senior Corps is a national service organization that provides retirees with opportunities to volunteer in their community. This site provides an overview of the program. It provides information on the program's successes and research on civic engagement by older people.

YourEncore

www.yourencore.com

This site describes a company that links corporations with retired experts. Corporations approach YourEncore with projects that they need to launch or with a problem they need solved. YourEncore searches its database for the best experts to fit the corporation's needs. An innovative approach to the use of retirees' expertise.

Seniors & Boomers Markets World Wide

www.thematuremarket.com/SeniorStrategic/contacts.php

This site offers information to seniors about a wide range of topics, including retirement, throughout the world. The site also provides information on conferences throughout the world related to retirement. One of the few sites that cover this topic from a global perspective.

Equal Employment Opportunity Commission

www.eeoc.gov

This site provides the text and regulations of the Age Discrimination in Employment Act. It also gives information on legal action, along with statistics on age discrimination charges and on the outcome of these charges. A good site to consult when researching age discrimination in the workplace.

The Sloane Center on Aging & Work at Boston College

http://bc.edu/research/agingandwork

This site provides a stream of reports and studies related to the aging workforce, older workers, older employees' views of work, and employer perceptions of older workers. An excellent source of quality research on older workers and the aging workforce.

chapter 10

HOUSING AND TRANSPORTATION

Mrs. Carrington lived alone after her husband died. She lived in the same one-bedroom apartment that they had shared. At first, this seemed fine, but after a few years she began to have trouble climbing the six flights of stairs to her apartment. She found it hard to go out for groceries. She even had trouble getting to her ground-floor mailbox every day. The building superintendent helped her with rides to the supermarket. He got her mail for her and did small repairs around her apartment. But this depended on his schedule and personal plans.

The apartment building mostly housed people in late middle age. They worked during the day, and Mrs. Carrington had few friends in the building. Her long-time friends kept in touch on the telephone daily, but they could get around less as they aged. She spent more and more of her time watching television, alone in her apartment. Her daughter, Ruth, who lived 2 hours away, spoke to her at least once a day.

Ruth noticed about this time that her mother's refrigerator contained almost no meat, vegetables, or milk. Mrs. Carrington's inability to get out meant that she could not get fresh food. Ruth began to worry about her mother's health. She decided to look for an apartment in a seniors' housing complex closer to her home. Mrs. Carrington resisted, but she finally agreed to move.

The new setting brought Mrs. Carrington out of isolation. The apartment had a recreation room, a lobby where people gathered in the afternoon, and social events like birthday parties. The apartment complex offered a bus service to a shopping center twice a week. The bus driver brought Mrs. Carrington's groceries to her door. Her first-floor apartment allowed her to go outside in the nice weather and she could easily walk to the lobby to sit with her new neighbors. The staff kept an eye on the tenants for signs of illness or other problems. The move improved the quality of Mrs. Carrington's life.

Many people, like Mrs. Carrington, prefer not to move. They feel anxious about the cost of new housing and about losing touch with their friends and neighbors. They also feel comfortable with the places and things they have lived with for many years. Studies show, however, that a move to a planned housing complex can improve morale, increase activity, and increase social interaction. People feel most satisfied if they move by choice and if the housing they move to suits their personal preferences.

The United States today offers older people a wide range of housing options. These options make it possible for people to live in the kind of housing they prefer. Still, problems with the housing supply exist. Some older people—those in inner cities and rural settings, for example—have few housing options. This chapter looks at (1) the continuum of housing options and living arrangements open to older people today, (2) new developments in housing and transportation for older people, and (3) the future of housing and transportation in an aging society.

LIVING ARRANGEMENTS

Noninstitutional living arrangements include living with a spouse, alone, with other relatives, or with nonrelatives. Most older people who lived in the community (54.6%) in 2008 lived with a spouse. But this differs for men and women. Seventy-two percent of older men live with a spouse, compared with only 42% of older women. This difference between men and women increases with age. For women age 75 and over, only 28.9% lived with a spouse. High rates of widowhood among very old women account for this. (See Figure 10.1.)

Almost one third (30.5%) of noninstitutionalized older persons in 2008 lived alone. This came to 39.5% of older women and 18.5% of older men. The propor-

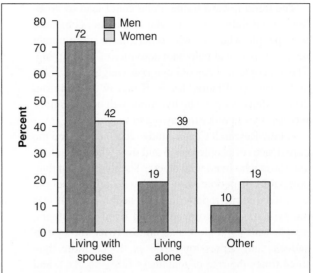

Compared to older women, a higher proportion of older men live with a spouse (72% vs. 42%). Note also that, compared to older men, older women have more than double the likelihood of living alone (39% vs. 19%). Higher rates of widowhood for older women explain most of this difference in living arrangements. The large proportion of older women who live alone poses challenges for the health care and social service systems. People who live alone tend to need more home care and have a higher risk of institutionalization.

FIGURE 10.1   Living Arrangements of Persons 65 and over, 2008

Source: Adapted from Administration on Aging. (2009). *A profile of older Americans: 2009.* Living arrangements. Citing U.S. Bureau of the Census including the 2008 Current Population Survey, Annual Social and Economic Supplement and the 2008 American Community Survey. Retrieved October 28, 2010, from www.aoa.gov/aoaroot/aging_statistics/Profile/2009/6.aspx.

tion of people who live alone increases with age. For example, half of women age 75 and over lived alone (Administration on Aging, 2009). Women outnumbered men in this category almost three to one.

Engelhardt and colleagues (Engelhardt, Gruber, Perry, & National Bureau of Economic Research, 2002) say that increased Social Security benefits in part account for an increase in older women living alone. Higher benefits give older women more living arrangement options. They can afford to live on their own.

The number of older people who live alone will likely increase in the future. Higher divorce rates in the middle and later years will add to the number of people who live alone, as will the increased number of people who choose never to marry. Also, older people today prefer what Rosenmayr and Kockeis (1963) first called "intimacy at a distance." They prefer to live near, but not with, their children.

The trend toward living alone could lead to problems in the future. People who live alone, compared with people who live with others, have more unmet needs for personal help with activities of daily living. These people in later old age risk weight loss, falls, and burns (LaPlante, Kaye, Kang, & Harrington, 2004). Many people who live alone will need community services in order to stay out of institutions.

A Pew Research Center Study (2009) compared the experiences of people age 65 and over who lived alone and those who lived with others. The study found that, compared to people who lived with others, people who lived alone reported poorer health and felt less happy. Compared to people who lived with others, people who lived alone had almost twice the rate of sadness and depression (26% vs. 15%), more than three times the rate of loneliness (28% vs. 8%), and more than twice the need for help with their affairs. Compared to women who live alone, men who live alone report lower rates of excellent or good health, lower rates of happiness, and higher rates of sadness.

People who live alone also spend less time with family members, less time involved in their community, and less time with grandchildren. On these measures, too, compared to older women, older men report less engagement with others. The older age of people who live alone and their poorer health account in part for these findings. Still, the findings show that living alone in old age leads to a lower quality of life for both men and women.

AN ECOLOGICAL MODEL OF HOUSING

Older people want to age in place. They want to stay in their homes as long as they can. The AARP (2006b) conducted a survey of community-dwelling people age 50 and over. The study found that in 2005, 89% of people age 50 and over say they want to stay in their current home as long as possible. The older the age group studied, the greater the desire to age in place. Eighty-four percent of people ages 55 to 64 said they preferred to age in place. This figure rose to 95% of people age 75 and over. Schaefer (1999, p. 8) concludes that "the vast majority of the elderly want to live out their lives in their homes."

An AARP survey (Bayer & Harper, 2000) found that 47% of people age 55 and over said they had lived at their current address more than 21 years. More than one quarter (28%) of this age group said they had lived at their current address for more than 30 years. The longer people lived in their current homes, the greater the likelihood that they preferred to age in place (Bayer & Harper, 2000). When older people move, they tend to stay in the same city or county. More than three quarters of older people who move do so within the same state.

A home means more than a physical place. To many older people, their home reminds them of their family and their past. The rooms, the decorations, and the neighborhood give a person a feeling of security and well-being (Shenk, Kuwahara, & Zablotsky, 2004). This is often particularly true in widowhood. "I just love it here," one widowed woman said of the house she and her husband had built together years before, "I have almost anything I want here" (Shenk et al., 2004, p. 165). For another widowed woman, her long-time home "contains many memories and much love" (p. 167).

Fogel (1992, p. 16) says that the meaning of home goes beyond logic. People give all the good reasons why they should move, "but then conclude that the only way they would leave their home would be in a box." **Aging in place** requires that a person have the capability to live in the setting they choose (Wagnild, 2001).

Lawton and Nahemow (1973; Lawton, 1990) created a model that describes the relationship between a person's capability and environmental demand. **Capability (competence)** refers to the total of a person's physical, mental, and social abilities. **Environmental demand (environmental press)** refers to the forces that, combined with need, lead a person to make a response. This model shaped housing policy in the United States over the past few decades. It continues to influence thinking about aging and housing today. Scheidt and Windley (2006, p. 108) call this "the most influential model for research and practice . . . in the field today."

This model shows that people function at their best when their capability suits the environment's demands. This allows them to fulfill their needs. If the environment demands too little or too much, the person feels out of balance and makes maladaptive responses. A healthy retiree who loves to garden and do home repairs but lives in a high-rise apartment may feel unchallenged. An older person who uses a walker may find life in a two-story house too demanding. People try to find a fit between what they can do and what the environment demands.

Parmelee and Lawton (1990) updated the person–environment fit model. They redefined competence as **autonomy**. They redefined environmental press as security. Autonomous people have the resources

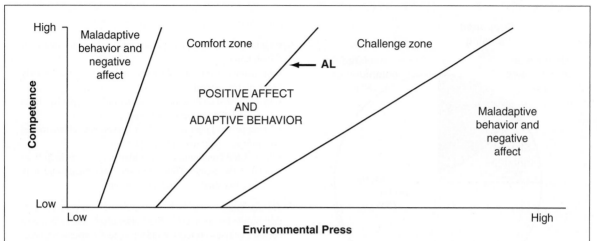

This figure describes the relationship between a person's ability and the demands of the person's environment. The line AL represents an average level of demand at a given level of competence. To the immediate left of the midpoint lies the comfort zone. People have enough competence here to easily get along in their environment. Here they feel most at ease. To the immediate right of the midpoint (line AL) lies the challenge zone. The environment makes the maximum demand on a person's ability.

As demand increases, adaptation takes place until environmental demand goes beyond the person's ability to adapt (right diagonal). As demand decreases below a person's adaptation level, the person will feel bored (left diagonal).

No matter how high the competence, at some level of demand a person will lose the ability to adapt. No matter how low the competence, a person will still have some adaptive ability.

The greater a person's competence, the greater the adaptive ability; the lower the competence, the lower the adaptive ability. A person with low competence can be challenged by

even a small increase in demand. Lawton calls this the "environmental docility" hypothesis. Likewise, a person with low competence can benefit from even small decreases in environmental demand.

This model shows that improvement in person–environment fit can take place in three ways: (1) A person can live in a less demanding environment. This may mean a move to a more supportive setting such as a nursing home. Or it can mean adaptation of the environment to suit a person's ability. A change in housing design (e.g., an entry ramp or lower countertops) can make a problem environment comfortable. (2) A person can improve competence (e.g., through physiotherapy). (3) A person can do both.

Too often improvements take the form of decreased demand. Professionals need to look at both sides of this model. Increased competence can also lead to better adaptation. Sometimes a single change, such as better lighting, can increase a person's competence and decrease environmental demand. This model encourages people to use their full ability within safe limits.

FIGURE 10.2   The Lawton-Nahemow Ecological Model

Sources: From "Ecology and the Aging Process" by M. P. Lawton & L. Nahemow (1973), in C. Eisdorfer & M. P. Lawton (Eds.), *Psychology of Adult Development and Aging.* Washington, D.C.: American Psychological Association. Copyright © 1973 by the American Psychological Association. Adapted with permission.

to pursue their goals. They have freedom of choice and action. A secure environment offers trustworthy physical and social resources. Autonomy and security, Parmelee and Lawton say, "form a dialectic that lies at the heart of person-environment relations in later life" (p. 466). People gain security, for example, when they move to a nursing home. But they lose autonomy. Likewise, people give up some security when they choose the autonomy of driving a car.

This model allows us to put housing options on a continuum from least to most demanding. We can

then look at the demands of each option and the adaptations needed to live in each setting.

HOUSING OPTIONS

A continuum of housing options exists today. (See Figure 10.3.) This continuum, in theory, offers older people a chance to match their abilities to an environment that maximizes their autonomy. Each type of housing has costs and benefits. An older person may move from one type of housing to another as abilities change.

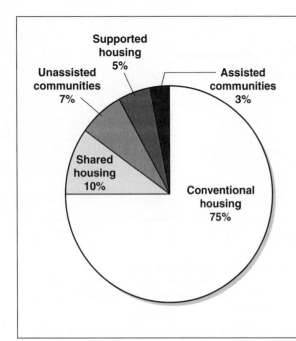

Supported housing 5%

Unassisted communities 7%

Assisted communities 3%

Shared housing 10%

Conventional housing 75%

Definitions:

- Older people in conventional housing tend to own their own homes.
- In shared housing, the older person lives with a nonelderly person for support.
- In unassisted communities, healthy older people live in an age-restricted setting without special supports.
- In supported housing, the older person gets either formal or informal help from outside the home.
- In assisted communities, the older person gets help from outside the home. This often includes meals and may include personal care and nursing services.

This figure shows that the large majority of older people live on their own in the community. Most older people live in their own homes. Eighty-two percent of older people in conventional housing live in owner-occupied homes. People tend to move to more supportive settings as they age. Also, people without children tend to live in supportive settings. Supportive settings provide help with ADL and may provide health care. This figure does not include people who live in nursing homes or other facilities.

FIGURE 10.3   Choice of Housing, Age 70 and Over

Source: Schaefer, R. (2000). *Housing America's seniors*, Chart 9, p. 10. Cambridge, MA: Joint Center for Housing Studies of Harvard University. Retrieved November 20, 2010, from http://www.jchs.harvard.edu/publications/seniors/housing_americas_seniors.pdf. Reprinted with permission.

Single-Family Homes

The Administration on Aging (2010) reports that of all households headed by older people, 80% lived in homes that they owned. Twenty percent lived in rented housing. Sixty-eight percent of older homeowners in 2007 lived mortgage free. Older people typically own homes valued less than the average for all homeowners.

Older people in nonmetropolitan settings, compared with city dwellers, more often own their own homes. But nonmetropolitan homeowners tend to live in older homes that, compared with city homes, have low market value. Older people lived in homes that were on average 4 years older than those of all householders (Administration on Aging, 2010e). These include problems with maintenance, plumbing, and kitchen equipment.

Older people live in older homes in part because they tend to age in place. Older homeowners stay put for a number of reasons. First, they enjoy the comfort and familiarity of their homes. A home means security and independence to older people. Second, selling a home may create an increase in taxes because of an increase in a person's liquid assets. Third, increased liquid assets may make a person ineligible for certain health or income supports. Some people have little choice but to stay in their homes.

People in good health report that they enjoy living where they do. But some older people find themselves overhoused. People with physical problems, for example, may have trouble getting around in a two-story, single-family home. And they may be unable to maintain it. About one third (35%) of respondents in an AARP housing modification study said they had trouble climbing up and down stairs. Another 30% had trouble walking or problems with arthritis, their back, or their legs (Bayer & Harper, 2000). Frail homeowners need help with repairs, chores, and home modifications (Pynoos, Cicero, & Nishita, 2010). They also need help managing and coordinating service providers. Repair and other services increase the cost of living in a home.

The philosophy of aging in place responds to older peoples' desire to stay out of a nursing home. Salomon (2010) reports that in a 2005 study, 89% of people age 50 and over said they wanted to stay in their homes "indefinitely." If that proved impossible, 85% said they wanted to stay in their local community as long as possible. Other studies support this finding.

A study of 402 community dwelling people age 65 and over (Clarity, 2007) asked about their housing preferences. More seniors in this study said they feared loss of independence (26%) and entering a nursing home (13%) than feared death (3%). A large majority of the seniors in the study (89%) said they wanted to age in place. But more than half (53%) feared that health problems, mental decline, and the inability to drive could all make aging in place a challenge.

About half the people in an AARP (2005a) study said their homes would not serve them "very well" as they age. Twelve percent said their homes would not serve them "well" or "not well at all." People who lived in poorly designed housing also engaged less with their community and felt isolated.

Aging in place as a philosophy has led the home design and housing industries to provide many options including home renovation, universal design, and adaptive housing.

A study of Americans age 55 and over (National Association of Home Builders, 2009) asked them about their future housing preferences. The results provide insight into Baby Boomers' thinking about their future needs. Respondents said they preferred suburban living, single-story homes, and high-speed Internet access. These Boomers didn't consider universal design (design to suit a person with a disability) a priority. Consumers also said they wanted to live close to shopping and medical services. Few said they would pay more for "green" homes.

These findings raise questions about Boomers' awareness of their future needs. Life in the suburbs will probably make access to amenities like shopping more difficult as people age in place. Like-

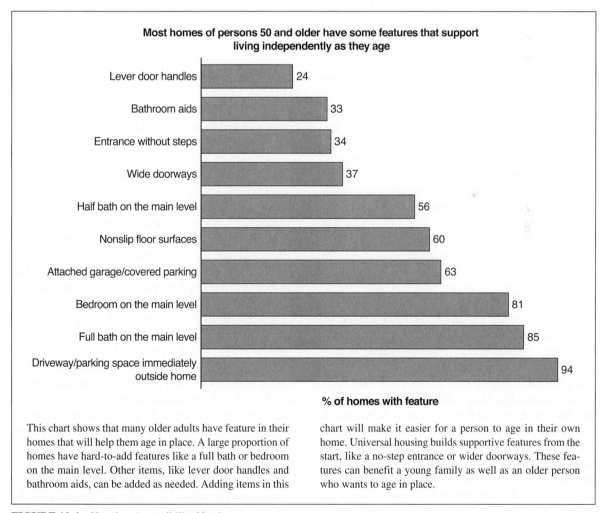

This chart shows that many older adults have feature in their homes that will help them age in place. A large proportion of homes have hard-to-add features like a full bath or bedroom on the main level. Other items, like lever door handles and bathroom aids, can be added as needed. Adding items in this chart will make it easier for a person to age in their own home. Universal housing builds supportive features from the start, like a no-step entrance or wider doorways. These features can benefit a young family as well as an older person who wants to age in place.

FIGURE 10.4 Housing Accessibility Needs

Source: AARP. (2005a). *Beyond 50.05: A report to the nation on livable communities.* Figure 8, p. 53. Retrieved October 19, 2010, from http://assets.aarp. org/rgcenter/il/beyond_50_communities.pdf. Reprinted with permission.

BOX 10.1
THE IMPACT OF THE HOUSING BUBBLE

Older people want to age in place. But the recent recession threatened many older people with the loss of their homes. Herd (2009) says that in the recent housing meltdown, housing prices fell by 30% from their peak in 2006. People in Florida and Arizona saw values fall by as much as 50%. During this fall in housing values, the loss in housing wealth came to $2.7 trillion.

Pynoos and Liebig (2009; also Brown, 2009) report on a housing survey conducted in December 2008. Fifteen percent of respondents age 65 and over in this survey said they faced problems in paying their mortgage or rent (Brown, 2009). Older residents also reported trouble paying for heating, cooling, and phone service.

Shelton (2008a) says that people age 50 and over made up more than one quarter (28%) of all people who were behind in their mortgage payments or faced foreclosure in the last quarter of 2007. Walters and Hermanson (2001) say that, compared to people age 35 and under, people age 65 and over held three times as many subprime mortgages. In the worst cases older homeowners find their property "under water"—they owe more on the mortgage than the home is worth.

For many older people the value of their home serves as a financial buffer in case of widowhood or a health care crisis. The Joint Center for Housing Studies of Harvard University (2009) says that home equity makes up 26% of household wealth for older people. Among poorer older people it makes up 59% of household wealth. The decline in housing values at this time threatens the financial security of many older homeowners.

---

wise, the lack of concern for universal design raises questions about Boomers' ability to live in their future ideal homes as they age. Sandra Timmerman, Director of the MetLife Mature Market Institute, says, "Aside from recognizing that one-story homes will be best for their later years, customers may be somewhat unrealistic."

Boomers' housing preferences may reflect a denial of aging and its effects in late old age. Or it may reflect a lack of information about the kind of housing that will allow someone to age in place. In either case, Boomers need more education about housing and the aging process.

Home Modification

Many people today live in "Peter Pan Housing"—housing designed as if the owners will never grow old. As many as 1 million older households need at least one modification such as a grab bar or ramp, but a small percent of older people's households have these modifications. The U.S. Public Health Service says that older people could prevent as many as two-thirds of falls by home modification (Ethel Percy Andrus Gerontology Center, 1995). Hare (1992, p. 36) says that if you choose to age in place, "your remodeler may be almost as important to you as your doctor."

About half of older people in a series of national studies (Newman, 2003) reported at least one home modification. Twenty-three percent said they had an unmet need for a modification, and about 14% said they had a house-related disability (e.g., they found it difficult to climb stairs at home). This study found that one half of the people who had made modifications still had an unmet need for modifications.

Aldwin, Spiro, and Park (2006) say that people often rearrange their homes to cope with disability. Sometimes a simple change makes a difference. For example, a person will arrange the furniture so that he or she can use a wall for support when walking. Nearly all of the respondents to the AARP home modification survey (86%) said they made some small change to their homes. These included nightlights, nonskid strips in the bathtub, and brighter light bulbs. But, aging in place may entail more extreme changes as people age and their physical conditions change (Bayer & Harper, 2000).

The AARP study also found that many people who aged in place made major modifications to their homes. People added lighting at the bottom or top of stairs (40%), made changes to allow them to live on a single floor (34%), used levers to replace knobs in the kitchen (25%), and added handrails on stairs and in the bathroom (25% and 23%, respectively). People with a health problem showed the greatest likelihood of modifying their homes.

Home modification can allow people to stay in their homes into late old age. And this seems like an increasingly popular way to help older people stay independent. Newman (2003) found that home modification nearly doubled between 1978 and 1995. People who have made changes report that this will allow them to stay in their homes at least 10 years longer (Bayer & Harper, 2000).

Journalist Jim Redden (2007) gives the example of Dave Heinlein, 58, of Portland, Oregon. Mr. Heinlein decided to make a change in his housing due to changes in his health. He began to have knee problems that made living in his two-story home a challenge. "It got to the point where the pain was so bad," he says, "I could barely make it up and down the stairs. I was only going up the stairs once at night to go bed, and only coming down once in the morning."

He decided to sell his two-story home and buy a one-story nearby. He hired a remodeling firm to make some changes to meet his future needs. The company removed some walls around the toilet, enlarged a shower door, and installed heavy-duty grab bars in both places. These small changes along with the move to a one-story home will allow Mr. Heinlein to age in place.

"Now," he says, "I can live in this house for the rest of my life. Even if I have to bring someone in to help me get around, there's plenty of room for them to help me get to the toilet and in and out of the shower."

Some people say they would like to modify their homes but haven't done so. Among those age 45 and over, about one third said that they didn't do the modification because they couldn't do it themselves. Another third said they couldn't afford to make the changes. Some people may resist home modification for another reason. Richard Duncan, an expert in adaptive design, says that "it's the first tangible expression of their aging, and often that's a shocking thing they have to contemplate" (cited in Sit, 1992, p. 74).

Home modification programs exist throughout the United States. Some of these programs use volunteers and donated material. Others use professionals to take on major construction projects. Some government agencies, such as the Rural Development–Rural Housing Service, provide loans to pay for repairs to fire hazards and plumbing.

This agency has also built apartment housing for older people who can no longer maintain their homes. In 1999, for example, the agency spent $32.5 million (two fifths of all funds lent) to build 49 apartment complexes for older people. This program served about 1,900 older people and people with disabilities. Older low-income women made up the majority of people served by this program (Rural Development, 2004).

The federal government announced in 2003 that it would provide $593 million to fund the construction or improvement of housing for low-income older people. This program will also subsidize rents for 5 years to ensure that low-income older people pay only 30% of their income for rent (National Resource Center, 2004). Pynoos and colleagues (Pynoos, Caraviello, & Cicero, 2009; Moulder, 2007) say that more than two thirds (68%) of city governments in the United States have home modification or maintenance programs.

Some housing experts propose a "universal" house. This would make home modifications unnecessary. The house would include a "wheelchair-accessible entryway, kitchens, and bathrooms; single-lever faucets; nonslip flooring; easy to reach temperature controls; anti-scald devices; and grab bars." A universal house (with anti-scald faucets, for example) has "transgenerational design" (Luscombe, 2003). It benefits children as well as older people. A young person with a sprained ankle, for example, will find the flat entryway easy to cross. A pregnant woman will find the adjustable countertops easy to work around. A person could move into a house like this with a young family and could stay there until late old age.

Universal design applies to an entire house that supports people of all ages and abilities. *Visitability* applies only to the first floor of a single-family home. It requires that an older resident or visitor with a disability be able to move barrier-free within the first floor of a single-family house.

Pynoos and colleagues (2010, p. 332, citing Nishita, Liebig Pynoos, Perelman, & Spegal, 2007) list four features of visitability. "A zero-step entrance, interior doors with a minimum width of 32 inches, an accessible route inside the house, and a half bathroom on the first floor." Visitability provides a welcoming environment for guests who may have mobility limitations. Pynoos and colleagues (2010) report that by 2008, 60 cities and states had adopted visitability codes. And developers had built 30,000 visitability homes.

Researchers at the University of Florida (Helal et al., 2008) use computer technologies to create supportive housing. The Gator Tech smart house, as it's called, includes a smart mailbox that senses when mail arrives and informs the person living in the house. The house includes a front door that uses a radio-frequency identification (RFID) tag to identify the owner, who can enter without a key. A smart laundry notifies residents when to do a wash. The master

---

BOX 10.2
DESIGNS FOR SAFETY AND COMFORT

The AARP, in conjunction with renowned architect Michael Graves, opened a universal design home in Washington, D.C. (Boniface, 2008). The home, named Andrus House, for the founder of the AARP, showcases design that suits the needs of older people. Features of the home include:

- Widened doorways, easy to use windows, lower light switches, grab bars, and raised electric outlets

- Lower stovetops, counters at varying levels to accommodate sitting or standing

- Cabinets with pull-out shelves, a raised dishwasher and oven are raised, and a double-sided refrigerator

- Cabinets have space underneath to accommodate someone in a wheelchair

- Appliances and temperature gauges can talk to help people with vision impairment

- A chairlift leads to the second floor

Companies will produce more products for older people in the future as the market grows. New technology will increase the ease and comfort of living at home and alone. For example, lights can now sense when a person enters or leaves a room. They go on and off without a touch. Remote control units and computer chips can control many appliances, including the television, radio, and fans. Home computers will give homebound older people access to the world. They will offer information, friendship, and entertainment.

Research engineers at Stanford, Carnegie Mellon, the University of Pittsburg, and the University of Michigan have applied computer technology to the needs of older people. They developed a walker with sonar detectors and mapping software to help frail older people get around. They also developed a first-generation robot named Pearl that will (in future generations of development) react to an older person's needs. The robot and other computerized devices will add to the support given by family members and professional caregivers (Rotstein, 2004).

Technology-enhanced designs make life easier for people of all ages. Door levers that help older people with arthritis, for example, also make it easier for children to enter and leave rooms. Elinor Ginzler, senior vice president, AARP Livable Communities Office of Social Impact, says, "a 34- or 36-inch doorway will help in all circumstances, whether you're an older person coming through in a wheelchair, a mom rolling a double stroller through, or anyone moving in an overstuffed chair or carrying an armful of groceries" (Boniface, 2008). Technology and invention will make houses safer and more enjoyable for everyone. Designs for older people can lead the way.

Are there other products that you know about or have seen that would help an older person live more comfortably? Can you suggest some home modification or invention that would make life easier for older people?

---

bathroom includes a toilet paper sensor and a soap dispenser that notify the owner when a refill is needed. A water temperature sensor prevents scalding.

Many of these and other innovations in the Gator Tech smart house will find their way into homes in the future. "Ultimately," the researchers say, "our goal is to create a 'Smart house in a box': off the shelf assisted technology for the home that the average user can buy, install, and monitor without the aid of engineers" (Helal et al., 2008, p. 708). Smart homes will help older people live more comfortably and safely.

Schaefer and Harvard University (2000; also Joint Center for Housing Studies, 2009) project an increase in major and minor modifications to housing units in the future. They report this trend for both owned and rented housing. They project that people age 85 and over will make the most home modifications.

Home Equity Conversion Loans (Reverse Mortgages)

Some people who want to stay in their homes find that they have excessive housing costs.[1] They may own a home worth $100,000 or more, but not have enough money for heat and taxes. These people live house rich, but cash poor. The lack of cash may force them to sell their home and move to more affordable housing. **Home equity conversion loans (HECs)**, sometimes called reverse mortgages, can provide homeowners with the income they need to age in place.

The U.S. Department of Housing and Urban Development says that very low income renters have excessive housing costs if they spend 30% of their before-tax income on housing (U.S. Department of Housing and Urban Development, 2011).

A study by Redfoot, Scholen, and Brown (2007) indicates that people most often use a reverse mortgage to retire an existing mortgage (19%), make home repairs and improvements (18%), improve the quality of life (14%), and pay for everyday expenses (10%). The use of federally insured reverse mortgages increased by 10% during 2008–09. The recent economic downturn may in part account for this increase as people use their home equity to shore up their incomes (Pynoos & Liebig, 2009).

A number of HEC programs exist. Through one program, a person gets a monthly loan based on the person's age, current interest rates, and the house's value. The person repays the loan on a set date. Another HEC is called a deferred payment loan. Through this method, people borrow against the value of their home. Their estate repays the loan when they die, or they repay it when they move and sell the home. Many variations on these two options exist.

The older the person, the greater the house's value, and the lower the interest rate, the better the income from an HEC. Critics of reverse mortgages say that banks get too large a share of the house's value. Also, the National Resource Center on Supportive Housing and Home Modification (2004; also Lafleur, 2009) says that reverse mortgages can include unexpected costs. These include "high set-up costs for the loans which include an origination fee, a monthly service charge of about $30 to $35, mortgage insurance premium, appraisal fee and other closing costs" (National Resource Center, 2004, n.p.).

Tara Coates (2011), writing for the AARP, lists a variety of fees charged for reverse mortgages. These include mortgage insurance, loan origination fees, closing costs, mortgage premiums, interest, and servicing fees. She gives an example of one typical charge for a reverse mortgage. She reports that a person who takes out a standard reverse mortgage will pay a 2% mortgage insurance premium on the total value of the home (not the amount borrowed). This means that a $400,000 home will cost $8,000 upfront just for mortgage insurance.

Coates's report on reverse mortgages includes many warnings. These include advice to put off taking out a reverse mortgage as long as possible. Donald Redfoot, an AARP policy expert, says, "Getting rid of a mortgage may seem like a good idea by freeing up income, but borrowers need to understand that they are trading future savings for current consumption. . . . Those who borrow early in retirement risk not having that equity available later in life when they may need it."

The Federal Housing Administration (FHA), a part of the U.S. **Department of Housing and Urban Development (HUD)**, has set up a program that overcomes some of the objections to reverse mortgages. The HUD program serves people age 62 or over who have paid off their homes or who have small mortgages. The FHA oversees and guarantees these reverse mortgages. HUD requires a free counseling session for people who want to take out an FHA-guaranteed reverse mortgage. The FHA assesses a person's situation—based on the person's age and home value—and will then tell a lender how much the FHA will guarantee (U.S. Department of Housing, 2007a).

So, for example, "based on a loan at today's interest rates of approximately 9%, a 65-year-old could borrow up to 26% of the home's value, a 75-year-old could borrow up to 39% of the home's value, and an 85-year-old could borrow up to 56% of the home's value" (U.S. Department of Housing, 2007a). The FHA puts limits on the cost of loans and guarantees that lenders will do what they promise (AARP, 2004b). (These limits will change at higher or lower interest rates.)

The AARP says that FHA-guaranteed mortgages cost less than other similar reverse mortgages, and this program lends older people the most money. This program also allows the most freedom in how a person can use the funds. A person can use the equity in his or her home to pay debts or live a more comfortable life. The funds can be distributed in a lump sum payment or monthly payments. The person can borrow against the full value of the home, but will not have to pay back more than the house is worth. If the house sells for more than the loan amount due, the estate gets to keep the profit.

Some people in financial need may still choose to avoid a reverse mortgage for several reasons: (1) the reverse mortgage uses up a large part of their estate, (2) they may not want to go into debt late in life, (3) income from a reverse mortgage can change a person's tax bracket and lower his or her government pension income, and (4) they may not understand the risks and gains. HUD offers free information on reverse mortgages on its Web site. Also, older people will want to consult with family members and financial advisors before deciding on whether a reverse mortgage works for them. Used wisely, a reverse mortgage can raise a person's standard of living and improve his or her sense of well-being.

The Older Women's League (1993) of Washington, DC, says that women often take out reverse mortgages because they need the cash. They care less about the high cost of the loans in the long run and more about maintaining their lifestyle now.

The United Seniors Health Council (2004) says that older people could use reverse mortgages to pay for health care and long-term care. Jacobs and Weissert (1987) report that reverse mortgages could finance long-term care for the lifetime of about half of high-risk single people. Likewise, about half of the high-risk single group could use their reverse mortgage payments to buy nursing home insurance. This would protect them against catastrophic health care costs.

Reverse mortgages have grown in popularity in the past few years. Between 2000 and 2009, the number of home equity conversion mortgages (HECMs) backed by the Federal Housing Association increased more than 20 times (from 6,637 in 2000 to 115,000 in 2009). Since 1990, HUD (cited in Reverse Mortgage Page, 2010) reports that 581,884 older homeowners have taken a HECM. The increase in home values during the early 2000s made HECMs more attractive than ever.

Home improvements and home equity conversion mortgages offer two ways for older homeowners to age in place. They expand a person's ability to maintain a home and to pay the high cost of maintenance and taxes.

Apartment Living

Apartments account for the greatest proportion of older people's housing after single-family homes. The Administration on Aging (2010) reports that apartment dwellers accounted for 20% of the households headed by older people in 2007. Renters tend to be older women, and they have about half the income of homeowners. Compared to homeowners, renters tend to spend a higher proportion of their income (more than 30%) on housing. Renters have fewer options than owners when it comes to home modification. Leases often limit the kinds of changes a person can make to an apartment. For this reason, many older people choose to move into apartment buildings already designed for older people.

Age Segregation Versus Age Integration

Age segregation refers to a setting where older people live only with people their own age. **Age integration** refers to a setting that includes people of all ages. Most older people live in age-integrated communities (as they have for most of their lives). But in 2006 about 2 million people, or 6% of the older population,

lived in an age-segregated setting (e.g., a high-rise apartment for seniors or a gated community) (Roy & Russell, 2006). Critics of age-segregated housing say that age segregation isolates older people from the rest of society. These critics fear that segregation will lead to loneliness and depression.

Research on age segregated housing found the opposite (Pynoos et al., 2010). Roy and Russell (2006) report that age-segregated housing helps people develop good relationships, allows for greater security, and offers more access to support services. Older people in age-segregated communities often create their own subcultures. People in these communities value one another's company, see the world in roughly the same way, and focus on activities they enjoy together. People in age-segregated housing also reported many links to networks outside their buildings. They belonged to clubs and organizations and maintained contacts with family and friends.

An Australian study (Davidson, Brooke, & Kendig, 2001, p. 123) compared older people in age-segregated housing with a similar group in mixed housing in the community. The researchers found that "the age-segregated sample had relatively more interaction with friends and had less risk of isolation from friends." This finding applied especially to people age 75 and over. The researchers conclude that age-segregated housing helps older people who have physical problems and can't easily visit others. People who lived in age-segregated housing, compared with those who lived in the community, received more visits from friends.

Lawton (1987) believes that older people do well in either age-segregated or age-integrated housing. The choice depends on what an individual prefers and on the individual's needs. It also depends on good design. Lawton says that the right design can make both age integration and age segregation enjoyable.

Normal Design Versus Special Design

Publicly sponsored apartment developments for older people in the past gave little thought to the issues raised by aging in place. They contained few supports for people as they aged. They assumed that as people needed more care, they would move to a nursing home. This rarely happens. Instead, people stay in their apartments, but they need more supports.

A large percentage of people in older persons' housing are age 80 and over. As one housing manager said to me, "We didn't expect it, but we've built high-rise nursing homes." These buildings now need to add supports for their tenants. Congregate housing meets this need.

Congregate Housing and Assisted (Apartment) Living

Housing can mean simply a roof and four walls, or it can mean a setting that enhances a person's well-being. Housing for some older people demands an integration of housing and services. The U.S. Department of Housing and Urban Development (2000b) says that about 10% of people ages 70 to 74 live in some kind of special care environments (either with another person or with some living assistance). This increases to approximately 60% at age 90. Enriched housing—also called congregate housing, **assisted living**, board and care homes, personal care homes, homes for the aged, and rest homes—provide one type of supportive environment.

Congregate Housing

Congregate housing offers private apartments where residents share recreational activities, transportation, and other services as they choose. Congregate housing reduces older residents' isolation and gives them a sense of safety and emotional security. Altus and Mathews (2002) surveyed people who live in congregate apartments. Tenants reported high satisfaction with their housing.

A **congregate (or enriched) housing** complex offers services such as meals, recreation programs, and in some cases health care and ADL support. But services and supports can vary widely between settings. Some settings offer many services, some offer few. Some offer privacy, others offer little privacy (Robinson et al., 2007).

A program in San Jose, California, titled Project Match helps local low-income seniors live in supportive housing. "The mission of Project Match is to develop safe, affordable housing with supportive services for seniors that enhance the abilities of seniors to live fully and well" (Volunteer Match, 2010).

In 2010, its Senior Group Residence Program consisted of 9 homes with 37 units of shared rental housing. Project Match provides furniture for common areas, cable TV, and phone service. Each resident has a private room. The program also provides services to residents. These include "needs assessment, psychosocial support, conflict management and linkages to community services."

Assisted Living Apartments

Assisted living apartments add personal services and some health care to congregate housing ameni-

ties. They provide services that optimize physical and psychological independence (Scheidt & Windley, 2006). The Assisted Living Federation of America (ALFA) (2000, 2009) reports that 36,000 assisted living communities exist nationwide. ALFA estimates that more than 1 million people live in assisted living settings.

Assisted living provides 24-hour care and supervision. Regnier (2003) reports that assisted living projects average 52.2 units. Most of the units (61%) are studio apartments. A study released in 2006 reported that female residents in assisted living quarters had a median age of 87 years and male residents 85 years. Residents had an average of two ADL limitations (Assisted Living Federation of America, 2006).

Regnier (2003) reports that a majority (65%) of people in assisted living arrangements need help bathing and more than one quarter (29%) need help toileting. Assisted living settings do not provide skilled nursing services. This reflects federal HUD policies on older persons' housing. On average in the United States in 2009, assisted living costs came to $37,572 per year. This came to less than half the cost of a single room in a nursing home ($79,935) (MetLife Mature Market, 2009a).

Unfortunately, in many cases congregate housing does not live up to its potential. First, cost cutting by HUD led to an absence of recreation, activity, and service space (like a dining room) in these buildings (Scott-Webber & Koebel, 2001). Second, HUD housing until recently assumed that older tenants had good health and could perform ADLs. Third, HUD policies assumed that supports led to dependency, so HUD-supported buildings provide little space and almost no services for older tenants. These policies created housing that failed to meet older tenants' needs.

Koff and Park (1993, p. 238) sum up the effects of public policy on older people's housing. "Too few federal housing policies for the elderly have considered the quality of life in the housing but instead have mainly focused on providing 'maintenance' environments that are only just adequate as shelter." Housing must offer older people services that enhance their autonomy, allow them to age in place, and provide them the chance for personal growth.

Subsidized Housing

The American Community Survey (2007) estimates that 53% of older renters pay more than 30% of their income for housing. Subsidized housing helps these poor older people live in affordable housing. More than 1.2 million people, most of them age 80 and over, live in subsidized housing. Golant (2003) found that many people who live in subsidized high-rise housing lack health and personal care supports. These people risk institutionalization.

The oldest people (age 85 and over), many of them women, face the greatest risk. A high proportion of these people have ADL and IADL deficiencies. They need help in maintaining themselves in the community. According to Golant, 12% of people in rent-assisted apartments have mental deficiencies that interfere with their everyday lives. These tenants need help with housekeeping and personal care. But relatively few subsidized buildings offer supports.

The federal government also provides rent subsidies to older people who live in nongovernment housing. HUD grants will subsidize rents for low-income older people for 5 years. The government does this through Section 8 of the federal Housing and Community Development Act. This program provides "housing choice vouchers" to low-income families. The vouchers allow a low-income renter to pay the difference between a fair market rent and their ability to pay. The family pays a percentage of their income for rent; the program pays the rest. This keeps very poor older tenants' rents at only 30% of their income (U.S. Department of Housing and Urban Development, 2011b).

The federal government, through HUD, has constructed more than 6,000 housing facilities for older people since 1959. This has meant an increase of 270,000 housing units for poorer older people. In the early 2000s, HUD produced about 5,800 housing units a year. HUD administers this program called "Section 202 Supportive Housing for the Elderly Program" under the National Affordable Housing Act of 1990. It is the only federal government-funded program focused solely on older people. Wardrip (2010) says that by 2010 roughly 300,000 units existed to support older adults.

Section 202 housing serves people at least 62 years old who have incomes below 50% of the median income in their area. On average, Section 202 residents were 79 years old in 2006. Residents have an average income of $10,018. Women make up 90% of the people in Section 202 housing.

Most people in Section 202 housing live in a one-bedroom unit. These units include grab bars, ramps, and other design features to make living safer and easier for residents. From 5% to 10% of these facilities serve people with disabilities (Pynoos et al., 2010).

Many facilities also provide housekeeping, transportation services, and Meals-on-Wheels. HUD has provided grants in recent years to service coordinators in these facilities. Bright (2005) says "such facilities provide security, community, and continuity."

In addition, an AARP study (Harrell, Brooks, & Nedwick, 2009) found that 250,000 subsidized units exist within half a mile of proposed or existing rail stations. The AARP report calls these "transit-oriented developments" (TODs). These units offer people mobility as well as a secure community. Harrell and colleagues (2009, p. 3) say, "Residents of affordable housing in compact neighborhoods benefited from dense urban development near amenities and were able to walk or take transit to the places they needed to go. In well-planned environments such as downtown Minneapolis, residents of all ages, including those 80 and older, were able to enjoy these benefits."

Older people who live in Section 202 housing stay for many years. Low turnover and high occupancy rates lead to long waiting lists. Renters in nonsubsidized housing age 75 and over, widows, and African American elders show some of the greatest housing need (Bright, 2005). But not enough subsidized housing exists to meet their needs. Pynoos and colleagues (2010, p. 326) say that "there are ten people on the waiting list for every one Section 202 unit."

A government commission estimates that the United States will need almost three quarters of a million more subsidized units by 2020 (Commission on Affordable Housing, 2002, cited in Perl, 2008). In 2005, HUD funded a program to help meet this demand. It awarded $741 million to develop or improve apartment housing for very low-income older people and people with disabilities. Of this total, $593 million went toward housing improvements for the very low-income elderly.

This added housing will still not meet the need for subsidized housing in the future. Bright (2005) says that HUD funding in 2005 fell below funding levels of the 1970s. She reports that between 1995 and 2004, for example, the number of new units declined by 29%. And in 2004, the number of new units came to 58% of the units produced in the early 1980s. An increase in the number of older people will mean an increased demand for subsidized housing.

Golant (2002) studied subsidized housing in Florida. He found that the state concentrated subsidized housing in certain counties. This meant that low-income older people who lived in other parts of the state had no access to this type of housing. Golant refs to this as "geographic inequality." Older people need subsidized housing distributed more fairly so they can make use of it.

Section 202 focuses on building housing for older people. Another option provides older people with vouchers so they can live where they choose. About 340,000 older renters use HUD Section 8 Tenant-Based Housing Choice Vouchers (McCarty, 2008). But rising housing prices and an end to government subsidies all threaten this resource. Harrell and colleagues (2009, p. 2) say that "more than two thirds of the federal subsidies that keep . . . apartments [near transit] affordable will expire within the next five years." A bipartisan Congressional commission pointed to this potential problem. The commission titled its report on senior subsidized housing "A Quiet Crisis in America" (Commission on Affordable Housing, 2002).

Wardrip (2010, p. 8) concludes that "when state- and locally subsidized properties are considered, it becomes obvious that government-subsidized housing plays a crucial role in the lives of a substantial number of older adults." He sees an increased need for subsidized housing for seniors in the future. And he cautions that communities need to maintain the subsidized units that exist.

Single Room Occupancy

The U.S. Department of Housing and Urban Development (2008) defines single room occupancy (SRO) as a unit, often within a multiple unit property, occupied by one person. These units may contain food preparation or sanitary facilities, or both.

Single room occupancy conjures up images of older people who live in run-down inner-city hotels. These hotels typically house men, over age 75, widowed or never married, and poor. Many of these men have lived in this kind of housing throughout their adult lives. SROs that house older men often lack services such as medical care and meals.

In the past few years, many central cities have torn down the old hotels that served as SRO housing. HUD sponsors a program for the creation of SRO housing and the subsidy of SRO resident rents. The program provides funds to local housing authorities to moderately restructure existing housing to serve SRO tenants. Buildings might include an old hotel, a YMCA or YWCA, an old school, or a vacant home. The funds come in the form of rental assistance to residents. Housing and Urban Development will provide rent subsidies that keep rent payments of residents to no

more than 30% of their income. HUD agrees to continue the subsidies for 10 years. The program plans to create housing for homeless people of all ages. But it would help the inner-city homeless older person as well (HUD, 2008).

Supportive Housing

Some housing options provide older people with assisted living: personal and health care supports. These options include board and care homes and nursing homes.

Board and Care Homes

Board and care homes go by the names of *adult care homes, halfway houses, shelter care homes, domiciliary care, personal care homes, community residence facilities, rest homes, assisted living facilities,* and *foster care homes.* These many names for the same type of housing can lead to confusion. Also, two places that use the same name can offer different services.

Most board and care homes "provide a room, meals, and help with daily activities. Some states will allow some nursing services to be provided" (Administration on Aging, 2004a). Board and care homes generally care for a small number of residents. These homes do not serve as medical facilities, but they do offer personal care services such as help with eating, bathing, and dressing. Residents in a board and care home eat together. The manager of the home takes responsibility for the residents' well-being.

Mollica, Johnson-Lamarche, and O'Keeffe (2005) found that, in 2004, the United States had 36,451 board and care and assisted living facilities (residential care facilities). These facilities served almost 1 million people, an increase of 16% over 2000. In 2004, three states—California, Florida, and Pennsylvania—accounted for one third of all beds in these homes. Board and care homes can range in size from 1 to more than 100 residents, although most homes have 30 or fewer residents. (In California, for example, more than 90% of homes have licenses for six or fewer people; California Registry, 2009.) Residents range in age from 60 to 75 years on average. More women than men live in these facilities.

Harrington and colleagues (Harrington, Chapman, Miller, Miller, & Newcomer, 2005) studied trends in the development of long-term care facilities and beds in the United States. The researchers found that the number of nursing home beds increased slightly (7%)

from 1990 to 2002. But assisted living facilities increased by 97% during this same time. This growth in assisted living facilities means more community-based care.

Residents often choose to live in a board and care home because they have too little income to pay for the services they need in their own homes. They need an affordable way to get personal care and supervision. The board and care home gives them service in a homelike setting. Most owners run board and care homes for profit. Homes vary widely in the services provided and in cost. All homes provide meals. Other services can range from help with eating to letter writing. Sometimes monthly fees include all services, sometimes not. All states license board and care homes.

Owners in some states must pass a test to get licensed. Most states have approval for Medicaid to cover service costs in board and care homes (Mollica et al., 2005). A board and care home can also solve a financial and housing problem for the manager/owner. Nell Stone, a 66-year-old retired home health aide, ran a board and care home in Teaneck, New Jersey. She gave care to two women, ages 95 and 76. The women lived in her home, and she provided them with meals, some personal care, and rides to services. Stone said the income from her boarders allowed her to maintain her home. "Without the ladies," she said, "I would have to move to a one-room apartment" (Gilman, 1994, p. 9C).

Many board and care homes now house people with cognitive impairments. This places new demands on home managers and on residents. Mollica and colleagues (2005) say that 44 states have set out requirements for homes that house people with Alzheimer's disease and other dementias. These requirements include trained staff, security, environmental design, and services that meet the needs of cognitively impaired residents. Still, some researchers raise questions about the ability of board and care homes to meet the needs of these seniors (Hawes, 1999).

A person who decides to live in a board and care home needs to know the details of life in the home. What services does the home provide? When and how often do meals get served? Does the home offer activities outside the building? Most people who live in board and care homes say they like where they live (Curtis, Sales, Sullivan, Gray, & Hedrick, 2005). They say their home offers a safe and private setting with the services they need.

Kane and Wilson (1993) studied assisted living programs (including board and care homes) in 21 states. They found that this type of program can offer care at moderate cost. The California Registry (2009) estimates that a board and care setting costs about half as much as a nursing home. It especially meets the needs of low-income and disabled older people. More and better community care options can help keep older people in the community and out of nursing homes (Muramatsu et al., 2007).

Nursing Homes

Nursing homes serve people who need medical care in addition to personal care. Nursing homes provide skilled nursing care. More than 15,000 Medicare and Medicaid certified nursing homes exist in the United States. A relatively small number of older people (1.4 million) lived in nursing homes in 2008 (Centers for Disease Control, 2010a; National Center for Health Statistics, 2009). This came to about 4% of the total older population. But the percentage of older people who live in nursing homes increases dramatically with age. For example, only 0.9% of people ages 65 to 74 lived in nursing homes in 2004. But this figure jumps to 13.9% of people age 85 and over (National Center for Health Statistics, 2010b).

Nursing homes care for frail and very old people. Many nursing home residents suffer from Alzheimer's disease. Nursing homes serve as an important resource for older people who can no longer live on their own. The quality of nursing homes has improved in the past few years. This improvement came about in part through stronger regulations and more government enforcement. The Omnibus Budget Reconciliation Act of 1987, called OBRA-87, nursing facility reform regulations, set out precise standards for nursing home care. These included the following requirements:

- All nursing homes must assess patients at least once a year. Assessments cover ADL as well as health care needs. The nursing home must create a detailed care plan based on this assessment.
- All nursing homes must inform residents orally and in writing about their legal rights. This includes the right to choose a doctor, the right to freedom from restraints, and the right to privacy and confidentiality.
- Staff must include a registered nurse for at least 8 hours each day and at least one licensed nurse at all times every day. Large facilities with 120 beds must have a full-time social worker. Nurses' aides must

---

BOX 10.3
A BOARDWALK BACK TO NATURE

"I'm going out," announced Clarence, early last winter, wearing his jacket and fedora. He was wheeling himself toward the door at the end of the "C" wing to go onto the boardwalk. "I try to get out some every day the weather lets me," he said to me that day, smiling broadly. Clarence was an avid hunter and outdoorsman all his life. Even though multiple sclerosis had totally debilitated his legs, Clarence continued his love affair with the outdoors. Propelling his wheelchair along the tree-lined boardwalk to the overlook at Knapps Creek, he savored the sights, sounds and smells of creation. . . .

For two years, my office window faced the boardwalk. Often I would look up from interminable paperwork at the nursing home to watch the action outside. Even now, memories of those days come back—of different faces and voices and qualities of light. Vernon, convinced that exercise would fend off aging, methodically walking twenty or more roundtrips a day, laying twigs on the handrail to count his progress. Charlie, struggling to maintain his own ambulatory ability, helping fellow resident Oleta to make it "all the way up and back." Volun-

teers pushing wheelchair residents along the slightly rough boards to explore once again the sensory mystery of sun and shade, gentle breeze, and the smell of the earth. . . .

It is a wintry day as I write this, but before long a day will arrive warm enough to ask Mrs. Harper for a "date."

Lulu Harper is past her mid-nineties now, with a narrow temperature comfort zone. But she is still the quintessential nature girl and possesses a sharp inquisitive mind.

On that special day, we'll roll out onto the boardwalk in her carriage. Like a prince, I will pluck for her fresh-born leaves, budding twigs, and dainty spring flowers. I may even bring back a handful of dank wood dirt from beneath the pines to present to this silver-haired queen of nature. And she will gently run her fingers over these jewels, while sunbeams dance on her cheeks.

The boardwalk, as you can tell, has affected us all— put us back in touch with our natures.

Source: A. Johnson (1994). A boardwalk back to nature. *Aging Magazine,* 366, 54–55. Reprinted with permission.

---

pass a training course of 75 hours. States must test the competency of aides.

- States must ensure that nursing homes comply with these new regulations.

Kane and Kane (2001, p. 417) call nursing homes "the most heavily regulated health industry." Due to past scandals over poor care and misuse of funds, "the nursing home industry has been viewed as one that must be closely overseen." Government regulations require that facilities meet "the highest practicable physical, medical and psychological well-being" of every resident (American Medical Directors Association, 2003).

Congress refined the original act in 1990, and debate goes on over new technical points. The legislation allows the government to take over the management of a facility that does not comply with the new policies. Or it can remove the nursing home from the Medicare or Medicaid program (according to U.S. Senate hearings cited in Koff & Park, 1993).

Older people in nursing homes value autonomy and privacy. Institutions should allow people to control some private space. Some nursing homes do this. They manage to create a homelike atmosphere. Older people in these settings build strong relationships with

staff and other residents. They decorate their rooms with mementos. They create a comfortable place for themselves. People with long-term illnesses may find more comfort in a good nursing home than in their former home.

Good nursing home design can also increase patient autonomy. Kitchens near living areas help cognitively impaired patients expect mealtime by the smell of cooking food. L-shaped rooms add to feelings of privacy in semiprivate rooms.

An award-winning facility called Woodside Place, in Pittsburgh, Pennsylvania, uses design to enhance the autonomy of patients with Alzheimer's disease. The facility houses 36 people in three 12-person houses. Each house has a different visual theme—star, tree, and house. The houses contain wallpaper borders, quilt designs, and old photos of Pittsburgh that use these themes. The themes give variety to the decor and help residents remember where they live (Deely & Werlinich, 1992; Arehart-Treichel, 2001). The small units give residents a feeling of place and a sense of home.

People with Alzheimer's disease and other forms of dementia pose a special problem for nursing home staff members. They tend to wander. They may walk out of a facility and get lost. Woodside solves this problem through design. The designers built an internal street that allows the residents to wander from space to space in the building freely and safely. The facility also has a fully fenced yard so that residents can go out without getting lost. Finally, each resident wears a name tag that contains a computer chip. This chip locks the entrance doors if a patient comes near.

Woodside Place shows that good design can support older people with special needs. This same attention to patient comfort and well-being can create a good environment in any nursing home.

Accessory Dwelling Units

Accessory dwelling units (ADUs), sometimes called elder cottages or in-law apartments (Medicare.gov, 2007), began under the name *granny flats* in the district of Victoria, Australia. They also go by the name *elder cottage housing opportunities (ECHO)*. An elder cottage is a small moveable cottage that sits in the yard of an adult child's house. The cottage attaches to the house's electrical and water systems. It contains a bathroom, kitchen, bedroom, and sitting area. The small size of the cottage allows the older person to save on maintenance. Some elder cottages fit into an attached garage next to a child's house. Elder cottages give older people the freedom to live on their own with the support of their family next door. The cottage gets moved when the older person dies or moves to a nursing home.

Accessory apartments exist within or are added onto a single-family home. An adult child may set up an accessory apartment for a parent. Or an older person may set one up and rent the space to another older person. The tenant gives the older owner companionship, and they may share services. The U.S. Census Bureau says that 2.5 million accessory apartments exist. Sometimes an accessory apartment produces income that allows an older person to keep his or her home (Chapman & Howe, 2001). For renters, accessory apartments provide affordable housing and companionship.

Because ADUs fit into local neighborhoods, they exist close to amenities and bus routes (Salomon, 2010). This makes them even more attractive to the older person who may no longer drive. But, Chapman and Howe (2001) say, elder cottages and accessory apartments often face zoning restrictions. The cottages decrease open space on lots, and apartments create multiple-family dwellings in residential neighborhoods. Neighbors fear that these options will lower housing values. Zoning laws that restrict accessory apartments have driven some people to develop them illegally.

Zoning laws may explain why few people have chosen accessory apartments and elder cottages. Chapman and Howe (2001) call these zoning laws counterproductive. They restrict the growth of a useful and effective housing alternative. Dyson (2010) reports that some cities (e.g., Santa Cruz, California, and Portland, Oregon) have modified their zoning laws to allow the placement of elder cottages. Virginia now allows the placement of a cottage on a single-home property with a doctor's order.

The United States has relied mostly on individual initiative and the private sector in the development of ADUs. But the cost of high-quality ADUs may create a barrier. A person has to pay for the cost of construction, building permits, and other fees. Add high-tech equipment and the cost can quickly get out of reach.

Lazarowich (1991) studied ECHO housing around the world. He found that in most places where ECHO housing has succeeded, families rent the units from the government. The government delivers the unit and arranges to move it when the older person dies or moves. This system controls the number of cottages in a community, their size, quality, and removal. Direct government support and grants to the private sector have led to the success of ECHO housing in a number of countries (Pollak & Gorman, 1989).

Home Sharing

Home sharing in the United States dates back to the 18th and 19th centuries (Jaffe, 1989). Home sharing most often takes place when an older homeowner rents out one or more rooms. The tenant pays rent and may help around the house as part of the payment. The homeowner and the tenant have separate bedrooms but share the kitchen, dining room, and living room.

Home sharers lose some of their privacy, but they gain companionship, help with housekeeping, and some income. "The money isn't essential," one home sharer said, "though it helps. I did it mainly for the company. I really don't like living alone. I like being with people" (Mantell & Gildea, 1989, p. 18). Stich (2000) reports that home sharers feel safer, less lonely, and healthier. They report eating and sleeping better than when they lived alone.

An AARP survey of 1,200 women age 45 and over found that one third expressed an interest in home sharing as long as they had some privacy. The study found that women who shared a home often enriched one another's lives (Mahoney & Rausser, 2007). Today, services exist to match homeowners with a person who wants to share living costs. These services often work as small nonprofit organizations, sometimes as part of a larger agency. They interview sharers and owners, check references, and help make the match work.

Stich (2000) sees home sharing as a growing option for single older people. She gives an example of this growth. An agency called Housemate Match (2010) began in 1984 in Atlanta, Georgia, by matching about 50 people per year. The program now matches 650 people per year. The National Shared Housing Resource Center (2010) exists to help people find a matching organization in their community or to start a shared housing program.

Home sharing appeals to only a small proportion of older people. Still, it meets the needs of the older person who wants companionship and a relatively low-cost housing option. And the recent downturn in the economy has led to increased interest in shared housing.

Retirement Communities

Retirement communities can take at least two forms: (1) naturally occurring retirement communities and (2) planned retirement communities.

Naturally Occurring Retirement Communities

About one quarter of older people live in a building or neighborhood where at least half the people are age 60 or over (Seniorresource.com, 2010b). Gerontologists call these **naturally occurring retirement communities (NORCs)**. The populations in most of these neighborhoods and apartment buildings grew older as people aged in place. People in these communities say they like living with older people. They say this keeps the neighborhood peaceful and quiet, they share common interests with neighbors, and they find their neighbors friendly and helpful.

Minority older people may find themselves in a NORC because of racial segregation. This applies to African American older people more than to any other group. Lifelong housing segregation has restricted where older African Americans could live. This has left many of them in inner cities or rural settings. Older African Americans tend to stay in place as they age, in part because they have little choice. Skinner

(1992, p. 50) says that "economic disadvantage from low incomes, racial segregation, and ageism join to create formidable barriers to housing and the free choice or movement to other housing options."

Inner-city neighborhoods or rural settings do not always turn into ideal NORCs. Many of these neighborhoods lack easy shopping, transportation, and safety. They can leave older people afraid and isolated in their homes. "With few options available to them, they are not only aging in place, they are stuck in place, prisoners in their own homes, without the ability to move to more appropriate housing" (Skinner, 1992, p. 51). Krause (2004a), for example, reports that people in inner-city neighborhoods may not have the resources available to help an older person. A run-down neighborhood can also create stress and health problems.

But this isn't true of all urban settings. Krause (2004a) notes that the lack of support may apply to only the worst neighborhoods. Some urban communities offer amenities that keep older people in place and attract others. For example, older people in inner-city neighborhoods live near the churches, shops, and neighbors they've known for years. This makes the local community an important resource for older minority group members. Krause (2004a) found that the amount of support available to an older person depended on the person's needs, the quality of the urban environment, and the amount of resources available in the neighborhood network.

Onolemhemhen (2009, p. 738) conducted an in-depth study of 15 poor older minority women in downtown Detroit. She found that these women made good use of their environment. Some of them stayed engaged in their church. One woman served as an usher and taught Sunday school. Another went to church several days a week.

Onolemhemhen (2009) found that nearly all these women preferred to stay in their homes in inner city Detroit. One woman said "Well, I don't want to live in the suburbs. . . . See, I've been in this house 50 years. I know the people here." Another woman said she preferred her city neighborhood because she liked the shopping and the stores. The density of urban environments make it easier for older people to shop, do their banking, and visit friends.

A program called Community Options in Cleveland, Ohio, helps people in NORCs age in place. A typical user of the program is an 82-year-old widow who has lived in her apartment for 12 years. The program offers activities and services. It links residents with one another and with community services. A survey of residents found that these services gave people a stronger sense of control over their lives (Anetzberger, 2010).

A similar program in St. Louis helps 600 members of a NORC to stay in their homes. Services in this program include home repair, social activities, and volunteer support. Members of this NORC pay a modest fee to belong (Moeller, 2009).

Moeller (2009) reports on one of the oldest members of the St. Louis NORC, 96-year-old Ida Seltzer. Ms. Seltzer attends knitting and crocheting groups and travels around her housing complex on a motorized wheelchair. She admits that loneliness can get her down. "Sometimes I get depressed and feel like giving up," she says, "but the NORC . . . makes me feel more like a person and keeps me in touch with other people."

Another resident, Bess Fine, age 90, agrees: "'Through the NORC, I have a much higher quality of life,' which includes frequent outings with other community members. 'I don't know what we'd do without it,' she says of the program" (Moeller, 2009).

Beacon Hill Village in downtown Boston serves as a model NORC that supports aging in place. The Village operates as a nonprofit organization with a board and a small professional staff. Members serve on the board and provide input on needed services. Scharlach (2009) considers this involvement the key to a quality community.

The Village provides three kinds of supports to its members: social activities, member services (e.g., meal delivery, a ride to a grocery store), and health care. Health care support includes exercise programs, flu shots, and home health care aides. Members pay a fee to belong to the Village ($600 per year for an individual, $800 for a couple). Low-income members pay a reduced rate. The community has formed partnerships with a local hospital, a residential services company, and a home health care provider.

McWhinney-Morse (2009, p. 85) says, "In order to promote healthy aging, the Village offers programs and services that address not only medical and housing needs but social, physical, emotional, and intellectual needs as well." Beacon Hill Village serves as the model for more than 50 Villages throughout the United States (Accius, 2010). These villages form a part of the Aging Friendly Communities movement (Scharlach, 2008).

Thomas and Blanchard (2009, pp. 15–17) call Beacon Hill Village a "spontaneous community" because local residents created it. The authors praise the social connectedness that Beacon Hill Village provides. This, they say, provides an alternative to the isolation in a single family home that can occur through aging in place.

Communities designed for social as well as physical support can provide a high quality of life. In one case a group of nuns, who left their order, formed a retirement community called "Elderspirit." They dedicated their community to personal growth, mutual support, and deepening their spiritual life. Thomas and Blanchard (2009, p. 17) call this an "intentional community." They propose that "aging in community" replace the concept of "aging in place." Aging in community, they say, "shifts the emphasis away from dwellings and toward relationships."

Marshall and Hunt (1999; also Hunt, Marshall, & Merrill, 2002) describe another type of NORC. These communities often occur in rural areas. They found that rural communities could become one of three types of NORC: amenity, convenience, and bifocal.

An *amenity community* attracted people who wanted the charm of a rural lifestyle and country environment. Amenity communities had younger, affluent, well-educated residents.

A *convenience community* attracted people who wanted the benefits of living in a community that could meet their health care and service needs. These communities, compared with those of amenity migrants, had older, less well-educated, and less wealthy residents.

A *bifocal community* attracted people who wanted amenities but also nearness to family and friends. Members of these communities shared characteristics of the other two groups.

People in all three types of communities tended to stay in a community that met their unique needs.

Planned Retirement Communities

Most newer **planned retirement communities** come about when a developer builds and sells houses to healthy active retirees. These communities supply health services, shopping centers, and recreation facilities. Communities range in size from towns, like Sun City, Arizona, with around 40,000 people, to small communities of 9,000 people, like Leisure World near Silver Spring, Maryland.

People who settle in these communities value the new homes, clean streets, easy access to shopping, and middle-class neighbors. The weather and relaxed lifestyle appeal to most migrants. They also look for safety and freedom from fear of crime. Many have left

A 95-year-old grandmother works in her rose garden at Leisure World in California.

northern communities where crime has increased. The new communities often have gates and guards, and residents in teams who watch out for strangers. They also have age restrictions that allow only people age 55 or older to move in.

Critics of these communities say they create barriers between older people and the rest of society. Kastenbaum (1993b, pp. 170–171) says that these communities can develop a "fortress mentality" and set up "barricades against physical or symbolic invasion." Only a small proportion of Americans choose to live in this kind of enclave, but those who do express satisfaction with their choice.

A new type of housing for older people has emerged—housing communities based on or near a university campus. Many campuses throughout the United States market themselves as retirement destinations. Retirees settle there because of the safe high-quality housing and because of the access to university facilities. Retirement community members use the campus fitness center, attend plays, and take classes.

As many as 50 to 100 housing centers for older people exist or are being built on U.S. university campuses. These include communities associated with the University of Indiana, Notre Dame, and Arizona State University. Simone and Scuilli (2005) say:

> At Lasell College in Massachusetts, for example, there is a waiting list to move into the residence, and the program requires its 200 residents to complete 450 hours of learning and fitness activities a year. "There is a mentality

about the future here rather than the past," says Paula Panchuck, the dean of Lasell Village. "Instead of, 'My life is over,' it's, 'What classes are coming up in the spring?'"

Projects that develop in partnership with a college or university integrate the residents with university life. These developments attract people interested in campus cultural offerings, in personal growth, or in getting a degree. Retired faculty and staff often choose this type of community so they can maintain contact with the campus. Campuses benefit from having older students in the classroom, from older residents' volunteer activities, and from donations from older residents.

Regnier (2003) reports that members of a community near Iowa State University donated $3 million to the university over a 5- to 6-year period. "Although this is a very small segment of the U.S. elder population, it nonetheless represents a growing and influential sector" (p. 109).

Continuing Care Retirement Communities

Nursing home costs can wipe out a person's savings and put the person's family in debt. To protect against these costs, some older people have moved to **continuing care retirement communities (CCRCs)**. "Continuing Care Retirement Communities (CCRCs) or communities offering Life Care are designed to offer active seniors an independent life-style and a private home from which to enjoy it, regardless of future medical needs" (Seniorresource.com, 2010a). Regnier (2003) reports that between 1,900 and 2,000 CCRCs exist in the United States.

Residents sign a binding lifelong contract when they enter a CCRC. Some communities ask for a payment up front and then monthly payment for services and medical expenses. These communities offer residents multiple care options (Seniorresource.com, 2010a). An AARP study (Ejaz, Schur, Fox, Blenkner, & AARP Andrus Foundation, 2003) found that most people moved to a CCRC because of their own or their spouse's health care needs.

Residents sign a contract with the facility that guarantees them access to housing and defined types of care for the rest of their lives. Helpguide.org (2007) describes three typical contracts:

1. *Life care/extensive contract.* This type of contract assures the resident of unlimited nursing care at no added cost for as long as needed. This contract provides the most insurance—but at the highest cost.
2. *Modified/continuing care contract.* This type of contract provides long-term care or nursing care for a limited time. After that time the resident pays the cost of care. This contract provides some security, and it costs less than the extensive contract.
3. *Fee-for-service contract.* This type of contract offers no prepaid care. The resident pays for long-term care services as needed. This contract provides no insurance against high long-term care costs in the future, but it costs the least at the start.

People in CCRCs live in private apartments that have kitchens, so residents can make their own meals. Some communities have common dining rooms where residents can eat if they choose. Most CCRCs provide transportation, fitness centers, and social activities. They also offer round-the-clock nursing care in a nursing home wing attached to the main building or in a separate building.

About 75% of CCRCs also offer long-term care in units without kitchens. These units have 24-hour nursing care and help with activities of daily living. Most CCRCs that offer this kind of help require that a person move from independent housing to a special unit.

Fees for long-term care services vary, depending on the CCRC's entrance fee and monthly charges. Most communities charge high entrance fees; all charge a monthly fee for rent and some services. CCRCs accept people who can live on their own, have good health,

and have the ability to pay higher monthly fees in the future. Entrance fees in most communities range from $40,000 to $90,000 for a one- or two-bedroom apartment. But they can run as high as $400,000 or more. Monthly fees average between $400 and $2,500 (AARP, 2004c; Helpguide.org, 2007).

Couples pay more than single people. Fees depend on the type of housing and the type of service chosen. Monthly fees can increase as the cost of services increases. Some communities will return a part of the entrance fee to a person's family or estate when the older person dies or leaves. Helpguide.org (2007) calls CCRCs "the most expensive long-term-care solution available to seniors."

Continuing care retirement communities attract older-old people. The typical resident is a single woman around 80 years old. These people want the security of future nursing home care. Moen and Erickson (2001) found that, compared with men, women showed the most overall satisfaction with life in a CCRC. One 80-year-old woman described her reasons for moving to a CCRC this way:

I have always done for myself. I have some very good friends and a dear house-mate, but I don't have any family nearby. Of course, my friends and house-mate are all in their eighties too. So, I realized that if I was going to continue doing for myself, I needed to make some changes. Here I have reliable backup. (Lavizzo-Mourey & Eisenberg, 1992, p. xvii)

Benefits aside, there are also some risks with CCRCs for older people. First, monthly payments can go up. Second, a person does not own the property. Third, the company that owns the community may go out of business. Older people can lose their investment and their housing if this happens. Some states regulate CCRCs, and the industry has set up an accreditation system. But even state regulation will not protect against future community failure. And the accreditation system does not ensure that a CCRC will fulfill its promises.

In the future, more people will fit the profile of current CCRC residents (single women, age 80 and older). They will want protection from crippling long-term care costs. But the high cost of entry into a CCRC will limit the number of people who can move to this type of housing. New types of CCRCs may emerge to meet the needs of a growing market. They will appear in more flexible forms with varied services. Potential residents will attempt to match a community with their assets, their needs, and their expectations about community life.

BOX 10.4
RETIREMENT COMMUNITIES WITH SPECIAL APPEAL

Deciding where to retire used to be like deciding on a summer camp—there were day camps and sleep-away camps, but the activities were pretty much the same. But just as summer camps now cater to interests ranging from archery to zoology, retirement communities are springing up that let you grow old in the company of people with similar backgrounds or mutual passions that go far deeper than a shared interest in golf.

They range from communities for gay men and lesbians to centers shaped for members of specific ethnic groups. Retired military officers have formed communities around the country. Sunset Hall in Los Angeles bills itself as a "home for free-thinking elders." Other examples include a residence for artists in the works in Manhattan; the Elder-Spirit Center, a co-housing retirement community based on spiritual principles . . . [in] Abingdon, VA; and an assisted-living center in Gresham, OR, for retirees who are deaf or blind, where the employees know sign language and there are rooms with door lights instead of bells.

Experts say that one force behind the trend is the lengthened lifespan of those retiring. Choosing where to live after work is no longer mostly a matter of deciding the best place to be when you fall apart.

Decades ago, the most common kind of partnership for a retirement community was with health care companies, said Bill Silbert, the marketing director for the Kendal Corporation, which runs retirement centers operating "in the Quaker tradition" near Cornell, Dartmouth, and Oberlin. Now the partnerships are often with universities. "Health care is an important part of the concept," Mr. Silbert said, "but it's not the reason to come."

Ron Manheimer, executive director of the North Carolina Center for Creative Retirement in Asheville, NC, said he expects to see more retirement communities in which older people can live among peers who share their specific interests and values. "These are pretty much the people you're going to end up living with for the rest of your life," he said. "People want to be with people they will be comfortable with and where there will be a high level of mutual trust."

"The whole idea that there's this homogenous group of elders is simply not true," he said. "There are cultures of aging, and there are more and more of them."

Robert G. Kramer, executive director of the National Investment Center for the Seniors Housing and Care Industries in Annapolis, MD, said the diversification is being driven in part by baby boomers seeking more options for their parents. This generation, he said, is used "to forcing the market to deliver what they want; they've done it all their life."

"What we see today," Mr. Kramer said, "will be absolutely nothing compared to what we'll see in 10 or 15 years."

Drew Leder, a professor at Loyola College in Maryland who has studied the spirituality of aging, agreed. "When the baby boomers were growing up there were three flavors of ice cream; now there are 1,000," he said. "Similarly, there are going to be 1,000 different flavors of retirement."

Here is a sampling of those flavors:

Jeanne Dolan, who bought land with her partner at Carefree Cove, a gated community for gay men and lesbians in Zionville, NC, said, "I think most people would like to retire with at least somewhat like-minded people, especially now that we're living a lot longer and going to be retired a lot longer."

But living in a community aimed at a specific group has its pros and cons. Pei Yang Chang, 88, lives with his wife, Rose, at Aegis Gardens, an assisted-living center in Fremont, CA, where everything from the food to the building design is Chinese. "The good thing," he said, "is there are so many old friends. The bad thing is we are out of touch with general public. We don't want to be too excluded."

Lorraine Carvalho dreamed of retiring in a community with other gay women. At 57, she learned about Carefree Cove, a gated community for gay men and lesbians in North Carolina's Blue Ridge Mountains. "I was like, 'Oh my God—there's my dream right there,'" Ms. Carvalho said.

Gay retirement living is a concept on the edge of a boom. The Palms of Manasota in Palmetto, FL, the first gay and lesbian retirement community, opened in 1998, and several others are being planned or close to breaking ground. Carefree Cove began selling lots in 2001.

David Aronstein, president of Stonewall Communities, a nonprofit corporation developing a cooperative in Boston for gay men and lesbians, said, "Especially for gay men and women who have spent their lives as a minority, the security of living with people with like-minded values is very valuable."

Aegis Gardens, a development for Chinese older people, shows how a housing development can adapt to the culture of its residents. The first street address assigned to the Aegis Gardens assisted-living center contained the number four. Chinese tradition associates the number with death, so Aegis Assisted Living petitioned for a change. Blue also connotes death, so the company's navy blue uniforms were changed to dark red, which means happiness. Brochures were printed in green, "a much more prosperous color," the president and chief executive, Dwayne J. Clark, said.

At Aegis Gardens, one of a small number of retirement centers catering to ethnic groups, the employees speak Mandarin or Cantonese. Activities include a daily tai chi exercise class, Chinese calligraphy and Chinese opera singing, as well as table tennis, mah jong and bingo.

To build Aegis Gardens, Mr. Clark said the company sought help from an advisory group of Chinese-Americans on details down to the size of the guardian lions at the entrance.

Mr. Clark, whose company runs a dozen retirement centers in the northwest, said a community aimed at Chinese retirees would not have been possible 10 or 15 years ago; tradition required adult children to care for their parents.

"As people become more Americanized, that's changing," he said. "The wives of Asian-Americans are working just like Americans that are born here."

Low-Income, Rural, and Minority Housing

A review of housing options shows that a wide range of options exists. But, compared to a person in a city, a person in a rural setting often has fewer housing options. Rural older people tend to live in single, detached houses that they own (Schaefer & Joint Center for Housing Studies of Harvard University, 2000). But some rural older people live in substandard housing—without hot water, a private toilet, or a private bathtub. Also, compared with urban residents, older rural residents have "a smaller and less diverse array of community-based supportive services" (Golant, 2004, p. 299). "Despite mental images of decaying urban neighborhoods and run-down boarding houses," Coward (1988, p. 170) says, "it is the rural elderly, as a whole, that seem to be disadvantaged." The housing continuum needs more options for low-income, minority, and rural older people.

Minority older people also need more access to the choices on the housing continuum. For example, minority members have made little use of alternative unsubsidized housing (e.g., home sharing or CCRCs). Few of these options suit poor older people. "If innovative housing alternatives remain untried among minority elderly," Lacayo (1991, p. 45) says, "then the disparity between their living arrangements and those of the dominant older population can only become more pronounced. This would mean increasing isolation and persistent poverty for minority elders."

Lacayo (1991) suggests a number of changes that would improve housing for minority older people:

- More funding for Section 202 loans to create housing for older people; more funding for home repair programs

- More subsidized housing in minority neighborhoods near services; government incentives to builders to create and maintain minority housing
- More innovative housing designed for minority older people; creative financing options for minority elders

Many older people cannot move along the housing continuum to find housing that meets their needs. Barriers to living in a supportive environment include the availability and affordability of options. Future housing policies need to ensure that options exist and that older people can choose the options that best suit their needs.

Homelessness

In an ideal world, a chapter on housing should not contain a section on homelessness. Homelessness should not exist. But it does. It affects young people, single people, families, and older people. The U.S. Health Resources and Services Administration (2010b) calls homeless seniors a "forgotten population."

Precise figures on homelessness among older people don't exist. The 2009 Annual Homeless Assessment Report to Congress (U.S. Department of Housing and Urban Development [HUD], 2010) provides the most accurate figures on homelessness. The report says that people age 51 and over made up nearly one quarter (22.1%) of all homeless sheltered adults. People age 62 and older made up between 2.8% and 3.6% of all homeless sheltered adults.

Supplemental Security Income (SSI), Social Security, Medicare, Medicaid, and assisted housing for older people keep most older people off the streets and out of shelters. Still, the HUD study found that homelessness has increased for people age 51 and over. And their dependence on shelters has also increased. In 2008, 30.6% of people age 51 and older in shelters stayed for more than 180 days. This figure jumped to 40.5% in 2009. The report calls this a "dramatic increase in the percentage of heavy users of emergency shelter" by people age 51 and over (HUD, 2010, p. 57).

Most experts agree that shelters don't suit the needs of older homeless people. Long lines, late entry and early exit, the lack of assurance of a bed each night, difficulty maintaining good hygiene, and potential robbery all make shelters unsuitable for older people. Still, some older people turn to shelters as their only option.

Homeless older people fall into two groups. The first group has experienced homelessness throughout their middle years. Most of these people are men. They aged in place and remained homeless. This group includes people with drug addictions and mental illness. The second group became homeless after retirement. The recent recession and loss of jobs forced some older people into homelessness. People near the poverty line and on a fixed income may also fall into homelessness if rents increase. This group lacks the street smarts of long-term homeless people. This exposes them to danger from other residents in shelters and even more danger on the streets.

Shelters often lack the medical and social service supports to help older people manage their health problems and prevent their health from getting worse (U.S. Department of Health and Human Services, Health Resources and Services, 2011). A study by the National Alliance to End Homelessness projects an increase in senior homelessness in the years ahead. The study estimates that senior homelessness will increase 33% by 2020 and by 50% by 2050 (Creamer, 2010). The older homeless person often has many medical problems and chronic illnesses.

The St. Mary's Center in Oakland, California, for example, provides support services to men and women age 55 and over. Trena Cleland interviewed clients of the St. Mary's Center to better understand the experience of homelessness. Cleland reports the story of Jeannette Hundley, a St. Mary's Center resident.

"My husband died about 20 months ago, when he was 60," Hundley says. "He had diabetes, then renal failure, and was on dialysis at the end. He went on disability and lost all insurance benefits, including life insurance for me. We had a lot of medical expenses; and not everything was covered by Medicare. We lost our major resources, including two homes. When he died, I was left penniless. I couldn't pay for our apartment.

"I stayed with my cousins in Oakland for over a year, but it seemed like I was going nowhere. Finally I got a job, so I got a little low-income hotel room. But the job didn't last, so I had to move out of the hotel. I couldn't go back to my relatives. I had to find a shelter." Hundley also suffers from mental illness. That makes it impossible for her to find work at this point in her life. St. Mary's provides her with a safe haven while she sorts out her life.

The city of Santa Barbara, California, an upscale community on the coast, took a unique approach to meeting the needs of homeless seniors. The city set up a dozen safe parking lots for older homeless people. These people can afford cars and gas and many of them have jobs. But they earn little and can't afford the high rents in the city. They live in their cars. Social workers patrol the lots to ensure the safety of people who live there. One woman says, "Just having a place to park added stability. . . . I felt safe."

Fleck (2008, pp. 22–24) tells the story of Barbara Harvey, 66, who sleeps in one of the lots reserved for women only. Harvey lost her job as a notary and couldn't afford her $2,150 per month rent. Social Security and a part-time job still didn't give her enough to pay her rent. She first stayed with relatives and in motels. But she ran out of choices. She knew the city and didn't want to leave. So, she chose to live in her car.

Other cities like Eugene, Oregon, offer similar safe parking programs. "Communities are recognizing the viability of people living in their vehicles," says Gary Linker, executive director of New Beginnings in Santa Barbara. ". . . You've got to accept this as an option for people." David Robbie, 57, a Vietnam veteran, told Fleck, "It's better than sleeping on the street."

This option works for a small number of people in moderate climates. It points to the resilience of older homeless people and to their need for help. But shelters and parking lots and other short-term options can't take the place of affordable housing. The rise of middle-class homelessness among older people has raised awareness of this issue. "Poverty," a social worker in Santa Barbara told Fleck, "has been going on for so long and people ignored it, but now it's hitting the middle class, and people are paying attention. We should've been trying to find solutions years ago."

Greater awareness of senior homelessness may lead to more support for poor older people. Supports should include quality low-cost housing, health care services, and Meals on Wheels service or other food service where needed. Supports should also include psychological and substance abuse services and case management to help people get the services they need.

THE FUTURE OF HOUSING

Improved housing in the future for all older people will depend on a better integration of housing and services. The key to aging in place often has little to do with the size and shape of a building. It has to do with the social and health care supports that allow people to stay in their homes. Some years ago Newcomer and Weeden (1986, p. 6) said, "Unfortunately, if integration or coordination occurs among [housing, health care, and social service] programs within any community, it is more likely by accident than design." This holds true in many cases today.

Newcomer and Weeden (1986) maintain that the lack of coordinated housing and services leaves many older people without the supports they need. They estimate that between 10% and 20% of nursing home residents could live outside institutions if they had supportive housing. The increase in assisted living facilities in the past few years will make life outside an institution possible for more people.

Regnier (1993, p. 46; 2003) studied supportive housing for older people in northern Europe. A number of countries (Sweden, Denmark, Norway) have developed something called the "mixed-use *service house*." This design provides services to older people in a housing complex and to people in the nearby community. Services include meals, recreation, and health treatment. One service house in Sweden shares space in a community center for middle school students. The students and older people share a crafts room and gymnasium. A restaurant serves residents, students, and the local community.

Another type of service house option puts older people's apartments over shops such as a pharmacy, cafe, and grocery store. These housing units often have balconies and courtyards linked to children's playgrounds. Service houses create links between older people and the community. Europeans, in their design of housing for older people, "integrate, connect, protect, overlook, enliven and facilitate" (Regnier, 1993, p. 51). This type of housing could serve as a model for supportive housing in the United States (Regnier, 2003). It would suit people, especially city dwellers, who want to stay in their communities but need help to do so.

The current generation of older people will need more supportive housing. This will include housing designed so people can age in place, and it will include more long-term care facilities. The future will see a blending of housing and services to help older people live as independently as possible.

TRANSPORTATION

Transportation gives older people a sense of independence and control over their lives. It allows them to visit friends, attend cultural events, go shopping, and receive health care. A lack of transportation can lead to isolation, poor health, and decreased well-being. A study of State Units on Aging asked about the importance of transportation. The respondents listed transportation as a top health issue for older people. Thirty-eight percent of the units said that poor transportation posed a barrier to promoting health among seniors (Government Accounting Office, 2004). All older people need access to transportation, but rural, suburban, and urban older people have different transportation options and needs.

Public Transportation

Public transportation and other forms of mobility (e.g., walking) account for only 8% of trips older people make outside their homes (Stutts, 2003). One study (Kochera, Straight, & Guterbock, 2003) reports that older people used public transport for only 1% of trips. Another study (Polzin & Chu, 2005) found that only 12% of older adults said they used public transportation in the past year.

Still, people who live in cities report the need to live near public transport. Low-income people who live alone and have health problems also express a need to live near public transport (AARP, 1993). Even older people who drive need public transportation at times. For example, they may need to make a trip at night, but hesitate to drive after dark.

Stutts (2003) says that American public transit options lag behind those in most European countries. And Bailey (2004) reports that more than half of older nondrivers (3.6 million people), on any given day, have to stay at home at least partly because they have no transportation options.

A good public transit systems allows older people to stay connected to their communities and to engage in activities they enjoy. One case illustrates the importance of housing linked to nearby transit:

> [An] 83-year-old resident of the Towers (an apartment complex in Minneapolis) . . . expressed great satisfaction

with her current location, noting that she could walk or take a short bus trip to restaurants, shopping, her church, and to Orchestra Hall to hear the Minneapolis Orchestra. She uses public transit two to three times a week, relying on the bus more than she used to, as walking has become more difficult, and takes the bus to the light rail that takes her to the Mall of America. With the passing of her husband, and now that she is older and less able to walk, her ability to take the bus allows her to maintain her independence and involvement in her community. (Harrell et al., 2009, p. 27)

Compared to older people in cities, older people in rural areas have fewer transportation options. Bailey (2004) reports that people in rural areas tend to make less use of public transportation (usually due to lack of available services). And, compared to people who live in cities, they tend to stay home more because they lack transportation. Fewer people in rural areas, compared with people in urban areas, have access to cars. And most towns under 10,000 people have no intercity bus line. Poor-quality rural roads and bridges make travel hard. And rural people pay more for public transportation due to large distances and the small numbers of users. All of these things increase the chance of isolation for rural older people.

Bailey (2004) recommends increases in federal funding to expand public transportation, especially in rural areas. She also recommends increased funding for special transportation services (such as Paratransit buses) to help older people with disabilities.

Many rural and urban older people need regular transportation services that accommodate disability. Buses that have platforms that come level with the ground help people with walkers or arthritis. Vehicles with lifts or ramps can serve the same function. For example, Amtrak stations in California that serve the Coast Starlight passenger train provide wayside lifts for people with disabilities.

Clear markings on the edges of stairs on buses and trains make for safer entry and exit. And wider aisles would make public buses easier for everyone to use (Hunter-Zaworski, 2008). Hunter-Zaworski goes on to suggest handholds and nonslip floor surfaces. Many older people would benefit from transportation services that they could contact on demand, rather than on services that follow a set route and schedule.

Paratransit services provide on-demand transport. Public agencies can also contract with taxi companies to provide service to people with disabilities

(Molnar & Eby, 2009). Harrell and colleagues (2009, p. 28) say "These services fill an important role because qualified riders can travel anywhere within the service area at a much lower cost than using a [normal] taxicab or other livery service." These services cost more than a normal bus service. Rosenbloom (2009) says that a typical bus trip costs $2.37. A comparable Paratransit trip costs over $35.00. This makes the expansion of Paratransit unlikely. It supports the case for better and more responsive public transit.

Transit needs to be accessible as well as available. Steep steps at train stations, for example, bar disabled or frail older people from access. Likewise, some people find that bus drivers fail to lower their buses to help them get on board. Other bus drivers simply bypass someone with a walker. Planners need to ensure that older people can get to and use transit in their neighborhoods.

Other alternative public transport programs include supplemental transportation programs (STPs) and independent transport networks (ITNs). STPs meet special mobility needs. They provide door-through-door service, escorts, and other types of personal support. Several hundred STPs exist throughout the country.

ITNs use paid and volunteer drivers in private cars. They offer door-through-door service, and drivers will help carry packages for passengers. Older users join an ITN for a low fee and get reduced rates on trips they take (Molnar & Eby, 2009). These and other transport options fill in the gaps left by conventional public transport systems. Communities that offer a "family of services" will best meet the needs of the older population.

The ITNPortland (2010) program in Maine offers a good example of the ITN model. The program lists the characteristics of its service:

- Available 24 hours a day, 7 days a week.
- Available for any type of ride within the service area, with no limitations on ride purpose.
- Rides are provided in private automobiles by trained drivers.
- People 60 years and older, and adults with visual impairments are eligible to join.
- Rides may be booked at any time; discounts are applied for shared rides and advance notice.

The ITN model can play a role in the transportation continuum from public to private transportation. It serves the needs of mobile older people who no longer can or want to drive their own cars. ITNs can benefit the rural older person who needs a flexible alternative to scheduled public transportation.

Will older people make more use of public transportation and alternative transport methods in the future? Molnar and Eby (2009; also Rosenbloom, 2009) don't think so. First, the use of alternative transportation systems has dropped over time. It dropped from 2.2% of all trips in 1995 to 1.3% in 2001. Second, national data show that, compared to younger people, older people make fewer trips on public transportation. Finally, aging Baby Boomers, who grew up in an automobile culture, will prefer to drive their own cars. Public transportation will play a part in the mix of options for older people. But older people now and in the future will use the private car as their primary means of transportation.

Private Transportation

A birthday card makes reference to the issue of driving later life. The front of the card says, "At my age I can't see very well, my reaction time is slow, and I don't have much strength in my hands." Open the card and it says "But thank goodness I can still drive."

The card makes us smile. Driving pushes the limits of safety for some older people (and for other drivers on the road).

Many of the physical changes that come with age affect a person's driving ability. The older person will more likely feel distracted by difficult situations, take a longer time to read signs, have trouble judging speed, have trouble seeing in low light conditions, and have slower reaction time.

Still, for many older people their car links them to the world outside their home. Few older people would willingly give up their driver's license.

Older people who live in rural areas and suburbs must drive to survive. These areas often have poor public transportation systems (Burkhardt, 2000). People need cars to get to friends, shops, and almost anywhere else. Suburban and rural buses and taxi services help older people get around, but they cannot overcome the isolation of living outside a city without a car.

Sweeney (2004) reports that in 2002, 89% of older people without a disability drove a car. And 56% of older people with one or more disabilities drove. People drive because it gives them a sense of freedom and control.

Molnar and Eby (2009, p. 189) say that "compared to previous cohorts, older drivers today drive more and longer into old age." They report that older people "made 77 percent more vehicle trips, spent almost 40 percent more time driving, and drove 98 percent more miles in 1995 than in 1983" (citing Rosenbloom, 2001). And this trend will likely continue as the Baby Boom generation enters old age.

Burkhardt (2000, p. 109) says that "even in areas where a variety of transportation options are available, the number one mode of transportation for older people remains the car, preferably with them as the driver." Stutts (2003) reports that two thirds of the time older people drive themselves when they take an automobile trip. And even people age 85 and over more often travel by car as a driver rather than as a passenger.

Travel by car accounts for 92% of trips made outside the home. And, compared with nondrivers, those who drive make twice as many trips outside the home each day. Stutts (2003) says that the trend toward more older drivers and more use of cars by older drivers will continue in the future.

Studies disagree on the effects of age on driving ability. Hakamies-Blomqvist (2004, cited in Scialfa & Fernie, 2006) reports that when judged by miles driven per year, except for very young drivers, older adults have the highest accident rate. But Molnar and Eby (2009) summarize a series of studies that dispute this finding. These studies show that the measure of accidents per miles driven works against older people. Older drivers tend to take shorter trips and drive on city streets. This boosts the risk of accidents. Studies that correct for this bias show similar accident rates for younger and older drivers.

Studies that use crashes per 1,000 drivers show that older people (even those age 75 and older) have the best safety records (Bryer, 2000). Compared with the crash rate of all other drivers, they have about half the rate of accidents (Stutts, 2003). But Stutts goes on to report that the fatality rate for the oldest drivers equals or surpasses that of the youngest drivers (ages 16 to 19). Other data show that, compared with younger drivers, older drivers more often bear the fault for an accident. And this tendency to be at fault increases with age.

Molnar and Eby (2009, p. 190) report that by 2025, "more than 40 percent of all fatal crashes may be associated with age-related frailties." According to Stutts (2003, p. 193), there is no question that physical changes in later life impair a person's ability to drive. Decreased vision, cognitive impairment, decreased strength and mobility, and slower reaction time all decrease a person's ability to drive safely.

Older people compensate for some of these declines (Rudinger & Jansen, 2003; Burkhardt, 2000). They may ride more often as passengers, they may limit their driving to the daytime, and they may limit their driving to familiar places in their neighborhoods. Sylvia Cornel, an 87-year-old widow in Lakewood, New Jersey, for example, continues to drive her car in her neighborhood. But she no longer takes long trips to see her daughter in a mountainous area where she might encounter snow. This kind of accommodation represents a trade-off between mobility and safety.

The concern over seniors' driving ability has led some states to test older drivers before reissuing licenses. Some states require vision tests for older drivers. Studies show that these states have lower fatal accident rates for drivers age 70 and over (Levy, Vernick, & Howard, 1995). A majority of states issue limited licenses for older people with a history of accidents. The license limits driving to daytime, low speeds, and near the person's home. The District of Columbia and the state of New Hampshire require that older people take a knowledge test after age 75 (Bruce, 1994). California requires that doctors report people with dementia who may have a problem driving (Stutts, 2003, citing Staplin, Lococo, Stewart, & Decina, 1998).

The AARP supports education for older drivers rather than age-based testing. It offers a course for older drivers called "55 Alive/Mature Driving." Several million people age 50 and over have taken the course, which includes discussions of how to adapt to physical changes. The American Automobile Association (AAA) offers a number of other programs for older drivers. A CarFit program, for example, has a technician adjust a car to make driving safer for the older person. Another program, Roadwise Review Online (AAA, 2011), helps people to assess their "driving health."

Other programs and information help a person cope with life after they give up their keys (AAA, 2009, 2010). A German study (Rudinger & Jansen, 2003) supports the value of these programs. It found that education and self-regulation lead to better results in regulating driving behavior than a general driving test based on a person's age.

The Federal Highway Administration has published a report with more than 100 recommendations for improvements to highways that will help the older driver. These include improvements in lighting on roads, larger and brighter signs, better signage at intersections, and clearer lines on roadways (Jovanis, 2003; Shahmehri, Chisalita, & Aberg, 2008; Stutts, 2003). These changes will give older drivers more confidence and better guidance and will allow them to drive more safely at later ages.

Auto engineers have also created designs that benefit the older driver. These include side airbags, lane change warning devices, and global positioning systems that use voice commands to give directions (Steinfeld, 2008a). These changes can reduce accidents and lower the fatality rate for older drivers. Future designs will include collision warning devices

---

BOX 10.5
CHANGING TIMES, CHANGING SIGNS

The federal government has issued new regulations on road signs. The Federal Highway Administration (FHWA) will give communities throughout the United States until 2015 to improve roadside signs so that seniors can more easily read them at night. The signs need to better reflect light back toward drivers from their headlights. The government also requires that communities change signs from all capital letters to both capital and lowercase letters. This makes for easier reading.

Victor Mendez, the FHWA administrator, told reporter Larry Copeland (2010), "As drivers get older, we want to make sure they're able to read the signs. . . . Research shows that older drivers are better able to read signs when they're written in both capital and small letters. [This change in policy], it's really driven by safety."

This new rule recognizes the changing abilities of older drivers. It also accepts that older people will continue driving into late old age. Roadways, automobile design, and signage will all need to adapt to the older driver.

and software to adjust speed in the presence of potential dangers (such as too short a distance between vehicles) (Färber, 2003; Jovanis, 2003).

Some manufacturers use "empathic design" methods or "human centered design" (Steinfeld, 2008b, p. 811). Engineers and designers work directly with end users to understand their needs. Human-centered designers use focus groups, observe how people use a product, and then create dramatizations of options for user comment. These methods create products better suited to users' real needs.

For example, an observation of older drivers shows that some older people have limited neck motion due to arthritis. This makes parking a problem. Designers have created sensors that alert a driver if he or she gets too close to a car at the rear. A more advanced tool, a video monitor in Toyota's Prius, gives the driver a view of the car's rear.

Older people in the United States link driving to freedom, competence, and youthfulness. A Florida woman expressed her frustration at life without a car: "I live alone and don't like to depend on friends. . . . I walk to the grocery, get rides from the Red Cross to the doctor's office. The logistics are driving me up a wall. If I had to do it over again, I wouldn't give up my car" (Burkhardt, 2000, p. 111). Education programs, changes in driving patterns, and better highway and auto designs can all extend the number of years an older person drives safely.

CONCLUSION

Dychtwald and Flower (1990) envision new forms of retirement communities in the future. These may include an Olympic village with nonstop athletic activities; a Tron center with high-tech computers, videos, and entertainment; and a time-share village where people can move from place to place every few years. These options may emerge to serve people with good incomes, good health, and a focus on leisure.

The large majority of older people, however, prefer to age in place. Many older people vacation in the Sun Belt. There they enjoy a relaxed lifestyle and leisure activities. But they prefer to live most of the year near lifelong neighbors, friends, and family. New housing options, including home modification—elder cottages and accessory apartments—can help older people achieve this goal.

Stafford (2009) predicts the development of an "elderburbia" as Baby Boomers age in place in the suburbs. He predicts new support services such as energy-efficient small buses and home help. He imagines the return of the retail store geared to the everyday needs of older people—including a delivery service. He notes that models like Beacon Hill Village already exist. And he envisions the growth of more communities like this, designed by and for community members. Stafford promotes a saying that may catch on in the years ahead as designers rethink the needs of an aging society: "from aging in place to aging in community" (p. 184).

Some older people will buck the suburban trend. They will give up the suburbs and move back to the city. They value the diversity and culture of city life. Smith (2004a, b) says that "whether they are new arrivals, savoring their liberation from lawn mowing and automobiles, or veteran urbanites, deeply rooted in communities they helped to build and surrounded by neighbors they have known all their lives, many older Americans find that the services they need and the amenities they enjoy are more plentiful and more accessible in the city."

Rosenbloom (2009, p. 39) says that in urban centers older people live near amenities like a grocery store, a dry cleaner, or a doctor's office. But older people complain of crowded sidewalks, broken sidewalks, ice, snow, and other barriers to walking. In addition, compared to drivers or passengers cars, older pedestrians face as much as a 15 times greater risk of injury.

Rosenbloom proposes a safer pedestrian environment. This includes "raised pavement markings, median islands, improved user-activated signal crossing devices, enhanced signals, and improved pedestrian crossings. Other possibilities include adopting traffic-calming devices such as narrowing streets, lowering speed limits, and using traffic circles to slow traffic." She proposes a more age-friendly environment that favors the person over the car. Pynoos and colleagues (2010) say that elder-friendly communities provide quality living spaces that benefit people of all ages.

Housing for older people in the future will focus less on age than on the needs of a diverse older population. Older people of all ages prefer to age in place and in community. This will mean something different for the active Baby Boomer and the frail 85-year-old. The AARP (Oberlink, 2008) says that housing and transport should create a livable community. "One that has affordable and appropriate housing, supportive community features and services, and adequate mobility options. Together these facilitate personal independence and the engagement of residents in civic and social life."

Housing and transport needs will range from more long-term care beds, to new types of housing developments with integrated services, to modified homes to allow people to stay in their homes longer, to new communities for active Baby Boomers. The continuum of housing and transportation for older people will expand in the future and will include more options than ever before.

SUMMARY

- Living arrangements include living with a spouse, alone, with other relatives, or with nonrelatives. Eighty-five percent of older people live alone or with a spouse. The rest live with another relative or with a nonrelative.
- The number of older people who live alone will increase in the future. Higher Social Security benefits, widowhood, and divorce all contribute to this trend.
- People who live alone report a high rate of chronic illness and activity limitation. As people age, their competence or ability may decline and environmental press or demand may increase. When this happens, people need supports to stay in their homes.
- Older people prefer to age in place. They want to stay in their homes as long as they can. Aging in place requires that people have the resources they need to live in the setting they choose. The ideal housing arrangement balances competence (a person's ability) with autonomy (their desire to pursue one's goals). It provides just the right amount of challenge and support.
- Many housing options exist for older people today. The most common types of housing, ranging from the most demanding to the least demanding environments, include (1) single-family homes, (2) apartments and condominiums, (3) life-care communities, (4) granny flats, (5) congregate housing, (6) shared housing, (7) assisted living, and (8) nursing homes. This housing continuum offers options that fit older people's varied needs.
- The large majority of people age 60 and over live in single-family homes. Most people own their homes, with the majority living mortgage free. Suburban homes, built for the families of the 1950s, create problems for older people. These homes may not suit the physical abilities of people who have aged in place. They may also leave a person isolated, with few transportation options.
- Home modifications can help a person stay in their own home. Modifications create a safer environment. Also, new transportation services can help older people stay in their suburban homes. To age in place, a person needs to adapt their home and transportation options to fit their changing abilities.
- Home equity loans can provide a person with the resources they need to age in place. The loan allows the person to tap their home's value in order to meet their current financial obligations. The federal government offers guidelines and policies to oversee the home equity loan business.
- Many people age 60 and over live in apartments. Renters tend to be older women with low incomes. They have fewer options when it comes to home modification. For this reason, older renters often choose to move into apartments designed for older people.
- Some older people require less demanding environments than single-family homes or apartments. They can choose from other options that offer more support and services. These options include congregate housing, subsidized housing, single rooms, and board and care homes.
- People who need nursing care (the oldest old) often live in a nursing home. Only a small proportion of older people need this option. And this proportion has decreased in recent years with the development of more community housing programs.
- Interest in new types of housing options will grow in the future. Designers have developed many new housing alternatives to meet the needs of people as they age. Some of these alternatives include elder cottages, home sharing, retirement communities, and continuing care retirement communities.
- Homeless older people, a very small proportion of people over age 65, have unique needs. Some communities have developed special programs to serve this population. The current economic slump drove some nonpoor older people into homelessness. This has increased the need for services to a new population of homeless people.
- Most older people today prefer to age in place. This depends on the integration of supportive housing, social services, transportation, and health care. Living arrangements will have to meet the needs of a diverse older population. These needs will range from long-term care in institutions to new communities for active Baby Boomers. Home modification can also help an older person age in place.
- As people age, they feel more need to live near public transportation. Improvements in the function and design of public transportation (wider aisles on buses, clearer markings on steps) would make public transportation more appealing to older people. Unique programs such as

independent transportation networks provide more personal service to older people.

• In spite of improvements in public transportation, older people prefer to drive their own cars. Physical changes can affect driving, but older drivers vary in their driving abilities. Education programs and new highway designs can help extend the number of years that older people can drive a car. This will allow seniors to live independently for a longer time.

DISCUSSION QUESTIONS

1. What types of living arrangements are available to older people? Arrange them on a continuum from least to most supportive housing.
2. What has led a greater proportion of older people than ever before to live alone? Why do gerontologists think this trend will continue?
3. Discuss some of the problems that an older person who lives alone can face. What are some methods for overcoming these problems?
4. Describe the relationship between a person's capability (competence) and environmental demand (press). How do these two things affect a person's ability to live alone?
5. What kinds of problems do older people face if they live in a single-family home? What kinds of home modifications can help a person live in safety and comfort?
6. Describe several housing options, besides single-family homes or apartments, that are available to older people today. How do these options differ from single-family homes and apartments?
7. What types of home modifications can help a person age in place? What inhibits people from having these modifications done?
8. List and describe several alternatives to traditional housing that are now available to older people. What benefits do they offer older residents? What risks do these alternatives present?
9. Explain the future trend in housing for older people. What kinds of things will help older people live independently in the future?
10. How does the lack of transportation affect older people? What kinds of services can society provide that will improve older people's access to transportation? What changes in policies and the environment would improve safety for older drivers?

SUGGESTED READING

Coughlin, J. F., & D'Ambrosio, L. A. (Eds.). (2010). *Aging America and transportation.* New York: Springer.

The MIT Age Lab developed the contents for this work. So it's not surprising that it places a lot of emphasis on technology. This includes discussions of vehicle design, transportation infrastructure, and innovations to improve mobility. The book also discusses challenges like driver safety in later life.

McCallion, P. (2007). *Housing for the elderly: Policy and practice issues.* Binghamton, NY: Haworth Press.

This book describes the full range of housing conditions for older people, from homelessness to communities for older people. The author looks at the latest research on naturally occurring retirement communities. The book examines the policies and strategies needed to create quality housing for older people.

Wahl, H.-W., Scheidt, R. J., & Windley, P. G. (Eds.). (2004). *Focus on aging in context: Socio-physical environments.* New York: Springer.

The editors have organized this collection around the ecological framework first proposed by Lawton and Nahemow and discussed in this chapter. The essays look at the fit between the person and the environment from various points of view. Topics include the effect of the environment on everyday life, competence, and problem solving; design of interior space; and the supportive neighborhood. The essays show the importance of looking at how a supportive environment can create the conditions for successful aging.

Websites to Consult

HUD.GOV 00 U.S. Department of Housing and Urban Development

http://portal.hud.gov/portal/page/portal/HUD

This portal provides federal government housing information. You can search by "audience group" (e.g., homeowners or home buyers). You can also search this site for research articles, public policies, and programs available for seniors.

U.S. Department of Housing and Urban Development—Information for Senior Citizens

http://portal.hud.gov/portal/page/portal/HUD/topics/information_for_senior_citizens

This page contains links to information about senior living situations. Links include ideas on how to live in a house during old age, how to search for an appropriate apartment, and how to choose an assisted living facility.

AARP—Home & Garden

www.aarp.org/home-garden

A popular site for the general public. This site contains information about current housing issues such as foreclosures, home maintenance, and new technology for the home. This site also reports on home modification and universal design. Some stories on this site also report on new car design.

National Center on Senior Transportation

http://seniortransportation.easterseals.com/site/PageServer?pagename=NCST2_homepage

This government portal provides news, data, and advice on senior transportation issues for caregivers, older Americans, and service providers. A good place to look for current audio conferences, webinars, and grant opportunities.

chapter 11

LEISURE, RECREATION, AND EDUCATION

I first met Sarah Bowles at a suburban YMCA. Sarah ran a fitness program for older adults called the Retired People's Participation Club. The program enrolled 215 members. It involved gym exercises, followed by a swim in the pool, with lots of time to kibitz and schmooze. "You want a political discussion," she once told me, "you'll find it in the sauna."

I first talked with Sarah as part of my research for my book *Successful Aging*. I considered Sarah a model of active living. She was 72 years old at the time. I decided to call Sarah again to see what she was doing 10 years later. How had this active, successfully aging woman fared over the years? I had no idea where to find her, so I tried the Y where I first visited with her.

"Yes," a receptionist said, "Sarah still works here. But she's gone for the day."

I left my number and Sarah called me back the next day. She told me that she still leads the club in the gym and swim program 5 days a week in the winter and 3 days a week in the summer. The program has now grown to more than 300 registrants, with about five new people enrolling each month. She has trained eight of the club members to work as instructors.

"The program must be benefiting people," she says, "because they just keep coming. As for me, I'm on nitro now. I keep working in the program because otherwise I would be at home stagnating."

"If I don't lead the program one day, my body doesn't work. I have a bad case of arthritis in both my wrists. So I wear a cast when I lead the gym session. I can barely get down on the mat because I broke both my knees some years ago and that bothers me. Plus, I'm afraid I might break my wrists. Last month I fell and cracked some ribs, so that bothered me for a while. But I still get down there. I do what I can. Sometimes I tell the people, 'Do as I say, not as I do.' I try the exercises out on me first. I hear some of them say, 'If she can do it, I can do it.'"

In addition to running her program, Sarah lectures to groups on health and fitness. She travels to small towns and teaches older people to lead fitness programs in their own communities. She also helps train university students in how to run fitness programs for older people. She does all this as a volunteer and says that dedication to her program keeps her fit and alert. "The program is the most important thing in my life," she says. "I feel guilty if I miss a day."

Many studies now support the value of active lifestyles like Sarah's. And the YMCA now offers "active older adult" programs in Ys throughout the United States. Research reports show that an active leisure lifestyle directly benefits health and helps buffer the influence of life events and illness.

This chapter looks at (1) the activity patterns of older people in the United States today, (2) some of the barriers that keep older people from active living, and (3) some model programs for overcoming barriers to active living.

LEISURE

The dictionary defines *leisure* as "freedom from time-consuming duties, responsibilities, or activities." It's no surprise that people have more leisure time once they retire. On an average day, for example, adults age 75 and over spent 7.8 hours on leisure and sports activities—more than any other age group. This came to almost double the leisure time spent by 35- to 44-year-olds (4.3 hours)—less than other age groups (American Time Use Survey, 2009). But what do older people do with this freedom? Do they take up new activities, maintain old activities, or become disengaged in later life?

Age and Leisure

Leisure activities differ by age. For example, researchers find that the rate of engagement in sports declines with age. This decline begins in midlife and gets more extreme as a person ages (Schoenborn, Vickerie, & Powell-Griner, 2006; Wilcox, 2002). In general, studies find that older people spend most of their leisure time alone and on sedentary **core leisure activities**. Horna (1994) defines *core activities* as those that need few resources, have a low cost, and have easy access. Core activities include reading, watching television, and visiting with family. Core leisure activities stay high for all age groups into late old age. Certain home-based activities like reading and watching TV increase with age.

Lee and King (2003) asked samples of community-dwelling men and women (age 49 and over) about their activities. Ninety-five percent of the people in the study reported talking on the phone and reading as frequent activities. Over 80% said they talked with friends, listened to the radio, or watched television. Compared with men, women spent more time on social activities and household maintenance.

The American Time Use Survey (ATUS) (2009) reports similar results. The ATUS found that compared to people age 75 and over people ages 15 to 19 spent four times more hours per day on sports, exercise, and recreation (0.8 vs. 0.2 hours). People age 75 and over, compared to 15- to 19-year-olds, spent almost twice as many hours per day watching television (4.2 vs. 2.2 hours). Compared to the younger group, the oldest group spent more time reading, relaxing, and thinking. The younger group spent more time socializing, communicating, and using the computer (often for computer games).

The Bureau of Labor Statistics Consumer Expenditure Survey (U.S. Department of Labor, Bureau of Labor Statistics, 2008) found that spending on leisure activities decreases from age 55 onward. Spending decreased on all categories measured—entertainment (including fees and admissions, audio and visual equipment and services, pets, toys, hobbies), personal care products and services, reading, education, and tobacco and smoking supplies. This may reflect a decrease in income after retirement. Or it may reflect a change in lifestyle.

Horna (1994) defines **peripheral leisure activities** as those that require more resources, take place outside the home, and need more effort. Peripheral activities include exercise, sports, outdoor recreation, and travel. Older people tend to avoid strenuous activities like swimming, running, and softball or baseball (Bureau of Labor Statistics, 2008b). For example,

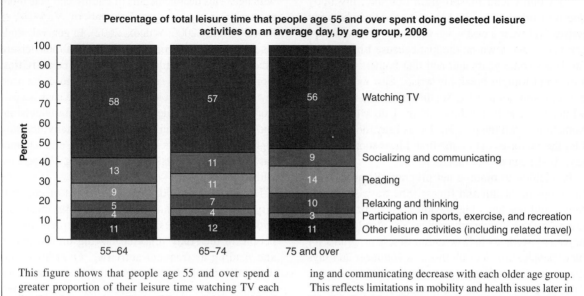

Percentage of total leisure time that people age 55 and over spent doing selected leisure activities on an average day, by age group, 2008

This figure shows that people age 55 and over spend a greater proportion of their leisure time watching TV each day than they spend on all other leisure activities combined. The proportion of time spent on some activities like socializ-

ing and communicating decrease with each older age group. This reflects limitations in mobility and health issues later in life. People in the oldest age group tend to engage in more solitary activities (relaxing and thinking).

FIGURE 11.1   Use of Time

Source: Federal Interagency Forum on Aging-Related Statistics. (2010f). *Older Americans 2010: Key indicators of well-being.* Indicator 28, p. 44. Washington, DC. Citing the Bureau of Labor Statistics, American Time Use Survey. Electronic version available at www.agingstats.gov.

29% of people ages 55 to 64 in 2007 reported regular leisure-time physical activity, compared to only 17.9% of people age 75 and over (Federal Interagency Forum, 2010d; National Center for Health Statistics, 2009). Frailty and decreased physical ability account for much of this decline.

This pattern of sedentary leisure activity seems resistant to change. Lee and King (2003) set up an intervention program to increase physical activity and change eating habits. They found that the intervention led to increased physical activity directly related to the program. But it did not change the other, more sedentary, patterns of leisure activity.

Wu (2000) found similar results in a survey of 136 older people in South Dakota. The people in the study reported that they most often engaged in visiting family or friends and watching movies or television. They said that they participated least in physical activities like tennis and skiing.

Housing can influence a person's leisure activities. Pruchno and Rose (2002) compared activities for three groups of frail older people. One group lived in a nursing home, a second group lived in an assisted living

facility, and a third group received home health care. The researchers found that the assisted living group spent more time than either group on housework. The frail older people in a nursing home tended to read less than the people in the other groups. But they engaged in more recreation activity than people who lived in their own homes. The nursing home provides opportunities for recreation and encourages this activity. People in assisted living or on their own had to spend more time on maintenance activities such as housework and shopping.

Gender and Leisure

Leisure participation differs by gender as well as age. Studies show that, compared to men, women have less leisure time in later life. They do more household tasks than men and often take on the role of caregiver to a spouse or relative.

The American Time Use Survey (Bureau of Labor Statistics, 2009) found that, compared to men age 65 and over, women in this age group spent one and a half times more hours on household activities.

This pattern carries over from earlier stages of life. The 2010 American Time Use Survey (Bureau of Labor Statistics, 2011) found that on an average day 20% of men did housework, including cleaning and laundry. But 49% of women did housework. Forty-one percent of men engaged in cooking or cleaning up. But 68% of women engaged in these activities. Compared to men, women spend more than twice as much time on child care (e.g., feeding or bathing a child)—66 minutes per day for women compared to 26 minutes per day for men.

Gender roles affect the kind of housework people do. Men, for example, show increases in time spent on yard work, repairs, and gardening. Men spend much less time than women on laundry and child care. Men and women also engage in different activities in retirement (as they did in their middle years). Men, for example, prefer sports activities and competition. Women tend to avoid sports and male-dominated activities. They prefer dance and aerobics (Horna, 1994). Garber and Blissmer (2002, p. 39; also Strain, Grabusic, Searle, & Dunn, 2002) say that "the socialization patterns established earlier in life appear to be salient into old age."

The National Health Interview Survey (Centers for Disease Control and Prevention, 2009c) found that only 16% of men and 11% of women age 75 and over engaged in regular leisure-time strengthening activity (e.g., lifting weights or calisthenics)—the lowest proportion of any age group. Satariano, Haight, and Tager (2000) studied the "avoidance of leisure time physical activity" in a sample of over 2,000 people age 55 and over in Sonoma, California. They found that, compared with men, women reported more limitations and avoidance of physical activity. But a large majority of both genders (81% of women and 73.5% of men) gave reasons why they limited or avoided physical activity.

Some people gave medical reasons for decreasing their activity, and this explanation increased with age. Nonmedical reasons accounted for about 20% to 30% of people who reported reduced activity. Nonmedical reasons included the absence of an exercise companion and no interest. The researchers suggest that interventions focus on nonmedical reasons (e.g., the lack of a companion). They suggest the creation of exercise teams or a buddy system to increase participation in activity programs.

Agahi and Parker (2008) studied a representative sample of 1,246 men and women ages 65 to 95. The study first questioned this group in 1991–1992. The researchers followed up 12 years later in 2004. They found that certain leisure activities led to longer life. Women who took part in organizational activities and study circles, compared to those who did not, tended to have lower mortality. The more leisure activities a woman took part in, the lower her mortality risk. Men, who showed lower mortality, focused on hobbies and gardening. This study suggests that leisure activity may lead to a longer life.

Minority Status and Leisure

Some studies find that leisure activity differs by race and ethnicity. For example, compared with whites and Asians, older African American and Hispanic minority group members report less participation in regular leisure-time physical activity (Garber & Blissmer, 2002; Schoenborn et al., 2006). Kamimoto and colleagues (Kamimoto, Easton, Maurice, Husten, & Macera, 1999, cited in Wilcox, 2002) found that 36% of white women ages 65 to 74 reported no leisure physical activity in the month before their study. But 53% of African American women in this age group reported inactivity.

These figures for inactivity rose to 47% for white women and 61% for African American women age 75 and over. Older African American women showed a lower rate of participation, compared with whites, when researchers in another study controlled for age, income, and education (Brown & Tedrick, 1993; also Wilcox, 2002). These women said that they lacked information about programs, family kept them from these activities, and they had transportation problems.

A study of 2,912 women age 40 and over looked at leisure activity by ethnic and racial group. The study found that, compared to white and Hispanic women, African American and American Indian/ Alaskan Native women showed the least likelihood of exercising. And, compared to white women, Hispanic women showed a greater tendency to exercise (Brownson et al., 2000). The study found that about one third of white, African American, and Hispanic American women reported no leisure activities (exercise, recreation, or physical activity) in the 2 weeks before the survey. About one half of American Indian/Alaskan Natives reported no leisure activity.

Cultural and economic barriers can keep minority members from enjoying active leisure. Low income may limit recreation options. For instance, the cost of transportation, equipment, or usage fees may keep poorer people from active leisure pursuits (e.g., membership in a health club). Also, minority members may fear prejudice, and they may lack experience with active leisure.

Gallagher and colleagues (2010) studied barriers to walking faced by African American inner-city residents. The study asked 21 people (2 men and 19 women) age 60 and over to comment on barriers to walking that they faced in their neighborhood.

The residents said that crowds, panhandlers, poor lighting, vacant lots, and criminal activity all discouraged walking.

But the presence of people encouraged walking. They said they enjoyed seeing neighbors, friendly people, and families with children. People in the study also listed quiet, peaceful surroundings and beautiful scenery as well as safety from crime as conditions that encouraged walking. Residents said that walking in the morning reduced barriers. Daylight and the quiet of the morning all encouraged walking.

Programs that intend to help minority elders stay fit need to take neighborhood barriers into account. The residents in this study suggest some ways to overcome barriers, such as walking in the morning or at times when they can be with other people.

Studies of minority leisure activities often compare minority and majority older people. They use majority behavior as the norm. This often makes minority members look deficient. But it ignores minority members' unique social context and values. A study of older African American women, for example, found that they have a unique view of leisure activity. They describe leisure as both freedom from work and a form of self-expression. They engaged in church work, attended senior centers, watched television, and did crafts. These women also engaged in self-care and care for others in their social network (Allen & Chin-Sang, 1990). They thought of caregiving as part of their leisure activities. They said that caregiving gives meaning to their lives and allows them to relate to others.

Tan and colleagues (2009, p. 308) studied the participation of 71 African American women in the Experience Corps—a mentoring program in Baltimore, where older people work with school-age students. The study compared these women with a group of women in the Women's Health and Aging

Studies (WHAS) program at Johns Hopkins University. The researchers found a significant increase in physical activity for the Experience Corps group compared to the WHAS group. The researchers conclude that "a high-intensity senior service program that is designed as a health promotion intervention can lead to significant long-term improvements in the level of physical activity in high-risk older adults."

The Experience Corps fits the type of volunteer work that African Americans prefer (Foster-Bey, Dietz, & Grimm, 2006). The increase in physical activity suggests that volunteer programs like the Experience Corps promote a more active lifestyle. And this benefits African American seniors who face a high risk of inactivity.

Leisure may also have a different meaning for people from other cultural backgrounds. For example, Wilcox (2002, p. 21) says, "Little is known about rates of [physical activity] in older Asian American women." On our campus in the early morning, for example, I see older Chinese men and women stretching and performing t'ai chi exercises. My observations of older groups in China and Japan suggests that these cultures value exercise in later life. And they have traditional forms of exercise that suit older people. I don't know of any research that has studied this informal activity.

Plonczynski (2003, p. 215) includes volunteer work and religious activities in her definition of physical activity. "These activities," she says, "are particularly important with older adults and minority older adults, respectively. This inclusion reflects the broad range of lifestyle physical activities within community life." Other studies of leisure need to take minority differences into account when studying the physical activity of older people and when assessing the minority person's leisure choices.

Leisure Education

Studies of older people's leisure attitudes show that they often formed their views of leisure in their childhoods. Many older men and women today were taught that play in adulthood meant wasted time. They learned that only young people should play sports or exercise. These attitudes work against an active leisure lifestyle. Older people today can learn the value of leisure activity. And they need to learn new ways to use their free time. Leisure education should include an appreciation of leisure as fun and enjoyment.

The people now entering the Third Age may need this type of education. An AARP study of people age 50 and over found that only about a quarter of this group engaged in regular leisure-time physical activity. The study also found a decrease in leisure-time physical activity for people ages 50 to 64 between 1997 and 2005 (AARP, 2007b). In this study, compared to the preceding year and to data from 10 years earlier, the proportion of obese and overweight people age 50 and over also increased.

McGuire, Dottavio, and O'Leary (1987a) studied data from a nationwide recreation survey. They identified two groups of older people, each with different leisure patterns. They called one group **contractors**. These people had stopped at least one outdoor activity in the past year and had not learned any new activity since age 65. At best, contractors continued the same activities they had learned in childhood. The researchers called the second group **expanders**. This group kept up their former activities but also had added at least one new outdoor activity since age 65. Expanders added new activities as their life circumstances changed.

The researchers say that leisure service providers need to create many options for older people. Leisure education programs can help contractors and expanders. Contractors can learn how to add new activities. Expanders can develop skills in the new activities they have begun.

NEW ACTIVITIES IN OLD AGE

Some older people have begun to explore new leisure activities. These people serve as role models for people in their middle years. Their discoveries will create new opportunities for aging in the future.

Outdoor Recreation

The federal government encourages older people to use outdoor recreation sites. It offers the "America the Beautiful—National Parks and Federal Recreational Lands Pass—Senior Pass," a lifetime pass for citizens and permanent residents age 62 and over. The pass costs $10 and allows free entry for the older person and companions to all U.S. national parks, historic sites, wildlife refuges, and recreation areas (National Park Service, 2010).

Many older people combine outdoor activity with travel. According to Willens (2003, p. 45), "Boomers live to travel. They travel quite frequently on vacation—and by astute financial planning, are seeking to guarantee the means to continue with this activity (as well as any other activities that may strike them)." He goes on to say that 60% of Baby Boomers have taken at least one vacation trip in the past 12 months and plan for another next year. Myers and Nielson (2003) report that people age 50 and over make up 80% of the luxury travel market (where people spend at least $350 per day). Compared to younger people, they take more trips (average three per year), stay longer at a vacation site, and spend 75% more money there.

MacNeil (2001) predicts a future interest in extreme sports by Baby Boom elders. These will include biking, skiing, water sports, and mountain climbing. Travel tour companies have caught on to this trend. They now offer challenging outdoor adventure tours to older people. These companies sponsor tours to the Amazon, the Galapagos Islands, and Antarctica. Some of the tours include hiking, climbing, rafting, and other demanding activities. Others include more support, such as a Jeep journey through the mountain passes of Tibet.

Lichtenstein (2007) says that some seniors combine extreme athletic competition with adventure travel. She describes the challenges that Jay Norman, 69, and Peter Spiller, 63, seek through ultramarathon running. Both compete in the Coastal Challenge race in Costa Rica—the Route of Fire. This race covers 230 kilometers (142.9 miles) over 6 days. The route goes past inland lakes, jungle, windswept highlands, and tropical forest. Norman says he does it "to do something that very few others ever attempt. The rewards are the memories of the experience."

Herb Schon, 76, told Lichtenstein that he plans to ride from San Francisco to Portsmouth, New Hampshire, on the America by Bicycle tour. The trip averages 82 miles a day. "Life," Schon says, "is a challenge and efforts are rewarded!"

A Web site, Seniors for Living, devotes a page to "11 Extreme(ly Old) Athletes: Seniors Who Defy Their Age & Inspire" (www.seniorsforliving.com/blog/2010/01/11/11-extremely-old-athletes-seniors-who-athletically-defy-their-age). The site provides video clips of seniors engaged in extreme sports. Clips include videos of a 48-person skydiving team, snowboarding, and "Banana" George Blair, now 92. Banana George holds the Guinness record as the oldest barefoot water-skier in the world.

Outdoor and adventure activity will attract more seniors in the future, especially people with good incomes and good health.

Fitness, Health, and Well-Being

Some years ago Kraus and Raab (1961) labeled disuse of the body in old age **hypokinetic disease**. This syndrome leads to physical decline in later life. Other gerontologists simply say, "Use it or lose it." Disuse leads to slow decline in the body. The National Health Interview Survey (National Center for Health Statistics, 2009) reports that in 2008, more than one quarter (26.6%) of people 60 and over were obese. The report found no significant difference in obesity between men and women.

Anderson and colleagues (Anderson, Franckowiak, Christmas, Walston, & Crespo, 2001) found

that overweight and obese people reported low levels of participation in leisure-time physical activity. The lack of activity puts these older people at risk for heart disease, osteoporosis, depression, and disability.

Even though older people would benefit from exercise, they show low participation rates in physical activity. And they generally show declines in physical activity with age (Plonczynski, 2003; Centers for Disease Control and Prevention, 2009c). The Centers for Disease Control and Prevention (cited in Center for Healthy Aging, 2004) reports that 28% to 34% of adults ages 65 to 74 engage in no leisure activity. This increases to 35% to 44% of people age 75 and over. Only 25% to 35% of older people engage in the recommended amounts of leisure activity. "It is clear," Kelly (1993, p. 123) says, "that no type of activity is as likely to be abandoned or avoided by the old as regular physical exercise."

Three gerontological theories give at least partial explanations for these findings: disengagement

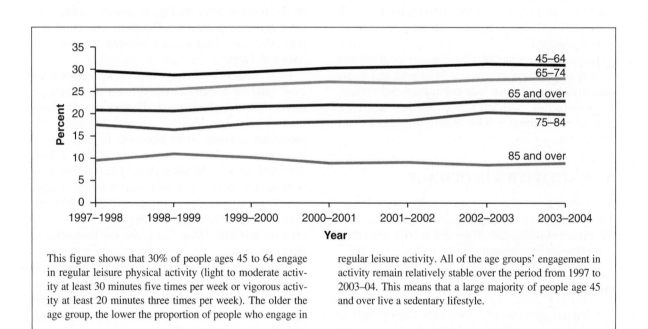

This figure shows that 30% of people ages 45 to 64 engage in regular leisure physical activity (light to moderate activity at least 30 minutes five times per week or vigorous activity at least 20 minutes three times per week). The older the age group, the lower the proportion of people who engage in regular leisure activity. All of the age groups' engagement in activity remain relatively stable over the period from 1997 to 2003–04. This means that a large majority of people age 45 and over live a sedentary lifestyle.

FIGURE 11.2 Percentage of Persons Age 45 and Over Who Reported Engaging in Regular Leisure Time Physical Activity, by Age Group, 1997–2004

Note: Data are based on 2-year averages. "Regular leisure time physical activity" is defined as "engaging in light-moderate leisure time physical activity for greater than or equal to 30 minutes at a frequency greater than or equal to 5 times per week, or engaging in vigorous leisure time physical activity for greater than or equal to 20 minutes at a frequency greater than or equal to 3 times per week." Reference population: These data refer to the civilian noninstitutionalized population.

Sources: Centers for Disease Control and Prevention, National Center for Health Statistics, National Health Interview Survey; Federal Interagency Forum on Aging-Related Statistics. (2006). *Older Americans, update 2006: Key indicators of well-being. Health risks and behaviors.* Indicator 24–Physical Activity. Retrieved November 17, 2007, from www.agingstats.gov/agingstatsdotnet/Main_Site/Data/2006Documents/Health_Risks&Behaviors.pdf.

theory, continuity theory, and age stratification theory.

1. Disengagement theory (Cumming & Henry, 1961) sees disengagement from activity as a natural process. It allows the older person to withdraw from social roles and activities prior to death.
2. Continuity theory (Atchley, 1999a) proposes that older people follow the same pattern of activity or inactivity in old age that they followed in middle age. Most people lead a sedentary life in middle age. They carry this pattern into later life.
3. **Age stratification theory** (Riley, 1971) says that society expects certain behaviors from people in later life. Society also offers older people a narrow range of social roles to play. An older person who wants to live an active lifestyle may feel out of step with social expectations. They will find few supports for an active lifestyle.

These theories point to social forces that can either encourage or inhibit an active lifestyle. Activity theory, a fourth major theory of aging, serves as a counterpoint to the three theories mentioned previously. Activity theory promotes the value of active living. It says that people experience high life satisfaction if they stay active. (See Chapters 2 and 6 for more details on these theories.)

Programs That Overcome Barriers to Active Living

Sport, leisure, and recreation programs can break the inertia of disengagement, continuity, and age stratification. To do this they need to attract sedentary older and middle-aged people.

For a start, older people need access to leisure and recreation programs. Disengagement theory views withdrawal as a normal social-psychological adaptation to aging. But disengagement may be as much a function of physical disability as of psychosocial withdrawal. A decline in health, for example, can challenge a person's ability to stay active. Poor health or activity limitation in part explains disengagement from a more active lifestyle with age. Interventions that help people overcome physical barriers show that, given the chance, even a person with a disability can stay physically active into late old age.

One woman, who had always wanted to tap dance, had arthritis in her legs and could barely stand. A recreation program that served homebound older people solved her problem. The program arranged for another senior, a dance instructor, to visit this woman. The instructor had the woman sit on a kitchen stool so she could tap dance without putting weight on her legs. This program helped fulfill this woman's lifelong wish. The program also ran special t'ai chi classes for people with visual impairments and other health challenges (Penning & Wasyliw, 1992).

Continuity theory says that people will follow patterns of activity in later life that they followed in their middle years. They do this in part to maintain a stable sense of self throughout life. People avoid leisure and recreation activities that might threaten their self-images or well-being. Continuity preserves self-esteem and self-worth. But continuity can also keep a person within boundaries that limit personal growth and development.

Women in the past, for example, had little exposure to sports. Their lower levels of participation (compared with men) suggest that they will continue to avoid these activities. Past prejudices and current fears keep them from activities that they might enjoy. Exercise and fitness programs need to take gender

Two women enjoy active leisure time at the beach.

differences into account. Some aerobics programs for women now introduce weight training into the program. By putting weight training within a women's aerobics class, the program makes this typically male activity available to women. And this can help women maintain bone strength as they age.

Continuity theory says that minority older people will tend to take part in programs that fit their understanding of leisure, recreation, and activity. Program designers need to understand how people from different cultures define leisure, recreation, and activity. They can also try to expand a person's leisure preferences. Some leisure programs need to provide instruction in languages other than English so that minority older people can take part in them.

Leisure and recreation programs must minimize physical and psychological risk to participants. Shephard (1990) presents a good discussion of the physical risk that exercise poses for people in their 70s and older. This includes injury, extreme fatigue, and in some cases, sudden death. Methods exist to avoid these dangers. Psychological risk includes fear of embarrassment, ridicule, and failure. People may fail to meet their own or others' expectations. This can even be true of former athletes who set unrealistic goals for themselves.

A program should allow people to take risks without fear of ridicule or failure. Programs should create a sense of **self-efficacy**. Self-efficacy refers to what people believe they can do. People with a strong sense of efficacy take on more challenging tasks and put out more effort. **Mastery accomplishments**, successful achievements, and knowledge of achievements all enhance efficacy (Cohen, 2005).

Sarah Bowles, described at the start of this chapter, traces the success of her program to the development of efficacy and self-confidence (although she doesn't use these terms). Sarah studies her people carefully. She listens to them, watches how they perform, and builds the program to suit their needs. Sarah's program reduces threats to members' self-worth. She has no music, no competition between class members, and no failures. People attend with walkers and canes if they need to. "Each person keeps their own time," she says. "I try out the exercises on me first. Over the years I've learned how fast to go and what's dangerous. It's amazing what people can do if the pace is right for their age."

Age stratification theory points to the societal pressures that keep people from an active lifestyle. This includes narrow notions of what older people should and shouldn't do. It also includes the absence of roles for active older people to play. We associate lawn bowling, walking, and golf with older people. Only recently have older people begun to break this mold by taking up swimming, aerobics, and gymnastics. Some senior athletes have set new records for their age group in track and field events.

Still, older athletes may seem like exceptions to the rule. Many people have imbibed the image of the older person as ill, at risk, and sedentary. Cousins and Burgess (1992) say that stereotypes of seniors' abilities exist among recreation specialists as well as the public. And due to stereotyping, professionals may underestimate seniors' abilities. The habit of typing people by age poses one of the greatest challenges to older people who want to live an active lifestyle. This can lead to programs that fail to challenge participants. This, in turn, reinforces stereotypes about seniors' lack of ability.

For example, 40 years ago, few people would have thought that t'ai chi would become one of the most popular activities among seniors. Older people who have taken up this ancient Chinese exercise often go on to develop great skill. Some have become amateur masters of this art and have become teachers. Activity programs should make the most of the abilities that older people have. Appropriate programs can help people develop a positive self-image and discover new potential as they age. Good program design can overcome other barriers that keep older people from living active lives.

Professionals who work with older people need to listen to participants. Good communication between a program leader and participants creates a successful program. Professionals can then set individual goals for clients, with realistic expectations. Older people need varied types of programs to suit their varied needs. Gentler activities, such as walking or swimming, may serve older people better than jogging or running.

A brisk walking program, for example, may best meet certain older people's needs. The growth of mall-walking programs in the past few years shows the appeal of walking as a form of exercise. I once arrived at a shopping mall at 7:30 A.M. on a frigid December morning in a northern city. I had a meeting in one of the offices attached to the mall. To my surprise, I found a group of senior mall-walkers already suited up and into their routine. Programs that fit the needs of their members and allow people to participate at their own pace will encourage attendance.

The National Recreation and Park Association started a walking program in 2007 in Phoenix, Arizona. The free program lasted 10 weeks. People who took part in the program got a step counter and a guide book and could join a walking group. The program also offered classes on nutrition and fitness.

Above all, program leaders must make programs enjoyable and rewarding. Cousins and Burgess (1992) say that instructors often speak too quickly, use slang or jargon, or start when the audience has not understood instructions. These researchers suggest that instructors break movements down into small units. Then the instructor should allow self-paced practice of the new skill.

Leaders should include participants in planning, assessing, and developing activity programs. This builds commitment to the program and leads to ongoing participation. Leaders also need to understand the life circumstances of the program members. Wilcox and King (2004) conducted a controlled study of an exercise program that enrolled 97 older people. The researchers found that negative life events (e.g., an illness) during the course of the program led to lower program attendance. The more negative life events, the greater the effect on attendance.

Many studies have found that seniors join and stay with a program if the program offers social interaction. Older people often take part in physical activities in order to be with others (Garber & Blissmer, 2002). Leaders need to ask people about their goals. They can then design the program to meet these goals. Older people's goals often differ from those of younger people in exercise, fitness, or sports programs.

Again, Sarah Bowles's program contains a principle that other professionals could apply. She puts people first. She gives people permission to enjoy themselves during their workout. "During the program, people just talk, and talk, and talk. Sometimes the noise is terrific," she says. "That has got a lot to do with the program's success."

Younger old people, compared with the very old, may have a more positive attitude toward exercise, fitness, and active living. This, in part, reflects a difference in the health of young-old and old-old people. Younger cohorts have better health and can still take part in many of the activities of their middle years.

Hanc (2010), citing a survey by the International Health, Racquet and Sportsclub Association, reports the "graying of the gym." The survey found that gym membership among older people rose from 1.5 million members in 1987 to 10.5 million members in 2008. This makes older exercisers the fastest-growing group in the health club population. Better incomes, better health, and new attitudes toward aging among younger cohorts account for this increase in gym membership.

A more positive attitude toward active living also probably reflects the effects of health promotion in recent years. Younger old people almost daily hear reports on the value of exercise for good health.

MacNeil (2001) predicts greater leisure activity among older people in the future. He says that this reflects lifestyle differences between Baby Boomers and the current generation of older people. Future cohorts of older people will come into old age with knowledge about the value of exercise and active living. They will bring a more positive attitude toward activity in later life. MacNeil says that these people will demand more recreation opportunities in later life.

Masters Athletes and the Senior Olympics

Sports leagues for older athletes have sprung up throughout the United States. The National Men's Senior Baseball League, for example, has 3,200 teams nationwide with 45,000 members. The league holds a World Series every fall, and its national tournaments host 650 teams. The league claims to hold the largest amateur baseball tournaments in the world (Men's Senior Baseball, 2010).

Older athletes, who range in age from 30 to their 70s, often refer to themselves as Masters. Masters cyclists now number more than 15,000. And more than 133,000 men and women compete in Masters tennis. These leagues hold local and national competitions. A Masters or senior division exists for nearly every sport.

The National Senior Games Association is "dedicated to motivating senior men and women to lead a healthy lifestyle through the senior games movement" (National Senior Games, 2010). It sanctions and coordinates sports and games activities for people age 50 and over throughout the country. Warren Blaney organized the first Youth Eternal Games (later called the Senior Olympics) in California in 1965 (Fishel, 2010). The program lasted 4 days and drew 175 participants to three events (marathon, swimming, and track and field).

By 1987, 50,000 people took part in regional Senior Olympic events in 50 cities in the United States. In that same year, the first National Senior Olympic games took place in St. Louis. Twenty-five hundred people competed and more than 100,000 people viewed the events. In 2010, the Summer Games took

---

BOX 11.1
THE WII WAY TO STAYING ACTIVE

Video games can keep a person entertained. But they don't do much to tone the body or encourage movement. Nintendo's Wii video game system gets players off the couch and into the action. Even someone with a disability can enjoy the challenge.

Journalist J Bertolucci interviewed Jack Bigelow, a former bowler and now a Wii master.

Jack Bigelow, a wiry, mustached 67-year-old, loves to bowl. But the retired Murrieta, Cal., resident walks with a cane these days and can't make it out to the lanes. Thanks to Nintendo Wii, a video game system, Bigelow can throw perfect strikes without throwing out his back.

"I used to bowl a lot," says Bigelow, who spent decades in the computer and retail hardware industries. "Since I can't get around much anymore," he says, the Wii "really intrigues me."

Bigelow was one of 20 seniors, two in wheelchairs, who filled a meeting room at Amanda Park, an independent-living community in Murrieta, 80 miles southeast of Los Angeles. They came for the facility's first-ever Nintendo Wii Tournament, a contest where neighbors battled good-naturedly for prizes.

Seniors playing video games? Yes, and not to bond with the grandkids, either. Rather the Wii bowling tournament was all about social interaction, exercise and even mental stimulation. As the seniors quickly learned, if you can hold a TV remote and wave it through the air, you're ready to bowl Wii-style.

The mood was fun yet competitive, the crowd cheering whenever someone bowled a virtual strike on the large-screen TV. Some shouted out light-hearted remarks during the action. Garnering a few laughs: "No smelly bowling shoes to put on" and "It's better than playing cards."

Much to the delight of Wii bowling enthusiast Jim Russell, 67, the James L. Brulte Senior Center in Rancho Cucamonga, about 55 miles north of Murrieta, has two Wii consoles. "It is absolutely wonderful," he says, noting that seniors "need something to keep them active, and something they can also enjoy."

Russell was introduced to the Wii by a few of his eleven grandkids. "Once you do get into it, and you practice it, oh yeah!" he says. "There's strategy the same as in a regular bowling game." The console costs about $250.

The Wii isn't limited to senior centers. Delbra Woodard, 56, bought the Wii so that she and her husband, Theodore, 57, could play together. "My husband is a couch potato, so I'm so grateful that he's not sitting around all day," says Woodard, laughing. She lives in Fontana, a few miles from the Rancho Cucamonga senior center, where she first heard about the Wii. Woodard's favorite Wii game is tennis, while her husband prefers Tiger Woods PGA Tour. . . .

Dr. Ronald Petersen, director of the Mayo Clinic Alzheimer's Disease Research Center in Rochester, Minn., calls the Wii "physically and intellectually engaging." And while he hasn't studied video games directly, he says they're probably beneficial to seniors, particularly "if you compare those activities to doing nothing or watching television."

These games require little athletic prowess, but players can overdo it. Russell recently endured a few aches after an intense Wii ping-pong battle. "Oh my lord! I got up the next morning and my shoulder was sore," he says. "My back was a little tweaked in places that I haven't felt before."

The Wii won't appeal to all seniors, although some will love it. After the tournament in Murrieta, five seniors kept playing. Among them was Bigelow, who steadied himself with his cane as he swung a virtual golf club through the air.

Source: Bertolucci, J. (2008, August 16). Wiiii! video game system bowls over seniors. *Kiplinger's Retirement Report,* 15(8). Reprinted with permission. Copyright © 2008, The Kiplinger Washington Editors, Inc. This material is published under license from the publisher through the Gale Group, Farmington Hills, Michigan. All inquiries regarding rights or concerns about this content should be directed to customer service (www.highbeam.com/contact_us.aspx).

---

place in the San Francisco Bay Area. The games attracted 10,000 athletes. Competition took place in 18 sports including cycling, badminton, triathlon, track and field, and basketball.

The National Senior Games Association (2010) says that the Summer Games have "grown to one of the largest multi-sport events in the world for seniors." The National Senior Games—The Senior Olympics encourages older people to stay active and make new friends. A study of senior Olympians found that they engaged in fitness programs to maintain their health and for the competition. People also mentioned recreation and social connection as reasons for taking part in the games (Merrill, Shields, Wood, & Beck, 2004).

Cardenas, Henderson, and Wilson (2009) studied 444 Senior Games participants in North Carolina. Respondents said they took part in the games to meet people and feel good about themselves. These people rated the

This older man takes part in a Nintendo Wii bowling tournament in New York City.

social benefits as more important than the health benefits (though health benefits still ranked high).

The Senior Games offer an opportunity for senior athletes to compete and achieve excellence in their sport. Heo and Lee (2010) call this "serious leisure." Athletes in the Australian Masters Games said that participation in competitive sport was an "expression of authentic self" and "reinforced their established identity" (Dionigi, 2002, p. 14).

The Senior Games attract a certain type of senior—mostly male, white, and highly educated. This fits with the male focus on competition and achievement throughout life. Few women or minority members compete in the Senior Games. Women and minority members may need other leisure outlets that suit their interests and cultural experience.

SENIOR CENTERS

Barriers to active living exist. These include negative attitudes toward exercise and poorly designed activity programs. But other more stubborn barriers to partici-

pation also exist. These include lack of transportation to programs, lack of money to take part in programs, fear of neighborhood crime, and bad weather. These barriers most often affect poorer old people. They may live in inner-city neighborhoods or in rural areas that lack easy access to programs and facilities.

Local senior centers help meet the needs of these older people. Senior centers in communities throughout the country include exercise, yoga, t'ai chi, and other fitness programs. These centers also offer transportation, meal programs, and social activities that attract older people who face barriers to active living.

Senior centers form the nearest thing to a nationwide recreation and service delivery program for older people. The National Council on Aging (2010) defines a **senior center** as "a *gateway* to the nation's aging network—connecting older adults to vital community services that can help them stay healthy and independent." The first club for older people began in Boston in 1870. New York City opened its first senior center more than 70 years later in 1943 (Leitner & Leitner, 1985).

By the year 2010, nearly 11,000 centers existed in the United States. They serve almost 1 million older people every day (National Council on Aging, 2010). The Older Americans Act provides some funding through service contracts to support more than 6,000 centers. Also, many centers today get funding from local governments and nonprofit agencies (such as the United Way). Senior centers provide services and activities that support independence and social contact. Most senior centers have a full-time administrator, an activity director, and volunteers.

The National Council on Aging (2010) reports that about 70% of participants are women. Half of them live alone. Whites make up the majority of center participants. But African Americans and other minority group members also use centers. A study of 734 centers found that participants ranged in age from 55 years to 93 years (mean age, 75). About one third of members were over age 80. Center users have lower incomes than nonusers. But they have better health and higher life satisfaction.

Centers must meet the needs of both frail and active older people in their communities. Most centers offer education programs in arts and the humanities, health services (such as foot care clinics and fitness activities), legal advice, and income counseling (National Council on Aging, 2010).

Centers also offer meal and nutrition programs. These serve a number of functions. They provide members with a hot meal once a day or several times a week, they bring people together to socialize, and they allow more able members to volunteer in meal preparation. Meal programs build camaraderie and an informal support network among members. Centers also link older people to other services in the community.

Standards exist for senior centers in the United States through the National Institute of Senior Centers. A National Senior Center Accreditation Board accredits centers nationwide. Some 116 centers met the Board's standards in 2007. Morgan (2007, 2010) has served on review teams for 10 centers. He says, "The average accredited center serves 3,700 participants each year, with an average daily attendance of 200. Two-thirds of participants are female, they are predominantly White and they are 60 to 74 years old." He also emphasizes that each center has a unique organizational structure and programs that meet local needs.

Wagner (1995) studied senior centers and found two models of center membership: the **social agency model** and the **voluntary organization model.** The

social agency model serves people with few resources, like single older people in poor health. These people use the center as a social service agency. They attend lunch or dinner programs and get health checkups. The voluntary organization model serves people with strong community contacts, like married older people in better health. They use the center as a social club.

Sabin (1993) used national data and found support for both models of center use. Senior centers of each type serve a specific clientele. But some groups rarely attend either type of center. Compared to older people in the city, rural older people tend to make less use of centers. They may find centers inaccessible or even unavailable. Where they do exist, centers serve an important function. In small towns, senior centers may offer the only chance for social contacts outside a person's family. Rural centers also tend to serve frail older people with in-home services.

Researchers need to look at racial differences in senior center use. Freysinger (1993) found that minority participation in senior centers depends on whether people feel a fit between their cultural identity and the staff, programs, and members at a center. Pardasani (2004) studied 220 senior centers in New York State. The study found that most centers had white administrators (86.2%) and attracted white participants (80%).

Multipurpose centers (that offered meals, recreation, education, and other programs) had a large proportion of minority participants (27.3%). Urban centers had the highest proportion of minority older people (41%). Programs that attracted minority older people tended to have minority staff and to offer linguistically and culturally diverse programs. This study points to the need for more diverse staffing and for culturally sensitive activities. Minority elders feel most comfortable in a setting that recognizes and respects their languages and cultures.

San Jose, California, has developed a number of successful senior center programs for Asian/Pacific Americans. San Jose now offers programs tailored to specific groups including Korean, Chinese, Indochinese, and East Indian older people. The centers help older immigrants with translation needs, health care, and legal help. The Yu-Ai Kai Japanese American Community Senior Service Center in San Jose's Japantown, for example, offers a range of social services (Yu-Ai Kai, 2010). These include a respite program for caregivers, a lunchtime meal program that offers Asian meals, and an exercise program.

Senior centers not only exist in the community but they also *create* a community for their members. Life in a thriving senior center reflects the backgrounds and needs of the people who belong to it and use it. A study of three rural senior centers in Minnesota found that people dropped by to socialize, relax, and drink coffee. They had a strong sense of ownership and control of their center (Havir, 1991). Many members volunteered their time to help make their center work.

Senior centers serve different purposes for ethnic, rural, frail, or isolated older people. They respond to the needs of the older people in their communities. But a study of 244 senior centers by the National Institute of Senor Centers found that the name "senior center" turned off Baby Boomers. Boomers link the term *senior center* with being old. And they didn't think of themselves as old.

A report in the *AARP Bulletin* (2007c, p. 8) says that 63% of center directors want to change the name of their program. And "60 percent don't believe the term 'senior center' will serve their community in the future." Like many of the institutions and services provided to older people today, senior centers will need to adapt to the needs of the Baby Boomers. This will challenge current centers and their leaders.

Milner (2007) asked senior center leaders about the needs of younger people in their programs. She found a shift in programming toward sports, wellness, and more physical activity. A consultant for Jewish community centers told her that people also want some spiritual content to link mind and body activities. A director of programs in Baltimore County says that Baby Boomers want fun, fitness, and adventure. He says the Baltimore centers must project vitality. These centers include wellness and travel programs to serve the needs of younger seniors.

A program director in Las Vegas notes the challenge that he faces today. Centers need to shape their programs to fit the interests and self-image of the new older population. At the same time they have to provide services to the oldest old and other older people who need current types of support.

Morgan (2007, 2010) in a report on senior centers today says that "senior centers are constantly evolving from *social centers* to *service centers* to *community centers* and even becoming *entrepreneurial centers* in order to adjust to the changing needs of the seniors they serve." The success of centers in the future will depend on their ability to listen to people in their communities. They can then create "facilities, programs, services and activities that meet the needs of this dynamic market."

EDUCATION

Formal Higher Education

Ruth approached me after class one day. "I've been meaning to tell you something," she said, after a talk I'd given on adult learning. "It took me 3 years before I had the courage to enroll in university." Ruth was in her early 40s. "I'd go to register each year. I'd see the young students in line to register and I'd walk away. I was afraid I couldn't compete with the young students. I was afraid of failing. I hadn't been in school for more than 20 years. I had no confidence in my ability. Finally, this year, I decided to sign up and I did. And now I feel I can do it."

Ruth's story has a happy ending. She did well in her courses that first year. And she went on to get her master's degree in counseling after completing her bachelor's degree. She then returned to her undergraduate university (where I first met her) and worked as a guidance counselor. She focused on helping mature students, especially older women.

An older person who wants to take a course at a university faces many barriers. First, the older student may face a long walk from a parking lot or bus stop to classes. The cost of parking and bad weather in some regions add to the problem of getting to class. Second, most classes take place in 1- or 2-hour time blocks. A person who wants to take one course may have to visit the university three times a week. Even a short commute can add 3 or more hours of travel to a 3-hour-per-week course (Lakin, Mullane, & Robinson, 2007).

Third, memories of schooling from childhood include competition and fear of failure. An older adult has to overcome these and other internal and external barriers. The American Council on Education (Lakin et al., 2007, p. 3) found a gap in our knowledge of "older adult learners and their postsecondary engagement." Educators need to better understand the older learner and the barriers they face.

The American Council on Education (ACE) began a series of studies to understand the older (50+) learner. The ACE (Lakin, Mullane, & Robinson, 2008; Lakin et al., 2007) produced two reports that summarize the studies. The most recent report found that in 2005 people age 50 and over made up only 3.8% of students in higher education programs. About half these students enrolled in community college programs. The study lists the most popular programs taken by older adults: fine arts/humanities, business management and entrepreneurship, human services and counseling, teacher education, and health services.

Except for fine arts/humanities, these programs focus on career development or new career preparation.

A focus group member in this study, "Elaine, 81, earned her certification as a nursing assistant, which led her into critical care work for hospices. As she ages, Elaine continues to gain skills—and new certifications—that open up opportunities for both paid and unpaid work" (Lakin et al., 2008, p. 9).

Not all older students come back to school to earn more money or advance in their careers. Some people have a good income, but they want personal fulfillment or they want to serve their community. A credential provides a sense of accomplishment and a new social identity. The ACE report points to the diversity among older learners and their many motives for returning to school.

A 71-year-old focus group member in the study expressed her desire to help others through her education. "My learning," she says, "is tied to wanting to help people in the community. Clothe the naked, feed the hungry. That's what I spend my time doing now" (Lakin et al., 2008, p. 8).

Will higher education respond to the needs of the older learner?

The study found that few institutions focus on the older adult student. The report suggests that institutions develop programs and services that fit older learners' life stage. This would include education in small chunks (the report calls these "skill-ettes"); accelerated programs to fit the older learner's lifestyle; credit for prior learning; internships; and career management counseling.

The ACE study (Lakin et al., 2008, p. 3) found that more than 40% of the institutions in the study said they "did not identify older adult students for purposes related to outreach, programs and services, or financial aid." This may explain why fewer than 10% of older adults make use of higher education programs and services. And only a handful of older adults make use of financial aid. The ACE study says that higher education has not yet defined its role in serving the older learner.

Universities in my experience focus primarily on traditional age students (18 to 22) and perhaps the slightly older group in the late 20s and early 30s. Campus life fits the life stage and lifestyle of the younger student. The ACE study shows the barriers that older adults face in higher education today. It also shows how higher education institutions could adapt to the older adult's needs.

Community colleges across the country take part in a program called the Plus 50 Initiative (American Association of Community Colleges, 2010). The Atlantic Philanthropies funded the 3-year initiative with a grant of $3.2 million. The program focuses on Baby Boomers who return to school for job training or to upgrade their skills. The initiative will expand campus programs for older learners including training and retraining, learning and enrichment, volunteer, and civic service activities.

Fifty-nine community colleges took part in the program in 2010. A first-year evaluation of the program in 2009 found that 72% of students said they got a job through workforce training in the program. Eighty-six percent of students explored new career options. More than 90% of students in volunteer roles said they felt useful and more connected to their communities.

The Plus 50 Initiative did an assessment of older learners' needs and preferences. The initiative then created programs tailored to the older learner. This included accelerated courses, convenient schedules, and participatory teaching styles that suit older learners (LFA Group, 2009).

One new learning opportunity may gain in popularity in the future: online learning. This may take some time to catch on among older learners. The ACE study found that today many older people prefer face-to-face learning (Lakin et al., 2007, 2008; also Eduventures, 2008). Some people said they lacked the computer skills for online learning. Many older adults want the sense of community that they get from face-to-face learning.

But this may change in the future. An Eduventures study (Guess, 2007, cited in Lakin et al., 2008, p. 21) found that "the demand for online learning rose by 21 percent among the 55- to 64-year-old age group in 2007, and by nearly 10 percent among those 65 and older." Online learning provides the flexibility in time and place that will suit the lifestyles of some older learners.

As new cohorts enter later life, they will bring the computer skills and confidence that will make online learning more attractive. Many Boomers will have taken classes or gone through an online training program at work. My university, for example, offers its driver certification program online (a course required in order to drive university vehicles). I took the class in small chunks at my desk when I had some free moments. This substituted for a class that would have used up a morning of my work time. Many similar learning experiences exist in workplaces today.

Online learning experience will improve as education programs use social media to deliver classes.

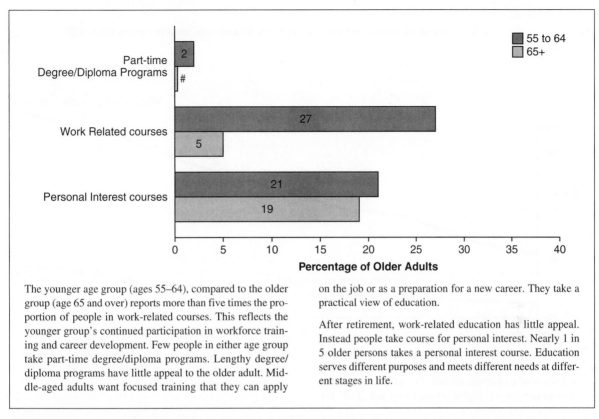

The younger age group (ages 55–64), compared to the older group (age 65 and over) reports more than five times the proportion of people in work-related courses. This reflects the younger group's continued participation in workforce training and career development. Few people in either age group take part-time degree/diploma programs. Lengthy degree/diploma programs have little appeal to the older adult. Middle-aged adults want focused training that they can apply on the job or as a preparation for a new career. They take a practical view of education.

After retirement, work-related education has little appeal. Instead people take course for personal interest. Nearly 1 in 5 older persons takes a personal interest course. Education serves different purposes and meets different needs at different stages in life.

FIGURE 11.3   Education Participation Among Older Adults, 2004–05

Estimate rounds to zero or zero cases in sample

Source: O'Donnell, K., & Chapman, C. (2006). *Adult education participation in 2004–05.* Table 1, p. 7. U.S. Department of Education. National Center on Education Statistics. Retrieved October 19, 2010, from http://nces.ed.gov/pubs2006/2006077.pdf.

An online class that uses video conferencing and social networking methods may prove as engaging as a face-to-face course. Tech-savvy seniors in the future will use the Internet for both formal and informal learning.

The younger the age group, the greater likelihood that someone will have a university education. In 2008, about 30% of people ages 55 to 59 held bachelor's degrees. This compares to 25% for people ages 60 to 69 and only 18% for people age 70 and over. The same pattern applies to community college credentials. Nine percent of people ages 55 to 59 hold an associate (2-year) degree. This compares to 7% for people ages 60 to 69 and only 5% for people age 70 and over (U.S. Census Bureau, 2006d, cited in Lakin et al., 2007).

This trend will lead to higher levels of education among future cohorts of older people. And the more education a person has, the greater the chance that he or she will enroll in an education program in later life.

This could lead to a boom in education programs for older people.

Informal Educational Options

Some time ago gerontologist Robert Atchley (1980, pp. 32–33) stated, "Only a very tiny portion of formal education . . . is devoted to the skills involved in enjoyment of living. . . . There is some question how relevant education is for the young, but there can be no question that most formal education programs have been irrelevant for older people." The data support this view. In 2004–05, for example, only 23% of older people said they had engaged in any formal educational activity in the past year (O'Donnell & Chapman, 2006).

Few people in the Third Age will return to school for formal job-related instruction. Most older adults want learning to meet their personal interests. This might include learning how to sail, ride a horse, ski,

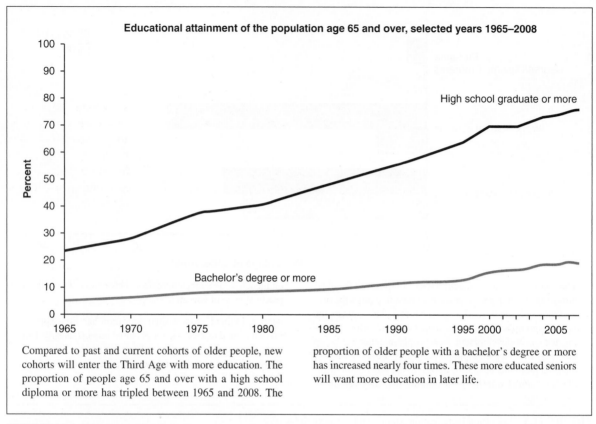

Compared to past and current cohorts of older people, new cohorts will enter the Third Age with more education. The proportion of people age 65 and over with a high school diploma or more has tripled between 1965 and 2008. The proportion of older people with a bachelor's degree or more has increased nearly four times. These more educated seniors will want more education in later life.

FIGURE 11.4   Educational Attainment

Note: A single question which asks for the highest grade or degree completed is now used to determine educational attainment. Prior to 1995, educational attainment was measured using data on years of school completed.

Reference population: These data refer to the civilian noninstitutional population.

Source: Federal Interagency Forum on Aging-Related Statistics. (2010c). *Older Americans 2010: Key indicators of well-being.* Indicator 4: Educational attainment, p. 6. Citing U.S. Census Bureau, Current Population Survey, Annual Social and Economic Supplement, 1966–2008. Washington, DC. Electronic version available at www.agingstats.gov.

learn to play piano, or learn a new hobby. Learning in the Third Age will take many forms, and few of them will look like learning in childhood or middle age.

A few authors have explored the content and purpose of learning in old age. Psychologist Carl Jung (1976), for example, saw the need for a unique educational experience in later life. Jung uses the image of the day to describe two phases of life: the morning and evening. Each phase, he says, has its specific purpose and content, and at each phase a person has specific educational needs. Jung says that in the morning of life (up to middle age), education prepares a person for a career and for participation in society.

Jung proposes that education in the evening of life serves self-discovery. He asks, "Are there perhaps colleges for forty-year-olds which prepare them for

the coming life and its demands as the ordinary colleges introduce our young people to knowledge of the world and of life?" He answers that no such colleges exist. These colleges would deal with what Jung calls "culture." They would explore spiritual issues and death and dying, and they would encourage self-discovery through the study of literature, art, and music.

Schools must adapt if they want to attract older students. First, they will have to offer courses in easy-to-reach places. Some schools already offer courses in shopping centers where students can park and get to class easily. Second, they will need to offer courses at more convenient times. Single 3-hour blocks, weekends, or even week-long courses better suit older learners' needs. Third, instructors will have to learn adult education methods. Older students have little patience with long lectures. They want to interact with their teachers and fellow students. They want to share their knowledge. Universities in the future will need to remove many of these barriers if they want to serve adult students. Some education programs have begun to do this.

Elderhostel

Elderhostel (now called Road Scholar) combines university education with European hostel programs. David Bianco and Martin Knowlton, a social activist and an educator, started the program in New Hampshire in 1975. They designed a series of challenging intellectual courses for older people. Then they arranged for the students to live on a university campus.

Elderhostel/Road Scholar began with 220 people age 55 and over enrolled in five schools. The program in 2007 enrolled 160,000 students at more than 8,000 programs in all 50 states and more than 90 countries (Elderhostel, 2007).

The original programs lasted 1 to 2 weeks—from Sunday night to Saturday morning. But today "traditional programs" (similar to the first programs offered by Elderhostel) in the United States can last from 3 to 12 days. Traditional programs typically include three academic courses that meet for 90 minutes each day. Students take all three courses. Programs include field trips and evening activities. Road Scholar tries to keep the class size small: Most courses enroll from 35 to 45 people at a time. The total fee for many of the 1-week programs in the continental United States in 2010—including food, rooms, course fees, and costs for extracurricular tours and activities—came to between $700 and $800.

Manheimer (2007, p. 222) says that new programs now compete with Road Scholar for seniors' education dollars. Some of these programs offer more expensive and luxurious programs. To meet this competition, Road Scholar has expanded beyond its traditional format. It now includes active outdoor programs, service programs, shipboard programs, and intergenerational programs (for grandparents and grandchildren).

International programs usually last 2 to 3 weeks. A 2-week program in Peru, for example, looks at pre-Colombian culture and includes a visit to Machu Picchu. Experts give lectures during the program, and students enjoy time in the capital city of Lima. The program costs about $3,500 (prices differ by time of year), not including airfare (Road Scholar, 2010b).

International programs can get expensive. A 1-month program in Australia costs more than $9,000 (Road Scholar, 2010b). This program uses train travel to see the country. Students learn about the ecology of the country, sample Australian wine at a local vineyard, learn about current social issues, and visit Sydney harbor and the Opera House.

In the United States, programs often play up local resources and points of interest. A 6-day program in northern California focuses on Monterey Bay and the California coast. The program explores the wine industry, the ocean ecology, and the legacy of author John Steinbeck, who lived in the region. The program also features live theatrical performances. Another program in the West explores the Grand Canyon's geology and the cultures of the people in the region.

Road Scholars who attend programs on university campuses share the joys and frustrations of student life. At some sites students share rooms; often they have to share bathrooms and eat in a university dining hall. A "Circumpolar Studies" program in Alaska and Siberia a few years ago came with the following warning set in bold type: "The sidewalks in Yakutsk and at the health resort are not well-maintained; cracked pavements and potholes are common. Walking over rough, unpaved roads is required for some field trips. Transportation during field trips will be via local school buses" (Elderhostel, 1995a, p. 6).

Road Scholar attracts older people for a number of reasons. Students say they take the programs to gain new knowledge, to try something new, and to visit a new place. Ruth Neleski (1995) reported that she took her first course, a canoe-study course in Maine, because she had a frequent flyer ticket that she wanted to use up. As a bonus, on the way to the course she met her husband-to-be in a Maine restaurant. They married 6 months later. Inez Ross (1995), a Road Scholar from Los Alamos, New Mexico, said that since taking an Elderhostel/Road Scholar course she has become one of the OPALS—Older Person with an Active Life-Style.

Road Scholar has grown stronger and more independent over time. It takes no money from the government, nor does it ask for any. It supports its programs through tuition and donations from alumni and other supporters. Moody (1988a, p. 205) traces Elderhostel/Road Scholar's success to its founders' insight that older people had "a potential for growth and continued learning."

Lifelong Learning Institutes

Elderhostel spawned a program called Institutes for Learning in Retirement (ILRs), now sometimes called lifelong learning institutes (LLIs). These programs attract students such as those who attend Road Scholar programs, but students in LLIs study in their own communities. The programs come in varied formats—lectures, seminars, and travel courses. In most cases, older people decide together on the topics they will study. Each institute has a distinct organizational structure, and members manage and run the program. These programs have grown rapidly throughout North America.

The New School for Social Research in New York started the first ILR in 1962 (Road Scholar, 2010a). By 1988, about 50 ILRs existed in the United States. These first ILRs had several things in common: First, they all had affiliations with universities to ensure academic integrity and to link the programs to campus life. Second, the programs encouraged learners to take ownership of their institutes, become members, and pay dues. Third, institutes encouraged members to manage the institute and in some cases teach classes.

Road Scholar estimates that about 500 ILRs affiliated with universities existed in North America in 2007. Elderhostel also estimates that another 300 to 500 education programs with high academic standards existed outside universities. Elderhostel set up an Elderhostel Institute Network (EIN) throughout North America. Network affiliates grew from 32 in 1988 to more than 300 by 2007. Over time, individual institutes grew more independent from Elderhostel. Road Scholar now provides services only via a Web site.

Elderhostel Institute Network affiliate programs offer more than 4,000 courses each term. Members of LLIs generally take two or three courses per term. Most programs offer two or three terms per year. About 200 to 300 people belong to a typical LLI. More than 100,000 people belong to a network-affiliated LLI (Road Scholar, 2010a). Road Scholar estimates that 10 to 20 new Institutes start each year. "It is quite clear," Elderhostel says, "that the future of the learning in retirement movement is very secure and will continue to grow, well into the 21st century" (Elderhostel, 2007b).

The Bernard Osher Foundation began a project in 2001 to set up and fund Osher Life Long Learning Institutes (OLLIs) throughout the United States. The foundation funds an OLLI for 4 years with $100,000 per year in startup funds (if the OLLI meets certain membership benchmarks). At the end of 4 years, if a program has 500 or more members it can apply for a $1 million endowment from the Bernard Osher Foundation. Large programs with more than 1,000 members can apply for a $2 million endowment.

The OLLI program began when the Bernard Osher Foundation funded the University of Southern Maine's Senior College. Sonoma State University, part of the California State University system, also received one of the early grants. Sonoma State hosts one of the largest OLLI programs on the West Coast. The program attracted 775 students in its first year, and it has grown larger since then.

The Osher Foundation requested proposals for OLLIs from schools in the California State University system, the University of California system, and other schools around the country. Later grants went to already-existing LLIs, including programs at Duke University, the University of Dayton, and George Mason University. Some of these programs received a double endowment of $2 million due to their large memberships and successful programs.

The Osher Life Long Learning Institute's network now includes more than 118 member institutions. The Bernard Osher Foundation also supports a journal, *The LLI Review*, dedicated to reporting on learning in later life. As these programs grow in numbers and as they attract younger retirees, they will serve the new educational interests of the Baby Boom generation.

Lifelong learning institutes (e.g., EIN programs, OLLI programs, and other independent programs) generally accept members age 55 and over and can take many forms. Some piggyback on already existing university classes. Some LLIs offer a unique set of courses that can include travel-study programs to China, history courses, or courses on foot massage and health maintenance.

Each LLI has its own culture. Members in some LLIs teach the classes. This provides the teachers with an outlet for their intellectual curiosity and talent. It provides the class with insights from a fellow member and someone from their generation. This builds esteem for the teacher and respect from the students. Sometimes students in the LLIs teach subjects far from their specialties. A retired chemical engineer, for example, may lead a class on mythologies of the Middle East. A dentist may lead a study group on opera. A group of five people in one class, with no experience in flying, built an ultralight aircraft.

Students will follow a gifted teacher from class to class. They tell friends and bring them along to the lectures or presentations. Groups and courses often grow this way through word of mouth and the enthusiasm of the members.

An LLI often feels like a club. Members know one another, they have serious discussions, and they feel committed to their LLI. Often they lunch together before or after classes. LLIs create a social bond that enriches people beyond their classroom instruction. Lamb and Brady (2005, p. 215) studied members of Osher Lifelong Learning Institutes. Members reported four benefits of the programs: "intellectual stimulation; participation in a supportive community; opportunities for enhancing self-esteem; and opportunities for spiritual renewal."

Research on social relations in LLIs shows the value and importance of these kinds of relationships in later life. Sociologists refer to these relations as **weak social ties**. They differ from the intimacy of family and friendship ties.

Family and friends tend to come from the same social and economic background. But weak social ties like those in an LLI link people from diverse backgrounds. Weak ties expose a person to new views and opinions.

Krause (2006, p. 190) says that "weak social ties may be an important source of informational support. Having a wider range of views may help older people select the best coping responses during difficult times. . . . Weak ties provide a context in which a person may experiment with new ideas and new behaviors with relatively low levels of accountability." Weak ties between LLI members make for stimulating classroom discussion.

Bea Carruthers, a 73-year-old widow, grew up in an Episcopalian family. Her straight posture and short gray hair make her look like a model of conservative values. When she talks about what she's learning in her LLI, she speaks mostly of her studies in massage, yoga, and holistic health.

"I've done deep breathing, of course," she says. "T'ai chi and yoga, foot massage and meditation—a little bit of everything. I'm very keen on exercise for older people.

"My friends think I'm a bit crazy. My sister, who's 82, and a couple of her friends have been introduced to foot massage. But my own friends won't let me touch them."

The classes in her LLI freed Bea from her friends' opinions. The classes provided her with an alternative support group and allowed her to experiment with new philosophies and new methods of self-care. Krause (2006, p. 190) says that the weak social ties that someone like Bea finds in her classes provide "anonymity, low accountability, and diversity of views . . . [and] cannot be found elsewhere." Life course changes such as retirement can remove a person from the social ties they enjoyed at work. Education programs can replace this important source of social support.

These programs don't appeal to everyone. Lamb and Brady (2005), for example, report that women make up between 66% and 75% of the students in LLIs. Programs in Australia and in Europe show the same pattern. Women in these programs often have more education and higher incomes than people who do not attend programs. This leaves open the question of why men tend not to join LLIs. It also raises the question of what educational options appeal to men in the Third Age.

Students in university-affiliated LLIs often give back to the university as much as they get. Some programs attract politicians, physicians, and business leaders. Some LLI students mentor undergraduates and may give lectures in required university courses. Members of other programs donate time to help the libraries at their institutions, or they may host dinners for foreign students. Students at California State University, Fullerton, built a 15,000-square-foot gerontology center for the university. The center includes space for research, teaching, and public outreach.

Studies show that the benefits of learning in the Third Age go beyond learning new facts or information. Lifelong learning also increases a person's confidence and the ability to do new things. Mehrotra (2003) calls this the "Can-do Factor." People feel more confident and more competent as they learn.

Cohen (2005, p. 179) reports on a study of older people in community arts programs: "Gaining a sense of mastery in one area can lead to feelings of empowerment that spread to other spheres of life, leading to more confidence, a willingness to take risks, and the energy for trying new things." People in these programs, compared to a control group, remained more socially involved a year into the study. Like the members of the OLLIs and other LLIs, the people in the arts programs supported one another socially. People felt a sense of belonging that enhanced their well-being.

Some people say that programs such as Elderhostel and LLIs segregate older people. Van der Veen (1990), for example, calls for "inter-age universities" that serve mixed age groups. These universities would take into account the special needs of older adults, but would mix older people with younger people in classes.

The American Council on Education study (Lakin et al., 2008, p. 4) of higher education used a focus group to explore the question of age segregation.

BOX 11.2
LIFELONG LEARNING

Second Age Learning	Third Age Learning
Work	Leisure
Professional development/training	Self-development
Nature	Culture
Social capital	Personal enrichment
Society subsidized	Individual pays
First career	Second career
Have to know	Want to know
Schooling	Education
Social purpose	Individual purpose
Career preparation	Learning for its own sake

These lists present an ideal type of education at two stages in life (young/middle adulthood and early old age). Education at each stage of life meets different social and individual needs. Educators have begun to design programs to meet the unique needs of Third Age learners. Programs include Elderhostel and Lifelong Learning Institutes.

Can you think of other concepts that define education at each of these life stages?

BOX 11.3
A CASE STUDY IN ADULT LEARNING

Carol Wahlberg, 56, started piano lessons in the 6th grade but only took lessons for 5 or 6 weeks. She came from a poor family, she says. And piano lessons were an expensive luxury. She began learning piano again "for real" about 10 years ago. "Music," she says, "has come into my life in the last few years."

Carol's a skilled learner with a doctorate in clinical psychology. She's taken courses and succeeded in classroom instruction throughout her life. But in learning the piano she follows a different path. She takes lessons, but plays the music, she says, "like a game." She plays for her own enjoyment, not to please a teacher, for a grade, or for any outside reward.

She takes lessons whenever she feels like it. "When I know I'm stuck, I take a lesson. . . . I don't practice for hours," Carol says. "But I'm able to concentrate more. I have to pay attention. It's good for my mind. It's enriching, my thinking about music."

Carol has immersed herself in music. She listens, plays, meets musicians, and develops friendships through music. Carol recently signed up for a DVD series of lectures on music. She's also taking community college music courses. She attends piano recitals. On one occasion she attended a rehearsal session of a well-known pianist. "I wouldn't leave the rehearsal," she says. "I sat on the floor near the door."

"I want to play more," she says. "Pay attention to how I play. Not for other people. Either it's enjoyable, or I don't want to do it. . . . It's internal motivation totally. It should only be enjoyment for me. That's enough."

Like many adult learners, Carol brings a lifetime of experience to her learning. She wants to explore new ideas and new approaches to learning. She also wants to explore new dimensions of herself. She consciously chooses the type of learning that suits her best. Sometimes that takes the form of classroom instruction. But often it takes other forms, like talks with professional musicians or shopping in the music stores during a recent visit to Salzburg, Austria.

Carol puts learning in the larger context of her life. And in this way her learning differs from childhood education. For Carol, the piano means more to her than just an instrument to play. It's more than a piece of furniture in her home. It resonates with a lifetime of memories that begin in her childhood. She thinks of music as a return to an unfinished chapter in her life. Playing the piano, whether she plays well or poorly, has meaning beyond the sounds she makes. Carol's music links her to her past, but it also draws her into the future.

Focus group members said they preferred intergenerational learning. They felt that younger and older students can learn from one another. They rejected the concept of what they called an "educational nursing home." In age-mixed settings older people will create role models for younger students. Universities will benefit if they include older people in their vision of the future.

Sadler (2006) sums up the value of learning in the Third Age: "All of the people whose lives illustrate growth and renewal have been committed learners. They have been learning more about themselves, about opportunities and challenges, about new areas they have not previously had the time to explore, and new skills." New generations of older people will develop new educational alternatives to meet their needs.

The Future of Education for Older People

Today it's impossible to avoid learning. We live immersed in a multimedia environment where information streams at us constantly. Watch people standing in line at the bank or waiting for a bus. They're on their mobile devices sending and receiving emails, Twittering, following, friending, watching CNN, and engaging in a host of learning activities.

The Pew Research Center (Jones & Fox, 2009) studied the use of computers by younger and older people. The researchers asked 2,253 adults in 2009 about their use of the Internet. They found that the proportion of Internet users in an age group declines with age. But every age group showed an increase in Internet use between 2005 and 2008. The study found that people ages 70 to 75 showed the greatest increase in Internet use during that time.

The study also found that the generations differed in their online activities. All age groups used email and search engines. People age 45 and older used the Internet to shop, to make travel arrangements, and to learn about health issues. Younger age groups use the Internet for recreation (games), entertainment, and social networking.

Lenhart (2009) reports that 75% of people ages 18 to 24 use social networks. This compares to only 7% of people age 65 and over. "At its core," Lenhart says, "use of online social networks is still a phenomenon of the young."

This may have been true in 2009. But a study published by AARP (Koppen, 2010), a year later, found that 27% of all people age 50 and over use social media Web sites. About a quarter of these people (23%) used Facebook. Among Internet users, nearly 2 in 5 (37%) used social networking sites. A third (31%) used Facebook. Adults age 50 and over mostly used social media to connect to children, grandchildren, and other relatives.

By the time you read this, the use of the Internet will have grown more common and popular among older people. In part this will happen because new cohorts will enter later life with computer skills and experience. Also, new uses for information technology will emerge. They will attract people of all ages. Finally, computers will get easier to use and less expensive. They will become a part of everyday life for older people.

The AARP study found, for example, that 83% of people age 50 and over had heard of the iPad (within a few months of its launch) and 11% of these people planned or wanted to buy one. Studies show that older adults use computers, have an interest in computer technology, and plan to explore new Internet tools and applications.

BOX 11.4
COMPUTER USE BY OLDER PEOPLE COMPARED TO YOUNGER PEOPLE

Sites with Highest Number of Visitors Age 55+	*Sites with Highest Number of Visitors Ages 25 to 34*
Games	Parenting
Obituaries	Family fun
Puzzles	Shopping
Investing	News
Genealogy	Invitations
Fantasy/sports	

Older and younger people share some interests on the Internet—for example, email and news. But some sites attract people from specific age groups. The listings above show some of the most popular sites for middle-aged and older Internet users.

These preferences show different interests of people at different stages of life. Do they also reflect generational (year of birth) differences? Do they reflect differences due to aging? Do they reflect differences due to the historical experiences of these two age groups? Do you think older people 20 years from now, familiar with online shopping and online news, will look more similar to younger/middle-aged people in their use of the computer?

Source: Klesius, M. (2007, May). *AARP Bulletin*, p. 29. Based on Hitwise.com findings of 500 most visited sites, February 2007.

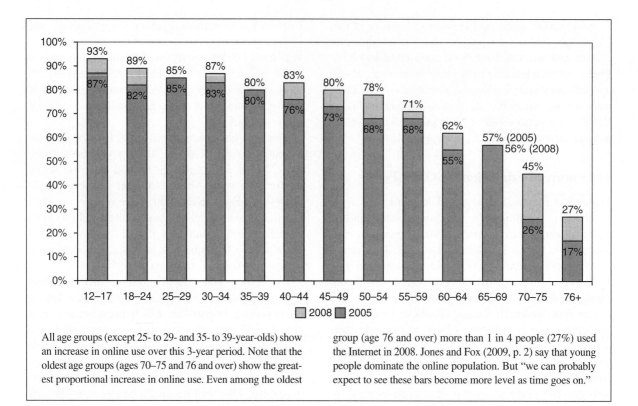

All age groups (except 25- to 29- and 35- to 39-year-olds) show an increase in online use over this 3-year period. Note that the oldest age groups (ages 70–75 and 76 and over) show the greatest proportional increase in online use. Even among the oldest group (age 76 and over) more than 1 in 4 people (27%) used the Internet in 2008. Jones and Fox (2009, p. 2) say that young people dominate the online population. But "we can probably expect to see these bars become more level as time goes on."

FIGURE 11.5 Percentage of Americans Online, by Age[a]

[a]*Note:* Teens, 12–17, Nov. 2007–Feb. 2008, margin of error ±3%. Adults, December 2008, margins of error differ by subgroup.

Source: Jones, S., & Fox, S. (2009). *Generations online in 2009.* Pew Internet Project Data Memo. Pew Internet & American Life Project, *p. 2.* Retrieved October 28, 2010, from www.pewinternet.org/~/media/Files/Reports/2009/PIP_Generations_2009.pdf. Reprinted with permission.

A nonprofit organization called SeniorNet helps people age 50 and over to use computer technology. The program began in San Francisco in 1986, funded by the Markle Foundation. Manheimer (2009) says that more than 240 SeniorNet centers exist in the United States and in other countries. SeniorNet has centers in public libraries, senior centers, and retirement communities. SeniorNet centers typically contain 6 to 10 computers (some have as many as 20). This program meets the needs of older people who have little experience with computers or who want to expand their skills.

The centers offer basic courses on word processing, the Internet, and email. More advanced courses deal with graphics, buying and selling on eBay, digital photography, and financial management on the computer (SeniorNet, 2010). Volunteer instructors teach most of the courses. SeniorNet claims to have educated more than 1 million older adults on computer and Internet use. SeniorNet also offers a large selection of online courses.

Cutler (2006) warns of a "digital divide" in the older population. People with more education and a better income will have access to and familiarity with computers. They will feel more comfortable using computers and will take advantage of the latest educational opportunities. Those with less education and income may get left out of this lifelong learning opportunity.

The decreasing cost of computers and the prevalence of computers in the workplace may help close the digital divide. Those with more formal education may use computers to take formal courses and training (a pattern that exists today in face-to-face instruction). Those with less formal education may use the Internet to gain information or to communicate with friends and relatives. Electronic media will benefit a person who can't get out of the house due to caregiving demands, illness, or disability.

Computers will become a part of everyday life for all age groups, much as the telephone did in the last century. The newness of computer technology in part

The first time she lost at Bookworm, Sister Jean-Marie Smith recalled, "I stood up and said, 'Me and this computer are going to have a talk.'" Seniors like Sister Jean-Marie play computer games for the mental and physical challenge.

creates the current digital divide. In the future, more people of all ages will make use of technology as a learning and communication tool.

Still, education programs, including Road Scholar and LLIs, risk serving an elite group of older people. Many students involved in Third Age education today have university degrees. Some have worked as educators. Older people, as a group, in the future will have better education than older people today, but the older population in the future will also show more diversity in education, income, racial and ethnic background, and health.

How will future education programs serve people with little education and low income? How will programs serve people who failed in school or who dislike formal education? How will future programs meet the needs of minority elders who speak little English? Manheimer (2009) worries about a "widening gap between the have and have-nots" in adult education. Will these groups miss out on new opportunities for personal growth through education as they age? Educators have to meet the educational needs of a diverse older population.

COMMUNITY SERVICE AND VOLUNTEER WORK

A survey conducted by the AARP (Silberman, Cantave Burton, & AARP, Knowledge Management, 2004) found that 43% of people age 65 and over work as volunteers. They do this for personal satisfaction and to help others. Another study found that older volunteers averaged 1 day a week, and one quarter of them said they would have volunteered more time if asked (Eldercare Volunteer, 1992).

The Bureau of Labor Statistics (2009) reports that volunteering declines with age. People ages 35 to 54 show the greatest tendency to volunteer. Nearly one third of people in this group (31.2%) spend some time volunteering. Only 23.9% of people age 65 and over report that they volunteer. Although the rate of volunteering declines with age, the oldest age group (age 65 and over) volunteers at a greater rate than people under age 35. Also, the rate of volunteering among people age 65 and over has increased from 14.3% in 1974 to 23.9% in 2009. Among people age 65 and over, women, compared to men, show a greater likelihood of volunteering.

Among older people, those ages 65 to 74 had the greatest percentage of volunteers (Silberman et al., 2004). The U.S. Department of Labor (2007) reports that, compared to younger volunteers, older volunteers tend to volunteer for religious organizations. Only 30.1% of volunteers ages 16 to 24 volunteered for a religious organization. But 44.7% of volunteers age 65 and over provided service to a religious organization.

Silberman and colleagues (2004) found similar results in a study of older volunteers in North Dakota.

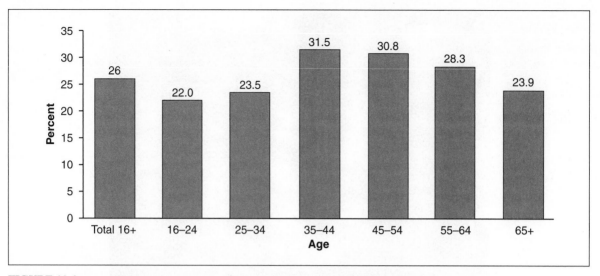

FIGURE 11.6 Volunteers by Selected Characteristics, September 2005 through September 2009

Note that the proportion of people who volunteer increases to a peak between ages 35 and 54. It tapers off in older age groups. Declines in health account for some of the drop-off in the oldest age group. But even in the 65-and-over group, nearly one quarter of this group reported that they volunteered.

Source: U.S. Department of Labor. (2010). *Volunteering in the United States, 2009.* Table A, Volunteers by selected characteristics, September 2005 through September 2009. Retrieved July 22, 2010, from www.bls.gov/news.release/volun.nr0.htm.

They found that religious organizations serve as the most popular context for volunteering in later life. Sixty-one percent of older volunteers worked for churches or religious organizations. About one quarter (27%) of older volunteers worked for civic organizations, and 22% worked for schools or educational organizations. (Respondents could work in more than one setting.) These people serve as resources in their communities and improve the quality of life for all age groups.

Tang (2009) used the multiwave Americans' Changing Lives survey to study the effects of volunteering on older people over time. Tang says that, compared with nonvolunteers, "older volunteers report better physical functioning, higher levels of life satisfaction and self-rated health, reduced depressive symptoms, and a lower mortality rate." Tang considers volunteering "a social approach to health maintenance." The University of Maryland Center on Aging asked Baby Boomers what would lead them to work as volunteers. People in the study said that as a volunteer they looked for "opportunities for personal growth, continued learning, participation in purposeful social networks working toward clearly defined goals, and activities that deepened their sense of meaning" (Manheimer, 2009). A better educated, healthier older population will take on more volunteer

work in the future if volunteer jobs offers these benefits. A few programs suggest ways to harness Boomers' energy.

Volunteer Opportunities

The Senior Corps

Lucy Williams, age 90, of Sonoma, California, works 4 hours a day, 5 days a week as a foster grandparent. She works with children who have a developmental disability. She has worked in institutions with these kinds of children for 28 years. At the age of 80 she volunteered to work in a local elementary school's special education classroom. She helps the students with reading, math, exercise, and social activities.

One teacher who worked with Lucy wrote, "Our students learn at a very slow pace so it requires much patience to work with them. Lucy has that patience. Grandma Lucy provides that little extra TLC that goes a long way in the lives of these kids. She is compassionate, caring and dedicated to making a difference for some very special kids."

Lucy Williams got her assignment through Senior Corps, a federal government program (part of the Corporation for National and Community Service).

This program offers volunteer opportunities to people age 55 and over. The program connects volunteers with people and organizations that need help. Help can take the form of mentoring, coaching, or serving as a companion to someone in need. Volunteers can serve on community projects or bring their expertise to local nonprofit, faith-based, or other organizations. Senior Corps began during the presidency of John F. Kennedy. It now links more than half a million people with service opportunities.

Senior Corps provides training to volunteers so that they can make the greatest contribution. Programs within Senior Corps include a Foster Grandparent Program for volunteers 60 years old and over. Through this program, more than 28,000 seniors serve as one-on-one mentors and tutors to young people at risk. The young people include abused and neglected children, troubled teens, premature infants, children with physical, mental and emotional disabilities, and children of incarcerated parents (Senior Corps, 2009).

A Senior Companion Program links over 15,000 volunteers age 60 and over with adults who need help with activities of daily living. The program served more than 68,000 older people in 2008. Volunteers help with shopping, interact with a doctor, or make a friendly visit.

An RSVP (Retired and Seniors Volunteer Program) links nearly 450,000 seniors with community groups that need their expertise. Opportunities can range from building houses to child immunization, to advising nonprofit organizations. RSVP volunteers serve in more than 1,500 counties throughout the United States. Senior Corps reports that volunteers worked on more than 1,300 projects. A Senior Corps "Fact Sheet" says that "94 percent of Senior Corps volunteers report that their service has improved their knowledge, health, or social connectedness" (Senior Corps, 2007).

The Peace Corps

The Peace Corps, a program that most often recruits young university graduates, also recruits and posts older volunteers. A Peace Corps spokesperson says

Seniors help one another as volunteers at a soup kitchen in Washington, DC.

that older volunteers bring a "demonstrated ability" to their work. "They've already gone through their careers and come to the Peace Corps with a wealth of experience" (Schlesinger, 2006, p. 26). Older Peace Corps volunteers can serve the typical 2-year assignment or they can serve on an emergency team for a shorter time. Currently people over age 50 make up 5% of all Peace Corps volunteers (Peace Corps, 2010).

Schlesinger (2006) reports that Roger Parent, a 67-year-old former mayor of South Bend, Indiana, served for 6 months in Thailand. He worked on an emergency team brought in after the 2004 tsunami. Parent has served four tours with the Peace Corps.

A married couple, Chuck and Marcia McBeath, 83 and 81 years old, from Seattle, have served six 2-year postings—the latest one in Kenya.

David Arnoldy, another Peace Corps volunteer, told Schlesinger (2006, p. 27) that the Peace Corps "was one of the most rewarding things we've done, and it gave us some very, very fresh perspectives to think about old things in a new way."

For a closer look at what motivates older Peace Corps volunteers, go to the Peace Corps multimedia site— http://multimedia.peacecorps.gov/multimedia/50plus/ index.html. There you can read their stories and hear older volunteers speak about their commitment to helping others.

All of these people and most other older volunteers report that volunteering gives added meaning to their lives. Greenfield and Marks (2004) found that volunteering helped people cope with the loss of major role identity. Other studies show that volunteering increases a person's self-esteem and enhances health and well-being (Krause, 2006).

The Experience Corps

The Experience Corps began in 1995 as a part of a larger program called Civic Ventures. The program now has independent status. This program has won awards for linking people age 55 and over with community needs throughout the United States. The program now exists in 22 cities across the country. More than 2,000 older people now serve as Experience Corps volunteers. About half the volunteers get a stipend for their work (between $3 and $5 per hour) (Experience Corps, 2010; McBride, Gonzales, Morrow-Howell, & McCrary, 2009).

Experience Corps members serve as tutors and mentors in elementary schools. They work with students on their homework and on reading and on writing skills. The Experience Corps trains volunteers in tutoring and mentoring. Volunteers serve at least 15 hours per week for an entire school year. Volunteers also work with teachers and administrators in schools to create projects to benefit students. Projects include parent involvement programs, library book drives, and other projects that meet a school's needs.

According to the Experience Corps, volunteers provided "more than 466,000 hours of tutoring and mentoring services to more than 20,000 students in the 2004–2005 school year." This work "boosts student academic performance, helps schools and youth-serving organizations become more successful, and enhances the well-being of the older adults in the process" (Experience Corps, 2007).

The Experience Corps (2007) reports the following results:

- In an independent survey of principals with Experience Corps teams in their schools, 90% reported significant improvement in student academic performance and readiness to learn.
- Nine out of ten Experience Corps members report an increased sense of usefulness and social connectedness since they joined the program.
- Johns Hopkins University medical school researchers compared Experience Corps Baltimore members and a control group. They found that those involved in Experience Corps saw meaningful improvements in their own mental and physical health and quality of life. Forty-four percent of Experience Corps participants reported feeling stronger, compared with 18% of controls. In addition, over the 2-year study period, 13% more Corps members reported their strength as very good to excellent, versus a 30% decline among controls. Over the same period of time, TV viewing decreased by 4% in volunteers and increased by 18% in the control group.

Raul Castaneda, an Experience Corps volunteer in San Francisco, says that when he retired he wanted something to do. "I saw an Experience Corps flyer at the library, and I called the organization. It's been a great experience working in the schools because I'm a bilingual tutor. . . . I have a student this year from Mexico. This last year I've been working with her one-on-one for 45 minutes every day, and she's more open and has friends. Also, last year, I worked with a third-grade boy. He had to go back to Mexico, and I visited him, bringing him letters from his old classmates. I want to visit him every year" (Experience Corps, 2010).

Volunteers express their personal benefit from volunteering. "I'm much happier," one volunteer says. "I have more ambition and I feel better about myself. That makes it easier on my family." Another volunteer says, "It was a revitalization of my first love—teaching. It makes me feel young again. . . . Back in the swing" (Morrow-Howell et al., 2008).

CONCLUSION

Today, a **structural lag** can exist between the changing lives of older people and the opportunity to live a successful old age. Research by Civic Ventures and MetLife Corporation found that many people in their 50s and 60s "don't think it will be very easy to find second careers doing good work." Riley and Riley (1994, p. 16) say that "there is a mismatch or imbalance between the transformation of the aging process . . . and the role opportunities, or places in the social structure, that could foster and reward people" in later life.

Many of the newest programs and activities respond to this mismatch. Master athlete programs, lifelong learning institutes, and innovative volunteer programs all respond to the growing leisure, recreation, and education needs of older people today. Better health among retirees and the desire for a meaningful retirement will call for more creative responses to leisure in the future.

Civic Ventures, in cooperation with the MetLife Corporation, conducted a survey in 2005 titled "The New Face of Work." The study asked 1,000 Americans ages 50 to 70 about the kind of work they preferred.

The study found that half the people surveyed (53%) plan to work in retirement. More than three quarters of those who plan to work (78%) want "to help the poor, the elderly, and other people in need." More than half of those who plan to work want to deal with health issues by working in a hospital or with an organization that fights a specific disease. Over half say they have an interest in teaching or another educational role. Forty-five percent expressed an interest in working with youth. Among leading-edge Boomers (between ages 50 and 60), 60% say they want work in retirement that serves the community and helps people in need (Princeton Survey, 2005).

These figures suggest that the Baby Boom generation will carry its social activism into later life. Freed from their first careers, many Boomers intend to stay active by serving society in encore careers (Freedman, 2007). This large group of engaged Boomers could use their skills and experience to tackle chronic social problems.

SUMMARY

- Gerontologists define *leisure* as free time. Most studies of leisure support the continuity theory of aging. This theory suggests that older people tend to maintain the leisure activities of their middle years. Retired people usually have more time for these activities. With enough time, income, and good health, retirees tend to show more continuity than change in their leisure activities.

- Older people spend most of their leisure time on core leisure activities like socializing and reading. These activities need few resources, have a low cost, and have easy access. Peripheral activities such as sports and exercise usually take place outside the home. They require more resources, effort, money, and time. Seniors today tend to avoid strenuous outdoor activities such as tennis, skiing, and swimming.

- Leisure participation differs by gender as well as by age and race. Studies show that men and women prefer different activities in retirement (as they did in their middle years). African American older people, compared with white older people, report less participation in outdoor activities. Gerontologists need to do more research on minority group members and leisure.

- Compared to young people in the past, young people today enjoy more leisure. They also have a greater interest in health, fitness, and activity. Many people will carry these characteristics into their old age. This will increase interest in leisure activity among older people in the future.

- Three social theories—disengagement, continuity, and age stratification—point to social forces that inhibit an active leisure lifestyle. Sport, leisure, and recreation programs for older people can overcome these barriers. Activity theory promotes an active lifestyle in old age.

- Senior centers provide recreation programs for older people. These centers offer varied programs and activities, including crafts, exercise, socializing, education, and meals. Centers will have to change their mix of programming if they hope to attract new retirees. People in the Third Age today want active and challenging programs.

- Studies show that people with more education have a greater tendency to enroll in education programs in later life. But an older person who wants to take a college course faces many barriers. A long commute to campus, long distances between buildings, and the lecture-style class do not appeal to most older people. Universities that want to attract older students will need to remove some of these barriers.

- Elderhostel (now Road Scholar) combines university education with the European hostel concept. The program typically consists of three academic courses that meet for one or two weeks. Road Scholar offers programs worldwide. This allows older people to combine travel with education. ILRs or LLIs offer older people a chance to learn in groups in their own communities. The Osher Life Long Learning Institutes form a national network of educational programs for Third Age adults.
- Computer technology opens new opportunities for learning in the Third Age. Learning takes place informally when a person searches for health information or reads a

newspaper online. Online education options will allow older people with disabilities to take classes from their homes. The use of the Internet will gain wider use as the Baby Boom generation enters later life.

- A high proportion of people age 60 and over do volunteer work. They do this mostly for personal satisfaction. Gerontologists predict that a more educated and affluent older population in the future will take on even more volunteer work. New volunteer options—such as the Senior Corps, the Peace Corps, the Experience Corps, and Civic Ventures—will open more opportunities for older people to serve their communities.
- In later life, people enjoy varied activities such as recreation, exercise, education, and volunteer work. These activities lead to physical, social, and spiritual well-being.

DISCUSSION QUESTIONS

1. Define the term *leisure* and explain the continuity theory of aging as it applies to leisure activities.
2. In general, how do older people spend their leisure time?
3. What effect does age have on participation in core and peripheral leisure activities? What accounts for this pattern?
4. What major factors influence an older person's choice of leisure activities?
5. Why do researchers predict a greater interest in leisure activities among older people in the future?
6. What benefits can people gain from exercise and physical activity?
7. List and describe the three sociological theories that explain why older people prefer to live sedentary lives.

How can older people learn to enjoy a more active lifestyle?

8. What services do senior centers provide for older people in the community? Why do some senior center directors want to move away from the name "senior center"?
9. Why do schools have a limited attraction for older people? Suggest some methods that can help older people learn better in a classroom situation. Describe the pros and cons of online learning for seniors.
10. Describe the Road Scholar, ILR, and OLLI programs. Give several reasons why they attract older people. Why do some gerontologists criticize such programs?
11. Suggest several ways to encourage older people to do more volunteer work.

SUGGESTED READING

Alfred, M. V. (2002). *Learning and sociocultural contexts: Implications for adults, community, and workplace education.* San Francisco: Jossey-Bass.

The author has collected nine essays on adult learning. The essays focus on how culture and context influence adult learning. This book sensitizes the reader to the issues that minority group learners face. Topics include cross-cultural mentoring, immigrant students' learning in adult education programs, and online learning. It is a stimulating look at the many contexts where adult learning takes place, including the workplace, online, and in professional practice.

Beisgen, B. A., & Kraitchman, M. C. (2003). *Senior centers: Opportunities for successful aging.* New York: Springer.

The authors base this book on 20 years' experience managing a senior center in Pittsburgh, Pennsylvania. They discuss how to create a successful center, design programs, and create a satisfying environment for older people. The book is filled with insights into the needs and interests of older center clients. Topics include

activities, education programs, and the future of senior centers. This book is practical guide written by people experienced in the field and a broad view of successful aging.

Freedman, M. (2007). *Encore: Finding work that matters in the second half of life.* New York: Public Affairs.

Author Marc Freedman presents a vision of retirement as a time to give back to the community and a time to discover new meaning in life. The book shows how America can use the skills and energy of the Baby Boom generation to address some of society's toughest problems. It presents inspiring stories of older volunteers and the differences they have made in their communities.

Websites to Consult

Elderhostel/Road Scholar: Adventures in Lifelong Learning

www.roadscholar.org

This site contains information about Road Scholar's not-for-profit, international, senior recreation and education program. It presents travel opportunities and recreation programs geared toward seniors' needs. The site gives insight into the kinds of activities appeal to older people today.

AARP Lifelong Learning

www.aarp.org/personal-growth/life-long-learning

This page provides information, current events, personal accounts, and learning opportunities related to lifelong learning. Another look at topics of interest to the current generation of seniors.

Civic Ventures

www.encore.org

This serves as a portal to all of the Civic Ventures programs including Encore Careers, The Purpose Prize, and the Experience Corps (now an independent organization). The site also provides stories about people who've taken up the volunteer challenge and changed their lives. An informative and inspiring site.

Meema, the pet name her grandchildren and great grandchildren call her, turned 89 last year. She stands about 5 feet 1 inch. She grew up in urban New Jersey and has been widowed for 40 years. She has the straight-at-you style of someone from that part of the world. And no one would place her accent south of Newark. She's free with advice and free to tell you she doesn't like something if she doesn't.

A photo taken of Meema at a grandson's wedding a few years ago shows her sitting in the front row.

Around her stand a crowd of her offspring—her daughters, their husbands, their children, her grandchildren, and in her lap her newest great-grandchild.

All of these family members support her in one way or another. Those farthest away on the West Coast call regularly and visit when they can. Those who live nearby remain in daily or weekly contact with her.

Meema speaks to her closest daughter, Sarah, every day. In the summer Sarah picks her up to take her to their boat at the Jersey Shore. At 89, Meema still drives her own car around town. She has three granddaughters within driving distance. Now she has five great-grandchildren less than an hour away. She drives to see them or they visit with her every few weeks. She's immersed in an ongoing series of birthday parties, graduations, and holiday celebrations. This year she'll go to her oldest granddaughter's house for Thanksgiving, where the whole New Jersey tribe will gather. She also has a daughter on the West Coast, three other grandchildren, and two more great-grandchildren. Meema lives in a complex web of loving relationships.

Her family monitors her health and well-being and supports her when she needs help. But support in her family flows both ways. She has provided babysitting services for decades, she helped one daughter financially when she needed to refurbish her home, she gives advice when asked, and she serves as the matriarch of the family. She's held in respect and treated with care and concern by all—even though the clan quarrels, argues, and often disagrees. It's never quiet at a family gathering.

Meema serves as a model of successful aging.

Is she typical of older family members today? Is this an unusual family? Research on families for the past several decades shows that most older people remain embedded in their extended families. Research long ago dispelled the myth of the family's decline. Studies show that older people get support from their families when needed. And they give to their families as much as they receive—sometimes more. Through help with child rearing, financial support, and good advice, older people enrich family life.

This chapter looks at three topics related to family life: (1) marital status (including marriage, widowhood, divorce, and lifelong singlehood); (2) sexuality and aging; and (3) grandparenting. The chapter concludes with a look at changing family structures and their impact on older people.

MARRIAGE AND WIDOWHOOD

Marital Status

Age-graded normative life events take place at expected times in a person's life. These events (e.g., high school graduation, religious confirmation, and retirement) mark entry into a new status or position in society. Marriage and widowhood are both age-graded normative life events.

Marriage leads to the status of being a married person in our society. It also leads to expectations about behavior such as monogamy, expressions of love, and sharing financial resources. Most people today marry for the first time in their 20s or early 30s. Goodwin, McGill, and Chandra (2009), in a study based on U.S. Census data, report that by age 40, about 81% of men and 86% of women have married. By age 50, this figure jumps to 94% (Kreider, 2005).

The Advantages and Disadvantages of Marriage

Marriage offers a number of advantages to people as they age.

First, married couples have more financial resources than single people. Married couples on average are younger than single older people, and one member of the couple may still work. Also, a number of lifelong trends account for why married people have more resources. Married couples tend to have a higher combined lifetime income than a single person, and they may have two pensions in old age. They also tend to spend less per person on food, rent, and other expenses because two people share the costs.

Kail, Quadagno, and Keene (2009) say that the difference in income between married couples and single people is due to differences in eligibility for pensions. Social Security, for example, provides both spouses with pension benefits. The wife of a pensioner will get her own pension if she has worked. Or she will get a pension worth half of her spouse's pension (if she hasn't worked or if her pension would be less than half his pension).

Also, married couples show greater participation in private pension plans. Single people are less likely to receive any private pension income, and those who do receive pension income tend to have defined contribution plans. These plans provide less security than defined benefit plans. Also, single women, compared to married couples and single men, tend to cash out their pension funds when they change jobs. This leaves them more at risk when they retire.

Second, compared to single people, married couples report greater life satisfaction and subjective well-being (Bennett, 2005; George, 2006). Pinquart and Sorensen (2001) conducted a meta-analysis of subjective well-being in 300 studies. They found that, compared to unmarried older people, married older people reported higher subjective well-being. Most older couples, especially those in good health, say

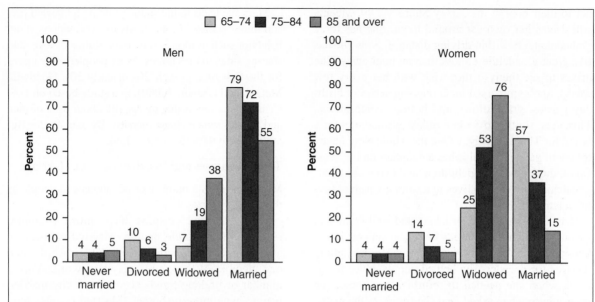

This figure shows 2008 data for the marital status of people age 65 and over. Only a small proportion of older men and women remained single throughout life. Also, only a small proportion of older people are divorced at any one time. (Some formerly divorced people now appear in the married column.)

This figure also shows the differences in marital status by age and the differences in marital status between men and women in later life. Note the large differences in widowhood and married percentages between older men and women at every age here. Women ages 65 to 74, for example, have 3.5 times the widowhood rate of men in this age group. By age 85 and over, more than three quarters of women live as widows (compared to about one third of men in that age group).

Marriage rates show the opposite effect. Seventy-nine percent of men ages 65 to 74 are married compared with just over half of women (57%) in this age group. Even in late old age (age 85 and over), more than half of men are married. Only 15% of women in this age group have a spouse. This figure shows the increase in widowhood with age for both men and women. But by late old age, nearly all women live as widows.

Some of the differences between men and women shown here will change in the future. Men will have longer life expectancies in the years ahead. This will lead to more married couples in later life and to a lower rate of widowhood for women.

FIGURE 12.1   Marital Status, Population Age 65 and Over, by Age Group and Sex, Percent, 2008

Note: *Married* includes married, spouse present; married, spouse absent; and separated. Data refer to civilian noninstitutionalized population.

Source: Federal Interagency Forum on Aging-Related Statistics. (2010g). *Older Americans 2010: Key indicators of well-being.* Indicator 3: Marital status. Washington, DC. Citing U.S. Census Bureau, Current Population Survey, Annual Social and Economic Supplement, 2008.

they are happy. And couples report greater satisfaction in later life than earlier in their marriages.

Studies find increases in love, intimacy, and bonding between married partners in the later years of marriage. Research shows, for example, that the "empty nest" leads to increased marital satisfaction. A Toyota ad tells this story with some humor. It shows a university-aged boy standing on his college dormitory lawn. He's surrounded by a pile of teenage gear. His parents' car sits in the background. The caption to the photo reads: "5:15 pm. Dropping the kid off at college. 5:17 pm. What kid?"

Empty-nest couples tend to spend more time together and to disagree less about issues such as parenting and household chores (Shiota & Levenson, 2007). They live adult-centered lives that allow them to travel, visit with friends, share work at home, and do things together. Couples at this stage of life focus more time and energy on themselves and each other.

BOX 12.1
THE WORLD'S LONGEST MARRIAGE OF A LIVING COUPLE

Herbert (age 104) and Zelmyra (age 101) Fisher celebrated their 85th wedding anniversary on May 19, 2009. The *Guinness Book of World Records* lists them as having the longest marriage of a living couple. They have 5 children, 10 grandchildren, and 9 great-grandchildren. They said they wouldn't change a thing if they had it to do over again. Oh, maybe one thing. They can't agree on watching baseball on TV. When the game comes on, Zelmyra leaves the room. On Valentine's Day in 2010 the couple tweeted messages about love and marriage to 4,400 followers.

Photos from Manogamy Movement Men (and Women for Manogamy). Retrieved: November 11, 2010, from www. manogamy.com/2010/02/couple-makes-guinness-record-for-longest-marriage-85-years.

Third, marriage leads to better adjustment to aging and to better health. A good marriage provides intimacy, greater life satisfaction, and more social support (Proulx, Helms, & Buehler, 2007). Marriage also provides emotional stability and a sense of security. Married older people, compared with single older people, live longer (especially men) and in better health (Brockmann & Klein, 2004). Vaillant (2002, p. 13) says, "A good marriage at age 50 predicted positive aging at 80. But surprisingly, low cholesterol levels at age 50 did not."

People who report a close relationship in their marriage also report reduced depression and anxiety, and higher self-esteem. Mancini and Bonanno (2006, p. 606) say, "Marital closeness is a vital resource in old age." Spouses offer one another a live-in support system in times of need. Couples have lower rates of hospitalization and nursing home placement. Couples in long-term marriages also have a lifetime of shared experiences to draw on. This can help the couple cope with physical and psychological changes in old age. Older married couples tend to rely more on each other than on outside social relations. They also report a greater likelihood than nonmarried older adults of having sexual relations.

Marriage may even help prevent mental decline in later life. Håkansson and colleagues (2009) studied a group of 1,449 people from midlife to old age. The study followed this group for 21 years from 1977 to

Marriage often leads to high life satisfaction in later life.

1998. The researchers found that people who lived with a partner in midlife (mean age 50.4) had a lower likelihood of cognitive impairment than any other group (single, separated, widowed). Divorced and separated people at the start and end of the study, compared to people with a partner, had three times the risk of mental decline. The researchers suggest that living with another person provides mental and social challenges that protect against cognitive impairment in later life.

Calasanti and Kiecolt (2007, p. 11) sum up the findings on long-term marriages. "Among couples married at least 50 years," they write, "most express high marital satisfaction, regardless of whether they share interests and values or lead more independent lives."

The previously mentioned findings apply to good marriages. A poor relationship will not necessarily improve over time. A relationship that includes bickering, fighting, and abuse may only get worse with age. Dissatisfaction in a marriage can lead to depression and illness (Choi & Marks, 2008).

Henry, Miller, and Giarrusso (2005) interviewed 105 older couples, who had been married an average of 42 years. This study shows that couples must deal with many issues that threaten their relationship. The couples in the study talked about difficulties, disagreements, and disappointments they had dealt with in their marriages over the previous few years. The three most common issues were: (1) leisure activities, (2) intimacy, and (3) finances.

Leisure issues involved a lack of sharing or interest in the other spouse's hobbies and activities; travel disagreements (for example, one spouse wanting to travel, the other wanting to stay home, or a difference in the desired destination); or disappointment with the lack of "quality time" together.

Intimacy challenges included both physical and emotional issues. There were "roadblocks to physical intimacy" for some couples because of changes in sexual desire or disagreements over sexual practices. Emotional intimacy challenges tended to center on communication problems—a spouse's lack of communication or negative style of communication.

Disagreements over spending habits tended to be the most common financial issue identified by these married people. Typically this involved a spouse either not wanting to spend money or spending too much money.

Other challenges facing a marriage include disagreements over social roles (Koppen & Anderson, 2008) and ill health later in life. This can lead to strains in marital satisfaction. Caregiving, for example, can strain a couple's romantic relationship. Caregiving can also strain the caregiver spouse's mental and physical health. (Caregiving forms a separate topic in Chapter 13.)

Couples in happy marriages were more likely to report fewer problems (or no problems) than were those in unhappy marriages. Koppen and Anderson (2008) say that the number of problems older couples face may not be as important as the types of problems husbands and wives identify. For example, they found that disagreements over household concerns (where to live and home repairs) and health problems (often related to a spouse's declining health and caregiving) showed up more often in unhappy marriages.

Studies need to look at the quality of a marriage to understand its impact on well-being. Married couples will live longer together than ever before, and long-term marriages face challenges in later life. Some couples will feel a decrease in marital satisfaction. These couples may benefit from professional counseling and other formal supports. Other marriages will have the resources to meet new challenges and thrive. Today, a good marriage provides an older person with a built-in support system, a companion, a friend, and a sexual partner.

Remarriage

Remarriage in later life is relatively uncommon. It is also more likely to occur for men than for women, and for divorced older adults than for the widowed (Calasanti & Kiecolt, 2007). The motivations to remarry in later life include loneliness (especially for men) and financial security (particularly for women). Many widowed women say they prefer to stay single. They enjoy their freedom, have fewer domestic chores than when they were married, and want to avoid potential spousal care in the future (Davidson, 2001).

Hurd Clarke (2005) asked women to compare their first marriages with their remarriage experiences. She found that most of the women reported a happy or happier second marriage. Some women whose first marriage ended in divorce said that they wished their second marriage had been their first. Many women reported a greater compatibility with their second partner and a fairer division of labor.

Some women talked about how the second marriage had "undone" some of the hurt and disappointment of the first marriage. For widowed women whose first marriage had been happy, the second marriage "complemented" the first. They said their first and second marriages fulfilled different needs. Romance and sexual fulfillment had been important in their first marriage (at a young age). In later life they valued marriage because it gave them companionship.

Hurd Clarke (2005) identifies a number of things that led these women to have a satisfying second marriage. First, the insights they gained from their first marriage helped them select a more compatible partner. Second, without child-rearing responsibilities (and, in the case of retirees, work commitments), couples had more time to invest in their relationship. They could also share domestic chores. Third, many of these women felt greater sexual freedom with their second or third husbands (Hurd Clarke, 2006, p. 138). This may be due to their increased willingness to express their sexual needs and their increased confidence—a confidence "acquired through age and experience."

Common-Law Unions and Cohabitation

Some older people choose to live together and not marry. For all adult age groups the rate of cohabitation has increased over time. Brown, Lee, and Bulanda (2006) used census data to estimate cohabitation among people age 51 and over. They estimate that just over 1 million people in this age group cohabited, less than 2% of the 51-and-over population.

Some older people decide to live together after the end of a first marriage. This may come before a remarriage. Or the couple may want an intimate relationship without the formal bonds of marriage (Leigh, 2000).

Living together (outside of marriage) may make economic sense for some older people. Ebeling (2007) says that remarriage can complicate estate planning, cost a new spouse alimony from the previous marriage, decrease Social Security benefits, and lose the newly married partner survivor benefits. A couple may need a financial planner to sort out the costs and benefits of marriage in later life. For this reason some people choose cohabitation.

Research by King and Scott (2005) compares the quality, purpose, and meaning of cohabitation for older and younger adults. They found a number of differences between these two age groups. First, compared to younger couples, older cohabiting couples report higher relationship quality, higher levels of fairness, fewer disagreements, and higher levels of happiness. Second, older couples report that they spend more time alone together, and they feel more confident that their relationship will last. Third, and consistent with earlier research, older couples saw cohabitation as an alternative to marriage. Researchers expect that the number of older adults who live together unmarried will increase in the future as more Baby Boomers enter old age.

Older adults now and in the future will have greater choice in the type of intimate relationships they form. Some unmarried couples today live in committed relationships, but they maintain separate households. These nonresident couples are known as LAT couples ("living apart together"). A LAT arrangement allows these couples to live in their own homes, but enjoy life with an intimate and committed partner. Karlsson and Borell (2005) studied a Swedish sample of LAT couples ages 60 to 90. They found that this arrangement gave women (who lived in their own homes) more freedom to manage their social relations. For example, when they chose, they could meet family and friends without their partner's presence. LAT relationships among older people add to the diversity of modern family life.

Divorce

Divorced or separated (including married/spouse absent) older persons represented only 11.6% of all older persons in 2008. But this percentage has increased since 1980, when 5.3% of the older population were divorced or separated/spouse absent (Administration on Aging, 2009). The increase in divorced or separated persons over time points to a greater willingness for people to dissolve an unsuccessful marriage.

Late-life couples often divorce because the marriage can no longer support the changing roles, needs, or desires of the individuals (Wu & Schimmele, 2007). Other reasons for divorce are similar for younger and older couples. They include problems of abuse, alcohol or drug addiction, and infidelity. Cohen (1999) says that people who divorce in middle or later life rarely remarry. But compared with women, men show a greater tendency to remarry after divorce.

Divorce in later life often means economic insecurity, particularly for women. For men, it often means loss of social contact with children and relatives. Divorced older men have the smallest social networks, the weakest ties to their families, and the lowest life satisfaction of any marital group. They are also less likely to receive support from their adult children (Lin, 2008).

Lifelong Singlehood

A small proportion (about 4%) of older people have never married (U.S. Census Bureau, 2006a). Little research exists on the lives and social relationships of lifelong single older people. People often believe that older never married people are unmarriageable, or that they feel lonely, live socially isolated lives, and feel disconnected from family. But many singles have chosen to remain unmarried. These individuals have made unique adaptations to aging. For example, they often play vital and supportive roles in the lives of siblings, older parents, and others.

Studies show that most older singles, particularly single women, develop strong and diverse social networks and have active ties with siblings, friends, and other family members (McDill, Hall, & Turell, 2006). They form friendships and other social relationships to provide themselves with supporters, confidants, and companions. For example, they may treat nieces and nephews as surrogate children.

One colleague, a lifelong single woman, gives support to two elderly aunts. She spends holidays with her sister's family, buys toy and clothes for her nieces and nephews, and takes them on outings. When she retired she sold her home and moved to another city to be near her sister and her younger relatives.

McDill and colleagues (2006) studied the singlehood experience of never-married women over the age of 40. They found that the majority of women in their study (65%) felt no social stigma related to their single status. Many said they had not married because they had not met the right person, not because of some personal shortcomings. These women were satisfied with their lives and felt particularly positive about the freedom their single status afforded them. They saw themselves as part of a "unique social stratum."

Overall, never-married older people report that they lead active lives and feel happy. They have good health and feel satisfied with their standard of living.

Singles feel they have freedom and control over their lives. In general, compared to single men, single women feel more satisfied with their lives (Barrett, 1999). Davies (1995) found that older single women reported greater psychological well-being than younger single women or older single men. Older single people do report more loneliness than married seniors. But, single people, particularly single women, tend to feel less lonely than divorced and widowed older people (Dykstra, 1995).

A study by Tamborini (2008), using Social Security data, found that never married older people (age 62 and over) had a high rate of poverty. Never-married people had twice the national rate of poverty (in 2004) and four times the rate of married people. They also had a higher poverty rate than divorced and widowed older people. This group also had more health risks than the national average or than married older people.

The literature on singlehood suggests that never-married people have good support networks (Connidis & McMullin, 1999). Still, compared with married couples, they lack spousal and child support in later life. This leads singles to use more formal supports and to develop more supportive friendships than married older people (Barrett & Lynch, 1999; Liebler & Sandefur, 2002). Older single people who need care are more likely to require institutional care because they lack a spouse or children.

Researchers project an increase in the proportion of old single people as Baby Boomers enter later life. These singles, as they age happily and in good health, may change societal attitudes about permanent singlehood. Future studies should look at the reasons for the health and financial problems some members of this group face. For example, does the experience of singlehood differ for different racial and ethnic group members? Studies can then learn about the coping strategies that never-married people use to maintain a high quality of life.

Widowhood

Nearly all adults (96%) in the United States marry at least once. But the proportion of people married at a given age decreases from middle age onward. Divorce accounts for only a small proportion of this decrease. On average, fewer than 2 older people per 1,000 divorce each year. Widowhood explains most of the decrease in marriage rates later in life. And the risk of widowhood differs for men and women.

There were more than four times as many older widows (8.8 million) as widowers (2.2 million) in the United States in 2008. Almost half of all older women were widows (42%) compared with only 14% of older men (Administration on Aging, 2009). Older women, particularly those age 75 and older, are more likely than older men to live their final years in widowhood, most often living alone. At least three things account for the higher rate of widowhood for women: (1) women tend to marry older men, (2) women have a longer life expectancy than men, and (3) men tend to remarry after loss of a spouse. Gerontologists describe widowhood as an expectable or age-graded normative life event (especially for women), one that creates a great deal of stress.

Male and Female Responses to Widowhood

Most studies of widowhood in the past focused on women. But recent studies look at how widowhood affects each gender (Bennett, 2007; Lee & DeMaris, 2007). Wolff and Wortman (2006) studied the effects of widowhood on nutrition and health. They report that, compared to women, men show a greater decline in health. Women in married couples often oversee the nutritional and health needs of the couple. For example, women tend to make doctor's appointments for medical checkups. The loss of a wife often leaves a man without the motivation to stay fit and healthy.

Research shows that widowed men, compared to women, find it harder to make new friends or to join self-help groups. Studies show that widowers suffer from isolation and loneliness after the loss of their spouse (Calasanti & Kiecolt, 2007). This in part reflects their low involvement in relationships outside marriage over the life course.

Some men may even experience elevated levels of depression *before* widowhood. They may experience depression because they anticipate the loss of their spouse. Women usually don't show this tendency (Lee & DeMaris, 2007). Widowers may increase smoking and drinking and will often change their diet and exercise routines (Wolff & Wortman, 2006).

Studies suggest that men experience more social isolation and have fewer sources of support than widows. Moore and Stratton (2002, p. 4) say that during their research they attended support group sessions for widows and widowers. They would often find only 2 men in a group of 100 women, even though census figures report about 76 men per 100 women.

"We had to wonder," they say: "Where were the men?" They found a similar lack of men at senior center activities. They believe that the older widower "may well be sitting at home watching TV, invisible to his neighbors, local service providers, national policy makers, and social science researchers."

Confidants (someone the widowed person can talk with and confide in) can contribute to good morale for widows and widowers. They can lessen anxiety, tension, and depression. Two reports from the Changing Lives of Older Couples (CLOC) study found that social support buffered the effects of widowhood. The CLOC study interviewed 1,532 married people age 65 and over. Richardson (2007) found that interaction with confidants improved well-being, especially for women, during the bereavement process. And Ha (2006) found that family and friends of the bereaved person increased positive support and decreased negative interactions.

Social support holds one key to life satisfaction for widowers. Carr (2004a), for example, reports that widowed men with strong social support (from friends and others) fare as well as widowed women in their adjustment to widowhood. Widowed men who have strong emotional support from friends can experience personal growth even in the face of spousal loss. Carr's research (2004b) finds that widowed men who have high levels of social support from friends are no more likely than widowed women to express a desire to remarry.

In part, the different life experiences of older men and women explain this difference in social support. Most older men spent their lives focused on their careers, while older women spent their lives focused on people. So, women have more close relationships than men in old age.

Because men have fewer supports than women, they more often experience loneliness after a spouse dies (Moore & Stratton, 2002). One man told Moore and Stratton (p. 100), "At night I stay home, but then the loneliness begins." Another man said, "Nights are endless." The researchers say that many of the men in their study said the same. Men also may experience a decline in their social functioning and mental health status. Chipperfield and Havens (2001) note that although life satisfaction declines for both men and women following the death of a spouse, men show a greater decline.

Studies show that wives link men to wider social networks. More often than men, women say they have close relationships with family and friends besides their husbands. A widowed woman with children will usually continue in the role of mother and grandmother.

Moore and Stratton (2002) found that, in spite of these challenges, some older widowed men bounce back from widowhood. The men in their study reestablished meaningful lives after the loss of their spouses. Many of them found companionship and got involved in social activities. Many widowed men remarry.

Moore and Stratton (2002) reviewed the literature on remarriage for older men. They found that (1) the smaller number of men in older age groups gives men an advantage in the marriage market; (2) compared to women, men marry sooner after widowhood; and (3) men tend to marry younger women, which gives them a large pool of potential mates. The researchers report that compared to older women, men have a remarriage rate that is six times higher. A widower loses a wife, a companion, and his link to other family and social ties. This may explain why many men rush into another marriage after they lose a spouse.

Compared with men, a smaller proportion of women remarry after their spouses die. This, in part, reflects the smaller number of eligible men compared with eligible women in later life. Women who do remarry say they want a companion and the feeling that they add to another person's happiness. Women who remarry tend to be younger, worry less about finances, and have a higher household income than widowed women who remain single (Moorman, Booth, & Fingerman, 2006). Wilcox and her colleagues (2003) report improved mental health and reduced depression in widowed women following their remarriage.

Sexual relations after the death of a spouse also differ by gender. Wolff and Wortman (2006, citing Hustins, 2001) say that only 7% of widows had some sexual relationship by the end of their first year of bereavement. By contrast, 54% of men reported a sexual relationship in this time. Even among older widowed men (age 65 and over), 31% said they had a sexual relationship within 2 years of bereavement. Only 4% of older widowed women reported a sexual relationship in this time (Davidson, 2001).

Many older widows report an interest in men, but not necessarily an interest in remarriage (Moorman et al., 2006). Some also reported negative attitudes toward remarriage and an increased enjoyment of their independence. Some women experience widowhood as a release. Widowhood allows them to rediscover parts of their identities they had lost in marriage. One woman I interviewed said she would not marry again (for the fourth time). "I'm tired of taking care of sick old men," she said. "I want to enjoy myself for a while." Widows sometimes set new goals, take up new activities, and take on new challenges (Silverman, 2004).

Future Research Questions

Some research suggests that men and women may have different social network needs and different types of relationships in later life. Studies in general have judged older men as less involved than older women in relationships. But self-reports by men show that they often see themselves as having strong bonds of affection and closeness to family members. Sometimes they rate higher than women on self-reports of closeness. Boxer, Cook, and Cohler (1986, p. 102) say, "By unquestioningly imposing a 'female model' of interpersonal relationships on men's experiences, investigators may be missing relevant information. . . . Male bonds may require more subtle measurement techniques and may manifest themselves in ways or in settings that are different from women's bonds."

These findings may reflect differences in how men and women develop relationships earlier in life. More research needs to look at the social lives of widows and widowers to understand how their needs differ. In particular, researchers need to include more men in their studies. This will create a more balanced view of widowhood.

Dating

Men tend to remarry after widowhood and women tend to stay single, but studies report little about how widows and widowers form new intimate relationships (Connidis, 2006).

Montenegro (2003) reports on an AARP study of 3,501 single men and women ages 40 to 69. She found that about one third of the people in the study had an exclusive dating arrangement. Another third had a nonexclusive dating arrangement. Nine percent expressed no interest in dating. Moore and Stratton (2002, p. 145) say that men in their study found dating stressful. One widower described dating as "akin to an hour on the rack" and "my worst nightmare." Another said he would only ask a woman out for one date in order not to get too involved.

Those people in Montenegro's study who dated regularly said they enjoyed the freedom of singlehood, but dating helped them cope with loneliness. Men and women said they looked for a dating partner

BOX 12.2
THE SHOCK OF WIDOWHOOD

I am sitting on a sofa, sipping tea with Joanna in her living room high above the city, in one of the wealthiest sections of town. Joanna has lived alone since her husband died 12 years ago. She describes the stress she felt as a caregiver at that time.

We had a comfortable middle-class life—two cars, a cottage, a house, children, and friends. We were involved in everything. Then he became ill with cancer of the brain.

Well, it was a matter of carrying on. I was going to stop working in real estate and be with my husband when he was sick, but I didn't. My supervisor thought it wasn't a good thing to dwell on it, to be at home a lot. He was right. So I carried on with my job. Of course, I had to do it well. It's part of the picture. You have to do it well. It has to be perfect.

I seemed to have this idea that I was going to carry it all on, that I could do it. I did for 2 years, and I ran myself into the ground, running up to the hospital at noon and helping him with his lunch, going up again after work. And then at night just sacking out so I could go on with another day. It was very hard.

I think all this running up to the hospital constantly wasn't really genuine. I did it. I cared for his suffering. But I was human. I wished someone else could be doing it. So I was not being true to myself. I think that led to a lot of things later.

Even after my husband died, I was determined to carry on as though nothing had happened. I was so determined that nothing like my husband's death was going to throw me, and I didn't allow myself a grievance time.

After his death, I traveled. At Christmas I went to Spain, Hawaii, or wherever. At Easter I went somewhere. I went to Europe. There was never a day—I didn't allow myself any time at all. Do you get the picture? No time to breathe.

It was unbelievable. No wonder I needed something. I didn't want to lean on people. I think I got hooked on a sleeping pill every night when my husband was sick, plus I drank a bit. Well, for a year after he died I was hospitalized off and on. I was using different kinds of pills. The doctor would change prescriptions, but I wouldn't discard the old one. I took more alcohol than I'd like to admit along with the pills. I was a very, very confused person. That was my way of coping, my way of standing the pain. I needed some kind of anesthetic. You finally have to get floored to realize you can't do it alone.

Well, I finally got floored. The last time I drove my car I drove right into a restaurant—right through the window.

I had the car washed that day. And I was parked in front of this pizza parlor having a cup of coffee. I thought the sidewalk was quite a distance from the front of the car. I didn't want it sticking out so I put it in low and just eased it up. I drove right through the window.

I just stepped out of the car—over these shards of plate glass, big pieces of plate glass on the road—and I said, "I'd like a cup of coffee." "Lady," the owner said, "you get back in that car." He was quite certain I was out of my tree. But I didn't get back. I just sat in the booth until the police came.

That's the last time I drove. That was getting near the end. I guess for me the change had to come in the form of a crisis. That's the only way I would accept it. I resist change, especially change imposed on me. Now, if I had to let it all go, I know I could do it. I have something here [pointing to herself] that I can be comfortable with.

Joanna took a year's leave of absence from her job, sold her house and car, and joined Alcoholics Anonymous. It took her 2 years to start a new life based on A.A., social commitments to groups she wants to help, and her family. Today Joanna has retired from work. She tutors young people after school, spends time cross-country skiing, and time alone at her cottage. She also has a strong relationship with her granddaughter.

Summing up her life today, Joanna says: "What really gives my life meaning now is inside. It's not external anymore. I have my inner resources—I always had them, but I didn't use them. For me widowhood was very painful at first because I resisted change. Now I'm changed and it's okay. I would say I have a new freedom."

---

with a good personality and a sense of humor. Many men in the study looked for physical attractiveness and sexual satisfaction in a dating partner. Most people in the study found dating prospects through friends, family, or work.

Older people say they date for several reasons: Some people want to find a marital partner. Others want to stay socially active. Older women say it increases their prestige. They believe that other women envy them for dating. Men say they date in order to talk about their personal concerns—but also for sexual satisfaction.

Dating also acts as a starting point for romance, sex, and love. More than one third of the daters in

Montenegro's (2003) study of regular daters reported that they had sexual intercourse at least once per month.

New approaches to dating arrived with the spread of the Internet and social networking. The AARP (Fisher, 2010) study of sexual activity among Americans age 50 and over found that, compared to past studies, more older singles in 2010 use dating services. Crary (2010) reports the case of a married couple in Cherry Hill, New Jersey, Tony Cost and his wife Rosemary. They met through the eHarmony online dating service in 2007 and married a year later. Rosemary had been divorced for about 10 years. Tony's wife had died a year earlier.

Tony says, "It was just a point in my life where I decided I wanted to do more than just sit. I wanted to look for someone to share the rest of my life with." The couple exchanged 55 emails before meeting at a restaurant for dinner. They talked for 5 hours. Rosemary says, "It was like we'd known each other forever."

This couple used the dating service to explore their interests before a first date. This approach may relieve some of the tension and mismatching that occurs when people meet face to face for the first time. A study of online personal ads supports this idea. A study of 600 Yahoo! personal ads found that people who placed the ads specified the types of people they wanted to meet. For example, older men wanted younger, attractive women. Women looked for status in their men until past age 70. Then they looked for older men (Alterovitz & Mendelsohn, 2009).

The trend toward the use of online connections by older people has just begun. Some older people already use the social media to screen potential partners. Others use Facebook and Twitter to maintain a large network of friends and acquaintances. Almost every Boomer can tell a story about a reconnection with a high school friend or lost relative. The use of social media may bring down some of the barriers to dating in later life. New seniors with a lifetime of experience using the Internet will feel comfortable with these new online options.

Sexuality

Sexual activity serves two functions: reproduction and pleasure. The Western tradition, from the Old Testament onward, emphasized reproduction. In the Judeo-Christian tradition, sex for pleasure is sinful and immoral. This view leaves little room for sex in later life and may have led to the notion that older people live (or should live) asexual lives.

And yet studies show that these beliefs have little basis in fact. For example, most people have an interest in sex throughout life. And, given good health and a partner, older people can (and do) have sexual relations into late old age (Elliott & Umberson, 2008; Fisher, 2010; Schlesinger, 1996). Roizen (1999) says that "[Sex] decreases stress, relaxes us, enhances intimacy, and helps form the foundation of strong and supportive personal relationships. No matter what your calendar age, nineteen or ninety, sex is a first rate age reducer."

Alex Comfort (1972), author of *The Joy of Sex,* says that most people give up sex for the same reason they give up riding a bicycle: (1) they think it looks silly (attitude); (2) they have arthritis and can't get on (health); and (3) they don't have a bicycle (widowhood).

Jacoby (1999, p. 41) refers to a "partner gap." She says that, compared with older women, older men are

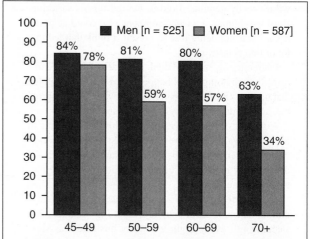

This chart shows that after age 50, compared to women, a significantly higher proportion of men in every age group have a sexual partner. Men report little decline in partner availability until later old age (70+). In the oldest age group, nearly twice the proportion of men, compared to women, have an available sexual partner. In part this reflects the tendency for men to have a spouse in later life.

FIGURE 12.2 The Partner Gap: Having a Regular Sexual Partner, by Sex and Age, Percent

Source: Fisher, L. L. (2010). Sex, romance, and relationships. *AARP Survey of Midlife and Older Adults*, p. 29. Retrieved November 11, 2010, from http://assets. aarp.org/rgcenter/general/srr_09.pdf. Reprinted with permission.

more likely to have sexual partners. And this difference between women and men increases with age. Widowhood or a husband's decision to stop having sex often puts an end to a woman's sexual activity. "The saddest truth," Jacoby says, ". . . is that for most (though not all) older widows, the loss of a husband translates into the end of sex" (p. 43).

Still, some people get around these barriers. A study of 166 lower-income older people in New Jersey ages 61 to 91 found that people had a variety of intimate experiences (Ginsberg, Pomerantz, & Kramer-Feeley, 2005). Many of them said they lacked a partner. But about 60% of the people in the study reported touching/holding hands, embracing/hugging, and kissing daily to at least once a month. The respondents said they wanted more frequent sexual activity.

A recent AARP survey, "Sex, Romance, and Relationships" (Fisher, 2010), looked at the sex lives of middle-aged and older adults. Fisher and a team of researchers surveyed 1,670 adults age 45 and over in 2009 (a representative sample of the U.S. population). The study found that people with a partner but not married had sex more often and with more satisfaction than married people. Pepper Schwartz, professor at the University of Washington and advisor to this study, says that "long-term married couples may get a little less interested [in sex]. . . . Older people in non-married relations work harder at it and enjoy it more."

People in this study reported satisfaction in a sexual relationship if: (1) they had a sexual partner, (2) they had frequent sexual intercourse (more than once a week), (3) the partners had good health, (4) the partners felt low levels of stress, and (5) the partners felt no financial worries.

This last point holds special meaning because this study took place during a major recession in the U.S. economy. Schwartz sees a link between the economy and the drop in sexual satisfaction reported in this study. "The economy has had an impact on these people," she says. "They're more liberal in their attitudes, yet they're having sex less often. The only thing I see that's changed in a negative direction is financial worries" (Crary, 2010).

Older people can have a satisfying marriage without an active sex life. But continued sexual activity leads to well-being and happiness for older couples. A qualitative study by Elliott and Umberson (2008, p. 396) explored how midlife and older married people experience and negotiate sex in long-term marriages. The married men and women in their study both saw sex as integral to a good marriage—"as a barometer of the health of their own marriage."

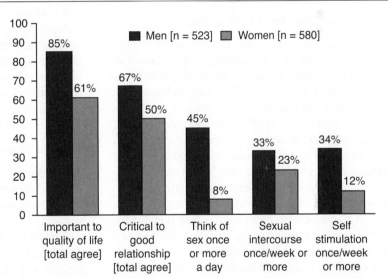

Men and women (age 45 and over) differ in their sexual attitudes and behavior. A higher proportion of older men, compared to older women, consider sexual thoughts and activities important to the quality of their lives and their relationships. More than five times the proportion of men, compared to women, think about sex once or more per day. Nearly three times the proportion of men, compared to women, engage in self-stimulation once or more per week. These findings give a picture of men, compared to women, as more focused on sexual thoughts and activities.

Do you think these results reflect a greater willingness of men, compared to women, to report their sexual activities? Do you think that future groups of older men and women will show these differences in attitudes toward sex and sexual behavior? Why do you think the results in the future will look the same or different from the results in this chart?

FIGURE 12.3 Gender Differences in Sexual Attitudes, Thoughts, and Behaviors, Percent

Source: Fisher, L. L. (2010). Sex, romance, and relationships. *AARP Survey of Midlife and Older Adults*, p. 5. Retrieved November 11, 2010, from http://assets.aarp.org/rgcenter/general/srr_09.pdf. Reprinted with permission.

But many couples experienced conflict around sex, often related to gender differences in desired frequency—typically husbands wanting to have sex more often than their wives. Couples often tried to "change their sexual selves"—to show greater or lesser interest in sex to better match their spouse's desires. This negotiation of their sexual relationship was done to reduce marital conflict, enhance marital intimacy, improve a spouse's self-esteem, or all three. The researchers call this "emotion work."

Cooley (2002, p. 2) says that "while expressing our sexuality isn't as essential for survival as food or water, it fulfills a need for affection and belonging." This in turn has a positive impact on our self-esteem and quality of life. Dr. Walter Bortz, past president of the American Geriatrics Society, offers a final word of wisdom. "If you stay interested, stay healthy, stay off medications, and have a good mate, then you can have good sex all the way to the end of life" (Stein, 2009).

Sexuality in Long-Term Care Settings

People in institutional settings face unique challenges to the expression of their sexuality. The structure of life in a long-term care facility allows people little privacy and little control over their time and activities. The views of the staff and facility policies can limit a person's sexual activity. Rheaume and Mitty (2008, p. 342) say that "in most long-term care settings, staff members tend to view resident's attempts at sexual expression as 'problem' behavior." Even married couples who share a room can feel inhibited (Kemp, 2008; Roach, 2004). Moss and Moss (2007) say that men who live in long-term care facilities may find it difficult to express their sexuality. And this can lead to a loss of their sense of masculinity.

Loue (2005) examined the literature on sexual intimacy of nursing-home residents. She found that the desire for sexual intimacy remains for many residents, including those with cognitive impairment. But many staff members and administrators feel uncomfortable when cognitively impaired residents express their sexuality. They also fear that the sexual intimacy of cognitively impaired residents may not be consensual. And this could lead to legal action against the facility. Research supports the need for more formal training programs that teach workers about the sexual needs and feelings of older residents.

Zeiss and Kasi-Godley (2001; also Reingold & Burros, 2004) call for programs that (1) give staff members information about sexuality in later life, (2) examine staff members' attitudes toward sexuality in later life, and (3) provide skill training so that staff members can work effectively with residents. Administrators can also encourage staff members to talk about issues and institutional policies (Kamel & Hajjar, 2003; Rheaume & Mitty, 2008).

Staff members need to consider residents' need for privacy, and to recognize other barriers to sexual expression that residents face. These include adverse effects of medication, physical limitations, and attitudes of staff and families (Hajjar & Kamel, 2003). Also, the increased number of residents with Alzheimer's disease or other forms of dementia raises the issue of consent. Staff members need to assess a cognitively impaired resident's ability to consent to sexual relations. Staff members need to protect dementia patients from sexual exploitation or abuse (Loue, 2005).

Attitudes of staff and older people toward sexuality will continue to change as new cohorts of people enter old age. Younger and midlife cohorts today have more open and accepting attitudes to sex. If they bring these attitudes with them into institutional settings, this will affect staff attitudes and policies. Training can heighten staff members' understanding of sexuality in later life. It can improve their ability to deal with sexual relations in their institution.

Physical Changes and Sexual Adaptations

Physical changes due to aging require adaptations in sexual performance. For example, with age a man's sexual response slows from first excitement through orgasm.

Sometimes illness can interfere with sexual function. Damage to blood vessels in the penis, for example, accounts for about half of all impotence in men past age 50. Also, hardening of the arteries can limit the flow of blood to the genitals. It can stop a man from having an erection and can lead to swelling of tissues in the vagina for women. Hypertension (high blood pressure) can interfere with sexual performance in both men and women (Woolston, 2009).

A heart attack, prostate surgery, or hysterectomy does not necessarily decrease sexual activity or enjoyment. But an illness may require an adjustment in sexual patterns or in lifestyle. Cooley (2002) says that good eating habits, weight control, limits on the use of alcohol, and an active sex life can all enhance and prolong sexual activity. Women can use vaginal jelly to decrease dryness during intercourse. Older people without a partner can masturbate for sexual pleasure. Masturbation can lead to a release of tension and increased well-being (Zeiss & Kasl-Godley, 2001). Counseling may help for nonmedical problems.

Willert and Semans (2000) recommend sex education to help couples cope with changes in sexual function. They propose that education include discussion of normal physical changes, chronic illness, and the myths people believe about sexuality in old age. Many books and videos exist that can help couples explore ways to adapt to these changes.

Drugs such as Viagra and Levitra now exist to restore or enhance sexual performance in older men. The AARP 2009 survey of people age 45 and over found that 10% of the men in the study, but none of the women, used "medications to improve sexual functioning" (Fisher, 2010, p. 16). Many men who use Viagra say it increases their sexual enjoyment. Their partners agree (Vares, Potts, Gavey, & Grace, 2007). But the AARP study shows that, compared to men, women have fewer resources to use if they feel a drop in their sexual interest or performance. The use of drug therapies and a greater interest in sexual activity among younger seniors will lead to more active sex lives among older adults in the future.

All of this talk about physical change and adaptation misses a key part of the sexual equation: the relationship of the people involved. People can adapt to many changes in their bodies and still enjoy a good sex life. But this requires knowledge about sex in later life and good communication between the partners. The National Institute on Aging (2010c) reminds us that sexuality includes emotional as well as physical response. The Institute says that a man's fear of impotence, for example, can create enough stress to cause it. A woman's feeling of lost beauty can interfere with enjoyment of sex.

Butler and Lewis (2002) say that older couples can develop a unique intimacy as they age. They refer to a "second language of sex"—increased intimacy and greater communication as a love relationship matures. Weg (1983a, p. 8) says that researchers too often ignore "the walking hand-in-hand or arm-in-arm; the caring for one another; the touching and holding, with or without intercourse."

Gott and Hinchliff, 2003, p. 73) report that being older "brought changes in the meaning of sex for women, with a shift in focus from reproduction to their own pleasure." Some older women see sexual intercourse as "the icing on the cake" (Hurd Clarke, 2006, p. 136). They emphasize cuddling and companionship more. As one remarried older woman said, "What is important is that we cuddle up . . . and then if there is sex on top of it, that's extra good."

This makes later life a good time to explore sexual potential. Touch, foreplay, a good setting, and mood can all enhance sex. Slower response time can lead to more intimacy and a deeper relationship. The Mayo Clinic Staff (2010b) gives some sound advice here: "To maintain a satisfying sex life, talk with your partner. Set aside time to be sensual and sexual together. When you're spending intimate time with your partner, share your thoughts about lovemaking. Tell your partner what you want from him or her. Be honest about what you're experiencing physically and emotionally."

Gay and Lesbian Older Adults

Cantor, Brennan, and Shippy (2004) note that few national surveys ask about sexual orientation or identity. And they say that surveys likely miss people who will not reveal their sexual orientation. So, only a rough estimate exists of the number of lesbian, gay, bisexual, or transgender (LGBT) older people in the United States. Cantor and colleagues conclude, from the few studies that do exist, that from 3% to 8% of the U.S. population have a LGBT orientation. The 2009 AARP national survey of sexuality among older Americans comes to a similar conclusion. It found that 3% of the respondents considered themselves gay, 1% lesbian, and 1% bisexual (Fisher, 2010).

This would mean that the United States has from 1 million to 2.8 million LGBT seniors. Cantor and colleagues (also de Vries, 2007) estimate that, as the older population increases, this figure could grow to between 2 million and 6 million LGBT seniors by 2030.

A myth exists that LGBT seniors live lonely, pathetic lives. The myth pictures them as ugly and rejected by young lovers. The myth assumes the gay or lesbian person is alone and lonely (Hostetler, 2004, p. 18).

Research findings on aging LGBTs fail to support this myth. Like heterosexuals, many older gays and lesbians have committed and enduring relationships and close ties to family and friends (O'Brien & Goldberg, 2005). Heaphy, Yip, and Thompson (2004) found that 40% of older gay men and 60% of older lesbians in their study were in couple relationships.

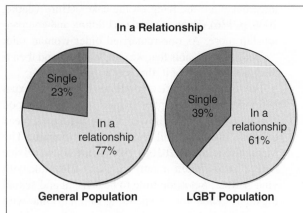

In a Relationship

Single 23%

In a relationship 77%

General Population

Single 39%

In a relationship 61%

LGBT Population

The MetLife and American Society on Aging study of LGBT relationships shows a similar proportion of LGBT and the general population in relationships. More than one-quarter of LBGT partners (ages 40–61) say they have gotten married (even though only five states grant marriage licenses to same-sex couples). Many LBGT people in this study say they would marry if federal or state law permitted.

FIGURE 12.4 Lesbian, Gay, Bisexual, and Transgender (LGBT) Relationships

Source: MetLife and American Society on Aging. (2010). *Still out, still aging: The MetLife study of lesbian, gay, bisexual, and transgender baby boomers.* Retrieved: November 11, 2010, from www.metlife.com/assets/cao/mmi/publications/studies/2010/mmi-still-out-still-aging.pdf. Reprinted with permission.

Studies also show that LGBT seniors play active roles in the gay and straight communities. Older LGBTs may play a parent or grandparent role to a younger person or play the role of caregiver to parents in their family (Cantor et al., 2004). Their single status, mobility, or willingness to live with a parent may select them for this role.

The MetLife and American Society on Aging (ASA) (2010) study of LGBT older people found that 1 person in 5 (21%) reported giving care to an adult family member or friend in the past 6 months. Studies of the general population find that only 17% of people report this type of caregiving. About one third of LGBT caregivers give care to a parent (33%); about one third give care to a partner (34%); the rest give care to friends (21%) and other nonrelatives.

Also, the MetLife ASA study found that the same proportion of men and women reported giving care (about 1 person in 5). The study found that gay men provided more hours of care per week (average 41 hours) than the lesbian or general population of men and women. These figures suggest that Baby Boom members of the LGBT community maintain strong social ties with their families and friends.

Blando (2001) conducted a review of the literature on gay and lesbian older people. Studies report satisfaction with long-term relationships, strong family ties, and a circle of friends. Cruz (2003) studied 125 gay and bisexual men ages 55 to 84. These men reported little depression and good health. Cahill, South, and Spade (2000) found that, compared to heterosexuals, gay men and lesbians may have stronger social networks.

Some older lesbians and gays are reluctant to use formal services. Instead they create their own support networks (Richard & Brown, 2006). Their friends often serve as surrogate families or "chosen families" (MetLife & American Society on Aging, 2010). These close friendships lead to good health and psychological well-being (de Vries & Blando, 2004). At the same time the reluctance of older lesbians and gays to use formal services can place an added burden on their caregivers (Brotman et al., 2007).

A MetLife study (MetLife Mature Market Institute, in conjunction with the Lesbian and Gay Aging Issues Network of the American Society on Aging and Zogby International, 2006b, p. 5; MetLife & American Society on Aging, 2010) also found that older gay men and lesbians are concerned about the same things as heterosexual older people—health, finances, end-of-life care, and caregiving. Women expressed a concern that they would outlive their finances. They also feared that the medical profession would not treat them with respect if they had a serious illness. Twelve percent of the lesbian respondents, for example, said that "they have absolutely no confidence that they will be treated respectfully." Men in this study feared dependence due to illness.

Gays and lesbians face certain unique problems as they age. First, the LGBT community, like the heterosexual community, values youth. Bergling (2004) reports that gay men have learned and believe many of the stereotypes of aging. Some writers (Hammond, 1987) say that lesbians feel less of this prejudice against age. Older African American gay men face the same issues as white gay men: homophobia, fear of discovery, and internal conflict. But they also experience racism. Burlew and Serface (2006) suggest that counselors provide culturally sensitive help to gay older African Americans. Counselors need to recognize that this group faces multiple forms of discrimination in later life.

Second, the law and social institutions generally do not recognize gay or lesbian relationships. This can lead to problems with legal custody of disabled partners, discrimination in housing, and barriers to the use of social services designed for heterosexual partnerships (Cahill & South, 2002). Hospitals, for example, sometimes limit access to intensive care units to family members. They may not recognize a gay or lesbian partner as family.

Federal law and many states give no legal status to same-sex marriage. De Vries (2007) cites 1,138 statutes where marriage determines federal government benefits. This leads to unequal treatment of gay and lesbian couples before the law. Consider the following economic challenges that gay and lesbian older couples face:

1. Compared to heterosexual couples, partners in a same-sex marriage cannot get death benefits from Social Security.
2. Same-sex couples face a heavy tax on retirement plans and they face an estate tax if the survivor inherits a home, even if it was jointly owned.
3. Same-sex partners risk losing a home when a partner enters a nursing home. Medicaid allows a married heterosexual spouse to remain in the couple's home (Bennett & Gates, 2004; Simmons & O'Connell, 2003).

Gay and lesbian couples also face practical and emotional challenges due to their unrecognized status. In one case, lesbian partners in a relationship held citizenship in two different countries—the United States and Scotland. The Scottish partner could not get U.S. citizenship as a spouse, even though the couple considered themselves married.

The Scottish partner's visa required that she leave the country every 6 months. So the couple had to move out of the United States for some time each year. Each time they came back they had to hope that immigration authorities would grant the Scottish partner a visa to stay in the United States for another 6 months. I asked this couple how long they would live this transient lifestyle. They said they had no idea how long they would keep doing this, but they were considering living outside the United States permanently in the future—something neither of them wanted to do.

Third, living in a homophobic and hostile environment causes some of the greatest stress for gay men and lesbians of any age. The controversy over gay marriage shows that many people oppose giving gay couples the same rights and recognition as heterosexual married couples. Older gay men and lesbians have suffered under this attitude for a lifetime. Self-help

groups, more research on gay and lesbian aging, and more societal acceptance will all lead to a better life for older gay men and lesbians in the future.

The double social stigma of being gay and being old increases the challenges that older gay men and lesbians face in later life. Essayist Tina Gianoulis (2004) writes, "If straight seniors must struggle against becoming invisible as they age, gay elders have been almost nonexistent in society's mirror."

Some writers believe that adaptation to living in a hostile society may improve the gay and lesbian person's ability to cope with aging. This can help them construct a positive image of themselves as they age (Jones & Nystrom, 2002). The MetLife American Society on Aging (2010; also MetLife, 2006b) study of LGBT older people supports this view. Three quarters of the people in the study said their sexual orientation helped prepare them for aging. And just over one quarter (29%) say that coping with discrimination in particular helped them prepare for aging. They said they "developed positive character traits, greater resilience, or better support networks as a consequence of being lesbian, gay, bisexual or transgender." More than one third of respondents (39%) said that their sexual orientation led to greater self-reliance.

Gays and lesbians also have experience in creating supportive relationships. This can help them create the support networks they need as they age. Many gays and lesbians have experience with political advocacy and will also be better able to defend their rights as they age. For example, some LGBTs have formed the Freedom to Marry Organization (2010). This group works "to end the exclusion of same-sex couples from the responsibilities, protections, and commitment of marriage." This activist experience can help aging gays and lesbians get the social supports they need in later life (Brotman, Ryan, & Cormier, 2002).

Research on gays and lesbians in later life has only begun. A number of research topics still need study. These include the longitudinal study of aging gay and lesbian couples, ethnic and cultural issues faced by gays and lesbians, gay widowhood, and the roles of aged gays and lesbians in their community. Researchers also need to study the relationships between gay older parents and their adult children and grandchildren.

Studies of gay and lesbian aging show that societal influences and past experiences shape a person's life in old age. They also show that sexuality plays an important part in gay and lesbian as well as heterosexual aging.

Some time ago Weg (1983b, p. 76) summarized the research on sexuality in later life:

There is no one way to love or to be loved; there is no one liaison that is superior to another. No one life-style in singlehood or marriage, heterosexual or homosexual, will suit all persons. Self-pleasuring, homosexuality, bisexuality, celibacy, and hetero-sexuality are all in the same human sexual reper-toire. . . . In a social climate that is more open and accepting, the reality of numbers is helping to return the "old" to the mainstream of living and sexuality to the elderly.

GRANDPARENTING

Francese (2009) estimates that the United States in 2009 had 70 million grandparents. He says that three in ten adults are grandparents—the highest proportion in history. Grandparents head 37% of U.S. households or 44 million households. People typically become grandparents in their 50s. And in 2009 more than half of grandparents (54%) were under age 65.

Most grandparents today work in the labor force and have good health. Francese says that grandparents today have disposable income and they spend some of this money on their grandchildren. "The grandparent population today," Francese says (2009, p. 4), "is larger, faster growing, better educated, more affluent and more economically active than any previous gen-eration of grandparents."

The number of grandparents in the population will increase as the Baby Boom ages. Uhlenberg (2009) estimates that by 2020 almost half of all 10-year-olds will have all grandparents alive. And 80% of those age 30 in 2020 will have at least one grandparent alive. Uhlenberg says that smaller family size today means fewer grandchildren per grandparent. For example, only 20% of grandparents will have more than two sets of grandchildren. This will allow grand-parents to invest more time and resources into a smaller pool of grandchildren.

Grandparents now play complex roles in the lives of their grandchildren. Some grandparents feel that they do enough by simply being present; others play a more active role as family arbitrators, watchdogs, or family historians. Grandparents often look out for the well-being of younger relatives, help them when they can, and create links between family members. The grandparent role offers older people one of the most satisfying and enjoyable ways to give to other family members.

Francese (2009), for example, estimates that grand-parents will spend $52 billion in 2009 on purchases for grandchildren. He estimates that in 2009 grandparents

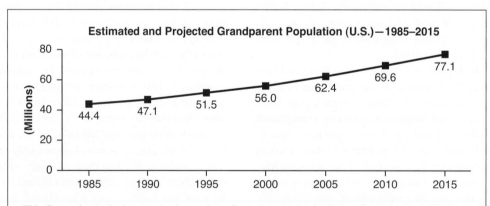

This figure shows the increase in the number of grandparents in the United States between 1985 and 2015 (estimated). The number almost doubles over the 30 years presented here.

What demographic forces account for this increase? Do you expect this trend to continue after 2015? What leads you to make this prediction?

FIGURE 12.5   Estimated and Projected Grandparent Population (U.S.)—1985–2015

Source: Adapted from Francese, P. (2009). *The grandparent economy. A study of the population, spending habits and economic impact of grandparents in the United States.* Figure 1, p. 4. Commissioned by Grandparents.com. Citing U.S. Census Bureau estimates & projections and 2004 Survey of Income & Program Participation. Retrieved November 12, 2010, from www. grandparents.com/binary-data/The-Grandparent-Economy-April-2009.pdf.

spent $32 billion on tuition and other educational expenses for grandchildren. A national survey of 1,077 grandparents in 2009 (MetLife, 2009) found that many grandparents set up college funds for grandchildren. Others help with tuition and loans.

Sandra Timmerman, Director of the MetLife Mature Market Institute, says, "Like grandparents in earlier generations, today's grandparents want to be involved in their grandchildren's lives. What may be different today is that grandparents are helping their children

and grandchildren to meet immediate financial needs." Grandparents have increased their support of grandchildren during the recent economic downturn. Many grandparents today would rather give direct support than save to leave a larger sum when they die.

The MetLife Mature Market Institute studied Asian Indian, Chinese, and African American grandparents (MetLife, 2010b). The study found that more than a quarter of the Asian Indian grandparents (28%) gave direct daily care to one or more grandchildren.

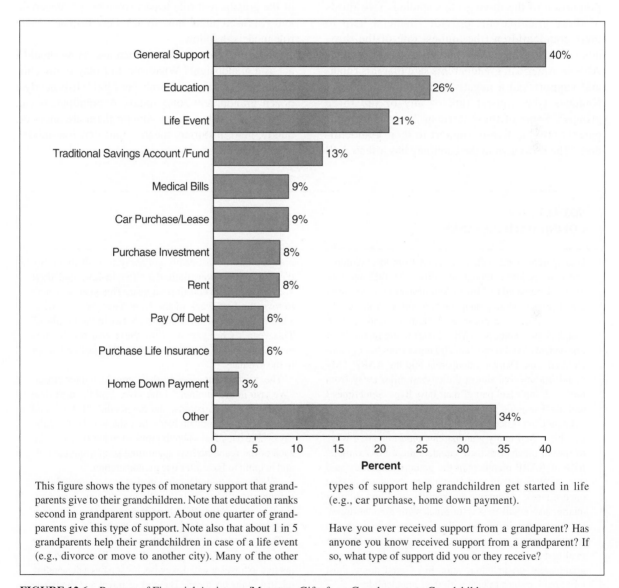

This figure shows the types of monetary support that grandparents give to their grandchildren. Note that education ranks second in grandparent support. About one quarter of grandparents give this type of support. Note also that about 1 in 5 grandparents help their grandchildren in case of a life event (e.g., divorce or move to another city). Many of the other types of support help grandchildren get started in life (e.g., car purchase, home down payment).

Have you ever received support from a grandparent? Has anyone you know received support from a grandparent? If so, what type of support did you or they receive?

FIGURE 12.6 Purpose of Financial Assistance/Monetary Gifts from Grandparents to Grandchildren

Source: MetLife. (2009). *2009 Grandparents: Generous with money, not with advice*. A MetLife QuickPOLL of American grandparents. MetLife Mature Market Institute. Retrieved November 12, 2010, from www.metlife.com/assets/cao/mmi/publications/quick-facts/mmi-grandparents-generous-money-not-advise.pdf. Reprinted with permission.

A similar proportion of the Chinese grandparents in this study reported caring for grandchildren. Both the Chinese and Asian Indian grandparents worked to instill cultural beliefs and the importance of their ancestry and heritage. About one third (31%) of the Asian Indian grandparents and 12% of the Chinese grandparents say they give financial help or money as gifts to grandchildren.

More than one third (36%) of African American grandparents in this study said they provide daily care for one or more grandchildren—the highest proportion of the three groups studied. Two thirds of these grandparents provide financial help to their grandchildren (the highest rate of the three ethnic/racial groups). About one third (32%) of the African American grandparents said that this financial support had a negative impact on their own finances (the highest rate of any of the three groups). Some of these African American grandparents provide live-in support to their grandchildren. The downturn in the economy has affected all of these groups and has forced some grandparents to cut back on support.

Not including grandparents who serve as surrogate parents, the grandparent role is an optional or open-ended role with few obligations or expectations attached. "Of all the roles in the nuclear and extended family," Westheimer and Kaplan (1998, p. 50) say, "none is as loosely defined as that of the grandparent. Fairy tales notwithstanding, no single dominant model exists of what a grandparent is supposed to do and how a grandparent is supposed to act." The openness of the grandparent role leaves some people uncertain and confused about how to act. Few Boomers have role models to follow.

Boomer grandparents may then ask: How should I act as a grandparent? What role do I play in my children's nuclear family? Kornhaber (2002) lists nearly a dozen grandparent roles today. A grandparent can play some or all of them. Among them are ancestor, buddy, hero, historian, mentor, nurturer, role model, spiritual guide, student, teacher, and wizard.

BOX 12.3
COPING WITH DISTANCE

Grandparents today often live apart from their children and grandchildren (though this differs by race and ethnicity). Compared to African American or other minority grandparents, white grandparents report a greater likelihood of living at a distance. A study of 1,500 AARP grandparent members (AARP, 2002) found that 45% of respondents lived more than 200 miles from their grandchildren. One Denver grandparent told the AARP, "My grandchildren live almost a thousand miles away from me. . . . I don't feel part of their busy lives. Sometimes I feel like I struggle just to be noticed."

Grandparents need to work at these long-distance relationships. And many grandparents report creative ways to stay in touch with their grandchildren. For example, 65% of AARP members in the grandparent study said they speak with their grandchildren on the phone at least once a week. A quarter use regular mail and another quarter use email to stay in touch with grandchildren. Improvements in phone and computer services make regular contact easier and relatively low cost. But the mail and media can only go so far in building a strong grandparent–grandchild relationship. Grandparents must take creative steps to visit with their grandchildren.

Wade Alister and his wife have a son who conducts genetic research on the East Coast. They live in California. Their son can't easily get away to visit them. So, they visit their son, their daughter-in-law, and their granddaughter several times a year. This year they plan to visit the first week of the New Year. Wade's wife, Julie, says, "We share Christmas between the families." This year it's her parents' turn. Next year the Alisters host Christmas in California. They all adjust and adapt to the distance.

The Alisters miss having their granddaughter closer. "We visit in the summer," Julie says, "and the next time we see her, at Christmas, she has teeth." "I did spend time with our granddaughter when she was born," Julie says. "The baby had a health problem in her first year. So each of the grandmothers spent time supporting the kids and helping to look after our granddaughter."

"We have a 'grandparent kit' that grandparents in our neighborhood share," Julie tells me. "It has a car seat, stroller, the works. We share it around among grandmothers in our neighborhood when the kids visit."

These grandparents all face the same issue. Families live scattered and busy lives today. Wade still works, so he's not free to travel at will. Likewise, his son has a demanding job that limits his travel. The cost of travel and the hassle with small children also make long-distance visits a challenge. Everyone adjusts to the demands of distance.

This last role may surprise you. Kornhaber says that societies in the past have often ascribed magical powers to elders. A modern grandparent can draw on this role to engage grandchildren in fantasy play. Kornhaber cites the case of a little girl who had an imaginary friend. Her grandparents set a place at the table for this friend when their granddaughter came to visit.

Grandparents can introduce grandchildren to the wonders of the natural world by taking hikes or camping in natural surroundings. They can pretend they are in some exotic location. Grandparents can have fun and don't have to abide by the rational rules that parents sometimes need to enforce. One 14-year-old grandchild told researchers, "Whenever I would sleep over at my grandparent's house they had this huge book of bedtime stories. So they always used to read that. It was cool!" (AARP, 2006a).

One grandfather said that if his grandson has a problem, "He'll come over to see me. . . . And if I need some help, like getting some screens down . . . for the summer, I'll get him to help me" (Cherlin & Furstenberg, 1985, p. 108). These findings suggest that grandparents and grandchildren can provide support and enjoyment for one another.

The Grandparent–Grandchild Relationship

Sanders and Trygstad (1993) studied the attitudes of college students toward their grandparents. They found that only about one quarter of the students saw their grandparents monthly or more. But the students considered their relationships with their grandparents important. They saw this relationship as a sign of family strength.

In another study, college students said they saw their grandparents (or significant elders) as parent surrogates, buddies, storytellers, and confidants (Franks, Hughes, Phelps, & Williams, 1993). A young man says about his grandmother, "It is great to be able to go round and complain about home or about dad being ridiculous or whatever. She will always be lovely and agree how stupid he is" (Jerrome, 1996, p. 91). Many students said that a grandparent babysat for them or cared for them in their youth. Most of these students said their grandparents had a strong influence on their values, goals, and choices in life. The students also felt that their grandparents created a link between the generations in their families. This gave students a sense of their history and roots.

Boon and Shaw (2007) studied grandchildren's feelings toward their grandparents. They found that grandchildren feel respect for their grandparents. They admire their strength and resilience in surviving the hardships and struggles of their younger years. Grandchildren also worry about the present-day health challenges their grandparents face. Novelli and Workman (2006, p. 69) say grandparents can serve as role models and mentors. "There's not much kids can't learn from grandparents," they say, "including strong moral values. Grandchildren will be the first to agree. They say their grandparents have taught them good manners, respect for others, and a strong work ethic."

Studies show that grandparents also learn from their grandchildren. Grandchildren can keep grandparents up to date on the latest films, music, and technologies. Grandchildren can also influence their grandparents' views on social issues, dress, and education (Kemp, 2004). Hagestad (1985, p. 41) calls this "reversed socialization."

Here a grandfather and grandson work together painting the family's summer cottage.

Grandparents and grandchildren can also travel together. For example, Road Scholar offers a number of vacations for grandparents and grandchildren. Short trips in the United States can cost less than $500 per person. A company called Grandtravel, in Washington, DC, offers vacation tours to exotic locations. First-class tours with unique activities can cost more than $5,000 per week per person. The Travel Industry Association of America reports that 30% of U.S. grandparents who travel for leisure have taken at least one vacation with their grandchildren (O'Brien, 2010). Travel creates special memories and encourages bonding between the generations.

Studies show that children's feelings about their grandparents depend, in part, on the relationship between the grandparents and the parents (Monserud, 2008). The closer the relationship between the parent and grandparent, the closer the tie between grandparents and grandchildren. The quality of the grandparents' relationship with their children-in-law may be of particular importance in influencing the quality of the grandparent–grandchild tie (Fingerman, 2004).

Holladay and colleagues (1997), for example, found that parental attitudes influenced teenaged granddaughters' feelings of closeness to their grandmothers. An absence of criticism of the grandmother by the parent and parents' comments on the importance of the grandmother led to greater feelings of closeness. Older grandchildren have closer ties with their grandparents if they see the relationship between their parents and grandparents as close.

Some researchers say that the importance of grandfathers has been underestimated (Mann, 2007). Roberto, Allen, and Blieszner (2001) studied male views of grandparenting. Some men in that study felt that grandfathers should take a "hands off" approach to caring for or disciplining their grandchildren. But other grandfathers felt that they should play an active role in the lives of grandchildren. "[These grandfathers] revealed that it is not enough to just *be* a grandfather; one must also *do*, in an active and involved way" (Roberto et al., 2001, p. 422).

Some researchers believe that "new norms of grandfatherhood" exist that focus on nurturing and mentoring (Mann, 2007). In general, research shows that although the bond between adult grandchildren and their grandparents remains high across the life course, the relationship involves continuity and change over time. Mills (1999) finds that as grandchildren age, they grow closer to grandmothers but less close to grandfathers.

Other research suggests that a gradual decline takes place in the relationship over time, with some increased closeness in the grandparents' later years (Silverstein & Long, 1998). Hodgson (1995) finds that grandchildren feel a continued closeness to grandparents over time, with some grandchildren reporting an increased appreciation for their grandparents as they themselves age. The literature shows that the grandparent role allows room for personal expression and that older people can use it as a source of emotional satisfaction.

Gender can also influence the quality of grandparent–grandchild relationships. For example, grandchildren tend to be closer to their maternal grandparents (Chan & Elder, 2000). The paternal grandfather will have the most distant relationship. Grandparents are closer to granddaughters than to grandsons. And grandmothers have closer and more active ties with both granddaughters and grandsons than do grandfathers (Silverstein & Long, 1998).

What a grandparent makes of the grandparent role also depends on the older person's gender, age, marital status, and relationship with his or her adult children.

Research by Kemp (2004) looks at the expectations grandparents and grandchildren have of themselves and each other within what she terms "grand" roles. She finds that although the roles and relationships are diverse, grandparents and grandchildren do have expectations related to behaviors and responsibilities within the relationship. For example, both grandparents and grandchildren feel that grandparents should provide love, support, encouragement, and assistance to grandchildren, but should not interfere in their lives unless asked for help or advice.

As one grandmother says, "I think being a grandparent is to listen and not to criticize" (Kemp, 2004, p. 11). A granddaughter says, "Grandparents are just supposed to be there when you need them and they always are. . . . They don't give advice unless you ask for it" (Kemp, 2004, p. 15). Grandparents were also seen as role models, teachers, and sources of family history and lived experience. Henderson (2001) studied grandparenting when adult children have divorced. He found that in the case of a divorce, attention from maternal grandmothers protects grandchildren from some of the negative effects of divorce. Stronger attachment to a maternal grandmother predicted better interpersonal competence and greater self-efficacy.

Grandchildren felt they should be respectful to grandparents and should give them their time and attention. They felt an obligation to give back to grandparents for all the love and support grandparents had given to the family. This came in the form of spending time with grandparents and doing things to make grandparents proud of their accomplishments. Grandparents also hoped that their grandchildren would spend time with them and be an important part of their lives.

Grandparents report feeling pride in their grandchildren, care and concern for their well-being, and a sense of continuity as they see their own values and purpose stretch into the future. Because grandparents don't have parenting responsibilities, they show a tolerance of grandchildren's actions.

The literature shows that the grandparent's role allows room for personal expression and that older people can use it as a source of emotional satisfaction. For both generations the tie is seen as "an unconditional latent reserve of support" or a "safety net" of support, should it be needed (Kemp, 2005, p. 173).

Grandparenting and New Family Structures

High divorce rates among children lead to new relationships for older people. A grandmother, for example, may stay in touch with her former daughter-in-law after her son's divorce in order to keep in contact with her grandchildren. She may even develop a close personal friendship with her former daughter-in-law. If her former daughter-in-law remarries, she may meet and get to know a new family of grandparents and children from this new marriage. This will expand her kinship and social network.

Grandparents may include step-grandchildren in their list of grandchildren. Some older people manage a complex system of relationships due to the marriage and remarriage of their children. These complexities increase as children marry and divorce, sometimes more than once.

Today we have nuclear, extended, blended, lesbian and gay families, as well as broken families. My wife and I recently attended a dinner at a friend's home. Our friend arranged the dinner to introduce us to his son and daughter-in-law, who were visiting from out of town. The young couple had six parents around the table. The son's two parents, the daughter-in-law's mother with her second husband, and the daughter-in-law's father with his male partner. A grandchild in this family will have six doting grandparents: one set in a long-term traditional marriage, a second set in a second marriage, and a third set in a gay relationship.

Things get more complicated if both parents in a second marriage have grandchildren—from children in former marriages and from their own marriage.

Likewise, if any of these children divorce and remarry, they may have children from more than one marriage. How will the parents relate to this collection of grandchildren—some distant in relation to them and some very close? Many older people will find themselves in these complex family structures. No rulebook exists to help sort out the right way to grandparent under these conditions.

Grandparent Visitation Rights

Grandparents' relationships with their grandchildren reflect their schedules, lifestyles, and interests. But grandparents must negotiate their relations with grandchildren through the child's parents. And parents may put boundaries on this relationship.

Gladstone (1987) studied 110 grandparents of families in which the parents had divorced or separated. He found that adult children can arrange or obstruct grandparents' visits. If the grandparents' former son- or daughter-in-law had custody, contact with grandchildren depended on the grandparent's relationship to the former son- or daughter-in-law. The issue of a grandparent's right to visit a grandchild has grown in importance with increases in the divorce rate.

Hilton and Macari (1997) found that, compared to paternal grandparents, maternal grandparents stay more involved in the grandparent role when their daughter gains custody of the children. The reverse takes place when a son gains custody of his children. Kruk (1995) found that denial of access by a son- or daughter-in-law, in the case of divorce, accounted for most cases of contact loss.

In the past, all 50 states (not including the District of Columbia) had some grandparent visitation statute. Advocacy groups helped set these in place. But the courts in many states have struck down these statutes (AARP, 2005c). In 2000, for example, the U.S. Supreme Court, in the case of *Troxel v. Granville*, overruled a Washington state statute that permitted grandparent visitation. The Supreme Court held that "fit parents" presumably act in the best interest of their children. The Court stated that the state should not interfere with "the private realm of the family." In states where permissive visitation statues exist, a grandparent can petition the courts for visitation rights. The statutes state under what conditions a grandparent can petition and how the courts should decide on granting rights.

But these statutes do not ensure that the court will grant this right. The court attempts to assess the child's best interest in deciding on visitation rights. And clear

"It's your grandparents, claiming their visitation rights."

legal guidelines do not exist on how to determine the child's best interests. States often allow petitions only in cases of divorce or death of a parent or if the child has lived with the grandparent for some time. The state court may require that grandparents show that harm will occur to the child if they do not get visitation rights.

Fernandez (1988) says that state statutes make vague statements that do not help judges make decisions. She proposes a model statute that assumes the autonomy of the nuclear family. It allows access only when access maintains a relationship that benefits the child. Fernandez proposes that a "substantial" relationship must exist between the child and grandparent as the basis for visitation. Court-ordered grandparent visitation risks constitutional infringement on the rights of parents to control access to a child. The U.S. Supreme Court holds

this view. Grandparents who go to court risk increasing the tension with the son- or daughter-in-law.

Today, grandparents have to show the courts why they should have access to their grandchildren. They also have to show that denying access would be harmful to grandchildren (Goldberg, 2003). Given the constitutional right of parents to control access to their children, it seems unlikely that grandparents will get any guaranteed visitation rights.

Advisors on this subject say that grandparents should maintain good relations with their son- or daughter-in-law in the case of a divorce. This provides the simplest means of access to grandchildren. The son- or daughter-in-law may fear that the grandparent will try to turn the child against the parent. A trusting relationship between the grandparent and the adult child can remove this fear. The AARP (2005c) says that a grandparent can use a trained mediator to improve a relationship between the grandparent and the grandchild's parent. This can sometimes resolve the issue without involving lawyers and the courts.

Grandparents as Surrogate Parents

Johnson and Schaner (2005a) report that almost 25% of people age 55 and over care for a grandchild. They provide supports that range from child-sitting in the afternoons and weekends to serving as legal guardians. Some older parents provide daily and lifelong care to children with disabilities (Joffres, 2002). Johnson and Schaner say that in the years between 1970 and 2003, grandparent care increased by 73%.

The U.S. Census (2009) reports that 6% of all children in the United States lived with a grandparent in the grandparent's home in 2009. More than 2.5 million grandparents say they provide basic support—food, clothing, and shelter—for the grandchildren who live with them. Two thirds of these grandparents work outside the home. Johnson and Schaner (2005b) estimate that unpaid grandparent care for grandchildren, if paid for, would have totaled $39 billion per year in 2002.

Skip-generation families (a grandparent and grandchild with no middle generation present) made up 6% of all multigenerational households in 2008. Skip-generation households made up 7% of white, 4% of Latino, and 1% of Asian American multigeneration households. Skip generation households made up 13% of African American multigeneration households—the highest rate among ethnic and racial groups.

Grandparents often care for their grandchildren because their own children cannot provide the care. This can occur because of divorce or separation, mental health difficulties, substance abuse, or the death of an adult child. Caring for a grandchild full time can create a close emotional bond, particularly for grandmothers (Bowers & Myers, 1999). Caregiving grandparents most often reported the rewards of caregiving if they felt a strong family bond and obligation to give care (Giarrusso, Silverstein, & Feng, 2000).

But grandparents in households where they care for a grandchild also face challenges (Pew Research Center, 2010). These can include worries about their own health, problems with social isolation, and financial difficulties (Sands & Goldberg-Glen, 2000). At a time of life when older people expect more freedom, these grandparents take on unexpected child-care responsibilities. And often they do this with high-risk grandchildren.

Minkler and Roe (1993, p. 83) studied African American grandmothers of crack cocaine–addicted children in Oakland, California. The researchers found that these grandmothers faced financial strain. Eighty-seven percent of the grandparents reported "significant financial difficulty since assuming full-time caregiving." One woman said, "We were doing so well before—now it's a disaster!"

Johnson (1992) says that in the case of divorce, a child (often a daughter) may return to her parents' home with her own children. Almost 40% of divorced children showed a pattern of return to parents' support. Grandparents in these cases will find themselves actively supporting two younger generations. Johnson found that about 75% of parents of divorced children provided them with financial aid. Almost 60% of the divorced children depended on their parents for their well-being. In these cases, the grandparents got involved in the day-to-day lives of their divorced children and grandchildren. Grandparents accepted the role, but often felt angry about this new responsibility.

Dolbin-McNabb (2006) says that skipped generation grandparents could benefit from parent education and training. This would build on their parenting experiences. But it would also help grandparents deal with the challenges of parenting grandchildren. Support groups, peer counseling, and respite services would also buffer grandparents' stress.

Many studies report the financial, emotional, and physical stresses that grandparents face when they care for a grandchild. Giarrusso and colleagues (2000, p. 88) call for a balanced view of the stresses and rewards of this role. They write, "Attention to only the stressful and obligatory nature of grandparent caregiving may mask the full social and psychological range of the experience and deny the underlying value and meaning that grandparents often attribute to this important societal role."

THE FUTURE OF THE FAMILY

Studies in the past looked at families with a husband, wife, and children from one marriage. Studies of widowhood, for example, generally refer to loss of a lifelong mate. But changes in the family today will change family life for older people in the years ahead.

An increase in studies of aging in alternative relationships will give a more varied picture of aging. Researchers need to do more studies of gay, lesbian, bisexual, and transsexual older people, of never-married older people, and of unmarried men.

People who enter old age today will bring with them more open attitudes toward sex. And these attitudes will shape their behavior in later life. Researchers need to look at changes in attitudes toward sexuality and the sexual behavior of new cohorts of older people.

Research on older people's family life has almost ignored the lives of certain types of people. Little research has been done on never-married older people (Baumbusch, 2004; Pudrovska, Schieman, & Carr, 2006), divorced older people (Lin, 2008; Wu & Schimmele, 2007), or the childless elderly (Dykstra & Hagestad, 2007). We also know little about gender differences in the social support needs of different marital status groups, including those who remarry in later life (Wister & Dykstra, 2000). Further research should also look at the social support needs and experiences of older LGBT couples and individuals (Connidis, 2003).

Few studies have compared family and social relations in different ethnic and racial groups. Researchers need to study cultural and social class differences that lead to unique social relationships. Researchers need to look more closely at minority family relations in later life. Some of this work has begun, for example, in the study of surrogate parenting in African American families. But researchers need to tease out the roles that cultural values and necessity play in these adaptations.

Studies of fictive kin and play siblings, for example, give insights into alternative cultural adaptations. The terms *fictive kin* and *play relatives* (a term used by older people themselves) refer to nonrelatives whom the older person thinks of as family. A study of 122 African Americans age 85 and over in Oakland, California, for example, found that 45% of the sample had fictive kin. And 80% of these people said they enjoyed these relationships (Johnson, 1999).

More studies need to look at male relationships in later life. Few studies exist on male friendships, male approaches to coping with widowhood, or grandfathers. More research needs to look at the stresses married people face in later life.

Longer life expectancy will also lead to relationships across more generations. Kornhaber (2002, p. 105) states, "Some great-grandparents do things they never dreamed of doing even when they were grandparents—and with flair. This attitude may indicate the emergence of a new characteristic in members of this generation who are surprised to find themselves so healthy at such advanced ages."

New patterns of family life have begun to emerge: gay relationships, serial monogamy (multiple marriages in a lifetime), widowhood, and remarriage. These all lead to more complex family structures in later life (Putney, Bengtson, & Wakeman, 2007). Grandparents will have grandchildren from several marriages of their children. They will have multiple in-laws from these marriages. Their grandchildren may in turn have several marriages. Older people themselves may have children, grandchildren, and great-grandchildren from their own multiple marriages. This will create a rich, complex, and uncertain family structure. We don't even have names for many of these relationships.

Will family (blood) bonds hold families together in the future? Or will people choose as relatives the people they like best? Will people invent new family structures to suit their needs? Or will people try to maintain traditional family structures? The changing family today will challenge all of us to rethink family relations.

CONCLUSION

A belief existed for many years that families in America abandon their older people. This myth included the idea that older people lived lonely, isolated lives. Research over the past several decades exploded this myth. We now know that most older people remain engaged in family life. They get support from their spouses, children, siblings, and members of their extended family. They also give support to family members. Sometimes they give more support than they receive.

Research also shows that older people play new roles in their families. For example, they sometimes care for grandchildren in skipped-generation families. They may also play a role in the lives of their grandchildren even if they live at a distance. New technologies—including low-cost long-distance phone calling—break down the barrier of distance. Computer technologies go even further in breaking down barriers. Systems like Skype allow for free or inexpensive face-to-face visits. Video games online allow grandparents and grandchildren to interact as if they lived in the same household.

Baby Boomers will bring new approaches to family life as they age. Some people will have children from more than one marriage. Others will come into old age childless. Gay individuals and couples will create new family relationships. Online dating and matchmaking systems create new opportunities for people to meet and bond. And Boomers' more liberal attitudes toward sex will overthrow the stereotype of the sexless older person.

Research today and in the future will teach us more about family life in an aging society. One thing seems certain: family will continue to evolve. It will take on new forms and will create new opportunities for relationships in later life.

SUMMARY

- Age-graded normative life events take place at expected times in a person's life. These events define a person's position in society. Expectable (normative) events, such as marriage or widowhood, often lead to a passage from one social role to another.

- The proportion of people married at a given age diminishes from middle age onward. Divorce accounts for only a small proportion of this decrease. Widowhood explains most of the reduction. Women, compared with men, have a greater chance of living as widows. Most men will live with spouses throughout their lives. Most women will live many years as widows.

- The advantages to marriage in later life include (1) a greater combined income and the benefits of sharing expenses, (2) greater life satisfaction, and (3) better adjustment to aging. The disadvantages of marriage in later life include the possibilities that (1) interests may diverge, (2) a relationship may suffer during a role change like retirement, and (3) ill health may strain a relationship.

- Relationships in later life can take forms other than a single lifetime of marriage. Alternatives include remarriage, common-law marriage, and cohabitation. Widowhood, divorce, and lifelong singlehood lead some older people to live a singles life.

- Women more than men risk widowhood as they age. Three major factors account for this: (1) women tend to marry older men, (2) women have a longer life expectancy than men, and (3) men tend to remarry after the loss of a spouse. Researchers call widowhood an expectable life event for older women.

- Men face some of the most difficulty in coping with widowhood. Widowhood often breaks their links to social networks. Compared to women, men tend to remarry after widowhood. Remarried people expressed satisfaction with their new spouses. Couples most often reported that they remarried for companionship and a strong need to love and be loved.

- People report an interest in sex into late old age. Substantial proportions of people remain sexually active until at least their 80s. Any decline in interest takes place gradually over many years. Studies show that the best predictor of a good sex life in old age is a good sex life in one's younger years.

- Most illnesses do not decrease sexual activity or enjoyment. Research shows that good eating habits, weight control, limiting alcohol, and an active sex life all enhance and prolong sexual activity.

- Gay and lesbian (LGBT) older people report unique relationships in later life and unique challenges as they age. Many LGBT elders have long-term relationships. The lack of legal sanction for gay marriage creates many challenges and hardships for LGBT older people.

- More older people will experience the grandparent role than ever before. Grandparents can shape this role to suit their lifestyle and interests. Grandchildren appreciate their grandparents and enjoy this special relationship. Grandparents have the best chance of a strong relationship with their grandchildren if they have good relations with their adult children. Some grandparents take on the role of surrogate parent. This creates unexpected stress late in life. But it can also lead to personal satisfaction.

- New patterns of family life have begun to emerge. Gay and lesbian relationships, divorce, and remarriage can lead to more complex family structures in later life. The older generation may have children, grandchildren, and great-grandchildren from their own and their children's multiple marriages. Changes in family life today will change family life for older people in the years ahead.

DISCUSSION QUESTIONS

1. Define the term *age-graded normative life event* and give several examples of this type of event.
2. Why does the proportion of married people decrease after middle age? How does the proportion of married people differ for men and women?
3. State the advantages and disadvantages to marriage in later life.
4. List the three major factors that account for the high rate of widowhood among women. Compare and contrast the different responses of men and women to widowhood.
5. In general, why do older people remarry? What do they report about their experience of remarriage?
6. What have researchers found out about older people's interest in sex?
7. What can older people do to improve their sex lives?
8. What unique issues do older LGBT individuals and couples face?
9. What models of grandparenting do researchers report? How do grandparenting styles change with age? What are the benefits that grandparents and grandchildren get from their relationships?

SUGGESTED READING

Caputo, R. K. (2005). *Challenges of aging on U.S. families.* Binghamton, NY: Haworth Press.

This collection looks at changing family structures in the United States. It describes the caregiving challenges faced by different family members, including grandparent caregivers. The text also reviews the economic impact of aging on families.

Kornhaber, A. (2002). *The grandparent guide.* Chicago: Contemporary Books.

The author charts the world of grandparenting today. He discusses the many roles that grandparents can and do play. He also describes the challenges grandparents face: grandparenting at a distance, keeping out of child-rearing disputes, and how to make the most out of a visit with a grandchild. Kornhaber also provides practical advice at the end of each chapter. Among his creative ideas: Build a memory chest. Create a container where grandparents can place objects of special meaning from the grandparent's and grandchild's experience.

Websites to Consult
AARP Friends and Family

www.aarp.org/relationships/friends-family

This site provides stories and information on a variety of relationship themes in later life. Topics include ways to stay active with grandchildren, how to make new friends, how to enjoy your role as an elder aunt or uncle. A lively site that changes often and provides insight into the latest topics of interest to older adults.

Legacy Project

www.legacyproject.org

This site supports linkages between the generations. It includes information on a program called "Across Generations." This program encourages closer connections between the young and the old. It includes activities, guides and workshops to support this goal.

State Fact Sheets for Grandparents and Other Relatives Raising Children

www.grandfactsheets.org/state_fact_sheets.cfm

This site provides data and information for grandparents who raise grandchildren. You can click on a particular state for information on that location. The sites include information on public policies, census data on grandparents who raise grandchildren, and a list of national programs and organizations. The sheet exists in English and Spanish.

chapter 13

SOCIAL SUPPORT

Glenda and Al care for Al's father, Mr. Simkin. Mr. Simkin has lived with them for the past 3 years since his wife died. Recently, Mr. Simkin's ability to care for himself has declined. He now relies on Glenda and Al for personal care like bathing and toileting. For the past 6 months, they have felt the strain.

For example, they can no longer leave Mr. Simkin alone. Al says they feel tied down, "like a mother to a baby." Glenda says they have begun to argue over Mr. Simkin's care and "we share a feeling of frustration because we can't escape from caregiving." Some nights Glenda sleeps on a mat on the floor in Mr. Simkin's room. She does this so she can get him water or help him to the bathroom in the middle of the night. Lately, she's begun to lose

patience with Mr. Simkin. Once she screamed, "I want a divorce from you, Pop."

Caregiving can put a strain on the caregiver and on family life. But Glenda will tell you that she loves Mr. Simkin, and she wants to care for him at home until he dies. Today, family members, like Glenda and Al, provide most of the support that older people get. Families provide income support, emotional support, social integration, and health care. The family also provides a network of social contacts that enhance the older person's self-image and sense of well-being.

Zunzunegui and colleagues (Zunzunegui, Alvarado, Del Ser, & Otero, 2003) found, for example, that the more relatives an older person saw each month, the better his or her mental functioning. They also found better mental functioning among older people who met with friends or relatives face to face.

This chapter examines two topics related to social support: (1) informal support given to older people from family members and friends, including the task of caregiving; and (2) elder abuse—the opposite of social support.

WHAT IS INFORMAL SOCIAL SUPPORT?

Social support refers to help and assistance we give to and receive from others. Gerontologists refer to the amount of resources available to a person, including social support, as their "life course capital" or "social capital" (O'Rand, 2006; Moren-Cross & Lin, 2006). The amount of **social capital** available to a person changes over time and differs for each individual.

In later life, for example, older people benefit from the support they get from family members and friends. This support takes the form of emotional support, companionship, help with household chores, and a range of other help.

But older family members also give help to others through financial support and help with child care. A survey of grandparents in 2009 (MetLife, 2009), for example, found that two thirds of grandparents had provided financial support to grandchildren in the past 5 years. One quarter of the grandparents in the survey say the economic downturn has caused them to increase the help they give to their grandchildren.

Older parents may also provide a home for unmarried, divorced, or unemployed adult children. In this way they provide "capital" or resources to their children (Putney, Bengtson, & Wakeman, 2007). For example, research shows that economic support most often flows from the older to the younger generation (Silverstein, 2006). And child-care support provided by older people to their grandchildren increases their children's economic status.

Family Life and Family Supports

Over the past 150 years, the family has changed in size and structure in the United States. In the past, one child, a "parent keeper," often stayed at home to look after aging parents (Hareven, 1992, p. 10). Hareven says that family members spent more time together and helped one another more. Even in the early years of industrialization, families often lived in multigenerational households.

Today, the family has gotten smaller as parents have fewer children, and children often move long distances from their parents in order to find or keep jobs. Even when parents and children live near one another, they rarely live in the same household. These and other changes in the family have led some writers to assume that families no longer support their older members. Frequent moves and the fast pace of modern life make it seem as if the family has abandoned its older members.

But studies in the United States find that families still provide most of the support for older people. Families help older members in times of illness, they exchange services with older members, and they often visit older relatives. Many adult children live within a short drive of their parents. Older people also keep in contact with family members through letters and by telephone. And now families keep in touch through the Internet.

Health care professionals and social services take on many jobs the family did in the past, but children often help their parents get access to these services (Neuharth & Stern, 2000). Children also monitor their parents' well-being and need for more help. Grandchildren may help a grandparent with household chores.

Summing up the research on family support based on a study of three generations, Brody (1995, p. 20) wrote, "Values about family care of elderly adults have not eroded despite demographic and socioeconomic changes. The old values were holding very firm indeed." And Shanas (1979), in a classic comment, called the idea of family breakdown a "hydra-headed myth." She said the myth persists, but the evidence doesn't support this view.

Informal Supports for Older People

Rosalynn Carter, former first lady, says, "There are four kinds of people in the world: those who have been caregivers; those who currently are caregivers; those who will be caregivers; and those who will need caregivers" (cited in Novelli & Workman, 2006, p. 74). Most of us will fill all of these roles, whether as caregivers to our children or to our parents or as people in need of care ourselves. Caregiving will create one of the challenges for children of aging parents in the future. *Formal support* refers to paid help from professional caregivers such as doctors, nurses, and social workers. *Informal support* refers to unpaid help given by friends, neighbors, and family. Informal support takes many forms, including advice, affection, companionship, helping older family members with transportation, and nursing care.

Bengtson (2001) estimates that almost 80% of informal care given to older people comes from family members. Gibson and Houser (2007) say that informal supports from family and friends came to an estimated $350 billion in 2006. To put this in perspective, this comes to the same amount as total Medicare payments in 2005 and more than four times the money spent on formal paid home care. The researchers estimate that about 34 million people age 18 and over provided informal care to older people with activity of daily living (ADL) limitations.

The researchers present a profile of the typical informal caregiver: a woman, 46 years old, works outside the home, and provides more than 20 hours per week of informal unpaid care.

Studies find that few older people who need help with daily chores or health care use only formal care. More often, people use both the formal and informal support systems (Penning, 2002; Spillman & Pezzin, 2000). Keating and colleagues (Keating, Fast, Connidis, Penning, & Keefe, 1997, p. 24) call this a "caring partnership." They say that social policies now favor this mix of informal and formal care. Bookman and Harrington (2007, p. 1005, cited in Gonyea, 2009) put this more bluntly. They say that family caregivers act as "geriatric case managers, medical record keepers, paramedics, and patient advocates to fill dangerous gaps in a system that is uncoordinated, fragmented, bureaucratic, and often depersonalizing."

Studies show that people usually turn to the formal system only after the informal system no longer meets their needs.

Four Models of Informal Support

Four models describe the roles of informal supporters:

1. The **task specificity model** says that various groups (spouse, child, neighbor) have different abilities and different resources to offer the older person (Litwak, 1985). Each group has a specific role to play in the older person's support system.
2. The **hierarchical compensatory model** says that supporters come first from the older person's inner family circle. Older people then move outward to get support from less intimate people as they need more help (Cantor & Little, 1985). This model says that married older people turn to a spouse first, then to a child (usually a daughter), then to a daughter-in-law (Putney et al.,

2007). Older people turn to friends, neighbors, and formal supports (in that order) if they still have unmet needs.
3. The **functional specificity of relationships model** (Simons, 1983–84) recognizes that "one tie may provide one type of support or a broad range of support, dependent on how that particular relationship has been negotiated" over the life course (Campbell, Connidis, & Davies, 1999, p. 118). For example, the gender, marital status, parenthood, and proximity of helpers all influence the amount and type of support a person will get.
4. The **convoy model of support** (Antonucci, Birditt, & Akiyama, 2009) sees people as having a dynamic network of close ties with family and friends. This model uses concentric circles to describe relationships around the older individual, with the strongest relationships in the closest circle. Outer circles show weaker relationships (Haines & Henderson, 2002). These relationships form a convoy that travels with individuals throughout life, exchanging social support and assistance. The relationships of people in this convoy grow and change with changing life circumstances.

Powers and Kivett (1992) found some support for the hierarchical compensatory model in a study of rural older adults. They discovered that older people expected more help from closer relatives and less help from more distant relations. They found less support for the task specificity model. Older people in this study expected all family members to visit and help during an illness.

Penning (1990) studied informal supports of people age 60 and over. She found that different groups of supporters did different tasks (supporting the task specificity model). But she found little support for the hierarchical compensatory model. People in this study used a variety of formal and informal supports at the same time.

Luckey (1994) studied African American elders' support networks. She found little support for the hierarchical compensatory model. Instead, she reports that African American elders drew on a broad range of kin for support. Their support systems included second and third generations of nieces, nephews, and grandchildren. These relatives provided a broad range of supports that complemented formal supports.

Feld and colleagues (2004) found similar results from a study of married white, African American, and Mexican American people age 70 and over. Results of the study showed that, compared to whites, African American older people had wider informal care networks. Compared to whites, they tended to get informal help from supporters other than their spouse.

Few studies have found strong support for the hierarchical compensatory model. This model may present too rigid a picture of the give and take of family life. It also fails to account for aging under different socioeconomic conditions. Low-income African American elders, for example, may lack the money to pay for a full hierarchy of supports. They also use substitute kin (e.g., nieces and nephews) to fill in for a missing spouse or children. This pattern differs from support system use among whites.

Campbell and colleagues (1999, p. 144) found support for the functional specificity of relationships model. They found that siblings provide a range of social support for certain groups, including single women, the childless, single men, and widowed women. However, siblings provide little support for divorced and married men. In general, siblings give support when they live nearby. Brothers and sisters also tend to serve as companions and confidants, and they more often provide practical support to sisters than to brothers. These findings show that particular groups of older adults develop supportive ties with siblings, "not as substitution or compensation for lost ties but based on a lifetime of negotiating unique ties with siblings."

Antonucci and colleagues (2009) report on the importance of social convoys for an older person's health. They say that among older men with less education, those who had larger social networks, reported higher-than-expected rates of good health. "Social relations," Antonucci and her colleagues say, "may provide a form of protection against the increased health risks common in this group" (p. 253). Convoys can provide a person with help when needed, affection and emotional support, and support for one's identity.

Sims-Gould and Martin-Matthews (2007) found support for the convoy model in a Canadian national study of caregivers. They found that older people often had a team of relatives and friends who supported them. Spouses and siblings often served as direct helpers to the older person. But adult children, other family members, and friends offered assistance as well. These helpers provided a web of support to their older relative or friend.

Putney and colleagues (2007) point to the rich resources that exist within a family structure. They refer to early work by Riley and Riley (1993; also Silverstein & Bengtson, 1997) who described a "latent-kin matrix." This refers to a family network that remains dormant until a need arises for support from a member. This network includes kin, ex-kin, and fictive kin (nonrelatives who can serve as supporters).

Haines and Henderson (2002) assessed the convoy model of social support. They found that although the model helps to identify supportive relationships, not all strong ties provide support. Weak ties, typically ignored in the convoy model of support, provide instrumental support, emotional support, and companionship.

The Role of Formal Supports

Older people also use formal supports along with informal supports. They do this for at least two reasons. First, an older person may have an incomplete informal network and need specific kinds of help (e.g., someone to do the shopping). Second, some older people who have intact networks have high health care needs. For example, caregivers who care for older family members with dementia use more in-home services than other caregivers (Hawranik, 2002). The informal and formal systems work together in these cases to share the overall load.

Ward-Griffin (2002; also Duner & Nordstrom, 2007) found that both formal and informal care providers perform physical and emotional care work. Formal care providers, specifically nurses in this study, have professional knowledge and skills that differentiate them from family care providers. However, as Ward-Griffin says, the boundary between professional and family caregivers blurs when family members develop caregiving skills and knowledge.

Other research findings add another dimension to this complexity. Living arrangements influence the type of supports older people use. For example, an older person who lives with someone will likely get support for ADL from that person. Shared living arrangements (between siblings or with friends) can help widowed or childless older people live in the community. Strain and Blandford (2003) find that caregivers who live with an older parent provide daily help with meal preparation and household chores.

A study of older adults ages 65 to 94 in rural Virginia found that living arrangements influenced the type of support older people used. Those who lived with others tended to use informal supports. People who lived alone tended to use formal supports. Also, people with better education, with less family contact, and with a preference for formal supports tended to use formal supports (Blieszner, Roberto, & Singh, 2001–02).

Ethnicity also influences the support an older person gets. Pinquart and Sorensen (2005) reviewed the results of 116 studies of caregivers. They found that African American and Hispanic care receivers had greater physical and cognitive impairment. Their caregivers, compared to white caregivers, provided higher levels of care. Compared to whites, minority care receivers (African American, Hispanic, and Asian) got more support from relatives, friends, and neighbors. The researchers say that strong minority cultural and communal values explain this difference.

Penning (1990, p. 227; also Montgomery & Kosloski, 2009) concludes that "the issue of who provides assistance to whom, of what type, and under what conditions is complex." Researchers need more sophisticated models to describe the reality of informal supports. More research on rural, minority, and low-income older people will also lead to more accurate models of social support.

Spousal Support

Studies show that spouses, if available, will take on the caregiving role. They most often served as **primary caregivers.** Johnson and Schaner report on results from the nationwide University of Michigan 2002 Health and Retirement Study (Johnson & Schaner, 2005a, p. 3). They found that almost 40% of both men and women age 55 and over spent time caring for a spouse.

This, Johnson and Schaner say, challenges "the conventional wisdom that family care is strictly the responsibility of women." The men in the study reported spending about 236 hours in that year on spousal caregiving and the women reported 231 hours (also MetLife & American Society on Aging, 2010). Hours of spousal caregiving for both men and women increased with age. People age 75 and over, compared to spouses ages 55 to 64, spent twice as many hours on spousal caregiving (886 hours a year). Three quarters of the time these older spouses spent on family care went to spousal care.

Calasanti (2006) found that husbands and wives differed in their approach to caregiving. Husbands took a pragmatic approach. They tended to see caregiving work as a job that they could master. Wives, on the other hand, saw caregiving as nurturing. They wanted to please their husbands and make them comfortable. This led to differences in coping styles. Men could distance themselves from unpleasant tasks by defining them as a form of work. Women found it harder to gain this distance. To them caregiving meant

the loss of their former relationship with their husbands. Calasanti's work shows that wives and husbands understand caregiving differently based on their lifelong gender roles.

Studies report that even after a spouse enters an institution, the community-dwelling spouse feels some stress (Garity, 2006). Majerovitz (2007) studied 103 family caregivers who cared for nursing home patients. She found that family caregivers often feel burdened and depressed. Older caregivers in poor health or with low income showed the highest risk, especially for depression. The more impaired the family member, the greater the risk of **caregiver burden**.

Spouses with a husband or wife in an institution report loneliness, a desire to get on with their lives, and feelings of guilt. They feel loyalty to the institutionalized spouse and yet feel the loneliness of widowhood. Novak and Guest (1989, 1992) studied caregivers of cognitively impaired older people. They found five dimensions of caregiver burden: time dependence, developmental burden, physical burden, social burden, and emotional burden.

Novak and Guest found that spouses of institutionalized older people, compared with adult children, feel more physical and developmental burden. *Physical burden* refers to the strain of long visits and travel to the institution. Hallman and Joseph (1999) found that women, compared with men, spend more time traveling to give care. *Developmental burden* refers to spouses' feelings of being unable to get on with life. Spouses felt that their focus on caregiving, even for an institutionalized spouse, blocked opportunities for personal growth.

Loos and Bowd (1997; also Garity, 2006) found that caregiver spouses felt guilty after institutionalization. One wife told Gladstone (1995, p. 56), "When you're apart after never being apart it has an effect on you. You seem to be in a turmoil. We'd known each other since we were 14 years old so we were together a long, long time."

Rosenthal and Dawson (1991) studied 69 wives of institutionalized men. They found that women went through a transition to "quasi-widowhood." During the first days following institutionalization, these women said they felt relief from the stress of caregiving at home. But they also displayed poor health, low morale, and depression. These women reported feeling guilty, sad, and lonely.

Most women over time adapt to having a spouse live in an institution. Some women accept the loss of their spouses as a friend and companion and restructure their lives outside the institution. Other spouses keep close ties to the institution. Ross, Rosenthal, and Dawson (1997a, b) found that more than 80% of the wives in their study visited their husbands at least several times a week. About 20% visited every day. But the researchers found that active visitors felt more depressed at the end of 9 months and felt dissatisfied with the care their husbands received.

This study suggests that wives who begin to give up the caregiver role do better after their husbands are institutionalized. The researchers found that about two thirds of spouses gave up some of their caregiving responsibility. These wives had cognitively impaired spouses. They visited less and allowed staff to take on the job of caring. This group felt less depressed and said they felt "sort of like a widow" (Ross, Rosenthal, & Dawson, 1994, p. 29). Healing began to take place as wives gained distance from the caregiver role.

The decision to move a relative into a long-term care home is a difficult one for families. Caron, Ducharme, and Griffith (2006) asked family members to talk about the process they went through to arrive at their decision. Three conditions influenced family members' decision: (1) the amount of care needed by the older relative; (2) the caregiver's ability to provide that amount of care; and (3) the formal supports available.

The placement decision can take a long time. Caron and colleagues (2006) say the decision took an average of 2 years from the family's first thoughts of placement until the actual move occurred. Many caregivers in this study said they did not receive the support they needed from health care professionals during this process.

Adult Children as a Source of Support

Spousal care declines with a person's age, but care from a child and other relatives increases with the age of the care receiver. Even among younger cohorts (ages 65 to 74) who need care, children and other relatives (often siblings and nieces) make up as much as two fifths of caregivers for men. Most adult children give secondary care; they serve as a backup and give respite to spousal caregivers. Children also serve as financial managers and provide links to formal services.

Some studies show that long before a parent begins to decline, adult children begin to monitor their parents' conditions. Phone calls and visits create opportunities to consciously or subconsciously check on parents' well-being.

Monitoring can turn into caregiving if a parent gets sick or begins to lose mental ability. Take the case of

Sam Kelso, age 61, who lives in Oregon. His mother lives in Tennessee. Sam is part of a caregiving team that includes his sister in New York and his brother in Los Angeles. Sam's mother's memory started failing a few years ago. At that point she moved from her single family home to a seniors' residence. There she lived a simpler life without having to care for a house. She could walk to the local senior center where she played cards and talked with the other members.

Her memory has worsened in the past year. This now places her health at risk. She skips meals and forgets to bathe. She also rejects the home help that Sam has tried to hire for her. She's fired several home helpers, and Sam's given up on this support for now.

Sam's mother's condition worries him. He visits several times a year to check on her and assess her needs. While there, he makes the rounds of the doctors and other professionals who give his mother support.

Dierdre, 62, flies back to St. Louis from Denver several times a year to help with care for her mother, who has Alzheimer's disease. Her father serves as the primary caregiver. He needs respite now and then. Recently he needed outpatient surgery on his knee. She flew back for a long weekend to help out while he recovered. Dierdre monitors her parents' well-being mostly by phone. But she knows that a drop in her father's health or a worsening of her mother's condition will mean a more active caregiver role for her.

Most Baby Boomers will go through some version of Sam's and Dierdre's dilemma. If children live close to a parent they may get involved in day-to-day issues related to caregiving. If they live far away they will need to manage care at a distance. This can include hiring a professional care manager to support an aging parent.

Widowhood will sometimes expose an aging parent's needs. For example, one member of a married couple may shore up the failing strength or mental ability of the other member. The death of a supportive spouse can put a parent at sudden risk. Add to this the grief a spouse will feel at loss of a long-time partner. The aging of the older population will mean that many Baby Boomers will provide some sort of care to aging parents.

Dupuis and Smale (2004) report that even older people who reside in long-term care institutions get informal help from their children. Garity (2006) found that adult children visited their parents often, helped with ADLs such as feeding, and monitored nursing care. Children also helped with laundry and clothing care as well as bill paying.

Mike Logan, 63, visits his mother in a nursing home several times a week. She has Alzheimer's disease and can't get out on her own. He'll take a long lunch and drive the hour-long round trip to take his mother out. They'll go to a Chinese restaurant nearby or to a local McDonald's. "Sometimes," Mike says, "she'll do some pretty inappropriate things. She'll loudly comment, 'That mother shouldn't talk like that to her child.' I have to ignore these comments and try to have a pleasant lunch with her."

Mike visits his mother even though she often doesn't remember he's been there. One time, he tells me, he forgot his hat in his mother's room after their lunch. He returned to pick it up and she welcomed him as if she hadn't seen him for some time. He immediately called his brother, who visits less often. "Hey, John," he joked, "today I got credit from Mom for two visits."

Of course, it's likely she won't remember either visit that day. Mike doesn't expect credit for his visits. He goes because his Mom enjoys the time they spend together. And he feels an obligation to visit her. While he's there he meets with the staff and generally sees that she's well cared for.

Children, like Mike, who help care for a parent in an institution say they feel a strong attachment to a parent and they recognize past help and support that they got (Keefe & Fancey, 2000). Mike may be unusual in one respect. Studies report that daughters, compared with sons, typically provide more care to parents. Daughters (more than sons) also report greater feelings of stress (Amirkhanyan & Wolf, 2006).

One caregiving daughter told Garity (2006, p. 45), "I use a lot of energy to keep everything balanced. When something happens [to my parent] post-placement like feeding or behavioral problems I let that structure my life as opposed to my having control over the things that I want to do." Another said, "My husband [who works out of town during week] has said we'd probably be divorced if he were at home because my father has absorbed . . . takes a lot of my time right now."

Daughters-in-law often provide care to their husbands' parents. They may feel responsible to give care even if they don't feel affection for the parent. Walker (1996) traces this fact to cultural pressures on women to give care. One woman put this simply: "Who else is going to do it?"

Keefe and Fancey (2002; Garity, 2006) found another reason daughters give care to their mothers: They felt obliged to return their mothers' earlier care. The researchers found that daughters recalled the past when their mothers provided help and support to them. This motivated them to give care in the present. Pillemer and Suitor (2006) studied mothers' expectations of care from their adult children. Mothers said they expected and preferred care from a daughter with whom they felt emotionally close.

The marital status of adult children influences their level of involvement with older parents (Sarkisian & Gerstel, 2008). Married sons and daughters are less likely than their single or divorced counterparts to stay in touch with parents. Married children less often provide parents with financial support, emotional support, or practical help. They are also less likely to receive these types of assistance from parents. The marital status of the parent can also influence their relationship with adult children, including the support they receive. For example, adult children provide about the same support to divorced or widowed mothers. But, they provide the least support to divorced fathers (Lin, 2008).

The Kaiser Women's Health Survey in 2004 (Salganicoff, Ranji, & Wyn, 2005) asked a nationally representative sample of 2,766 women age 18 and over about their caregiving experience. The study assessed the types of work female caregivers do for their care receiver (a disabled or sick family member), and the amount of time they spend on caregiving. Nearly all of the women (91%) said they helped with housework, shopping, errands, and meals. Another large proportion of women (83%) said they helped with transportation. More than half the sample said they helped with finances (bill paying, etc.) and medical decisions. Forty-two percent said they helped with physical care (dressing, bathing, etc.). These findings show that a high proportion of adult women serve as caregivers to a needy relative.

These women juggle many responsibilities in addition to caregiving. Forty percent have children under age 18. And more than half (56%) work outside the home. Nearly half of these caregivers (46%) have their own chronic health condition. One quarter (24%) report their own health as fair to poor.

Many of these women spend so much time caregiving that they cannot work at a job for pay. Nearly one third (29%) of these women spend more than 40 hours a week on caregiving. More than 2 in 5 (44%) of the poorest women in this sample (with family incomes under 200% of the poverty line) spend more than 40 hours on caregiving.

The study also shows that many women engage in health care tasks. This includes giving medications, giving injections, and adjusting medical equipment.

Few informal caregivers have training for these tasks. They learn them on their own.

Nearly three quarters of these caregivers (72%) say they feel "very concerned" or "somewhat concerned" about balancing their caregiver responsibilities with other demands. They felt that caregiving took time away from their other family responsibilities. And caregiving caused them concern about their own health.

This national survey supports a large body of research on caregivers and the challenges they face. The study calls women "health care leaders for their families." It goes on to propose "social supports, workplace flexibility, and assistance with long-term care" as approaches needed to help women who give care (p. 49).

Even though adult children provide care to their parents, parents often report that they receive less support from their children than is true. Early work by Bengtson and Kuypers (1971) referred to this as differences in the **developmental stake** or (more recently) **generational stake** (Mandemakers & Dykstra, 2008). This theory says that, compared with their children, older people feel a greater stake in having good parent–child relations. This leads older parents to emphasize family harmony and solidarity. They may deemphasize the support their children give them in order not to see themselves as a burden. This difference in perception can create family tensions. Adult children can feel that their parents do not appreciate what they do for them, even though the children do as much as they can.

Recent research from the Netherlands (Mandemakers & Dykstra, 2008) finds limited and mixed support for the generational stake hypothesis. This study reports discrepancies in parents' and adult children's reports of contact and support. But *both* parents and their adult children misjudge the amount of support given and received. Parents underestimate the amount of support they receive and children overestimate the amount of support they provide. Better-educated parents and children seemed to more accurately estimate relationship contact and support.

Mandemakers and Dykstra (2008, p. 504) also find that parents and adult children in high-quality relationships tend to overestimate the support and contact in their relationship. The authors suggest there may be value in having such a "sunny" outlook on a relationship. They conclude that, "People in close relationships harbor 'positive illusions' about each other. They emphasize their partners' virtues, and are motivated to overlook their faults. A certain level of favorable deception seems to be basic to happy relationships."

Siblings as a Source of Informal Support

Most older people have at least one living brother or sister. Siblings can serve as an important source of social support for older people. The support provided by a sibling will vary by individual need. For example, a married older person with many children nearby may make little use of sibling support. Single people and women make the most use of sibling supports (Barrett & Lynch, 1999).

Consider the following case. Ann Whitlea, a 75-year-old widow, stood next to her shopping cart waiting for the bus to take her back to her housing complex. She leaned forward to rest on the cart for support, but the cart scooted out from under her. Ann fell and caught herself on her outstretched hand. The weight of the fall caused her wrist to snap and caused a bruise on her knee. She fell forward onto her face and damaged her teeth.

An ambulance rushed her to the hospital, where they put a cast on her wrist and gave her first aid for cuts on her face. She would have to see her dentist about her teeth. Ann could have returned to her apartment later that day, but the shock of the injuries, the pain, and the cast on her wrist made it hard for her to stay by herself. Ann called her brother, who came over immediately. He arranged for her to move in with her younger sister in a nearby town for 2 weeks until she felt better. Ann's daughter arranged for doctors' appointments and helped set her up in her apartment again.

Ann relies on a network of kin that includes her children and her siblings. Because her children live several hours away and have their own demanding schedules, she often relies on her brother and sister when she needs help. Her brother takes her shopping for special items like clothes or furniture. Her sister has her over for holidays and family dinners.

Older people who have at least one remaining brother or sister report frequent interaction with their siblings. Spitze and Trent (2006) studied adult sibling ties in two-child families. They found that sisters exchanged advice and kept in touch by phone more often than did other pairs of siblings. Their closeness rests, in part, on their shared experience of aging. Older sisters, for example, may have experienced widowhood. They often form close friendship bonds and provide emotional support to one another (Miner & Uhlenberg, 1997).

Supports for Childless Older People

Some older people have never married. Others, who married, had no children. These people adapt to aging without the support of adult children. They create a network of supportive family and friends. For example, childless older people, compared with people who have children, set up more supportive ties with their siblings. Childless older people tend to get more support from siblings when they get ill. They also tend to give support to their brothers and sisters. Childless women often build relationships with nieces, nephews, and the children of nonrelatives.

Those who have chosen to remain childless report high life satisfaction and happiness (Connidis & McMullin, 1999). Still, the social networks of older childless people offer less support when the older person becomes sick. Childless older people who report disadvantages point to a lack of companionship, missed experiences, and incompleteness.

This group tends to be disadvantaged in other ways as well. They tend to be less financially secure, to be in poorer health, and to live alone. Widows in particular feel disadvantaged if childless. Because childless older people may lack informal support, they may need more formal supports than do older parents. For example, compared to people with children, childless older people face a greater risk of institutionalization (Aykan, 2003).

Research often ignores childless adults. Or research views their lives "through a lens of deficiency" or as the "other" category (Dykstra & Hagestad, 2007, p. 1291). As a result, compared to what we know about older people with children, we know less about the social networks and relationships of childless older people. We also know less about the varied responses people make to childlessness. Dykstra and Hagestad (p. 1301) say that for some people, "life without children can have particular advantages, in others it can have disadvantages, and in yet others, no effects at all." They say that research should explore "when childlessness matters and when it does not."

Friends and Neighbors

Older people without families often rely on friends and neighbors for support. Lilly, Richards, and Buckwalter (2003) found that friends provided emotional support and social integration.

Dependence on friends and neighbors prevents isolation and loneliness. Studies find that friends and neighbors make up from 5% to 24% of caregivers. This fits the estimate of most national studies. By this estimate, about 140,000 frail older people have nonkin caregivers.

Studies show that friends' social and emotional support improves the well-being of older people. This especially applies to older people who have no spouse

These friends attend an inner-city nutrition site in San Francisco for lunch each day. At the site they meet people, enjoy sociability, and share an understanding based on their life experience.

or whose children live far away. Friends do more than provide services to older people. Older people use friends for social and emotional support (Lilly et al., 2003). Krause (2007), for example, studied the effect over time of anticipated support from friends—support a person expects if he or she needs help. He found that anticipated support from friends led to a deeper meaning in life over time.

Moremen (2008a) asked older women in her study to choose the person they felt closest to, and explain how that person contributed to their health. Half of the women named friends as their closest confidants. Female friends were more likely to be named as confidants than were male friends or daughters. Many of these women said that they would turn to their friend to discuss physical health concerns or when they felt sad or lonely. But, they did not feel comfortable sharing concerns about mental health issues or financial problems. And they didn't call on their friends for personal care. These women felt their close confidants kept them healthy. They provided diet and exercise advice, provided meals and transportation, shared fun and laughter, and helped them feel good about themselves.

Researchers say that friendships can help older people overcome problems caused by lost work roles and the lost spouse role in old age (Field, 1999). A widowed woman told Blieszner (2001) in a study of friendship, "Well, a lot of times, I'll just call her. . . . She'll be on my heart and I'll call her. It's a good time to talk with her. Maybe she needs a word of encouragement."

Friends support a person's self-worth. But relations with family members don't always have this effect. Compared to family, friends have this effect because the older person chooses friendship ties voluntarily. Friends provide a support that family cannot give. For example, friends provide companionship and "may facilitate and encourage self-expression, thereby helping people feel productive in late life" (Krause, 2006, p. 190).

This suggests that different people in the older person's social network play various support roles. A spouse or child will help with household chores. But friends serve as social partners. They help each other cope with life difficulties and stressful events. Friends who are the same age often share the same physical limits, the same interests, and the same historical background. Lifelong friends also share experiences and memories.

Although friends can play a vital role in the support network of older people, friendships in later life can also involve tensions and disappointments. Moremen (2008b) terms this the "downside of friendship." Some of the women in Moremen's study reported "disruptions" in their friendships. Disruptions occurred when friends did not share their interests, habits, and other friends. A loss of trust in the relationship, dishonesty, or exploitation could also put strain on the friendship.

For some women, differences in marital status, socioeconomic status, or geographic location (when a friend moved away) could create stress. Women said they felt anger, betrayal, disappointment, resentment, and sadness when these situations occurred. Many women used an avoidance strategy to deal with strains and problems in the relationship. This often meant not confronting the problem or keeping hurt or angry feelings inside. But sometimes these feelings ended the friendship. Some women resolved these tensions by talking about them. Some used humor or they agreed to disagree.

Research shows the importance of close and supportive friendships in the lives of older adults (Davidson, Daly, & Arber, 2003; de Jong Gierveld, 2003). A variety of relationships, including friendships, create a full and satisfying support network.

Pets as a Source of Social Support

Few people think of pets as a source of social support. But pets provide their owners with companionship, affection, and friendship. Researchers have studied the potential social support and health benefits pets can provide to older people. This includes older people who live in the community and those in long-term care settings (Banks, Gonser, & Banks, 2001; Wood, Giles-Corti, & Bulsara, 2005). Pet ownership increases social contact, positive interaction with neighbors, and community involvement. Human-pet interaction can help people deal with stress, loneliness, and bereavement (Allen, Blascovich, & Mendes, 2002). Pet ownership can also protect a person from cardiovascular disease, improve blood pressure, and increase physical activity.

Compared to owners of other pets, dog owners get the most physical benefit from pet ownership (Thorpe et al., 2006). Studies show that dog owners do more recreational walking than non-dog owners. Dogs can also act as a "catalyst for social interaction" (Wood et al., 2005). Compared to people who walk alone, people who walk their dogs tend to engage in conversation with neighbors, other dog owners, or even strangers. Dogs can also precipitate the exchange of favors between neighbors.

These casual social exchanges do not generally turn into sources of social support. Still, as Wood and colleagues (2005, p. 1162) say, "Dogs have the greatest capacity to facilitate social interaction and contact as they are the type of pet most likely to venture with their owners into the broader community."

Animal-assisted therapy has been used as an effective therapy for older residents in long-term care homes. This therapy introduces pets, such as dogs, cats, rabbits, or birds, into nursing homes or other residential care settings. Research finds that pets can bring pleasure and comfort to residents in long-term care homes. Banks and Banks (2002) found that pets reduced the loneliness of residents. One study found that having an aquarium in the dining room stimulated residents to eat more at mealtime and to gain weight.

Filan and Llewellyn-Jones (2006) conducted a review of literature on the use of animal-assisted therapy for dementia residents. They found that quiet interaction between residents and dogs lowered blood pressure and increased feelings of relaxation and bonding for residents. Studies suggest that the presence of a dog can reduce agitation and aggression in residents with dementia. Dogs also promote positive social behavior.

Research supports the value of pets in long-term care settings. But pet visits may not suit all residents. Some residents may have allergies. Others may fear dogs, birds, or other animals. An aggressive patient may mishandle or harm an animal. Residents and staff in long-term care homes must see that pets in these settings get good care and treatment.

Minority Differences in Social Support

Pinquart and Sorensen (2005) analyzed 116 studies of minority group caregivers. They found that, compared to white caregivers, minority caregivers gave more informal care and expressed more commitment to parental care. Asian American caregivers, compared to whites, tended to use fewer formal supports. This may reflect the cultural commitment of Asian adult children to care for their parents. African American caregivers, compared to whites, expressed less caregiver burden. All minority group members (Asian, Hispanic, and African American), compared to whites, reported poorer health.

Research suggests that African Americans offer strong support to their older members. Dilworth-Anderson (1992) describes the African American family as a mutual aid system that expresses many of the traditional values of the African American community. For example, black families absorb needy members and give them help to survive in harsh economic times. The National Long Term Care Demonstration Project found that African American families give their older members medical care supports (White-Means, 1993).

Older African Americans also rely on the church for support. Church membership gives older black people a group of friends and confidants in addition to their families. Krause (2002) reports that older African Americans who actively take part in church activities report more spiritual and emotional support from their fellow parishioners. Spurlock (2005) found that spiritual well-being can buffer caregiver stress. Spurlock suggests that intervention programs include support for spiritual development.

Gibson and Jackson (1992) say that the oldest old African Americans (age 85 and over) made the most use of both family and church supports. Walls (1992) reports that African American elders rely on the family for emotional support and the church for instrumental support. People with strong family and church networks felt a sense of well-being. Yoon and Lee (2007) propose that intervention programs take into account and encourage caregivers' religious and spiritual practices.

Kivett (1993) found that African American grandmothers, compared with white grandmothers, give and receive more support from their grandchildren. African American grandmothers sometimes play the role of surrogate parents for grandchildren. Older African Americans also provide needy adult children with shelter, food, and money.

Minkler and Fuller-Thomson (2005) analyzed U.S. Census data on older (45+) African American grandparents. The data show that more than 500,000 African Americans age 45 and over raised grandchildren in 2000. Most of these grandparents were women. Many of them lived in poverty and got public assistance. But four fifths of those in poverty got no public assistance. Compared to grandfather caregivers, grandmother caregivers had more functional limitation and tended to live in poverty. These grandparent caregivers themselves face stress and hardship in addition to the demands of caregiving. Mbanaso, Shavelson, and Ukawuilulu (2006) say that older African American caregivers need more information about resources and government services.

Hispanic families also show a strong interdependence of older and younger members. Sotomayor and

Randolph (1988) say that Hispanic families (in most Hispanic subgroups) value mutual support between the generations. They report that the family still plays an important role in supporting older people. A study by Tomaka and colleagues (2006) confirms this view. They compared social supports reported by 755 Hispanic and white older people ages 60 to 92. They found that, compared to whites, Hispanics reported more family support. They also found that Hispanic older people with family support reported lower rates of diabetes, kidney disease, and arthritis.

Sotomayor and Randolph (1988, p. 155) studied family support for Puerto Rican and Mexican American elders. They found that Hispanic families engage in mutual support "when ill, making important decisions, and handling financial problems." The researchers say that older members, when ill, get more help from their families than the family expects the older person to give. Older Hispanics rely on their children for help with shopping, transportation, and home maintenance.

Most older Hispanics in this study (about 70%) said that their children both love and respect them. They say they know this because their children visit them and check on their needs. These older people also said they give more advice than they get. Some of them said they take unemployed children into their homes, babysit for grandchildren, and give religious instruction to young family members (Sotomayor & Randolph, 1988). Sotomayor and Randolph say that for these elders "the extended family is a vital social support system that includes a special role for the elderly family members" (p. 143).

Cultural values, love, and respect in part explain the supports that younger Hispanic family members give to their elders. But Sotomayor and Randolph (1988) say that poverty and a lack of suitable social services sometimes force Hispanic elders to rely on their families. Bastida (1988) studied Puerto Rican elders and found that none of them considered formal services as a major source of support.

Past research has idealized the informal supports available to minority older people. But Lockery (1991) says that these beliefs create a simplistic view of minority aging. Some families do give support. But other families lack the resources to give support. And this may create stress for older family members. Diversity within minority groups leads to different amounts and types of support to older members. Also, changing social and economic conditions create new challenges for minority families.

Longer life expectancies, poverty, and declining health in later life will place a greater burden on African American and Hispanic families in the years ahead. This feeling of strain within minority families may already have begun. Eggebeen (1992), for instance, reported that Mexican Americans showed no greater exchange between the generations than whites. And African Americans showed lower levels of intergenerational help than either Mexican Americans or whites.

Eggebeen (1992, p. 49) notes that demands on minority families have increased at the same time that resources have shrunk. "Perhaps," he says, "these data point to how much has changed among black families in the past decade more than they correct erroneous characterizations drawn from past ethnographic work."

Lockery (1991, p. 61) proposes that future studies of minority supports need to focus on the needs of each minority group. Future policies must take care "not to perpetuate the myth that racial and ethnic minorities take care of their own. Not only may their elderly need more caregiving services, they may also lack the primary support systems that many assume are there."

Technology and Social Support

The rise of the Internet has changed social interaction for nearly everyone in the United States today. Instant messaging, email, and social websites (e.g., Facebook and Twitter) offer new channels for interaction and social support. Young people use these methods to keep in touch with one another throughout the day and night. They allow people at long distances to interact and form communities.

Some studies show that time spent on virtual relationships substitutes for face-to-face time spent with family and friends (Nie, Hillygus, & Ebring, 2002). Other studies find that the Internet leads to membership in wider social networks and greater interaction with others. Internet users can take part in communities of interest outside the boundaries of local space and time.

Fox (2004) found that 94% of older people who used the Internet said they used it for email and to keep in touch with children and grandchildren. Cutler (2006) says that caregivers also use the Internet for information and to take part in support groups. Many caregivers cannot get to a face-to-face support group. The Internet allows caregivers to give and get support at a time convenient to them and from their own home.

One study found that 25% of caregivers used the Internet to get information on their care receiver's condition, on available services, and on health care facilities (National Alliance for Caregiving, 2009). People who use these supports find that they reduce caregiver strain. And, when combined with family therapy, they reduce depression (Eisdorfer et al., 2003).

Future generations of older people will feel more comfortable using the Internet. Digital forms of communication will bridge time and space barriers to family and friends. Grandparents, for example, will interact with grandchildren through real-time video connections. Let me give a real-world example of this.

While writing this section, I received a call on the Skype system from my son in Santa Fe, New Mexico. We connected via video and I had a chance to visit with him and his family. His wife stopped by the computer to say hello as she went about her chores. My grandchildren shared their schoolwork with me and their latest craft projects. We were able to look together at the pictures and videos from their recent Christmas trip to the East Coast.

I don't think of this as "social support." But it is. The use of technology enriches my life and keeps me in close touch with family members far away. I expect that technology will play an important role in our family life in the years ahead. Improvements in technology and lower costs will make family contacts like this easier for everyone in the future.

CAREGIVING

Gender Roles and the Challenge of Caregiving

Harris (2005) reports that sons make up 10% to 12% of primary caregivers to elderly parents. They make up as many as 52% of secondary caregivers. Husbands make up about 13% of all caregivers. But we know less about these male caregivers than about women who give care.

Kramer (2002) reports that, compared to women, men may feel more isolated in their caregiving roles because they have fewer close friends. Men often rely on their spouse for social and emotional support. When they have to give care to their spouse they may have fewer social resources to call on.

A qualitative study shows how sons view their care to older parents. L. D. Campbell (2002, p. 500; also Campbell & Carroll, 2007) collected data on 58 adult sons who provide care to older parents. She found some common themes in the experiences of these sons. For example, most men provided care out of a sense of commitment to family. They felt a strong bond to their parents and a desire to repay them for past support. Many sons talked about how providing care had brought them emotionally closer to their parent.

Men experienced a mixture of emotions, including feelings of love, compassion, and responsibility, as well as sadness, frustration, and guilt. As one 40-year-old married son said about caring for his mother: "I love my mum [but] sometimes it is frustrating and sometimes it's overwhelming. . . . [There's] a sense of feeling very spread out. I'm using very emotional terms, but, you know, yeah, so emotionally overwhelming sometimes."

Many sons felt that no matter how difficult the tasks might be, they just did what needed to be done. As one son said, "Just deal with it . . . do what you have to do and move on" (Campbell & Carroll, 2007, p. 498). Sons say they feel good about caregiving and that caregiving gives them a chance to give back to their parents for past support they received.

Compared to older women, older men more often get care from a spouse. Still, husbands play a significant role in caring for their wives in later life (Calasanti, 2006; Calasanti & Bowen, 2006). Men make up about 40% of spousal caregivers. Studies also find that husbands and wives provide about the same amount and types of care. Research suggests that husbands often see caregiving as an extension of their work role—like a "new career," or a continuation of their authority in the marital relationship (Ribeiro, Paúl, & Nogueira, 2007). Husbands often bring problem-solving strategies from their work role to their care role (Harris, 2005).

Calasanti (2006) studied the different experiences of 22 husband and wife caregivers (9 men [average age 72] and 13 women [average age 67]). She found that husbands and wives did similar caregiving tasks. But they thought of their tasks differently. Calasanti speaks of different "caregiving styles" (p. 276).

Men, she says, approached caregiving by "rationally identifying and mastering tasks." One husband likened his caregiving work to a job. Men, she found, took great pleasure in successfully completing their work. Men distanced themselves emotionally from their caregiving tasks. One husband described how he learned to do caregiving work: "You just have to pick it up like you do a trade. Like laying brick or finishing concrete" (Calasanti, 2006, p. 277).

Men took a problem-solving approach to unpleasant tasks like toileting. This distanced them emotionally from the task. Women took a more empathic approach to their work. They performed tasks similar to those of men, but they defined their work as nurturing.

BOX 13.1
WHO ARE THE CAREGIVERS?

In 2009 the National Alliance for Caregiving (2009) in cooperation with AARP conducted a national study of caregiving in the United States. The study interviewed 1,480 family caregivers age 18 and over. Of these caregivers, 1,397 looked after someone age 50 and over. Structured telephone interviews asked caregivers about their experience in the past 12 months. Key findings included the following points.

- An estimated 61.8 million people in the United States provide unpaid care to an adult family member.

- More than 1 in 4 U.S. households (29.4%) report at least one person who served as a caregiver for an adult in the past 12 months. An estimated 34.3 million households have a caregiver for an adult relative.

- Most caregivers of adults are female; average age 49.2. Seven in 10 caregivers in this study give care to someone age 50 and over. The typical adult care receiver is a woman. The average age of a care receiver is 69.3. Eighty-six percent of caregivers care for a relative; 36% care for a parent. Twenty-six percent care for an elderly mother. Caregivers age 65 and over have given care an average of 7.2 years.

- Old age and Alzheimer's top the reasons that caregivers give care. Other reasons include illnesses of old age (e.g., heart disease and stroke). More than one quarter of caregivers (26%) said their care receiver suffered from dementia. Alzheimer's caregivers have high levels of caregiver burden.

- One third (31%) consider caregiving emotionally stressful; half of caregivers (53%) say caregiving takes time from friends and other family members.

- Two thirds of caregivers for adults (65%) say they have "gone in late, left early, or taken time off during the day to deal with caregiving issues" (p. 9); 1 in 5 caregivers took a leave of absence at some time while giving care.

These findings support and reinforce the findings of the many quantitative and qualitative studies of caregiving in the United States and elsewhere. This study also explored caregivers' unmet needs. More than three quarters (78%) of caregivers said they need more information or help with their caregiving. In particular they wanted to know more about safety, stress management, and finding time for themselves. More than half of all caregivers (53%) say they used the Internet in the past year to get information related to caregiving.

Calasanti (2006) calls this "emotion work" (p. 277). Wives tried to smooth over tensions and unpleasantness. They wanted to make their husbands happy. Wives linked their caregiving to their earlier role as mothers. One woman said, "I am basically a caretaker at heart, so it's kind of my nature." Another woman put this simply: "I was a mom."

Some men feel uncomfortable providing care that involves "traditionally female" tasks, such as domestic work and personal care. These men report "role incongruence." Many are not prepared for the caregiving role and need to learn new and unfamiliar skills (Harris, 2005). Still, they feel satisfaction and a sense of accomplishment in being able to provide care to their spouses (Kirsi, Hervonen, & Jylhä, 2004).

One husband told Calasanti (2006, p. 283) "I . . . hated making meals, but I have gotten used to that. It's more routine. . . . I didn't think I could handle incontinence, but I guess I can. So on you go." Another husband talked about the problem he faces when he has to clean up his wife's bowel movements: ". . . and then you have to . . . fix it, you know."

Calasanti and Bowen (2006) conducted in-depth interviews with spousal caregivers to learn more about gender and its effect on caregiving. They found that both men and women "crossed gendered boundaries" in their caregiving.

First, husbands and wives assumed responsibility for domestic and household tasks that were typically done by the other spouse. For example, women took responsibility for the household finances, learned outside home maintenance, or learned how to maintain the car. One woman said: "I never had to put gas in a car, I never had to check the tires, I never had to do anything about an automobile because he did everything. And now I have that and that is hard" (Calasanti & Bowen, 2006, p. 257). Caregiving husbands took on tasks typically done by their wives. Husbands had to do many of these tasks, like cooking and cleaning, every day. "I found out how difficult it is to do all these things [that she used to do]," one husband said (p. 258).

Second, spouses "crossed gender boundaries" when they helped their partner with personal care. Caregivers helped their partners maintain their gendered identity as a man or woman. They did this, for example, by helping their spouses with bathing and grooming. They saw that their spouses wore clean and attractive clothing. Wives experienced this as an extension of familiar tasks. Husbands experienced personal care for their spouses as new and unfamiliar. Still, the authors say, husbands "strove to insure their wives looked like the 'ladies' they had been" (Calasanti & Bowen, 2006, p. 259).

Family, friends, and the broader society often praise men for taking on care work, particularly tasks typically performed by women (Milne & Hatzidimitriadou, 2003). Ribeiro and his colleagues (2007) call this "perceived social honour." Milne and Hatzidimitriadou (2003) use the phrase "isn't he wonderful." Yet, Russell (2007) found that while men got praised for special care tasks, they got little recognition for "unheroic" daily caregiving chores.

Many husbands felt their spousal care was invisible, and that others around them did not appreciate how much of their lives was consumed by the demands of caregiving. "For many [men], the locus of care work, the home, represented a location in which they became as invisible as the work they performed" (Russell, 2007, p. 311). This invisibility contributed to an increased sense of social isolation.

Studies find that sons will get involved in care primarily in the absence of a female caregiver. But sons, compared with daughters, get less involved in their parents' emotional needs and less often get involved in routine household work. They seem better at setting limits on how much help they give. They also feel less guilty about setting these limits. Male caregivers rely more on formal help for their care receivers. Studies of caregiving husbands and sons show that gender roles influence caregiving activities. Men favor a more administrative, managerial role. Women more often give emotional support and personal care.

Caregiver Burden

Many studies report that giving care to a physically disabled or cognitively impaired older person leads to *caregiver burden*. This refers to problems and stress due to caregiving. Longer life expectancy now and in the future will lead to more older people needing support for more years. This will place an increased demand on more family caregivers. It may lead to more cases where caregivers feel extremely stressed.

Schulz and Martire (2004) found that an older person with many chronic conditions or a cognitive impairment can stretch the limits of a caregiver's energy, health, and emotions (National Alliance for Caregiving, 2009). This can lead to depression, anxiety, and emotional exhaustion. Garand and colleagues (Garand, Dew, Eazor, DeKosky, & Reynolds, 2005) found that even in cases of mild dementia, caregivers report increased feelings of depression and anxiety. Caregiving often restricts the caregiver's social contacts outside the home. It can lead caregivers to feel trapped and at a dead end in life.

Family caregivers report that they feel a loss of control and autonomy. One caregiver says, "I feel like, like now, I'm all on tenterhooks. I feel like I'm on a treadmill, all the time, all the time, and I can't get off this thing" (O'Connor, 1999, p. 226). Family caregivers also report stress due to tasks like cleaning, doing laundry, and shopping. Still, many spouse caregivers refuse to use outside help. They feel an obligation to their spouses and they feel that they can give the best care.

Caring for someone with Alzheimer's disease (and other cognitive impairments) can put the greatest strain on an informal caregiver. Caregivers feel the physical strain of caregiving, but also the emotional strain of seeing someone they love deteriorate. Writers have described caregiving for an Alzheimer's patient as a "36-hour day" (Mace & Rabins, 1981). A person with Alzheimer's disease may wander the house all night or wander outside. One caregiver reported that her husband got out of the house at night with the car keys. He drove for 100 miles before the car ran out of gas and someone found him wandering near a farmhouse in his pajamas.

This woman, like many caregivers of cognitively impaired spouses, lives in constant anxiety. She suffers from a lack of sleep and physical exhaustion. This has led to a decline in her health. Her doctor has advised her that she may need medical help unless she gets some respite from her caregiving chores.

MacLean (2008) conducted in-depth interviews with older wives whose husbands with dementia waited for placement in a long-term care setting. The study found that wives experience multiple "layers of loss." First, wives talked about the loss of communication with their husbands. Women missed having a partner to talk to about household finances or other every day issues. They even missed simple dinner conversations. They felt that their husband's "true self" had gone.

Second, wives identified the loss of their marriage partnership. In taking on the physical care of their spouse, as well as his household tasks and responsibilities, these women felt their relationship was no longer a "give-and-take" partnership. One woman said: "Well, granted, I'm still his wife, but he's not like my husband . . . my husband isn't there" (MacLean, 2008, p. 53).

Third, many of the women felt a loss of personal freedom. This involved the loss of contact with friends, or the inability to attend social activities. They missed the everyday freedoms like running down to the mailbox to mail a letter or going shopping. As one woman described it: "I feel I'm sort of tied down . . . I'm pretty well trapped" (MacLean, 2008, p. 53).

These women, at times, also lost patience with their spouses. To cope with their situation, they drew on their internal strengths, such as thinking positively. They also remembered their spouse's former self. They relied on religious teachings to gain patience. And they used external resources like formal care services, or support from friends and family.

Most of these women just tried to get through the day—one day at a time. As MacLean (2008) explains: "With this simple and primary goal, these women demonstrated their clear understanding that longer term goals are inappropriate when caregiving for a person whose illness experience changes minute to minute, hour to hour, and day after day" (p. 104).

Caregiving also leads to conflicting demands on the caregiver. Caregiving children often feel intense pressure as they try to meet the demands of work, their children, and caregiving (Neal, Wagner, Bonn, & Niles-Yokum, 2008). Some caregiving daughters quit their jobs, give up promotions, or take time off from work to give care. Daughters also gave up vacations and leisure activities.

A daughter in one caregiver study said, "I wouldn't want to put my kids through what I am going through." Another caregiver said that a person who had "to work a full day, raise a family, and take care of an impaired relative would be susceptible to suicide, parent-abuse and possibly murder." A daughter-in-law in this study said, "I hope I die before I have her kind of problems" (Lund, 1993a, p. 60).

Adult children often need to negotiate parent care within their sibling network. Connidis and Kemp (2008) found that in general adult children with fewer family and work responsibilities, and greater proximity to their parents, most often get selected by their siblings to serve as caregiver. Sisters more often than brothers serve in this role. Hequembourg and Brallier (2005) found that caregiving roles among siblings get divided like the domestic tasks in a traditional marriage.

Research shows that wives, daughters, and other female relatives give most of the informal support to older family members. Women do the domestic chores and provide the personal care that a parent or spouse may need. But the trend toward more women working outside the home and having less time available to provide care to older parents can create a caregiving crunch. Working women feel the crunch because society expects women to serve as caregivers. These women experience more stress and greater absenteeism from work (Matthews & Campbell, 1995). Researchers say that caregivers need to work out family strategies to cope with stress. They also need job flexibility and community supports to help them stay at work.

The Rewards of Caregiving

Caregiver research often focuses on burden and the costs of caregiving. But some caregivers report feelings of satisfaction and achievement. Some people who feel committed to the caregiver role report a sense of well-being (Pierce, Lydon, & Yang, 2001). Pinquart and Sorensen (2004; also Carpenter & Mak, 2007) reviewed 103 studies and found that greater involvement with a care receiver can lead to greater reward. Cohen, Colantonio, and Vernich (2002) found that 73% of caregivers could identify at least one positive thing about caregiving. An additional 7% identified more than one positive thing.

Caregivers enjoyed helping their care receiver feel better. They also felt duty and love toward their care receiver (Ross et al., 1997a). These caregivers respond to the demands of caregiving "with a sense of challenge and . . . in fact, seem to thrive in the situation" (Chiriboga, Weiler, & Nielsen, 1990, p. 135).

Some people say that caregiving made them more caring and compassionate toward others. They say they learned patience and learned to value life more (Lund, 1993a). Sometimes these people carry heavy loads of caregiver demand, but they view caregiving as a calling, a responsibility, and an expression of their love for their care receiver. Heru, Ryan, and Iqbal (2004) found that caregivers of moderately impaired family members showed the least burden if they had a supportive family.

Research shows that caregivers who have positive feelings about caregiving have lower depression, less burden, and better self-reported health (Cohen et al., 2002). Lund (1993a) says that successful caregivers (1) provide good care, (2) want to give care, (3) protect their own well-being, and (4) develop new skills and abilities. The research on successful family caregiving shows that informal caregivers in general do better when they use formal care services (Chiriboga et al., 1990). A flexible system of services can support the work of informal caregivers and provide the care that the older person needs.

Care for the Caregiver

A number of researchers have proposed ways to ease caregiver burden.

1. Family counseling. Counseling works best when it takes into account the entire family system— the caregiver's spouse, children, and siblings, as well as the older person. It can help caregivers deal with moral conflicts about how much protection to give a care receiver. Counseling or psychotherapy can also help a caregiver deal with stress and depression. Caregivers also benefit from skill training such as how to bathe a person or take blood pressure.

   Gonyea, O'Connor, and Boyle (2006) trained 80 caregivers to use behavior modification techniques in response to care receivers' neuropsychiatric symptoms. They compared this group to a control group that got education about psychological problems. Compared to the control group, the group that learned the behavior modification techniques reported less stress related to care receiver symptoms. The techniques also led to some reduction in care receivers' symptoms.

   Specific training can lead to more effective care and to less stress related to specific care receiver symptoms. A program in southern Illinois used the telephone to provide knowledge and skills to rural caregivers (Dollinger, Chwalisz, & O'Neill Zerth, 2006). The program found that, compared to a control group, caregivers in the tele-health program felt reduced feelings of psychological stress and better social functioning. Interventions that combine knowledge and behavior management methods can reduce caregiver stress. The researchers say that this type of intervention especially helps highly stressed and overburdened caregivers.

2. Support groups give caregivers information about how to cope with caregiving demands. They also give caregivers emotional support. The Alzheimer's Society, hospitals, and churches offer support groups. Some groups offer support based on a specific disease (e.g., dementia or cancer). Some of these groups have a professional leader; others work as self-help groups. People in support groups often report feelings of relief and greater ability to manage as caregivers (Hagen, Gallagher, & Simpson, 1997).

Harris (2005) found that caregiving husbands in her study, but not sons, were interested in talking to other men who provided care. They wanted to know how other men dealt with the stress and challenges. Caregiving sons were interested in short-term educational workshops. Education through workshops or support groups help caregivers place their own experience in a context. They can see that what they experience is normal. And this helps them adjust to the caregiver role (Carpenter & Mak, 2007).

Smith and Toseland (2006) found that a telephone support group reduced depression and burden in adult children caregivers. But this did not help spousal caregivers. One study looked at weekly telephone support given by experienced family caregivers to new or newly vulnerable caregivers. The new caregivers reported increased satisfaction with support, improved coping skills, and increased caregiving competence. They also reported less caregiver burden and decreased loneliness (Stewart et al., 2006). Different types of caregivers appear to benefit from different types of group support.

3. Respite services in the community give caregivers a break from the demands of caregiving. These services range from friendly visitors who stay with the care receiver for a few hours, to full-day adult day care, to longer institutional respite. Institutional respite programs can last from several days to several weeks, allowing caregivers to take vacations, deal with personal needs such as medical treatment, or simply rest. One respite method uses a video to distract the attention of the care receiver for an hour or so (Lund, Wright, & Caserta, 2005).

4. Eldercare programs at work can also help family caregivers cope. These programs include counseling services, information on community services and supports, and flexible work schedules.

Good programs and creative interventions cannot completely do away with all feelings of burden, nor should we expect them to. Spouses and children feel loss, anger, and frustration as they see a person close to them suffer through an illness. These feelings reflect a legitimate response to a parent's or spouse's suffering. But interventions can help caregivers understand caregiving, they can help caregivers cope with the everyday demands of care, and they can give caregivers social and emotional support.

Lawrence Goldstein, (center), and Mollie Simon on the Culture Bus, a Chicago Alzheimer's support group. Support groups help relieve the stress and tension that come with round-the-clock caregiving.

The Future of Informal Support

Some time ago Brody (1995, p. 17) said, "The needs of the old for care have far exceeded the capacity of the family to fulfill." Changes in family structure will make this even more the case in the future. First, families now have more generations alive than ever before. Families have a vertical or **bean-pole family structure**. Each generation will have fewer members and fewer potential supporters from within their own generation. Family members will have to support one another across generational lines.

Second, kin networks are becoming top-heavy. An average married couple today and in the future will have more parents than children. Many middle-aged couples will spend more years with parents over 65 than with children under age 18.

Third, some members of the oldest generation in a family will be age 85 and over. These people will need a lot of support. Many of them will be widowed, and some of their adult children will need care themselves. Caregiving will move to later ages as older people stay healthy until late old age. Add to these changes the fact that many traditional family

caregivers, middle-aged and older women, now work in the labor force. Many more women in the future will stay in the labor force past age 65. They will not have the time or energy to serve as caregivers to older relatives.

Fourth, supports for older people tend to decline over time due to the death of a spouse and cohort attrition. This change leads older people to use their remaining ties (typically their children) to meet their needs. This could put future pressure on the children of the Baby Boom. In the third and later decades of this century, middle-aged children may find themselves challenged by their parents' care needs.

Caregiving demands today peak in later middle age. And for the working middle-aged adult, caregiving demands put a strain on an already busy schedule. Caregivers often struggle to maintain a balance between work and family responsibilities (Johnson & Lo Sasso, 2000). More than one quarter (28%) of women in one study reported quitting work to care for an older relative. Another quarter thought about quitting. More women in the future may decide to stay at work and hire help rather than care for a parent.

BOX 13.2
KEEPING MOTHER GOING

Researcher Elaine Brody (1981) coined the term *woman in the middle* to describe the strains felt by middle-aged women who care for children, a spouse, and an elderly parent. Mary Anne Montgomery describes the pressures she faced caring for three generations.

> For Mother the fracture was catastrophic. I was appalled that a "minimal fracture" behind the knee could have such a devastating effect on the entire mind and body. Mother seemed like a balloon that had been pricked and lost all its air. She lay, sometimes pale and listless, other times in pain, with periods of confusion, disorientation, and memory loss. I often found myself visiting an eighty-year-old, helpless, sad, whiney child who barely resembled the mother I knew. The brief episodes when she looked at me strangely and didn't recognize me were eerie and frightening. . . .
>
> For me those weeks were full of new experiences, responsibilities, uncertainties, decisions to be made, and always, pressures. The trip to the hospital twice a day left little time or energy for household matters. As one who owned four different books on organizing and using one's time wisely, I couldn't find time to read them; I was swamped with work to be done. The house was a mess. Our beloved twelve-year-old basset hound suddenly developed incontinence problems, creating additional chores. I longed for just one full day at home alone to work and gather my thoughts in peace. Yet I seemed always to be driving—to see

Mother, or to do errands for her or for my family of five. The children frequently needed to be chauffeured here and there or to be watched in this school program or that game. With the Christmas shopping season upon us, there were family gifts to be purchased. Mother began to have shopping requests for me, too. The physical demands on my time plus the emotional strains of dealing with an unpredictable and different mother reduced me almost to a state of shock. I was mentally and physically numbed.

> Numbness was no help in trying to figure out the complexities of Medicare, doctor, and hospital bills or in making plans for Mother's extended care when I didn't know where to turn for guidance. Her own files and health insurance records were a jumble. The policies seemed to be lost. Household and medical bills arrived at her apartment daily, and I found her check-book stubs a mystery of incompleteness. Having so many tasks and responsibilities dumped on me all at once was terribly difficult. Not even my husband, Mike, truly understood the enormity of the pressures I felt. (He was busy trying to cope with the children, the meals, and the household work I had neglected.) From way back in my childhood came to mind the cry for rescue: "Mother! Please help me!" But of course it was my turn to help Mother.

Source: Montgomery, M. A. (1988). Keeping Mother going. In J. Norris (Ed.), *Daughters of the elderly: Building partnerships in caregiving* (pp. 51–64). Bloomington: Indiana University Press. Reprinted with permission.

All of these changes will increase the need for supports to older people. They will also reduce the amount of informal support available. In the future, informal supporters will rely on formal supports to help them care for older family members. These formal programs need to offer flexible services—like adult day care, night care, respite care, and support groups—to meet the needs of individual families.

Policy makers often speak of partnerships between state programs and informal supports. But a number of researchers ask whether this new focus on the family will provide better care or simply shift the burden of care to families. Putney and colleagues (2007, p. 136) say that budgetary pressures and policy changes put new emphasis on family care. But this takes place "as families are less able to care for their elderly members."

Harlton, Keating, and Fast (1998) found that older people and policy makers differed in their view of care to older people. Policy makers thought that family and neighborhood (informal) supports gave older people more control over their lives. But older people felt that family support made them more dependent and a burden on their families. They did not feel that family members should provide housing, financial support, or personal care (Kemp & Denton, 2003). They preferred state-funded supports, believing that these supports gave them the most control over the services they received.

More than a decade ago, Rosenthal (1994, p. 421) said that formal support should play the central part in social support. Families (mostly middle-aged women) could then decide how much or how little of this support they need. "We should not overestimate the availability or quality of family care," Rosenthal said. "Some older people do not have family members who are able to provide care." Others may have family members who do not have the time or energy to give more than emotional support. Still others may prefer professional help to family care. Policy makers need to learn more about the views of older clients and their families to create programs that meet older people's needs. Kunemund and Rein (1999) find that generous state-funded social and health care supports strengthen rather than weaken family solidarity.

Eldercare and the Workplace

Eldercare can range from calling a parent once a week to providing personal care such as bathing or feeding. Eldercare can create stress for a middle-aged person who also has a family and a job. According to Dinger (2007, p. 1), "This caregiving role may interfere with their role as employee—through absenteeism, early departure from work, late arrival to work, personal phone calls, and emotional distraction." A MetLife (2006) study estimated a cost of $17.1 billion to

---

BOX 13.3
ELDERCARE AND WORK: A BALANCING ACT

Many middle-aged workers have to work and care for an older relative. The following case study shows the effects of caregiving on a person's work life. It also shows how an employee assistance plan can help a worker cope with the stress of caregiving.

Ron, a 35-year-old editor for a large publishing firm, provides care for his mother who has Alzheimer's disease. During the day, Ron's mother, Alice, attends an adult day program 3 days a week and has a paid caregiver who comes to the apartment 2 days a week. Ron and his mother live in Manhattan in a small rent-controlled apartment that has been their home since Ron was a child. Once the disease was diagnosed and it became clear that living alone was a dangerous proposition for Alice, Ron moved back into his childhood home to manage the everyday needs of his mother.

For the past three years, Ron has come home from work in time to pick up his mother at the day program or relieve the paid caregiver, and he spends his evenings on domestic chores and caregiving tasks. Lately Ron has taken to sleeping in the same room as his mother because of her sleep problems and fear that she might injure herself when she gets up in the night. Ron's cousin, who helps on the weekend, has encouraged Ron to begin to look for care facilities for his mother. While he realizes that moving Alice to a facility is inevitable, Ron has delayed making a decision based upon frequent conversations he had with his mother over the years about her fear of moving to a care facility in old age. Like many other caregivers of persons with cognitive impairment, Ron is distressed by the changes he observes in his mother and feels guilty and conflicted about providing care for his mother and managing the beginning of his career as an editor.

Ron has curtailed all of his work-related travel and often has to leave work early or come in late in order to take his mother to doctor's appointments. Lately, on the days after his mother has had a difficult night he has also noticed that he is making small mistakes at work because of his fatigue. He hasn't spoken to his supervisor or co-workers about his mother or his caregiving situation. After hearing them speak about a woman on their team who is also caring for her mother, he was concerned that he might be viewed as lacking the proper attitude and commitment for work if he brought his family life into the office. He did, however, use the 800 number available to employees for advice on eldercare because it was confidential and he didn't have to give his name. The phone call resulted in a list of adult day programs and phone numbers that eventually led to the services his mother is now using. Ron feels increasingly isolated in his work and in his caregiving tasks—and all too aware of the fact that relief will only come when it becomes necessary for him to break a promise he made to his mother many years ago.

Wagner, the author of this case study, published by Family Caregiver Alliance, estimates that as many as 15% of workers care for chronically ill relatives. The number of people who face this challenge will increase in the years ahead as more women are in the workforce, the United States has more older people in the population, and families have fewer adult children to care for aging parents.

What are some of the ways that businesses can help workers cope with the dual demands of eldercare and work?

Source: From Wagner, D. L. (2003). *Workplace programs for family caregivers: Good business and good practice.* Retrieved November 25, 2004, from www.caregiver.org/caregiver/jsp/content/pdfs/op_2003_workplace_programs.pdf. Family Caregiver Alliance/National Center on Caregiving. Reprinted with permission.

employers who have full-time employees with intense caregiving responsibilities. An estimate of the costs for all full-time employees who give care (not just the most intense cases) came to $33.6 billion. This included employee replacement costs, absenteeism, workday interruptions, and other adjustments to full-time work.

Dinger (2007) on behalf of the AARP surveyed 587 companies in South Carolina to learn about eldercare issues faced by workers. The companies reported that almost two-thirds of their employees (64%) provided care to an older person in the past two years. And 56% of the companies said that caregiving had an effect on worker performance. Half of workers at these companies (52%) had asked for time off to give eldercare. Thirty-four percent asked for time off under the Family Medical Leave Act. This requires employers to offer up to 12 weeks of unpaid leave to workers who need time off for family care.

A MetLife (2007) study of caregivers found that at least 6 in 10 had to make some adjustments at work due to caregiving responsibilities. Also, 52% of women and 34% of men said that caregiving for older relatives led to interruptions in their work (Neal & Hammer, 2006). Studies estimate that between 10% and 31% of caregiver workers leave their jobs because of caregiving demands. Some people retire early. Others quit their jobs (National Alliance for Caregiving, 2009; MetLife, 2006).

Gottlieb and Kelloway (1995, p. 339) found that people who give eldercare cut back on "leisure, continuing education, and volunteer activities." The researchers found that caregivers who gave personal care, such as nursing care, and those who gave dual care (who care for children and an older person) showed the greatest tendency to cut back on personal activities. Gottlieb and Kelloway say, "Paradoxically, it appears that, in their efforts to balance family demands and job responsibilities, employees are cutting back on those activities that afford relaxation, rejuvenation, and personal or career development."

MetLife (2006) reports that only about one third of large employers in the United States offer an eldercare program. Services include counseling referrals, support groups, and adult day care. Some companies offer employee assistance programs where a worker can get help from a professional counselor outside the company (Dinger, 2007). Mid-sized and smaller companies tend not to offer these programs.

But even simple, low-cost options such as flex time, seminars on eldercare, and more information about services help. They lower stress and lead to more job satisfaction. Wagner (2003) notes that the most progressive companies offer a "decision-support model." This model offers employees access to a care manager. The manager helps employees with care planning and with insurance and legal issues. The employer may hire a care manager or retain a company to supply this service.

More companies might offer these programs if they knew of the benefits to their workers and if they understood the potential savings in lost employee productivity. MetLife provides an "eldercare calculator" [www.eldercarecalculator.org] to help employers measure the productivity costs of caregiving. This may convince some companies to institute or expand their eldercare programs.

Older People as Family Supporters

Most of the research on older people in families focuses on their needs and on what other people do for them. But studies also find that older people give help to their families (Keefe & Fancey, 2002). Very early work by Shanas (1967) found that "far from being the passive recipients of their adult children's bounty, reciprocal help is given in the form of home services, monetary assistance, assistance in time of illness and other crisis situations and, in addition, older parents often provide childcare services."

Johnson and Schaner (2005a) say that almost 2 of 5 people age 55 and older, and about half of people ages 55 to 64, provided family care in 2002. Even among people age 75 and over, nearly one fifth provide care to family members. These older caregivers averaged almost 900 hours of care per year (or about 20 hours per week).

Researchers find that over a lifetime, parents give more support than they receive. Stone, Rosenthal, and Connidis (1998, p. 24) state, "If we had included the monetary value of services provided informally by one generation to another we would increase markedly the relative size of the figure for flows that benefit the young." Support from older parents to their children includes more than money. They often help their children with health care and daily chores. This can include help with housework or yard work.

Older people in families often play the role of kinkeeper. Kinkeepers keep family members in touch with one another. They form a hub of family communication. In our family, my mother played the role of kinkeeper. She kept in touch with her brothers and sisters weekly. She heard from my aunts and uncles on my father's side of the family a few times a year. She attended weddings and birthdays. Cousins, who live throughout the United States, called once or twice a year to keep my mother up to date on their lives. When I called, my mother would relay the latest news of family members' relationships, careers, and health. When I came to visit, my mother would arrange a dinner and invite our extended family. These people rarely saw one another except on these occasions.

A woman usually takes on the role of kinkeeper. Often a kinkeeper's daughter will take her place when the kinkeeper dies. Troll and Bengtson (1992) say that a younger woman may serve as an assistant kinkeeper when the kinkeeper gets feeble. Sometimes more than one person takes on this role and they become co-kinkeepers.

Troll and Bengtson (1992, p. 43) note that even the oldest old have a role to play in their families. Very old family members may withdraw from active roles like kinkeeping. They then serve to strengthen family solidarity. They give to their families "the memory of what they did for them and the model of how the next generation can carry on the pattern. . . . Their contribution to the young is perhaps also more symbolic than instrumental."

Family roles can give meaning and purpose to an older person's life. Research finds that older people have the highest emotional well-being when they give as well as receive support. Reciprocity makes older people feel useful, independent, and worthwhile.

Research shows that giving support to others—family, friends, and neighbors—even leads to longer life (Brown, Nesse, Vinokur, & Smith, 2003).

These findings overall show that most older people live interdependently with family, neighbors, and friends. They give and receive help with practical activities, finances, and advice throughout their lives. Older people's supportive roles can strengthen intergenerational ties and create more fulfilling relationships between parents and their children, as well as their grandchildren.

Elder Abuse

Until the late 1980s, few studies existed on elder abuse. Studies often used small convenience samples. Estimates on the amount of abuse ranged from 4% (Block & Sinott, 1979, cited in Pillemer & Finkelhor, 1988) to as low as 1.5% (Gioglio & Blakemore, 1983, cited in Pillemer & Finkelhor, 1988). Pillemer and Finkelhor (1988) conducted the first large random sample survey of elder abuse in the United States. The study took place in the Boston metropolitan area and included interviews with more than 2,000 older people in the community. The study focused on physical abuse, psychological abuse, and neglect. The study found an elder abuse rate for all types of abuse of 32 per 1,000, a physical violence rate of 20 per 1,000, a verbal aggression rate of 11 per 1,000, and a neglect rate of 4 per 1,000.

BOX 13.4
TYPES OF ELDER ABUSE

Writing and research on abuse and neglect typically include the following categories:

- Emotional or psychological abuse—mental intimidation, verbal or non-verbal aggression

- Neglect of yourself/neglect by your caregiver—improper use of medicine, poor eating habits, poor hygiene

- Financial exploitation—unauthorized use of funds or resources that belong to an older person

- Physical abuse—physical force that results in injury, pain, or impairment

- Sexual abuse—nonconsensual contact with an older person

- Exploitation—theft, fraud, misuse, or neglect of authority, use of influence to gain control of an older person's money or property

- Abandonment—desertion by someone responsible for care (National Center on Elder Abuse, 2007)

How common is each type of abuse? The state of Texas Area Agency on Aging of the Capital Area (2010) reports that neglect tops the list. Nearly 3 in 5 abuse cases (58.5%) arose from neglect. Physical abuse followed, making up 15.7% of cases. Financial abuse made up 12.3% of cases, emotional abuse 7.3%, and sexual abuse 0.4%. Other types and unknown cases made up the rest of the cases. Researchers (Pillemer & Finkelhor, 1988) estimated that in family settings (not counting self-neglect) only 1 in 14 incidents of abuse get reported. Another report (Wasik, 2000) estimated that only 1 in 25 cases of financial abuse gets reported.

TABLE 13.1 Who Perpetrates Abuse?

The following table, developed from data from 30 states in the mid-1990s, gives a picture of who perpetrates abuse.

Adult children	35.0%	Grandchildren	5.9%
Spouse	13.4%	Other relatives	13.6%
Service provider	6.2%	Friend/neighbor	5.2%
All others	10.3%	Unknown	7.4%
Sibling	2.9%		

Most abuse takes place within the family. In all, more than 7 in 10 abusers come from the abused elder's family—with adult children topping the list. Many researchers see elder abuse as a continuation of family violence that has gone on for years (Area Agency on Aging of the Capital Area, 2010).

Source: Area Agency on Aging of the Capital Area. (2010). *Elder abuse.* Retrieved November 20, 2010, from www.aaacap.org/eldabuse.html.

The *incidence of abuse* refers to the number of new abuse cases in a given time period, usually 1 year. In the late 1990s, Congress requested a study of elder abuse in the United States (National Center for Health Statistics, 2003). The government released the study, titled the "National Elder Abuse Incidence Study," in the fall of 1998. The study estimated that in 1996, 450,000 people age 60 and over in domestic settings experienced abuse or neglect (a rate of about 10 per 1,000). This figure fits with data collected in a 1999 study of all types of elder abuse in 17 states. That study found a rate of 8.6 per 1,000 older adults (Jogerst et al., 2003).

Prevalence refers to the total number of people who have experienced abuse or neglect in the population in a selected time period. This measure estimates how common a condition is in a population over a period of time. The National Center on Elder Abuse (2005, p. 1; National Research Council Panel, 2003) reports, "According to the best available estimates, between 1 and 2 million Americans age 65 or older have been injured, exploited, or otherwise mistreated by someone on whom they depended for care or protection."

The 1998 national incidence study found that only about one fifth of all cases got reported to an official agency. In other words, reported cases represent only a small portion (about 20%) of the actual cases of abuse in the United States. The national incidence study also found that, compared to men, women experienced a higher rate of abuse. Women made up 58% of the older population, but they made up 76% of emotional/psychological abuse cases, 71% of physical abuse cases, 63% of financial exploitation cases, and 60% of neglect cases. And very old people (age 80 and over) were abused or neglected at two to three times their proportion of the older population.

Black older people were abused at roughly twice their proportion of the older population. Ninety percent of the time the abuser was a family member. And of these family members, two thirds were adult children or spouses. Neglect most often occurred with people who were depressed, isolated, confused, or frail (National Center on Elder Abuse, 2010).

The study found that men accounted for 83.4% of abandonment incidents and 62.6% of physical abuse cases. Most perpetrators were between the ages of 36 and 59. Nearly one third of abusers were age 60 and over (Carp, 2000; National Center on Elder Abuse, 1998; Teaster, 2000). These findings and others have led to a number of theories of elder abuse. Some of these theories focus on family violence.

Theories of Abuse

Researchers have developed a number of theories to explain the causes of elder abuse (Carp, 2000). Theories of abuse focus on the causes of abuse. Quinn and Tomita (1997) describe five of the most common explanations in the literature: (1) the dependency of the older person; (2) caregiver stress; (3) learned violence in the family; (4) impairment of the abuser (by alcohol, drugs, mental retardation, etc.); and (5) societal attitudes toward older people, the disabled, and women.

Aronson, Thornewell, and Williams (1995; also Hightower, 2004) take a feminist view of elder abuse. They say that elder abuse reflects women's lack of power throughout life. Quinn and Tomita (1997) find that some studies support the theory that elder abuse is a continuation of spousal abuse into later life.

Theories of abuse are not mutually exclusive. Abuse can arise from more than one cause. A stressed caregiver may also come from a violent family and may be an alcoholic. A caregiver may hold both ageist and sexist views, and the stress of caregiving may trigger violence. Research shows that a number of conditions—the relationship of the caregiver to the older person, a history of family violence, lack of support for the caregiver, the gender of the caregiver, and caregiver competence—all play a role in determining whether abuse occurs.

Responses to Abuse

Researchers and practitioners disagree over the definition of *elder abuse* (Carp, 2000). They apply the term to many types of unhappy family relationships. This has led to confusion over what counts as elder abuse and to disagreement about the prevalence of abuse. Lachs and Pillemer (1995) say that arguments over the

---

BOX 13.5
CASE STUDIES OF ELDER ABUSE

The following case studies show the impact of elder abuse and neglect on vulnerable older people.

RUBY was a 71-year old widow who lived with her son Wayne. A neighbor stated that her friend Ruby seemed more and more depressed as time went by. In a recent conversation between the two women, Ruby told her friend that, at night, after she was in bed, Wayne sat next to her bed and read to her. After turning out the light, he slipped his hand under the bed covers and into her pants. Then, he fondled her private parts for nearly half an hour, and the time was increasing both in duration and in frequency. When Ruby told the story to her neighbor, both women cried.

GLENDA, age 83, was admitted to the hospital with a ruptured left eye due to untreated glaucoma. Her hair was matted, and her clothes were soiled. She had sores on her legs. Her toenails were so long that they curved over and under her feet. Glenda lived with a daughter who had a history of mental illness. Their home was infested with roaches and cluttered with trash both inside and out.

HARRY, age 72, was hospitalized due to the amputation of his leg. He signed over a power of attorney to his son, John. John did not have a job, nor did his wife. Harry had an estate of $400,000, plenty of money to support all of them. The son and his wife moved in and took over, including remodeling the house and spending significant amounts of money on luxury items. Though they said they remodeled a bathroom for Harry, the bathroom was not wheelchair accessible, and no ramps were built to enable Harry to come and go from the house. Harry was very capable of making his own decisions but was told whom he could see and was never included in making decisions about how his money was to be spent. Kept hostage in his own home, he never telephoned anyone because his son and daughter-in-law would listen in on the conversation and then yell at him. Other family members were told that they could not visit Harry unless they made prior arrangements with John, who summarily denied all of them contact.

(Note: Names are changed in order to protect confidentiality.)

Source: Teaster, P. B. (2000). *A response to the abuse of vulnerable adults: The 2000 Survey of State Adult Protective Services.* Washington, DC: National Center on Elder Abuse, pp. 1-2. Retrieved: July 3, 2010, from www.ncea.aoa.gov/NCEAroot/Main_Site/pdf/research/apsreport030703.pdf. Reprinted with permission.

National Center on Elder Abuse
1201 15th Street NW, Suite 350
Washington, DC 20005-2800
(202) 898-2586
Fax: (202) 898-2583
NCEA@nasua.org
www.elderabusecenter.org

---

definition of abuse overlooks the needs of the victims. They say that physical frailty, devalued social status, and elder abuse do exist, and that practitioners don't need to get hung up in this debate. They should focus on the needs of abuse victims.

Pillemer and Finkelhor (1988) suggest three responses to elder abuse: (1) professionals who work with older people need to know more about the prevalence of abuse and potential abusers (see also Cook-Daniels, 2004); (2) older people need to know more about abuse and what they can do about it; and (3) responses to abuse need to focus on parental and spousal abuse.

Studies show that the type of abuse depends on the physical and mental conditions of the abuser and the abused. It depends on the past and present relationship of the abuser and the abused. It also depends on social supports in the environment the abuser and abused live in. Interventions can improve these conditions and decrease the rate of abuse.

Elder Abuse Interventions and Policies

Policy refers to regulations and guidelines on how to deal with elder abuse. Policies can include criminal court action, mandatory reporting, guardianship and power of attorney, and mediation to resolve disputes. These methods use public means (by a social worker or police) to improve a family relationship. These methods intend to protect the older person. But this course of action often fails. The law assumes that two people in a dispute have only a limited relation to each other. But an abused spouse or parent often has a long-term relationship with his or her abuser, and he or she may want to maintain this relationship (sometimes at personal risk).

Legal action may do little to improve the abused person's life. A legal outcome, such as removing the abused person from a setting, may cause more stress to the abused person. Likewise, abused people may

---

BOX 13.6
WHAT ARE YOUR ATTITUDES AND BELIEFS ABOUT ELDER ABUSE?

Researcher Michael J. Stones created a research tool, the Elder Abuse Aptitude Test (EAAT), to study attitudes and beliefs about elder abuse. Fill out the EAAT below and total your score to assess your attitudes and beliefs. The EAAT will also sensitize you to the many types of abuse that older people can face.

The following statements refer to how people sometimes act toward older adults. They refer only to behavior by someone an older adult has reason to trust. That person could be a relative or someone who takes care of the older person. That person could also be someone paid to help or look after the older person's affairs, such as a doctor, nurse, homemaker, or lawyer. The questions do not refer to how strangers treat older people. Do you understand the kinds of people the questions refer to?

Please indicate whether the actions below are (1) not abusive, (2) possibly abusive, (3) abusive, (4) severely abusive, or (5) very severely abusive toward an older person if done by someone that person has reason to trust. Remember that the questions don't apply to an act by a stranger. Circle a number next to each statement, given that:

1 means Not Abusive
2 means Possibly Abusive
3 means Abusive
4 means Severely Abusive
5 means Very Severely Abusive

    A person a senior has reason to trust who

1. Steals something a senior values   [1]   [2]   [3]   [4]   [5]

2. Makes a senior pay too much for things like house repairs or medical aids   [1]   [2]   [3]   [4]   [5]

3. Pushes or shoves a senior   [1]   [2]   [3]   [4]   [5]

4. Lies to a senior in a harmful way   [1]   [2]   [3]   [4]   [5]

5. Opens a senior's mail without permission   [1]   [2]   [3]   [4]   [5]

6. Pressures a senior to do paid work when that senior doesn't want to   [1]   [2]   [3]   [4]   [5]

7. Doesn't take a senior places that senior has to go (like a doctor's appointment)   [1]   [2]   [3]   [4]   [5]

8. Withholds information that may be important to a senior   [1]   [2]   [3]   [4]   [5]

9. Unreasonably orders a senior around   [1]   [2]   [3]   [4]   [5]

10. Doesn't provide a senior with proper clothing when needed   [1]   [2]   [3]   [4]   [5]

11. Tells a senior that he or she is "too much trouble"   [1]   [2]   [3]   [4]   [5]

12. Fails to provide proper nutrition for a senior   [1]   [2]   [3]   [4]   [5]

13. Disbelieves a senior who claims to be abused without checking that claim   [1]   [2]   [3]   [4]   [5]

Add the numbers you circled and divide the total by 13. How did you score? How did your classmates score? Stones reported average scores of 4.07 for 22- to 40-year-olds, 3.83 for 41- to 64-year-olds, and 3.50 for 65- to 93-year-olds.

Sources: Stones, M. J. (1994). *Rules and tools: The meaning and measurement of elder Abuse: A manual for milestones*. Newfoundland; also Stones, M. J., and Pittman, D. (1995). Individual differences in attitudes about elder abuse: The Elder Abuse Attitude Test (EAAT). *Canadian Journal on Aging, 14*(Suppl 2), 61–71. Reprinted with permission from the Canadian Association of Gerontology, www.utpjournals.com. Also Stones, M. J., and Bédard, M. (2002). Higher thresholds for elder abuse with age and rural residence. *Canadian Journal on Aging, 21*(4), 577–586.

---

reject legal remedies such as jailing an abusing child or spouse because they depend on that person for help. Abused elders often fear reprisals from their abuser (Beaulaurier, Seff, Newman, & Dunlop, 2007).

Beaulaurier and colleagues (2007) examined the external barriers that older women face when they seek help from domestic abuse. Most women in this study felt that their families would not support them if they reported abuse. And the research bore this out. Families typically denied abuse or blamed the victim. One abused woman's mother said, "You married him knowing he was like that . . . so deal with it" (p. 750).

Women also lacked faith in the justice system. They did not feel they would get the help and support they needed. They feared that by reporting abuse they face greater jeopardy. One woman said: "A restraining order is [a court order] asking him to stay away from you, but it doesn't keep him away from you" (Beaulaurier et al., 2007, p. 751). Some women did talk to a member of the clergy for guidance (or said they would do so). But none of the women who talked to their clergy had been referred later to social services or the police. The authors found that most clergy encouraged these women to maintain "the status quo while offering little practical help" (p. 750).

Many women did not know where to go for community support, or felt no help existed. This applied especially to older victims of domestic violence. Beaulaurier and his colleagues (2000) say that "law enforcement responders need to . . . involve community providers of domestic violence and elder services in any intervention to create a viable safety net" (p. 754).

Nahmiash and Reis (2000) examined the effectiveness of intervention strategies in cases of abuse. The most successful strategies involved concrete help from nurses and other medical professionals as well as homemaking services. Other successful interventions helped to empower older people. These included support groups, volunteers who acted as advocates, and information about a person's rights and available resources (also World Health Organization & International Network for the Prevention of Elder Abuse, 2002).

Safe apartments in congregate housing and self-help groups for older abused spouses can help. Florida, for example, funds a statewide system of shelters for abused family members. More use could be made of these shelters.

Mason (2003) describes a 12-week program called SEAM—Stop Elder Abuse and Mistreatment. This program helps abusers change their behavior. It discusses their past unacceptable behavior and helps them develop acceptable alternatives.

Barriers exist to implementing these changes. For example, Wolf (2001) finds that many victims of family violence refuse to join a support group. She suggests that support groups have an older group leader or co-leader, someone familiar with issues these older people face. Many abused older people refuse services that might reduce stress. These include medical services, home care assistance, daycare centers, and respite programs. Roberto, Teaster, and Duke (2004) found that, compared with white women, African American older women tended to refuse intervention even though they ran a higher risk of repeated abuse.

Future Issues in Elder Abuse

Elder abuse and neglect have existed throughout history. What, then, accounts for the sudden interest in abuse and neglect? Four social changes explain this interest: (1) the growth in size of the older population, (2) the increased political power of older people, (3) the women's movement and a critical analysis of the family, and (4) the state's willingness to intervene in family life.

Wolf and Pillemer (1989) see health and social service professionals' intervention in child abuse and in elder abuse as parallel. In both cases, professionals, on behalf of the state, set out to protect a vulnerable minority (Otto, 2000). Through this process, elder abuse has become a legitimate social problem. Wolf and Pillemer see this attention as a first step in creating social policies to protect abused older people. Today, for example, in most states a health care professional must report suspected abuse or face criminal charges. These range from fines to time in jail.

Researchers have explored the causes, theories, and responses to elder abuse. More research is needed on the role of race, ethnicity, and culture in the abuse and neglect of older people. More research is also needed on elder abuse in institutional settings. Glendenning (1999) reviewed the literature on abuse and neglect in long-term care settings. This review found that the facility environment, the characteristics of the resident, and the characteristics of the staff (including the problem of staff burnout) all influenced the existence of abuse.

In 2003, State Long Term Care Ombudsman programs nationally investigated 20,673 complaints of abuse (National Ombudsman, 2003). They studied cases of gross neglect and exploitation on behalf of nursing-home and board-and-care residents. Among seven types of abuse categories, physical abuse was the most common type reported. Researchers say that professionals need more education about abuse and the tools to assess and detect abuse (Almoque, Beloosesky, Marcus, & Weiss, 2009; Cook-Daniels, 2004).

The large majority of older people do not experience abuse. Still, the number of abuse cases will grow in the future as the older population expands. This makes elder abuse an ongoing concern. Future studies should propose policies and practices to help ensure the safety of a growing and diverse older population.

THE FUTURE OF SOCIAL SUPPORTS

Studies in the past looked at families with a husband, wife, and children from one marriage. Studies of widowhood, for example, generally refer to loss of a lifelong mate. But changes in the family today will change family life for older people in the years ahead.

Married couples, for example, tend to make little use of formal supports. Even in late old age, when people have severe functional problems, compared with unmarried older people, married people have a much lower rate of institutionalization. Caregiving spouses may feel that the use of a nursing home, respite care, or other services means that they have failed. A couple may ignore the buildup of stress in their relationship until abuse or some other form of breakdown occurs. Studies can look more closely at couples and how they manage as they age.

Putney and colleagues (2007) speak of the "modified extended family" today. They see strength in multigenerational bonds, longer lives lived together, and complex family structures. This development provides rich supports for all family members—old and young. Distance and infrequent face-to-face contact challenges family members to stay in touch. But new technologies—computers and mobile phones, text messaging, Facebook, and Twitter—help bridge these distances.

Gonyea (2009, p. 217) questions this picture of the supportive mixed and fractured family. "Others argue," she says, "that while the step-kin or half-kin gained through marriage or remarriage may increase the size or number of members in one's latent network, this does not necessarily translate into willingness to provide needed support or care. In fact, there is mounting evidence that divorce and blended families tend to weaken ties between generations." Davey (Temple University, 2007) found that adult children of divorced parents reported less involvement in the everyday care of their aging parents (especially fathers). The obligations of these distant kin and almost-kin to care for one another and for older family members remains unclear.

Gonyea (2009) predicts a future crisis in care for older people. Increases in chronic illness among the old-old (85+) generation will put a strain on formal and informal care systems. Adult children of these older people say they intend to work for more years past retirement. This will reduce the number of family members available to support very old family members. In addition, Baby Boomers may feel financially strapped as they help their own children and grandchildren and provide support to their aging parents. Gonyea (p. 224) calls these Boomers the "club sandwich generation." Divorce, remarriage, and widowhood among the young-old will also reduce supports for their aging parents. These events will probably reduce supports in the future for Baby Boomers as well.

Who will feel obligated to support whom in the future? What will motivate older and younger people to care for one another? The changing needs of older people will pose new challenges for all of us as we age and depend on social support.

CONCLUSION

Research shows that older people provide support to family members and receive support in turn. Older people provide financial support, child care, and even housing to younger family members. They receive support when they face health problems or in cases of dementia.

The study of social support in later life finds strong links between the generations. It also shows that tensions can arise when an older person's support needs go beyond what a family can provide. In those cases, formal supports can take pressure off family members.

Most families today and in the future will rely on a combination of formal and informal supports to care for their older members. This will require a flexible system of formal supports that will include respite care, home care, and institutional care where needed. It will also include counseling and other interventions when an older person faces abuse from a caregiver.

SUMMARY

- In the past, at least one child stayed home to look after aging parents. Today, children move long distances from their families to find and keep jobs. In addition, families have gotten smaller as parents have fewer children. These changes in the family have led people to assume that families no longer support their older members. But studies show that families still provide most of the support for older people.

- Relatives provide most of the care for older people even when formal (paid or professional) care exists. Studies show that a spouse, if available, will take on the caregiving role.

- Women often take on the work of informal support for older family members. Male caregivers tend to feel less distress and depression than female caregivers. Men, compared with women, seem better at setting limits on their caregiving. Spouses and children provide most of the informal support for older people today. Siblings, friends, and neighbors provide emotional support.
- Sociologists describe the African American family as a mutual aid system. Older African Americans receive support from family members and help these members in turn. They also turn to the family for emotional and financial support. Additionally, the church is important for instrumental support for African Americans. People with strong family and church ties feel a sense of well-being.
- Caregivers of older family members with chronic conditions or with cognitive impairments often feel caregiver burden. Many caregivers find the role rewarding, but few find it easy. Successful informal caregiving entails (1) providing good care, (2) wanting to give care, (3) protecting one's own well-being, (4) developing new skills and abilities, and (5) using formal care systems when necessary. Older people and their caregivers need flexible services that they can tailor to their specific needs.
- Companies can help workers cope with caregiving demands. Eldercare programs can provide counseling, advice, and flexible work schedules. These programs would reduce caregiver stress and would improve productivity in the workplace.
- Families in the future will need to rely on formal supports to supplement informal caregiving. Pressures on the family in the future will include (1) more generations alive at one time, (2) top-heavy kin networks, (3) older members living to a very old age, and (4) more middle-aged women (traditional caregivers) in the labor force.
- Many caregivers report feelings of distress and burden. This applies especially to caregivers who care for someone with Alzheimer's disease. These caregivers can face time dependence burden, developmental burden, physical burden, social burden, and emotional burden. Spouses face some of the greatest challenges as they cope with a cognitively impaired mate.
- Researchers have discovered many types of elder abuse. Studies show that the type of abuse depends on the physical, mental, and environmental conditions of the abuser and the abused. It also depends on the past relationships of these people and the social supports available to them. Education programs and shelters for abused family members can help decrease the rates of abuse.

DISCUSSION QUESTIONS

1. What does research show about the existence of family support for older people?
2. Who provides most of the routine support for older people in their families? What other family members will older people typically depend on?
3. What type of system best describes how African American families provide support for their older members? What other informal supports, besides the family, do African American people use?
4. What types of strains do many female caregivers face today? Why do male caregivers, compared with female caregivers, feel less distress and depression?
5. What predictions do gerontologists make about the availability of family caregiver supports in the future?

How can companies help their employees cope with caregiving demands?
6. Describe some of the major changes in family structure that occurred in the 20th century. How has the system of informal supports changed due to this change in structure?
7. State at least three beliefs about elder abuse that the first large studies of elder abuse called into question. How can society help reduce the rate of elder abuse?
8. What effect will changing patterns in family life today have on older people in the future?

SUGGESTED READING

Kramer, B. J., & Thompson, E. H. (2002). *Men as caregivers: Theory, research, and service implications.* New York: Springer.

The authors say that caregiving research has generally looked at female caregivers. They note that, compared with women, male caregivers see caregiving differently, responding to the needs of their care receivers in unique ways. Men need different supports to fulfill the caregiving role. This book suggests new approaches to research on male caregiving.

Starkman, E. M. (1993). *Learning to sit in the silence: A journal of caretaking.* Watsonville, CA: Papier-Mache.

This book is based on a 10-year journal kept by a daughter-in-law caregiver. She describes the everyday feelings of satisfaction and frustration in her role. This unique and valuable book looks at the inner world of caregiving. Starkman concludes that families need to talk more about caregiving decisions.

Web Sites to Consult
The Caregiver's Home Companion

www.caregivershome.com

This site contains information for caregivers. The site's core belief is that caregiving can be stressful and difficult, but that it can also be rewarding and satisfying. The site provides information that helps caregivers reduce the stress and increase the joy of eldercare.

National Family Caregivers Association and the National Alliance for Caregiving

www.familycaregiving101.org

This site provides practical advice on caregiving for caregivers of ill and disabled elders. The site reviews the stages of caregiving, techniques on how to manage, and information on social supports.

This site serves as an example of the information on the Web available to caregivers.

National Center on Elder Abuse

www.ncea.aoa.gov/ncearoot/Main_Site/index.aspx

This site contains information on identifying and stopping elder abuse in a number of settings. It also includes white papers and peer-reviewed publications on the subject.

New York Times—The New Old Age

http://newoldage.blogs.nytimes.com

Stories and information on "caring and coping," nursing homes, dementia, and other topics of current interest. The site also provides listings of Web sites on specific aging-related topics such as government, caregiving, and end-of-life issues. A good source for up-to-date information.

chapter 14

DEATH AND DYING

Draw a line across a piece of paper. Put the word *birth* at the left end of the line. Put the word *death* at the right end of the line. Now put a dot for today's date. Put the date of your birth under the word *birth*. Now put the date you project for your death under the word *death*.

How did you feel about fixing a date for your death? How did you come up with a date? Do people of different ages think the same way about death? Do you look forward to your next birthday? Or do you think about how few years you have left to do the things you want to do? How do older people think and feel about death?

Have you discussed death within your family? Do people in your family or among your friends talk about a "good" death, about their preferences for

burial or cremation, or about their feelings about death and dying? This chapter looks at death in old age. It focuses on (1) attitudes toward death and on where death takes place, (2) ethical questions about death and dying, and (3) mourning and grief.

DEATH AND SOCIETY

Aiken (2001) says that social attitudes toward death fall on a continuum. Some societies see death as an enemy, something people fight with all their power. Other societies welcome death and even see it as a transition to a better, even blissful, world. Still others, in the middle, see death as a mystery.

BOX 14.1
DEATH AND DYING AMONG THE HUTTERITES

In an article on aging and death, Joseph W. Eaton reprinted the following letter from a Hutterite farmer to his sister. The letter describes the death of their younger brother.

Dear sister, our dear brother came home on September 8, on a Wednesday morning about 5 o'clock. He said that he had a fairly nice trip. He cried a great deal because of pains. He stated that distress teaches one to pray. I went immediately the following day to visit with him. I could hardly look at him, it was so painful to me; he looked so terrible that it made my heart almost break. However, I remained with him until he died, and until the funeral was over.

Two evenings before his death, his home was full of people, approximately 25 were there. He expressed a heavenly pleasure when he saw them all and said he could not express his pleasure in seeing them. It struck me almost as a miracle when I saw this starved and weak body lying there, telling us such a strong story. We listened to him, warned him not to talk so much because it may do him harm. However, he stated, "while I am still alive, I can speak. When I will be dead, then, of course, I won't be able to tell you what I have to say." . . .

He stated that dying does not cause him any difficulty; he said that he had a clear conscience and is in peace with God and all people. He asked many people in my presence whether they had something against him. However,

everybody replied in the negative. They said to him that they themselves were in peace with him. . . .

[Just before his death] his children stood around him with a sad heart, and all realized that his departure will be soon. He called his oldest son, gave him his hand and pressed a kiss on his forehead, and advised him how he should behave in the future. Among other words he told him he should obey his preacher, the boss and the field boss, and if the community entrusted a position to him, he should execute same as well as he could, and not only superficially. . . .

[He then calls to his side his daughter, the colony business manager, his wife and his brother.] He said, "I am at peace with God and with all people. I have a clear and good conscience. I am ready to depart, but now everything goes so slow. I have only one desire and that is to go to my Lord." He said quite frequently how good it is to have a clear and peaceful conscience. He advised us also that we should prepare ourselves, because the pleasure was inexpressible.

So I have described to you the events and experiences which I have seen with my own eyes, and it is my request and my wish that we all should prepare ourselves. Blessed by God.

Source: Joseph W. Eaton (1964), "The art of aging and dying," *Gerontologist* 4:94–112. Reproduced with permission of the Gerontological Society of America, 2000.

Kastenbaum (1999, p. xv) says he misses the old days—"the really old days." In the ancient past, he says, people saw death as a mysterious transition. They created myths and stories to explain death to themselves. The Greek Hades, the Christian Heaven or Hell, and the Muslim Paradise all show humans grappling with the meaning of death. For some societies, death meant an eternity of darkness and shadow. For others, as Dante describes in his *Inferno,* it could mean punishment for an evil life. And for Muslims, death means a life of ease and pleasure for believers. As Kastenbaum says, "Death was clearly something BIG." The power of the stories, their central role in religion and culture, tell us that people have always wondered about death.

But times have changed, and we have a new view of death and dying (one that coexists with some of our traditional views). Science and technology extend life and push death and dying to late old age.

Death remains abstract and foreign to most of us. We see graphic scenes of death in the movies and on television, but these images distance us from death. They have little impact on our daily lives. We can turn off the television or leave the theater if the images scare or depress us. We rarely have a direct experience of death.

Today, death challenges our moral and ethical codes. Our legal system grapples with the issue of physician-assisted suicide, our health care system deals with the long trajectory toward death that we call long-term care, and families cope with institutions such as hospitals and nursing homes where death most often occurs.

Death may still fill us with fear. But more often it confronts us with practical choices: To die in an institution or at home? To prolong care or end treatment? To opt for burial, cremation, or freezing the body until science finds a cure? We still hear the old stories through our religious traditions and literature. But they lack mystery and sound more like fantasy. Discussions of death and dying today often focus on death and dying in old age.

DEATH IN OLD AGE

In the past, high infant mortality, childhood diseases, and high female death rates during childbearing years made death among all age groups a common event. Today, most infants will live to old age. Life expectancy at birth in the United States for 2006 stood at 80.2 years for females and 75.51 years for males. Even at age 65 a woman can expect to live to age 84.7 and a man could expect to live to age 82 (Arias, 2010).

Longer life expectancy today means that death most often takes place in old age. Johnson (2009) says that in Europe people age 65 and older make up 80% of all deaths. This same figure holds for the United States (National Center for Health Statistics, 2010a). Today, most people die of the diseases of old age—cancer, heart disease, stroke, and lung disease. These diseases result from a lifetime of accumulated stress, genetic predisposition, or environmental attack. The trajectory of death from these diseases differs from dying in the past. People died at younger ages in the past and they often died quickly of an acute illness (e.g., influenza, pneumonia) or due to an accident.

Today, people often die from more than one chronic illness (Bern-Klug, Gessert, & Forbes, 2001). People often experience a slow decline along with intense crises that lead to death. Dying can include pain, delirium, swallowing problems, loss of mental function, and other forms of discomfort (Ross, MacLean, Cain, Sellick, & Fisher, 2002). Dying in old age makes special demands on health care providers, family members, and older people themselves.

Lynn (2005) describes three typical death trajectories in later life based on a study of more than 10,000 very ill patients in five hospitals from 1989 to 1994. The study showed that (1) about 20% of Americans will die from a fatal illness (e.g., cancer) after a long period of maintenance with good function and a rapid decline before death; (2) about 25% of Americans will die from an illness (e.g., emphysema) after a long slow decline with periods of crisis and a sudden death; and (3) about 40% of Americans will die from an illness (e.g., dementia) after a long-term decline in function that will need years of personal care. (The rest will die from other causes such as a heart attack, stroke, or complications from surgery.) Each group has unique health care, service, and social support needs. Lynn says that the health care system could serve people best by understanding each trajectory and providing each type of patient with appropriate care.

The Experience of Dying

Only a small number of studies have looked at how older people experience dying (Cicirelli, 2002). Gerontological theories suggest a number of alternative attitudes toward death in later life.

According to *activity theory,* for example, people want to stay active throughout their lives. They substitute new roles and activities for ones that they lose as they age. When people retire, activity theory says that they will have the highest life satisfaction if they find new things to do. This theory says nothing about death.

Disengagement theory says that people want to disengage from social roles as they age. This theory also says that retirement and withdrawal from social responsibilities leads to high life satisfaction. According to this theory, an awareness of impending death starts the process of disengagement. People know that they will die soon, so they ease out of social life.

Disengagement produces a smooth transition of power and responsibility from one generation to the next. Death has a less disruptive effect on society if older people disengage from social roles as they age. This theory focuses on the social effects of dying, but it says little about death as a personal experience or about how older people feel about death.

Erikson's (1963, p. 268) *theory of ego development* says that the last stage of life leads to a life review. A person looks over his or her life, ties up loose ends, and prepares for death. Erikson describes this as **ego integrity**. "It is the acceptance of one's one and only life cycle as something that had to be and that, by necessity, permitted of no substitutions." The integrated person accepts his or her biography and culture, and with this acceptance "death loses its sting."

These theories say that older people respond to death in more than one way: Some people deny it, some accept it, and some embrace it. The few studies that have tested these theories have found complex combinations of acceptance and rejection of death (Cicirelli, 2002).

Koster and Prather (1999) report that people at the end of life had five concerns: avoiding a drawn-out death, getting pain relief, having control of treatment options, staying in touch with loved ones, and fear of becoming a burden. People feared that they would burden their family with physical care, that family members would have to witness their deaths, and that family members would have to make decisions about life-sustaining treatment.

Studies that compare older and younger people find that older people think about death more but feel less afraid of death than the young. Cicirelli (1999), for example, studied 388 adults with an average age of 73. He found that younger people in this group reported more fear of death. A survey conducted for AARP in 2000 asked 1,815 people age 45 and older about their attitudes toward death (cited in Vierck, 2002). The study found that the older the person, the less she or he felt afraid of dying and of pain at the end of life. Both Cicirelli and the AARP study found that women, compared with men, expressed more fear of dying. Women also expressed more fear of pain and of having artificial means used to keep them alive.

A study of the oldest-old (people age 85 and over) found that people in this age group understood that life had come near its end. They considered death a part of living, and they felt that they needed to make decisions as they prepared for death. The loss of friends and the many changes in the world around them made it easier for them to accept death (Johnson & Barer, 1997).

Cicirelli (2002) studied the meaning of death for 109 older people between the ages of 70 and 97. The sample included people of both high and low socio-economic status and African Americans as well as whites. Cicirelli found that death held four meanings for this group. It meant (1) eventual meeting with God or nonexistence; (2) continued involvement in earthly life; (3) preparation to leave a legacy, something people would remember them for; and (4) a limited time left to do the things they wanted or needed to do. Some people felt more strongly about some of these items than others. And people often expressed all or more than one of these meanings at the same time. Cicirelli says, "In short, personal meanings of death influenced both how older adults lived now and how they expected to exist beyond death" (p. 79).

Cicirelli (2002) found a relatively low fear of death among the people in his study. Women scored higher than men on the four fear-of-death scales in this research. Cicirelli also found that fear of the process of dying and fear of the unknown peaked in the late 1970s and early 1980s. He suggests that at this age, people have not yet accepted the inevitability of death and have not come to a personal understanding of death.

Studies of the fear of death find that people with mild or uncertain religious belief fear death most, whereas those with strong religious beliefs or no belief at all deal with death best. Those who believe in hell also expressed a fear of death (Koppen & Anderson, 2007). People who believe in hell may have reason to fear their future. Those with an uncertain religious belief may accept enough of religion to believe in an afterlife, but not enough to feel they will have a good one.

Ardelt and Koenig (2006) studied 122 healthy older people, including 19 **hospice** patients. (Hospice care focuses on the quality of the dying person's life. It provides patients with pain relief and helps them maintain clear mental awareness.) The researchers in this study found that people who felt a strong personal relationship with God reported a better acceptance of death. Nakashima (2007) studied a small sample of hospice patients ages 65 to 103. She found that people who reported spiritual well-being (by feeling a closeness to divine existence) coped best with dying.

INSTITUTIONAL DEATH

Religious belief and a sense of purpose can help buffer the fear of death, but how and where a person expects to die also affects how he or she feels about death. In the past, most people died at home, surrounded by family, friends, and neighbors. Some cultures still ensure this kind of death. But in the United States, a large majority of deaths (for people of all ages) takes place in hospitals or nursing homes (Weitzen, Teno, Fennell, & Mor, 2003).

Between 14% and 22% of people in residential care or assisted living setting die each year (Golant, 2004; Zimmerman et al., 2005). And 34% of nursing-home residents die within the first year after they move in. About one quarter of all deaths in the United States in a year take place in a nursing home (Bercovitz, Decker, Jones, & Remsburg, 2008).

Many more people die in hospitals. About 50% of older people transferred from a nursing home to a hospital die within 4 days (Levy, Eilertsen, & Kramer, 2002b). The National Hospice and Palliative Care Organization (NHPCO) (2004) reports similar figures. Hospitals will take in more and more dying patients as the population ages. But studies show that many doctors and nurses in hospitals feel uncomfortable with dying patients. Ross and colleagues (2002) say that acute-care hospitals often marginalize older dying patients. Staff members see them as practical problems or bed blockers. The medical model, based on technology and cure, often fails to meet the needs of the dying older person.

A study of medical textbooks, for example, found that more than half the textbooks contained no information about pain management, psychological issues at the end of life, fear of death, or spirituality (Bronner, 2003). The Robert Wood Johnson Foundation has provided large grants to improve teaching about end-of-life treatment to physicians. The foundation has also supported changes in medical textbooks so that they contain more content on end-of-life care.

The foundation reports that more needs to be done. Nurses, pharmacists, and other health care professionals also need more training in **palliative care**. A study of pharmacy programs in the United States, for example, found that only 62% of pharmacy programs provide classroom instruction in end-of-life care (Herndon, Jackson, Fike, & Woods, 2003).

Medical staff members sometimes feel guilty or angry about dying patients. And they may misunderstand patients' preferences for end-of-life care. Wenger and colleagues (2000) report that in 54% of cases, physicians misunderstood patients' preference to forgo cardiopulmonary resuscitation. These patients had a lower chance of getting a "do not resuscitate" order on their charts and therefore had a lower chance of getting the treatment they preferred.

Because they have spent all of their professional lives learning to keep people alive, doctors tend to think of death as a failure. They may avoid dying patients or respond less quickly to their needs. Health care professionals need knowledge about pain management and about the unique needs of minority older people (Ross et al., 2002).

Dubler (2007) adds another challenge to the mix. In the recent past, risk-averse hospital administrators and risk-averse lawyers supported extreme measures to keep people alive. Dubler notes that these decisions took place without reference to patients' or their families' wishes. Recently patients and their families have begun to challenge the practice of keeping people alive almost without limit. The rise of palliative care medicine, hospice care, and the legalization in some states of physician-assisted suicide have all opened alternatives to limitless medical intervention. Public debate, patients' voices, and family concerns now shape the dialogue around end-of-life care.

CHANGES IN THE TREATMENT OF THE DYING

The health care system has begun to change its approach to dying patients of all ages. Two doctors more than any others—Elisabeth Kübler-Ross in the United States and Dame Cicely Saunders in England—started this reform.

Stages of Death and Dying

Kübler-Ross (1969) described five stages that her patients went through before they died. First, she says, people deny that they are dying. They say, "Not me." They may believe that the doctor has the wrong x-rays or someone else's tests. Perhaps they will go from specialist to specialist, looking for a new diagnosis. They may not even hear the doctor tell them they have a fatal illness.

Second, she says, people feel angry. They begin to believe that they will die. "Why me?" they ask. At this point, people blame the doctors or their spouses or God for their illnesses.

Third, people begin to bargain. They say, "Yes, me, but . . ." and try to make deals with the hospital staff. They may promise to be a good patient and to follow their doctor's orders, if only they will get better. They may bargain with God, promising to go to worship or to live a more pious life, or asking God for one more summer at the cottage, or for enough time to see a child married, a grandchild born, or their next birthday.

Fourth, people feel depressed. Their illness gets worse, and they know they will die. They say, "Yes, me," and they feel a great sadness. Kübler-Ross says that depression has two stages. In the first stage, people mourn present losses—the loss of family, career, and the things they love, such as a home, car, or cottage. In the second stage, they mourn future losses— the loss of good times to come, the chance to see children or grandchildren grow up, and other future events. People begin to say good-bye in this stage.

Fifth, people accept death. They say, "My time is close now . . . it's okay." They say good-bye to family and friends and die in peace.

Kübler-Ross says that at every stage, a person holds on to hope. At first, a person may hope the doctor has made a mistake; later, there may be hope for a remission if the person has cancer; and later still, there may be hope for a painless death.

Some writers question the number of Kübler-Ross's stages or their order. Shneidman (1984, p. 199) rejects Kübler-Ross's stage theory—"the notion that human beings, as they die, are somehow marched in lock step through a series of stages of the dying process"—on clinical grounds. He reports a wide range of emotions, needs, and coping methods that dying people use. "A few of these in some people, dozens in others—experienced in an impressive variety of ways." Kübler-Ross (1969) herself says that patients can skip stages, stages can overlap, and people can go back over the same stage many times. Some responses, such as anger, come up again and again.

Also, different illnesses create different trajectories of death or different patterns of response. Kübler-Ross based her model on cancer patients in a hospital, but cancer patients who have remissions may go through these stages more than once. People with other illnesses show other trajectories. Sometimes, a person can have long plateaus between times of decline. However, someone who dies shortly after an auto accident may not go through any of these stages.

Northcott and Wilson (2001) say that the dying process depends on many things—a person's age, the illness, the individual's will to live, and the treatments used to fight or manage the disease. Lawton (2001, citing Institute of Medicine, 1997; also Kaufman, 2002), for example, notes that "sudden death, steady decline, and episodic decline" all have unique death trajectories.

All sides of this debate share one thing: They have brought discussion and thinking about death into public life. People who have to cope with death and dying—patients, their families, and medical staff—now have a number of ways to think and talk about death. This has helped free many people from the silence that surrounded death and dying only a few years ago.

Hospice Care

The idea of a hospice dates back to at least the Middle Ages in Europe. Hospices at that time took in travelers who needed food, shelter, and care. Hospices today meet the special needs of dying patients. Dame Cicely Saunders opened the first modern hospice, St. Christopher's Hospice, in London, England, in 1967.

St. Christopher's has 52 beds, inpatient and outpatient services, a home visiting program, a day-care center for the children of staff, and private rooms for older people. The hospice welcomes visitors, including children, and allows families to cook for their dying relatives if they want to. Rooms are available for relatives who want to stay overnight. St. Christopher's does not attempt to extend life; it tries to relieve symptoms and to help patients enjoy their last days.

Hospice Program Goals

Saunders says that a "hospice is a program, not a place" (Canadian Medical Association, 1987, p. 34). First, a hospice controls pain. People fear death for many reasons, but often they fear the pain that may accompany death more than death itself. Pain relief ensures that the person will die in comfort, thus relieving much of the fear and anxiety. St. Christopher's pioneered the pain relief techniques now used by hospices around the world.

St. Christopher's created the Brompton mix—a mixture of heroin or morphine, cocaine, Stemetil syrup, and chloroform water—to relieve chronic pain. Medical staff base pain control on two techniques:

First, they adjust drug dosage until it relieves a patient's pain. "The aim," Saunders (1984, p. 268) says, "is to titrate the level of analgesia against the patient's pain, gradually increasing the dose until the patient is pain free." Then, the nurses give the next dose before the previous one has worn off. Hospitals often wait until a person shows signs of pain before they give the next dose of pain reliever. By giving the analgesic "before the patient may think it necessary [usually every 4 hours] . . . it is possible to erase the memory and fear of pain."

Patients cared for by this method need lower dosages to maintain a pain-free state because the drug does not have to overcome the pain that has begun. Lower dosages mean that patients stay more alert. A study conducted by the AARP (cited in Vierck, 2002) found that the public supports pain control at the end of life. Three fourths of people age 45 and over in this study said that doctors should be able to use controlled substances to control pain at the end of life.

The state of Oregon enacted legislation to support this view. The state passed the Intractable Pain Act in 1995. This act allows doctors to use controlled substances (e.g., morphine) to manage patients' pain at the end of life. The act relieves doctors of the fear of censure for prescribing pain-relieving drugs.

Dr. Susan Tolle, director of the Center for Ethics in Health Care at Oregon Health and Science University (cited in Ostrom, 2000), says the Intractable Pain Act has improved the treatment of dying people. She reports that Oregon, compared with the nation as a whole, has the lowest in-hospital death rate, better attention to advance planning, more referrals to hospices, fewer barriers to prescribing narcotics, and a smaller percentage of dying patients in pain (34% vs. 50% nationally).

Second, a hospice allows a person to die a simple death. The hospice does not use respirators or resuscitators to keep someone alive. Staff members make dying a part of life in the hospice. They leave the curtains open around a dying person's bed so that patients can see that their roommates have died. Patients also know they have a say in their treatment; they can ask for medication when they feel they need it, and they can ask to die at home. Saunders (1984) reports that people who die at home can feel more pain than people who die in the hospice, and caregivers often feel burdened by the demands of care. St. Christopher's (and other hospices) agree to re-admit patients whenever the patient or the family needs more support.

Third, a hospice gives people love and care. Johnson (2009) says that the hospice philosophy combines modern medical technique with Christian and secular spirituality. Staff members provide pain control, but also focus on the comfort of the patient, taking the time to touch patients and hold them. The hospice will serve special foods that patients like or give them soothing scented baths. The hospice also helps patients do as much for themselves as they can; this increases patients' well-being by giving them a sense of control over their treatment. The family members of dying patients also receive care. The Family Service Project at St. Christopher's offers help to families who find it hard to cope with their grief. Saunders (1984, p. 269) says that "staff and volunteers visit to assess the need and to offer support, and if more specialized help is indicated, this can be arranged."

Hospices spread to North America during the 1970s and early 1980s. More than 1,000 hospices opened in the United States between 1974 and 1984. The NHPCO (2004) says that in 1977, the United States had fewer than 100 hospices. By 2007, the number had grown to an estimated 4,700 hospice programs. Between 2000 and 2007 the number of nonprofit and government hospice programs remained fairly stable. But in that time the number of for-profit hospice programs more than doubled (from 700 to 1,600 programs) (NHPCO, 2009b).

The NHPCO (2007, 2010) reported that by 2008, 1.45 million people had used hospice care in the United States. More than a half million people worked as hospice volunteers in 2008, putting in 25 million hours of service. Most of that time they spent on direct patient care—spending time with patients and their families. A typical volunteer averaged 20 visits to hospice patients.

The NHPCO (2009) says that in 2008, 38.5% of all deaths in the United States took place within a hospice

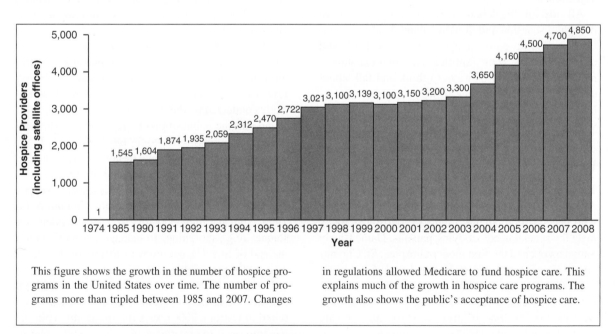

This figure shows the growth in the number of hospice programs in the United States over time. The number of programs more than tripled between 1985 and 2007. Changes in regulations allowed Medicare to fund hospice care. This explains much of the growth in hospice care programs. The growth also shows the public's acceptance of hospice care.

FIGURE 14.1 Growth in U.S. Hospice Programs: 1974–2007

Source: National Hospice and Palliative Care Organization. (2009b). *Facts and figures: Hospice care in America.* Alexandria, VA: NHPCO. Retrieved July 24, 2010, from www.nhpco.org/files/public/Statistics_Research/NHPCO_GraphUSHospicePrograms_Nov2007.pdf.

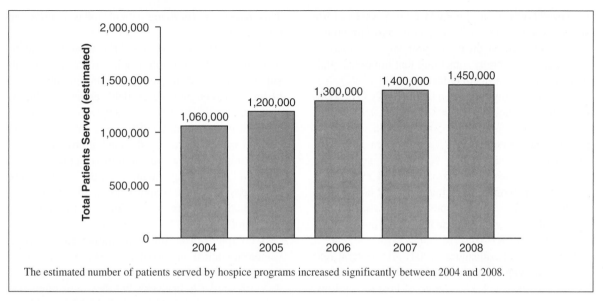

The estimated number of patients served by hospice programs increased significantly between 2004 and 2008.

FIGURE 14.2 Total Hospice Patients Served, by Year

Source: National Hospice and Palliative Care Organization. (2009b). *Facts and figures: Hospice care in America.* Alexandria, VA: NHPCO. Retrieved July 24, 2010, from www.nhpco.org/files/public/Statistics_Research/NHPCO_facts_and_figures.pdf.

program. Four fifths of all hospice patients (83.2%) in 2008 were age 65 and over. Thirty-eight percent of patients were age 85 and over. Hospices tend to serve people with three types of illnesses: cancer, kidney disease, and Alzheimer's. These illnesses put the most burden on caregivers. Hospices help relieve the increased strain of caregiving near the end of life.

At least four types of hospices existed in the United States in 2008: (1) freestanding/independent hospice facilities (57.5% of all hospices); (2) part of a hospital emphasizing relief of pain (21.8%); (3) part of a home health agency (19.4%); and (4) part of a nursing home (1.4%) (NHPCO, 2009b).

Hospice users report satisfaction with all of these programs. The Medicare Payment Advisory Commission (MedPAC) (2008), an independent federal body that advises Congress, found that families of cancer patients gave hospice care an excellent rating 77.9% of the time and a very good/good rating 20.5% of the time. Dementia patient family members gave hospices similarly high ratings.

Hospice care has taken the place of hospitals and nursing homes as the preferred place for cancer patients to die. The number of cancer patients who died in a hospice program doubled between 1992 and 2000. A report by the NHPCO (2009b) says that cancer patients make up almost 2 in 5 (38.3%) hospice admissions.

The 1982 decision to allow Medicare to support hospice care in part explains this shift in the location of deaths (Rybarski, 2004). The Centers for Disease Control and Prevention (CDC) (2007) says, "To qualify for the Medicare hospice benefit, terminally-ill patients must have a terminal diagnosis, a life-expectancy of 6 months or less, and [be] willing to forgo further treatments." Medicare spending for hospice care rose from $118 million in 1988 to over $10 billion in 2007 (Bernstein et al., 2003). The Office of the Actuary *2008 Trustees Report* (2008) projects a doubling of this amount for hospice care to $21 billion by 2018.

End-of-life care uses a high proportion of health care dollars. Surgeon and writer Atul Gawande (2010, p. 38) says that 25% of Medicare expenses go to 5% of patients at the end of their lives. And most of the cost comes in the last few months of life with "little apparent benefit." The medical model of care throws costly resources at incurable diseases to try to keep a person alive. "But, ultimately," Gawande says, "death comes, and no one is good at knowing when to stop." Hospice care offers one way for the health care system to cope with the high cost of dying.

Does hospice care save money? A study done at Duke University (2007; Taylor, Ostermann, Van Houtven, Tulsky, & Steinhauser, 2007; also MedPAC, 2008) found that hospice care reduced Medicare costs by $2,309 per patient. Hospice reduced Medicare costs for cancer patients who used up to 233 days of care. For noncancer patients, hospice reduced costs for patients who used care up to 154 days. Patients who used hospice care for the last 7 to 8 weeks of life show the best cost savings. Taylor and colleagues (2007) say, "The Medicare program appears to have a rare situation whereby something that improves quality of life also appears to reduce costs."

A national study sponsored by the NHPCO (2009b) found that hospice use in 2008 varied by age, gender, and race. People under age 65 make up 16.8% of hospice patients. People age 75 and over make up the majority of patients (67%). And people age 85 and over make up nearly 2 in 5 patients (37.8%). Compared to men, women had a higher rate of hospice use (56.6% vs. 43.4%). And, compared to whites, other racial and ethnic groups made less use of hospice care (81.9% vs. 18.1%).

Bernstein and colleagues (2003) give several reasons for this gap in hospice use by race. Older African Americans may lack knowledge of hospice options, they may lack a case manager (for instance, a regular doctor) to admit them to a hospice program, or they may lack the copayments required by Medicare to make use of the Medicare Hospice Benefit program. This difference in hospice use may also reflect cultural differences in preferred end-of-life care.

The gap between white and African American use of hospice care has grown over time. If this gap reflects socioeconomic inequality, these facts call for an improvement in Medicare policies. Policies need to recognize the unique economic and social conditions of many African American elders.

Critics of the hospice model say that it promotes a "good death" or "well-managed death." It defines a good death as a quiet and peaceful passing. The hospice, critics say, has institutionalized death. Western society has once again tried to bring death under systematic control. And some cultural and ethnic groups reject this approach to death.

Still, hospices provide an important alternative to death in a normal hospital or nursing home. Given the choice, cancer patients say they prefer hospice care to other institutional care options. Hospices, Johnson says (2009, p. 271) "proved to be a powerful and refreshing mix [of medical and religious ideals]." People can talk openly about dying and can feel some sense of control in their final days.

Palliative Care

The CDC (2007) says, "As many as 50% of dying persons with cancer or other chronic illnesses experience unrelieved symptoms during their final days."

This makes care for dying patients today an important clinical issue.

Moon (2006, p. 175) says, "For those who do not want to formally enroll in hospice, some services outside a hospice setting (such as counseling about end-of-life issues) ought to be available as well." Palliative care can play this role. It offers a way to ease suffering due to a chronic illness. "Palliative care, also called comfort care, is primarily directed at providing relief to a terminally-ill person through symptom management and pain management. The goal is not to cure, but to provide comfort and maintain the highest possible quality of life for as long as life remains" (Growth House, 2007).

A complete program of palliative care includes symptom control and spiritual support as well as bereavement support and education. Palliative care units do work similar to hospices, but they most often exist within a large acute-care hospital. And they may treat someone for months or years (vs. the hospice that treats people near death). Some programs now provide palliative care for patients in their homes. Workers in palliative care programs include nurses, physiotherapists, psychologists, and volunteers. The number of palliative care programs across the United States almost doubled from 632 in 2000 to 1,240 in 2005. Palliative care asks doctors and nurses to rethink their approach to pain and end-of-life care (Kenen, 2007).

Palliative Care for the Elderly

Studies show that palliative care can help older people as well as younger people, but some older patients have unique needs.

Brumley and colleagues (2007) conducted a controlled study of 297 older community dwelling palliative care patients (average age 73.8 years). These patients all had a terminal illness with an expectation of less than 1 year to live. They all lived at home and all received home health services. One group received normal care—home health service visits, acute care, and hospice care. The palliative care group got these services plus a team that provided relief of pain and symptoms, family education, training, and other supports. The palliative care group reported increased satisfaction with care and, compared to the control group, were more likely to die at home. They also made fewer visits to the emergency room and had fewer hospital admissions. The researchers say that this program resulted in cost savings to the health care system.

Palliative care turns some assumptions of the health care system upside down. First, palliative care acknowledges the limits of curative medicine. It accepts death as part of life. Second, palliative care follows the natural course of an individual's death. Palliative health services adapt to suit each person's needs. Third, palliative care treats the whole person—this includes the person's caregivers and social support system. Palliative care calls for a different kind of health care practice, one that broadens the health care options for dying patients.

A number of challenges face palliative care programs. First, funding of the health care system limits some palliative care services. For example, hospitals cannot claim reimbursement for services to caregivers. Also, only some palliative programs cover bereavement counseling. And physicians get low pay for home visits, a condition that limits their interest in palliative home care.

Second, health care workers and the public need more knowledge about palliative care. The public needs to know what this option offers. Professionals must know how to work effectively on a palliative care team. They need better primary training and more frequent continuing education.

Third, palliative care challenges some core beliefs that people hold today. Many people believe in the curative power of modern medicine. They may think that palliative care admits defeat and gives up on the patient. They may feel guilty about choosing palliative care for a dying parent or spouse. Northcott and Wilson refer to the "California daughter syndrome" (2001, p. 68). A child, who may not have seen a parent for many years, refuses to accept the imminent death of the parent. The child then demands maximum medical treatment. Gawande (2010), a physician, reports the following case.

> [A woman] in her eighties, with end-stage respiratory and kidney failure, had been in the unit for 2 weeks. Her husband had died after a long illness, with a feeding tube and a tracheotomy, and she had mentioned that she didn't want to die that way. But her children couldn't let her go, and asked to proceed with the placement of various devices: a permanent tracheotomy, a feeding tube, and a dialysis catheter. So now she just lay there tethered to her pumps, drifting in and out of consciousness. (p. 38)

Northcott and Wilson suggest one way to deal with a family's reluctance to end curative treatment. They call for the gradual use of palliative care measures as a person approaches death. This, they say, may avoid the appearance that treatment has ended when palliative care has begun.

A program at a skilled nursing facility in western Pennsylvania applies this approach (Capitosti, 2007). The program enrolls people in a palliative care program in two stages. A person enters the first stage if an interdisciplinary team cannot say for sure when the person's life will end. The second stage begins when the care team feels the person has less than 1 month to live.

All patients in the program (at either level) and their families have agreed to forgo attempts to cure the patient's illness. The team then designs a program that includes creation of a detailed **advance directive** and pain management plan.

Fourth, nurses in one study said that the health care system often made it hard for them to deliver palliative care at home (Ross & McDonald, 1994). They blamed bureaucracy, fragmented services, and too much focus on efficiency. These forces interfered with the quality of care they wanted to provide. It kept them from giving patients the emotional support they wanted to give. This study points to the tension between the values of palliative care and the model of efficiency and cost savings that drives the health care system.

Fifth, many older people will have no one at home to provide palliative care outside the institution. Community-based palliative care programs favor people with a primary caregiver. Older women, many of them widowed, often lack a primary caregiver. This makes them ineligible for home-based palliative care. Also, multiple pathologies in an older patient may make pain control more complex.

Frail older people on palliative home care may need the use of respite beds and a day hospital. Palliative care at home places more demands on family caregivers. And some caregivers of older patients in palliative care programs report feeling stressed and exhausted (Ross et al., 2002). Families need health care and social support to carry out home-based palliative care.

Home care workers can help with cleaning and shopping. Respite care can help family caregivers get the rest they need. Quality community-based end-of-life care depends on a partnership between formal and informal caregivers. It also depends on the support of institutional care when needed. In Great Britain, for example, most end-of-life care takes place at home, but people often go to a hospital for a short (1- to 3-day) stay before they die (Eastaugh, 1996, cited in Northcott & Wilson, 2001).

The Last Acts organization (2002, 2003), originally funded by a grant from the Robert Wood Johnson

Foundation, studied palliative programs in all 50 states and the District of Columbia. The study found that more programs exist today than in the past. And people throughout the country show more awareness of end-of-life issues. But the study also saw room for improvements. The research found that only about 25% of dying patients die at home. Most people still die in hospitals and nursing homes. Many of these people would benefit from home-based palliative care. The study also found that the country needs more health care professionals trained in pain management.

Other studies support the need for more professional training in palliative care. One study, for example, found that primary care physicians created the most barriers to fulfilling palliative care goals (such as pain control) (Ryan, Carter, Lucas, & Berger, 2002). In another study, 66% of physicians trained as geriatric fellows felt that they could use more training in hospice and palliative care (Medina-Walpole, Barker, & Katz, 2004).

Training of fellows in geriatric medicine continues to improve. Pan and colleagues (2005) conducted a survey of 188 (of 296) new geriatric medicine fellows in 2002. Nearly all of the respondents (95%) said they felt physicians should know how to care for dying patients. Seventy percent of the fellows reported that they had taken a rotation that dealt with end-of-life care. The fellows reported satisfaction with their end-of-life training and confidence in their ability to care for dying patients. Those who had taken a palliative care or end-of-life rotation felt the most confidence in their ability. Training topics included learning how to

say good-bye to patients. These findings suggest that geriatric medicine recognizes the importance of end-of-life care. Training programs have begun to provide doctors with the skills they need.

ETHICAL ISSUES

Palliative care and other approaches to the treatment of dying patients raise a variety of ethical questions. Is it ethical to stop actively treating a person's illness? Does the decision not to put someone on a respirator or not to use a heroic lifesaving measure contribute to the person's death? Philosophers, physicians, and legal experts have looked at these and other issues related to dying today.

Two ethical questions come up again and again in the writing on death and dying. First, how much information should health care providers give a dying person about his or her conditions? Second, when should a doctor allow a person to die?

Advance Directives

Some years ago, experts debated whether to tell dying patients about their condition or keep this knowledge from them. Today, most experts support an open awareness context. They agree that patients have a right to know about the choice of treatment the physician has made and about alternative treatments, including the choice of no treatment. Advance directives (statements of a patient's wishes) empower the patient and remind physicians to include patients in planning

---

BOX 14.2
PRINCIPLES OF QUALITY PALLIATIVE CARE

A study titled "Last Acts," originally funded by the Robert Wood Johnson Foundation, looked at the experience of death and dying in America. The program involved more than 400 organizations in producing the following guidelines for quality palliative care.

The following Five Principles of Palliative Care describe what care can and should be like for everyone facing the end of life. Some of these ideas may seem simple or just common sense. But together they give a new and more complete way to look at end-of-life care.

1. Palliative care respects the goals, likes, and choices of the dying person.

2. Palliative care looks after the medical, emotional, social, and spiritual needs of the dying person.

3. Palliative care supports the needs of the family members.

4. Palliative care helps gain access to needed health care providers and appropriate care settings.

5. Palliative care builds ways to provide excellent care at the end of life.

Source: A vision for better care at the end of life. Retrieved December 13, 2004, from www.partnershipforcaring.org/Resources/prineng.html.

their care. Perkins (2007, p. 52) says that advance directives prod "people to overcome their aversions and to face the hard decisions about dying."

Patients need to communicate their preferences for end-of-life treatment to their health care providers. At present, a person who lacks the mental competence to refuse treatment must rely on someone else to act for him or her. Family members, a friend, or a medical doctor often must make this decision. Even if a person has told someone what he or she wishes or has written a statement of the wish to end treatment at a certain point, these instructions have no binding effect on a decision maker. Yet the clearer a person's wishes, the more information caregivers have when they need to make a decision.

Directives most often take the form of the **power of attorney** or a **living will**. The **power of attorney** gives someone (often a lawyer, but also a child, spouse, other family member, or a health care provider) the right to make financial or health care decisions on behalf of the older person if the person loses his or her mental capacity. The **living will** refers to health care wishes at the end of life. The Mayo Clinic (2009) defines a *living will* as a written, legal document that states the types of medical treatment or life sustaining measures you do or don't want. These would include the use of mechanical breathing devices, tube feeding, dialysis, or resuscitation.

Some states call the living will a "health care declaration" or "**health care directive**." Each state has a preferred form for an advance directive. A Web site called Caring Connections (www.caringinfo. org/googlehealth) provides free advance directives for each state. In the past 3 years, Caring Connections has distributed more than 2.5 million advance directive forms.

The NHPCO (2009a) partnered with Google Health for a new way to access and store advance directives. A person can now go online and download an advance directive, scan the form to their computer file, upload the file to a Google Health profile, and share their profile with family members and caregivers. (See http://googleblog.blogspot.com/2009/07/plan-ahead-document-and-share-your.htmll). NHPCO and Google want to make advance directives accessible to caregivers when needed.

Advance directives state who can make health care decisions on the older person's behalf, if the older person can't make decisions on his or her own. Advance directives allow the older person to maintain autonomy. They state what medical actions a person wants

under what conditions. The CDC (2007) encourages families to have conversations about end-of-life issues. Directives can help avoid court intervention in decision making.

The federal government and state laws govern advance directives. Each state has its own statutes. All but a few states authorize the use of the living will and the medical power of attorney. Most states allow family members and in some cases close friends to make health care decisions for an incapacitated person.

Unfortunately, state statutes sometimes conflict with one another. And even within a state, advance directive statutes may conflict with other laws. In 1993, the National Conference of Commissioners on Uniform State Laws (2010) passed a draft of a Uniform Health-Care Decisions Act. The commissioners proposed that states pass this act to bring uniformity to statutes across the country. At this writing, only some states have passed this act.

A more powerful boost to the use of advance directives came from the federal government. The federal government passed the Patient Self-Determination Act in 1990. This act encourages people to choose the type of medical care and the extent of medical care they want at the end of life. The Patient Self-Determination Act says that hospitals, nursing homes, and other health agencies that get Medicare or Medicaid payments must recognize the living will and health care powers of attorney. The Patient Self-Determination Act affirms a person's right to make his or her own end-of-life decisions. Health care agencies must ask people whether they have advance directives. They must also give people educational materials about their rights under state law.

Family members and physicians sometimes differ in their judgment of the person's will to live and in their judgment of the person's end-of-life preferences. This potential for conflict supports the need for an advance directive. An advance directive allows a person to think about his or her preferences while in a sound state of mind. It allows people to control their own destinies. The courts will honor advance directives. But a person's relatives or friends need to make health care professionals aware of the directive and what it says. Emanuel (2008) says that physicians would appreciate this kind of guidance from patients.

Cramer, Tuokko, and Evans (2001) report that most people have heard of advance directives, but relatively few people have them. In their study, they found that only 28% of their sample had made out a power of attorney for finances. Only 19% said they had a living will for health services. People with more education tended to have these documents in place.

Dubler (2007, p. 23, citing Zeleznick et al., 1999) found that only 1.5% of people age 65 and over who entered a hospital had an advance directive. She calls this a "failed policy" because it fails to work in practice. Cramer and colleagues (2001) say that advance directives work best when the older person has discussed preferences with the person's surrogate. But "most patients," Dubler (p. 25) says, "do not prepare for death by telling others what they want. Most patients slip slowly into the process of dying depending on family and medical providers to act for them and in their best interest."

The literature on advance directives comes back again and again to the need for conversations between a person and their family and physician. Gawande (2010) says that, compared to patients who did not discuss their end-of-life care goals, those who did had fewer trips to the intensive care unit, less often had cardiopulmonary resuscitation, and less often ended up on a ventilator. Those who enrolled in a hospice program suffered less, maintained their physical ability longer, and continued to interact with others. People who discussed their wishes with their doctor died at peace and spared their families distress.

Some research shows that people put off creating an advance directive. They may not know about them, may not know their value, or may not want to think about poor health or death (Hamer, Guse, Hawranik, & Bond, 2002). Galambos (1998), for example, reports that relatively few people—15% to 20% of the population—make advance directives. She reports that only 35% of people age 75 and over have such a document. Upper-class whites show the greatest likelihood of having an advance directive. Minorities show the least likelihood.

Minorities and Advance Directives

Hopp and Duffy (2000) studied the end-of-life decisions of 540 people age 70 and over. The study included 86 African Americans and 454 whites. The researchers found that, compared with African Americans, whites tended to discuss their preferences for treatment before their deaths. Whites tended to have a living will and to identify a **durable power of attorney**. In addition, whites tended to make decisions about limiting care and withholding treatment at the end of life. African Americans tended to desire all possible treatments to extend life.

McAuley and Travis (2003) studied the use of advance directives in long-term care settings—specifically, living wills and orders that limited treatment. They found that, compared with the rest of the sample, African Americans were least likely to have either type of advance directive. Austin and Fleisher (2003) say that minority group members' choices at the end of life reflect their earlier experiences with the health care system. They report that minority group members feel distrust in the health care system. Minority group members also face cultural barriers. These include language barriers and attitude differences between minority patients and white health care providers (Krakauer, Crenner, & Fox, 2002).

These conditions account for the high proportion of African American elders who die in a hospital (Berger, Pereira, Baker, O'Mara, & Bolle, 2002). A study of African Americans' end-of-life preferences (Johnson, Kuchibhatia, & Tulsky, 2008) found that, compared to whites, they had expressed less trust in the health care system. They held less favorable views of hospice care and felt more discomfort discussing death. They also preferred more aggressive care. Minority members who feel that the system has excluded them in the past tend to want all available treatment at the end of their lives (Owen, Goode, & Haley, 2001).

Also, spiritual beliefs may conflict with the goals of palliative care. Johnson and colleagues (2008, p. 1953) compared African American and white attitudes toward palliative care. They found that compared to whites, "African Americans were more likely to express discomfort discussing death, want aggressive care at the end of life, have spiritual beliefs that conflict with the goals of palliative care, and distrust the healthcare system." African Americans also tended to agree that "those who believe in God do not have to plan for end-of-life care" (p. 1956).

Yeo (2009) says that palliative care, advance directives, hospice, open discussions of death, and other Western end-of-life approaches may not suit minority cultures. She says that health care professionals need to take cultural differences into account. Yeo says that family members in Asian cultures, for example, may demand that everything be done to keep an older parent alive. The values of filial piety and a belief in the will of God requires this.

Also, members of Navajo and Chinese cultures may not feel comfortable discussing death. These cultures feel that if a person knows that they are dying, they will give up hope. The family may ask the physician not to inform the older person about his or her condition.

Modern medicine can feel proud of recent advances in end-of-life care. But, as Yeo (2009) cautions, minority cultural values may clash with the latest thinking in Western medicine. The ethnic and racial diversity of the older population requires sensitivity to cultural differences.

Yeo proposes that: (1) health care settings bring in people from ethnic populations to provide more culturally and linguistically appropriate services. These people can serve as "cultural guides, brokers, and navigators." Respected clergy, educators, clan leaders, and interpreters can all serve in this role. They can bridge the cultural gap between minority patients and the health care setting. And (2) health care settings need to provide training and continuing education to nonminority health care professionals. This will increase professionals' awareness of patients' diversity and their cultural preferences.

A final point on the diversity of views related to end-of-life care: Some people oppose active and passive euthanasia on moral, ethical, and religious grounds. Someone with this view considers artificial nutrition and hydration as essential to life—not as a form of medical treatment. This view, for example, would not allow a third party to end artificial nutrition or hydration (unless the patient authorized this in an advance directive). A group called the National Right to Life Committee (NRLC) offers an alternative to the standard living will. They call this a "Will to Live." (You can find a copy of the "Will to Live" at www.nrlc.org/euthanasia/willtolive/index.html.)

This discussion of advance directives shows that people differ in their attitudes toward end-of-life treatment and decisions. A more diverse older population in the future will mean more diversity in attitudes toward death and dying. Health care professionals will need to take this diversity of views into account in their treatment of older patients.

Beyond Advance Directives: The Importance of Communication

In spite of their value, advance directives pose problems that need public discussion. First, most people don't fill out an advance directive. Mezey and colleagues (Mezey, Mitty, Bottrell, Ramsey, & Fisher, 2000) found that only 51% of nursing-home residents had written advance directives. Some studies find that people prefer to let family members make end-of-life decisions for them. They may decide not to fill out an advance directive in order to give family members more freedom.

Second, in some cases people change their minds about treatment as they near death, but they may not get a chance to change their advance directive. Lawton (2001) reviewed studies of end-of-life preferences. He found support for this concern. The research showed that about 30% of people change their preferences over time. Some want more intervention (10%) and others less (20%). He concludes that people need the chance to review and, if necessary, revise their advance directive as they approach death.

Third, subtle forms of coercion may influence an older person's instructions in an advance directive. Older people may propose an end to treatment because they feel that they will burden others with their care. Also, a health care provider, due to conscience or institutional policy, may refuse to abide by the older person's wishes.

BOX 14.3

A DIVERSE OLDER POPULATION HAS DIVERSE VIEWS ON END-OF-LIFE CARE

The study of minority groups shows the variety of preferences for end-of-life treatment. Some groups accept the modern approach that includes the patient in end-of-life decisions, other groups prefer that the family make decisions for the dying person. Some groups prefer to end extreme treatment, other groups prefer that everything be done to keep a person alive. The following case told to Professor George Dickinson shows that a person's social group can influence end-of-life treatment. In this case the man's pain gave meaning to his dying.

An elderly male patient with cancer would not take his pain medication. The nurse asked to talk to him. She learned that he was in the landing of Normandy in World War II and endured much pain and hardship. Many of his comrades died in the invasion. Out of his feelings for those comrades and those memories of the landing, he told the nurse that he could/would endure the pain. The pain brought back memories, and he must "bear it" out of respect for those fallen fellow soldiers.

Told to George Dickinson by a nurse in the spring of 1999 in Sheffield, England.

Source: Listening to the voices. Enduring pain. In Leming, M. R., & Dickinson, G. E. (2007). *Understanding dying, death, and bereavement* (6th ed., p. 213). Belmont, CA: Thomson Wadsworth.

Fourth, health care professionals may not know an advance directive exists. Or they may not think it applies in a specific case. Finally, the advance directive may be too vague to guide action. "As a result," Hickman and colleagues (Hickman, Sabatino, Moss, & Nester, 2008, p. 119) say, "Advance directives typically do not affect patient care."

These issues point to the need for better methods of communication between dying people and their caregivers (Teno, Gruneir, Schwartz, Nanda, & Wetle, 2007). Bern-Klug and colleagues (2001) say that older people, families, and health providers need to have more than a written advance directive. They need to have in-depth discussions about an older person's preferences for end-of-life care.

Teno and colleagues (2007) explored the impact of advance directives. The researchers interviewed a sample of 1,587 people who died in a nursing home, in a hospital, or at home. They found that 70.8% of the people who died had an advance directive. The presence of an advance directive led to less use of feeding tubes and respirators in the last month of life. Also, relatives of those with an advance directive felt more satisfied with physician communication.

Still, the researchers found the need for more attention to end-of-life care. For example, they found that 1 in 4 of the respondents said that the deceased relative had unmet pain needs. One in 2 reported inadequate emotional support for the patient. And 1 in 3 said the patient lacked enough family emotional support. The researchers conclude that advance directives led to greater use of hospice care and better communication. But the study also points to the need for attention to the quality of end-of-life care.

Perkins (2007, p. 51) says that even with the best planning, death and dying create unexpected demands. Physicians "should warn patients and families that momentous, unforeseeable decisions lie ahead." Perkins stresses "honest communication, preparation of patients and families for death's harsh and unpredictable reality, mutual support, nonformulaic, individualized care, and courageous decision making despite uncertainties" (p. 55). Physicians and other health care workers should provide guidance and emotional support to family members.

Tulsky (2005), a physician, sums up the importance of advance directives and their limitations. "Advance care planning," he says, "remains a useful tool for approaching conversations with patients about the end of life." But planning must respond to "patient and family emotions." The patient and family, their comfort and wishes, must be the focus of quality care.

New Methods of Communication

Dubler (2007, p. 28) says the legal reliance on advance directives (and their typical absence) leads to "far more aggressive care . . . than the physicians think is appropriate or than the family wants." Dubler proposes a legal process that would come into play when the patient has not left a clear preference for end-of-life care. This process would end disputes over patient treatment.

The state of Texas (2004), for example, enacted a law to resolve disputes between family members and physicians over care. The law provides for the involvement of an ethics committee, possible transfer to another health care setting, and final appeal to a court. If disagreement remains, the hospital may stop treatment over the family's objection. Dubler (2007, p. 31) supports this "new, open, transparent, and engaged process." Researchers will study the effectiveness and acceptance of this process.

The state of Oregon developed a Physician Orders for Life-Sustaining Treatment (POLST) Paradigm Program. This program ensures that communication takes place between health care providers and patients. The POLST paradigm turns "patient goals and preferences for care into medical order" (Center for Ethics in Health Care, 2010). The POLST program helps health care professionals work up treatment plans that fit patients' wishes.

The patient and physician fill out and sign a formal and highly visible (bright pink in some cases) form that states the patient's wishes in detail. The form includes a Do Not Attempt Resuscitation/DNR option. But it also includes specific treatment options—the patient's preferred level of medical intervention (e.g., comfort care only), the patient's choice related to the use of antibiotics, and the patient's choice related to artificial feeding. (Each state has its own laws and regulations. See Figure 14.3 for an example of the Oregon POLST form.)

The POLST form now serves as an accepted standard of care in Oregon. All hospices and more than 95% of nursing homes in Oregon use the form. Other states adopted programs similar to the one in Oregon. Early adopters include New York, Pennsylvania, Washington, West Virginia, and Wisconsin. Other states have since enacted laws to support the POLST paradigm program. The term *POLST paradigm* refers to these programs and to the specific process that they follow.

POLST forms do not take the place of advance directives. Advance directives appoint a surrogate in

HIPAA PERMITS DISCLOSURE OF POLST TO OTHER HEALTH CARE PROFESSIONALS AS NECESSARY

Physician Orders
for Life-Sustaining Treatment (POLST)

First follow these orders, then contact physician, NP, or PA. This is a Physician Order Sheet based on the person's medical condition and wishes. Any section not completed implies full treatment for that section. Everyone shall be treated with dignity and respect.

Last Name	
First Name/ Middle Initial	
Date of Birth	

A *Check One*

CARDIOPULMONARY RESUSCITATION (CPR): Person has no pulse and is not breathing.

☐ Attempt Resuscitation/CPR ☐ Do Not Attempt Resuscitation/DNR (Allow Natural Death)

When not in cardiopulmonary arrest, follow orders in **B**, **C** and **D**.

B *Check One*

MEDICAL INTERVENTIONS: Person has pulse and/or is breathing.

☐ **Comfort Measures Only** Use medication by any route, positioning, wound care and other measures to relieve pain and suffering. Use oxygen, suction and manual treatment of airway obstruction as needed for comfort. ***Do not transfer** to hospital for life-sustaining treatment.* ***Transfer** if comfort needs cannot be met in current location.*

☐ **Limited Additional Interventions** Includes care described above. Use medical treatment, IV fluids and cardiac monitor as indicated. Do not use intubation, advanced airway interventions, or mechanical ventilation. ***Transfer** to hospital if indicated. Avoid intensive care.*

☐ **Full Treatment** Includes care described above. Use intubation, advanced airway interventions, mechanical ventilation, and cardioversion as indicated. ***Transfer** to hospital if indicated. Includes intensive care.*

Additional Orders: ______________________

C *Check One*

ANTIBIOTICS

☐ No antibiotics. Use other measures to relieve symptoms.
☐ Determine use or limitation of antibiotics when infection occurs.
☐ Use antibiotics if life can be prolonged.

Additional Orders: ______________________

D *Check One*

ARTIFICIALLY ADMINISTERED NUTRITION: Always offer food by mouth if feasible.

☐ No artificial nutrition by tube.
☐ Defined trial period of artificial nutrition by tube.
☐ Long-term artificial nutrition by tube.

Additional Orders: ______________________

E

REASON FOR ORDERS AND SIGNATURES

Discussed with:
☐ Patient
☐ Parent of Minor
☐ Health Care Representative
☐ Court-Appointed Guardian
☐ Other:______________

My signature below indicates these orders are consistent with the person's preferences, if known. See medical record for further documentation.

Print Physician/NP/PA Name and Phone Number ( )	Office Use Only
Physician/NP /PA Signature (mandatory) / Date	

SEND FORM WITH PERSON WHENEVER TRANSFERRED OR DISCHARGED

This relatively simple form provides specific end-of-life health care preferences. It also states who has agreed to these preferences, and it includes the physician's signature. This shows that the patient has discussed his or her preferences with a health care provider. The bright pink color of most POLST forms alerts staff to the presence of the form.

FIGURE 14.3 A Sample POLST Paradigm Form from Oregon

Source: Center for Ethics in Health Care, Oregon Health & Science University, 3181 Sam Jackson Park Rd., UHN-86, Portland, OR, 97239-3098. Phone: 503-494-3965. Reprinted with permission.

case a patient can no longer make decisions. The advance directive also expresses the person's values. An advance directive complements a POLST form. The POLST form ensures that the person has discussed medical options and made informed choices along with his or her physician. A report by the National Quality Forum (2006, p. 43) says that "compared with other advance directives programs, POLST more accurately conveys end-of-life preferences and yields higher adherence by medical professionals."

Fitzpatrick and Fitzpatrick (2010, p. 165) say that POLST forms, as they observe their use in Oregon, have their limitations. They say that the forms "are routinely ignored by nursing homes." Some homes require a terminal illness diagnosis from two doctors before they will act on a POLST form. This can lead to treatment that the patient does not want. The POLST paradigm program (and any other program) depends for its success on the willingness of health care providers to abide by the patient's wishes.

Legal barriers can also stand in the way of POLST form use. Hickman and colleagues (2008) reviewed state laws that influence the use of POLST forms. They found that some states define medical conditions (e.g., a diagnosis of terminal illness by at least two doctors) that must exist before a POLST form can come into play. Also, some states require a specific witness before health care providers can use the POLST form. Finally, some experts consulted in this study had trouble interpreting the application of state laws to end-of-life care.

The ability of modern medicine to keep us alive has raised ethical and practical issues. Gawande (2010, p. 42) speaks of the "unstoppable momentum of medical treatment." He goes on to say "We've created a multi-trillion-dollar edifice for dispensing the medical equivalent of lottery tickets—and have only the rudiments of a system to prepare patients for the near certainty that those tickets will not win."

The current legal and health care systems struggle to ensure individual choice and quality end-of-life care. People can use advance directives, POLST forms, and communication with their health care providers to make their end-of-life wishes known. This requires thoughtful decisions communicated to others before terminal illness or dementia occur.

Euthanasia and Physician-Assisted Suicide

Doctors sometimes face ethical conflicts when they treat dying patients. Medical ethics say that a doctor should heal and cure patients, but the Hippocratic oath also says that a doctor should first "do no harm." What should a doctor do when machines, surgery, or drugs that extend a person's life also prolong that person's suffering? What should a doctor do when a patient asks to die? And what does the law say about **euthanasia** (actively helping someone achieve a painless death)?

First, when is a person dead? When he or she stops breathing? When the heart stops beating? Or when the brain waves stop? Current laws adopted by most U.S. states use the Uniform Determination of Death Act (UDDA) as a definition of death. The UDDA states that "an individual who has sustained either (1) irreversible cessation of circulatory and respiratory functions, or (2) irreversible cessation of all functions of the entire brain, including the brain stem, is dead" (Stanford Encyclopedia of Philosophy, 2007, citing the President's Commission, 1981, p. 119). But what if a machine keeps someone breathing, or a heart pump keeps someone's heart beating, or medication keeps someone alive? Are these people alive or dead? When does a family or a doctor have the right to end treatment?

Current laws leave many questions open. Once treatment has begun, for instance, some laws inhibit a doctor from discontinuing treatment. The doctor may know, through an advance directive, that after some time the patient would want treatment discontinued. But, by discontinuing the treatment, the doctor risks legal action. In addition, family members may insist that treatment continue even if a person has no chance of regaining consciousness. The law generally supports the decision of a family surrogate.

Active euthanasia presents a more controversial case. Most laws and medical ethics reject **active euthanasia** or **physician-assisted suicide (PAS)**—actively helping someone end his or her life either because the person asks for death or to relieve suffering (Steinbock, 2005).

In a 2007 Associated Press poll (MSNBC, 2007), more than two thirds of Americans said that under certain conditions a patient should be allowed to die. But the public shows ambivalence about PAS. Forty-eight percent of the respondents said PAS should be legal (as it is in Oregon). Forty-four percent said it should be illegal.

A Pew Research Center (2006) poll of 1,500 adults found similar results. The respondents showed strong support for the right to die. Eighty-four percent supported right-to-die laws. And 70% said, "patients should sometimes be allowed to die." But this poll

---

BOX 14.4
A FAMILY'S RESPONSE TO DEATH AND DYING

The academic discussions of the right to decide on pro-longing life often focus on medical and legal issues. But every day, people, along with their physicians and nursing staff, make decisions about their older family members. These decisions, at their best, take place within a context of openness and trust between families and health care professionals. The following case shows how one family decided against aggressive treatment.

Mrs. Walker, age 78, moved into an apartment in the Beth Sharon Senior Complex in early December. The complex offered her a supportive environment. It had a security system, access for a wheelchair, and a chance to socialize with other residents.

Mrs. Walker had played an active part in her community for many years as a hospital volunteer and business-person. So, when she moved into her apartment complex, she joined the Beth Sharon Seniors Group and regularly attended their afternoon teas in a nearby center. On January 10, as she left for the tea, she lost her balance, fell down a flight of stairs, and severely injured her head. When an ambulance arrived, she was found to be unconscious and was taken to a nearby hospital for emergency treatment.

Mrs. Walker's daughter, Phyllis, a nurse, rushed to the hospital when she was called. The neurosurgeon on staff had already completed a CT scan and showed it to Phyllis. "I don't like the look of this," he said. "There appears to be severe bleeding at the base of the brain stem. She's not likely to be well again, or indeed function on her own."

Phyllis left the ward to talk with her sister and other family members. They agreed that they would not press for an operation to remove the blood clot. Surgery would almost certainly lead to the necessity of a respirator and other artificial means of life support. Over the next few days, as the family waited for some change in their mother's condition, Phyllis would suggest various actions or ask for another test. Each time the surgeon in charge would ask a simple question, "Would your mother like us to do that?" And each time Phyllis agreed that her mother would not want aggressive treatment to prolong her life.

The decision to wait became harder to sustain as Mrs. Walker's breathing faltered. But the family stayed with its decision, based on Mrs. Walker's many discussions with them. Family members and close friends supported the family's decision to follow their mother's wishes.

Sixteen days after entering the hospital, and without regaining consciousness, Mrs. Walker died. She was cremated, in accordance with her request, and her family held a memorial service to celebrate her life.

---

also showed a division in views over PAS. Forty-six percent of the respondents supported laws that permit doctors to help patients die. Forty-five percent opposed such laws.

People's views on these issues differed by race, age, and religion. Fifty-one percent of African Americans, for example, felt that "doctors and nurses should always do everything possible to save a patient" (40% disagreed). More than one third (35%) of people ages 18 to 29 said everything should be done to keep a patient alive (a higher percentage than any other age group). African Americans and younger people also said they would personally want everything done to save their life. Only 16% of nonreligious people agreed that everything should be done to keep someone alive. But 26% of evangelical Protestants felt this way.

People generally support stopping the treatment for someone else. But more than a third of respondents (34%) said they would tell their doctor to do everything possible to save their own life. Thirty-eight percent said they would want everything done to save them even if they had to rely totally on someone else for their care.

St. John and Man-Son-Hing (2002) found that a request for active euthanasia most often comes from someone in pain or with depression. Symptom control can make dying less painful and can reduce the request for active euthanasia. If medicine could control pain, would the person still ask for death? Doctors disagree on how much a physician should assist a person who wishes to die.

In PAS, a doctor gives a person the means to commit suicide or advice on how to commit suicide. The patients take the action themselves. Controversy exists over this practice. Recent cases in the United States have (at least for now) settled the issue. The courts have ruled PAS illegal.

The case of Dr. Jack Kevorkian kept the issue of physician-assisted suicide in the news for several years. Michigan courts acquitted Kevorkian of murder three times in cases where he helped patients commit suicide. But in 1999, a jury convicted Kevorkian of

---

BOX 14.5
THE CASE OF TERRI SCHIAVO

Terri Schiavo, age 41, died on March 31, 2005. She suffered from brain damage and survived on life support, including a feeding tube, for over 15 years. Michael Schiavo, Terri's husband and legal guardian, said in October 2004 that his wife did not want artificial life support. "This is Terri's wish, this is Terri's choice," he said. "And I'm going to follow that wish if it's the last thing I can do for Terri." Michael Schiavo ordered his wife's feeding tube removed in mid-March 2005. Less than 2 weeks later, Terri died.

This ended a series of court battles over Terri Schiavo's treatment that began in 1998 between Michael Schiavo and Terri's parents, Bob and Mary Schindler. Terri's parents argued before the courts for 5 years to keep Terri on life support. They succeeded periodically in having the tube reinserted after her husband ordered it removed. The Schindlers argued that Terri might recover from her vegetative state. Her husband argued that she would have wanted an end to artificial life support. Finally, the courts ruled against Terri's parents. In the end the U.S. Supreme Court refused to hear the case (for the sixth time since 2001). That ended Terri's parents' hope for reinstatement of life support through the courts.

This case went beyond a family dispute or even a legal dispute. The press picked up the story, and soon the country buzzed with debate over end-of-life treatment. The Congress, the President of the United States, and even the Pope expressed opinions about the case. Commentators brought out legal, religious, moral, ethical, and practical arguments to support their positions.

Three days after doctors removed Terri Schiavo's feeding tube, Congress passed a bill that moved jurisdiction of the case from the Florida state court to a U.S. District Court. President Bush signed this law the next day. This brought the case under the review of a federal judge. But the federal courts upheld the state courts' decisions.

Terri Schiavo did not have a living will or other advance directive. A young person seldom thinks about the need for one. But in the absence of an advance directive, her husband, parents, doctors, and the courts lacked specific knowledge of her wishes. This case and its messy conclusion show the value of advance directives. A directive expresses in writing a clear wish about end-of-life treatment. An advance directive might have prevented some of the distress that this family experienced.

---

murder. Supporters and critics of PAS often argue about the issue of consent. Supporters of physician-assisted suicide say that the patient's right to accept or refuse treatment will protect people from misuse of PAS. Critics of PAS fear that this will lead to mercy killing without a patient's consent.

Krauthammer (1996; also Patel, 2004) reports that this type of mercy killing occurred in the Netherlands, where legalized PAS exists. Also, some doctors may consent to patient requests too quickly. Medical associations have begun to review their standards in light of recent court actions and social changes.

Public debate on this issue will continue to grow. Physicians now have the ability to prolong life through technology. This could mean more years of pain and suffering for some patients. Also, the cost of keeping people alive on machines and with expensive medications will increase. Some people will support active euthanasia on economic grounds. Many people see the choice of active euthanasia (under conditions of pain and suffering with no hope for improvement) as a right in modern society (Pew Research Center, 2006; Yankelovich & Vance, 2001).

A few countries today allow voluntary euthanasia or PAS. And the experience in these countries gives some idea of the issues that legalized PAS raises. Humphry (2000) reports that Swiss law has allowed assisted suicide since 1937 as long as it relieves suffering and has a humanitarian purpose. But social sanctions in Switzerland keep most doctors from assisting with suicide.

The Constitutional Court of Colombia on May 20, 1997, legalized euthanasia. The court ruled that "no person can be held criminally responsible for taking the life of a terminally ill patient who has given clear authorization to do so." As of 2000, the ruling had not gone before the country's Congress for adoption (Humphry, 2000, p. 49).

In only a few places does assisted suicide have legal support—Switzerland, the Netherlands, Belgium, the state of Oregon, and (as of March 5, 2009) the state of Washington.

The Netherlands' legal statutes (Articles 293 and 294 of the Penal Code) prohibit euthanasia and PAS. But a legislative act makes an exception to these articles under specific conditions. On April 1, 2002,

Dr. Jack Kevorkian and his suicide machine.

The Netherlands passed the Termination of Life on Request and Assisted Suicide (Review Procedures) Act. Under this law, PAS is legal if a series of conditions are met. For example, the patient's suffering must be unbearable and the patient must have no hope for improvement. The person must make an informed choice. And a second doctor must agree with the first doctor's assessment. Doctors have to report a case when they have assisted with a suicide.

In 2009 doctors in The Netherlands reported a total of 2,636 cases of PAS. In 80% of the cases people died at home after their doctors administered a lethal dose of drugs. This compares to 2,331 reported deaths by euthanasia in 2008 (a 10% increase over 2007) (Caldwell, 2010). This may indicate a rise in actual numbers or a greater willingness of doctors to report cases.

Oregon enacted the Death with Dignity Act on October 27, 1997. This act bans voluntary euthanasia (mercy killing), but it supports PAS in cases of advanced terminal illness. It allows physicians to prescribe drugs that help a person end his or her life. The law lays out a detailed process for patients and physicians to follow. The process includes a number of safeguards, including at least a 15-day waiting period before the doctor can write a prescription. The federal government challenged this law, but lost the case.

A report in 2009 on the Oregon policy (Oregon, 2009) found that 95 people got legal prescriptions for medication that year (compared to 88 in 2008). Fifty-three used the medicine. Six people who had earlier prescriptions died in 2009. This brought the total of deaths under this policy to 59 in 2009.

During the year, 55 doctors wrote 95 prescriptions. Since 1997, 460 people have died under the Death

with Dignity Act. Most of these patients died at home (98.3%) and most enrolled in hospice care (91.5%). (The state of Washington produces a similar report.) Hedberg, Hopkins, and Kohn (2003), in a 5-year report on PAS in Oregon, note that the number of people who use PAS has increased over time. But the number of people who use PAS "remains small relative to the overall number of deaths."

Studies in Oregon show the need for education about end-of-life options. Silveira and colleagues (Silveira, DiPiero, Gerrity, & Feudtner, 2000), for example, studied 728 outpatients in four Oregon clinics. They found that only 23% understood assisted suicide and only 32% understood active euthanasia. Sixty-two percent of the people in the study did not know the difference between the two. The researchers say that people need education about their options before they can make intelligent decisions about end-of-life care.

Many groups and individuals oppose euthanasia and PAS. They see this as a move toward unregulated killing of old and disabled people. Others say that with proper regulation PAS can end suffering for thousands of people who choose to end their lives.

The debate over physician-assisted suicide and euthanasia will continue as Americans sort out the implications of these practices. At the same time other approaches to end-of-life illness, such as hospice care and palliative care, will grow in importance. People need to learn more about advance directives so that they can get the end-of-life care that they want.

MOURNING AND GRIEF

When an older person dies, he or she often leaves behind children, sometimes a spouse, and other family members (such as grandchildren or siblings). These survivors need to adjust to the loss, and society can help with this adjustment. Funeral practices and rituals structure the grieving process. They prescribe what mourners should say, what they should wear, and in some cultures even how they should sit.

Mourners in Christian cultures wear black; mourners in some Asian cultures wear white. North American society values silent, unemotional grieving; some Chinese families hire professional mourners to make loud wailing noises at the funeral. Jewish tradition requires that the family sit *shivah* for 7 days after a funeral. According to this custom, mourners tear their clothes, sit on low chairs to deny themselves physical comfort, cover the mirrors in their home, and light a candle that burns for 1 week. The mourning family accepts visitors throughout the week, and 10 men gather at the house each day for prayer. Mourning continues in less intense stages for a year until the unveiling of a commemorative stone on the grave of the deceased. Orthodox Judaism forbids mourning after the year has passed.

Each culture has its own funeral rituals and mourning practices, but all of them have a common purpose: to help the bereaved family cope with grief and to reestablish community bonds after the loss of a community member. Regardless of the culture a person belongs to or the type of funeral he or she attends, each bereaved person has to work through personal feelings of grief.

Bereavement refers to the feeling of loss and sorrow at the death of a loved one. Bereavement often leads to grief. This refers to the deep mental anguish a person feels at the loss of a loved one. Some research in North America shows that mourners go through stages of grief. Early work by Lindemann (1944) describes three such stages: an initial response phase, an intermediate phase, and a recovery phase. First, the bereaved person feels shock and disbelief. He or she may report feeling cold and numb, and some people say they feel dazed, empty, and confused. These feelings protect a person from feelings of sorrow. People in this phase often fear that they will break down in public. This phase can last for several weeks.

Second, the person begins to review what has happened. This takes three forms: (1) The bereaved person obsessively reviews one or two scenes related to the death, or may be very self-critical about something that should have been said or done. (2) The bereaved person searches for a meaning for the death. Religious people may find solace in knowing that God willed this death. (3) The bereaved person searches for the deceased. This may mean that a widow goes to places where she expects to see her spouse. She may also feel his presence while watching television, eating dinner, or lying in bed. Some people even call out to their spouses and expect an answer. This phase lasts about a year.

Third, the bereaved person begins to recover. Survivors look for social contacts. They may join a club or go on a cruise. They feel that they have come through an ordeal and say they feel stronger and more competent than before. This stage begins around the second year after the death.

Kastenbaum (2001) says that grief affects a person's physical as well as psychological well-being. Some research shows that grief throws the body's neuroendocrine system out of balance. Acute grief can lead to illness and may even lead to death. Grief affects a person's entire life, including his or her social relations.

Not everyone makes a smooth trip through the grieving process. Sometimes a person shows a delayed emotional response to a parent's or a spouse's death. The person seems to cope well, displaying lots of zest and energy, but he or she may have internalized the grief. This delay can lead to emotional upset and physical illness later.

Only a small percentage of bereaved people go through morbid grieving. But research shows that people who have problems with grieving may turn to alcohol and drugs (Connor, 1998). They may also feel sorrow, anger, bitterness, rage, and despair (Northcott & Wilson, 2001, citing Clark, 1993a). These grief reactions may come in waves and can last two years or more.

Researchers note that stage models can include up to seven stages of grief and mourning (Aiken, 2001). But many people deviate from these patterns of grieving. Stages may overlap, a person may go through some stages more than once, stages can come in a different order than predicted, or a person may only go through some of the stages. O'Rourke (2010, pp. 67–68) in a review of literature on grieving says that "grief and mourning don't follow a checklist; they're complicated and untidy processes, less like a progression of stages and more like an ongoing process— sometimes one that never fully ends."

Northcott and Wilson (2001) say that the pattern of grieving by survivors depends in part on how the person died, whether the death took place suddenly or over time, and how old the person was. A young person's death in a fatal accident can produce a severe grief reaction. Princess Diana's death in an auto crash, for example, set the whole world mourning. People felt grief at this sudden loss of life. But an expected death after a long illness may produce a less extreme immediate reaction (Almberg, Grafstrom, & Winblad, 2000).

The research on grief and grieving finds some common experiences among mourners—such as the feeling of loss and sorrow, yearning for the person no longer there. But it also shows the many individual reactions to death. Grief can depend on the relationship to the dead, the personality of the mourner, and community rituals. These and other conditions make grief and mourning an unpredictable experience.

Widowhood and Bereavement

Silverman (2004) reports that the death of a spouse in most cases causes a shock. Older widows, for example, compared with younger widows, tend to show a less intense immediate grief response. But they may show intense grief months after the death (Aiken, 2001; Mancini, Pressman, & Bonanno, 2006).

Widows and widowers face some common problems. These include not enough time to grieve, a lack of emotional support after the official mourning period, and lack of support from adult children during grieving. Forewarning about a spouse's death may allow a person to work out some grief. Surviving spouses can then plan for the future, and this eases adjustment to widowhood.

Burton, Haley, and Small (2006) found that a sudden death led to a greater risk of depression. They also found that strong emotions may come and go for many months after a spouse's death, especially among highly stressed caregivers. Feelings of grief can include disbelief, shock, numbness, sadness, or guilt. A person can also feel abandoned, isolated, angry, and depressed.

Many widows report that widowhood stripped them of their identities. Van den Hoonaard (1997) calls this "identity foreclosure." Widowhood signals the end of a woman's former identity (as a wife) and begins the need to build a new identity. MacDougall (1998, pp. 1–2), a widow, says that "part of the pain has to do with our sense of self; without our life-long partner, it becomes necessary to redefine our place in the world. When one has been part of a couple for a very long time, the adjustment can seem impossible."

Bereavement can go on months after the formal mourning period. Some widowed women find or reestablish meaning in their lives through holding on to memories of their role as wife and mother. They continue personal rituals and routines as mother and homemaker, and keep their attachment to their marital home and possessions (Shenk, Kuwahara, & Zablotsky, 2004). As one widowed woman explained: "I do a lot of things [the same], you get into the habit over 50 years of marriage. . . . I think it sort of keeps you connected" (p. 167).

Many women hold on to the wife role for years after their husbands' deaths. Onrust and Cuijpers (2006) reviewed 11 studies for evidence of depression and anxiety in widowhood. The studies contained data on 3,481 widows and 4,685 nonwidows. They found a high rate of major depressive disorder among the widows in the first year of widowhood. Almost 22% of the widowed group showed high rates of depression and 12% showed posttraumatic stress disorder.

The Changing Lives of Older Couples (CLOC) study included more than 1,500 people before widowhood (Mancini et al., 2006). The researchers then conducted a three-wave longitudinal study at 6, 18, and 48 months after the death of a study participant's spouse. This study, because it looked at preloss mental health, could assess the effect of loss on psychological well-being over time.

The study found five responses to the loss of a spouse: (1) chronic grief (low preloss depression, high postloss depression after 6 to 18 months); (2) common grief or recovery (low preloss depression and high postloss depression at 6 months with improvement at 18 months); (3) resilience (low pre- and low postloss depression at 6 and 18 months); (4) depressed-improved (high preloss depression and low postloss depression at 6 and 18 months); and (5) chronic depression (high preloss depression and high postloss depression at 6 and 18 months).

Only a small group (about 15.6%) showed chronic grief—low pre-loss depression but high post-loss depression. This study distinguished these people from those who showed chronic depression—high pre- and high postloss depression. This group made up 7.8% of the study population. The largest group in this study (45.7%) reported low pre- and low postloss depression after 6 to 18 months. This result shows that those in good mental health before a spouse's death cope reasonably well with their grief.

Some people, the depressed-improved group, felt less depressed after the death of their spouses. These people may have suffered through an unpleasant marriage. Or they may have felt burdened by caregiving before their spouse's death. Death may have come as a relief. The study found that a majority of spouses either recovered from their grief (10.7%) after 6 to 18 months or coped well with their grief and showed low depression at 6 to 18 months (45.7%). This study, for the first time, detailed the frequency and variety of reactions to a spouse's death.

Martin and Elder (1993) see grieving as a long-term process. They say that grief may come and go in cycles over many years. Northcott and Wilson (2001, p. 156) say that "grief is never truly over." An older person may need support long after his or her spouse's death.

Baker (1991) reports that spouses who have died continue to influence the living in many ways. People sometimes talk to dead spouses, ask them for advice, or try to imagine what they would do in a situation the surviving spouse is facing. One woman said she felt her husband lie down next to her in bed some months after his funeral. Widows or widowers sometimes decide against remarriage because of the close ties that still exist with their dead spouses. Moss and Moss (1984–85, p. 204) consider this a normal response to widowhood in old age and "a nourishing link to the past." More research on bereavement in old age will show how this experience differs from bereavement in younger people.

CONCLUSION

This chapter has touched on some of the complex issues related to death and dying. Each religion has its own views on issues such as euthanasia, funeral practices, and mourning. Each culture shapes its members' beliefs about the meaning of death, about life after death, and about care for the sick and dying. People will respond in unique ways to their own death and to the deaths of people they know and love.

Today, changes in technology, the management of terminal illness, and the meaning of death raise new questions about death and dying. The study of death and dying can help people to understand these issues and make better choices for themselves. An incident from my life made this clear to me.

After my father's funeral, my mother, my sister, my father's brothers, and I got into a rented limousine and drove to the cemetery. The funeral director stopped the cars in the funeral procession at the cemetery gate. We saw the hearse pull ahead and stop a hundred yards away. I turned around to talk to one of my uncles in our car.

A few minutes later, the director waved all the cars on. We stopped behind the hearse and got out. It was empty. The director led us to the graveside. We stood close to the grave, but we could not see the coffin or any earth. A blanket of fake grass covered the earth that had come from the grave. Another blanket covered the coffin. Relatives and friends gathered to the side and behind us. The director said some prayers and a few kind words. My mother, my sister, and I stood and stared at the fake grass.

I think we were supposed to leave. But I motioned to the director to pull the grass back. He looked surprised. I told him to pull the grass back. He did. We saw the corner of the coffin and the corner of the grave, and we started to cry.

I tell this story because my knowledge of death and dying gave me the confidence to act. I felt I should do something to make my father's death real and begin the grieving process. And I knew what I had to do.

Those of us in the field of aging use our knowledge of aging each day. We use it to better understand our families and friends. And we use it to understand the changes we go through as we age. Knowledge about death and dying allows us to plan for our future with less fear and denial. The study of aging can make old age a better time of life for each of us and for the people we love.

SUMMARY

- Attitudes to death vary by age, religion, and culture. Older people generally accept death more than younger people. Like younger people, older people say they want to continue living, if they feel their life has meaning.
- People with either no religious belief or a very strong belief seem to cope with death best.
- Death occurs more often in old age today than in the past, and it also occurs more often in an institution. These trends will increase as the population ages.
- Elisabeth Kübler-Ross reports five stages of dying. Not everyone goes through all of these stages in the order Kübler-Ross describes, but her writings encouraged a more open discussion of death and dying when they first appeared.
- Cicely Saunders opened the first modern hospice in England in 1967. St. Christopher's Hospice offers an alternative to hospital care for the dying. Hospices offer pain control and a homelike setting for death. Hospice programs have grown in number in the United States, and they serve more people than ever before.

- Palliative care units in hospitals offer the same comfort and care as a hospice. Some of these units will help patients die in their own homes. They also ensure that patients can return to the hospital at any time. Health care professionals need more training in how to care for dying patients.
- Most experts and patients prefer an open awareness context for dying. They agree that patients have a right to know about the choice of treatment the physician has made and about alternative treatments, including the choice of no treatment. Doctors today need to understand their own feelings about death and dying, so they can give their patients the kind of care that their patients prefer.
- Advance directives (e.g., power of attorney or living will) state a person's health care preferences at the end of life. A person can make his or her wishes clear in an advance directive. This gives guidance to family members and health care providers when making end-of-life decisions. Google provides a Web site (Google Health) for storing and sharing advance directives among caregivers. People

need to share their end-of-life wishes if they want to get the care they prefer.

- Minority groups differ from one another and from the majority in their views of death, dying, and end-of-life care. Traditional religious and cultural beliefs may oppose modern approaches death and dying. Some minority groups, for example, see pain and suffering as a part of the dying process. They may view palliative care as interference with their ideal of a good death. Health care providers need to understand different cultural views of death and dying.

- New methods of communicating end-of-life wishes exist. The POLST program provides a system for patients to express their wishes. It requires that the person share those wishes with their physician. It alerts health care workers to the patient's wishes and provides directions for treatment.

- Doctors say that proper pain control would end the fear that leads people to ask for euthanasia. The law today does not require doctors to take heroic measures to keep a terminally ill patient alive. Many people support a person's right to die. But the public remains divided on the issue of physician-assisted suicide (PAS). Clearer guidelines would help doctors decide about stopping treatment for people in certain situations. The law prohibits active euthanasia.

- The state of Oregon legalized PAS in cases of advanced terminal illness. The law provides safeguards for the use of this practice. Safeguards include a 15-day waiting period before a doctor will prescribe lethal medication to a terminally ill person who requests it. Oregon monitors its policy and reports on cases of PAS. The number of people who use PAS has increased over time, but relatively few people take this option.

- Death leads to grief and mourning for survivors. Culture and religion help people cope with feelings of grief. Funerals, for example, bring the community together and give mourners support. Still, each person has to work through feelings of grief in his or her own way. Some researchers say that mourners go through stages of grief. Other writers feel that grief and mourning take many complicated paths.

- The study of widowhood shows that it can create distress and the need to rethink one's role in life. The Changing Lives of Older Couples (CLOC) study found that most people cope with loss and get on with their lives. The study found several patterns of distress and coping. The largest group in the study reported low pre- and low post-loss depression after 6 to 18 months.

- Knowing about death and dying can help you and your family cope better with loss, grief, and mourning.

DISCUSSION QUESTIONS

1. Researchers have proposed three theories that describe how older people respond to death. List and explain each of these theories.

2. Describe the means that older people use to buffer their fear of death.

3. How has population aging changed the context of dying?

4. Describe how Elisabeth Kübler-Ross and Cicely Saunders each influenced thinking about death and dying.

5. Explain the main function of a hospice. What methods do hospices use to help people enjoy their last days?

6. Compare and contrast palliative care units and hospices. Why do researchers think that, compared with a normal hospital, palliative care units cost less money to care for dying patients?

7. Discuss the differences between active and passive euthanasia. Discuss the pros and cons of physician-assisted suicide.

8. How do advance directives help guide physicians and families in end-of-life decisions for family members and patients? How do minority groups differ in their views of end-of-life treatment?

9. Discuss the issues around the legalization of physician-assisted suicide (PAS). What are the pros and cons for legalizing this practice?

10. Does grief follow a pattern or set of stages? Discuss the evidence that supports or rejects stage theories of grief.

11. What are some of the typical responses to the death of a spouse? What do studies tell us about widows' ability to adapt to loss?

SUGGESTED READING

Kastenbaum, R. J. (2001). *Death, society, and human experience* (7th ed.). Boston: Allyn & Bacon.

A classic text in the field, this book offers information on hospice care, end-of-life decisions, euthanasia, and bereavement. The book also covers unusual topics such as survival after death. The book is well written, with good summaries of the research on death and dying.

Morgan, J. D., & Laungani, P. (2002). *Death and bereavement around the world. Volume I: Major religious traditions.* Amityville, NY: Baywood.

One of five volumes that analyze the way different cultures deal with death, dying, and grief. The first volume compares the religious traditions and national value systems as they influence death and dying. This book can inform professionals who work with people from diverse cultural backgrounds.

Web Sites to Consult

The Hospice Foundation of America

www.hospicefoundation.org

This site includes service information, publications, videos, and news stories about hospice care in America. It also includes an excellent e-newsletter that discusses current events and writings related to hospice care.

Beth Israel University Department of Pain Medicine & Palliative Care

www.stoppain.org/palliative_care

This site contains the latest news and information on palliative care strategies. Its ready-made fatigue quiz can help you collect quantitative data about how fatigue affects older people. It is an excellent resource for research papers. Heavily oriented toward medical treatment.

National Hospice and Palliative Care Organization

www.nhpco.org/templates/1/homepage.cfm

This site provides information on professional resources, end-of-life care, advance directives, and careers. It includes a job board for employers and employees in the field of hospice and palliative care. The site also has a section in Spanish.

American Bar Association

www.americanbar.org/groups/law_aging/resources/consumer_s_
    toolkit_for_health_care_advance_planning.html

This site offers a toolkit to aid in creating a health care advance directive. It includes step-by-step advice and assistance on creating a document that expresses a person's wishes. The site encourages good communication between individuals, their families, and their care providers.

chapter 15

POLITICS AND POLICIES

Maggie Kuhn started her career as a senior activist in 1972 at the age of 67. She helped create and promote the causes of the **Gray Panthers**, a vocal and activist group. Through protests, speeches, and appearances on national television, she showed that older people have intelligence, energy, and political savvy. They also have experience that society needs and can use.

The Gray Panthers use "the experience and survival knowledge of old people and the idealism and energy of young people to change attitudes and social policy. Our

long range goals," Kuhn said, "are directed toward social change and in the direction of a more humane and just society" (Kuhn, 1976, p. 88; Kuhn, 1975, p. 360). Kuhn lived these ideals until the end of her life on April 22, 1995. In its May–June 1995 issue, *Aging Today* wrote: "Young and old will remember her spirit as galvanizing the intergenerational movement she helped to foster."

Maggie Kuhn chose the activist's role. But older people stay politically involved in other ways, too. Gerontologists study older people, politics, and policies

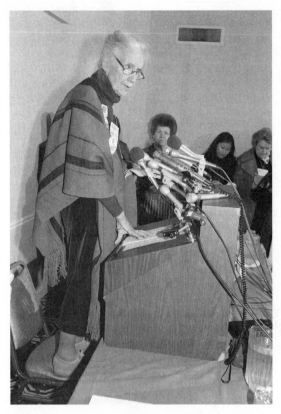

Maggie Kuhn, founder of the Gray Panthers, at a conference in Washington, DC. She inspired others with her desire to improve social life for the young and old.

from at least three points of view. First, they study voting patterns, political attitudes, and the age of people in public office. Second, they study advocacy, activism, and group conflict. This includes the study of lobby groups and interest groups. Third, they look at the policies and structures of government that serve older people.

This chapter looks at (1) political action, including voting, attitudes, and office holding; (2) advocacy and activism; and (3) government policies and structures. The chapter concludes with a look at the future of aging, politics, and policy in America.

VOTING

Older people take part in politics in many ways. They listen to public affairs shows on radio and television, they give money to political parties, and they work on political campaigns (Binstock, 2009b). They also vote, run for office, and engage in political advocacy and activism. Some of these activities demand more involvement than others. Voting, for example, takes the least effort but allows for the involvement of the most older people. Studies in the 1960s reported that

the proportion of people voting peaked in middle age and dropped off in older age groups (Milbrath, 1965). These studies supported the idea that older people disengage from social and political life.

More recent studies of voting report that older people stay engaged even into later old age. And they consider voting an important obligation. Love (2004) conducted a survey for the **AARP** (see Table 15.1).

TABLE 15.1   Political Activity in Later Life

In this table you will find results from a 2004 AARP survey of political activity among middle-aged and older Americans.

24. How politically active would you say you are, are you very active, somewhat active, not very active, or not active at all?

	40–57	*58–69*	*70+*
Very active	7%	6%	9%
Somewhat active	43	45	41
Not very active	31	31	27

30. These days, many people are so busy they can't find time to register to vote, or move around so often that they don't get a chance to re-register. Are you now registered to vote in your precinct or election district or haven't you been able to register so far?

	40–57	*58–69*	*70+*
Registered to vote	84%	92%	91%
Haven't registered	16	8	9

33. Do you, yourself, plan to vote in the election this November (2004)?

	40–57	*58–69*	*70+*
Yes	90%	93%	92%
No (skip to 35)	7	5	5
Don't know (skip to 35)	3	2	2

34. How certain are you that you will vote (in the election this November 2004)? Are you absolutely certain, fairly certain, or not certain?

	40–57	*58–69*	*70+*
Absolutely certain	83%	87%	85%
Fairly certain	13	9	11
Not certain	5	4	3
Don't know	—	1	1

The findings show, overall, that political activity and interest either show little difference between older and younger age groups or increase in older age groups. Older people show roughly the same commitment to voting as do younger age groups. Seventeen percent of the people in the 70-plus group said they would like to be more politically active. But they had "difficulty getting around." These findings show that people stay politically active into late old age. And in many cases only health limitations keep them from being more active.

Source: Love, J. (2004). *Political behavior and values across the generations.* AARP Strategic Issues Research, 2004. Retrieved July 13, 2011, from http://assets.aarp.org/rgcenter/general/politics_values.pdf. © 2004, AARP. Reprinted with permission.

He found that 89% of people ages 40 to 69 considered voting "a very important obligation." Ninety-three percent of people age 70 and over held this view. This survey asked people whether they considered themselves "politically active." Seven percent of people ages 40 to 57 considered themselves "very active." Six percent of people ages 58 to 69 gave this same response. Nine percent of people age 70 and over considered themselves "very active" politically.

The U.S. Census Bureau (2005b) reports that in the November 2004 election a large majority of older people registered and voted. For example, 76.9% of people ages 65 to 74 registered to vote and 70.8% voted. In that same year, 76.8% of people age 75 and over registered to vote and 66.7% voted. These figures show that older people stay active and engaged in political life into late old age. Only among people age 75 and over do declines in voting occur, mostly due to poor health or disability (see Figure 15.1).

Binstock (2009b) studied voting behavior of people age 65 and over in the 2004 presidential election. He found that, compared to younger people, older people showed a higher voter turnout. Sixty-nine percent of people age 65 and over voted in that election.

This compares to 58% for the overall rate of voter turnout. To say this another way, older people made up 19% of all the voters in the 2004 election even though they made up only 16% of the population old enough to vote.

People age 65 and over also show the highest proportion of voters of any age group (File & Crissey, 2010). Hudson (2009a) says that only the older age group has shown an increase in voter participation in presidential elections in the past 40 years. During this time other age groups' voting participation declined. As a result, older people "now have higher participation rates than any other age-group" (Hudson, 2009a, p. 541). Binstock (2009b, p. 136) says, "There is little doubt that older Americans are highly engaged in political participation today."

Why do older people turn out to vote in such large numbers? In part, they vote because they feel a strong link to a political party. And people with strong political affiliations tend to vote. Also, compared to younger people, older people report a greater interest in public life, read more about current events, and tend to follow political campaigns (Binstock, 2006–07, 2009b). Their interest in political campaigns and their

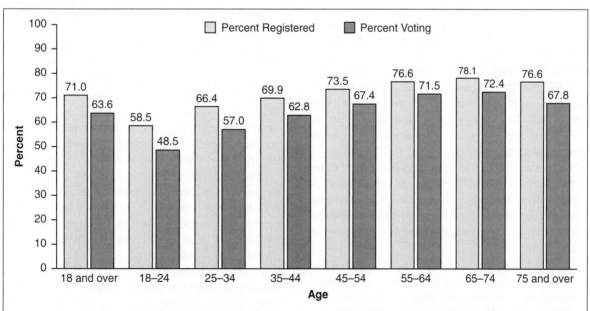

This figure shows the proportion of people in various age groups who registered to vote and then voted in the November 2008 election. The figures show that both registration and percent voting increase with age until age 75. After age 75, both registration to vote and the percentage of people who vote drops off. This table shows that older people maintain their interest in political life into late old age. A decline in the physical ability accounts for the decline in voting later in life.

FIGURE 15.1 Reported Voting and Registration, by Sex and Age, U.S. citizens: November 2008.

Source: Adapted from U.S. Census Bureau (2010h). *Voting and registration in the election of November 2008.* Detailed tables. Current population survey. Table 1. Reported voting and registration, selected ages, November 2008. Washington, DC, 2000. Retrieved November, 24, 2010.

knowledge of public affairs continues into late old age. Cox (1993, p. 379) says that older people are "interested and better informed about political developments and are more likely to participate actively in the process themselves."

Hudson (2009a, p. 542; 2010c) says that the presence of a large older population probably doesn't shape public policy. And their voting patterns may not directly lead to age-related policies. But "they are there, and they are aware," and this may keep certain policy options off the public agenda. They also pay attention to issues of importance to them, like Social Security and Medicare. Politicians tread carefully on these issues. Elected officials often express support for these and other core programs for seniors.

Older people have more time than younger people to stay informed about political issues and to take part in the political process. Of the older people who registered to vote, those that didn't vote gave illness or disability as their primary reason for not voting (File & Crissey, 2010).

For whom do older people vote? Binstock (2009b) looked at exit poll data. He found that older people voted for candidates in roughly the same proportions as the rest of the population (also see Hudson, 2005). "*To date,*" Binstock says, "*older Americans have not shown any tendency to vote as a bloc*" (p. 139, emphasis in the original). For example, social class differences split the older Democratic vote in the 2008 presidential election. Older white working-class and middle-class voters tended to back Hillary Clinton. Higher income, well-educated whites tended to vote for Barack Obama (Lynch, 2010). This diversity of the older population dampens seniors' influence on election outcomes.

Binstock (2009b) notes that older voters share some common interests, such as the preservation of strong Social Security and Medicare programs. And this makes them a good target for political campaigns. But, he says, politicians can't take their vote for granted:

> There is no sound reason to expect that a birth cohort diverse in economic and social status, labor force participation, gender, race, ethnicity, religion, education, health status, family status, residential locale, political attitudes, partisan attachments and every other characteristic in American society—would suddenly become homogenized in self-interests and political behavior when it reaches the old age category. Old age is only one of many personal characteristics of old people, and only one of many with which they may identify themselves. (p. 140)

Participation Trends Among Older Voters

Among older voters, compared with women, men have a higher proportion of registrants and a higher proportion of voters. Also, compared with women, older men show less decline in registration and less decline in voting with increased age. For example, men show no decline in registration even after age 75 (U.S. Census Bureau, 2005a).

Studies of voting show that voting participation increases with education (File & Crissey, 2010). Among those age 65 and over, only 51.9% of people with less than a high school diploma voted in the November 2008 election. But in this same age group, 82% of people with a college degree or more voted. Among the oldest age group (age 75 and over) in 2004, those with 5 years or more of college voted at almost twice the proportion of people with less than a grade 9 education (82.9% compared with 42.9%) (U.S. Census Bureau, 2005b). Also, the higher a person's level of education, the greater the likelihood the person will work for a campaign and for a political party (Jirovec & Erich, 1992).

People with higher incomes also show greater tendencies to vote. Only 61.2% of people ages 65 to 74 who reported a family income under $10,000 voted in November 2004. But 80.7% of people in this age group who earned $150,000 or more voted. Even among the oldest age group (age 75 and over), the wealthiest group voted at almost 1.5 times the rate of the poorest group (U.S. Census Bureau, 2005b).

Educated, affluent people tend to understand the political system. They also see a strong link between voting and social policies such as taxation. This gives them a reason to vote and to believe that their vote will make a difference. Voting also gives them more influence over the electoral system and public policy.

Minority group elders have lower rates of voting than the general population. Among older people, compared with African Americans and Hispanics, a higher proportion of whites report that they vote. The gap between the proportion of white and minority voters grows with age. The oldest Hispanic women (age 75 and over), for example, had the lowest turnout. Only 42.8% of this group voted in the November 2004 election (compared with 66.8% of white women in this age group). Asian seniors had the lowest voting rates of all groups (U.S. Census Bureau, 2005a; File & Crissey, 2010).

Culture, language, and literacy barriers may keep some minority older people from voting. Also, minority elders may feel less hopeful than whites that their vote will improve their lives. Still, compared to

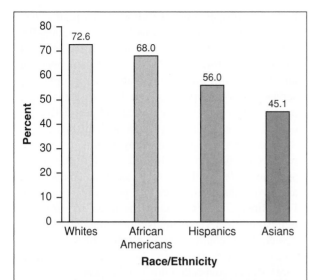

Voter participation rates differ by race and ethnicity. This pattern has held true for two recent national elections (2004 and 2008). Economic status influences voting behavior. Minorities that typically earn less than whites have lower voter turnout. Language and culture also influence voting behavior. Little or no ability to speak English or immigration from a country without a democratic system will also inhibit voting.

FIGURE 15.2 Older Voter (65+) Participation Rates by Race and Ethnicity, 2008 (Percent)

Source: File and Crissey (2010). Data source: U.S. Census Bureau, *Current population survey*, November 2004 and 2008.

younger minority group members, senior minority group members show greater voter participation (U.S. Census Bureau, 2005b).

Love (2004) found that voter participation reflects the values of older people today. Older people don't necessarily believe that voting gives them a say in how the government runs things. Only 37% of those age 70 and over strongly agreed with this statement. But they do feel that a person should vote "regardless of how they feel about the candidates." For example, 76% of people age 70 and over consider voting "an act of patriotism."

The oldest age group also believes in the democratic electoral process. Compared with younger age groups, older people report more commitment to the two major political parties (Vierck, 2002). Historical events have shaped these views. People age 70 and over today grew up in a more patriotic age. Compared with younger people today, older people feel more respect for the government. They may also identify their own sense of self-worth with the social order they helped create and maintain. Does this mean that older people take a conservative stance on political issues?

The AARP study shows some evidence of this. Love (2004) found that members of the oldest age group are "largely conservative on economic (59%) and social (49%) issues, and about one-third of them say they have become more conservative on economic, social, foreign policy, moral, and legal issues as they have aged."

On the other hand, the oldest group (age 70 and over), like the middle-aged groups, showed support for more welfare programs to help the poor and support for more environmental protection. The AARP study shows that older people's views differ by issue. Compared with middle-aged people, they seem conservative. They tend to favor prayer in schools and increased military defense. But on other issues they take a liberal stance. For example, they favor strong, government-run Social Security and Medicare systems. A Gallup poll (Barry & Duka, 2002) found that older people, more than other age groups, considered Social Security and a Medicare drug benefit as top national priorities.

Love (2004) says that issues such as environmental protection and Medicare may not reflect conservative or liberal views. They may reflect self-interest and an interest in the good of the larger community.

Binstock (2009a) studied voting patterns among older people in the 2008 national election. He found that "older voters were the only age-group that gave a majority to McCain." People age 60 and over gave 51% of their vote to McCain and 47% to Obama. Older people in this case voted for the loser of the election. This has happened only twice in the past 10 presidential elections.

Binstock (2009a, p. 698) asks why older people voted as they did. He proposes three reasons for this outcome. (1) The cohort now in its late 60s tends to vote Republican. Binstock calls them Eisenhower Republicans because they were "socialized to politics during the 8 years of Dwight Eisenhower's presidency." (2) People ages 65 to 74 identified with McCain, age 72. Finally, (3) white voters age 30 and over gave McCain a majority of their votes.

Voter preferences reflected older white voters' preference for a white candidate. But in addition, voters' life experiences and their life stage led them to support McCain. This study shows that older people do not vote as a bloc. Researchers must look at different subgroups and different cohorts within the older population to understand voting behavior.

What will future voting patterns look like as the Baby Boom generation enters old age? Binstock's (2009a) study and others suggest that cohort and period effects influence voter choices. Baby Boomers, for example, came of age politically during the Democratic presidencies of John F. Kennedy and Lyndon B. Johnson. As a group, compared to older cohorts, they report a slightly more liberal tendency on economic and social issues. For example, on economic issues 16% of Baby Boomers rate themselves as "moderately liberal." This compares with 12% of the group ages 58 to 69 and 11% of the 70-plus group. This same trend holds for social issues. Nineteen percent of Baby Boomers rated themselves as "moderately liberal" compared with 16% of the 58- to 69-year-olds and 11% of the 70-plus group.

The Baby Boomers, more than the two other age groups, felt that they had become more conservative as they aged. This may reflect their starting point. As children of the 1960s social revolution, they may feel a strong contrast between their more moderate views today and the radical views they held in the past. On the other hand, this group may continue to grow more conservative over time and may come to share the views of many seniors today.

Most studies of voting today use cross-sectional methods. They compare the voting patterns of younger and older age groups at one point in time, so they cannot tell us whether voting patterns change as people age. Probably voting behavior reflects some increase in commitment to the social order with age. It probably also reflects attitudes toward government and authority that people develop in their early years. New cohorts of older people may feel less commitment to the system and to party politics.

The AARP study reported that, compared with older cohorts, the Baby Boomers feel they owe the least obligation to the country (Love, 2004). They feel the least obligation to pay attention to the political process. They also report the strongest feelings of self-interest. The Baby Boom cohorts that came of age in the 1960s, compared with the World War II generation, will probably take a more liberal view of social policies. But they also feel skeptical of the traditional political process. This group may take part in other kinds of political action, like protests and lobbying.

Will Older People Form a Voting Bloc?

Binstock (2000) reports that older people have a greater impact on election results today than in the past. He found that as a proportion of the total votes cast in presidential elections, the proportion of votes cast by older people increased.

Some writers predict that this high voter turnout and the growing number of older people will create a power bloc. They fear that older people will gain control of local and national politics (and of government budgets). Rosenbaum and Button (1989, p. 301) call this the "gray peril hypothesis." Binstock (2006–07; 2009a) questions this assumption and the myth of "gray power." Binstock (2005a) says that the image of an older voting bloc scapegoats older people and serves as another type of ageism. It suggests that older people will form a self-interested and destructive social force. But this doesn't square with the facts.

True, when all of the Baby Boom generation reaches age 65 they will make up 27% of the voting age population. And they may cast between one-third and two-fifths of all votes in a presidential election. But, Binstock (2005a) says, the large and growing number of older voters holds more symbolic than real power. They could sway an election by voting as a bloc on a specific issue (e.g., Social Security or Medicare). But he doubts that this will happen.

Instead, he says, people age 65 and over hold varied political beliefs. Older people's views differ by social class, race, and gender. Members of different groups within the older population have different concerns (Binstock, 2009b). A study of voting patterns related to Social Security, for example, showed that, compared with wealthier voters, lower-income voters showed a stronger concern for and commitment to the Social Security system. This reflects the lower-income person's dependence on Social Security. A. L. Campbell (2002) says that this shows the power of self-interest in shaping voting preferences. Older voters choose a candidate for many reasons. They rarely vote for someone based on one issue, such as age-related policies.

Even on age-related issues, older people differ in their views and vote for different candidates. Social class, for example, plays a bigger role in voting behavior than age. A wealthy man may decide to vote against a program to help poor older women if the program increases his taxes. The poorest 20% of older people rely on Social Security for 83% of their income. But Social Security makes up only 20% of the income of those in the highest income bracket. These two groups have different stakes in the strength of the Social Security program. And they may vote differently on issues related to this program (Schulz & Binstock, 2006).

Differences in ethnicity, lifelong attachment to a political party, and urban and rural differences all fragment the older vote. Older people often look at an issue with an eye to how their vote will affect their children and grandchildren.

Robert Blendon of the Harvard University School of Public Health agrees. He says that older Americans could certainly "drive a change in Congress if they just focused on seniors' issues. But with everything else going on, they may vote on other things" (cited in Barry & Duka, 2002). The economy, the state of the stock market, corporate scandals, the fear of terrorism, and patriotism all shape older people's choices on election day.

Even large organizations such as the AARP, with more than 38 million members, cannot deliver blocks of votes. Binstock (2009b) says that in the 1980 presidential election, for example, the majority of older people (54%) voted for Ronald Reagan. Reagan, once elected, froze Social Security's annual cost-of-living increases. He also proposed more permanent cuts. Still, in 1984 Reagan increased his share of the senior vote to 60% (about the same percentage as the overall vote).

Binstock (1978) says,

> There is little reason to believe that a phenomenon termed "senior power" will significantly increase the proportion of the budget devoted to the aging, or redirect that portion of the budget toward solving the problems of the severely disadvantaged. Whatever senior power exists is held by organizations that cannot swing decisive voting blocs.

Still, older people as a group have influenced legislation in the recent past, although not generally through voting. Lobbying efforts, for example, helped pass the Medicare legislation of 1965. Protests to Congress also helped repeal the Medicare Catastrophic Coverage Act in 1989. The growing number of older people means that politicians cannot ignore their concerns. In 1983, for example, a year when Social Security cuts looked possible, 1 in 5 older persons contacted their representatives in Washington. This may have influenced the amendments that protected the program (Binstock, 2009b). Torres-Gil (1992, p. 75) says that "senior citizens might not always have been the principal player [in policy decisions], but they have been an important one."

HOLDING POLITICAL OFFICE

In the United States, older people make up a high proportion of political officeholders, and the highest political posts often have the oldest people in them. This happens, in part, because a politician tends to move to higher positions over time.

Schlesinger (1996, cited in Williamson, Evans, Powell, & Hesse-Biber, 1982) found that the younger a person's age, the less important was the office held. For example, election to the U.S. House of Representatives will tend to come at an earlier age than election as governor. And this tends to come earlier than election as a U.S. senator. Presidents often get elected late in their careers. Many have passed age 65 in office, although the United States has elected only two presidents over age 65—William Henry Harrison and Ronald Reagan.

BOX 15.1
THE ACCOMPLISHMENTS OF SOME VERY OLD POLITICIANS

Slate, the online magazine, publishes a yearly listing titled "80 Over 80" (Slate, 2010). *Slate* calls this a "list of the most powerful octogenarians in America." The list includes many politicians who serve in Washington. These officials hold important positions in the Senate and Congress due to their seniority and experience. Here you can read about some of these elder statesmen.

Daniel Inouye, 85. *Slate* ranks this senior Senator, a Democrat from Hawaii, as the third most influential person on its list (after number 1, Thomas S. Monson, 82, President of the Church of Jesus Christ of Latter-day Saints; and number 2, John Paul Stevens, 89, Supreme Court Justice). Inouye has served in the Senate for 47 years and is the second-most-senior member. He has served in Congress since Hawaii became a state. Inouye won his eighth Senate term with 76% of the vote. He heads the powerful Senate Committee for Appropriations.

Robert Byrd, 92. *Slate* ranks Senator Byrd, a Democrat from West Virginia, number 10 on its list. Byrd died on June 28, 2010, after serving 51 years in the Senate and 6 years in the House of Representatives. He served as senator longer than anyone in U.S. history. He was also the oldest member of the Senate. He served as president pro tempore of the Senate. This put him third in line for the presidency. President Obama called him "a voice of principle and reason."

John Dingell, 83. *Slate* ranks Congressman Dingell, a Democrat from Michigan, number 28 on its list. Dingell is currently the longest-serving member in the House of Representatives. He is also the longest-serving Congressman in U.S. history. He serves as the chair emeritus of the Energy and Commerce Committee. He supports social welfare reform and a national health insurance system.

Note: No women appear on *Slate*'s list of influential octogenarians in national political office. This reflects the smaller number of women in national elected offices. It also reflects the barriers that existed for women who wanted to enter politics at the time when these men first got elected.

Exceptions to older officeholders do occur. John F. Kennedy, Bill Clinton, George W. Bush, and Barack Obama show a trend toward younger ages for U.S. presidents. This could reflect the Baby Boomers' desire to elect presidents from their own cohort.

As Boomers age, the trend toward older presidents could return. The system favors the older officeholder. Older members of the Senate and House of Representatives, for example, have more power than younger members. They serve on and chair the most powerful committees due to Congress's seniority system. These powerful leaders can shape legislation to serve their states and districts. This gives voters an incentive to reelect older politicians, and it keeps some members of Congress in their jobs into their 80s. Supreme Court justices also tend to stay in office past age 65. Justices usually get appointed in their late 50s. Some stay on the court past age 90.

This gives a select group of older people direct access to power and influence. Does this mean that older politicians promote older people's concerns? Not necessarily. Spivack (1992) assessed Washington lobbyists' views of politicians. Lobbyists ranked some of Congress's oldest senators as opponents of programs for older people.

ADVOCACY

Advocacy is working within the system through lobbying and presentations to government to achieve political change. Senior advocacy groups have played an important role in national politics in the past half-century. The earliest advocacy groups, in the 1930s, set the stage for the Social Security system. More recently, in the mid-1960s, advocacy groups promoted Medicare and Medicaid legislation. They succeeded in getting this legislation passed over the protests of powerful groups such as the American Medical Association. Today, senior advocacy groups lobby government officials to maintain and expand current programs for older people.

Gerontologists disagree over how best to describe senior advocacy. One perspective views older people's political actions as a form of social movement. A social movement forms when a group (1) comes together around a set of issues, (2) creates a media image of itself as concerned and important, (3) places pressure on government and policy decision makers, and (4) has expertise and can raise money or votes to support its issues (Hendricks & Hendricks, 1986). Gerontologists disagree on whether age can form the basis of a social movement.

The Leadership Council of Aging Organizations, made up of 64 old-age interest groups, attempts to create an age-based social movement. The coalition focuses on age-related issues, positions itself as concerned about these issues, and pressures government through briefings and letter-writing campaigns. Groups within the coalition may raise money and attempt to sway votes. But Schulz and Binstock (2006) point out that these groups sometimes disagree with one another on important policy issues (e.g., Medicare hospital catastrophic coverage). This lack of cohesiveness limits the influence of this coalition. The diversity of philosophies and goals among these organizations makes collective action unpredictable.

A second perspective sees older people's political influence as an example of "interest group pluralism" (Williamson, Evans, Powell, & Hesse-Biber, 1982, p. 12). This perspective views public policy as the "outcome of competition among a variety of groups." Each group expresses the interests of its members, advocates for its position, and competes with other groups for scarce public resources. Most experts agree that older people's organizations have played this role for at least 60 years.

Binstock (2005b) describes three forms of political power available to senior advocacy groups. First, these groups have access to elected officials in Congress, to government policy makers, and sometimes to the White House. They can present their views on legislation and policy issues.

The National Institute of Senior Centers and the National Council on the Aging (1993), for example, developed an advocacy manual for senior organization board members, coordinators of programs, and senior services volunteers. The manual instructs readers on how to influence local, state, and national political decisions. The manual contains instructions on how to meet with a legislator, how to influence state or national legislative bills, and how to lobby within legal limits. The manual targets increased support for senior services under the Older Americans Act.

Other groups such as the Coalition of Women in Long Term Care lobby for improvements in the long-term care system. This group claims more than 200 groups as members, including nursing-home owners, nurses, and representatives of the home health industry (Flippen, 1998).

Second, senior advocacy groups have access to the media. Large and influential groups such as the AARP can speak out at congressional hearings and conferences and can play a role in national policy forums like the White House Conferences on Aging. Third, advocacy groups can use what Schulz and Binstock (2006) call "the electoral bluff." Groups, such as the AARP, can claim to deliver millions of votes on an age-related issue (though they may lack this power). Politicians may believe this claim. They then treat age-related issues seriously because they do not want to offend a large group of potential supporters.

Senior advocacy groups first gained national attention in the United States in the 1930s. Writer Upton Sinclair proposed a plan in California to give people age 60 and over a $50 per month pension. Another California group, called Ham and Eggs, proposed a weekly pension for unemployed people age 50 and over. This group held marches and rallies and sponsored radio shows. It claimed 300,000 members. Both Sinclair's program and Ham and Eggs folded before achieving their goals.

A third advocacy group, the Townsend movement, began at the same time in California. This group committed itself to legislative reform. The Townsend plan (named after the founder of the movement, Dr. Francis Townsend) proposed that the government pay older people in the United States $200 a month. Older people who got the money would agree to stay out of the labor force and would spend the money within 30 days. Townsend designed this plan to give older people an income and to stimulate the economy during the Depression. As many as 2 million people joined this movement by the mid-1930s (Burg, 1999).

The Townsend movement flexed its political muscles only once, in 1934. It successfully defeated an incumbent congressman who showed little concern for aging issues. The movement put its own candidate, John McGroarty, 72 years old, into office. McGroarty had no success in getting the Townsend plan adopted in Washington, and the Townsend movement never reached its goal of a monthly wage for older people.

The movement's success at the polls, however, led to national recognition of its goals. Hudson (2009a, p. 536) says, "Nowhere else have older people ever been organized to such a degree." Scholars disagree on the exact impact of the Townsend movement on Social Security legislation. But, Hudson says, Roosevelt's Committee on Economic Security "was keenly aware of its presence." Wallace and his colleagues (Wallace, Williamson, Lung, & Powell, 1991, p. 98) say that from this point on, "the elderly promised to be a significant force in American politics."

Today, senior advocacy groups have greater access to politicians and to Congress than ever before.

Achenbaum (2000b) notes the recent growth in size and influence of lobby groups that serve older people. These include more than 100 organizations that advocate for older adults or represent professionals who work with older people.

The National Committee to Preserve Social Security and Medicare (NCPSSM), for example, supports the Social Security and Medicare programs. Policy analysts and lobbyists who work for the NCPSSM meet with members of Congress. They present the National Committee's position and suggest approaches to current legislation. The NCPSSM also supports candidates who show support for the Social Security and Medicare programs (National Committee, 2010).

Gray lobby groups such as the AARP set out legislative agendas, open offices in state capitals, and gain pledges from lawmakers to support senior issues. They can even threaten to oppose lawmakers who renege on their pledges or fail to support senior issues (Serafini, 2002). "Whatever AARP chooses to do (or not do)," Binstock says, "tends to define the overall position of the old-age lobby" (1997, p. 65).

A 2009–2010 publication titled *The Policy Book: AARP Public Policies 2009–2010* begins with a statement of its strength. "AARP's membership comprises 40 million Americans age 50 and over. Our members include workers and retirees, individuals in their 50s at the peak of their earning years and those over 80 living alone, people with comfortable standards of living and those struggling with minimal resources" (AARP, 2008b). *The Policy Book* covers the landscape of public policy, including the national budget, taxation, retirement income, health, and civic engagement (to list only a few of its topics). This publication expresses the breadth of AARP's political concerns. The publication implies that its large membership holds a common view on these issues.

The AARP gets its power from the claim that it represents millions of older people. Its national campaign titled "Divided We Fail," for example, aimed to shape the debate for the 2008 presidential election. An editorial in the *AARP Bulletin* (2007c) stated the association's position and its approach to electoral politics:

> The over-50 voters form the battleground in the looming 2008 national election because they cast the majority of votes in the last election. They are impatient—and independent. No group of voters shifted their political support from Republicans to Democrats more sharply last November than did the 50-plus voters. That means that candidates will be forced to deal with their concerns, and candidates will be taken to task if they don't deliver.

Achenbaum (2000b) predicts that in the future, gray lobby groups will create links to women's groups and groups that represent people with disabilities. Some of these groups already belong to the Leadership Council of Aging Organizations. These groups share concerns that overlap with those of the older population.

A recent response to nonprofit lobby groups suggests the influence of older people on Congress. Lieberman (2000) reports on the work of a conservative think tank, the Capital Research Center. This group attempted to discredit the AARP to weaken its ability to influence Social Security and Medicare legislation. The think tank criticized the AARP's size, its support of liberal causes, and the size of its office in Washington.

This attack led to Senate hearings on the organization's finances and practices. The attack weakened the AARP's lobbying efforts for a time and led the organization to soften its support for Social Security and Medicare. The attempt by conservative forces to discredit AARP points its key role in the political process. AARP weather this attack and has continued its activist stance.

Future debates over health care costs will keep senior lobby groups at the center of political action. A closer look at these groups will describe their goals, the people they serve, and how they influence lawmakers.

The AARP

The AARP (formerly the American Association of Retired persons) "is dedicated to enhancing quality of life for all as we age. We lead positive social change and deliver value to members through information, advocacy and service." The association envisions "a society in which everyone ages with dignity and purpose, and in which AARP helps people fulfill their goals and dreams" (AARP, 2003). The AARP has more than 3,200 local chapters and more than 40 million members—second in membership only to the Roman Catholic Church in the United States (Gilleard & Higgs, 2009). It has offices in all 50 states, the District of Columbia, Puerto Rico, and the U.S. Virgin Islands. Students of aging politics have called the AARP everything from "the most fearsome force in politics" (Birnbaum, 1997, p. 122) to an "800 pound gorilla" (Rix, 1999, p. 181; Binstock, 2004).

The AARP grew out of the National Retired Teachers Association (NRTA), which began in 1947. In 1955, the NRTA began to offer group life insurance to its members. This program grew so popular that in 1958 the NRTA formed the AARP so that people other than retired teachers could get this insurance. By 1982, the NRTA had become a division of the larger AARP.

The AARP attracts its large membership for at least two reasons. First, it has a low membership fee. Membership for 1 year (in 2010) cost $16.00 for a person age 50 and over (the person's spouse gets membership for free). This includes a subscription to *AARP: The Magazine* and the *AARP Bulletin* (the AARP also prints *AARP Segunda Juventud,* a quarterly newspaper in Spanish). Second, the AARP offers services to its members, including life and health insurance, a discount pharmacy service, special credit card rates, travel advice, education programs, and other services.

Gilleard and Higgs (2009) say that the AARP functions day-to-day less as an "advocacy organization and more as a consumers' movement whose concern is for the great American middle classes." AARP's annual report gives some support to this view.

In its 2009 annual report, the AARP stated that it earned $1.42 billion in revenue in that year. AARP earned this revenue from membership dues, royalties, advertising, insurance, grants, programs, and contributions. About two thirds of this total came from membership fees ($246 million) and royalties ($657 million). Another $113 million came from advertising fees in AARP publications (AARP, 2009b). Earnings from fees, insurance, and services allow the AARP to maintain a lobbying and public affairs staff.

Research also makes up part of the AARP agenda. For example, the association joined with the National Council on the Aging to produce a study titled *American Perceptions of Aging in the 21st Century* (Cutler, Whitelaw, & Beattie, 2002). This study surveyed Americans' attitudes toward aging.

The AARP supports an in-house Public Policy Institute (PPI). The PPI publishes research reports and analyses throughout the year. It circulates these reports to policy makers and government officials. The PPI includes teams that focus on economics, health, consumer issues, and independent living/long-term care. Publications in 2009 include reports on chronic care, health reform, Social Security, housing, and community planning. Between its retail activities and its attention to social policy AARP mixes "consumerism with civic-mindedness" (Gilleard & Higgs, 2009).

The AARP takes a neutral stance toward both major political parties. It engages in lobbying on behalf of broad issues like Social Security and Medicare. The

AARP spent $101 million, or about 7% of its total budget, on policy research and legislative lobbying in 2009. A neutral political stance broadens the association's membership base, keeps the association's tax-free status, and keeps both parties anxious to please. The organization also supports lobby groups in every state and promotes political organization in all of the U.S. congressional districts.

The organization keeps members up to date on aging issues through reports and bulletins. It also attempts to shape members' opinions on current issues. "Even if most AARP members may initially join the organization for nonpolitical reasons," Binstock (2009b, p. 142) says, "a by-product is that the organization heightens political awareness among its members."

An article in the January 2005 issue of the *AARP Bulletin,* for example, contained an analysis of President George W. Bush's plan to reform Social Security (Goozner, 2005). The article reviewed the administration's plan to allow workers to set up private savings accounts with their Social Security payroll taxes. The plan would allow workers to invest their money in the stock market and take advantage of potential gains in market value.

The AARP warned that this approach would put workers' retirement savings at risk. If the market performed poorly, many older Americans could find themselves with little or no pension savings. The analysis presented the facts about the proposed policy. But it also attempted to sway the opinion of AARP's large membership against the proposal.

The article ends with a picture of army troops in a line getting ready to lob grenades at an enemy outside the picture's frame. An invitation under the photo reads: "Call to Action! Call AARP's hotline . . . and tell your members of Congress to oppose private accounts that take money out of Social Security" (AARP, 2005b, p. 15). (Note: The plan to privatize Social Security never got off the ground in Congress. The general public, in addition to AARP, did not support this proposal. The fall in stock prices a few years later reinforced, for many people, the wisdom of publicly held Social Security accounts).

Binstock (2009b, p. 143) says that large senior organizations like the AARP have "symbolic legitimacy." This provides them with access to political decision makers. Through these meetings politicians show their interest in seniors' issues. Politicians can claim that they hear the voice of millions of older people through these meetings. The AARP also gets asked to attend government-sponsored forums and congressional hearings. Santangelo (2005–06; also Moon, 2006) says that the AARP played a role in shaping recent health care legislation including the Medicare Catastrophic Coverage Act and the Medicare Prescription Drug, Improvement and Modernization Act of 2003 (MMA). For example, in preparation for the MMA the Bush administration "entered into negotiations with the crucial congressional committees and interest groups such as AARP" (Santangelo, 2005–06, p. 32).

Through its publications, the AARP can influence the thinking of large numbers of older people. This gives the organization some clout in its dealing with lawmakers. Politicians fear offending older people and fear their anger at the polls. Binstock (2009b, p. 143) says, "The perception of being powerful is, in itself, a source of political influence for these organizations."

The AARP spends about 6% of its revenue on membership development. But it will face a challenge as its membership grows. A larger membership will increase the association's potential influence, but it will also increase differences in members' views on issues. The diversity of the AARP's membership will make focused advocacy more difficult in the future. An organization with a diverse membership such as the AARP has a hard time speaking for its members' many interests (let alone the interests of all older people) (Gilleard & Higgs, 2009).

Many other advocacy groups for older people exist. They include the National Council on the Aging, the National Active and Retired Federal Employees Association (NARFE), and minority group organizations such as the National Hispanic Council on Aging and the National Caucus and Center on Black Aged, Inc. Smaller groups, such as the Older Women's League, lobby on behalf of specific constituencies. All of these groups educate, provide information, and make government agencies aware of their members' needs. Some groups sponsor model social programs and support research on aging. All of them claim to speak on behalf of some group of older people.

The Limits of Advocacy

Senior advocacy groups can influence policy, but they have limited political power (Hudson, 2009b). In the past, senior organizations played only a supporting role in creating social policy. Hudson (2009b, p. 127) says that the AARP, for example, "had virtually no

---

BOX 15.2
SILVER-HAIRED LEGISLATURES

Many lobbyists have expense accounts, $1,000 suits, and expensive watches. Behind them stand large corporations such as oil and gas companies or telecommunications giants. But a more modest breed of lobbyist also exists. These people work the state legislatures on behalf of older people. Some of them are older people themselves. Legislators respect them for their commitment to their cause and their knowledge of the issues.

More than 30 states in the United States have created channels for this activity. Most states call these groups *Silver-Haired Legislatures (SHL)*. The first Silver-Haired Legislature began in 1973 in Missouri.

SHLs consist of seniors who are elected by their peers and in some cases supported by the Local Area Agency on Aging, Title VI American Indian Programs, and the Older Americans Act. SHLs work closely with area elected legislators and others to advocate for changes in legislation to improve conditions for the aged.

People age 55 and over can serve in these legislatures. But Vierck (2002) says that the members' average age is 80. Members include teachers, doctors, and business people. These representatives meet with state legislators to express their constituents' concerns. They also keep their constituents up to date on legislation.

Silver-Haired Legislatures in most cases meet for a few days each year. They then prepare and present a list of priority proposals to their legislators.

Are these groups effective in creating policies that serve seniors? Some evidence suggests that they are. Silver-Haired Legislators in Missouri, for example, worked to pass more than 60 bills that have gone on to become state law. This group worked with actual legislators to create the Nursing Home Reform Law, the Missouri Senior Prescription Drug Program, and laws that ensure that Missouri seniors are exempt from taxes on Social Security and pension benefits (Kinder, 2010; Missouri Department of Health and Senior Services, 2010).

---

political presence until the 1970s" (a time of expansion in programs for older people). The creation of policies in the 1960s and early 1970s gave advocacy groups a focus for their activities.

A study of 43 advocacy groups found that more than half of them came into existence after 1965—the year that Congress passed Medicare, Medicaid, and the Older Americans Act. Walker (1983, p. 403), the author of this study, says, "In all of these cases, the formation of new groups was one of the *consequences* of major new legislation, not one of the *causes* of its passage." A more recent study by Campbell (2003) came to the same conclusion. She compared public opinion and voting data with the expansion of the Social Security program. She concludes:

Senior mass membership groups did not create Social Security policy. Rather, the policy helped create the groups. Social Security's effects on the individual—the increase in income, free time due to retirement, and political interest—enhance the likelihood of group membership. Social Security created a constituency for interest group entrepreneurs to organize, just as it defined a group for political parties to mobilize. (p. 77)

Pratt (1983) notes that at least three things stifle the impact of senior advocacy groups. First, many members join these groups for personal reasons—to get insurance

benefits or discount drugs. They do not support the group's political aims. An AARP poll, for example, found that 40% of members join for cheap insurance and other benefits. Only 14% join to support lobby efforts. Only a small percentage of members plays an active part in policy debates. As a result, a group like the AARP cannot deliver the votes of its members.

Second, senior groups show surges and declines in support from members. Surges often occur when federal benefits (like Social Security or Medicare) get threatened. Otherwise, most members show relatively little interest in policy issues.

Third, senior **lobby groups** have to spread their lobbying efforts in Washington. They do this because many congressional committees and government agencies deal with senior-related issues (housing, health, pensions). This means that senior advocacy groups cannot focus their efforts on one or two key players involved in aging policy.

Advocacy on behalf of older people has more impact on public policy than does voting. But, in the case of both lobbying and voting, the diversity of the older population dampens seniors' clout. Walker (2006, p. 349) calls gray power "a myth." Advocacy groups show their greatest strength, Pratt (1983) says, "When it comes to defending the sanctity of existing public programs . . . it tends to be easier to veto change than to initiate it successfully" (p. 165). The case of the Medicare Catastrophic Coverage Act (MCCA) makes this clear.

THE MEDICARE CATASTROPHIC COVERAGE ACT AND THE MEDICARE MODERNIZATION ACT: TWO CASE STUDIES IN SENIOR ADVOCACY

The Medicare Catastrophic Coverage Act

The story of the Medicare Catastrophic Coverage Act (MCCA), points to a shift in government support for age-related programs. Hudson (2009b) calls the period of the 1960s and early 1970s an "expansionary" phase. This period saw the start of Medicare, Medicaid, and the passage of the Older Americans Act in 1965. The period from the mid-1970s onward he calls a "restrictive" phase. The MCCA story shows the impact of this shift in policy.

It shows the government's concern for older people, the limits of government support for older people's programs, and the potential for class conflict within the older population.

Holstein and Minkler (1991, p. 189) call the MCCA of 1988 "the greatest expansion of Medicare since the program's establishment in 1965." This act (1) put a cap on hospital and physician expenses; (2) granted more coverage for prescription drugs, and some new Medicaid payments by the states; (3) included a small expansion of long-term care coverage; (4) protected some spousal assets from the spend-down required for Medicaid-sponsored nursing home care; and (5) created a commission to study long-term care and health care for uninsured people.

The MCCA funded these benefits by asking older people to pay more for Medicare (up to $800 per year). The act also required an added Medicare payment from older people with incomes over $25,000 a year. Congress passed this legislation by a large majority. Members of both parties supported the MCCA. So did major senior lobby groups like the AARP. President Reagan held a signing ceremony in the White House Rose Garden on July 1, 1988, to celebrate the bill's passage. To Congress's surprise, the act raised a storm of protest from groups of (mostly well-off) older people.

Older people rejected this legislation for several reasons. First, the legislation improved benefits for cases of acute illness but did not include relief from the costs of long-term care. For instance, the act did not cover nursing-home costs, an average cost of $29,000 a year. This left middle-class and wealthier older people without protection for one of their greatest present and future health care expenses. It failed to relieve the fear that a long-term illness could wipe out a lifetime of savings.

Second, many middle-class people had their own insurance coverage for acute care, or they had coverage through their retirement plans. Some upper-income older people thought, erroneously, that they already had coverage for catastrophic hospital costs (Schulz & Binstock, 2006). These people saw little advantage to the new legislation.

Third, wealthier older people rejected the idea of an extra tax on their Medicare payments.

Groups in Florida, California, and the Southwest began to protest this legislation. The National Committee to Preserve Social Security and Medicare led a national drive to repeal the MCCA. This organization grew to 5 million people during the campaign. Older people from across the country wrote to Congress. Six thousand members of the AARP resigned from that organization to protest its support of the MCCA. The AARP (in a reversal of its earlier position) turned against the MCCA. By mid-1989, Congress felt enough pressure to repeal the MCCA. The repeal passed Congress by Thanksgiving of 1989.

This case study teaches at least three lessons about politics and policies for older people today. First, Congress sent a message to older people by passing the MCCA. This legislation symbolically said that Congress will support improvements in programs such as Medicare, but only if older people pay for these improvements themselves. The MCCA symbolized an end to the growth of government-supported programs for older people.

Second, the repeal of the MCCA shows the strong social class divisions that exist within the older population. This legislation would have charged wealthier older people more for benefits. Poorer older people would have paid less. Wealthier older people then acted on the basis of their class interests. They rejected the legislation. And they succeeded in having it repealed. This case shows that older people can, and will, act to protect their interests. But in this case, they acted to protect common social class interests, rather than age identity interests.

Middle-class older people defeated a plan that would have helped poorer older people. Congressman Pete Stark, an author of the repeal, said, "We are being stampeded by a small group to deny benefits to everyone else" (Binstock, 1992, p. 404). "By all accounts," Binstock says, "a relatively small, unrepresentative proportion of comparatively well-off older persons who were upset by having to pay a new progressively scaled surtax were able to cow their congressional representatives into repealing [the MCCA]" (p. 404).

Third, this case makes it clear that large lobby groups such as the AARP do not speak for all older people. The AARP supported the MCCA because its leadership supports more benefits for older people. But the AARP membership, mostly middle-class people, rejected the plan. When the AARP called for a repeal of the MCCA, it lost its chance to speak for poorer older people. Poorer people stood to gain the most from this act. But the AARP decided in the end to support its middle-class members.

This incident caused the AARP to review its ability to shape policy for its membership. Due to this loss of member support, "from about 1995 to 2003, AARP assumed a withdrawn public posture" (Schulz & Binstock, 2006, p. 215). The association took cautious stances on policy issues during this period, and it reemerged only in the mid-2000s to again flex its policy muscles. Gilleard and Higgs (2009) conclude that "AARP lobbies to ensure that those older than 50 remain a constituency deserving a place in the wider market and that AARP itself continues to command a large section of that market."

The MCCA case shows the complexity of policy making for older people today. **Compassionate ageism** in the past assumed that all older people suffered from low income, poor health, and lack of services. This led to legislation that improved Social Security, created Medicare, and put in place the Older Americans Act. But older people as a group no longer live at the bottom of the income scale. The older group has diverse needs, and sometimes these needs clash. The needs of middle-class, working-class, and poor older people may differ. Middle-class people, for example, want lower taxes. Poorer people want more government services. Minority group needs may differ from those of the majority, and differences in need may exist between minority groups. Policy in the future must take these diverse interests into account.

The Medicare Modernization Act

The story of the Medicare Modernization Act (MMA) contains some of the same drama as MCCA tale, but with a different outcome. The MMA legislation provided $410 billion over 10 years to support Medicare coverage of outpatient prescription drugs. Later analysis suggested a price tag of $534 billion (Moon, 2006). Hudson (2010a, p. 9) calls this "the most significant expansion of Medicare since its inception." Morgan (2010) says this was the first time Medicare beneficiaries had to sign up with a private insurer to receive a portion of their Medicare benefits.

The legislation faced some criticism because it promoted further privatization of Medicare (dubbed Medicare Advantage). In particular it provided incentives for Medicare recipients to choose managed care organizations over the traditional fee-for-service Medicare plan. The legislation set up a competition between fee-for-service Medicare and private-sector Medicare programs. Binstock (2005a) says the legislation favored the private sector.

This situation posed a dilemma for the AARP (and for other senior advocacy groups). The AARP felt compelled to support the expansion of Medicare through the prescription drug plan. At the same time the AARP and other senior groups expressed concern about the erosion of the traditional Medicare program. Binstock (2005a) reports that the AARP sent "an eight-page letter to members of Congress." In the letter AARP threatened to oppose the legislation unless Congress made changes to the bill. But the bill emerged without significant change, and several senior organizations (but not the AARP) opposed it.

The AARP finally endorsed the bill and gave it full support. The AARP organized rallies to inform its members about the bill. And it spent $7 million on advertising to support passage of the law. This set AARP apart from other mass membership organizations that opposed the bill. Binstock (2005b, p. 284) says that "by all accounts . . . AARP's endorsement was decisive in enabling the bill to pass the Senate."

AARP probably took this route for at least two reasons. First, the MMA would help many older people to afford the drugs they need. And it would expand Medicare coverage. Second, support of MMA would sound good to members, who look to AARP to support senior benefits.

This plan only partially succeeded. About 45,000 AARP members resigned over its position. But, as Binstock (2005b) says, AARP might have lost millions of members if it failed to support prescription drug coverage within Medicare. After MMA's passage, AARP defended its action to members and promised to work on improving the new law.

BOX 15.3
INTEREST GROUP COALITIONS

Wallace and colleagues (1991) call senior power "no more dangerous than a lamb in wolf's clothing." They say that older people as a group do not have the power to bring about social reform. Instead, older people most often succeed in creating change when they link their interests to those of other lobby groups.

Williamson and colleagues (1982) support this view. They studied the start of Medicare and found that interest-group coalitions formed over the ideological issue of growing state programs to redistribute services to the needy. The coalition in favor of Medicare supported more services to people in need. The coalition against Medicare opposed any transfer of funds from tax revenues. The lists present the most influential members of the two groups.

These coalitions support different social class interests. The unions and working-class groups supported Medicare. Business and organized medicine opposed Medicare. Powerful pressure groups such as organized

labor won the day. The overlap of labor's interests and those of older people led to success. Ironically, medical doctors and hospitals (opponents of Medicare) got some of the largest financial benefits from the program.

For Medicare	*Against Medicare*
AFL-CIO	American Medical Association
American Nurses Association	American Hospital Association
Council of Jewish Federations and Welfare Funds	Life Insurance Association of America
American Association of Retired Workers	National Association of Manufacturers
National Association of Social Workers	National Association of Blue Shield Plans
National Farmers Union Federation	American Farm Bureau
The Socialist Party	The Chamber of Commerce
American Geriatrics Society	The American Legion

This case shows the power of senior advocacy by a mass membership organization as large as AARP. Binstock (2005b, p. 283) says that AARP's "impact on this process may have been the most influential that any old age interest group has had in U.S. politics."

Both cases (the MCCA and the MMA) show that the AARP considers the reaction of its members when it makes policy decisions. It relies on a large membership for its revenue and for its ability to impress and sway legislators. But members within such a diverse organization hold diverse views. AARP needs to consider the costs and benefits of its actions in relation to members' concerns.

In the case of the MCCA, AARP misjudged its wealthier members' concerns and had to backtrack to keep their support. In the case of the MMA, the organization could feel more confident in supporting the legislation. The unappealing part of the legislation would offend only a small group of people who understood Medicare policy and the cost of privatization. All social classes within AARP would gain some benefit from the new law. AARP could count on general membership support for its actions.

Politicians cannot ignore older people's needs. The size of the older population, its voting record, the large amount of the federal budget that goes to age-related programs, and the organized voice of advocacy groups

give the older population a major role in American politics. But experts debate whether advocacy groups directly can or will shape public policy. Or exactly how much influence they have. These cases also show the contentious and complex political environment that advocacy groups live in today.

ACTIVISM

Some years ago Alex Comfort (1976, p. 29) gave the following advice to people entering old age:

> You are about to join an underprivileged minority. There is no way of avoiding this at present. The remedies available to you will be those available to other minorities—organization, protest and militancy. Don't get trapped into aging alone if you can help it. The time to organize and get into a posture to resist is before the floor falls out.

Activism complements the work of advocacy groups. Advocacy largely works within the system to reform or support existing programs. Rarely do advocacy groups speak out on broad social issues such as inequality in later life. Activists, by contrast, work for fundamental social change. Often this change goes beyond narrow issues related to pensions and health care.

The Gray Panthers embody Comfort's call to action. The Gray Panthers calls itself "an intergenerational, multi-issue organization working to create a society that puts the needs of people over profit, responsibility over power and democracy over institutions" (Gray Panthers, 2010). The organization defines itself as "Age and Youth in Action."

At the organization's high point in the 1970s and 1980s, it raised senior activism to a fine art. "Their approach to nursing-home reform, for example, was to stage a street play at the AMA Convention in Atlantic City in which a doctor sold patients to the Kill 'Em Quick Nursing Home; doctors' wives were reported to have glared in disapproval at what the old folks were doing" (Hapgood, 1978, p. 353).

The first leader of the Gray Panthers, Maggie Kuhn, founded the organization in 1972 with six other retirees when her employer (a church in Philadelphia) forced her to retire. This group made a commitment to use their retirement years for public service. Maggie Kuhn's appearances on television and at rallies throughout the United States led to rapid growth in Gray Panther membership. At that time, the group claimed 50,000 members in 100 networks throughout the country.

Maggie Kuhn's charisma and energy accounted for much of the Panthers' success. But this strength also points to the group's weaknesses. First, new leadership did not develop after Maggie Kuhn's death in 1995. This created a crisis that threatened the group's future. Second, the Panthers lack formal organization. The group in 2007 claims active local chapters in 13 states, but it lacks a strong central office. It also lacks long-term professional staff. Third, most Panther members want more power for older people, but they no longer get the press coverage for their views.

In 1997, the organization appointed a new board of directors and a new chair. Today, the Gray Panthers take a critical view of social policies, but they look more like an advocacy group than an activist group. The group holds conventions and sells bumper stickers, buttons, and T-shirts. It raises awareness of senior issues on its Web site, criticized the proposed privatization of Social Security, and supports improvements in Medicare (Gray Panthers, 2010).

A relatively small number of older people took part in senior activism in the past, and even fewer do so today. But more people may choose this approach in the future. Baby Boom cohorts that protested in the 1960s and 1970s may feel more comfortable using an activist approach to social change. They may also use these methods to protest poverty, pollution, and other social problems.

BOX 15.4
HOUSE PANEL LEADER JEERED BY ELDERLY IN CHICAGO

Older people rarely take an activist stance. But they can get riled over attempts to change Social Security or Medicare policies. An Associated Press report tells the story of one Congressman who dared to tinker with the Medicare program. This article appeared in *The New York Times* shortly after the incident occurred.

CHICAGO, AP Aug. 19 [1989]—Representative Dan Rostenkowski of Illinois, one of the most powerful members of Congress, was booed and followed down the street by a group of screaming elderly people Thursday as he left a meeting with community leaders opposed to his stance on a program intended to protect the elderly from the high costs of extended illnesses.

Several dozen people shouted "Liar!" "Impeach!" and "Recall!" when Mr. Rostenkowski, the Democrat who heads the House Ways and Means Committee, left a community center in the North Side district of Chicago that he has represented for 30 years.

The group briefly blocked his car, hitting it with picket signs and pounding on the windows. Mr. Rostenkowski got out of the car and walked briskly down the street for about a block, with the protesters in pursuit. The driver then drove the car to a gasoline station, the Congressman got back in and the car sped away.

As he walked down the street, Mr. Rostenkowski said, "I don't think they understand what's going on. That's too bad."

The incident occurred after Mr. Rostenkowski discussed his support for the Catastrophic Coverage Act of 1988 in a private meeting with representatives of six organizations for the elderly.

Source: Associated Press, *New York Times*. (1989, August 19). *House panel leader jeered by elderly in Chicago*. Retrieved: July 14, 2011, from www.nytimes.com/1989/08/19/us/house-panel-leader-jeered-by-elderly-in-chicago.html

GOVERNMENT AND AGING POLICY

Federal, state, and local governments now have a web of agencies, policies, and programs to serve older people. Some programs serve all older people; others target specific groups (Supplemental Security Income, for example, serves low-income older people). Some programs offer benefits for people to use as they wish (e.g., Social Security); others offer direct services, such as senior centers. These programs grew without a plan into what became the **aging network**. Hudson (2010a, p. 6) calls this "an array of public and private sector planning and service agencies that now blanket the nation."

The Older Americans Act

The Older Americans Act (OAA) has served as the basis of federal government aging policy for over 40 years. Congress introduced the OAA in 1965 with the goal of "assuring the well-being of the elderly." No other federal program has this single broad purpose.

Funding for the act grew from $6.5 million in 1965 to $1.73 billion in 2009. This increase in funding reflects the OAA's increased responsibility for setting up a national service network for older people. The OAA also set up the Administration on Aging (AoA) within the federal Department of Health and Human Services.

The Older Americans Act charges the AoA (2010d) with the responsibility "to develop a comprehensive, coordinated and cost-effective system of home and community-based services that helps elderly individuals maintain their health and independence in their homes and communities." The AoA is the official federal agency charged with looking after federal aging policy. It coordinates programs and services, puts policy into practice, and conducts research on aging.

The AoA works with federal, state, local, and tribal agencies in the National Network on Aging. The National Network on Aging serves about 7 million older people and caregivers. The Network has "56 State Units on Aging (SUAs); 629 Area Agencies on Aging; 244 Tribal organizations and 2 Native Hawaiian organizations." The network includes nearly 20,000 service providers and thousands of volunteers (AoA, 2007b, 2010f).

The AoA includes both small and large agencies. Their budgets range from $150,000 to $250 million. The numbers of clients they serve range from 91 to 128,945. And the numbers of employees in agencies range from 1 to 650 (Kunkel & Lackmeyer, 2008). Some agencies exist in small rural communities, others in large cities. Some agencies operate as private nonprofits; others exist as part of a government or tribal entity.

The National Network on Aging provides services to all older people, but most programs target poorer older people—people who live in isolation and people with severe health problems. Older Americans Act programs managed by the AoA include supportive services and senior centers, nutrition services, health, prevention, and wellness services, the National Family Caregiver Support Program, services that protect older people from abuse, and services to Native Americans. These and a variety of other services get state and local support as well as federal funding.

The federal government reauthorized the Older Americans Act in 2000 and again in 2006. The 2006 reauthorization will extend all programs through 2011. The reauthorization in 2000 provided for a new program—the National Family Caregiver Support Program. This program focuses support on family caregivers for ill or disabled older people. It recognizes the important role that family caregivers play in community long-term care. The program provided $125 million per year to state agencies on aging. The funding will provide information, counseling, support groups, respite care, and other supports to family caregivers (AoA, 2004d).

Some critics blame the AoA for not coordinating government aging policies and programs. But the position of the AoA within the federal government makes program oversight impossible. In the

Congressmen and seniors meet at a Capitol Hill press conference to discuss prescription drug benefits to seniors under the Medicare program.

United States, many age-related policies and programs (e.g., housing) come under other government departments. And each department has its own priorities and programs.

Hudson (2010b, pp. 307–308) says that in some cases Area Agencies "have become major players . . . in the design an implementation of home and community-based services." Some people suggest that the Area Agencies on Aging should coordinate all community programs, but all aging programs will probably never come under one authority. Instead, all parts of the government in the future will need to take the aging population into account. They will need to adjust programs to meet older people's needs.

Burgess and Applebaum (2009) say that an increase in the older population, especially people age 85 and over, means more demand for services. At the same time, "the aging network is being asked to serve an ever increasing older population with shrinking federal, state, and private support."

A shortage of funds has led to a shift in the Older Americans Act's focus. The OAA stated a broad vision of service to improve the health and general well-being of older people (including social and emotional well-being). The OAA shifted recently to focus on the chronically ill. Hudson (2010b) points to three related trends in service delivery to older people: (1) targeting specific groups of older people, (2) narrowing the scope of services, and (3) focusing on health-related concerns.

These changes channel resources to the most needy people. Hudson (2010b, p. 320) considers this focus on the most needy one of "the principal successes of the aging services network." This has meant a shift toward keeping frail older people in the community and out of institutions. And this has also meant a shift away from social programs like senior centers and recreation.

This shift of resources to the most needy has led to programs that serve all people in an area based on need rather than age. This includes younger disabled people. A health care agency, for example, might set up a community health clinic in a Hispanic neighborhood. This program would serve all poorer people in the neighborhood. The program might serve fewer older people than a clinic for all older people (since some older people might have incomes too high to qualify for the service). But it would see that health care resources went to the people who needed them most.

Programs such as this could use a means test to ensure that only people with financial need got the service. Or programs could use a functional test and make services only available to the frail elderly. Some writers reject this approach. They say that need-based programs would single out the poor and needy and could give basic services the stigma of welfare.

Torres-Gil (1992, p. 145) says that "means-testing benefits should be a last resort." Instead, he proposes higher ages for entitlement. This would restrict use of government programs to people in older age groups. Binstock (2009b, p. 149) says that any changes to programs for older people will probably have "long transition periods." This minimizes the effect on the current generation of older people and makes change politically acceptable.

The debate over age-based versus needs-based programs has gone on for years and will continue. So will the tension between funding for programs that support an active engaged lifestyle and services that meet the needs of the frail elderly. These tensions will heat up in the future as the government tries to serve a growing older population with limited funds. As the large Baby Boom generation enters old age, Hudson (2009b, p. 127) says, it will "face a political arena that will be both more inclusive and more contentious than any that older people have faced to this point."

GENERATIONAL EQUITY

News articles and media reports link the rising numbers of older people in the United States to the high cost of social and health care services. Some policy analysts propose that a large older population will burden young people with crushing debt. They describe the growth of the older population as a "tidal wave," a burden, or a source of intergenerational conflict. Some writers use population projections to warn about a coming crisis in American society.

David M. Walker, Comptroller General of the Government Accountability Office (GAO), warns that an aging U.S. population "will absorb a larger and ultimately unsustainable share of the federal budget and economic resources" (Walker, 2002, p. 6; cited in Novelli, 2005).

In another context Walker (2004) linked the aging of the Baby Boom generation to "fiscal imbalance [that] will test the nation's spending and tax policies." The gap in our ability to pay, he says, "is now so large that we will not be able simply to grow our way out of the problem. Difficult choices are inevitable." William D. Novelli (2005), former CEO of the American Association of Retired Persons (AARP), takes a more balanced view. But he, too, ends his remarks on a

---

BOX 15.5
THE WHITE HOUSE CONFERENCE ON AGING (WHCoA), 2005

Once a decade since 1961 the White House has held a Conference on Aging (WHCoA). As of this writing, the most recent conference took place December 11 to 14, 2005, in Washington, DC. Governors from each of the states and territories, members of Congress, and the National Congress of American Indians selected delegates to the conference. Some at-large delegates, selected for their expertise and work in the field of aging, attended as well. In all, 1,200 delegates, the majority over age 55, attended the conference. Delegates make recommendations to the president and to Congress to shape policy over the next 10 years.

The theme of the 2005 conference was "The Booming Dynamics of Aging." The conference focused on current and future age-related issues, including the entry of the Baby Boom generation into later life.

The conference asked for and received several dozen resolutions from large and small interest groups. These included resolutions from the AARP, National Council on the Aging, and Generations United. The WHCoA considered 73 resolutions during its meetings. Some of these resolutions may find their way into policy through executive order of the president. Others may work their way onto the legislative agenda.

The following list presents the top 10 resolutions (out of 73) that the delegates passed in 2005. I follow this list with the list from the 1995 WHCoA. Both lists are ranked with the item receiving the highest number of votes at the top.

Top Ten Resolutions, 2005

1. Reauthorize the Older Americans Act within the first six months following the 2005 White House Conference on Aging.
2. Develop a coordinated, comprehensive long-term care strategy by supporting public and private sector initiatives that address financing, choice, quality, service delivery, and the paid and unpaid workforce.
3. Ensure that older Americans have transportation options to retain their mobility and independence.
4. Strengthen and improve the Medicaid program for seniors.
5. Strengthen and improve the Medicare program.

6. Support geriatric education and training for all health care professionals, paraprofessionals, health profession students, and direct care workers.
7. Promote innovative models of non-institutional long-term care.
8. Improve recognition, assessment, and treatment of mental illness and depression among older Americans.
9. Attain adequate numbers of health care personnel in all professions who are skilled, culturally competent, and specialized in geriatrics.
10. Improve state and local based integrated delivery systems to meet 21st-century needs of seniors.

Top Ten Resolutions, 1995

1. Keeping Social Security sound, now and for the future
2. Preserving the integrity of the Older Americans Act
3. Preserving the nature of Medicaid
4. Ensuring the future of the Medicare program
5. Preserving advocacy functions under the Older Americans Act
6. Ensuring the availability of a broad spectrum of services
7. Financing and providing long-term care and services
8. Acknowledging the contribution of older volunteers
9. Assuming personal responsibility for the state of one's health
10. Strengthening the federal role in building and sustaining a well-trained work force grounded in geriatric and gerontological education

Note the similarities and differences in these two lists. What issues have remained the same over the 10 years between conferences? What new issues have emerged? Do these lists suggest that some issues will remain permanent parts of the social policy landscape? Do you think these resolutions will have an impact on national public policy?

You can find out more about the resolutions passed as well as the proposed implementation strategies by going to the White House Conference on Aging Web site at www.whcoa.gov.

---

disturbing note. He says "America is facing a dramatic change propelled by the increased longevity of its citizens and the coming retirement of the boomers. . . . Can America afford to grow older with intergenerational fairness—without sticking our children and grandchildren with the bill?"

Historically American society has treated its older people generously compared to other age groups. Hudson (2009a) notes a number of policy firsts directed at older people: Civil War pensions for Northern veterans (1862), old-age assistance and insurance (1935), disability insurance for people over age 50

BOX 15.6
FEDERAL GOVERNMENT INITIATIVES ON AGING

Since the 1950s, the federal government has put into place a number of agencies, committees, and programs that develop and provide services for older people. The following list gives some of the most important developments in the aging network.

1959	U.S. Senate Special Committee on Aging established
1961	First White House Conference on Aging
1965	Older Americans Act passed; Medicare and Medicaid
1965	Administration on Aging established as an operating agency of the Department of Health, Education, and Welfare
1967	Age Discrimination in Employment Act signed into law
1971	Second White House Conference on Aging
1973	Older Americans Comprehensive Services Amendments (the Older Americans Act) passed; Area Agencies on Aging developed to plan services for older people statewide
1974	National Institute on Aging created
1978	Legislation raised mandatory retirement age from 65 to 70
1981	Third White House Conference on Aging
1986	Mandatory retirement eliminated
1987	Omnibus Budget Reconciliation Act set new standards for nursing home care

1988	Medicare Catastrophic Coverage Act passed
1989	Medicare Catastrophic Coverage Act repealed
1995	Fourth White House Conference on Aging
1997	Congress creates the Roth IRA
2003	Medicare Modernization Act (MMA) passed
2005	Medicare prescription drug reimbursement implemented
2005	Deficit Reduction Act passed to realign Medicaid incentives to provide community-based, long-term care
2005	Fifth White House Conference on Aging
2010	Patient Protection and Affordable Care Act passed

The greatest legislative activity on behalf of older people took place during the 1970s. The public supported these programs because they saw older people as poor and needy. By the 1980s, public opinion shifted and older people came to be seen as relatively well off. Recent attempts to create policies to help older people have met resistance due to this view. McKenzie (1993) suggests that supports for older people have peaked. He sees a trend toward higher taxes on Social Security benefits, higher costs for medical care, and a decline in older people's income.

Sources: Based on R. B. McKenzie, "Senior Status: Has the Power of the Elderly Peaked?" *American Enterprise, 4*(3) (1993): 74–80. www.TAEmag.com. See also R. Rosenblatt, "The WHCOA and Lower Expectations," *Aging Today, 16*(2) (1995): 2.

(1956), Medicare (1965), and Supplemental Security Income (1972) for poor old, blind, and disabled people. These policies assumed that older people were poor and frail and too weak to earn a living. Sympathy for the old drove public support for these policies. But this sympathy for the old may have come to an end.

The cost of programs for older people has led some critics to ask whether older people get too much support. Schulz and Binstock (2006) call these the "merchants of doom." Hudson (1997, p. 39; also Hudson, 2007) says that in the eye of public policy critics, old age policy in the past few decades has gone from "'We can't do enough' to 'Have we done too much?'" Discussions of support for older people, given the costs of age-based programs, often come down to the issue of the fair distribution of resources to the older and younger generations. Terms like "greedy geezers" portray older people as well off and anxious to grab more benefits if they can (Fairlie, 1988).

Rosenzweig (1991), for example, dealt with this topic in an address given at the annual meeting of the Gerontological Society of America some years ago. He said that unless older people willingly give up some of their current benefits in a time of scarcity, they will create a "disastrous" effect on society. "Of every nondefense, noninterest dollar in the federal budget [in the United States]," he said, "47 cents is spent on programs for people age 65 and over." And he projected that the government will spend more than half of its budget on older people in the years ahead.

Rosenzweig predicted that these costs will lead to a conflict between retirees and the rest of society, including future retirees. And he said that leaders of interest groups ought to help their members "shape a conception of their interests that fits their own immediate needs into the needs of the larger community on whose overall well-being their own ultimately depends."

BOX 15.7
OLDER AMERICANS ACT OF 1965, AS AMENDED 2000

TITLE 42—THE PUBLIC HEALTH AND WELFARE
CHAPTER 35—PROGRAMS FOR OLDER
AMERICANS
SUBCHAPTER I—DECLARATION OF
OBJECTIVES AND DEFINITIONS
SEC. 3001. CONGRESSIONAL
DECLARATION OF OBJECTIVES

The Congress hereby finds and declares that, in keeping with the traditional American concept of the inherent dignity of the individual in our democratic society, the older people of our Nation are entitled to, and it is the joint and several duty and responsibility of the governments of the United States, of the several States and their political subdivisions, and of Indian tribes to assist our older people to secure equal opportunity to the full and free enjoyment of the following objectives:

1. An adequate income in retirement in accordance with the American standard of living.

2. The best possible physical and mental health which science can make available and without regard to economic status.

3. Obtaining and maintaining suitable housing, independently selected, designed and located with reference to special needs and available at costs which older citizens can afford.

4. Full restorative services for those who require institutional care, and a comprehensive array of community-based, long-term care services adequate to appropriately sustain older people in their communities and in their homes, including support to family members and other persons providing voluntary care to older individuals needing long-term care services.

5. Opportunity for employment with no discriminatory personnel practices because of age.

6. Retirement in health, honor, dignity—after years of contribution to the economy.

7. Participating in and contributing to meaningful activity within the widest range of civic, cultural, education and training and recreational opportunities.

8. Efficient community services, including access to low-cost transportation, which provide a choice in supported living arrangements and social assistance in a coordinated manner and which are readily available when needed, with emphasis on maintaining a continuum of care for vulnerable older individuals.

9. Immediate benefit from proven research knowledge which can sustain and improve health and happiness.

10. Freedom, independence, and the free exercise of individual initiative in planning and managing their own lives, full participation in the planning and operation of community-based services and programs provided for their benefit, and protection against abuse, neglect, and exploitation.

Source: U.S. Code Online via GPO Access, wais.access.gpo.gov. Laws in effect as of January 7, 2003. Document not affected by Public Laws enacted between January 7, 2003 and February 12, 2003. CITE: 42USC3001. Retrieved January 11, 2005, from http://frwebgate.access.gpo.gov/cgi-bin/getdoc.cgi?dbname=browse_usc&docid=Cite:+42USC3001.

In part, these views reflect changes in the treatment of older people and improvements in their financial status. Policy changes between 1965 and the 1990s led to rapid improvements in older people's lives. The government promoted Medicare, Medicaid, four large increases in Social Security, cost-of-living adjustments to Social Security, a Supplemental Security Income program, housing subsidies, and expanded community care.

This led to a rapid decrease in poverty rates among older people, one of the great social achievements of this century. Between 1959 and the mid-1990s, for example, the poverty rate for older people dropped by two thirds, from 39% to around 13% (Hudson, 1996; also Hudson, 2009a). "Social Security," Hudson (1997, p. 5) says, "has done more to alleviate poverty and inequality among old people than either the tax system or other social programs, including welfare."

The media during the 1980s and 1990s created a new stereotype of older people. It described them as healthy, fun-loving, affluent, and living a life of luxury and ease—all at the expense of their children and grandchildren. As late as 2003, Chapman wrote an article for *Slate,* an online magazine, titled "Meet the Greedy Grandparents" (cited in Schulz & Binstock, 2006).

Three assumptions underlie the generational equity debate: (1) older people get an unfair share of the nation's resources, (2) a larger older population will place an intolerable burden on younger people, and

(3) younger people pay high taxes for Social Security today but will get little benefit from the system when they retire. Each of these points focuses on the distribution of resources to younger and older people.

At the same time that poverty has decreased for older people, poverty among children has increased. Some writers make a connection between these two facts. Smith (1992, p. 68), for example, says that "in order to pay for the oldsters' Big Rest, other worthy causes, most critically investment in children, increasingly get pushed aside." He suggests that money for old-age programs go to expand Head Start, vaccination, and school lunch programs for children.

Lacayo (1990, p. 40) agrees. He says that the government should "trim spending on affluent older people to free up funds for nutrition, schooling and health care for impoverished kids." Lacayo suggests that the government create a means test for Social Security and Medicare.

The issue of **generational equity** has sparked debate and controversy. It led to the creation of a group called Americans for Generational Equity (AGE). This group believes that young and middle-aged people cannot pay the high costs for services to older people.

The AGE Web site contains the following assessment of generational relations in the years ahead:

> The typical boomer is preparing to embark on a retirement averaging 21 years with illiquid home equity and financial assets sufficient to replace barely one year's pre-retirement income. With medical bills significantly higher than those of today's retirees, boomers will be more dependent on their children than any generation before them.
>
> What does this mean for our young? At a minimum, they will devote a much larger share of their incomes to taxes and healthcare. They may also need to save much more, in anticipation that today's unsustainable benefit promises eventually will be trimmed. (AGE, 2007)

Americans for Generational Equity proposes cuts to programs for older people to free up money for the young. For example, it proposes to replace Social Security in the United States with a system of welfare for the poorest older people (Quadagno, 1991). Other U.S. groups, such as the Concord Coalition, propose a means test for Social Security and Medicare. The coalition says that only people who earn under $40,000 per year should get Social Security and Medicare.

Cruikshank (2003, p. 27) reports that in 1999, the Concord Coalition "took out a full-page ad in the *New York Times* to attack a proposal to use part of the budget surplus to strengthen Social Security and Medicare." Groups like AGE and the Concord Coalition gather support by pitting the interests of older people against those of the young. Townson (1994, p. 14) says the media have taken up the cause of "kids versus canes." Hudson (1993, p. 79) says that "the aged find themselves transformed into an overindulged and singularly greedy population."

Generational equity supporters assume that most older people no longer need Social Security and other government programs. This view ignores the diversity of the older population. Large proportions of the very old, minority older people, and older women still live near or below the poverty line. It also ignores the fact that Social Security accounts for the current modest standard of living enjoyed by most older people. A decrease in Social Security support would plunge many people into poverty.

Kail, Quadagno, and Keene (2009) say that little relationship exists between spending on older people and spending on children. Poverty exists among children because social policies and policy makers allow it to exist. Critics of childhood poverty should emphasize society's failure to deal with this issue. Poor children, for example, live in poor families. Often, women with low incomes head these families. Quadagno (1989), for example, shows that the increase in the number of single mothers in America explains the increase in childhood poverty and not Social Security payments. Reduced support for older people will not solve the problem of poverty in youth. It will only lead to a return to high poverty rates at the latter end of life.

Binstock (2005a) says that politicians and officials target programs for older people as they search for solutions to budget deficits. This, he says, scapegoats the elderly and makes them seem the source of economic problems. Other sources of national debt—expensive overseas military ventures and the need for a Wall Street bailout—seem beyond political control.

The argument that a larger older population will place an intolerable burden on younger people assumes that older people will demand more resources and that younger people will have to pay for them. It further assumes that younger people will find these increased costs burdensome. This view assumes that nothing will change either in the economy or in public policy in the future.

But a stronger economy would make programs for older people more affordable, and containment of health care costs (the cause of much of the increase in program costs for older people) would make programs for older people less expensive. Public policies related to health care and Social Security need to change now to prepare for future demands. Changes will include the adjustment of benefit levels, an increase in the retirement age, and an increase in payments into the system. (See Chapter 8 for a detailed discussion of Social Security reform.)

Some of these changes have begun to take place. For example, the 1986 amendments to the federal Age Discrimination in Employment Act abolished mandatory retirement. This protects workers in the public and private sector from forced retirement. It allows workers to choose to stay at work longer. Recent increases in workforce participation by older workers shows that many people now choose this option. And many Baby Boomers say they intend to work past age 65.

Federal policy has raised the age for full Social Security eligibility from age 65 to age 67 by the year 2027. This policy will encourage people to stay at work longer. The government has also increased Social Security taxes. These two policy changes will allow the Social Security trust fund to grow and meet the needs of a large older population.

Further increases in payroll taxes could cover Social Security costs over the next 75 years without an intolerable burden on the young. Goozner (2005, p. 12) says, "According to the Social Security trustees, if the tax on wages today were raised by less than 1% each for employee and employer (from the current rate of 6.2% each), Social Security would be solvent through 2077."

The facts about Social Security do not support the argument that young people pay high taxes for Social Security today but will get little benefit from the system when they retire. A solvent system to 2077 will ensure that all workers today benefit from the system.

Also, many of the people who get income from the Social Security system today are younger men, women and children, dependents, survivors, and disabled people. In 2010, for example, children, young people, and adults under age 64 made up 30% of all people who received Social Security benefits. This came to over 16 million people. This includes 10 million disabled workers and their dependents who get benefits from the Social Security system (Social Security Online, 2010a).

Social Security policies may change in the future. Some authors have suggested a means test for Social Security. This would limit Social Security benefits to poor older people. But such a move would erode support for Social Security among more affluent older

Claude Pepper served as a congressman from Florida into his late 80s. He fought for many years to improve services and programs for older people. In 1990, the Pepper Commission proposed improved home care and long-term care insurance to protect older people from poverty.

people. And this would weaken the system and lower benefits for the poor.

A strong Social Security program will benefit middle-class workers by providing them with income security in later life. Wealthier older people may see some reduction in benefits, but they will still benefit from the system. Poor people, in particular, will benefit from a strong Social Security system. A weakened Social Security system would reverse the achievements of "America's most effective poverty-reduction program" (Marmor, Mashaw, & Harvey, 1990).

Conflict Ahead?

Studies of intergenerational relations find little support for predictions of intergenerational conflict in the future. The AARP (2004f), for example, conducted a nationwide telephone survey in 2004 to assess Americans' attitudes toward older people. The study created an index of "intergenerational conflict" that included questions about the share of government benefits that older people get and the impact of older people on the community. The study "found that 91% of Americans believe that older Americans receive about or less than their fair share of local government benefits and 89% of Americans believe that older persons have the right amount or too little influence in this country." The report states that the same index was created in 1994, and the average index value was almost the same as in 2004. These studies show little support for the existence of intergenerational conflict.

Kohli (2006, citing Hicks, 2001) reports that, in the United States, 86% of the population say that the government should ensure a decent standard of living for older people. Even people under age 30 in this national study support government oversight for Social Security. Younger people fear above all that the system will not exist to serve them.

"Contrary to what the lively public discourse in the United States would suggest," Kohli (2006, p. 470)

says, "the age gap is almost nonexistent in this country." He goes on to say that between 1996 and 2001, support for a state-managed Social Security system grew even stronger. In another study, Cutler and colleagues (2002) found that in a national survey only 6% of the people age 18 and over considered older people "greedy geezers." Curiously, older people agreed with this statement at more than twice the rate of other age groups. These authors concluded, "There is more evidence of a generation consensus than a generation gap" (p. 64).

Kohli (2006, p. 474) calls for "intergenerational interdependence." A coalition group called Generations United (GU) takes this approach. Generations United began with the National Council on the Aging and the Child Welfare League of America as co-chairs. The group represents more than 100 national, state, and local organizations, including the United Way and Volunteers of America (Generations United, 2010). It claims to speak for over 70 million Americans.

BOX 15.8
AGING IN CALIFORNIA: CONFLICT IN THE MAKING?

The generational equity debate predicts potential future conflict between older and younger people. The demographics of California add an ethnic dimension to this potential conflict. Census data show that California's Anglo population decreased from 79% to 43.8% of the population between 1970 and 2005.

At the same time, the Latino population grew from 10.9% to 35.2% of the population. These figures point to a potential clash over the state's resources.

Hayes-Bautista (1991) called attention to this issue some years ago. It's an issue that other states and regions may face in the years to come.

The Latino population has a higher birth rate than the Anglo population. As a result, Latinos will have a young population compared to Anglos. This will mean that this younger Latino population will pay taxes to support a relatively large older Anglo population. Hayes-Bautista (1991, 2004; also Burr, Mutchler, & Gerst, 2010; Lynch, 2010) sees the potential for generational conflict in this situation. He bases his view on the demographic and social conditions of these two groups. "The shrinking Anglo population," he says, "lives a world apart from the growing, youthful Latino community." He notes that Anglos, compared to Latinos, have about 1.5 times the years of education and more than 1.5 times the median family income. Latinos have 3 times the poverty rates of Anglos. Latino children have 3 times the poverty rate of Anglo children.

"On the surface," Hayes-Bautista (1991) says, "it would appear that the conditions for a very bitter interethnic and intergenerational conflict exist: a well-educated elderly Anglo population that has rarely experienced poverty expecting to be supported in its retirement by a poorly educated, younger Latino population for which poverty is a common occurrence."

Can a conflict be avoided?

Hayes-Bautista holds out hope for a win-win outcome. Support for Anglos in old age, he says, depends on the economic success of young Latinos. Older Anglos and young Latinos will both win through support of good education and a strong economy. "The key step," he says, "will be to forge alliances across ethnic groups and across generations."

Sources: U.S. Census Bureau, *State and County Quick Facts.* Retrieved November 18, 2007, from http://quickfacts.census.gov/qfd/states/06000.html; Burr, J. A., Mutchler, J. E., & Gerst, K. (2010). Public policies and older populations of color. In R. B. Hudson (Ed.). *The new politics of old age policy* (2nd ed., pp. 160–182). Baltimore: The Johns Hopkins University Press; Lynch, F. R. (2010). Political power and the baby boomers. In R. B. Hudson, (Ed.). *The new politics of old age policy* (2nd ed., pp. 87–107). Baltimore: The Johns Hopkins University Press; Hayes-Bautista, D. E. (1991, Fall–Winter). Young Latinos, older Anglos, and public policy: Lessons from California. *Generations,* pp. 37–39; Palmer, J., Song, Y., & Lu, H.-H. (2002). *The changing face of child poverty in California.* National Center for Children in Poverty. Retrieved November 18, 2007, from www.nccp.org/publications/pub_482.html.

Generations United works to unite age-based groups in a common cause.

> GU promotes an *intergenerational approach* to framing public policies that impact children, youth and elderly issues. While popular perception suggests that advocates of each respective interest group are at different ends of the policy spectrum, we contend otherwise. . . . Our goal is for others to understand that generational interdependence—the giving and receiving of resources over time—is crucial to promoting social progress. (Generations United, 2007)

GU supports an expansion of funding for the National Senior Service Corps and policy changes that would allow more older people to serve as foster grandparents. GU also supports training programs that would teach Housing and Urban Development workers about the needs of grandparents who raise children in public housing. GU sponsors a project called Seniors4kids. It enlists people age 50 and over to develop programs that connect children and older people. In one project, volunteers age 50 and over work to develop quality pre-kindergarten programs.

Generations United maintains a Web site that informs people about intergenerational issues. It sponsors meetings and conferences that bring the generations together. It publishes a journal on intergenerational issues titled *Together*. Organizations such as GU help buffer potential conflict between the generations.

The debate over the cost of an older population will go on in the years ahead. But, Hudson (2009b, p. 130) says, "There is no sociological or anthropological literature suggesting deep-seated animosity among older and younger people." Research shows the opposite. Cook (2002) reports that over 90% of people in all age groups support Social Security in its present form or in an expanded version.

Ideology and Aging Policy

The debate over the cost of programs for older people has grown more ideological in recent years (Hudson, 2004). Conservative Republicans, for example, support the privatization of the Social Security system and competition in health care services. They want to shift more responsibility for financial resources, health care, and caregiver services to the individual, the family, and the community. This neoconservative approach aims to reduce government support of programs for older people. It looks to the private sector to provide services to older people.

Liberal Democrats, on the other hand, propose improvements in the current system. They propose an increase in the retirement age, an increase in contributions to Social Security, and a focus on serving the poorest older people. The liberal view looks for ways to control Medicare and Medicaid costs. Liberal Democrats look for ways to maintain and support the current network of social supports.

"Absent a real (or manufactured) crisis atmosphere," Hudson (2009b, p. 132) says, "it seems likely that the contending forces will be at loggerheads [over aging policy], and such stalemate may well put off the day of reckoning." This contentious atmosphere will also stand in the way of sound policy reform.

The growing size of the older population will draw attention to the costs of public pensions, health care, and other services. It will deepen the divide between these two views of social policy and practice. But blaming older people for an increase in their need for Social Security and health care services will not lead to a better life for older or younger people.

The public needs good information about the costs and the benefits of social policies. We all have parents and grandparents. We will all be old someday. And we want a society that cares for people at every age.

CIVIC ENGAGEMENT

Historian Andrew Achenbaum (2006, p. 19) traces the history of civic engagement by older people throughout American history. "Elders," he says, "have been leaders in galvanizing voluntary associations." They played a role in the abolitionist movement before and after the Civil War, they fought for women's rights, and they led the development of the labor movement in the early 1900s.

Today, older people work to better society through thousands of voluntary organizations. Some of these organizations affiliate with religious bodies, others affiliate with political parties. Some groups have a social service function, like Rotary and Kiwanis. These organizations enlist the voluntary support of adults, including older people, for the improvement of society.

An organization called Civic Ventures enlists older volunteers for specific projects. Civic Ventures helped establish Experience Corps, a program that recruits older people to serve as tutors and mentors in the schools. Civic Ventures also helps community groups develop projects served by older volunteers. It runs an award program, called the "Purpose Prize."

BOX 15.9
THE PURPOSE PRIZE

In 2006, Civic Ventures (2007b) first offered "The Purpose Prize." The prize went to "social innovators," people age 60 and over, who use their talents to address pressing social issues. Civic Ventures awards five $100,000 prizes and ten $10,000 prizes to people who have demonstrated "uncommon vision, determination and entrepreneurialism in addressing community and national problems." Two foundations support this program: the Atlantic Philanthropies and the John Templeton Foundation. The program (a 3-year project) intends to build a national network of "Purpose Prize Winners and Fellows." The program will highlight the achievements of older social entrepreneurs. In 2006, Civic Ventures awarded 15 Purpose Prize Winners and 40 Purpose Prize Fellows.

The following example provides a sample of the Purpose Prize Winners' achievements:

Hispanics will soon be the second largest segment of the U.S. labor force. But their lagging rates of educational attainment threaten both their own chance of success and our country's ability to compete economically in the global markets. *Jose-Pablo Fernandez,* former director of the Mexican Institute of Houston, knew he needed to do something. But what? In 2002 Fernandez created a program to teach computer technology in Spanish to parents at the same schools their children attend. The 16-week, 96-hour program equips parents with marketable computer skills, while teaching them strategies to encourage their children to stay in school and go on to college. Today, the program is offered in 110 schools and community centers in Houston, San Antonio and Beaumont. More than 4,000 Hispanic adults have graduated from the program, and parental involvement in the participating schools has dramatically increased. In 2007, Fernandez set up CCA Alliance, Inc. to partner with nonprofit organizations in cities across the United States to replicate the success he had in Houston.

Purpose Prize winners will serve as a resource to others who want to engage in social action and community service. Civic Ventures intends to hold an annual meeting of prize winners and fellows called the Purpose Prize Innovation Summit. This meeting will bring together Purpose Prize Fellows along with scholars, activists, and funders. The Summit will hold workshops, panel presentations, and cultural events to stimulate social entrepreneurship (Civic Ventures, 2007b).

You can learn more about the Purpose Prize and see video clips of all the prize winners at www.encore.org/prize.

Prizes (up to $100,000) go to outstanding social entrepreneurs over age 60 to encourage their work. The Atlantic Philanthropies and the John Templeton Foundation sponsor these prizes. Examples of Purpose Prize winners include a psychiatrist who asks fellow therapists to volunteer as counselors to returning veterans and their families; a telecom executive who arranges broadband connections for poor farm communities in Appalachia; and a professor who creates safe "green" bricks from toxic waste. (See www.encore.org/prize for more information on this program.) Civic Ventures encourages people to explore "encore careers" in their Third Age. It sets the stage for Baby Boomers to find meaning in later life through volunteerism.

THE FUTURE OF AGING, POLITICS, AND POLICY

No one can predict with assurance the future of the politics of aging. New social conditions in the future may give rise to new forms of political action. Still, it seems likely that Baby Boomers will have a unique influence on political life. Schulz and Binstock (2006) predict that, compared to the proportion of older people who vote today, Boomers will probably make up a higher proportion of voters in national elections in the future. Will they form a voting bloc in the future? This seems as unlikely in the future as it does today.

Under dire economic conditions in the future, faced with a threat to old age benefits, Boomers could come together in a single voice. But in most cases in the future they will not vote as a bloc. Boomers could form a political party or support one to advance their interests. Is this possible? Yes. "But," Schulz and Binstock (2006, p. 227) say, "in our opinion not likely." In the absence of radical change in old age benefits, Boomers will likely show the same diversity of views and political affiliations that they show today.

Older people in the future will probably not control political decision making through voting, advocacy, or activism. Even in the best case of advocacy (support for the prescription drug legislation), the AARP and other groups rode a wave of support from business and the pharmaceutical industry.

Still, in the future older people, by their sheer presence, will influence public policy. Pampel and

Williamson (1989, cited in Wallace et al., 1991) studied the effects of an aging population on welfare spending in 18 societies, including the United States. They found that an increased older population leads to more money spent on pensions and medical care. This held true in spite of social class and governmental differences in these countries.

Hudson (1988) studied developed nations, including Sweden, Canada, France, Great Britain, West Germany, and the United States. He found increases in expenditures on social security in all of these countries between the mid-1950s and the late 1970s. All of these societies will see an increase in the number of older people who get a public pension. This will increase the amount of money devoted to programs for older people. This, in turn, will lead to more lobbying and debate around seniors' issues. Wallace and colleagues (1991, p. 108) say that "numbers alone will give the elderly considerable power in the basic operation of the society."

Two images of older people in the future emerge from the literature. One is an image of selfish, mean-spirited bullies willing and able to sway social programs and policies to serve their needs. The other is an image of wise, intelligent people able to look at broad societal needs and to the future. Minkler (1991) proposes the ideal of generational *interdependence* (rather than generational equity) as a way to view relations between different age groups. The younger and older generations need one another.

The old need the young to provide social resources for them in old age. The young need the old to plan for the well-being of future generations. Some programs need the support of all generations. The proposed changes to national health insurance coverage in the United States, for example, will benefit people of all ages and backgrounds.

Hudson (1994) sees the diversity of the older population as a source of generational interdependence. He says that on certain issues, such as antipoverty programs, some older people have more in common with younger people than with people in their own age group. Other writers think that age may no longer serve as a useful way to think about the needs of the population. Torres-Gil (1992, pp. 90–91; also Achenbaum, 2000b) proposes "vertical alliances" across age groups based on common needs. "The poor, the disabled, minorities, women, and other disadvantaged groups of all ages will find more in common with each other than with those who simply share their age."

The ideal of generational interdependence changes the discussion of aging, politics, and policy. Voting and the interest group perspective look at politics as a competition between age groups. In a time of scarce resources, this leads to conflict and makes everyone poorer. Interest group politics have also created a deadlock on social policy reform.

For example, Medicare costs grow each year, but no politician wants to tamper with the program. The concept of generational interdependence calls for rethinking our image of older people as a homogeneous group in need. Instead policy should serve people in need from every age group.

Maggie Kuhn (Kerschner, 1976, cited in Hessel, 1977, p. 93) offered some wisdom on this point. She said that she and the Gray Panthers "have worked through and gone beyond the so-called 'Senior Power' view of ourselves. . . . We do not wear Senior Power buttons or think of ourselves as special pleaders for the cause of old people and old people's campaigns." She said that older people should do more than argue for cheap travel fares and lower taxes for themselves. Instead, they should become advocates and activists for a better society. They can serve both young and old in this role.

CONCLUSION

Older people take an active part in political life even in late old age. They vote, hold public office, work as advocates for social causes, and take an activist stance on social issues. Older people advise the government on policy (through Silver-Haired Legislatures and participation in White House Conferences on Aging). They also form coalitions with other groups (such as unions) to pass legislative reform.

Older people have succeeded in improving their condition through political action. Government programs such as Social Security, Medicare, and the Older Americans Act have all improved the quality of life in old age. Political action and its outcomes have transformed the image of older people. The public once saw seniors as weak and needy. It now sees them as powerful and sometimes greedy. Neither image fits reality. But the image of a wealthy and powerful older generation could lead to a backlash against programs for older people. This would hurt the poorest older people most.

Gerontologists propose a more balanced view of older people and their role in political life. Instead of unique programs for older people to take part in, some writers propose generational interdependence. This view joins older and younger people around issues that will create a better society for all.

SUMMARY

- Gerontologists study aging and politics from three points of view: (1) voting patterns, (2) activism, and (3) the policies of government that serve older people. Older people take part in politics in many ways. They give money to political parties, work in political campaigns, vote, run for office, and engage in advocacy and activism.

- Studies show that the proportion of people who vote increases with age and declines only in late old age. The increasing number of older people and their tendency to vote adds to their influence on government policy. This influence has its limits because older people do not vote as a single bloc.

- Minority older people have lower rates of voting than the general population. Culture, language, and literacy barriers prevent some of these older people from voting. Also, they may feel less hopeful that their votes will have an effect.

- The elderly differ by social class, race, gender, and age. They also differ in their views, and they vote for different candidates as well. Research shows that social class, for example, plays a bigger role in voting behavior than age. Older people will probably not form a voting bloc in the future.

- In the United States, older people make up a high proportion of officeholders. This occurs because a person tends to move to higher positions over time.

- Gerontologists disagree about whether older people can and will form a social movement. Older people form interest groups that compete with other groups for public resources.

- Senior advocacy groups have access to three forms of political power. First, these groups have access to elected officials. Second, they have access to national media. Third, they can use "the electoral bluff," the idea that they can sway votes for or against a politician. Senior lobby groups use all of these methods to influence national and local policies.

- The AARP takes a neutral position toward both major political parties. It supports lobby groups in every state and promotes political organization in all the U.S. congressional districts.

- The AARP has a diverse membership, which makes it difficult to express a single unified view on issues. As the AARP membership grows larger, its diversity will increase. This will increase its presence in political life. But it will make it hard for the organization to speak with one voice for its entire membership. The AARP must walk a fine line between advocating for senior benefits and keeping in step with its core middle-class membership.

- Senior advocacy groups such as the AARP attract many members for personal reasons (like discounts on travel). Most members have little interest in political advocacy. Interest in advocacy surges when the government threatens programs like Social Security.

- Older people most often succeed in creating social change when they link their interests to other lobby groups.

- Coalitions form around interests that serve social class interest. The Medicare Catastrophic Coverage Act (MCCA) brought social class conflict to the surface within the older population. Middle-class and wealthier seniors objected to a program that would have helped the poor.

- Activism complements the work of advocacy groups. Advocacy works within the system to reform or support existing programs. Activists work for fundamental social change. They use methods such as protest and scrutiny of corporate practices to bring about change.

- Federal funding for the elderly has more than doubled since the 1960s. This reflects the increased number of older people and the increase in services and programs for older people. These programs and services form a social safety net that ensures a minimum standard of health care and income for all older people.

- The Older Americans Act has served as the basis of federal government aging policy since 1965. The Older Americans Act attempts to ensure the well-being of older people. It does this through a national network of services. The Administration on Aging has the job of carrying out the Older Americans Act. It coordinates programs and services, sets policies, and conducts research on aging.

- Federal government policy has led to improvements in the well-being and financial status of older people. Some groups, such as Americans for Generational Equity and the Concord Coalition, say that too much of the national budget goes to older people. They call for more funding for children's programs and cutbacks to programs for the elderly.

- Three assumptions underlie the generational equity debate: Older people get an unfair share of the nation's resources; a large older population places an intolerable burden on younger people; and young people pay taxes for Social Security but will get few benefits when they retire. Gerontologists find little evidence to support these assumptions. They also find little evidence for the generational conflict that some observers predict.

- A group called Generations United (GU) promotes intergenerational programs and policies. Minkler (1991) calls for generational interdependence as a way to view generational relations.

- Older people have begun to view civic engagement as a way to stay engaged in social life. Programs such as Civic Ventures offer older people the opportunity to give back to their communities. This role uniquely suits the older person who has the time, the knowledge, and the skills to serve others. Civic engagement turns the older population into a valuable social resource.

- Gerontologists suggest at least two ways to avoid generational conflict. First, the government should offer programs based on need, not age. Second, older people can show support for non–age-based programs and for programs that benefit other age groups.

DISCUSSION QUESTIONS

1. Gerontologists study at least three types of senior political activity. List them and give several examples of these activities.
2. Describe the voting patterns of older people. How does this influence their political decisions?
3. Explain why older minority group members have a lower voting rate than the general population.
4. Why don't older people vote as a bloc? What plays the biggest role in determining how people vote?
5. Why do some gerontologists think that older people can and will form a social movement? Why do other gerontologists disagree?
6. What methods do older people use to influence national and local policies?
7. What does the AARP do? What strengths does this organization have? What weaknesses? How does the AARP differ from the National Council of Senior Citizens?
8. What type of advocacy has the most impact on public policy?
9. Explain the term *interest group coalition*. How do these coalitions help older people?
10. How do activist groups differ from advocacy groups? What issues do advocacy groups deal with? How do groups like the Gray Panthers achieve their goals?
11. Why has federal funding for the elderly increased over the years? Explain how federal programs benefit older people.
12. Discuss the social class conflict that lay beneath the controversy over the Medicare Catastrophic Coverage Act (MCCA). Why did the Medicare Modernization Act (MMA) face less opposition?
13. List and explain the objectives of the Older Americans Act. What government agency carries out these objectives?
14. Will the United States see conflict between the older and younger generations in the future? Give reasons to support your answer.
15. What assumptions underlie the generational equity debate? How might conflict be avoided? What alternatives do gerontologists give to the concept of generational equity?
16. What is Civic Ventures? How does it use the talents of older people to improve social life for all? What role will programs like this play in the future?

SUGGESTED READING

Freedman, M. (2002). *Prime Time: How Baby Boomers will revolutionize retirement and transform America*. New York: Public Affairs.

The author, CEO of Civic Ventures, expands the discussion of aging beyond issues of health care and Social Security costs. This book points to the value of a well-educated, healthy older population. Older Americans can put their skills and energy to work for the good of their communities. *Prime Time* profiles older people and programs that exemplify this model of social service in later life. It is a stimulating and inspiring book.

Schulz, J. H., & Binstock, R. H. (2006). *Aging nation: The economics and politics of growing older in America*. Westport, CT: Praeger.

Two of the best-known (and most readable) writers in the field of aging social policy provide a critical look at aging in America today. They take a hard look at the demographic doomsayers and debunk the "phony threat of population aging." They also look at the shift from the state to the individual, from collective support to individual risk. The book takes on a theme the authors have discussed before—the unlikely development of a senior power bloc. This thought-provoking book is filled with information and insight into social policy issues today.

Wilson, L. B., & Simson, S. P. (Eds.). (2006) *Civic engagement and the Baby Boomer generation: Research, policy, and practice perspectives*. Binghamton, NY: Haworth Press.

Readings in this book describe models of civic engagement recognized by the National Council on Aging and the American Public Health Association for their excellence. Articles include discussion on the scope of civic engagement in the United States, the link between civic engagement and lifelong learning institutes, and volunteerism worldwide. This is an excellent overview of the latest developments on this emerging movement.

Web Sites to Consult

The American Bar Association Commission on Law and Aging
www.americanbar.org/groups/law_aging.html

This site contains information and publications on legal issues related to aging. It also provides a bimonthly journal on age-related legal topics.

Generations United
www.gu.org

This site promotes intergenerational strategies, programs, and policies. The site includes fact sheets on intergenerational topics, resources for policy makers, and links to Web sites on intergenerational topics.

Global Action on Aging
www.globalaging.org/index.htm

This site follows international stories on aging, health, elder rights, and the politics associated with aging. A fascinating look at aging issues around the world.

The Gray Panthers
www.graypanthers.org

This multi-issue activist organization's Web site contains a "soapbox blog" that provides news from the Gray Panthers' unique and proactive perspective on aging.

WORKS CONSULTED

A4M (American Academy for Anti-Aging Medicine). (2006). *About A4M.* Retrieved July 13, 2007, from www.worldhealth.net/p/96.html.

Aadlandsvik, R. (2007). Education, poetry, and the process of growing old. *Educational Gerontology, 33*(8), 665–678.

Aaron, H. J., Blinder, A., Munnell, A., & Orszag, P. (2001). *Perspectives on the draft interim report of the President's Commission to Strengthen Social Security.* Center on Budget and Policy Priorities. www.cbpp.org.

AARP (American Association of Retired Persons). (1992). *Making wise decisions for long-term care.* [Pamphlet]. Washington, DC: Author.

AARP (American Association of Retired Persons). (1993). *Understanding senior housing: For the 1990's.* Washington, DC: Author.

AARP (American Association of Retired Persons). (1999). *Consumer behavior, experiences, and attitudes: A comparison by age groups.* Princeton, NJ: Princeton Survey Research Associates. Retrieved December 20, 2004, from http://research.aarp.org/consume/d16907_behavior.pdf.

AARP (American Association of Retired Persons). (2002). *The Grandparent Study 2002 Report.* Data collected by AARP; data prepared by Roper ASW; report prepared by Curt Davies with the assistance of Dameka Williams. Washington, DC: AARP's Grandparent Information Center. Retrieved June 15, 2007, from http://research.aarp.org.

AARP (American Association of Retired Persons). (2003). *Annual report 2002.* Retrieved December 6, 2004, from http://assets.aarp.org/www.aarp.org_/articles/aboutaarp/annual report2002_f.pdf.

AARP. (2004a). *A chartbook.* Washington DC: The AARP Public Policy Institute. Retrieved August 26, 2007, from http://assets.aarp.org/rgcenter/econ/ip_ch2004.pdf.

AARP (American Association of Retired Persons). (2004b). *Federally insured loans. Eligibility and repayment.* Retrieved October 3, 2004, from www.aarp.org/Articles/a2003-03-21-elig.html.

AARP (American Association of Retired Persons). (2004c). *Housing choices. Continuing care retirement communities.* Retrieved November 7, 2004, from www.aarp.org/life/housingchoices/Articles/a2004-02-26-retirement-community.html.

AARP (American Association of Retired Persons). (2004d). *Staying ahead of the curve: The AARP Work and Career Study.* Washington, DC: Author. Retrieved September 17, 2004, from www.research.aarp.org/econ/multiwork.html.

AARP (American Association of Retired Persons). (2004e). *Synthesis of AARP research in physical activity: 1999–2003.* Washington, DC: Author.

AARP (American Association of Retired Persons). (2004f). *Intergenerational conflict? Think again!* Retrieved: July 14, 2011, from www.aarp.org/about-aarp/press-center/info-2004/aging_1.html.

AARP (American Association of Retired Persons). (2005a). *Beyond 50.05: A report to the nation on livable communities.* Washington, DC: AARP Public Policy Institute.

AARP (American Association of Retired Persons). (2005b). Call to action! *AARP Bulletin, 46*(1).

AARP (American Association of Retired Persons). (2005c). *Caring for your grandchild.* Retrieved January 7, 2005, from www.aarp.org/life/grandparents/grandchild/Articles/a2004-09-01-grandparents-visitation.html.

AARP (American Association of Retired Persons). (2005d). *Multicultural study: 2004: Perspectives past, present, and future: Traditional and alternative financial practices of the 45+ community.* Retrieved November 3, 2007, from http://assets.aarp.org/rgcenter/general/2004_perspectives_1.pdf.

AARP (American Association of Retired Persons). (2005e). *Reimagining America: How America can grow old and prosper.* Washington, DC: Author. Retrieved November 11, 2007, from http://assets.aarp.org/www.aarp.org_/articles/legpolicy/reimagining_200601.pdf.

AARP (American Association of Retired Persons). (2006a). *Grandparenting: The joys and challenges.* Retrieved October 11, 2007, from http://assets.aarp.org/www.aarp.org_/articles/families/joys_challenges_english.pdf.

AARP (American Association of Retired Persons). (2006b). *The state of 50+America: 2006.* Washington, DC: AARP Public Policy Institute. Retrieved July 5, 2011, from www.globalaging.org/elderrights/us/2006/fiftyplus.pdf.

AARP (American Association of Retired Persons). (2006c). *Workers 50+: Age discrimination: What employers need to know.* Washington, DC: Author.

AARP (American Association of Retired Persons). (2007a). *AARP profit from experience: Perspectives of employers, workers and policymakers in the G7 countries on the new demographic realities.* Retrieved March 22, 2008, from http://assets.aarp.org/rgcenter/econ/intl_older_worker.pdf.

AARP (American Association of Retired Persons). (2007b). *The state of 50+ America 2007.* Retrieved September 28, 2007, from http://assets.aarp.org/rgcenter/econ/fifty_plus_2007.pdf.

AARP (American Association of Retired Persons). (2007c, July–August). Now hear this: Name game. *AARP Bulletin,* p. 8.

AARP (American Association of Retired Persons). (2008a). *Staying ahead of the curve. The AARP work and career study.* Washington, DC: AARP. Retrieved June 4, 2011, from http://assets.aarp.org/rgcenter/econ/work_career_08.pdf.

AARP (American Association of Retired Persons). (2008b). *The policy book: AARP public policies 2009–2010.* Introduction. Retrieved August 6, 2010, from http://assets.aarp.org/www.aarp.org_/articles/legpolicy/2008/Introduction.pdf.

AARP (American Association of Retired Persons). (2009a). *Bulletin survey on retirement savings. Executive summary.* Retrieved May 22, 2010, from http://assets.aarp.org/rgcenter/econ/bulletin_retiresavings.pdf.

AARP (American Association of Retired Persons). (2009b). *Consolidated statement of activities. Year ended December 31, 2009* (p. 3). Retrieved August 6, 2010, from http://assets.aarp.org/www.aarp.org_/cs/misc/2009_aarp_consolidated_financial_statements_12_31_09.pdf.

AARP (American Association of Retired Persons). (2010). *Social Security 75th anniversary survey report: Public opinion trends.* Retrieved July 18, 2011, from http://assets.aarp.org/rgcenter/econ/social_security_75th.pdf.

AARP Public Policy Institute. (2009). *The social compact in the twenty-first century.* Washington, DC: AARP Public Policy Institute.

AARP and the University of Southern California. (2004). *Images of aging in America 2004: A summary of selected findings.* Retrieved December 20, 2004, from http://research.aarp.org/general/images_aging.pdf.

Abdulrazak, B., & Mokhtari, M. (2008). Assistive robotics for independent living. (pp. 355–374). In Helal, A. (S.), Mokhtari, M., & Abdulrazak, B. (Eds.), *The engineering handbook of smart technology for aging, disability, and independence.* Hoboken, NJ: Wiley.

Aboderin, I. (2006). *Intergenerational support and old age in Africa.* New Brunswick, NJ: Transaction.

Accius, J. C. (2010). The Village: A growing option for aging in place. *Fact Sheet 177.* Washington, DC: AARP Public Policy Institute. Retrieved July 12, 2010, from www.aarp.org/home-garden/housing/info-03-2010/fs177-new.html.

Achenbaum, W. A. (1983). *Shades of gray: Old age, American values, and federal policies since 1920.* Boston: Little, Brown.

Achenbaum, W. A. (1987). Can gerontology be a science? *Journal of Aging Studies, 1,* 3–18.

Achenbaum, W. A. (2000a). Afterword. In T. R. Cole, R. Kastenbaum, & R. E. Ray (Eds.), *Handbook of the humanities and aging* (2nd ed., pp. 419–431). New York: Springer.

Achenbaum, W. A. (2000b). The elderly's future stake in voluntary associations. *Journal of Aging and Social Policy, 11*(2–3), 41–47.

Achenbaum, W. A. (2006). A history of civic engagement of older people. *Generations, 30*(3), pp. 18–23.

Achenbaum, W. A., & Cole, T. R. (2007). Transforming age-based policies to meet fluid life-course needs. In R. A. Pruchno & M. A. Smyer (Eds.), *Challenges of an aging society: Ethical dilemmas, political issues* (pp. 238–267). Baltimore: Johns Hopkins University Press.

Ackerman, P. L. (2008). Knowledge and cognitive aging. In F. I. M. Craik & T. A. Salthouse (Eds.), *The handbook of aging and cognition* (3rd ed., pp. 445–489). New York: Psychology Press.

Adams, C., Smith, M. C., Pasupathi, M., & Vitolo, L. (2002). Social context effects on story recall in older and younger women: Does the listener make a difference? *Journals of Gerontology Series B: Psychological Sciences and Social Sciences, 57,* 28–40.

Adams, P. F., Heyman, K. M., & Vickerie, J. L. (2009). *Summary health statistics for U.S. population: National Health Interview Survey, 2008.* National Center for Health Statistics. *Vital and Health Statistics, 10* (243).

Aday, R. H., & Austin, B. S. (2000). Images of aging in the lyrics of American country music. *Educational Gerontology, 26*(2), 135–154.

Administration for Children and Families. (2010). *2009/2010 HHS Poverty Guidelines.* LIHEAP Clearinghouse. U.S. Department of Health and Human Services. Retrieved October 19, 2010, from http://liheap.ncat.org/profiles/povertytables/FY2010/popstate.htm.

Administration on Aging. (2002). *A profile of older Americans.* Retrieved November 24, 2004, from www.aoa.gov/prof/Statistics/profile/3.asp.

Administration on Aging. (2003). *A profile of older Americans: 2003.* Washington, DC: U.S. Department of Health and Human Services. Retrieved September 6, 2004, from www.aoa.gov/prof/Statistics/profile/2003/2003profile.pdf.

Administration on Aging. (2004a). *Board and care.* Retrieved October 31, 2004, from www.aoa.gov/eldfam/housing/housing_services/board_care.asp.

Administration on Aging. (2004b). *Fact sheets—Challenges of global aging.* Washington, DC: U.S. Department of Health and Human Services. Retrieved March 15, 2004, from www.aoa.gov/press/fact/alpha/fact_global_aging.asp.

Administration on Aging. (2004c). *GAO, IG & U.S. Senate hearings.* Retrieved December 10, 2004, from www.aoa.gov/prof/research/research.asp.

Administration on Aging. (2004d). *Older Americans Act.* Retrieved December 10, 2004, from www.aoa.gov/about/legbudg/oaa/legbudg_oaa.asp.

Administration on Aging. (2007a). *Older women.* Retrieved August 26, 2007, from www.aoa.gov/naic/may2000/factsheets/olderwomen.html.

Administration on Aging. (2007b). *Welcome. Mission.* Retrieved October 28, 2007, from www.aoa,gov/about/over/over_mission.asp.

Administration on Aging. (2008a). *A statistical profile. Facts on Asian and Pacific Islander Elderly.* Retrieved January 31, 2010, from www.aoa.gov/AoARoot/Aging_Statistics/Minority_Aging/Facts-on-API-Elderly2008-plain_format.aspx.

Administration on Aging (2008b). *A statistical profile of American Indian and Alaskan Native older Americans aged 65+.* Retrieved January 31, 2010, from www.aoa.gov/AoARoot/Aging_Statistics/Minority_Aging/Facts-on-AINA-Elderly2008-plain_format.aspx.

Administration on Aging. (2008c) A statistical profile of Hispanic older Americans aged 65+. Retrieved January 31, 2010, from www.aoa.gov/AoARoot/Aging_Statistics/Minority_Aging/Facts-on-Hispanic-Elderly-2008.aspx.

Administration on Aging. (2009). *A profile of older Americans: 2009.* Washington, DC: U.S. Department of Health and Human Services. Retrieved May 17, 2010, from www.aoa.gov/AoARoot/Aging_Statistics/Profile/2009/5.aspx; also www.aoa.gov/AoARoot/Aging_Statistics/Profile/2009/3.aspx; also www.aoa.gov/aoaroot/aging_statistics/Profile/2009/6.aspx.

Administration on Aging. (2010a). *A statistical profile of black older Americans aged 65+.* Facts. Retrieved October 8, 2010, from www.aoa.gov/aoaroot/Press_Room/Products_Materials/fact/pdf/FS_BlackAmericansAged65.pdf.

Administration on Aging. (2010b). *A statistical profile of black older Americans aged 65+.* Retrieved May 17, 2010, from www.aoa.gov/AoARoot/Aging_Statistics/minority_aging/Facts-on-Black-Elderly-plain_format.aspx.

Administration on Aging. (2010c). *About AoA.* Retrieved August 7, 2010, from www.aoa.gov/aoaroot/about/index.aspx.

Administration on Aging. (2010d). *Older Americans Act.* Retrieved August 7, 2010, from www.aoa.gov/AoARoot/AoA_Programs/OAA/index.aspx.

Administration on Aging. (2010e). *A profile of older Americans: 2010.* Housing. Retrieved: July 5, 2011, from www.aoa.gov/AoARoot/Aging_Statistics/Profile/2010/11.aspx.

Administration on Aging. (2010f). *National Aging Network.* Retrieved July 14, 2011, from www.aoa.gov/AoARoot/AoA_Programs/OAA/Aging_Network/Index.aspx.

Administration on Aging. (n.d.) *Achieving cultural competence.* Retrieved March 29, 2010, from www.docstoc.com/docs/29384529/US-Administration-on-Aging.

Agahi, N., & Parker, M. G. (2006). Continuity of leisure participation from middle age to old age. *Journals of Gerontology: Series B: Psychological Sciences and Social Sciences, 61B*(6), S340–S346.

Agahi, N., & Parker, M. G. (2008). Leisure activities and mortality: Does gender matter? *Journal of Aging and Health, 20*(7), 855–871.

Agree, E. M., & Freedman, V. A. (2000). Incorporating assistive devices into community-based long-term care: An analysis of the potential for substitution and supplementation. *Journal of Aging and Health, 12*(3), 426–450.

Aiken, L. R. (2001). *Dying, death, and bereavement* (4th ed.). Mahwah, NJ: Erlbaum.

Alberta Heritage Foundation for Medical Research. (2009). *Research finds older women who are physically fit have better cognitive function. Want to stay sharp as you age? Then get moving.* News release. Retrieved February 27, 2010, from www.ahfmr.ab.ca/press/2009-01-08.php.

Aldwin, C. M., & Gilmer, D. F. (2004). *Health, illness, and optimal aging: Biological and psychosocial perspectives.* Thousand Oaks, CA: Sage.

Aldwin, C. M., Spiro III, A., & Park, C. L. (2006). Health, behavior, and optimal aging: A live span developmental perspective. In J. E. Birren & K. W. Schaie (Eds.), *Handbook of the psychology of aging* (6th ed., pp. 85–104). Burlington, MA: Elsevier Academic Press.

Alexander, C. N., Langer, E. J., Newman, R. I., Chandler, H. M., & Davies, J. (1989). Transcendental meditation, mindfulness, and longevity: An experimental study with the elderly. *Journal of Personality & Social Psychology, 57,* 950–964.

Allen, K., Blascovich, J., & Mendes, W. (2002). Cardiovascular reactivity and the presence of pets, friends and spouses: The truth about cats and dogs. *Psychosomatic Medicine, 64*(5), 727–739.

Allen, K. R., & Chin-Sang, V. (1990). A life time of work: The context and meanings of leisure for aging African American women. *The Gerontologist, 30*(6), 734–740.

Allen, K. R., & Walker, A. J. (2009). Theorizing about families and aging from a feminist perspective. In V. L. Bengtson, M. Silverstein, M. M. Putney, & D. Gans (Eds.), *Handbook of theories of aging* (pp. 517–528). New York: Springer.

Allen, P. A., Bucur, B., & Murphy, M. D. (2006). Information-processing theory. In R. Schulz, S. L. S. Noelker, K. Rockwood, & R. L. Sprott, eds., *The Encyclopedia of Aging* (4th ed., pp. 588–591). New York: Springer.

Alliance for Aging Research. (2010). *Geriatric training.* Retrieved January 24, 2010, from www.agingresearch.org/content/topic/detail/1016; also www.agingresearch.org/content/topic/detail/?id=1016&template=position.

Almberg, B. E., Grafstrom, M., & Winblad, B. (2000). Caregivers of relatives with dementia: Experiences encompassing social support and bereavement. *Aging and Mental Health, 4*(1), 82–89.

Almoque, A., Beloosesky, Y., Marcus, E., & Weiss, A. (2010; in press 2009). Attitudes and knowledge of medical and nursing staff towards elder abuse. *Gerontology and Geriatrics, 51,* 86–91.

Alterovitz, S. S., & Mendelsohn, G. A. (2009). Partner preferences across the life span: Online dating by older adults. *Psychology and Aging, 24*(2), 513–517.

Altman, N. J. (2007). *Protecting Social Security's beneficiaries: Achieving balance without benefit cuts.* The Economic Policy Institute, Briefing Paper No. 206. Retrieved November 23, 2007, from www.sharedprosperity.org/bp206.html.

Altus, D. E., & Mathews, R. M. (2002). Comparing the satisfaction of rural seniors with housing co-ops and congregate apartments: Is home ownership important? *Journal of Housing for the Elderly, 16*(1–2), 39–50.

Alwin, D. F., Hofer, S. M., & McCammon, R. J. (2006). Modeling the effects of time integrating demographic and developmental perspectives. In R. H. Binstock & L. K. George (Eds.), *Handbook of aging and the social sciences* (6th ed., pp. 20–38). Burlington, MA: Academic Press.

Ambrosius, G. R. (1994, July–August). Virtual marketing and the deyouthing of America. *Aging Today,* p. 11.

American Association of Community Colleges. (2010). *Rewired.* Retrieved July 22, 2010, from http://plus50.aacc.nche.edu.

American Association of Suicidology. (2009). *Elderly suicide fact sheet.* Retrieved June 25, 2011, from www.suicidology.org/c/document_library/get_file?folderId=232&name=DLFE-242.pdf.

American Automobile Association. (2009). Good directions. *Via Magazine,* p. 8.

American Automobile Association. (2010). *For individuals and families.* Retrieved July 6, 2011, from http://lpp.seniordrivers.org/notdriving/notdriving.cfm.

American Automobile Association. (2011). *Roadwise Review online.* Retrieved July 5, 2011, from www.seniordrivers.org/driving/driving.cfm?button=roadwiseonline.

American Community Survey. (2007). Table B25072. Retrieved December 15, 2010, from www.factfinder.census.gov.

American Diabetes Association. (2011). *Diabetes statistics.* Retrieved July 15, 2011, from www.diabetes.org/diabetes-basics/diabetes-statistics.

American Heart Association. (n.d.). *Cigarette smoking and cardiovascular disease,* citing the 1990 Surgeon General's Report. Retrieved December 29, 2005, from www.americanheart.org/presenter.jhtml?identifier=4545.

American Library Association. (1989). *Presidential Committee on Information Literacy: Final report.* Chicago: Author.

American Medical Directors Association. (2003). *Synopsis of federal regulations in the nursing facility: Implications for attending physicians and medical directors.* Retrieved November 6, 2004, from www.amda.com/federalaffairs/regulations_synopsis.htm.

Americans for Generational Equity. (2007). *Organization.* Retrieved October 28, 2007, from http://www.nndb.com/org/319/000168812/

American Time Use Survey. (2009). *American Time Use Survey—2009 results.* News release. Bureau of Labor Statistics, United States Department of Labor. Retrieved July 15, 2010, from www.bls.gov/news.release/pdf/atus.pdf.

Amirkhanyan, A. A., & Wolf, D. A. (2006). Parent care and the stress process: Findings from panel data. *Journals of Gerontology: Series B: Psychological Sciences and Social Sciences, 61B*(5), pp. S248–S255.

Amoss, P. T. (1981). Coast Salish elders. In P. T. Amoss and S. Harrell (Eds.), *Other ways of growing old: Anthropological perspectives* (pp. 227–247). Stanford, CA: Stanford University Press.

Anderson, J. W., Liu, C., & Kryscio, R. J. (2008). Blood pressure response to Transcendental Meditation: A meta-analysis. *American Journal of Hypertension, 21*(3), 310–316.

Anderson, R. E., Franckowiak, S., Christmas, C., Walston, J., & Crespo, C. (2001). Obesity and reports of no leisure time activity among older Americans: Results from the Third National Health and Nutrition Examination Survey. *Educational Gerontology, 27,* 297–306.

Andrews, G. J., Gavin, N., Begley, S., & Brodie, D. (2003). Assisting friendships, combating loneliness: Users' view on a "befriending" scheme. *Ageing and Society, 23*(3), 349–362.

Andrews, J. (1989). *Poverty and poor health among elderly Hispanic Americans.* Baltimore, MD: Commonwealth Fund Commission on Elderly People Living Alone.

Anetzberger, G. J. (2010). Community options of greater Cleveland, Ohio: Preliminary evaluation of a naturally occurring retirement community program. *Clinical Gerontologist, 33*(1), 1–15.

Angel, R. J., & Angel, J. L. (2006). Diversity and aging in the United States. In R. H. Binstock & L. K. George (Eds.), *Handbook of aging and the social sciences* (6th ed., pp. 94–110). Burlington, MA: Academic Press.

Antonucci, T. C., Birditt, K. S., & Akiyama, H. (2009). Convoys of social relations: an interdisciplinary approach. In V. L. Bengtson, M. Silverstein, M. M. Putney, & D. Gans (Eds.), *Handbook of theories of aging* (pp. 247–260). New York: Springer.

AON Consulting. (2007). Retirement and the aging workforce. Retrieved June 6, 2010, from www.cfo.com/whitepapers/index.cfm/download/10492691.

Apt, N. (1998). Keynote address. *Bulletin on Aging, 1&2,* 13–15.

Ardelt, M. (2000). Antecedents and effects of wisdom in old age. *Research on Aging, 22*(4), 360–394.

Ardelt, M., & Koenig, C. S. (2006). Role of religion for hospice patients and relatively healthy older adults. *Research on Aging, 28*(2), 184–215.

Area Agency on Aging of the Capital Area. (2010). *Elder abuse.* Retrieved July 3, 2010, from www.aaacap.org/eldabuse.html.

Arehart-Treichel, J. (2001). Innovative Alzheimer's residence tries new models of care. *Psychiatric News, 36*(9), 14.

Argue, A., Johnson, D. R., & White, L. K. (1999). Age and religiosity: Evidence from a three-wave panel analysis. *Journal for the Scientific Study of Religion, 38,* 423–435.

Arias, E. (2010). United States life tables, 2006. *National Vital Statistics Reports, 58*(21). Retrieved July 22, 2010, from www.cdc.gov/nchs/data/nvsr/nvsr58/nvsr58_21.pdf.

Aristotle. (1941). *The basic works of Aristotle.* R. McKeon (Ed.). New York: Random House.

Arking, R. (1991). *Biology of aging: Observations and principles.* Englewood Cliffs, NJ: Prentice-Hall.

Aronson, J., Thornewell, C., & Williams, K. (1995). Wife assault in old age: Coming out of obscurity. *Canadian Journal on Aging, 14*(Suppl), 72–88.

Assisted Living Federation of America. (2000). *ALFA's overview of the assisted living industry.* Fairfax, VA: Author.

Assisted Living Federation of America. (2006). *Comprehensive assisted living data released.* Retrieved September 15, 2007, from www.alfa.org/i4a/pages/Index.cfm?pageID=3808.

Assisted Living Federation of America. (2009). *Assisted living today—A brief overview of senior living care.* Retrieved July 12, 2010, from www.alfa.org/alfa/About_ALFA.asp?SnID=1636759120.

Atchley, R. C. (1980). *The social forces in later life: An introduction to social gerontology* (3rd ed.). Belmont, CA: Wadsworth.

Atchley, R. C. (1989). A continuity theory of normal aging. *The Gerontologist, 29,* 183–190.

Atchley, R. C. (1994). *The social forces in later life* (7th ed.). Belmont, CA: Wadsworth.

Atchley, R. C. (1999a). *Continuity and adaptation in aging: Creating positive experiences.* Baltimore: Johns Hopkins University Press.

Atchley, R. C. (1999b). Continuity theory, self, and social structure. In V. W. Marshall & C. D. Ryff (Eds.), *The self and society in aging processes* (pp. 94–121). New York: Springer.

Austad, S. N. (2001). Concepts and theories of aging. In E. J. Masoro & S. N. Austad (Eds.), *Handbook of the biology of aging* (5th ed., pp. 3–22). San Diego, CA: Academic Press.

Austad, S. N. (2009). Making sense of biological theories of aging. In V. L. Bengtson, M. Silverstein, M. M. Putney, & D. Gans (Eds.), *Handbook of theories of aging,* (pp. 147–162). New York: Springer.

Austin, B. J., & Fleisher, L. K. (2003). *Financing end-of-life care: Challenges for an aging population.* Academy of Health. Retrieved December 13, 2004, from www.hcfo.net/pdf/eolcare.pdf.

Aykan, H. (2003). Effect of childlessness on nursing home and home health care use. *Journal of Aging and Social Policy, 15*(1), 33–53.

Bach, P. B., Pham, H. H., Schrag, D., Tate, R. C., & Hargraves, J. L. (2004). Primary care physicians who treat blacks and whites. *New England Journal of Medicine, 351*(6), 575–584.

Bäckman, L., Hill, R. D., & Stigsdotter-Neely, A. (Eds.). (2000). *Cognitive rehabilitation in old age.* New York: Oxford University Press.

Bäckman, L., Small, B. J., & Wahlin, A. (2001). Aging and memory: Cognitive and biological perspectives. In J. E. Birren & K. W. Schaie (Eds.), *Handbook of the psychology of aging* (5th ed.). San Diego, CA: Academic Press.

Bäckman, L., Small, B. J., Wahlin, A., & Larsson, M. (2000). Cognitive functioning in very old age. In F. I. M. Craik & T. A. Salthouse (Eds.), *The handbook of aging and cognition* (2nd ed., pp. 499–558). Mahwah, NJ: Erlbaum.

Bailey, L. (2004). *Aging Americans: Stranded without options.* Washington, DC: Surface Transportation Policy Project. Retrieved October 31, 2004, from www.transact.org/library/reports_html/seniors/aging.pdf.

Baker, L., & Gringart E. (2009). Body image and self-esteem in older adulthood. *Ageing & Society, 29,* 977–995.

Baker, L. A., & Silverstein, M. (2008). Preventive health behaviors among grandmothers raising grandchildren. *Journals of Gerontology: Social Sciences, 63,* S304–S311.

Baker, P. M. (1991). Socialization after death: The might of the living dead. In B. Hess & E. Markson (Eds.), *Growing old in America* (4th ed.). New York: Transaction Books.

Baldridge, D. (2002). Indian elders. In D. L. Infeld (Ed.), *Disciplinary approaches to aging: Vol. 4. Anthropology of aging* (pp. 255–267). New York: Routledge.

Baldridge, D. (2004, Spring). Double jeopardy: Advocating for Indian elders. *Generations.* Retrieved October 9, 2010, from www.asaging.org/generations/gen28-1/article.cfm.

Ball, K., Berch, D. B., Helmers, K. F., Jove, J. B., Leveck, M. D., Marsiske, M., et al. (2002). Effects of cognitive training interventions with older adults. *Journal of the American Medical Association, 288,* 2271–2281.

Ball, M. M., Perkins, M. M., Whittington, F. J., Connell, B. R., Hollingsworth, C., King, S. V., et al. (2004). Independence in assisted living. *Journals of Gerontology: Series B: Psychological Sciences and Social Sciences, 59B*(4), S202–S212.

Baltes, M. M., & Carstensen, L. L. (2003). The process of successful aging: Selection, optimization, and compensation. In U. M. Staudinger & U. Lindenberger (Eds.), *Understanding human development: Dialogues with life-span psychology* (pp. 81–104). Dordrecht, The Netherlands: Kluwer Academic.

Baltes, P. B. (1992, February). Wise, and otherwise. *Natural History, 26,* 50–51.

Baltes, P. B. (1997). On the incomplete architecture of human ontogeny: Selection, optimization, and compensation as foundations of developmental theory. *American Psychologist, 52,* 366–380.

Baltes, P. B., & Baltes, M. M. (1990). Psychological perspectives on successful aging: The model of selective optimization with compensation. In P. B. Baltes & M. M. Baltes (Eds.), *Successful aging: Perspectives from the behavioral sciences* (pp. 1–34). Cambridge, England: Cambridge University Press.

Baltes, P. B., & Willis, S. L. (1982). Plasticity and enhancement of intellectual functioning in old age: Penn State's Adult Development and Enrichment Project (ADEPT). In F. I. M. Craik & S. E. Trehub (Eds.), *Aging and cognitive processes* (pp. 353–389). New York: Plenum.

Bank, D. (2009). Encore careers and the economic crisis. *Generations, 33*(3), 69–73.

Banks, M., Gonser, P., & Banks, W. (2001). Animal assisted therapy in the treatment of loneliness in long-term care facility residents. *The Gerontologist, 57A*(7), M428–M432.

Banks, M. R., & Banks, W. A. (2002). Effects of animal-assisted therapy on loneliness in an elderly population in long-term care facilities. *Journals of Gerontology: Series A: Biological Sciences and Medical Sciences, 57A*(7), M428–M432.

Banks, W. A., & Banks, M. R. (2003). Putting more heart in the nursing home: What we learned from the dogs. *Geriatrics and Aging, 6*(2), 66.

Barer, M. L., Hertzman, C., Miller, R., & Pascali, M. V. (1992). On being old and sick: The burden of health care for the elderly in Canada and the United States. *Journal of Health Politics, Policy and Law, 17*(4), 763–782.

Barnes, D. E., Tager, I. B., Satariano, W. A., & Yaffe, K. (2004). The relationship between literacy and cognition in well-educated elders. *Journals of Gerontology Series B: Psychological Sciences and Social Sciences, 59,* M390–M395.

Barnes, P. M., Adams, P. F., & Powell-Griner, E. (2010). *Health characteristics of the American Indian or Alaska Native adult population: United States, 2004–2008.* National health statistics reports; no. 20. Hyattsville: MD: National Center for Health Statistics.

Barresi, C. M. (1990). Ethnogerontology: Social aging in national, racial, and cultural groups. In K. F. Ferraro (Ed.), *Gerontology: Perspectives and issues* (pp. 247–265). New York: Springer.

Barrett, A. E. (1999). Social support and life satisfaction among the never married. *Research on Aging, 21*(1), 46–72.

Barrett, A. E., & Lynch, S. M. (1999). Caregiving networks of elderly persons: Variations by marital status. *The Gerontologist, 39*(6), 695–704.

Barry, P. (2010, May). A user's guide to health care reform. *AARP Bulletin,* pp. 19–26.

Barry, P., & Duka, W. (2002). Older vote carries clout. Experts say it could sway elections, set future course for critical issues. *AARP Bulletin Online, 43*(9), 3–6. Retrieved December 6, 2004, from www.aarp.org/bulletin/news/Articles/a2003-08-26-clout.html.

Bartels, S. J., & Smyer, M. A. (2002, Spring). Mental disorders of aging: An emerging public health crisis? *Generations,* 14–20.

Bartke, A., & Lane, M. (2001). Endocrine and neuroendocrine regulatory functions. In E. J. Masoro & S. N. Austad (Eds.), *Handbook of the biology of aging* (5th ed., pp. 297–323). San Diego, CA: Academic Press.

Barzilai, N., & Gabriely, I. (2001). The role of fat depletion in the biological benefits of caloric restriction. *Journal of Nutrition, 131,* 903S–906S.

Basak, C., Boot, W. R., Voss, M. W., & Kramer, A. F. (2008). Can training in a real-time strategy video game attenuate cognitive decline in older adults? *Psychology and Aging, 23*(4), 765–777.

Bass, D., McClendon, M., Brennan, P., & McCarthy, C. (1998). The buffering effect of a computer support network on caregiver strain. *Journal of Aging and Health, 10,* 20–43.

Bastida, E. (1988). Reexamining assumptions about extended families: Older Puerto Ricans in a comparative perspective. In M. Sotomayor & H. Curiel (Eds.), *Hispanic elderly: A cultural signature* (pp. 163–183). Edinburg, TX: Pan American University Press.

Basting, A. (2003). Reading the story behind the story: Context and content in stories by people with dementia. *Generations, 23*(3), 25–29.

Bates, C. J., Benton, D., Biesalski, H. K., Stachelin, H. B., van Staveren, W., Stehle, P., et al. (2002). Nutrition and aging: A consensus statement. *Journal of Nutrition, Health and Aging, 6*(2), 103–116.

Baumbusch, J. L. (2004). Unclaimed treasures: Older women's reflections on lifelong singlehood. *Journal of Women and Aging, 16*(1–2), 105–121.

Baumgarten, M., Lebel, P., Laprise, H., Leclerc, C., & Quinn, C. (2002). Adult day care for the frail elderly. *Journal of Aging and Health, 14*(2), 237–259.

Bayer, A.-H., & Harper, L. (2000). *Fixing to stay: A national survey of housing and home modification issues.* Washington, DC: AARP. Retrieved September 15, 2007, from http://assets.aarp.org/rgcenter/il/home_mod.pdf.

Beard, R. L. (2004). In their voices: Identity preservation and experiences of Alzheimer's disease. *Journal of Aging Studies, 18*(4), 415–428.

Beaulaurier, R. L., Seff, L. R., Newman, F. L., & Dunlop, B. (2007). External barriers to help seeking for older women who experience intimate partner violence. *Journal of Family Violence, 22,* 747–755.

Beck, M. (1990b, April 23). What do we call . . . them? *Newsweek.*

Becker, B. (2001). Challenging "ordinary pain": Narratives of older people who live with pain. In G. Kenyon, P. Clark, & B. de Vries (Eds.), *Narrative gerontology: Theory, research, and practice* (pp. 91–112). New York: Springer.

Beehr, T. A., & Adams, G. A. (2003). Concluding observations and future endeavors. In G. A. Adams & T. A.

Beehr (Eds.), *Retirement: Reasons, processes, and results* (pp. 293–298). New York: Springer.

Beisgen, B. A., & Kraitchman, M. C. (2003). *Senior centers: Opportunities for successful aging.* New York: Springer.

Belden, R., & Stewart Research/Strategy/Management. (2001). *In the middle: A report on multicultural boomers coping with family and aging issues: A national survey conducted for AARP.* Washington, DC: AARP. Retrieved July 14, 2004, from http://research.aarp.org/il/in_the_middle.pdf.

Belgrave, L. L, & Bradsher, J. E. (1994). Health as a factor in institutionalization: Disparities between African Americans and whites. *Research on Aging, 16*(2), 115–141.

Bengtson, V. L. (1993). Is the "contract across generations" changing? Effects of population aging on obligations and expectations across age groups. In V. L. Bengtson & W. A. Achenbaum (Eds.), *Changing contract across generations* (pp. 3–23). New York: A. de Gruyter.

Bengtson, V. L. (2001). Beyond the nuclear family: The increasing importance of multigenerational relationships in American society. The 1998 Burgess Award Lecture. *Journal of Marriage and the Family, 63*(1), 1–16.

Bengtson, V. L., Burgess, E. O., & Parott, T. M. (1997). Theory, explanation, and a third generation of theoretical development in social gerontology. *Journals of Gerontology: Series B: Psychological Sciences and Social Sciences, 52*(2), S72–S88.

Bengtson, V. L., Gans, D., Putney, N. M., & Silverstein, M. (2009). Theories about age and aging. In V. L. Bengtson, M. Silverstein, M. M. Putney, & D. Gans (Eds.), *Handbook of theories of aging* (pp. 3–23). New York: Springer.

Bengtson, V. L., & Kuypers, J. A. (1971). Generational differences and the developmental stake. *International Journal of Aging and Human Development, 2,* 249–260.

Bengtson, V. L., Rice, C. J., & Johnson, M. L. (1999). Are theories of aging important? Models and explanations in gerontology at the turn of the century. In V. L. Bengtson & K. W. Schaie (Eds.), *Handbook of theories of aging* (pp. 3–20). New York: Springer.

Bengtson, V. L., M. Silverstein, M. M. Putney, & D. Gans (Eds.), *Handbook of theories of aging.* New York: Springer.

Bennett, D. A., Schneider, J. A., Aranitakis, Z., Kelly, J. F., Aggarwal, N. T., Shah, R. C., et al. (2006). Neuropathology of older persons without cognitive impairment from two community-based studies. *Neurology, 66*(12), 1837–1844.

Bennett, K. M. (2005). Psychological wellbeing in later life: the longitudinal effects of marriage, widowhood and marital status change. *International Journal of Geriatric Psychiatry, 20*(3), 280–284.

Bennett, K. M. (2007). "No sissy stuff": Towards a theory of masculinity and emotional expression in older widowed men. *Journal of Aging Studies, 21,* 347–356.

Bennett, L., & Gates, G. (2004). *The cost of marriage inequality to gay, lesbian, and bisexual seniors.* A Human Rights Campaign Foundation Report. Washington, DC: Urban Institute. Retrieved June 28, 2010, from www.urban.org/url.cfm?ID=410939.

Bensing, K. M. (2006). A guide to information resources on aging and gerontology. *Medical Reference Services Quarterly, 25*(2), 69–79.

Bercovitz, A., Decker, F. H., Jones, A., & Remsburg, R. E. (2008). *End-of-life care in nursing homes: 2004.* National Nursing Home Survey. National health statistics reports; no 9. Hyattsville, MD: National Center for Health Statistics.

Berg, C. A. (2008). Everyday problem solving in context. In S. M. Hofer & D. F. Alwin (Eds.), *Handbook of cognitive aging: Interdisciplinary perspectives* (pp. 207–223). Los Angeles: Sage.

Berg, C. A., & Sternberg, R. J. (2002). Multiple perspectives on the development of adult intelligence. In J. Demick & C. Andreoletti (Eds.), *Handbook of adult development* (pp. 121–130). New York: Kluwer Academic/Plenum.

Berg, C. A., & Sternberg, R. J. (2003). Multiple perspectives on the development of adult intelligence. In J. Demick & C. Andreoletti (Eds.), *Handbook of adult development* (pp. 103–119). New York: Kluwer Academic.

Berger, A., Pereira, D., Baker, K., O'Mara, A., & Bolle, J. (2002). Commentary: Social and cultural determinants of end-of-life care for elderly persons. *The Gerontologist, 42* (Special Issue 3), 49–53.

Berger, P., & Luckmann, T. (1967). *The social construction of reality.* Garden City, NY: Anchor.

Bergling, T. (2004). *Reeling in the years: Gay men's perspectives on age and ageism.* New York: Harrington Park.

Bern-Klug, M., Gessert, C., & Forbes, S. (2001). Need to revise assumptions about the end of life: Implications for social work practice. *Health and Social Work, 26*(1), 38–48.

Bernstein, A. B., Hing, E., Moss, A. J., Allen, K. F., Siller, A. B., & Tiggle, R. B. (2003). *Health care in America: Trends in utilization.* Hyattsville, MD: National Center for Health Statistics.

Beyene, Y., Becker, G., & Mayen, N. (2002). Perception of aging and sense of well-being among Latino elderly. *Journal of Cross-Cultural Gerontology, 17*(2), 155–172.

Bharucha, A. J. (2003). Late-life suicide. In J. M. Ellison & V. Sumer (Eds.), *Depression in later life: A multidisciplinary psychiatric approach* (pp. 297–305). New York: Marcel Dekker.

Biggs, S., Hendricks, J., & Lowenstein, A. (2003). The need for theory in gerontology: Introduction. In S. Biggs, A. Lowenstein, & J. Hendricks (Eds.), *The need for theory: Critical approaches to social gerontology* (pp. 1–12). Amityville, NY: Baywood.

Biggs, A. G., & Springstead, G. R. (2008). Alternate measures of replacement rates for Social Security benefits and retirement income. *Social Security Bulletin, 68*(2). Retrieved May 17, 2010, from www.ssa.gov/policy/docs/ssb/v68n2/v68n2p1.pdf.

Binstock, R. H. (1978, November 11). Federal policy toward the aging—Its inadequacies and its politics. *National Journal,* pp. 1838–1845.

Binstock, R. H. (1983). The aged as scapegoats. *The Gerontologist, 23*(2), 136–143.

Binstock, R. H. (1992). The oldest old and "intergenerational equity." In R. M. Suzman, D. P. Willis, & K. G. Manton (Eds.), *The oldest old* (pp. 394–417). New York: Oxford University Press.

Binstock, R. H. (1993). Healthcare costs around the world: Is aging a fiscal "black hole"? *Generations, 17*(4), 37–42.

Binstock, R. H. (1997). The old-age lobby in a new political era. In R. B. Hudson (Ed.), *The future of age-based public policy* (pp. 56–74). Baltimore, MD: Johns Hopkins University Press.

Binstock, R. H. (2000). Older people and voting participation: Past and future. *The Gerontologist, 40*(1), 18–31.

Binstock, R. H. (2004). Advocacy in an era of neoconservatism: responses of national aging organizations. *Generations, 28*(1), 49–54.

Binstock, R. H. (2005a). Old-age policies, politics, and ageism. *Generations, 29*(3), 73–78.

Binstock, R. H. (2005b). The contemporary politics of old age policies. In R. B. Hudson (Ed.), pp. 265–293. *The new politics of old age policy.* Baltimore: Johns Hopkins University Press.

Binstock, R. H. (2006). Older voters and the 2004 election. *The Gerontologist, 46*(3), 382–382.

Binstock, R. H. (2006–07). Older people and political engagement: from avid voters to "cooled-out marks." *Generations, 30*(4), 24–30.

Binstock, R. H. (2007). Is responsibility across generations politically feasible? In R. A. Pruchno & M. A. Smyer (Eds.), *Challenges of an aging society* (pp. 285–308). Baltimore: Johns Hopkins University Press.

Binstock, R. H. (2009a). Older voters and the 2008 election. *The Gerontologist, 49*(5), 697–701.

Binstock, R. H. (2009b). The Boomers in politics: Impact and consequences. In R. B. Hudson (Ed.). *Boomer Bust? Economic and political issues of the graying society. Perspectives on the Boomers* (Vol. 1, pp. 135–152). Westport, CT: Praeger.

Binstock, R. H., Fishman, J. R., & Johnson, T. E. (2006). Anti-aging medicine and science: Social Implications. In R. H. Binstock & L. K. George (Eds.), *Handbook of aging and the social sciences* (6th ed., pp. 436–455). Burlington, MA: Academic Press.

Binstock, R. H., & George, L. K. (2006). *Handbook of aging and the social sciences* (6th ed.). Burlington, MA: Academic Press.

Binstock, R. H., & Kahana, J. (1988). An essay on setting limits: Medical goals in an aging society. *The Gerontologist, 28*(3), 424–426.

Birnbaum, J. (1997, May 12). Washington's second most powerful man. *Fortune,* pp. 122–126.

Birren, J. E., & Schaie, K. W. (Eds.). (2006). *Handbook of the psychology of aging* (6th ed.). Burlington, MA: Elsevier Academic Press.

Black, S. A., Ray, L. A., & Markides, K. S. (1999). The prevalence and health burden of self-reported diabetes in older Mexican American: Findings from the Hispanic established populations for epidemiologic studies of the elderly. *American Journal of Public Health, 89*(4), 546–552. Retrieved June 28, 2011, from http://ajph.aphapublications.org/cgi/reprint/89/4/546.

Blackburn, J. A., & Dulmus, C. N. (Eds.). (2007). *Handbook of gerontology: Evidence-based approaches to theory, practice, and policy.* Hoboken, NJ: Wiley.

Blanchard-Fields, F., & Abeles, R. P. (1996). Social cognition and aging. In J. E. Birren & K. W. Schaie (Eds.), *Handbook of the psychology of aging* (4th ed., pp. 159–161). San Diego, CA: Academic Press.

Blando, J. A. (2001). Twice hidden: Older gay and lesbian couples, friends, and intimacy. *Generations, 25*(2).

Blazer, D. G. (2003). Depression in late life: Review and commentary. *Journals of Gerontology Series A: Biological Sciences and Medical Sciences, 58,* M249–M265.

Blieszner, R. (2001). "She'll be on my heart": Intimacy among friends. *Generations, 25*(2).

Blieszner, R., Roberto, K. A., & Singh, K. (2001–02). Helping networks of rural elders: Demographic and social psychological influences on service use. *Aging International, 27*(1), 89–119.

Block, M. R., & Sinnott, J. D. (1979). *Battered elder syndrome—An exploratory study.* Administration on Aging Report. Retrieved July 12, 2011, from www.ncjrs.gov/App/Publications/abstract.aspx?ID=70678

Bluestone, B., & Melnik, M. (2010). *After the recovery: Help needed. The coming labor shortage and how people in encore careers can help solve it.* San Francisco: Civic Ventures and MetLife Foundation.

Board of Trustees. (2009). *2009 Annual Report of the Boards of Trustees of the Federal Hospital Insurance and Federal Supplementary Medical Insurance Trust Funds.* Washington, DC: Boards of Trustees.

Board of Trustees. (2011). *2011 Annual Report of the Board of Trustees of the Federal Old-Age and Survivors Insurance and Federal Disability Insurance Trust Funds.* Retrieved July 1, 2011, from www.ssa.gov/oact/TR/2011/tr2011.pdf.

Boeri, M. M., & Baunach, D. M. (2002). Effects of education on retirement: A continuity perspective. *Southwest Journal on Aging, 17*(1–2), 15–21.

Boniface, R. (2008). AARP unveils universal design home in Washington, DC *AIArchitect, 15*(June 27). Retrieved November 20, 2010, from http://info.aia.org/aiarchitect/thisweek08/0627/0627p_aarp.cfm.

Bookman, A., & Harrington, M. (2007). Family caregivers: A shadow workforce in the geriatric health care system? *Journal of Health Politics, Policy & Law, 32,* pp. 1005–1041.

Boon, S. D., & Shaw, M. J. (2007) Grandchildren's perceptions of grandparents' health: Worries and impact on their own lives. *Journal of Intergenerational Relationships, 5*(1), 57–78.

Booth, M., Fralich, J., & Sucier, P. (1997). *Integration of acute and long-term care for dually eligible beneficiaries through managed care.* Portland, ME: Muskie School of Public Service, University of Southern Maine.

Botwinick, J. (1984). *Aging and behavior* (3rd ed.). New York: Springer.

Bowannie, T., & Leekity, K. (2008). Long-term care services: Coordination and collaboration in Zuni Pueblo. *Journal of Native Aging and Health, 3*(1), 25–26.

Bowd, A. D. (2003). Stereotypes of elderly persons in narrative jokes. *Research on Aging, 25*(1), 22–35.

Bowers, B. F., & Myers, B. J. (1999). Grandmothers providing care for grandchildren: Consequences of various levels of caregiving. *Family Relations, 48*(3), 303–311.

Boxer, A. M., Cook, J. A., & Cohler, B. J. (1986). Grandfathers, fathers, and sons: Intergenerational relations among men. In K. A. Pillemer & R. S. Wolf (Eds.), *Elder abuse: Conflict in the family* (pp. 93–121). Dover, MA: Auburn House.

Boyle, M. (2005, December 26). Help! My company keeps changing my 401(k). *Fortune,* pp. 107–110.

Brach, J. S., Simonsick, E. M., Kritchevsky, S., Yaffe, K., & Newman, A. B. (2004). Association between physical function and lifestyle activity and exercise in the Health, Aging and Body Composition Study. *Journal of the American Geriatrics Society, 52*(4), 502–509.

Bradley, D. E., & Longino, C. F. (2001). How older people think about images of aging in advertising and the media. *Generations, 25*(3), 17–21.

Bradshaw, J., & Klein, W. C. (2007). Health promotion. In J. A. Blackburn & C. N. Dulmus (Eds.), *Handbook of gerontology: Evidence-based approaches to theory, practice, and policy* (pp.171–200). Hoboken, NJ: Wiley.

Braun, P., & Sweet, R. (1983–84). Passages: Fact or fiction? *International Journal of Aging and Human Development, 18,* 161–176.

Braver, T. S., & West, R. (2008). Working memory, executive control, and aging. In F. I. M. Craik & T. A. Salthouse (Eds.), *The handbook of aging and cognition* (3rd ed., pp. 311–372), New York: Psychology Press.

Bravo, G., Dubois, M.-F., Charpentier, M., De Wals, P., & Emond, A. (1999). Quality of care in unlicensed homes for the aged in the eastern townships of Quebec. *Canadian Medical Association Journal, 160*(10), 1441–1448.

Breytspraak, L. M. (1995). The development of self in later life. In M. Novak (Ed.), *Aging and society: A Canadian reader* (pp. 92–103). Toronto: Nelson Canada.

Bright, K. (2005). *Section 202 Supportive Housing for the Elderly.* Research Report. Washington, DC: AARP Public Policy Institute. Retrieved November 10, 2007, from www.aarp.org/research/housing-mobility/accessibility/fs65r_housing.html#SECOND.

Brockmann, H., & Klein, T. (2004). Love and death in Germany: The marital biography and its effect on mortality. *Journal of Marriage and Family, 66*(3), 567–581.

Brody, E. (1981). "Women in the middle" and family help to older people. *The Gerontologist, 21*(5), 471–480.

Brody, E. (1983). Women's changing roles and help to elderly parents: Attitudes of three generations of women. *Journal of Gerontology, 38,* 597–607.

Brody, E. (1995). Prospects for family caregiving: Response to change, continuity, and diversity. In R. A. Kane & J. D. Penrod (Eds.), *Family caregiving in an aging society* (pp. 15–28). Thousand Oaks, CA: Sage.

Bronner, E. (2003). *The foundation's end-of-life programs: Changing the American way of death.* Retrieved December 13, 2004, from www.rwjf.org/publications/publications Pdfs/anthology2003/chapter_04.html.

Bronnum-Hansen, H., & Juel, K. (2001). Abstention from smoking extends life and compresses morbidity: A population based study of health expectancy among smokers and never smokers in Denmark. *Tobacco Control, 10*(3), 273–278.

Brotman, S., Ryan, B., Collins, S., Chamberland, L., Cormier, R., Julien, D., et al. (2007). Coming out to care: Caregivers of gay and lesbian seniors in Canada. *The Gerontologist, 47* (4), 490–503.

Brotman, S., Ryan, B., & Cormier, R. (2002). Mental health issues of particular groups: Gay and lesbian seniors. In *Writings in gerontology: Mental health and aging* (pp. 56–67). Cat. No. H71–s2/1–18–2002E. Ottawa: Minister of Public Works and Government Services Canada.

Brown, A. (1989). A survey on elder abuse at one Native American tribe. *Journal of Elder Abuse and Neglect, 1*(2).

Brown, C. M., & Gibbons, J. L. (2008). Taking care of our elders: An initial study of an assisted-living facility for American Indians. *Journal of Applied Gerontology, 27*(4), 523–531.

Brown, D. (2006). Road less traveled: Providing home care in rural communities. *Caring, 25*(1) pp. 7–11.

Brown, H. W. (2009). *Boomer women's long-term care planning: Barriers and levers.* Washington, DC: AARP Knowledge Management.

Brown, K. (2009). *A year-end look at the economic slowdown's impact on middle-aged and older Americans.* Washington, DC: AARP. Retrieved June 6, 2010, from http://assets.aarp.org/rgcenter/econ/economic_slowdown_09.pdf.

Brown, M. B., & Tedrick, T. (1993). Outdoor leisure involvements of black older Americans: An exploration of ethnicity and marginality. *Activities, Adaptation and Aging, 17*(3), 55–65.

Brown, S. C., & Park, D. C. (2003). Theoretical models of cognitive aging and implications for translational research in medicine. *The Gerontologist, 43,* 57–67.

Brown, S. K. (2003). *Staying ahead of the curve 2003: The AARP working in retirement study.* Washington, DC: AARP Knowledge Management. Retrieved September

13, 2007, from http://assets.aarp.org/rgcenter/econ/multiwork_2003.pdf.

Brown, S. L., Lee, G. R., & Bulanda, J. R. (2006). Cohabitation among older adults: A national portrait. *Journals of Gerontology: Series B: Psychological Sciences and Social Sciences, 61B*(2), pp. S71–S79.

Brown, S. L., Nesse, R. M., Vinokur, A. D., & Smith, D. M. (2003). Providing social support may be more beneficial than receiving it: Results from a prospective study of mortality. *Psychological Science, 14*(4), 320.

Brownson, R. C., Eyler, A. A., King, A. C., Brown, D. R., Shyu, Y. L., & Sallis, J. F. (2000). Patterns and correlates of physical activity among U.S. women 40 years and older. *American Journal of Public Health, 90,* 264–270.

Bruce, J. (1994). To drive or not to drive. *Aging, 366,* 49–51.

Brugman, G. M. (2006). Wisdom and aging. In J. E. Birren & K. W. Schaie (Eds.), *Handbook of the Psychology of Aging* (6th ed., pp. 445–476). Burlington, MA: Elsevier Academic Press.

Brumley, R., Enguidanos, S., Jamison, P., Seitz, R., Morgenstern, N., Saito, S., et al. (2007). Increased satisfaction with care and lower costs: Results of a randomized trial of in-home palliative care. *Journal of the American Geriatrics Society, 55*(7), 993–1000.

Bryant, D. P., & Bryant, B. R. (2003). *Assistive technology for people with disabilities.* Boston: Pearson.

Bryer, T. (2000). Characteristics of motor vehicle crashes related to aging. In K. W. Schaie & M. Pietrucha (Eds.), *Mobility and transportation in the elderly* (pp. 157–206). New York: Springer.

Buettner, D. (2005, November). The secrets of living longer. *National Geographic Magazine,* pp. 2–27.

Buettner, D. (2008) *The blue zone.* Washington, DC: National Geographic.

Buettner, D. (2010). *The blue zones: lessons for living longer from the people who've lived the longest.* Washington, DC: National Geographic Society.

Bugos, J. A., Perlstein, W. M., McCrae, C. S., Brophy, T. S., & Bedenbaugh, P. H. 2007. Individualized piano instruction enhances executive functioning and working memory in older adults. *Aging and Mental Health, 11*(4), 464–471.

Bull, C. N., & Bane, S. D. (1993). Growing old in rural America: New approach needed in rural health care. *Aging Magazine, 365,* 18–25.

Bulow, J. I., & Summers, L. H. (1986). A theory of dual labor markets with application to industrial policy, discrimination, and Keynesian unemployment. *Journal of Labor Economics, 4*(3, part 1), 376–414.

Bumiller, E. (2005, January 12). Bush presses his argument for Social Security change. *The New York Times,* p. A18.

Bureau of Labor Statistics. (2008a). *Older workers. Spotlight on statistics.* Retrieved May 22, 2010, from www.bls.gov/spotlight/2008/older_workers.

Bureau of Labor Statistics. (2008b). *Sports and exercise activities among various age groups.* Spotlight on statistics. Sports and exercise. Retrieved July 20, 2010, from www.bls.gov/spotlight/2008/sports.

Bureau of Labor Statistics. (2011). *American Time Use Survey—2010 results.* Retrieved July 8 2011, from www.bls.gov/news.release/pdf/atus.pdf.

Bureau of Labor Statistics. Department of Labor. Office of Publications & Special Studies. (2010). Chart 1. Average health care spending shares of total annual expenditures by age of reference person, Consumer Expenditure Interview Survey, 1998, 2003, 2008. *Consumer Expenditure Survey, Volume 1,* No. 8. Retrieved October 10, 2010, from www.bls.gov/opub/focus/volume1_number8/cex_1_8_chart1_data.htm.

Burg, S. B. (1999). *Gray crusade: Townsend Movement, old age politics, and the development of Social Security.* Ann Arbor, MI: UMI Dissertation Services.

Burgess, M., & Applebaum, R. (2009, Fall). The aging network in today's economy. *Generations.* Retrieved August 10, 2010, from http://findarticles.com/p/articles/mi_7543/is_200910/ai_n49420965/.

Burggraf, V. (2000). Older woman: Ethnicity and health. *Geriatric Nursing, 21*(4), 183–187.

Burkhardt, J. E. (2000). Limitations of mass transportation and individual vehicle systems for older persons. In K. W. Schaie & M. Pietrucha (Eds.), *Mobility and transportation in the elderly* (pp. 97–123). New York: Springer.

Burlew, L. D., & Serface, H. C. (2006). Tricultural experience of older, African American, gay men: Counseling implications. *Adultspan Journal, 5*(2), 81–90.

Burr, J. A., & Mutchler, J. E. (2003). English language skills, ethnic concentration, and Household composition: Older Mexican immigrants. *Journals of Gerontology Series B: Psychological Sciences and Social Sciences, 58,* S83–S92.

Burr, J. A., Mutchler, J. E., & Gerst, K. (2010). Public policies and older populations of color. In R. B. Hudson (Ed.), *The new politics of old age policy* (2nd ed., pp. 160–182). Baltimore: Johns Hopkins University Press.

Burrows, N., Geiss, L., Engelgau, M., & Acton, K. (2000). Prevalence of diabetes among Native Americans and Alaskan Natives, 1990–1997. *Diabetes Care.* Retrieved April 15, 2002, from www.findarticles.com/cf_0/mOCUH/12_23/68322723/p1/articlejhtml.

Burton, A. M., Haley, W. E., & Small, B. J. (2006). Bereavement after caregiving or unexpected death: Effects on elderly spouses. *Aging and Mental Health, 10*(3), 319–326.

Burton, L., & DeVries, C. (1992, Summer). Challenges and rewards: African American grandparents as surrogate parents. *Generations,* 51–54.

Bush, G. W. (2005, February 3). Transcript: President Bush's State of the Union address. *New York Times.*

Business Communications Company, Inc. (2005). *Anti-aging products & services.* Norwalk, CT: Author.

Butler, R. N. (1969). Age-ism: Another form of bigotry. *The Gerontologist, 9,* 243–246.

Butler, R. N. (1974). The creative life and old age. In E. Pfeiffer (Ed.), *Successful aging.* Durham, NC: Center for the Study of Aging and Human Development, Duke University.

Butler, R. N. (1975). *Why survive? Being old in America.* New York: Harper & Row.

Butler, R. N. (1987). Ageism. In G. Maddox (Ed.), *The encyclopedia of aging.* New York: Springer.

Butler, R. N. (1993). Dispelling ageism: The cross-cutting intervention. *Generations, 17*(2), 75–78.

Butler, R. N., & Lewis, M. I. (1988). *Love and sex after sixty.* New York: Harper & Row.

Butler, R. N., & Lewis, M. I. (2002). *New love and sex after 60* (3rd rev. ed.). New York: Ballantine Books.

Butts, D. M., & Lent, J. P. (2009). Better together: Generational reciprocity in the real world. In R. B. Hudson (Ed.), *Boomer bust? Economic and political issues of the graying society. The Boomers and their future* (Vol. 2, pp. 145–165). Westport, CT: Praeger.

Cahill, S., & South, K. (2002). Policy issues affecting lesbian, gay, bisexual, and transgender people in retirement. *Generations, 26*(2), 49–54.

Cahill, S., South, K., & Spade, J. (2000). *Outing age: Public policy issues affecting gay, lesbian, bisexual and transgender elders.* New York: The Policy Institute of the Gay and Lesbian Task Force.

Calasanti, T. (2002). Work and retirement in the 21st century: Integrating issues of diversity and globalization. *Ageing International, 27*(3), 3–20.

Calasanti, T. (2004a). Feminist gerontology and old men. *Journal of Gerontology: Social Sciences, 59B*(6), S305–S314.

Calasanti, T. (2004b). New directions in feminist gerontology: an introduction. *Journal of Aging Studies, 18* (1), 1–8.

Calasanti, T. (2006). Gender and old age: Lessons from spousal care work. In T. M. Calasanti & K. F. Slevin (Eds.), *Age matters: Realigning feminist thinking* (pp. 269–294). New York: Routledge Taylor & Francis.

Calasanti, T. (2008). A feminist confronts ageism. *Journal of Aging Studies, 22,* 152–157.

Calasanti, T. (2009). Theorizing feminist gerontology, sexuality, and beyond: intersectional approach. In V. L. Bengtson, M. Silverstein, M. M. Putney, & D. Gans (Eds.), *Handbook of theories of aging* (pp. 471–485). New York: Springer.

Calasanti, T., & Bowen, M. E. (2006). Spousal caregiving and crossing gender boundaries: Maintaining gendered identities. *Journal of Aging Studies, 20,* 253–263.

Calasanti, T., & Kiecolt, K. J. (2007). Diversity among late-life couples. *Generations, 31*(3), 10–17.

Calasanti, T., & Slevin, K. F. (Eds.). (2006). *Age matters: realigning feminist thinking.* New York: Routledge.

Caldera, S. (2009, April). *Social Security: Ten facts that matter.* Fact Sheet 154. Washington, DC: AARP Public Policy Institute. Retrieved December 15, 2010, from www.aarp.org/ppi.

Caldwell, S. (2010, June 20). Euthanasia cases in Holland rise by 13 per cent in a year. *Telegraph.* Retrieved July 22, 2010, from www.telegraph.co.uk/news/worldnews/europe/netherlands/7841696/Euthanasia-cases-in-Holland-rise-by-13-per-cent-in-a-year.html.

California Registry. (2009). *Residential care homes (AKA board and care homes).* Retrieved July 12, 2010, from www.calregistry.com/housing/bce.htm.

Calkins, M. P. (2003). Lighting for older eyes. *Nursing Homes Long Term Care Management, 52*(11), 68+.

Callahan, D. (1987). *Setting limits: Medical goals in an aging society.* New York: Simon & Schuster.

Callahan, J. J. (2009). New challenges for old warriors. *Aging Today, 30*(3), 3–4.

Campbell, A. L. (2002). Self-interest, Social Security, and the distinctive participation patterns of senior citizens. *American Political Science Review, 96*(3), 565–574.

Campbell, A. L. (2003). *How policies make citizens: Senior political activism and the American welfare state.* Princeton, NJ: Princeton University Press.

Campbell, L. D. (2002). *Men who care: Exploring the male experience of filial caregiving.* Paper presented at the International Symposium on Reconceptualising Gender and Ageing, University of Surrey, Guildford, UK, June 25–27.

Campbell, L. D., & Carroll, M. P. (2007). The incomplete revolution: Theorizing gender when studying men who provide care to aging parents. *Men and Masculinities, 9*(4), 491–508.

Campbell, L. D., Connidis, I. A., & Davies, L. (1999). Sibling ties in later life: A social network analysis. *Journal of Family Issues, 20*(1), 114–148.

Canadian Medical Association. (1987). *Health care for the elderly: Today's challenges, tomorrow's options.* Ottawa: Canadian Medical Association.

Cantor, M. H., & Brennan, M. (2000). *Social care of the elderly: The effects of ethnicity, class and culture.* New York: Springer.

Cantor, M. H., Brennan, M., & Shippy, R. A. (2004). *Care giving among older lesbian, gay, bisexual, and transgender New Yorkers.* New York: National Gay and Lesbian Task Force Policy Institute.

Cantor, M. H., & Little, V. (1985). Aging and social care. In R. H. Binstock & E. Shanas (Eds.), *Handbook of aging and social sciences* (pp. 745–781). New York: Van Nostrand Reinhold.

Capelli, P. (2010, orig. 2003). Will there really be a labor shortage? Retrieved May 22, 2010, from http://aoaconsulting.com/yahoo_site_admin/assets/docs/Will_There_Really_Be_A_Labor_Shortage.190155250.pdf. Originally published in *Organizational Dynamics* (2003, August).

Capitosti, S. G. (2007). Managing patients at end of life. *Provider, 33*(5), 37–40.

Carcagno, G. J., & Kemper, P. (1988). Evaluation of the National Long Term Care Demonstration: Overview of the channeling demonstration and its evaluation. *Health Services Research, 23*(1), 1–22.

Cardenas, D., Henderson, K. A., & Wilson, B. E. (2009). Physical activity and Senior Games participation: Benefits, constraints, and behaviors. *Journal of Aging and Physical Activity, 17,* 135–153.

Caro, F. (2003). *Long-term care: Informed by research.* AARP: Academy Health. Retrieved May 6, 2010, from www.academyhealth.org/files/publications/ltcresearch.pdf.

Caron, C. D., Ducharme, F., & Griffith, J. (2006). Deciding on institutionalization for a relative with dementia: The most difficult decision for caregivers. *Canadian Journal on Aging, 25*(2), 193–205.

Carp, F. M. (2000). *Elder abuse in the family: An interdisciplinary model for research.* New York: Springer.

Carpenter, B. D., & Mak, W. (2007, Fall). Caregiving couples. *Generations,* pp. 47–53.

Carr, D. (2004a). Gender, preloss marital dependence, and older adults' adjustment to widowhood. *Journal of Marriage and Family, 66*(1), 220–235.

Carr, D. (2004b). The desire to date and remarry among older widows and widowers. *Journal of Marriage and Family, 66*(4), 1051–1068.

Carrns, A. (2008, May 3–4). Excess exercise. *Wall Street Journal,* p. R12.

Carstensen, L. L., Mikels, J. A., & Mather, M. (2006). In J. E. Birren & K. W. Schaie (Eds.), *Handbook of the psychology of aging* (6th ed., pp. 343–362). Burlington, MA: Elsevier Academic Press.

Cataldo, J. K. (2003). Smoking and aging: Clinical implications. Part 1: Health and consequence. *Journal of Gerontological Nursing, 29*(9), 15–20.

Cattell, M. G. (1994). "Nowadays it isn't easy to advise the young": Grandmothers and granddaughters among Abaluyia of Kenya. *Journal of Cross-Cultural Gerontology, 9,* 157–178.

Cattell, R. B. (1963). Theory of fluid and crystallized intelligence: An initial experiment. *Journal of Educational Psychology, 54,* 105–111.

Cecil, A., & Heo, J. (2009). Senior athletes and active sport tourism: A case of Senior Olympic Games. *Indian Journal of Gerontology, 23*(3), 302–314.

Center for Healthy Aging. (2004). *Best practices in physical activity.* Retrieved November 23, 2004, from http://healthyagingprograms.org/content.asp?sectionid=31&ElementID=144.

Center for Medicare Advocacy, Inc. (2010). *Quick reference Medicare facts & statistics.* Retrieved April 25, 2010, from www.medicareadvocacy.org/InfoByTopic/QuickStatistics.htm.

Center on Budget and Policy Priorities. (2011, April 15). *Policy basics: Where do our federal tax dollars go?* Retrieved June 30, 2011, from www.cbpp.org/cms/index.cfm?fa=view&id=1258.

Centers for Disease Control and Prevention. (2007). *End of life issues.* Retrieved October 15, 2007, from www.cdc.gov/aging/EOL.htm.

Centers for Disease Control and Prevention (CDC). (2009a). *CDC Features: Number of adults reporting disability is increasing.* Retrieved June 6, 2009, from http://cdc.gov/Features/DisabilityCauses/.

Centers for Disease Control and Prevention. (2009b). *Injury prevention & control: Violence prevention.* National suicide statistics at a glance. Percentage of suicides among persons ages 65 years and older, by race/ethnicity and mechanism, United States, 2002–2006. Retrieved March 12, 2010, from www.cdc.gov/violenceprevention/suicide/statistics/mechanism05.html.

Centers for Disease Control and Prevention. (2009c, September 4). QuickStats: Percentage of adults aged 18 years of over who engaged in leisure-time strengthening activities, by age group and sex—National Health Interview Survey, United States 2008. *MMWR Weekly, 58*(34), 955. Retrieved July 8, 2011, from www.cdc.gov/mmwr/preview/mmwrhtml/mm5834a6.htm?s_cid=mm5834a6_e.

Centers for Disease Control and Prevention. (2010a). *Nursing home care.* Retrieved July 12, 2010, from www.cdc.gov/nchs/fastats/nursingh.htm.

Centers for Disease Control. (2010b). *Understanding suicide.* Fact Sheet. Retrieved March 12, 2010, from www.cdc.gov/violenceprevention/pdf/Suicide-FactSheet-a.pdf.

Centers for Disease Control and Prevention. (2011). *A report of the Surgeon General. Physical activity and health. Older adults.* Retrieved June 25, 2011, from www.cdc.gov/nccdphp/sgr/pdf/olderad.pdf.

Centers for Disease Control and Prevention and The Merck Company Foundation. (2007). *The state of aging and health in America 2007.* Washington, DC: Centers for Disease Control.

Centers for Medicare & Medicaid Services. (2009). *Medicare & Medicaid statistical supplement.* Details for personal health care expenditures. Tables 1.1–1.4. Retrieved October 10, 2010, from www.cms.gov/MedicareMedicaidStatSupp/LT/itemdetail.asp?filterType=dual,%20keyword&filterValue=2009&filterByDID=0&sortByDID=3&sortOrder=ascending&itemID=CMS1232664&intNumPerPage=10.

Centers for Medicare & Medicaid Services. (2010a). *List of PACE provider organizations.* Retrieved May 6, 2010, from www.cms.gov/PACE/LPPO/list.asp#TopOfPage.

Centers for Medicare & Medicaid Services. (2010b). *Medicare & you 2011.* Washington, DC: Department of Health & Human Services. Retrieved November 13, 2010, from www.medicare.gov/Publications/Pubs/pdf/10050.pdf.

Centers for Medicare & Medicaid Services. (2010c). *National health expenditures 2009 highlights.* Retrieved August 21, 2010, from www.cms.gov/NationalHealthExpendData/downloads/highlights.pdf.

Centers for Medicare & Medicaid Services. (2010d). *Projected health expenditures.* Retrieved October 10, 2010, from www.cms.gov/NationalHealthExpendData/03_NationalHealthAccountsProjected.asp#TopOfPage.

Centers for Medicare & Medicaid Services. (2010e). National Health Expenditure Projections 2009–2019. Retrieved October 10, 2010, from www.cms.gov/NationalHealthExpendData/downloads/proj2009.pdf.

Centers for Medicare & Medicaid Services and Office of the Assistant Secretary for Planning and Evaluation. (2007). *An overview of the U.S. health care system chart book.* Retrieved November 4, 2007, from www.cms.hhs.gov/TheChartSeries/Downloads/Chartbook_2007_pdf.pdf.

Cerella, J. (1990). Aging and information-processing rate. In J. E. Birren & K. W. Schaie (Eds.), *Handbook of the psychology of aging* (3d ed., pp. 201–221). San Diego, CA: Academic Press.

Cerella, J., Rybash, J., Hoyer, W., & Commons, M. L. (Eds.). (1993). *Adult information processing: Limits on loss.* San Diego, CA: Academic Press.

Cerpa, H. (1989). The effects of clinically standardized meditation on Type II diabetics. *Dissertation Abstracts International 49*(8–B), 3432.

Chan, C. G., & Elder, G. H. Jr. (2000). Matrilineal advantage in grandchild-grandparent relations. *The Gerontologist, 40*(2), 179–190.

Chan, L. (2003). Is spirituality healthful? *Wellness Options, 4*(12), 26–27.

Chandler, C. (2006, September 18). Changing places. *Fortune,* p. 62.

Chapman, N. J., & Howe, D. A. (2001). Accessory apartments: Are they a realistic alternative to ageing in place? *Housing Studies, 16*(5), 637–650.

Chappell, N. L., & Blandford, A. (1991). Informal and formal care: Exploring the complementarity. *Ageing and Society, 11*(Pt. 3), 299–317.

Chappell, N. L., Strain, L. A., & Blandford, A. A. (1986). *Aging and health care: A social perspective.* Toronto, ON: Holt, Rinehart and Winston of Canada.

Charness, N. (1981). Aging and skilled problem solving. *Journal of Experimental Psychology: General, 110*(1), 21–38.

Charness, N., & Krampe, R. T. (2008). Expertise and knowledge. In S. M. Hofer & D. F. Alwin (Eds.), *Handbook of cognitive aging: Interdisciplinary perspectives* (pp. 244–258). Los Angeles: Sage.

Chatterji, P., Burstein, N. R., Kidder, D., & White, A. J. (1998). *Evaluation of the Program of All-Inclusive Care for the Elderly (PACE).* Cambridge, MA: Abt Associates.

Chatters, L., & Taylor, R. (1993). Intergenerational support: The provision of assistance to parents by adult children. In J. S. Jackson, L. M. Chatters, & R. J. Taylor (Eds.), *Aging in African American America* (pp. 69–83). Newbury Park, CA: Sage.

Chen, Y.-P. (2001). Social Security benefits for the family: An issue in social protection. In F. L. Ahearn (Ed.), *Issues in global aging* (pp. 17–23). New York: Haworth.

Cheong, J. M. K., Johnson, M. A., Lewis, R. D., Fischer, J. G., & Johnson, J. T. (2003). Reduction in modifiable osteoporosis-related risk factors among adults in the Older Americans Nutrition Program. *Family Economics and Nutrition Review, 15*(1), 83–91.

Cherlin, A., & Furstenberg, F. F. (1985). Styles and strategies of grandparenting. In V. L. Bengtson & J. F. Robertson (Eds.), *Grandparenthood* (pp. 97–116). Beverly Hills: Sage.

Chernoff, R. (2002). Health promotion for older women: Benefits of nutrition and exercise programs. *Topics in Geriatric Rehabilitation, 18*(1), 59–67.

Chipperfield, J. G., & Havens, B. (2001). Gender differences in the relationship between marital status transitions and life satisfaction in later life. *Journal of Gerontology: Psychological Sciences, 56B*(3), P176.

Chiriboga, D. A., Weiler, P. G., & Nielsen, K. (1990). The stress of caregivers. In D. E. Biegel & A. Blum (Eds.), *Aging and caregiving: Theory, research, and policy* (pp. 121–138). Newbury Park, CA: Sage.

Choi, H., & Marks, N. F. (2008). Marital conflict, depressive symptoms, and functional impairment. *Journal of Marriage and Family, 70*(2), 377–390.

Choi, N. G., Wyllie, R. J., & Ransom, S. (2009). Risk factors and intervention programs for depression in nursing residents: Nursing home staff interview findings. *Journal of Gerontological Social Work, 52*, 668–685.

Christensen, H., Anstey, K. J., Leach, L. S., & Mackinnon, A. J. (2008). Intelligence, education, and the brain reserve hypothesis. In F. I. M. Craik & T. A. Salthouse (Eds.), *The handbook of aging and cognition* (3rd ed., pp. 133–189). New York: Psychology Press.

Christensen, K., Doblhammer, G., Rau, R., & Vaupel, J. W. (2009). Ageing populations: The challenges ahead. *Lancet, 374*(9696), 1196–1208. Retrieved August 11, 2010, from http://pubget.com/paper/19801098?title=Ageing+populations%3A+the+challenges+ahead.

Cicirelli, V. G. (1999). Personality and demographic factors in older adults' fear of death. *The Gerontologist, 39*(5), 569–579.

Cicirelli, V. G. (2002). *Older adults' views on death.* New York: Springer.

Civic Ventures. (2007a). *New face of work survey.* Retrieved September 29, 2007, from www.civicventures.org/publications/surveys/new-face-of-work.cfm.

Civic Ventures. (2007b). *The purpose prize.* Retrieved October 21, 2007, from www.purposeprize.org/purposeprize/why_the_prize.cfm.

Clarity. (2007, August). *Attitudes of seniors and Baby Boomers on aging in place.* Retrieved July 9, 2010, from www.clarityproducts.com/research/ClarityAging_in_Place_2007.pdf and www.slideshare.net/clarityproducts/clarity-2007-aginig-in-place-in-america-2836029?from=share_email.

Clark, D. O., Stump, T. E., & Damush, T. M. (2003). Outcomes of an exercise program for older women recruited through primary care. *Journal of Aging and Health, 15*(3), 567–585.

Clark, P. G. (1993a). Moral discourse and public policy in aging: Framing problems, seeking solutions, and "public ethics." *Canadian Journal on Aging, 12*(4), 485–508.

Clark, R. L. (1993b). Population aging and retirement policy: An international perspective. In A. M. Rappaport & S. J. Schieber (Eds.), *Demography and retirement: The twenty-first century* (pp. 255–284). Westport, CT: Praeger.

Clarke, L. C. H. (2002). Beauty in later life: Older women's perceptions of physical attractiveness. *Canadian Journal on Aging, 21*(3), 429–442.

Clarke, L. H., Griffin, M., & Maliha, K. (2009). Bat wings, bunions, and turkey wattles: body transgressions and older women's strategic clothing choices. *Ageing and Society, 29*, 709–726.

Clarke, P., & Colantonio, A. (2005). Wheelchair use among community-dwelling older adults: Prevalence and risk factors in a national sample. *Canadian Journal on Aging, 24*(2), 191–198.

Clifford, J. C. (1989). What DRGs mean to the patient and the provider. *Journal of Geriatric Psychiatry, 22*(2), 201–210.

Coates, T. (2011, February 11). *10 things you should know about reverse mortgages.* AARP. Retrieved July 5, 2011, from www.aoa.gov/AoARoot/Aging_Statistics/Profile/2010/11.aspx.

Cohen, C. A., Colantonio, A., & Vernich, L. (2002). Positive aspects of caregiving: Rounding out the caregiver experience. *International Journal of Geriatric Psychiatry, 17*(2), 184–188.

Cohen, E. S. (2001). Complex nature of ageism: What is it? Who does it? Who perceives it? *The Gerontologist, 41*(5), 576–577.

Cohen, G. D. (1994). Journalistic elder abuse: It's time to get rid of fictions, get down to facts. *The Gerontologist, 34*(3), 399–401.

Cohen, G. D. (1999). Marriage and divorce in later life: Editorial. *American Journal of Geriatric Psychiatry, 7*, 185–187.

Cohen, G. D. (2005). *The mature mind: The positive power of the aging brain.* New York: Basic Books.

Cohen, G. D., Perlstein, S., Chapline, J., Kelly, J., Firth, K. M., & Simmens, S. (2006). Impact of professionally conducted cultural programs on the physical health, mental health, and social functioning of older adults. *The Gerontologist, 46*(6), 726–734.

Cohen, G. D., Perlstein, S., Chapline, J., Kelly, J., Firth, K. M., & Simmens, S. (2007). Impact of professionally conducted cultural programs on the physical health, mental health, and social functioning of older adults—2-year results. *Journal of Aging, Humanities and the Arts, 1*(1–2), 5–22.

Coile, C. (2003). *Retirement incentives and couples' retirement decisions.* Chestnut Hill, MA: Center for Retirement Research at Boston College. Retrieved September 17, 2004, from www.bc.edu/centers/crr/papers/wp_2003-04.pdf.

Cole, T. R., Achenbaum, W. A., Jakobi, P. L., & Kastenbaum, R. (Eds.). (1993). *Voices and visions of aging: toward a critical gerontology.* New York: Springer.

Cole, T. R., & Ray, R. E. (2000). Introduction. In T. R. Cole, R. Kastenbaum & R. E. Ray (Eds.), *Handbook of the humanities and aging* (2nd ed., pp. xi–xxii). New York: Springer.

Comfort, A. (1972). *The joy of sex.* New York: Crown.

Comfort, A. (1976). *A good age.* New York: Simon & Schuster.

Commission on Affordable Housing and Facility Needs for Seniors in the 21st Century. (2002). *A quiet crisis in America.* Report to Congress, submitted to the Committee on Financial Services, Committee on Appropriations, U.S. House of Representatives & the Committee on Banking, Housing and Urban Affairs, Committee on Appropriations, U.S. Senate, June 30. Retrieved July 12, 2010, from http://govinfo.library.unt.edu/seniorscommission/pages/final_report/finalreport.pdf.

Concord Coalition. (1993). *The zero deficit plan: A plan for eliminating the federal budget deficit by the year 2000.* Washington, DC: Author.

Concord Coalition. (2004). *Facing facts: Social Security reform—Facing up to the real trade-offs.* Retrieved September 12, 2004, from www.concordcoalition.org/facing_facts/alert_v10_n1.html.

Congressional Budget Office. (2004). *Financing long-term care for the elderly.* Washington, DC: Congressional Budget Office.

Congressional Budget Office. (2011). *CBO's 2011 long-term budget outlook.* A CBO report. Retrieved July 1, 2011, from www.cbo.gov/ftpdocs/122xx/doc12212/06-21-Long-Term_Budget_Outlook.pdf.

Connidis, I. A. (2003). Bringing outsiders in: Gay and lesbian family ties over the life course. In S. Arber, K. Davidson, & J. Ginn (Eds.), *Gender and ageing: Changing roles and relationships* (pp. 79–94). Maidenhead, UK: Open University Press.

Connidis, I. A. (2006). Intimate relationships: Learning from later life experiences. In T. M. Calasanti, & K. F. Slevin (Eds.), *Age matters: Realigning feminist thinking* (pp. 123–153). New York: Routledge.

Connidis, I. A., & Kemp, C. L. (2008). Negotiating actual and anticipated parental support: Multiple sibling voices in three-generation families. *Journal of Aging Studies, 22*, 229–238.

Connidis, I. A., & McMullin, J. A. (1999). Permanent childlessness: Perceived advantages and disadvantages among older persons. *Canadian Journal on Aging, 18*(4), 447–465.

Connor, S. R. (1998). *Hospice: Practice, pitfalls, and promise.* Washington, DC: Taylor & Francis.

Consumer Reports. (2008, February). *12 money mistakes that can cost you $1,000,000,* pp. 16–21.

Conway, P., & Shuster, L. (2007). Reciprocal relationships between grandparent caregivers and their grandchild's parent. *Journal of Native Aging and Health, 2*(1), 19–30.

Conwell, Y. (2001). Suicide in later life: A review and recommendations for prevention. *Suicide and Life-Threatening Behavior, 31*(1, Suppl. S), 32–47.

Conwell, Y., Duberstein, P. R., Connor, K., Eberly, S., Cox, C., & Caine, E. D. (2002). Access to firearms and risk for suicide in middle-aged and older adults. *American Journal of Geriatric Psychiatry, 10*(4), 407–416.

Cook, F. L., & Welch, A. S. (1994). *Economic hardship and the coping strategies of middle-aged and elderly low income women.* Paper presented at the annual meeting of the Gerontological Society of America, November 18–20, Atlanta, GA.

Cook, F. L., with Jacobs, L. (2002). Assessing assumptions about Americans' attitudes about Social Security: Popular claims meet hard data. In P. Edleman & L. L. Salisbury (Eds.), *The future of social insurance* (pp. 82–110). Washington DC: Brookings Institution Press.

Cook-Daniels, L. (2004). Training of adult protective services workers: A survey report. *Victimization of the Elderly and Disabled, 7*(3), 37+.

Cooke, M. (2006). Policy changes and the labour force participation of older workers: Evidence from six countries. *Canadian Journal on Aging, 25*(4), 387–400.

Cooley, M. E. (2002). Sex over sixty. *Expression: Bulletin of the National Advisory Council on Aging, 15*(2).

Copeland, C. (2007a). 401(k)-type plans and individual retirement accounts (IRAs). *EBRI Notes, 28*(10).

Copeland, C. (2007b). IRA assets, contributions, and market share. *EBRI Notes, 28*(1), 8–14.

Copeland, C. (2008). Ownership of individual retirement accounts (IRAs) and 401(k)-type plans. *EBRI Notes, 29*(5). Retrieved August 12, 2008, from www.ebri.org/pdf/EBRI_Notes_05-2008.pdf.

Copeland, C. (2009, November). *Employment-based retirement plan participation: Geographic differences and trends, 2008.* EBRI Issue Brief No. 336. Employee Benefit Research Institute. Retrieved May 17, 2010, from www.ebri.org/pdf/briefspdf/EBRI_IB_11-2009_No336_Ret-Part.pdf.

Copeland, C. (2010a). *Employment status of workers ages 55 or older, 1987–2008.* Percentage of workers age 55 or older working part-time, full-year, by age, 1987–2008. Figure 4. Vol. 31(3), p. 4. Notes. Employee Benefit Research Institute. Retrieved November 20, 2010, from www.ebri.org/pdf/notespdf/EBRI_Notes_03-Mar10.EmptStat.pdf.

Copeland, C. (2010b). Labor force participation rates: The population age 55 and older, 2008. *Notes, 31*(2). Washington, DC: Employee Benefit Research Institute. Retrieved December 15, 2010, from http://ebri.org/pdf/notespdf/EBRI_Notes_02-Feb10.LF-Prtcp.pdf.

Copeland, L. (2010, October 21). ALL CAPS? Not OK on road signs, federal government says. *USA Today.* Retrieved October 29, 2010, from www.usatoday.com/news/nation/2010-10-21-road-signs-all-caps-lowercase_N.htm?csp=usat.me.

Corbett, D. (with R. Higgins). (2007). *Portfolio life.* San Francisco: Wiley.

Corley, C. (2009, November 20). *Black males hit extra hard by unemployment.* National Public Radio. Retrieved June 6, 2010, from www.npr.org/templates/story/story.php?storyId=120351534.

Coronel, S. (2004). *Long-term care insurance in 2002.* Washington, DC: America's Health Insurance Plans.

Corr, C. A., Nabe, C. M., & Corr, D. M. (1994). *Death and dying, life and living.* Pacific Grove, CA: Brooks/Cole.

Costa, D. L. (1998). *The evolution of retirement.* Chicago: University of Chicago Press.

Cotman, C. W., & Berchtold, N. C. (2002). Exercise: A behavioral intervention to enhance brain health and plasticity. *Trends in Neuroscience, 25,* 295–301.

Coupland, J. (2009). Discourse, identity and change in mid-to-late life: Interdisciplinary perspectives on language and ageing. *Ageing & Society, 29*(6), 849–861.

Cousins, S. O., & Burgess, A. (1992). Perspectives on older adults in physical activity and sports. *Educational Gerontology, 18,* 461–481.

Coward, R. T. (1988). Aging in the rural United States. In E. Rathbone-McCuan & B. Havens (Eds.), *North American elders: United States and Canadian perspectives* (pp. 161–178). New York: Greenwood.

Cowgill, D. O., & Holmes, L. D. (Eds.). (1972). *Aging and modernization.* New York: Appleton-Century-Crofts.

Cowley, M. (1980). *The view from 80.* New York: Viking Press.

Cox, H. (1993). Political beliefs and activities. In R. Kastenbaum (Ed.), *Encyclopedia of adult development* (pp. 377–381). Phoenix, AZ: Oryx.

Craik, F. I. M. (2000). Age-related changes in human memory. In D. C. Park & N. Schwarz (Eds.), *Cognitive aging: A primer* (pp. 75–92). Philadelphia: Taylor & Francis.

Craik, F. I. M., & Salthouse, T. A. (Eds.). (2008). *The handbook of aging and cognition* (3rd ed.). New York: Psychology Press.

Cramer, K., Tuokko, H., & Evans, D. (2001). Extending autonomy for health care preferences in late life. *Aging Neuropsychology and Cognition, 8*(3), 213–224.

Crary, D. (2010). *Health news—Blame the recession? AARP survey says sex for 45-and-older set is less frequent, less fun.* Retrieved June 28, 2010, from http://blog.taragana.com/health/2010/05/06/blame-the-recession-aarp-survey-says-sex-for-45-and-older-set-is-less-frequent-less-fun-22618/.

Creamer, A. (2010, April 6). Study warns more senior citizens will become homeless. *The Sacramento Bee,* p. 2B.

Crews, D. E. (1993). Biological aging: Book review essay. *Journal of Cross-Cultural Gerontology, 8,* 281–290.

Crimmins, I. M., & Saito, Y. (2001). Trends in healthy life expectancy in the United States, 1970–1990: Gender, racial, and educational differences. *Social Science and Medicine, 52*(11), 1629–1641.

Crimmins, I. M., Saito, Y., & Ingegneri, D. (1989). Changes in life expectancy and disability-free life expectancy in the United States. *Population and Development Review, 15,* 235–267.

Crowley, C., & Lodge, H. S. (2004). *Younger next year.* New York: Workman Publishing.

Cruikshank, M. (2003). *Learning to be old: Gender, culture, and aging.* Lanham: Rowman & Littlefield.

Cruz, J. M. (2003). *Sociological analysis of aging: The gay male perspective.* New York: Harrington Park.

Cukrowicz, K. C. (2009). Course of suicide ideation and predictors of change in depressed older adults. *Journal of Affective Disorders, 113*(1–2), 30–36.

Cullen, L. T. (2006, February 27). Not quite ready to retire. *Time,* pp. 48–49.

Cumming, E., & Henry, W. E. (1961). *Growing old: The process of disengagement.* New York: Basic Books.

Cummings, J., Sproul, L., & Keisler, S. (2002). Beyond hearing: Where real-world and online support meet. *Group Dynamics: Theory, Research and Practice, 6,* 78–88.

Curley, L. (1987). Native American aged. In G. L. Maddox (Ed.), *The encyclopedia of aging* (pp. 469–470). New York: Springer.

Curtin, S. (1972). *Nobody ever died of old age.* Boston: Little, Brown.

Curtis, L. (2006, April). Partnering with faith communities to provide elder fraud prevention, intervention, and victim services. *OVC (Office for Victims of Crime) Bulletin.* Retrieved September 25, 2010, from www.ojp.usdoj.gov/ovc/publications/bulletins/elderfraud_case/pg3.html.

Curtis, M. P., Sales, A. E. B., Sullivan, J. H., Gray, S. L., & Hedrick, S. C. (2005). Satisfaction with care among community residential care residents. *Journal of Aging and Health, 17*(1), 3–27.

Cutler, N. E., Whitelaw, N. A., & Beattie, B. L. (2002). *American perceptions of aging in the 21st century. A myths and realities of aging chartbook.* Washington, DC: National Council on the Aging and the AARP Foundation.

Cutler, S. J. (2006). Technological change and aging. In Robert H. Binstock & Linda K. George (Eds.), *Handbook of aging and the social sciences* (6th ed., pp. 257–276). Burlington, MA: Academic Press.

Dabelko, H. I., & Zimmerman, J. A. (2008). Outcomes of adult day services for participants: A conceptual model. *Journal of Applied Gerontology, 27,* 78–92.

Dall, T. M., Zhang, Y., Chen, Y. J., Quick, W. W., Yang, W. G., & Fogli, J. (2011). The economic burden of diabetes. *Health Affairs, 30*(6). Retrieved June 24, 2011, from http://content.healthaffairs.org/content/29/2/297.abstract.

Dancy, J. Jr. (1997). *The Black elderly: A guide for practitioners: with comprehensive bibliography.* Ann Arbor, MI: Institute of Gerontology, University of Michigan— Wayne State University.

Dancy, J. Jr., & Ralston, P. A. (2002). Health promotion and Black elders: Subgroups of greatest need. *Research on Aging, 24*(2), 218–242.

Davidson, K. (2001). Late life widowhood, selfishness and new partnership choices: A gendered perspective. *Aging and Society, 21,* 297–317.

Davidson, K. (2009). Ageing societies: a comparative introduction. *Ageing and Society, 29*(Part 6), 1002–1003.

Davidson, K., Daly, T., & Arber, S. (2003). Exploring the social worlds of older men. In S. Arber, K. Davidson, & J. Ginn (Eds.), *Gender and ageing: Changing roles and relationships* (pp. 168–185). Maidenhead, UK: Open University Press.

Davidson, S., Brooke, E., & Kendig, H. (2001). Age-segregated housing and friendship interaction for older people. In L. A. Pastalan & B. Schwarz (Eds.), *Housing choices and well-being of older adult: Proper fit* (pp. 123–135). New York: Haworth.

Davies, L. (1995). A closer look at gender and distress among the never married. *Women and Health, 23*(2), 13–30.

Davis, K. (2004, June 5). *Long-term care policy: Time for attention.* Keynote address delivered at the Long-Term Care Colloquium, Annual Meeting of Academy Health, San Diego, CA.

De Jong Gierveld, J. (2003). Social networks and social well-being of older men and women living alone. In S. Arber, K. Davidson, & J. Ginn (Eds.), *Gender and ageing: Changing roles and relationships* (pp. 95–110). Maidenhead, UK: Open University Press.

De la Vega, R., & Zambrano, A. (2003). Topic interview: Professor Yaakov Stern, cognitive reserve [on-line]. *La Circunvalación del hipocampo, September.* Retrieved: February 27, 2010, from www.hipocampo.org/entrevistas/ystern.asp.

De Luce, J. (2001). Silence at the newsstands. *Generations, 25*(3), 39–43.

De Vries, B. (2007, Fall). LGBT couples in later life: A study in diversity. *Generations,* pp. 18–23.

De Vries, B., & Blando, J. A. (2004). The study of gay and lesbian aging: Lessons for social gerontology. In G. Herdt & B. de Vries (Eds.), *Gay and lesbian aging: Research and future directions* (pp. 3–28). New York: Springer.

Deely, B., & Werlinich, K. (1992). Woodside Place: A personal care home for people with Alzheimer's disease. *Aging, 363–364,* 35–36.

Del Balso, Michael, & Alan D. Lewis. (2008). *First steps: A guide to social research* (4th ed.). Toronto: Nelson.

DeNavas-Walt, C., Proctor, B. D., & Smith, J. C. (2009). *Income, poverty, and health insurance coverage in the United States: 2007.* U.S. Census Bureau, Current Census Reports, P60–236. Washington, DC: U.S. Government Printing Office.

Dennis, W. (1968). Creative productivity between the ages of 20 and 80 years. In B. L. Neugarten (Ed.). *Middle age and aging* (pp. 106–114). Chicago: University of Chicago Press.

Dentinger, E., & Clarkberg, M. (2002). Informal caregiving and retirement timing among men and women: Gender and caregiving relationships in later midlife. *Journal of Family Matters, 23,* 857–879.

Denton, M. A., Kemp, C. L., French, S., Gafni, A. Joshi, A., Rosenthal, C. J., et al. (2004). Reflexive planning for later life. *Canadian Journal on Aging, 23*(Supplement1), S71–S82.

Deren, J. M. (1990). Challenges and constraints: Creating nationally available programs for midlife women. In C. L. Hayes & J. M. Deren (Eds.), *Pre-retirement planning for women: Program design and research* (pp. 77–88). New York: Springer.

Dergance, J. M., Calmbach, W. L., Dhanda, R., Miles, T. P., Hazuda, H. P., & Mouton, C. P. (2003). Barriers to and benefits of leisure time physical activity in the elderly: Differences across cultures. *Journal of the American Geriatrics Society, 51,* 863–868.

Der-McLeod, D., & Hansen, J. C. (1992). On Lok: The family continuum. *Generations, 17*(3), 71–72.

Diamond, P. A., & Orszag, P. R. (2007). A summary of *Saving Social Security: A Balanced Approach.* In R. A. Pruchno & M. A. Smyer (Eds.), *Challenges of an aging society: Ethical dilemmas, political issues* (pp. 346–395). Baltimore: Johns Hopkins University Press.

Dickens, W. T., & Lang, K. (1985). A test of dual labor market theory. *American Economic Review, 75*(4), 792–805.

Digiovanna, A. G. (2000). *Human aging: Biological perspectives* (2nd ed.). Boston: McGraw-Hill.

Dilworth-Anderson, P. (1992, Summer). Extended kin networks in black families. *Generations,* pp. 29–32.

Dilworth-Anderson, P., Williams, I. C., & Williams, S. W. (2001). Urban elderly African Americans. In L. K. Olson (Ed.), *Age through ethnic lenses: Caring for the elderly in a multicultural society* (pp. 95–102). London: Rowman & Littlefield.

Dinger, E. (2007). *AARP South Carolina Caregiving in the Workplace Survey.* Washington, DC: AARP Knowledge Management. Retrieved October 6, 2007, from http://assets.aarp.org/rgcenter/econ/sc_caregiving_2007.pdf.

DiNubile, N. A. (2005). *Framework.* Rodale.

Dionigi, R. (2002). Leisure and identity management in later life: Understanding competitive sport participation among older adults. *World Leisure Journal, 44*(3), 4–15.

Dittmann, M. (2003). Fighting ageism. *Monitor on Psychology 34*(5), 50.

Dixon, R. A., Backman, L., & Nilsson, L.-G. (Eds.). (2004). *New frontiers in cognitive aging.* Oxford, U.K.: Oxford University Press.

Dixon, R. A., & Cohen, A.-L. (2001). The psychology of aging: Canadian research in an international context. *Canadian Journal on Aging, 20*(Suppl. 1), 125–148.

D'Mello, D. A. (2003). Epidemiology of late-life depression. In J. M. Ellison & V. Sumer (Eds.), *Depression in later life: A Multidisciplinary psychiatric approach* (pp. 1–26). New York: Marcel Dekker.

Dobell, L. G., & Newcomer, R. J. (2008). Integrated care: incentives, approaches, and future considerations. *Social Work in Public Health, 23*(4), 25–47.

Dobrow, L. (2005, March 21). Boomers, electronics hold promise of prime growth. *Advertising Age,* p. S4.

Doi, Emi. (2007, April 1). Japan faces mass retirements of "Boomers." *San Jose Mercury News,* p. 19A.

Dolbin-McNabb, M. L. (2006). Just like raising your own? Grandmothers' perception of parenting a second time around. *Family Relations, 55,* 564–575.

Dollinger, S. C., Chwalisz, K., & O'Neill Zerth, E. (2006). Tele-help line for caregivers (TLC), A comprehensive telehealth intervention for rural family caregivers. *Clinical Gerontologist, 30*(2), 51–64.

Domitrovich, A. (1986). Thoughts on aging. In J. Alexander (Ed.), *Women and aging: An anthology by women* (pp. 131–133). Corvallis, OR: Calyx Books.

Donlon, M. M., Ashman, O., & Levy, B. R. (2005). Revision of older television characters: a stereotype-awareness intervention. *Journal of Social Issues, 61*(2), 307.

Dorfman, L. T., Murty, S. A., Ingram, J. G., Evans, R. J., & Power, J. R. (2004). Intergenerational service-learning in five cohorts of students: Is attitude change robust? *Educational Gerontology, 30*(1), 39–55.

Dowd, J. J. (1975). Aging as exchange: A preface to theory. *Journal of Gerontology, 30,* 584–594.

Dowd, J. J. (1980). *Stratification among the aged.* Monterey, CA: Brooks/Cole.

Doyle, D. P. (1990). Aging and crime. In K. F. Ferraro (Ed.), *Gerontology: Perspectives and issues* (pp. 294–315). New York: Springer.

Draganski, B., Gaser, C., Busch, V., Schuierer, G., Bogdahn, U., & May, A. (2004, January 22). Changes in gray matter induced by training. *Nature, 427,* 311–312.

Drucker, P. F. (2001, November 3). The next society. *The Economist.*

Du Bois, B. C., Yavno, C. H., & Stanford, E. P. (2001). Care options for older Mexican Americans: Issues affecting health and long-term care service needs. In L. K. Olson (Ed.), *Age through ethnic lenses: Caring for the elderly in a multicultural society* (pp. 71–85). London: Rowman & Littlefield.

Duberstein, P. R., Conwell, Y., Seidlitz, L., Denning, D. G., Cox, C., & Caine, E. D. (2000). Personality traits and suicidal behavior and ideation in depressed inpatients 50 years of age and older. *Journals of Gerontology Series B: Psychological Sciences and Social Sciences, 55*(1), P18–P26.

Dubler, N. N. (2007). Legal aspects of end-of-life decision making. In R. A. Pruchno & M. A. Smyer (Eds.), *Challenges of an aging society: Ethical dilemmas, political issues* (pp. 19–33). Baltimore: Johns Hopkins University Press.

Duke University. (2007). *Hospice use saves money for Medicare, Duke study finds*. Retrieved July 24, 2010, from http://news.duke.edu/2007/11/hospice.html.

Duner, A., & Nordstrom, M. (2007). Roles and functions of the informal support networks of older people who receive formal support: a Swedish qualitative study. *Ageing and Society, 27*(1), 67–85.

Dupuis, S. L., & Smale, B. J. A. (2004). *In their own voices: Dementia caregivers identify the issues*. Final report prepared for the Ministry of Health and Long-Term Care and the Ontario Senior's Secretariat as part of Initiative No. 6 of Ontario's Alzheimer Strategy. Waterloo, ON: Murray Alzheimer Research and Education Program.

Duque, G., & Troen, B. R. (2008, May). Understanding the mechanisms of senile osteoporosis: new facts for a major geriatric syndrome. *Journal of the American Geriatrics Society, 56*(5), 935–941.

Durkheim, E. (1951). *Suicide: A study in sociology*. New York: Free Press.

Dustman, R. E., & White, A. (2006). Effect of exercise on cognition in older adults. In L. W. Poon, W. Chodzko-Zajko, & P. D. Tomporowski (Eds.), *Active living, cognitive functioning, and aging* (Vol. 1, pp. 51–74). Champaign, IL: Human Kinetics.

Dychtwald, K., & Flower, J. (1990). *Age wave: The challenges and opportunities of an aging America*. New York: Bantam Books.

Dykstra, P. A. (1995). Loneliness among the never and formerly married: The importance of supportive friendships and a desire for independence. *Journal of Gerontology: Social Sciences 50B*, S321–S329.

Dykstra, P. A., & Hagestad, G. O. (2007). Roads less taken: Developing a nuanced view of older adults without children. *Journal of Family Issues, 28*(10), 1275–1310.

Dyson, T. (2010, July–August). A portable alternative to nursing homes. *AARP Bulletin*, p. 6.

Eaker, E. D., Sullivan, L. M., Kelly-Hayes, M., D'Agostino, R. B. Sr., & Benjamin, E. J. (2005). Tension and anxiety and the prediction of the 10-year incidence of coronary heart disease, atrial fibrillation, and total mortality: The Framingham Offspring Study. *Psychosomatic Medicine, 67*, 692–696.

Easom, L. R. (2003). Concepts in health promotion: Perceived self-efficacy and barriers in older adults. *Journal of Gerontological Nursing, 29*(5), 11–19.

Eastaugh, A. M. (1996). Approaches to palliative care by primary health care teams: A survey. *Journal of Palliative Care, 12*(4), 47–50.

Easterlin, R. A. (1987). *Birth and fortune* (2nd ed.). Chicago: University of Chicago Press.

Ebeling, A. (2007). Second match. *Forbes, 180*(10), 86–87+.

Economist, The. (2007a, February 17). An American epidemic, p. 37.

Economist, The. (2007b, February 10). Fiscal frustrations, p. 28.

Economist, The. (2007c, March 31). Retire to be rehired, p. 83.

Edmonds, M. M. (1993). Physical health. In J. S. Jackson, L. M. Chatters, & R. J. Taylor (Eds.), *Aging in African American America* (pp. 151–166). Newbury Park, CA: Sage.

Eduventures, Inc. (2008). *The adult learner: An Eduventures perspective—Who they are, what they want, and how to reach them*. Boston, MA: Author. https://www.vtrenz.net/imaeds/ownerassets/884/EV_WP_Adultlearners.pdf.

Effros, R. B. (2001). Immune system activity. In E. J. Masoro & S. N. Austad (Eds.), *Handbook of the biology of aging* (5th ed., pp. 324–350). San Diego, CA: Academic Press.

Effros, R. B. (2009). The immunological theory of aging revisited. In V. L. Bengtson, M. Silverstein, M. M. Putney, & D. Gans (Eds.), *Handbook of theories of aging* (pp. 163–178). New York: Springer.

Eggebeen, D. J. (1992, Summer). From generation unto generation: Parent-child support in aging American families. *Generations*, 45–49.

Eglit, H. C. (1986). *Age discrimination* (Vol. 2, p. 40). Colorado Springs, CO: Shepard's/McGraw-Hill.

Ejaz, F. K., Schur, D., Fox, K., Blenkner, M., & AARP Andrus Foundation. (2003). *Consumer satisfaction in continuing care retirement communities*. Cleveland, OH: Margaret Blenkner Research Institute.

Ekerdt, D. J. (1986). The busy ethic: Moral continuity between work and retirement. *The Gerontologist, 26*(3), 239–244.

Elder, G. H. (1999). *Children of the great depression: Social change and life experience*. Boulder, CO: Westview.

Elder, G. H., Jr. (2000). The life course. In E. F. Borgatta & R. J. V. Montgomery (Eds.), *The encyclopedia of sociology* (2nd ed., Vol. 3, pp. 939–991). New York: Wiley.

Elder, G. H., & Johnson, M. K. (2003). The life course and aging: Challenges, lessons, and new directions. In R. A. Settersten (Ed.), *Invitation to the life course: Toward new understandings of later life* (pp. 49–81). Amityville, NY: Baywood.

Elder, G. H., & Pavalko, E. K. (1993). Work careers in men's later years: Transitions, trajectories, and historical change. *Journal of Gerontology, 48*(4), S180.

Eldercare Volunteer Corps begins recruitment drive. (1992). *Aging, 363–364*, 54–60.

Elderhostel. (1995, July). *Elderhostel: International catalogue*. Boston: Author.

Elderhostel. (2007). *About us*. Retrieved September 28, 2007, from www.elderhostel,org/about/default.asp.

Elias, C. J., & Inui, T. S. (1993). When a house is not a home: Exploring the meaning of shelter among chronically homeless older men. *The Gerontologist, 33*(3), 396–402.

Elliott, S., & Umberson, D. (2008). The performance of desire: Gender and sexual negotiation in long-term marriages. *Journal of Marriage and Family, 70*, 391–406.

Ellis, E. R., Roberts, D., Schwartz, T., & Rousseau, D. M. (2010). *Medicaid enrollment in 50 states. December 2008 data update.* The Kaiser Commission on Medicaid and the Uninsured. Retrieved October 10, 2010, from www.kff.org/medicaid/upload/7606-05.pdf.

Elo, I. T., & Preston, S. H. (1997). Racial and ethnic differences in mortality at older ages. In L. Martin & B. J. Soldo (Eds.), *Racial and ethnic differences in the health of older Americans.* Washington, DC: National Academies Press.

Emanuel, L. L. (2008). Advance directives. *Annual Review of Medicine, 59,* 187–198. Retrieved July 22, 2010, from http://arjournals.annualreviews.org/doi/abs/10.1146/annurev.med.58.072905.062804.

Employee Benefit Research Institute. (2004). *The 2003 Minority Retirement Confidence Survey.* Retrieved September 18, 2004, from www.ebri.org/rcs/2003/03mrcssf.pdf.

Employee Benefit Research Institute. (2007). *2007 minority retirement confidence survey fact sheet.* Retrieved September 9, 2007, from www.ebri.org/files/MRCS07.FS4_Final.pdf.

Employee Benefit Research Institute. (2009). Aggregate trends in defined benefit and defined contribution retirement plan sponsorship, participation, and vesting. In *EBRI databook on employee benefits,* Chapter 10. Washington, DC. Retrieved May 17, 2010, from www.ebri.org/pdf/publications/books/databook/DB.Chapter%2010.pdf.

Employee Benefit Research Institute. (2010a). *EBRI databook on employee benefits.* Retrieved May 17, 2010, from www.ebri.org/publications/books/index.cfm?fa=databook.

Employee Benefit Research Institute. (2010b, April 28). *How many workers are delaying retirement? Why?* Fast Facts No. 162. Retrieved November 20, 2010, from www.ebri.org/pdf/FFE162.28April10.RetDelay-RCS.Final.pdf.

Employee Benefit Research Institute. (2010c). *The sources of income of elderly men and women (age 65 and older).* Fast Facts. Retrieved October 23, 2010, from www.ebri.org/pdf/FFE176.30Sept10.IncEld-Gndr.Final.pdf.

Eng, C., Pedulla, J., Eleazer, G. P., McCann, R., & Fox, N. (1997). Program of All-inclusive Care for the Elderly (PACE), an innovative model of integrated geriatric care and financing. *Journal of the American Geriatric Society, 45,* 223–232.

Engelhardt, G. V., Gruber, J., Perry, C. D., & National Bureau of Economic Research. (2002). *Social Security and elderly living arrangements.* Cambridge, MA: National Bureau of Economic Research.

Engelman, M. (2000). Here's to the Belleville Ladies: Creativity in aging. *Activities, Adaptation and Aging, 24*(4), 19–26.

Ephron, N. (2006). *I feel bad about my neck: And other thoughts on being a woman.* New York: Knopf.

Erikson, E. H. (1959). Identity and the life cycle: Selected issues. *Psychological Issues, 1,* 50–100, Appendix.

Erikson, E. H. (1963). *Childhood and society* (2nd ed.). New York: W. W. Norton.

Erikson, E. H. (1982). *The life cycle completed.* New York: W. W. Norton.

Erikson, E. (2005, orig. 1959). The eight ages of man. In Jenks, C. (Ed.), *Childhood: Critical concepts in sociology* (Vol. 1, pp. 313–325). New York: Taylor & Francis.

Ernst & Young. (2006). *The aging of the U.S. workforce: Employer challenges and responses, January 2006.* Retrieved May 22, 2010, from www.cfo.com/whitepapers/index.cfm/download/10422375.

Eshbaugh, E. M. (2009). The role of friends in predicting loneliness among older women living alone. *Journal of Gerontological Nursing, 35*(5), 13–16.

Estes, C. L. (1979). *The aging enterprise.* San Francisco: Jossey-Bass.

Estes, C. L. (2000). The uncertain future of home care. In R. H. Binstock & L. E. Cluff (Eds.), *Home care advances* (pp. 239–256). New York: Springer.

Estes, C. L. (2003). Theoretical perspectives on old age policy: A critique and a proposal. In S. Biggs, A. Lowenstein, & J. Hendricks (Eds.)., *The need for theory: Critical approaches to social gerontology* (pp. 219–243). Amityville, NY: Baywood.

Ethel Percy Andrus Gerontology Center. (1995, Winter). Research update: Home safe home. *Vitality,* pp. 4–5.

Etnier, J. L. (2009). Physical activity programming to promote cognitive function. Are we ready for prescription? In W. Chodzko-Zajko, A. F. Kramer, & L. W. Poon (Eds.), *Enhancing cognitive functioning and brain plasticity* (pp. 159–175). Champaign, IL: Human Kinetics.

Even, W. E., & Macpherson, D. A. 2004. When will the gender gap in retirement income narrow? *Southern Economic Journal 71*(1), 182–200.

Evensky, H. (2005, July 11). Get real about your future. *Fortune, 11,* 42.

Experience Corps. (2007). *Fact sheet.* Retrieved September 29, 2007, from www.experiencecorps.org/about_us/factsheet.cfm.

Experience Corps. (2010). *About us.* Retrieved July 17, 2010, from www.experiencecorps.org/about_us/about_us.cfm.

Eyetsemitan, F. E., & Gire, J. T. (2003). *Aging and adult development in the developing world: Applying Western theories and concepts.* Westport, CT: Praeger.

Fair, J. M. (2003). Cardiovascular risk factor modification: Is it effective in older adults? *Journal of Cardiovascular Nursing, 18,* 161–168.

Fairlie, H. (1988). Talkin' 'bout my generation. *New Republic, 198*(13), 19–22.

Färber, B. (2003). Microinterventions: Assistive devices, telematics, and person-environment interactions. In K. W. Schaie, H.-W. Wahl, H. Mollenkopf, & F. Oswald (Eds.), *Aging independently: Living arrangements and mobility* (pp. 248–262). New York: Springer.

Feder, J., Komisar, H. L., & Niefeld, M. (2001). The financing and organization of health care. In R. H. Binstock &

L. K. George (Eds.), *Handbook of aging and the social sciences* (5th ed., pp. 387–405). San Diego, CA: Academic Press.

Federal Bureau of Investigation (FBI). (2010). Common fraud schemes. Retrieved September 25, 2010, from www.fbi.gov/majcases/fraud/fraudschemes.htm.

Federal Interagency Forum on Aging-Related Statistics. (2004, November). *Older Americans 2004: Key indicators of well-being.* Washington, DC: U.S. Government Printing Office.

Federal Interagency Forum on Aging-Related Statistics. (2008). *Older Americans 2008: Key indicators of well-being.* Washington, DC: U.S. Government Printing Office.

Federal Interagency Forum on Aging-Related Statistics. (2010a). Indicator 16: Chronic health conditions. *Older Americans 2010: Key indicators of well-being* (p. 27). Washington, DC: U.S. Government Printing Office.

Federal Interagency Forum on Aging-Related Statistics. (2010b). Indicator 23: Diet quality. *Older Americans 2010: Key indicators of well-being* (p. 38). Washington, DC: U.S. Government Printing Office.

Federal Interagency Forum on Aging-Related Statistics. (2010c). *Older Americans 2010: Key indicators of well-being* (p. 6). Indicator 4: Educational attainment. Washington, DC: U.S. Government Printing Office.

Federal Interagency Forum on Aging-Related Statistics. (2010d). *Older Americans 2010: Key indicators of well-being* (p. 39). Indicator 24: Physical activity. Washington, DC: U.S. Government Printing Office.

Federal Interagency Forum on Aging-Related Statistics. (2010e). *Older Americans 2010: Key indicators of well-being* (p. 40). Indicator 25: Obesity. Chronic health conditions. Washington, DC: U.S. Government Printing Office.

Federal Interagency Forum on Aging-Related Statistics. (2010f). *Older Americans 2010: Key indicators of well-being* (p. 44). Indicator 28: Use of time. Washington, DC: U.S. Government Printing Office.

Federal Interagency Forum on Aging-Related Statistics. (2010g). *Older Americans 2010: Key indicators of well-being.* Indicator 3: Marital status. Washington, DC. Citing U.S. Census Bureau, Current Population Survey, Annual Social and Economic Supplement, 2008.

Federal Interagency Forum on Aging-Related Statistics. (2010h). *Older Americans 2010: Key indicators of well-being* (p. 82). Indicator 7: Poverty. Washington, DC: U.S. Government Printing Office.

Federal Trade Commission. (2010). *Web scams.* Retrieved September 25, 2010, from www.ftc.gov/bcp/menus/consumer/tech/scams.shtm.

Feld, S., Dunkle, R. E., & Schroepfer, T. (2004). Race/ethnicity and marital status in IADL caregiver networks. *Research on Aging, 26*(5), 531–558.

Feldman, D. C. (2003). Endgame: The design and implementation of early retirement incentive programs. In G. A. Adams & T. A. Beehr (Eds.), *Retirement: Reasons, processes, and results* (pp. 83–114). New York: Springer.

Fernandez, P. S. (1988). Grandparent access: A model statute. *Yale Law and Policy Review, 6*(88), 109–136.

Ferraro, K. F. (1989). Reexamining the double jeopardy to health thesis. *Journal of Gerontology: Psychological Sciences, 44*(1), S14–S16.

Ferraro, K. F. (1990). The gerontological imagination. In K. F. Ferraro (Ed.), *Gerontology: Perspectives and issues* (pp. 3–18). New York: Springer.

Ferraro, K. F. (2006). Health and aging. In R. H. Binstock & L. K. George (Eds.), *Handbook of aging and the social sciences* (6th ed., pp. 238–256). Burlington, MA: Academic Press.

Ferraro, K. F., & Farmer, M. M. (1993). *Double jeopardy to health for black older Americans?: A longitudinal analysis.* Report. West Lafayette, IN: Purdue University.

Ferraro, K. F., & Kelley-Moore, J. A. (2003). Cumulative disadvantage and health: Long-term consequences of obesity? *American Sociological Review, 68,* 707–729.

Ferraro, K. F., LaGrange, R. L., & McCready, W. C. (1990). *Are older people afraid of crime? Examining risk, fear, and constrained behavior.* DeKalb, IL: Northern Illinois University.

Ferraro, K. F., Shippee, T. P., & Schaefer, M. H. (2009). Cumulative inequality theory for research on aging and the life course. In V. L. Bengtson, M. Silverstein, M. M. Putney, & D. Gans (Eds.), *Handbook of theories of aging* (pp. 413–435). New York: Springer.

Ferrucci, L., Izmirlian, G., Léveillé, S. G., Phillips, C. L., Corti, M. C., Brock, D. B., et al. (1999). Smoking, physical activity, and active life expectancy. *American Journal of Epidemiology, 149*(7), 645–653.

Field, D. (1999). Continuity and change in friendships in advanced old age: Findings from the Berkeley older generation study. *International Journal of Aging and Human Development, 48*(4), 325–346.

Fierst, E. U., & Campbell, N. D. (Eds.). (1988). *Earnings sharing in Social Security: A model for reform.* Washington, DC: Center for Women Policy Studies.

Filan, S. L., & Llewellyn-Jones, R. H. (2006). Animal-assisted therapy for dementia: A review of the literature. *International Psychogeriatrics, 18*(4), 597–611.

File, T., & Crissey, S.(2010). *Voting and registration in the election of November 2008. Population characteristics.* Current population reports, P20–562. U.S. Census Bureau. Retrieved August 1, 2010, from www.census.gov/prod/2010pubs/p20-562.pdf.

Fillit, H. (1994). Challenges for acute care geriatric inpatient units under the present Medicare prospective payment system. *Journal of the American Geriatrics Society, 42*(5), 553–558.

Fingerman, K. L. (2004). The role of offspring and in-laws in grandparents' ties to their grandchildren. *Journal of Family Issues, 25*(8), 1026–1049.

Fishel, D. (2010, April 17). Column: Senior Olympics offer chances for activities, fun. *The Daily Courier.* Retrieved July 19, 2010, from www.dcourier.com/main.asp?Sectio

nID=2&SubSectionID=2&ArticleID=80039&TM=
20727.83.

Fisher, L. L. (2010). *Sex, romance, and relationships: AARP Survey of midlife and older adults.* Washington, DC: AARP. Retrieved June 28, 2010, from http://assets.aarp.org/rgcenter/general/srr_09.pdf.

Fiske, A., & Arbore, P. (2000–01). Future directions in late life suicide prevention. *Omega: Journal of Death and Dying, 42*(1), 37–53.

Fitts, S. S., & Phelan, E. A. (2008). What is the optimal duration of participation in a community-based health promotion program for older adults? *Journal of Applied Gerontology, 27*(2), 201–214.

Fitzpatrick, J., & Fitzpatrick, E. M. (2010). *A better way of dying.* New York: Penguin.

Fleck, C. (2008, October). No place to call home. *AARP Bulletin,* pp. 22–24.

Fleck, C. (2010, May). Forced to retire. *AARP Bulletin,* pp. 14–15.

Flippen, C., & Tienda, M. (2000). Pathways to retirement: Patterns of labor force participation and labor market exit among the pre-retirement population by race, Hispanic origin, and sex. *Journals of Gerontology Series B: Psychological Sciences and Social Sciences, 55*(1), S14–S27.

Flippen, S. (1998). Why there's a coalition for women in long-term care. *Nursing Homes Long Term Care Management, 47*(1), 54–56.

Fogel, B. S. (1992, Spring). Psychological aspects of staying at home. *Generations,* 5–19.

Ford, G. S., & Ford, S. G. (2009). *Internet use and depression among the elderly.* Phoenix Center Policy Paper No. 38. Phoenix Center for Advanced Legal & Economic Public Policy Studies.

Foster-Bey, J., Dietz, N., & Grimm, R., Jr. (2006). *Volunteers mentoring youth: Implications for closing the mentoring gap.* Washington, DC: Cohen Corporation for National & Community Service.

Foundations Project. (1980). Foundations for gerontological education. *The Gerontologist, 20,* Pt. II.

Fowler, L. (1990). Colonial context and age group relations among Plains Indians. *Journal of Cross-Cultural Gerontology, 5,* 149–168.

Fox, S. (2004). *Older Americans and the Internet.* Retrieved June 22, 2007, from Pew Internet & American Life Web site: www.pewinternet.org/pdfs/PIP_Seniors_Online_2004.pdf.

Fozard, J. L., & Gordon-Salant, S. (2001). Changes in vision and hearing with age. In J. E. Birren & K. W. Schaie (Eds.), *Handbook of the psychology of aging* (5th ed., pp. 241–266). San Diego, CA: Academic Press.

Francese, P. (2009) *The grandparent economy. A study of the population, spending habits and economic impact of grandparents in the United States.* Commissioned by Grandparents.com. Retrieved November 12, 2010, from www.grandparents.com/binary-data/The-Grandparent-Economy-April-2009.pdf.

Franco, O. H., de Laet, C., Peeters, A., Jonker, J., Mackenbach, J., & Nusselder, W. (2005). Effects of physical activity on life expectancy with cardiovascular disease. *Archives of Internal Medicine,165,* 2355–2360. Retrieved May 4, 2007, from http://archinte.ama-assn.org/cgi/content/full/165/20/2355?maxtoshow=&HITS=10&hits=10&RESULTFORMAT=&fulltext=Franco&searchid=1&FIRSTINDEX=0&resourcetype=HWCIT.

Frankl, V. (1984). *Man's search for meaning.* New York: Washington Square Press. (Originally published 1946)

Frankl, V. (1990). Facing the transitoriness of human existence. *Generations, 15*(4), 7–10.

Franks, L. J., Hughes, J. P., Phelps, L. H., & Williams, D. G. (1993). Intergenerational influences on Midwest college students by their grandparents and significant elders. *Education Gerontology, 19*(3), 265–271.

Freedman, M. (2007). *Encore: Finding work that matters in the second half of life.* New York: Public Affairs.

Freedom to Marry. (2010). *Freedom to marry.* Retrieved July 1, 2010, from www.freedomtomarry.org.

Freeman, J. T. (1979). *Aging: Its history and literature.* New York: Human Sciences.

Freid, V. M., Prager, K., MacKay, A. P., & Xia, H. (2003). Chartbook on trends in the health of Americans. Health, United States, 2003. Hyattsville, MD: National Center for Health Statistics.

Freidenberg, J. N. (2000). *Growing old in El Barrio.* New York: New York University Press.

French, H. W. (2006, June 30). As China ages, a shortage of cheap labor looms. *New York Times,* nyTimes.com. Retrieved April 26, 2007, from www.nytimes.com/2006/06/30/world/asia/30aging.html?_r=1&scp=1&sq=&oref=slogin.

Frere-Jones, S. (2005, January 17). When I'm sixty-four. *The New Yorker,* 94ff.

Freysinger, V. J. (1993). The community, programs, and opportunities. In J. R. Kelly (Ed.), *Activity and aging* (pp. 211–163). Newbury Park, CA: Sage.

Friedland, R. B., & Summer, L. (1999). *Demography is not destiny.* Washington, DC: National Academy on an Aging Society.

Friedman, M. (1992). Confidence swindles of older consumers. *Journal of Consumer Affairs, 26*(1), 20–46.

Fries, J. F. (1980). Aging, natural death, and the compression of morbidity. *New England Journal of Medicine, 303,* 130–136.

Fries, J. F. (1987a). Disease postponement and the compression of morbidity. In G. L. Maddox (Ed.), *The encyclopedia of aging* (pp. 183–186). New York: Springer.

Fries, J. F. (1990). Medical perspectives upon successful aging. In P. B. Baltes & M. M. Baltes (Eds.), *Successful aging: Perspectives for the behavioral sciences* (pp. 35–49). Cambridge, U.K.: Cambridge University Press.

Fry, C. L. (2003). The life course as a cultural construct. In R. A. Settersten, Jr. (Ed.), *Invitation to the life course: Toward new understandings of later life* (pp. 269–294). Amityville, NY: Baywood.

Fryar, C. D., Hirsch, R., Porter, K. S., Kottiri, B., Brody, D. J., Louis, T., et al. (2006). *Smoking and alcohol behaviors reported by adults, United States, 1999–2002*. Advance data from vital and health statistics; no. 378. Hyattsville, MD: National Center for Health Statistics.

Funderburk, B., Damron-Rodriguez, J., Storms, L. L., & Solomon, D. (2006). Endurance of undergraduate attitudes toward older adults. *Educational Gerontology, 32*(6), pp. 447–462.

Gafni, A. (2001). Protein structure and turnover. In E. J. Masoro & S. N. Austad (Eds.), *Handbook of the biology of aging* (5th ed., pp. 59–83). San Diego, CA: Academic Press.

Galambos, C. M. (1998). Preserving end-of-life autonomy: The Patient Self-Determination Act and the Uniform Health Care Decisions Act. *Health and Social Work, 23*(4), 275–281.

Galenson, D. W. (2006). *Old masters and young geniuses: the two lifecycles of artistic creativity*. Princeton: Princeton University Press.

Galinsky, E., Bond, J. T., & Sakai, K. (with Kim, S. S., & Giuntoli, N. (2008). *2008 National Study of Employers*, p. 3. Retrieved June 6, 2010, from http://familiesandwork.org/site/research/reports/2008nse.pdf.

Galinsky, E., Eby, S., & Peer, S. L. (2008). *2008 guide to bold new ideas for making work*. Families and Work Institute. Retrieved June 13, 2010, from http://familiesandwork.org/3w/boldideas.pdf.

Gallagher, N. A., Gretebeck, K. A., Robinson, J. C., Torres, E. R., Murphy, S. L., & Martyn, K. K. (2010). Neighborhood factors relevant for walking in older, urban, African American adults. *Journal of Aging and Physical Activity, 18*, 99–115.

Gallegos, J. S. (1991). Culturally relevant services for Hispanic elderly. In M. Sotomayor (Ed.), *Empowering Hispanic families: A critical issue for the '90s* (pp. 173–190). Milwaukee, WI: Family Service America.

Gallo, W. T., Bradley, E. H., Liegel, M., & Kasl, S. V. (2000). Health effects of involuntary job loss among older workers: Findings from the Health and Retirement Survey. *Journals of Gerontology Series B: Psychological Sciences and Social Sciences, 55*, S131–S140.

Galston, W. A. (2009). My view. In AARP Public Policy Institute, *The social compact in the twenty-first century* (p. 6). Washington, DC: AARP Public Policy Institute.

Gandy, M., Westeyn, T., Brashear, H., & Starner, B. (2008). Wearable systems design issues for aging or disabled users. In Helal, A. (S.), Mokhtari, M., & Abdulrazak, B (Eds.), *The engineering handbook of smart technology for aging, disability, and independence* (pp. 317–338). Hoboken, NJ: Wiley.

Gans, D. (2009). The future of theories of aging. In V. L. Bengtson, M. Silverstein, M. M. Putney, & D. Gans (Eds.), *Handbook of theories of aging* (pp. 723–737). New York: Springer.

Garand, L., Dew, M. A., Eazor, L. R., DeKosky, S. T., & Reynolds, C. F., III. (2005). Caregiving burden and psychiatric morbidity in spouses of persons with mild cognitive impairment. *International Journal of Geriatric Psychiatry, 20*(6), 512–522.

Garber, C. E., & Blissmer, B. J. (2002). The challenge of exercise in older adults. In P. M. Burbank & D. Riebe (Eds.), *Promoting exercise and behavior change in older adults* (pp. 29–56). New York: Springer.

Garcia, C. (1993). What do we mean by extended family? A closer look at Hispanic multigenerational families. *Journal of Cross-Cultural Gerontology, 8,* 137–146.

Garfinkel, H. (1967). *Studies in ethnomethodology*. Englewood Cliffs, NJ: Prentice-Hall.

Garity, J. (2006). Caring for a family member with Alzheimer's disease: Coping with caregiver burden post-nursing home placement. *Journal of Gerontological Nursing, 32*(6), 39–48.

Garrett, M. D., & Black, K. F. (2006). Healthy-aging: lessons from Isleta Pueblo elders. *Journal of Native Aging and Health, 1*(2), 5–16.

Garroutte, E. M., & Beals, J. (2008). Perceptions of medical interactions between healthcare providers and American Indian older adults. *Social Science and Medicine, 67*(4), 546–556.

Gatza, C., Hinkal, G., Moore, L., Dumble, M., & Donehower, L. A. (2006). P53 and mouse aging models. In E. J. Masoro & S. N. Austad (Eds.), *Handbook of the biology of aging* (6th ed., pp. 149–180). Burlington, MA: Elsevier.

Gaugler, J. E., & Zarit, S. H. (2001). The effectiveness of adult day services for disabled older people. *Journal of Aging & Social Policy, 12*(2), 23–47.

Gavrilov, L. A., & Gavrilova, N. S. (1991). *The biology of life span: A quantitative approach* (Revised and updated English edition, V. P. Skulachev, Ed.; J. Payne & L. Payne, Trans.). New York: Harwood Academic.

Gavrilov, L. A., & Gavrilova, N. S. (2001). Reliability theory of aging and longevity. *Journal of Theoretical Biology, 213*(4), 527–545.

Gavrilov, L. A., & Gavrilova, N. S. (2006). Reliability theory of aging and longevity. In E. J. Masoro & S. N. Austad (Eds.), *Handbook of the biology of aging* (6th ed., pp. 3–42). Burlington, MA: Elsevier.

Gawande, A. (2007, April 30). The way we age now. *The New Yorker*, pp. 50–59.

Gawande, A. (2010, August 2). Letting go. *The New Yorker*, pp. 36–49.

Gelfand, D. (Ed.). (2003). *Aging and ethnicity: Knowledge and services* (2nd ed.). New York: Springer.

Gendell, M. (2008, January). Older workers: Increasing their labor force participation and hours of work. *Monthly Labor Review*, p. 42. Retrieved May 22, 2010, from www.bls.gov/opub/mlr/2008/01/art3full.pdf.

Generations United. (2007). *About us*. Retrieved October 28, 2007, from www.gu.org/about.asp.

Generations United. (2010). *About Generations United*. Retrieved August 8, 2010, from www.gu.org/about.asp.

Genworth Financial. (2010). *2010 Cost of Care Survey*. Retrieved May 6, 2010, from www.genworth.com/content/etc/medialib/genworth_v2/pdf/ltc_cost_of_care.Par.14625.File.dat/2010_Cost_of_Care_Survey_Full_Report.pdf.

George, L. K. (2006). Perceived quality of life. In R. H. Binstock & L. K. George (Eds.), *Handbook of aging and the social sciences* (6th ed., pp. 320–336). Burlington, MA: Academic Press.

Gerber, J., Wolff, J., Klores, W., & Brown, G. (1989). Lifetrends: The future of baby boomers and other aging Americans. New York: Macmillan.

Gianoulis, T. (2004). *GLBTQ: An Encyclopedia of Gay, Lesbian, Bisexual, Transgender, & Queer Culture*. Chicago: glbtq.

Giarrusso, R., Silverstein, S., & Feng, D. (2000). Psychological costs and benefits of raising grandchildren: Evidence from a national survey of grandparents. In C. B. Cox (Ed.), *To grandmother's house we go and stay* (pp. 71–90). New York: Springer.

Gibson, M. J., & Houser, A. (2007, June). Valuing the invaluable: A new look at the economic value of family caregiving. AARP Policy Institute. *PPI Issue Brief, 82,* pp. 1–12. Retrieved October 5, 2007, from http://assets.aarp.org/rgcenter/il/ib82_caregiving.pdf.

Gibson, R. C. (1986). Outlook for the black family. In A. Pifer & L. Bronte (Eds.), *Our changing society* (pp. 181–197). New York: W. W. Norton.

Gibson, R. C. (1987). Reconceptualizing retirement for black Americans. *The Gerontologist, 27,* 691–698.

Gibson, R. C. (1991). Subjective retirement of black Americans. *Journals of Gerontology, 46*(4), S204.

Gibson, R. C. (1993). The black American retirement experience. In J. S. Jackson, L. M. Chatters, & R. J. Taylor (Eds.), *Aging in Black America* (pp. 277–297). Newbury Park, CA: Sage.

Gibson, R. C., & Jackson, J. S. (1992). The black oldest old: Health, functioning, and informal support. In R. M. Suzman, D. P. Willis, & K. G. Manton (Eds.), *The oldest old* (pp. 321–340). New York: Oxford University Press.

Gilleard, C., & Higgs, P. (2009). The power of silver: Age and identity politics in the 21st century. *Journal of Aging & Social Policy, 21*(3), 277–295.

Gillen, M., & Kim, H. (2009). Older women and poverty transition. *Journal of Applied Gerontology, 28*(3), 320–341.

Gillum, R. F. (1997). Sudden cardiac death in Hispanic Americans and African Americans. *American Journal of Public Health, 87,* 1461–1466.

Gilman, E. (1994, February 20). Matching the elderly with foster families. *New York Times*, Section NJ, p. 9C.

Ginsburg, I. F. (2009). On-site mental health services for PACE (Program of All-inclusive Care for the Elderly) Centers. *Journal of the American Medical Directors Association, 10*(4), 277–280.

Gioglio, G. R., & Blakemore, P. (1983). *Elder abuse in New Jersey: the knowledge and experience of abuse among older New Jerseyans*. Unpublished manuscript. Department of Human Services, Trenton, NJ.

Gist, Y. J. (1994). Aging trends—Southern Africa. *Journal of Cross-Cultural Gerontology, 9,* 255–276.

Gladstone, J. W. (1987). Factors associated with changes in visiting between grandmothers and grandchildren following an adult child's marriage breakdown. *Canadian Journal on Aging, 6,* 117–127.

Gladstone, J. W. (1995). The marital perceptions of elderly persons living or having a spouse living in a long-term care institution in Canada. *The Gerontologist, 35*(1), 52–60.

Gladwell, M. (2005), *Blink: The power of thinking without thinking. New York:* Little, Brown and Company.

Glendenning, F. (1999). Elder abuse and neglect in residential settings: The need for inclusiveness in elder abuse research. *Journal of Elder Abuse and Neglect, 10*(1–2), 1–11.

Gluck, M. E. (Ed.), Reno, V. P. (Ed.), & National Academy of Social Insurance (U.S.). (2001). *Reflections on implementing Medicare* (2nd ed.). Washington, DC: National Academy of Social Insurance.

Goggin, J. (2009). Encore careers for the twenty-first-century aging-friendly community. *Generations, 33*(2), 95–97.

Golant, S. (2002). Geographic inequalities in the availability of government-subsidized rental housing for low-income older persons in Florida. *The Gerontologist, 42,* 100–109.

Golant, S. (2003). Political and organizational barriers to satisfying low-income U.S. seniors' need for affordable rental housing with supportive services. *Journal of Aging & Social Policy, 15*(4), 21–48.

Golant, S. (2004). The urban-rural distinction in gerontology: An update of research. In H.-W. Wahl, R. J. Scheidt, & P. G. Windley (Eds.), *Annual review of gerontology and geriatrics: Vol. 23, 2003. Focus on aging in context: Socio-physical environments* (pp. 280–312). New York: Springer.

Gold, R., Michael, Y. L. Whitlock, E. P., Hubbell, F. A., Mason, E. D., Rodriguez, B. L., et al. (2006). Race/ethnicity, socioeconomic status, and lifetime morbidity burden in the Women's Health Initiative: A cross-sectional analysis. *Journal of Women's Health, 15*(10), 1161–1173.

Goldberg, D. L. (2003). *Grandparent-grandchild access: A legal analysis*. Paper presented to Family, Children, and Youth Section, Department of Justice Canada. Minister of Justice and Attorney General of Canada.

Golden, F. (2004, January 19). Still sexy after sixty. *Time*.

Gonidakis, S., & Longo, V. D. (2009). Programmed longevity and programmed aging theories. In V. L. Bengtson, M. Silverstein, M. M. Putney, & D. Gans (Eds.), *Handbook of theories of aging* (pp. 215–228). New York: Springer.

Gonyea, J. G. (2009). Multigenerational bonds, family support, and Baby Boomers: Current challenges and future prospects for eldercare (pp. 213–232). In R. B. Hudson (Ed.), *Boomer Bust? Economic and political issues of the graying society. The Boomers and their future* (Vol. 2). Westport, CT: Praeger.

Gonyea, J. G., O'Connor, M. K., & Boyle, P. A. (2006). Project CARE: A randomized controlled trial of a behavioral intervention group for Alzheimer's disease caregivers. *The Gerontologist, 46*(6), 827–832.

Goodwin, P., McGill, B., & Chandra, A. (2009). *Who marries and when? Age at first marriage in the United States*, 2002. NCHS Data Brief, No. 19. Hyattsville, MD: National Center Health Statistics. Retrieved June 30, 2010, from www.cdc.gov/nchs/data/databriefs/db19.pdf.

Goozner, M. (2005). Don't mess with success. *AARP Bulletin, 46*(1), 12–15.

Gosselin, P. G. (2005, May). Experts are at a loss on investing. *Los Angeles Times*. Retrieved May 20, 2006, from www.latimes.com/news/printedition/from/la-na-nobel11,1,1607625.story?coll=la-headlines-front-page.

Gott, M., & Hinchliff, S. (2003). Sex and ageing: A gendered issue. In S. Arber, K. Davidson, & J. Ginn (Eds.), *Gender and ageing: Changing roles and relationships* (pp. 63–78). Maidenhead, U.K.: Open University Press.

Gottlieb, B. H., & Kelloway, E. K. (1995). Eldercare and employment. In M. Novak (Ed.), *Aging and society: A Canadian reader* (pp. 336–341). Scarborough, ON: Nelson Canada.

Government Accounting Office. (2004). *Transportation-disadvantaged seniors*. GAO-04-971. Retrieved July 15, 2010, from www.gao.gov/new.items/d04971.pdf.

Graham, N. P. (2010, January–February). Aging's not optional. *AARP—The Magazine*, p. 4.

Gray Panthers. (2010). *Gray Panthers are*. Retrieved August 8, 2010, from www.graypanthers.org.

Greene, R., & Galambos, C. (2002). Social work's pursuit of a common professional framework: Have we reached a milestone? *Journal of Gerontological Social Work, 39*(1–2), 7–23.

Greenfield, E. A., & Marks, N. F. (2004). Formal volunteering as a predictive factor for adults' psychological well-being. *Journals of Gerontology: Series B: Psychological Sciences and Social Sciences, 59B*(5), S258–S264.

Greer, G. (1991). *The change: Women, aging and the menopause*. Toronto: Alfred A. Knopf.

Greisman, L. C. (2005). *Identifying and fighting consumer fraud against older Americans*. Prepared statement of the Federal Trade. Division of Planning and Information, Bureau of Consumer Protection. Presented before the Special Committee on Aging on July 17, 2005. Washington: Federal Trade Commission.

Grief, G. L. (2009). Understanding older men and their male friendships: A comparison of African American and White men. *Journal of Gerontological Social Work, 52*(6), 618–632.

Griffin, Kelly. (2005, November–December). Diabetes denial. *AARP Magazine*. Retrieved November 2, 2007, from www.aarpmagazine.org/health/diabetes.html.

Groeneman, S. (2008). *Staying ahead of the curve 2007. The AARP Work and Career Study*. Washington, DC: AARP Knowledge Management.

Grogan, C. M., & Andrews, C. M. (2010). The politics of aging within Medicaid. In R. B. Hudson (Ed.), *The new politics of old age policy* (2nd ed., pp. 275–306). Baltimore: Johns Hopkins University Press.

Gross, D. (2006, March). The big freeze. *AARP Bulletin*.

Grossman, I., Na, J., Varnum, M. E. W., Park, D. C., Kitayama, S., & Nisbett, R. E. (2010). Reasoning about social conflicts improves into old age. *Proceedings of the National Academy of Sciences*. Retrieved August 28, 2010, from www.pnas.org/content/early/2010/03/23/1001715107—also Supporting information, from www.pnas.org/content/suppl/2010/03/24/1001715107.DCSupplemental/pnas.201001715SI.pdf.

Growth House. (2007). *Palliative care*. Retrieved October 15, 2007, from www.growthhouse.org/palliat.html.

Grune, T., & Davies, K. J. A. (2001). Oxidative processes in aging. In E. J. Masoro & S. N. Austad (Eds.), *Handbook of the biology of aging* (5th ed., pp. 25–58). San Diego, CA: Academic Press.

GSA Task Force on Minority Issues in Gerontology. (1994). *Minority elders: Five goals toward building a public policy base* (2nd ed.). Washington, DC: Gerontological Society of America.

Gubrium, J. F. (1993). Voice and context in a new gerontology. In T. R. Cole, W. A. Achenbaum, P. L. Jakobi, & R. Kastenbaum (Eds.), *Voices and visions of aging* (pp. 46–63). New York: Springer.

Gubrium, J. F., & Holstein, J. A. (1999). Constructionist perspectives on aging. In V. L. Bengtson & K. W. Schaie (Eds.), *Handbook of theories of aging* (pp. 287–305). New York: Springer.

Guess, A. (2007, November 28). Geography emerges in distance ed. *Inside Higher Education*. Retrieved December 15, 2010, from www.insidehighered.com/news/2007/11/28/online.

Guinness Book of World Records. (1988). *Guinness book of world records* (27th ed.). New York: Sterling.

Gutner, T. (2004, July 25). Getting psyched to retire. *BusinessWeek*, pp. 88–90.

Guttman, M. (2008, September 6). The aging brain. www.usc.edu/hsc/info/pr/hmm/01spring/brain.html—retrieved January 25, 2009.

Haber, C. (1993, Spring/Summer). "And the fear of the poorhouse": Perceptions of old age impoverishment in early twentieth-century America. *Generations*, 46–50.

Haber, C. (2000). Historians' approach to aging in America. In T. R. Cole, R. Kastenbaum, & R. E. Ray (Eds.), *Handbook of the humanities and aging* (2nd ed., pp. 25–40). New York: Springer.

Haber, C. (2001–02). Anti-aging: why now? A historical framework for understanding the contemporary enthusiasm. *Generations*, 25(4), 9–14.

Haber, C. (2004). Life extension and history: The continual search for the fountain of youth. *Journals of Gerontology: Series A: Biological Sciences and Medical Sciences, 59A*(6), 515–522.

Haber, D. (2010). *Health promotion and aging: Practical applications for health professionals* (5th ed.). New York: Springer.

Hacker, J. S. (2006). *The great risk shift.* New York: Oxford University Press.

Hagen, B., Gallagher, G. M., & Simpson, S. (1997). Family caregiver education and support programs: Using humanistic approaches to evaluate program effects. *Educational Gerontology, 23*(2), 129–142.

Hagestad, G. O. (1985). Continuity and connectedness. In V. L. Bengtson & J. F. Robertson (Eds.), *Grandparenthood.* Beverly Hills, CA: Sage.

Hahn, R., & Eberhardt, S. (1995). Life expectancy in four U.S. racial/ethnic populations: 1990. *Epidemiology, 6,* 352–356.

Haines, V. A., & Henderson, L. J. (2002). Targeting social support: A network assessment of the convoy model of social support. *Canadian Journal on Aging, 21*(2), 243–256.

Hajjar, R. R., & Kamel, H. K. (2003). Sexuality in the nursing home, part 1: Attitudes and barriers to sexual expression. *Journal of the American Medical Directors Association, 4*(3), 152–156.

Hakamies-Blomqvist, L. (2004). Safety of older persons in traffic. In *Transportation in an aging society: A decade of experience.* Washington, DC: National Academy of Sciences, Transportation Research Board.

Håkansson, K., Rovio, S., Helkala, E.-L, Vilska, A.-R., Winblad, B., Soininen, H., et al. (2009). Association between mid-life marital status and cognitive function in later life: population based cohort study. *BMJ, 339,* 2462. Retrieved November 11, 2010, from www.bmj.com/content/339/bmj.b2462.full?sid=79df263a-adbf-4ab1-b55e-5371e3145da3.

Hall, M., & Havens, B. (2002). Social isolation and social loneliness. In *Writing in gerontology: Mental health and aging,* No. 18, pp. 33–44. Ottawa: National Advisory Council on Aging.

Hallman, B. C., & Joseph, A. E. (1999). Getting there: Mapping the gendered geography of caregiving to elderly relatives. *Canadian Journal on Aging, 18*(4), 397–414.

Hamer, C. F., Guse, L. W., Hawranik, P. G., & Bond, J. B. Jr. (2002). Advance directives and community dwelling older adults. *Western Journal of Nursing Research, 24*(2), 143–158.

Hammond, D. B. (1987). *My parents never had sex.* Buffalo, NY: Prometheus Books.

Hanc, J. (2010). *In America's gyms, more than a touch of gray.* Retrieved August 28, 2010, from www.nytimes.com/2010/03/04/business/retirementspecial/04GYM.html.

Hao, Y. (2008). Productive activities and psychological well-being among older adults. *Journals of Gerontology: Series B: Psychological Sciences and Social Sciences, 63B*(2), S64–S72.

Hapgood, D. (1978). The aging are doing better. In R. Gross, B. Gross, & S. Seidman (Eds.), *The new old* (pp. 345–363). Garden City, NY: Anchor.

Haralson, D., & Parker, S. (2003, January 21). Age and job searching. *USA Today.*

Hardy, M. (2006). Older workers. In R. H. Binstock & L. K. George (Eds.), *Handbook of aging and the social sciences* (6th ed., pp. 201–218). Burlington, MA: Academic Press.

Hare, P. H. (1992, Spring). Frail elders and the suburbs. *Generations,* pp. 35–39.

Hareven, T. K. (1992, Summer). Family and generational relations in the later years: A historical perspective. *Generations,* pp. 7–12.

Harlton, S. V., Keating, N., & Fast, J. (1998). Defining eldercare for policy and practice: Perspectives matter. *Family Relations, 47*(3), 281–288.

Harman, S. M., Metter, E. J., Metter, J., Tobin, J. D., Pearson, J., & Blackman, M. R. (2000). Longitudinal effects of aging on serum total and free testosterone levels in healthy men. *Journal of Clinical Endocrinology & Metabolism, 86*(2), 724–731.

Harrell, R., Brooks, A., & Nedwick, T. (2009). *Preserving affordability and access in livable communities: Subsidized housing opportunities near transit and the 50+ population.* Washington, DC: AARP Public Policy Institute. Retrieved July 12, 2010, from www.hud.gov/offices/cpd/about/conplan/pdf/preservingaffordable housingNeartransit.pdf.

Harrington, C., Chapman, S., Miller, E., Miller, N., & Newcomer, R. (2005). Trends in the supply of long-term-care facilities and beds in the United States. *Journal of Applied Gerontology, 24*(4), 265–282.

Harris, D. K., Changas, P. S., & Palmore, E. B. (1996). Palmore's first Facts on Aging Quiz in a multiple-choice format. *Educational Gerontology, 22*(6), 575–589.

Harris, L. (1991). 1.9 million seniors ready and able to go back to work. *Aging, 362,* 51.

Harris, L. M (Ed.). (2003a). *After fifty: How the Boomers will redefine the mature market.* Ithaca, NY: Paramount Market Publishing.

Harris, L. M. (2003b). An introduction: Connecting with the Boomers. In L. M. Harris (Ed.), *After fifty: How the Baby Boom will redefine the mature market* (pp. 1–8). Ithaca, NY: Paramount Market Publishing.

Harris, P. B. (2005). The voices of husbands and sons caring for a family member with dementia. In B. J. Kramer & E. H. Thompson, Jr. (Eds.), *Men as caregivers* (pp. 213–233). Amherst, NY: Prometheus Books.

Hartley, A. (2006). Changing role of the speed of processing construct in the cognitive psychology of human aging. In J. E. Birren & K. W. Schaie (Eds.), *Handbook of the psychology of aging* (6th ed., pp. 183–207). Burlington, MA: Elsevier Academic Press.

Harvard University & MetLife. (2004) *Reinventing retirement: Baby Boomers and civic engagement.* Cambridge,

MA: Harvard School of Public Health and MetLife Foundation, President and Fellows of Harvard College.

Havens, B., & Hall, M. (2001). Social isolation, loneliness, and the health of older adults in Manitoba, Canada. *Indian Journal of Gerontology, 15*(1–2), 1126–1144.

Havir, L. (1991). Senior centers in rural communities: Potentials for serving. *Journal of Aging Studies, 5*(4), 359–374.

Hawes, C. (1999). Key piece of the integration puzzle: Managing the chronic care needs of the frail elderly in residential care settings. *Generations, 23*(2), 51–55.

Hawranik, P. (2002). Inhome service use by caregivers and their elders: Does cognitive status make a difference? *Canadian Journal on Aging, 21*(2), 257–272.

Hayes-Bautista, D. E. (1991, Fall–Winter). Young Latinos, older Anglos, and public policy: Lessons from California. *Generations*, pp. 37–39.

Hayes-Bautista, D. E. (2004). *La nueva California: Latinos and California Society, 1940–2040.* Berkeley: University of California Press.

Hayes-Bautista, D. E., Hsu, P., Perez, A., & Gambon, C. (2002). The "browning" of the graying of America: Diversity in the elderly population and policy implications. *Generations, 26*(3), 15–22.

Hayflick, L. (1981). Prospects for human life extension by genetic manipulation. In D. Danon, N. W. Shock, & M. Marois (Eds.), *Aging: A challenge to science and society* (pp. 162–179). Oxford, U.K.: Oxford University Press.

Hayflick, L. (1996). *How and why we age.* New York: Ballantine.

Hayflick, L., & Moorehead, P. S. (1961). The serial cultivation of human diploid cell strains. *Experimental Cell Research, 25*, 585–621.

Hayslip, B. Jr., Shore, R. J., & Henderson, C. E. (2000). Perceptions of grandparents' influence in the lives of their grandchildren. In B. Hayslip & R. Goldberg-Glen (Eds.), *Grandparent raising grandchildren: Theoretical, empirical, and clinical perspectives* (pp. 35–46). New York: Springer.

He, W., Sangupta, M., Velkoff, V. A., & De Barros, K. A. (2005). *65+ in the United States: 2005.* U.S. Census Bureau, Current Population Reports, P23–209. Washington, DC: U.S. Government Printing Office. Retrieved July 14, 2007, from www.census.gov/prod/2006pubs/p23-209.pdf.

Healey, T. J. (2010, May 22). Plan sponsors: Time to face the PBGC music. Pensions and Investments. Retrieved May 22, 2010, from www.pionline.com/article/20100125/REG/100129949.

Health and Human Services Administration. (2010). *National HealthService Corps.* Retrieved May 6, 2010, from http://nhsc.hrsa.gov.

Health Resources and Services Administration. (2010). *Homeless and elderly: Understanding the special health care needs of elderly persons who are homeless.* Retrieved July 17, 2010, from http://bphc.hrsa.gov/policy/pal0303.htm.

Healthy People Consortium. (2010). *Healthy People. Washington, DC: U.S. Department of Health and Human Services.* Retrieved January 31, 2010, from www.healthypeople.gov/Document/tableofcontents.htm#volume1.

Heaphy, B., Yip, A. K. T., & Thompson, D. (2004). Ageing in a non-heterosexual context. *Ageing & Society, 24*, 881–902.

Hedberg K., Hopkins D., & Kohn M. (2003, March 6). Five years of legal physician-assisted suicide in Oregon. Correspondence. *New England Journal of Medicine, 348*, 961–964. Retrieved July 25, 2010, from www.nejm.org/doi/full/10.1056/NEJM200303063481022.

Hedlund, A. L. (1999). Give-and-take: Navajo grandmothers and the role of craftswomen. In M. M. Schweitzer (Ed.), *American Indian grandmothers: Traditions and transitions* (pp. 53–77). Albuquerque: University of New Mexico Press.

Heisel, M. J. (2006). Suicide and its prevention among older adults. *Canadian Journal of Psychiatry, 51*(3), 143–154.

Helal, S., Bose, R., Pickles, S., Elzabadani, H., King, J., & Kaddourah, Y. (2008). The Gator Tech smart house: A programmable pervasive space. In Helal, A. (S.), Mokhtari, M., & Abdulrazak, B (Eds.), *The engineering handbook of smart technology for aging, disability, and independence* (pp. 695–709). Hoboken, NJ: Wiley.

Helman, R., Copeland, C., & VanDerhei, J. (2010). *The 2010 retirement confidence survey: Confidence stabilizing, but preparations continue to erode.* Employee Benefit Research Institute, Issue Brief, No. 340. Washington, DC: Employment Benefit Research Institute.

Helman, R., Greenwald, M., & Associates, Van Derhei, J., & Copeland, C. (2007, June). *Minority workers remain confident about retirement, despite lagging preparations and false expectations.* Employee Benefit Research Institute, Issue Brief, No. 306. Retrieved September 9, 2007, from www.ebri.org/pdf/briefspdf/EBRI_IB_06-2007.pdf.

Helpguide.org. (2007). *Continuing care retirement communities (CCRCs).* Retrieved November 10, 2007, from www.helpguide.org/elder/continuing_care_retirement_communities.htm.

Henderson, C. E. (2001). *Grandparent-grandchild attachment as a predictor of psychological adjustment among youth from divorced families.* Ann Arbor, MI: UMI Dissertation Services.

Hendricks, J. (1997). Bridging contested terrain: Chaos or prelude to a theory. *Canadian Journal on Aging, 16*(2), 197–217.

Hendricks, J. (1999). Creativity over the life course—A call for a relational perspective. *International Journal of Aging and Human Development, 48*(2), 85–111.

Hendricks, J., & Hendricks, C. D. (1986). *Aging in mass society: Myths and realities* (3rd ed.). Boston: Little, Brown.

Hendrix, L. R. (2003). Intercultural collaboration: An approach to long term care for urban American Indians. *Care Management Journals, 4*(1), 46–52.

Henry, R. G., Miller, R. B., & Giarrusso, R. (2005). Difficulties, disagreements, and disappointments in late-life marriages. *International Journal of Aging and Human Development, 61*(3), 243–264.

Heo, J., & Lee, Y. (2010). Serious leisure, health perception, dispositional optimism, and life satisfaction among Senior Games participants. *Educational Gerontology, 36*(2), 112–126.

Hequembourg, A., & Brallier, S. (2005). Gendered stories of parental caregiving among siblings. *Journal of Aging Studies, 19,* 53–71.

Herd, P. (2009). The two-legged stool: The reconfiguration of risk in retirement income security [Part of a special issue: *The Great Recession: Implications for an aging America*]. *Generations, 33*(3), 12–18.

Herd, P., & Kingson, E. R. (2005). Reframing Social Security: Cure worse than the disease. In R. B. Hudson (Ed.). *The new politics of old age policy* (pp. 183–204). Baltimore: The Johns Hopkins University Press.

Herndon, C. M., Jackson, K. II, Fike, D. S., & Woods, T. (2003). End-of-life care education in United States pharmacy schools. *American Journal of Hospice and Palliative Care, 20*(5), 340–344.

Heron, M., Hoyert, D. L., Murphy, S. L., Xu, J., Kochanek, K. D., & Tejada-Vera, B. (2009, April 17). Deaths: Final data for 2006. *Vital Statistics Reports, 57*(14). Retrieved December 20, 2009, from www.cdc.gov/nchs/data/nvsr/nvsr57/nvsr57_14.pdf.

Heru, A. M., Ryan, C. E., & Iqbal, A. (2004). Family functioning in the caregivers of patients with dementia. *International Journal of Geriatric Psychiatry, 19*(6), 533–537.

Hess, B. B. (1987). Poverty. In G. L. Maddox (Ed.), *The encyclopedia of aging* (pp. 530–532). New York: Springer.

Hess, T. M. (2006). Attitudes toward aging and their effects on behavior. In J. E. Birren & K. W. Schaie (Eds.), *Handbook of the psychology of aging* (6th ed., pp. 379–406). Burlington, MA: Elsevier Academic Press.

Hess, T. M., Auman, C., Colcombe, S. J., & Rahhal, T. A. (2003). The impact of stereotype threat on age differences in memory performance. *Journals of Gerontology, Series B, Psychological Sciences and Social Sciences. 58B*(1), 3–11.

Hess, T. M., Rosenberg, D. C., & Waters, S. J. (2001). Motivation and representational processes in adulthood: The effects of social accountability and information relevance. *Psychology and Aging, 16*(4), 629–642.

Hessel, D. (Ed.) (1977). *Maggie Kuhn on aging: A dialogue.* Philadelphia: Westminster Press.

Hewitt Associates. (2008, July 30). Retiring boomers prompt increased employer interest in phased retirement programs, according to Hewitt survey [Press release]. Retrieved August 28, 2010, from http://hiringsolutionsllc.com/RetiringBoomersPrompt.html.

Hey, R. P. (1995). Cuts loom for Medicare enrollees. *AARP Bulletin, 36*(6), 1ff.

Hickman, S. E., Sabatino, C. P., Moss, A. H., & Nester, J. W. (2008, Spring). The POLST (Physician Orders for Life- Sustaining Treatment) paradigm to improve end-of-life care: Potential state legal barriers to implementation. *Journal of Law, Medicine & Ethics, Religions and Cultures of East and West: Perspectives on Bioethics,* pp. 119–140.

Hicks, P. (2001). *Public support for retirement income reform.* OECD Labour Market and Social Policy Occasional Papers No. 55.

Hightower, J. (2004). Age, gender and violence: Abuse against older women. *Geriatrics and Aging, 7*(3), 60–63.

Hill, E. T. (2002). Labor force participation of older women: Retired? Working? Both? *Monthly Labor Review, 125*(9), 39–48.

Hilton, J. M., & Macari, D. P. (1997). Grandparent involvement following divorce: A comparison in single-mother and single-father families. *Journal of Divorce and Remarriage, 28*(1–2), 203–224.

Hirth, V., & Dever-Bumba, M. (2009). Program of all-inclusive care (PACE), past, present, and future. *Journal of the American Medical Directors Association, 10*(3), 155–160.

Hobson, K. (2010). Wisdom of the ages: Sailing past 90 with lots left to do. *U.S. News & World Report.* February, 32–37.

Hodgson, L. G. (1995). Adult grandchildren and their grandparents: The enduring bond. In J. Hendricks (Ed.), *The ties of later life* (pp. 155–170). Amityville, NY: Baywood.

Hoenig, H., Taylor, D. H., & Sloar, F. A. (2003). Does assistive technology substitute for personal assistance among the disabled elderly? *American Journal of Public Health, 93*(2), 330–337.

Hofer, S. M., & Sliwinski, M. J. (2006). Design and analysis of longitudinal studies on aging. In J. E. Birren & K. W. Schaie (Eds.), *Handbook of the psychology of aging* (6th ed., pp. 15–37). Burlington, MA: Elsevier Academic Press.

Hoffman, J. P. (1998). Confidence in religious institutions and secularization: Trends and implications. *Review of Religious Research, 39,* 321–343.

Hogan, R., Perrucci, C. C., & Wilmoth, J. M. (Eds.). (2000). Gender inequality in employment and retirement income: Effects of marriage, industrial sector, and self-employment. In *Advances in Gender Research* (Vol. 4, pp. 27–54). Stamford, CT: JAI.

Holden, K., & Hatcher, C. (2006). Economic status of the aged. In R. H. Binstock & L. K. George (Eds.), *Handbook of aging and the social sciences* (6th ed., pp. 219–237). Burlington, MA: Academic Press.

Holladay, S., Denton, D., Harding, D., Lee, L., Lackovich, R., & Coleman, M. (1997). Granddaughters' accounts of the influence of parental mediation on relational closeness with maternal grandmothers. *International Journal of Aging and Human Development, 45*(1), 23–38.

Holmen, K., Ericsson, K., Andersson, L., & Winblad, B. (1992). Loneliness among elderly people living in Stockholm: A population study. *Journal of Advanced Nursing, 17*(1), 43–51.

Holstein, M. (2005). A normative defense of universal age-based public policy. In R. B. Hudson, ed., *The new politics of old age policy.* Baltimore; Johns Hopkins University Press.

Holstein, M., & Minkler, M. (1991). The short life and painful death of the Medicare Catastrophic Coverage Act. In M. Minkler & C. L. Estes (Eds.), *Critical perspectives on aging: The political and moral economy of growing old* (pp. 189–206). Amityville, NY: Baywood.

Holt, J. (1978). *Never too late: My musical life story.* New York: Delacorte Press.

Homans, G. C. (1961). *Social behavior: Its elementary forms.* New York: Harcourt Brace Jovanovich.

Honig, M. (1999). Minorities face retirement: Work-life disparities repeated? New York: International Longevity Center. Retrieved September 6, 2004, from www.ilcusa.org/_lib/pdf/publicationsminoritiesface.pdf.

Hooker, S. P., & Wicks, L. (2007). Walkable neighborhoods for seniors: The Alameda County experience. *Journal of Applied Gerontology, 26*(2), 157–181.

Hopp, F. P., & Duffy, S. A. (2000). Racial variations in end-of-life care. *Journal of the American Geriatrics Society, 48*(6), 658–663.

Horn, J. L. (1982). The aging of human abilities. In B. B. Wolman (Ed.), *Handbook of developmental psychology* (pp. 847–870). Englewood Cliffs, NJ: Prentice-Hall.

Horn, J. L., & Cattell, R. B. (1966). Age differences in primary mental ability factors. *Journal of Gerontology, 21*, 210–220.

Horn, J. L., & Cattell, R. B. (1967). Age differences in fluid and crystallized intelligence. *Acta Psychologia, 26*, 107–129.

Horna, J. (1994). *The study of leisure: An introduction.* Toronto, Ontario: Oxford University Press.

Hostetler, A. J. (2004). Old, gay, and alone? The ecology of well-being among middle-aged and older single gay men. In G. Herdt & B. de Vries (Eds.), *Gay and lesbian aging: Research and future directions.* New York: Springer.

Housell, C., & Riojas, A. M. (2006). Older women face tarnished "golden years." *Aging Today, 27*(2), 7–9.

Housemate Match. (2010). *Housemate match.* Retrieved October 19, 2010, from www.atlantajcc.org/index.php?src=gendocs&ref=SV-HS-HousemateMatch&category=Services.

Howard, D. J., & Woodring, B. K. (2009). *Labor force participation rate of people 65 years and older: 2008 American Community Survey.* Washington, DC: U.S. Census Bureau. Retrieved June 5, 2009, from www.census.gov/prod/2009pubs/acsbr08-9.pdf.

Hoyer, W. J., & Verhaeghen, P. (2006). Memory aging. In J. E. Birren & K. W. Schaie (Eds.), *Handbook of the psychology of aging* (6th ed., pp. 209–232). Burlington, MA: Elsevier Academic Press.

Hubert, H. B., Block, D. A., Oehlert, J. W., & Fries, J. F. (2002). Lifestyle habits and compression of morbidity. *Journals of Gerontology: Series A: Biological Sciences and Medical Sciences, 57A*(6), M347–M351.

Hudson, R. B. (1988). Social policy in the United States. In E. Rathbone-McCuan & B. Havens (Eds.), *North American elders: United States and Canadian perspectives* (pp. 55–68). New York: Greenwood.

Hudson, R. B. (1993). "Graying" of the federal budget revisited. *Generations, 17*(2), 79–82.

Hudson, R. B. (1994). The "graying" of the federal budget revisited. In D. Shenk & W. A. Achenbaum (Eds.), *Changing perceptions of aging and the aged* (pp. 145–153). New York: Springer.

Hudson, R. B. (1996). Changing face of aging politics. *The Gerontologist, 36*(1), 33–35.

Hudson, R. B. (1997). The history and place of age-based public policy. In R. B. Hudson (Ed.), *The future of age-based public policy* (pp. 1–12). Baltimore: Johns Hopkins University Press.

Hudson, R. B. (2004). Advocacy and policy success in aging. *Generations, 28*(1), 17–24.

Hudson, R. B. (2005). Election '04 and politics '05. *Public Policy and Aging Report, 15*(1), 1–23.

Hudson, R. B. (2007). The political paradoxes of thinking outside the life-cycle boxes. In R. A. Pruchno & M. A. Smyer (Eds.), *Challenges of an aging society: Ethical dilemmas, political issues* (pp. 268–284). Baltimore: Johns Hopkins University Press.

Hudson, R. B. (2009a). From industrialization to institutionalism: Theoretical accounts of aging policy development in the United States. In V. L. Bengtson, M. Silverstein, M. M. Putney, & D. Gans (Eds.), *Handbook of theories of aging* (pp. 531–553). New York: Springer.

Hudson, R. B. (2009b). Public policy and the Boomers: An expanding scope of conflict. In R. B. Hudson (Ed.). *Boomer bust? Economic and political issues of the graying society. Perspectives on the Boomers* (Vol. 1, pp. 113–134). Westport, CT: Praeger.

Hudson, R. B. (2010a). Contemporary challenges to aging policy. In R. B. Hudson (Ed.). *The new politics of old age policy* (2nd ed., pp. 3–20). Baltimore: Johns Hopkins University Press.

Hudson, R. B. (2010b). The Older Americans Act and aging services network. In R. B. Hudson (Ed.). *The new politics of old age policy* (2nd ed., pp. 307–323). Baltimore: Johns Hopkins University Press.

Hudson, R. B. (2010c). Theoretical approaches to the development of aging policy in the United States. In R. B. Hudson (Ed.), *The new politics of old age policy* (2nd ed., pp. 108–138). Baltimore: Johns Hopkins University Press.

Hughes, M. E., Waite, L. J., LaPierre, T. A., & Luo, Y. (2007). All in the family: The impact of caring for grandchildren on grandparents' health. *Journals of Gerontology: Social Sciences, 2,* S108–S119.

Hughes, S. L., & Bazzarre, T. (2009). Best-practice physical activity programs for older adults: Findings from the National Impact Study. *American Journal of Public Health, 99*(2), 362–368.

Hummer, B., Benjamins, M. R., & Rogers, R. G. (2004). Racial and ethnic disparities in health and mortality among U.S. elderly population. In N. B. Anderson, R. A. Bulatao, & B. Cohen (Eds.). *Critical perspectives on racial and ethnic differences in health in late life* (pp. 53–94). Washington, DC: National Academies Press.

Hummert, M. L., Garstka, T. A., & O'Brien, L. (2002). Using the implicit association test to measure age differences in implicit social cognitions. *Psychology and Aging, 17*, 482–495.

Humphry, D. (2000). *Supplement to final exit*. Junction City, OR: Norris Lane Press.

Hunt, M. E., Marshall, L. J., & Merrill, J. L. (2002). Rural areas that affect older migrants. *Journal of Architectural and Planning Research, 19*(1), 44–56.

Hunter-Zaworski, K. M. (2008). Accessible public transportation services in America. In Helal, A. (S.), Mokhtari, M., & Abdulrazak, B (Eds.), *The engineering handbook of smart technology for aging, disability, and independence* (pp. 519–534). Hoboken, NJ: Wiley.

Hurd Clarke, L. (2005). Remarriage in later life: Older women's negotiation of power, resources, and domestic labour. *Journal of Women & Aging, 17*(4), 21–41.

Hurd Clarke, L. (2006). Older women and sexuality: Experiences in marital relationships across the life course. *Canadian Journal on Aging, 25*(2), 29–140.

Hustins, K. (2001). Gender differences related to sexuality in widowhood. Is it a problem for the male bereaved? In D. A. Lund (Ed.), *Men coping with grief: Death, value, and meaning series* (pp. 207–213). Amityville, NY: Baywood.

Hutchens, R. (2003). *The Cornell study of employer phased retirement policies: A report on key findings*. Retrieved May 22, 2010, from www.ilr.cornell.edu/extension/files/20031219112155-pub1251.pdf.

Hutchens, R. (2007). Phased retirement: Problems and prospects. Retrieved August 25, 2010, from http://crr.bc.edu/images/stories/Briefs/wob_8.pdf?phpMyAdmin=43ac483c4de9t51d9eb41.

Huttman, E. (1987). Continuum of care. In G. L. Maddox (Ed.), *The encyclopedia of aging* (pp. 145–147). New York: Springer.

Ibe, H. (2000). *Aging in Japan*. New York: International Longevity Center–USA, Ltd.

IBIS World. (2011). Gym, health & fitness clubs. Retrieved June 24, 2011, from www.ibisworld.com/industry/default.aspx?indid=1655.

Ibrahim, S. A., Whittle, J., Bean-Mayberry, B., Kelley, M. E., Good, C., & Conigliaro, J. (2003). Racial/ethnic variations in physician recommendations for cardiac revascularization. *American Journal of Public Health, 93*(10), 1689–1693.

Idler, E. (2006). Religion and aging. In R. H. Binstock & L. K. George (Eds.), *Handbook of aging and the social* sciences (6th ed., pp. 277–300). Burlington, MA: Academic Press.

Institute of Medicine. (1997). *Approaching death*. Washington, DC: National Academies Press.

Institute for Women's Policy Research. (2005). *Fact sheet: Who are Social Security beneficiaries?* Retrieved August 25, 2007, from http://womenandsocialsecurity.org/Women_Social_Security/pdf/D461.pdf.

Internal Revenue Service. (2009a). *401(k) resource guide—plan participants—limitation on elective deferrals*. Retrieved May 17, 2010, from www.irs.gov/retirement/participant/article/0,id=151786,00.html.

Internal Revenue Service. (2009b). *Choosing a retirement plan: Defined benefit plan*. Retrieved May 17, 2010, from www.irs.gov/retirement/article/0,id=108950,00.html.

International Longevity Center. (2006). *Ageism in America*. New York: Author. Retrieved January 23, 2010, from www.ilcusa.org/media/pdfs/Ageism%20in%20America%20-%20The%20ILC%20Report.pdf.

International Longevity Center & AARP. (2003). Unjust desserts: Financial realities of older women. New York: ILC and AARP. Retrieved September 6, 2004, from www.ilcusa.org/_lib/pdf/unjustdesserts.pdf.

International Longevity Center–USA. (2003). The International Longevity Center–USA calls for a new Men's Health Initiative to determine the true effects of testosterone replacement therapy. Retrieved July 23, 2007, from www.ilcusa.org/_lib/pdf/andropauserel5.30.03.pdf.

Iso-Ahola, S. E. (1993). Leisure lifestyle and health. In D. Compton & S. Iso-Ahola (Eds.), *Leisure and mental health*. Park City, UT: Family Development Resources.

ITNPortland. (2010). *Dignified transportation for seniors*. Retrieved October 19, 2010, from www.itninc.org.

Jackson, J. J. (1972). African American women in a racist society. In C. Willie, B. Kramer, & B. Brown (Eds.), *Racism and mental health* (pp. 185–268). Pittsburgh, PA: University of Pittsburgh Press.

Jackson, J. S., Chatters, L. M., & Taylor, R. J. (1993a). Status and functioning of future cohorts of African-American elderly: Conclusions and speculations. In J. S. Jackson, L. M. Chatters, & R. J. Taylor (Eds.), *Aging in African American America* (pp. 301–318). Newbury Park, CA: Sage.

Jackson, J. S., Taylor, R. J., & Chatters, L. M. (1993b). Roles and resources of the African American elderly. In J. S. Jackson, L. M. Chatters, & R. J. Taylor (Eds.), *Aging in African American America* (pp. 1–20). Newbury Park, CA: Sage.

Jackson, R., Howe, N., Center for Strategic International Studies (Washington, DC), & Watson Wyatt Worldwide. (2003). *Aging vulnerability Index: An assessment of the capacity of twelve developed countries to meet the aging challenge*. Washington, DC: Center for Strategic International Studies (Washington, DC) & Watson Wyatt Worldwide.

Jacobs, B., & Weissert, W. (1987). Home equity financing of long-term care for the elderly. In J. A. Hancock (Ed.), *Housing the elderly* (pp. 151–176). New Brunswick, NJ: Center for Urban Policy Research.

Jacobs, S.-E. (1999). Being a grandmother in the Tewa world. In M. M. Schweitzer (Ed.), *American Indian grandmothers: Traditions and transition* (pp. 125–144). Albuquerque: University of New Mexico Press.

Jacoby, S. (1999, October). Great sex: What's age got to do with it? *Modern Maturity*, pp. 41ff.

Jaffe, D. J. (1989). An introduction to elderly shared housing research in the United States. In D. J. Jaffe (Ed.), *Shared housing for the elderly* (pp. 3–12). New York: Greenwood.

Janelli, L. M., & Sorge, L. (2001). Portrayal of grandparents in children's storybooks: A recent review. *Gerontology and Geriatrics Education, 22*(2), 69–88.

Jerrome, D. (1996). Continuity and change in the study of family relationships. *Ageing and Society, 16*(1), 93–104.

Ji, L. L., & Hollander, J. (2000). Antioxidant defence: effects of ageing and exercise. In Z. Radak (Ed.), *Free radicals in exercise and ageing* (pp. 35–72). Champaign, IL: Human Kinetics.

Jirovec, R. L., & Erich, J. A. (1992). Dynamics of political participation among the urban elderly. *Journal of Applied Gerontology, 11*(2), 216–227.

Joffres, C. (2002). Barriers to residential planning: Perspectives from selected older parents caring for adult offspring with lifelong disabilities. *Canadian Journal on Aging, 21*(2), 303–311.

Jogerst, G. J., Daly, J. M., Brinig, M. F., Dawson, J. D., Schmuch, G. A., & Ingram, J. G. (2003). Domestic elder abuse and the law. *American Journal of Public Health, 93*(12), 2131–2136.

John, R. (1994). The state of research on American Indian elders' health, income security, and social supports. In J. S. Jackson (Ed.), *Minority elders: Five goals toward building a public policy base* (2nd ed., pp. 46–58). Washington, DC: Gerontological Society of America.

John, R., Hennessy, C. H., & Denny, C. H. (1999). Preventing chronic illness and disability among Native American elders. In M. L. Wykle & A. B. Ford (Eds.), *Serving minority elders in the 21st century* (p. 51). New York: Springer.

Johnson, C. (1999). Fictive kin among oldest old African Americans in the San Francisco Bay area. *Journals of Gerontology: Series B: Psychological Sciences and Social Sciences, 54B*(6), S368–S375.

Johnson, C. L. (1992, Summer). Divorced and reconstituted families: Effects on the older generation. *Generations*, pp. 17–20.

Johnson, C. L. (2000). Kinship and gender. In D. H. Demo, K. R. Allen, & M. A. Fine (Eds.), *Handbook of family diversity* (pp. 128–148). New York: Oxford University Press.

Johnson, C. L., & Barer, B. M. (1990). Families and networks among older inner-city African Americans. *The Gerontologist, 30*(6), 726–733.

Johnson, J. C., & Smith, N. H. (2002). Health and social issues associated with racial, ethnic, and cultural disparities. *Generations, 26*(3), 25–32.

Johnson, K. S., Kuchibhatia, M., & Tulsky, J. A. (2008). What explains racial differences in the use of advance directives and attitudes toward hospice care? *Journal of the American Geriatrics Society, 56*(10), 1953–1958. Retrieved July 22, 2010, from www3.interscience.wiley.com/journal/121394326/abstract.

Johnson, M. L. (2009). Spirituality, finitude, and theories of the life span. In V. L. Bengtson, M. Silverstein, M. M. Putney, & D. Gans (Eds.), *Handbook of theories of aging* (pp. 659–674). New York: Springer.

Johnson, N. E. (2000). The racial crossover in comorbidity, disability, and mortality. *Demography, 37*(3), 267–284.

Johnson, R. W. (2008, December 17). *How is the recession affecting older workers?* Fact sheet on retirement policy. Washington, DC: Urban Institute. Retrieved July 16, 2011, from www.urban.org/publications/411804.html.

Johnson, R. W., & Lo Sasso, A. T. (2000). *Parental care at midlife: Balancing work and family responsibilities near retirement.* Retirement Project Brief No. 9. Washington, DC: The Urban Institute.

Johnson, R. W., & Mommaerts, C. (2010). *Will health care costs bankrupt aging boomers?* Washington, DC: The Urban Institute.

Johnson, R. W., & Schaner, S. G. (2005a, July). Many older Americans engage in caregiving activities. The Retirement Project. The Urban Institute. *Perspectives on Productive Aging, 3.* Retrieved October 6, 2007, from www.urban.org/UploadedPDF/311203_Perspectives3.pdf.

Johnson, R. W., & Schaner, S. G. (2005b, September). Value of unpaid activities by older Americans tops $160 billion per year. The Retirement Project. The Urban Institute. *Perspectives on Productive Aging, 4.* Retrieved October 6, 2007, from www.urban.org/UploadedPDF/311227_older_americancs.pdf.

Johnson, R. W., & Soto, M. (2009). *50+ Hispanic workers: A growing segment of the U.S. workforce.* Washington, DC: AARP Knowledge Management.

Johnson, T. (2006, December 13). China fears aging population will strain benefits system. *San Jose Mercury News*, pp. 20A.

Joint Center for Housing Studies of Harvard University. (2009). *The state of the nation's housing 2009.* Cambridge, MA: President and Fellows of Harvard College.

Jones, A. L., Dwyer, L. L., Bercovitz, A. R., & Strahan, G. W. (2009). *The National Nursing Home Survey: 2004 overview.* National Center for Health Statistics. *Vital and Health Statistics, 13*(167).

Jones, R. N., Marcantonio, E. R., & Rabinowitz, T. (2003). Prevalence and correlates of recognized depression in U.S. nursing homes. *Journal of the American Geriatric Society, 51*(10), 1404–1409.

Jones, S., & Fox, S. (2009). *Generations online in 2009.* Retrieved July 19, 2010, from www.pewinternet.org/Reports/2009/Generations-Online-in-2009.aspx.

Jones, T. C., & Nystrom, N. M. (2002). Looking back . . . looking forward: Addressing the lives of lesbians 55 and older. *Journal of Women and Aging, 14*(3–4), 59–76.

Jordan-Marsh, M., & Harden, J.T. (2005). Fictive kin. *Journal of Gerontological Nursing, 31*(2), 25–31.

Jorenby, D. E. (2001). Smoking cessation strategies for the 21st century. *Circulation, 104,* e51. Retrieved December 2, 2006, from http://circ.ahajournals.org/cgi/content/full/104/11/e51.

Jovanis, P. P. (2003). Macrointerventions: Roads, transportation systems, traffic calming, and vehicle design. In K. W. Schaie, H.-W. Wahl, H. Mollenkopf, & F. Oswald (Eds.). *Aging independently: Living arrangements and mobility* (pp. 234–247). New York: Springer.

Jung, C. G. (1976). The stages of life. In J. Campbell (Ed.), *The portable Jung.* Harmondsworth, England: Penguin.

Kahana, E., & Kahana, B. (2003). Contextualizing successful aging: New directions in an age-old search. In R. A. Settersten (Ed.), *Invitation to the life course: Toward new understandings of later life* (pp. 225–255). Amityville, NY: Baywood.

Kahana, E., Kahana, B., & Kercher, K. (2003). Emerging lifestyles and proactive options for successful aging. *Ageing International, 28*(2), 155–180.

Kahn, K. L., Draper, D., Keeler, E. B., Rogers, W. H., & Rubenstein, L. V. (1992). *Effects of the DRG-based prospective payment system on quality of care for hospitalized Medicare patients: Final report.* Report prepared by RAND, Santa Monica, CA, for the Health Care Financing Administration.

Kail, B. L., Quadagno, J., & Keene, J. R. (2009). The political economy perspective of aging. In V. L. Bengtson, M. Silverstein, M. M. Putney, & D. Gans (Eds.), *Handbook of theories of aging* (pp. 555–571). *New York: Springer.*

Kaiser Commission. (2004). *Uninsured workers in America.* The Kaiser Commission on Medicaid and Uninsured Workers. Retrieved August 14, 2004, from www.kff.org/uninsured/7117.cfm.

Kaiser Family Foundation. (2003). *The Kaiser Family Foundation DC Health Care Access Survey, 2003.* Retrieved December, 29, 2004, from www.kff.org/minority health/loader.cfm?url=/commonspot/security/getfile.cfm&PageID=23624.

Kaiser Family Foundation and Health Research & Education Trust. (2009). *Employer health benefits: 2009 summary of findings.* Retrieved April 25, 2010, from http://ehbs.kff.org/pdf/2009/7937.pdf.

Kaiser Slides. Kaiser Commission on Medicaid and the Uninsured. (2010). *Medicaid expenditures by service, 2008.* Retrieved October 10, 2010, from http://facts.kff.org/chart.aspx?ch=472.

Kalish, R. A. (1979). The new ageism and the failure models: A polemic. *The Gerontologist, 19,* 398–402.

Kamel, H. K., & Hajjar, R. R. (2003). Sexuality in the nursing home, part 2: managing abnormal behavior—legal and ethical issues. *Journal of the American Medical Directors Association, 4,* 203–206.

Kane, R. A., & Kane, R. L. (1987). *Long-term care: Principles, programs and policies.* New York: Springer.

Kane, R. A., & Wilson, K. B. (1993). *Assisted living in the United States: A new paradigm for residential care for frail older persons?* Report. AARP, Public Policy Institute.

Kane, R. L. (1991). SHMO outlook: Is the cup half full or half empty? Comments in response to "Adding long-term care to Medicare: The Social HMO experience." *Journal of Aging and Social Policy, 3*(4), 89–92.

Kane, R. L. (1999). Setting the PACE in chronic care. *Contemporary Gerontology: A Journal of Reviews and Critical Discourse, 6*(2), 47–50.

Kane, R. L., Arling, G., Mueller, C., Heid, R., & Cooke, V. (2007). A quality-based payment strategy for nursing home care in Minnesota. *The Gerontologist, 47*(1), 108–115.

Kane, R. L., Illston, L. H., & Miller, N. A. (1992). Qualitative analysis of the program of all-inclusive care for the elderly (PACE). *The Gerontologist, 32*(6), 771–780.

Kane, R. L., & Kane, R. A. (2001). Emerging issues in chronic care. In R. H. Binstock & L. K. George (Eds.), *Handbook of aging and the social sciences* (5th ed., pp. 406–425). San Diego, CA: Academic Press.

Kang, T. S., & Kang, G. E. (1983). Adjustment patterns of the Korean-American elderly: Case studies of ideal types. *Journal of Minority Aging, 8*(1–2), 47–55.

Kaplan, F. S. (1987). *Osteoporosis: Pathophysiology and prevention.* Clinical Symposia, No. 4 (Canada). Mississauga, ON: Ciba-Geigy.

Karlawish, J. (2004). Ethics of research in dementia. In S. Gauthier, P. Scheltens, & J. L. Cummings (Eds.), *Alzheimer's disease and related disorders annual 2004* (pp. 123–136). London: Martin Dunitz.

Karlsson, S. G., & Borell, K. (2005). Home of their own. Women's boundary work in LAT-relationships. *Journal of Aging Studies, 19*(1), 73–84.

Karmarkar, A., Chavez, E., & Cooper, R. A. (2008). Technology for successful aging and disabilities. In Helal, A. (S.), Mokhtari, M., & Abdulrazak, B (Eds.), *The engineering handbook of smart technology for aging, disability, and independence* (pp. 29–48). Hoboken, NJ: Wiley.

Kart, C. S. (1990). Diversity among aged African American males. In Z. Harel, E. A. McKinney, & M. Williams (Eds.), *African American aged: Understanding diversity and service needs* (pp. 100–113). Newbury Park, CA: Sage.

Kassner, E. [Updated by Lina Walker] (2009). LTCI fact sheet 2009. Washington, DC: AARP Public Policy Institute. Retrieved May 1, 2010, from www.aarp.org/research/ppi/ltc/ltc-ins/articles/LTCI_fact_sheet_2009_08.html www.aarp.org/ppi.

Kastenbaum, R. (1993b). Encrusted elders: Arizona and the political spirit of postmodern aging. In T. R. Cole, W. A. Achenbaum, P. L. Jakobi, & R. Kastenbaum (Eds.), *Voices and visions of aging: Toward a critical gerontology* (pp. 160–183). New York: Springer.

Kastenbaum, R. J. (1999). Foreword. In B. de Vries (Ed.), *End of life issues* (pp. xv–xvii). New York: Springer.

Kastenbaum, R. J. (2001). *Death, society, and human experience*. Boston: Allyn & Bacon.

Kastenbaum, R. J., & Candy, S. (1973). The four percent fallacy: A methodological and empirical critique of extended care facility program statistics. *Aging and Human Development, 4,* 15–21.

Katz, S. (2001–2002). Growing older without aging? Positive aging, anti-ageism, and anti-aging. *Generations, 25*(4), 27–32.

Katz, S. (2003). Critical gerontological theory: Intellectual fieldwork and the nomadic life of ideas. In S. Biggs, A. Lowenstein, & J. Hendricks (Eds.), *The need for theory: Critical approaches to social gerontology* (pp. 15–31). Amityville, NY: Baywood.

Katz, S. (2008). Thinking of age: personal reflections on critical gerontology. *Journal of Aging Studies, 22*(2), 140–146.

Katz, S., & Marshall, B. (2003). New sex for old: Lifestyle consumerism, and the ethics of aging well. *Journal of Aging Studies, 17*(1), 3–16.

Kaufman, A. V., Scogin, F. R., Burgio, L. D., Morthland, M. P., & Ford, B. K. (2007). Providing mental health services to older people living in rural communities. *Journal of Gerontological Social Work, 48*(3), 349–365.

Kaufman, S. R. (1993, Spring/Summer). Reflections on "the ageless self." *Generations*, pp. 13–16.

Kaufman, S. R. (2002). Commentary: Hospital experience and meaning at the end of life. *The Gerontologist, 42*(Special Issue 3), 34–39.

Keating, N. C., Fast, J. E., Connidis, A., Penning, M., & Keefe, J. (1997). Bridging policy and research in eldercare. *Canadian Journal on Aging/Canadian Public Policy, 16*(Suppl.), 22–41.

Keefe, J. M., & Fancey, P. (2000). Care continues: Responsibility for elderly relatives before and after admission to a long-term care facility. *Family Relations, 49*(3), 235–244.

Keefe, J. M., & Fancey, P. J. (2002). Work and eldercare: Reciprocity between older mothers and their employed daughters. *Canadian Journal on Aging, 21*(2), 229–241.

Keegan, C., Gross, S., Fisher, L., & Remez, S. (2002). *Boomers at midlife: The AARP Life Stage Study.* Washington, DC: AARP.

Keith, A. (2004) *Aging is not an option.* Plano, TX: Ageless Publishing.

Kellerman, V. (1994, April 24). Other end of spectrum: AIDS strikes elderly. *New York Times,* pp. L1, 12.

Kelley-Moore, J. A., & Ferraro, K. F. (2004). Black/white disability gap: Persistent inequality in later life? *Journals of Gerontology: Series B: Psychological Sciences and Social Sciences, 59B*(1), S34–S43.

Kelly, J. R. (1993). Varieties of activity. In J. R. Kelly (Ed.), *Activity and aging* (pp. 119–124). Newbury Park, CA: Sage.

Kemp, C. (2004). "Grand" expectations: The experiences of grandparents and adult grandchildren. *Canadian Journal of Sociology, 29*(4), 499–525.

Kemp, C. (2005). Dimensions of grandparent–adult grandchild relationships: From family ties to intergenerational friendships. *Canadian Journal on Aging, 24*(2), 161–178.

Kemp, C. (2008). Negotiating transitions in later life: Married couples in assisted living. *Journal of Applied Gerontology, 27*(3), 231–251.

Kemp, C. L., & Denton, M. (2003). The allocation of responsibility for later life: Canadian reflections on the roles of individuals, government, employers, and families. *Ageing and Society, 23*(6), 737–760.

Kemper, P., Brown, R., Carcagno, G. J., Applebaum, R. A., Christianson, J. B., Corson, W., et al. (1998). The evaluation of the National Long-Term Care Demonstration. *Health Services Research, 23*(1), special issue.

Kemper, P., Spillman, B., & Murtaugh, C. (1991). A lifetime perspective on proposals for financing nursing home care. *Inquiry, 28*(4), 333–344.

Kendis, R. J. (1989). *An attitude of gratitude: The adaptation to aging of the elderly Japanese in America.* New York: AMS Press.

Kenen, J. (2007). Big idea: The comfort connection. *AARP: The Magazine.* Retrieved November 12, 2007, from www.aarpmagazine.org/health/big_idea_palliative_care.html.

Kerschner, P. A. (Ed.). (1976). *Advocacy and age: Issues, experiences, strategies.* Los Angeles: Ethel Percy Andrus Gerontology Center.

Kim, J., & Lauderdale, D. S. (2002). The role of community context in immigrant elderly living arrangements: Koran American elderly. *Research on Aging 24*(6), 630–653.

Kim, P. K. H., & Kim, J. S. (1989). Curriculum development for social work with Asian-American elderly. *Gerontology and Geriatrics Education, 10,* 89–98.

Kinder, P. D. (2010). *Missouri Silver Haired Legislature directory.* Missouri Department of Health and Senior Services. Retrieved August 1, 2010, from www.dhss.mo.gov/SilverHaired/SHLPictureDirectory.pdf.

King, V., & Scott, M. E. (2005). A comparison of cohabiting relationships among older and younger adults. *Journal of Marriage and Family, 67*(2), 271–285.

Kinsella, K., & Velkoff, V. A. (2001). An aging world: 2001. U.S. Census Bureau, Series P95/01–1. Washington, DC: U.S. Government Printing Office. Retrieved February 10, 2005, www.census.gov/prod/2001pubs/p95-01-1.pdf.

Kirk, A. B., Waldrop, D. P., & Rittner, B. A. (2001). More than a meal: The relationship between social support and quality of life in daytime meal program participants. *Journal of Gerontological Social Work, 35*(1), 3–20.

Kivett, V. R. (1993). Grandparenting: Racial comparisons of the grandmother role: Implications for strengthening the family support system of older black women. *Family Relations, 42*(2), 165–172.

Klees, B. S., Wolfe, C. J., & Curtis, C. A. (2009a). Brief summaries of Medicare and Medicaid. *Health Care Financing*

Review, 2009 statistical supplement. Washington, DC: Centers for Medicare and Medicaid Services, Department of Health and Human Services. Retrieved May 1, 2010, from www.cms.gov/MedicareMedicaidStatSupp/downloads/2009BriefSummaries.pdf.

Klees, B. S., Wolfe, C. J., & Curtis, C. A. (2009b). Brief summaries of Medicare and Medicaid. Title XVIII and Title XIX of The Social Security Act. Baltimore: Office of the Actuary, Centers for Medicare & Medicaid Services, Department of Health and Human Services. Retrieved September 5, 2010, from www.cms.gov/MedicareProgramRatesStats/downloads/MedicareMedicaidSummaries2009.pdf.

Kleyman, P. (2002). Journalism's age-beat continues steady heartbeat despite ageist media economics. *Contemporary Gerontology: A Journal of Reviews and Critical Discourse, 8*(4), 115–118.

Knapp, J. l., & Stubblefield, P. (2000). Changing students' perceptions of aging: The impact of an intergenerational service learning course. *Educational Gerontology, 26*(7), 611–621.

Knight, B. G., & Laidlaw, K. (2009). Transitional theory: A wisdom-based model for psychological interventions to enhance well-being in later life. In V. L. Bengtson, M. Silverstein, M. M. Putney, & D. Gans (Eds.). *Handbook of theories of aging. (pp. 693–703)*. New York: Springer.

Knight, B. G., Kaskie, B., Shurgot, G. R., & Dave, J. (2006). Improving the mental health of older adults. In James E. Birren & K. W. Schaie (Eds.), *Handbook of the psychology of aging* (6th ed., pp. 407–424). Burlington, MA: Elsevier Academic Press.

Knight, J., & Traphagan, J. W. (2003). The study of the family in Japan: Integrating anthropological and demographic approaches. In J. W. Traphagan & J. Knight (Eds.), *Demographic change and the family in Japan's aging society* (pp. 3–24). Albany: State University of New York Press.

Koch, T. (2000). *Age speaks for itself: Silent voices of the elderly.* Westport, CT: Praeger.

Kochera, A., Straight, A., & Guterbock, T. (2005). *Beyond 50.05: A report to the nation on livable communities; creating environments for successful aging.* Washington, DC: AARP.

Koff, T. H., & Park, R. W. (1993). *Aging and public policy: Bonding the generations.* Amityville, NY: Baywood.

Kohli, M. (2006). Aging and justice. In R. H. Binstock & L. K. George (Eds.), *Handbook of aging and the social sciences* (6th ed., pp. 456–478). Burlington, MA: Academic Press.

Kolb, P. J. (2000). Continuing to care: Black and Latina daughters' assistance to their mothers in nursing homes. *Affilia, 15*(4), 502–525.

Koncelik, J. A. (2003). The human factors of aging and the micro-environment: Personal surroundings, technology and product development. *Journal of Housing for the Elderly, 17*(2), 117–134.

Koppen, J. (2010). *Social media and technology use among adults 50+.* Washington, DC: AARP.

Koppen, J., & Anderson, G. (2007). *Thoughts on the afterlife among U.S. adults 50+.* Washington, DC: AARP. Retrieved July 31, 2010, from http://assets.aarp.org/rgcenter/general/afterlife.pdf.

Koppen, J., & Anderson, G. (2008). *Retired spouses: A national survey of adults 55–75.* Washington, DC: AARP, Knowledge Management.

Korczyk, S. M., & Public Policy Institute, AARP. (2002). Back to which future: The U.S. aging crisis revisited. Washington, DC: Public Policy Institute, AARP.

Kornhaber, A. (2002). *The grandparent guide.* Chicago: Contemporary Books.

Koster, J., & Prather, J. (1999, April). *Around the world: Canada.* AARP Global Aging e-Report. Email communication.

Krakauer, E. L., Crenner, C., & Fox, K. (2002). Barriers to optimum end-of-life care for minority patients. *Journal of the American Geriatrics Society, 50*(1), 182–190.

Kramer, A. F., Babiani, M., & Colcombe, S. J. (2006). Contributions of cognitive neuroscience to the understanding of behavior and aging. In J. E. Birren & K. W. Schaie (Eds.), *Handbook of the psychology of aging* (6th ed., pp. 57–83). Burlington, MA: Elsevier Academic Press.

Kramer, D. A. (2003). The ontogeny of wisdom in its variations. In J. Demick & C. Andreoletti (Eds.), *Handbook of adult development* (pp. 131–151). New York: Kluwer Academic.

Kramer, J. B. (1992). Serving American Indian elderly in cities: An invisible minority. *Aging, 363–364*, 48–51.

Krampe, R. T., & Ericsson, K. A. (1996). Maintaining excellence: Deliberate practice and elite performance in younger and older pianists. *Journal of Experimental Psychology: General 125*, 331–359.

Kraus, H., & Raab, W. (1961). *Hypokinetic disease.* Springfield, IL: Charles C. Thomas.

Krause, N. (2002). Church-based social support and health in old age: Exploring variations by race. *Journals of Gerontology: Series B: Psychological Sciences and Social Sciences, 57B*(6), S332–S347.

Krause, N. (2004a). Neighborhoods, health, and well-being in late life. In H.-W. Wahl, R. J. Scheidt, & P. G. Windley (Eds.), *Annual review of gerontology and geriatrics: Vol. 23, 2003. Focus on aging in context: Socio-physical environments* (pp. 223–249). New York: Springer.

Krause, N. (2004b). Stressors in highly valued roles, meaning in life, and the physical health status of older adults. *Journal of Gerontology: Social Sciences, 59*, S287–S297.

Krause, N. (2006). Social relationships in late life. In R. H. Binstock & L. K. George (Eds.), *Handbook of aging and the social sciences* (6th ed., pp. 181–200). Burlington, MA: Academic Press.

Krause, N. (2007). Longitudinal study of social support and meaning in life. *Psychology and Aging, 22*(3), 456–469.

Krause, N. (2009). Deriving a sense of meaning in late life: An overlooked forum for the development of interdisciplinary theory. In V. L. Bengtson, M. Silverstein, M. M. Putney, & D. Gans (Eds.). *Handbook of theories of aging* (pp. 101–116). New York: Springer.

Krause, N. M. (2006). Exploring race and sex differences in church involvement during late life. *International Journal for the Psychology of Religion, 16*(2), 127–144.

Krauthammer, C. (1996, April 15). First and last, do no harm. *Time,* p. 61.

Kreamer, A. (2007, September 10). The gray wars. *Time,* pp. 71–74.

Kreider, R. M. (2005). *Number, timing, and duration of marriages and divorces: 2001.* Current Population Reports, P70–97. Washington, DC: U.S. Census Bureau. Retrieved October 14, 2007, from www.census.gov/prod/2005pubs/p70-97.pdf.

Krueger, B. (2001). How aging is covered in the print media. *Generations, 25*(3), 10–12.

Kruk, E. (1995). Grandparent-grandchild contact loss: Findings from a study of "grandparent rights" members. *Canadian Journal on Aging, 14*(4), 737–754.

Kübler-Ross, E. (1969). *On death and dying.* New York: Macmillan.

Kuh, D., Ben-Shlomo, Y., Lynch, J., Hallqvist, J., & Power, C. (2003). Life course epidemiology. *Journal of Epidemiological Community Health, 57,* 778–783. Retrieved June 25, 2011, from www.ncbi.nlm.nih.gov/pmc/articles/PMC1732305/pdf/v057p00778.pdf.

Kuhl, D., & Westwood, M. (2001). A narrative approach to integration and healing among the terminally ill. In G. Kenyon, P. Clark, & B. de Vries (Eds.), *Narrative gerontology: Theory, research, and practice* (pp. 311–330). New York: Springer.

Kuhn, M. (1975). Learning by living. *International Journal of Aging and Human Development, 8*(4), 359–365.

Kuhn, M. (1976). What old people want for themselves and others in society. In P. Kerschner (Ed.), *Advocacy and age.* Los Angeles: University of California Press.

Kunemund, H., & Rein, M. (1999). There is more to receiving than needing: Theoretical arguments and empirical explorations of crowding in and crowding out. *Ageing and Society, 19*(1), 93–121.

Kung, H. C., Hoyert, D. L., Xi, J., & Murphy, S. L. (2008). Deaths: Final data for 2005. *National Vital Statistics Reports, 56*(10). Retrieved June 24, 2011, from www.cdc.gov/nchs/data/nvsr/nvsr56/nvsr56_10.pdf.

Kunkel, S. R., & Lackmeyer, A. (2008). Evolution of the aging network: Modernization and long-term care initiatives. *Public Policy and Aging Report, 18*(3), 19–25.

Kvavilashvili, L., & Fisher, L. (2007). Is time-based prospective remembering mediated by self-initiated rehearsals? Effects of incidental cues, ongoing activity, age and motivation. *Journal of Experimental Psychology: General, 136,* 112–132.

Kyomen, H. H., & Gottlieb, G. L. (2003). Barriers to the safe and effective treatment of late-life depression. In J. M. Ellison & V. Sumer (Eds.), *Depression in later life: A multidisciplinary psychiatric approach* (pp. 27–53). New York: Marcel Dekker.

Lacayo, C. G. (1991, Fall–Winter). Living arrangements and social environment among ethnic minority elderly. *Generations,* pp. 43–46.

Lacayo, R. (1990, October 29). The generation gap. *Time,* p. 40.

Lachman, M. E. (2000). Promoting a sense of control over memory aging. In J. N. Lahey, *Do older workers face discrimination?* Issue Brief No. 33. Chestnut Hill, MA: Boston College Center for Retirement Research.

Lachs, M. S., & Pillemer, K. (1995). Abuse and neglect of elderly persons. *New England Journal of Medicine, 332,* 437–443.

Laditka, J. M. M., & Laditka, S. B. (2000). Morbidity compression debate: Risks, opportunities, and policy options for women. *Journal of Women & Aging, 12*(1–2), 23–38.

Lafleur, D. P. (2009). *Supervisory insights.* Federal Deposit Insurance Corporation. Retrieved July 12, 2010, from www.fdic.gov/regulations/examinations/supervisory/insights/siwin08/reverse_mortgages.html.

Lahey, J. (2006). *Age, women, and hiring: An experimental study.* Work Opportunities for Older Americans Series Working Paper No. 4. Chestnut Hill, MA: Center for Retirement Research at Boston College.

Laise, E. (2009, February 27). *The incredible shrinking employer 401(k) match. The Wallet* (a blog of *The Wall Street Journal*). http://blogs.wsj.com/wallet/2009/02/27/the-incredible-shrinking-401k-employer-match/.

Lakin, M. B., Mullane, L., & Robinson, S. P. (2007). *Framing new terrain: Older adults & higher education. First report: Reinvesting in the third age: Older adults and higher education.* Washington, DC: American Council on Education (ACE).

Lamb, R., & Brady, E. M. (2005). Participation in lifelong learning institutes: What turns members on? *Educational Gerontology, 31,* 207–224.

Lamdin, L., & Fugate, M. (1997). *Elderlearning: New frontier in an aging society.* Phoenix, AZ: Oryx Press.

Land, K. C., & Yang, Y. (2006). Morbidity, disability, and mortality. In R. H. Binstock & L. K. George (Eds.), *Handbook of aging and the social sciences* (6th ed., pp. 41–58). Burlington, MA: Academic Press.

Lantz, M. S., & Giambanco, V. (2001). Key to treating older smokers? Don't quit helping. *Geriatrics, 56*(5), 58–59.

LaPlante, M. P., Kaye, S. H., Kang, T., & Harrington, C. (2004). Unmet need for personal assistance services: Estimating the shortfall in hours of help and adverse consequences. *Journals of Gerontology: Series B: Psychological Sciences and Social Sciences, 59B*(2), S98–S108.

Larkin, M. (2001). Aging brains put both hemispheres to work on complex tasks. *The Lancet, 358*(9282), 644. Retrieved

October 1, 2010, from www.thelancet.com/journals/lancet/article/PIIS0140-6736(01)05820-2/fulltext.

Laslett, P. (1976). Societal development and aging. In R. H. Binstock & E. Shanas (Eds.), *Handbook of aging and the social sciences*. New York: Van Nostrand.

Last Acts. (2002). *Means to a better end: A report on dying in America today*. Washington, DC: Last Acts National Program Office.

Last Acts Campaign. (2003). State-by-state report card on care for the dying finds mediocre care nationwide. *Journal of Pain and Palliative Care Pharmacotherapy, 17*(2), 111–115.

Lavizzo-Mourey, R., & Eisenberg, J. M. (1992). Foreword. In A. R. Somers & N. L. Spears (Eds.), *The continuing care retirement community: A significant option for long-term care?* (pp. xvii–xx). New York: Springer.

Lawlor, E. F. (2009). Medicare in the image of the Baby-Boom generation. In R. B. Hudson (Ed.), *Boomer bust? Economic and political issues of the graying society. Perspectives on the Boomers* (Vol. 1, pp. 215–225). Westport, CT: Springer.

Lawton, M. P. (1987). Housing. In G. L. Maddox (Ed.), *The encyclopedia of aging* (pp. 333–336). New York: Springer.

Lawton, M. P. (1990). Residential environment and self-directedness among older people. *American Psychologist, 45*(5), 638–640.

Lawton, M. P. (2001). Quality of life and the end of life. In J. E. Birren & K. W. Schaie (Eds.), *Handbook of the psychology of aging* (5th ed.). San Diego, CA: Academic Press.

Lawton, M. P., & Nahemow, L. (1973). Ecology and the aging process. In C. Eisdorfer & M. P. Lawton (Eds.), *Psychology of adult development and aging* (pp. 619–674). Washington, DC: American Psychological Association.

Lazarowich, N. M. (Ed.) (1991). *Granny flats as housing for the elderly: International perspectives*. New York: Haworth.

Lazenby, H. C., & Letsch, S. W. (1990, Winter). National health expenditures 1989. *Health Care Financing Review, 12*, 1–26.

Lee, G. R., & DeMaris, A. (2007). Widowhood, gender, and depression. *Research on Aging, 29*(1), 56–72.

Lee, J., Yeo, G., & Gallagher-Thompson, D. (1993). Cardiovascular disease risk factors and attitudes towards prevention among Korean-American elders. *Journal of Cross-Cultural Gerontology, 8,* 17–33.

Lee, J. J. (1992). *Development, delivery, and utilization of services under the Older Americans Act: A perspective of Asian American elderly*. New York: Garland.

Lee, J. S. (2002). Aging curriculum and research capacity in schools of social work: A national survey. *Educational Gerontology, 28*(9), 805–815.

Lee, R. E., & King, A. C. (2003). Discretionary time among older adults: How do physical activity promotion interventions affect sedentary and active behaviors? *Annals of Behavioral Medicine, 25*(2), 112–119.

Lehman, H. C. (1953). *Age and achievement*. Princeton, NJ: Princeton University Press.

Lehman, H. C. (1968). The creative production rates of present versus past generations of scientists. In B. L. Neugarten (Ed.). *Middle age and aging.* (pp. 99–105). Chicago: University of Chicago Press.

Leigh, G. K. (2000). Cohabiting and never-married families across the life course. In S. J. Price, P. C. McKenry, & M. J. Murphy (Eds.), *Families across time: A life course perspective* (pp. 77–89). Los Angeles: Roxbury.

Leitner, M. J., & Leitner, S. F. (1985). *Leisure in later life*. New York: Haworth.

Lenhart, A. (2009). *Adults and social network websites*. Pew Internet. Retrieved July 17, 2010, from www.pewinternet.org/Reports/2009/Adults-and-Social-Network-Websites.aspx.

Leutz, W., Abrahams, R., & Capitman, J. (1993). Administration of eligibility for community long-term care. *The Gerontologist, 33*(1), 92–104.

Levin, D. P. (1994, February 20). The graying factory. *New York Times,* Section 3, p. 1.

Levitt, S. D., & Dubner, S. J. (2005). *Freakonomics*. New York: William Morrow.

Levitz, J., & Shishkin P. (2009). More workers cite age bias after layoffs. *Wall Street Journal* (March 10), A1.

Levy, B. R., Slade, M. D., Kunkel, S. R., & Kasl, S. V. (2002a). Longevity increased by positive self-perceptions of aging. *Journal of Personality and Social Psychology, 83*(2), 261–270.

Levy, C., Eilertsen, T., & Kramer, A. (2002b). Hospital versus nursing home: A comparison of nursing home residents who die in the hospital rather than the nursing home. *Journal of the American Geriatrics Society, 50*, 41.

Levy, D. T., Vernick, J. S., & Howard, K. A. (1995). Relationship between driver's license renewal policies and fatal crashes involving drivers 70 years or older. *Journal of the American Medical Association, 274*(13), 1026–1030.

Lewin Group. (2001, September 19–October 3). *AoA caregiver listserv: Respite services for caregivers*. Retrieved August 18, 2007, from www.aoa.gov/prof/aoaprog/caregiver/careprof/progguidance/research/respite-services-caregiver.pdf.

LFA Group. (2009). *Plus 50: Year one evaluation report*. Retrieved July 22, 2010, from http://plus50.acc.nche.edu/docs/pr/Plus50_Year_One_Evaluation_Report.pdf.

Lichtenstein, G. (2007). *Senior fit for adventure*. Retrieved July 20, 2010, from http://senior-travel-adventures.suite101.com/article.cfm/adventure_tours_for_fit_seniors.

Lieberman, T. (2000). *Slanting the story: The forces that shape the news*. New York: New Press.

Liebler, C. A., & Sandefur, G. D. (2002). Gender differences in the exchange of social support with friends, neighbors, and co-workers at midlife. *Social Science Research, 13*(3), 364–391.

Lilly, M. L., Richards, B. S., & Buckwalter, K. C. (2003). Friends and social support in dementia caregiving: Assessment and intervention. *Journal of Gerontological Nursing, 29*(1), 29–36.

Lin, I.-F. (2008). Consequences of parental divorce for adult children's support of their frail parents. *Journal of Marriage and Family, 70*(1), 113–128.

Lincoln, Y., & Guba, E. (2000). Paradigmatic controversies, contradictions, and emerging confluences. In N. Denzin & Y. Lincoln (Eds.), *Handbook of qualitative research* (2nd ed., pp. 163–187). Thousand Oaks, CA: Sage.

Lindberg, D. H. (2005). Integrative review of research related to meditation, spirituality and the elderly. *Geriatric Nursing, 26*(6), 372–377.

Lindemann, E. (1944). Symptomatology and management of acute grief. *American Journal of Psychiatry, 101,* 141–148.

Lindenberger, U., & Baltes, P. D. (1997). Intellectual functioning in old and very old age: Cross-sectional results from the Berlin Aging Study. *Psychology and Aging, 12,* 410–432.

Lindenberger, U., Scherer, H, & Baltes, P. B. (2003). The strong connection between sensory and cognitive performance in old age: Not due to sensory acuity reductions operating during cognitive assessment. *Psychology & Aging, 16,*196–205.

Lippert, B., & Scott, Z. (2003). What's wrong with this picture? *My Generation, 12,* 48ff.

Litwak, E. (1985). *Helping the elderly: The complementary roles of informal networks and formal systems.* New York: Guilford.

Liu, L. L., & Park, D. C. (2003). Technology and the promise of independent living for adults: A cognitive perspective. In N. Charness & K. W. Schaie (Eds.), *Impact of technology on successful aging* (pp. 262–289). New York: Springer.

LiveScience. (2010). Boomers beset with disabilities. Retrieved November 6, 2010, from www.livescience.com/health/baby-boomer-mobility-disability-100408.html.

Lockery, S. A. (1991, Fall/Winter). Family and social supports: Caregiving among racial and ethnic minority elders. *Generations,* pp. 58–62.

Long, M. V., & Martin, P. (2000). Personality, relationship closeness, and loneliness of oldest old adults and their children. *Journals of Gerontology Series B: Psychological Sciences and Social Sciences, 55,* P311–P319.

Longino, C. F., & Powell, J. L. (2009). Toward a phenomenology of aging. In V. L. Bengtson, M. Silverstein, M. M. Putney, & D. Gans (Eds.), *Handbook of theories of aging* (pp. 375–387). New York: Springer.

Longino, C. F. Jr., & Bradley, D. E. (2006). Internal and international migration. In R. H. Binstock & L. K. George (Eds.), *Handbook of aging and the social sciences* (6th ed., pp. 76–93). Burlington, MA: Academic Press.

Loos, C., & Bowd, A. (1997). Caregivers of persons with Alzheimer's disease: Some neglected implications of the experience of personal loss and grief. *Death Studies, 21*(5), 501–514.

Loue, S. (2005). Intimacy and institutionalized cognitively impaired elderly. *Care Management Journals, 6*(4), 185–190.

Love, J. (2004). *Political behavior and values across the generations.* AARP Strategic Issues Research. Retrieved December 5, 2004, from http://research.aarp.org/general/politics_values.pdf.

Lovell, D. I., Cuneo, R., & Gass, G. C. (2010). Can aerobic training improve muscle strength and power in older men? *Journal of Aging in Physical Activity,18,* 14–26.

Luanaigh, C., & Lawlor, B. A. (2008). Loneliness and the health of older people. International *Journal of Geriatric Psychiatry, 23,* 1213–1221.

Luckey, I. (1994). African American elders: The support network of generational kin. Families in society. *Journal of Contemporary Human Services, 75*(2), 82–89.

Lugaila, T. (1998). *Marital status and living arrangements: March 1997.* Current Population Reports, P20–154. Washington, DC: U.S. Census Bureau.

Lund, D. A. (1993a). Caregiving. In R. Kastenbaum (Ed.), *Encyclopedia of adult development* (pp. 57–63). Phoenix, AZ: Oryx.

Lund, D. A. (1993b). Widowhood: The coping response. In R. Kastenbaum (Ed.), *Encyclopedia of adult development* (pp. 537–541). Phoenix, AZ: Oryx.

Lund, D. A., Wright, S. D., & Caserta, M. S. (2005). Respite services: Enhancing the quality of daily life for caregivers and persons with dementia. *Geriatrics and Aging, 8*(4), 60–65.

Luscombe, B. (2003, September–October). This bold house. *AARP: The Magazine.* Retrieved September 15, 2007, from www.aarpmagazine.org/lifestyle/Articles/a2003-08-28-bold_house.html.

Luttropp, N. (1995). Minnie Mouse matures. *Aging Today, 16*(4), 5.

Lynch, F. R. (2010). Political power and the baby boomers. In R. B. Hudson (Ed.). *The new politics of old age policy* (2nd ed., pp. 87–107). Baltimore: Johns Hopkins University Press.

Lynn, J. (2005). Living long in fragile health: The new demographics shape end of life care. Special report. *Hastings Center Report, 35*(6), S14–S18.

MacDougall, B. (1998). A time to grieve. *Expression, 12*(1), 1–2.

Mace, N., & Rabins, P. (1981). *The 36-hour day.* Baltimore: Johns Hopkins University Press.

MacKnight, C., & Powell, C. (2001). Effect of a home visit on first year medical students' attitude towards older adults. *Geriatrics Today, 4*(4), 182–185.

MacLean, E. (2008). *Getting through the day: A coping process of drawing upon resources while caring for a spouse with dementia awaiting long term care placement.* Master's Thesis, School of Nursing, McMaster University, Hamilton, ON, Canada.

MacNeil, R. D. (2001). Bob Dylan and the Baby Boom generation: The times they are a changin'—again. *Activities, Adaptation and Aging, 25*(3–4), 45–58.

Madden, D. J. (2001). Speed and timing of behavioral processes. In J. E. Birren & K. W. Schaie (Eds.), *Handbook of the psychology of aging* (5th ed.) San Diego, CA: Academic Press.

Maddox, G. L., & Campbell, R. T. (1985). Scope, concepts, and methods in the study of aging. In R. H. Binstock & E. Shanas (Eds.), *Handbook of aging and the social sciences* (2nd ed., pp. 3–31). New York: Van Nostrand.

Maguire, E., Frackowiak, R., & Firth, C. (1997). Recalling routes around London: Activation of the right hippocampus in taxi drivers. *Journal of Neuroscience, 17,* 7103–7110.

Mahoney, D., Tarlow, B., & Jones, R. (2003). Effects of an automated telephone support system on caregiver burden and anxiety: Findings from the REACH TLC intervention study. *The Gerontologist, 43,* 556–567.

Mahoney, S., & Rausser, S. (2007, July–August). New housemates. *AARP The Magazine, 50*(4B), 50–53ff.

Maeda, D. (2009). Japan. In E. Palmore, F. Whittington, & S. Kunkel (Eds.), *The international handbook on aging* (3rd ed., pp. 321–329). Santa Barbara, CA: ABC-CLIO.

Majerovitz, S. D. (2007). Predictors of burden and depression among nursing home family caregivers. *Aging and Mental Health, 11*(3), 323–329.

Malveaux, J. (1993). Race, poverty, and women's aging. In J. Allen & A. Pifer (Eds.), *Women on the front lines: Meeting the challenge of an aging America* (pp. 167–190). Washington, DC: Urban Institute Press.

Mancini, A. D., & Bonanno, G. A. (2006). Marital closeness, functional disability, and adjustment in late life. *Psychology and Aging, 21*(3), 600–610.

Mancini, A. D., Pressman, D. L., & Bonanno, G. A. (2006). Clinical interventions with the bereaved. In D. Carr, R. M. Nesse, & C. B. Wortman (Eds.), *Spousal bereavement in late life* (pp. 255–278). New York: Springer.

Mandemakers, J. J., & Dykstra, P. A. (2008). Discrepancies in parent's and adult child's reports of support and contact. *Journal of Marriage and Family, 70,* 495–506.

Manheimer, R. J. (2007). Allocating resources for lifelong learning for older adults. In R. A. Pruchno & M. A. Smyer (Eds.), *Challenges of an aging society: Ethical dilemmas, political issues* (pp. 217–237). Baltimore: Johns Hopkins University Press.

Manheimer, R. J. (2009). Gearing up for the big show: Lifelong learning programs are coming of age. In R. B. Hudson (Ed.). *Boomer bust? Economic and political issues of the graying society. Perspectives on the Boomers* (Vol. 1, pp. 99–112), Westport, CT: Springer.

Mann, R. (2007). Out of the shadows?: Grandfatherhood, age and masculinities. *Journal of Aging Studies, 21,* 281–291.

Mantell, J., & Gildea, M. (1989). Elderly shared housing in the United States. In D. J. Jaffe (Ed.), *Shared housing for the elderly* (pp. 13–23). New York: Greenwood.

Manton, K. G., & Gu, X.-L. (2001, May 8). *Dramatic decline in disability continues for older Americans.* Proceedings of the National Academy of Sciences of the United States of America. Cited in National Institutes of Health. Retrieved May 4, 2004, from www.nia.nih.gov/news/pr/2001/0507.htm.

Manton, K., Gu, X., & Lamb, V. L. (2006, November 28). Change in chronic disability from 1982 to 2004/2005 as measured by long-term changes in function and health in the U.S. elderly population. *Proceedings of the National Academy of Sciences of the United States of America, 103*(48). Retrieved November 2, 2007, from www.pnas.org/cgi/reprint/103/48/18374.

Markides, K. S., & Coreil, J. (1986). The health of southwestern Hispanics: An epidemiologic paradox. *Public Health Reports, 101,* 253–265.

Markides, K. S., Timbers, D. M., & Osberg, J. S. (1984). Aging and health: A longitudinal study. *Archives of Gerontology and Geriatrics, 3,* 33–49.

Markides, K. S., & Wallace, S. P. (2007). Minority elders in the United States: Implications for public policy. In R. A. Pruchno, & M. A. Smyer (Eds.). *Challenges of an aging society: Ethical dilemmas, political issues* (pp. 193–216). Baltimore: Johns Hopkins University Press.

Marler, P. L., & Hadaway, C. K. (2002). "Being religious" or "being spiritual" in America: A zero-sum proposition? *Journal for the Scientific Study of Religion, 41,* 289–300.

Marmor, T. R., Mashaw, J. L., & Harvey, P. L. (1990). Attack on Social Security. In T. R. Marmor, J. L. Mashaw, & P. L. Harvey (Eds.), *America's misunderstood welfare state: Persistent myths, enduring realities* (pp. 128–174). New York: Basic Books.

Marshall, L. (2007). Kiss of the spider woman: Native American storytellers and cultural transmission. *Journal of Aging, Humanities, and the Arts, 1*(1–2), 35–52.

Marshall, L. J., & Hunt, M. E. (1999). Rural naturally occurring retirement communities: A community assessment procedure. *Journal of Housing for the Elderly, 13*(1–2), 19–34.

Marshall, V. W. (2009). Theory informing public policy: The life course perspective as a policy tool. In V. L. Bengtson, M. Silverstein, M. M. Putney, & D. Gans (Eds.), *Handbook of theories of aging* (pp. 573–593). New York: Springer.

Marsiske, M., & Margrett, J. A. (2006). In J. E. Birren & K. W. Schaie (Eds.), *Handbook of the psychology of aging* (6th ed., pp. 315–342). Burlington, MA: Elsevier Academic Press.

Martin, K., & Elder, S. (1993). Pathways through grief: A model of the process. In J. D. Morgan (Ed.), *Personal care in an impersonal world: A multidimensional look at bereavement* (pp. 73–86). Amityville, NY: Baywood.

Martin, L. G., & Kinsella, K. (1994). Research on the demography of aging in developing countries. In L. G. Martin & S. H. Preston (Eds.), *Demography of aging* (pp. 356–397). Washington, DC: National Academies Press.

Martin, P. P. (2007). Hispanics, Social Security, and Supplemental Security Income. *Social Security Bulletin, 67*(2), 73–100.

Martinez, I. L. (2002). Elder in the Cuban American family: Making sense of the real and ideal. *Journal of Comparative Family Studies, 33*(3), 359–375.

Marx, K. (1967, orig. 1867–1895). *Das Kapital.* New York: International Publishers.

Mason, A. (2003). S.E.A.M., Stop Elder Abuse and Mistreatment: A psycho-educational program for abusers of the elderly. *Victimization of the Elderly and Disabled, 5*(5), 67.

Masoro, E. J. (2001). Dietary restriction: An experimental approach to the study of the biology of aging. In E. J. Masoro & S. N. Austad (Eds.), *Handbook of the biology of aging* (5th ed., pp. 396–420). San Diego, CA: Academic Press.

Masoro, E. J. (2006). Are age-associated diseases an integral part of aging? In E. J. Masoro & A. N. Austad (Eds.), *Handbook of the biology of aging* (6th ed., pp. 43–62). Burlington, MA: Elsevier.

Masoro, E. J., & Austad, S. N. (Eds.). (2006). *Handbook of the biology of aging* (6th ed.). Burlington, MA: Elsevier.

Matsumoto, Y. (2009). Dealing with life changes: Humor in painful self-disclosures by elderly Japanese women. *Ageing and Society, 29*(6), 929–952.

Matthews, A. M., & Campbell, L. D. (1995). Gender roles, employment and informal care. In S. Arber & J. Ginn (Eds.), *Connecting gender and aging: A sociological approach* (pp. 129–143). Buckingham, U.K.: Open University Press.

Mayer, C. (2009, March 12). Ten ideas changing the world right now: 5. Amortality. *Time.* Retrieved December 21, 2009, from www.time.com/time/specials/packages/article/0,28804,1884779_1884782_1884758,00.html.

Mayo Clinic. (2009). *Living wills and advance directives for medical decisions.* Retrieved July 22, 2010, from www.mayoclinic.com/health/living-wills/HA00014.

Mayo Clinic. (2010a). *Menopause. Definition.* Retrieved November 5, 2010, from www.mayoclinic.com/health/menopause/DS00119.

Mayo Clinic Staff. (2010b). Sexual health and aging: Keep the passion alive. *Healthy Aging.* Retrieved July 1, 2010, from www.mayoclinic.com/health/sexual-health/HA00035.

Mbanaso, M. U., Shavelson, J., & Ukawuilulu, J. (2006). Elderly African Americans as intragenerational caregivers. *Journal of Gerontological Social Work, 47*(1–2), 3–15.

McAdams, D. P. (1996). Narrating the self in adulthood. In J. E. Birren et al. (Eds.), *Aging and biography: Exploration in adult development* (pp. 31–148). New York: Springer.

McAuley, W. J., & Travis, S. S. (2003). Advance care planning among residents in long-term care. *American Journal of Hospice and Palliative Care, 20*(5), 353–359.

McBride, A. M., Gonzales, E., Morrow-Howell, N., & McCrary, S. (2009). *The case for stipends in volunteer service.* CSD Working Papers No. 09–12. Retrieved July 19, 2010, from http://csd.wustl.edu/Publications/Documents/WP09-12.pdf.

McBride, T. D. (1988). *Retirement behavior of women: Findings from the 1982 new beneficiary survey* (Working Paper No. 3063–01). Washington, DC: Urban Institute.

McCall, N., Petersons, A., Moore, S., & Korb, J. (2003). Utilization of home health services before and after the Balanced Budget Act of 1997: What were the initial effects? *Health Services Research, 38*(1, Part 1), 85–106.

McCann, L., & Ventrell-Monses, C. (2010). Age discrimination in employment. In R. B. Hudson (Ed.), *The new politics of old age policy* (2nd ed., pp. 356–372). Baltimore: Johns Hopkins University Press.

McCarty, M. (2008). *An overview of the Section 8 housing programs.* Congressional Research Service Report to Congress RL32284. Washington, DC: Congressional Research Service, Library of Congress.

McCrae, R. R., & Costa, P. T., Jr. (1990). *Personality in adulthood.* New York: Guilford.

McDaniel, M. A., Einstein, E. O., & Jacoby, L. L. (2008). New considerations in aging and memory: The glass may be half full. In F. I. M. Craik & T. A. Salthouse (Eds.), *The handbook of aging and cognition* (3rd ed., pp. 251–309). New York: Psychology Press.

McDill, T., Hall, S. K., & Turell, S. C. (2006). Aging and creating families: Never married heterosexual women over forty. *Journal of Women & Aging, 18*(3), 37–50.

McDonald, L. (2006). Gender and family—Major dimensions of retirement research. In L. O. Stone (Ed.), *New frontiers of research on retirement* (pp. 129–136). Ottawa: Minister of Industry. Statistics Canada. Cat. No. 75–511-XIE.

McDonald, L. R., Ludtke, R. L., & Muus, K. J. (2006). Health risk factors among American Indian and Alaska Native elders. *Journal of Native Aging and Health, 1*(2), 17–24.

McDonald, L. R., & Muus, K. J. (2006). Health risk factors among American Indian and Alaska Native elders. *Journal of Native Aging and Health, 1*(2), 17–24.

McDougall, G. J. (2000). Memory improvement in assisted living elders. *Mental Health Nursing, 21*(2), 217–233.

McGarry, K., & Schoeni, R. F. (1995). *Transfer behavior within the family: Results from the asset and health dynamics survey.* Working Paper No. 5099. Cambridge, MA: National Bureau of Economic Research.

McGuire, F. A., Dottavio, F. D., & O'Leary, J. T. (1987a). The relationship of early life experiences to later life leisure involvement. *Leisure Sciences, 9,* 251–257.

McGuire, F. A., O'Leary, J. T., Alexander, P. B., & Dottavio, F. D. (1987b). Comparison of outdoor recreation preferences and constraints of black and white elderly. *Activities, Adaptation and Aging, 9*(4), 95–104.

McKenzie, R. B. (1993). Senior status: Has the power of the elderly peaked? *American Enterprise, 4*(3), 74–80.

McKinlay, J. B. (1985). A case for refocusing upstream: The political economy of illness. In P. Conrad & R. Kern (Eds.), *The sociology of health and illness: Critical perspectives* (pp. 484–498). New York: St. Martin's Press.

McLeod, D. (1995). Fake bank examiners bilk the unsuspecting. *AARP Bulletin, 36*(5), 1, 14.

McMellon, C. A., & Schiffman, L. G. (2002). Cyber senior empowerment: How some older individuals are taking control of their lives. *Journal of Applied Gerontology, 21*(2), 157–175.

McMullin, J. A., & Berger, E. D. (2006). Gendered ageism/ag(ed) sexism. In T. M. Calasanti & K. F. Slevin (Eds.), *Age matters: realigning feminist thinking* (pp. 201–223). New York: Routledge.

McWhinney-Morse, S. (2009). Beacon Hill Village. *Generations, 33*(2), 85–86.

Mead, G. H. (1934). In C. W. Morris (Ed.), *Mind, self, and society: From the standpoint of a social behaviorist.* Chicago: University of Chicago Press.

Meade, M. L., & Park, D. C. (2009). Enhancing cognitive function in older adults. In W. Chodzko-Zajko, A. F. Kramer, & L. W. Poon (Eds.), *Enhancing cognitive functioning and brain plasticity* (pp. 35–47). Champaign, IL: Human Kinetics.

Medicare. (2004a). *Medicare plan choices.* Retrieved July 25, 2004, from www.medicare.gov/Choices/Overview.asp.

Medicare. (2004b). *Alternatives to nursing home care: About PACE.* Retrieved February 28, 2004, from www.medicare.gov/Nursing/Alternatives/Pace.asp?PrinterFriendly=rue.

Medicare.gov. (2007). *Types of long-term care. In-law apartments.* Retrieved October 19, 2010, from www.medicare.gov/longTermCare/static/AccessoryDwelling.asp.

Medicare Payment Advisory Commission. (2002). *Report to Congress: Assessing Medicare benefits.* Washington, DC: MedPAC.

Medicare Payment Advisory Commission. (2003). Social health maintenance organization (S/HMO): Recommendations for the future of the demonstration. Retrieved May 6, 2010, from www.medpac.gov/publications/congressional_reports/Aug03_SHMO%20Report.pdf.

Medicare Payment Advisory Commission. (2004). *Report to Congress: New approaches in Medicare.* Washington, DC: MedPAC.

Medicare Payment Advisory Commission. (2008). *Caring. MedPAC examining Medicare Hospice Benefit Reimbursement system.* Retrieved July 31, 2010, from www.nahc.org/haa/attachments/HF-June08.doc.

Medina-Walpole, A., Barker, W. H., & Katz, P. R. (2004). Strengthening the fellowship training experience: Findings from a national survey of fellowship trained geriatricians 1990–1998. *Journal of the American Geriatrics Society, 52*(4), 607–610.

MedlinePlus. (2004a). *Medical encyclopedia.* Retrieved May 7, 2004, from www.nlm.nih.gov/medlineplus/ency/article/004013.htm#Information.

MedlinePlus. (2004b). *Menopause. Medical encyclopedia.* Retrieved May 7, 2004, from www.nlm.nih.gov/medlineplus/ency/article/000894.htm#Symptoms.

Mehrotra, C. M. (2003). In defense of offering educational programs for older adults. *Educational Gerontology, 29,* 645–655.

Melenhorst, A., Fisk, A., Mynatt, E., & Rogers, W. (2004). Potential intrusiveness of aware home technology: Perceptions of older adults. *Proceedings of the Human Factors and Ergonomics Society, 48,* 266–270.

Men's Senior Baseball League. (2010). *About us.* Retrieved July 19, 2010, from www.msblnational.com/main.aspx?action=doc&doc_id=2.

Mermelstein, R., Miller, B., Prohaska, T., Benson, V., & Van Nostrand, J. F. (1993). In J. F. Van Nostrand, S. E. Furner, & R. Suzman (Eds.), *Health data on older Americans: United States, 1992* (pp. 9–21). Hyattsville, MD: National Center for Health Statistics.

Merrill Lynch. (2006a). *New retirement survey: A perspective from the baby boomer generation.* Retrieved December 14, 2006, from http://askmerrill.ml.com/pdf/RetirementSurveyReport.pdf.

Merrill Lynch. (2006b). *The 2006 Merrill Lynch new retirement study: A perspective from individuals and employers.* Washington, DC. Retrieved August 14, 2010, from www.ml.com/media/66482.pdf.

Merrill, R. M., Shields, E. C., Wood, A., & Beck, R. E. (2004). Outcome expectations that motivate physical activity among world Senior Games participants. *Perceptual and Motor Skills, 99,* 1277–1289.

Merzenich, M. (2006). Engage your brain: Improving our thinking and learning. Retrieved February 27, 2010, from www.aarp.org/health/healthyliving/articles/engage_your_brain.html.

MetLife. (2006). *The MetLife caregiving cost study: Productivity losses to U.S. business.* Westport, CT: MetLife Mature Market Institute and National Alliance for Caregiving.

MetLife. (2009). *2009 grandparents: Generous with money, not with advice. A MetLife QuickPOLL of American grandparents.* MetLife Mature Market Institute. Retrieved November 12, 2010, from www.metlife.com/assets/cao/mmi/publications/quick-facts/mmi-grandparents-generous-money-not-advise.pdf.

MetLife. (2010a). *8th annual study of employee benefits trends.* Findings from the national survey of employers and employees. New York: MetLife. Retrieved August 24, 2010, from www.metlife.com/assets/institutional/services/insights-and-tools/ebts/Employee-Benefits-Trends-Study.pdf.

MetLife (2010b). *From generation to generation: Grandparents imparting lessons, legacy, and love.* Westport, CT: MetLife Mature Market Institute. Retrieved November

12, 2010, from www.metlife.com/assets/cao/mmi/publications/studies/2010/mmi-grandparents-imparting-lessons-legacy-love.pdf.

MetLife & American Society on Aging. (2010). *Still out, still aging: The MetLife study of lesbian, gay, bisexual, and transgender Baby Boomers.* Retrieved November 11, 2010, from www.metlife.com/assets/cao/mmi/publications/studies/2010/mmi-still-out-still-aging.pdf.

MetLife Mature Market Institute. (2007). *It's not your mother's retirement: A MetLife study of women & generational differences.* Retrieved August 26, 2007, from www.wiserwomen.org/pdf_files/notmothersretirement.pdf.

MetLife Mature Market Institute. (2009a). *Market survey of long-term care costs.* Waltham, MA: MetLife.

MetLife Mature Market Institute. (2009b). *The 2009 MetLife market survey of nursing home, assisted living, adult day services, and home care costs.* Retrieved May 6, 2010, from www.nadsa.org/assets/library/292_2009marketsurveymetlife.pdf.

MetLife Mature Market Institute, in conjunction with Meyer, B. J. F., & Pollard, C. K. (2006a). Applied learning and aging: A closer look at reading. In J. E. Birren & K. W. Schaie (Eds.), *Handbook of the psychology of aging* (6th ed., pp. 233–260). Burlington, MA: Elsevier Academic Press.

MetLife Mature Market Institute, in conjunction with the Lesbian and Gay Aging Issues Network of the American Society on Aging and Zogby International. (2006b). *Out and aging: The MetLife study of lesbian and gay Baby Boomers.* Westport, CT: MetLife Market Institute. Retrieved October 4, 2007, from www.metlife.com/WPSAssets/76429144001164722419V1FOut and Aging.pdf.

Meyer, B. J. F., & Pollard, C. K. (2006). Applied learning and aging: A closer look at reading. In J. E. Birren & K. W. Schaie (Eds.), *Handbook of the psychology of aging* (6th ed., pp. 233–260). Burlington, MA: Elsevier Academic Press.

Meyer, M. H. (2010). Shifting risk and responsibility: The state and inequality in old age. In R. B. Hudson (Ed.). *The new politics of old age policy* (2nd ed., pp. 21–41). Baltimore: Johns Hopkins University Press.

Miedema, B., & Tatemichi, S. (2003). Gender, marital status, social networks and health: Their impact on loneliness in the very old. *Geriatrics Today, 6*(2), 95–99.

Milbrath, L. W. (1965). *Political participation: How and why do people get involved in politics?* Chicago: Rand McNally.

Miller, A. M., & Iris, M. (2002). Health promotion attitudes and strategies in older adults. *Health Education and Behavior, 29*(2), 249–267.

Miller, B. G. (1999). Discontinuities in the statuses of Puget Sound grandmothers. In M. M. Schweitzer (Ed.), *American Indian grandmothers: Traditions and transitions* (pp. 103–124). Albuquerque: University of New Mexico Press.

Miller, W. D., Levell, T. S., & Mazachek, J. (2004). Stereotypes of the elderly in U.S. television commercials from the 1950s to the 1990s. *International Journal of Aging and Human Development, 58*(14), 315–340.

Millett, C., Everett, C. J., Matheson, E. M., Bindman, A. B., & Mainous, A. G. III. (2010). Impact of Medicare Part D on seniors' out-of-pocket expenditures on medications. *Archives of Internal Medicine, 170*(15), 1325–1330.

Mills, T. L. (1999). When grandchildren grow up: Role transition and family solidarity among baby boomer grandchildren and their grandparents. *Journal of Aging Studies, 13*(2), 219–239.

Milne, A., & Hatzidimitriadou, E. (2003). "Isn't he wonderful?": Exploring the contributions and conceptualization of elder husbands as carers. *Ageing International, 28,* 389–407.

Milner, J. (2007). Recreation and the age wave. *Journal on Active Aging, 6*(2), 72–77.

Miner, S., & Uhlenberg, P. (1997). Intergenerational proximity and the social role of sibling neighbors after midlife. *Family Relations, 46*(2), 145–153.

Minkler, M. (1991). Generational equity or interdependence? *Generations, 15*(4), 36ff.

Minkler, M., & Estes, C. L. (Eds.). (1999). *Critical gerontology: Perspectives from political and moral economy.* Amityville, NY: Baywood.

Minkler, M., & Fadem, P. (2002). "Successful aging." A disability perspective. *Journal of Disability Policy Studies, 12,* 229–235.

Minkler, M., & Fuller-Thomson. (2005). African American grandparents raising grandchildren: A national study using the Census 2000 American Community Survey. *Journals of Gerontology: Series B: Psychological Sciences and Social Sciences, 60B*(2), S82–S92.

Minkler, M., & Roe, K. M. (1993). *Grandmothers as caregivers: Raising children of the crack cocaine epidemic.* Newbury Park, CA: Sage.

Mireles, D. E., & Charness, N. (2002). Computational explorations of the influence of structured knowledge on age-related cognitive decline. *Psychology and Aging, 17*(2), 245–259.

Missouri Department of Health and Senior Services. (2010). *Silver Haired Legislature.* Retrieved August 1, 2010, from www.dhss.mo.gov/SilverHaired.

Moberg, D. O. (1997). Religion and aging. In K. F. Ferraro (Ed.), *Gerontology: Perspectives and issues* (2nd ed., pp. 193–220). New York: Springer.

Moberg, D. O. (2001). The reality and centrality of spirituality. In D. O. Moberg (Ed.), *Aging and spirituality* (pp. 3–20). New York: Haworth.

Modigliani, F., & Muralidhar, A. (2004). *Rethinking pension reform.* Cambridge, UK: Cambridge University Press.

Moeller, P. (2009, October 7). Unique havens for an aging America. *U.S. News and World Report, 146*(6). Retrieved January 19, 2011, from http://money.usnews.com/money/personal-finance/articles/2009/10/07/norcs-unique-havens-for-an-aging-america?PageNr=2.

Moen, P., & Erickson, M. A. (2001). Decision-making and satisfaction with a continuing care retirement community. In L. A. Pastalan & B. Schwarz (Eds.), *Housing choices and well-being of older adult: Proper fit* (pp. 53–69). New York: Haworth.

Moen, P., Erickson, W. A., Agarwal, M., Fields, V., & Todd, L. (2000). *The Cornell Retirement and Well-Being Study.* Ithaca, NY: Cornell University.

Moen, P., & Roehling, P. (2005). *The career mystique: Cracks in the American dream.* Boulder, CO: Rowman & Littlefield.

Moen, P., & Spencer, D. (2006). *Converging divergences in age, gender, health, and well-being: Strategic selection in the third age.* In R. H. Binstock & L. K. George (Eds.), *Handbook of aging and the social sciences* (6th ed., pp. 127–144). Burlington, MA: Academic Press.

Mollica, R., Johnson-Lamarche, H., & O'Keeffe, J. (2005). *State residential care and assisted living policy: 2004.* U.S. Department of Health and Human Services. Retrieved October 19, 2010, from http://aspe.hhs.gov/daltcp/reports/04alcom.htm.

Molnar, L. J., & Eby, D. W. (2009). Getting around: Meeting Boomers' mobility needs. In R. B. Hudson (Ed.), *Boomer bust? Economic and political issues of the graying society. The Boomers and their future* (Vol. 2, pp. 189–211). Westport, CT: Praeger.

Monserud, M. A. (2008). Intergenerational relationships and affectual solidarity between grandparents and young adults. *Journal of Marriage and Family, 70,* 182–195.

Montenegro, X. P., & AARP. (2003). *Lifestyles, dating and romance: A study of midlife singles for AARP The Magazine.* Knowledge Management. National Member Research, Knowledge Networks, Inc. Washington, DC: AARP, Knowledge Management, National Member Research.

Montepare, J. M., & Zebrowitc, L. A. (2002). A social developmental view of ageism. In T. D. Nelson (Ed.), *Ageism: Stereotyping and prejudice against older persons* (pp. 77–128). Cambridge, MA: Massachusetts Institute of Technology.

Montgomery, A., Barber, C., & McKee, P. (2002). Phenomenological study of wisdom in later life. *International Journal of Aging and Human Development, 54*(2), 139–157.

Montgomery, R. J., & Kosloski, K. (2009). Caregiving as a process of changing identity: Implications for caregiver support. *Generations, 33*(1), 47–52.

Moody, H. R. (1976). What philosophical justification is there for educating older adults? *Educational Gerontology, 1,* 1–16.

Moody, H. R. (1988a). *Abundance of life: Human development policies for an aging society.* New York: Columbia University Press.

Moody, H. R. (1993). Overview: What is critical gerontology and why is it important? In T. R. Cole, W. A. Achenbaum, P. L. Jakobi, & R. Kastenbaum (Eds.), *Voices and visions of aging* (pp. xv–xli). New York: Springer.

Moody, H. R. (1998b). Toward a critical gerontology: The contribution of the humanities to theories of aging. In J. E. Birren & V. L. Bengtson (Eds.), *Emergent theories of aging* (pp. 19–40). New York: Springer.

Moon, M. (2005) Sustaining Medicare as an age-related program. In R. B. Hudson (Ed.), *The new politics of old age policy* (pp. 205–218). Baltimore: Johns Hopkins University Press.

Moon, M. (2006). *Medicare: A policy primer.* Washington, DC: The Urban Institute.

Moore, A. J., & Stratton, D. C. (2002). *Resilient widowers: Older men speak for themselves.* New York: Springer.

Moore, S. L., Metcalf, B., & Schow, E. (2006). Quest for meaning in aging. *Geriatric Nursing, 27*(5), 293–299.

Moorman, S. M., Booth, A., & Fingerman, K. L. (2006). Women's romantic relationships after widowhood. *Journal of Family Issues, 27*(9), 1281–1304.

Moremen, R. D. (2008a). Best friends: The role of confidantes in older women's health. *Journal of Women & Aging, 20*(1–2), 149–167.

Moremen, R. D. (2008b). The downside of friendship: Sources of strain in older women's friendships. *Journal of Women & Aging, 20*(1–2), 169–187.

Moren-Cross, J. L., & Lin, N. (2006). Social networks and health. In R. H. Binstock & L. K. George (Eds.), *Handbook of aging and the social sciences* (6th ed., pp. 111–126). Burlington, MA: Academic Press.

Morgan, J. (2007). *Accredited senior centers: A snapshot.* Retrieved September 28, 2007, from www.ncoa.org/content.cfm?sectionID=369&detail=1307.

Morgan, J. (2010). *Accredited senior centers: A snapshot.* Retrieved July 16, 2010, from www.ncoa.org/strengthening-community-organizations/senior-centers/nisc/accredited-senior-centers-a.html.

Morrell, R. W., Dailey, S. R., & Rousseau, G. K. (2003). Applying research: The NIHSeniorHealth.gov Project. In N. Charness & K. W. Schaie (Eds.), *Impact of technology on successful aging* (pp. 134–161). New York: Springer.

Morrow, D. (2003). Technology as environmental support for older adults' daily activities. In N. Charness & K. W. Schaie (Eds.), *Impact of technology on successful aging* (pp. 290–305). New York: Springer.

Morrow, D. G. (2009). A contextual approach to aging and expertise. In W. Chodzko-Zajko, A. F. Kramer, & L. W. Poon (Eds.), *Enhancing cognitive functioning and brain plasticity* (pp. 49–60). Champaign, IL: Human Kinetics.

Morrow-Howell, N., McCrary, S., Gonzales, E., McBride, A., Hong, S.-I., & Blinne, W. (2008). Experience Corps: Benefits of volunteering. Retrieved July 19, 2010, from http://csd.wustl.edu/Publications/Documents/RB08-23.pdf.

Morton, D. J., Stanford, E. P., Happersett, C. J., & Molgaard, C. A. (1992). Acculturation and functional impairment among older Chinese and Vietnamese in San Diego County, California. *Journal of Cross-Cultural Gerontology, 7,* 151–176.

Moss, M. S., & Moss, S. Z. (1984–85). Some aspects of the elderly widow(er)'s persistent tie with the deceased spouse. *Omega, 15*, 195–206.

Moss, S. Z., & Moss, M. S. (2007). Being a man in long term care. *Journal of Aging Studies, 21*(1), 43–54.

Moulder, E. (2007). The maturing of America: How local governments are preparing for a wave of retirees. In *The Municipal Yearbook*. Washington, DC: International City/County Management Association.

MSNBC. (2007). *Americans still split on doctor-assisted suicide.* Retrieved July 25, 2010, from www.msnbc.msn.com/id/18923323/.

Muennig, P. A., & Glied, S. A. (2010). What changes in survival rates tell us about U.S. health care. *Health Affairs, 29*(11), 2105–2113.

Munnell, A. (2009). *An update on 401(k) Plans: Insights from the 2007 SCF.* Issue in Brief No. 9–5. Chestnut Hill, MA: Center for Retirement Research at Boston College.

Munnell, A. H., & Quinby, L. (2009). *Pension coverage and retirement security.* No. 9–26. Chestnut Hill, MA: Center for Retirement Research at Boston College.

Munnell, A. H., & Sundén, A. (2004). *Coming up short: The challenge of 401(k) plans.* Washington, DC: Brookings Institution Press.

Munnell, A. H., Wu, A., & Hurwitz, J. (2010, September). *Why did poverty drop for the elderly?* No. 10–16. Chestnut Hill, MA: Center for Retirement Research at Boston College. Retrieved November 20, 2010, from http://crr.bc.edu/images/stories/Briefs/IB_10-16.pdf.

Muramatsu, N., Yin, H., Campbell, R. T., Hoyem, R. L., Jacob, M. A., & Ross, C. O. (2007). Risk of nursing home admission among older Americans: Does states' spending on home- and community-based services matter? *Journals of Gerontology: Series B: Psychological Sciences and Social Sciences, 62B*(3), S169–S178.

Murray, T. M. (1996). Mechanisms of bone loss. *Journal of Rheumatology, 23*(Suppl. 45), 6–10.

Murtaugh, C. M., McCall, N., Moore, S., & Meadow, A. (2003). Trends in Medicare home health care use: 1997–2001. *Health Affairs, 22*(5), 146–156.

Mutchler, J. E., & Burr, J. (2009). Boomer diversity and well-being: Race, ethnicity, and gender. In R. B. Hudson (Ed.). *Boomer bust? Economic and political issues of the graying society. The Boomers and their future* (Vol. 2, pp. 23–45). Westport, CT: Praeger.

Myers, A., & Nielson, J. (2003). Baby Boom travel emphasizes adventure and relaxation. In L. M. Harris (Ed.), *After fifty: How the Baby Boom will redefine the mature market* (pp. 55–92). Ithaca, NY: Paramount Market Publishing.

Myers, G. C. (1990). Demography of aging. In R. H. Binstock & L. K. George (Eds.), *Handbook of aging and the social sciences* (3rd ed., pp. 19–44). San Diego, CA: Academic Press.

Myles, J. (1984). *Old age in the welfare state: The political economy of public pensions.* Boston: Little, Brown.

Myles, J. (1991). Postwar capitalism and the extension of Social Security into a retirement wage. In M. Minkler & C. L. Estes (Eds.), *Critical gerontology: Perspectives from political and moral economy* (pp. 293–309). Amityville, NY: Baywood.

Myles, J. (2010). What justice requires: Normative foundations for U.S. pension reform. In R. B. Hudson (Ed.). *The new politics of old age policy* (2nd ed., pp. 64–86). Baltimore: Johns Hopkins University Press.

Nahmiash, D., & Reis, M. (2000). Most successful intervention strategies for abused older adults. *Journal of Elder Abuse and Neglect, 12*(3–4), 53–70.

Nakashima, M. (2007). Positive dying in later life: Spiritual resiliency among sixteen hospice patients. *Journal of Religion, Spirituality and Aging, 19*(2), 43–66.

Narushima, M. (2005). "Payback time": Community volunteering among older adults as a transformative mechanism. *Ageing and Society, 25*(4), 567–584.

National Academy on Aging. (1995a, May). Facts on Social Security: The Old Age and Survivors Trust Fund. *Gerontology News*, pp. 6–7.

National Academy on Aging. (1995b, October). Facts on Medicare: Hospital insurance and supplementary medical insurance. *Gerontology News*, pp. 9–10.

National Advisory Council on Aging. (1993). *The NACA position on the image of aging.* Cat. No. H71–2/5–1993. Ottawa: Minister of Supply and Services.

National Alliance for Caregiving. (2009). *Caregiving in the U.S. 2009.* Washington, DC: NAC and AARP.

National Association for Home Care & Hospice. (2008). *Basic statistics about home care.* Retrieved August 11, 2008, from www.nahc.org/facts/08HC_Stats.pdf.

National Association for Home Care & Hospice. (2010). *Basic statistics about home care.* Updated 2010. Retrieved July 1, 2011, from www.nahc.org/facts/10hc_stats.pdf.

National Association of Home Builders & MetLife Mature Market Institute. (2009). *Housing trends update for the 55+ market.* Retrieved January 19, 2011, from www.metlife.com/mmi/research/55-housing-trends-update.html#findings.

National Center for Health Statistics. (2003). *Health, United States, 2003.* Hyattsville, MD: Author.

National Center for Health Statistics. (2004a). *Fast facts A to Z.* Table 96. Nursing home residents 65 years of age and over, according to age, sex, and race: United States, 1973–74, 1985, 1995, and 1999. Retrieved December 28, 2004, from www.cdc.gov/nchs/data/hus/tables/2003/03hus096.pdf.

National Center for Health Statistics. (2004b). *Health, United States, 2004.* With chartbook on trends in the health of Americans. Hyattsville, MD: U.S. Government Printing Office.

National Center for Health Statistics. (2004c). *National Nursing Home Survey.* Retrieved September 16, 2007, from www.cdc.gov/nchs/data/nnhsd/nursinghomefacilities2006.pdf#01.

National Center for Health Statistics. (2007a). *Early release of selected estimates based on data from the January–March 2007 National Health Interview Survey*. Retrieved September 28, 2007, from www.cdc.gov/nchs/data/nhis/earlyrelease/200709_06.pdf.

National Center for Health Statistics. (2007b). *Vital and health statistics. Summary health statistics for U.S. adults: National Health Interview Survey, 2006*. Series 10: Data from the National Health Interview Survey, No.235. Hyattsville, MD: U.S. Department of Health and Human Services.

National Center for Health Statistics. (2009). *Health, United States, 2008 with chartbook*. Hyattsville, MD: Author.

National Center for Health Statistics. (2010a). *FastStats. Deaths and mortality*. Retrieved July 22, 2010, from www.cdc.gov/nchs/fastats/deaths.htm.

National Center for Health Statistics. (2010b). *Health, United States, 2009: With special feature on medical technology*. Hyattsville, MD: Author.

National Center for Health Statistics. (2010c). *Health, United States, 2009*. National health expenditures . . . and percent distribution, by type of expenditure: United States, selected years 1960–2007, Table 126, p. 397.

National Center for Health Statistics. (2011). *Health, United States, 2010: With special feature on death and dying*. Hyattsville, MD: Author.

National Center on Elder Abuse. (1998). *The National Elder Abuse Incidence Study*. Retrieved January 7, 2005, from www.aoa.gov/eldfam/Elder_Rights/Elder_Abuse/ABuseReport_Full.pdf.

National Center on Elder Abuse. (2005). *Elder abuse prevalence and incidence. What do the studies say? Fact sheet*. Retrieved October 14, 2007, from www.ncea.aoa.gov/ncearoot/Main_Site/pdf/publication?FinalStatistics050331.pdf.

National Center on Elder Abuse. (2007). *Major types of abuse*. Retrieved July 3, 2010, from www.ncea.aoa.gov/NCEAroot/Main_Site/FAQ/Basics/Types_Of_Abuse.aspx.

National Center on Elder Abuse. (2010). *Frequently asked questions*. Retrieved July 6, 2010, from www.ncea.aoa.gov/NCEAroot/Main_Site/FAQ/Questions.aspx.

National Committee to Preserve Social Security and Medicare. (2009). *Facts about Medicare*. Retrieved April 24, 2010, from www.ncpssm.org/medicare/fastfactm.

National Committee to Preserve Social Security and Medicare. (2010). *Our history*. Retrieved August 4, 2010, from www.ncpssm.org/history.

National Consumers League. (2004). New survey reveals consumers confused about, but overwhelmingly use, antiaging products and procedures. Washington: National Consumers League. Retrieved January 24, 2010, from www.nclnet.org/news/2004/antiaging.htm.

National Council on the Aging. (2000, May 9). *National study says retirement not determined by work status or age*. Retrieved September 18, 2004, from www.ncoa.org/content.cfm?sectionID=105&detail=42.

National Council on the Aging. (2010). *Senior centers: Fact sheet*. Retrieved July 8, 2011, from www.ncoa.org/pressroom/fact-sheets/senior-centers-fact-sheet.html.

National Hospice and Palliative Care Organization. (2004). *Hospice facts and figures*. Retrieved December 13, 2004, from www.nhpco.org/files/public/Hospice_Facts_110104.pdf.

National Hospice and Palliative Care Organization. (2007). *New study sheds better light on hospice use across America*. Retrieved October 15, 2007, from www.nhpco.org/i4a/pages/Index.cfm?pageID=5317.

National Hospice and Palliative Care Organization. (2009a). *Caring Connections and Google Health press release*. Retrieved July 22, 2010, from www.nhpco.org/i4a/pages/index.cfm?pageID=5946.

National Hospice and Palliative Care Organization. (2009b). *NHPCO facts and figures: Hospice care in America*. Retrieved July 24, 2010, from www.nhpco.org/files/public/Statistics_Research/NHPCO_facts_and_figures.pdf.

National Hospice and Palliative Care Organization. (2010). *History of hospice care*. Retrieved July 22, 2010, from www.nhpco.org/i4a/pages/index.cfm?pageid=3285&openpage=3285.

National Institute of Mental Health. (2009). Suicide in the U.S.: Statistics and Prevention. Retrieved March 12, 2010, from www.nimh.nih.gov/health/publications/suicide-in-the-us-statistics-and-prevention/index.shtml#adults.

National Institute of Population and Social Security Research. (2002–2003). *Social security in Japan 2002–03*. Retrieved March 15, 2004, from www.ipss.go.jp/English/Jasos2002/Jasos2002.html.

National Institute of Population and Social Security Research (Japan). (2004). *Key learning from the 2nd public opinion survey on population issues in Japan*. Retrieved March 15, 2004, from www.ipss.go.jp/English/pospi_2nd/chosa.html.

National Institute of Senior Centers & National Council on the Aging. (1993). *Making your voice heard: an advocacy manual for board members and staff of programs and services for older Americans*. Washington, DC: Author.

National Institute on Aging. (2002, June 25). *Diet rich in foods with vitamin E may reduce Alzheimer's disease risk. NIA News: AD Research Update*. Retrieved May 14, 2004, from www.alzheimers.org/nianews/nianews47.html.

National Institute on Aging. (2004a). *Hearing loss*. Age page. Health information. Retrieved April 25, 2004, from www.niapublications.org/engagepages/hearing.asp.

National Institute on Aging. (2004b). *HIV, AIDS, and older people*. Age page. Health information. Retrieved April 25, 2004, from www.niapublications.org/engagepages/aids.asp.

National Institute on Aging. (2007). *Dietary supplements: More is not always better*. Age page. Retrieved July 13, 2007, from www.niapublications.org/agepages/supplements.asp.

National Institute on Aging. (2008a). *2008 progress report on Alzheimer's Disease: Moving discovery forward.* Washington, DC: U.S. Department of Health and Human Services.

National Institute on Aging. (2008b). *Alzheimer's disease fact sheet.* Age page. Retrieved August 8, 2008, from www.nia.nih.gov/HealthInformation/Publications/hiv-aids.htm.

National Institute on Aging (2008c). *HIV, AIDS, and older people.* Age page. Retrieved August 8, 2008, www.nia.nih.gov/HealthInformation/Publications/hiv-aids.htm.

National Institute on Aging. (2009a). *Glaucoma.* Retrieved January 19, 2011, from http://nihseniorhealth.gov/glaucoma/toc.html.

National Institute on Aging. (2009b). *Hearing loss.* Age page. Retrieved January 19, 2010, from www.nia.nih.gov/healthinformation/publications/hearing.htm.

National Institute on Aging. (2010a). *Baltimore Longitudinal Study of Aging.* National Institutes of Health. Retrieved October 25, 2010, from www.grc.nia.nih.gov/branches/blsa/blsanew.htm.

National Institute on Aging. (2010bTips). *Can we prevent aging? Tips from the National Institute on Aging.* Retrieved November 5, 2010, from www.nia.nih.gov/HealthInformation/Publications/preventaging.htm.

National Institute on Aging. (2010c). *Sexuality in later life.* Age page. Retrieved July 1, 2010, from www.nia.nih.gov/HealthInformation/Publications/sexuality.htm.

National Institute on Aging. (2010d). *Menopause.* Age page. Retrieved June 24, 2011, from www.nia.nih.gov/healthinformation/publications/menopause.htm.

National Institute on Aging and National Institutes of Health. (2007). *Growing older in America: The Health & Retirement Study.* Washington, DC: U.S. Department of Health and Human Services.

National Institutes of Health. (1993). *In search of the secrets of aging.* Washington, DC: Department of Health and Human Services.

National Ombudsman Reporting System. (2003). *Data tables.* Washington, DC: U.S. Administration on Aging.

National Park Service. (2010). *America the beautiful—National parks and federal recreational lands pass.* Retrieved July 20, 2010, from www.nps.gov/fees_passes.htm.

National Quality Forum. (2006). *A national framework and preferred practices for palliative and hospice care quality: A consensus report.* Washington, DC. Retrieved July 30, 2010, from www.qualityforum.org/Publications/2006/12/A_National_Framework_and_Preferred_Practices_for_Palliative_and_Hospice_Care_Quality.aspx.

National Research Council Panel to Review Risk and Prevalence of Elder Abuse and Neglect. (2003). *Elder mistreatment: Abuse, neglect and exploitation in an aging America.* Washington, DC.

National Resource Center on Supportive Housing and Home Modification. (2004). *Home modification.* Retrieved October 2, 2004, from www.homemods.org.

National Senior Games Association. (2010). *Who we are.* Retrieved July 16, 2010, from www.nsga.com/about-nsga/who-we-are.

National Shared Housing Resource Center. (2010). *Shared housing.* Retrieved October 19, 2010, from www.nationalsharedhousing.org/.

Neal, M. B., Wagner, D. L., Bonn, K. J. B., & Niles-Yokum, K. (2008). Caring from a distance: Contemporary care issues. In A. Martin-Matthews and J. E. Phillips (Eds.), *Aging and caring at the intersection of work and home life* (pp. 107–128). New York: Psychology Press.

Neal, M. B., & Hammer, L. B. (2006). *Working couples caring for children and aging parents.* Mahwah, NJ: Erlbaum.

Neleski, R. (1995, May). A funny thing happened on the way to Elderhostel. In *Elderhostel: United States and Canada catalogue.* Boston: Elderhostel.

Neugarten, B. L., Havighurst, R. J., & Tobin, S. (1968). Personality and patterns of aging. In B. L. Neugarten (Ed.), *Middle age and aging.* Chicago: University of Chicago Press.

Neuharth, T. J., & Stern, S. (2000). *Shared caregiving responsibilities of adult siblings with elderly parents.* Retrieved November 25, 2004, from www.people.virginia.edu/~sns5r/resint/ltcstf/tennille2.pdf.

Neuman, W. L. (2003). *Social research methods: Qualitative and quantitative approaches* (5th ed.). Boston: Allyn & Bacon.

Neuman, W. L., & K. Robson. (2009). *Basics of social research: Qualitative and quantitative approaches, Canadian edition.* Toronto: Pearson Education Canada.

Newcomer, R. J., & Weeden, J. P. (1986). Perspectives on housing needs and the continuum of care. In R. J. Newcomer, M. P. Lawton, & T. O. Byerts (Eds.), *Housing an aging society: Issues, alternatives, and policy* (pp. 3–9). New York: Van Nostrand Reinhold.

Newcomer, R., Harrington, C., & Kane, R. (2002). Challenges and accomplishments of the second-generation Social Health Maintenance Organization. *The Gerontologist, 42*(6), 843–852.

Newman, S. (2003). Living conditions of elderly Americans. *The Gerontologist, 43*(1), 99–109.

Newport, F. (2006). *Religion most important to blacks, women, and older Americans.* Gallup News Service. Retrieved June 25, 2011, from www.gallup.com/poll/25585/Religion-Most-Important-Blacks-Women-Older-Americans.aspx.

New York Times News Service. (2007, March 23). China faces economic dilemma as boomers near early retirement. *Wire-International,* p. A3. Source LexisNexis Academic.

Nie, N., Hillygus, D., & Ebring, L. (2002). Internet use, interpersonal relations, and sociability. In B. Wellman & C. Haythornthwaite (Eds.), *The Internet in everyday life* (pp. 215–243). Malden, MA: Blackwell.

Nishita, C. M., Liebig P. S., Pynoos, J., Perelman, L., & Spegal, K. (2007). Promoting basic accessibility in the home:

analyzing patterns of diffusion of visitability legislation. *Journal of Disability Policy Studies, 18*(1), 2–13.

Norrick, N. (2009). The construction of multiple identities in elderly narrators' stories. *Ageing and Society, 29*(6), 905—921.

Northcott, H. C., & Wilson, D. M. (2001). *Dying and death in Canada.* Aurora, ON: Garamond.

Novak, M. (1985). *Successful aging: The myths, realities, and future of aging in Canada.* Markham, ON: Penguin.

Novak, M. (1985–86). Biography after the end of metaphysics. *International Journal of Aging and Human Development, 22*(3), 189–204.

Novak, M., & Guest, C. (1989). Application of a multidimensional caregiver burden inventory. *The Gerontologist, 29*(6), 798–803.

Novak, M., & Guest, C. (1992). A comparison of the impact of institutionalization on spouse and non-spouse caregivers. *Journal of Applied Gerontology, 11,* 379–394.

Novelli, B. (2005, December). Reimagining America. *AARP Bulletin,* pp. 5, 30.

Novelli, B., & Workman, B. (2006). *50+: Igniting an evolution to reinvent America.* New York: St. Martin's Press.

Nyberg, L., Sandblom, J., Jones, S., Stigsdotter Neely, A., Petersson, K. M., Ingvar, M., et al. (2003). Neural correlates of training-related memory improvement in adulthood and aging. *Proceedings of the National Academy of Sciences, USA, 100,* 13728–13733.

O'Brien, C., & Goldberg, A. (2005). Lesbians and gay men inside and outside families. In V. Zawilski & C. Levine-Rasky (Eds.), *Inequality in Canada: A reader on the intersections of gender, race, and class* (pp. 126–146). Don Mills, ON: Oxford University Press.

O'Brien, S. (2010). Grand travel: Ideas for travel with grandchildren. Ask.com: Senior living. http://seniorliving.about.com/od/travelsmart/a/grandtravel.htm.

O'Connor, D. (1999). Living with a memory-impaired spouse: (Re)cognizing the experience. *Canadian Journal on Aging, 18*(2), 211–235.

O'Donnell, K., & Chapman, C. (2006). *Adult education participation in 2004–05.* Table 1. p. 7. U.S. Department of Education. National Center on Education Statistics. Retrieved October 19, 2010, from http://nces.ed.gov/pubs2006/2006077.pdf.

O'Rand, A. M. (2006). Stratification and the life course: Life course capital, life course risks, and social inequality. In R. H. Binstock & L. K. George (Eds.), *Handbook of aging and the social sciences* (6th ed., pp. 145–162). Burlington, MA: Academic Press.

O'Rourke, M. (2010, February 1). Good grief. *The New Yorker,* pp. 66–72.

OASDI Board of Trustees (2009). *Highlights. 2009 OASDI Trustees Report.* Retrieved May 9, 2010, from www.ssa.gov/OACT/TR/2009/II_highlights.html#76460.

Oberlink, M. R. (2008). *Opportunities for creating livable communities.* Washington, DC: AARP.

Oduaran, A., & Molosi, K. (2009). Botswana. In E. Palmore, F. Whittington, & S. Kunkel (Eds.). *The international*

handbook on aging (3rd ed., pp. 119–129). Santa Barbara, CA: ABC-CLIO.

Office of Retirement and Disability Policy. (2009). Annual statistical supplement, 2009. U.S. Social Security Administration. Retrieved May 9, 2010, from www.ssa.gov/policy/docs/statcomps/supplement/2009/highlights.html.

Okura, T., & Langa, K. M. (2010). Prevalence of neuropsychiatric symptoms and their association with functional limitations in older adults in the United States: The aging, demographics, and memory study. *Journal of the American Geriatrics Society, 58* (2), 330–337.

Older Women's League. (1993). *Room for improvement: The lack of affordable, adaptable and accessible housing for midlife and older women.* Washington, DC: Author.

Olshansky, S. J., Rudberg, M. A., Carnes, B. A., Casse, C. A., & Brody, J. A. (1991). Trading off longer life for worsening health: The expansion of morbidity hypothesis. *Journal of Aging and Health, 3,* 194–216.

On Lok SeniorHealth. (2004). *Our vision.* Retrieved August 14, 2004, from www.onlok.org/content.asp?catid=240000182&scatid=240000189.

On Lok SeniorHealth. (2007). *Home page.* Retrieved August 18, 2007, from www.onlok.org/seniorhealth/index.asp.

Online Dictionary of the Social Sciences. (2004). *Social institutions.* Retrieved December 17, 2004, from http://bitbucket.icaap.org/dict.pl?action=about.

Onolemhemhen, D. N. (2009). Meeting the challenges of urban aging: Narratives of poor elderly women of Detroit, Michigan. *Journal of Gerontological Social Work, 52*(7), 729–743.

Onrust, S. A., & Cuijpers. (2006). Mood and anxiety disorders in widowhood: a systematic review. *Aging and Mental Health, 10*(4), 327–334.

Oregon. (2009). *2009 summary of Oregon's Death with Dignity Act.* Retrieved July 22, 2010, from www.oregon.gov/DHS/ph/pas/docs/year12.pdf.

Organization for Economic Co-operation and Development. (2009). *OECD health at a glance 2009: Key findings for the United States.* Retrieved April 25, 2010, from www.oecd.org/document/21/0,3343,en_2649_34631_44219221_1_1_1_1,00.html.

Orsega-Smith, E., Payne, L. L., & Godbey, G. (2003). Physical and psychosocial characteristics of older adults who participate in a community-based exercise program. *Journal of Aging and Physical Activity, 11*(4), 516–531.

Orszag, P. (2008). *Congressional Budget Office testimony: Growth in health care costs.* Delivered before the Committee on the Budget, United States Senate, January 31.

Orzechowski, S., & Sepielli, P. (2003). *Net worth and asset ownership of households: 1998 and 2000.* Household Economic Studies. Washington, DC: U.S. Census Bureau. Retrieved September 5, 2004, from www.census.gov/prod/2003pubs/p70-88.pdf.

Osgood, N. J., Brant, B. A., & Lipman, A. (1991). *Suicide among the elderly in long-term care facilities.* New York: Greenwood.

Osnos, E. (2007, January 30). China's getting old before it becomes rich. *San Jose Mercury News,* p. 7A.

Ostbye, T., & Taylor, D. H. Jr. (2004). Effect of smoking on years of healthy life (YHL) lost among middle-aged and older Americans. *Health Services Research, 39*(3), 531–551.

Ostrom, C. M. (2000, May 14). The war on pain; Oregon leads the nation in push to improve quality of life for chronically ill and dying patients. *Seattle Times.* Retrieved December 16, 2004, from http://archives.seattletimes. nwsource.com/cgibin/texis.cgi/web/vortex/display?slug =4021141&date=20000514&query=ostrom.

Otto, J. (2000). The role of adult protective services in addressing abuse. *Generations, 24,* 33–38.

Ovrebo, B., & Minkler, M. (1993). The lives of older women: Perspectives from political economy and the humanities. In T. R. Cole, W. A. Achenbaum, P. L. Jakobi, & R. Kastenbaum (Eds.), *Voices and visions of aging: Toward a critical gerontology* (p. 289). New York: Springer.

Owen, J. E., Goode, K. T., & Haley, W. E. (2001). End of life care and reactions to death in African-American and white family caregivers of relatives with Alzheimer's disease. *Omega: Journal of Death and Dying, 43*(4), 349–361.

Pagan, J. (2002). Home care comes of age. *Contemporary Long Term Care, 25*(5), 12.

Page, S. (2010). Poll: Health care plan gains favor. *USA Today,* March 23. Retrieved May 1, 2010, from www. usatoday.com/news/washington/2010-03-23-health-poll-favorable_N.htm.

Palmer, J., Song, Y., & Lu, H.-H. (2002). *The changing face of child poverty in California.* National Center for Children in Poverty. Retrieved November 18, 2007, from www.nccp. org/publications/pub_482.html.

Palmore, E. B. (1977). Facts on Aging: A short quiz. *The Gerontologist, 18,* 315–320.

Palmore, E. B. (1981). The Facts on Aging Quiz: Part two. *The Gerontologist, 21,* 431–437.

Palmore, E. B. (1998). *Facts on aging quiz* (2nd ed.). Springer: New York.

Palmore, E. B. (2001). Ageism survey: First findings. *The Gerontologist, 41*(5), 572–575.

Pampel, F. C., & Williamson, J. B. (1989). *Age, class, politics and the welfare state.* New York: Cambridge University Press.

Pan, C. X., Carmody, S., Leipzig, R. M., Granieri, E., Sullivan, A., Block, S. D., et al. (2005). There is hope for the future: National survey results reveal that geriatric medicine fellows are well-educated in end-of-life care. *Journal of the American Geriatrics Society, 53*(4), 705–710.

Paradiso, R., Taccini, N., & Loriga, G. (2008). Textile sensing and e-textiles (smart textiles). In Helal, A. (S.), Mokhtari, M., & Abdulrazak, B. (Eds.), *The engineering handbook of smart technology for aging, disability, and independence* (pp. 673–692). Hoboken, NJ: Wiley.

Pardasani, M. P. (2004). Senior centers: Increasing minority participation through diversification. *Journal of Gerontological Social Work, 43*(2–3), 41–56.

Park, D. C. (2000). The basic mechanisms accounting for age-related decline in cognitive function. In D. C. Park & N. Schwarz (Eds.), *Cognitive aging: A primer* (pp. 3–21). Philadelphia: Taylor & Francis.

Park, D. C., & Gutchess, A. H. (2000). Cognitive aging and everyday life. In D. C. Park & N. Schwarz (Eds.), *Cognitive aging: A primer* (pp. 217–232). Philadelphia: Taylor & Francis.

Park, D. C., & Meade, M. L. 2006. Memory: Everyday. In R. Schulz, S. L. S. Noelker, K. Rockwood, & R. L. Sprott (Eds.), *The encyclopedia of aging* (4th ed., pp. 744–747). New York: Springer.

Parkinson, D. (2002). *Voices of experience: Mature workers in the future workforce.* New York: The Conference Board.

Parmelee, P. A., & Lawton, M. P. (1990). The design of special environments for the aged. In J. E. Birren & K. W. Schaie (Eds.), *Handbook of the psychology of aging* (3rd ed., pp. 464–488). San Diego, CA: Academic Press.

Parsons, T. (1951). *The social system.* New York: Free Press.

Patel, K. (2004). Euthanasia and physician-assisted suicide policy in the Netherlands and Oregon: A comparative analysis. *Journal of Health and Social Policy, 19*(1), 37–55.

Peace Corps. (2010). *FAQ—While serving abroad.* Retrieved July 22, 2010, from http://multimedia.peacecorps. gov/multimedia/50plus/index.html.

Pearman, A., & Storandt, M. (2004). Predictors of subjective memory in older adults. *Journals of Gerontology Series B: Psychological Sciences and Social Sciences, 59,* P4–P6.

Pearson, M. (2009). *Written statement to Senate Special Committee on Aging. On behalf of the Organization for Economic Co-operation and Development.* Retrieved April 25, 2010, from www.oecd.org/dataoecd/5/34/ 43800977.pdf.

Peek, M. K., Coward, R. T., & Peek, C. W. (2000). Race, aging, and care. *Research on Aging, 22*(2), 117–142.

Peng, D., & Hui, Y. China. (2009). In Palmore, E., Whittington, F., & Kunkel, S. (Eds.), *The international handbook on aging* (3rd ed., pp. 145–157). Santa Barbara, CA: ABC-CLIO.

Penman, S. (2000). *Honor the grandmothers.* St. Paul: Minnesota Historical Society.

Penning, M. (1990). Receipt of assistance by elderly people: Hierarchical selection and task specificity. *The Gerontologist, 30,* 220–227.

Penning, M. (2002). Hydra revisited: Substituting formal for self- and informal in-home care among older adults with disabilities. *The Gerontologist, 42*(1), 4–16.

Penning, M., & Wasyliw, D. (1992). Homebound learning opportunities: Reaching out to older shut-ins and their caregivers. *The Gerontologist, 32,* 704–707.

Pennington, H. R., Pachana, N. A., & Coyle, S. L. (2001). Use of the Facts on Aging Quiz in New Zealand: Validation of questions, performance of a student sample, and effects of a don't know option. *Educational Gerontology* 27(5), 409–416.

Penninx, B., Leveille, S., Ferrucci, L., van Eijk, J., & Guralnik, J. (1999). Exploring the effect of depression on physical disability: Longitudinal evidence from the Established Populations for Epidemiologic Studies of the Elderly. *American Journal of Public Health, 89*, 1346.

Pension Benefit Guarantee Corporation. (2009). *2009 Annual management report*. Retrieved May 17, 2010, from www.pbgc.gov/docs/2009_annual_report.pdf.

Pension Benefit Guaranty Corporation. (2010a). *PBGC's guarantees for single-employer pension plans*. Retrieved May 22, 2010, from www.pbgc.gov/media/key-resources-for-the-press/content/page13542.html.

Pension Benefit Guaranty Corporation. (2010b). *Maximum monthly guarantee tables*. Retrieved May 22, 2010, from www.pbgc.gov/workers-retirees/benefits-information/content/page789.html.

Perfect, T. J., & Dasgupta, Z. R. R. (1997). What underlies the deficit in reported recollective experience in old age? *Memory and Cognition 25*(6), 849–858.

Perkins, H. S. (2007). Controlling death: The false promise of advance directives. *Annals of Internal Medicine, 147*, 51–57.

Perkins, K. (1993). Recycling poverty: From the workplace to retirement. *Journal of Women and Aging, 5*(1), 5–23.

Perl, L. (2008). *Section 202 and other HUD rental housing programs for low-income elderly residents*. CRS Report to Congress. Retrieved July 12, 2010, from http://aging.senate.gov/crs/aging13.pdf.

Perron, R. (2010a). *African American experiences in the economy: Recession effects more strongly felt*. Washington, DC: AARP.

Perron, R. (2010b). *Recessions takes toll on Hispanics 45+: Boomers particularly hard hit*. Washington, DC: AARP Knowledge Management.

Peterson, P. G. (1999, January–February). Gray dawn: The global aging crisis. *Foreign Affairs*. www.foreignaffairs.org.

Pew Research Center for the People and the Press. (2006). *Strong public support for right to die*. Retrieved July 25, 2010, from http://people-press.org/report/266/strong-public-support-for-right-to-die.

Pew Research Center for the People and the Press. (2010). *The return of the multi-generational family household*. Retrieved July 3, 2010, from http://pewsocialtrends.org.

Phillips, L. H., Kliegel, M., & Martin, M. (2006). Age and planning tasks: the influence of ecological validity. *International Journal of Aging and Human Development, 62(2), 175–184.*

Pienta, A. M., & Hayward, M. D. (2002). Who expects to continue working after age 62? The retirement plans of couples. *Journals of Gerontology Series B: Psychological Sciences and Social Sciences, 57,* S199–S208.

Pierce, T., Lydon, J. E., & Yang, S. (2001). Enthusiasm and moral commitment: What sustains family caregivers of those with dementia. *Basic and Applied Social Psychology, 23*(1), 29–41.

Piktialis, D. S. (2009). Redesigning work for an aging labor force: Employer and employee perspectives. In R. B. Hudson (Ed.), *Boomer bust? Economic and political issues of the graying society. The Boomers and their future* (Vol. 2, pp. 17–31). Westport, CT: Praeger.

Pillemer, K., & Finkelhor, D. (1988). The prevalence of elder abuse: A random sample survey. *The Gerontologist, 28*(1), 51–57.

Pillemer, K., & Suitor, J. J. (2006). Making choices: a within-family study of caregiver selection. *The Gerontologist, 46*(4), 439–448.

Pinquart, M., & Sorensen, S. (2001). Gender differences in self-concept and psychological well-being in old age: A meta-analysis. *Journal of Gerontology: Psychological Sciences, 56B*, P195–P213.

Pinquart, M., & Sorensen, S. (2004). Associations of caregiver stressors and uplifts with subjective well-being and depressive mood: A meta-analytic comparison. *Aging and Mental Health, 8*, 438–449.

Pinquart, M., & Sorensen, S. (2005). Ethnic differences in the caregiving experience: implications for interventions. *Geriatrics and Aging, 8*(10), 64–66.

Plonczynski, D. J. (2003). Physical activity determinants of older women: What influences activity? *Medical Surgical Nursing, 12*(4), 213–223.

Polacca, M. (2001). American Indian and Alaska Native elderly. In L. K. Olson (Ed.), *Age through ethnic lenses: Caring for the elderly in a multicultural society* (pp. 113–122). London: Rowman & Littlefield.

Pollak, P. B., & Gorman, A. N. (1989). *Community-based housing for the elderly: A zoning guide for planners and municipal officials*. Chicago: American Planning Association.

Polzin, S. E., & Chu, X. (2005). *Public transit in America: Results from the 2001 national household travel survey*. Tampa: National Center for Transit Research, Center for Urban Transportation Research, University of South Florida.

Poon, L., & Harrington, C. A. (2006). Commonalities in aging- and fitness-related impact on cognition. In L. W. Poon, W. Chodzko-Zajko, & P. D. Tomporowski, (Eds.), *Active living, cognitive functioning, and aging* (Vol. 1, pp. 33–50). Champaign, IL: Human Kinetics.

Poon, L. W. (1985). Differences in human memory with aging: Nature, causes, and clinical implications. In J. E. Birren & K. W. Schaie (Eds.), *Handbook of the psychology of aging* (2nd ed.). New York: Van Nostrand.

Pope, E. (2008). Highlights and implications. *Staying ahead of the curve: The AARP work and career study*. Washington, DC: AARP Knowledge Management.

Powers, E. A., & Kivett, V. R. (1992). Kin expectations and kin support among rural older adults. *Rural Sociology, 57*(2), 194–215.

Pratt, H. J. (1976). *The gray lobby.* Chicago: University of Chicago Press.

Pratt, H. J. (1983). National interest groups among the elderly: Consolidation and constraint. In W. P. Browne & L. K. Olson (Eds.), *Aging and public policy: The politics of growing old in America* (pp. 145–179). Westport, CT: Greenwood.

President's Commission for the Study of Ethical Problems in Medicine and Biomedical and Behavioral Research. (1981). *Defining death: Medical, legal and ethical issues in the determination of death.* Washington, DC: U.S. Government Printing Office.

Princeton Survey Research Associates International. (2005). *New face of work survey.* Executive summary. Retrieved September 29, 2007, from www.civicventures.org/publications/surveys/new_face_of_work/nfw_exec_summary.pdf.

Prohaska, T., Mermelstein, R., Miller, B., & Jack, S. (1993). Functional status and living arrangements. In J. F. Van Nostrand, S. E. Furner, & R. Suzman (Eds.), *Health data on older Americans: United States, 1992* (pp. 23–39). Hyattsville, MD: National Center for Health Services.

Proulx, C., Helms, H., & Buehler, C. (2007). Marital quality and personal well-being: A meta-analysis. *Journal of Marriage and Family, 69*(3), 576–593.

Pruchno, R. A., & Rose, M. S. (2002). Time use by frail older people in different care settings. *Journal of Applied Gerontology, 21*(1), 5–23.

Pudrovska, T., Schieman, S., & Carr, D. (2006). Strains of singlehood in later life: Do race and gender matter? *Journal of Gerontology SS, 61B*(6), S315–S322.

Puner, M. (1979). *Vital maturity.* New York: Universe Books.

Putnam, M. (2009). Long-term care policy as an investment in Baby Boomers and future generations. In R. B. Hudson (Ed.). *Boomer bust? Economic and political issues of the graying society. Perspectives on the Boomers. Volume 1.* (pp. 227–240). Westport, CT: Springer.

Putney, N. M., Bengtson, V. L., & Wakeman, M. A. (2007). The family and the future. In R. A. Pruchno & M. A. Smyer (Eds.), *Challenges of an aging society: Ethical dilemmas, political issues* (pp. 117–155). Baltimore: Johns Hopkins University Press.

Pynoos, J., Caraviello, R., & Cicero, C. (2009). Lifelong housing: The anchor in aging-friendly communities. *Generations, 33*(2), 26–32.

Pynoos, J., Cicero, C., & Nishita, C. M. (2010). New challenges and growing tends in senior housing. In R. B. Hudson (Ed.). *The new politics of old age policy* (2nd ed., pp. 3–20). Baltimore: Johns Hopkins University Press.

Pynoos, J., & Liebig, P. (2009). Changing work, retirement, and housing patterns. *Generations, 33*(3), 20–26.

Quadagno, J. (1989). Generational equity and the politics of the welfare-state. *Politics & Society, 17,* 353–376.

Quadagno, J. (1991). Generational equity and the politics of the welfare state. In B. B. Hess & E. W. Markson (Eds.), *Growing old in America* (4th ed., pp. 341–351). New Brunswick, NJ: Transaction.

Quadagno, J. (2005). *One nation uninsured: Why the U.S. has no national health insurance.* New York: Oxford University Press.

Quadagno, J. (2007). Book review—*Aging nation: The economics and politics of growing older in America. Journal of Health Politics, Policy and Law, 32*(5), 887–889.

Quadagno, J., & Reid, J. (1999). The political economy perspective in aging. In V. L. Bengtson & K. W. Schaie (Eds.), *Handbook of theories of aging* (pp. 344–358). New York: Springer.

Qualls, S. J. (2002, Spring). Defining mental health in later life. *Generations,* pp. 9–13.

Quetelet, L. A. J. (1835). *Sur l'homme el le developpement de ses facultes.* Bruxelles: L. Hauman et compe.

Quinn, J. F., Burkhauser, R. V., & Myers, D. A. (1990). *Passing the torch: The influence of economic incentives on work and retirement.* Kalamazoo, MI: W. E. Upjohn Institute for Employment Research.

Quinn, M. J., & Tomita, S. K. (1997). *Elder abuse and neglect: Causes, diagnosis, and intervention strategies* (2nd ed.). New York: Springer.

Ragan, A. M., & Bowen, A. M. (2001). Improving attitudes regarding the elderly population: The effects of information and reinforcement for change. *The Gerontologist, 41*(4), 511–515.

Rahhal, T. A., Hasher, L., & Colombe, S. J. (2001). Instructional manipulations and differences in memory: Now you see them, now you don't. *Psychology & Aging, 16*(4), 697–706.

Randall, W. L., & Kenyon, G. M. (2004). Time, story, and wisdom: Emerging themes in narrative gerontology. *Canadian Journal on Aging, 23*(4), 333–346.

Rao, N. (2001). *Public pension fund management in India.* Conference on Public Pension Fund Management, September 24–26, 2001. Retrieved December 20, 2009, from www.google.com/search?hl=en&q=public+pension+plan+in+India&btnG=Search&aq=f&oq=&aqi=.

Rawson, N. E. (2003). Age-related changes in perception of flavor and aroma. *Generations, 27*(1), 20–26.

Ray, Ruth E. 2003a. The perils and possibilities of theory. In S. Biggs, A. Lowenstein, & J. Hendricks (Eds.), *The need for theory: Critical approaches to social gerontology* (pp. 33–44). Amityville, NY: Baywood.

Ray, R. E. (2003b). Uninvited guest: Mother/daughter conflict in feminist gerontology. *Journal of Aging Studies, 17*(1), 113–128.

Ray, R. E. (2008). Coming of age in critical gerontology: Introduction. *Journal of Aging Studies, Special Issue, 22*(2), 97–100.

Ray, R. O., & Heppe, G. (1986). Older adult happiness: The contributions of activity breadth and intensity. *Physical and Occupational Therapy in Geriatrics, 4*(4), 31–43.

Rayman, P., Allshouse, K., & Allen J. (1993). Resiliency amidst inequity: Older women workers in an aging

United States. In J. Allen & A. Pifer (Eds.), *Women on the front lines: Meeting the challenge of an aging America* (pp. 133–166). Washington, DC: Urban Institute Press.

Raz, N. (2000). Aging of the brain and its impact on cognitive performance: Integration of structural and functional findings. In F. I. M. Craik & T. A. Salthouse (Eds.), *The handbook of aging and cognition* (2nd ed., pp. 1–90). Mahwah, NJ: Erlbaum.

Rebok, G. W., Carlson, M., Glass, T. A., McGill, S., Hill, J., Wasik, B., et al. (2004). Short-term impact of Experience Corps participation on children and schools: Results from a pilot randomized trial. *Journal of Urban Health, 81*(1), 79–93.

Redden, J. (2007, June 26). Fixes keep seniors in homes. Industry focuses on housing suitable for aging. *The Portland Tribune*. Updated October 30, 2009. Retrieved July 17, 2010, from www.portlandtribune.com/rethinking/story.php?story_id=118272195530913500.

Redfoot, D. L., Scholen, K., & Brown, S. K. (2007). *Reverse mortgages: Niche product or mainstream solution? Report on the 2006 AARP National Survey of Reverse Mortgage Shoppers*. Washington, DC: AARP Public Policy Institute.

Reeves, T. J., & Bennett, C. E. (2004). *We the people: Asians in the United States*. Census 2000 Special Reports. U.S. Census Bureau. U.S. Department of Commerce, Economics and Statistics Administration. Retrieved August 26, 2007, from www.census.gov/prod/2004pubs/censr17.pdf.

Regnier, V. (1993, June). Innovative concepts in assisted housing. *Ageing International*, pp. 46–51.

Regnier, V. (2003). Purpose-built housing and home adaptations for older adults: The American perspective. In K. W. Schaie, H.-W. Wahl, H. Mollenkopf, & F. Oswald (Eds.), *Aging independently: Living arrangements and mobility* (pp. 99–117). New York: Springer.

Reichl, R. (2005). *Garlic and sapphires*. New York: Penguin.

Reingold, D., & Burros, N. (2004). Sexuality in the nursing home. *Journal of Gerontological Social Work, 43*(2–3), 175–186.

Rendell, P. G., & Thomson, D. M. (2002). Aging and prospective memory: Differences between naturalistic and laboratory tasks. *Journals of Gerontology Series B: Psychological Sciences and Social Sciences, 57*, P3–P10.

Reuters (Health). (2005). Tension, anxiety boost risk of death. *The Epoch* Times, p. 12. October 28–November 3, 2005. Retrieved June 24, 2011, from www.daikynguyen.com/eet/print_archive/united_states/los_angeles/2005/10-Oct/28/12_EET.indd.pdf.

Revell, J. (2003, March 17). Bye-bye pension. *Fortune*, pp. 65–74.

Reverse Mortgage Page. (2010). Retrieved July 12, 2010, from www.reversemortgagepage.com/2008/11/hecm-reverse-mortgage-statistics.

Rheaume, C., & Mitty, E. (2008). Sexuality and intimacy in older adults. *Geriatric Nursing, 29*(5), 342–349.

Rhoades, D. A., Welty, T. K., Wang, W., Yeh, F., Devereux, R. B., Fabsitz, R. R., et al. (2007). Aging and the prevalence of cardiovascular disease risk factors in older American Indians: The Strong Heart Study. *Journal of the American Geriatrics Society, 55*(1), 87–94.

Ribeiro, O., Paúl, C., & Nogueira, C. (2007). Real men, real husbands: Caregiving and masculinities in later life. *Journal of Aging Studies, 21,* 302–313.

Rich, M. L. (1999). PACE model: Description and impressions of a capitated model of long-term care for the elderly. *Care Management Journals, 1*(1), 62–70.

Rich, S. (1991, March 8). 900,000 could need long-term care. *The Washington Post*, p. 2.

Richard, C. A., & Brown, A. H. (2006). Configurations of informal social support among older lesbians. *Journal of Women & Aging, 18*(4), 49–65.

Riediger, M., Li, S. C., & Lindenberger, U. (2006). In J. E. Birren & K. W. Schaie (Eds.), *Handbook of the psychology of aging* (6th ed., pp. 289–313). Burlington, MA: Elsevier Academic Press.

Riegel, K. F. (1979). *Foundations of dialectical psychology*. New York: Academic Press.

Riley, M. W. (1971). Social gerontology and the age stratification of society. *The Gerontologist, 11*, 79–87.

Riley, M. W. (1985). Age strata in social systems. In R. H. Binstock & E. Shanas (Eds.), *Handbook of aging and the social sciences* (2nd ed., pp. 369–411). New York: Van Nostrand.

Riley, M. W. (1987). On the significance of age in sociology. *American Sociological Review, 52*, 1–14.

Riley, M. W., Foner, A., & Riley, J. W., Jr. (1999). The aging and society paradigm. In V. L. Bengtson & K. W. Schaie (Eds.), *Handbook of theories of aging* (pp. 327–343). New York: Springer.

Riley, M. W., Johnson, M. E., & Foner, A. (Eds.). (1972). *Aging and Society: Vol. 3. A sociology of age stratification*. New York: Russell Sage Foundation.

Riley, M. W., & Riley, J. W. (1993). Connections: Kin and cohort. In V. L. Bengtson and W. A. Achenbaum (Eds.), *The changing contract across generations* (pp. 169–189). New York: Aldine de Gruyter.

Riley, M. W., & Riley, J. W., Jr. (1994). Structural lag: Past and future. In M. W. Riley, R. L. Kahn, & A. Foner (Eds.), *Age and structural lag* (pp. 15–36). New York: Wiley.

Rivlin, A. (2010, July 21). *The right reason for saving Social Security*. Brookings. Retrieved July 17, 2011, from www.brookings.edu/opinions/2010/0722_saving_social_security_rivlin.aspx.

Rix, S. (1993). Women and well-being in retirement: What role for public policy? *Journal of Women and Aging, 4*(4), 37–56.

Rix, S. (1999). The politics of old age in the United States. In A. Walker & G. Naegele (Eds.), *The politics of old age in Europe* (pp. 178–196). Buckingham, U.K.: Open University Press.

Rix, S. (2002). The labor market for older workers. *Generations, 26*(2), 25–30.

Rix, S. E. (2004). *Aging and work: A view from the United States.* Washington, DC: AARP Public Policy Institute. Retrieved September 17, 2004, from http://research.aarp.org/econ/2004_02_work.pdf.

Rix, S. (2006). *Update on the aged 55+ worker: 2005.* Washington, DC: AARP Public Policy Institute. Retrieved December 8, 2006, from http://assets.aarp.org/rgcenter/econ/dd136_worker.pdf.

Rix, S. (2008). *Update on the aged 55+ worker: 2007.* Washington, DC: AARP Public Policy Institute. Retrieved May 22, 2010, from http://assets.aarp.org/rgcenter/econ/fs142_worker.pdf.

Rix, S. (2009a). *Little to cheer about: Unemployment and the older worker—December 2008.* AARP Public Policy Institute. Retrieved June 1, 2010, from www.aarp.org/work/working-after-retirement/info-01-2009/fs150_worker.html.

Rix, S. (2009b). Will the Boomers revolutionize work and retirement? In R. B. Hudson (Ed.), *Boomer bust? Perspectives on the Boomers* (Vol. 1, pp. 77–94). Westport, CT: Praeger.

Roach, S. M. 2004. Sexual behaviour of nursing home residents: Staff perceptions and responses. *Journal of Advanced Nursing, 48*(4), 371–379.

Road Scholar. (2010a). *Facts about the Elderhostel Institute Network.* Retrieved July 16, 2010, from www.roadscholar.org/ein/factsheet.asp.

Road Scholar. (2010b). *Find a program.* Retrieved July 16, 2010, from www.roadscholar.org/about/what_program.asp.

Roberto, K. A., Allen, K. R., & Blieszner, R. (2001). Grandfathers' perceptions and expectations of relationships with their adult grandchildren. *Journal of Family Issues, 22*(4), 407–426.

Roberto, K. A., Teaster, P. B., & Duke, J. O. (2004). Older women who experience mistreatment: Circumstances and outcomes. *Journal of Women and Aging, 16*(1–2), 3–16.

Roberts, E., Takenaka, J. I., Ross, C. J., Chong, E. H., & Tulang, J. I. (1989). Hawaii Asian-American response to the Staying Healthy After Fifty program. *Health Education Quarterly, 16*(4), 509–527.

Robinson, T., Popovich, M., Gustafson, R., & Fraser, C. (2003). Older adults' perceptions of offensive senior stereotypes in magazine advertisements: Results of a Q method analysis. *Educational Gerontology, 29*(6), 503–519.

Robison, J., Gruman, C., Shugrue, N., Kellett, K., Porter, M., & Reed, I. (2007). *University of Connecticut Health Center.* Retrieved November 10, 2007, from www.cga.ct.gov/coa/PDFs/Part%201%20Survey%20results%20FINAL_July%202%202007.pdf.

Roff, S. (2001). Suicide and the elderly: Issues for clinical practice. *Journal of Gerontological Social Work, 35*(2), 21–36.

Roizen, M. F. (1999). *Real age.* New York: Cliff Street Books.

Roring, R. W., & Charness, N. (2007). A multilevel model analysis of expertise in chess across the lifespan. *Psychology and Aging, 22,* 291– 299.

Rose, M. R. (1993). Evolutionary gerontology and critical gerontology: Let's just be friends. In T. R. Cole, W. A. Achenbaum, P. L. Jakobi, & R. Kastenbaum (Eds.), *Voices and visions of aging: Toward a critical gerontology* (pp. 64–75). New York: Springer.

Rosenbaum, W. A., & Button, J. W. (1989). Is there a gray peril? Retirement politics in Florida. *The Gerontologist, 29*(3), 300–306.

Rosenbloom, S. (2009). Meeting transportation needs in an aging-friendly environment. *Generations, 33*(2), 33–43.

Rosenmayr, L., & Kockeis, E. (1963). Propositions for a sociological theory of aging and the family. *International Social Science Journal, 15,* 410–426.

Rosenthal, C. J. (1994). Editorial: Long-term care reform and "family" care: A worrisome combination. *Canadian Journal on Aging, 13*(3), 419–427.

Rosenthal, C. J., & Dawson, P. (1991). Wives of institutionalized elderly men: The first stage of the transition to quasi-widowhood. *Journal of Aging and Health, 3*(3), 315–334.

Rosenzweig, R. M. (1991, January). Generational conflict brewing, GSA members warned. *Gerontology News.*

Ross, I. (1995, May). Step aside, yuppies. Here come "opals." In *Elderhostel: United States and Canada catalogue.* Boston: Elderhostel.

Ross, J. L., & Upp, M. M. (1993, Fall). Treatment of women in the U.S. Social Security system, 1970–1988. *Social Security Bulletin, 56,* 56–67.

Ross, M. M., MacLean, M. J., Cain, R., Sellick, S., & Fisher, R. (2002). End of life care: The experience of seniors and informal caregivers. *Canadian Journal on Aging, 21*(1), 137–146.

Ross, M. M., & McDonald, B. (1994). Providing palliative care to older adults: Context and challenges. *Journal of Palliative Care, 10*(4), 5–10.

Ross, M. M., Rosenthal, C. J., & Dawson, P. (1994). The continuation of caregiving following the institutionalization of elderly husbands. In National Advisory Council on Aging, *Marital disruption in later life,* 23–32. Cat. No. H71–3/17–1994E. Ottawa: Minister of Supply and Services.

Ross, M. M., Rosenthal, C. J., & Dawson, P. G. (1997a). Spousal caregiving in the institutional setting: Task performance. *Canadian Journal on Aging, 16*(1), 51–69.

Ross, M. M., Rosenthal, C. J., & Dawson, P. G. (1997b). Spousal caregiving in the institutional setting: Visiting. *Journal of Clinical Nursing, 6*(6), 473–483.

Roth, D. (2005). Culture change in long-term care: Educating the next generation. *Journal of Gerontological Social Work, 45*(1–2), 233–248.

Rovner, J. (1995, June). Ending the great terror of life. *AARP Bulletin: Special Report,* p. 1ff.

Rowe, J. W., & Kahn, R. L. (1991). Human aging: Usual and successful. In Harold Cox (Ed.), *Aging* (7th ed.). Guilford, CT: Dushkin. (Originally published in 1987, *Science, 237,* 143–149.)

Rowe, J. W., & Kahn, R. L. (1998). *Successful aging.* New York: Dell.

Roy, H., & Russell, C. (2006). Housing, age-segregated. *The encyclopedia of aging & the elderly.* Retrieved July 13, 2010, from www.medrounds.org/encyclopedia-of-aging/2006/01/housing-age-segregated.html.

Rudinger, G., & Jansen, E. (2003). Self-initiated compensations among older drivers. In K. W. Schaie, H.-W. Wahl, H. Mollenkopf, & F. Oswald (Eds.), *Aging independently: Living arrangements and mobility* (pp. 220–233). New York: Springer.

Ruffenach, G. (2007, November 17–18). In search of a purpose. *Wall Street Journal.*

Ruhm, C. (1991). *Bridge employment and job stopping in the 1980s* (American Over 55 at Work Program, Background Paper Series, No. 3). New York: Commonwealth Fund.

Rural Development Rural Housing Service. (2004). *Rural housing options for elderly people.* Retrieved October 2, 2004, from www.rurdev.usda.gov/rd/pubs/pa1662.htm.

Russell, C. (1999). Interviewing vulnerable old people: Ethical and methodological implications of imagining our subjects. *Journal of Aging Studies, 13*(4), 403–417.

Russell, C. (2001). *The baby boom, Americans aged 35 to 54* (3rd ed.). Ithaca, NY: New Strategist Publication.

Russell, R. (2007). The work of elderly men caregivers: From public careers to an unseen world. *Men & Masculinities, 9*(3), 298–314.

Ruth, J., & Coleman, P. (1996). Personality and aging: Coping and management of the self in later life. In J. E. Birren & K. W. Schaie (Eds.), *Handbook of the psychology of aging* (4th ed., pp. 308–322). San Diego, CA: Academic Press.

Ryan, A., Carter, J., Lucas, J., & Berger, J. (2002). You need not make the journey alone: Overcoming impediments to providing palliative care in a public urban teaching hospital. *American Journal of Hospice and Palliative Care, 19*(3), 171–180.

Rybarski, M. (2004). Boomers after all is said and done: A generation that rewrites all the rules takes on death. *American Demographics, 16*(5), 32–34.

Ryff, C., & Keyes, C. L. (1996). The structure of psychological well-being revisited. *Journal of Personality and Social Psychology, 69,* 719–727.

Ryff, C. D., Kwan, C. M. L., & Singer, B. H. (2001). Personality and aging: Flourishing agendas and future challenges. In J. E. Birren & K. W. Schaie (Eds.), *Handbook of the psychology of aging* (5th ed., pp. 477–499). San Diego, CA: Academic Press.

Ryff, C. D., Magee, W. J., Kling, K. C., & Wing, E. H. (1999). Forging macro-micro linkages in the study of psychological well-being. In C. D. Ryff & V. W. Mar-

shall (Eds.), *The self and society in aging processes* (pp. 247–278). New York: Springer.

Saarnio, R., & Isola, A. (2009). The use of physical restraint in institutional elderly care in Finland. *Research in Gerontological Nursing, 2*(4), 276–286.

Sabin, E. P. (1993). Frequency of senior center use: A preliminary test of two models of senior center participation. *Journal of Gerontological Social Work, 20*(1–2), 97–114.

Sadler, W. A. (2006, Fall). Changing life options: Uncovering the riches of the Third Age. *The LLI Review, The Annual Journal of the Osher Life Long Learning Institutes, 1,* 11–20. Retrieved December 16, 2006, from www.usm.maine.edu/olli/national/pdf/LLI-Review.pdf.

Salganicoff, A., Ranji, U., & Wyn, R. (2005). *Women and health care: A national profile.* Kaiser Family Foundation. Retrieved July 2, 2010, from www.kff.org/women shealth/upload/Women-and-Health-Care-A-National-Profile-Key-Findings-from-the-Kaiser-Women-s-Health-Survey.pdf.

Salholz, E., Clift, E., Thomas, R., & Bingham, C. (1990, October 29). Blaming the voters. *Newsweek,* p. 36.

Salomon, E. (2010). Housing policy solutions to support aging in place. Fact sheet 172. Washington, DC: AARP Public Policy Institute. Retrieved July 6, 2010, from www.hebrewseniorlife.org/workfiles/HSL/AAPR-aging-in-place.pdf.

Salthouse, T. A. (1996). Processing-speed theory of adult age differences in cognition. *Psychological Review, 103,* 403–428.

Salthouse, T. A. (2006). Theoretical issues in the psychology of aging. In J. E. Birren & K. W. Schaie (Eds.), *Handbook of the psychology of aging* (6th ed., pp. 3–13). Burlington, MA: Elsevier Academic Press.

Sanchez, A. (2008). Native American long-term care. *Journal of Native Aging and Health, 3*(1), 27–29.

Sanchez, C. D. (2001). Puerto Rican elderly. In L. K. Olson (Ed.), *Age through ethnic lenses: Caring for the elderly in a multicultural society* (pp. 86–94). London: Rowman & Littlefield.

Sanders, G. F., & Trygstad, D. W. (1993). Strengths in the grandparent-grandchild relationship. *Activities, Adaptation and Aging, 17*(4), 43–53.

Sands, R., & Goldberg-Glen, R. S. (2000). Factors associated with stress among grandparents raising their grandchildren. *Family Relations, 49*(1), 97–105.

Santangelo, M. (2005–06). Historical perspective on adding drugs to Medicare. *Health Care Review, 27*(2), 25–33.

Sarkisian, C. A., Prohaska, T. R., Wong, M. D., Hirsch, S., & Mangione, C. M. (2005). The relationship between expectations for aging and physical activity among older adults. *Journal of Internal Medicine, 20*(10), 911–915.

Sarkisian, N., Gerena, M., & Gerstel, N. (2007). Extended family integration among Euro and Mexican Americans: Ethnicity, gender, and class. *Journal of Marriage and Family, 69,* 40–54.

Sarkisian, N., & Gerstel, N. (2008). Till marriage do us part: Adult children's relationships with their parents. *Journal of Marriage and Family, 70*(2), 360–376.

Sastry, M. L. (1992). Estimating the economic impacts of elderly migration: An input-output analysis. *Growth and Change, 23*(1), 54–79.

Satariano, W. A., Haight, T. J., & Tager, I. B. (2000). Reasons given by older people for limitation or avoidance of leisure time physical activity. *Journal of the American Geriatrics Society, 48*(5), 505–512.

Sattelmair, J. R., Kurth, T., Buring, J. E., & Lee, I.-M. (2010). Physical activity and risk of stroke in women. *Stroke, 41,*1243–1250. Retrieved August 21, 2010, from http://stroke.ahajournals.org/cgi/content/abstract/41/6/1243.

Satter, D. E., & Wallace, S. P. (2010). *Health disparities: American Indian health: Critical information for researchers and policymakers.* Los Angeles: Author.

Saunders, C. (1984). St. Christopher's Hospice. In E. S. Shneidman (Ed.), *Death: Current perspectives* (3rd ed.). Palo Alto, CA: Mayfield.

Savishinsky, J. S. (2000). *Breaking the watch: The meanings of retirement in America.* Ithaca: Cornell University Press.

Schaefer, J. L. (2010). Voices of older baby boomers students: Supporting their transitions back into college. *Educational Gerontology, 36*(1), 67–90.

Schaefer, R. (1999). *Housing America's elderly population.* W99–4. Cambridge, MA: Joint Center for Housing Studies, Harvard University. Retrieved November 7, 2004, from www.jchs.harvard.edu/publications/seniors/schaefer_W99-4.pdf.

Schaefer, R., & Joint Center for Housing Studies of Harvard University. (2000). *Housing America's seniors.* Cambridge, MA: Joint Center for Housing Studies of Harvard University.

Schaie, K. W. (1990). Intellectual development in adulthood. In J. E. Birren & K. W. Schaie (Eds.), *Handbook of the psychology of aging* (3rd ed., pp. 291–309). San Diego, CA: Academic Press.

Scharlach, A. (2008). Good places to grow old: New realities for an older America. *Aging Today, 29*(1), 6, 8.

Scharlach, A. (2009). Creating aging-friendly communities. *Generations, 33*(2), 5–11.

Scheibe, S., Kunzmann, U., & Baltes, P. B. (2007). Wisdom, life longings, and optimal development. In J. A. Blackburn & C. N. Dulmas (Eds.). *Handbook of gerontology: evidence-based approaches to theory, practice, and policy* (pp. 117–142). Hoboken, NJ: Wiley.

Scheidt, R. J., & Windley, P. G. (2006). Environmental gerontology: Progress in the post-Lawton era. In J. E. Birren & K. W. Schaie (Eds.), *Handbook of the psychology of aging* (6th ed., pp. 105–125). Burlington, MA: Elsevier Academic Press.

Schieber, F. (2003). Human factors and aging: Identifying and compensating for age-related deficits in sensory and cognitive function. In N. Charness & K. W. Schaie (Eds.), *Impact of technology on successful aging* (pp. 42–77). New York: Springer.

Schieber, F. (2006). Vision and aging. In J. E. Birren & K. W. Schaie (Eds.), *Handbook of the psychology of aging* (6th ed., pp. 129–161). Burlington, MA: Elsevier Academic Press.

Schlesinger, B. (1996). Sexless years or sex rediscovered. *Journal of Gerontological Social Work, 26*(1–2), 117–131.

Schlesinger, R. (2006, March 26–27). Giving peace a chance. *AARP Bulletin.*

Schmidt, K. F. (1993, March 8). Science and society: Old no more. *U.S. News and World Report,* pp. 67–73.

Schneider, E. L. (1992, Fall/Winter). Biological theories of aging. *Generations, 17,* 7–10.

Schneider, E. L., & Miles, E. (2003). *AgeLess: Take control of your age and stay youthful for life.* Emmaus, PA: Rodale.

Schneider, R., Nidich, S., Kotchen, J. M., Kotchen, T., Grim, C., Rainforth M., et al. (2009). Effects of stress reduction on clinical events in African Americans with coronary heart disease: A randomized controlled trial. *Circulation, 120,* S461. Retrieved June 24, 2011, from http://circ.ahajournals.org/cgi/content/meeting_abstract/120/18_MeetingAbstracts/S461-a.

Schoenbom, C. A., Adams, P. F., Barnes, P. M., Vickerie, J. L., & Schiller, J. S. (2004). Health behaviors of adults: United States, 1999–2001. *Vital and Health Statistics, 10*(219). Hyattsville, MD: National Center for Health Statistics.

Schoenbom, C. A., Vickerie, J. L., & Powell-Griner, E. (2006). *Health characteristics of adults 55 years of age and over: United States, 2000–2003.* Advance data from Vital and Health Statistics No. 370. Hyattsville, MD: National Center for Health Statistics.

Schooler, C. (2009). The effects of the cognitive complexity of occupational conditions and leisure-time activities on the intellectual functioning of older adults. In W. Chodzko-Zajko, A. F. Kramer, & L. W. Poon (Eds.). *Enhancing cognitive functioning and brain plasticity* (pp. 15–34). Champaign, IL: Human Kinetics.

Schulmerich, S. C. (2000). Public policy and the crisis in home care. *Caring, 19*(9), 42–45.

Schulz, J. H. (1988). *The economics of aging* (4th ed.). Dover, MA: Auburn House.

Schulz, J. H. (2001). *The economics of aging* (7th ed.). Westport, CT: Auburn House.

Schulz, J. H., & Binstock, R. H. (2006). *Aging nation: The economics and politics of growing older in America.* Westport, CT: Praeger.

Schulz, J. H., & Borowski, A. (2006). Economic security in retirement: Reshaping the public-private pension mix. In R. H. Binstock & L. K. George (Eds.), *Handbook of aging and the social sciences* (6th ed., pp. 360–379). Burlington, MA: Academic Press.

Schulz, R., & Martire, L. M. (2004). Family caregiving of persons with dementia: Prevalence, health effects, and support strategies. *American Journal of Geriatric Psychiatry, 12*(3), 240–249.

Schulz-Hipp, P. L. (2001). Do spirituality and religiosity increase with age? In D. O. Moberg (Ed.), *Aging and spirituality* (pp. 85–98). New York: Haworth.

Schutz, A. (1967). *The phenomenology of the social world* (G. Walsh & F. Lehnert, Trans.). Evanston, IL: Northwestern University Press.

Schweitzer, M. M. (Ed.). (1999). *American Indian grandmothers: Traditions and transitions.* Albuquerque: University of New Mexico Press.

Scialfa, C. T., & Fernie, G. R. (2006). Adaptive technology. In J. E. Birren & K. W. Schaie (Eds.), *Handbook of the psychology of aging* (6th ed., pp. 425–441). Burlington, MA: Elsevier Academic Press.

Scott, V. J., Gordon, S., Hargreaves, M., Periyakoil, V. S., Perweiler, E. A., Lieto, J., et al. (2010). Health and health care for African American elders. In *Curriculum in ethnogeriatrics* (2nd ed.). Retrieved January 31, 2010, from www.stanford.edu/group/ethnoger/.

Scott-Webber, L., & Koebel, T. (2001). Life-span design in the near environment. In L. A. Pastalan & B. Schwarz (Eds.), *Housing choices and well-being of older adult: Proper fit* (pp. 97–122). New York: Haworth.

Seeman, T. E., Dubin, L. F., & Seeman, M. (2003). Religiosity/spirituality and health: A critical review of the evidence for biological pathways. *American Psychologist, 58,* 53–63.

Selye, H. (1956). *The stress of life.* New York: McGraw-Hill.

Senior Corps. (2007). *What is Senior Corps?* Retrieved September 29, 2007, from www.seniorcorps.gov/about/sc/index.asp.

Senior Corps. (2009). *Fact sheet.* Retrieved July 17, 2010, from www.seniorcorps.gov/pdf/factsheet_seniorcorps.pdf.

SeniorNet. (2010). *About learning centers.* Retrieved August 14, 2010, from www.seniornet.org/index.php?option=com_content&task=view&id=66&Itemid=181.

Seniorresource.com. (2010a). *Housing choices.* Retrieved October 19, 2010, from www.seniorresource.com/house.htm#ccrc.

Seniorresource.com. (2010b). *What is a NORC?* Retrieved July 12, 2010, from www.seniorresource.com/ageinpl.htm#norc.

Sennott-Miller, L. (1994). Research on aging in Latin America: Present status and future directions. *Journal of Cross-Cultural Gerontology, 9,* 87–97.

Serafini, M. W. (2002). AARP's new direction. *National Journal, 34*(1), 28–32.

Settersten, R. A. (2003). Propositions and controversies in life-course scholarship. In R. A. Settersten (Ed.), *Invitation to the life course: Toward new understandings of later life* (pp. 15–45). Amityville, NY: Baywood.

Settersten, R. A. (2006). Aging and the life course. In R. H. Binstock & L. K. George (Eds.), *Handbook of aging and the social sciences* (6th ed., pp. 3–19). Burlington, MA: Academic Press.

Seufert, R. L., & Carrozza, M. A. (2002). Test of Palmore's Facts on Aging Quizzes as alternate measures. *Journal of Aging Studies, 16*(3), 279–294.

Sevak, P., Weir, D., & Willis, R. (2004). The economic consequences of a husband's death: Evidence from the HRS and AHEAD. *Social Security Bulletin, 65*(3), 31–44.

Sevick, M. A., McConnell, T., & Muender, M. (2003). Conducting research related to treatment of Alzheimer's disease. *Journal of Gerontological Nursing, 29*(2), 6–12.

Shahmehri, N., Chisalita, I., & Aberg, J. (2008). People with special needs and traffic safety. In Helal, A. (S.), Mokhtari, M., & Abdulrazak, B (Eds.), *The engineering handbook of smart technology for aging, disability, and independence* (pp. 459–477). Hoboken, NJ: Wiley.

Shanas, E. (1967). Family help patterns and social class in three societies. *Journal of Marriage and the Family, 29,* 257–266.

Shanas, E. (1979). The family as a social support system in old age. *The Gerontologist, 19*(2), 169–174.

Shapira, N., Barak, A., & I., Gal. (2007). Promoting older adults' well-being through Internet training and use. *Aging & Mental Health, 11*(5), 477–484.

Shedlock, D. J., & Cornelius, S. W. (2003). Psychological approaches to wisdom and its development. In J. Demick & C. Andreoletti (Eds.), *Handbook of adult development* (pp. 153–167). New York: Kluwer Academic.

Sheehy, G. (1992). *The silent passage: Menopause.* New York: Random House.

Shelton, A. (2008a). A first look at older Americans and the mortgage crisis. *Insight on the Issues 9.* Washington, DC: AARP Public Policy Institute.

Shelton, A. (2008b). Reform options for Social Security. *Insight on the Issues.* Washington, DC: AARP Public Policy Institute.

Shenk, D., Kuwahara, K., & Zablotsky, D. (2004). Older women's attachments to their home and possessions. *Journal of Aging Studies, 18,* 157–169.

Shenk, D., & Schmid, R. M. (2002). A picture is worth . . . : The use of photography in gerontological research. In G. D. Rowles & N. E. Schoenberg (Eds.), *Qualitative gerontology* (2nd ed., pp. 241–262). New York: Springer.

Shephard, R. J. (1990). The scientific basis of exercise prescribing for the very old. *Journal of the American Geriatric Society, 38*(1), 62–70.

Shibata, T., & Wada, K. (2008). Robot therapy and elder care institutions: effects of long-term interaction with seal robots. In Helal, A. (S.)., Mokhtari, M., & Abdulrazak, B (Eds.), *The engineering handbook of smart technology for aging, disability, and independence* (pp. 405–418). Hoboken, NJ: Wiley.

Shibusawa, T., Lubben, J., & Kitano, H. H. L. (2001). Japanese American elderly. In L. K. Olson (Ed.), *Age through ethnic lenses: Caring for the elderly in a multicultural society* (pp. 32–44). London: Rowman & Littlefield.

Shiota, M. N., & Levenson, R. W. (2007). Birds of a feather don't always fly farthest: Similarity in big five personality predicts more negative marital satisfaction trajectories in long-term marriages. *Psychology and Aging, 22*(4), 666–675.

Shneidman, E. S. (1984). Malignancy: Dialogues with life-threatening illnesses. In E. S. Shneidman (Ed.), *Death: Current perspectives* (3rd ed.). Palo Alto, CA: Mayfield.

Shomaker, D. (1990). Health care, cultural expectations and frail elderly Navajo grandmothers. *Journal of Cross-Cultural Gerontology, 5*, 21–34.

Shringarpure, R., & Davies, K. J. A. (2009). Free radicals and oxidative stress in aging. In V. L. Bengtson, M. Silverstein, M. M. Putney, & D. Gans (Eds.), *Handbook of theories of aging,* (*pp. 229–244*). *New York: Springer.*

Signorielli, N. (2001). Aging on television: The picture in the nineties. *Generations, 25*(3), 34–38.

Silveira, M. J., DiPiero, A., Gerrity, M. S., & Feudtner, C. (2000). Patients' knowledge of options at the end of life: Ignorance in the face of death. *Journal of the American Medical Association, 284*(19), 2483–2488.

Silverman, P. R. (2004). *Widow to widow* (2nd ed). New York: Brunner-Routledge.

Silverstein, M. (2006). Intergenerational family transfers in social context. In R. H. Binstock & L. K. George (Eds.), *Handbook of aging and the social sciences* (6th ed., pp. 165–180). Burlington, MA: Academic Press.

Silverstein, M., & Bengtson, V. L. (1997). Intergenerational solidarity and the structure of adult-parent relationships in American families. *American Journal of Sociology, 103*, 429–460.

Silverstein, M., & Long, J. D. (1998). Trajectories of grandparents' perceived solidarity with adult grandchildren: A growth curve analysis over 23 years. *Journal of Marriage and the Family, 60*(4), 912–923.

Simmons, T., & O'Connell, M. (2003). *Married-couple and unmarried-partner households: 2000.* Washington, DC: U.S. Census Bureau.

Simone, P., & Scuilli, M. (2005). Cognitive benefits of participation: Lifelong Learning Institutes. *OLLI Journal, 1*(1), 48–49.

Simons, R. L. (1983–84). Specificity and substitution in the social networks of the elderly. *International Journal of Aging and Human Development, 18*, 121–139.

Simonton, D. K. (1977). Creative productivity, age, and stress: a biographical time-series analysis of 10 classical composers. *Journal of Personality and Social Psychology, 35*(11), 791–804.

Simonton, D. K. (1988). Age and outstanding achievement: what do we know after over a century of research? *Psychological Bulletin, 104*, 251–267.

Simonton, D. K. (1990). Creativity and wisdom in aging. (pp. 320–329). In J. E. Birren & K. W. Schaie (Eds.).

Handbook of the psychology of aging (3rd ed.). San Diego, CA: Academic Press.

Simonton, D. K. (2006). Creativity. (pp. 269–270). In R. Schulz, S. L. S. Noelker, K. Rockwood, & R. L. Sprott (Eds.), *The encyclopedia of aging* (4th ed). New York: Springer.

Sims-Gould, J., & Martin-Matthews, A. (2007). Family caregiving or caregiving alone: who helps the helper? *Canadian Journal on Aging, 26*(Suppl. 1), 27–45.

Sinai, T., & Souleles, N. (2007). *Net worth and housing equity in retirement.* Working paper no. 07–33. Research Department, Federal Reserve Bank of Philadelphia.

Sinclair, D. A., & Howitz, K. T. (2006). Dietary restriction, hormesis, and small molecule mimetics. In E. Masoro, J. Edward, & S. N. Austad (Eds.), *Handbook of the biology of aging* (6th ed., pp. 63–104). Burlington, MA: Elsevier.

Singer, B. H., & Ryff, C. D. (1999). Hierarchies of life histories and associated health risks. In N. D. Adler, B. S. McEwen, & M. Marmot (Eds.), Socioeconomic status in industrialized countries. *Annals of the New York Academy of Sciences, 896*, 96–115.

Singleton, J. F., Forbes, W. F., & Agwani, N. (1993). Stability of activity across the lifespan. *Activities, Adaptation and Aging, 18*(1), 19–27.

Sit, M. (1992). With elders in mind: A home can be made more suitable. *Generations, 19*(2), 73–74.

Sixsmith, A. (2008). Modeling the well-being of older people. In Helal, A. (S.), Mokhtari, M., & Abdulrazak, B. (Eds.), *The engineering handbook of smart technology for aging, disability, and independence* (pp. 569–584). Hoboken, NJ: Wiley.

Ska, B., & Nespoulous, J.-L. (1988). Encoding strategies and recall performance of a complex figure by normal elderly subjects. *Canadian Journal on Aging, 7*, 408.

Skinner, J. H. (1992, Spring). Aging in place: The experience of African American and other minority elders. *Generations*, pp. 49–51.

Slate. (2010). *80 over 80. Slate's 2009 list of the most powerful octogenarians in America.* Retrieved August 8, 2010, from www.slate.com/id/2199926/.

Slevin, K. F. (2005). Intergenerational and community responsibility: Race uplift work in the retirement activities of professional African American women. *Journal of Aging Studies, 19*(3), 309–326.

Slevin, K. F. (2006). The embodied experiences of older lesbians. In T. M. Calasanti & K. F. Slevin (Eds.), *Age matters: Realigning feminist thinking* (pp. 247–268). New York: Routledge.

Small, B. J., & McEvoy, C. L. (2008). Does participation in cognitive activities buffer age-related cognitive decline? In S. M. Hofer & D. F. Alwin (Eds.), *Handbook of cognitive aging: Interdisciplinary perspectives* (pp. 575–586). Los Angeles: Sage.

Smith, A. D. (1996). Memory. In J. E. Birren & K. W. Schaie (Eds.), *Handbook of the psychology of aging* (4th ed., pp. 236–250). San Diego, CA: Academic Press.

Smith, D. G. (1992). *Paying for Medicare: The politics of reform.* New York: Aldine de Gruyter.

Smith, K. E., Soto, M., & Penner, R. G. (2009). *How seniors change their asset holding during retirement.* The Urban Institute. The Retirement Policy Program. Discussion Paper 09–06. Retrieved May 17, 2010, from www.urban.org/uploadedpdf/412006_howseniorschange.pdf.

Smith, T. L., & Toseland, R. W. (2006). The effectiveness of a telephone support program for caregivers of frail older adults. *The Gerontologist, 46*(5), 620–629.

Smith, V., Gifford, K., Ellis, E., Wiles, A., Rudowitz, R., & O'Malley, M. (2005). Medicaid budgets, spending and policy initiatives in state fiscal years 2005 and 2006: Results from a 50–state survey. Kaiser Commission on Medicaid and the uninsured. Available at www.kff.org/medicaid/upload/Medicaid-Budgets-Spending-and-Policy-Initiatives-in-State-Fiscal-Years-2005-and-2006-report-executive-summary.pdf.

Smith, W. (2004a). Good life in the big city. *AARP Bulletin, 45*(6), 4ff.

Smith, W. (2004b). The good life in the big city: Empty nesters join older urbanites where the lights are brighter. *AARP Bulletin Online.* Retrieved November 6, 2004, from www.aarp.org/bulletin/yourlife/Articles/a2004-05-26-goodlife.html.

Smyer, M. A., Besen, E., & Pitt-Catsouphes, M. (2009). Boomers and the many meanings of work. In R. B. Hudson (Ed.). *Boomer bust? Economic and political issues of the graying society. The Boomers and their future* (Vol. 2, pp. 5–15). Westport, CT: Praeger.

Snowdon, D. (2001). *Aging with grace: What the nun study teaches us about leading longer, healthier, and more meaningful lives.* New York: Bantam Books.

Sobczak, J. (2002). Staying stronger longer. *Quality in Aging, 3*(2), 6–10.

Social Security Administration. (1997). *Social Security programs in the United States.* Washington, DC: Office of Research, Evaluation and Statistics. SSA Publication No. 13–11758.9. Retrieved September 4, 2004, from www.ssa.gov/policy/docs/progdesc/sspus/sspus.pdf.

Social Security Administration. (2004a). *Fact sheet Social Security: Social Security basic facts.* Washington, DC: Author. Retrieved September 4, 2004, from www.ssa.gov/pressoffice/factsheets/basicfact-alt.htm.

Social Security Administration. (2004b). *Full retirement benefits.* Washington, DC: Author. Retrieved September 4, 2004, from www.ssa.gov/retirement/1960.html.

Social Security Administration. (2004c). *Retirement and Medicare: Qualify and apply.* Washington, DC: Author. Retrieved September 4, 2004, from www.ssa.gov/r&m2.htm.

Social Security Administration. (2004d). *Social Security's future—FAQs.* Washington, DC: Author. Retrieved September 4, 2004, from www.ssa.gov/qa.htm.

Social Security Administration. (2004e). *Social Security online. Benefits planner. Frequently asked questions.* Retrieved September 11, 2004, from www.ssa.gov/planners/faqs.htm.

Social Security Administration. (2005). *Full retirement age is increasing. Find your retirement age.* Retrieved June 5, 2005, from www.ssa.gov/retirechartred.htm.

Social Security Administration. (2007). *Social Security fact sheet.* Retrieved August 23, 2007, from www.ssa.gov/legislation/2007+%20factsheet.pdf.

Social Security Administration. (2009). *Social Security basic facts.* Retrieved May 9, 2010, from www.ssa.gov/pressoffice/basicfact.htm.

Social Security Administration. (2010a). *Annual statistical supplement to the Social Security Bulletin, 2009.* SSA Publication No. 13–11700. Washington, DC: Office of Retirement and Disability Policy. Office of Research, Evaluation, and Statistics.

Social Security Administration. (2010b). *History. Historical background and development of Social Security.* Retrieved May 9, 2010, from www.ssa.gov/history/briefhistory3.html.

Social Security Administration. (2010c). *Income of the population 55 or older, 2008.* Office of Retirement and Disability Policy. Office of Research, Evaluation, and Statistics. Retrieved October 23, 2010, from www.ssa.gov/policy/docs/statcomps/income_pop55/2008/incpop08.pdf.

Social Security Administration. (2010d). *Monthly statistical snapshot, March 2010.* Office of Retirement and Disability Policy. Retrieved May 9, 2010, from www.ssa.gov/policy/docs/quickfacts/stat_snapshot/.

Social Security and Medicare Board of Trustees. (2004). *Status of the Social Security and Medicare programs. A summary of the 2004 Annual Reports.* Retrieved December 28, 2004, from www.ssa.gov/OACT/TRSUM/trsummary.html.

Social Security Online. (2010a). *Beneficiary data. Number of Social Security beneficiaries.* Retrieved August 8, 2010, from www.ssa.gov/OACT/ProgData/icpGraph.html.

Social Security Online. (2010b). *Proposal addressing trust fund solvency. Actuarial publications.* Retrieved May 9, 2010, from www.ssa.gov/OACT/solvency/index.html.

Social Security Online. (2010c). *Retirement benefits.* Retrieved May 9, 2010, from www.ssa.gov/pubs/10035.html.

Social Security Online. (2010d). *Social Security income, outgo, and assets. Trust fund data.* Retrieved May 9, 2010, from www.ssa.gov/policy/docs/statcomps/supplement/2009/highlights.html.

Social Security Online. (2010e). *SSI federal payment amounts for 2011. Automatic increases.* Retrieved October 19, 2010, from www.ssa.gov/OACT/COLA/SSI.html.

Social Security Online. (2010f). *Supplemental Security Income (SSI) in New York.* SSA Publication No. 05–11146. Retrieved May 22, 2010, from www.ssa.gov/pubs/11146.html#pay.

Social Security Online. (2010g). *Supplemental Security Income (SSI) in California. SSA Publication No. 05–11125.* Retrieved May 22, 2010, from www.ssa.gov/pubs/11125.html#pay.

Social Security Online. (2010h). *The earnings test for people at full retirement age. Find an answer to your question.* Retrieved October 19, 2010, from http://ssa-custhelp. ssa.gov/app/answers/detail/a_id/295/related/1.

Social Security Online. (2011). *Supplemental Security Income (SSI). Rules for getting SSI.* Retrieved July 1, 2011, from www.socialsecurity.gov/pubs/11000.html.

Sokolovsky, J. (2000, February 8–10). *Living arrangements of older persons and family support in less developed countries.* Paper presented at the Technical Meeting on Population Ageing and Living Arrangements of Older persons: Critical Issues and Policy Responses. New York: United Nations Secretariat. New York.

Sorrell, J. (2006). Developing programs for older adults in a faith community. *Journal of Psychosocial Nursing and Mental Health Services, 44*(11), 15–18.

Sotomayor, M., & Randolph, S. (1988). A preliminary review of caregiving issues and the Hispanic family. In M. Sotomayor & H. Curiel (Eds.), *Hispanic elderly: A cultural signature* (pp. 137–160). Edinburg, TX: Pan American University Press.

Spillman, B. C., & Pezzin, L. E. (2000). Potential and active family caregivers: Changing networks and the sandwich generation. *Milbank Quarterly, 78*(3). Retrieved November 25, 2004, from www.milbank.org/quarterly/7803feat.html.

Spirduso, W. W., Francis, K. L., & MacRae, P. G. (2005). *Physical dimensions of aging.* Champaign, IL: Human Kinetics.

Spirduso, W. W., Poon, L. W., & Chodzko-Zajko, W. (2008). Conclusions and future research directions. In W. W. Spirduso, L. W. Poon, & W. Chodzko-Zajko (Eds.), *Exercise and its mediating effects on cognition* (pp. 211–219). Champaign, IL: Human Kinetics.

Spitze, G., & Trent, K. (2006). Gender differences in adult sibling relations in two-child families. *Journal of Marriage and Family, 68*(4), 977–992.

Spivack, M. S. (1992). Washington politicians who favor seniors—And those who don't. *New Choices for Retirement Living, 32*(7), 26–29.

Spurlock, W. R. (2005). Spiritual well-being and caregiver burden in Alzheimer's caregivers. *Geriatric Nursing, 26*(3), 154–161.

St. John, P., & Man-Son-Hing, M. (2002). Requests for physician-assisted suicide in older persons: An approach. *Geriatrics Today, 5*(2), 81–83.

Stafford, P. B. (2009). Living large while living small: The spatial life of aging Boomers. In R. B. Hudson (Ed.). *Boomer bust? Economic and political issues of the graying society. The Boomers and their future* (Vol. 2, pp. 169–189). Westport, CT: Praeger.

Stanford, E. P. (1990). Diverse African American aged. In Z. Harel, E. A. McKinney, & M. Williams (Eds.), *African American aged: Understanding diversity and service needs* (pp. 33–49). Newbury Park, CA: Sage.

Stanford Encyclopedia of Philosophy. (2007). *The definition of death.* Retrieved November 5, 2010, from http://plato.stanford.edu/entries/death-definition/#1CurMaiVieWhoBraApp.

Staplin, L., Lococo, K. H., Stewart, J., & Decina, L. E. (1998). *Safe mobility for older people notebook.* Report No. DTNH22–96–C-05140. Washington, DC: U.S. Department of Transportation, National Highway Traffic Safety Administration.

Statehealthfacts.org. (2010). *Medicaid payments per enrollee, FY2001.* Retrieved October 10, 2010, from www.statehealthfacts.org/comparetable.jsp?ind=183&cat=4.

Statistics Canada. (2000a). Stress and well-being. *Health Reports, 12*(3). Cat. No. 82–003. Retrieved May 27, 2005, from www.statcan.ca/english/freepub/82-003-XIE/art2.pdf.

Statistics Canada. (2000b). Stress and well-being. *Health Reports 12*(3), 21–32. Cat. No. 82–003-XIE. Retrieved November 23, 2003, from www.statcan.ca/english/freepub/82-003-XIE/art1.pdf.

Stearns, S. C., & Partridge, L. (2001). The genetics of aging in *Drosophila.* In E. J. Masoro & S. N. Austad (Eds.), *Handbook of the biology of aging* (5th ed., pp. 353–368). San Diego, CA: Academic Press.

Stein, L. (2009). *Special report: Sexuality after 60. Health after 60.* Retrieved July 1, 2010, from www.ahealthyme.com/topic/srsex.

Steinbock, B. (2005). The case for physician assisted suicide: Not (yet) proven. *Journal of Medical Ethics, 31*(4), 235–241.

Steinfeld, A. (2008a). Smart systems in personal transportation. In Helal, A. (S.), Mokhtari, M., & Abdulrazak, B. (Eds.), *The engineering handbook of smart technology for aging, disability, and independence* (pp. 737–747). Hoboken, NJ: Wiley.

Steinfeld, A. (2008b). Universal design/design for all: practice and method. In Helal, A. (S.)., Mokhtari, M., & Abdulrazak, B. (Eds.), *The engineering handbook of smart technology for aging, disability, and independence* (pp. 803–818). Hoboken, NJ: Wiley.

Stern, L. (1993, February–March). Nothing ventured. *Modern Maturity,* pp. 52–83.

Stern, Y. (2002). What is cognitive reserve? Theory and research application of the reserve concept. *Journal of the International Neuropsychological Society, 8,* 448–460.

Stern, Y. (Ed.). (2007). *Cognitive reserve: theory and applications.* New York: Taylor & Francis.

Stettner, A., & Wenger, J. (2003). *The broad reach of long-term unemployment.* EPI Issue Brief No. 194. Washington, DC: The Economic Policy Institute.

Stevens-Long, J., & Michaud, G. (2003). Theory in adult development. In J. Demick & C. Andreoletti (Eds.),

Handbook of adult development (pp. 3–22). New York: Kluwer Academic/Plenum.

Stewart, M., Bamfather, A., Neufeld, A., Warrne, S., Letourneau, N., & Liu, L. (2006). Accessible support for family caregivers of seniors with chronic conditions: From isolation to inclusion. *Canadian Journal on Aging, 25*(2), 179–192.

Stich, S. (2000). Room for a housemate? *New Choices: Living Even Better After, 50, 40*(8), 51–53.

Stine-Morrow, E. A. L., Parisi, J. M., Morrow, D. G., Greene, J., & Park, D. C. (2007). Engagement model of cognitive optimization through adulthood. *Journals of Gerontology: Series B: Psychological Sciences and Social Sciences, 62B*(Special Issue 1), 62–69.

Stoller, E. P., & Gibson, R. C. (2000). *Worlds of difference: Inequality in the aging experience* (3rd ed.). Thousand Oaks, CA: Pine Forge Press.

Stone, L. O., Rosenthal, C. J., & Connidis, I. A. (1998). *Parent–child exchanges of supports and intergenerational equity.* Cat. No. 89–557-XPE. Ottawa: Ministry of Industry.

Stone, R. (1989). The feminization of poverty among the elderly. *Women's Studies Quarterly, 17*(1–2), 20–34.

Stone, R. I. (2006). Emerging issues in long-term care. In Robert H. Binstock & Linda K. George (Eds.), *Handbook of aging and the social sciences* (6th ed., pp. 397–418). Burlington, MA: Academic Press.

Stowell-Ritter, A. (2005). *Strategies to support home and community-based long-term care: A New Jersey survey.* Washington, DC: AARP, Knowledge Management.

Strain, L. A., & Blandford, A. A. (2003). Caregiving networks in later life: Does cognitive status make a difference? *Canadian Journal on Aging, 22*(3), 261–273.

Strain, L. A., Grabusic, C. C., Searle, M. S., & Dunn, N. J. (2002). Continuing and ceasing leisure activities in later life: a longitudinal study. *The Gerontologist, 42*(2), 217–223.

Strehler, B. (1977). *Time, cells and aging* (2nd ed.). New York: Academic Press.

Stuart-Hamilton, I., & Mahoney, B. (2003). Effect of aging awareness training on knowledge of and attitudes towards older adults. *Educational Gerontology, 29*(3), 251–260.

Stutts, J. C. (2003). The safety of older drivers: The U.S. perspective. In K. W. Schaie, H.-W. Wahl, H. Mollenkopf, & F. Oswald (Eds.), *Aging independently: Living arrangements and mobility* (pp. 192–204). New York: Springer.

Sung, K. (2000). Respect for elders: Myths and realities of East Asia. *Journal of Aging and Identity, 5*(4), 231–239.

Surgeon General of the United States. (2004). *2004 Surgeon General's report—The health consequences of smoking.* Centers for Disease Control. Retrieved June 24, 2011, from www.cdc.gov/tobacco/data_statistics/sgr/2004/index.htm.

Sutton, D. (2002, Winter) Medical and everyday assistive device use among older adults with arthritis. *Canadian Journal on Aging, 21*(4), 535–548.

Sweeney, M. (2004). *Travel patterns of older Americans with disabilities.* Working paper 2004–001-OAS. Bureau of Transportation Statistics. Retrieved June 23, 2007, from www.bts.gov/programs/bts_working_ papers/2004/paper_01.

Swinburn, B., & Sager, R. (2003). Promotion of exercise prescriptions in general practice for older populations. *Geriatrics and Aging, 6*(7), 20–23.

Szanto, K., Gildengers, A., Mulsant, B. H., Brown, G., Alexopoulos, G. S., & Grynolds, C. F. III. (2002). Identification of suicidal ideation and prevention of suicidal behaviour in the elderly. *Drugs and Aging, 19*(1), 11–24.

Szinovacz, M. (1983). Beyond the hearth: Older women and retirement. In E. W. Markson (Ed.), *Older women: Issues and prospects.* Lexington, MA: D. C. Heath.

Szinovacz, M. (2003). Contexts and pathways: Retirement as institution, process, and experience. In G. A. Adams & T. A. Beehr (Eds.), *Retirement: Reasons, processes, and results* (pp. 6–52). New York: Springer.

Szinovacz, M. (2006). Families and retirement. In L. O. Stone (Ed.), *New frontiers of research on retirement* (pp. 165–198). Statistics Canada. Cat. No. 75–11-XIE. Ottawa: Minister of Industry.

Takamura, J. (2002). Social policy issues and concerns in a diverse aging society: Implication of increasing diversity. *Generations, 26*(3), 33–38.

Tamborini, C. (2008). Never-married in old age: Projections and concerns for the near future. *Social Security Bulletin, 67*(2), 25–40.

Tammeveski, P. (2003). Making of national identity among older Estonians in the United States. *Journal of Aging Studies, 17*(4), 399–414.

Tan, E. J., Rebok, G. W., Yu, Q., Frangakis, C. E., Carlson, M. C., Wang, T., et al. (2009). The long-term relationship between high-intensity volunteering and physical activity in older African American women. *Journal of Gerontology: Social Sciences, 64B*(2), 304–311.

Tang, F. (2009). Late-life volunteering and trajectories of physical health. *Journal of Applied Gerontology, 28*(4), 524–533.

Taylor-Jones, A. (2006). Connections in the gold years: Social support networks of African American elders. *International Journal of Cognitive Technology, 11*(2), 17–26.

Taylor, D. H., Ostermann, J., Van Houtven, C. H., Tulsky, J. A., & Steinhauser, K. (2007). What length of hospice use maximizes reduction in medical expenditures near death in the U.S. Medicare program? *Social Science & Medicine, 65,* 1466–1478.

Taylor, M. A., & Doverspike, D. (2003). Retirement planning and preparation. In G. A. Adams & T. A. Beehr (Eds.), *Retirement: reasons, processes, and results* (pp. 53–82). New York: Springer.

Taylor, R. J., Chatters, L. M., Bullard, K. M., Wallace, J. M., & Jackson, J. S. (2009). Organizational religious behavior among older African Americans. *Research on Aging, 31*(4), 440–462.

Taylor, R. J., Keith, V. M., & Tucker, M. B. (1993). Gender, marital, familial, and friendship roles. In J. S. Jackson, L. M. Chatters, & R. J. Taylor (Eds.), *Aging in African American America* (pp. 49–68). Newbury Park, CA: Sage.

Teaster, P. B. (2000). *A response to the abuse of vulnerable adults: The 2000 Survey of State Adult Protective Services.* Washington, DC: The National Center on Elder Abuse. Retrieved July 3, 2010, from www.ncea.aoa.gov/NCEAroot/Main_Site/FAQ/Questions.aspx.

Teno, J. M., Gruneir, A., Schwartz, Z., Nanda, A., & Wetle, T. (2007). Association between advance directives and quality of end-of-life care: A national study. *Journal of the American Geriatrics Society, 55*(2), 189–194. Retrieved July 22, 2010, from www3.interscience.wiley.com/journal/117995713/abstract?CRETRY=1&SRETRY=0.

Texas. (2004). Health and Safety Code, Title 2, Subtitle J. Public Health Provisions, Chapter 166 Advance Directives, Subchapter B, Directive To Physicians. Tex. Health and Safety Code Ann. Article166.039.

Theroux, P. (2003). *Dark star safari: Overland from Cairo to Capetown.* Boston: Houghton Mifflin.

Thomas, J. L., Sperry, L., & Yarbrough, M. S. (2000). Grandparents as parents: Research findings and policy recommendations. *Child Psychiatry and Human Development, 31*(1), 3–22.

Thomas, W. H., & Blanchard, J. M. (2009). Moving beyond place: Aging in community. *Generations, 33*(2), 12–17.

Thomas, W. I., & Thomas, D. S. (1928). *The child in America: Behavior problems and programs.* New York: Knopf.

Thompson, M. E., & Forbes, W. F. (1990). The various definitions of biological aging. *Canadian Journal on Aging, 9,* 91–94.

Thornton, R., & Light, L. L. (2006). Language comprehension and production in normal aging. In J. E. Birren & K. W. Schaie (Eds.), *Handbook of the psychology of aging* (6th ed., pp. 261–267). Burlington, MA: Elsevier Academic Press.

Thorpe, R. J. Jr., Kreisle, R. A., Glickman, L. T., Simonsick, E. M., Newman, A. B., & Kritchevsky, S. (2006). Physical activity and pet ownership in Year 3 of the Health ABC Study. *Journal of Aging and Physical Activity, 14*(2), 154–168.

Tierney, M. C., & Charles, J. (2002). The care and treatment of people with dementia and cognitive impairment: An update. *Writings in gerontology: Mental health and aging* (pp. 97–112). Ottawa: National Advisory Council on Aging.

Tomporowski, P. D. (2006). Physical activity, cognition, and aging: A review of reviews. In L. W. Poon, W. Chodzko-Zajko, & P. D. Tomporowski (Eds.), *Active living, cognitive functioning, and aging* (Vol. 1, pp. 15–32). Champaign, IL: Human Kinetics.

Toossi, M. (2005). Labor force projections to 2014: Retiring boomers. *Monthly Labor Review Online, 128*(11). Retrieved December 14, 2010, from www.bls.gov/opub/mlr/2005/11/art3full.pdf.

Tornstam, L. (1999). Late-life transcendence: A new developmental perspective on aging. In L. E. Thjomas & S. A. Eisenhandler (Eds.), *Religion, belief, and spirituality in late life* (pp. 178–202). New York: Springer.

Tornstam, L. (2005). *Gerotranscendence: A developmental theory of positive aging.* New York: Springer.

Torres-Gil, F. M. (1992). *The new aging: Politics and change in America.* New York: Auburn House.

Tournier, P. (1972). *Learning to grow old.* London: SCM Press.

Townson, M. (1994). *The social contract and seniors: Preparing for the 21st century.* Ottawa: National Advisory Council on Aging.

Tran, T. V., Ngo, D., & Sung, T. H. (2001). Caring for elderly Vietnamese Americans. In L. K. Olson (Ed.), *Age through ethnic lenses: Caring for the elderly in a multicultural society* (pp. 59–70). London: Rowman & Littlefield.

Troll, L. E., & Bengtson, V. L. (1992, Summer). The oldest-old in families: An intergenerational perspective. *Generations,* pp. 39–44.

Trombley, J., Thomas, B., & Mosher-Ashley, P. (2003). Massage therapy for elder residents. *Nursing Homes Long Term Care Management, 52*(10), 92ff.

Trust for America's Health (TFAH). (2007). *F as in fat: How obesity policies are failing in America, 2007.* Retrieved September 9, 2007, from http://healthyamericans.org/reports/obesity2007/Obesity2007Report.pdf.

Tsiantar, D. (2007, April 16). Wrinkles in living color. *Time, Global,* pp. 1–2.

Tulandi, T., & Lal, S. (1985). Menopausal hot flash. *Obstetrics Gynecology Survey, 40,* 553–563.

Tulsky, J. A. (2005). Beyond advance directives. Importance of communication skills at the end of life. *Journal of the American Medical Association, 294*(3), 359–365.

Tumlinson, A., Aguiar, C., & Watts, M. O. (2009). *Closing the long-term care funding gap: The challenge of private long-term care insurance.* The Kaiser Commission on Medicaid and the Uninsured. Retrieved August 13, 2010, from www.kff.org/insurance/upload/Closing-the-Long-Term-Care-Funding-Gap-The-Challenge-of-Private-Long-Term-Care-Insurance-Report.pdf.

Tumulty, K., Pickert, K., & Park, A. (2010, April 5). America, the doctor will see you now. *Time,* pp. 24–32.

Turvey, C. L., Conwell, Y., Jones, M. P., Phillips, C., Simonsick, E., Pearson, J. L., et al. (2002). Risk factors for late-life suicide: A prospective, community-based study. *American Journal of Geriatric Psychiatry, 10*(4), 398–406.

U.S. Census Bureau. (2001). *Poverty in the United States: 2000.* Retrieved June 10, 2002, www.census.gov/prod/2001pubs/p60-214.pdf.

U.S. Census Bureau. (2002). *Statistical abstract of the United States: 2002.* Retrieved April 26, 2004, from www.census.gov/prod/2004pubs/03statab/pop.pdf.

U.S. Census Bureau. (2003a). *Statistical abstract of the United States. Income, expenditures, and wealth.* No. 697. Retrieved July 13, 2004, from www.census.gov/prod/2004pubs/03statab/income.pdf.

U.S. Census Bureau. (2003b). *Statistical abstract of the United States.* Population. No. 13. Retrieved July 13, 2004, from www.census.gov/prod/2004pubs/03statab/pop.pdf.

U.S. Census Bureau. (2005a). *Reported voting and registration by race, Hispanic origin, sex, and age groups 1964 to 2004.* Retrieved July 7, 2005, from www.census.gov/population/www/socdemo/voting.html.

U.S. Census Bureau. (2005b). *Voting and registration in the election of November 2004. Current population survey, November 2004.* Retrieved October 27, 2007, from www.census.gov/population/www/socdemo/voting/cps2004.html.

U.S. Census Bureau. (2006a). *America's families and living arrangements: 2006.* Table A1. Marital status of people 15 years and over, by age, sex, personal earnings, race, and Hispanic origin/1, 2006. Retrieved September 30, 2007, from www.census.gov/population/www/socdemo/hh-fam/cps2006.html.

U.S. Census Bureau. (2006b). *Current population reports.* P60–231. Income, poverty, and health insurance coverage in the United States: 2005. Washington, DC: U.S. Government Printing Office. Retrieved August 23, 2007, from www.census.gov/prod/2006jpubs/p60-231.pdf.

U.S. Census Bureau. (2006c). *Current population survey, annual social and economic supplement, 2005.* CPS Table Generator. Retrieved July 18, 2011, from http://www.census.gov/hhes/www/cpstc/apm/example_apm.html.

U.S. Census Bureau. (2006d). *Current population survey: Educational attainment in the United States: 2006.* Washington, DC: Author. Retrieved July 17, 2011, from http://www.census.gov/hhes/socdemo/education/data/cps/2006/tables.html.

U.S. Census Bureau. (2007a). *Table INC RD-AEI 3.* Median income of households by selected characteristics and income definition: 2005 and 2006. Current Population Survey (CPS). Annual Social and Economic (ASEC) Supplement. Retrieved October 19, 2010, from http://pubdb3.census.gov/macro/032007/altinc/newinc03_000.htm.

U.S. Census Bureau. (2007b). *The 2007 statistical abstract, the national data book.* Table 44. Social and economic characteristics of the Hispanic population: 1995 to 2005. Retrieved June 9, 2007, from www.census.gov/compendia/statab/population/.

U.S. Census Bureau. (2008a). *POV01: Age and sex of all people, family members and unrelated individuals iterated by income-to-poverty ratio and race: 2007.* Below 100% of poverty—all races. Annual Social and Economic (ASEC) Supplement. Current Population Survey (CPS). Retrieved May 17, 2010, from http://pubdb3.census.gov/macro/032008/pov/new01_100_01.htm.

U.S. Census Bureau. (2008b). *U.S. population projections. National population projections.* Released 2008 (based on Census 2000). Summary tables (with projections of the population by race, ethnicity, age, and sex for the United Sates, 2010 to 2050). Washington, DC: U.S. Department of Commerce. Retrieved August 29, 2010, from www.census.gov/population/www/projections/summarytables.html.

U.S. Census Bureau. (2009). *Statistical abstract of the United States.* Population, social and economic characteristics of the Hispanic population: 2008. Table No. 39. Retrieved November 7, 2010, from www.census.gov/prod/2009pubs/10statab/pop.pdf.

U.S. Census Bureau. (2010a). *Current population survey, 2008 annual social and economic supplement.* Retrieved January 24, 2010, from http://pubdb3.census.gov/macro/032008/pov/new01_100_01.htm.

U.S. Census Bureau. (2010b). *Percent of workers participating in retirement benefits by worker characteristics: 2005 to 2008.* The 2010 statistical abstract. Retrieved May 22, 2010, from www.census.gov/compendia/statab/cats/social_insurance_human_services/social_security_retirement_plans.html.

U.S. Census Bureau. (2010c). *POV01: Age and sex of all people, family members and unrelated individuals iterated by income-to-poverty ratio and race: 2008.* Source: U.S. Census Bureau, Current Population Survey, 2009 Annual Social and Economic Supplement. Retrieved May 9, 2010, from www.census.gov/hhes/www/cpstables/032009/pov/new01_100_01.htm.

U.S. Census Bureau. (2010d). *Poverty.* Retrieved May 9, 2010, from www.census.gov/hhes/www/poverty/threshld/thresh09.html.

U.S. Census Bureau. (2010e). *The 2010 statistical abstract.* Births, deaths, marriages, & divorces: Life expectancy. Table 105. Expectation of life and expected deaths by race, sex, and age: 2006. Retrieved September 4, 2010, from www.census.gov/compendia/statab/2010/tables/10s0105.pdf.

U.S. Census Bureau. (2010f). *The 2010 statistical abstract.* Family net worth—mean and median net worth in constant (2007) dollars by selected family characteristics: 1998 to 2007. Table 705. Retrieved May 17, 2010, from www.census.gov/compendia/statab/2010/tables/10s0705.pdf.

U.S. Census Bureau. (2010g). *The 2010 statistical abstract. The national data book.* Labor force, employment, & earnings: Labor force status. Civilian labor force and participation rates with projections: 1980 to 2016. Retrieved July 17, 2011, from http://www.census.gov/prod/2009pubs/10statab/labor.pdf

U.S. Census Bureau. (2010h). *Voting and registration in the election of November 2008.* Detailed tables. Current population survey. Table 1. Reported voting and registration, selected ages, November 2008. Washington, DC, 2000. Retrieved November, 24, 2010, from www.census.gov/population/www/socdemo/voting/cps2008.html.

U.S. Department of Agriculture and U.S. Department of Health and Human Services. (2010). *Dietary guidelines for Americans* (7th ed.). Washington, DC: U.S. Government Printing Office.

U.S. Department of Health and Human Services. (2003). Summary health statistics for the U.S. population: National Health Interview Survey, 2001. *Vital and Health Statistics, 10*(217).

U.S. Department of Health and Human Services. (2007). *Growing older in America: The Health & Retirement Study*. Retrieved December 14, 2010, from www.nia.nih.gov/ResearchInformation/ExtramuralPrograms/Behavioral AndSocialResearch/HRS.htm.

U.S. Department of Health and Human Services, Baltimore Longitudinal Study of Aging. (1993). *With the passage of time: The Baltimore Longitudinal Study of Aging,* NIH Pub. No. 93–3685. Washington, DC: U.S. Department of Health and Human Services. Retrieved January 4, 2005, from www.grc.nia.nih.gov/branches/blsa/blsa.htm.

U.S. Department of Health and Human Services. Health Resources and Services Administration. Primary Care. (2011). *Understanding the special health care needs of elderly persons who are homeless*. Program assistance letter 2003–03. Retrieved July 5, 2011, from http://bphc.hrsa.gov/policiesregulations/policies/pal200303.html.

U.S. Department of Health and Human Services, National Institute on Aging (NIA). (1993, June 17). *Health and retirement study*. Press release. Washington, DC: NIA.

U.S. Department of Health and Human Services, Social Security Administration, Office of Research and Statistics. (1993). Social Security programs in the United States. *Social Security Bulletin, 56*(4). Washington, DC: U.S. Government Printing Office.

U.S. Department of Housing and Urban Development (2000a). *Homes and communities. Community planning and development. SRO terms.* Retrieved October 30, 2004, from www.hud.gov/offices/cpd/homeless/library/sro/understandingsro/terms.cfm.

U.S. Department of Housing and Urban Development (2000b). *Trends in elderly housing. Urban Research Monitor, 5*(2), 1. Retrieved October 29, 2004, from www.huduser.org/periodicals/urm/urm_07_2000/urm1.html and www.huduser.org/periodicals/urm/urm_07_2000/urm2.html.

U.S. Department of Housing and Urban Development (2007a). *Home equity conversion mortgage program*. Retrieved September 15, 2007, from www.hud.gov/offices/hsg/sfh/hecm/hecmdf.cfm.

U.S. Department of Housing and Urban Development (2007b). *More than 300,000 seniors benefiting from HUD reverse mortgages*. Retrieved September 15, 2007, from www.hud.gov/news/release.cfm?content=pr07-089.cfm.

U.S. Department of Housing and Urban Development (2007c). *Single room occupancy program (SRO)*. Retrieved September 16, 2007, from www.hud.gov/offices/cpd/homeless/prorams.sro/.

U.S. Department of Housing and Urban Development (2008). *Single room occupancy (SRO)*. Retrieved July 12, 2010, from www.hud.gov/offices/cpd/homeless/programs/sro/.

U.S. Department of Housing and Urban Development. (2010). *The 2009 annual homeless assessment report to Congress*. Washington, DC. Retrieved July 17, 2010, from www.hudhre.info/documents/5thHomelessAssessmentReport.pdf.

U.S. Department of Housing and Urban Development. (2011a). *Data sets. Frequently asked questions: FY 2011 income limits*. Retrieved July 5, 2011, from www.huduser.org/portal/datasets/il/il11/faq_11.html.

U.S. Department of Housing and Urban Development. (2011b). *Housing choice vouchers fact sheet*. Retrieved July 5, 2011, from http://portal.hud.gov:80/hudportal/HUD?src=/topics/housing_choice_voucher_program_8.

U.S. Department of Labor. (2004). *Women and retirement savings*. Washington, DC: U.S. Government Printing Office.

U.S. Department of Labor. (2007). *Volunteering in the United States, 2006*, Table A. Retrieved November 27, 2007, from www.bls.gov/news.release/volun.nr0.htm.

U.S. Department of Labor. (2009). *Quick stats on women workers, 2009*. Retrieved October 19, 2010, from www.dol.gov/wb/stats/main.htm.

U.S. Department of Labor, Bureau of Labor Statistics. (2002, August). Worker displacement, 1999–2001. *News, USDL 02–483*. Washington, DC: U.S. Government Printing Office.

U.S. Department of Labor, Bureau of Labor Statistics. (2008). *Consumer Expenditure Survey—2008*. Expenditure Tables—Table 3. Age of reference person: Average annual expenditures and characteristics, Consumer Expenditure Survey, 2008—Continued. Retrieved July 19, 2010, from www.bls.gov/cex/2008/Standard/age.pdf.

U.S. Department of Labor, Women's Bureau. (2007). *Quick stats on women workers, 2007*. Retrieved August 25, 2007, from www.dol.gov/wb/stats/main.htm.

U.S. Department of Labor, Women's Bureau (2009). *Quick stats on women workers, 2009*. Retrieved July 2, 2011, from www.dol.gov/wb/stats/main.htm.

U.S. Government Accountability Office. (2007). *Private pensions. Increased reliance on 401(k) plans calls for better information on fees*. Retrieved May 22, 2010, from www.gao.gov/new.items/d07530t.pdf.

U.S. News and World Report. (2009). *Simple exercise keeps brain at top of its game—In older women, being more fit helps cognitive function, study shows*. Retrieved October 1, 2010, from http://health.usnews.com/articles/health/healthday/2009/01/20/simple-exercise-keeps-brain-at-top-of-its-game.html.

U.S. Senate Hearing. (2001). Hearing testimony on anti-aging medicine. Special Senate Committee on Aging. September 10. Retrieved August 21, 2011, from http://www.quackwatch.org/01QuackeryRelatedTopics/Hearing/witness.html

UCLA Center for Health Policy Research. (2003). *California health interview survey, 2003.*

Uhlenberg, P. (2009). Children in an aging society. *Journal of Gerontology: Social Sciences, 64B*(4), 489–496.

Unilever. (2010). *Beauty has no age limit.* Retrieved September 25, 2010, from www.unilever.com/brands/hygieneandwelbeing/beautyandstyle/articles/beautyhasnoagelimit.aspx.

United Nations (2002a). *World population ageing: 1950–2050.* Department of Economic and Social Affairs. Population Division. Retrieved December 19, 2009, from www.un.org/esa/population/publications/worldageing19502050/regions.htm.

United Nations. (2002b). World population aging: 1950–2050. Department of Economic and Social Affairs. Population Division. Retrieved September 25, 2010, from www.un.org/esa/population/publications/worldageing19502050/pdf/sources_web.pdf.

United Seniors Health Council (A Program of the National Council on the Aging). (2004). *Private long-term care insurance: To buy or not to buy?* Retrieved October 3, 2004, from www.ncoa.org/attachments/LTC.pdf.

University of North Dakota. School of Medicine and Health Sciences. Center for Rural Health. (2003). *National family caregiver support program: North Dakota's American Indian caregivers.* Grand Forks, ND: Center for Rural Health, University of North Dakota, School of Medicine and Health Sciences.

Vaillant, G. E. (2002). *Aging well.* Boston: Little, Brown.

van den Hoonaard, D. K. (1997). Identity foreclosure: Women's experiences of widowhood as expressed in autobiographical accounts. *Ageing and Society, 17*(5), 533–551.

Van der Veen, R. (1990). Third age or inter-age universities? *Journal of Educational Gerontology, 5*(2), 96–105.

Van Ellett, T. (1993). Social health maintenance organizations: An American experiment. *Aging International, 20*(2), 39–41.

Van Praag, H. (2009). Exercise and the brain: something to chew on. *Trends in Neurosciences, 32*(5), 283–290.

Vares, T., Potts, A., Gavey, N., & Grace, V. M. (2007). Reconceptualizing cultural narratives of mature women's sexuality in the Viagra era. *Journal of Aging Studies, 21,* 153–164.

Verhaeghen, P., & Cerella, J. (2008). Everything we know about aging and response times: A meta-analytic integration. In S. M. Hofer & D. F. Alwin (Eds.), *Handbook of cognitive aging: Interdisciplinary perspectives* (pp. 134–150). Los Angeles: Sage.

Vesperi, M. D. (2002). Seeing the unseen: Literary interpretation in qualitative gerontology. In G. D. Rowles & N. E. Schoenberg (Eds.), *Qualitative gerontology* (2nd ed., pp. 263–278). New York: Springer.

Vierck, E. (2002). *Growing old in America.* Farmington, MI: Gale Group, Thomson Learning.

Vijg, J. (2000). Somatic mutations and aging: A re-evaluation. *Mutation Research, 447,* 117–135.

Villa, V. M., & Aranda, M. P. (2000). Demographic, economic, and health profile of older Latinos: Implications for health and long-term care policy and the Latino family. *Journal of Health and Human Services Administration, 23*(2), 161–180.

Vita, A. J., Terry, R. B., Hubert, H. B., & Fries, J. F. (1998). Aging, health risks, and cumulative disability. *New England Journal of Medicine, 338,* 1035–1041.

Vogler, G. P. (2006). Behavior genetics and aging. In J. E. Birren & K. W. Schaie (Eds.), *Handbook of the psychology of aging* (6th ed., pp. 41–55). Burlington, MA: Elsevier Academic Press.

Volunteer Match. (2010). Project Match, Inc. Retrieved July 14, 2010, from www.volunteermatch.org/search/org30406.js.

von Zglinicki, T., Nilsson, E., Docke, W. D., & Brunk, T. T. (1995). Lipofuscin accumulation and aging of fibroblasts. *Gerontology, 41*(Suppl. 2), 95–108.

Wagner, D. L. (1995). Senior center research in America: An overview of what we know. In D. Shollenberger (Ed.), *Senior centers in America: A blueprint for the future.* Washington, DC: National Council on the Aging and National Eldercare Institute on Multipurpose Senior Centers and Community Focal Points.

Wagner, D. L. (2003). *Workplace programs for family caregivers: Good business and good practice.* Retrieved November 25, 2004, from www.caregiver.org/caregiver/jsp/content/pdfs/op_2003_workplace_programs.pdf.

Wagner, L. S., & Wagner, T. H. (2003). Effect of age on the use of health and self-care information: Confronting the stereotype. *The Gerontologist, 43*(3), 318–324.

Wagnild, G. (2001). Growing old at home. In L. A. Pastalan & B. Schwarz (Eds.), *Housing choices and well-being of older adult: Proper fit* (pp. 71–84). New York: Haworth.

Walford, R. L. (1983). *Maximum life span.* New York: W. W. Norton.

Walker, A. (1996). Intergenerational relations and the provision of welfare. In A. Walker (Ed.), *The new generational contract: Intergenerational relations, old age and welfare* (pp. 10–36). London: UCL Press.

Walker, A. (2006). Aging and politics. In R. H. Binstock & L. K. George (Eds.), *Handbook of aging and the social sciences* (6th ed., pp. 339–359). Burlington, MA: Academic Press.

Walker, D. (2002, March 21). *Statement to the U.S. Special Committee on Aging,* p. 6.

Walker, D. (2004, February 4). The debt no one wants to talk about. *The New York Times.* www.nyTimes.com/2004/02/04/opinion/04WALK.html.

Walker, E. (2002). The needs of Indian elders: A hearing by the Senate Committee on Indian Affairs. Retrieved July 6, 2004, from www.nicoa.org/policy_walker.html.

Walker, J. (1983). The origins and maintenance of interest groups in America. *American Political Science Review, 77,* 390–406.

Wallace, S. P., & Castaneda, X. (2008). *Migration and health: Latinos in the United States.* Los Angeles:

National Council of the Government of Mexico (CONAPO) and the University of California.

Wallace, S. P., Mendez-Luck, C., & Castaneda, X. (2009). Heading south: Why Mexican immigrants in California seek health services in Mexico. *Medical Care, 47*(6), 662–669. Retrieved March 29, 2010, from http://journals. lww.com/lww-medicalcare/Abstract/2009/06000/ Heading_South__Why_Mexican_Immigrants_in.8.aspx.

Wallace, S. P., & Smith, S. E. (2009). *Half a million older Californians living alone unable to make ends meet.* Policy brief. Los Angeles: Insight Center for Community Economic Development. Retrieved March 29, 2010, from www.healthpolicy.ucla.edu/pubs/files/Older_CAs_ PB_0209.pdf.

Wallace, S. P., Williamson, J. B., Lung, R. G., & Powell, L. A. (1991). A lamb in wolf's clothing? The reality of senior power and social policy. In M. Minkler & C. L. Estes (Eds.), *Critical perspectives on aging: The political and moral economy of growing old* (pp. 95–114). Amityville, NY: Baywood.

Walls, C. T. (1992, Summer). The role of church and family support in the lives of older African Americans. *Generations,* pp. 33–36.

Walters, N., & Hermanson, S. (2001). *Subprime mortgage lending and older borrowers.* Report. Washington, DC: AARP Public Policy Institute. Retrieved October 19, 2010, from www-static-w2-md.aarp.org/research/credit-debt/mortgages/aresearch-import-182-DD57.html.

Wannell, T. (2007). Public Pensions and Work. *Perspectives on Labour and Income, 8*(8), 12–19.

Wapner, S., & Demick, J. (2003). Adult development. In J. Demick & C. Andreotti (Eds.), *Handbook of adult development* (pp. 63–83). New York: Kluwer.

Ward-Griffin, C. (2002). Boundaries and connections between formal and informal caregivers. *Canadian Journal on Aging, 21*(2), 205–216.

Wardrip, K. (2010, March). Strategies to meet the housing needs of older adults. *Insight on the Issues, 38.* Washington, DC: AARP Public Policy Institute. Retrieved July 12, 2010, from http://assets.aarp.org/rgcenter/ppi/ liv-com/i38-strategies.pdf.

Wasik, J. F. (2000, March–April). The fleecing of America's elderly. *Consumers Digest.*

Watson, C., & Hall, S. E. (2001). Older people and the social determinants of health. *Australian Journal on Ageing, 20*(3), 23–26.

Weaver, D. A. (1994). Work and retirement decisions of older women: A literature review. *Social Security Bulletin, 57*(1), 3–24.

Weber, M. (1955). *The Protestant ethic and the spirit of capitalism.* New York: Charles Scribner's Sons. (Original work published in 1905.)

WebMD. (2010). *Arthritis.* Retrieved January 16, 2010, from http://arthritis.webmd.com.

Weeks, L. (2009, April 3). *Looking for a full-time job can be a full-time job.* National Public Radio. Retrieved June 6, 2010, from www.npr.org/templates/story/story. php?storyId=102395801.

Weg, R. B. (1983a). Introduction: Beyond intercourse and orgasm. In R. B. Weg (Ed.), *Sexuality in the later years: Roles and behavior* (pp. 1–10). New York: Academic Press.

Weg, R. B. (1983b). The physiological perspective. In R. B. Weg (Ed.), *Sexuality in the later years: Roles and behavior* (pp. 39–80). New York: Academic Press.

Weg, R. (1987). Menopause: Biomedical aspects. In G. L. Maddox (Ed.),*The Encyclopedia of Aging* (pp. 433–437). New York: Springer.

Weibel-Orlando, J. (1990). Grandparenting styles: Native American perspectives. In J. Sokolovsky (Ed.), *The cultural context of aging: Worldwide perspectives* (pp. 109–125). New York: Bergin & Garvey.

Weindruch, R., & Walford, R. L. (1988). *The retardation of aging and disease by dietary restriction.* Springfield, IL: Charles C. Thompson.

Weinstein, M. H. (1988). Changing picture in retiree economics. *Statistical Bulletin, 69*(3), 2–7.

Weitzen, S., Teno, J. M., Fennell, M., & Mor, V. (2003). Factors associated with site of death: A national study of where people die. *Medical Care, 41*(2), 323–335.

Wenger, N. S., Phillips, R. S., Teno, J. M., Oye, R. K., Dawson, N. V., Liu, H., et al. (2000). Physician understanding of patient resuscitation preferences: Insights and clinical implications. *Journal of the American Geriatrics Society, 48*(5, Suppl), S44–S51.

Westheimer, R. K., & Kaplan, S. (1998). *Grandparenthood.* New York: Routledge.

Wheeler, J. R. C. (2003). Can a disease self-management program reduce health care costs? The case of older women with heart disease. *Medical Care, 41*(6), 706–715.

White-Means, S. I. (1993). Informal home care for frail black elderly. *Journal of Applied Gerontology, 12*(1), 18–33.

Whitfield, C. (2001). Benign or malign? Media stereotyping. *Nursing Older People, 13*(6), 10–13.

Wiener, J. M., & Harris, K. M. (1990, Fall). Myths & realities: Why most of what everybody knows about long-term care is wrong. *The Brookings Review,* pp. 29–34.

Wikipedia. (2011). *Wikipedia: About.* Retrieved June 10, 2011, from http://en.wikipedia.org/wiki/Wikipedia: About.

Wilcox, S. (2002). Physical activity in older women of color. *Topics in Geriatric Rehabilitation, 18*(1), 21–33.

Wilcox, S., Evenson, K. R., Aragaki, A., Wassertheil-Smoller, S., Mouton, C. P., & Loevinger, B. L. (2003). Effects of widowhood on physical and mental health, health behaviours, and health outcomes: The Women's Health Initiative. *Health Psychology, 22*(5), 513–522.

Wilcox, S., & King, A. C. (2004). Effects of life events and interpersonal loss on exercise adherence in older adults. *Journal of Aging and Physical Activity, 12*(2), 117–130.

Willens, H. (2003). Current boomer behavior and attitudes: What the surveys show. In L. M. Harris (Ed.), *After fifty: How the baby boom will redefine the mature market* (pp. 39–54). Ithaca, NY: Paramount Market Publishing.

Willert, A., & Semans, M. (2000). Knowledge and attitudes about later life sexuality: What clinicians need to know about helping the elderly. *Contemporary and Family Therapy, 22*(4), 415–435.

Williams, D. R., & Wilson, C. M. (2001). Race, ethnicity, and aging. In R. H. Binstock & L. K. George (Eds.), *Handbook of aging and the social sciences* (pp. 160–178). San Diego, CA: Academic Press.

Williamson, J., & Pahor, M. (2010). Evidence regarding the benefits of physical exercise. *Archives of Internal Medicine, 170*(2), 124–125.

Williamson, J. B. (2007). Social Security reform and responsibility across the generations. In R. A. Pruchno & M. A. Smyer (Eds.), *Challenges of an aging society: Ethical dilemmas, political issues* (pp. 311–331). Baltimore: Johns Hopkins University Press.

Williamson, J. B., Evans, L., Powell, L. A., & Hesse-Biber, S. (1982). *The politics of aging: Power and policy.* Springfield, IL: Charles C. Thomas.

Willis, S. L., Tennstedt, S. L., Marsiske, M., Ball, K., Elias, J., Koepke, K. M., et al., for the ACTIVE Study Group. (2006). Long-term effects of cognitive training on everyday functional outcomes in older adults: The ACTIVE Study. *Journal of the American Medical Association, 296,* 2805–2814. Retrieved December 14, 2010, from www.nia.nih.gov/Alzheimers/ResearchInformation/NewsReleases/Archives/PR2006/PR20061219ACTIVE.htm.

Willis, S. L., Schaie, K. W., & Martin, M. (2009). Cognitive plasticity. In V. L. Bengtson, M. Silverstein, M. M. Putney, & D. Gans (Eds.), *Handbook of theories of aging* (pp. 295–322). New York: Springer.

Wilmoth, J. M. (2001). Living arrangements among older immigrants in the United States. *The Gerontologist, 41*(2), 228–238.

Wilson, R. S., de Leon, C. F., Barnes, L. L., Schneider, J. A., Bienias, J. L., Evans, D. A., et al. (2002). Participation in cognitively stimulating activities and risk of incident Alzheimer disease. *JAMA 287*(6), 742–748.

Winkler, M. G. (1992). Walking to the stars. In T. R. Cole, D. D. Van Tassel, & R. Kastenbaum (Eds.), *Handbook of the humanities and aging* (pp. 258–284). New York: Springer.

Wister, A. V., & Dykstra, P. A. (2000). Formal assistance among Dutch older adults: An examination of the gendered nature of marital history. *Canadian Journal on Aging, 19*(4), 508–535.

Wister, A. V., & Strain, L. A. (1986). *Social support and well-being: A comparison of older widows and widowers.* Paper presented at the 21st annual meeting of the Canadian Sociology and Anthropology Association, Winnipeg, MB.

Wolf, R. S. (2001). Support groups for older victims of domestic violence. *Journal of Women and Aging, 13*(4), 71–83.

Wolf, R. S., & Pillemer, K. A. (1989). *Helping elderly victims: The reality of elder abuse.* New York: Columbia University Press.

Wolff, K., & Wortman, C. B. (2006). Psychological consequences of spousal loss among older adults. In D. Carr, R. M. Nesse, & C. B. Wortman (Eds.), *Spousal bereavement in late life* (pp. 81–115). New York: Springer.

Wolff, S. J., Kabunga, E., Tumwekwase, G., & Grosskurth, H. (2009). "This is where we buried our sons": people of advanced old age coping with the impact of the AIDS epidemic in a resource-poor setting in rural Uganda. *Ageing and Society, 29*(Part 1), 115–134.

Women's Institute for a Secure Retirement. (2000). *Instead of golden years, America's minority women face bleak retirement in poverty, new report finds.* Retrieved September 11, 2004, from www.wiser.heinz.org/prminority retirement.html.

Women's Institute for a Secure Retirement. (2006). *Unique challenges faced by women in preparing for and managing their retirement years.* Retrieved May 17, 2010, from www.wiserwomen.org/index.php?id=250&page=WISER_Report:_Women_Face_Unique_Challenges_When_Planning_for_Retirement#_ftn6.

Wong, R. (2002). Migration and socioeconomic conditions of older adults. *Demos: carta demografica sobre Mexico (DEMOS: A demographic letter concerning Mexico), 14.* Retrieved September 18, 2004, from www.ssc.upenn.edu/mbas/Papers/3.pdf.

Wood, J. B., & Estes, C. L. (1990). Impact of DRGs on community-based service providers: Implications for the elderly. *American Journal of Public Health, 80*(7), 840–843.

Wood, S., Giles-Corti, B., & Bulsara, M. (2005). The pet connection: Pets as a conduit for social capital? *Social Science & Medicine, 61,* 1159–1173.

Woodruff, D. S., & Birren, J. E (Eds.). (1975). *Aging: Scientific perspectives and social issues.* New York: Van Nostrand.

Woodruff-Pak, D. S. (1989). Aging and intelligence: Changing perspectives in the twentieth century. *Journal of Aging Studies, 3,* 91–118.

Woolston, C. (2009). *Sex and high blood pressure. Ills & conditions.* Retrieved July 1, 2010, from www.ahealthyme.com/topic/bpsex.

World Health Organization & International Network for the Prevention of Elder Abuse. (2002). *Missing voices: Views of older persons on elder abuse.* Geneva, Switzerland: World Health Organization.

Wright, W., & Davies, C. (2007). *Retirement security survey report* Washington, DC: AARP Knowledge Management.

Wu, K. (2003). *Income and poverty of older Americans in 2001: A chartbook.* Washington, DC: American Association of Retired Persons. Retrieved September 6, 2004, from http://research.aarp.org/econ/ip_cb2001.pdf.

Wu, K. (2006a). *Income and poverty of older Americans in 2004*. www.census.gov/hhes/www/poverty/histpov/histpov3.html.

Wu, K. (2006b). *Income and poverty of older Americans in 2004: A chartbook*. Washington, DC: AARP Public Policy Institute. Retrieved May 9, 2010, from http://assets.aarp.org/rgcenter/econ/ip_cb2004.pdf.

Wu, M.-T. (2000). *Factors that influence the participation of senior citizens in recreational and leisure activities*. Ann Arbor, MI: UMI Dissertation Services, ProQuest Information and Learning.

Wu, Z., & Schimmele, C. M. (2007). Uncoupling in later life. *Generations, 31*(3), 41–46.

Wykle, M., & Kaskel, B. (1994). Increasing the longevity of minority older adults through improved health status. In *Minority elders: Five goals toward building a public policy base* (2nd ed., pp. 32–39). Washington, DC: Gerontological Society of America.

Xu, J., Kochanek, K. D., Murphy, S. L., & Tejada-Vera, B. (2010). Deaths: Final data for 2007. *National Vital Statistics Reports, 28*(19). Hyattsville, MD: National Center for Health Statistics.

Xu, J., Kochanek, K. D., Tejada-Vera, B. (2009, August 19). Deaths: Preliminary data for 2007. *National Vital Statistics Reports, 58*(1). Retrieved December 20, 2009, from www.cdc.gov/nchs/data/nvsr/nvsr58/nvsr58_01.pdf).

Yahnke, R. E. (2000). Intergeneration and regeneration: The meaning of old age in films and videos. In T. R. Cole, R. Kastenbaum, & R. E. Ray (Eds.), *Handbook of the humanities and aging* (2nd ed., pp. 293–323). New York: Springer.

Yankelovich, D., & Vance, C. R. (2001). Final request. *American Demographics, 23*(4), 22.

Yee, D. L. (1999). Preventing chronic illness and disability: Asian Americans. In M. L. Wykle & A. B. Ford (Eds.), *Serving minority elders in the 21st century* (pp. 37–50). New York: Springer.

Yeo, G. (2009). How will the U.S. healthcare system meet the challenge of the ethnogeriatric imperative? *Journal of the American Geriatrics Society, 57*(7), 1278–1285. Retrieved July 23, 2010, from www3.interscience.wiley.com.libaccess.sjlibrary.org/journal/122475454/issue.

Yoon, D. P., & Lee, E-K. O. (2007). Impact of religiousness, spirituality, and social support on psychological well-being among older adults in rural areas. *Journal of Gerontological Social Work, 48*(3–4), 281–298.

YourEncore. (2010). *Your Encore*. Retrieved May 22, 2010, from www.yourencore.com.

Yu-Ai Kai. (2010). *Programs and services*. Retrieved October 19, 2010, from www.yuaikai.org/index.php?option=com_content&view=article&id=1&Itemid=4.

Zacks, R. T., Hasher, L., & Li, K. Z. H. (2000). Human memory. In F. I. M. Craik & T. A. Salthouse (Eds.), *The handbook of aging and cognition* (2nd ed., pp. 293–357). Mahwah, NJ: Erlbaum.

Zarit, S. H. (2009). A good old age: Theories of mental health and aging. (pp. 675–690). In V. L. Bengtson, M. Silverstein, M. M. Putney, & D. Gans (Eds.), *Handbook of theories of aging* (pp. 573–593). New York: Springer.

Zarit, S. H., Femia, E. E., Watson, J., Rice-Oeschger, L., & Kakos, B. (2004). Memory club: A group intervention for people with early-stage dementia and their care partners. *The Gerontologist, 44*(2), 262–269.

Zawadski, R. T., & Eng, C. (1988). Case management in capitated long term care. *Health Care Financing Review, Annual Supplement*, pp. 75–81.

Zeiss, A., & Kasl-Godley, J. (2001). Sexuality in older adults' relationships. *Generations, 25*(2), 18–25.

Zeleznick, J., Post, L. F., Mulvhill, M., Jacobs, L. G., Burton, W. B., & Dubler, N. N. (1999). The doctor-proxy relationship: Perception and communication. *Journal of Law, Medicine and Ethics, 13,* 17.

Zhang, A. (2001, July 19). China faces the challenge of an aging society. *Beijing Review*, pp. 12–15.

Zielenziger, M. (2009a, July 1). Fresh start: Jobless auto workers go back to school. *AARP Bulletin*, pp. 18–20.

Zielenziger, M. (2009b). From job loss to Peace Corps. *AARP Bulletin*. Retrieved November 19, 2010, from www.aarp.org/giving-back/volunteering/info-09-2009/from_job_loss_to_peace_corps.htmls.

Zimmerman, L., Mitchell, B., Wister, A., & Gutman, G. (2000). Unanticipated consequences: A comparison of expected and actual retirement timing among older women. *Journal of Women and Aging, 12*(1–2), 109–128.

Zimmerman, S., Sloane, P. D., Eckert, J. K., Gruber-Baldini, A. L., Morgan, L. A., Hebel, J. R., et al. (2005). How good is assisted living? Findings and implications from an outcomes study. *Journal of Gerontology: Social Sciences, 60B,* S195–S204.

Zsembik, B. A., & Singer, A. (1990). The problem of defining retirement among minorities: The Mexican Americans. *The Gerontologist, 30*(6), 749–757.

Zunzunegui, M., Alvarado, B. E., Del Ser, T., & Otero, A. (2003). Social networks, social integration, and social engagement determine cognitive decline in community-dwelling Spanish older adults. *Journal of Gerontology: Social Sciences, 58B,* S93–S100.

GLOSSARY OF TERMS

AARP (formerly the American Association of Retired Persons) The largest senior advocacy group in the United States. The AARP lobbies government, supports research on older people, and informs members about political issues.

absolute deprivation Refers to the minimal income needed to buy food, clothing, shelter, and health care. People who lack this minimum income are poor. The government sets a poverty level each year based on this minimum.

absolute number of older people The total number of older people in a society.

accessibility A health care service or program is accessible if a person can get to it.

active euthanasia Intervening actively to end a person's life.

activism Working outside the system through protest, monitoring elected officials' behaviors, and street theater.

activities of daily living (ADLs) Basic activities needed to live alone or to live a good quality of life. Examples include toileting, preparing food, and bathing.

activity theory The belief that activity leads to the highest satisfaction in later life.

acute illness Short-term illness or condition; treatment often leads to full recovery. Examples include measles, influenza, and a sprained ankle.

ADL Activities of daily living, a way to measure a person's ability to care for himself or herself.

adult day care A program that provides socializing, recreation, and meals for older people outside their homes in a group setting.

advance directive A precise statement of the desired treatment and care, including what medical actions to be taken under what conditions and a declaration of who has the right to decide.

advocacy Working within the system through lobbying and presentations to government to achieve political change.

age cohort A group of people born at about the same time.

age effects The effect of the passage of time on the body and the self.

age-graded normative life events Life events linked to a specific age or stage of development. Society often structures these events (a graduation, a wedding) to mark a status passage.

age integration Housing for many age groups—for example, an apartment building that houses people of all ages from children to retirees.

age-irrelevant society A society that judges people by who they are and what they can do, rather than their age.

age segregation Housing for only one age group—for example, an apartment complex for older people.

age stratification system The system of age grades that every society has. People move through these grades as they age.

age stratification theory Society provides older people with specific roles to play and with expectations about activity in later life.

ageism "A process of systematic stereotyping and discrimination against people because they are old" (Butler, 1987, p. 22).

aging enterprise The complex of professional services (many of them government sponsored) that serve the older population.

aging network The collection of programs and services that provide supports to older people.

aging in place Living in the same location, usually a home or apartment, until late old age or death.

amenity migration A move in retirement in order to enjoy the lifestyle in a new location. People in the colder northern United States might make amenity migrations to the Sunbelt.

anti-aging medicine and science An approach to slowing, stopping, or reversing the effects of aging. The anti-aging movement often promotes methods of health care that stand outside the standards of Western science and medicine.

assimilation continuum Ramon Valle's idea that minority assimilation ranges from very traditional (nonassimilation) to bicultural to very assimilated.

assisted living Provides personal care such as meals and bathing, and 24-hour supervision.

autodidacts People who take charge of their own learning.

autonomy Similar to capability; the ability of a person to independently carry out daily activities.

availability A health care service or program is available if it exists.

bean-pole family structure A family that has many generations alive at the same time, but with few people in each generation.

birth rates   The numbers of live births per 1,000 population.

bridge job   The job a person holds after a career job, but before full retirement. Bridge jobs include part-time work, second careers, and self-employment after retirement.

busy ethic   The flip side of the work ethic, this ethic values the active life in retirement. It allows people to justify retirement in terms of mainstream social beliefs and values.

capability (competence)   A measure of a person's ability to live comfortably in an environment.

capitated payments   A set amount (usually per month) that a program such as an HMO gets to serve each of its patients. The HMO must use its resources to provide services for this amount or less in order to make a profit.

care manager   Someone who coordinates health care for an individual.

caregiver burden   The feeling of physical and emotional exhaustion that caregivers sometimes feel.

chore services   Paid household help.

chronic illness   Long-term illness or condition, often a lifelong problem; treatment controls symptoms but seldom leads to full recovery. Examples include arthritis, asthma, and hypertension.

cognitive reserve   Individuals have a reserve mental capacity. This allows a person to function well in later life even in the face of decline in brain function. Education, for example, can increase a person's cognitive reserve. Also, people can enhance their reserve through training and activities that challenge the mind.

cohort effects   Effects of year of birth on a person's life. People born around the same time have many of the same experiences in life.

cohort flow   As cohorts age (and members die), cohorts replace one another in society's age structure. New groups of people enter each age grade over time.

coinsurance   Payments the patient makes to cover part of a health care bill. For example, a person may pay 20% of all health care costs (in addition to paying a yearly deductible).

compassionate ageism   The belief that older people are needy and deserve special policies to help them.

compassionate stereotype   A stereotype that attempts to arouse sympathy or pity for older people.

competence   A person's skill at real-world tasks.

compression of morbidity   The idea that modern science can push chronic illness and disability to a time shortly before death.

congregate (or enriched) housing   Housing that provides amenities such as meals on site for residents.

congregation   of a population takes place when people of all ages move to an area, but older people arrive at the fastest pace. Florida, Arizona, and North Carolina fit this pattern.

continuing care retirement communities (CCRCs)   Offer health and social services to members for a fee.

continuity theory   The belief that people adapt to change by integrating new experience with past history and moving forward.

contractors   People who do not take up new activities in later life to replace activities of their younger years.

convoy model of support   This model of support uses an image of concentric circles to describe relationships with the older person. The strongest relationships exist in the closest circle. Outer circles show weaker relationships. These rings of relationships follow a person (like a ship convoy) throughout life. The relationships of people in this convoy grow and change with changing life circumstances.

copayments   Like coinsurance; the portion of a medical bill that the patient has to pay.

core leisure activities   Activities such as reading and socializing, often home based and inexpensive.

correlation   A relationship between two things (e.g., age and intelligence scores). It does not show that one thing causes another. For example, age only partly accounts for low intelligence scores among older people. Education differences between young and older people also influence these scores.

critical gerontology   The theory attempts to expose the effects of positivism on older people. Critical researchers attempt to empower people by giving them an understanding of the forces that shape their lives.

cross-linking   Damage to DNA and proteins due to free radical attack and other types of chemical attack (such as glycation).

crystallized intelligence   Abilities such as vocabulary, association of past and present ideas, and technical ability, which depend on a person's education or store of information.

cultural competence   An older minority person's ability to function in the wider society.

cumulative disadvantage theory   Refers to the inequalities that build up over the course of a person's life and lead to inequality in old age.

death rates   The numbers of deaths per 1,000 people of a given age. Demographers translate this into life expectancy at a given age.

deductible   The amount of money a person has to pay before health care insurance begins to cover health care bills. For example, a person may pay the first $100 per year of health care expenses.

defined benefit plans   Pension plans that state how much a worker will get out of the plan when he or she retires. This may be phrased as a proportion of the best 5 or 10 years of salary.

defined contribution plans   Pension plans that state how much a worker pays in. The amount that a worker gets depends on the economic conditions at the time of the worker's retirement.

demographers   People who study population dynamics. The study of population dynamics is demography.

demographic changes   Changes in the structure and dynamics of the population. This includes changes in birth, death, and migration rates.

demographic transition   The transition from a society that has high birth and death rates to one with low birth and death rates.

demography   The study of the size, structure, and development of human populations.

Department of Housing and Urban Development (HUD)   A primary source of subsidized housing for older people in the United States.

developed nations   Countries that have industrial economies and modernized social institutions and have gone through the demographic transition. The developed nations are the nations of North America and Europe, including the former Soviet Union, as well as Japan, Australia, and New Zealand.

developing nations   Nations that have begun to industrialize, have begun to develop modern social institutions (such as schools and hospitals), and have begun to go through the demographic transition. The developing nations are all nations not listed under **developed nations**.

developmental intelligence   Cohen calls this an "advanced style of cognition." Three styles characterize this type of thinking: relativistic thinking, dualistic thinking, and systematic thinking.

developmental stake   *See* **generational stake**.

diagnosis-related groupings (DRGs)   System in which hospitals categorize patients by medical condition. Medicare reimburses hospitals for a fixed number of days of care according to the patient's DRG.

disability-free life expectancy   The number of years a person will live without a severe or moderate disability.

discouraged workers   Workers who give up looking for work often because they can't find work or they can't find work in their field or at a pay rate that makes working worthwhile. Older workers may give up rather than face discrimination in employment.

discrimination   Unfair treatment based on prejudice rather than on merit.

disengagement theory   The belief that as people age, social interaction naturally decreases.

displaced workers   People who have lost their jobs due to economic slowdowns, plant closings, or an end to their positions.

dominant group   The racial or ethnic group with the most power in society. This group may or may not have a numerical majority of the population.

durable power of attorney   The power that gives someone—usually a lawyer, child, friend, or other family member—the right to make decisions on behalf of the ill person.

ego integrity   The acceptance of the notion that one's life cycle is something complete and unique.

elderly dependency ratio   The ratio of people aged 65 and over to the population aged 15 to 64.

elderly support ratio   The number of people age 65 and over per 100 people ages 20 to 64 years old.

elderspeak   A specialized speech register resembling baby talk sometimes used in addressing older adults.

employment pensions   Pensions from people's place of work. Workers pay into this plan during their working years. The employer often pays into this plan as well.

encoding   Learning information, preparing it for storage in the mind.

encore careers   Careers that older people take up in retirement. Often these new jobs fulfill a higher purpose, such as volunteering to help others and the community.

environmental demand (environmental press)   A measure of the demand that an environment places on an older person.

euthanasia   Ending the life of someone suffering a terminal illness or incurable condition.

expanders   People who begin new activities later in life to replace activities from their younger years.

extrinsic aging   Changes in the body due to the impact of the environment or lifestyle choices such as sunlight, smoking, or noise.

fertility   As defined by demographers, fertility is the number of live births per 1,000 women aged 15 to 44.

fertility rate   The number of live births regardless of age of mother per 1,000 women aged 15 to 44.

fictive kin   Friends, neighbors, and service workers whom an older person views as family members.

fluid intelligence   Activities such as creative design, quick response to a question, or mental rearrangement of facts, which rely on how well the central nervous system works.

formal support systems   Health care and social service systems, often run by the government or some large institution. The client pays for the service (or someone pays on the client's behalf).

free radicals   Oxygen radicals that bond with chemicals in the body and cause damage to cell and body functions.

functional capacity   People's ability to function on their own.

functional specificity of relationships model   This model of support to older people recognizes that a person may provide one type of support or a broad range of support. This will depend on how the relationship between the supporter and the older person has developed over time. Gender, marital status, parenthood, and geographical closeness or distance all play a role in deciding the kind of support a person can give.

generations   Groups of people who share an awareness of their common historical or cultural experiences, but who may come from different age cohorts.

generational equity   Refers to the concern that middle-aged people will be burdened with the costs of caring for a large older population (e.g., high Social Security, Medicare, and other service costs). Some groups propose cuts to programs for older people to free up money for the young.

generational event theory   Attitudes form for a generation in their teens. People who grow up at the same time in the same society share the same attitudes.

generational life course   Within generational life courses, the life plan is to mature into adulthood, have a family, work in subsistence, and simply live.

generational stake   Compared with their children, older people feel a greater stake in having good parent–child relations. This leads older parents to emphasize family harmony and solidarity.

gerontology   The social or natural scientific study of aging. *Geriatrics* refers to the medical practice of care for older people.

gerotranscendence   The self expands its boundaries and reflects on the meaning of human life and death. It includes a deepening spirituality and a greater sense of intergenerational community.

glycation   A process that occurs due to the long-term exposure of proteins to glucose (sugar) molecules. This leads to cross-linking and chemical malfunctions in the body.

Gray Panthers   Founded in 1972 as a multiage activist group. The Panthers used protests and street theater to achieve their goals.

Hayflick limit   The maximum number of times a cell can divide. This differs for each organism.

health care directive   Instructions with specific information for family members and doctors about the amount of treatment the person prefers under different conditions.

health maintenance organizations (HMOs)   Health care programs that provide members with all or most of their health care needs for a set fee.

hierarchical compensatory model   The idea that caregivers come from the care receiver's closest relations first (spouse and children). Then caregiving responsibilities move outward in a hierarchy from closer to more distant relatives and friends.

home equity conversion loans (HECs)   Methods for freeing up the equity (or value) of a home.

homemaker credits   This program would, if enacted, give homemakers pension credit based on the estimated income they would earn from their work at home. The plan would pay pensions out of general revenue, or homemakers might pay into the plan.

hospice   A health care service that meets the special needs of dying patients.

hypokinetic disease   Poor health related to lack of movement.

IADL   Instrumental activity of daily living, such as banking and cooking.

industrialization   A social process leading from a rural economy based on animal power and relatively low productivity to a market economy based on steam and electrical power with high productivity.

in-migration   Migration into a country, region, or state.

institutional completeness   The amount of institutional support available to an older minority person. More complete communities have an array of formal supports available to older people.

institutionalized life course   The life course that emerged in the late 19th and early 20th centuries in the United States. It is shaped by modern education and industrialization.

instrumental activities of daily living (IADLs)   Activities that enhance a person's quality of life. Examples include shopping, using the phone, and light housework.

intrinsic aging   Physical decline due to the normal working of the body (such as the Hayflick limit).

least developed nations   Refers to nations that have the lowest indicators of socioeconomic development among nations, such as the lowest per capita income, poorest health, and lowest literacy.

less developed nations   Refers to nations that have a low rating among nations on measures of socioeconomic development, such as low life expectancy at birth, low educational level, and low standard of living.

leveling   A decrease in the gap between minority and dominant group members as they age. For example, the income gap between minority and dominant group members closes with age.

life course perspective   The idea that life unfolds from birth to death in a social, cultural, and historical context. This perspective looks at how people are affected by social institutions, historical periods and events, personal biography, life cycle stage, life events, and resources.

life expectancy   The number of additional years a person can expect to live at a given age (e.g., life expectancy at birth, or life expectancy at age 65).

life portfolio   This consists of a person's commitments to specific activities and relationships. These include family, community service, spiritual development, recreation, and in some cases work.

life span   The maximum number of years a specific organism can live.

lipofuscin   A fatty deposit that builds up in the cells with age.

living will   A legal document that specifies the limits of health care treatment desired in case of a terminal illness.

lobby groups   Groups that attempt to influence politicians' behavior on certain issues.

macro-level theories   Theories of large-scale social phenomena such as the impact of the government or social policy on older people.

macrophages   Immune system cells that seek out invading or noxious molecules, engulf them, destroy them, and send them to the kidneys for elimination. This protects the body from processes such as glycation and cross-linking.

mastery accomplishments   Achievements that demonstrate skill and ability. This leads to feelings of self-efficacy.

median age   The midpoint of a population. One-half the population is above and one-half below the median age.

Medicaid   The federal government health care program for low-income Americans of all ages.

Medicare   The federal government health care program for all people who receive Social Security. Medicare contains two parts: hospital insurance (Part A) and medical insurance (Part B).

melting pot   The idea that the United States takes in immigrants and transforms them into typical Americans. The melting pot concept assumes that immigrants give up their minority status and ethnic identity over time.

micro-level theories   Studies of small-scale social phenomena such as personal interactions and small groups.

migration Movement into or out of a country or other area. Internal migration can take place from one region of a country to another.

modernization The transformation from a preindustrial to an industrial society.

mortality The death rate generally measured as the number of deaths per 1,000 population for a given age group. For infants it is measured as the number of deaths per 1,000 live births.

mortality crossover Minority group members show shorter life expectancies than whites until old age, and then in later old age they show greater life expectancies than whites. This is the crossover.

multiple jeopardy The theory that the negative effect of being a member of one risk group is increased if you are also a member of another risk group. For example, gerontologists say that older minority women may suffer the effects of multiple jeopardy.

naturally occurring retirement community (NORC) A building or neighborhood with at least half the people aged 60 or over. This occurs without conscious planning as people in a community age in place.

near poverty Family income between 100% and 199% of the poverty level.

new ageism Stereotyping old age as a time of loss and decline to justify help for older people. *See* **compassionate stereotype**.

off time Refers to life events that occur at a time other than when society has programmed them to occur (e.g., a first birth for a woman at age 50).

Older Americans Act The government act passed in 1965 (and amended since then) that established programs and services for older people nationwide.

on time Refers to life events that occur when society has programmed them to occur (e.g., a high school graduation in the later teen years).

out-migration Movement out of a country, region, or state.

overmedicalized service Use of the medical model to treat chronic illness and functional problems. For example, the use of sleeping pills to help someone sleep when more exercise during the day would do the same thing.

palliative care Care directed toward improving the quality of life for the dying, including symptom control and spiritual support as well as bereavement support and education.

paradigms Frameworks used to think about and organize an understanding of natural or social phenomena. They define what questions scientists ask and how they conduct their studies.

pay-as-you-go plan A pension plan such as Social Security that funds current benefits to retirees from current workers' payments.

period effects Effects on a person in a study due to the period in which the study takes place. An economic downturn during a study of retirement, for example, will influence people's decision to retire.

peripheral leisure activities Activities such as sports and travel; they often take place outside the home and at some expense.

personal care Community services such as help with bathing or toileting.

phase III phenomenon The buildup of debris in the cell and the decline in cell function.

physician-assisted suicide (PAS) Actively helping someone end his or her life either because the person asks for death or to relieve suffering.

planned retirement communities A community planned, usually by a developer, to house and serve older people.

plasticity The ability to change and adapt with age.

play siblings A type of fictive kin; nonrelatives (e.g., neighbors or formal care workers) who bond with an older person and are considered a best friend or sibling.

pleiotropic genes Genes that have a positive function at one point in life but that may harm the body through their action later in life.

pluralistic society A society in which many racial and ethnic groups exist side by side. People maintain their racial and ethnic heritage and still take part in the wider society. (This contrasts with the concept of U.S. society as a melting pot.)

political economy A perspective that looks at social organization and how political and economic conditions shape life experiences such as retirement.

population aging An increase in the number of older people in a society, an increase in a society's median age, or an increase in the proportion of older people in a society.

portability This allows a person to transfer the money value of his or her pension to another plan.

positivism Employs the methods of natural science—mathematical measurement, statistical methods, and cause-and-effect models.

postindustrial society A society that has a large service sector, many complex social institutions, and a high standard of living. Contemporary U.S. society is postindustrial.

poverty Family income less than 100% of the poverty level. The poverty line depends on the size of the family and the number of children in the family.

power of attorney Gives someone (often a lawyer, but also possibly a child, spouse, other family member, or health care provider) the right to make financial or health care decisions on behalf of the older person if the person loses his or her mental capacity.

prejudice A negative judgment made about someone based on a trait or on his or her membership in a particular group.

preretirement education (PRE) Programs and information that help a person plan for retirement.

primary caregiver The person who takes on most of the responsibility for caring for an older person.

Prospective Payment System (PPS) System in which hospitals are paid a predetermined amount for treatment of each patient disorder.

qualitative methods "Look at social life from multiple points of view and explain how people construct identities" (Neuman, 2003, p. 146).

quantitative methods Relationships between and among factors (variables) are emphasized through numerical measurement (quantity, amount, frequency).

recomposition of a population takes place when older people move into an area that younger people leave. For example, some older people move to rural areas to retire. Arkansas and Missouri fit this pattern.

rectangularization of the life curve The idea that more and more people will live the full, natural life span. This idea also assumes that humans have a fixed and unchangeable life span.

relative deprivation Defines a person as poor in relation to people who have more money. This definition would say that the bottom 10th of income earners are poor.

respite care Short-term relief for caregivers of chronically ill patients.

retrieval The recall of information from mental storage.

sarcopenia The decrease in muscle and bone content that comes with age.

scapegoating Blaming a person or group (such as older people) for a complex and hard-to-solve social problem (such as the national debt).

second career A new career after retirement; a career shaped by a person's interests and passions.

secondary labor market Jobs that offer low pay and few benefits and require physical labor; common in the retail and service industries. These jobs often lead to disability.

selective optimization with compensation (SOC) A description of how people who age successfully respond to life's challenges. They select activities that optimize their abilities. They compensate for changes by setting new priorities.

self-efficacy People's belief that they can meet environmental demands.

semantic memory Our store of factual information.

senior center A place where older adults come together for services and activities.

sex ratio The ratio of men to women in the older population.

skilled nursing facility A facility that provides medical care by licensed nursing staff.

social agency model The use of a senior center as an agency that provides social and health care services.

social capital The resources available to a person, including social supports.

social gerontology Psychosocial, socioeconomic-environmental, and practice-related studies of aging are included. It views aging from the perspective of the individual and the social system.

social health maintenance organizations (SHMOs) HMOs with social services such as counseling.

social institutions Sociologists define social institutions as organized patterns of social behavior.

Social Security The U.S. retirement income system. Workers pay into this system throughout their lives and collect a pension when they retire.

Social Security (OASDI) Old Age, Survivors, and Disability Insurance. The federal government pension plan begun in 1935.

stereotyping A stereotype usually has some basis in reality, but it represents an overgeneralization about a person or group. A stereotype leads us to treat older people in terms of a general pattern or characteristic, rather than as unique individuals.

storage Saving learned information for retrieval at a later time.

structural lag Change in social structures (such as educational institutions) lags behind individual change; for example, few educational organizations today respond to the educational preferences of older people.

successful aging (As defined by Rowe & Kahn, 1991) refers to people who show good physical function in later life.

Supplemental Security Income (SSI) Program started in 1972 to help the poorest blind, disabled, and older people. SSI gets paid out of general revenues.

task specificity model The idea that people take on caregiving roles according to their ability to perform a task.

Thomas theorem Sociologist W. I. Thomas said, "If people define situations as real, they are real in their consequences."

three-legged stool A description of the U.S. retirement income system. The system includes public pensions, private pensions, and savings (the legs of the stool).

total dependency ratio The ratio of the population 0 to 14 years plus the population aged 65 and older to the population aged 15 to 64.

trajectories Long-term patterns of stability and change.

transitions Changes in social status or social roles (in particular, when those changes occur, how long they last, etc.).

underfunded pension plans A pension plan that does not have enough money in it to meet its future obligations to workers.

urbanization An increase in the size of cities and in the concentration of people in cities. Urbanization often goes along with modernization and industrialization.

vesting This means that workers will get all or part of their earned benefit from a company when they leave. They will get this benefit even if they have moved to a different company.

voluntary organization model The use of a senior center as social club.

weak social ties Weak social ties link people from diverse backgrounds, exposing them to new views and opinions.

working memory This type of memory selects, manipulates, and stores recent information.

youth dependency ratio The ratio of the population 0 to 14 to the population aged 15 to 64.

INDEX

A

AAA. *see* American Automobile Association (AAA)
AARP. *see* American Association of Retired Persons (AARP)
Abdulrazak, B., 101
Abeles, R. P., 140
Aberg, J., 319
Abnormal aging, 148–154
Aboderin, I., 58, 59
Abrahams, R., 222
Absolute deprivation (poverty), 243
Absolute number of older people, 54
Accessibility
  housing needs, 297
  for poor/old, 214
  of services, 230
Accessory apartments, 308
Accessory dwelling units (ADUs), 308
Accius, J. C., 310
Accumulation, 71
ACE. *see* American Council on Education (ACE)
Achenbaum, W. A., 20, 27, 44, 46, 50, 443, 444, 459, 461
Ackerman, P. L., 125, 130
Acquired immune deficiency syndrome (AIDS)
  African Americans, 96
  Hispanic Americans, 96
  and older people, 96
Active living, 331–333
Activism, 449–450
Activities of daily living (ADLs), 93–99, 202, 219, 386
  limitations, 383
Activity theory, 144, 412
Acton, K., 189
Acute illness, 231
AD. *see* Alzheimer's disease (AD)
Adams, C., 127
Adams, G. A., 271
Adams, P. F., 103, 189, 190
Aday, R. H., 6
ADEA. *see* Age Discrimination in Employment Act (ADEA)
ADLs. *see* Activities of daily living (ADLs)

Administration for Children and Families, 261
Administration on Aging (AoA), 451
Adult children
  caregiving, 396
  marital status of, 387
  parents and, 388
  social support from, 386–388
Adult day care, 201
  programs, 223
ADUs. *see* Accessory dwelling units (ADUs)
Advance directive, 419–422
  communication and, 423–426
  minorities and, 422–423
Advertisements. *see also* Media
  and older people, 20
Advocacy, 442–444
  AARP, 444–445
  gray lobby groups, 443
  interest group coalitions, 449
  limits of, 445–447
  Medicare Catastrophic Coverage Act, 447–448
  Medicare Modernization Act, 448–449
Aerobic exercise, 106
Africa, population aging in, 59
African Americans, 171–178
  advance directive, 422
  amenity migration, 72
  Asian American *vs.*, 186–187
  care receivers, 385
  family/community life, 173–175
  future of aging, 177–178
  grandparents, 175, 372, 391
  health, 167, 171–172
  hospice care, 418
  hypertension, 93
  income, 172–173
  life course perspective, 169
  life expectancy, 10
  men, 175–177
  minority older people, 160
  mortality rate, 10, 65
  population growth in, 70, 71
  rates of disability for, 95
  religion and, 143, 176
  retirement, 272–276
  risk of AIDS and, 96
  secondary labor market, 273

social support, 175–176, 391
stress reduction approach, 110
subgroups, 164
support networks, 383–384
traditional values of, 391
Transcendental Meditation, 110
women, 173, 175
Agahi, N., 145, 327
Agarwal, M., 279
AGE. *see* Americans for Generational Equity (AGE)
Age cohort, 33, 35
Age discrimination, workplace and, 12–14
Age Discrimination Act, 1975, 22
Age Discrimination in Employment Act (ADEA), 12, 22, 268
Age effects, 40
Age-graded normative life events, 147–148, 361
Age grades, 32–33
Age integration, 302
Age-irrelevant society, 20
Ageism, 3–4
  ageless self and, 14–16
  compassionate, 3, 448
  culture as source of, 4–9
  defined, 3
  and discrimination at workplace, 12–14
  lack of knowledge and, 8–9
  media as source of, 5–8
  responses to, 16–17
  and retail sales, 6
  self-esteem and, 141
  and workplace, 12–14
Ageism in America, 6
Ageless self, 14–16
Age/period/cohort (APC) problem, 40
Age segregation, 302
Age stratification theory, 33, 34, 147, 331, 332
  criticisms of, 34–36
Aggarwal, N. T., 133
Aging
  African Americans, future of, 177–178
  American Indians, future of, 192–193
  Asian Americans, future of, 188–189
  education programs, 20–21
  enterprise, 3
  federal government initiatives on, 454

Dunkle, R. E., 383
Dunlop, B., 405, 406
Dunn, N. J., 327
Dupuis, S. L., 386
Duque, G., 89
Durable power of attorney, 422
Durkheim, E., 153
Dustman, R. E., 136
Dwyer, L. L., 222
Dychtwald, K., 320
Dykstra, P. A., 360, 378, 388, 389
Dyson, T., 308

E

EAAT. *see* Elder Abuse Aptitude Test
   (EAAT)
Eaker, E. D., 108
Early retirement, 277
Easom, L. R., 102, 227
Eastaugh, A. M., 419
Easterlin, R. A., 65, 147
Eazor, L. R., 395
Ebeling, A., 359
Eberhardt, S., 186
Eberly, S., 152
EBRI. *see* Employee Benefit Research Insti-
   tute (EBRI)
Ebring, L., 392
Eby, D. W., 317, 318
Eby, S., 280
ECHO. *see* Elder cottage housing opportuni-
   ties (ECHO)
Eckert, J. K., 413
Education programs
   elderhostel, 341
   formal higher, 337–339
   future of, 345–347
   gerontology/geriatric, 20–21
   informal educational options, 339–341
   leisure, 328–329
   lifelong learning institutes, 341–345
   seniors, 337–347
EEOC. *see* Equal Employment Opportunity
   Commission (EEOC)
Effros, R. B., 86, 87
Eggebeen, D. J., 392
Eglit, H. C., 14
Ego integrity, 412
Eilertsen, T., 413
Einstein, E. O., 123, 127, 130
Eisenberg, J. M., 312
Ejaz, F. K., 312
Ekerdt, D. J., 283
Elder, G. H., 33, 34, 148, 279
Elder, G. H., Jr., 35, 374
Elder, S., 432
Elder abuse, 402–406
   attitudes/beliefs about, 405
   case studies of, 404
   interventions/policies, 404–406
   responses to, 403–404

theories of, 403
types of, 402
Elder Abuse Aptitude Test (EAAT), 405
Eldercare
   programs, 397
   and workplace, 400–401
Elder cottage housing opportunities
   (ECHO), 308
Elder cottages, 308
Elderhostel, 341
Elderly dependency ratio, 77. *see also*
   Dependency ratios
Elderly support ratio, 57
Elderspeak, 6
Elderspirit, 310
Eleazer, G. P., 226
Electric scooters, 101
Electronic media, and fraud, 12
Elias, J., 134
Elliott, S., 364, 365
Ellis, E. R., 206, 214
Elo, I. T., 168
Elzabadani, H., 299, 300
Emanuel, L. L., 421
Emond, A., 49
Emotion work, 394
Employee Benefit Research Institute
   (EBRI), 273
Employee Retirement Income Security Act
   (ERISA), 1974, 245, 247, 262
Employer-sponsored health care plans,
   207–208
Employment Act, 1967, 22
Employment pensions, 238, 244–249
Encoding, information, 122
Encore Careers, 281–282
Endocrine/immunological theory, biological
   aging, 85–87
End-of-life care, 417
   diversity on, 423
Eng, C., 226
Engaged caregivers, 184
Engelgau, M., 189
Engelhardt, G. V., 293
Engelman, M., 483
Enguidanos, S., 418
Environmental demand, 294
Environmental improvements, for older peo-
   ple, 101–102
Ephron, N., 483
Equal Employment Opportunity Commis-
   sion (EEOC), 13
Erich, J. A., 438
Erickson, M. A., 312
Erickson, W. A., 279
Ericsson, K. A., 126, 151
Erikson, E. H., 139, 412
ERISA, 1974. *see* Employee Retirement
   Income Security Act (ERISA), 1974
Error theories, of biological aging, 87–88
   cross-linking theory, 87

free radicals theory, 87–88
   somatic mutation theory, 87
Eshbaugh, E. M., 151
Estes, C. L., 3, 36, 38, 213
Ethical issues
   death/dying, 420–429
   in research, 47–49
Ethnicity
   early retirement and, 277
   minority groups and, 158–160 (*see also*
      specific ethnic groups)
   and support for older people, 385
Etnier, J. L., 136
Euthanasia, 426–429
Evans, D. A., 134, 421, 422
Evans, L., 441, 442, 449
Evensky, H., 263
Evenson, K. R., 362
Everett, C. J., 203, 204
Exercises, 105–108, 330
   and brain function, 136
   and fitness programs, 229
Expanders, 329
Experience Corps, 328, 350–351
Experimental designs, research, 39–40
Extended families, 174
Extrinsic aging, 84
Eyetsemitan, F. E., 140
Eyler, A. A., 327

F

Fabsitz, R. R., 189
Facts on Aging Quiz (FAQ), 8
Faculty early retirement program (FERP),
   280
Fadem, P., 113
Fair, J. M., 104
Fairlie, H., 455
Family care, 259
Family/community life, 354–378
   African Americans, 173–175
   American Indians and Alaskan Natives,
      190–192
   Asian Americans, 187–188
   future of, 377–378
   grandparenting (*see* Grandparents)
   Hispanic Americans, 184–186
   marriage (*see* Marriage)
   and support for older people, 382
   widowhood (*see* Widowhood)
Family Service Project, 416
Family supporters, older people as, 401–402
Fancey, P., 387, 401
FAQ. *see* Facts on Aging Quiz (FAQ)
Färber, B., 320
Fast, J. E., 383, 399
Fear, of crime, 12
Feder, J., 203, 207, 212
Federal government
   initiatives on aging, 454
Federal Highway Administration, 319

PHOTO CREDITS